CONSTITUTIONAL RIGHTS AND STUDENT LIFE:

VALUE CONFLICT IN LAW AND EDUCATION

CASES AND MATERIALS

By

FRANK R. KEMERER

Professor of Educational Law and Administration
North Texas State University

and

KENNETH L. DEUTSCH

Associate Professor of Political Science
State University of New York at Geneseo

———

Introductory Comment by
The Honorable David L. Bazelon

ST. PAUL, MINN.
WEST PUBLISHING CO.
1979

Library of Congress Cataloging in Publication Data

Kemerer, Frank R
    Constitutional rights and student life.

    Bibliography: p.
    Includes index.
    1. Students—Legal status, laws, etc.—United States. 2. Educational law and legislation—United States. 3. Civil rights—United States. I. Deutsch, Kenneth L., joint author. II. Title.
II. Title.
KF4150.K46   344′.73′0793   79–13935
ISBN 0-8299-2051-X

K. & D. Const.Rights & Student Life MCB

To our families and our students, and to the
spirit of communication among the academic disciplines.

*

INTRODUCTORY COMMENT

When I entered law school a number of years ago, I assumed I would acquire legal knowledge like most law students—learn to decipher the mystery of complex cases, memorize technical rules, and learn the meaning of obscure Latin phrases. I expected the study of law to yield objective standards by which human behavior could be measured and conflicts resolved.

One of my professors, Leon Green, quickly taught me otherwise. He persisted in asking those complex questions which lay behind the case decisions and the fixed rules we studied. The prospect of these questions was terrifying; for if the law was merely what we made it, then what was it, after all?

Of course, legal rules provide necessary consistency in resolving human conflict. They embody the prudence of the long view, that judgment cannot lurch after the day's passing fancy. Yet my primary lesson from Professor Green—that values underlie legal rules and surround legal controversies—has been reinforced countless times over the years in the cases coming before my court.

I recall Supreme Court Justice Benjamin Cardozo's words, "If judges have woefully misinterpreted the mores of their day, or if the mores of their day are no longer those of ours, they ought not to tie, in helpless submission, the hands of their successors." But when should legal rules be followed and when should they be changed?

Today, the admonition of Justice Cardozo is more relevant than ever. Litigation has become a way of life, as people struggle to achieve a more just society. Nor is the educational institution immune. With the exception of the family, no institution so profoundly influences our development as individuals and as a society. It is appropriate, therefore, that it too become part of the struggle to achieve a more just society. I believe the growing tendency to resort to lawyers and the courts is not merely a symptom of our quarrelsome nature, but is in part a healthy indication of our commitment to extending liberty and fairness. Nevertheless, the hard questions persist: What is liberty? What is fairness? How can these values best be achieved?

This book is written with the express purpose of confronting you with many of the same difficult questions I have faced as a judge. Your authors have sought to strip away the mask of certainty from constitutional issues and ask you to confront a dark and seemingly anarchic landscape. You will, like judges and lawyers, struggle to identify and respond to the underlying questions inherent in the cases and situations coming before you.

INTRODUCTORY COMMENT

Those of you who will eventually enter the legal profession will continue to ponder the issues discussed here throughout your legal careers. Those of you who intend to devote your life's work to education will be better prepared to forestall legal disputes and can help those of us in the legal profession think creatively about the resolution of disputes involving your profession.

Regardless of your chosen field of study, *Constitutional Rights and Student Life* will help you see that the law is not something confined to the law school and the court but is pervasively involved in our lives. Its strengths are our strengths, and its shortcomings are a measure of the road we have before us to a just and humane society. As Judge Tuttle of the Fifth Circuit has observed, "the only way the law has progressed from the days of the rack, the screw and the wheel is by the development of moral concepts."

DAVID L. BAZELON
Senior Circuit Judge,
United States Court of Appeals
for the District of Columbia
Circuit

PREFACE

A. *Purpose and Scope*

Given the natural interest of students in student life, and given the growing interest of academic professionals in the development of interdisciplinary studies, we have joined efforts to produce this integrated textbook primarily for undergraduates in law-related courses and for professional school students planning a career in education.*

We have found that traditional undergraduate courses in civil liberties and constitutional law can be made much more attractive and meaningful to students if cases involving their own milieu are included to illustrate concepts and principles. Despite the fact that students spend nearly one-quarter of their lives in educational institutions, few courses ever provide them with much insight into their status within these organizations. The use of student cases, in combination with doctrinal cases from the larger political and social setting, enriches traditional courses by adding a new dimension focusing on the application of the law within a complex organization and has the added advantage of appealing directly to student interests.

We have also found that most students in professional schools of education are abysmally ignorant of the growing involvement of the judiciary in the affairs of educational institutions. Existing educational law courses are usually aimed at a narrow clientele, primarily those intending to become educational administrators. Unfortunately, most graduates of schools and colleges of education consider the law to be at once a mystery and a threat. This textbook, which bridges the gap between several distinct but related disciplines, provides the ideal subject-matter for a legal foundations course open to all students regardless of academic concentration. Since many education students will become faculty members in schools and colleges, parallel legal developments involving academic professionals have been included.

Constitutional Rights and Student Life is much more than a student rights textbook. This book brings readers face-to-face with key cases and basic questions concerning constitutional rights in society, the involvement of courts in resolving issues within a complex organization, and the role of values in decision making. In short, through the experience of the student, we have attempted to combine the legal, political science, and education disciplines into a meaningful whole.

---

*Instructors are urged to consult the *Instructor's Manual* for suggestions on ways in which this book can be most effectively used in political science, law and society, and educational law courses.

Specifically, the objectives of *Constitutional Rights and Student Life* are:

1. To review through case law the development of constitutional rights in the American political and social setting;

2. To examine the problems and issues of applying these same rights to students;

3. To present the current state of the law concerning student constitutional rights;

4. To encourage the reader to consider basic value questions related to legal and educational issues in general, and the involvement of the judiciary in educational affairs in particular.

The chapter formats generally follow the pattern of these objectives.

B. *Content Overview*

Part I begins with an exploration of major issues. What are the dominant value positions concerning constitutional rights? What should be the mission of educational institutions? Who should decide conflicts over student rights? How do judges reach decisions? How have courts decided issues involving the establishment of schools and student attendance? Through narrative, court cases, and hypothetical situations, the first two chapters constituting Part I are designed to prod the reader into thinking about basic value questions underlying court decisions presented and discussed in the rest of the book.

Part II explores the developing law of rights of expression, religious freedom, due process, and equal protection through a number of important constitutional rights cases. With the help of provocative questions and hypothetical situations, the narrative links educational law with parallel developments in the larger political and social setting. The student is continually forced to confront the major issues discussed in Part I. And in one chapter we provide the reader with a case study of our legal system in operation by following a student constitutional rights dispute from the time it arises until it is finally settled by the U.S. Supreme Court.

Part III focuses on emerging student rights of privacy and concludes with a general reconsideration of the basic issues raised in Part I.

For students unfamiliar with legal terms, with briefing cases, and with legal research, we have included appendices covering these topics. For ease of reference, the appendix also includes a copy of the United States Constitution. Finally, we have provided an annotated bibliography for those interested in further reading and research.

Some further words about format: we have attempted to avoid sexist labels by randomly changing pronoun genders throughout the book. In effect, we have adopted a consistent policy of inconsistency! Our own footnotes are numbered consecutively in each chapter; footnotes within case excerpts retain their original numbers. In most instances, we have deleted the case references from excerpted decisions. However, we have provided case citations within our text as an aid to those who may wish to engage in further study; in the interest of space and ease of reading, unexcerpted U.S. Supreme Court cases are cited only to the official reporter and state cases to the West National Reporter System. Finally, as part of our effort to confront students with decision-making opportunities, we have offered a number of lengthy hypothetical situations which attempt as nearly as possible to portray the complexity of real-life situations.

Constitutional Rights and Student Life does not attempt to indicate the one "best" value position on any of the topics discussed. Rather, it is the goal of this book to help readers develop their own positions on constitutional issues within the educational setting by providing alternative viewpoints through a variety of cases, questions, and comments.

C. *Acknowledgements*

Since this book is largely about students, it seemed fitting that they play a substantial role in voicing views about what should be included. We applaud those students in our classes who so patiently waded through labored early drafts of many of the chapters. We hope their efforts to comprehend, reflect, and react were not in vain.

The development of this interdisciplinary book was also considerably assisted by numerous professionals in the fields of law, political science, and education. Upon completion, each of the chapters was sent to one or more acknowledged experts for reaction and comment. Chapter One was reviewed in its earliest stages by Stanford University education professors Henry M. Levin and David Tyack, and by J. Victor Baldridge, Senior Research Associate at the Higher Education Research Institute at Los Angeles. After being convinced not to write the entire book in the first chapter, we sent a considerably shortened and revised version of Chapter One to Theodore R. Sizer, Headmaster at Phillips Academy, Andover, Massachusetts, for his comments. Patricia A. Hollander, Director of the Program in Law and Social Science at SUNY-Buffalo's Survey Research Center; Walter C. Hobbs, Professor of Higher Education at SUNY-Buffalo; and James Lieberman, Staff Attorney for the U.S. House of Representatives Select Committee on Population, reviewed Chapter Two.

We are indebted to Loren Beth, Professor and Department Chairman of Political Science at the University of Georgia, who consented to review Chapters Three and Four. John R. Carrell, Professor of Business Administration and Law at North Texas State University, also reviewed Chapter Three, and Professor David W. Leslie of the University of Virginia's Center for the Study of Higher Education reviewed Chapter Five.

PREFACE

Chapter Six could not have been written without the cooperation of the Harvard Center for Law and Education, which provided most of the documents associated with *Goss v. Lopez,* the case dissected in that chapter. The attorneys who argued Goss contributed many hours of their time to reviewing drafts of the chapter and adding comments enriching the case study. We are particularly indebted to Denis R. Murphy and Peter Ross, who argued on behalf of Dwight Lopez, and to Thomas Bustin, who was chief legal counsel for the school officials. Gary Pavela, Director of Judicial Programs at the University of Maryland, and Roosevelt Washington, Associate Professor of Educational Administration at North Texas State University, reviewed Chapter Six. We are also indebted to Robert Weinstein, Tom Cronmiller, and Jody Carra, three students who waded through the many documents and papers to develop an initial documentary outline of the case.

Chapter Seven was reviewed by Walter McCann, chairman of Programs in Administration, Planning, and Social Policy at the Harvard University Graduate School of Education and by Peter Roos, Director of Education Litigation for the Mexican American Legal Defense and Educational Fund (MALDEF) in San Francisco.

Chapter Eight was reviewed by Jon Bible, Attorney for the Texas Association of School Boards.

When all the chapters were revised based on comments from the reviewers, we submitted the entire manuscript to D. Parker Young, Professor of Higher Education at the University of Georgia and a frequent writer and commentator on educational law. Dr. Young provided many suggestions for improving both coverage and consistency of style across chapters.

We also wish to acknowledge the efforts of our hard-working research assistant, Richard Tubiolo, who is now attending law school at St. John's University. Louella Schumaker and Sandy Behrens, our persistent typists are to be commended for their good spirits in typing and retyping the manuscript countless times.

Finally, we thank The Honorable David L. Bazelon for his introductory comments. For over thirty years, Judge Bazelon has served as a member of the U.S. Circuit Court of Appeals in Washington, D.C., sixteen of those years as its chief judge. He is well known for his persistent questioning in search of the complex human factors which underlie the cases coming before his court. Throughout his legal career, Judge Bazelon has endeavored to reach across the disciplines to better fathom human behavior.

While many persons have helped us develop this book in addition to those specifically mentioned above, we absolve them all of any responsibility for its shortcomings. As authors, that is a burden we must shoulder. We hope, however, that our readers will not judge us too unkindly for

PREFACE

having undertaken the task of looking across departments and divisions to provide better perspective to the vagaries of constitutional law within the educational setting as well as within society-at-large.

FRANK R. KEMERER

KENNETH L. DEUTSCH

June, 1979

*

SUMMARY OF CONTENTS

TABLE OF CONTENTS

PART I. THE MAJOR ISSUES AND THEMES

TABLE OF CONTENTS

TABLE OF CONTENTS

TABLE OF CONTENTS

TABLE OF CONTENTS

TABLE OF CONTENTS

TABLE OF CONTENTS

TABLE OF FIGURES

(References are to Pages)

*

TABLE OF CASES

The principal cases are in italic type. Cases cited or discussed are in roman type. References are to pages.

TABLE OF CASES

TABLE OF CASES

TABLE OF CASES

*

TABLE OF CASES

*

CONSTITUTIONAL RIGHTS
AND
STUDENT LIFE

Part I

THE MAJOR ISSUES AND THEMES

Chapter One

"Constitutional rights do not mature and come into being magically only when one attains the state-defined age of majority. Minors, as well as adults, are protected by the Constitution and possess Constitutional rights."

Justice Harry A. Blackmun
Planned Parenthood v.
Danforth, 1976.

"RIGHTS, RESPONSIBILITIES, AND THE EDUCATIONAL ENVIRONMENT"

The subject of student constitutional rights is a complex mixture of legal and educational concerns. Consider a typical example from everyday life in schools and colleges. An educational official receives information from an anonymous source—a student has a cache of drugs with her and intends to sell them on the campus. The educator is immediately faced with a number of problems. Should the anonymous tip be ignored or should the student be confronted? Should a warrantless search of the student then be conducted or should a search warrant first be obtained with police brought to the scene? If drugs are found, should the student be subject to internal disciplinary procedures? Or has the educator a duty to turn the student and the evidence over to the police?

Suppose the educator, concerned about his responsibilities to other students, parents, and society, decides to search the student, and, finding drugs, turns her over to the police, followed by internal disciplinary procedures. The student later sues the educator, claiming a violation of the constitutional rights of privacy, protection from unreasonable searches and seizures, and procedural due process. Should the judge decide the case by tailoring the ruling to the particular factual circumstances of this situation? Or should a more general ruling be applied—one which could be

1

used in future cases? Should the judge consider precedents developed in the larger political and social setting?

This introductory chapter and the next will raise the underlying issues which must inevitably be confronted before decisions can be reached about the rights of individuals, in general, and students, in particular. Temporarily, we will defer wrestling with the specifics of constitutional rights and related court cases to succeeding chapters.

I. THE CONTINUING DEBATE OVER RIGHTS AND RESPONSIBILITIES

Any discussion of student constitutional rights must first include a review of the different conceptions of rights that exist in the general political and social setting. The goal of any educational institution, as a subunity of society is to prepare students to live within that society. Thus, the themes of society at large will be reflected in the functioning of educational institutions.

What are "rights"? If a street-corner census were conducted in any large American city, this question would yield a variety of definitions and examples. A "right" to one person may or may not be a "right" to another. Similarly, in educational institutions, what "rights" students should have depends largely upon who is asked. Individual values vary widely. It is these differences in individual values which provoke a variety of responses to questions about rights and responsibilities.

A. The Sources of Rights

The chief source of American constitutional rights is the Bill of Rights, which incorporates elements of the English common law as well as liberties the framers of the Amendments wished to protect from government abuse in America.* Of the ten amendments, only the first eight actually convey specific rights. Of these eight, the First Amendment is generally considered the most important. Other amendments, in addition to the Bill of Rights, which are important sources of rights are the Thirteenth, Fourteenth, Fifteenth, Nineteenth, and Twenty-Sixth. Article One, Sections 9 and 10, and Article Four of the Constitution also contain important provisions protecting individual rights.

Constitutional rights guarantee basic protection from governmental tyranny and despotism. The Constitution established a government bound by carefully delineated procedures and rules, which severely limit governmental authority over individuals and provide for fairness in such areas as criminal trials. While the Declaration of Independence, implicitly, and the Bill of Rights, explicitly, provide the cultural and legal foundation of constitutional rights, neither translates rights into practice. Political institutions such as the Supreme Court, the President, Congress, and state legislatures are required to implement and protect them.

Constitutional rights also emanate from state constitutions. Through legislation passed both by Congress and state legislatures, existing consti-

---

* The Constitution of the United States is reprinted in Appendix C.

tutional rights can be broadened and other rights added, e. g., section five of the Fourteenth Amendment empowers Congress to enact "appropriate legislation" to enforce its various provisions. Just after the Civil War, a federal law (42 U.S.C.A. § 1983), based on this provision was passed, which provided citizens of the United States with a civil remedy against state officials who deprive them of their Fourteenth Amendment rights. Thus, Congress translated the general rights prescribed by the amendment into concrete protections, particularly for blacks.

Similarly, the President has the power of "executive order," through which he can promulgate rules of executive and administrative performance. President Franklin D. Roosevelt issued an executive order in 1941 requiring defense contractors not to discriminate against any worker "because of race, creed, color, or national origin," thereby initiating the intricate process of expanding rights to fair treatment in employment for blacks and other disenfranchised groups.

The United States Supreme Court has been the primary institutional arbiter and definer of rights and responsibilities. It has the historic responsibility and authority for defining the Constitution and the Bill of Rights, and determining whether Congress, the President, and state officials are properly exercising their powers. We will focus on the Supreme Court's attempts to authoritatively determine what constitutional rights mean and how extensively they can be applied in specific situations.

B. Defining Freedom, Justice and Equality

Constitutional rights encompass the protection of three basic values— "freedom", "justice," and "equality". Men and women have fought for the implementation of these values through vociferous debate, dissent, and even political revolution. The legitimacy of the American political and legal system stems mainly from these fundamental values. However, in practice, their meaning is highly contested. The First Amendment's use of the term "freedom" in the context of religion, speech, press, and assembly, and the terms "due process of law" (justice) in the Fifth and Fourteenth Amendments and "equal protection of the laws" in the Fourteenth Amendment, are subject to widespread differences in interpretation. Constitutional clauses are not self-explanatory. Their meaning is translated into political, legal, and educational reality largely by the Supreme Court, which has historically shifted its position on the meaning and content of these phrases.

(1) Freedom of Expression: The Problem of Limits

Should we give a public forum to Nazis to espouse the view that certain racial groups are genetically inferior to others? Should the government place limits on publications and films which are pornographic? At the center of the controversy over freedom of expression is the question of *limits*. The difficulty lies in devising a precise formula to indicate when freedom has exceeded rightful bounds. Some have argued that damaging another's reputation is an unwarranted exercise of the right of expression and, consequently, support laws against libel and slander as legitimate limits to freedom of speech and press. Others claim that national security requires limits on freedom of expression.

Students in all educational settings experience limits on freedom of expression. Should students be permitted to express their political views in their respective educational institutions? Or should they be subject to limits not applicable outside the school because an orderly environment is a prerequisite for effective teaching and learning? These questions form the basis for a seminal student rights case, *Tinker v. Des Moines School Dist.*, 393 U.S. 503 (1969),* one of the First Amendment cases to be examined in Chapter Three.

(2) Justice and the Rights of the Accused: The Problem of Fairness

The Anglo-American approach has been to treat those accused of a crime "fairly" or with "due process of the law"—but what is "fairness"? What is "due process of law"? "Fairness" for some means procedural justice, that is, proceedings conducted according to established and predictable rules. Others criticize the "coddling" of criminals and believe justice should mean quick retribution to provide security for persons and property—"law and order." Still others view justice as equalizing legal resources in the criminal justice system, giving every person, rich or poor, the same treatment.

The problem is complicated in the educational setting because of continuing social pressure for more student discipline, the fear that due process procedures will undermine the student-teacher relationship by superimposing the criminal law adversary system on the school, and the problem of deciding whether due process should be required when challenges arise over academic decisions such as grading, tracking, and academic dismissals.

During the past two decades, the Supreme Court has attempted to specify in detail the nature of due process requirements guaranteed to those accused of crime. Recently, the Court has decided student cases involving temporary school suspensions, corporal punishment, and academic dismissal from a public medical school. Chapter Five presents these and other student cases along with several of the more important cases dealing with due process for adult offenders and juvenile delinquents. The controversial student suspension case, *Goss v. Lopez,* 419 U.S. 565 (1975), generally regarded as the most supportive of student due process rights, serves as the focus for Chapter Six, "Anatomy of a Student Rights Case."

(3) Equality: The Problem of Distributing Burdens and Benefits

The proposition that all people are created equal has never meant that all possess the same abilities, interests, or talents. The problem arises in determining which differences are relevant to differential treatment. Most agree that, other things being equal, it is never appropriate to discriminate on the basis of race, sex, religion, or national origin. However, some claim that it is necessary to re-distribute societal resources by taking from advantaged groups and giving to the disadvantaged, so that all may acquire the essentials of food, shelter, access to employment, medical care, and education. The controversy over what equality should mean

---

* Readers unfamiliar with the case citation system are urged to read the first section of Appendix B "Researching the Law" at this point. Appendix D "Legal Terminology" will also be helpful in defining unfamiliar terms.

has surfaced in the issue of preferential treatment for minorities. Should the government establish programs to aid minority groups in the competition for jobs and higher education? Are these programs legitimate forms of "compensatory treatment" for past racial discrimination or are they a form of unwarranted "reverse discrimination" against whites? The Supreme Court recently dealt with this perplexing issue in an educational context in the case of *Bakke v. Regents of the State of California* (1978), which is among the cases included in Chapter Seven.

II. RIGHTS, RESPONSIBILITIES, AND EDUCATION: THREE PERSPECTIVES

Tinker v. Des Moines School Dist. is a case involving several public school students (ages 16, 15, 13, 11 and 8) who decided to demonstrate their opposition to the Vietnamese war by wearing black armbands to school. Fearing disruption of the educational process and possible violence, school officials invoked a hastily enacted school rule against such demonstrations, which suspended the students until they removed their armbands. The students contested their suspensions. Should the students have been allowed to carry their demonstration into the school? Or did they have a responsibility to observe the rules set forth by the school officials, who have a legal obligation to safeguard the welfare of others and to ensure an orderly environment within which teaching and learning can take place?

In response to this question, three major ideological positions about rights and the role of educational institutions are outlined.

A. The Liberal Endorsement of Social Pluralism

The liberal view of constitutional government and corporate economics consists of:

1. Open access to the political arena: there are no barriers to a group's getting a hearing; participation is open;

2. A constitutional democracy which operates within clearly defined rules and restraints;

3. A sufficiently large number of political and economic groups so that no one group can dominate the political power structure;

4. The belief (on the part of some liberals) that disadvantaged groups should be given certain additional resources in order to be able to compete in the political and economic arenas.

Power in society is tamed, balanced, and civilized by open competition for scarce resources. James Madison, the principal author of the Federalist Papers and the Bill of Rights, believed that the best way to prevent class warfare was to allow so large a number of parties and interests to exist that one of them could never constitute a majority.[1] Fragmentation of interest groups coupled with representative government, itself divided by a separation of powers and a system of checks and balances, would assure the preservation of natural rights. Politics for the liberal is free access

---

1. Edward McNall Burns, "The Philosophy of History of the Founding Fathers," 14 *Historian* 142, Spring, 1954, at p. 167.

to the political arena in a context of limited government and procedural justice. Legal rules exist to preserve these political norms and moderate political conflicts.

The kind of educational environment that serves the political norms of the liberal has perhaps been most lucidly expressed by the liberal philosopher and educator, John Dewey:

> It is the aim of progressive education to take part in correcting unfair privilege and unfair deprivation, not to perpetuate them.
>
> *   *   *
>
> An education which should *   *   * unify the disposition of the members of society would do much to unify society itself.[2]

If schools did function this way, Dewey believed they could be in the forefront of societal change:

> When this happens schools will be the dangerous outposts of a humane civilization. But they will also begin to be supremely interesting places.[3]

If politics and education were joined, Dewey claimed that "politics will have to be in fact what it now pretends to be, the intelligent management of social affairs." [4]

Dewey was an advocate of scientific progress, linking scientific method to the values of individual freedom, competition, and democracy. For Dewey and many contemporary liberals, if the schools' main purpose were to instill respect for traditional values, students would become appendages to the machines they operate or to the authorities they vote into office. Instead, children's instincts need to be "trained in social directions, enriched by historical interpretation, controlled and illuminated by scientific methods" so that they can cope effectively with change. Knowledge should not be viewed as an "immobile solid", solely the province of the elite; knowledge is "actively moving in all the currents of society itself." Therefore, the students' learning process should not be a passive one—it should be dynamic and involve real-life situations which build on students' tendencies "to make, to do, to create, to produce, whether in the form of utility or of art." [5]

A more contemporary view of the mission of educational institutions is expressed by R. Freeman Butts, an educator long identified with the liberal view. Butts argues that the highest priority should be placed on "the educational search for a viable, inclusive, and just political community." He proposes a civic liberal education for all schools with the goal of dealing

2. John Dewey, *Democracy and Education: An Introduction to the Philosophy of Education* (New York: The Macmillan Co., 1920), at pp. 140 and 305.

3. As quoted in Joseph Ratner (Ed.), *Characters and Events: Popular Essays in Social and Political Philosophy* (New York: Henry Holt and Co., 1929), Vol. 11, at p. 781.

4. *Id.*

5. John Dewey, "The School and Society," in Martin S. Dworkin (Ed.), *Dewey on Education* (New York: Teachers College, Columbia, 1961), at pp. 46–47.

with *all* students in ways calculated to motivate them and enable them to play their parts as informed, responsible, and effective members of the democratic political system. This is to be achieved by developing within them the values, the knowledge, and the skills of participation required for making deliberate choices among real alternatives.[6]

Another liberal perspective on the purpose of educational institutions suggests that the educational system has no higher function than to help people develop a sense of identity and self-direction. The president of a liberal arts college recently suggested that his sister institutions break away from the usual pattern by focusing on student self-development:

A central purpose (of liberal arts colleges) should be to identify the values influencing our behavior, to use our reason to appraise those values, and then to reconsider them in light of their validity and their consequences for both the individual and society. * * * The undergraduate years are the one time when people can come to understand something of themselves and the world around them, when they can begin to reach beyond themselves "to touch the world at unnumbered points." That spirit of curiosity and concern, that sensibility to the meaning of life, must prevail.[7]

B. The Conservative Quest for Order

Conservatives are generally those who oppose political coalitions favoring regulation of private wealth, extensive social welfare legislation, and popular control over the reins of political power. Ideologically, they accept and defend those values and institutions of Western tradition which include deference to enlightened and educated elites; civility in political expression; the awareness of social responsibilities and restraints as well as freedom of expression; and the insistence on slow change grounded in commitment to social and political order.

American conservatives consider the great English statesman, Edmund Burke, as their intellectual father. His primary concern was controlling the passions of individuals who could potentially destroy the economic and spiritual resources of society. Conservatives believe that government and the legal process exist for a very specific purpose—that freedom means accepting those necessary restraints on one's passions which if unregulated can endanger or destroy the delicate fabric of social order. In effect, the concept of order is implicit in their concept of freedom.

Everyone is entitled to fair and equal treatment under the law, "but not to equal things," said Burke. In society, those individuals with greater knowledge, talents, and resources should not be leveled to the lowest common denominator. Conservatives see private property as the bastion of "ordered liberty," since property and wealth provide a suitable base for the security required by a talented and well-educated populace. With em-

6. R. Freeman Butts, "Once Again the Question for Liberal Public Educators: Whose Twilight?" 58 *Phi Delta Kappan*, September, 1976, at p. 12. Emphasis in original.

7. Theodore D. Lockwood, "Liberal Arts Colleges in the Cause of Humanity", *The Chronicle of Higher Education*, March 25, 1974.

phasis on the three R's, the gifted student is encouraged, while the mediocre are channeled towards technical curricula.

Conservatives see the educational system as an integral part of the
social, economic, and political life of the nation. The cooperation of educational facilities is essential to maintaining national stability, security,
and economic well-being. Interactions within this framework could include: science faculties working with government to develop space technology or new weapons; political scientists and economists cooperating
with the State Department or Defense Department to meet national security needs; psychologists aiding prison authorities in helping to rehabilitate inmates, etc.

During the last decade, there has been increasing concern about the
steady national decline in student performance on standardized tests of
verbal and arithmetic skills, which has reduced public faith in academic
programs. Inevitably, many link the decline to a lack of discipline by
school officials. In a 1978 Gallup Poll, "a poor curriculum" ranked high
on a list of major problems confronting the schools. The most popular
suggestions about how to improve the quality of schools were to "enforce
stricter discipline" and "devote more attention to teaching basic skills."

A recent study [8] by Frank E. Armbruster, which represents the largely
conservative back-to-the-basics movement, contends that, in spite of continually increasing levels of expenditures, elementary and secondary
schools are teaching less and less. The percentage of gross national product spent in public education has more than doubled since 1950, but standardized tests continue to document a decline in basic skills. (However,
while GNP percentages devoted to education have increased, so have the
percentage of school age population and the time students spend in educational institutions.) According to Armbruster, too much time has been
spent on fads and concern for the welfare of teachers and administrators,
while discipline in the classroom has deteriorated. His solution is to return
to the basics:

> Syllabuses and courses used in some states today may simply be
> inadequate tools to impart the knowledge many children current-
> ly lack, which they used to acquire under the old system. Just
> as the "new math" courses and syllabuses are beginning to be
> dropped in primary schools in favor of traditional ways of teach-
> ing mathematics, the same action may be required in the social
> studies area in high school. "Asian and African Culture Studies"
> is huge in scope from the viewpoint of centuries of time, and geo-
> graphic, historic and cultural diversity, but has little depth and
> is simply no substitute for Ancient History in ninth grade. Such
> modern writings as *Soul on Ice* simply do not impart the impor-
> tant elements which substantial amounts of classical American
> and English Literature do (to say nothing of the civilizing process
> which we wish to see advanced in our high schools). Nor are
> "rap sessions" about a current movie a class has viewed any sub-

8. Frank E. Armbruster, *The U. S. Primary
and Secondary Educational Process* (New
York: Hudson Institute, 1975).

stitute for teacher-scrutinized and corrected written book reports or themes.[9]

Openly critical of such educational practices as team teaching, open classrooms, automatic grade promotion, ethnic studies, the acceptance of "street English," faculty tenure, new math and busing, Armbruster maintains that "scholastically richer courses" and the reduction of "enrichment" and "mini courses" will raise academic achievement, improve academic decorum, and reduce costly equipment inventories and inflated salary costs for unnecessary administrators and teachers.

C.   The Radical Vision of Democratization

Radicals place great critical emphasis on the inequality of economic resources, the repression of dissenters who question the *status quo,* and the gross inadequacy of democratic control over the political, economic, and educational systems.   These problems of society require a root transformation.   Radical socialists have characterized our socio-political system as:

1.   a system dominated by a small elite who own or control the most important areas of private property (the productive capacity of a society which provides goods and services);

2.   a military-industrial complex that is outside popular control, unaccountable and unresponsive to the society at large;

3.   a legal system that discriminates against the poor segments of society through high bail, inadequate legal services, and discriminatory sentencing;

4.   an educational system whose quality differs from neighborhood to neighborhood according to socio-economic status, and whose curricula and methods channel students into the capitalist economic system of private profit.

Michael Parenti, a radical political scientist, believes that any political or power structure serves those who own and control the resources of the country.   Social prestige, money, time, and expertise—all influence the attention of political decision makers:

> Indeed, our political system works well for the large producer and corporate interests that control the various loci of power in the state and federal legislatures and bureaucracies.   One can find no end to the instances in which public agencies have become the captives of private business interests.   Economic power is to political power as fuel is to fire,   *   *   *   for political power when properly harnessed becomes a valuable resource in expanding the prerogatives of those economic interests that control it.[10]

Radicals such as Parenti believe that the liberals' view of government as a broker or referee amid a vast array of competing groups is

9.   *Id.,* at p. 295; footnotes deleted.

10.   Michael Parenti, "The Possibilities for Political Change," in Dorothy Buckton

James, *Outside Looking In: Critiques of American Policies and Institutions Left and Right* (New York: Harper and Row, 1972), at p. 357.

naive. They claim that access to the political system and society's resources, including education, is inherently unequal, that the process of
policy-making and the distribution of scarce resources is neither neutral
nor in the interest of the masses. Access to education is based on the
students' socio-economic background—students from different classes and
neighborhoods receive different symbolic messages as to what "democracy" means, different kinds of courses, and different kinds of teacher-
student relationships. The result is that schools and colleges reproduce
existing economic inequalities into the next generation.

Some radicals argue that student-centered learning can occur only
in an unstructured, permissive learning environment—hence the rise of the
"free school." Others suggest that such learning should take place outside of school and call for the "deschooling of society." Ivan Illich would
abolish all state-established schools and outlaw discrimination in the job
market based on degrees, certificates, and other indications of school attendance. Instead of schools, Illich suggests establishing skill centers
where students can go for job training at public expense and a computerized networking system to match up learners and teachers.[11]

Radicals have also joined those who advocate a voucher system to replace the contemporary elementary and secondary educational system. In
its most common form, state-backed school vouchers given to parents and
children are, theoretically, redeemable at any of a variety of institutions in
return for approved educational services. These institutions can range
from traditional local public schools to prestigious private institutions to
innovative "store-front" schools. To counteract the possibility that
wealthy parents could send their children to the most expensive schools,
while the poor would have few choices, some radical reformers have recommended that the amount of the voucher vary inversely with wealth, so
that diversity of choice in the school setting would be guaranteed.

On the basis of these three brief descriptions of opposing ideologies,
how would a representative of each group decide the issue central to
Tinker v. Des Moines School Dist., i. e., the appropriateness of wearing
armbands to school as a symbol of protest?

III. STUDENT RIGHTS DECISION MAKING

A critical factor in the *Tinker* situation is the *age* of the students. If
the same situation had occurred at a four-year college, would each of the
representatives from the dominant ideologies decide the same way? What
if the protest had occurred at an elementary school or outside of the school
setting altogether?

A. How Much and at What Age?

Those below the traditional demarcation line separating childhood
from adulthood (generally considered to be between ages 16 and 21) are
granted rights that differ only in extent from those enjoyed by adults.
Justice Blackmun, speaking for the majority of the Supreme Court in the

11. Ivan Illich, *Deschooling Society* (New
York: Harper and Row, 1970), Chapter 6,
"Learning Webs."

1976 abortion case, *Planned Parenthood v. Danforth,* 428 U.S. 52, reiterated the Court's long-held position:

> Constitutional rights do not mature and come into being magically only when one attains the state-defined age of majority. Minors, as well as adults, are protected by the Constitution and possess constitutional rights. (At p. 74).

However, the Court added that the State has broad authority to regulate the activities of children; parents also have broad authority to direct the upbringing of their children. Thus, those below the "state-defined age of majority" in reality have few rights. The rights of children are most likely to be found in areas which do not conflict with the rights of federal, state, and local governments to pass protective regulations on behalf of children, e. g., child labor laws, curfew laws, compulsory school laws, etc.; and do not conflict with the rights of adults to function effectively as parents. Exactly what these rights are will be subsequently discussed.

As far as the "state-defined age of majority" is concerned, the Supreme Court ruled in 1975 in the case of *Stanton v. Stanton,* 421 U.S. 7, that the state cannot set different ages at which men and women are considered adults under the law. In this case Utah had set the age of adulthood at 18 for women and 21 for men, reasoning that men need a longer period of parental support to secure an education. Justice Blackmun wrote for the majority, "No longer is the female destined solely for the house and the rearing of family and only the male for the marketplace and the world of ideas" (at pp. 14–15). Justice Rehnquist was the sole dissenter.

The rights of young people in educational institutions may differ from their rights in the political and social setting, e. g., all young people have certain rights if accused of a crime, but public high school students have a limited version of these rights when threatened with a temporary suspension. *Goss v. Lopez* (1975). In the same case, the U. S. Supreme Court recognized that public high school students may have a greater claim to due process where long-term suspensions and expulsions are concerned, although it was not specific. The *Goss* protections are not extended to students in private schools and colleges because of the unique nature of these institutions (see the next chapter). The Court has not indicated if *Goss* applies to public elementary school students and has refused to apply the *Goss* ruling to cases of corporal punishment in public educational institutions. *Ingraham v. Wright,* 425 U.S. 990 (1977). Neither has the Court, to date, ruled that students attending public educational institutions are entitled to due process rights when threatened with suspension or expulsion for academic reasons, even though the consequences for the student are the same as those resulting from disciplinary action. Both *Goss v. Lopez* and *Ingraham v. Wright* are prime examples of the judicial dilemma of balancing the interests of student rights against the interests of academic decorum and professional educational responsibilities.

If guidelines can be established which define the nature of rights guaranteed to a student, at what age should they be protected? Should stu-

dents be given certain rights at age 13 which will be extended at age 18?
Edward T. Ladd believes that:

> * * * we should classify students into groups correspond-
> ing roughly to the progress they should have made and should now
> be making in freeing themselves from adult direction, and * * *
> we should set up different regulations and requirements for each
> group; we should, in short, stair-step regulations and require-
> ments, so that they facilitate, and, even force, the transition
> * * *

> * * *

> * * * it would seem to make sense to build four-year steps,
> bracketing students in our schools as "younger children", aged
> 6–9; "older children", aged 10–13; "youth", aged 14–17; and
> adults, aged 18 and older.

> * * *

How might we stair-step freedom?

> * * * wouldn't it be a good idea to say that younger chil-
> dren will be allowed to move freely around in the rooms to which
> they are assigned but not to leave them without permission; older
> children will be allowed to move around the school building * *
> on their own, and youths will be allowed to sign out and leave the
> building at will?

> Wouldn't it be a good idea to say that students will be allowed
> to say almost anything they want—by word of mouth or in writ-
> ing, at any time * * * except in the infrequent situations
> where doing so would clearly and substantially interfere with
> people's rights to engage in their own affairs or to be let alone?
> Along the same lines, why wouldn't it be a good idea to allow stu-
> dents to move their furniture around at will and to sit, stand, lie,
> or squat wherever and with whomever they choose? [12]

Would it be preferable to accord certain rights to a student when she
actually reaches a certain level of maturity, regardless of age?

B. Who Should Decide What Rights Students Have?

Courts decide constitutional issues, with definitive rulings emanating
from the U. S. Supreme Court. However, traditionally, courts have been
reluctant to consider the constitutional rights of students because student
concerns often conflict with the interests of others, chiefly parents, state
governments, and professional educators. These various factions contending for the power to resolve issues of student rights may each make
a strong case at different levels in the educational process.

(1) The Case for State Governments

States are responsible for establishing public educational institutions
and determining graduation requirements. States have set up systems
of public education because it is commonly accepted that the social bene-

---

12. Edward T. Ladd, "Civil Liberties for
Students—At What Age?" 3 *J.Law and
Educ.* 255, April, 1974, at pp. 255–258.

fits generated outweigh costs. Challenges to the plenary power of the state over public education are not likely to be successful. In *Sapp v. Renfroe,* 372 F.Supp. 1193 (N.D.Ga.1974), a federal district court ruled against a student whose parents brought a suit on his behalf challenging a mandatory ROTC requirement in the public schools. The court noted that:

> * * * the * * * compulsory ROTC program * * * serves a valid educational purpose and bears a rational connection to the fulfillment of the state school system's position of *parens patriae* by teaching students discipline, leadership, personal hygiene, and first aid. The additional topics of military sciences, military organization, firearms safety and marksmanship also serve valid educational goals * * *. (At p. 1196).

The concept of *"parens patriae"* (roughly, 'parent of the country') referred to in the court's decision underlies the basic right of all governments to pass laws protecting the welfare of citizens and society as a whole. In *Planned Parenthood v. Danforth* (1976), which overturned a statutory parental consent requirement for persons below the age of 18 seeking abortions, U. S. Supreme Court Justice Stevens defined this concept in his dissent from the majority decision:

> The State's interest in the welfare of its young citizens justifies a variety of protective measures. Because he may not foresee the consequences of his decisions, a minor may not make an enforceable bargain. He may not lawfully work or travel where he pleases, or even attend exhibitions of constitutionally protected adult motion pictures. Persons below a certain age may not marry without parental consent. * * * The State's interest in protecting a young person from harm justifies the imposition of restraints on his or her freedom even though comparable restraints on adults would be constitutionally impermissible. (At p. 102).

The state thus assumes the role of a father as head of the family.

(2) The Case for the Parent

The U. S. Supreme Court first recognized the right of parents to control the upbringing of their children in *Meyer v. Nebraska,* 262 U.S. 390 (1923). In *Meyer* the court reversed a teacher's conviction for teaching German contrary to a state law prohibiting the teaching of foreign languages to children in public schools. Acting *parens patriae,* the state had passed the law as a means of fostering a homogeneous society. Considered one of the most conservative justices who have ever sat on the Court, Justice McReynolds ruled that the Nebraska law interfered "with the calling of modern language teachers, with the opportunities of pupils to acquire knowledge, and with the power of parents to control the education of their own." (At p. 401).

The forces tending toward state dominance have grown. The spiraling divorce rate, the influence of television, efforts to bring compensatory education to the pre-schoolers of poverty families, the rising costs of living which force both parents into the job market are a few of the forces moving control over children away from the family. Alternatively, there are counterforces: a guaranteed family income, educational vouchers, and attacks on compulsory school attendance laws favor the family over the state. Proponents argue that these devices provide control by individuals and families, rather than remote social workers and impersonal state officials. Parental control and family autonomy are felt to be the best guarantee of societal pluralism.

John E. Coons, a law professor at the University of California, Berkeley, believes that the sovereignty of parents is to be preferred to the sovereignty of the state:

> By virtue of its size, intimacy, and continuity, the family is the forum in which the child's voice on any issue affecting him is most likely to reach adult ears, informing their decisions with that combination of objective and affective knowledge that is unattainable by large-scale institutions. The family is also the sovereign likely to care the most about the child's personal well being and development; whatever its motivation, it must after all live with him, and therefore has a stake in his achieving personal autonomy. * * * this assumes that parents no less than professionals want children to become autonomous; certainly parents have the stronger economic interest in eliminating dependencies. * * * these qualities make the family a plausible agent for rescuing the child from serious misassignment within systems of treatment, care, or education. Left to a large-scale sovereign, change of assignment can be a difficult affair. Given the power to reject the decision of the system, the family is at the very least an effective backstop for the child overlooked by the Leviathan.[13]

Coons recognizes the need for "legal minimums" to safeguard the child from despotic parents, although courts have always favored parents over potential challengers to their authority except in cases of demonstrable child abuse.

He advocates emancipation and responsibility for the adolescent at some arbitrary age—even though this tends to extend parental power—rather than the idealistic "age neutrality" concepts for conveying rights to children based on maturity. In the case of the latter, too little liberty may subject the mature child to the autonomy of the parent, as in the case of a 16-year-old who is forced to attend a nonpublic school against his will. Too much liberty for the young adolescent may free the child and subject the parents: for example, the 15-year-old who can drive a car but whose parents must guarantee insurance. "It is ironic but true that the most autocratic of our institutions remains in ultimate terms a source of liberty." [14]

(3) The Case for Educators

The learning-teaching-counseling process is very complex, characterized by low technology and high dependence on trained specialists. At all

13. John E. Coons, "Law and the Sovereigns of Childhood," 58 *Phi Delta Kappan*, September, 1976, at p. 24.

14. *Id.*

levels of education, those persons charged with academic and administrative duties consider themselves professionals and demand the prerogatives enjoyed by professionals in other occupations such as law and medicine. Therefore, educators demand control over curricular decisions, professional evaluation and reward systems, and client participation. Armed with sophisticated research studies and mounting evidence of child neglect in our society, many educators are not at all reluctant to challenge the control of parents over the education of America's children. A recent study by Burton L. White of Harvard found that 90 percent of American families fail to help their children develop their full social and intellectual capabilities during the first three years of life and concluded that the day care center was one solution.[15] White recognized that his findings raise immense public policy issues, particularly for lower-income, single-parent families, intensifying the debate about the role of the state vis-a-vis the private family, as more concern is focused on the critical importance of early childhood in human development. But he also concluded that in the entire history of Western education, there has never been a society that adequately recognized the critical importance of the education of very young children.

Educational professionalism is most pronounced in higher education where subject specialization has produced academic departments with considerable curricular control. The greater the training and experience of the educator, so the argument goes, the greater his right to decision-making power. Indeed, college and university faculties often assert that "we *are* the university." While this syndrome is less pronounced in elementary and secondary education, where local communities through their school boards and administrators are more influential, faculty members at these levels continue to seek greater decision-making power through professional bodies and academic unions.

The case for professional elitism was well made several years ago in an editorial in the *New York Times* by John R. Silber, President of Boston University. While Silber was speaking primarily of postsecondary education, his thesis still basically applies to elementary and secondary schools.

> Democracy is * * * counterfeited by the claim that every institution in a democracy ought to be democratic. * * *
>
> In fact, most institutions ought to be run on an elitist basis—that is, decisions within them ought to be made by those most qualified to make them. * * *
>
> Indeed, life itself may depend on it. All would agree that the practice of surgery should be restricted to persons of extraordinary knowledge and skill. * * * No one would give consent to be operated on by a surgeon who intended to poll those in the operating room before deciding on a procedure. We recognize that the surgeon's opinion should prevail without any plebiscite be-

15. Burton L. White, *The First Three Years of Life* (Englewood Cliffs, N.J.: Prentice-Hall, 1975).

cause it is better than the opinion of the nurse, the medical student, the intern, or the patient.

As long as intelligence is better than stupidity, knowledge than ignorance, and virtue than vice, no university can be run except on an elitist basis. A university that strives for the commonplace and is content with mediocrity would be roughly comparable to a Supreme Court on which seats were reserved for mediocrity. Thus handicapped, these institutions could not fulfill their missions in society.[16]

(4) The Case for Students

As young people have gained more rights, status, and privileges in modern society, a corresponding student drive for greater power in educational institutions has developed, first becoming evident with the growth of student activism in the 1960s. "Student Power" was a slogan borrowed from Black Power advocates of the same era. Initially, it meant a demand for more autonomy in the social areas of formal education. Today, it is not uncommon for students to sit on faculty, administrative, and even governing board committees at both secondary and postsecondary institutions. Students have become less interested in such participation as an apparent apathy has replaced activism at many institutions. Whether the apathy is only surface-deep and thus transitional is undetermined.

Students have also urged emancipation from parental control. While the general legal tendency to defer to parental power in the absence of emancipation legislation has already been noted, the Supreme Court has been willing to consider the interests of children, e. g., the Court ruled in 1976 that a state cannot prohibit females under the age of 18 from getting an abortion without the consent of their parents.

A more extreme case for student power in educational institutions has been expressed by those who embrace a purely student-centered concept of education. A student leader in New York State has argued that students need to assert control of the educational system:

> * * * If the present educational system is authoritarian, then radical transformation and overthrowing of the system is necessary. Present liberal reform efforts aimed at putting students on governing boards, revisions in the curriculum and grading system, etc., take the existing system and structure for granted. What is needed is radical, structural reform to alter the power relationships in the existing structure and to transform the system itself.[17]

Renewal of student radicalism could well result from widespread student unemployment and subsequent disillusionment with the educational system. By the mid-1970s, reports from several European countries

---

16. John R. Silber, "Above the Rabble," *New York Times*, September 1, 1976, at p. 35. © by the New York Times Company. Reprinted by permission.

17. Ray Glass, "Unionism: Beyond Student Governments, Beyond Collective Bargaining," in *Student Unionization: Perspectives in Establishing a Union of Students* (Washington: National Student Association, 1975), at p. 29.

showed student frustration growing to alarming levels. In Italy it was reported that only 30 percent of the 72,000 university graduates would find jobs in 1977; the others would join the 240,000 degree holders still out of work. Many of these graduates vented their frustration by major uprisings which forced the periodic closing of the country's higher educational institutions. In the United States, continued high unemployment of college graduates is a matter of concern.

(5) The Case for Courts

Some argue that courts ought to become more involved in student rights issues other than merely drawing lines beween the claims of the various adult contenders as in *Meyer v. Nebraska*. These commentators would have the judges themselves decide what rights students have or defer only to student wishes. In *Wisconsin v. Yoder,* 406 U.S. 205 (1971), Justice William O. Douglas' dissent listed the instances of Supreme Court intervention on the side of the child and urged similar action in the case under consideration. *Wisconsin v. Yoder* involved the refusal of the Old Order Amish to enroll their children in public or private high schools despite the state compulsory school attendance law. Two of the children involved in the case were 15 years of age and one was 14. Said Douglas:

> Where the child is mature enough to express potentially conflicting desires (with those of the parents), it would be an invasion of the child's rights to permit such an imposition without canvassing his views. * * * As the child has no other effective forum, it is in this litigation that his rights should be considered. (At p. 242; bracketed material added).

Edward J. Meade, Jr., in charge of public education programs for the Ford Foundation, claims that the courts have become involved in internal educational matters because there is no other remedy for "countless violations of due process in disciplining students * * *."[18] The impact of court action, he maintained, has not been negative but positive.

> * * * the intent of these new legal decrees and interpretations is to extend democracy. * * * they are making more explicit what we formerly thought was implicit in our society and our schools: * * * equity and justice.[19]

Meade's thesis may be illustrated by the problems in the large urban elementary and secondary schools—underfinanced, overcrowded, and frequently the scene of racial and cultural tensions, these institutions have a questionable educational impact on their students. According to Ira Glasser and Alan H. Levine, "willful resistance" by school officials has been the primary threat to the rights of students in the New York public school system. The only hope these students have are the courts and supportive interest groups such as the New York Civil Liberties Union. They concluded that, "At the very least, the availability of legal help has apparently begun to redress the one-sided balance of power which has traditionally

18. Edward J. Meade, Jr., "Is Law Polluting Our Schools?" 59 *Phi Delta Kappan*, February, 1977, at p. 478.

19. *Id.*

resulted in students' rights being subordinated to those of every other organized group in the school system." [20]

C. What Standards Should Be Used?

All contenders for the power to decide issues of student rights have pre-conceived views about the purpose of educational institutions. They seek to bolster their credibility by basing their decisions on objective information. However, when student constitutional rights are concerned, securing objective data is often hindered by the complexity of the educational process. Suppose a court is asked to rule against local financing of public schools because the interdistrict variance in per pupil expenditures denies students living in poor districts the right to an equal education. Is education "a right?" What is "an equal education?" To what extent can social science research be used to convince the court to rule against the local financing system?

Extensive research has been conducted on the impact of the educational process on students. The first massive study, the Coleman Report,[21] surfaced in the mid-1960s and served as the major reference point for most of the later studies. Through extensive testing of 600,000 pupils enrolled in a sample of 4,000 elementary and secondary schools in 1965, Coleman found that variations in the resources of schools made little difference in the achievement levels of students. School *quality* (with the possible exception of teachers) had little to do with educational outcomes. Coleman's study served to undermine the social reforms its sponsors were actively pursuing: compensatory educational programs designed to help the schools foster equal educational opportunity for the poor and for members of racial minorities.

In 1972 an even greater blow to liberal reformers came in the form of a Harvard study which re-examined the Coleman data and added additional tests designed to assess the impact of schooling.[22] Christopher Jencks and associates at the Center for Educational Policy Research at Harvard, showed that schooling *per se* has little to do with later economic success. Thus, even if schools were completely equal, vast inequalities would remain in society. Jencks concluded: "even if we went beyond 'equal opportunity' and allocated resources disproportionately to schools whose students now do worst on tests and are least likely to acquire credentials, this would not improve these students' prospects very much." [23]

Jencks' research represented an extension of the earlier Coleman study by demonstrating that not only do differences among schools have little relationship to student achievement levels, but in general, schooling has only a remote relationship to future income levels. According to Jencks, "adult success must depend on a lot of things besides family background, schooling, and the cognitive skills measured by standardized

20. Ira Glasser and Alan H. Levine, "Bringing Student Rights to New York City's School System," 1 *J.Law and Educ.* 213, April, 1972, at p. 229.

21. James S. Coleman *et al.*, *Equality of Educational Opportunity* (Washington, D.C.: Government Printing Office, 1966).

22. Christopher Jencks, *et. al.*, *Inequality: A Reassessment of the Effect of Family and Schooling in America* (New York: Basic Books, 1972).

23. Mary Jo Bane and Christopher Jencks, "The Schools and Equal Opportunity," 55 *Sat. Review of Educ.*, September 16, 1972.

tests." [24] He admitted that he had no idea what these things are, although "luck" seemed to figure prominently in his thinking. The implications of the Jencks research were: if schools have little "melting pot" effect, and only peripheral influence on future economic success, relying on them to reduce inequality in society would be a waste of time and money.

However, Samuel Bowles and Herbert Gintis, two radical economists, maintained in their book, *Schooling in Capitalist America*,[25] that schools actually have a great effect on students. Jencks had simply misunderstood the role of the American educational system.

> The error in Jencks' method and the main shortcoming of the entire debate on the efficacy of equal education to achieve economic goals may be traced to the theory of education which places it outside of society, an instrument to be independently manipulated for the better or ill by enlightened reformers, selfish elites, or mindless bureaucrats.[26]

In actuality the educational system functions very effectively indeed by perpetrating the characteristics of the American capitalist economy.

> Schools foster legitimate inequality through the ostensibly meritocratic manner by which they reward and promote students, and allocate them to distinct positions in the occupational hierarchy. They create and reinforce patterns of social class, racial and sexual identification among students which allow them to relate "properly" to their eventual standing in the hierarchy of authority and status in the production process. Schools foster types of personal development compatible with the relationship of dominance and subordinacy in the economic sphere, and finally, schools create surpluses of skilled labor sufficiently extensive to render effective the prime weapon of the employer in disciplinary labor—the power to hire and fire.[27]

A facet of the Bowles-Gintis thesis relates to the impact of school classification on students. David Kirp, a University of California-Berkeley professor, has expressed concern over primary school grouping, the placement of secondary school students in educational tracks, and particularly the role of the state and the school system in determining which students are to be treated as "special" or "exceptional."

> Such students by no means resemble one another. They may have intellectual, physical, or emotional handicaps; they may not speak English as their native language; they may simply be hungry or unhappy with their particular school situation. The number and variety of differentiating characteristics is large; overlapping among the characteristics (multiple differences) further complicates the pattern.[28]

24. *Id.*, at p. 41.

25. Samuel Bowles and Herbert Gintis, *Schooling in Capitalist America* (New York: Basic Books, 1976).

26. *Id.*, at p. 248.

27. *Id.*, at p. 11.

28. David L. Kirp, "Student Classification, Public Policy, and the Courts," in *The Rights of Children* (Cambridge, Mass.: Harvard Educ.Rev., 1974), at p. 283.

In order to accommodate these students, the school develops classifications which attempt to group students with similar characteristics simply because every student cannot be offered an individualized program. Those students who cannot be classified, e. g., aliens illegally residing in the country, are often excluded. Because of imprecise assessment techniques, Kirp asserts that many students are misclassified and thus damaged for life. Like Bowles and Gintis, Kirp assumes that the educational institution does have a substantial effect on adult success.

Sociologists Hyman, Wright, and Reed published a study about the same time as the Bowles and Gintis work, which sought to demonstrate the relationship between formal education and the accumulation of knowledge and exercise of learning-related skills, such as reading. From complex statistical analyses of some 50 opinion polls of American adults conducted between 1949–1974, they concluded that "education produces large, pervasive and enduring effects on knowledge and receptivity to knowledge." [29] They found that 7 to 10 percent of the elementary school educated were reading a book at the time they were surveyed, while 46 to 60 percent of the college graduates reported doing so. In addition, the more formal schooling one has, the more one is likely to follow newspaper and magazine accounts of public affairs.

The Hyman, Wright, and Reed study documented a degree of credibility for the educational system unrelated to income levels. However, the study was not without its weaknesses, e. g., controls for family life and social class were relatively weak, leading to speculation that the researchers may have over-estimated the impact of formal schooling. As a class, college graduates differ from high school graduates in family social status and probably in motivation and learning ability. The study also ignored the *quality* of the learning incurred in schools. While demonstrating that individuals with more formal education read more (not how *well* they read), the study showed that the college graduates' depth of knowledge is quite shallow. Nevertheless, the study did bolster faith in the efficacy of the educational system after a decade of devastating assessments.

However, it is important to note that the work of Hyman, Wright, and Reed does not contradict the findings of other researchers. The authors went to great length to point out that their study does not conflict with Coleman's, since the two studies were examining different things. Rather, they suggested that their findings are quite compatible with Coleman's—variations among schools seem to have little effect on the knowledge of the learner in the long run. Jencks' conclusions remain unassailed, since he dealt with the economic consequences of schooling, not the impact of schooling on knowledge. The Bowles and Gintis study was neither discussed nor contradicted. Both groups of researchers agree that schools inculcate habits and knowledge. Bowles and Gintis consider this impact to be negative; Hyman, Wright, and Reed do not.

The Jencks research, in particular, came as a great shock to the educational world. While the socio-economic status and home life of students were generally accepted as important influences in learning (largely

29. Herbert H. Hyman, Charles R. Wright,   *of Education* (Chicago: University of Chi-
    and John S. Reed, *The Enduring Effects*   cago Press, 1975), at p. 109.

due to the earlier research by James Coleman) few suspected that the school had such minimal effect on adult success. Even fewer were prepared for the overall conclusion that economic success depends primarily on chance factors only remotely related to one's class of origin, genes, or schooling.

The Jencks study added to the growing reluctance to allocate more resources to poorly financed schools in order to produce greater equality of opportunity. If equalizing school expenditure does nothing to reduce inequality, why spend the money? Liberals in particular were enraged with these findings. They believed that while school reform may not be as successful in reducing inequality as reconstituting our economic and political system, it is the only realistic alternative. Liberals were particularly displeased that this research should surface just as the U. S. Supreme Court was about to rule on the constitutionality of unequal financing of local schools. Confirming their worst fears, in *San Antonio Independent School Dist. v. Rodriquez*, 411 U.S. 1 (1973) (excerpted in Chapter Seven), the Supreme Court ruled that unequal school financing does not deprive students of the equal protection of the laws. Part of the majority's conclusion rested on the conflicting research findings.

All of the studies demonstrate the complexity of the educational process which makes the impact of schooling hard to assess. An interesting and thought-provoking reaction to the publication of both the Jencks and the Bowles and Gintis studies came from fellow-radical economist and frequent critic of the schools, Henry M. Levin. In an article published shortly after the appearance of the Jencks book, Levin charges social science with "an objectivity gap": "Using similar data and techniques of analysis, Jencks' colleagues at Harvard, Herbert Gintis and Samuel Bowles, have found powerful support for the theory that social class and income inequality are indeed transmitted from generation to generation by * * * both family background and schools." [30] Levin asserted that these researchers came to conflicting conclusions, not because of their data, but because of their own differing values. He also suggested several techniques Jencks apparently used to play down the impact formal education has on income levels.

Levin concludes that leeway for interpretation, combined with different prospectives, creates a situation in which:

> To a substantial degree the social scientist is himself a product of the very forces he wishes to study. Long before he has received his professional training he is exposed to such phenomena as class, race, family structure * * *, and more. His perspective of the world is largely a cumulative result of his role as a child, student, sibling, * * *, and so on. All of these roles have defined the boundaries of experience which in turn mold his social reality. * * * the social scientist who studies the effects of schooling on achievement has been socialized to a large degree by his own particular experiences during his education.[31]

30. Henry M. Levin, "The Social Science Objectivity Gap," 55 *The Sat. Review of Educ.*, November 11, 1972, at p. 51.

31. Henry M. Levin, "Education, Life Chances, and the Courts: The Role of Social Science Evidence," 39 *Law and Con-*

Levin went on to note that researchers are not usually assigned to projects; they pick their own topics. Government and other decision makers are also inclined to choose those researchers who are known to have a certain "outlook" on the subject to be studied. Consequently, truly "objective" social science evidence is nearly impossible to obtain.

Judges appear to be increasingly reluctant to accept the conclusions of "expert" witnesses in complex cases. Consider the following comments by U. S. Court of Appeals Judge J. Skelly Wright on the utilization of social science evidence in an adversary proceeding.

> Plaintiffs' motion for an amended decree and for further enforcement has now been argued and reargued * * * for one full year. During this time the * * * tendency has been to lose sight of the disadvantaged young students on whose behalf this suit was first brought in an overgrown garden of numbers and charts and jargon like "standard deviation of the variable," statistical "significance," and "Pearson product moment correlations." The reports by the experts—one noted economist plus assistants for each side—are less helpful than they might have been for the simple reason that they do not begin from a common data base, disagree over crucial statistical assumptions, and reach different conclusions. Having hired their respective experts, the lawyers in this case had a basic responsibility, which they have not completely met, to put the hard core statistical demonstrations into language which * * * concerned laymen could * * * understand. Moreover, the studies by both experts are tainted by * * * data shopping and scanning to reach a preconceived result; and the court has had to reject parts of both reports as unreliable because biased. Lest * * * this litigation itself should consume the capital of the children in whose behalf it was brought, the court has been forced back to its own common sense approach to a problem which, though admittedly complex, has certainly been made more obscure than was necessary.[32]

What comprises the "common sense approach" advocated by Judge Wright? Should the courts rely on their own views of the appropriate mission for educational institutions? Or should they defer to educators, parents, or students?

No clear set of standards has emerged to guide judicial decision makers in all situations. One commentator has pointed out that, "The dilemma of judicial ignorance of the realities of today's schools, compounded by the need for judicial intervention, portends grave difficulties in the development of a constitutional law of expression for young adults." [33] Others would broaden the comment to apply to the development of a constitutional

temporary Problems, 217, Spring, 1975, at pp. 232–233.

32. *Hobson v. Hansen*, 327 F.Supp. 844 (D. C.D.C.1971), at p. 859.

33. Mark Tushnet, "Free Expression and the Young Adult: A Constitutional Framework," 1976 *University of Illinois Law Forum* 746, 1976, at p. 762.

law in general for all students. Nevertheless, an outline of such a constitutional doctrine has emerged from recent rulings. Just how appropriate recent legal intervention has been, is a matter which will be left to the reader.

––––––

HYPOTHETICAL: *Parents v. Acme Township School Bd.*

A school board election was recently held in the Acme Township School District. All residents over 18 years of age in Acme Township are eligible to vote in school board elections whether they have children or not, since a large portion of property taxes are used for school support. Acme District is composed of three elementary schools, two high schools, and a community college.

Only 40 percent of the eligible voters participated in the recent election. A well-organized group of conservative citizens, consisting of parents and non-parents, were able to place enough representatives of their views on the Board to assert majority control. Professing a "return to the basics" doctrine, the newly-elected conservative school board members voted at their first meeting to ask the district superintendent to implement a comprehensive slate of objectives.

One of the objectives was to remove a number of allegedly subversive and controversial books "harmful to the development of the young people of Acme District" from the library shelves of the elementary and secondary schools; among them was J. D. Salinger's *Catcher in the Rye*. The district superintendent opposed the removal of books but agreed to implement the directive. Several parents and their high school age children brought suit against the school board, demanding a court order prohibiting the removal of the books.

––––––

Place yourself in the position of the judge as you consider the following:

1. How would you decide this case? Would you:
    a. Demand social science evidence that the works are "harmful" ?
    b. Defer to the wishes of the majority on the school board?
    c. Defer to the professional views of the school officials and teachers?
    d. Decide on the basis of your own knowledge about child rearing and the educational process?
    e. Decide the case wholly on the basis of legal precedent related to the Bill of Rights from the political and social setting?
2. Would you distinguish between the elementary school and the high school? Suppose the book removal order had applied to the community college. Would these students have a better chance

to assert rights? Should the judge make an effort to ascertain the views of students in this case?

3. If the teachers had brought a suit against the school board, would they have a better chance of winning their case than the students and their parents? What might be their argument? Again, how would you decide the case?

IV. SUMMARY

We began with an exploration of the source and nature of constitutional rights, and continued with a review of the three major ideological viewpoints (liberal, conservative, and radical) on rights in the educational framework. Each has a position as to whether young persons have rights, and at what age (if at all), they should be granted.

The major contenders for making decisions about student rights were identified, along with a brief discussion of the rationale for their positions. We then noted that there is little consensus even among experts about the nature and functioning of educational institutions. Two reasons emerged for the lack of consensus: the complexity of the learning-teaching-counseling process, and the diverse value systems and ideologies of educators, students, parents, judges, and the public at large.

This diversity results in no set parameters for the rights of students. The nature and extent of student rights depends upon: individual interpretation given to concepts such as "freedom," "justice," and "equality;" the way one views the purpose and functioning of educational institutions within their respective communities; and the identity of the decision makers.

Chapter Two

"Scarcely any political question arises in the United States that is not resolved, sooner or later into a judicial question."

Alexis DeToqueville
Democracy in America

"The fundamental theory of liberty upon which all governments in this Union repose excludes any general power of the State to standardize its children by forcing them to accept instruction from public teachers only."

Justice James C. McReynolds
Pierce v. Society of Sisters, 1925

"THE LEGAL ENVIRONMENT AND THE DEVELOPMENT OF EDUCATIONAL INSTITUTIONS"

We begin by examining the role of the judiciary in the establishment and functioning of a legal system. The primary focus is on the United States Supreme Court since it has final responsibility for deciding constitutional issues in the political and social setting, as well as in the educational setting. An examination of the federal Bill of Rights and particularly the 14th Amendment follows, emphasizing its critical role in conveying constitutional rights to students and in the development of public and private educational institutions. As we will see, the distinction between "public" and "private" is not always easy to maintain. Ultimately, it is the judiciary which must define the difference and resolve disputes over the nature and scope of student rights in both sectors. Those already familiar with the judicial system and the Fourteenth Amendment may wish to skim the material in sections I and II.

Section III utilizes case law to illustrate the judicial response to the development of educational institutions, and section IV focuses on the rights of students in the nonpublic sector. An extended discussion of the rights of students in private education has been included in this chapter since the status of these rights relates directly to the public/private dichotomy inherent in the U. S. Constitution.

I. THE JUDICIARY AND THE LAW

Law can be viewed in a number of ways: rules, custom, order, natural or moral obligations, power, elite domination, the pronouncements of legislatures. According to Martin P. Golding, a legal system exists in a society only if certain conditions are satisfied:

1. There are laws;
2. There exists an agency for changing and making the laws;
3. There exists an agency for determining the infractions of the laws;

4.   There exists an agency for upholding the laws;

5.   There exists an agency for settling disputes between individuals.[1]

The agency for upholding laws and settling disputes in our society is the judiciary. Judges are guided in carrying out their responsibilities by authoritative standards set forth in written constitutions. Both the state constitutions and the federal Constitution contain fundamental principles of government. By including bills of rights and by defining the specific power of governmental institutions, constitutions are designed to limit the chances of abuse of governmental power.

A.   Federal and State Judicial Systems

(1)   The Federal Court System

The structure of the federal judiciary is outlined in Article III, Section I, of the U. S. Constitution.* This article specifically establishes the U. S. Supreme Court, and delegates to Congress the power to establish other courts. Congress has set up the first-level district courts (99 trial courts with original jurisdiction) and the second-level courts of appeal (eleven appeal courts with appellate jurisdiction) [Figure 2–1 illustrates the location of the latter.] Since there are far more district courts, the authority of each is confined to a smaller geographic region. Congress has also established a series of special courts and quasi-judicial tribunals.

The rulings of the appellate and district courts apply only to their own areas, e. g., a decision of the Eighth Circuit Court of Appeals is controlling only for seven midwestern states. It is possible that appellate courts in other parts of the country may resolve a given issue differently from the Eighth Circuit. Thus, the law would vary, depending upon where one lives. Court decisions about student hair length in public elementary and secondary schools are representative of this variance in legal norms. By the mid-1970s, about half the federal courts of appeal had decided that hair length is a fundamental right inherent in the Constitution, while the other half had decided it is not. The issue can be resolved for the whole country only by the U. S. Supreme Court, which to date has not heard a case on this point.

The jurisdiction of the federal judiciary is outlined in Article III, Section II, of the U. S. Constitution. In general, federal courts handle two categories of cases: those involving "federal questions" and those that relate to particular characteristics of the parties. The categories are wholly independent of one another. Those involving a "federal question" refer to cases pertaining essentially to the Constitution and to federal laws and treaties. Those depending on certain characteristics of the parties include cases in which the federal government is a party, as well as those in which a state is a party. Also included are cases between citizens of different states (diversity of citizenship). In the latter instance, Congress has decided that these cases must involve $10,000, or more. Since state courts also are open to some of these cases, parties often have a choice of courts,

---

1.   Martin P. Golding, *Philosophy of Law* (Englewood Cliffs, N.J.: Prentice-Hall, 1975), at p. 11.

* The Constitutional provisions cited in this section are contained in Appendix C.

although they must stay within their selection once made. However, cases involving federal questions, may be appealed to the U. S. Supreme Court. (See Figure 2–2 on page 31).

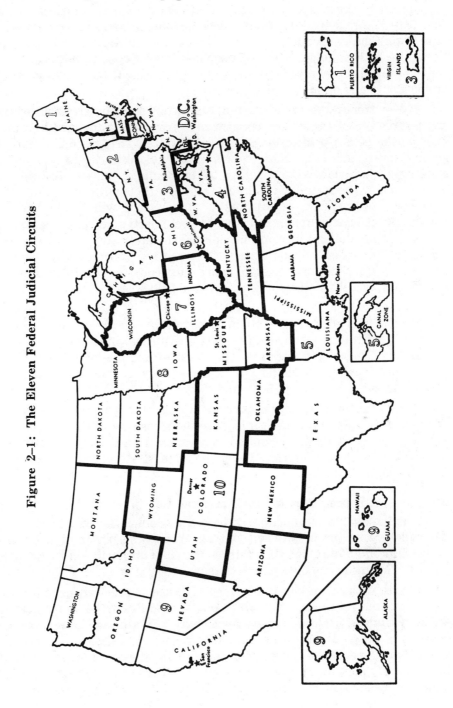

Figure 2–1: The Eleven Federal Judicial Circuits

(2) The State Court System

The federal judiciary represents one legal system; the state systems represent 50 others. Not all state court systems are alike, although they are similar in their arrangement to the federal system, which some pre-date (See Figure 2–2). The highest level of state systems is often known as "the State Supreme Court;" but this is not always the case, e. g., in New York, the highest court is the "New York State Court of Appeals." The Appellate Division of the Supreme Court comes next, followed by the Supreme Court and other courts of record.

The existence and jurisdiction of state courts are determined by state legislatures under the "reserved powers" provision of the Tenth Amendment to the U. S. Constitution. Generally, state courts handle all matters arising under state law. State courts have final authority in interpreting state laws, and federal courts adhere to their rulings, unless a federal issue is involved, or the state law, as interpreted, conflicts with the Constitution or a congressional law. Occasionally, state courts will handle cases involving a state law which also raise a federal question, e. g., if a suspended student claims that his suspension violated the state education code (law) *and* his rights under the Due Process Clause of the Fourteenth Amendment to the U. S. Constitution, the state court must consider the applicable state law or laws, as well as relevant constitutional principles.

The federal courts and the U. S. Supreme Court are thus *not* superior to state courts in all matters, only in those that involve federal law, treaties, and the Constitution. Article VI of the Constitution, the so-called "Federal Supremacy Clause," provides that the Constitution, the laws of the United States, and treaties "shall be the supreme Law of the Land" and that "Judges in every State shall be bound thereby."

Finally, as in the federal judicial system, the geographic extent of state court jurisdiction is determined by their position in the judicial hierarchy. Lower courts have limited geographic range; higher courts are responsible for larger areas. Thus, the highest state court hears cases from throughout the state.

B.   The U. S. Supreme Court: Its Power and Limits

It is impossible to understand the tremendous influence of judges and the judiciary in our society without examining the power of the United States Supreme Court, for the Court is the final authority on the meaning of the Constitution and laws passed pursuant to it.

Words, the grist of law, can never be framed so precisely as to preclude differing interpretations. Yet, the Court's reading of the words framing the Constitution or laws passed by Congress, state legislatures, or city councils is final. If, in an attempt to promote civil order, a federal law sets criminal penalties for persons moving in interstate travel with the intention of "inciting to riot," the Supreme Court could ultimately determine the meaning of the phrase "inciting to riot" and its constitutionality in light of the First Amendment guarantees of free speech and assembly.

In ascertaining the meaning of words in a federal statute, Supreme Court Justices have a choice of several different techniques that have evolved over the years. They may try to learn the intent of the lawmakers from what was said in the general sessions, in committees or at hearings; they may engage in a semantic inquiry as to the "real" meaning of the words; they could conduct historical research into the problem that gave rise to the law in the first place; or, they could take a pragmatic approach to the need to solve contemporary problems. Where state statutes are involved, the Court usually defers to the definitive construction provided by state courts, then passes upon the constitutionality of the statute "as construed." State judges, like their federal counterparts, employ similar techniques in interpreting legislation.

Closely related to the problem of interpreting statutory language is the power of *judicial review*, which deals with defining the actual words of the Constitution in terms of the legitimate exercise of governmental authority. Any federal or state court may declare a statute or government act to be "contrary to the manifest tenor of the Constitution" and therefore void. But the Supreme Court has the decisive last word. The Constitution is silent on the power of judicial review. Yet, James Madison, the father of the Constitution, in *Federalist Paper* No. 78 argued clearly that the Courts should have such power:

> * * * the courts were designed to be an intermediate body between the people and the legislature * * *, to keep the latter within the limits assigned to their authority. The interpretation of the laws is the proper and peculiar province of the courts. A constitution is, in fact, and must be regarded by the judges, as a fundamental law. It therefore belongs to them to ascertain its meaning, as well as the meaning of any particular act proceeding from the legislative body.[2]

It was Chief Justice John Marshall who was to solidify the Supreme Court's power of judicial review in the landmark case, *Marbury v. Madison*, 5 U.S. (1 Cranch) * 137 (1803). To Marshall, the particular phraseology of the Constitution as fundamental, paramount law confirmed and strengthened the principle which is "supposed to be essential to all written constitutions, that a law repugnant to the Constitution is void; and that courts, as well as other departments, are bound by that instrument." (At p. 180). To illustrate why the Supreme Court should be the ultimate authority for what the Constitution says and what governmental acts are contrary to the Constitution and therefore void, Marshall's reasoning took the form of a syllogism:

Major Premise: The Constitution is the supreme law of the land—"the paramount law"—and judges take an oath to support and defend the Constitution.

Minor Premise: It is the responsibility of the Judiciary in Article III of the Constitution to interpret the law.

2. *The Federalist* (New York: Modern Library, 1937), at p. 506.

* The early volumes containing the reported decisions of the Supreme Court are known by the last names of their recorders. The Cranch volumes were the first devoted exclusively to U. S. Supreme Court decisions.

Conclusion: Judges must not enforce a statute they consider to be contrary to a provision of the Constitution. They must declare it null and void.

Many have attacked Marshall's reasoning. But few can deny Marshall's assumption of power and status for the Supreme Court, the most powerful and independent court in the world.

Later, the Court assumed the same power over state laws. The power of judicial review is rarely used over actions of Congress and the President, e. g., from 1789 to 1960, only 73 acts of Congress were judged unconstitutional by the Court. However, in the same time span hundreds of state laws have been so declared. The only effective way to cancel out the Supreme Court's ruling that a law is unconstitutional is to pass a constitutional amendment overturning the decision pursuant to the terms of Article V. However, the task is arduous—only a handful of proposed amendments has ever been ratified.

Among the reasons for the Court's reluctance to use the power of judicial review are: (1) it is not specifically granted to the Court in the Constitution; (2) the Court needs public support to function; (3) the Justices don't wish to upset the delicate governmental balance (as nearly happened in the 1930s); and (4) of the three branches of government, the Court is the most remote from the people. In reality, it is the least democratic.

The Supreme Court makes decisions on the basis of majority vote, but the dissenting opinions are important in pointing out issues of law and public policy that should be explored further. In many instances, today's dissenting opinions turn out to be tomorrow's majority decisions.

When it overrules a lower court, the Supreme Court will often "vacate" the lower court decision and "remand" the case back to the trial court for proceedings "not inconsistent" with its decision. If a state court were to ignore the Supreme Court and decide again the same way, the alternatives open to the Court are few, given its lack of enforcement power. Ultimately, the Justices depend upon the enforcement power of the President to deal with defiance of their rulings.

The routes to the Supreme Court are complex.   (Figure 2–2).

Figure 2–2.   Interrelationships between Federal and State Courts

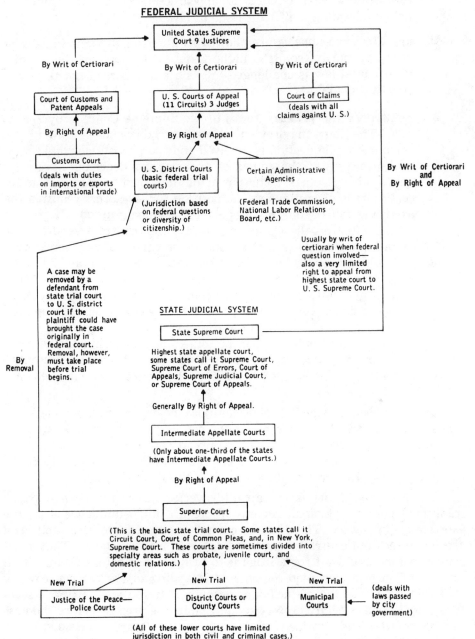

Source: William T. Schantz, *The American Legal Environment* (St. Paul, Minn.: West Publishing Co., 1976), p. 141.

[B3053]

Generally, the Supreme Court hears appellate cases coming to it in the following manner (cases arising under the Court's original jurisdiction are too few to warrant discussion here):

1. **certificate:** federal courts of appeal (rarely) ask the Court for help on deciding a difficult issue of law.

2. **appeal:** some appeals are allowed as a matter of right in selected cases, primarily from the highest state courts where the validity of a federal law is challenged or a state law is held not to be unconstitutional.

3. **certiorari:** the primary route to the Supreme Court is by *certiorari.* The Court may review on *certiorari* decisions of state courts when a federal question is involved and there exists no right of appeal, decisions of the courts of appeals, and decisions of several quasi-judicial courts. The power of the Court to issue grants of *certiorari* is discretionary. A petition for *certiorari* requires the assenting vote of four Justices before it can be granted. If granted —and few are—the Court directs a lower court to send up the record in a given case because one of the parties alleges some error in the lower court's handling of the case. (Note: some 3500 petitions may be filed in a year.) If the Court does agree to hear the case, it may issue a brief announcement of its decision in the form of an unsigned *per curiam* opinion * or write a lengthy opinion signed by one of the Justices after hearing oral argument. Frequently, signed opinions will be joined by concurring and dissenting opinions reflecting the views of the other Justices. Presently, some 90 percent of the cases before the Court come via the *certiorari* route.

The workload of the Supreme Court is heavy, a frequent criticism Chief Justice Burger has made about the country's entire judicial system, state and federal. The Court itself hears relatively few of the many cases coming before it and each year renders full opinions in about 140 cases. Approximately two-thirds of these are civil, the rest criminal.

The Supreme Court is not an all-powerful institution even with its traditional power of judicial review; there are important checks on the exercise of its power. The Justices cannot go into the political and legal arena and seek out controversies that happen to interest them. They must remain passive and wait for a litigant to bring a case before them. Such technical Court-derived requirements as "standing to sue" (a controversy entertained because the plaintiff has actually suffered an injury or an infringement upon a legally protected right) must be present before the case can be heard. The President must enforce the Court's decisions—they are not self-enforcing. Congress can alter the appellate jurisdiction of the

* There is considerable criticism of the Court's resort to *per curiam* decisions. For example, when the Court issues summary affirmance of a lower court decision, it affirms the judgment only, not necessarily the reasoning by which it was reached. In fact, where several different issues are involved and different views expressed, it is often unclear what part of the lower court's judgment is being affirmed. For a critical comment on summary action by the Supreme Court, see Note, "Supreme Court Per Curiam Practice: A Critique," 69 *Harvard L.Rev.* 707 (1956).

Court under the Constitution. Congress may refuse to appropriate funds that may be necessary for effective enforcement of a Supreme Court decision. Congress can propose a constitutional amendment to overturn the Court's use of judicial review. Public opinion may influence future Supreme Court appointments. Even though the Supreme Court does not follow the election returns directly, it is not unaware of sustained public sentiment on a particular issue. In short, the Supreme Court of the United States does not operate in a vacuum.

Given its extensive power and the many checks on its power, it is not surprising that members and analysts of the Court will proffer a variety of strategies and value positions on how the Court should exercise its power properly and communicate its reasoning and arguments to the outside world most effectively. The history of the Supreme Court provides countless examples to support Justice Holmes' famous remark: "We are very quiet here, but it is the quiet of a storm center, as we all know."[3]

C. The Continuing Debate Over Judicial Power

For over a century and a half, it has been debated whether or not the Supreme Court should exercise the power of judicial review and circumscribe the activities of popularly elected officials.[4] This debate assumes that there is an automatic dichotomy between an elitist Supreme Court—nine persons selected for life, who are unaccountable to the public—and public officials, who are representatives of the people, and popularly elected. Our political culture seems to thrive on this tension between the guardians of our legal rights and the representatives of our changing interests. Archibald Cox once posed the question in the following manner: "Should the Court play an active, creative role in shaping our destiny, equally with the executive and legislative branches? Or should it be characterized by self-restraint, deferring to the legislative branch whenever there is room for policy judgment and leaving new departures to the initiative of others? "[5]

The long-standing debate on judicial power and action has defined three discrete approaches to judicial decision-making that still claim many contemporary advocates: the judicial neutralists, the judicial activists, and the judicial self-restraintists. Since these three interpretations of the role of the Supreme Court Justice, and judging in general, are crucial to understanding judicial influence in resolving student rights disputes, they will be reviewed here.

(1) The Judicial Neutralists

The blindfolded Greek goddess of justice holding scales symbolizes the venerable notion of the judge as an objective and passionless vehicle for the application of the laws to the particular facts of a case. The judge

3. Oliver W. Holmes, "Law and the Court," in *The Occasional Speeches of Justice Oliver Wendell Holmes*, Mark Wolfe Howe, Ed. (Cambridge: The Belknap Press of Harvard University Press, 1962), at p. 168.

4. See, for example, Howard E. Dean, *Judicial Review and Democracy* (New York: Random House, 1966) for an analysis and evaluation of the argument that judicial review is undemocratic.

5. Archibald Cox, *The Warren Court* (Cambridge, Mass.: Harvard University Press, 1968), at p. 2.

finds the law; he or she does not make it. Morris Cohen once referred to this approach as the "phonograph theory of the judicial function", [6] which assumes that the judge is simply an oral repetition of the word of the law (or the Constitution, or the legal culture) that has been recorded into him. This mechanical image of the purely objective, passionless, and logical judge assumes the law to be a coherent system of definite, consistent rules that are readily obtainable and can be easily expressed in a clear decision.

Supreme Court Justice Owen Roberts, a leading proponent of the neutralist approach, sat on the Court during the tempestuous days of the 1930s New Deal. He explained his approach to deciding whether or not laws are constitutional in these terms:

> When an act of Congress is appropriately challenged in the courts as not conforming to the constitutional mandate, the judicial branch of the government has only one duty: to lay the article of the Constitution which is invoked beside the statute which is challenged and to decide whether the latter squares with the former. All that the Court does or can do, is to announce its considered judgment upon the question. The only power it has, if such it may be called, is the power of judgment.[7]

This approach to the judicial function appears to give the Supreme Court a modest role in the judicial process. But it fails to explain how a judge faced with a constitutional issue is to proceed in the face of uncertainty. For example, does "reverse discrimination" admissions criteria at public educational institutions *violate* the equal protection of the laws or serve as one means to *provide* equal protection of the laws?

One recent commentator on the role of the judiciary believes that when in doubt, Supreme Court Justices should always prefer the values of the Framers of the Constitution over their own. Raoul Berger, in defending the "look-it-up-in-the-library" approach to judicial decision making, states,

> * * * if it is not rooted in the Constitution, "it is not a constitutional principle and the Court has no business imposing it."
> * * * Our system is committed to "Equal Justice *Under* Law," not to "Justice Above the Law." They were not authorized to revise the Constitution in the interests of "justice." [8]   (Emphasis in original.)

The amendment process outlined in Article V of the Constitution, according to Berger's thinking, is sufficient for updating the Constitution to modern times. The formulators of judicial neutralism vigorously defend the notion that law is apart from and above the petty clashes of politics. Judges have a special obligation to act against other organs of government when principles of justice are violated. The most important issue for the neutralists is not whether courts should involve themselves in major contested issues of public concern, but what *rationale* for their actions is

---

6. Morris Cohen, *Law and Social Order* (New York: Harcourt, Brace, 1933), at p. 113.

7. *U. S. v. Butler*, 297 U.S. 1 (1936), at pp. 62–63.

8. Raoul Berger, *Government by Judiciary* (Cambridge, Mass.: Harvard University Press, 1977), at pp. 285 and 289.

legally and logically consistent. They argue that the prestige and authority of courts, especially the Supreme Court, are enhanced to the degree that the public believes that decisions are reached by the consistent application of fundamental and eternal principles.

(2) The Judicial Activists

The "activist" judge views the court as a dynamic political force for resolving contemporary issues. There are a number of variations on the activist theme, depending largely on the ideology of the judge, i. e., liberal, conservative, or radical. Early in the 20th century, *conservative* activists dominated the federal judiciary and consistently preferred *economic freedom* of individuals and private corporations over state social regulation. Recently, *liberal* activists have been more prevalent, requiring the government to show a compelling reason for restricting individual *political and social rights* under the Bill of Rights. Whether conservative or liberal, the "activist" judge has a particular role orientation, according to Murphy and Pritchett:

> The activist judge may be described as goal-oriented. His interest in achieving the "right" result in the controversies that come before him is stronger than his interest in the process by which the court arrives at the result. His tests for the rightness of a decision are whether it is politically and morally acceptable and whether its effects will be beneficial to society. Since he views law as one form of social control, he will be more creative in developing new legal doctrines to support his conclusions about public policy and more willing to overrule precedents that stand in the way of desired results. He is less hesitant to challenge the political branches and less fearful of becoming involved in controversy.[9]

The activists see their role as guarding the American political conscience, protecting basic values against the occasional onslaught of popularly elected representatives or even the people themselves. Justice Hugo Black has expressed these sentiments:

> * * * when judges have a constitutional question in a case before them, and the public interest calls for its decision, refusal to carry out their duty to decide would not, I think, be the excuse of an enviable "self-restraint." Instead I would consider it to be an evasion of responsibility. * * * In such circumstances I think "judicial self-restraint" is not a virtue but an evil.[10]

Finally, the activist judge does not view himself as a prisoner of previous precedent. *Stare decisis*—the rule of precedent—does provide some "moorings" for the judge; it serves to take the capriciousness out of the law and to give some stability to society. However, *stare decisis* should not let the Constitution freeze in the pattern that one generation may give

9. Walter F. Murphy and C. Herman Pritchett, *Courts, Judges and Politics* Second Ed. (N.Y.: Random House, 1974), at p. 31.

10. Hugo Black, *A Constitutional Faith* (N. Y.: Knopf, 1969), at p. 20.

to it. Justice William O. Douglas expressed the activist approach to *stare decisis* and precedent when he stated:

> The decisions of yesterday or of the last century are only the starting points. * * * A judge looking at a constitutional decision may have compulsions to revere the past history and accept what was once written. But he remembers above all else that it is the Constitution which he swore to support and defend, not the gloss which his predecessors may have put on it. So he comes to formulate his own views, rejecting some earlier ones as false and embracing others. He cannot do otherwise unless he lets men long dead and unaware of the problems of the age in which he lives do his thinking for him.[11]

The activist judge, then, assumes a profound obligation to be a creative interpreter and adaptor of constitutional principles to the pressing problems of our times.

(3) The Judicial Self-Restraintists

The history of the Supreme Court is replete with frontal attacks on judicial activism and its expansive use of judicial review, with the most serious criticisms coming from the advocates of "judicial self-restraint." These critics recommend judicial modesty and deference to the legislative and executive policy-makers, who are elected by the people. The classic formulation of this particular approach was developed by Professor James Bradley Thayer during his many influential years at Harvard Law School. Thayer argued that judicial review is contrary to the representative form of government; it deprives the people and their representatives of the right to develop legislation that meets the specific requirements of a complex society. "Under no system can the power of courts go far to save a people from ruin; our chief protection lies elsewhere * * *."[12] The Courts should operate under a rule of self-restraint, urged Thayer. "An Act of the legislature is not to be declared void unless the violation of the constitution is so manifest as to leave no room for reasonable doubt."[13] A statute can be declared unconstitutional only when those who have the right to make laws have not merely made a mistake, but have made a very clear one—so clear that it is not open to rational question.

Many advocates of judicial self-restraint view the Supreme Court as the non-democratic organ of our government, adding that the powers exercised by this Court are inherently oligarchic or elitist. Justice Felix Frankfurter argued this position forcefully when he claimed that members of the Court should not strike down legislation they consider to be unwise. The wisdom of a statute is a matter for legislators to debate and decide; they are the elected representatives of the people. In his concurring opinion in *Dennis v. U. S.*, Justice Frankfurter asserted:

> Free-speech cases are not an exception to the principle that we are not legislators, that direct policy-making is not our province. How best to reconcile competing interests is the business of legislatures,

11. William O. Douglas, "Stare Decisis", *The Record*, N.Y.C.Bar Assoc., April 1949, at pp. 153–154.

12. Cited in Howard E. Dean, *Judicial Review and Democracy*, *supra*, at p. 112.

13. *Id.*, at p. 113.

and the balance they strike is a judgment not to be displaced by ours, but to be respected unless outside the pale of fair judgment.[14]

To Frankfurter, courts are not representative bodies and they are poorly designed to be a good reflection of the complexities of a society or of its democratic procedures. Moreover, he strongly felt that they seriously jeopardize their independence when they become embroiled in the passions of the day and assume responsibility for choosing between competing political, economic, and social pressures. Although Frankfurter was not quite as emphatic as Thayer, he would "set aside the judgment of those whose duty it is to legislate only if there is no reasonable basis for it." [15] When the Justices reject judicial self-restraint, efforts to attack and weaken the Court invariably arise.

Total commitment to judicial self-restraint would prevent courts from becoming involved with major social issues. Justice Frankfurter was consistent with this position when he authored the Supreme Court opinion upholding the compulsory classroom flag salute against the objections of Jehovah's Witnesses, who consider the flag a "graven image" in terms of Exodus XX, 4:

> Perhaps it is best   *   *   *   to give the least popular sect leave from conformities like those here in issue. But the courtroom is not the arena for debating issues of educational policy.   *   *   * So to hold would in effect make us the school board for the country. That authority has not been given to this Court, nor should we assume it.[16]

Although the Frankfurter opinion was overturned two years later, it raises a serious question about the doctrine of judicial self-restraint: should the classroom and the educational environment be immune from judicial scrutiny?

D. Implications for Student Rights Decision Making

It may be appropriate at this point to insert a word of caution about labelling. We may find judges and educators with the same value orientation to the nature of individual rights coming to opposite conclusions about the resolution of a rights dispute. For example, a liberal judge may agree with a liberal educator that it is desirable to eradicate inter-district differences in public school financing but may not take advantage of an opportunity to do so because of a belief that the matter should be decided by the legislature, not the judiciary. Such a self-restraintist approach is reflective of the judge's view of the judicial function. In this way, different professional orientations can separate persons with similar ideologies. The commitment of educators and judges to their respective professions may stand in the way of cooperative action in resolving disputes over the rights of students.

Until recently, judicial self-restraint was the dominant approach to educational matters involving the rights of students and teachers. Judges

14. 341 U.S. 494 (1951), at pp. 539–540.

15. *Id.*, at p. 525.

16. *Minersville School Dist. v. Gobitis*, 310 U.S. 586 (1940), at p. 598.

believed that the courtroom was an inappropriate place for resolving disputes occurring within the educational institution. Since state legislatures establish and control educational institutions through a variety of state-level and local agencies, schools were considered a legislative, not judicial, responsibility. Further contributing to judicial reluctance was the prevailing view that students simply had no constitutional rights. At home, students were controlled by their parents and at school they were controlled by educational authorities. Only if that control were exercised unreasonably would courts reluctantly intervene.

This judicial self-restraint still colors the views of many judges, e. g., four Justices of the Supreme Court dissented in the 1975 landmark case, *Goss v. Lopez*, arguing that the Court has no business involving itself in due process disputes over school discipline, a matter they asserted should be left to state legislators and school officials. Whether liberal or conservative, judicial self-restraintists consider the proper role of courts to be the overriding consideration. Thus, even though a judge may prefer a particular desired result, he or she may very well rule against mandating it because the U. S. Constitution does not require it, or because it is not the proper role of the court to do so.

But judges have not always hesitated to involve themselves in educational disputes. One of the earliest and most significant Supreme Court decisions, *Pierce v. Society of the Sisters of the Holy Names of Jesus and Mary*, a 1925 case reviewed later in this chapter, is representative of judicial activism. There, a conservative Court overruled the efforts of a state legislature to require all students to attend public schools. The Court maintained such a requirement worked against the interests of private school operators to exercise their constitutional property rights. More recently, judicial activism has been exercised on behalf of liberal values. In 1969 the Supreme Court extended rights of free expression to students within the public schools in *Tinker v. Des Moines School Dist.* This decision was part of the liberal activist record of the Warren Court (Chief Justice Earl Warren served from 1953 to 1969).

Because activist judges can be either liberal or conservative, many prefer courts to practice self-restraint or judicial neutralism so as not to undermine consistency in the law, leaving policy formulation to legislatures and school boards. Yet, critics of the restraintist approach point out that it prevents judges from living up to their responsibility to say what the Constitution means and what the law is. By default they end up approving repressive practices. Critics of judicial neutralism believe judging from this approach places more emphasis on procedure than results, thereby shielding judges from wrestling with the really complex issues. It should be obvious that none of the approaches provides the perfect solution to the dilemma of judicial functioning: to uphold the Constitution and the Bill of Rights, and at the same time, to maintain the separation of powers of government and public support for the judiciary.

Beginning with the appointment of Chief Justice Warren Burger in 1969, the Supreme Court became more middle-of-the-road in its approach. While a few liberal activist Justices continue to serve on the Court, the majority appear to be conservative in their orientation to individual freedom and lean toward judicial self-restraint. Nevertheless, several significant gains in student rights were realized by decisions of the Burger Court.

Since the Justices, including the Chief Justice, are appointed by the President with the advice and consent of the Senate, a change in personnel can have significant effects on the ideological approach of the entire Court. The same is true of the lower federal courts.

II. THE BILL OF RIGHTS AND THE FOURTEENTH AMENDMENT

The discussion so far has centered on the character of the judiciary in general, with special focus on the role of the U. S. Supreme Court. Before turning to an examination of judicial involvement in the development of educational institutions, the primary constitutional sources of civil liberties will be reviewed. We begin by noting a critical feature of the American system of government: the clear distinction between public and private sectors.

A. The Public-Private Dichotomy

The first eight amendments * to the United States Constitution convey rights which only the *federal* government cannot invade. In the early case of *Barron v. Baltimore*, 32 U.S. (7 Peters) 243 (1833), Chief Justice John Marshall said, "Had the framers of these amendments intended them to be limitations on the powers of the state governments, they would have imitated the framers of the original Constitution, and have expressed that intention." (At p. 250). Thus, under the original Bill of Rights, state governments and private citizens conceivably can violate the specific personal liberties guaranteed therein with impunity. In *Barron* the private owner of a wharf could not recover damages when Baltimore city officials diverted a stream and thereby rendered the wharf useless.

The Ninth Amendment to the United States Constitution, which states, "The enumeration in the Constitution, of certain rights, shall not be construed to deny or disparage others retained by the people," has rarely been used by the Supreme Court. And the Tenth Amendment specifically illustrates the principle of federalism by stating that the powers which are not delegated to the central government are reserved to the states, unless the Constitution specifically prohibits the states from exercising a particular power.

However, the Fourteenth Amendment, which was added along with the Thirteenth and Fifteenth Amendments in the post-Civil War period, pertains directly to actions by *state governments*. Since states and local governments are responsible for the establishment and operation of public schools, the terms of the Fourteenth Amendment are particularly important. Not only are the rights of students intimately related to the terms of the Fourteenth Amendment, so too are the property rights of those who establish and operate nonpublic educational institutions. Its provisions are broader than the Thirteenth and the Fifteenth. The Thirteenth Amendment specifically prohibits slavery and involuntary servitude

---

* We suggest the reader review the provisions of the Bill of Rights and the post-   Civil War Amendments in Appendix C in conjunction with reading this section.

from existing in the United States, while the Fifteenth restricts both the central government and the state governments from denying voting rights to citizens of the United States on the basis of race, color, or previous condition of servitude. The last section of each of the post-Civil War Amendments shows that Congress has the power to enforce their terms by enacting appropriate legislation. Many of our modern federal civil rights laws are based on this broad power of enforcement.

Section I is the heart of the Fourteenth Amendment, and is stated in much more sweeping terminology than either the Thirteenth or Fifteenth. It contains three important clauses which restrict state governments from infringing on individual liberty: "No state shall make or enforce any law which shall abridge the privileges or immunities of citizens of the United States; nor shall any state deprive any person of life, liberty, or property, without due process of law; nor deny to any person within its jurisdiction the equal protection of the laws."

It is also significant that the Fourteenth Amendment's prohibitions are directed at *states*. The word "state" encompasses state *officials* as well as units of government. Local governmental units and officers are also included, since they draw their power from the Tenth Amendment reserved powers of states. *For the Fourteenth Amendment to apply to a given situation, then, there must be some evidence of state or local governmental involvement. This requirement has come to be known as "state action." The coming chapters will be most concerned with the Fourteenth Amendment because public educational institutions are maintained either at the local or state level and school officials are considered "state agents."*

Since the Fourteenth Amendment does not apply specifically to private individuals, the actions of private individuals are not covered. This point was clarified in the *Civil Rights Cases*, 109 U.S. 3 (1883), involving racial discrimination by private organizations when Justice Bradley said, " * * it is proper to state that civil rights, such as are guaranteed by the Constitution against State aggression, cannot be impaired by the wrongful acts of individuals, unsupported by State authority in the shape of laws, customs, or judicial or executive proceedings." (At p. 17). Since the Court has ruled that the Constitution generally does not protect a citizen whose legal rights are violated by other citizens, the only recourse would be to sue them under federal or state law. However, if no laws have been passed enabling such suits to be brought, the chances of relief from the courts are limited. Indeed, this was the situation during the Reconstruction period in the South when there were no specific state laws designed to protect the civil rights of blacks from state, much less private, discrimination.

It is important to note, however, that a strict separation of the public from the private sector has not always been maintained. In some situations, the Supreme Court has been inclined to imply "state action" as required by the Fourteenth Amendment, even where the state was only indirectly involved. For example, in *Shelley v. Kraemer*, 334 U.S. 1 (1948), the Supreme Court ruled that state enforcement of agreements among property owners to prevent persons of a certain race from buying houses violated the Fourteenth Amendment's Equal Protection Clause. In a few situations, the Court has even gone so far as to rule that what appears to be *wholly* private action is really public and thus covered by the terms of the Fourteenth Amendment. A prime example is *Marsh v. Alabama*, 326 U.S. 501 (1946), where the Court held that when a company-maintained town has the same characteristics as a public city or town, it is covered by the terms of the Fourteenth Amendment. In this case, company officials were considered the functional equivalents of public officials, and the Court ruled that as such, they, like their public counterparts, could not prevent Jehovah's Witnesses from exercising their religious freedoms within the town. This trend reached its apex in *Amalgamated Food Employees Union Local 590 v. Logan Valley Plaza, Inc.*, 391 U.S. 308 (1968), when the Court extended the same principle to peaceful labor picketing in the driveways and parking areas of private shopping centers.

Beginning in 1972, the Court began to draw back, apparently fearing total emasculation of the private sector. In *Lloyd Corp., Ltd. v. Tanner*, 407 U.S. 551 (1972), Justice Powell for the majority expressed grave concern that the trend of considering some types of private property to be the equivalent of the public sector could very well result in a deprivation of private property rights. The 1972 case involved the arrest of persons who were peacefully distributing anti-draft Vietnam leaflets inside a private shopping mall in Portland, Oregon, for trespassing on private property. Said Justice Powell:

> * * * it must be remembered that the [Fourteenth Amendment] * * * safeguard(s) the rights of free speech and assembly by limitations on *State* action, not on action by the owner of private property used nondiscriminatorily for private purposes only. The Due Process Clauses of the Fifth and Fourteenth Amendments are also relevant to this case. They provide that "no person shall * * * be deprived of life, liberty, or property, without due process of law." There is the further proscription in the Fifth Amendment against the taking of "private property * * * for public use, without just compensation. * * * "
>
>   * * *
>
> * * * property [does not] lose its private character merely because the public is generally invited to use it for designated purposes. * * * The essentially private character of a store and its privately owned abutting property does not change by virtue of being large or clustered with other stores in a modern shopping center. (At pp. 567 and 569; emphasis in original, material in brackets added).

In the Spring of 1976, in the case of *Hudgens v. NLRB*, 424 U.S. 507 (1976), the Supreme Court consolidated this reversal of views by overruling its decision in the 1968 *Logan Valley* case. Thus, except for the area of racial discrimination, the Fourteenth Amendment is limited to action by state and local governments and their agents, and does not cover invasions of civil rights by private persons or organizations, including nonpublic educational institutions.

B. What Rights Does the Fourteenth Amendment Protect from Hostile State Action?

As already noted, the first section of the Fourteenth Amendment has three essential provisions: the "privileges or immunities" clause; the "deprivation of life, liberty, or property without due process" clause; and the clause guaranteeing "equal protection of the laws." The last section of the Fourteenth Amendment enables Congress to enact statutes to enforce the terms of the amendment. This fifth section in itself is significant, since it represents a reversal of views about the function of state and federal governments in the area of civil rights. Up to this time, state governments were considered to be protectors of citizens against hostile action by the central government. It was they who insisted upon the addition of the first ten Amendments to the Constitution as a condition for ratifying the document. Now, the roles are reversed. The central government has become the friend of the individual, protecting her against hostile action by state and local governments.

It is from these three provisions that the rights of individuals to protection from hostile state action have been deprived. How the Supreme Court interprets these clauses, not only for the citizen in society in general but also for the student in the educational world, will be investigated in the pages and chapters which follow.

The first of the three clauses, the "privileges or immunities" clause, was relegated to secondary importance by *The Slaughterhouse Cases*, 83 U.S. (16 Wallace) 36 (1873), where, in a complex opinion, the Court chose a narrow interpretation. In effect, this case and a later case, *Maxwell v. Dow*, 176 U.S. 581 (1900), established quite clearly that the provisions of the first eight amendments of the Bill of Rights were not incorporated into the "privileges or immunities" clause and did not apply to the states. Thus, the clause does not protect individuals from hostile state action related to the kinds of rights and liberties contained in the federal Bill of Rights, i. e., freedom of speech, right to be free from unreasonable searches and seizures, and so on. Essentially, this relatively narrow interpretation has continued to the present day.

With the "privileges or immunities" clause relegated to secondary importance, the deprivation of "life, liberty, or property without due process" clause assumes greater significance. (A discussion of the Equal Protection Clause is deferred). Was the wording of the Due Process Clause meant to carry over *all* of the specific Bill of Rights freedoms to protect persons from hostile state actions? There have traditionally been two views on this question. The first suggested that the provisions of the entire Bill of Rights were meant by the framers of the Fourteenth Amendment to apply automatically to the states. This "incorporation view" was most ardently supported by Justice Hugo Black. However, Justice Black's view was never adopted by a majority on the Supreme Court.

The alternative "independent view" was the one the Court subsequently endorsed. Rather than incorporating the provisions of the Bill of Rights, the Fourteenth Amendment was determined by the Supreme Court to be independent of them. But, in fact, as time has gone on, most of the specific freedoms and protections in the Bill of Rights have been "absorbed" through the Fourteenth Amendment to apply to the states. Therefore, *it is important to remember that when we discuss our "First Amendment rights" in the state setting, we are really saying "our First Amendment rights as applied to the states and their subdivisions through the first section of the Fourteenth Amendment."*

Our primary concern in this book will be: what is the meaning of deprivation of "life, liberty, or property without due process" and "equal protection of the laws" when applied to real-life situations?

III. COURTS AND THE ESTABLISHMENT OF EDUCATIONAL INSTITUTIONS

A. The Establishment and Operation of Schools

The U. S. Constitution does not specifically delegate the power to set up schools to the federal government. In fact, the Constitution nowhere mentions the word "education." Therefore, under our federal system of government, control over education is a matter for the states under the so-called "reserved" powers of the Tenth Amendment.

Governments throughout history have utilized educational institutions as socialization devices. When public schooling and compulsory attendance laws were widely adopted in 19th-century America, the rationale was that the public school provided the best means to socialize the disparate ethnic groups comprising the country and to provide everyone with an equal means to advance economically.

Private schools, once the dominant mode of elementary and secondary schooling, became alternatives to public schools for those who could afford them and provided specialized services that the public schools were not able to offer, such as concentrated college preparation or religious instruction. Statistically, the private share of the nation's elementary and secondary enrollment dropped quickly to roughly 10 percent at the turn of the century and has not deviated very much from that figure since.

State constitutions often indicate that the legislature has the power and responsibility to develop public education, and legislatures have typically responded by establishing elaborate sets of education laws or "codes." Most legislatures, however, leave the implementation of broad state policy on education to state and local administrative agencies.

One feature of all state-controlled schooling systems is that part of public education is compulsory. The first state to pass a compulsory school law was Massachusettes in 1852. By 1918 all states had such laws. At a given age, public schooling becomes voluntary, usually between the ages of 16 and 18, although states and localities continue to recognize the public benefits of formal education by subsidizing postsecondary education. Thus, it is still considerably less expensive to attend a state college or university than a private one.

At about the same time the public school movement blossomed, the great land-grant universities were developed. As more and more students aspired to a college education, the public sector of higher education grew, particularly after World War II. By the 1970s, three-fourths of all students and two-thirds of all faculty were in public institutions. Today, over half the high school population continues on to college.

(1) Who Controls School Operation?

The primary role of the state in the operation of elementary and secondary schools is to develop broad policy guidelines through legislation and through the activities of the state board of education and the state office of education, whose head is the superintendent of public instruction. Members of state boards are usually appointed by the governor, and superintendents of public instruction are usually appointed either by the governor or the state board. However, in about ten states, members of the state board are popularly elected, and in double that number, the superintendent is chosen by popular vote. Thus, politics plays an important role in the operation of many public educational institutions.

Public elementary and secondary schools are primarily funded and operated at the local level. The "neighborhood school" is a tradition in American life, even though differences in local tax bases may produce great inequality in school finance. These differences, as Chapter Seven illustrates, have furnished the grounds for recent suits based on the Equal Protection Clause of the Fourteenth Amendment. With the exception of Hawaii, each state is divided into numerous school districts, each with its own board of education, or "school board," which oversees school operation. Presently there are about 16,000 school districts in the country. Members of these school boards are usually elected and thus reflect the wishes, values, and norms of their constituencies.

Four-year and graduate institutions, and increasingly community colleges as well, are funded and frequently controlled exclusively at the state level. The inclusion of public postsecondary institutions in state-wide "systems" of education is increasingly characteristic of higher education, but private institutions have not entirely avoided regulation. Many states have developed centralized "coordinating" agencies which regulate both public and private postsecondary institutions in light of financial and market conditions. Not surprisingly, this trend toward centralization has resulted in great tension as local communities, and particularly college administrators and faculty, perceive an erosion of institutional autonomy.

Aside from these centralized administrative agencies in higher education, most state boards and offices of public education are confined to record-keeping, data dissemination, and policy formulation over such issues as compulsory attendance, certification of teachers, building and equipment standards, and graduation requirements. Curriculum decision-making has usually been left to local districts, except where states have mandated the teaching of specific courses such as American or state history, driver education, the dangers of alcohol and drugs, and physical education. To some extent, state laws and policy regulations also set forth guidelines for pupil and faculty discipline, although many of these matters are also under the control of the local districts.

Some states, notably California and New York, have begun to assert more and more control through both the legislature and the state board of education, and its administrative arm, the state office of education. States are also becoming increasingly involved in supplementing local financing of schools to eliminate inter-district inequities and, particularly in postsecondary education, in approving or disapproving new academic programs. A contributing factor to centralization has been the growth of powerful teacher unions in many states. Over a quarter of the nation's school districts and over 20 percent of higher education institutions are now unionized.

(2) Points of Tension

The present structure and operation of the American educational system contain numerous built-in points of potential conflict. Public institutions are established by the state but still largely operated and financed at the local level. Partisan politics play a role at all levels of school operation. There are tensions within a given community as to the purposes and functioning of educational institutions, tensions between students and educational officials, tensions between the general public and the professionals who work in schools, tensions between local and state bureaucracies, tensions between faculty unions and school authorities, and tensions between public and private institutions.

Even the federal government, which contributes less than 10 percent of school funding and can only influence schools indirectly, has come to play a large and controversial role in education by providing federal aid for specific purposes. The "strings" attached to these federal dollars frequently constitute a source of tension. For example, in *Lau v. Nichols*, 414 U.S. 563 (1974), the U. S. Supreme Court agreed that officials of the San Francisco School District had violated HEW guidelines prohibiting discrimination in federally-assisted school systems by not providing Chinese students with instruction in the English language. The federal agency had developed the regulations as part of its responsibility to enforce federal civil rights laws. Said Justice Douglas for the Court, "The Federal Government has power to fix the terms on which its money allotments to the States shall be disbursed." (At p. 569). One wonders if the outcome would have been the same in the absence of the statute.

These tensions have led to court challenges on numerous occasions. There has always been an uneasy balance between the general academic and socialization functions of educational institutions on the one hand, and the needs and interests of individuals within those institutions on the other. There have been several prominent periods within our legal history when the courts were especially active in adjudicating educational disputes. This book will focus on two: the first coinciding with the development of public schools, and the second beginning with the civil rights movement in the 1950s. The latter reached a level of intensity in the late 1960s which has not abated. Most of the legal developments involving students and teachers in the public sector have occurred primarily within the past 20 years. Thus, the whole subject of student constitutional rights is of comparatively recent origin.

B.   The Right of the State to Set Up Public Schools

Courts have long recognized the power of states and their subdivisions to establish schools for academic and socialization purposes. For example, in the early 1870s, taxpayers in Kalamazoo, Michigan, filed suit against the collection of taxes assessed against them for support of the local high school.[17] By majority vote the people of Kalamazoo had agreed to support such an institution. The Supreme Court of Michigan recognized the broader implications in the case, noting that "the real purpose of the suit * * * seeks a judicial determination of the right of school authorities * * * to levy taxes upon the general public for support of what in this state are known as high schools, and to make free by such taxation the instruction of children in other languages than the English." (At pp. 70–71). The plaintiffs believed that high schools should not be supported by the general public but only by those who wished to attend them because the benefits of such education accrue primarily to the students. After a careful review of state constitutional and legislative history, the court concluded "We content ourselves with the statement that neither in our state policy, in our constitution, or in our laws, do we find the primary school districts restricted in the branches of knowledge which their officers may cause to be taught, or the grade of instruction that may be given, if their voters consent in regular form to bear the expense and raise the taxes for the purpose." (At pp. 84–85). The court noted a state policy to provide free schools in which education, including "the elements of classical education," could be extended to all children of the state.

Similarly, courts have recognized the legality of compulsory attendance laws. One famous early case involved a demand that a New Hampshire school district furnish transportation to a nine-year-old boy living four miles from the school. In agreeing that this district had an obligation to provide at least some transportation during the school year, the New Hampshire Supreme Court commented: "Free schooling furnished by the state is not so much a right granted to pupils as a duty imposed upon them for the public good. If they do not voluntarily attend the school provided for them, they may be compelled to do so." *Fogg v. Board of Educ.*, 82 A. 173 (New Hampshire, 1912), at p. 175. In effect, this "duty" means that students have no choice but to attend school in the face of state-mandated school attendance.

As noted in the previous chapter, the state has great power to determine what rights young people have and the age at which they can enjoy them. No lesser authority than the U. S. Supreme Court has acknowledged the *parens patriae* power of government. In *Prince v. Commonwealth of Massachusetts*, 321 U.S. 158 (1944), the Court upheld a State law making it a crime for a girl under the age of 18 or boy under the age of 12 to sell newspapers in public places, even though the child involved claimed her religion made it her duty to do so, and was thus an activity protected under the Free Exercise of Religion Clause of the First Amendment. The child's mother supported her case, citing parental rights. In spite of the

17.   *Stuart v. School Dist. No. 1 of the Village of Kalamazoo*, 30 Mich. 69 (Michigan, 1874).

child's invoking of a specific constitutional right and the parent's assertion of a right to control the upbringing of the child, the Court ruled against the child and in favor of the law. Wrote Justice Rutledge for the majority:

> The state's authority over children's activities is broader than over like actions of adults. * * * A democratic society rests, for its continuance, upon the healthy, well-rounded growth of young people into full maturity as citizens, with all that implies. It may secure this against impeding restraints and dangers within a broad range of selection. Among evils most appropriate for such action are the crippling effects of child employment, more especially in public places, and the possible harms arising from other activities subject to all the diverse influences of the street. It is too late now to doubt that legislation appropriately designed to reach such evils is within the state's police power, whether against the parent's claim to control of the child or one that religious scruples dictate contrary action.

> It is true children have rights, in common with older people, in the primary use of highways. But even in such use streets afford dangers for them not affecting adults. And in other uses, whether in work or in other things, this difference may be magnified. This is so not only when children are unaccompanied but certainly to some extent when they are with their parents. What may be wholly permissible for adults therefore may not be so for children, either with or without their parents' presence. (At pp. 168–169).

Prince is important also because it clearly states that parental rights to control their children's lives are limited. Elsewhere in the opinion Justice Rutledge noted that:

> * * * the family itself is not beyond regulation in the public interest * * *. Acting to guard the general interest in youth's well being, the state as *parens patriae* may restrict the parent's control by requiring school attendance, regulating or prohibiting the child's labor and in many other ways. Its authority is not nullified merely because the parent grounds his claim to control the child's course of conduct on religion or conscience. (At p. 166).

It is important to note that states do make exceptions to compulsory school laws. For example, the choice of a comparable nonpublic school is preserved in all states by the *Pierce* case discussed in the next section. In addition, some states allow for private tutoring and education in the home. But even in these instances, the state continues to assert its interest in providing all children with a common school experience by stipulating the minimum standards these alternative educational modes must meet. A good example of the way courts handle non-constitutional challenges to state control is the following 1974 New York case.[18]

---

18. For a discussion of how to read court cases and develop outlines or "briefs" of their contents, consult Appendix A.

IN RE H.

Family Court, Yates County, 1974.
78 Misc.2d 412, 357 N.Y.S.2d 384.

FREDERICK D. DUGAN, Judge.

The three children of the respondents were enrolled for the school year 1972–73 in the Gorham-Middlesex Central School District where respondents and the children reside. The children were not enrolled for school in September, 1973 and none have attended upon instruction at that school during the year 1973–74.

Had they gone to school, John, age 12, would have attended sixth grade, Thomas, age 13, eighth grade and Robert, age 10, fifth grade.

The respondent parents contend that they are adequately instructing these children at home.

* * *

Part I, Article 65 of the New York State Education Law (Compulsory Education) provides that each minor, age 6 to 16, shall attend upon full time instruction.

It is the statutory duty of the parents to cause such minor to attend upon instruction as required under Part I, Article 65.

Where a minor is not attending upon instruction at a public or parochial school in the district where the parents reside, it is the duty of such parent to furnish proof that the minor is attending upon required instruction elsewhere. Failure to furnish such proof is presumptive evidence that the minor is not attending.

While the Family Court has jurisdiction to hear, try and determine charges of violation of the provisions of Part I of Article 65, contemplating penalties of fine and imprisonment, the petitions herein * * * (allege) each child is neglected in that he is not allowed to attend school in accord with Part I, Article 65 of the Education Law.

Under Article 10 of the Family Court Act, a neglected child is one less than eighteeen years of age whose physical, mental or emotional condition has been impaired or is in imminent danger of becoming impaired as a result of the failure of his parent to exercise a minimum degree of care in supplying the child with education in accordance with provisions of Part I of Article 65 of the Education Law.

The Compulsory Education provisions of Article 65 thus are incorporated by reference in Article 10 of the Family Court Act.

This Court holds that Article 65 establishes the statutory duty of the parent to cause such minor to attend upon full time instruction and that proof that a minor is not attending upon instruction at a school in the district where the parent resides is *prima facie* proof that such minor is a neglected child * * *.

The burden of then going forward with the proof shifts to the respondent-parents to overcome the presumption that the minor is not attending with proof that the minor is attending upon required instruction "elsewhere".

Ed.L. § 3204, subdivision 1, states that a minor "may attend at a public school or elsewhere". Subdivision 2 specifies that the instruction may be given only by a competent teacher and, if given elsewhere than at a public school, it shall be at least substantially equivalent to the instruction given to minors of like age and attainments at the public schools of the district where the minor resides.

Under Subd. 3, par. a(1) of Ed.L. § 3204, the course of study for the first eight years of full time public day school shall provide for instruction in at least the twelve common school branches of arithmetic, reading, spelling, writing, the

English language, geography, United States history, civics, hygiene, physical training, the history of New York State and science. The Department of Education Regulations require the same subjects with the addition of music and visual arts.

Under Ed.L. § 3204, subd. 4, par. a, a full time day school or class, except as otherwise prescribed, shall be in session for not less than 190 days each year, inclusive of legal holidays that occur during the term of said school and exclusive of Saturdays.

Here, respondent parents in carrying forward this burden of proof contend the instruction provided by them to these children at home satisfies the instructional requirements under Ed.L. § 3204.

* * *

In respondents' proof several references were made to "free school" and "alternate school" and the instruction given by respondents to these children was regularly referred to as "your school". However, no proof was offered or suggested that the instruction given by respondents had been registered under regulations of the Commissioner of Education as required for private schools * * *.

We turn now to assess the preponderance of competent, material and relevant evidence that these children are attending upon required instruction elsewhere.

The respondent-father holds two degrees, one an advanced degree in literature from a well known university. He has taught English and literature in at least three school systems and in 1974 received permanent certification by the State of New York to teach English, 7th through 12th grades. He once taught in the 6th grade. He has studied at six universities and colleges, and here states that he is a college teacher.

The mother, who has worked as a librarian, majored in English and science when she attended a small college in a nearby state for two years. She takes a substantial responsibility in the instruction of the children and keeps the record of attendance required under Ed.L. § 3211(1).

There are six children now living with the family. Janet, the eldest, is a senior attending the central school. Douglas, age 16, who does not attend school, is interested in mechanics and spends most of his time working on machinery at the family farm. Faye, the 15 year old sister, does not attend public school but receives instruction at home with the three younger brothers. She is not included in the instant application.

The family resides on a 100 acre farm in the Town of Middlesex. There are some 20 tillable acres, the balance being wooded. They keep about a dozen chickens and last year a cow was sold. There was testimony that corn might be planted on the tillable acreage.

The father left a teaching position on August 31, 1973 and now draws unemployment insurance. He testifies that he works 6 or 7 hours a day on the farm, representing 50% to 75% of the time. He hopes that someday the farm will be a source of substantial income, but at this point it is not the livelihood of the family.

He states that he is directly in contact with one or another of these children in excess of 5 or 6 hours a day. He testified that "on a formal basis the only thing I teach (the three children) is math. The rest of what we teach in our school is taken care of in our daily activities. * * * " He expresses a concept of education that the classroom should not be limited to 9 to 3, but should be a normal, natural day with instructions in a total environment by the example of adults who are themselves growing in some way. Apparently reflecting his training and experience, he hopes to start a school with an emphasis that would be environmental; real activities producing a living on a farm and being interested in things going on around us. With this in mind, he and his wife set up the instruction of these children. The father objects to the public school system and states, "schools can't touch creativity in our way".

Besides arithmetic, the father testified that he and his wife instruct the children in English language, reading together, writing plays and acting them out, writing newspapers and compositions.

Spelling and grammar are included in these projects. They talk about spelling and the parents read everything the children write. While the parents state that they discuss all of the children's work with them and review it, there is intentionally no attempt to mark or grade their work or performance.

Arithmetic is taught by the father through certain workbooks which were not presented as part of the exhibits herein or otherwise identified. In this regard, while the psychological evaluation of all three children by the Mental Health Clinic (copies of which were provided confidentially to the law guardian and both attorneys prior to the hearing) indicate that all three have above average intellectual ability and advanced reading skills, two of the children scored below grade level in arithmetic and one below grade level in spelling.

The academic skills and ability of these bright youngsters may reflect the professional teaching they received when they attended school more than the teaching efforts of their parents. The 1972–73 school records of the children stipulated in evidence show each to be an "A" student.

The testimony on science instruction indicates that the topics of animal husbandry, gardening, botany, zoology and astronomy are contemplated without detail on the material or the quality of the instruction involved.

United States history and the history of New York State are admittedly not "done too much with" except that they are talked about "when it comes up". One of the boys does have a keen interest in the Civil War.

Testifying on the content of geography instruction, the father advises that maps and atlases are available in the house and that they plan a lot of trips. The family has attended the planetarium, the library and the theater in Rochester and visited Central Park in New York City. It does not appear from the testimony that there is any systematic program to teach geography.

The family raises much of its own food and one of the boys is evidently interested in organic gardening. All three of the children know how to cook. The family involve themselves in playing football, volleyball, folk dancing and hiking. These interesting and pleasurable activities are presented as the curriculum in hygiene and physical training.

The testimony is that the children are learning to play the guitar and that they sing individually and with the family.

The father testified that "school" was held 5 days a week, and that the classroom was the total environment of the farm although it appears that some instruction was given in the living room of the dwelling, at least in the morning.

The mother described the daily schedule. After breakfast and chores inside and outside the home and normally at 9:00 A.M. the children meet for instruction. Some three mornings a week they have math instruction from their father lasting about an hour. Then they turn to something else; writing letters, listening to music or plays, or reading. The given project, according to the testimony, "grows naturally out of what our interests are at the time", such as planting seedlings for the garden or baking bread. The children apparently are involved in preparing lunch. There was no description of a typical afternoon's instruction or activity.

Magazines like ORGANIC GARDENING, PSYCHOLOGY TODAY and NATIONAL GEOGRAPHIC are available for the children in the home. Reading lists for each of the children bear out their advanced reading skills. The home library contains textbooks on geometry and algebra, botany, field guides, dictionaries, encyclopedias, atlases and anthologies of poetry and prose, gardening books, health and nutrition books, children's fiction, science fiction, a section of unidentified workbooks and books on religion, Indians, sociology, literature, music, art and an unidentified series of Time-Life books. During the five month period of September, 1973 to February, 1974, the mother testified that the children had made four or five trips to libraries in Canandaigua and Rochester and that they had use of a mobile library, but the frequency of its use was not specified.

The attendance record required under Ed.L. § 3211 and as kept by the mother, indicates that each of the children was "present" on apparently every school day from September 5, 1973 to February 27, 1974. There is no indication that any of the children were ever "absent", but the mother testified that she considered trips taken to Syracuse to be "school days" and marked the children as "present".

Attendance elsewhere than at a public school is provided for under Ed.L. § 3210(2). The hours of attendance shall be at least for as many hours and within the hours specified for the public school. Absences shall be permitted only for causes allowed by the general rules and practices of the public schools. Holidays and vacations shall not exceed in total amount and number those allowed by public schools.

Under Paragraph d, Ed.L. § 3210(2), a shorter school day or a shorter school year, or both, are authorized, but there is no proof here that the instruction given to these children has been approved by the school authorities as being substantially equivalent in amount and quality to that required under Part I, Article 65 of the Education Law.

Indeed, the instruction required under Ed.L. § 3204(2) elsewhere than at a public school must be at least substantially equivalent to the instruction given to minors of like age and attainments at public schools of the district where the minor resides. While the respondent parents may have the background and qualifications as competent teachers as evidenced by their familiarity with the fourteen branches of instruction covered in their testimony, their proof does not preponderantly show the home instruction here to be substantially equivalent to the instruction given at the district school in all fourteen branches.

Nor does the proof show their compliance with the 190 day length of school session under Ed.L. § 3204(4a) or the daily hours of attendance required under Ed.L. § 3210(2a).

The proof here shows a lack of consistent quality in subject instruction, if not an absence of instruction in some areas and it shows the absence of a systematic approach to the course of study of the branches specified in the statute and regulations. These instructions are not adequate and the program, viewed as a whole, constitutes an attempt to evade the Compulsory Education Law.

The Court makes a finding of fact that each of the respondents' children, Thomas, John and Robert, each being less than eighteen years of age, is a neglected child whose physical, mental or emotional condition has been impaired or is in imminent danger of becoming impaired as a result of the failure of the respondents and each of them to exercise a minimum degree of care in supplying the child with education in accordance with the provisions of Part I of Article 65 of the Education Law in that they, and each of them, failed to cause each child to attend upon instruction as required by law at the Gorham-Middlesex Central School where said respondents and children resided during the school year 1973–74 or to provide at least substantially equivalent instruction to them elsewhere.

An Order of Protection is entered herein that the respondents and each of them shall cause each said child to attend upon full time instruction at a public school in the district where they reside. The said respondents and each of them are placed under the supervision of the Yates County Probation Department for a period of eighteen months from the date hereof.

NOTES AND QUESTIONS

1. Do you agree with the decision in the case? Do you believe the education the parents were providing their children was the equivalent of that provided by the school? Review briefly the various conceptualizations in Chapter One about what schools should be doing; note that your answer largely depends upon which of the approaches you endorse. Which of the approaches does the judge endorse?

2. If the parents were able to show that the value of the public school in their district was zero, should the judge then overrule the compulsory education requirement? If the public school officials were unable to show that education in the home was any more or less effective than that offered in school, would this be enough to convince the judge that the compulsory education law is unreasonable? Where social science evidence is conflicting at best, what stance should courts take?

3. Parents are occasionally successful at challenging the authority exerted by school officials under the doctrine of *ultra vires,* i. e., actions beyond the express and implied powers granted to a corporation or agency such as the school board or administration. Examples of successful challenges of school officials for exceeding their statutory authority to prescribe rules pertaining to school operation include: the establishment of a dress code, *Alexander v. Thompson,* 313 F.Supp. 1389 (C.D.Cal.1970); punishing a student for possession of heroin off school grounds, *Howard v. Clark,* 299 N.Y.S.2d 65 (New York 1969); off-campus drinking, *Bunger v. Iowa High School Athletic Ass'n,* 197 N.W.2d 555 (Iowa, 1972); exclusion of a married student with a child from school, *Alvin Ind. School Dist. v. Cooper,* 404 S.W.2d 76 (Texas, 1966); and excessive or unfair punishments such as a reduction in grades for each day a student is suspended, *Dorsey v. Bale,* 521 S.W.2d 76 (Kentucky 1975).

In some of these situations, had the legislature or other appropriate rule making body granted school officials the power to make such rules, the outcomes may have been different. On the other hand, occasionally the *ultra vires* argument is accompanied by the effective charge of state or federal constitutional violations, and thus the grant of authority by statute may make no difference.

It should also be understood that not every *ultra vires* claim is meritorious. Legislatures and courts are frequently inclined to allow school and college authorities broad professional discretion in carrying out their duties, even when the expression of such authority may intrude upon what students and their parents may regard as their domain. Note, for example, the broad scope of power conferred on school boards by this Iowa education statute:

> * * * [t]he board shall make rules for its own government and that of the directors, officers, teachers, and pupils, and for the care of the schoolhouse, grounds, and property of the school corporation, and aid in the enforcement of the same, and require the performance of duties by said persons imposed by law and the rules." Iowa Code § 279.8 (1972).

Augmenting the power of both school and college authorities is the legal assumption that these officials act "in place of the parent" and possess similar powers (the *in loco parentis* doctrine further explored below).

4. Until well into the 20th century, compulsory school laws were not very effective. Gradually, more stringent enforcement increased the percentage of youngsters attending school. At the same time, the period of compulsory school attendance has increased. For example, in 1870 the average number of days per year spent in school was 132.2. A hundred years later, the figure reached almost 180 days per year. Students also are required to spend more years in school. In most states, the compulsory law covers students until they are 16 or 17 years old. Why do you suppose students are required to spend more time in school today? Are the reasons solely educational? What economic arguments could be cited as well? Current criticism of education has fueled the debate over compulsory schooling. Do you think many courts today would endorse the argument that compulsory school laws constitute an unreasonable and insidious restriction on the freedom of young people?

5. Occasionally, an expanded hypothetical situation will be presented to provide readers with an opportunity to consider a realistic, involved situation. The first such situation follows.

HYPOTHETICAL: *In the Matter of the Smith Family*
(Family Court)

The Smith Family consists of Sam, Sr., aged 42; Susan, aged 41; Mary, aged 17; and Sam, Jr., aged 16. Sam, Sr., has his doctorate in psychology from a nationally known private university. Susan has no formal education beyond the eighth grade. In 1970 Sam decided to quit his teaching position, buy a small farm and live off the land in Acme County, Minnefornia. The family income consists primarily of royalties Sam receives from sales of two textbooks he authored on child-rearing. Neither Sam nor Susan is willing to apply for unemployment insurance. Both admit they "dropped out" of mainstream America because of their antagonism toward the "growing permissiveness of society and the misplaced reliance on social interaction." As Sam puts it, "Our desire is to be by ourselves in a world of our own making."

Since leaving the 8th grade, neither Sam, Jr., nor Mary have attended school. For the past several years, first the children and then the family have been engaged in a number of skirmishes with school officials in Acme county and with state officials from the Department of Education. As it now stands, officials of the State Education Department backed by appropriate legal forces are demanding that the Smiths cease their home educational program and send their children to public school. In Minnefornia, all students must attend a public school or "substantially equivalent" nonpublic school until they are 18 years of age. If the Smiths refuse, the state and school officials request that the children be removed from the Smith home, placed in foster homes, and be sent to public school.

The home environment can best be characterized as authoritarian. The parents believe that children should be reared in a disciplined, structured environment. Neither Sam, Jr., nor Mary are considered to have "freedoms" by their parents. Sam's two books and his own structured homelife speak to child-rearing from his theoretical position. According to Sam and Susan, when a person is born, he is controlled by "basic need stimuli." Thus, a child is dependent on the mother for food, the air for oxygen, and so on. As a youngster, the child learns about and accepts these facts of life. This period Sam labels "Step I"; it concludes at age 5. Once Step I is passed, children are ready to learn the basic skills of reading, writing and arithmetic. These, Sam and Susan believe, are best learned in the elementary division of the county-wide school district. They consented to send their children to the public elementary school because the classroom situation is quite structured and discipline is maintained.

But with the conclusion of eighth grade, the learning experience outside the home environment or "Step II" should be over, according to Sam and Susan. Thus, they brought their own children back into the home environment and assumed control of their education. Through daily three-hour "search and discover" sessions, the parents are seeking to teach their children self-discipline and the value of self-reliance. They particularly emphasize the importance of the family unit, the "only social group that counts," they assert. The textbooks and exercises used in the home for this purpose have been written and assembled by Sam.

At the same time, the parents continue to place great emphasis on the skills of mathematical manipulation, reading, and writing. Their home records show spending another three-hour session daily on these subjects. All learning is conducted in a very strict, authoritarian environment. For example, there are no breaks scheduled; the children must receive permission to go to the bathroom.

School officials refuse to approve the home instruction as "substantially equivalent" to that offered in the public high scool. They assert that the home learning "experiments" of Sam and Susan are inconsistent and are detrimental to the children. The officials point out that in the local high school, students have a wide variety of course selection, with much time devoted to extra-curricular activities of the students' choice. They emphasize that unlike Sam and Susan, the high school stresses the importance of developing a healthy attitude toward contemporary society, the necessity to live comfortably within social norms, and the value of social relationships among a diversity of groups. Included within the school program are compensatory programs which school officials maintain provide every student with the maximum of equality of opportunity for social and economic mobility, a mandatory guidance program to assure that students develop self-actualization, and a civil liberties course designed to assist students understand their rights within the educational and societal setting.

Sam and Susan find these three aspects of the school program particularly objectionable. They argue that their children will be far better off relying on their own inner strengths and skills and the strengths of the family unit than relying on others in a permissive society. Sam adds that the high school is really brain-washing parents and children when it tries to accomplish something which is clearly impossible. "Ask them how they know their program really works," Sam often declares. In any case, he maintains that social and economic mobility is irrelevant since his children "are never going to enter the rat-race."

The children themselves have contradictory views about their home life and educational environment. Mary wishes to go to a modern art academy on the West Coast, while Sam wishes he could stay at home with his parents but "be allowed to play football, basketball, and baseball at school."

Based on previous discussion and cases, what arguments would you make for each side? If you were to decide this hypothetical case, what decision would you reach?

C. The Right to Have Private Schools: The Pierce Case

Pierce v. Society of the Sisters of the Holy Names of Jesus and Mary, 268 U.S. 510 (1925), the landmark decision upholding the right of nonpublic elementary and secondary schools to exist as alternatives to public schooling, has a unique, even bizarre background. The case grew out of the conservative backlash to the internationalism of World War I and the changing American social environment of the 1920s. The seeds were sown for the legal battle when the Ku Klux Klan, the white-robed crusaders for racial purity and religious fundamentalism, championed a voter initiative in Oregon requiring all children between eight and 18 years of age to attend public schools. The Klan chose Oregon for its crusade for a state monopoly on education because independent and religiously-affiliated private schools in the state were few in number and support for public schools strong.

It is ironic that the Klan with its racial separation bias, should have become the leading advocate for the common school, for the initiative would have the effect of placing all religious and ethnic elements together in the same educational setting. But like many of today's liberal educational theorists, Klan members subscribed to the "melting pot" view of schooling. Said the Oregon KKK Grand Dragon and chief sponsor of the school bill: "Somehow these mongrel hordes must be Americanized; failing that, deportation is the only remedy." [19] Similarly, the common school would be the vehicle to convert the Catholics to American Protestantism.

Against the Klan were arrayed a variety of constituencies including many religious leaders, businessmen who anticipated higher taxes, minority groups, and citizens who feared encroaching government. One Oregonian saw passage of the bill as a step toward socialism: The next thing, "Some

19. As quoted in David B. Tyack, "The Perils of Pluralism: The Background of the *Pierce* Case," 74 *American Historical Review* 74, 1968, at p. 79.

self-appointed patriots calling themselves 100 percent will come along with a petition requesting that all babes must be removed from the home from the mother's breast lest the babes hear some unpatriotic lullaby song, * * * and (be) placed in a state institution." [20]

In spite of the opposition, the bill passed by a narrow margin. Fearing a tyranny of the majority in the making, those opposed to the compulsory public school measure took their case to court. Two schools, the Society of the Sisters of the Holy Name of Jesus and Mary and the Hill Military Academy (one of whose students had been the son of the KKK Grand Dragon), brought suit in 1922 against Oregon Governor Walter Pierce, an ardent supporter of the new law and a favorite of the Klan, and several other state officials. The suit was brought in spite of the fact that the law would not take effect until 1926.

In briefs filed before the federal court, defense lawyer Wallace Mc-Cammant argued the "melting pot" theory of public schooling:

"The great danger overshadowing all others which confront the American people is the danger of class hatred. History will demonstrate the fact that it is the rock upon which many a republic has been broken and I don't know any better way to fortify the next generation against that insidious poison than to require that the poor and the rich, the people of all classes and distinction, and of all different religious beliefs, shall meet in the common schools, which are the great American melting pot, there to become * * * the typical American of the future." [21]

For the plaintiffs, Dan Marlarkey argued that the public school could never be a melting pot because of the way schools are established.

"You don't mingle the rich and poor. You have your schools established in districts; you have your school out here by Riverside, a public school that is as aristocratic an institution as ever existed anywhere. Why? Because the people that live in that neighborhood are people that are well to do. Their children go to the public schools. They don't mix with the poor * * *. The character of the children that go to the schools is determined by the neighborhood in which the school is located. You talk about foreigners. I haven't the figures but I will venture to say that there is less than five per cent of all the children that go to all the schools of this plaintiff who are foreign born." [22]

The three-judge federal court ruled in favor of the Sisters and the proprietors of the military academy. On appeal to the Supreme Court, the lawyers argued their point with renewed vigor. The brief for Governor Pierce predicted that if the Oregon school law were ruled unconstitutional, then "the great centers of population in our country will be dotted with elementary schools which instead of being red on the outside will be red on the inside." [23] Can there be no way, questioned the lawyer, "in which a state can prevent the entire education of a considerable proportion of its

20. *Id.*, at p. 84.   22. *Id.*, at p. 94.

21. *Id.*, at p. 93.   23. *Id.*, at p. 96.

future citizens from being controlled and conducted by bolshevists, syndicalists and communists?"

For appellants, attorney Louis Marshall pointed out that much more was at stake than the existence of nonpublic schools.

"Fundamentally * * * the questions in these cases are: May liberty to teach and to learn be restricted? Shall such liberty be dependent upon the will of the majority? Shall such majority be permitted to dictate to parents and to children where and by whom instruction shall be given? If such power can be asserted, then it will lead inevitably to the stifling of thought." [24]

As you read the Supreme Court's opinion, consider whether it was a victory for educational pluralism or for state control of education.

PIERCE v. SOCIETY OF THE SISTERS OF THE HOLY NAMES OF JESUS AND MARY

Supreme Court of the United States, 1925.
268 U.S. 510, 45 S.Ct. 571, 69 L.Ed. 1070.

Mr. Justice McREYNOLDS delivered the opinion of the Court.

* * *

The challenged Act, effective September 1, 1926, requires every parent, guardian or other person having control or charge or custody of a child between eight and sixteen years to send him "to a public school for the period of time a public school shall be held during the current year" in the district where the child resides; and failure so to do is declared a misdemeanor. * * * without doubt enforcement of the statute would seriously impair, perhaps destroy, the profitable features of appellees' business and greatly diminish the value of their property.

Appellee, the Society of Sisters, is an Oregon corporation, organized in 1880, with power to care for orphans, educate and instruct the youth, establish and maintain academies or schools, and acquire necessary real and personal property. It has long devoted its property and effort to the secular and religious education and care of children, and has acquired the valuable good will of many parents and guardians. It conducts interdependent primary and high schools and junior colleges, and maintains orphanages for the custody and control of children between eight and sixteen. In its primary schools many children between those ages are taught the subjects usually pursued in Oregon public schools during the first eight years. Systematic religious instruction and moral training according to the tenets of the Roman Catholic Church are also regularly provided. All courses of study, both temporal and religious, contemplate continuity of training under appellee's charge; the primary schools are essential to the system and the most profitable. It owns valuable buildings, especially constructed and equipped for school purposes. The business is remunerative—the annual income from primary schools exceeds thirty thousand dollars—and the successful conduct of this requires long time contracts with teachers and parents. The Compulsory Education Act of 1922 has already caused the withdrawal from its schools of children who would otherwise continue, and their income has steadily declined. The appellants, public officers, have proclaimed

24. *Id.*, at p. 97.

their purpose strictly to enforce the statute.

After setting out the above facts the Society's bill alleges that the enactment conflicts with the right of parents to choose schools where their children will receive appropriate mental and religious training, the right of the child to influence the parents' choice of a school, the right of schools and teachers therein to engage in a useful business or profession, and is accordingly repugnant to the Constitution and void. And, further, that unless enforcement of the measure is enjoined the corporation's business and property will suffer irreparable injury.

Appellee, Hill Military Academy, is a private corporation organized in 1908 under the laws of Oregon, engaged in owning, operating and conducting for profit an elementary, college preparatory and military training school for boys between the ages of five and twenty-one years. The average attendance is one hundred, and the annual fees received for each student amount to some eight hundred dollars. The elementary department is divided into eight grades, as in the public schools; the college preparatory department has four grades, similar to those of the public high schools; the courses of study conform to the requirements of the State Board of Education. Military instruction and training are also given, under the supervision of an Army officer. It owns considerable real and personal property, some useful only for school purposes. The business and incident good will are very valuable. In order to conduct its affairs long time contracts must be made for supplies, equipment, teachers and pupils. Appellants, law officers of the State and County, have publicly announced that the Act of November 7, 1922, is valid and have declared their intention to enforce it. By reason of the statute and threat of enforcement appellee's business is being destroyed and its property depreciated; parents and guardians are refusing to make

contracts for the future instruction of their sons, and some are being withdrawn.

The Academy's bill states the foregoing facts and then alleges that the challenged Act contravenes the corporation's rights guaranteed by the Fourteenth Amendment and that unless appellants are restrained from proclaiming its validity and threatening to enforce it irreparable injury will result. The prayer is for an appropriate injunction.

*   *   *

No question is raised concerning the power of the State reasonably to regulate all schools, to inspect, supervise and examine them, their teachers and pupils; to require that all children of proper age attend some school, that teachers shall be of good moral character and patriotic disposition, that certain studies plainly essential to good citizenship must be taught, and that nothing be taught which is manifestly inimical to the public welfare.

The inevitable practical result of enforcing the Act under consideration would be destruction of appellees' primary schools, and perhaps all other private primary schools for normal children within the State of Oregon. These parties are engaged in a kind of undertaking not inherently harmful, but long regarded as useful and meritorious. Certainly there is nothing in the present records to indicate that they have failed to discharge their obligations to patrons, students or the State. And there are no peculiar circumstances or present emergencies which demand extraordinary measures relative to primary education.

Under the doctrine of *Meyer v. Nebraska,* we think it entirely plain that the Act of 1922 unreasonably interferes with the liberty of parents and guardians to direct the upbringing and education of children under their control. As often heretofore pointed out, rights guaranteed by the Constitution may not be abridged by legislation which has no reasonable relation to some purpose within the competency of the State. The fundamental theory of liberty upon which all governments in this Union repose excludes any general power of the State to standardize its children by forcing them to accept instruction from public teachers only. The child is not the mere creature of the State; those who nurture him and direct his destiny have the right, coupled with the high duty, to recognize and prepare him for additional obligations.

Appellees are corporations and therefore, it is said, they cannot claim for themselves the liberty which the Fourteenth Amendment guarantees. Accepted in the proper sense, this is true. But they have business and property for which they claim protection. These are threatened with destruction through the unwarranted compulsion which appellants are exercising over present and prospective patrons of their schools. And this court has gone very far to protect against loss threatened by such action.

Generally it is entirely true, as urged by counsel, that no person in any business has such an interest in possible customers as to enable him to restrain exercise of proper power of the State upon the ground that he will be deprived of patronage. But the injunctions here sought are not against the exercise of any *proper* power. Plaintiffs asked protection against arbitrary, unreasonable and unlawful interference with their patrons and the consequent destruction of their business and property. * * *

The suits were not premature. The injury to appellees was present and very real, not a mere possibility in the remote future. If no relief had been possible prior to the effective date of the Act, the injury would have become irreparable. Prevention of impending injury by unlawful action is a well recognized function of courts of equity.

The decrees below are affirmed.

* * *

NOTES AND QUESTIONS

1. The Due Process Clause of the Fourteenth Amendment states that "nor shall any State deprive any person of life, liberty, or property, without due process of law." The Fifth Amendment—which, like all of the first eight Amendments, provides safeguards only against the actions of the federal government—contains a similar clause. During the late 19th and early 20th centuries, the Supreme Court used both Due Process Clauses to void many federal and state regulatory laws. The Court was very much concerned that no law unfairly deny a person, or more particularly a corporation (which the Court had earlier decided was a "person" under the Fourteenth Amendment and entitled to the same protections), the full use of private property. If laws did restrict the use of property, then they were subject to close scrutiny under the Due Process Clauses. The largely conservative Court actively supported these two essential civil rights— "sanctity of private property" and the *laissez-faire* free enterprise system.

A careful reading of the *Pierce* case will produce this central issue: "Whether a state law requiring all children to attend public schools deprives those operating a private school of their property without due process of law under the Fourteenth Amendment to the United States Constitution." * It is important to note that the case was decided on the basis of the rights of the nonpublic school operators to operate their schools, i. e., enjoy their rights of private property without state interference, and not on the rights of parents to send their children to nonpublic schools, though this was a consideration in the decision. Since neither parents nor children were parties to the suit, no judgment could have been rendered for them.

With the Court's retreat from an aggressive use of the Fourteenth Amendment Due Process Clause to challenge regulatory legislation during the New Deal 1930s, the *Pierce* case has often been utilized by nonpublic school advocates to support an alleged right of parents to choose nonpublic alternatives to public schooling. It is significant that this was not the primary basis upon which the case was decided in 1925.

2. Note also that Justice McReynolds mentions *Meyer v. Nebraska*, 262 U.S. 390 (1923), in his opinion. More than *Pierce, Meyer* has affirmed that the word "liberty" in the Fourteenth Amendment Due Process Clause gives parents the right to control the upbringing of their children. (This case was referred to in Chapter One, regarding the argument for parents to make decisions about student rights.) While *Meyer* is frequently cited to support the right of parents to control their children's upbringing, that right is not absolute, as *Prince v. Massachusetts,* (1940), mentioned earlier in this chapter, attests.

Both *Pierce* and *Meyer* have been relied on in recent years by parents who seek to challenge school regulations. Typical of these cases is *Citizens for Parental Rights v. San Mateo County Bd.,* 124 Cal.Rptr. 68 (California, 1975). In this case, a group of parents sought to challenge the family life and sex education programs in the five school districts of San Mateo County. The courses were taught objectively, with teachers instructed not to interpret what they were teaching or assign value judgments ("good" or "bad," etc.), but to acknowledge that some topics were "controversial." The significant fact here is that parents and guardians had the right under the sex education regulations to withhold or withdraw their children from the program on moral or religious grounds.

The three-judge state appellate court rejected all of the parents' contentions, including their assertion of parental rights to control the upbringing of their children under the Fourteenth Amendment. Distinguishing *Meyer* and *Pierce,* the court wrote that parents do not have the right to

* * * preclude other students who may voluntarily desire to participate in a course of study under the guise that the objector's liberty, personal happiness or parental authority is somehow jeopardized or impaired. To adhere to such a concept would use judicial constitutional authority to limit inquiry to conformity, and to limit knowledge to the known. (At p. 91).

---

* Note: From this point onward, the term "nonpublic" rather than "private" will be used to describe these institutions, since the word "nonpublic" encompasses both independent and religiously-affiliated private institutions. Note that both types of institutions were involved in the *Pierce* case.

Similarly, courts have upheld compulsory education requirements in the face of constitutional challenges based on the parental rights doctrine.   In *Scoma v. Chicago Bd. of Educ.*, 391 F.Supp. 452 (N.D.Ill.1974), the parents sought to secure the right to educate their children in their homes by asserting a wide-ranging definition of parental rights under the word "liberty" of the Fourteenth Amendment including, "(the) right and duty to educate their children adequately but as they see fit; to rear their children in accordance with their determination of what best serves the family's interest and welfare; to be protected in their family privacy and personal decision-making from governmental intrusion; to distribute and receive information; and to teach and to ensure their children's freedom of thought and inquiry." (At p. 460).   The court rejected such an expansive interpretation of parental rights.   Noting that *Pierce* pertained only to the property rights of the operators of the nonpublic schools, the court concluded that the "right" claimed by the parents "merely provides parents with an opportunity to seek a reasonable alternative to public education for their children."   The court went on:

> The plaintiff's asserted right to educate their children "as they see fit" and "in accordance with their determination of what best serves the family's interest and welfare" does not rise above a personal or philosophical choice and cannot claim to be within the bounds of Constitutional protection.   Aside from claims based on the exercise of religion clause, compulsory attendance statutes have generally been regarded as valid.   The courts have held that the state may constitutionally require that all children attend some school, under the authority of its police power.   (At p. 461).

Courts appear to be reluctant to extend the *Pierce* and *Meyer* precedents too far lest judges themselves become involved in decisions traditionally left to legislative bodies or educational experts, e. g., the literacy merit of a book, the value of compulsory education requirements, or the value of an innovative instructional program.   For the same reason, courts have not been eager to entertain parent or student suits charging failure of school programs.   As one commentator notes:

> * * * a parent's attempt to insulate his child from exposure to a certain book may conflict with a teacher's interest in discussing it or with another student's interest in reading it. When confronted with such a dispute, courts frequently conclude that the best way to protect the rights of unrepresented groups is to defer to the school board, whose judgment ostensibly represents the best interests of the entire community.[25]

But why might such a resolution be ineffective?   Obviously, there are situations where parental resort to the political process may prove fruitless.   And, of course, while parents may seek a remedy through the political process, children cannot.   What action should a court take when there is reason to believe that parents and their children do not agree?

---

25.   Project, "Education and the Law: State Interests and Individual Rights," 74 *Mich. L.Rev.* 1373, June, 1976, at p. 1421.

Parental challenges to school authority are particularly evident when schools serve communities of mixed ethnic and social groups and when respect for education is low. Thus, in recent years parental challenges in the interests of their children have multiplied. As a general rule, however, courts have become involved only when a *specific* parental or student constitutional or statutory right has been affected.

As illustrated in later chapters, charges of infringement of religious liberty and of racial discrimination have most frequently triggered judicial involvement in internal educational decision-making.

3. Frequently, it is asserted that for the state to affirm a right and then deny the means to secure this right is in reality a denial of the right. As applied to the right of a parent to have access to nonpublic schools, the argument suggests the state has an *obligation* to see that those without adequate means can attend nonpublic schools if they wish. Does the *Pierce* case carry such an implication? Should it? If a state places postsecondary education on a cost basis, could a poor student successfully sue to gain entrance to college? This "affirmative action" posture will be explored in discussing the Fourteenth Amendment Equal Protection Clause.

4. It should be noted that the Pierce case does *not* undermine the state's right to educate and socialize the child. Rather, it asserts that the state has no authority to *standardize* the educational experience by maintaining a monopoly. At the same time, however, the state does have the power "reasonably to regulate all schools, to inspect, supervise, and examine them, their teachers and their pupils; to require that all children of proper age attend some school, that teachers shall be of good moral character and patriotic disposition, that certain studies plainly essential to good citizenship must be taught, and that nothing be taught which is manifestly immoral to the public welfare." This so-called "police power" is related to the *parens patriae* power of states under the Tenth Amendment. How far does it go?

> a. Can a state prohibit a nonpublic school from violating a student's right to free speech?
>
> b. Can a state require nonpublic schools to provide students with a hearing prior to taking disciplinary action against them?
>
> c. Can a state require a nonpublic school to integrate?
>
> d. Can a state refuse to allow a free school or alternative college to open because it does not meet state standards?

In each of the above, what arguments are the operators of nonpublic schools likely to make against such state regulation? How successful would they be? How would you rule in each instance?

5. Was *Pierce* a liberal, conservative, or radical decision? Compare how the decision might have been viewed when it was rendered with how it is viewed today. Does this tell you something about "labelling"? Note the following comment: " 'Conservative' judges have been just as willing as 'liberal' ones to use judicial position and power to defend according to

their convictions what they consider to be 'right' public policy or constitutional doctrine." [26]

6.　Given what we know—or do not know—about the impact of schools on students from the discussion in Chapter One, do you think the Court should have become involved in the *Pierce* case or should it have left the matter to the legislators and the people of Oregon to resolve? How might a judicial activist, neutralist, or self-restraintist approach this legal issue? Which was the approach Justice McReynolds used?

[26]. Stephen T. Early, Jr., *Constitutional Courts of the U.S.* (Totowa, N.J.: Littlefield, Adams, 1977) at p. 138.

IV. STUDENT RIGHTS: THE NONPUBLIC EDUCATIONAL SETTING

So far only indirect reference has been made to student rights. At this point, a direct examination of the status of student rights in the educational setting begins. It will help to identify the sources of student rights for both public and nonpublic sectors. Figure 2–3 illustrates the variety of sources from which student rights and privileges can emanate.

Figure 2–3. Sources of Student Rights

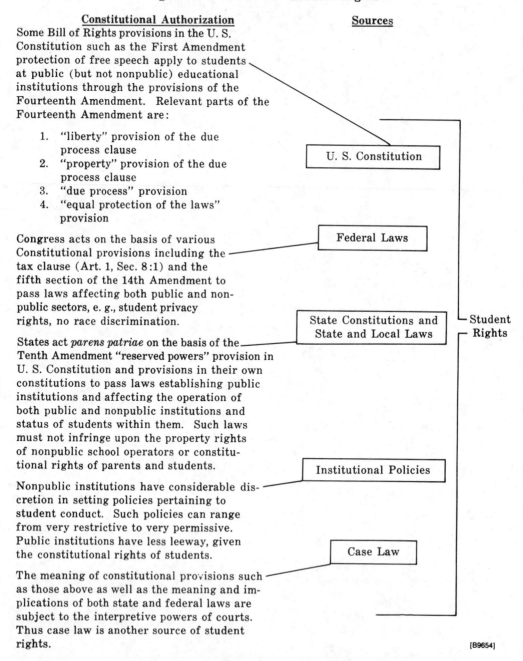

Constitutional Authorization

Some Bill of Rights provisions in the U. S. Constitution such as the First Amendment protection of free speech apply to students at public (but not nonpublic) educational institutions through the provisions of the Fourteenth Amendment. Relevant parts of the Fourteenth Amendment are:

1. "liberty" provision of the due process clause
2. "property" provision of the due process clause
3. "due process" provision
4. "equal protection of the laws" provision

Congress acts on the basis of various Constitutional provisions including the tax clause (Art. 1, Sec. 8 :1) and the fifth section of the 14th Amendment to pass laws affecting both public and nonpublic sectors, e. g., student privacy rights, no race discrimination.

States act *parens patriae* on the basis of the Tenth Amendment "reserved powers" provision in U. S. Constitution and provisions in their own constitutions to pass laws establishing public institutions and affecting the operation of both public and nonpublic institutions and status of students within them. Such laws must not infringe upon the property rights of nonpublic school operators or constitutional rights of parents and students.

Nonpublic institutions have considerable discretion in setting policies pertaining to student conduct. Such policies can range from very restrictive to very permissive. Public institutions have less leeway, given the constitutional rights of students.

The meaning of constitutional provisions such as those above as well as the meaning and implications of both state and federal laws are subject to the interpretive powers of courts. Thus case law is another source of student rights.

Sources

- U. S. Constitution
- Federal Laws
- State Constitutions and State and Local Laws
- Institutional Policies
- Case Law

Student Rights

[B9654]

Rights do not emanate from the U. S. Constitution alone; legislation is an equally important source. For example, most challenges brought in federal courts against the actions of public educational officials are filed pursuant to a civil rights law, 42 U.S.C.A. § 1983, which is an example of Congress' power to enforce the terms of the Fourteenth Amendment. This important law will be covered in more depth in later chapters. Congress can also use its fiscal power by setting conditions for the receipt of federal funds. For example, the Family Educational Rights and Privacy Act of 1974 (Buckley Amendment), granting students and parents with access to their educational records, provides that failure of educational officials to comply with the law may trigger curtailment of federal funding.

Similarly, state constitutions, state laws, and the policies of administrative agencies such as the state board of education are sources of student rights. The best examples are provisions providing for the establishment of educational institutions and the access of students to them through direct and indirect financial aid. Compulsory education laws thus can be viewed as sources of student rights because they entitle the student to an education. Educational institutions themselves are also sources of student rights through the rules and policies they develop.

While all of these sources are relevant and have authorization in the U. S. Constitution, the rights of students which stem *directly* from the U. S. Constitution are of prime significance. Thus, an understanding of the provisions of the Constitution, particularly the Bill of Rights and the Fourteenth Amendment, as well as the case law interpreting them is necessary. It will be useful to review the constitutional provisions contained in Appendix C now and periodically thereafter. Frequent reference to Figure 2–3 is also advised to keep in perspective the many sources of student rights.

A. The Current Nonpublic Student-Institution Relationship

Nonpublic students have few rights beyond those granted by the institution, because the concept of private property rights discussed above in relation to the Fifth and Fourteenth Amendments and again with regard to the *Pierce* case places a good deal of autonomy in the hands of those who maintain and operate nonpublic educational institutions. As will be seen in later chapters, however, private property rights have had to yield to other interests in some situations, particularly those involving elimination of racial discrimination. At the same time, it is important to point out that most nonpublic colleges and universities, and many nonpublic elementary and secondary schools, have voluntarily developed internal policies recognizing student rights. The point is, however, that this action has been done voluntarily, not on a court-mandated basis.

The student-institutional relationship in the nonpublic sector is thus inherently quite different from that in the public. Two leading cases illustrate this fact. The first, *Gott v. Berea College*, upholds the *in loco parentis* power of nonpublic school officials and the second, *Greene v. Howard Univ.*, outlines the nature of the contractual relationship between students and nonpublic schools.

(1) In Loco Parentis

GOTT v. BEREA COLLEGE

Court of Appeals of Kentucky, 1913.
156 Ky. 376, 161 S.W. 204.

NUNN, J. The appellant, J. S. Gott, about the 1st of September, 1911, purchased and was conducting a restaurant in Berea, Ky., across the street from the premises of Berea College. A restaurant had been conducted in this same place for quite a long while by the party from whom Gott purchased. For many years it has been the practice of the governing authorities of Berea College to distribute among the students at the beginning of each scholastic year a pamphlet entitled "Students Manual," containing the rules and regulations of the college for the government of the student body. Subsection 3 of this manual, under the heading "Forbidden Places," enjoined the students from entering any "place of ill repute, liquor saloons, gambling houses," etc. During the 1911 summer vacation, the faculty, pursuant to their usual practice of revising the rules, added another clause to this rule as to forbidden places, and the rule was announced to the student body at chapel exercise on the first day of the fall term, which began September 11th. The new rule is as follows: "(b) Eating houses and places of amusement in Berea, not controlled by the college, must not be entered by students on pain of immediate dismission. The institution provides for the recreation of its students, and ample accommodation for meals and refreshment, and cannot permit outside parties to solicit student patronage for gain."

Appellant's restaurant was located and conducted mainly for the profits arising from student patronage. During the first few days after the publication of this rule, two or three students were expelled for its violation, so that the making of the rule and its enforcement had the effect of very materially injuring, if not absolutely ruining, appellant's business because the students were afraid to further patronize it.

On the 20th day of September appellant instituted this action in equity and procured a temporary restraining order and injunction against the enforcement of the rule above quoted, and charging that the college and its officers unlawfully and maliciously conspired to injure his business by adopting a rule forbidding students entering eating houses. For this he claimed damages in the sum of $500. By amended petitions he alleged that in pursuance of such conspiracy the college officers had uttered slanderous remarks concerning him and his business and increased his prayer for damages to $2,000. The slanderous remarks were alleged to have been spoken at chapel and other public exercises to the student body as a reason for the rule, and were to the effect that appellant was a bootlegger, and upon more than one occasion had been charged and convicted of illegally selling whisky. Berea College answered and denied that any slanderous remarks had been made as to appellant, or that they had conspired maliciously or otherwise, or that the rule adopted was either unlawful or unreasonable. In the second paragraph the college affirmatively set forth that it is a private (incorporated) institution of learning, supported wholly by private donations and its endowment and such fees as it collects from students or parents of students who desire to become affiliated with said institution and abide by and conform to the rules and regulations provided by the governing authorities of the college for the conduct of the students; that every student upon entering said institution agrees, upon pain of dismissal, to conform to such rules and regulations as may be from time to time promulgated; that the institution aims to furnish an education to inexperienced country, mountain boys and girls of very little means at the lowest possible cost; that practically all of the students are from rural districts and unused to the ways of even a village the size of Berea; and that they are of very limited means. It is further alleged that they have been compelled from time to time to pass rules tending to prevent students from wasting their time and money and to keep them wholly occupied in study; that some of the rules prohibit the doing of things not in themselves wrong or unlawful, but which the governing authorities have found and believe detrimental to the best interest of the college and the student body. For these reasons the rule in question was adopted, but they say at the time that they had no knowledge that the plaintiff owned or was about to acquire a restaurant, and that the rule was in no way directed at the plaintiff. * * *

* * * The larger question, and the one we are called here to pass upon, is whether the rule forbidding students entering eating houses was a reasonable one and within the power of the college authorities to enact, and the further question whether, in that event, appellant Gott will be heard to complain. That the enforcement of the rule worked a great injury to Gott's restaurant business cannot well be denied; but unless he can show that the college authorities have been guilty of a breach of some legal duty which they owe to him, he has no cause of action against them for the injury.

One has no right of action against a merchant for refusal to sell goods, nor will an action lie, unless such means are used as of themselves constitute a breach of legal duty, for inducing or causing persons not to trade, deal, or contract with another; and it is a well-established practice that, when a lawful act is performed in the proper manner, the party performing it is not liable for mere incidental consequences injuriously resulting from it to another.

College authorities stand in loco parentis concerning the physical and moral welfare and mental training of the pupils, and we are unable to see why, to that end, they may not make any rule or regulation for the government or betterment of their pupils that a parent could for the same purpose. Whether the rules or regulations are wise or their aims worthy is a matter left solely to the discretion of the authorities or parents, as the case may be, and, in the exercise of that discretion, the courts are not disposed to interfere, unless the rules and aims are unlawful or against public policy. Section 881 of the Kentucky Statutes, applicable to corporations of this character, provides that they may "adopt such rules for their government and operation, not inconsistent with law, as the directors, trustees, or managers may deem proper." The corporate charter of Berea College empowers the board of trustees to "make such by-laws as it may deem necessary to promote the interest of the institution, not in violation of any laws of the state or the United States." This reference to the college powers shows that its authorities have a large discretion, and they are similar to the charter and corporate rights under which colleges and such institutions are generally conducted.

Having in mind such powers, the courts have without exception held to the rule which is well settled in 7 Cyc. 288: "A college or university may prescribe requirements for admission and rules for the conduct of its students, and one who enters as a student impliedly agrees to conform to such rules of government." The only limit upon this rule is as to institutions supported in whole or in part by appropriations from the public treasury. In such cases their rules are viewed somewhat more critically; but, since this is a private institution, it is unnecessary to notice further the distinction.

A further consideration of the power of school boards is found in Mechem on Public Officers, § 730, from which we quote: "There is no question that the power of school authorities over pupils is not confined to schoolroom or grounds, but to extend to all acts of pupils which are detrimental to the good order and best interest of the school, whether committed in school hours, or while the pupil is on his way to or from school, or after he has returned home." Of course this rule is not intended to, nor will it be permitted to, interfere with parental control of children in the home, unless the acts forbidden materially affect the conduct and discipline of the school.

There is nothing in the case to show that the college had any contract, business, or other direct relations with the appellant. They owed him no special duty; and, while he may have suffered an injury, yet he does not show that the college is a wrongdoer in a legal or any sense. Nor does he show that in enacting the rule they did it unlawfully, or that they exceeded their power, or that there was any conspiracy to do anything unlawful. Their right to enact the rule comes well within their charter provision, and that it was a reasonable rule cannot be very well disputed. Assuming that there were no other outside eating houses in Berea, and that there never had been a disorderly one, or one in which intoxicating liquors had been sold, still it would not be an unreasonable rule forbidding students entering or partronizing appellant's establishment. In the first place, the college offers an education to the poorest, and undertakes to offer them the means of a livelihood within the institution while they are pursuing their studies, and at the same time provides board and lodging for a nominal charge. Whatever profit was derived served to still further reduce expenses charged against the pupil. It stands to reason that when the plans of the institution are so prepared, and the support and maintenance of the students are so ordered, there must be the fullest co-operation on the part of all the students, otherwise there will be disappointment, if not failure, in the project. It is also a matter of common knowledge that one of the chief dreads of college authorities is the outbreak of an epidemic and against which they should take the utmost precaution. These precautions, however, may wholly fail if students carelessly or indiscriminately visit or patronize public or unsanitary eating houses. Too often those operating such places are ignorant of, or indifferent to, even the simplest sanitary requirements. As a safeguard against disease infection from this source, there is sufficient reason for the promulgation of the rule complained of.

But, even if it might be conceded that the rule was an unreasonable one, still appellant Gott is in no position to complain. He was not a student, nor is it shown that he had any children as students in the college. The rule was directed to and intended to control only the student body. For the purposes of this case the school, its officers and students, are a legal entity, as much so as any family, and, like a father may direct his children, those in charge of boarding schools are well within their rights and powers when they direct their students what to eat and where they may get it, where they may go, and what forms of amusement are forbidden. * * *

* * *

Considering the whole case, the judgment of the lower court is affirmed.

NOTES AND QUESTIONS

1. According to the opinion, Berea College enacted the rule prohibiting students from patronizing restaurants, including Gott's, located off campus. Why did the college enact the rule? If the college had said the primary reason was to force students to spend their funds at college-operated facilities because such financial support was essential to continued college operation, would it have made a difference? Does the opinion indicate *any* restraints at all on the rule-making power of Berea College officials? If the state had passed a law saying all incorporated educational institutions must allow students the option of off-campus room and board, what constitutional arguments could college officials have made? How successful do you think they would have been in having the law struck down in light of the *Pierce* case?

2. Judge Nunn's argument depends heavily on the doctrine of *in loco parentis*, which literally means "in place of the parent." (Some say it really translates to mean "crazy like the parent"!) It is an old common law concept that in effect gives anyone—guardians, stepparents, grandparents—who stands in place of the parent the same rights, responsibilities, and liabilities that the true parent possesses over his own children. In the educational milieu, the doctrine extends to the educator the power of surrogate parent. *Gott* illustrates its application at the time of that decision to the college setting. Until recently, the doctrine characterized student-institutional relationships in both public and nonpublic educational sectors. Note in this connection the reference Judge Nunn makes to the power of public school boards as found in the passage from Mecham's treatise on public officers.

It is not surprising that *in loco parentis* should have been imported from England to the American college and university. As the American historian, Henry Steele Commanger, has noted:

> "(*In loco parentis*) was transferred from Cambridge to America, and caught on here more strongly for very elementary reasons: College students were, for the most part, very young. A great many boys went up to college in the colonial era at the ages of 13, 14, 15. They were, for most practical purposes, what our high school youngsters are now. They did need taking care of, and the tutors were *in loco parentis*." [27]

Today, even when applied full force as in the elementary school setting, the doctrine does not give the educator the same panoply of power as, for example, the student's legal guardian. The school official has only as much power *in loco parentis* as necessary to carry out his responsibilities, i. e., educate the child. To go beyond this is to invite legal challenges. The most frequent exercise of *in loco parentis* is related to student discipline, particularly student searches and corporal punishment.

Unless incorporated into statutory law, or set forth in school rules, *in loco parentis* parameters are determined by common law. It is im-

---

27. As quoted in Van Alstyne "Procedural Due Process and State University Students," 10 *U.C.L.A.Law Rev.* 368, 1963, at pp. 377–378.

portant to remember, however, that in the public educational setting today *in loco parentis* has declined in significance as a rationale for the authority of educators. In part this decline reflects a conscious decision by educators to place more responsibility on students at an earlier age than in the past. It also reflects the inroads made by legislation and court decisions in support of student rights in curtailing the discretionary authority of educators. The latter factor has been felt primarily in the public sector. In the nonpublic sector, though, most educators have willingly recognized the quickened maturation of American youth and have limited the use of *in loco parentis* accordingly through their own rules and regulations set forth in student handbooks and the like. At best, *in loco parentis* has always been a vague, even nebulous, doctrine as applied to the educational setting. Nevertheless, as a legal doctrine, it continues to exist and is still available as a rationale for many actions by educational officials.

3. If Gott were a student who had challenged the college rules, could he have asserted a denial of his freedom? What response would college officials have made? Under the Berea rule, what penalty would a student who had violated the rule receive? Do you think this is fair? The issue of student complaints about rules in the nonpublic sector is illustrated in the more recent *Greene* case below.

(2) The Contract Theory

GREENE v. HOWARD UNIV.

United States District Court, District of Columbia, 1967.
271 F.Supp. 609.

HOLTZOFF, District Judge.

The primary question presented in these * * * cases is whether the relations between a University and its students, and between a University and its faculty, are subject to judicial control; specifically, whether the termination by a University of the status of a student, or of a member of the faculty, is subject in whole or in part to judicial review.

The defendant in these cases is Howard University an institution of higher learning located in Washington, D. C. The plaintiffs may be divided into two classes. Some of them are students, whose status was terminated by the University as of the close of the academic year ending June 30, 1967. Others are members of the faculty, who held temporary appointments for a specific period only, and whose appointments the University declined to renew. This action is brought to require the University to restore the plaintiffs to their former status.

The matter is before the Court at this time on motions for a preliminary injunction to reinstate the plaintiffs pending the trial of this action.

In view of the disposition of the issues about to be made by this Court, it would be superfluous to review in detail the incidents that led to the action taken by the University against the plaintiffs. Suffice it to say that it arose out of a series of disorders that took place on the campus of Howard University. In one instance, the head of the Selective Service System of the United States had been invited to make a speech at the University. A group of students created such a disturbance as made it impossible for him to address the audience. At another time the University authorities were about to conduct a hearing on charges of misconduct against a student. A group composed of some students and of some members of the faculty created such a commotion and uproar as to render it impracticable for the hearing to proceed. Threatening utterances were heard on the campus. Several fires took place. The University authorities concluded, after a careful and thorough investigation, that the student plaintiffs, as well as those plaintiffs who were members of the faculty, actively participated in creating these chaotic conditions and disorder. Accordingly, in an effort to bar a continuation and repetition of such disruptive incidents, the University in June 1967, sent a formal letter to each of the student plaintiffs, notifying him that he would not be permitted to return to the institution for the next academic year. The other plaintiffs were instructors, or junior professors, who had only temporary appointments without any permanent tenure. If such appointments were not renewed, their connection with the faculty would be automatically terminated at the expiration of the academic year. The University, again in June 1967, sent a letter to each of this group of plaintiffs formally notifying him that his appointment, which was about to expire on June 30, 1967, would not be renewed.

As the questions of law relating to the two types of plaintiffs are somewhat different, we shall deal with each category separately. We shall first consider the student plaintiffs. Their complaint is predicated on the contention that they were not accorded their alleged Constitutional right to receive notices of charges and a hearing, but were dismissed from the University by *ex parte* decisions. The relief that they seek is to require the University to vacate its action and to give them notices of charges and a hearing.

This contention is based on a misconception of the scope of the Bill of Rights. The procedural safeguards and the privileges accorded by the Constitution of the United States are confined solely to judicial and quasi-judicial proceedings, either in the courts or before administrative agencies. They are directed solely against Governmental action. They do not extend to any other relation in life, such as that of parent and child, teacher and pupil, or employer and employee. These relations are of a private character. While some of them, such as that of employer and employee, may be circumscribed by contract or by statute, they are not controlled by the Constitution. * * *

* * * Howard University is not a governmental body. It is a private corporation created by an Act of Congress. True, a large percentage of its expenses are paid by annual appropriations made by Congress. As a condition of receiving such money, the Secretary of Health, Education and Welfare is given authority to visit and inspect Howard University and to control and supervise the expenditures of those funds which have been appropriated by Congress. In addition, the President and Directors of Howard University are required to file an annual report with the Secretary. No Government officer, however, is a member of the Board of Trustees of the Institution, nor is any control over the institution vested in the Federal Government.

The status of Howard University is not open for determination by this Court, for it has already been held by the Court of Appeals for this Circuit that the University is a private corporation and is not a public institution, Maiatico Const. Co. v. United States. Speaking for a unanimous bench, Groner, J., in that case wrote as follows:

Howard University is a private corporation. It was incorporated under an act passed March 2, 1867 and its charter gives it all the rights and powers usually vested in private corporations, including the right to purchase and sell real estate, and the right to contract and to sue and to be sued.

Judge Groner then referred to the fact that in 1928, a statute was enacted enabling Congress to make annual appropriations for the support of the University. Judge Groner continued:

This amendment of the charter of the university goes no farther than its terms. If it successfully legalizes the appropriation out of the Treasury of money of the government in aid of a private institution, it does not, nor does it purport to, change the fundamental character of the institution or make it any the less private; for Congress has passed no law giving the Secretary of the Interior or any other officer of the government control of the university, and we think it is obvious it could not do so without the consent and approval of the corporate authorities of that institution. Hence, in the view we take, the generosity of the government is not enough in itself to change a private into a public institution.

The *Maiatico* case was cited with approval and its doctrine reaffirmed and applied in Irwin v. United States. It is clear, therefore, that the principle which counsel for the plaintiffs seek to invoke, namely, that a Government college or university may not expel its students without notice of charges and an opportunity to be heard, is not applicable to Howard University, for it is not a public institution nor does it partake of any governmental character.

It would be a dangerous doctrine to permit the Government to interpose any degree of control over an institution of higher learning, merely because it extends financial assistance to it. There are numerous colleges in this country, whose establishment was made financially possible by grants of land by the Federal Government. It is inconceivable that for this reason every "land grant college", as such institutions are generally denominated, should to some degree be subject to the control of the Federal Government, or that the Federal courts should be empowered to interfere with the administration of discipline, or the appointment of members of the faculty in such schools. In recent years, numerous universities, colleges and technical schools have received Governmental aid of various kinds by being granted funds to carry on scientific research projects. Surely it should not be held that any institution by entering into a contract with the United States for the conduct of some project of this sort and receiving funds for that purpose, has placed its head in a noose and subjected itself to some degree of control by the Federal Government. Such a result would be intolerable, for it would tend to hinder and control the progress of higher learning and scientific research. Higher education can flourish only in an atmosphere of freedom, untrammelled by Governmental influence in any degree. The courts may not interject themselves into the midst of matters of school discipline. Such discipline cannot be administered successfully in the same manner as governs the trial of a criminal case or a hearing before an administrative agency.

Students entering Howard University are formally advised by the University authorities that attendance at the institution is not a right but a privilege. In that important respect, among many others, Howard University differs from some State colleges. It is further indicated that this privilege may be withdrawn by the authorities if in their own judgment a student, who has been accepted for admission, does not conform to standards of conduct that the University exacts from its student body. Nowhere is it stated directly or by implication that a student would be accorded a hearing before his connection with the University could be terminated.

The University catalog, which is available to all prospective students and to members of the student body, as well as to the general public, enunciates the relation between the University and its students as follows:

Attendance at Howard University is a privilege. In order to protect its standards of scholarship and character the University reserves the right, and the student concedes to the University the right, to deny admission to and to require the withdrawal of any student at any time for any reason deemed sufficient to the University. Admission to and enrollment in the University include obligations in regard to conduct, both inside and outside the classroom, and students are expected to conduct themselves in such a manner as to be a credit both to themselves and to the University. They are amenable to the laws governing the community as well as to the rules and orders of the University and University officials, and are expected to conform to the standards of conduct approved by the University.

In this important respect, among many others, Howard University differs from some State institutions to which all qualified residents of the State are entitled to be admitted. As indicated in its catalog, this is not the case at Howard University, which partakes of the character of a private institution. If there is any contractual relation between the University and its students, the foregoing provisions are part of the contract.

The conclusion necessarily follows that the student plaintiffs had no constitutional, statutory, or contractual right to a notice of charges and a hearing before they could be expelled or their connection with the University could be otherwise severed. It was entirely within the discretion of the University authorities to grant or withhold a hearing. Consequently, the student plaintiffs are not entitled to any relief requiring the University to reinstate them until they have received a notice of charges and a hearing.

* * * the appointments of the faculty plaintiffs were not renewed as of the end of the academic year ending June 30, 1967. They were so notified prior to the expiration date. In following this course the University was entirely within its legal rights.

It is claimed in behalf of plaintiffs in this category, however, that under what are asserted to be regulations of the University, they were entitled to notice prior to specified dates that their appointments would not be renewed, and that failure to give such notice, required the University to renew the appointments. This contention is lacking in merit.

The Faculty Handbook of Howard University, which embodies regulations affecting members of the faculty and which is available to all of them, contains the following significant provision in regard to a renewal of term appointments in Section V, paragraph B, p. 19:

> The University shall be under no obligation to renew term appointments and therefore holders of academic positions under term appointments should have neither presumption of permanence nor expectancy of automatic reappointment.

Counsel for the faculty plaintiffs relies on Section IX of the same Handbook.
* * *

* * *

It is contended by counsel that Section IX constitutes an obligation to give notice of an intention not to renew a term appointment not later than a specified date, and in case of failure to give such a notice, the appointment must be deemed renewed. To construe Section IX in this manner would do violence to its very language. That regulation provides that it will be the practice of the University *without contractual obligation to do so,* to give written notice prior to specified dates. Section IX and Section V must be read together. Instructors and professors holding term appointments are expressly warned that there is no obligation to renew term appointments and holders of such positions should have neither presumption of permanence nor expectancy of automatic reappointment. While Section IX sets forth a practice of giving advance notice of intention not to reappoint, it is expressly provided that there is no contractual obligation to do so. It is entirely conceivable that a situation may arise subsequently to the specified date that would lead the University not to renew a term appointment. Such were the circumstances in this instance.

The conclusion is inescapable that the faculty plaintiffs were not entitled to a renewal of their appointments as a matter of law, and that the University had a legal right not to reappoint them. Complete discretion in the matter is vested in the University authorities.

* * *

The intellectual history of Western Europe and the United States is marked by the establishment and gradual growth of universities that are self-governing, in the selection of their faculties, in prescribing their curriculum, and in administering discipline of their student bodies. This history demonstrates that centers of higher learning can best develop and flourish in an atmosphere of liberty and independence, where they are free from governmental influence in any respect as to any aspect of their activities. A glance at this history is convincing. Universities in Italy, such as Bologna; universities in France, such as Paris; and Universities of Oxford and Cambridge in England, all of which originated in the Middle Ages, were from their very inception and always have remained independent bodies, unfettered by any intrusion on the part of any governmental agency, or of the courts. In this country with the early establishment of Harvard, William and Mary, Yale, Princeton, and King's College (later Columbia), this tradition was continued and has prevailed. Such institutions have been free of governmental control. One attempt to the contrary was defeated by the decision of the Supreme Court in the *Dartmouth College* case, in which the college was eloquently and forceably represented by Daniel Webster as counsel. Fortunately, even State universities in this country, which came later, particularly the larger institutions, have been left singularly free of governmental control or interference.

It would be a sad blow to institutions of higher learning and to the development of independent thought and culture if the courts were to step in and control and direct the administration of discipline and the selection of members of the faculty in universities and colleges. An entering wedge seemingly innocuous at first blush, may lead step-by-step to a serious external domination of universities and colleges and a consequent damper and hindrance to their intellectual development and growth.

In the light of the foregoing considerations, the motions for a preliminary injunction are denied.

* * *

NOTES AND QUESTIONS

1. In the famous *Dartmouth College Case* [*The Trustees of Dartmouth College v. Woodward*, 17 U.S. (4 Wheaton) 518 (1819)] referred to by Judge Holtzoff, Chief Justice John Marshall strongly supported the concept of private property by holding that New Hampshire could not modify the original charter establishing Dartmouth College.

* * * Dartmouth is an eleemosynary [charitable] institution incorporated for the purpose of perpetuating the application of the bounty of the donors, to the specified objects of that bounty; that its trustees or governors were originally named by the founder, and invested with the power of perpetuating themselves; that they are not public officers, nor is it a civil institution, participating in the administration of government; but a charity school, or a seminary of education, incorporated for the preservation of its property, and the perpetual application of that property to the objects of its creation. (At pp. 640–641; material in brackets added).

Marshall argued that the charter was in effect a contract and that Article I, Section 10:2 of the U. S. Constitution prevents states from passing laws "impairing the Obligation of Contracts." That New Hampshire had done this by reorganizing Dartmouth into a public institution under the control of an enlarged board of public officials was clear.

[The Founders of Dartmouth College] contracted for a system, which should, as far as human foresight can provide, retain forever the government of the literary institution they had formed, in the hands of persons approved by themselves. This system is totally changed. The charter of 1769 exists no longer. It is re-organized; and re-organized in such a manner, as to convert a literary institution, moulded according to the will of its founders, and placed under the control of private literary men, into a machine entirely subservient to the will of government. This may be for the advantage of this college in particular, and may be for the advantage of literature in general; but it is not according to the will of the donors, and is subversive of that contract, on the faith of which their property was given. (At pp. 652–653).

In effect, Marshall ruled that the constitutional protection accorded in Article I, Section 10 limited the Tenth Amendment powers of the state. This case raises some interesting questions. For instance, if the donors had established an institution with other than noble goals, e. g., a school for pickpockets or prostitutes, should such an organization be allowed to function?

The power to incorporate belongs to the state under the Tenth Amendment. (Dartmouth represents an unusual situation, since the College was chartered by the English King prior to the American Revolution.) Presumably, states could refuse to issue charters of incorporation to organizations appearing to operate contrary to the public welfare. Moreover, charters of incorporation usually contain clauses reserving to the state the power to amend them in the future. Through these devices, states retain sufficient authority to prevent abuses beyond reach of government action.

Nevertheless, questions arise. For example, should a private university or school, which admittedly performs a public function, be able to deny its students basic constitutional liberties such as freedom of association as in *Gott*, or the right to due process of law, as in *Greene*, when a public university or school, perhaps located across the street, cannot? Even when tax exemption and other types of government assistance enable the private university to continue to function? Do taxpayers have a right to demand that those institutions benefiting from public funds adhere to the public law? On the other hand, to what extent would restrictions of this type constitute invasions of the property rights of those establishing and operating charitable organizations?

When there is such a blending of public and private interests, serious issues arise under the Fourteenth Amendment, as the final section in this chapter will show.

2.   Judge Holtzoff asserts that Howard University is a private institution. In coming to this conclusion, he places little weight on the fact that Howard was created by an Act of Congress and receives considerable federal funding in order to operate. He chooses instead to rely on the *Maiatico* decision reached by the court of appeals that Howard is private, an illustration of the reliance placed by our legal system on prior decisions through the concept of *stare decisis,* or "rule by precedent."

Do you think that Howard University is sufficiently "public" to be governed by the same rules that apply to a state university? Should Judge Holtzoff have ignored the *Maiatico* decision?

3.   According to the opinion, attendance at a nonpublic institution is a privilege. Presumably, students waive their rights when they accept admission to these institutions. Do you think a person should be able to waive rights? What conditions should apply to acts of waiver?

4.   Judge Holtzoff ends his opinion by somewhat dramatically suggesting what might happen if the autonomy of nonpublic institutions were subject to court or legislative interference. Frequently decision makers, including judges, seek to bolster the rationale for their actions by picturing the evils attendant on a different ruling. Legal commentators sometimes label this technique "the parade of imaginary horribles." Are the evils Judge Holtzoff projects convincing?

5.   The faculty fared no better than the students in the district court proceeding. Like the students, the relationship of the faculty members to Howard University is viewed as contractual. No constitutional rights are involved because Howard is considered a nonpublic institution, despite its relationship to the federal government.

On appeal to the United States Court of Appeals for the District of Columbia Circuit, the students won a temporary restraining order pending court disposition of their appeal, preventing enforcement of the dismissals. The students were able to continue their studies, and when the case was decided two years later, they had graduated. The court, therefore, dismissed the action as moot with a proviso expunging the students' records of any mention of the expulsions. 412 F.2d 1128 (1969).

With regard to the faculty members, the appeals court ruled that they had stated a cause of action and would, upon proof, be entitled to monetary damages for breach of contract. Judge McGowan concluded that, considering all dimensions of the employment relationship at the university, the faculty members were entitled to be heard before being dismissed:

> The employment contracts of appellants here comprehend as essential parts of themselves the hiring policies and practices of the University as embodied in its employment regulations and customs. The very phrase relied upon by the District Court is in a Faculty Handbook which is replete with other provisions in conflict with the spirit of the use of that phrase now sought to be made. Those provisions seem to us to contemplate a hearing be-

fore separating from the academic community for alleged misconduct one who, although a non-tenured employee, has acquired a
different dimension of relationship because of the expectations inherent in the University's failure to give notice as contemplated by
its own regulations. (At p. 1135).

Judge McGowan noted that contracts in the academic setting "are
written and are to be read, by reference to the norms of conduct and expectations founded upon them" and added that precedents from the commercial world "are not invariably apt in this non-commercial context." (*Id.*)

This approach to contractual interpretation in the nonpublic educational setting, coupled with Judge McGowan's comment in a footnote that cases
like *Maiatico* are "far removed from the matter at hand", suggests greater judicial activism in the nonpublic sector than in the past. While only a
few courts have opted for greater involvement to date, the number may
grow. From the standpoint of the student, the following section explores
some of the approaches courts might employ to this end.

B. Theories of Expansion

The theories which have been advanced in recent years to justify judicial involvement in the relationship between student and nonpublic educational institutions can be categorized as follows: the public function—state
action theory, the contract-of-adhesion theory, the fiduciary theory, the
rights-of-common-law theory, and the legislative action theory. Each
of these will be discussed briefly, illustrated by case law and commentary.
Consider as you read which of the theories best reflects your own view
or whether you prefer a continuation of Judge Holtzoff's approach in
Greene.

(1) Public Function-State Action Theory

In its broadest sense, this approach envisions treating the nonpublic
educational institution as the legal equivalent of the public institution.
Thus, all of the same rights now enjoyed by students in public education
would automatically be carried over to the student in the nonpublic sector.
There are two versions of the theory, the first viewing all institutions as
performing public functions, and the second applying a more discriminating
"state action" test before considering the nonpublic institution the legal
equivalent of the public.

In 1960, the U. S. Supreme Court found that a privately endowed
park for whites only was subject to the terms of the Fourteenth Amendment because the park served a public function. *Evans v. Newton*, 382 U.S.
296 (1966). This case also reaffirmed the right recognized in *Pierce* to
establish and operate non-public schools. Thus, like the shopping center
cases, the public function concept has limited applicability in the educational setting, even though most nonpublic educational institutions, particularly those that have no religious affiliation, are largely identical to
their public counterparts in goals, curricula, and functioning.

Closely related to the public function concept is the state action theory,
which is less abstract than the former, focusing on actual state involvement
in the activities of educational institutions. The epitome to date of the

state action theory is a New York State case, *Ryan v. Hofstra Univ.*, 324 N.Y.S.2d 964, supplemented 328 N.Y.S.2d 339 (New York, 1971). The case involved a student who was dismissed from the university without notice or a hearing after he had been apprehended throwing a rock through a plate glass window at the campus bookstore. Ryan was suspected by university officials of having engaged in previous violent conduct. The state court, in reasoning contrary to Judge Holtzoff's in *Greene v. Howard Univ.*, reinstated Ryan after it found Hofstra so entangled with governmental activities as to be subject to the due process terms of the Fourteenth Amendment. Said the court,

> The responsiveness of private universities to constitutional inhibition is a lively current topic. Because of the essential need for academic freedom, a justly careful watch must be kept on outside interference in educational institutions. Yet the principle of personal right is also an essential need of democratic society. In this competition of principle, a constitutional domino theory is occasionally advanced [see, *Greene v. Howard Univ.*] under which any collegiate restriction is viewed as an opening fall which will surely tumble the entire institutional array. (At p. 977; bracketed material in original).

Noting that private organizations are often performing public functions and as such may be subject to constitutional requirements, the court examined the ties of Hofstra to the state and federal government:

> Hofstra has the major state governmental presence of the New York Dormitory Authority. According to the testimony, over half of the total book value of Hofstra University consists of assets not only constructed but owned by the Dormitory Authority.

> Formed under the provisions of the New York Public Authorities Law, the Dormitory Authority constructs dormitories and other buildings for universities, state operated, statutory and contract colleges, as well as other higher educational institutions such as Hofstra. Under the statutes, the State owns the facilities and leases them to universities authorized to confer degrees by the State Board of Regents. This includes Hofstra. The construction money comes from municipal bonds issued by the public authority upon the guaranty of the public authority. The Authority is, of course, tax exempt.

> * * * the Dormitory Authority, which is a state public body, has the power to insist upon rules and regulations for the operation of the Hofstra facilities.

> * * *

> The acts complained of in the disciplinary proceeding took place on Dormitory Authority property.

> *Other governmental financial participation*

> The public participation is not solely measured by the relationship with the Dormitory Authority.

Consider the following additional governmental financial aspects:

(a) Over $1,000,000 of the Hofstra $25,000,000 operating budget comes directly from governmental grants.

(b) The large majority of Hofstra students are New York State residents receiving State scholarship awards and incentives of various amounts under the New York State Education Law. No computation was offered of the exact amount of the Hofstra receipts from State scholarships and incentives.

(c) During the past five years, Hofstra has received over $3,000,000 in direct federal construction grants.

(d) Hofstra received a donation, conditioned upon educational use, from the federal government of 125 acres of land which forms over half its campus.

(e) The total book value of Hofstra is estimated to be $61,-000,000, of which $31,500,000 is supplied by the Dormitory Authority. $4,000,000 comes from government grants and $3,500,000 from private gifts, which are largely facilitated by income tax deductions. Only about one-third of the Hofstra plant comes from funds generated by Hofstra over the years, presumably through operations. However, it is unknown just how much of this operational surplus stems from prior availability of governmental funding or contract money for governmental services.

(f) The total acreage of Hofstra is 225 acres in the heart of Nassau County, with 1,600,000 square feet of building space. Being a tax-exempt organization, it pays no real estate taxes on its education use properties. Taking judicial notice of the tax rates and assessments in the surrounding area of land and buildings, it is necessary to conclude that a substantial percentage of its total revenues would have to be paid in public real estate taxes if Hofstra were fairly and currently assessed and tax paying.

(g) An Internal Revenue Service Training Center is operated by the Government prominently on campus in a separate leased building. Hofstra also operates a Police Training program for Nassau County. (At pp. 979–980)

* * *

The court concluded that Hofstra is in reality largely a governmental operation and thus subject to the same legal requirements to accord students due process rights as public institutions.

The *Ryan* case has not found much of a following, however. Though no institution will really know whether the state action principle applies to it or not until taken to court, most state and federal courts have been reluctant to extend the state action concept beyond cases where the entire institutional budget is supplied by the government. A good illustration of the current posture regarding the public function—state action theory is a recent case decided by the U. S. Court of Appeals for the Seventh Circuit. Judge John Paul Stevens wrote the opinion in *Cohen v. Illinois Institute of Technology*, 524 F.2d 818 (7th Cir. 1975) just prior to his appointment to the Supreme Court. Not only must there be substantial state support, wrote Judge Stevens, but the state must also be *directly tied* to the action being challenged.

> The facts that I.I.T. was chartered by the State and includes the word "Illinois" in its title do not lend any support to the claim that I.I.T. acts under color of state law. Every private corporation, whether profitable or charitable, is chartered by the States; unless the charter contains a special authorization or directive to engage in the challenged conduct, the fact that it is granted by the State is of no significance. * * *

> The State of Illinois provides support for I.I.T. in various ways. The Institute may benefit from the State's eminent domain [take private property for public use] powers; its students are allowed to use the facilities of various state agencies in certain study programs; its students receive financial support in the form of loan guarantees and scholarships; and, under the State Grant Program, funds are provided directly to the school. At most, however, the funds contributed by the State represent only a small fraction of the cost of educating the students for whom the grants are paid.

* * *

> The same analysis is applicable to the allegations describing the State's comprehensive regulation of the Institute. The regulation encompasses a wide variety of matters, from physical plant to course content and faculty qualifications. It is settled, however, that the mere existence of detailed regulation of a private entity does not make every act, or even every regulated act, of the private firm, the action of the State. Unless it is alleged that the regulatory agency has encouraged the practice in question, or at least given its affirmative approval to the practice, the fact that a business or institution is subject to regulation is not of decisive importance. (At pp. 824–826; material in brackets added).

Cohen's claim of sex discrimination against IIT in denying faculty promotion and tenure was dismissed. The decision was affirmed by the U. S. Supreme Court in April of 1976. In cases involving racial discrimination, however, the line between public and nonpublic sectors is not so carefully drawn, as the discussion in Chapter Seven shows.

(2) The Contract-of-Adhesion Theory

This theory, like the theories that follow, is much more limited in scope. It would accord nonpublic students only the right to *some* form of procedural due process, or basic fairness, in serious disciplinary matters. Thus, unlike the public function—state action theory, this approach would not grant nonpublic students the same civil liberties that students attending public educational institutions have, i. e., expression, press, association, etc.

As it is now understood to apply to the student enrolled at a nonpublic institution, the contract relationship is no different from any contractual relationship. Students who come to nonpublic institutions pay tuition (or their families do) in return for educational services. In this exchange of money for services, there are certain policies and rules that are either explicitly or implicitly agreed to. These policies and rules are found in catalogues, bulletins, letters of agreement, and so on. If the student does not observe the rules, he or she may be asked to go elsewhere. If the institution does not follow these rules or misrepresents them, then the student has a right to sue the institution for breach of contract.

There are some problems with present relationships, however. For one thing, the public school student usually has the same contractual rights as the nonpublic school student but in addition has certain constitutional guarantees which cannot be easily removed and are considered part of the contract, e. g., right to due process in disciplinary proceedings. Should students be entitled to similar rights in disciplinary actions when they attend nonpublic educational institutions? Consider another famous New York state case, *Anthony v. Syracuse Univ.*, 231 N.Y.S. 435 (New York, 1928). Susan Anthony signed a waiver upon matriculation giving the school the right to demand a student's withdrawal at any time for whatever reason. Plaintiff was dismissed from the university without any procedural due process after authorities had heard rumors about her and after her sorority sisters had reported that Susan was not "a typical Syracuse girl." Susan challenged the university action as arbitrary and unjust. The judge who wrote the New York Court of Appeals opinion concluded that:

> I can discover no reason why a student may not agree to grant to the institution an optional right to terminate the relations between them. The contract between an institution and a student does not differ in this respect from contracts of employment. * *

* * *

> * * * The regulation, in my judgment, does not reserve to the defendant an absolute right to dismiss the plaintiff for any cause whatever. Its right to dismiss is limited, for the regulation must be read as a whole. The University may only dismiss a student for reasons falling within two classes, one in connection with safeguarding the University's ideals of scholarship, and the other in connection with safeguarding the University's moral atmosphere. When dismissing a student, no reason for dismissing need be given. The University must, however, have a reason, and that reason must fall within one of the two classes mentioned above. Of course, the University authorities have wide discretion in determining what situation does and what does not fall within the classes mentioned, and the courts would be slow indeed in disturbing any decision of the University authorities in this respect.

When the plaintiff comes into court and alleges a breach of contract, the burden rests upon her to establish such breach. She must show that her dismissal was not for a reason within the terms of the regulation. The record here is meager on this subject. While no adequate reason was assigned by the University authorities for the dismissal, I find nothing in the record on which to base a finding that no such reason existed. She offered no testimony, either as to her character and relation with her college associates, or as to her scholarship and attention to her academic duties. The evidence discloses no reason for her dismissal not falling within the terms of the regulation. It follows, therefore, that the action fails. (At pp. 439–440).

Thus, while the court did say the university must have a reason for its action to escape a charge of arbitrariness, the burden was on the student to show that no reason existed. The court also rejected Susan's charge that she had not read the "fine print" in the catalogue and that the university regulation was contrary to public policy.

This decision points out the critical weakness of the traditional approach to student-institutional contractual arrangements. A student is not the equal of the university or school and cannot really "negotiate" a contract with the institution. It is really a "take it or leave it" proposition. Under these circumstances students who wish to attend nonpublic schools and colleges may have little choice but to waive rights available to them in the public sector on the basis of such "reservation clauses."

There are other weaknesses also. Usually, a student at a nonpublic institution does not sign a contractual document which sets forth the rules and regulations of the institution. In fact, the rules and regulations may be among the materials distributed to the student at various times after he or she has been granted admission, e. g., policy statements in catalogues, student handbooks, fee statements, and so on. As a result, the student is probably unaware of many of the binding terms of the "contract," including the often "reserved right" of the institution to dismiss the student at any time without stating reasons. Yet most courts will assume that the student knows the terms of the agreement. Furthermore, most courts will saddle the student, not the institution, with the burden of proving the institution's action not to be within the terms of the agreement. This is particularly true in disputes over grades or curriculum where courts feel they do not possess the expertise to reverse decisions made by educators. As one judge recently put it, "Educating young minds is not the same thing as building a house."

Proponents of a revised contract rationale to guarantee basic rights to nonpublic school students have sought to read into the student-institution agreement an obligation for the institution to accord the student at all times a duty of fundamental fairness regardless of the "fine print." John Beach, who, interestingly, was an attorney for Syracuse University at the time he wrote his article, has argued most persuasively for an updated contract theory to secure fairness for nonpublic students.

The contract approach, despite all the one-sided decisions from a prior age, seems preferable * * *. * * * it is time to ac-knowledge—or re-acknowledge—a *public policy* favoring funda-mental fairness in the contractual relationship between student and private educational institution. * * *

* * *

* * * But the egregious case of arbitrary deprivation of a student's reasonable expectations should have a court and a remedy open to it. And since the contractual approach *is* the more general theory, it is perfectly capable of absorbing this sub-stance of what fundamental fairness requires. In fact it is per-fectly capable of application to public institutions—as well as to the private institutions. Even though constitutional doctrines do not apply to private institutions without untoward aberrations in "state action" concepts, the reverse is not true. The college-student relationship has always been deemed at least contractual regardless of whether the college involved was private or public. Once it is well established that contract law, informed by public policy, requires fundamental fairness in the student-college con-tract, we shall have identified the one durable shield against ar-bitrary fiat at private institutions. To boot we shall have added an alternative shield against arbitrary fiat at *public* institutions.

It is an important task. I urge the bar and the state courts to fashion a contract law of fundamental fairness for private col-lege and university disciplinary and expulsion cases, since for good reason the Constitution doesn't quite reach.[28]

Beach adds that insofar as *Anthony* is concerned:

We would no longer expect to be upheld (at Syracuse University) in expelling a student for no stated reason, even if we still slip-ped language of consent to such action into the forms signed by the student at registration. More to the point, we would expect to lose it on grounds of contract law, and not on constitutional grounds.[29]

The approach suggested by Beach has been followed in situations where one party controls the drafting of the contract. Such contracts are called "contracts of adhesion" and require courts to construe ambiguous terms in favor of the weaker party and generally see that the weaker party is treated fairly.

The contract-of-adhesion theory does recognize institutional diversity insofar as educational mission and student rights are concerned. It is particularly evident in the nonpublic sector that student rights are closely related to the philosophy of the institution: one would expect the rights of students in a military academy to differ from the rights of students

---

28. John A. Beach, "Fundamental Fairness in Search of a Legal Rationale in Private College Student Discipline and Expulsions," 2 *J.Coll. & Univ.L.* 65, Fall, 1974, at pp. 80–81. (Emphasis in original).

29. *Id.*, at p. 69.

in a free school. Since the nonpublic sector is composed of many types of schools, this limited approach would likely be more compatible with its characteristics than would be the public function-state action theory.

Recently, several courts have begun to read into the contractual relationship between the student and the nonpublic institution the kind of fundamental fairness criteria urged by Beach. For example, in *Wisch v. Sanford School, Inc.*, 420 F.Supp. 1310 (D.C.Del.1976), the federal district court rejected the state action theory as applied to Sanford School, a nonpublic school with an enrollment of 375 students. But the court did suggest that because of "the very special nature of the relationship between a student and the school and the primary importance of education" the school had a duty to act fairly and reasonably in disciplinary matters. (At p. 1315). However, in this case the court concluded that the institutions had acted fairly, and thus the student lost.

To date, aside from a few cases, the contract-of-adhesion approach has not commanded a great deal of judicial support. Courts continue by and large to adhere to the *Gott-Syracuse-Greene* approach deciding in favor of the institution except where institutions have acted arbitrarily and without regard to the contract or have failed to deliver what was clearly and specifically promised in the contract. Consumer suits, of course, can be brought by both nonpublic and public school students and constitute a growing area of educational law. To date, however, courts are reluctant to interfere to any great degree with the freedom of contract, a right long associated with the word "liberty" in the Fourteenth Amendment and historically significant in the economic development of the country. The more basic issue of fundamental fairness at nonpublic institutions has not been extensively addressed via the contract theory.

(3) The Fiduciary Theory

The fiduciary theory as applied to the educational setting assumes that students are simply too young and unversed to protect their own interests in making agreements with educational institutions. They therefore place their trust in the wisdom and integrity of the institution, which is presumed to have a duty to act in their best interests. A fiduciary relationship is said to exist where there is special trust placed in one who is bound to act in good faith and with due regard to the interests of the person placing the trust. Fiduciary responsibilities are found in such relationships as those between husband and wife, attorney and client, trustee and beneficiary, clergyman and parishioner, doctor and patient, and corporate director and stockholder.

As a consequence of the fiduciary relationship, the judiciary holds the fiduciary (the party in whom trust is placed) to a high standard of conduct, one untainted by selfish actions. In effect, the burden of proving good faith conduct is always placed on the fiduciary, rather than the dominated party, when conflicts arise in the relationship.

A leading proponent of the fiduciary theory in education states:

> Given the proposition that there is a fiduciary relationship between student and university, it becomes apparent that, contrary to past practice, the courts have a positive duty to scrutinize

carefully any action which might blemish the high standard of conscience and honor which should govern the conduct of a fiduciary (the university) in dealing with entrusters (its students). Consistent with the usual rule of fiduciary relations, the institution, not the student, should carry the evidentiary burden of proving the fiduciary quality of its conduct. Since the school's central role, by dedication, declaration and tradition, is to be a citadel of free inquiry in the disciplined but unfettered search for truth, any examination of its conduct should be posed in terms of its fidelity to that function. Similarly, as a fiduciary, the university has the burden of establishing that it acted in a just and reasonable manner toward its students. Moreover, as a fiduciary it must disclose fully all relevant facts in any transaction with the student.[30]

Goldman asserts that adopting a fiduciary approach would eliminate the dichotomous judicial treatment of public and nonpublic educational institutions, since it applies equally well to both.

But the fiduciary theory has not been accepted by either educators or the judiciary. In the first place, students at the high school or postsecondary level can hardly be considered the dominated party. To characterize students in this fashion constitutes a return to the *in loco parentis* doctrine. In reality students beyond elementary school are often very capable decision makers and active participants in the learning process. Under these circumstances, the institution cannot always be held responsible for student-initiated actions such as academic failure, destruction of property, or anti-social behavior. Secondly, the standards under which the fiduciary approach would be applied in the educational setting are unclear. Since no case law has been built up, the fiduciary approach suffers from considerable ambiguity about its exact nature and application.

(4) The Rights-of-Common Law Theory

The rights-of-common law theory is based on the proposition that students, whether at public or nonpublic institutions, have a sufficient investment or interest in their education to warrant procedural safeguards against its denial. The interest of the student in his education is in the nature of a property right. Under English common law, membership in a nonpublic association such as a medical club was considered sufficiently important to the individual to require fair procedure before termination. Failure to accord members such fairness could result in legal liability for damages. In the United States, several courts have similarly required minimum standards of fairness before members of organizations such as trade unions and social clubs can be expelled, even when the bylaws are silent on the issue or expressly *deny* such a right to fair procedure.*

---

30. Alvin L. Goldman, "The University and the Liberty of Its Students—A Fiduciary Theory," 54 *Kentucky L. Journal* 643, 1966, at p. 674.

* In the United States many associations tightly control employment conditions and thus have great power over their members. In *Law Students Civil Rights Research Council, Inc. v. Wadmond*, 401 U.S. 154 (1971), for example, the U. S. Supreme Court decided in a narrow 5–4 vote that state bar organizations do not violate the Constitution in insisting that applicants

The rights-of-common law theory would simply add the educational institution to the list of associations in which the individual's membership has been considered a property interest by the courts. But the theory would apply only where denial of membership is at stake.

> Since the rationales for protecting the student's interest are based largely on guarding against the external effects of discipline arbitrarily imposed, or against actions which effectively deny the student the intrinsic educational benefits associated with the status of student, the court's *jurisdiction* would be limited to those instances where the sanction which the university imposes amounts to an effective expulsion, in the sense that his pursuit of an education and an eventual diploma, to which his status entitles him, are substantially frustrated. Minor matters of discipline which do not significantly impede the student's pursuit of his education and degree would not, therefore, fall within the court's jurisdiction regardless of how unfair or unreasonable the punishment may be.[31]

So far, the rights-of-common law theory has not been adopted by the courts to apply to disciplinary actions at nonpublic schools and colleges. Its promise for the future, therefore, is dim.

(5) The Legislative Action Theory

Frequently one hears the admonition, "Don't depend on the courts to grant you rights; seek them from the legislature." There is much validity in the statement, for many courts are reluctant to act, or even appear to act, as legislative bodies. Student rights, as we have seen, can emanate from the action of legislative bodies. Most students enjoy the protections of the 1974 Family Educational Rights and Privacy Act (Buckley Amendment), for example, because Congress saw fit to pass the law.

It has been suggested that legislatures pass laws extending an array of rights to students attending nonpublic educational institutions. The danger is that such laws would be open to attack as an interference in the institutions' internal affairs. Rights of private property, including the freedom of contract, are jealously guarded in the United States. Such laws, even if acknowledged as meritorious, would be considered dangerous precedents and potentially destructive of the healthy diversity nonpublic institutions contribute to the overall American educational system. For example, laws in the form of financial aid programs may not appear to threaten private property rights because nonpublic institutions are free to reject them. In reality, economic pressures may dictate their acceptance.

be of good moral character and loyal to the Constitution. Loyalty to the Constitution in this case meant required sworn support for state and federal constitutions and a statement concerning any membership in organizations advocating violent overthrow of the government. State agencies may also exert similar controls. Recent Supreme Court decisions have upheld state requirements that in order to be employed, teachers must swear to support state and federal constitutions, *Connell v.*

Higginbotham, 403 U.S. 207 (1971), and that all state employees also take an oath against overthrow of the government by force or violence. *Cole v. Richardson*, 405 U.S. 676 (1972).

31. Comment, "Common Law Rights for Private University Students: Beyond the State Action Principle," 84 *Yale L. Journal* 120, 1974, at pp. 147–148. Emphasis in original.

Institutional autonomy, as well as individual privacy, have become major rallying points for those who decry big government's encroaching regulation, whether direct or indirect. In short, it seems questionable whether legislative action will be a major source for increasing student rights in the nonpublic sector.

NOTES AND QUESTIONS

1. Should courts become more involved in the operation of nonpublic educational institutions? Recall that Judge Holtzoff in the *Greene* case asserted that "history demonstrates that centers of higher learning can best develop and flourish in an atmosphere of liberty and independence, where they are free from governmental influence in any respect as to any aspect of their activities." On the other hand, while we may wish to preserve the diversity and independence of nonpublic education, should the policies and rules of these educational institutions take precedence over state and federal constitutional provisions insofar as student rights are concerned? If you believe the judiciary ought to be involved in extending rights to the nonpublic student, where should the line between institutional autonomy and judicial involvement be drawn? What principles might guide the drawing of such a line? Which should be given more weight: freedom of contract or a prescribed set of student rights in nonpublic educational institutions?

2. In our discussion of the first section of the Fourteenth Amendment above, we noted that the U. S. Supreme Court extended the protections of the Amendment to residents of the company town because officials running the town performed essentially the same functions as their public counterparts. Could the same reasoning be used to apply to the nonpublic sector? Might it be easier to extend the analogy to nonpublic colleges and universities than to nonpublic elementary and secondary schools?

3. The dichotomous treatment courts accord public and nonpublic educational institutions, respectively, yields some bizarre results. For example, in *Powe v. Miles*, 407 F.2d 73 (2nd Cir. 1968), several students were suspended from Alfred University, a nonpublic institution in New York, for disrupting an ROTC ceremony. The students challenged the action as a denial of their Fourteenth Amendment rights, asserting that the action of Alfred officials constituted state action. The U. S. Court of Appeals for the Second Circuit ruled that those suspended students who were enrolled in the Liberal Arts College of Alfred University were not entitled to Fourteenth Amendment rights because Alfred is a private institution. However, the suspended students enrolled in the College of Ceramics *did* have Fourteenth Amendment rights because of the agreement the State of New York had made with Alfred University to operate the Ceramics College. Specifically, the court cited relevant sections of the Education Law to show that the state had not relinquished ownership of the college property, of the tuition and other fees paid by students enrolled in the college, or of its operating budget.

Some commentators have noted that nonpublic institutions may increasingly be considered quasi-public because of growing state involvement in their internal affairs. For example, state efforts to coordinate the future growth and operation of both public and nonpublic postsecondary educational institutions tend to curtail institutional autonomy. Federal and state financial aid programs testify to public involvement in maintaining the viability of the nonpublic sector. Nonpublic institutions which increasingly are feeling a financial pinch may have little choice but to accept state regulations and assistance. To the extent this is true, they take on features of public institutions.

If a state statute grants a statutory right to nonpublic educational officials to use complete discretion in disciplining students, is such a law merely recognizing the independence of nonpublic institutions or forming a partnership with them? Would such a partnership transfer all discipline procedures at these institutions from private to state acts, subject to court review under the Fourteenth Amendment? In *Coleman v. Wagner College*, 429 F.2d 1120 (2d Cir. 1970), the Second Circuit was sufficiently unsure about the intent behind such an Indiana statute that it overruled a lower court dismissal of a student complaint and remanded the case for further hearings.

It would appear that many nonpublic campuses may eventually find themselves "between a rock and a hard place." Do you think courts ought to look beyond the indices of state involvement to decide what should be considered the equivalent of state action? Should they base their conclusions on institutional philosophy and mission?

4.   HYPOTHETICAL: *The Case of the Suspicious Test Scores*

Stephen Student was disappointed with his score on the aptitude test for graduate school. So he decided to take the test again. This time his score jumped over 200 points. His total score on the second test was sufficiently high to place him in a very competitive position for admission to the finest graduate schools in his field. He lost no time in filling out applications to a number of institutions nationally recognized for their quality and degree of selectivity.

Several weeks after notification of his second test score, Stephen received a letter from the private testing agency, informing him that his score on the second test had been cancelled and that the agency had informed all of the institutions to which Stephen had reported the test results that the agency was taking this action "because we have serious doubts as to the authenticity of the score." The agency offered to provide Stephen with a third opportunity to take the test, this time free of charge. However, in order for the high score achieved on the second test to be valid, Stephen had to come within 50 points of it on the retest.

Stephen was furious. He hired an attorney to represent him in a suit against the testing agency for reinstatement of the score, a retraction of the reason for the cancellation, and money damages for the injury to his reputation and to his chances for a successful career in his chosen field. He also testified under oath that he had not cheated.

The private testing agency claimed that Stephen had apparently failed to read the application form carefully. The application form contained this phrase: "We reserve the right to cancel any test score if, in our sole opinion, there is adequate reason to question its validity." Stephen countered with the assertion that he had no choice but to sign up for the test with the agency and pay the necessary fee because there were no competing testing agencies to which he could turn. This particular aptitude test was the standard test for Stephen's field.

Based on previous discussion and cases, how would you decide the case if you were the judge? What principles would guide you to your decision?

V. SUMMARY

This chapter and the one preceding it have covered a lot of territory. Chapter One focused on the dominant value positions held in our society about the relationship of the individual to government and the corresponding mission of educational institutions. The current state of social science research on the impact of schools was reviewed, as was the case for each of several contenders for deciding student rights.

This chapter examined the dominant judicial approaches to the role of the courts in American society and reviewed how courts have adjudicated disputes arising from the development of our public and nonpublic educational systems.

The purpose of these two chapters has been to illustrate the complexity of student rights issues. There are no easy resolutions. Decisions about rights involve an intricate interplay of factors. Value positions about the nature of the individual and the role of government have a bearing on one's conceptions about freedom, justice, and equality. Subsequent chapters will develop this point. The orientation of the decision maker to the educational environment, its constituencies, and its mission, constitutes another set of variables. The answer to the question "What rights should students have?" is directly related to how one views the purpose of the educational institution in which the students are enrolled.

Where judges are the decision makers, their orientation to the role of the court may be critical to judicial involvement. An activist approach is more likely to induce a judge to become involved in sensitive and controversial matters in the interest of establishing reforms than adherence to either judicial self-restraint or judicial neutralism.

Figure 2–4 below illustrates these concerns as they relate to judicial decision making about student rights. It is important to understand, however, that these variables are not so closely patterned as to allow the prediction of outcomes when courts confront student rights issues. On the contrary, the interplay of variables is far too subtle and complex for this to be possible. The purpose of the diagram is only to bring some degree of order to the many components involved in judicial resolution of student rights disputes.

Figure 2–4: Variables Involved in Judicial Decision Making About Student Rights

Value Position on the Individual and the Government $\Longrightarrow$ Value Position on Freedom, Justice, and Equality $+$ Orientation to the Educational Environment $+$ Orientation to the Role of the Court $=$ DEGREE OF INVOLVEMENT IN STUDENT RIGHTS DISPUTES

Example:

Liberal Emphasis on Social Pluralism	(To Be Explored in Forthcoming Chapters)	Marketplace of Ideas
Conservative Emphasis on Social Order		Inculcate Self-Discipline and Social Values

Example:

Example:

Active Involvement to Solve Social Problems

Self-Restraint and Deferral to Others (Legislators, Parents, Educators)

Part II

THE DEVELOPING LAW

Chapter Three

"First Amendment rights, applied in light of the special characteristics of the school environment, are available to teachers and students. It can hardly be argued that either students or teachers shed their constitutional rights at the schoolhouse gate."

Justice Abe Fortas
Tinker v. Des Moines School Dist., 1969

"RIGHTS OF SPEECH, PRESS, AND ASSEMBLY"

The cornerstone of American civil liberties is the First Amendment. It provides that "Congress shall make no law respecting an establishment of religion, or prohibiting the free exercise thereof; or abridging the freedom of speech, or of the press; or the right of the people peaceably to assemble, and to petition the Government for a redress of grievances."

This chapter reviews the application of the First Amendment to the political and social setting, and notes specifically and in some detail its application to the student in public educational institutions. To provide the reader with a framework for understanding how the First Amendment has been interpreted over time, the dominant approaches in our society to defining "freedom" and the variety of approaches used by members of the U. S. Supreme Court in applying the terms of the First Amendment to specific situations will be examined first.

This chapter will focus on freedoms of speech, press, and assembly. Religious freedoms will be deferred until the next chapter.

I. THE JUDICIARY AND THE FIRST AMENDMENT

Freedom of communication has long been a cherished value in American political life. The nineteenth century British philosopher, John Stuart Mill, advanced the classic argument for the freedom to communicate and the need for diversity of opinion in his work *On Liberty*: "Though the silenced opinion be an error, it may and very commonly does contain a portion of truth, and since the general or prevailing opinion on any subject is rarely or never the whole truth, it is only in the collision of adverse opinions that the remainder of the truth has any chance of being supplied."[1] Freedom to speak, believe, publish, or associate is considered a pivotal value in our approach to pluralist democratic politics. As Justice Benja-

1. John Stuart Mill, *On Liberty*, (New York: Appleton Century Crofts, 1947), at p. 50.

min N. Cardozo once wrote, freedom of thought and of speech is "the matrix, the indispensable condition, of nearly every other form of freedom." [2]

But what is freedom? What kinds of behavior are included in this "matrix of nearly every other form of freedom?" What are the limits within which these freedoms may be exercised? Who determines what limits should be set?

A. Freedom: How Much and For Whom?

The definition of "freedom" has always been a problematic issue. To say that Mr. X or Ms. Y is free poses the questions: "Free *from* what? Free to *do* what?" Assuming that freedom is possible, political and legal commentators disagree about its importance in human affairs. Some argue that it is dangerous. Others contend that it is the supreme aim of human existence. Still others insist that it is meaningless without a prior guarantee of material security. Obviously, there is no one right view of "freedom," but three basic images have evolved, each with its attendant problems for political and legal action.

(1) Negative Freedom: The Absence of Governmental Restraint

The practical person views human freedom as a product of social and political structure. People are free to the extent that they are allowed to pursue certain interests without the imposition of external restraints. A free political system is considered one which encourages the development of conditions favorable to the pursuit of individual interests, and permits the natural expression of those interests by limiting the authority of those who govern.

This conception of freedom is frequently referred to as *negative freedom*—freedom exists when there are no restraints. The wording of the First Amendment is considered the ultimate embodiment of this view, namely "Congress *shall make no law* respecting an establishment of religion," and so on. As Justice Hugo Black frequently said, "No law means no law."

(2) Positive Freedom: Government Support for Individual Growth and Social Pluralism

An opposing faction contends that freedom as the absence of restraint is an improper value position, that being "free" must include possessing the resources necessary to develop one's capabilities, talents, skills, and interests. Freedom from restraint in speaking one's mind is useless without the intellectual skills or financial resources necessary for effective expression. The government must take positive action to guarantee basic minimal resources to all individuals in a society if each is to have equal opportunity of expression in a competitive political and social setting. To advocates of "positive freedom" educational institutions are particularly significant. Since a knowledge of facts and possession of skills are always relevant to the making of intelligent and effective choices, the ex-

2. *Palko v. Connecticut*, 302 U.S. 319 (1937),
at p. 327.

tent of a society's educational facilities will provide an empirical index of its support for freedom. The kind of knowledge educational facilities offer through the curriculum and the manner in which it is taught will influence the extent to which individuals can effectively pursue their interests. In a system concerned with individual positive freedom, some clear distinction, of course, must be made between indoctrination and teaching.

Those who advocate positive freedom frequently claim that if a society is genuinely commited to working for the development of individual capabilities, some restraint may be necessary. It may, for example, be necessary to tax (or restrain) the economic resources of some in order to provide more extensive physical protection or educational opportunities for others. Therefore, negative freedom cannot be considered an absolute because it must always be balanced against other interests such as public order, the right to a fair hearing, or equality of opportunity.

(3) Freedom as Necessity: Truth as a Prerequisite

Not everyone views the good life as being primarily dependent on the existence of certain social interests and values. Some political writers assert that human beings have spirtual needs that neither negative nor positive freedom can satisfy. For these advocates, being "free" means fulfilling these needs rather than immediate impulses or urges. Religious observers use this conception of freedom when they say that "the truth shall make you free." A person is considered free when he or she acts in conformity with God's law—that which is objectively and irrefutably true.

Other uses of this conception of "freedom as necessity" are the Marxist philosophy of universal economic equality and the conservative view that the "true" freedom lies in obeying and defending the societal rules, traditions, and regulations that preserve peace and order. The radical Marxist and the conservative view of "freedom" or "being free" means conforming to the basic values of human nature. The significant issue raised by the freedom as necessity theory is that political pluralism is not a particular virtue. For Marxists and arch-conservatives alike (strange bedfellows indeed) truth is truth, and compromise and pluralism may mean that human beings are not meeting the needs of their "real" or "true" nature. For these political actors, only *their* "truth" in effect makes us "free."

B. Background to First Amendment Freedoms: Judicial Approaches

As the previous chapter demonstrated, many people are opposed to judicial activism, yet no one denies that courts have the authority to interpret and adjudicate issues that deal with constitutional questions. In judicial terms, freedom of expression has generally meant the freedom to communicate without prior restraint, that is to say, without prior censorship of what one intends to say or write. Permissible prior restraints, as noted later in this chapter, are confined to special situations, one of which relates to the student press.

Subsequent punishment, rather than prior restraint, has been the preferred way to regulate expression. The problem, however, centers on deciding exactly what expression should subject the speaker to punishment. Freedom of expression as defined in the First Amendment is far from clear to everyone. Shouting "fire" in a crowded theater, to cite Justice Holmes' famous example, is a lawful exercise of freedom of speech if there actually is a fire; but if there is no fire, it represents an abuse of freedom of speech. Trying to distinguish between what is lawful communication and what is unlawful agitation, what is artistic expression and what is unprotected obscenity, what is a political speech and what is illegal slander, is the very substance of judicial interpretation and adjudication. It is up to the judges to decide whether yelling "fire", "dirty Fascist," or "goddamn Communist" is freedom of expression or an abuse of that freedom which society has a right to restrain or regulate in the public interest.

To come to grips with these issues in a consistent manner, the members of the Supreme Court have developed several approaches over the years to interpreting the meaning of the First Amendment. These approaches range from an "anything goes" view supportive of negative freedom to a middle-of-the-road balancing of interests view in harmony with positive freedom to a conservative orientation designed to assure that freedom of expression is not used in anti-social ways. Since these approaches help individual judges achieve some consistency in dealing with diverse free expression cases and are as applicable in the educational setting as in society-at-large, it is important to review them briefly.

(1) The Absolute-Literalist Approach [3]

In its purest form, this approach has never been wholly embraced by the Supreme Court. An absolute interpretation of the First Amendment would prevent the passage of any law or the imposition of any punishment restricting expression. While no member of the Supreme Court has taken this extreme view of rights of expression, Justice Hugo Black perhaps came closest to it when he flatly asserted that "no law means no law." This strict constructionist position does not provide exceptions for types of expression such as obscene movies or seditious utterances. For Justice Black, no form of oral communication could be forbidden. As he expressed it:

> It is my belief that there *are* "absolutes" in our Bill of Rights, and they were put there on purpose by men who knew what words meant, and meant their prohibitions to be "absolutes." * * * I am primarily discussing here whether liberties *admittedly* covered by the Bill of Rights can nevertheless be abridged on the ground that a superior public interest justifies the abridgement. I think the Bill of Rights made its safeguards superior. (Emphasis in original) [4]

The implications of Black's absolutist position are that all existing obscenity, sedition, and libel laws would have to be repealed or declared

---

3. For a detailed discussion of judicial standards associated with the First Amendment, see Craig R. Ducat, *Modes of Constitutional Interpretation* (St. Paul, Minn.: West Publishing Co., 1978).

4. Hugo L. Black, "The Bill of Rights," 35 *N.Y.Univ.L.R.* 865, April, 1960, at pp. 866–867.

unconstitutional. In this area, Justice Black is the judicial activist *par excellence.*

Although Justice Black viewed the prohibition against regulation of First Amendment freedoms as absolute, he took the words of the Amendment literally. Thus, in his view, "speech" should be literally interpreted as verbal expression only. Writing in *A Constitutional Faith* in 1968, Justice Black categorically denied that picketing is a protected right under the First Amendment. "Marching back and forth, though utilized to communicate ideas, is not speech and therefore is not protected by the First Amendment." [5] Thus here is advanced the "literalist" aspect of the absolute-literalist standard.

In essence, the absolutists have concluded that those who live in a free society choose to govern themselves, even though self-government may result in slipping into error. The absolutists claim that those who live in a free socity choose not to be protected against erroneous opinions but to assume the responsibility of searching continuously for the truth. As another great absolutist and civil libertarian, Alexander Meiklejohn, put it:

> We have adopted it (i. e., the search for truth) as our "way of life," our method for doing the work of governing for which, as citizens, we are responsible. Shall we, then, as practitioners of freedom, listen to ideas which, being opposed to our own, might destroy confidence in our form of government? Shall we give a hearing to those who hate and despise freedom, to those who, if they had the power, would destroy our institutions? Certainly! Yes! Our action must be guided, not by their principles, but by ours. We listen, not because they desire to speak, but because we need to hear. If there are arguments against our theory of government, our policies in war or in peace, we, the citizens, we, the rulers, must hear and consider them for ourselves. That is the way of public safety. It is the program of self-government.[6]

If the First Amendment were to be interpreted as Justice Black and Professor Meiklejohn have argued, negative freedom would indeed be a political reality. But Justice Black and the few others who have embraced the so-called absolute-literalist approach have maintained that while the *content* of expression can not be regulated, the *time, place,* and *manner* in which expression is exercised, can. In an interview with Professor Edmund Cahn of New York University Law School in 1962, Justice Black outlined his view of legal restraints on expression:

> Nobody has ever said that the First Amendment gives people a right to go anywhere in the world they want to go or say anything in the world they want to say. * * * We have a system of property in this country which is also protected by the Constitution. * * * For instance, I would feel a little badly if somebody were to try to come into my house and tell me that he had a con-

5. Hugo Black, *A Constitutional Faith* (New York: Alfred Knopf, 1968) at p. 54.

6. Alexander Meiklejohn, *Political Freedom: The Constitutional Powers of the People* (New York: Harper, 1960) at p. 57.

stitutional right to come in there because he wanted to make a speech against the Supreme Court. I realize the freedom of people to make a speech against the Supreme Court, but I do not want him to make it in my house.

> This is a wonderful aphorism about shouting "fire" in a crowded theater. But you do not have to shout "fire" to get arrested. If a person creates a disorder in a theater, they would get him there not because of *what* he hollered but because he *hollered.* (Emphasis in original).[7]

Justice Black's *Tinker* dissent presented later in this chapter will reveal that he considered the educational institution an inappropriate place for exercise of rights of expression by students.

With the addition of time, place, and manner qualifications, this approach moves closer to the positive freedom concept discussed earlier since it obligates the judiciary to take positive action in supporting those basic or fundamental freedoms found in the First Amendment on the one hand and societal order on the other. The time, place, and manner approach will be examined at greater length below.

(2) The Preferred Position Approach

Under this approach, First Amendment freedoms are preferred above all other clauses of the Constitution as well as the right of the federal government and state governments to pass restrictive laws. This approach is most reflective of recent Court decisions indicating a greater tolerance for pluralism and dissent both in educational institutions and in society-at-large. An early illustration is the 1944 case, *Thomas v. Collins,* 323 U.S. 516, where a Texas statute requiring registration of labor organizers was used to enjoin a pro-labor speech in a public hall. Said Justice Rutledge for the majority in overturning the conviction of Thomas:

> The case confronts us again with the duty our system places on this Court to say where the individual's freedom ends and the State's power begins. Choice on that border, now as always delicate, is perhaps more so where the usual presumption supporting legislation is balanced by the preferred place given in our scheme to the great, the indispensable democratic freedoms secured by the First Amendment. That priority gives these freedoms a sanctity and a sanction not permitting dubious intrusions. And it is the character of the right, not of the limitation, which determines what standard governs the choice. (At pp. 529–530).

Drawing much of their inspiration from Justice Cardozo's observation in *Palko v. Connecticut* (1937), that basic liberties constitute the "matrix" of democratic society, preferred position advocates insist on the need for special, positive protection of First Amendment freedoms. Frequently the argument for this extra measure of protection invokes the need for some added weight to tip the scales of justice. C. Herman Pritchett com-

---

7. "Justice Black and First Amendment 'Absolutes': A Public Interview" 37 *N.Y.Univ. L.Rev.* 549, June, 1962, at p. 558.

pares the preferred freedoms approach to "the butcher who consistently weighs his thumb with the meat." [8] *How much* preference is to be given when the rights of dissenters come into conflict with the needs of social order has never been precisely described. Thus it is not always clear exactly what a judge has in mind when utilizing this approach.

(3) The Time, Place, Manner Approach

The time, place, manner approach asserts that while the *content* of expression may not be regulated, the *time, place,* and *manner* surrounding it can be. Such regulations must be "content-neutral," that is, based on reasons other than content, otherwise the approach is a subterfuge for restricting certain kinds of expression. The Supreme Court is always alert to possible discriminatory applications of allegedly content-neutral regulations such as parade permits, curfew regulations, and disturbing the peace ordinances.

An early representative of time, place, and manner cases is *Kovacs v. Cooper,* 336 U.S. 77 (1949), where the Court sustained a Trenton, New Jersey, ordinance designed to regulate the use of loudspeakers on city streets. Justice Reed for the majority acknowledged that "Absolute prohibition within municipal limits of all sound amplification, even though reasonably regulated in place, time, and volume, is undesirable and probably unconstitutional as an unreasonable interference with normal activities." (At pp. 81–82). Here, however, the regulation was designed only to prohibit the use of sound trucks which emit "loud and raucous noises" from the streets of Trenton. The dissenters objected to the statute, considering it a ready means of unconstitutional censorship.

Judges frequently use the time, place, and manner approach in the company of one of the other more permissive approaches (most often preferred position) to uphold curtailment of rights of expression. They will go out of their way to assert that one *does* have a constitutional right to speak, to picket, or to march, but *not* at the time, at the place, or in the manner of the situation under review. The problem is to ascertain whether specific applications of time, place, and manner regulations are *really* content-neutral or rather are devices for the suppression of unpopular expression.

(4) The Balancing Approach

The balancing approach is perhaps the most illustrative of positive freedom because it assumes that the judge must weigh the rights of others or of the state against the exercise of expression. This approach places the onus squarely on the judge not to delude the public or the legal community that these matters are easily resolved. The judge is central to the interpretation of conflicting rights, values, and interests, determining the validity of governmental actions against First Amendment freedoms by "a balancing * * * of the competing private and public interest at stake in the particular circumstances shown." [9]

8. C. Herman Pritchett, *Civil Liberties and the Vinson Court* (Chicago: University of Chicago Press, 1954), at p. 249.

9. *Barenblatt v. U. S.,* 360 U.S. 109 (1959), at p. 126.

In *Lehman v. Shaker Heights,* 418 U.S. 298 (1974), the Supreme Court concluded that a city could constitutionally prohibit political advertisements from display in city buses. Justice Douglas, concurring in the result, wrote:

> While petitioner clearly has a right to express his views to those who wish to listen, he has no right to force his message upon an audience incapable of declining to receive it. In my view the right of the commuters to be free from forced intrusions on their privacy precludes the city from transforming its vehicles of public transportation into forums for the dissemination of ideas upon this captive audience. (At p. 307).

The balancing approach seems to operate on the premise that freedom of communication is valued but not presumptively preferred. Other values such as a right to privacy, national security, and equality of opportunity may be entitled to greater protection in a given situation. No precise test can be outlined. Each case must be weighed on its merits. During the 1950s McCarthy era the Court typically determined that the government's interest in guaranteeing national security outweighed the Communists' rights of association. In 1968 the Court ruled in *United States v. O'Brien,* 391 U.S. 367, that the interest of the state in assuring that each draft registrant has a draft card justifies whatever infringement on speech might be involved in the prohibition of draft card burning. And until 1969 it was generally assumed that the interests of educational officials in providing an educational environment conducive to teaching and learning outweighed any right students might have to freedom of expression in that setting.

Balancing suggests the use of "judicial scales" in which conflicting interests or values are weighed to determine which is of greater importance. The technique is also indicative of the individual judge's view of the Court's overall role. Judicial self-restraintists, such as Justice Felix Frankfurter, have used a balancing of interests standard to abridge free expression rather than challenge the authority of Congress or the state legislatures. Judicial activists such as Justice Douglas have used it to elevate the interest of free expression over the interests of national security or domestic peace. The balancing approach, paradoxically then, appears to give judges considerable discretionary power. How they use the standard depends upon (1) which political value they give particular weight to (freedom, security, etc.) and (2) which approach to judicial power they endorse (neutralism, activism, restraintism).

A modern variation of the balancing approach is a relatively new concept, the *two-level theory.* The two-level approach is, like balancing, illustrative of the concept of positive freedom. It is also an indication that the exercise of freedom should be related to specific societal norms or ideals. According to the advocates of this standard, some varieties of expression are entitled to more constitutional protection than others. Thus in a 1976 case, *Young v. American Mini Theatres,* 427 U.S. 50, Justice John Paul Stevens for the majority ruled that stricter zoning ordinance could be applied to threatres showing erotic films than to theatres not showing such films, even though the erotic films were not considered constitutionally obscene. Had they been considered constitutionally obscene, their showing would have been entitled to no constitutional protection at all and could be effectively banned. Wrote Justice Stevens,

> *   *   *   we recognize that the First Amendment will not tolerate the total suppression of erotic materials that have some arguably artistic value *   *   *   [however] it is manifest that society's interest in protecting this type of expression is of a wholly different, and lesser, magnitude than the interest of untrammeled political debate *   *   *. Whether political oratory or philosophical discussion moves us to applaud or to despise what is said, every schoolchild can understand why our duty to defend the right to speak remains the same. But few of us would march our sons and daughters off to war to preserve the citizen's right to see "Specified Sexual Activities" exhibited in the theaters of our choice. (At p. 70; material in brackets added).

Only four Justices on the Court endorsed the two-level theory in this case. Dissenting Justice Brennan, embracing the preferred position approach, argued that the provisions of the First Amendment were developed primarily to protect the unpopular minority from majority control. Discrimination against theaters showing erotic films, he argued, is just such majority control.

A major criticism lodged against the two-level theory is that it serves to complicate an already complicated area by introducing another largely subjective variable—the *degree* of entitlement to First Amendment protection. Some types of expression such as erotic films are considered to be of less value than other types of expression such as political debate, and therefore are subject to more restriction. Deciding whether expression is constitutional or unconstitutional is difficult enough. Deciding in addition to what degree of constitutional protection certain forms of expression are entitled complicates the decision process even more.

(5) The Clear and Present Danger Approach

This approach represents a greater concern for the interests of social order and national security than do those previously discussed. It was first articulated in *Schenck v. United States*, 249 U.S. 47 (1919), by Justice Oliver Wendell Holmes:

> The question in every case is whether the words used are used in such circumstances and are of such a nature as to create a clear and present danger that they will bring about the substantive evils that Congress has a right to prevent. It is a question of proximity and degree. When a nation is at war many things that might be said in time of peace are of such a hindrance to its effort that their utterance will not be endured so long as men fight, and that no Court could regard them as protected by any constitutional right. (At p. 52).

The clear and present danger approach is intended to distinguish between abstract or general discussion which is considered constitutionally protected and discussion which is uttered in such circumstances and is of such a nature as to create a "clear and present danger" to the order or security of society. It places heavy emphasis on the context in which speech is uttered. It examines, in effect, the *circumstances* surrounding the exercise of expression rights.

While essentially a more explicitly formulated version of balancing, the clear and present danger approach is considered by critics to be an incomplete enumeration of the many factors that should be considered. These commentators contend that far too little attention is given to the significance of the speech uttered in a particular situation or the seriousness of the actual "danger" or "evil" that allegedly results.

(6) The Bad Tendency Approach

At the opposite end of the spectrum from the absolute-literalist view is the bad tendency approach which some judges use to highlight the importance of assuring social order and national security. This approach is similar to clear and present danger, except that it requires less of an immediate threat of substantive evil. A *tendency* to cause harm is sufficient to justify restraint or state regulation of speech.

The bad tendency standard was first articulated in *Gitlow v. New York,* 268 U.S. 652 (1925) by Justice Sanford, speaking for the majority:

> It is a fundamental principle, long established, that freedom of speech and of the press * * * does not confer an absolute right to speak or publish, without responsibility, whatever one may choose, or an unrestricted and unbridled license that gives immunity for every possible use of language, and prevents the punishment of those who abridge this freedom. * * *
>
> * * *
>
> * * * That utterances inciting to the overthrow of organized government by unlawful means present a sufficient danger of substantive evil to bring their punishment within the range of legislative discretion is clear. Such utterances, by their very nature, involve danger to the public speech and to the security of the State. They threaten breaches of the peace and ultimate revolution. And the immediate danger is none the less real and substantial because the effect of a given utterance cannot be accurately foreseen. The state cannot reasonably be required to measure the danger from every such utterance in the nice balance of a jeweler's scale. A single revolutionary spark may kindle a fire that, smoldering for a time, may burst into a sweeping and destructive conflagration. It cannot be said that the state is acting arbitrarily or unreasonably when * * * it seeks to extinguish the spark without waiting until it has enkindled the flame or blazed into the conflagration. * * * it may, in the exercise of its judgment, suppress the threatened danger of its incipiency. (At pp. 666–669).

In this case, Benjamin Gitlow's conviction under the New York Criminal Anarchy Act of 1902 for distributing a document similar to the Communist Manifesto was upheld.

The bad tendency approach is the most conservative of the freedom of expression approaches. Proponents assume that freedom of expression must be exercised in harmony with social ideas. This freedom as necessity orientation gives primary weight to social order and national security.

However, after the *Gitlow* case, the Court gradually moved away from this conservative posture to a greater tolerance of political and social pluralism. In most contemporary cases involving rights of expression, the Supreme Court has tended to use the preferred position or balancing approach to uphold expression, and the content-neutral time, place, and manner approach to justify restriction. Nevertheless, the special characteristics of the educational environment have prompted some judges to resurrect the clear and present danger approach and the bad tendency approach for application in this setting.

Figure 3–1, p. 102, illustrates the approaches of interpretation just discussed. Admittedly, the value of categorizing First Amendment decision making is limited. Judges vary in their approaches, given the variety of backdrops against which they are used. And, too, the approaches are so subjective that a decision maker can claim consistency by putting forth a particular rationale, yet actually embrace quite a different set of values. Despite these limitations, the spectrum of approaches to First Amendment decision making outlined in Figure 3–1 does help uncover some of the major concerns involved in the process of deciding and helps explain why some cases are handled one way and other cases handled differently. As you read the remainder of this chapter, reflect on which approach you would take in a given situation and, should you vary in your stance, what factors prompt your change. It will be readily apparent that judges often shift their approach when dealing with student and teacher expression cases because of the nature of the educational environment.

Figure 3-1: Standards of Interpreting Constitutional Rights of Expression

	Absolute-Literalist	Preferred Position	Time, Place, Manner	Balancing	Clear and Present Danger	Bad Tendency
Definition	The words of the First Amendment are to be taken literally. Thus "speech" means oral communication and "no law" means no law. So construed, the 1st Amendment constitutes an absolute ban on government regulation of rights of expression	Rights of expression in the First Amendment and 14th Amendment are preferred above other sections of the Constitution. Government regulation bears a heavy burden of justification	While content of expression cannot be regulated, the time, place, and manner of expression may be. Thus, content-neutral regulations, such as breach of the peace laws, parade permits, trespass laws, and the like are constitutional.	Weighing of interests of other persons or the state against exercise of expression.	Expression which is used in such circumstances and is of such a nature to create a substantive evil which the government has the duty to prevent.	A variation of the Clear and Present Danger standard. Requires less of an immediate threat of substantive evil. A "tendency to injure" is enough to justify regulation.
Relation to Concept of Freedom	Negative Freedom (the absence of restraint)	Negative Freedom (if emphasis on absence of restraint) - or - Positive Freedom (toleration for pluralism)	Positive Freedom (toleration for pluralism)	Positive Freedom (Toleration for pluralism)	Positive Freedom (toleration for pluralism) - or - Negative Freedom (must be in harmony with certain societal ideals)	Freedom as Necessity (must be in harmony with certain societal ideals)
Representative Case	None. Justice Black came closest to this view, though he endorsed regulating the time, place and manner of expression as opposed to its content	Thomas v. Collins, 323 U.S. 516, (1944) reversing conviction of a labor organizer for giving a speech in a public hall before registering with the state as required by law.	Kovacs v. Cooper, 336 U.S. 77, (1949) upholding a city ordinance limiting the use of sound trucks in public streets.	(Other Persons) Lehman v. Shaker Heights, 418 U.S. 298 (1974) protecting "captive audiences" in city buses from political advertisements (State) U.S. v. O'Brien, 391 U.S. 367 (1968), upholding state prosecution of a draft card burner protesting the Vietnam War.	Schenck v. U. S., 249 U.S. 47 (1919) upholding federal conviction of a person circulating leaflets critical of U. S. entry into World War I and of the draft.	Gitlow v. N. Y., 268 U.S. 652 (1925), upholding conviction of a person for distributing a document similar to the Communist Manifesto.
Major Criticism	At its purest, this posture would eliminate all laws designed to protect abuses of expression, e.g., libel, slander, obscenity.	Unclear as to what factors are to be considered in sustaining a government regulation.	Can be a guise for regulating content if applied indiscriminately.	Unclear as to what factors are to be considered in balancing.	How clear and how present must the substantive evil be? Unclear as to what factors are to be considered.	Same as Clear and Present Danger with greater emphasis on the subjectivity of the standard.

NOTE: This standard is frequently used to justify restraints of expression under the Preferred Position and Balancing Standards

Rights of expression are contained in the First Amendment to the U.S. Constitution. They have been extended to apply to state governments and their subdivisions through the word "liberty" of the first section of the 14th Amendment. Note that neither the First nor the 14th Amendment apply to actions by private persons or organizations.

[B9658]

II. THE DEVELOPMENT OF FREEDOM OF SPEECH

A. Freedom of Speech in the Political and Social Setting

The first major test of the First Amendment freedom of speech took place during the Administration of President John Adams. Congress passed the Alien and Sedition Laws of 1798, which were designed to suppress criticism of officials of the federal government. These laws provided for the deportation of aliens and the imprisonment and fining of citizens who criticized the national government. A prime example was made of Congressman Matthew Lyon of Vermont, who published some pejorative remarks about John Adams. Lyon was fined $1,000 and sent to jail for four months. The Supreme Court was never requested to rule on the constitutionality of these acts, though several of the Justices indicated that they thought the laws were constitutional. Thomas Jefferson and James Madison later waged a successful campaign for the repeal of this repressive law.

(1) The Early Years

The Supreme Court first tackled the problem of the First Amendment freedoms of expression in the immediate post-World War I period (1919–20).[10] As we have seen, the tensions of the war years produced many laws intended to curtail expression that might hinder the war effort. The first major case, *Schenck v. United States,* 249 U.S. 47 (1919), was concerned with a prosecution for interference with the operation of the armed forces by the distribution of pamphlets urging men to reject the draft call. Schenck was convicted under the Espionage Act of 1917. He defended himself on the grounds that his right of expression was protected under the First Amendment. Justice Holmes, speaking for the Supreme Court, affirmed the conviction, using, as we have seen, the clear and present danger approach. For Holmes, expression allowable in peacetime may not be protected during periods of war.

In his classic dissenting opinion in *Abrams v. United States,* 250 U.S. 616 (1919), Holmes found that the "best test of truth is the power of the thought to get itself accepted in the competition of the market * * *." (At p. 630). A group of Bolsheviks who advocated strikes in munitions plants with the alleged aim of frustrating American interference with the Russian Revolution did not pose for Holmes and Brandeis a clear and present danger. Although a majority of the Court was convinced of the evil intent of this group, Holmes and Brandeis claimed that the prosecution failed to demonstrate that their words constituted enough of a threat to justify punishment under the clear and present danger standard.

In 1927, the Supreme Court announced the bad tendency approach in *Gitlow v. New York,* rejecting the clear and present danger standard. *Gitlow* was also important because it was the first case in which the Supreme Court held that the speech and press provisions of the First Amendment were incorporated in the word "liberty" of the Due Process Clause of the

---

10. For a more comprehensive history of the Supreme Court's position on the First Amendment, see Jonathan D. Casper, *The* *Politics of Civil Liberties* (New York: Harper and Row, 1972), at pp. 30–86.

Fourteenth Amendment and thereby applicable to state governments. The Court upheld Gitlow's conviction.

The late 1930s saw the development of the "preferred position" approach, denying to restrictive legislation dealing with First Amendment political freedoms the presumption of constitutionality enjoyed by other types of legislation.

(2) World War Two and Its Aftermath

During World War II one important case did emerge in the freedom of expression area. In *Chaplinsky v. New Hampshire,* 315 U.S. 568 (1947), the Supreme Court came to terms with the problem of "fighting words" and their constitutional protection. The case involved a confrontation between a Jehovah's Witness and a police officer. After an intense altercation, Chaplinsky called the police officer a "damned Fascist". As a result of this statement, he was arrested, charged, and convicted under a New Hampshire statute which prohibited utterances that have a "direct tendency to cause acts of violence by the persons to whom, individually, the remark is addressed." The Supreme Court upheld the statute, advancing the doctrine that "fighting words," by their very utterance, inflict injury or tend to incite an immediate breach of the peace, and therefore are not considered protected speech. Use of such words may be punished without violation of the Constitution. The Court stated categorically:

> There are certain well-defined and narrowly limited classes of speech, the prevention and punishment of which have never been thought to raise any Constitutional problem. These include the lewd and obscene, the profane, the libelous, and the insulting or "fighting" words—those which by their very utterance inflict injury or tend to incite an immediate breach of the peace. It has been well observed that such utterances are no essential part of any exposition of ideas, and are of such slight social benefit as a step to truth that any benefit that may be derived from them is clearly outweighed by the social interest in order and morality. (At pp. 571–572).

In 1940, just prior to America's entry into World War II, Congress passed the Smith Act, 18 U.S.C.A. § 2385 (1969), giving the government strong authorization to deport, refuse citizenship to, or take away the U. S. citizenship of aliens who engaged in certain activities deemed detrimental to the interests of the United States. In 1940, the primary concern was Nazi infiltration and subversion. Included in the act was a briefly debated clause which was to become the focus of attention for several decades. The clause prohibited knowingly or willfully advocating or teaching the duty, necessity, desirability, or propriety of overthrowing the government of the United States by force or violence. Also prohibited was the intent to cause such overthrow by organizing a group for this purpose.

The first test of the Smith Act occurred in 1948 when eleven leaders of the American Communist Party were convicted for engaging in these proscribed activities. Their tempestuous trial is reminiscent of the more recent conspiracy trials of Angela Davis and of the Chicago Seven. Continuing prosecutions of numerous Communist Party leaders in the late 1940s eventually set the stage for a Supreme Court decision.

In *Dennis v. United States,* 341 U.S. 494 (1951), the Supreme Court upheld the conviction of the eleven leaders of the Communist Party for organizing and leading a party (a "conspiracy") that advocates overthrow of the United States government by force or violence. In effect, the Court affirmed the constitutionality of the Smith Act. Although a majority of the Court affirmed the conviction, none of the several opinions written could secure majority support. Three of the opinions in particular merit attention as indicative of how different First Amendment approaches were applied to the same case.

Chief Justice Fred M. Vinson (joined by three other Justices) invoked a version of the bad tendency approach to assert that the government did not have to wait until the revolution is about to begin. The Communists were a menace which had to be effectively controlled. His test, borrowed from Chief Judge Learned Hand, who was a member of the lower court, was whether the "gravity of the 'evil', discounted by its improbability, justifies such invasion of free speech as is necessary to avoid the danger." (At p. 510). Vinson removed the "immediacy" of danger requirement, deemed crucial by Justice Brandeis. For Vinson and his three colleagues, the Communist leadership posed a clear danger. And that was enough.

Justice Felix Frankfurter concurred in the affirmation of conviction. However, his reasoning clearly differed from that of his four colleagues. He rejected their reliance upon "clear and present danger" approaches and declined to weigh the competing interests of societal security and individual freedom, preferring to base his decision on the doctrine of judicial restraint.

> Free-Speech cases are not an exception to the principle that we are not legislators, that direct policy-making is not our province. How best to reconcile competing interests is the business of legislatures, and the balance they strike is a judgment not to be displaced by ours, but to be respected unless outside the pale of fair judgment. (At pp. 539–540).

Justices William O. Douglas and Hugo Black dissented. Rejecting the use of the clear and present danger approach as a basis for conviction, Douglas claimed that the eleven defendants only *taught* the doctrines of Marx and Lenin. He disagreed with the majority's conclusion that the Communist Party was a real danger to the security of the United States, claiming that since its doctrines had been so thoroughly exposed in this nation, its few adherents created no real threat. Black argued against the conviction even more directly by claiming the unconstitutionality of the Smith Act. Utilizing the absolute-literalist approach, Black stated that:

> These petitioners were not charged with an attempt to overthrow the Government. They were not charged with overt acts of any kind to overthrow the Government. They were not even charged with saying anything or writing anything designed to overthrow the Government. The charge was that they

agreed to assemble and to talk and publish certain ideas at a later date: The indictment is that they conspired to organize the Communist Party and to use speech or newspapers and other publications in the future to teach and advocate the forcible overthrow of the Government. No matter how it is worded, this is a virulent form of prior censorship of speech and press, which I believe the First Amendment forbids. (At p. 579).

By 1957, in *Yates v. United States,* 354 U.S. 298, the Court required a stricter standard of proof before individuals could be convicted under the Smith Act. Convictions could not be upheld unless there was evidence of personal participation in specific acts directed at the overthrow of government. The Department of Justice was thus forced to work harder to secure conspiracy convictions under the Smith Act. Four years later the Supreme Court ruled in *Scales v. United States,* 367 U.S. 203 (1961), that a provision of the Smith Act punishing "knowing" membership in an organization which advocated violent overthrow of the government was constitutional. In a companion case, *Noto v. United States,* 367 U.S. 290 (1961), the Court emphasized that there must be proof that the accused was an "active member" and had undertaken personally to accomplish the group's unlawful objectives. Thus construed, the Smith Act was constitutional.

At about the same time the Court was deciding cases dealing with the Smith Act, it was confronted with challenges to loyalty oaths in public employment. Many involved the teaching profession. In *Wieman v. Updegraff,* 344 U.S. 183 (1952), the Court unanimously declared an Oklahoma loyalty oath law unconstitutional because it disqualified a person from public employment for membership in a subversive organization even if the person did not know at the time of membership of its purposes and activities. In 1966 the Court applied the same requirements announced in *Scales* and *Noto* to loyalty oaths. In *Elfbrandt v. Russell,* 384 U.S. 11, the Court in a 5 to 4 vote ruled that a member of a subversive organization could suffer no penalties unless it could be shown that he joined with the specific intent to further its unlawful purposes or had actually engaged in them. As Justice Douglas noted for the majority:

> We recognized in *Scales v. United States* that "quasi-political parties or other groups * * * may embrace both legal and illegal aims." We noted that a "blanket prohibition of association with a group having both legal and illegal aims" would pose "a real danger that legitimate political expression or association would be impaired. * * * "
>
> * * *
>
> Those who join an organization but do not share its unlawful purposes and who do not participate in its unlawful activities surely pose no threat either as citizens or as public employees. Laws such as this which are not restricted in scope to those who join with the "specific intent" to further illegal action impose,

in effect, a conclusive presumption that the member shares the unlawful aims of the organization. (At pp. 15–16).

In 1968 the Court affirmed a lower court decision in *Knight v. Board of Regents,* 269 F.Supp. 339 (S.D.N.Y.1967), *aff'd* 390 U.S. 36, upholding a provision in the New York Education Law requiring public and private school teachers and professors to swear allegiance to the state constitution and the U.S. Constitution.[11]

(3) The 1960s and Brandenburg

During the 1960s, the Supreme Court developed what many analysts consider to be the definitive statement on the permissible limits of the government's power to restrict pure speech. Central to the recent Court's position on public speech and association is *Brandenburg v. Ohio,* 395 U.S. 444 (1969). It is a case which brings together many of the themes examined so far in this chapter.

In 1966, Clarence Brandenburg invited a Cincinnati newscaster to attend a Ku Klux Klan meeting in Hamilton County, Ohio. The newscaster and his crew made two films, sections of which were broadcast locally as well as nationally. One film showed 12 hooded figures, burning a large wooden cross. Some were carrying guns and most were expressing racially derogatory statements such as, "Bury the niggers" and "Send the Jews back to Israel." In the last section, Brandenburg appears in full Klan regalia to state:

> "This is an organizers meeting. We have had quite a few members here today which are—we have hundreds, hundreds of members throughout the State of Ohio. * * * We're not a revengeful organization but if our President, our Congress, our Supreme Court, continues to suppress the white, Caucasian race, · it's possible there might have to be some revengence taken.

> We are marching on Congress July the Fourth four hundred thousand strong. From there we are dividing into two groups, one to march on St. Augustine, Florida, the other group to march on Mississippi. Thank you." (At p. 446).

The second film showed Brandenburg repeating his speech in the presence of five hooded Klansmen, some with guns, in which he left out the word "revengence" and added: "Personally, I believe the nigger should be returned to Africa, the Jew returned to Israel."

On the evidence of these two films, Brandenburg was arrested, tried, and convicted under a 1919 Ohio criminal syndicalism statute which prohibited "advocat(ing) * * * the duty, necessity, or propriety of crime, sabotage, violence, or unlawful methods of terrorism as a means of accomplishing industrial or political reform" and "voluntarily assembl(ing) with any society, group or assemblage of persons formed to teach or advocate the doctrines of criminal syndicalism". He was fined $1,000 and

11. In 1971 the Court used *Knight* as precedent in unanimously approving part of a similar Florida statute. *Connell v. Higginbotham,* 403 U.S. 207 (1971). The Court struck down a portion of the oath, however, requiring the signer to pledge that he does not believe in overthrow of the government by force or violence since the provision did not provide for notice and a hearing prior to dismissal.

sentenced from one to ten years imprisonment. Brandenburg went through two appeals in Ohio. Each appellate court upheld his conviction.

During the appellate process, the Ohio and American Civil Liberties Unions became interested in the case. They claimed that the Ohio criminal syndicalism statute violated the First and Fourteenth Amendment's freedom of speech guarantees and therefore Brandenburg's conviction should be appealed to the United States Supreme Court. The Court agreed to hear the case. It is interesting to note that one of the major briefs supporting Brandenburg's right to freedom of speech was the one by Eleanor Holmes Norton, a Black ACLU attorney.

The Court overruled the conviction on the basis that the Ohio statute was unconstitutional. In his concurring opinion, Justice Douglas offered perhaps the clearest exposition to date of the limits to which a government is empowered to invade the individual's freedom of thought and speech.

BRANDENBURG v. OHIO

Supreme Court of the United States, 1969.
395 U.S. 444, 89 S.Ct. 1827, 23 L.Ed.2d 430.

(Per Curiam)

* * *

The Ohio Criminal Syndicalism Statute was enacted in 1919. From 1917 to 1920, identical or quite similar laws were adopted by 20 States and two territories. In 1927, this Court sustained the constitutionality of California's Criminal Syndicalism Act, the text of which is quite similar to that of the laws of Ohio. *Whitney v. California,* 274 U.S. 357 (1927). The Court upheld the statute on the ground that, without more, "advocating" violent means to effect political and economic change involves such danger to the security of the State that the State may outlaw it. But *Whitney* has been thoroughly discredited by later decisions. See *Dennis v. United States,* (1951). These later decisions have fashioned the principle that the constitutional guarantees of free speech and free press do not permit a State to forbid or proscribe advocacy of the use of force or of law violation except where such advocacy is directed to inciting or producing imminent lawless action and is likely to incite or produce such action. As we said in *Noto v. United States,* (1961), "the mere abstract teaching . . . of the

moral propriety or even moral necessity for a resort to force and violence, is not the same as preparing a group for violent action and steeling it to such action." A statute which fails to draw this distinction impermissibly intrudes upon the freedoms guaranteed by the First and Fourteenth Amendments. It sweeps within its condemnation speech which our Constitution has immunized from governmental control.

Measured by this test, Ohio's Criminal Syndicalism Act cannot be sustained. * * * Neither the indictment nor the trial judge's instructions to the jury in any way refined the statute's bald definition of the crime in terms of mere advocacy not distinguished from incitement to imminent lawless action.

Accordingly, we are here confronted with a statute which, by its own words and as applied, purports to punish mere advocacy and to forbid, on pain of criminal punishment, assembly with others merely to advocate the described type of action. Such a statute falls within the condemnation of the First and Fourteenth Amendments. The contrary teaching of *Whitney v. California,* cannot be supported, and that decision is therefore overruled.

Reversed.

Mr. Justice BLACK, concurring.

I agree with the views expressed by Mr. Justice DOUGLAS in his concurring opinion in this case that the "clear and present danger" doctrine should have no place in the interpretation of the First Amendment. I join the Court's opinion, which, as I understand it, simply cites *Dennis v. United States*, (1951), but does not indicate any agreement on the Court's part with the "clear and present danger" doctrine on which *Dennis* purported to rely.

Mr. Justice DOUGLAS, concurring.

While I join the opinion of the Court, I desire to enter a *caveat*.

The "clear and present danger" test was adumbrated by Mr. Justice Holmes in a case arising during World War I—a war "declared" by the Congress, not by the Chief Executive. The case was *Schenck v. United States,* where the defendant was charged with attempts to cause insubordination in the military and obstruction of enlistment. The pamphlets that were distributed urged resistance to the draft, denounced conscription, and impugned the motives of those backing the war effort. The First Amendment was tendered as a defense. Mr. Justice Holmes in rejecting that defense said:

"The question in every case is whether the words used are used in such circumstances and are of such a nature as to create a clear and present danger that they will bring about the substantive evils that Congress has a right to prevent. It is a question of proximity and degree."

* * *

(Justice Douglas reviews the World War I "clear and present danger" cases.)

Those, then, were the World War I cases that put the gloss of "clear and present danger" on the First Amendment. Whether the war power—the greatest leveler of them all—is adequate to sustain that doctrine is debatable. The dissents * * * show how easily "clear and present danger" is manipulated to crush what Brandeis called "[t]he fundamental right of free men to strive for better conditions through new legislation and new institutions" by argument and discourse even in time of war. Though I doubt if the "clear and present danger" test is congenial to the First Amendment in time of a declared war, I am certain it is not reconcilable with the First Amendment in days of peace.

The Court quite properly overrules *Whitney v. California,* which involved advocacy of ideas which the majority of the Court deemed unsound and dangerous.

Mr. Justice Holmes, though never formally abandoning the "clear and present danger" test, moved closer to the First Amendment ideal when he said in dissent in *Gitlow v. New York:*

"Every idea is an incitement. It offers itself for belief and if believed it is acted on unless some other belief outweighs it or some failure of energy stifles the movement at its birth. The only difference between the expression of an opinion and an incitement in the narrower sense is the speaker's enthusiasm for the result. Eloquence may set fire to reason. But whatever may be thought of the redundant discourse before us it had no chance of starting a present conflagration. If in the long run the beliefs expressed in proletarian dictatorship are destined to be accepted by the dominant forces of the community, the only meaning of free speech is that they should be given their chance and have their way."

We have never been faithful to the philosophy of that dissent.

* * *

Out of the "clear and present danger" test came other offspring. Advocacy and teaching of forcible overthrow of government as an abstract principle is immune from prosecution. *Yates v. United States.* But an "active" member, who has a guilty knowledge and intent of the aim to overthrow the Government by violence, *Noto v. United States,* may be prosecuted. *Scales v. United States.* And the power to investigate, backed by the powerful sanction of contempt, includes the power to determine which of the two categories fits the particular witness. *Barenblatt v. United States.* And so the investigator roams at will through all of the beliefs of the witness, ransacking his conscience and his innermost thoughts.

Judge Learned Hand, who wrote for the Court of Appeals in affirming the judgment in *Dennis,* coined the "not improbable" test, which this Court adopted and which Judge Hand preferred over the "clear and present danger" test. Indeed, in his book, The Bill of Rights 59 (1958), in referring to Holmes' creation of the "clear and present danger" test, he said, "I cannot help thinking that for once Homer nodded."

My own view is quite different. I see no place in the regime of the First Amendment for any "clear and present danger" test, whether strict and tight as some would make it, or free-wheeling as the Court in *Dennis* rephrased it.

When one reads the opinions closely and sees when and how the "clear and present danger" test has been applied, great misgivings are aroused. First, the threats were often loud but always puny and made serious only by judges so wedded to the *status quo* that critical analysis made them nervous. Second, the test was so twisted and perverted in *Dennis* as to make the trial of those teachers of

Marxism an all-out political trial which was part and parcel of the cold war that has eroded substantial parts of the First Amendment.

Action is often a method of expression and within the protection of the First Amendment.

Suppose one tears up his own copy of the Constitution in eloquent protest to a decision of this Court. May he be indicted?

Suppose one rips his own Bible to shreds to celebrate his departure from one "faith" and his embrace of atheism. May he be indicted?

* * *

The act of praying often involves body posture and movement as well as utterances. It is nonetheless protected by the Free Exercise Clause. Picketing, as we have said on numerous occasions, is "free speech plus." That means that it can be regulated when it comes to the "plus" or "action" side of the protest. It can be regulated as to the number of pickets and the place and hours, because traffic and other community problems would otherwise suffer.

* * *

One's beliefs have long been thought to be sanctuaries which government could not invade. *Barenblatt* is one example of the case with which that sanctuary can be violated. The lines drawn by the Court between the criminal act of being an "active" Communist and the innocent act of being a nominal or inactive Communist mark the difference only between deep and abiding belief and casual or uncertain belief. But I think that all matters of belief are beyond the reach of subpoenas or the probings of investigators. That is why the invasions of privacy made by investigating committees were notoriously unconstitutional. That is the deep-seated fault in the infamous loyalty-security hearings which, since 1947 when President Truman launched them, have processed 20,000,000 men and women. Those hearings were primarily concerned with one's thoughts, ideas, beliefs, and convictions. They were the most blatant violations of the First Amendment we have ever known.

The line between what is permissible and not subject to control and what may be made impermissible and subject to regulation is the line between ideas and overt acts.

The example usually given by those who would punish speech is the case of one who falsely shouts fire in a crowded theatre.

This is, however, a classic case where speech is brigaded with action. They are indeed inseparable and a prosecution can be launched for the overt acts actually caused. Apart from rare instances of that kind, speech is, I think, immune from prosecution. Certainly there is no constitutional line between advocacy of abstract ideas as in *Yates* and advocacy of political action as in *Scales*. The quality of advocacy turns on the depth of the conviction; and government has no power to invade that sanctuary of belief and conscience.

NOTES AND QUESTIONS

1. The *Brandenburg* decision placed the contemporary Court in a position where the constitutional guarantees of free speech and free association do not permit a state to prohibit or limit speech advocating unpopular ideas or the use of force, except where such advocacy clearly causes lawless actions or incites such actions. In effect, the Supreme Court legitimated freedom of association for many unpopular political groups and accepted their broad right to advocate the overthrow of the government as an abstract doctrine. Do you agree with the decision? Had the same factual situation occurred in the educational environment, would you decide the same way?

2. What approach did the Supreme Court use in *Brandenburg?* What practical impact does this decision have for the pluralistic political debate in the nation? How do you think liberals, conservatives, and radicals reacted to this decision?

3. In 1969 the Supreme Court decided by a 5 to 4 vote in *Street v. New York,* 394 U.S. 576, that a state law which makes it a crime to "cast contempt" upon the American flag by words or acts is unconstitutional. The decision reversed the conviction of Street, who burned the American flag in public to show his contempt for the shooting of a black civil rights leader. Street himself was black. Justice Harlan, speaking for the majority, argued that "we are unable to sustain a conviction that may have rested on a form of expression, however distasteful, which the Constitution tolerates and protects." (At p. 594). Chief Justice Warren and Justices Black, Fortas, and White dissented, on the basis that *acts* such as flag desecration are not constitutionally protected as is speech, and thus can be restrained or prohibited entirely by the government.

The Court refined its *Street* precedent in a 1974 decision, *Smith v. Goguen,* 415 U.S. 566. There Justice Powell claimed that a state law which made it a crime to "treat contemptuously the flag of the United States" lacks specificity and thus infringes on the right of free speech. Powell claimed that the law failed "to draw reasonably clear lines between the kinds of non-ceremonial treatment that are criminal and those that are not." (At p. 574). Thus, a man who wore a small American flag on the seat of his jeans was not subject to arrest, since the guidelines did not clearly distinguish ceremonial from non-ceremonial display. What kind of "clear lines" would you find acceptable to a "balancing of interests" approach that would regulate the expression of those who treat the flag of the United States contemptuously? Would you consider the wearing of the flag on the seat of one's jeans to be constitutionally protected "symbolic speech"?

(4) The Contemporary Scene

The Vietnam War and the dissent against it introduces the final problem of free speech. The protesters sometimes burned the flag or associated it with the trident peace symbol. Many were outraged by what they felt to be the misuse or desecration of this honored symbol of our country. During this period prosecutions under federal and state flag misuse laws occurred frequently. In the Vietnam context, a major case emerged to pose some crucial civil liberties questions. Do the First Amendment freedoms of speech and press include only spoken and written forms of communication, or do they cover *conduct* intended to communicate ideas? Can purely symbolic gestures such as the burning of one's draft card constitute a form of speech, protected under the First Amendment? Or, should they be construed as actions which the legislature has a right to regulate on public interest grounds?

These questions provided the basis for *United States v. O'Brien,* 391 U.S. 367 (1968). In an act of protest against the draft and the Vietnam War policy, O'Brien burned his draft card on the steps of South Boston Courthouse. O'Brien was convicted under a Federal statute which prohibits the deliberate destruction of Selective Service registration certificates. The Supreme Court used the balancing of interest approach to uphold the conviction, reasoning that the government had a substantial interest in ensuring the continued availability of Selective Service certificates and that the legislation was a means of protecting this interest. The legislation dealt only with the noncommunicative impact of the act—the burning of the certificate—which O'Brien's defense claimed represented "symbolic speech" against the war.

Chief Justice Warren, speaking for a 7–1 majority, stated: "We cannot accept the view that an apparently limitless variety of conduct can be labeled 'speech' whenever the person engaging in the conduct intends thereby to express an idea." (At p. 376). As Warren indicated, even if this were considered communication, Congress' power to establish a registration system and require the public to cooperate with it constituted a "sufficiently important government interest" to override O'Brien's intent to communicate by his act. Certainly the basic questions this case raised are whether there is some element of physical action in all forms of communication and whether the primary feature of this particular symbolic gesture is the expression of an idea or action.

The development of freedom of speech in the political and social setting demonstrates that judicial decision-making on First Amendment rights is related to: (1) a judge's value positions on "freedom" and the relationship of the individual to the government; (2) the approach articulated on the First Amendment; and (3) the judicial orientation on the court's role in society. The figure below is intended to illustrate these relationships. A careful study of it will help to sort out the variety of factors impinging on judicial decision-making.

Figure 3–2: Judicial Support for Freedom of Expression

DIRECTION OF INFLUENCE

INFLUENCING VARIABLES		Promoting	Retarding	Uncertain
	Value Position on Individual and Government	Support for Social Pluralism	Support for Societal Order	
	Value Position on Freedom	Negative Freedom Some Form of Positive Freedom	Freedom as Necessity (conservative interpretation)	
	Approach to First Amendment	Absolute-Literalist Preferred Position	Balancing Bad Tendency	Time, Place, Manner Clear and Present Danger
	Orientation to Role of Court	Activism	Restraintism	Neutrality

[B9656]

It is important to realize that in any situation the value system of a particular decision-maker may often contain conflicting values. It may work to promote unrestrained freedom of speech for adults in the political system, yet retard this kind of freedom for young people in the educational environment. Therefore, developing a framework of relevant factors serves only to help organize an understanding of the decision-making process in the interpretation and application of First Amendment rights in the political system and in the educational environment. It is not meant to be a means of predicting outcomes.

B. Freedom of Speech for Students in the Public Educational Setting

Almost all major cases dealing with the First Amendment rights of young people involve the public educational setting. This isn't really surprising, since young people spend much of their waking time in public school. There are two leading cases involving the First/Fourteenth Amendment rights of students. The first, *West Virginia State Bd. of Educ. v. Barnette,* 319 U.S. 624, was decided by the U. S. Supreme Court in 1943 and involves the right of students to refuse to salute the flag when doing so would violate their religious beliefs. The implications of *Barnette* are great, for Justice Jackson spoke in sweeping terms about the value of free expression in the educational setting. This case will be explored in the next chapter, which relates directly to freedom of religion.

The second doctrinal case, *Tinker v. Des Moines School Dist.* was decided by the U. S. Supreme Court in 1969, one year after the *O'Brien* case. It concerns the right of all students in the public educational setting to free expression and thus represents an extension of *Barnette*. The *Tinker* decision, which is reprinted below, does not, however, accord students the *same* rights of expression that adults enjoy. The Justices were obviously conscious of the age factor present in the case and the unique setting. Thus, they tailored their decision to apply to what they considered are the special circumstances of youth in the school. As you read the decision, consider whether it represents a reasonable accommodation between the rights of students and the interests of educational institutions. Consider also why John and Mary Beth Tinker's educational context *does* permit their "symbolic speech," while David O'Brien's Vietnam War and Selective Service Registration context *does not* permit his "symbolic speech."

TINKER v. DES MOINES INDEPENDENT COMMUNITY SCHOOL DIST.

Supreme Court of the United States, 1969.
393 U.S. 503, 89 S.Ct. 733, 21 L.Ed.2d 731.

Mr. Justice FORTAS delivered the opinion of the Court.

Petitioner John F. Tinker, 15 years old, and petitioner Christopher Eckhardt, 16 years old, attended high schools in Des Moines, Iowa. Petitioner Mary Beth Tinker, John's sister, was a 13-year-old student in junior high school.

In December 1965, a group of adults and students in Des Moines held a meeting at the Eckhardt home. The group determined to publicize their objections to the hostilities in Vietnam and their support for a truce by wearing black armbands during the holiday season and by fasting on December 16 and New Year's Eve. Petitioners and their parents had previously engaged in similar activities, and they decided to participate in the program.

The principals of the Des Moines schools became aware of the plan to wear armbands. On December 14, 1965, they met and adopted a policy that any student wearing an armband to school would be asked to remove it, and if he refused he would be suspended until he returned without the armband. Petitioners were aware of the regulation that the school authorities adopted.

On December 16, Mary Beth and Christopher wore black armbands to their schools. John Tinker wore his armband the next day. They were all sent home and suspended from school until they would come back without their armbands. They did not return to school until after the planned period for wearing armbands had expired—that is, until after New Year's Day.

This complaint was filed in the United States District Court by petitioners, through their fathers, under § 1983 of Title 42 of the United States Code. It prayed for an injunction restraining the respondent school officials and the respondent members of the board of directors of the school district from disciplining the petitioners, and it sought nominal damages. After an evidentiary hearing the District Court dismissed the complaint. It upheld the constitutionality of the school authorities' action on the ground that it was reasonable in order to prevent disturbance of school discipline. The court referred to but expressly declined to follow the Fifth Circuit's holding in a similar case that the wearing of symbols like the armbands cannot be prohibited unless it "materially and substantially interfere[s] with the requirements of appropriate discipline in the operation of the school." *Burnside v. Byars*, 363 F.2d 744, 749 (1966).[1]

On appeal, the Court of Appeals for the Eighth Circuit considered the case *en banc*. The court was equally divided, and the District Court's decision was accordingly affirmed, without opinion. We granted certiorari.

I.

The District Court recognized that the wearing of an armband for the purpose of expressing certain views is the type of symbolic act that is within the Free Speech Clause of the First Amendment. As we shall discuss, the wearing of armbands in the circumstances of this case was entirely divorced from actually or potentially disruptive conduct by those participating in it. It was closely akin to "pure speech" which, we have repeatedly held, is entitled to comprehensive protection under the First Amendment.

First Amendment rights, applied in light of the special characteristics of the school environment, are available to teachers and students. It can hardly be argued that either students or teachers shed their constitutional rights to freedom of speech or expression at the schoolhouse gate. *   *   *

*   *   *

1. In *Burnside*, the Fifth Circuit ordered that high school authorities be enjoined from enforcing a regulation forbidding students to wear "freedom buttons." It is instructive that in *Blackwell v. Issaquena County Board of Education*, 363 F.2d 749 (1966), the same panel on the same day reached the opposite result on different facts. It declined to enjoin enforcement of such a regulation in another high school where the students wearing freedom buttons harassed students who did not wear them and created much disturbance.

The school officials banned and sought to punish petitioners for a silent, passive expression of opinion, unaccompanied by any disorder or disturbance on the part of petitioners. There is here no evidence whatever of petitioners' interference, actual or nascent, with the schools' work or of collision with the rights of other students to be secure and to be let alone. Accordingly, this case does not concern speech or action that intrudes upon the work of the schools or the rights of other students.

Only a few of the 18,000 students in the school system wore the black armbands. Only five students were suspended for wearing them. There is no indication that the work of the schools or any class was disrupted. Outside the classrooms, a few students made hostile remarks to the children wearing armbands, but there were no threats or acts of violence on school premises.

The District Court concluded that the action of the school authorities was reasonable because it was based upon their fear of a disturbance from the wearing of the armbands. But, in our system, undifferentiated fear or apprehension of disturbance is not enough to overcome the right to freedom of expression. Any departure from absolute regimentation may cause trouble. Any variation from the majority's opinion may inspire fear. Any word spoken, in class, in the lunchroom, or on the campus, that deviates from the views of another person may start an argument or cause a disturbance. But our Constitution says we must take this risk; and our history says that it is this sort of hazardous freedom—this kind of openness—that is the basis of our national strength and of the independence and vigor of Americans who grow up and live in this relatively permissive, often disputatious, society.

In order for the State in the person of school officials to justify prohibition of a particular expression of opinion, it must be able to show that its action was caused by something more than a mere desire to avoid the discomfort and unpleasantness that always accompany an unpopular viewpoint. Certainly where there is no finding and no showing that engaging in the forbidden conduct would "materially and substantially interfere with the requirements of appropriate discipline in the operation of the school," the prohibition cannot be sustained.

In the present case, the District Court made no such finding, and our independent examination of the record fails to yield evidence that the school authorities had reason to anticipate that the wearing of the armbands would substantially interfere with the work of the school or impinge upon the rights of other students. Even an official memorandum prepared after the suspension that listed the reasons for the ban on wearing the armbands made no reference to the anticipation of such disruption.[3]

On the contrary, the action of the school authorities appears to have been based upon an urgent wish to avoid the controversy which might result from the expression, even by the silent symbol of armbands, of opposition to this Nation's part in the conflagration in Vietnam.[4]

* * *

It is also relevant that the school authorities did not purport to prohibit the wearing of all symbols of political or controversial significance. The record shows that students in some of the schools wore buttons relating to national political campaigns, and some even wore the Iron Cross, traditionally a symbol of Nazism. The order prohibiting the wearing of armbands did not extend to these. Instead, a particular symbol— black armbands worn to exhibit opposition to this Nation's involvement in Vietnam—was singled out for prohibition. Clearly, the prohibition of expression of one particular opinion, at least without evidence that it is necessary to avoid material and substantial interference with school work or discipline, is not constitutionally permissible.

In our system, state-operated schools may not be enclaves of totalitarianism. School officials do not possess absolute authority over their students. Students in school as well as out of school are "persons" under our Constitution. They are possessed of fundamental rights which the State must respect, just as they themselves must respect their obligations to the State. In our system, students may not be regarded as closed-circuit recipients

---

3. The only suggestions of fear of disorder in the report are these:

　　"A former student of one of our high schools was killed in Viet Nam. Some of his friends are still in school and it was felt that if any kind of a demonstration existed it might evolve into something which would be difficult to control."

　　"Students at one of the high schools were heard to say they would wear arm bands of other colors if the black bands prevailed."

Moreover, the testimony of school authorities at trial indicates that it was not fear of disruption that motivated the regulation prohibiting the armbands; the regulation was directed against "the principle of the demonstration" itself. School authorities simply felt that "the schools are no place for demonstrations," and if the students "didn't like the way our elected officials were handling things, it should be handled with the ballot box and not in the halls of our public schools."

4. The District Court found that the school authorities, in prohibiting black armbands, were influenced by the fact that "[t]he Viet Nam war and the involvement of the United States therein has been the subject of a major controversy for some time. When the armband regulation involved herein was promulgated, debate over the Viet Nam war had become vehement in many localities. A protest march against the war had been recently held in Washington, D. C. A wave of draft card burning incidents protesting the war had swept the country. At that time two highly publicized draft card burning cases were pending in this Court. Both individuals supporting the war and those opposing it were quite vocal in expressing their views."

of only that which the State chooses to communicate. They may not be confined to the expression of those sentiments that are officially approved. In the absence of a specific showing of constitutionally valid reasons to regulate their speech, students are entitled to freedom of expression of their views. * * *

In *Meyer v. Nebraska,* Mr. Justice McReynolds expressed this Nation's repudiation of the principle that a State might so conduct its schools as to "foster a homogeneous people." He said:

"In order to submerge the individual and develop ideal citizens, Sparta assembled the males at seven into barracks and intrusted their subsequent education and training to official guardians. Although such measures have been deliberately approved by men of great genius, their ideas touching the relation between individual and State were wholly different from those upon which our institutions rest; and it hardly will be affirmed that any legislature could impose such restrictions upon the people of a State without doing violence to both letter and spirit of the Constitution."

This principle has been repeated by this Court on numerous occasions during the intervening years. In *Keyishian v. Board of Regents,* 385 U.S. 589, Mr. Justice BRENNAN, speaking for the Court, said:

" 'The vigilant protection of constitutional freedoms is nowhere more vital than in the community of American schools.' *Shelton v. Tucker,* [364 U. S. 479,]. The classroom is peculiarly the 'marketplace of ideas.' The Nation's future depends upon leaders trained through wide exposure to that robust exchange of ideas which discovers truth 'out of a multitude of tongues, [rather] than through any kind of authoritative selection.' "

The principle of these cases is not confined to the supervised and ordained discussion which takes place in the classroom. The principal use to which the schools are dedicated is to accommodate students during prescribed hours for the purpose of certain types of activities. Among those activities is personal intercommunication among the students. This is not only an inevitable part of the process of attending school; it is also an important part of the educational process. A student's rights, therefore, do not embrace merely the classroom hours. When he is in the cafeteria, or on the playing field, or on the campus during the authorized hours, he may express his opinions, even on controversial subjects like the conflict in Vietnam, if he does so without "materially and substantially interfer [ing] with the requirements of appropriate discipline in the operation of the school" and without colliding with the rights of others. But conduct by the student, in class or out of it, which for any reason—whether it stems from time, place, or type of behavior—materially disrupts classwork or involves substantial disorder or invasion of the rights of others is, of course, not immunized by the constitutional guarantee of freedom of speech.

Under our Constitution, free speech is not a right that is given only to be so circumscribed that it exists in principle but not in fact. Freedom of expression would not truly exist if the right could be exercised only in an area that a benevolent government has provided as a safe haven for crackpots. The Constitution says that Congress (and the States) may not abridge the right to free speech. This provision means what it says. We properly read it to permit reasonable regulation of speech-connected activities in carefully restricted circumstances. But we do not confine the permissible exercise of First Amendment rights to a telephone booth or the four corners of a pamphlet, or to supervised and ordained discussion in a school classroom.

If a regulation were adopted by school officials forbidding discussion of the Vietnam conflict, or the expression by any student of opposition to it anywhere on school property except as part of a prescribed classroom exercise, it would be obvious that the regulation would violate the constitutional rights of students, at least if it could not be justified by a showing that the students' activities would materially and substantially disrupt the work and discipline of the school. In the circumstances of the present case, the prohibition of the silent, passive "witness of the armbands," as one of the children called it, is no less offensive to the Constitution's guarantees.

As we have discussed, the record does not demonstrate any facts which might reasonably have led school authorities to forecast substantial disruption of or material interference with school activities, and no disturbances or disorders on the school premises in fact occurred. These petitioners merely went about their ordained rounds in school. Their deviation consisted only in wearing on their sleeve a band of black cloth, not more than two inches wide. They wore it to exhibit their disapproval of the Vietnam hostilities and their advocacy of a truce, to make their views known, and, by their example, to influence others to adopt them. They neither interrupted school activities nor sought to intrude in the school affairs or the lives of others. They caused discussion outside of the classrooms, but no interference with work and no disorder. In the circumstances, our Constitution does not permit officials of the State to deny their form of expression.

We express no opinion as to the form of relief which should be granted, this being a matter for the lower courts to determine. We reverse and remand for further proceedings consistent with this opinion.

Reversed and remanded.

Mr. Justice STEWART, concurring.

Although I agree with much of what is said in the Court's opinion, and with its judgment in this case, I cannot share the Court's uncritical assumption that, school discipline aside, the First Amendment rights of children are co-extensive with those of adults. Indeed, I had thought the Court decided otherwise just last Term in *Ginsberg v. New York,* 390 U.S. 629. I continue to hold the view I expressed in that case: "[A] State may permissibly determine that, at least in some precisely delineated areas, a child— like someone in a captive audience—is not possessed of that full capacity for individual choice which is the presupposition of First Amendment guarantees."

Mr. Justice WHITE, concurring.

While I join the Court's opinion, I deem it appropriate to note, first, that the Court continues to recognize a distinction between communicating by words and communicating by acts or conduct which sufficiently impinges on some valid state interest; and, second, that I do not subscribe to everything the Court of Appeals said about free speech in its opinion in *Burnside v. Byars,* a case relied upon by the Court in the matter now before us.

Mr. Justice BLACK, dissenting.

The Court's holding in this case ushers in what I deem to be an entirely new era in which the power to control pupils by the elected "officials of state supported public schools * * *" in the United States is in ultimate effect transferred to the Supreme Court. The Court brought this particular case here on a petition for certiorari urging that the First and Fourteenth Amendments protect the right of school pupils to express their political views all the way "from kindergarten through high school." Here the constitutional right to "political expression" asserted was a right to wear black armbands during school hours and at classes in order to demonstrate to the other students that the petitioners were mourning because of the death of United States soldiers in Vietnam and to protest that war which they were against. Ordered to refrain from wearing the armbands in school by the elected school officials and the teachers vested with state authority to do so, apparently only seven out of the school system's 18,000 pupils deliberately refused to obey the order. One defying pupil was Paul Tinker, 8 years old, who was in the second grade; another, Hope Tinker, was 11 years old and in the fifth grade; a third member of the Tinker family was 13, in the eighth grade; and a fourth member of the same family was John Tinker, 15 years old, an 11th grade high school pupil. Their father, a Methodist minister without a church, is paid a salary by the American Friends Service Committee. Another student who defied the school order and insisted on wearing an armband in school was Christopher Eckhardt, an 11th grade pupil and a petitioner in this case. His mother is an official in the Women's International League for Peace and Freedom.

As I read the Court's opinion it relies upon the following grounds for holding unconstitutional the judgment of the Des Moines school officials and the two courts below. First, the Court concludes that the wearing of armbands is "symbolic speech" which is "akin to 'pure speech'" and therefore protected by the First and Fourteenth Amendments. Secondly, the Court decides that the public schools are an appropriate place to exercise "symbolic speech" as long as normal school functions are not "unreasonably" disrupted. Finally, the Court arrogates to itself, rather than to the State's elected officials charged with running the schools, the decision as to which school disciplinary regulations are "reasonable."

Assuming that the Court is correct in holding that the conduct of wearing armbands for the purpose of conveying political ideas is protected by the First Amendment, the crucial remaining questions are whether students and teachers may use the schools at their whim as a platform for the exercise of free speech —"symbolic" or "pure"—and whether the courts will allocate to themselves the function of deciding how the pupils' school day will be spent. While I have always believed that under the First and Fourteenth Amendments neither the State nor the Federal Government has any authority to regulate or censor the content of speech, I have never believed that any person has a right to give speeches or engage in demonstrations where he pleases and when he pleases. This Court has already rejected such a notion. * * *

While the record does not show that any of these armband students shouted, used profane language, or were violent in any manner, detailed testimony by some of them shows their armbands caused comments, warnings by other students, the poking of fun at them, and a warning by an older football player that other, nonprotesting students had better let them alone. There is also evidence that a teacher of mathematics had his lesson period practically "wrecked" chiefly by disputes with Mary Beth Tinker, who wore her armband for her "demonstration." Even a casual reading of the record shows that this armband did divert students' minds from their regular lessons, and that talk, comments, etc., made John Tinker "self-conscious" in attending school with his armband. While the absence of obscene remarks or boisterous and loud disorder perhaps justifies the Court's statement that the few armband students did not actually "disrupt" the classwork, I think the record overwhelmingly shows that the armbands did exactly what the elected school officials and principals foresaw they would, that is, took the students' minds off their classwork and diverted them to thoughts about the highly emotional subject of the Vietnam war. And I repeat that if the time has come when pupils of state-supported schools, kindergartens, grammar schools, or high schools, can defy and flout orders of school officials to keep their minds on their own schoolwork, it is the beginning of a new revolutionary era of permissiveness in this country fostered by the judiciary. The next logical step, it appears to me, would be to hold unconstitutional laws that bar pupils under 21 or 18 from voting, or from being elected members of the boards of education.

* * *

In my view, teachers in state-controlled public schools are hired to teach there. Although Mr. Justice McReynolds may have intimated to the contrary in *Meyer v. Nebraska, supra,* certainly a teacher is not paid to go into school and teach subjects the State does not hire him to teach as a part of its selected curriculum. Nor are public school students sent to the schools at public expense to broadcast political or any other views to educate and inform the public. The original idea of schools, which I do not believe is yet abandoned as worthless or out of date, was that children had not yet reached the point of experience and wisdom which enabled them to teach all of their elders. It may be that the Nation has outworn the old fashioned slogan that "children are to be seen not heard," but one may, I hope, be permitted to harbor the thought that taxpayers send children to school on the premise that at their age they need to learn, not teach.

* * *   Here the Court should accord Iowa educational institutions the * * * right to determine for themselves to what extent free expression should be allowed in its schools * * *. But even if the record were silent as to protests against the Vietnam war distracting students from their assigned class work, members of this Court, like all other citizens, know, without being told, that the disputes over the wisdom of the Vietnam war have disrupted and divided this county as few other issues ever have. Of course students, like other people, cannot concentrate on lesser issues when black armbands are being ostentatiously displayed in their presence to call attention to the wounded and dead of the war, some of the wounded and the dead being their friends and neighbors. It was, of course, to distract the attention of other students that some students insisted up to the very point of their own suspension from school that they were determined to sit in school with their symbolic armbands.

Change has been said to be truly the law of life but sometimes the old and the tried and true are worth holding. The schools of this Nation have undoubtedly contributed to giving us tranquility and to making us a more law-abiding people. Uncontrolled and uncontrollable liberty is an enemy to domestic peace. We cannot close our eyes to the fact that some of the country's greatest problems are crimes committed by the youth, too many of school age. School discipline, like parental discipline, is an integral and important part of training our children to be good citizens—to be better citizens. Here a very small number of students have crisply and summarily refused to obey a school order designed to give pupils who want to learn the opportunity to do so. One does not need to be a prophet or the son of a prophet to know that after the Court's holding today some students in Iowa schools and indeed in all schools will be ready, able, and willing to defy their teachers on practically all orders. This is the more unfortunate for the schools since groups of students all over the land are already running loose, conducting break-ins, sit-ins, lie-ins, and smash-ins. Many of these student groups, as is all too familiar to all who read the newspapers and watch the television news programs, have already engaged in rioting, property seizures, and destruction. They have picketed schools to force students not to cross their picket lines and have too often violently attacked earnest but frightened students who wanted an education that the pickets did not want them to get. Students engaged in such activities are apparently confident that they know far more about how to operate public school systems than do their parents, teachers, and elected school officials. It is no answer to say that the particular students here have not yet reached such high points in their demands to attend classes in order to exercise their political pressures. Turned loose with lawsuits for damages and injunctions against their teachers as they are here, it is nothing but wishful thinking to imagine that young, immature students will not soon believe it is their right to control the schools rather than the right of the States that collect the taxes to hire the teachers for the benefit of the pupils. This case, therefore, wholly without constitutional reasons in my judgment, subjects all the public schools in the country to the whims and caprices of their loudest-mouthed, but may be not their brightest, students. I for one, am not fully persuaded that school pupils are wise enough, even with this Court's expert help from Washington, to run the 23,390 public school systems in our 50 States. I wish therefore, wholly to disclaim any purpose on my part to hold that the Federal Constitution compels the teachers, parents, and elected school officials to surrender control of the American public school system to public school students. I dissent.

Mr. Justice HARLAN, dissenting.

I certainly agree that state public school authorities in the discharge of their responsibilities are not wholly exempt from the requirements of the Fourteenth Amendment respecting the freedoms of expression and association. At the same time I am reluctant to believe that there is any disagreement between the majority and myself on the proposition that school officials should be accorded the widest authority in maintaining discipline and good order in their institutions. To translate that proposition into a workable constitutional rule, I would, in cases like this, cast upon those complaining the burden of showing that a particular school measure was motivated by other than legitimate school concerns—for example, a desire to prohibit the expression of an unpopular point of view, while permitting expression of the dominant opinion.

Finding nothing in this record which impugns the good faith of respondents in promulgating the armband regulation, I would affirm the judgment below.

NOTES AND QUESTIONS

1. By stating that rights do not stop at the schoolhouse gate, the Court by implication recognizes that students have a constitutional right to free expression *outside* the school as well. Justice Stewart, however, points out in his concurring opinion that the Court previously decided that student First Amendment rights are not "co-extensive with those of adults." Justice Stewart cites *Ginsberg v. New York,* 390 U.S. 629 (1968), one of the few cases involving the rights of young people outside the educational arena. In *Ginsberg,* the Court in an opinion written by Justice Brennan repeated its view expressed in *Prince v. Massachusetts* (1944), as already noted, that the state may exert more authority over children than it may exercise over adults. In *Ginsberg,* the Court upheld a New York criminal law prohibiting the sale to minors of material considered to be obscene as applied to them even though it might not be obscene as applied

to adults. Justice Fortas, along with Justices Douglas and Black, dissented in that case.

Review Figure 3–1 summarizing judicial approaches to First/Fourteenth Amendment decision making. Which of the approaches does the majority appear to take? Which the two dissenters?

2. What role do the attitudes of the Justices about the mission of educational institutions play in this decision? As noted earlier in this chapter, Justice Black was one of the most ardent supporters of rights of expression. It is apparent that Figure 3–2 is incomplete insofar as judicial First/Fourteenth Amendment decision making in the educational area is concerned. Contrast this figure with Figure 3–3 on page 222.

Justice Black's view is almost diametrically opposed to that of the majority. Less extreme is the dissent by Justice Harlan. He would place the burden of proof on the plaintiffs to show that "a particular school measure was motivated by other than school concerns." Do you think that Justice Harlan's solution is workable? What might be potential drawbacks?

Note Justice Black's comments on the 18 year old voting issue. Interestingly, one year later he wrote the opinion in *Oregon v. Mitchell,* 400 U.S. 112, upholding Congressional authority to lower the voting age in national elections (but not state elections) to 18 years of age. His personal views evidently did not stand in the way of sanctioning the constitutional authority of Congress to take this action.*

3. Some have asserted that *Tinker* relates only to rights outside of the classroom setting, that is, to rights of expression in the lunchroom, on the campus grounds, and so on. Is this an accurate reading of the majority opinion? Suppose a student is extremely critical of the way the class textbook deals with the causes of World War II. Based on *Tinker,* does he have a constitutional right to express an opinion in the classroom over the objections of the teacher? If a school board regulation requires that the history of the Vietnam War be taught from reading the assigned textbook only and that there be no opportunity for comment by students or teachers, would *Tinker* apply? Should it?

In a series of cases, the Supreme Court has recognized the right of faculty members in the public educational setting to "remain free to inquire, to study and to evaluate, to gain new maturity and understanding." *Sweezy v. New Hampshire,* 354 U.S. 234 (1957), at p. 250. Several of those cases are referred to in the majority opinion. This concept of "academic freedom" judged inherent in the First Amendment has consistently found its greatest judicial support when applied to the public postsecondary classroom setting. Judicial support, coupled with the policies of such national organizations as the American Association of University Professors, has given college professors a good deal of classroom control in the public educational setting. Faculty members cannot be punished for exercising constitutional rights.

* On July 1, 1971, the Twenty-Sixth Amendment to the U. S. Constitution was ratified by the requisite number of states under the provisions of Article V of the Constitution. That Amendment lowers the voting age in all national and state elections to 18.

In the public elementary and secondary setting, academic freedom is less secure, primarily because it often conflicts with the plenary control school boards have over the curriculum as Justice Black maintains in his *Tinker* dissent and as we will see expressed again and again in numerous court decisions. However, some courts are recognizing a "market place of ideas" or "open forum" character of the elementary and secondary school classroom and are more inclined to support academic freedom for the public school teacher in some situations. Illustrative of this evolving judicial approach is *Parducci v. Rutland,* 316 F.Supp. 352 (M.D.Ala.1970), which is the first case to use the "material and substantial interference with school work or discipline" standard from *Tinker* in the context of teacher free speech. *Parducci* involved an eleventh grade English teacher who was dismissed for teaching Kurt Vonnegut, Jr.'s "Welcome to the Monkey House." The district court, noting that the Supreme Court has emphasized that academic freedom is fundamental to a democratic society, concluded that:

> Since the defendants have failed to show either that the assignment was inappropriate reading for high school juniors, or that it created a significant disruption to the educational processes of this school, this Court concludes that plaintiff's dismissal constituted an unwarranted invasion of her First Amendment right to academic freedom. (At p. 356).

A number of caveats need to be expressed about this case. There were no standards to guide teachers in selecting books for classes, published school reading lists included works with more controversial language and philosophies than the Vonnegut story, and the actions of school officials appeared arbitrary. The general judicial tendency remains to defer to the *parens patriae* power of state legislatures and local school boards except where actions are clearly arbitrary or work to stifle healthy classroom discussion and debate.[12]

However, outside of school, the Supreme Court has ruled that teachers have the same rights of expression as other citizens, so long as state-

12. See generally S. H. Nahmod "Controversy in the Classroom: The High School Teacher and Freedom of Expression," 39 *Geo.Wash.L.Rev.* 1032 (1971); S. H. Nahmod "First Amendment Protection for Learning and Teaching: The Scope of Judicial Review," 18 *Wayne L.Rev.* 1479 (1972); Note, "Academic Freedom in the Public Schools: The Right to Teach," 48 *N.Y.Univ.L.Rev.* 1179 (1977); *cf.* Stephen R. Goldstein, "The Asserted Constitutional Right of Public School Teachers to Determine What They Teach," 124 *U.Penn.L.Rev.* 1293 (1976). See also *Cary v. Board of Educ. of Adams-Arapahoe School Dist.*, 427 F.Supp. 945 (D.C.Col.1977). In *Cary,* the court came close to recognizing some entitlement of public high school teachers to academic freedom in selecting classroom teaching materials, asserting that:

Effective citizenship in a participatory democracy must not be dependent upon advancement toward college degrees. Consequently, it would be inappropriate to conclude that academic freedom is required only in the colleges and universities. (At p. 953).

But the court did not choose to decide whether the school board or teachers ought to prevail in a dispute over materials to be taught in certain elective courses. The court ruled that while the school board had itself consented to allow student and teacher the freedom to explore contemporary literature by allowing the courses to be taught as electives, the teachers had bargained away their freedom over classroom instructional materials in collective negotiations. Suppose the course had been required and the teachers nonunionized?

ments made in relation to the school are not made recklessly or with knowledge of their falsity and do not impede school operations. *Pickering v. Board of Educ.,* 391 U.S. 563 (1968). In 1976 the Court extended the *Pickering* principle in a unanimous decision upholding a teacher's right to speak at a school board meeting about employment matters even though the teacher is a member of the collective bargaining unit. Traditionally, only the bargaining agent can communicate about matters related to collective bargaining. Chief Justice Burger noted that when the school board meets in public meetings, "it may not be required to discriminate between speakers on the basis of their employment, or the content of their speech." *City of Madison Joint School Dist. No. 8 v. Wisconsin Employment Relations Comm'n,* 429 U.S. 167 (1976), at p. 176.

Two other recent U.S. Supreme Court decisions involving teacher rights of expression should be noted here. The first, *Mt. Healthy v. Doyle,* 429 U.S. 274 (1977), held that while a teacher cannot be denied reemployment for the legitimate exercise of constitutional rights, the teacher has the burden of proving that the action taken against him stemmed primarily from the exercise of the right. In the words of Justice Rehnquist, who spoke for the Court,

> A borderline or marginal candidate should not have the employment question resolved against him because of constitutionally protected conduct. But that same candidate ought not to be able, by engaging in such conduct, to prevent his employer from assessing his performance record and reaching a decision not to rehire on the basis of that record, simply because the protected conduct makes the employer more certain of the correctness of its decision. (At p. 286).

Mt. Healthy involved a teacher who, in addition to other incidents occurring within the school, made comments critical of the school over a local radio station. The case was remanded for further proceedings consistent with the Court's opinion.

The second decision, *Givhan v. Western Line Consolidated School Dist.,* 47 U.S.L.W. 4102 (1979), involved private communication between a public school teacher and a school principal. In a unanimous reversal of the Fifth Circuit Court of Appeals, the Supreme Court ruled that private, as well as public, expression is protected by the First Amendment in the context of the public employment. Justice Rehnquist for the Court stated that,

> The First Amendment forbids abridgement of the "freedom of speech." Neither the Amendment itself nor our decisions indicate that this freedom is lost to the public employee who arranges to communicate privately with his employer rather than to spread his views before the public. (At p. 4104).

Nevertheless, the Court repeated its caveat expressed in *Pickering* that a teacher does not have an absolute right to free expression. If the expression is recklessly made, impedes the performance of the teacher's duties, or interferes with school functioning, the expression loses its protection and action may be taken against the teacher. The Court added that since subordinate-superior relations are particularly sensitive, the *content* of what is said in private expression, as well as the time, place, and manner in which it is said, can be taken into account in deciding what is and is not constitutionally protected. The Court remanded the *Givhan* case to determine if the decision not to reappoint would have been made even if the protected encounters with the school principal had never occurred.

These three cases taken together do provide the public school teacher with some degree of constitutional protection for exercising rights of expression. However, they neither accord the teacher academic freedom in the classroom nor carte blanche in criticising superiors. Furthermore, they place the burden on the teacher to prove that the legitimate exercise of a constitutional right was a substantial factor in whatever sanctions are imposed. Once this is proven (usually through a lawsuit), the school then must show that even if the protected communication had never occurred, the same action would have been taken against the teacher.*

4. Are you disturbed that the Court treats a 13 year old, a 15 year old, and a 16 year old in the same way? To what extent is each student reflecting his or her own view about the Vietnam War? Note that the parents and their children had previously engaged in protest activities. What does this suggest about the impact of schooling vis-a-vis the family on attitudes and behaviors of students?

5. Which of the following are constitutionally protected forms of expression based on *Tinker* and which are not? (Hint: ask yourself what is being expressed.)

   a. Student wears a military uniform to school.

   b. There is a peaceful rally by students in the school cateteria against the math requirement.

   c. Kindergartners conduct a protest during school against the 15 minute morning nap period.

   d. Student speakers use profanity at a junior high school assembly.

   e. Student wears mickey mouse ears to his high school commencement.

   f. College students walk backwards through the library.

C. Regulating Student Expression

After *Tinker,* attention was focused on *what kinds* of student expression are entitled to constitutional protection under the First/Fourteenth Amendments and *to what extent* such protected expression can be regulated when it "materially disrupts classwork or involves substantial disorder or invasion of the rights of others."

Note that *Tinker* concerns student *expression.* Obviously, there are many educational rules which have nothing to do with expression. They may regulate or even prohibit certain conduct, e. g., smoking on school

---

* For a recent review of the decisions since *Pickering,* see George R. Steven's, "Balancing Speech and Efficiency: The Educator's Freedom of Expression after *Pickering*" 8 J.Law and Educ. 223, April, 1979. As Stevens notes, School districts have been successful in most of the cases.

grounds. Or they may require certain conduct, e. g., school attendance to age 18. In order to carry out their functions, educational officials have inherent authority to make campus rules which do not conflict with state or federal laws, the rulings of courts and administrative agencies (for example, a board of education), or state or federal constitutional provisions. In most instances one has little choice but to follow these rules or seek to have them changed. Legal challenges are unlikely to be successful because no constitutional or statutory right is being adversely affected and because those who have authority are presumed to exercise it responsibly. In these situations, the burden is generally upon parents and students to show that authority is being exercised in an arbitrary and unlawful manner.

However, both in the political and social setting and in the public educational setting, when the exercise of authority restricts fundamental rights such as freedom of speech, the burden of showing an overriding need to regulate shifts to public officials. Generally, it can be said that *the closer a public school or college regulation comes to affecting protected constitutional or statutory rights, the greater the burden of justification placed by courts on educators.* Of course, the line between what is and is not a protected right is never easy to draw. Even the *Tinker* case itself involves the wearing of symbolic armbands and not "pure speech." Contrast the *Tinker* ruling with that in the *O'Brien* case where the Court refused to recognize symbolic draft card burning as protected expression.

This section investigates the prevailing court approach to educational rules. Whether involving protected rights or not, educational institutions, like all organizations and society itself, need rules to assure orderly functioning. As one commentator has noted:

> The trustees indeed have an affirmative *duty* to protect the well-being of * * * students, at least while they are under the jurisdiction of the school, by adopting policies and regulations designed to ensure a safe educational environment, and by taking appropriate action against students who violate the board policies or who pose a threat to the safety of the other students or to the school property.[13]   (Emphasis in original)

As already noted, few judges believe that even protected constitutional rights are absolute. There are situations where protected rights must give way in the interest of order, as Justice Fortas points out in *Tinker.* However, for authority to be exercised fairly—particularly where protected rights are involved—there must be clearly stated rules which are communicated to all. Like citizens in society-at-large, unless students are aware of what the rules are, they cannot be expected to live up to their responsibilities as members of educational institutions. *The presence of clearly stated rules is a fundamental feature of all law-abiding societies.* Their presence is particularly important where rights of expression are involved because our society, particularly educators and judges, places a high premium on individual expression. Recent U. S. Supreme Court decisions suggest that the First Amendment occupies a "preferred position"

13.   Jon Bible, *Student Rights and Responsibilities: A New Generation of Law* (Austin,   Texas: Texas Association of School Boards, Spring, 1977), at p. 27.

over other constitutional guarantees. Because this is so, the imposition of sanctions without rules or in the presence of rules which are vague or overbroad, is legally suspect.

The first case in this section, *Soglin v. Kauffman,* a 1969 federal court of appeals decision, discusses the importance of having clearly stated rules in the educational setting. Though it is really a procedural due process case and perhaps belongs more appropriately in Chapter Five, it is included here to illustrate the prevailing judicial approach to rules affecting protected rights of expression.

The next two cases following *Soglin* illustrate the complexities of deciding what behavior falls into the "materially disrupts classwork or involves substantial disorder or invasion of the rights of others" standard announced by Justice Fortas in *Tinker*.

(1) Avoiding Vague and Overly Broad Rules

SOGLIN v. KAUFFMAN

United States Court of Appeals, Seventh Circuit, 1969.
418 F.2d 163.

CUMMINGS, Circuit Judge.

*   *   *

The named plaintiffs are ten students at the Madison campus of the University of Wisconsin and the Madison chapter of the Students for a Democratic Society. * * * The defendants are various officials of the University of Wisconsin, the State of Wisconsin and the City of Madison allegedly involved in disciplinary actions on the Madison campus. The final complaint alleges the following pertinent facts:

On October 18, 1967, plaintiffs and others were protesting the presence of recruiting representatives of the Dow Chemical Corporation on the Madison campus. On the following day, the defendant Dean of Student Affairs wrote two of the plaintiffs and other "members of their class" that they were "suspended from the University pending a hearing before the Administrative Division of the Committee on Student Conduct and Appeals." The ground for the suspension was stated to be violation of Chapter 11.- 02 of the Laws and Regulations of the University of Wisconsin, and the students were informed that a hearing date

would be set at a later time. By letter of October 21, 1967, the chairman of the Administrative Division advised them that the hearing would be held on November 2, and that they would be permitted to attend classes and write examinations in the interim.

On November 1, some of the plaintiffs, as well as other individuals, received "Amended Charges" from the chairman of the Administrative Division. These charges specifically described the offensive conduct ascribed to plaintiffs, including the denial of others' rights to job interviews with the Dow Chemical Corporation by physical obstruction of the doorways and corridors of a university building. This behavior was characterized as "misconduct" * * *.

The complaint further alleged that some of the defendants had previously expelled two plaintiffs and another member of their class "by application of the doctrine of 'misconduct'," and were threatening to suspend or expel others for "misconduct." This doctrine was alleged to be so vague and overbroad as to violate the rights of plaintiffs under the First and Fourteenth Amendments. The complaint requested a declaratory judgment that the defendants' misconduct doctrine on its face violated the United States Constitution and prayed for an injunction against further application of that doctrine as the basis for disciplinary proceedings.

For their part, defendants answered that the term "misconduct" "as a standard for disciplinary action by the University" did not violate any of the provisions of the federal Constitution.

The district court, in a scholarly opinion, held that the standard of misconduct alone may not serve as the foundation for the expulsion or suspension of students for any significant time. The court concluded that "misconduct", as so used, violates the Due Process Clause of the Fourteenth Amendment by reason of vagueness or, in the alternative, violates the First Amendment (as applied to the states by the Fourteenth Amendment) by reason of vagueness and overbreadth. * * *

* * *

Turning to the merits, defendants contend that the "misconduct" doctrine does not constitute a "standard" of conduct and that it was not employed as such. They argue that "misconduct" represents the inherent power of the University to discipline students and that this power may be exercised without the necessity of relying on a specific rule of conduct. This rationale would justify the *ad hoc* imposition of discipline without reference to any preexisting standards of conduct so long as the objectionable behavior could be called misconduct at some later date. No one disputes the power of the University to protect itself by means of disciplinary action against disruptive students. Power to punish and the rules defining the exercise of that power are not, however, identical. Power alone does not supply the standards needed to determine its application to types of behavior or specific instances of "misconduct."

As Professor Fuller has observed: "The first desideratum of a system for subjecting human conduct to the governance of rules is an obvious one: there must be rules." Fuller, Law and Morality, p. 46 (2d printing, 1965). The proposition that government officers, including school administrators, must act in accord with rules in meting out discipline is so fundamental that its validity tends to be assumed by courts engaged in assessing the propriety of specific regulations. The doctrines of vagueness and overbreadth, * * * presuppose the existence of rules whose coherence and boundaries may be questioned. * * *

* * * These same considerations also dictate that the rules embodying standards of discipline be contained in properly promulgated regulations. * * * Consequently, in the present case, the disciplinary proceedings must fail to the extent that the defendant officials of the University of Wisconsin did not base those proceedings on the students' disregard of university standards of conduct expressed in reasonably clear and narrow rules.

* * * The use of "misconduct" as a standard in imposing the penalties threatened here must therefore fall for vagueness. The inadequacy of the rule is apparent on its face. It contains no clues which could assist a student, an administrator or a reviewing judge in determining whether conduct not transgressing statutes is susceptible to punishment by the University as "misconduct." Since the misconduct standard is invalid on its face, it was unnecessary for the district court to make any findings with respect to plaintiffs' activities on October 18, 1967. * * *

It is not an adequate answer to contend, as do defendants, that the particular conduct which is the object of university discipline might have violated an applicable state or local law or otherwise merited punishment. The issue here is not the character of the student behavior but the validity of the administrative sanctions. Criminal laws carry their own definitions and penalties and are not enacted to enable a university to suspend or expel the wrongdoer absent a breach of a university's own rule. Nor is "misconduct" necessarily confined to disruptive actions covered by criminal codes. The ability to punish "misconduct" *per se* affords no safeguard against the imposition of disciplinary proceedings overreaching permissible limits and penalizing activities which are free from any taint of impropriety. Hence we feel compelled to strike down the University's reliance on the doctrine of misconduct in order to ensure that "reasonable regulation of speech-connected activities [of students remains confined to] carefully restricted circumstances." Tinker v. Des Moines School District.

Pursuant to appropriate rule or regulation, the University has the power to maintain order by suspension or expulsion of disruptive students. Requiring that such sanctions be administered in accord with preexisting rules does not place an unwarranted burden upon university administrations. We do not require university codes of conduct to satisfy the same rigorous standards as criminal statutes. We only hold that expulsion and prolonged suspension may not be imposed on students by a university simply on the basis of allegations of "misconduct" without reference to any preexisting rule which supplies an adequate guide. The possibility of the sweeping application of the standard of "misconduct" to protected activities does not comport with the guarantees of the First and Fourteenth Amendments. The desired end must be more narrowly achieved.[7]

Affirmed.

NOTES AND QUESTIONS

1. The doctrines of vagueness and overbreadth have become important features of constitutional law. In the rights of expression area, they have much the same meaning, though there is one technical difference. A rule which is overbroad may be very clearly stated and thus not be vague. For example, a rule at a public high school prohibiting the distribution of any non-school printed material on campus while school is in session is very specific but may be overly broad in denying entirely the constitutional right to freedom of the press. Such a rule bears a heavy presumption against its validity. This is not to say, however, that there may not be circumstances justifying the rule. Can you foresee a situation where such a rule might be justified?

7. The Annual Report of the Committee on Student Conduct and Appeals of October 2, 1967, recognized this in stating:

"*Student Conduct Code.* In recent years it has become clear that a college education is of such significance that disciplinary action which prevents or interrupts that educational opportunity must be handled with great care and due process. However, at present the University disciplinary rules are unclear, consisting of a patchwork of special regulations and broad statements of standards, often developed on an ad hoc basis, which fail to give students adequate notice. One means of approaching these goals of care and due process might be the development of a student conduct code, clearly setting out the duties and responsibilities of students and the disciplinary procedures applicable in case of violation. A number of other universities have developed such student codes. Therefore, the Committee recommends that desirability and feasibility of such a code for the Madison campus be studied, perhaps in relation to studies of the rule of student government which are now underway."

Here, "misconduct" is certainly a vague rule, and it may have the effect of "chilling" the exercise of rights of expression. Not knowing what expression is permissible and what is not, only the boldest students may risk possible punishment by continuing to express themselves.

The vagueness/overbreadth arguments have been used to strike down a great number of statutes and rules aimed at regulating speech-making, parades, the circulation of leaflets, and so on. They have also become a standard feature of challenges to the rules of public educational institutions.

2. Do you agree with the court that "it is not an adequate answer to contend, as do defendants, that the particular conduct which is the object of university discipline might have violated an applicable state or local law or otherwise merited punishment"? Do you think that a public high school or university should be able to discipline students for off-campus behavior under any circumstances? If so, what are the implications for rule-making in the educational institution? There will be occasions in later chapters to explore the relationship between the school as a community and the larger societal setting.

3. Note that the court specifically states that "We do not require university codes of conduct to satisfy the same rigorous standards as criminal statutes." Prior to his appointment to the Supreme Court, Justice Blackmun stated in *Esteban v. Central Missouri State College,* 415 F.2d 1077 (8th Cir. 1969), a campus disruption case, that college students are presumed "to possess some minimum intelligence" and are perfectly capable of understanding what kind of conduct constitutes " 'mob misconduct' " and " 'gatherings which might be considered unruly.' " (At pp. 1088 and 1082). Once again, the issue becomes one of line-drawing and subjective judgment.

Which of the following would you consider proper rules for the public educational institution and which would you say are unconstitutionally vague and/or overbroad? Assume each begins with the phrase, "Students at this public educational institution will be subject to disciplinary action for:"

a. hazing in all forms.

b. picnicking on school grounds during school hours.

c. talking in the library.

d. interference with the personal liberty of a fellow student.

e. disorderly disturbance or course of conduct directed against the administration or policies of the college.

f. upbraiding, abusing, or insulting any member of the instructional staff on school property or in the presence of the pupils at a school activity.

g. organizing, instigating, inciting, directing, and/or participating in student picketing on school grounds while school is in session.

h. improper or disrespectful conduct in the classroom.

i. conduct which leads to a criminal conviction for engaging in force, disruption, or the seizure of university property where such crime was of a serious nature and contributed to a substantial disruption of the administration of the institution.

j.   violating a rule or order announced by a school official acting in his or her official capacity.

It is quite apparent that the development of rules and regulations, particularly where rights of expression are likely to be affected, is a very complex and controversial process in and out of the educational setting. One knowledgeable commentator has questioned whether the concept of overbreadth has any real value at all.

> How many people   *   *   *   read the statutes and ordinances closely enough to be deterred from constitutionally protected speech by an over-broad law, and then follow the law reports with such care as to be reassured by a Supreme Court decision declaring the law unconstitutional on its face unless and until it is saved by a narrowing construction by the State's highest tribunal? And how many check for narrowing State court interpretations? Nor has the [Supreme] Court given any sign that it has faced the problems of the draughtsmen and has some notion of how to write a law which covers the endless variety of conduct that may disturb public order or decency yet cannot be twisted to reach some constitutionally protected form of expression. (Material in brackets added).[14]

The same criticism can be applied to the concept of vagueness.

4.   Given *Soglin,* how would you advise educational officials to develop their student codes in the future? Would you advise them to include a "blanket" provision to cover a variety of situations or to enumerate the situations where the rules will be applied?

(2) What is "Materially Disruptive?" The Shanley and Siegel Cases

Just what Justice Fortas meant in *Tinker* by the phrase "materially disrupts classwork or involves substantial disorder or invasion of the rights of others" is unclear from the opinion. One way to clarify what he had in mind is to outline the factors in *Tinker* under which free expression was allowed. The *Tinker* ruling applies to a situation with these characteristics:

a.   Involvement of children of various ages.

b.   Peaceful symbolic protest signified by wearing armbands.

c.   Occurring on public school grounds and in public school classrooms.

d.   Occurring during regular school hours.

e.   Occurring before a high school and junior school audience.

f.   Reaction of others limited to sporadic signs of disapproval but not serious overt actions.

g.   Specific and clearly communicated school rule.

---

14.   Archibald Cox, *The Role of the Supreme Court in American Government* (New York: Oxford University Press, 1976), at p. 45.

To construct a situation where the "materially disrupts" and "substantial disorder or invasion of the rights of others" standards apply, what circumstances would have to be different? It is this issue which the courts tried to come to grips with in the two cases below.

SHANLEY v. NORTHEAST INDEPENDENT SCHOOL DIST.

Federal Court of Appeals for the 5th Circuit, 1972.
462 F.2d 960.

GOLDBERG, Circuit Judge:

It should have come as a shock to the parents of five high school seniors in the Northeast Independent School District of San Antonio, Texas, that their elected school board had assumed suzerainty over their children before and after school, off school grounds, and with regard to their children's rights of expressing their thoughts. We trust that it will come as no shock whatsoever to the school board that their assumption of authority is an unconstitutional usurpation of the First Amendment.

Appellants, Mark S. Shanley, Clyde A. Coe, Jr., William E. Jolly, John A. Alford, and John Graham, were seniors at MacArthur High School in the Northeast Independent School District of San Antonio. At least they were students there save for a period of three days during which they were suspended for violating a school board "policy." Each of the students here was considered a "good" or "excellent" student. All were in the process of applying for highly competitive slots in colleges or for scholarships. The three days of zeros that resulted from the suspensions substantially affected their grade averages at a critical time of their educational careers.

The occasion of the suspension was the publication and distribution of a so-called "underground" newspaper entitled "Awakening." The newspaper was authored entirely by the students, during out-of-school hours, and without using any materials or facilities owned or operated by the school system. The students distributed the papers themselves during one afternoon after school hours and one morning before school hours. At all times distribution was carried on near but outside the school premises on the sidewalk of an adjoining street, separated from the school by a parking lot. The students neither distributed nor encouraged any distribution of the papers during school hours or on school property, although some of the newspapers did turn up there. There was absolutely no disruption of class that resulted from distribution of the newspaper, nor were there any disturbances whatsoever attributable to the distribution. It was acknowledged by all concerned with this case that the students who passed out the newspapers did so politely and in orderly fashion.

The "Awakening" contains absolutely no material that could remotely be considered libelous, obscene, or inflammatory. In fact, the content of this so-called "underground" paper is such that it could easily surface, flower-like, from its "underground" abode. As so-called "underground" newspapers go, this is probably one of the most vanilla-flavored ever to reach a federal court.

The five students were suspended by the principal for violation of school board "policy" 5114.2 which reads in pertinent part:

"Be it further resolved that *any* attempt to avoid the school's established procedure for administrative approval of activities such as the production for distribution and/or distribution of petitions or printed documents of *any* kind, sort, or type without the specific approval of the principal shall be cause for suspension and, if in the judgment of the principal, there is justification, for referral to the office of the Superintendent with a recommendation for expulsion * * * "

Northeast Independent School District "policy" 5114.2 at 2–3, adopted November 20, 1969 [emphasis added].

The students requested a hearing before the full school board, which was transcribed by a court reporter at the students' request and expense. Counsel for the students and the school board were present at the hearing. The students argued before the board that, after consulting with an attorney and a professor at a local law school, they had concluded that the regulation in question simply did not apply to conduct exercised entirely outside school hours and off school premises.

The school board affirmed the suspensions one day later.

Objecting to the school board's bootstrap transmogrification into Super-Parent, the parents of the five affected students sought both temporary and permanent injunctive relief as next-friends in the federal courts, requesting that the school board be enjoined from entering the zeros into the students' permanent records and from prohibiting the distribution of the "Awakening" off campus and outside school hours. The district court denied all relief, dismissing the case on its own motion as "wholly without merit." The district court also denied the students' request for an injunction pending appeal to this court, and the students immediately appealed. On an emergency basis this court expedited the appeal and enjoined the school board from entering the zeros that resulted from the suspensions into the students' records and from refusing to afford the students a reasonable opportunity to complete and submit

for academic credit the work that they had missed as a result of the suspensions pending this appeal.

* * *

It is clear * * * that the authority of the school board to balance school discipline against the First Amendment by forbidding or punishing off-campus activity cannot exceed its authority to forbid or punish on-campus activity. Therefore, we must first examine the authority of the school board to order the actions of students *on* school grounds and *within* school hours.

While a school is certainly a market place for ideas, it is just as certainly not a market place. The educational process is thwarted by the milling, mooing, and haranguing, along with the aggressiveness that often accompanies a constitutionally-protected exchange of ideas on the street corner. There is, of course, a substantive difference between schools and the street corner in terms of weighing the sometimes competing interests of a completely free flow of any and all expression with the requirement that there be order and discipline. Thus, this court has endeavored to give "careful recognition to the differences between what are reasonable restraints in the classroom and what are reasonable restraints on the street corner." Because high school students and teachers cannot easily disassociate themselves from expressions directed towards them on school property and during school hours, because disciplinary problems in such a populated and concentrated setting seriously sap the educational processes and because high school teachers and administrators have the vital responsibility of compressing a variety of subjects and activities into a relatively confined period of time and space, the exercise of rights of expression in the high schools, whether by students or by others, is subject to reasonable constraints more restrictive than those constraints that can normally limit First Amendment freedoms.[6]

* * *

When the constitutionality of a school regulation is questioned, it is settled law that the burden of justifying the regulation falls upon the school board. The test for curtailing in-school exercise of expression is whether or not the expression or its method of exercise "materially and substantially" interferes with the activities or discipline of the school. * * *

* * *

When the standards are applied to this case, it is beyond serious question that the activity punished here does not even approach the "material and substantial" disruption that must accompany an exercise of expression, either in fact or in reasonable forecast. As a factual matter there were no distruptions of class; there were no disturbances of any sort, on or off campus, related to the distribution of the "Awakening." Disruption in fact is an important element for evaluating the reasonableness of a regulation screening or punishing student expression. * * * One week after *Tinker* the Supreme Court denied certiorari in a case that had involved rather violent and disruptive activity by some college students. The district court found that the students had exceeded their constitutional privileges of free expression. In the Supreme Court's denial of review, Mr. Justice Fortas, who wrote for the majority in *Tinker,* observed in concurrence that "the petitioners . . . engaged in an aggressive and violent demonstration, and not in peaceful nondisruptive expression." Barker v. Hardway, 1969.

One of the great concerns of our time is that our young people, disillusioned by our political processes, are disengaging from political participation. It is most important that our young become con-

vinced that our Constitution is a living reality, not parchment preserved under glass. * * *

* * *

Although the students urge the argument, we do not feel it necessary to hold that *any* attempt by a school district to regulate conduct that takes place off the school ground and outside school hours can never pass constitutional muster. * * * We do note, however, that it is not at all unusual to allow the geographical location of the actor to determine the constitutional protection that should be afforded to his or her acts. For example, the now-proverbial "fire" might be constitutionally yelled on the street corner, but not within the theater; or a march down the middle of a street might be protected activity, while a march down the hallway of a building might not. By the same token, it is not at all unusual in our system that different authorities have responsibility only for their own bailiwicks. An offense against one authority that it perpetrated within the jurisdiction of another authority is usually punishable only by the authority in whose jurisdiction the offense took place. Thus, contrary to the district court's opinion, the width of a street might very well determine the breadth of the school board's authority. Students, as any other citizens, are subject to the civil and criminal laws of the community, state, and nation. A student acting entirely outside school property is potentially subject to the laws of disturbing the peace, inciting to riot, littering, and so forth, whether or not he is potentially subject to a school regulation that the school board wishes to extend to off-campus activity. In our case the distribution of the "Awakening" was entirely off-campus and was effected only before and after school hours. The distribution was orderly and polite, and no disruption ac-

6. For example, we doubt that a school board could not restrain the sort of inflammatory and vitriolic exhortation that was protected by the Supreme Court in

Terminiello v. Chicago, 1949, 337 U.S. 1, in the context of a speaking engagement before paying adults.

tually occurred or was reasonably foreseeable under the circumstances. Thus, we hold here only that the exercise of disciplinary authority by the school board under the aegis of "policy" 5114.2 was unconstitutionally applied to prohibit and punish presumptively-protected First Amendment expression that took place entirely off-campus and without "substantial and material" disruption of school activities, either actual or reasonably-foreseeable. Therefore, the Northeast Independent School District is enjoined from entering any zeros upon the permanent records of these five students that resulted from the unlawful suspensions or from preventing the students from making up work missed during the suspensions. We decline to enjoin the school board from prohibiting distribution of the "Awakening" under any and all circumstances, and we see no need under the traditional bases of equitable remedies to issue a protective injunction against the board. As we have made clear in this opinion, the balancing of expression and discipline is an exercise in judgment for school administrations and school boards, subject only to the constitutional requirement of reasonableness under the circumstances. We decline to attempt to conjure and transcribe every possible permutation of circumstances regarding the distribution of the "Awakening," and we have complete faith that the school board and the school administration will make every effort to abide by the Constitution.

* * *

Tinker's dam to school board absolutism does not leave dry the fields of school discipline. This court has gone a considerable distance with the school boards to uphold its disciplinary fiats where reasonable. *Tinker* simply irrigates, rather than floods, the fields of school discipline. It sets canals and channels through which school discipline might flow with the least possible damage to the nation's priceless topsoil of the First Amendment. Perhaps it would be well if those entrusted to administer the teaching of American history and government to our students began their efforts by practicing the document on which that history and government are based. Our eighteen-year-olds can now vote, serve on juries, and be drafted; yet the board fears the "awakening" of their intellects without reasoned concern for its effect upon school discipline. The First Amendment cannot tolerate such intolerance. This case is therefore reversed for entry of an order not inconsistent with this opinion.

Reversed.

CLARK, Circuit Judge (specially concurring).

* * *

NOTES AND QUESTIONS

1. In *Shanley* the school reserved to itself the right to review materials such as the "Awakening" prior to their distribution. The issue of prior restraints in the educational setting is the subject of the next section, and therefore that part of the opinion has been deleted. The focus of attention is on possible limits to the scope of educational regulations.

From your reading of Northeast Independent School District policy 5114.2, would you assume it applied to the exercise of rights of expression occurring wholly out of school? In a later section of his opinion, Judge Goldberg ruled that section 5114.2 is both overly broad and vague and therefore unconstitutional. At the same time, Judge Goldberg refuses to accept the students' argument that school regulations can *never* regulate behavior occurring outside of school.   He acknowledges that the location of the act in question is important in deciding whether constitutional protections apply or not.   If students were to shout derogatory comments about school policy on the public sidewalk outside of the school building during school hours, should they be subject to disciplinary action by school officials?   Or would it be better if the police were called to handle this situation?   Which do you think would be in the best interest of the school? Of the students?   Which would you prefer?   If the police are called, should students also be subject to school disciplinary action?

2.   In general, courts are reluctant to entertain suits by students and/ or their parents unless existing school administrative procedures have been fully utilized first.   However, where there are no procedures, as is apparently the case here, or where the utilization of those procedures which are in place would clearly be an empty and useless gesture, courts will be more inclined to hear cases challenging educational policies and actions.   The burden, however, is on the plaintiffs to show why they have failed to pursue existing administrative remedies before coming to court.   Recall from the previous chapter that most judges subscribe to judicial self-restraint, particularly where judicial review is involved and where their expertise is open to question, as in disputes between students and educational officials.

3.   Why do you suppose the federal district court dismissed the action as "wholly without merit?"   Obviously, the facts haven't changed, yet the court of appeals quite clearly reaches the opposite conclusion.   Once again, views about the public educational setting clearly affect court involvement—or lack of involvement—in student rights cases.   Note that *Shanley* is precedent only for this particular federal circuit, though most courts have followed the *Shanley* pattern.

4.   One of the most important parts of the *Shanley* decision are the comments about the school as a market-place for ideas.   Like Justice Fortas in *Tinker,* Judge Goldberg endorses the value of free expression in the public educational setting.   The school rule in *Shanley* is simply too restrictive for Judge Goldberg to accept.   Yet, also like Justice Fortas, Judge Goldberg indicates that public educational institutions do have an interest in preserving order so that the educational process can continue. Judge Goldberg asserts that the burden is upon the educational institution to fashion rules which are not unduly restrictive, which do serve the legitimate function of preserving order, and which are specific enough to be clearly understood.

Obviously, time, place, and manner regulations, which are not based on the *content* of what is expressed, serve these considerations most effectively.   Since the *Tinker* decision, and lower court decisions such as *Soglin* and *Shanley* which are based on it, educational institutions have struggled to develop legally defensible time, place, and manner regulations and to discipline students who violate them only when clearly warranted. Courts have upheld many of these rules.   For example, in 1975 a California lower court upheld a university policy prohibiting door-to-door voter registration in campus dormitories since the policy was designed to protect the privacy of residents and did allow registration in dormitory lobbies.   *National Movement for Student Vote v. Regents of the Univ. of Cal.,* 123 Cal.

Rptr. 141 (California, 1975). And a U. S. Supreme Court case excerpted later in this chapter upheld an anti-noise ordinance restricting expression in the vicinity of a high school while classes were in session. *Grayned v. Rockford*, 408 U.S. 104 (1972).

While both Justice Fortas and Judge Goldberg value freedom of expression in public educational institutions, they nevertheless distinguish the educational setting from the non-educational. Judge Goldberg elaborates on the caveats about the extent of student rights of expression by Justice Fortas in *Tinker* with his reference to the *Terminiello* case. In *Terminiello* the U. S. Supreme Court reversed Terminiello's conviction under a breach of the peace statute for having delivered a provocative address under riotous conditions in a Chicago public auditorium. Writing for the majority, Justice Douglas found that the trial judge's interpretation of the breach of the peace statute to include speech which "stirs the public to anger, invites disputes, brings about a condition of unrest, or creates a disturbance" violated freedom of expression. On the contrary, Justice Douglas noted that it is a function of free speech under our system to *invite* disputes.

Unlike the situation in Terminiello, the student in the educational setting may be subject to punishment if in the exercise of expression rights, she provokes a disturbance. Do you agree that greater restraints are probably necessary in the educational environment?

5. Not all judges, of course, would endorse the views expressed by Judge Goldberg. For example, in *Jones v. Board of Regents of the Univ. of Arizona*, 436 F.2d 618 (9th Cir. 1970), Judge Ely was particularly disturbed that campus police had arrested a protestor rather than his protagonists. In this instance, the protestor, who was wearing a sandwich board sign announcing his opposition to the Vietnam War and distributing handbills with a similar message at the University of Arizona campus at Tucson, was assaulted by two bystanders, who tore off the signs from his back and chest, and destroyed them. Jones was forcibly removed from the campus. At the time, a crowd of twenty-five to thirty persons had gathered. Said Judge Ely:

> Neither the regulation [a blanket prohibition on handbilling] nor the police action in this particular case can be justified by the fact that two members of the crowd were moved to tear the sandwich boards from Jones' body or that certain unidentified members of the community had threatened to remove him from the campus if the police failed to do so. Jones was lawfully and nonviolently exercising rights guaranteed to him by the Constitution of the United States. It is clear to us that the police had the obligation of affording him the same protection they would have surely provided an innocent individual threatened, for example, by a hoodlum on the street. A politically motivated assault is no less illegal than assaults inspired by personal vengeance or by any other unlawful motive. Indeed, in this case, the action of the police was misdirected. It should have been exerted so as to prevent the infringement of Jones' constitutional right by

those bent on stifling, even by violence, the peaceful expression of ideas or views with which they disagreed. (At p. 621; material in brackets added.)

Do you suppose the fact that a college setting was involved in *Jones* rather than a high school setting as in *Shanley* accounts for the different judicial attitudes? What else might account for the difference?

SIEGEL v. REGENTS OF THE UNIV. OF CAL.

United States District Court for the Northern District of California, 1970.
308 F.Supp. 832.

SWEIGERT, District Judge.

* * *

The facts shown by the record are in substance and effect that plaintiff Siegel is a student enrolled at the School of Law on the Berkeley Campus of the University of California. On May 15, 1969, he was president-elect of the Associated Students, University of California, designated by the Chancellor of the Berkeley Campus as the student government organization at that campus.

As of May 15, 1969, certain real property belonging to defendant The Regents, and situated in the vicinity of the Berkeley Campus, had been forcibly seized and occupied by persons not acting under the control or direction of defendant Regents. On the morning of May 15, 1969, The Regents caused a fence to be erected on the perimeter of said property.

On the same day a rally was held at the noon hour in Sproul Plaza on the Berkeley Campus. Several thousand persons were in attendance. Plaintiff Siegel addressed the rally and concluded his remarks as follows:

"Now, we have not yet decided exactly what we are going to do. But there is some plans, I have a suggestion, let's go down to the Peoples Park, because we are the people. But a couple of things, a couple of points I would like to make. If we are to win this thing, it is because we are making it more costly for the University to put up its

fence than it is for them to take down their fence. What we have to do then is maximize the cost to them, minimize the cost to us. So what that means, is people be careful. Don't let those pigs beat the shit out of you, don't let yourselves get arrested on felonies, *go down there and take the park.*" (emphasis added.)

Immediately thereafter, several thousand persons proceeded from the rally down Telegraph Avenue toward the aforementioned property where they were met by law enforcement officers. Violence ensued resulting in the next few days in one death, numerous injuries and many arrests.

By letter dated May 20, 1969, defendant Shotwell, Coordinator of Facilities and Regulations, advised plaintiff in writing that he was charged with violating certain specified regulations, copies of which were enclosed, by reason of his actions on May 15, 1969 in urging his audience to "go down there and take the park."

Plaintiff was also advised that a hearing had been set before the Berkeley Campus Committee on Student Conduct for May 29, 1969, and he was asked to state whether or not he would be represented by legal counsel. At plaintiff Siegel's request the hearing was reset for June 5, 1969. Defendants refused an additional postponement.

On May 29, 1969, a preliminary hearing was held by defendant Williams,

Dean of Students, at which University counsel and plaintiff and his counsel were present. Plaintiff and his counsel reviewed videotapes and audiotapes taken of plaintiff's speech of May 15, 1969.

The hearing was held on June 5, 1969, before the Berkeley Campus Student Faculty Committee. Plaintiff was represented by his counsel and presented witnesses. * * *

The Committee on Student Conduct found and concluded:

" * * * that the action of Mr. Siegel did constitute violations of the University's regulations on the Standard of Conduct by exposing the University and its people to mob formation and its attendant potential consequence of violence. Therefore the Committee as a whole agrees that disciplinary action is warranted."

A majority of the Committee also concluded that Siegel:

" * * * knowingly spoke at a rally in reckless disregard of the tense and angry nature of the crowd without regard to the foreseeable consequences. At best, his conduct exhibits inexcusable ignorance of the dangerous circumstances."

A majority of the Committee also decided that Siegel:

" * * * by his initiation of the march to the 'Park' through his reckless words, greatly inflamed the situation at Haste and Telegraph by sending a great crowd to join another smaller one which was described in great detail by the defense counsel in such words as 'unruly', 'hostile', 'aggressive', 'undisciplined', 'angry', etc."

A majority of the Committee also found that Siegel's:

" * * * reckless choice of words spoken in an angry and highly excited tone, nevertheless, lose significance as an appeal to reason or aggressive persuasion. They become instead part of the instrument of force and violence. Such disorderly and disruptive conduct which endangers the welfare and safety of any members of the campus community *is* a violation of University regulations."

The Committee recommended that the Chancellor approve the placing of Siegel on disciplinary probation, including exclusion from participation in all privileges or extracurricular activities and specifically from serving as President of the student government.

By letter dated July 2, 1969 defendant Williams advised plaintiff of the Chancellor's acceptance of the recommendations of the Committee on Student Conduct and informed Siegel that he was placed on probation for a one-year period, the terms of probation permitting plaintiff the privileges of a student and privileges incidental to his studies, but prohibiting him from holding student government office or engaging in other extracurricular activities.

The preliminary injunction sought by plaintiff would enjoin defendants from imposing any discipline on plaintiff for his speech of May 15, 1969 and would require defendants to restore plaintiff forthwith to full student status with all rights and privileges thereof, including the right to hold and occupy the office of President of the Associated Students.

Plaintiff contends that the University regulations promulgated by the University, an agency of the State of California, are constitutionally invalid in that they are "overbroad" and "vague" restrictions upon the right of free speech protected by the First Amendment.

* * *

The regulations under which plaintiff was disciplined and which are attacked upon constitutional grounds by plaintiff, are as follows: [1]

1. (1) University of California Policies Relating to Students and Student Organizations, Use of University Facilities and Non-Discrimination (March 17, 1969): Sec.

SUBSTANTIALITY OF CONSTITU-TIONAL CONTENTIONS

Although First Amendment rights of expression, applied in the light of the special characteristics of school environment, are available to teachers and students (who, of course, do not shed their constitutional rights to freedom of speech or expression at the schoolhouse gate), school officials, nevertheless, have comprehensive authority to prescribe and control, consistently with constitutional safeguards, conduct which intrudes upon the work of the school.

It is well settled that even speech or expression, which materially and substantially intrudes upon the work of the school by interfering with the requirements of appropriate discipline in its operation, may be prohibited.

II, Part A, Standard of Conduct, Pars. 3, 4, 7, 10, 12; Sec. III, Part A, Campus Regulations, Par. 1.

Section II, Part A, Standard of Conduct, provides that a student enrolling in the University assumes an obligation to conduct himself in a manner compatible with the University's functions as an educational institution, and that misconduct for which students are subject to discipline falls into the following categories:

Paragraph 3 prohibits obstruction or disruption of administration or other University activities, including its public service functions, or of other authorized activities on University premises.

Paragraph 4 prohibits physical abuse of any person on University owned or controlled property or conduct which threatens or endangers the health or safety of any such person.

Paragraph 7 refers generally to violation of University policies or of campus regulations concerning the use of University facilities. (Note: Berkeley Campus Regulations, Sec. III, infra, prohibits unauthorized uses of University facilities).

Paragraph 10 prohibits disorderly conduct on University owned or controlled property.

Paragraph 12 prohibits conduct which adversely affects the student's suitability as a member of the academic community.

Section III, Part A, Campus Regulations, Par. 1, provides that University facilities

Regulations for these purposes, which reasonably set forth what conduct is expected from students, are sufficient and need not be tested by the strict standards applicable to criminal statutes or proceedings.

It will be noted that the regulations in question here are on their face directed, not to speech or mere expression of opinion, but to conduct.

There is nothing in these regulations that could be fairly said to have a "chilling effect" upon a student's exercise of First Amendment rights of free speech or expression because of "vagueness" or "overbreadth" or otherwise.

Nor is the record such as to show that the regulations have been applied with that effect as to this particular plaintiff.

shall not be used for the purpose of organizing or carrying out unlawful activity. This item of the charge was for some reason eliminated on 6/3/69.

(2) Berkeley Campus Regulations, Implementing University-wide Policies, Sec. III–1, Revised 1/2/68. This regulation prohibits unauthorized uses of University facilities.

(3) Emergency Regulations, Office of the Chancellor, 2/24/69. This emergency regulation recites a declaration of the Regents that interim suspension shall be imposed immediately in all cases where there is reasonable cause to believe that during a campus disturbance a student has violated University or campus regulations by acts such as physical violence or threats thereof, wilful destruction of University property, wrongful blocking of access to University facilities or other disruptive activities and, further, the regulation recites a policy of the Regents and of the University, that in the light of an emergency University facilities shall not be used for the purpose of organizing or carrying out unlawful activity. The regulation concludes to the effect that the use or threat of physical force to coerce persons using University facilities or engaged in administration or University related activities on campus is a fundamental violation of conditions of membership in an academic community and that any student found to have engaged in such misconduct shall be disciplined.

The complaint, itself, sets forth the exhortation by plaintiff at the close of his speech to "Go down and take the park" and the circumstances under which those words were uttered.

Although the complaint alleges that this exhortation by plaintiff was intended by him as mere rhetoric and not for the purpose of directing a physical seizure of the park [2] the complaint, nevertheless, discloses that plaintiff, President-elect of the Associated Students addressing 2,000 students already aroused over the park situation, told them to "Go down and take the park."

The record also shows that plaintiff has admitted by his own testimony at the hearing (and as quoted in the Committee Report) that he attempted to make his comments sound militant so he wouldn't be turned off; that he couldn't say simply "Now stay away from the police" because they would have told him to sit down; that he couldn't say it in those words because a moderate sounding statement "wouldn't have any effect on them, whereas a statement made in their own language would have a modifying effect on them, I hoped."

Under the circumstances shown by the record that statement transcends mere expression of opinion and becomes *conduct* —a distinct, affirmative *verbal act*— overt conduct for which plaintiff could be properly called to account under the regulations whatever might be his claim as to his subjective purpose and intent.

Illegal conduct is not protected merely because it is in part initiated, evidenced or carried out by language. Utterance in a context of violence, involving a clear and present danger, can lose its significance as an appeal to reason and become part of an instrument of force and as such unprotected by the Constitution. * * *

Obviously, such conduct, according to any reasonable, educational standard, would materially and substantially intrude upon University administration within the meaning of *Tinker*.

* * *

The court concludes that the constitutional issues raised by plaintiff concerning the regulations in question are insubstantial * * *.

* * *

CONCLUSION AND ORDER

For the foregoing reasons we conclude that the record does not present even a prima facie showing that plaintiff has been deprived of any constitutional right * * *.

Accordingly, plaintiff's motion for a preliminary injunction should be and is hereby denied, and defendants' motion to dismiss the action should be and is hereby granted upon the ground that the complaint, considered as a whole and with the exhibits attached thereto, fails to state a claim upon which relief could be granted in this action.

---

2. We have well in mind that plaintiff's suit cannot be and should not be, treated as a mere petition for review of the university's proceedings. * * * However, the issue raised by this civil rights complaint is, not whether plaintiff was in fact guilty of violating university rules or any other law, nor whether his subjective intent was, in fact, innocent and therefore, a defense to the charges, nor whether the university hearing board's findings on the evidence before it were correct, but, rather, and only whether the university in charging, trying and disciplining plaintiff under the circumstances shown on the face of the complaint, deprived plaintiff of any federally protected constitutional right.

NOTES AND QUESTIONS

1. Note discussion here of the clear and present danger standard. Has Judge Sweigert effectively applied the clear and present danger standard in the educational setting or has he used an approach closer to the bad tendency standard? Suppose upon hearing the remark, "Go down there and take the park," the police arrested Siegel and the crowd didn't go down to the park. Should he still be disciplined for violating campus rules? Suppose Siegel had made his statement on property other than the Berkeley campus; should he be treated in the same way or not?

The court in *Siegel* states that in certain circumstances a "statement transcends mere expression of opinion and becomes conduct * * *." What might be the circumstances? Would it be preferable to say that in certain circumstances speech cannot be protected because it presents a clear and present danger that substantive evil will occur rather than saying that speech can become conduct?

2. Assume in the following hypothetical situations that the rules and procedures under which action was taken by educational administrators or law enforcement personnel are fair. Review Figure 3–1 on page 102 to select the decision-making standard you think to be most appropriate for judging student expression cases. Then, given the legacy of *Tinker*, consider how you would decide the following situations if they were contested by the students affected. Will your conclusions be similar to those of your fellow students? Be prepared to argue why your views should prevail. (Assume all institutions are public.)

a. School officials, fearing racial violence at a football game, ban demonstrations of any kind.

b. Students are disciplined for a sit-in at the admissions office when applicants and their parents complain about the intrusion.

c. Black students are disciplined for walking out of a pep rally when "Dixie" is played by the school band. Suppose attendance at the rally was required?

d. Students peacefully picket an area where other students are engaging in violence and are being arrested. The picketing students are arrested when they refuse to obey an order to leave the area.

e. Tom wears a Nazi uniform to school and speaks to anyone who will listen in the corridors of the school about the growing numbers of Jewish students in the school—he calls it the "Zionist power menace." Jewish students, twenty percent of the student body, demand he cease his attack or they will show him what Zionist power can do. School officials discipline Tom.

f. Students planned a rally where violence occurred. The student planners did not take part in the violence but were present. They are disciplined along with those engaging in violence.

g. Students are disciplined after they silently sat at a table in the college library with arms folded every day for a week. Other students complained to the school officials that the silent vigil was distracting.

What would have to be evident in each of these situations for you to uphold the decision of educational officials to discipline the students? How would you design institutional rules to cover these situations? Would you merely copy the words of Justice Fortas in *Tinker*? Or should you provide examples of what you mean?

3. HYPOTHETICAL: *Students v. Officials of El Gruncho Community College*

Carl Concern and Rick Rights, members of the El Gruncho Public Community College Student Council, wanted to lead an all-campus rally discussing their differences of opinion with the faculty and administration over a variety of topics. They decided on a date and went around campus putting up posters announcing the rally. The setting was to be a quad right outside the college union. In addition to the union, the quad was composed of two academic buildings and the administration building. The rally was set for a Friday at 3 P.M. when a few classes were still in session.

As the rally began, the crowd was small. Carl and Rick grew more fervent in the style and substance of their speeches. As a result, the crowd soon grew to several hundred persons. The entrance to the union became largely blocked by the crowd; only by pushing and shoving could one enter or leave the building. A few students attending classes in the nearby academic buildings became distracted and began peering out of the windows and doorways of the classrooms to see what was going on.

The dean of students was working in the administration building. She came down to the rally to ask Rick and Carl to stop what they were doing and help disperse the crowd. They refused. She then offered to let the students continue the rally in the administration conference room, which seats 50 people. As an alternative, she suggested they move the rally to a vacant playing field on the other side of the campus (about a mile away). Again, the offers were refused. Saying she had no choice but to summon security officials to disperse the crowd, the dean left. Upon hearing this threat, the students began leaving. The rally soon broke up completely.

The following Monday, Rick and Carl received notice they were being charged with violating a college rule which said in part that any student "causing or tending to cause disruptive behavior of El Gruncho students and thereby inhibiting the conduct of legitimate college business shall be subject to disciplinary action." After a hearing, they were suspended from the college for the remainder of the term. Later, they brought suit against the college.

––––––

Based on previous discussion and cases, what arguments would you make for each side? If you were to decide this hypothetical case, what decision would you reach?

4. Based on our lengthy elaboration of the material disruption test, would you agree with Judge Goldberg that *Tinker* "sets canals and channels through which school discipline might flow with the least possible damage to the nation's priceless topsoil of the First Amendment"? Or

do you still seem troubled by what is and is not permissible? Note the following comment:

> * * * (I)t is impossible to know when * * * education is disrupted unless it is first known what education is. In this area, confusion reigns supreme.[15]

III. THE DEVELOPMENT OF FREEDOM OF THE PRESS

A. Freedom of the Press in the Political and Social Setting

The value of a press free of governmental interference and censorship has been a major political and legal norm in American society. It is obvious that the press can be an effective means for exposing corruption, error, or folly on the part of government officials, and it is just as important that it serves as a vehicle to express a variety of views on all phases of social life. Amid the conformist trends of mass society, a free press may be one of the few ways still available for dissident opinions to reach a broad audience. At the same time, control of the press means that a good deal of power is in the hands of relatively few persons and raises the question whether the mass media really does present dissident opinions even if free. Thus fairness and a sense of responsibility on the part of those who have control of the press are also of great concern.

(1) The Near Decision

The Supreme Court has generally but not invariably taken the position that no censorship through a system of prior restraints is permissible under the First Amendment. The federal and state governments cannot prohibit a book or newspaper from being published. A license cannot be required for a publisher to operate. Special taxes cannot be levied that discriminate against publishers vis-a-vis other business enterprises. The Court has largely accepted the legal principle of Sir William Blackstone that "The liberty of the press is indeed essential to the nature of a free state; but this consists in having no previous restraints upon publications, and not in freedom from censure for criminal matter when published."

The principal doctrinal decision which deals with the question of censorship of the press is *Near v. Minnesota*, 283 U.S. 697 (1931). Because of its importance, the case is excerpted below. In *Near* the County Attorney of Hennepin County brought an action under Minnesota's so-called "gag law" to enjoin publication of a periodical known as "The Saturday Press." Nine editions of the newspaper had been printed in 1927, all of them critical of public officials in Minneapolis. The articles charged that a Jewish gangster was in control of racketeering in the city and that law enforcement personnel were ineffective in controlling crime because they had been bought. The newspaper demanded a special grand jury and prosecutor be appointed to investigate the situation, including the shooting of one of the defendants after publication of the initial issue of "The Saturday Press." At the trial the defendants denied the articles were malicious, scandalous,

---

15. Peter J. Riga, "*Yoder* and Free Exercise," 6 *J.Law and Educ.* 449, October, 1977, at p. 455 (footnote 45).

or defamatory. They claimed freedom of the press protection under the First/Fourteenth Amendment. The trial court issued a permanent injunction against further publication of the newspaper. The Minnesota Supreme Court upheld the lower court, noting that defendants had not indicated a desire "to conduct their business in the usual and legitimate manner." Thereupon, defendant Near appealed to the U.S. Supreme Court.

NEAR v. MINNESOTA

Supreme Court of the United States, 1931.
283 U.S. 697, 51 S.Ct. 625, 75 L.Ed. 1357.

Mr. Chief Justice HUGHES delivered the opinion of the Court.

Chapter 285 of the Session Laws of Minnesota for the year 1925 provides for the abatement, as a public nuisance, of a "malicious, scandalous and defamatory newspaper, magazine or other periodical."

Section one of the Act is as follows:

"Section 1.   Any person who as an individual, or as a member or employee of a firm or association or organization, or as an officer, director, member or employee of a corporation, shall be engaged in the business of regularly or customarily producing, publishing or circulating, having in possession, selling or giving away.

(a) an obscene, lewd and lascivious newspaper, magazine, or other periodical or

(b) a malicious, scandalous and defamatory newspaper, magazine or other periodical,
is guilty of a nuisance, and all persons guilty of such nuisance may be enjoined, as hereinafter provided. * * *

* * *

This statute, for the suppression as a public nuisance of a newspaper or periodical, is unusual, if not unique, and raises questions of grave importance transcending the local interests involved in the particular action. It is no longer open to doubt that the liberty of the press, and of speech, is within the liberty safeguarded by the due process clause of the Fourteenth Amendment from invasion by state action. * * * In maintaining this guaranty, the authority of the State to enact laws to promote the health, safety, morals and general welfare of its people is necessarily admitted. * * * Liberty of speech, and of the press, is * * * not an absolute right, and the State may punish its abuse. Liberty, in each of its phases, has its history and connotation and, in the present instance, the inquiry is as to the historic conception of the liberty of the press and whether the statute under review violates the essential attributes of that liberty.

* * *

The question is whether a statute authorizing such proceedings in restraint of publication is consistent with the conception of the liberty of the press as historically conceived and guaranteed. In determining the extent of the constitutional protection, it has been generally, if not universally considered that it is the chief purpose of the guaranty to prevent previous restraints upon publication. * * *

* * * (I)t is recognized that punishment for the abuse of the liberty accorded to the press is essential to the protection of the public, and that the common law rules that subject the libeler to responsiblity for the public offense, as well as for the private injury, are not abolished by the protection extended in our constitutions. The law of criminal libel rests upon that secure foundation. There is also the conceded authority of

courts to punish for contempt when publications directly tend to prevent the proper discharge of judicial functions. In the present case, we have no occasion to inquire as to the permissible scope of subsequent punishment. For whatever wrong the appellant has committed or may commit, by his publications, the State appropriately affords both public and private redress by its libel laws. As has been noted, the statute in question does not deal with punishments; it provides for no punishment, except in case of contempt for violation of the court's order, but for suppression and injunction, that is, for restraint upon publication.

The objection has also been made that the principle as to immunity from previous restraint is stated too broadly, if every such restraint is deemed to be prohibited. That is undoubtedly true; the protection even as to previous restraint is not absolutely unlimited. But the limitation has been recognized only in exceptional cases: "When a nation is at war many things that might be said in time of peace are such a hindrance to its effort that their utterance will not be endured so long as men fight and that no Court could regard them as protected by any constitutional right." *Schenck v. United States.* No one would question but that a government might prevent actual obstruction to its recruiting service or the publication of the sailing dates of transports or the number and location of troops. On similar grounds, the primary requirements of decency may be enforced against obscene publications. The security of the community life may be protected against incitements to acts of violence and the overthrow by force of orderly government. * * * These limitations are not applicable here. * * *

The exceptional nature of its limitations places in a strong light the general conception that liberty of the press, historically considered and taken up by the Federal Constitution, has meant, princi-

pally although not exclusively, immunity from previous restraints or censorship. The conception of the liberty of the press in this country had broadened with the exigencies of the colonial period and with the efforts to secure freedom from oppressive administration. That liberty was especially cherished for the immunity it afforded from previous restraint of the publication of censure of public officers and charges of official misconduct. * * *

The fact that for approximately one hundred and fifty years there has been almost an entire absence of attempts to impose previous restraints upon publications relating to the malfeasance of public officers is significant of the deep-seated conviction that such restraints would violate constitutional right. Public officers, whose character and conduct remain open to debate and free discussion in the press, find their remedies for false accusations in actions under libel laws providing for redress and punishment, and not in proceedings to restrain the publication of newspapers and periodicals. * * *

The importance of this immunity has not lessened. While reckless assaults upon public men, and efforts to bring obloquy upon those who are endeavoring faithfully to discharge official duties, exert a baleful influence and deserve the severest condemnation in public opinion, it cannot be said that this abuse is greater, and it is believed to be less, than that which characterized the period in which our institutions took shape. Meanwhile, the administration of government has become more complex, the opportunities for malfeasance and corruption have multiplied, crime has grown to most serious proportions, and the danger of its protection by unfaithful officials and of the impairment of the fundamental security of life and property by criminal alliances and official neglect, emphasizes the primary need of a vigilant and courageous press, especially in great cities. The fact that the liberty of the press may be abused by miscreant purveyors of scandal does not make any the less necessary the immunity of the press from previous restraint in dealing with official misconduct. Subsequent punishment for such abuses as may exist is the appropriate remedy, consistent with constitutional privilege.

In attempted justification of the statute, it is said that it deals not with publication *per se*, but with the "business" of publishing defamation. If, however, the publisher has a constitutional right to publish, without previous restraint, an edition of his newspaper charging official derelictions, it cannot be denied that he may publish subsequent editions for the same purpose. He does not lose his right by exercising it. If his right exists, it may be exercised in publishing nine editions, as in this case, as well as in one edition. If previous restraint is permissible, it may be imposed at once; indeed, the wrong may be as serious in one publication as in several. Characterizing the publication as a business, and the business as a nuisance, does not permit an invasion of the constitutional immunity against restraint. Similarly, it does not matter that the newspaper or periodical is found to be "largely" or "chiefly" devoted to the publication of such derelictions. If the publisher has a right, without previous restraint, to publish them, his right cannot be deemed to be dependent upon his publishing something else, more or less, with the matter to which objection is made.

Nor can it be said that the constitutional freedom from previous restraint is lost because charges are made of derelictions which constitute crimes. With the multiplying provisions of penal codes, and of municipal charters and ordinances carrying penal sanctions, the conduct of public officers is very largely within the purview of criminal statutes. The freedom of the press from previous restraint has never been regarded as limited to such animadversions as lay outside the range of penal enactments. Historically, there is no such limitation; it is inconsistent with the reason which underlies the privilege, as the privilege so limited would be of slight value for the purposes for which it came to be established.

The statute in question cannot be justified by reason of the fact that the publisher is permitted to show, before injunction issues, that the matter published is true and is published with good motives and for justifiable ends. If such a statute, authorizing suppression and injunction on such a basis, is constitutionally valid, it would be equally permissible for the legislature to provide that at any time the publisher of any newspaper could be brought before a court, or even an administrative officer (as the constitutional protection may not be regarded as resting on mere procedural details) and required to produce proof of the truth of his publication, or of what he intended to publish, and of his motives, or stand enjoined. If this can be done, the legislature may provide machinery for determining in the complete exercise of its discretion what are justifiable ends and restrain publication accordingly. And it would be but a step to a complete system of censorship. The recognition of authority to impose previous restraint upon publication in order to protect the community against the circulation of charges of misconduct, and especially of official misconduct, necessarily would carry with it the admission of the authority of the censor against which the constitutional barrier was erected. The preliminary freedom, by virtue of the very reason for its existence, does not depend, as this Court has said, on proof of truth.

Equally unavailing is the insistence that the statute is designed to prevent the circulation of scandal which tends to disturb the public peace and to provoke assaults and the commission of crime.

Charges of reprehensible conduct, and in particular of official malfeasance, unquestionably create a public scandal, but the theory of the constitutional guaranty is that even a more serious public evil would be caused by authority to prevent publication. * * * There is nothing new in the fact that charges of reprehensible conduct may create resentment and the disposition to resort to violent means of redress, but this well-understood tendency did not alter the determination to protect the press against censorship and restraint upon publication. * * * The danger of violent reactions becomes greater with effective organization of defiant groups resenting exposure, and if this consideration warranted legislative interference with the initial freedom of publication, the constitutional protection would be reduced to a mere form of words.

For these reasons we hold the statute, so far as it authorized the proceedings in this action under clause (b) of section one, to be an infringement of the liberty of the press guaranteed by the Fourteenth Amendment. We should add that this decision rests upon the operation and effect of the statute, without regard to the question of the truth of the charges contained in the particular periodical. The fact that the public officers named in this case, and those associated with the charges of official dereliction, may be deemed to be impeccable, cannot affect the conclusion that the statute imposes an unconstitutional restraint upon publication.

Judgment reversed.

Mr. Justice BUTLER dissented in an opinion in which Justices VAN DEVANTER,   McREYNOLDS,   and SUTHERLAND concurred.

* * *

(2) The Pentagon Papers Case

In 1971 some of the possible limitations of a free press raised in the context of criticism of the government in Chief Justice Hughes' *Near* opinion came to the Court's attention. The Nixon Administration sought an injunction against the *New York Times* and the *Washington Post* to prevent their continued publication of the so-called "Pentagon Papers." These papers were part of 47 volumes made at the direction of the Department of Defense to learn how the United States became involved in the war in Vietnam. The report was classified as secret. However, copies were eventually provided to these newspapers in violation of security regulations. The government claimed that publication would hinder the war effort and the possibilities of effective negotiations with the enemy. The two newspapers claimed the right to publish without prior restraint. The case was expedited to the Supreme Court, where it was heard and decided in record time, a fact disturbing to some of the Justices. The Court issued a *per curiam* decision, followed by individual opinions from all nine Justices. The opinions revealed that the Justices split 6–3 on the issue of prior restraint. The opinions also revealed major differences among the Justices in their views about freedom of the press and the role of the judiciary.

NEW YORK TIMES CO. v. UNITED STATES

Supreme Court of the United States, 1971.
403 U.S. 713, 91 S.Ct. 2140, 29 L.Ed.2d 822.

Per Curiam.

We granted certiorari in these cases in which the United States seeks to enjoin the New York Times and the Washington Post from publishing the contents of a classified study entitled "History of U. S. Decision-Making Process on Viet Nam Policy."

"Any system of prior restraints of expression comes to this Court bearing a heavy presumption against its constitutional validity." The Government "thus carries a heavy burden of showing justification for the imposition of such a restraint." The District Court for the Southern District of New York in the New York Times case and the District Court for the District of Columbia and the Court of Appeals for the District of Columbia Circuit in the Washington Post case held that the Government had not met that burden. We agree.

The judgment of the Court of Appeals for the District of Columbia Circuit is therefore affirmed. The order of the Court of Appeals for the Second Circuit is reversed and the case is remanded with directions to enter a judgment affirming the judgment of the District Court for the Southern District of New York. The stays entered June 25, 1971, by the Court are vacated. The judgments shall issue forthwith.

So ordered.

Mr. Justice BLACK, with whom Mr. Justice DOUGLAS joins, concurring.

* * * I believe that every moment's continuance of the injunctions against these newspapers amounts to a flagrant, indefensible, and continuing violation of the First Amendment. * * * In my view it is unfortunate that some of my Brethren are apparently willing to hold that the publication of news may sometimes be enjoined. Such a holding would make a shambles of the First Amendment.

* * *

In the First Amendment the Founding Fathers gave the free press the protection it must have to fulfill its essential role in our democracy. The press was to serve the governed, not the governors. The Government's power to censor the press was abolished so that the press would remain forever free to censure the Government. The press was protected so that it could bare the secrets of government and inform the people. Only a free and unrestrained press can effectively expose deception in government. And paramount among the responsibilities of a free press is the duty to prevent any part of the government from deceiving the people and sending them off to distant lands to die of foreign fevers and foreign shot and shell. In my view, far from deserving condemnation for their courageous reporting, the New York Times, the Washington Post, and other newspapers should be commended for serving the purpose that the Founding Fathers saw so clearly. * * *

* * *

Mr. Justice DOUGLAS, with whom Mr. Justice BLACK joins, concurring.

* * *

The dominant purpose of the First Amendment was to prohibit the widespread practice of governmental suppression of embarrassing information. It is common knowledge that the First Amendment was adopted against the widespread use of the common law of seditious libel to punish the dissemination of material that is embarrassing to the powers-that-be. * * * The present cases will, I think, go down in history as the most dramatic illustration of that principle. A debate of large proportions goes on in the Nation over our posture in Vietnam. That debate antedated the disclosure of the contents of the present documents. The latter are highly relevant to the debate in progress.

Secrecy in government is fundamentally anti-democratic, perpetuating bureaucratic errors. Open debate and discussion of public issues are vital to our national health. On public questions there should be "uninhibited, robust, and wide-open" debate. * * *

* * *

Mr. Justice BRENNAN, concurring.

* * *

* * * The entire thrust of the Government's claim throughout these cases has been that publication of the material sought to be enjoined "could," or "might," or "may" prejudice the national interest in various ways. But the First Amendment tolerates absolutely no prior judicial restraints of the press predicated upon surmise or conjecture that untoward consequences may result. Our cases, * * *, have indicated that there is a single, extremely narrow class of cases in which the First Amendment's ban on prior judicial restraint may be overridden. Our cases have thus far indicated that such cases may arise only when the Nation "is at war," during which times "[n]o one would question but that a government might prevent actual obstruction to its recruiting service or the publication of the sailing dates of transports or the number and location of troops." Near v. Minnesota. Even if the present world situation were assumed to be tantamount to a time of war, or if the power of presently available armaments would justify even in peacetime the suppression of information that would set in motion a nuclear holocaust, in neither of these actions has the Government presented or

even alleged that publication of items from or based upon the material at issue would cause the happening of an event of that nature. * * *

Mr. Justice STEWART, with whom Mr. Justice WHITE joins, concurring.

* * *

In the absence of the governmental checks and balances present in other areas of our national life, the only effective restraint upon executive policy and power in the areas of national defense and international affairs may lie in an enlightened citizenry—in an informed and critical public opinion which alone can here protect the values of democratic government. For this reason, it is perhaps here that a press that is alert, aware, and free most vitally serves the basic purpose of the First Amendment. For without an informed and free press there cannot be an enlightened people.

Yet it is elementary that the successful conduct of international diplomacy and the maintenance of an effective national defense require both confidentiality and secrecy. Other nations can hardly deal with this Nation in an atmosphere of mutual trust unless they can be assured that their confidences will be kept. And within our own executive departments, the development of considered and intelligent international policies would be impossible if those charged with their formulation could not communicate with each other freely, frankly, and in confidence. In the area of basic national defense the frequent need for absolute secrecy is, of course, self-evident.

I think there can be but one answer to this dilemma, if dilemma it be. The responsibility must be where the power is. If the Constitution gives the Executive a large degree of unshared power in the conduct of foreign affairs and the maintenance of our national defense, then under the Constitution the Executive must have the largely unshared duty to determine and preserve the degree of internal security necessary to exercise that power successfully. It is an awesome responsibility, requiring judgment and wisdom of a high order. I should suppose that moral, political, and practical considerations would dictate that a very first principle of that wisdom would be an insistence upon avoiding secrecy for its own sake. For when everything is classified, then nothing is classified, and the system becomes one to be disregarded by the cynical or the careless, and to be manipulated by those intent on self-protection or self-promotion. I should suppose, in short, that the hallmark of a truly effective internal security system would be the maximum possible disclosure, recognizing that secrecy can best be preserved only when credibility is truly maintained. But be that as it may, it is clear to me that it is the constitutional duty of the Executive— as a matter of sovereign prerogative and not as a matter of law as the courts know law—through the promulgation and enforcement of executive regulations, to protect the confidentiality necessary to carry out its responsibilities in the fields of international relations and national defense.

* * *

* * * in the cases before us we are asked neither to construe specific regulations nor to apply specific laws. We are asked, instead, to perform a function that the Constitution gave to the Executive, not the Judiciary. We are asked, quite simply, to prevent the publication by two newspapers of material that the Executive Branch insists should not, in the national interest, be published. I am convinced that the Executive is correct with respect to some of the documents involved. But I cannot say that disclosure of any of them will surely result in direct, immediate, and irreparable damage to our Nation or its people. That being so, there can under the First Amendment be but one judicial resolution of the issues before us. I join the judgments of the Court.

Mr. Justice WHITE, with whom Mr. Justice STEWART joins, concurring.

I concur in today's judgments, but only because of the concededly extraordinary protection against prior restraints enjoyed by the press under our constitutional system. I do not say that in no circumstances would the First Amendment permit an injunction against publishing information about government plans or operations. * * *

But I * * * agree that the United States has not satisfied the very heavy burden that it must meet to warrant an injunction against publication in these cases, at least in the absence of express and appropriately limited congressional authorization for prior restraints in circumstances such as these.

* * *

It is not easy to reject the proposition urged by the United States and to deny relief on its good-faith claims in these cases that publication will work serious damage to the country. But that discomfiture is considerably dispelled by the infrequency of prior-restraint cases. Normally, publication will occur and the damage be done before the Government has either opportunity or grounds for suppression. So here, publication has already begun and a substantial part of the threatened damage has already occurred. The fact of a massive breakdown in security is known, access to the documents by many unauthorized people is undeniable, and the efficacy of equitable relief against these or other newspapers to avert anticipated damage is doubtful at best.

What is more, terminating the ban on publication of the relatively few sensitive documents the Government now seeks to suppress does not mean that the law either requires or invites newspapers or others to publish them or that they will be immune from criminal action if they do. Prior restraints require an unusually heavy justification under the First Amendment; but failure by the Government to justify prior restraints does not measure its constitutional entitlement to a conviction for criminal publication. That the Government mistakenly chose to proceed by injunction does not mean that it could not successfully proceed in another way.

* * *

* * * Congress has addressed itself to the problems of protecting the security of the country and the national defense from unauthorized disclosure of potentially damaging information. It has not, however, authorized the injunctive remedy against threatened publication. It has apparently been satisfied to rely on criminal sanctions and their deterrent effect on the responsible as well as the irresponsible press. I am not, of course, saying that either of these newspapers has yet committed a crime or that either would commit a crime if it published all the material now in its possession. That matter must await resolution in the context of a criminal proceeding if one is instituted by the United States.

Mr. Justice MARSHALL, concurring.

* * *

* * * The Constitution provides that Congress shall make laws, the President execute laws, and courts interpret laws. It did not provide for government by injunction in which the courts and the Executive Branch can "make law" without regard to the action of Congress. * * *

* * *

* * * it is clear that Congress has specifically rejected passing legislation that would have clearly given the President the power he seeks here and made the current activity of the newspapers unlawful. When Congress specifically declines to make conduct unlawful it is not

for this Court to redecide those issues— to overrule Congress. * * *

* * *

Mr. Chief Justice BURGER, dissenting.

So clear are the constitutional limitations on prior restraint against expression, that from the time of Near v. Minnesota, we have had little occasion to be concerned with cases involving prior restraints against news reporting on matters of public interest. There is, therefore, little variation among the members of the Court in terms of resistance to prior restraints against publication. Adherence to this basic constitutional principle, however, does not make these cases simple. In these cases, the imperative of a free and unfettered press comes into collision with another imperative, the effective functioning of a complex modern government and specifically the effective exercise of certain constitutional powers of the Executive. * * *

* * *

The newspapers make a derivative claim under the First Amendment; they denominate this right as the public "right to know"; by implication, the Times asserts a sole trusteeship of that right by virtue of its journalistic "scoop." The right is asserted as an absolute. Of course, the First Amendment right itself is not an absolute, as Justice Holmes so long ago pointed out in his aphorism concerning the right to shout "fire" in a crowded theater if there was no fire. There are other exceptions, some of which Chief Justice Hughes mentioned by way of example in Near v. Minnesota. There are no doubt other exceptions no one has had occasion to describe or discuss. Conceivably such exceptions may be lurking in these cases and would have been flushed had they been properly considered in the trial courts, free from unwarranted deadlines and frenetic pressures. An issue of this importance should be tried and heard in a judicial atmosphere conducive to thoughtful, reflective deliberation, * * *.

* * *

* * * As I see it we have been forced to deal with litigation concerning rights of great magnitude without an adequate record, and surely without time for adequate treatment either in the prior proceedings or in this Court. It is interesting to note that counsel on both sides, in oral argument before this Court, were frequently unable to respond to questions on factual points. Not surprisingly they pointed out that they had been working literally "around the clock" and simply were unable to review the documents that give rise to these cases and were not familiar with them. This Court is in no better posture. * * *

* * *

We all crave speedier judicial processes but when judges are pressured as in these cases the result is a parody of the judicial function.

Mr. Justice HARLAN, with whom The Chief Justice and Mr. Justice BLACKMUN join, dissenting.

* * *

* * * I agree that, in performance of its duty to protect the values of the First Amendment against political pressures, the judiciary must review the initial Executive determination to the point of satisfying itself that the subject matter of the dispute does lie within the proper compass of the President's foreign relations power. * * * Moreover, the judiciary may properly insist that the determination that disclosure of the subject matter would irreparably impair the national security be made by the head of the Executive Department concerned—here the Secretary of State or the Secretary of Defense—after actual personal consideration by that officer. * * *

But in my judgment the judiciary may not properly go beyond these two inquiries and redetermine for itself the probable impact of disclosure on the national security.

* * *

* * * I can see no indication in the opinions of either the District Court or the Court of Appeals in the Post litigation that the conclusions of the Executive were given even the deference owing to an administrative agency, much less that owing to a co-equal branch of the Government operating within the field of its constitutional prerogative.

* * *

Mr. Justice BLACKMUN, dissenting.

* * *

The First Amendment, * * * is only one part of an entire Constitution. Article II of the great document vests in the Executive Branch primary power over the conduct of foreign affairs and places in that branch the responsibility for the Nation's safety. Each provision of the Constitution is important, and I cannot subscribe to a doctrine of unlimited absolutism for the First Amendment at the cost of downgrading other provisions. First Amendment absolutism has never commanded a majority of this Court. What is needed here is a weighing, upon properly developed standards, of the broad right of the press to print and of the very narrow right of the Government to prevent. Such standards are not yet developed. The parties here are in disagreement as to what those standards should be. But even the newspapers concede that there are situations where restraint is in order and is constitutional. * * *

I therefore would remand these cases to be developed expeditiously, of course, but on a schedule permitting the orderly presentation of evidence from both sides * * *.

NOTES AND QUESTIONS

1. All the Justices, as Chief Justice Burger points out, are suspicious of governmental prior restraints on what the press, including the electronic media, may communicate. But their views range from the absolute prohibition Justice Black sees in the First Amendment to the balancing of press freedom against Article II of the Constitution endorsed by Justice Blackmun. Note that some of the Justices base their views on deference to Congress, while the dissenters suggest that the judiciary limit its investigation to seeing that the action complained of is a proper assertion of the powers of the President. Which view most nearly approximates your own?

2. Note as well that some of the Justices are concerned about the proper role of the judiciary. Thus Justice Harlan suggests the Court play a limited role while Justices Black, Douglas, and Brennan would have the Court take an activist stance in defending freedom of the press. Where highly charged political issues involving the three branches of government are involved, the Justices often are noticeably less inclined toward judicial activism, primarily because the Court has little power outside of legal and moral suasion. This same hesitancy is evident but for different reasons when the Court confronts issues involving the internal affairs of educational institutions. What are the reasons?

The *Pentagon Papers Case* is an excellent illustration of how the sets of variables outlined in Figure 3–2 on p. 113 impinge on judicial resolution of complex disputes. Each of the Justices comes to his decision from a different route, largely dependent on how he views the various considerations reflected in the figure.

3. Justices White and Marshall are most vocal in urging deference to Congress. They appear to imply that had Congress authorized the use of injunctions to prevent disclosure of potentially damaging information, they would view the case differently. Suppose Congress had passed a law sanctioning such prior restraints. Based on the comments in Note 2 above, why do you suppose some of the Justices might look more favorably on prior restraint of the press under these circumstances? Should they? Suppose a school board or college board of trustees enacted a rule authorizing educational administrators to review all material to be included in a student newspaper in order to screen out potentially damaging information. Should judges hesitate before striking down the prior restraint as an infringement on freedom of the press because of the existence of the rule?

4. Justice White notes that the government "mistakenly chose to proceed by injunction" and suggests that subsequent punishment is still an available option. This fact is important to note. Just because prior restraints are ruled out does not mean that other remedies are unavailable. The important point is that the sanctions are applied *after* the illegal act has been committed, not before. Why might subsequent punishment be preferred to prior restraints? What drawbacks exist?

5. The Federal Communication Commission's "fairness doctrine" was instituted to give individuals and groups with opposing views an opportunity to articulate their respective positions, particularly when they come into conflict with the views expressed by the television networks them-

selves. In 1973 the U. S. Supreme Court decided the case of *Columbia Broadcasting System, Inc. v. Democratic Nat. Committee,* 412 U.S. 94. Chief Justice Burger wrote the opinion in which he indicated that neither the First Amendment nor the FCC's "fairness doctrine" requires broadcasters to accept paid editorial advertisements from individuals and groups who wish to express their views on public issues through the mass media. The majority found that such a requirement might work contrary to the public interest in a fair presentation of the news. Do you agree? If you see this situation as a classic conflict between these two basic rights, speech and press, which right should prevail? Under what circumstances?

(3) Rights and Responsibilities of News Reporters

In recent years two important issues have been raised that deal with the rights and responsibilities of reporters. One issue concerns comments made about public officials; the other pertains to reporters' keeping their sources of information confidential from governmental officials. These issues are not only major concerns to persons involved in maintaining the business of gathering and disseminating information; they also have a major impact on the free flow of information and the public's right to be informed.

The landmark case dealing with the right to comment on public officials is *New York Times Co. v. Sullivan,* 376 U.S. 254 (1964). In this decision the Court overturned a libel judgment against a newspaper for printing a full page advertisement by Black clergymen, charging local officials in Montgomery, Alabama, with perpetuating a "wave of terror" against civil rights demonstrators. Although some of the material in the advertisement turned out to be false, the Court stated that public officials could not recover damages because the printed statement was not made with "actual malice," which is to say, with knowledge that it was false or with reckless disregard of whether it was false or not. "Erroneous statements honestly made" cannot be punished as libel when dealing with public officials. The Court reasoned that "debate on public issues should be uninhibited, robust, and wide-open, and that it may well include vehement, caustic, and sometimes unpleasantly sharp attacks on public officials." (At p. 270).

In *Rosenbloom v. Metromedia, Inc.,* 403 U.S. 29 (1971), the Court took this position a step further in holding that this rule includes some private individuals as well. A dealer in nudist magazines, arrested but found innocent of obscenity charges in Court, was held not to have been libeled by radio station broadcasts that referred to him as a "smut peddler."

The press lost an important case in 1972 which pertained to their right to keep certain sources of information confidential from government officials and courts of law. In *Branzburg v. Hayes,* 408 U.S. 665 (1972), Justice White for the five-man majority balanced the interests of the press with those of grand juries, striking the balance for the latter:

> * * * we perceive no basis for holding that the public interest in law enforcement * * * is insufficient to override the consequential, but uncertain, burden on news gathering that is said to result from insisting that reporters, like other citizens, respond

to relevant questions put to them in the course of a valid grand jury investigation or criminal trial. (At pp. 690–691).

The press decried this decision, claiming that such compulsion to testify about their confidential sources would dry up sources of information, making the press an investigative arm of the government. By 1978, twenty-six states had adopted so-called shield laws, which give reporters the privilege of refusing to disclose in legal proceedings any information gained in the course of news gathering. Their effectiveness, however, is uncertain; the Supreme Court will likely be called on again to clarify the law in this sensitive area.

In a decision more favorable to the press in 1974, the Court ruled that a Florida statute requiring newspapers which comment pejoratively on a political candidate to afford free space for reply purposes was an unconstitutional intrusion into the editorial function. *Miami Herald Pub. Co. v. Tornillo,* 418 U.S. 241 (1974). And in 1976 the Court ruled in *Nebraska Press Ass'n v. Stuart,* 427 U.S. 539, that court-imposed "gag orders" forbidding news reporters to report about pre-trial proceedings in a mass murder case violated the First Amendment. The Court indicated a heavy presumption against the constitutionality of gag orders, noting that " * * prior restraint on publication (is) one of the most extraordinary remedies known to our jurisprudence." (At p. 562).

The press lost another important case in 1978 involving police searches of newsrooms. The case, *Zurcher v. Stanford Daily,* 436 U.S. 547 (1978), concerned a police search pursuant to a search warrant of the Stanford University student newspaper office. The police were looking for photographs of persons who attacked a group of policemen at a political demonstration near the university. The newspaper claimed that the Fourth Amendment search warrant process provides insufficient protection to the press since it enables the police to enter news offices unannounced and conduct an extensive investigation of files, desks, and so on. Such unrestrained searches, claimed the newspaper, are not only disruptive but also violate the freedom of the press because they dry up confidential news sources, thus hampering gathering and reporting the news. The paper opted for the use of subpoenas. The subpoena process affords due process rights to the subjects of searches, unlike search warrants. In a decision soundly attacked by radio, television, and newspapers across the country, Justice White ruled in a 5 to 3 decision (Justice Brennan took no part in the case) that the press has no special right under the Fourth Amendment search and seizure provision. The search warrant provided for in that Amendment affords sufficient protection.

Justice Stewart in his dissenting opinion noted that the Court's refusal to authorize the subpoena process for searches of news offices "requires no blind leap of faith to understand that a person who gives information to a journalist only on the condition that his identity will not be revealed will be less likely to give that information if he knows that, despite the journalist's assurance, his identity may be disclosed." (At p. 1985). Justice Stewart added that it is not accurate to say that the press is entitled to no more protection than any other person or business under the Constitution, for only the press is guaranteed explicit protection in that document.

In April, 1979, the Court split 6 to 3 in ruling in *Herbert v. Lando,* 99 S.Ct. 1635, that *New York Times* and its progeny do not prohibit public officials and public figures in libel actions from inquiring into the state of mind and the editorial processes of defendant news reporters and publishers. Dissenting Justices Brennan and Marshall argued that editorial deliberations should be constitutionally privileged lest fear of lengthy and expensive legal proceedings mute rigorous exchange of ideas among news reporters. Not surprisingly, the decision was soundly criticized by the press.

Both the *Zurcher* and the *Herbert* decisions will likely prompt the press to seek passage of statutory protection from Congress and state legislatures.

B. Freedom of the Press for Students in the Public Educational Setting

How free should the press be in the public educational setting? The issue is complex, partly because of the differing age groups involved, partly because of the uniqueness of the educational environment, and partly because the educational institution itself may be involved in varying degrees in student press activities. "The press" could mean any number of variations of the following: a campus newspaper or yearbook financed by the institution and operated under the auspices of an academic department, a newspaper or literary magazine funded by mandatory student fees but otherwise independent of the institution, an "underground" flyer or paper printed at the expense of the editor and distributed on or off the campus, or a commercial publication distributed by students.

How much control should the educational institution exert, if any, over these publications? What variables must we take into consideration in answering this question? For example, should institutional control vary inversely with the age and grade level of the students? Should the "materially disruptive" test of *Tinker* apply? What effect does the funding of campus newspapers by mandatory student fees have on institutional control? Should standards of good taste be a valid institutional concern?

These and other issues are explored below, beginning with a case which illustrates present general legal attitudes about freedom of the press in the public educational setting.

(1) Freedom of the Student Press

In *Dickey v. Alabama State Bd.,* Gary Dickey, editor of the Troy State College student newspaper, *The Tropolitan,* was suspended for one academic year over a dispute concerning an editorial he wished to include in the paper. Dickey sought to print an editorial supportive of the president of the University of Alabama, who was then under attack in the state legislature for his refusal to censor a student publication entitled "Emphasis 67, A World in Revolution." Both the faculty advisor and the president of Troy State College, Ralph Adams, refused to approve the editorial. The basis for their refusal was a college rule called the "Adams Rule," which said in effect that editorials or articles critical of state officials could not be printed in the college newspaper. The rule did not prohibit laudatory material, however. The faculty advisor gave Dickey an essay entitled

"Raising Dogs in North Carolina" to be used in place of the restricted editorial. Dickey refused to print the essay and instead left the space in the newspaper blank with the exception of the single word "Censored." He then mailed the banned editorial to a newspaper in Montgomery. He was suspended for willful and deliberate insubordination.

DICKEY v. ALABAMA STATE BD. OF EDUC.

United States District Court for the Middle District of Alabama, 1967.
273 F.Supp. 613.

JOHNSON, Chief Judge.

* * *

It is basic in our law in this country that the privilege to communicate concerning a matter of public interest is embraced in the First Amendment right relating to freedom of speech and is constitutionally protected against infringement by state officials. The Fourteenth Amendment to the Constitution protects these First Amendment rights from state infringement, and these First Amendment rights extend to school children and students insofar as unreasonable rules are concerned. West Virginia State Board of Education v. Barnette. Boards of education, presidents of colleges, and faculty advisers are not excepted from the rule that protects students against unreasonable rules and regulations. This Court recognizes that the establishment of an educational program requires certain rules and regulations necessary for maintaining an orderly program and operating the institution in a manner conducive to learning. However, the school and school officials have always been bound by the requirement that the rules and regulations *must be reasonable.* Courts may only consider whether rules and regulations that are imposed by school authorities are a reasonable exercise of the power and discretion vested in those authorities. Regulations and rules which are necessary in maintaining order and discipline are always considered reasonable. In the case now before this Court, it is clear that the maintenance of order and discipline of the students attending Troy

State College had nothing to do with the rule that was invoked against Dickey. As a matter of fact, the president of the institution, President Adams, testified that his general policy of not criticizing the Governor or the State Legislature under any circumstances, regardless of how reasonable or justified the criticism might be, was not for the purpose of maintaining order and discipline among the students. On this point, President Adams testified that the reason for the rule was that a newspaper could not criticize its owners, and in the case of a state institution the owners were to be considered as the Governor and the members of the Legislature.

With these basic constitutional principles in mind, the conclusion is compelled that the invocation of such a rule against Gary Clinton Dickey that resulted in his expulsion and/or suspension from Troy State College was unreasonable. A state cannot force a college student to forfeit his constitutionally protected right of freedom of expression as a condition to his attending a state-supported institution. State school officials cannot infringe on their students' right of free and unrestricted expression as guaranteed by the Constitution of the United States where the exercise of such right does not "materially and substantially interfere with requirements of appropriate discipline in the operation of the school." Burnside v. Byars, 363 F.2d 744 (5 Cir. 1966). The defendants in this case cannot punish Gary Clinton Dickey for his exercise of this constitutionally guaranteed right by cloaking his expulsion or suspension in the robe of "insubordination." The attempt to characterize Dickey's conduct, and the basis for their action in expelling him, as "insubordination" requiring rather severe disciplinary action, does not disguise the basic fact that Dickey was expelled from Troy State College for exercising his constitutionally guaranteed right of academic and/or political expression.

The argument by defendants' counsel that Dickey was attempting to take over the operation of the school newspaper ignores the fact that there was no legal obligation on the school authorities to permit Dickey to continue as one of its editors. As a matter of fact, there was no legal obligation on the school authorities to operate a school newspaper. However, since this state-supported institution did elect to operate The Tropolitan and did authorize Dickey to be one of its editors, they cannot as officials of the State of Alabama, without violating the First and Fourteenth Amendments to the Constitution of the United States, suspend or expel Dickey from this state-supported institution for his conduct as that conduct is reflected by the facts presented in this case.

*   *   *

Defendants' argument that Dickey's readmission will jeopardize the discipline in the institution is superficial and completely ignores the greater damage to college students that will result from the imposition of intellectual restraints such as the "Adams Rule" in this case. The imposition of such a restraint as here sought to be imposed upon Dickey and the other students at Troy State College violates the basic principles of academic and political expression as guaranteed by our Constitution. Dr. Rose recognized the importance of this academic and constitutional principle when he determined that as to the University of Alabama, such freedoms must be permitted to flourish. As

the Supreme Court stated in Sweezy v. State of New Hampshire, 354 U.S. 234, 250:

> "We believe that there unquestionably was an invasion of petitioner's liberties in the areas of academic freedom and political expression—areas in which government should be extremely reticent to tread.

> "The essentiality of freedom in the community of American universities is almost self-evident. No one should underestimate the vital role in a democracy that is played by those who guide and train our youth. To impose any strait jacket upon the intellectual leaders in our colleges and universities would imperil the future of our Nation. No field of education is so thoroughly comprehended by man that new discoveries cannot yet be made. Particularly is that true in the social sciences, where few, if any, principles are accepted as absolutes. Scholarship cannot flourish in an atmosphere of suspicion and distrust. Teachers and students must always remain free to inquire, to study and to evaluate, to gain new maturity and understanding; otherwise our civilization will stagnate and die."

In accordance with the foregoing, it is the order, judgment and decree of this Court that the action taken by Troy State College, acting through its Student Affairs Committee, on Friday, August 25, 1967, which action denies to Gary Clinton Dickey admission to Troy State College beginning with the fall quarter of 1967, be and the same is hereby declared unconstitutional, void, and is rescinded.

It is further ordered that the defendants immediately reinstate Gary Clinton Dickey as a student in Troy State College, commencing September 11, 1967.

It is further ordered that the defendants, and each of them, their agents, servants, employees, and others acting in concert or participation with them, be and each is hereby enjoined and restrained from denying, upon the basis of his conduct as herein discussed, Gary Clinton Dickey admission to Troy State College as a student and from refusing to allow him to attend as such for the academic year commencing September 11, 1967.

It is further ordered that the costs incurred in this proceeding be and they are hereby taxed against the defendants, for which execution may issue.

NOTES AND QUESTIONS

1. Would it have made any difference if President Adams had only suspended Dickey as editor of the newspaper, allowing him to remain in school? Should it?

2. President Adams asserted that since the newspaper was "owned" by the Governor and members of the legislature, it could not criticize their actions without their consent. Why does the court refuse to accept this analogy? Is President Adams correct, however, insofar as the nonpublic educational sector and boards of trustees are concerned?

3. Note that since *Tinker v. Des Moines School Dist.* had yet to be decided, the court cites *West Virginia State Bd. of Educ. v. Barnette* in stating that First Amendment rights extend to "school children and students." The court also cites *Sweezy v. State of New Hampshire*, a 1957 U. S. Supreme Court case involving the right of faculty members at public institutions to academic freedom.

4. Should press rights be granted greater protection under the First/ Fourteenth Amendment than speech rights? Consider the following comment by Harvard Law Professor S. H. Nahmod:

> (In press cases) in comparison with the worn symbol in *Tinker,* there is a more explicit and a more articulate attempt to inform and persuade. Arguments made and positions taken in print are more conducive to rational thought or, at least, to some reflective thought. Since what such students say is in print and can later be referred to and checked, printing will often—not always—exert a moderating influence on the authors.[16]

While courts have not specifically endorsed this approach, there does appear to be strong legal support for student press rights, even when the institution itself is intimately involved in student journalism operations. Note Chief Judge Johnson's comments that the college has no legal obligation to operate a school newspaper, but that once the privilege is extended, it cannot be compromised by suspending Dickey for the reason cited. Recently, this same principle has been applied to a public high school in Virginia. In *Gambino v. Fairfax County School Bd.*, 429 F.Supp. 731 (E.D.Va.1977), a federal district court ruled that school officials could not suppress the publishing of an article entitled "Sexually Active Students Fail to Use Contraceptives" in *The Farm News* because of a school board rule prohibiting the teaching of sex education. Like President Adams,

16. Sheldon H. Nahmod, "First Amendment Protection for Learning and Teaching: The Scope of Judicial Review," 18 *Wayne L.Rev.* 1479, 1972, at p. 1489.

school officials argued that the paper was not entitled to First Amendment protection because it was established and partially subsidized by the school board. Furthermore, the faculty advisor was paid a salary supplement, and students received academic credit for working on the paper. While the court agreed that the school board has substantive control of curricular matters in the school, it disagreed that the paper was anything other than a student activity. "Once a publication is determined to be in substance a free speech forum, constitutional protections attach and the state may restrict the content of that instrument only in accordance with First Amendment dictates." (At p. 734).

The school argued further that the high school environment is different from the collegiate and that in the absence of controls, irresponsible and uncontrollable publication might occur. The court agreed that the age of the students could be a factor, but in this instance, the school had simply concluded that the First Amendment didn't apply. No evidence was introduced to show that the publication was harmful to younger children in the school, nor was there an effective regulatory scheme for making such a determination. And insofar as there was no evidence of irresponsible journalism, the court rejected the argument as speculative.

The district court decision was affirmed in a brief *per curiam* opinion by the Fourth Circuit Court of Appeals in 1977. (564 F.2d 157). Judge Donald Russell dissented. He maintained the decision made "a plain mockery" of school board curricular control:

> A school administration certainly has a legitimate concern in eliminating from its curriculum material which may reasonably be considered as conducive to immorality and not appropriate to proper academic education; by the same token, it would seem equally clear that it would not be required to wink at the same material being taught in a backhanded way through the columns of a school paper, sponsored and largely financed by it. (At p. 158).

What if the parents of the students had argued that they wanted the school officials to review the publication before distribution in the school? Should the court still intervene in the case on the side of the students and against both school officials and parents?

5. Note the use of the "free speech forum" concept in the *Gambino* case above. Since the concept deprives educational officials of substantial regulatory power, under what circumstances are free speech forums likely to exist? What if the school officials in *Gambino* had argued that the paper represents an extension of the classroom learning experience and thus is "co-curricular"? Could this have made a difference? Suppose the paper is produced by the journalism class as a class assignment. Would school board control over curriculum then apply? Should it?

Could a school board assert control over the titles of books housed in the library? Or would you agree with the federal court of appeals in *Minarcini v. Strongsville City School Dist.*, 541 F.2d 577 (6th Cir. 1976), that once a library is created, neither the state nor the school board may "place conditions on the use of the library which (are) related solely to the social or political tastes of school board members."?   (At p. 582). Why not?   (Apply this ruling to the hypothetical at the end of Chapter One.)[17]   One commentator offers this rationale:

> It has been suggested that [curriculum] prohibitions are more suspect that requirements because of interference with the student's access to information and knowledge.   Translated into the judicial function, this means that the state's burden of justification should be greater for curriculum prohibition than for a requirement.   For the latter, a party attacking the requirement should have the burden of proving it has no rational educational basis.   For the former, perhaps the state should have the burden of proving its purpose is not to prevent controversy and its prohibition is not based only on "apprehension of disorder" found insufficient in *Tinker*.   When prohibitions are scrutinized, considerations of vagueness, overbreadth, and balance may also be judicially useful.[18]   (Material in brackets added).

Is the classroom itself a free speech forum?   To conclude that it is directly threatens traditional school board control of curricular matters and also challenges the traditional hierarchical relationship between teacher and student.   Like students, teachers in recent years have been more inclined to challenge the authority of school boards and administrators. As noted earlier in this chapter, teachers at the elementary and secondary level do not enjoy the same rights to academic freedom as college professors.   Most courts are reluctant to address these difficult issues, primarily because of the inherent social and educational policy questions judges feel unqualified to resolve.   Thus school boards and administrators retain considerable control over curricular matters and over classroom conduct by teachers and students.

(2) Validity of Prior Restraints

In the *Dickey* case, Chief Judge Johnson stated that "* * * they cannot as officials of the State of Alabama, without violating the First and Fourteenth Amendments to the Constitution of the United States, suspend or expel Dickey from this state-supported institution for his conduct as that conduct is reflected by the facts presented in this case."   The Chief Judge left open the possibility that under certain other circumstances, the editor *could* be suspended.   And in *Gambino,* the court implicitly agreed that under certain conditions and with certain procedures, school officials could exercise some control over the school newspaper.

What are those circumstances?   What procedures must be followed? Can disciplinary action be exercised *before* the literature in question has been distributed or only *after* the fact?   What impact do the ages and grade levels of the students involved have?   The next two cases present two quite different responses to these questions.

17. For a penetrating analysis of *Minarcini* and the student's "right to know" together with a 1972 decision by the Second Circuit reaching the opposite conclusion (*President's Council, Dist. 25 v. Community School Bd. No. 25*, 457 F.2d 289), see Note, "Constitutional Aspects of Removing Books from School Libraries," 66 *Kentucky L. Journal* 127, 1977–78.

18. *Id.*, at p. 1513.

EISNER v. STAMFORD BD. OF EDUC.

United States Court of Appeals, Second Circuit, 1971.
440 F.2d 803.

IRVING R. KAUFMAN, Circuit Judge:

The deceptively simple facts in this case generate legal problems which summon up many centuries of political and social thought and action concerning the relation between the rights and powers of men, women, and children, and their government. To resolve this problem we are required to consider principles and concepts which courts have fashioned over several decades of this century, giving concrete effect to the proscription of the first amendment against any law abridging freedom of expression, and apply them to the unique social structure prevailing in a public system of secondary schools.

The Board of Education of the City of Stamford, Connecticut, on November 18, 1969, adopted the following "policy":

"Distribution of Printed or Written Matter

"The Board of Education desires to encourage freedom of expression and creativity by its students subject to the following limitations:

"No person shall distribute any printed or written matter on the grounds of any school or in any school building unless the distribution of such material shall have prior approval by the school administration.

"In granting or denying approval, the following guidelines shall apply.

"No material shall be distributed which, either by its content or by the manner of distribution itself, will interfere with the proper and orderly operation and discipline of the school, will cause violence or disorder, or will constitute an invasion of the rights of others."

Plaintiffs are students at Rippowam High School in Stamford. They wish to distribute free of the restraint imposed by the quoted policy, or of any other similar restraint, a mimeographed newspaper of their own creation and other printed and written literature. The district court agreed with their contention that the Board's policy violates their right to freedom of expression. Limiting the issue to the constitutional validity of the requirement that the *contents* of "the literature be submitted to school officials for approval prior to distribution" (the validity of reasonable regulation concerning time, place, and manner of distribution being conceded by plaintiffs), the court reasoned that the policy imposed a "prior restraint" on student speech and press, invalid under Near v. Minnesota ex rel. Olson (1931) in the absence of even "a scintilla of proof which would justify" the restraint. As an independent ground for granting plaintiffs' and denying defendants' motions for summary judgment, the court found the policy fatally defective for lack of "procedural safeguards," citing Freedman v. Maryland, 380 U.S. 51 (1965). Specifically, Judge Zampano faulted the policy because it does "not specify the manner of submission, the exact party to whom the material must be submitted, the time within which a decision must be rendered; nor * * * provide for an adversary proceeding of any type or for a right of appeal." The court therefore declared the policy unconstitutional and enjoined defendants from enforcing any requirement that students obtain prior approval before publishing or distributing literature within the Stamford public schools.

We affirm the decision below, insofar as it declares unconstitutional and enjoins the enforcement of the Board's policy of

November 18, 1970, but we do so, as will shortly appear, with some reservations and for reasons significantly different from those advanced by the court below. * * *

I.

Consideration of the judicial interpretations enunciated over the years in this highly complex free speech-press area are a necessary backdrop to our discussion. In *Near,* the Supreme Court struck down a statute which if analogized to the instant case would place a prior restraint upon distribution of literature by any student who had in the past regularly distributed material deemed by school authorities to be obscene, lewd, and lascivious, or malicious, scandalous, and defamatory. * * * But Chief Justice Hughes made it clear that his opinion was not to be read as invalidating all "previous restraints." He took pains to catalogue several varieties of "exceptional cases" which would justify a "previous restraint." Thus, it was well established then as it is now that "[t]he constitutional guaranty of free speech does not 'protect a man from an injunction against uttering words that may have all the effect of force'." Nor did it question that "the primary requirements of decency may be enforced against obscene publications."

A listing of permissible prior restraints did not have its genesis nor end in *Near.* We are aware of the warning sounded in Kingsley Books, Inc. v. Brown, 354 U.S. 436 (1957), quoted and put to use by Times Film Corp. v. City of Chicago, 365 U.S. 43 (1961), that "[t]he phrase 'prior restraint' is not a self-wielding sword. Nor can it serve as a talismanic test." In *Times Film,* the Court instructed that the First Amendment does not guarantee "complete and absolute freedom to exhibit, at least once, any and every kind of motion picture," relying in part on the dictum in Chaplinsky v. New Hampshire, 315 U.S. 568 (1942), that

governments may with appropriate measures either punish or prevent the dissemination of "the lewd and obscene, the profane, the libelous, and the insulting or 'fighting' words—those which by their very utterance inflict injury or tend to incite an immediate breach of the peace." The earlier dictum and the holding in *Times Film* were sifted and refined again in Freedman v. Maryland, 380 U.S. 51, (1965), when the Court laid down three specific procedural safeguards "designed to obviate the dangers of a censorship system," safeguards which we shall shortly discuss in more detail.

The sensitive analysis of the constitutional validity of previous restraints of speech suggested by these cases requires that we address ourselves to the following questions. First, is the Board's policy justified as included within one or more of the categories of exceptional cases to which previous restraints are permissible? Second, is the policy as narrowly drawn as may reasonably be expected so as to advance the social interests that justify it or, to the contrary, does it unduly restrict protected speech, to an extent "greater than is essential to the furtherance of" those interests? In light of *Freedman,* the latter question might usefully be addressed, alternatively, to the substantive and to the procedural aspects of the policy—that is, first to the criteria by which school officials are permitted to bar literature from the school and second to the means by which the bar is to be effected.

II.

We agree with appellants that we need not and should not concern ourselves with the content or disruptive potential of the specific issue of the newspaper which plaintiffs sought unsuccessfully to distribute on school property. The students are challenging the policy "on its face" and not as applied to their particular publication.

Moreover, we cannot ignore the oft-stressed and carefully worded dictum in the leading precedent. Tinker v. Des Moines School District, that protected speech in public secondary schools may be forbidden if school authorities reasonably "forecast substantial disruption of or material interference with school activities."

*   *   *

III.

The policy criteria by which school authorities may prevent students from distributing literature on school property departs in no significant respect from the similarly very general and broad instruction of *Tinker* itself. Although the policy does not specify that the foreseeable disruption be either "material" or "substantial" as *Tinker* requires, we assume that the Board would never contemplate the futile as well as unconstitutional suppression of matter that would create only an *im*material disturbance. Thus, the regulation tracks the present state of the authoritative constitutional law, and while we realize this does not end the matter it does save the regulation from the charge that it is on its face fatally overbroad, since the policy statement does not purport to authorize suppression of a significant class of protected activity.
*   *   *

Absence of overbreadth, of course, does not in itself absolve the policy statement of the plaintiffs' charge that it is also unduly vague. The phrase "invasion of the rights of others" is not a model of clarity or preciseness. But several factors present here lessen or remove the familiar dangers to first amendment freedoms often associated with vague statutes. Thus, the statement does not attempt to authorize *punishment* of students who publish literature that under

the policy may be censored by school officials. If it did, students would be left to guess at their peril the thrust of the policy in a specific case and the resultant chill on first amendment activity might be intolerable. Also, because any ban that school authorities may impose would apply only to students *on school property,* the policy statement does not threaten to foreclose, e. g., from the publisher of a newspaper, a significant market or block of potential buyers should the publisher guess wrongly as to the kind of literature that a school principal will tolerate under particular circumstances. The policy does not in any way interfere with students' freedom to disseminate and to receive material outside of school property; nor does it threaten to interfere with the predominate responsibility of *parents* for their children's welfare. The statement is, therefore, in many ways narrowly drawn to achieve its permissible purposes, and indeed may fairly be characterized as a regulation of speech, rather than a blanket prior restraint.[5]

In sum, we believe that the Board's policy statement is neither overbroad nor unconstitutionally vague, so far as it prescribes *criteria* by which school officials may prevent the distribution on secondary school property of written or printed matter. *   *   *

IV.

Since however, the policy statement is in other ways constitutionally deficient, it would not be remiss for us to observe that greater specificity in the statement would be highly desirable. The Board would in no way shackle school administrators if it attempted to confront and resolve in some fashion, prior to court intervention, some of the difficult constitutional issues that will almost inevitably be

---

5. Because of such factors as the larger size of university campuses, and the tendency of students to spend a greater portion of their time there, the inhibitive effect of a similar policy statement might be greater on the campus of an institution of higher education than on the premises of a secondary school and the justifications for such a policy might be less compelling in view of the greater maturity of the students there.

raised when so broad a rule is applied to particular cases. For example, to what extent and under what circumstances does the Board intend to permit school authorities to suppress criticism of their own actions and policies? Similarly, does the Board anticipate that school officials will take reasonable measures to minimize or forestall potential disorder and disruption that might otherwise be generated in reaction to the distribution of controversial or unpopular opinions, before they resort to banishing the ideas from school grounds? See Terminiello v. City of Chicago (1949).[6] The Board might also undertake to describe the kinds of disruptions and distractions, and their degree, that it contemplates would typically justify censorship, as well as other distractions or disorders that it would consider do not justify suppression of students' attempts to distribute literature. At the same time it would be wise for the Board to consider the areas of school property where it would be appropriate to distribute approved material.

Refinements of the sort we mention would lessen the possibility that the policy statement under attack here because of its tendency to over-generalization, will be administered arbitrarily, erratically, or unfairly. By grappling with some of the difficult issues suggested, the Board might also succeed in demonstrating its conscientious intent to formulate policy not only within the outer limits of constitutional permissibility, but also with a sensitivity to some of the teaching reflected in relevant constitutional doctrine and to the dangers lurking in improper and unconstitutional administration of a broad and general standard.

Finally, greater specificity might reduce the likelihood of future litigation and thus forestall the possibility that federal courts will be called upon again to intervene in the operation of Stamford's public schools. It is to everyone's advantage that decisions with respect to the operation of local schools be made by local officials. The greater the generosity of the Board in fostering—not merely tolerating—students' free exercise of their constitutional rights, the less likely it will be that local officials will find their rulings subjected to unwieldy constitutional litigation.

V.

Although the Board's regulation passes muster as authorizing prior restraints, we believe it is constitutionally defective in its lack of procedure for prior *submission* by students for school administration approval, of written material before "distribution." In Freedman v. Maryland (1965), the Court instructed that strict procedural formalities must be observed whenever a state attempts to enforce a requirement that motion picture exhibitors submit a film to a state board of censors for clearance before the film is shown to the public. In order "to obviate the dangers of a censorship system" the state must:

(1) assume the burden of proving that a film is obscene in the constitutional sense and hence unprotected by the first amendment;

(2) secure a judicial determination of the film's obscenity before it may "impose a valid final restraint"; and

---

6. * * * The difficult constitutional problems raised by "the heckler's veto," becomes particularly acute in a public school, where the threshold of disturbance which may justify official intervention is relatively low.

We do not imply by the suggestion in the text to which this footnote is appended,

that school authorities must tolerate and indeed protect distribution on secondary school property of the kind of racial or religious slander involved in *Terminiello*. * * * We only mean to recommend that school authorities address themselves to these delicate issues and resolve them administratively before federal courts are called upon to do so.

(3) reach a final decision whether to restrain the showing of the film "within a specified brief period."

For the reasons we have already set forth, we do not regard the Board's policy as imposing nearly so onerous a "prior restraint" as was involved in *Freedman*. Also, we believe that it would be highly disruptive to the educational process if a secondary school principal were required to take a school newspaper editor to court every time the principal reasonably anticipated disruption and sought to restrain its cause. Thus, we will not require school officials to seek a judicial decree before they may enforce the Board's policy. As for the burden of proof, *Tinker* as well as other federal cases, establish that, if students choose to litigate, school authorities must demonstrate a reasonable basis for interference with student speech, and that courts will not rest content with officials' bare allegation that such a basis existed. We believe that this burden is sufficient to satisfy the intent of *Freedman* in the special context of a public secondary school. Of course, this standard is a matter for courts to enforce and need not be reflected in the policy statement.

We see no good reason, however, why the Board should not comply with *Freedman* to the extent of ensuring an expeditious review procedure. The policy as presently written is wholly deficient in this respect for it prescribes no period of time in which school officials must decide whether or not to permit distribution. To be valid, the regulation must prescribe a definite brief period within which review of submitted material will be completed.

The policy is also deficient in failing to specify to whom and how material may be submitted for clearance. Absent such specifications, students are unreasonably proscribed by the terms of the policy statement from distributing *any* written material on school property, since the statement leaves them ignorant of clearance procedures. Nor does it provide that the prohibition against distribution without prior approval is to be inoperative until each school has established a screening procedure.

Finally, we believe that the proscription against "distributing" written or printed material without prior consent is unconstitutionally vague. We assume that by "distributing" the Board intends something more than one student passing to a fellow student his copy of a general newspaper or magazine. Indeed, this assumption underpins most of our discussion concerning the constitutional validity of the policy statement, apart from the deficiencies we describe here. If students are to be required to secure prior approval before they may pass notes to each other in the hallways or exchange Time, Newsweek or other periodicals among themselves, then the resultant burden on speech might very likely outweigh the very remote possibility that such activities would ever cause disruption. We assume, therefore, that the Board contemplates that it will require prior submission only when there is to be a *substantial* distribution of written material, so that it can reasonably be anticipated that in a significant number of instances there would be a likelihood that the distribution would disrupt school operations. If the Board chooses to redraft its policy in light of what we have said in this opinion, it must make its intentions in this respect clear. Once it does, courts may better evaluate the potential "chill" of the policy on speech. The Board would be wise to be mindful of this danger zone.

For the reasons stated above, we affirm the declaratory judgment by the district court that the Board's policy statement is unenforceable. Because we disagree with the district court's conclusion that under all circumstances, any system for prior submission and restraint would be unconstitutional, the district court must modify its grant of injunctive relief so as to restrain only the enforcement of this particular policy. We therefore affirm and remand the case to the district court for entry of an appropriate judgment in accordance with this opinion.

NOTES AND QUESTIONS

1. Note that this is *not* a time, place, or manner case. Plaintiffs agreed that these considerations were fair. Rather *Eisner,* like *Near v. Minnesota* and *Freedman v. Maryland,* pertains to prior restraints based on the *contents* of the literature in question. *Eisner* is the leading case on prior restraints in the educational setting. Do you find *Eisner* to be a thoughtful and sensitive approach to applying rulings dealing with prior restraints in the political and social setting to the educational environment? Do you think that precedents from the former should be applied to the educational setting, as both Judge Zampano of the district court and Judge Kaufman of the court of appeals assumed?

2. Note that Judge Kaufman acknowledges that his ruling might have been different if a public university rather than a high school had been involved. Courts occasionally recognize a distinction between high school and postsecondary education. Among the areas where this distinction appears to arise most frequently are disputes over freedom of the press. Consider, for example, the statement below from a New York federal district court decision upholding the right of public school officials to suspend a student who disobeyed orders not to distribute an underground newspaper on campus.

> A special note should be taken that the activities of high school students do not always fall within the same category as the conduct of college students, the former being in a much more adolescent and immature stage of life and less able to screen fact from propaganda. *Schwartz v. Schuker,* 298 F.Supp. 238 (E.D. N.Y., 1969), at p. 242.

Would you agree? Does the assertion above justify prior restraints in a senior high school but not in a community college, even though the ages of the students in both institutions will not differ very much? Could a more convincing argument be made for prior restraints at the junior high level? Would it make any difference if the school were in an urban rather than a rural setting? Are judges sufficiently knowledgeable to decide these issues?

3. Judge Kaufman agrees that the answer to the first issue in the case is affirmative, that is, the school is justified in seeking to control the content of expression falling into the categories for which prior restraints have been judged appropriate. This is so because "the regulation tracks the present state of the authoritative constitutional law." Thus, the regulation is not overbroad. Judging from the "reasonable forecast of substantial disruption" test from *Tinker,* the "fighting words" test from *Chaplinsky,* and the "primary requirements of decency" standard of *Near,*

do you agree the regulation is not overbroad? Can you tell what specifically it is that the school wishes to restrain on the basis of contents alone? Note that after Judge Kaufman concludes that the regulation is not unconstitutionally overbroad or vague, he offers a number of suggestions to school officials designed to specify what is meant by such terms as "interfere with the proper and orderly operation and discipline of the school" and "rights of others." In light of these suggestions, do you think Judge Kaufman decided the first issue correctly?

4. While Judge Kaufman found the substantive aspects of the school regulation constitutional, he upholds the lower court in invalidating the rule because of its procedural flaws. If the regulation had had the procedural qualities Judge Kaufman suggests are necessary, would you uphold the regulation as constitutional? In *Baughman v. Freienmuth,* 478 F.2d 1345 (4th Cir. 1973), Judge Craven outlined what he considers the four essential features of a system of prior restraint in the public high school setting:

(d) A prior restraint system, even though precisely defining what may not be written, is nevertheless invalid unless it provides for:

(1) A definition of "Distribution" and its application to different kinds of material;

(2) Prompt approval or disapproval of what is submitted;

(3) Specification of the effect of failure to act promptly; and,

(4) An adequate and prompt appeals procedure. (at p. 1351).

Are these procedural guarantees sufficient? Would you add more? Would you apply the same procedures to the junior high school? The elementary school?

5. Assuming that all procedural safeguards are met, who is to decide what constitutes "substantial disruption of or material interference with school activities" and what factors are involved in reasonably forecasting such disruption or interference? Should judges leave this to school officials? An excellent illustration of the controversy surrounding this issue is a recent case also decided by the Second Circuit in which the majority relied on the standard announced by Judge Kaufman in *Eisner.* Recall that Judge Kaufman concluded that if challenged, "school authorities must demonstrate a reasonable basis for interference" with student rights of expression. In *Trachtman v. Anker,* 563 F.2d 512 (2nd Cir. 1977), the court of appeals used this approach to conclude that school authorities could prohibit staff members of a student newspaper from distributing an optional sex questionnaire to students attending Stuyvesant High School in New York City and publishing the results in the paper. The lower court had enjoined the distribution of the survey to ninth and tenth graders but approved submitting the questionnaire to eleventh and twelfth graders. The Board of Education for New York City argued against conducting the survey because the students did not possess the expertise to administer such a questionnaire, did not guarantee anonymity to respondents, and made no provision for parental consent. Furthermore, school officials argued that the survey could result in harm to students who participated in it since many high school students are only beginning to develop sexual

identities and having to respond to complex issues of this nature could force emotionally immature individuals to face psychological pressures prematurely.

The three-judge appeals court recognized that the First Amendment freedom of the press was involved in the case but, relying on its decision in *Eisner,* concluded that school officials had a reasonable basis to foresee potential disruption and harm resulting from the administration of the questionnaire. The court noted the testimony from several medical experts to this effect. The opinion of the majority concluded that "where school authorities have reason to believe that harmful consequences might result to students, while they are on the school premises, from solicitation of answers to questions, then prohibition of such solicitation is not a violation of any constitutional rights of those who seek to solicit." (At p. 520).

Judge Mansfield dissented, arguing that fear of psychological harm is too nebulous and speculative to justify restraints of constitutional rights. He pointed out that the survey was optional and that a number of medical experts not employed by the school had testified that the survey was not harmful but in fact useful in helping students cope with their sex-related anxieties. He noted as well that other circuits had approved the distribution of sex-related materials in school, and he asserted that students were not likely to be upset by the questionnaire when they are "literally bombarded with explicit sex materials on public newsstands on the way to and from school * * *." (At p. 526). The latter comment is representative of the so-called "inconsistency doctrine" which courts occasionally use to thwart censorship of student literature, drama productions, and the like. Simply stated, the doctrine means that regulation is considered unwarranted when material in the library, the curriculum, and the communications media contains similar objectionable passages. Judge Mansfield worried that the protective attitude of the school officials with regard to the sensitivities of other students might be used in the future to justify similar restraints of constitutional rights:

> * * * If school officials are permitted to ban a questionnaire of the type here at issue because of possible "psychological" harm, they could prohibit the dissemination of a broad range of other articles on school premises on the same theory, even though the publications were readily available elsewhere and the information in them was instructive. (At p. 521).

The U. S. Supreme Court refused to review the court of appeal's decision in 1978. Compare the *Trachtman* decision with the *Gambino* ruling discussed in the preceding section. Are the respective federal circuits involved consistent in their approaches? Why do they come to different conclusions?

Consider the difficulties associated with this type of balancing approach to the exercise of student rights in the educational setting as you read the next case, which presents quite a different view.

FUJISHIMA v. BOARD OF EDUC.

United States Court of Appeals, Seventh Circuit, 1972.
460 F.2d 1355.

SPRECHER, Circuit Judge.

This suit challenges the constitutionality of section 6–19 of the rules of the Chicago Board of Education:

No person shall be permitted * * * to distribute on the school premises any books, tracts, or other publications, * * * unless the same shall have been approved by the General Superintendent of Schools.

Plaintiffs are three high school students who were disciplined for violation of section 6–19. * * *

Plaintiffs Burt Fujishima and Richard Peluso were seniors at Lane Technical High School. They were suspended for four and seven days respectively for distributing about 350 copies of *The Cosmic Frog,* an "underground" newspaper they and another student published. The papers were distributed free both before and between classes and during lunch breaks.

Plaintiff Robert Balanoff, a sophomore at Bowen High School, was suspended for two days for giving another student an unsigned copy of a petition calling for "teach-ins" concerning the war in Viet Nam. The exchange occurred in May of 1970 in a school corridor between classes.

In October 1970, Balanoff was suspended for five days for distributing leaflets about the war to 15 or 20 students. This distribution took place during a fire drill, while Balanoff and his classmates were in their assigned places across the street from the school.

I

Plaintiffs appealed. Defendants' primary theory on the appeal is that section 6–19 is constitutionally permissible because it does not require approval of the content of a publication before it may be distributed. Unfortunately for defendants' theory, that is neither what the rule says nor how defendants have previously interpreted it. The superintendent must approve "the same," which refers back to "any books, tracts, or other publications." The superintendent cannot perform his duty under the rule without having the publication submitted to him. The principals believed the rule requires approval of the publication itself: the Fujishima and Peluso suspensions were for "distribution of unauthorized material in the school"; the Balanoff suspensions were for "distribution of unauthorized materials in the school building" and for "distributing unapproved literature in class during fire drill."

Because section 6–19 requires prior approval of publications, it is unconstitutional as a prior restraint in violation of the First Amendment. This conclusion is compelled by combining the holdings of Near v. Minnesota ex rel. Olson, (1931), and Tinker v. Des Moines Independent Community School District (1969). *Tinker* held that, absent a showing of material and substantial interference with the requirements of school discipline, schools may not restrain the full First-Amendments rights of their students. *Near* established one of those rights, freedom to distribute a publication without prior censorship.

Other courts have held unconstitutional similar restraints on student distribution of underground newspapers and political literature. * * *

* * *

The district court in Eisner v. Stamford Board of Education, reached the same result in invalidating a rule which required prior approval. On appeal the Second Circuit affirmed the invalidation, but modified the lower court's opinion so extensively as to obliterate it. The court allowed prior submission of publications if accompanied by elaborate procedural safeguards.

We believe that the court erred in *Eisner* in interpreting *Tinker* to allow prior restraint of publication—long a constitutionally prohibited power—as a tool of school officials in "forecasting" substantial disruption of school activities. In proper context, Mr. Justice Fortas' use of the word "forecast" in *Tinker* means a prediction by school officials that existing conduct, such as the wearing of arm bands—if allowed to continue—will probably interfere with school discipline. *Tinker* in no way suggests that students may be required to announce their intentions of engaging in certain conduct beforehand so school authorities may decide whether to prohibit the conduct. Such a concept of prior restraint is even more offensive when applied to the long-protected area of publication.

* * *

The *Tinker* forecast rule is properly a formula for determining when the requirements of school discipline justify *punishment* of students for exercise of their First-Amendment rights. It is not a basis for establishing a system of censorship and licensing designed to *prevent* the exercise of First-Amendment rights.

Because we believe *Eisner* is unsound constitutional law, and because defendants in effect concede that they cannot require submission of publications before approval of distribution, we declare section 6–19 unconstitutional and remand the case for entry of an injunction against its enforcement.

Such injunction will not prevent defendants from promulgating reasonable, specific regulations setting forth the time, manner and place in which distribution of written materials may occur. This does not mean, as defendants' brief suggests, that the board may require a student to obtain administrative approval of the time, manner and place of the particular distribution he proposes. The board has the burden of telling students when, how and where they may distribute materials. The board may then punish students who violate those regulations. Of course, the board may also establish a rule punishing students who publish and distribute on school grounds obscene or libelous literature.

II

Plaintiff Balanoff's second suspension remains on his record. He was punished under section 6–19 for distributing leaflets to classmates during a fire drill. Because the rule is unconstitutional, his suspension under it cannot stand.

Defendants argue that the justification for the suspension is "self-evident" from the record. All that appears in the record are the following allegations by plaintiffs:

> At no time during the fire drill was there any disorder. The distribution of said leaflets did not disrupt classes; nor did it interfere with any other proper school activity, including the fire drill. At no time during the distribution was the Plaintiff asked to stop distributing the leaflets by any member of the Bowen faculty or administration.

Neither in the district court nor on appeal have defendants suggested that evidence exists to challenge those factual assertions.

* * *

The board might issue a rule prohibiting distribution of literature during a fire drill as a regulation of time and place, but it could not apply such a rule *ex post facto* to Balanoff.

The district court's order shall include a direction to expunge Balanoff's second suspension from his record.

* * *

NOTES AND QUESTIONS

1. Circuit Judge Sprecher in *Fujishima* reads *Near* and *Tinker* to ban entirely prior restraints based on content. According to Judge Sprecher, students can only be disciplined *after* distribution, not before. He reads the use of the word "forecast" in *Tinker* quite differently from Judge Kaufman. Which do you think is the correct reading of the *Tinker* decision? With which view do you most agree? Apply the *Fujishima* rationale to the sex survey issue in *Trachtman v. Anker* cited in the notes and questions following *Eisner*. Would the outcome be the same? Which of the two approaches to freedom of the press within elementary and secondary schools do you prefer? Why?

The *Fujishima* decision represents the most extreme version on prior restraints in the public educational setting. Even this circuit appears uncertain about the decision, for in *Jacobs v. Board of Com'rs*, 490 F.2d 601 (1973), the Seventh Circuit used a void-for-vagueness approach rather than the blanket prohibition of *Fujishima*. Since the three judges in *Jacobs* were not the same as in *Fujishima* (membership on each of the eleven circuits varies; currently the Seventh Circuit has 11 judges assigned to it), the Seventh Circuit may themselves be uncertain.

Interestingly, while the *Eisner* approach seems to be preferred, at least for the secondary school setting, to date most challenges to prior restraints in the public educational setting have been successful, either because of policy defects or inappropriate policy applications.

2. Should school officials be able to require that publications circulated on campus be signed? In 1960 the U. S. Supreme Court ruled that a public ordinance forbidding distribution of unsigned handbills was unconstitutional. The Court reasoned that unpopular and persecuted groups may have no choice but to communicate their views anonymously. *Talley v. California*, 362 U.S. 60 (1960). The cases involving educational institutions have gone both ways. Once again, however, it is clear that if unique circumstances in the school setting require identification of publications, the rules and procedures establishing the identification policy must be specifically drawn. In short, the burden of proof is on school officials to show that the school setting does present unique circumstances, and that the rules and procedures requiring identification of anonymous publications are necessary and appropriate in light of those circumstances.

3. The following bill was introduced into the California Legislature in 1977. Note that there are provisions for both content-based prior restraints and content-neutral time, place, and manner regulations. If you were asked to render an opinion on the constitutionality of this proposed law, what would you decide?

48916. Students of the public schools shall have the right to exercise freedom of speech and of the press including, but not limited to, the use of bulletin boards, the distribution of printed materials or petitions, the wearing of buttons, badges, and other insignia, and the right of expression in official publications, whether or not such publications or other means of expression are supported financially by the school or by use of school facilities, except that expression shall be prohibited which is obscene, libelous, or slanderous. Also prohibited shall be material which so incites students as to create a clear and present danger of the commission of unlawful acts on school premises or the violation of lawful school regulations, or the substantial disruption of the orderly operation of the school.

Each governing board of a school district and each county board of education shall adopt rules and regulations in the form of a written publications code, which shall include reasonable provisions for the time, place, and manner of conducting such activities within its respective jurisdiction.

Student editors of official school publications shall be * * * responsible for assigning and editing the news, editorial, and feature content of their publications subject to the limitations of this section. However, it shall be the responsibility of a journalism adviser or advisers of student publications within each school to supervise the production of the student * * * staff, to maintain professional standards of English and journalism, and to maintain the provisions of this section.

There shall be no prior restraint of material prepared for official school publications except insofar as it violates this section. School officials shall have the burden of showing justification without undue delay prior to any limitation of student expression under this section.

"Official school publications" shall refer to material produced by students in the journalism, newspaper, yearbook, or writing classes and distributed to the student body either free or for a fee.

Nothing in this section shall prohibit or prevent any governing board of a school district to adopt otherwise valid rules and regulations relating to oral communication by students upon the premises of each school.

4. Consider the following hypothetical situation.

HYPOTHETICAL: *Parents v. Learned*

The editors of the student newspaper at West Thumper Public High School have never been involved in any major dispute with school officials. The editorial staff of the newspaper, which is subsidized by the school, operates under the general supervision of the chairman of the English Department. The chairman, however, has rarely intervened, leaving the student staffers largely on their own.

The principal of West Thumper recently resigned. Replacing him is John Learned, a young man embarking on his first major administrative position. Mr. Learned assumed his new position July 1st. Early in August, seniors Steve Smith and Carla Jones, co-editors of the newspaper, met with the principal to discuss their plans for a special new student edition. The special edition would be sent prior to the opening of school to the newly entering ninth grade students and to other new students transferring into the upper grades. Approximately 1000 newspapers were to be printed and circulated, 800 of them to freshmen.

Mr. Learned liked the idea of the orientation newspaper. However, he wanted the students to work under the direction of the English Department chairman. The students pointed out that the department chairman was out of town and would not return until the start of school. Mr. Learned then said that he personally wanted to review the paper before it was sent. Steve and Carla noted that they intended to portray the school and its staff honestly. They stated emphatically that they did not want to put together a "public relations" paper. They asked the principal if he might censor some of the material. Mr. Learned responded that since the paper would be read by parents as well as students, he wanted to be sure that the positive features of the school were portrayed. He said that he did not favor censorship, but that he reserved the right to make sure that a balanced view was presented.

Steve and Carla were not pleased, indicating that in their view, Mr. Learned's position was unfair and "probably illegal." However, they resolved to go ahead with the project, hoping that the principal would find the orientation edition acceptable.

Two weeks later, they brought the first copy of the paper to Mr. Learned. After reading the stories and viewing the photos, he ordered that the paper not be circulated because of its general "gossipy" tone, the absence of stories pertaining to the academic side of school life, and the generally sloppy writing and paste-up.

After efforts to reach an accommodation failed, the parents of the students brought suit against Mr. Learned and other school officials who approved his action.

———

Based on previous discussion and cases, what arguments would you make for each side? If you were to decide the hypothetical case, what decision would you reach?

5. In 1976 the Supreme Court ruled in *Virginia State Bd. of Pharmacy v. Virginia Citizens Consumer Council*, 425 U.S. 748, that "commercial speech" is protected by the First Amendment in the political and social setting. Does the mission of the educational institution serve to restrict the application of this ruling in the educational institution? Can education officials prohibit outright the distribution of commercial publications on campus? Would the purpose for which the funds are sought make a difference, e. g., selling magazine subscriptions or the magazines themselves to finance a student publication or to raise funds for a political candidate? Is such solicitation "conduct" and, if so, is it constitutionally unprotected or is it so intimately related to First and Twenty-Sixth Amendment rights that the institution cannot prohibit it? At one public college, political fundraising for candidates and parties external to the campus was banned because, in the words of one administrator,

It would encourage political parties and pressure groups to view the campus not as an open forum for ideas and intellectual contact but as a fertile territory in which to seek a base of partisan campaign operations and exploit a residential group created by the people for educational purposes. It would also employ the property and resources of the State and its people as a whole in the service of selfish political and financial interests clearly distinguishable from the interests of academic educational opportunity.

How viable is this argument? Might it be more convincing if made in reference to the public secondary sector? What about the assertion that the Twenty-Sixth Amendment to the U. S. Constitution conveys a special status to political solicitation that is not present in other types of situations, such as, for example, solicitation to finance a student's education? Note that insofar as politically-related fundraising is concerned, the view one has of the mission of the educational institution takes on new significance.

(3) The Complicating Factor of Mandatory Student Activity Fees

Many institutions, mostly in postsecondary education, impose a mandatory student activity fee in addition to tuition and other fees on all students to help defray the costs of various campus extracurricular activities. The proceeds of the mandatory student activity fee may be used to support a single activity such as the athletic program or may be widely dispursed to a variety of campus organizations. Since the fee is mandatory, it is a condition of enrollment. Failure to pay usually results in a late penalty fee; sustained failure to pay will prompt impoundment of grades and transcripts and may even jeopardize continued enrollment.

There often is a tug-of-war between student government and institutional officials for control of mandatory student activity fee expenditures. Student governments demand control because the purpose of the funds is said to be uniquely related to the function of student governments to broaden student opportunities outside of the classroom. Control of the funds not only places a good deal of power over campus activities in the hands of student leaders, it also contributes to the legitimacy of student government. Educational officials, on the other hand, worry about delegating substantial control over mandatory fees to students. According to most statutory and institutional guidelines establishing mandatory student activity fee programs, the funds may only be used to broaden and enrich the educational experience. Use of the funds for other purposes would undermine the rationale for their collection on a mandatory basis. Officials are reluctant to function merely as a collection agency when the use of funds may antagonize other students, members of the governing board, the general public, or the state legislature.

Litigation has arisen over mandatory fee programs at public institutions in several contexts. Some students are opposed in principle to mandatory student activity fee programs, particularly as tuition and board costs have escalated. They assert that the collection of these fees on a mandatory basis infringes their property rights without due process of law under the Fourteenth Amendment. Courts have generally upheld the legality of these programs, viewing them as no different from mandatory fees for health services, athletic privileges, and so on. See, for example, *Veed v. Schwartzkopf*, 353 F.Supp. 149 (D.C.Neb.1973), *aff'd mem.* 478 F.2d 1407 (8th Cir. 1973), *cert. denied* 414 U.S. 1135 (1974). Legal challenges may also assert that the expenditure of mandatory student activity fees abridges student First/Fourteenth Amendment rights by forcing them to support organizations advocating ideas and practices contrary to their beliefs.

A third source of litigation represents the other side of the dilemma. To what extent can an institution which is responsible for monitoring a mandatory student activity fee program exercise control over student organizations receiving funds? If colleges and universities require newspapers, speakers bureaus, film clubs, and the like to present a balanced format of views, the student organizations and their members may, like Dickey, sue the institution for violating their freedom of expression. Conversely, the *absence* of controls may trigger suits by segments of the student body who accuse both the student organizations and the educational institution of infringing on *their* freedom of expression and due process rights. In short, both courts and campus officials appear to be "between a rock and a hard place" where mandatory student activity fee programs are concerned.

In the case below, six students at the University of North Carolina at Chapel Hill brought suit against the Chancellor of the University, Ferebee Taylor, and other University officials, claiming that the portion of the mandatory student fee used to defray part of the expenses of the student newspaper, *The Daily Tar Heel,* deprived them of their rights of expression. At the time, *The Daily Tar Heel* was exclusively a student-run newspaper. That portion of its funds from student activity fees was appropriated by students through the Campus Governing Council. The University acted primarily as a collection agency. There was no procedure by which a student at the University who disagreed with the editorial or reportorial positions taken by *The Daily Tar Heel* could be excused from paying that portion of the fee disbursed to the newspaper. If the mandatory student fees were not paid in full, the student was charged a late payment penalty. Continued nonpayment resulted in the withholding of grades, transcript of credits, or a diploma.

ARRINGTON v. TAYLOR

United States District Court, M.D. North Carolina, Durham Division, 1974.
380 F.Supp. 1348.

GORDON, Chief Judge.

*   *   *

Plaintiffs in this case are students in good standing at the University of North Carolina at Chapel Hill. As such they are required to pay, and have paid, a Student Activities Fee in addition to tuition and other costs. Funds from this fee are appropriated to *The Daily Tar Heel*; it is this expenditure of the Student Activities Fee which is challenged by the plaintiffs. Plaintiffs have shown an immediate and direct interest in the outcome of this litigation. If they prevail in their contentions, the defendants will be enjoined from any further efforts to exact compulsory fees for *The Daily Tar Heel* and plaintiffs will be entitled to reimbursement of funds already paid by them for that purpose. If the defendants prevail, plaintiffs will, of course, be entitled to no relief and must continue to pay the Student Activities Fee as a condition of attending the University. It is, therefore, concluded that the plaintiffs have alleged "such a personal stake in the outcome of the controversy as to assure that concrete adverseness which sharpens the presentation of issues upon which the court so largely depends for illumination of difficult constitutional questions * * * "

* * *

* * * Plaintiffs contend in this action that their First Amendment rights of free speech are abridged by requiring them, as students of the University, to pay a Student Activities Fee (hereafter Fee), a portion of which is used to subsidize a University publication, The Daily Tar Heel, which takes positions and advocates ideas contrary to those held by the plaintiffs.

* * *

* * * Plaintiffs allege with particularity specific positions taken by The Daily Tar Heel with which they disagree. During the period that the University newspaper expounded these views, the plaintiffs were required to tender monies to the University which were used to support this publication.

* * *

Any contention that the mandatory fee exacted from the plaintiffs, only a portion of which is used to support The Daily Tar Heel, reduces their economic ability to further their positions is unsupportable. Economic capacity and First Amendment rights are only remotely related, if related at all. Moreover, to allow a taxpayer to refuse to pay that portion of his taxes which is used for informational purposes would undermine the entire tax collection system. This princi-

ple seems fully applicable here. Plaintiffs' economic capacity to advocate their views has been only incidentally lessened, and this slight infringement is not of such proportions as to render the procedure unconstitutional.

* * *

The fear on the part of the plaintiffs that the use of their funds to support views with which they disagree will "drown out" their own voices is the corollary of the diminished economic capacity effect already discussed. * * * The Daily Tar Heel, although it advocates positions on various matters, speaks only for those which control its content at any given time. It does not speak on behalf of a group with which the plaintiffs are identified, i. e., the student body. Rather, it provides a forum for those who operate it to express their views. The positions advocated in The Daily Tar Heel are no more permanent than the brief tenure of its editors and writers. Moreover, The Daily Tar Heel is much more than a forum for its staff. It not only prints timely local and national news items, but also invites and prints views contrary to expressions by those in control. Plaintiffs' voices have not been drowned relative to that of a group to which they belong. There is no group, and plaintiffs have available an additional forum to express themselves in opposition to views set forth therein.

Finally, positions adopted and presented by The Daily Tar Heel are not imposed upon the plaintiffs because they are required to provide financial support to it. * * *

* * * The University subsidizes The Daily Tar Heel for several purposes, none of which involves the desire to propagate a particular position or point of view. The publication is a useful device to inform the student body of noteworthy campus activities. It also prints pertinent local, national and international news. Perhaps its most important func-

tion is to complement classroom education by exposing the student body to various points of view on significant issues, and to allow students to express themselves on those issues. Far from being a "predictable conduit" upon which the state can depend to express its views, *The Daily Tar Heel* has published diverse views on a variety of issues, often conflicting with and criticizing governmental policies. There is simply no factual basis for concluding that the University's motives in maintaining financial support for *The Daily Tar Heel* are other than laudable.

Under the foregoing analysis, it is concluded that requiring the plaintiffs to pay a mandatory fee, a portion of which is used to subsidize *The Daily Tar Heel* does not violate First Amendment rights guaranteed to the plaintiffs. 　*　*　*

What authority there is on the specific issue now under consideration supports the result reached herein. In a recently decided case factually indistinguishable from the case now at bar, Judge Urbom held that use of mandatory student fees to subsidize a student newspaper, a student association, and a guest-speaker program did not violate the First Amendment rights of students who disagreed with opinions expressed in those activities. *Veed v. Schwartzkopf.* Judge Urbom recognized that the activities complained of were meaningful parts of the educational process and complemented formal classroom instruction, and reasoned that to subsidize these activities from student fees violated no constitutional rights of the students. Significantly, the opinion in *Veed* recognized that there was no legal distinction between a student newspaper and a college speaker program. Each provides a forum whereby differing views on controversial subjects are presented. The resulting stimulant to student participation and discussion is at the core of the educational process. Indeed, there is really no difference once the student moves inside the classroom. Teachers, with salaries paid in part from tuition, present differing views on pertinent subjects in an educational setting. That a teacher may present one viewpoint as more meritorious than another surely does not deny to students in that classroom their constitutional rights.

*　*　*

Defendants financially support *The Daily Tar Heel* in two ways. First, defendants levy student fees and make the funds derived from these fees available for appropriation to the newspaper. Secondly, defendants make available, rent-free, University (therefore state owned) office space and other facilities. Plaintiffs contend that it follows that this results in the establishment by the State of particular viewpoints and religious beliefs in violation of the First Amendment.

To resolve this issue, it is probably sufficient to repeat what has been stated earlier in this opinion. There has been no factual showing that *The Daily Tar Heel* was created for, or has ever been used for, the furtherance of a particular governmental position or program. *　*　* *The Daily Tar Heel* is almost exclusively a student publication. There has been no satisfactory showing that defendants have attempted to regulate the newspaper nor use it to further their own interests. When we speak of the "state" in the context of abridging First Amendment rights, we certainly do not mean to include a campus newspaper which exists primarily for the benefit of, and controlled by, the students themselves. Simply classifying *The Daily Tar Heel* as a state agency for purposes of evaluating its activity in certain circumstances, see Joyner v. Whiting, cannot dictate the conclusion that it is, therefore, the organ and creature of the state for all purposes. For instance, when *The Daily Tar Heel* adopts a position on a given subject, it acts more as an independent newspaper than as a state agency. The position is that of its editors and writers and not that of the University or state government. By contrast, if the editors of *The Daily Tar Heel* practiced racial discrimination in hiring staff members, such conduct would constitute state action and would violate the Fourteenth Amendment. Joyner v. Whiting.

* * *

For the reasons heretofore stated, it is concluded that the practice of supporting *The Daily Tar Heel* with funds derived from mandatory student fees and by providing University facilities without charge violates no rights of the plaintiffs guaranteed to them under the First and Fourteenth Amendments to the United States Constitution. Accordingly, defendants may continue to impose and collect the Student Activities Fee and authorize funds derived from this source to be appropriated to *The Daily Tar Heel*. An appropriate judgment and order incorporating these findings will be entered.

However, the Court is constrained to observe that when one considers the magnitude of the operation of *The Daily Tar Heel*, that is, a paid Editor, advertising revenues of approximately $84,000.00 in

1972–73, a subscriber to United Press International News Service, occupancy of 1125 square feet of office space, with considerable sales of subscriptions off-campus in competition with the local press, there is reasonable cause for the plaintiffs to question why *The Daily Tar Heel* should be subsidized by providing it rent-free space and substantial funds. Obviously, *The Daily Tar Heel's* operation is on a par with the other news media, and its concern goes beyond campus news and gossip or service as a public relations medium for the University. Objective and serious news coverage will ordinarily bring independence of operation. Some of the advantages of independence, among others, are: (1) efficient operations are essential to survival and thus a better training ground is provided for those interested in news media careers; (2) the paper must gain the support of the public and, therefore, those who control the operation are compelled to be more professional; and (3) by reason of the lack of ties with the University, greater acceptance is enjoyed in that suspicion by subscribers of control is eliminated.

* * *

NOTES AND QUESTIONS

1. Note the discussion at the beginning of the opinion about the plaintiffs' "immediate and direct interest in the outcome of this litigation." Standing to sue is a prerequisite of judicial action. The reason is clearly outlined by Chief Judge Gordon.

2. Note that Chief Judge Gordon discusses each of the arguments advanced by the plaintiffs, then asserts that for purposes of rights of expression, there is no requisite state action. That is, the student newspaper is not an agency of the state where rights of expression are concerned, and therefore the plaintiffs have no constitutional grounds on which to sue. If the University had attempted to interfere with the editorial and reportorial policies of *The Daily Tar Heel*, then the student editors of the newspaper would have had a constitutional claim against the University for interference with their freedom of the press. Why do you suppose Chief Judge Gordon didn't simply dismiss the action on these grounds rather than discuss the substance of plaintiffs' arguments first?

One of the reasons relates to *Joyner v. Whiting*, 477 F.2d 456 (4th Cir. 1973), which Chief Judge Gordon discusses later in his opinion. *Joyner v. Whiting* was initially decided by Chief Judge Gordon's court. In that decision, his court concluded that the student newspaper at North Carolina Central University, *The Campus Echo, was* an agent of the state.

> Any organization, association or group which has been established under the authority of North Carolina Central University and pursuant to its regulations, and which has received financial aid and support from North Carolina Central University, whether from funds received from North Carolina directly, out of taxes and escheats, or from funds collected by North Carolina Central University under the authority of North Carolina, or both, is an agency of North Carolina Central University and, therefore, indirectly, of North Carolina itself. *The Campus Echo* was established by North Carolina Central University, and, until September 24, 1971, was financially supported by North Carolina Central University. It received a portion of the student fee which North Carolina Central University required each student to pay as a prerequisite to registration. The Editor-in-Chief received a salary, though it is not clear whether this is paid from funds received through the student fee or from funds received through tuition and the contributions of North Carolina. *The Campus Echo*, as a matter of law, is an agency of North Carolina Central University and of North Carolina. The Editor-in-Chief of *The Campus Echo* is a salaried official of both North Carolina Central University and of North Carolina. (341 F.Supp. 1244, at p. 1247)

There is little difference between the financial support for *The Campus Echo* and *The Daily Tar Heel*. Yet, Chief Judge Gordon's court departs from the earlier decision in *Arrington* because the Court of Appeals for the Fourth Circuit, with one judge dissenting, reversed the lower court ruling in *Joyner*, asserting that where freedom of the press is at issue, the institution cannot withdraw funds as a punishment.*

> * * * It may well be that a college need not establish a campus newspaper, or, if a paper has been established, the college may permanently discontinue publication for reasons wholly unrelated to the First Amendment. But if a college has a student newspaper, its publication cannot be suppressed because college officials dislike its editorial comment. (477 F.2d 456, at p. 460)

At the same time, however, the appeals court acknowledged that for other purposes, a student newspaper subsidized in the fashion of *The Campus Echo* and presumably *The Daily Tar Heel* is not completely independent of the state.

> A college newspaper's freedom from censorship does not necessarily imply that its facilities are the editor's private domain. When a college paper receives a subsidy from the state, there are strong arguments for insisting that its columns be open to the expression of contrary views and that its publication enhance, not inhibit, free speech.

---

* The Fourth Circuit affirmed *Arrington* without comment in 1975.

* * * Campus organizations claiming First Amendment rights must comply with valid campus regulations * * *. (At pp. 462 and 463).

One of the regulations to which the campus newspaper must comply in *Joyner* prohibited racial discrimination. The court of appeals thus agreed that student newspapers have *some* characteristics of public forums and that the institution may have *some* obligation to see that the newspaper's "columns be open to the expression of contrary views * * *." One commentator has suggested that the paid advertisement section, the announcement section, and the letters-to-the-editor page provide the best examples of public forums within a campus newspaper, areas over which student editors would have less control.

> If any part of a campus newspaper is identified as a public forum, the right of access of potential contributors must be reconciled with the first amendment rights of the student editors. Within the public forum, student editors may not interfere with the right of access of other contributors. The university has an affirmative duty to maintain access to the forum. In non-forum sections of the paper, student editors enjoy the rights of private publishers including the right not to publish.[19]

One important case, however, rejects this approach. In *Mississippi Gay Alliance v. Goudelock*, 536 F.2d 1073 (5th Cir. 1976), the Mississippi Gay Alliance, an informal association of homosexuals in the state, sought to force the editor of *The Reflector*, the student newspaper at Mississippi State University, to accept their paid advertisement. The Alliance claimed that the refusal of the editor to do so constituted a denial of First/Fourteenth Amendment rights. The Fifth Circuit Court of Appeals held that even though mandatory fees were used to defray the cost of the newspaper, the newspaper was not related to the state and "in the absence of state action the student newspaper editor could 'accept or reject such material as he saw fit.'" (At p. 1075). The U. S. Supreme Court refused to grant certiorari in 1977, and so the appeals court decision was left standing. It is binding only within that circuit, of course, though other circuits and other federal and state courts may cite it as precedent.

Other courts have been less inclined to acknowledge the independence of campus newspapers. For example, in *Larson v. Board of Regents*, 204 N.W.2d 568 (Nebraska, 1973), the Nebraska Supreme Court ruled that "Where a university newspaper is supported by mandatory student fees, or by other university funds, reasonable supervision is required by the university authorities with a view to promoting and permitting the reflection of a broad spectrum of university life and reasonable representation of the various aspects of student thought and action." (At p. 571). And in *Kiluma v. Wayne State Univ.*, 250 N.W.2d 81 (Mich.1977), the university itself was held to be the sole defendant in a libel action involving an allegedly defamatory article in *The Southend*, the campus newspaper. The Court of Appeals of Michigan observed in a footnote:

> Since *The Southend* is not a separate legal entity, but merely a student activity within the university, we consider Wayne State

---

19. Lisa Newell, "A Right of Access to Student Newspapers at Public Universities," 4 *J.Coll. & Univ.L.* 209, Spring, 1977, at p. 220.

University as the sole defendant presently before the court. (At p. 81).

3. For an institution either required (as in *Arrington*) or simply preferring to avoid any regulatory control over the student press on campus, would it make sense to require that a disclaimer be printed in the masthead of the student periodical? This was the suggestion of the U. S. Court of Appeals for the Fifth Circuit in *Bazaar v. Fortune*, 489 F.2d 225 (1973). In an interesting dissenting opinion in that case, Circuit Judge Griffin Bell, later U. S. Attorney General during the Carter Administration, questioned whether the University of Mississippi has a right to *refuse to sponsor* a free speech forum—in this case, a literary magazine. He would have preferred to remand the case for a full hearing on the issue of sponsorship.

Could an institution simply refuse to continue to support a mandatory student activity fee program? Could an institution insist that a student newspaper or other periodical be housed and printed off campus and show no tie to the institution, i. e., no use of the campus seal, etc.? What if, under these circumstances, the student newspaper failed? Is there a student right to a free press forum or does freedom of press begin only *after* there is a forum?

4. *Maryland Public Interest Research Group v. Elkins*, 430 F.Supp. 387 (D.C.Maryland, 1976), rev'd, 565 F.2d 864 (4th Cir. 1977), involved the interesting issue of whether a university could prohibit a student organization from using mandatory student fees to hire attorneys in order to engage in litigation, including action against the university. The lower court, noting that access to the courts is a civil right inherent in the First Amendment, ruled that the university had shown no valid justification for restricting the use of mandatory fees for this purpose. But the U. S. Court of Appeals for the Fourth Circuit reversed that decision on the grounds that MaryPIRG's access to the courts had not been cut off, only the use of state funds to that end: "There is no affirmative commandment upon the University to activate MaryPIRG's exercise of First Amendment guarantees; the only commandment is not to infringe their enjoyment." (At p. 866). The court also noted that the group had outside funding available for covering litigation costs. Even assuming there might be some infringement on First Amendment freedoms, the appeals court asserted that the University has a compelling interest in seeing that mandatory fees are not used to finance causes which other students may find distasteful and which may saddle the institution with additional costs. The Supreme Court refused to hear the case in 1978, thus leaving the appeals court decision in place.

More than any other activity, the financing of suits against the state and the institution itself by mandatory student activity fee funds underscores the confusion over the exact nature of the money. Are the funds really *student* funds? If so, why shouldn't the students collect and dispurse the funds themselves, leaving the institution out of it altogether?

The reason, of course, is that without the assistance of the educational institution, a mandatory policy could never be enforced. Once the institution becomes involved in establishing a mandatory student activity fee program, to what extent do the funds become "public" in nature? This is the essence of the problem, and the cases demonstrate that so far, there has been no adequate answer.

5. Based on the discussion and cases in this section how would you resolve the following hypothetical cases?

a. Editor of a campus newspaper at a state college submits to the printer an issue with an editorial comment by the Neo-Nazi party. The editorial is derogatory of Jews and blacks. The publisher refuses to print the newspaper unless the overseeing student-faculty advisory group officially approves the editorial.

(1) What advice would you give the advisory group?

(2) Suppose the group refuses to sanction the editorial and the campus president orders mandatory fees to be withheld so that the issue cannot be printed? Is the president acting legally?

(3) Suppose the group does sanction the editorial but the president of the college overrules them and withholds funds?

b. A group of students bring suit against a public college because the campus newspaper, funded by mandatory fees which the college collects, consistently supports leftist causes to which the group is opposed.

(1) Would the students be successful in their suit? Should they be?

(2) Does the campus administration have an obligation in this situation to the student body in general?

c. Public college administation has a policy of allowing the student newspaper complete freedom, but does provide space and heat, and collects and disperses mandatory fees.

(1) Teacher brings libel suit against the newspaper and the administration. Should the administration bear part of the liability if the teacher is successful?

(2) Student brings a libel suit. Should the administration bear part of the liability if the student is successful?

6. Suppose an educational institution had turned student fee disbursement over entirely to the student government, which then (a) refused to support a student newspaper or (b) regulated its contents. Would the constitutional answers differ from those in cases in which the university itself took these actions?

7. Given the complexities of student mandatory fees, what advice would you give college administrators regarding campus newspapers: (1) sever all relations with a student-run newspaper, (2) assume total control of the newspaper, or (3) maintain control over some aspects of the paper's operation? If the third option, what areas of operation should be regulated by college officials? How would your answers differ if you were considering nonpublic institutions only?

IV. SPEECH, PRESS, AND STANDARDS OF GOOD TASTE

A. Obscenity in the Political and Social Setting

Censorship of art and written materials can be traced back as far as ancient Greece and Rome. State censorship of "obscene" materials is a product of modern technology, with the introduction of the printing press in England at the end of the 15th century. In the subsequent two centuries, European societies experienced a growing concern about the problem of public morals and pornographic materials.

The word "obscene" is said by some to be derived from the Latin *obscenum*, which supposedly related to *caenum*—"dirt". Others have claimed that "obscene" may refer to that which is "out of the scene," that which should not be allowed on stage because of its lewd or lascivious content. However one might define the phenomenon of obscenity, in ordinary usage it has a pejorative meaning: it refers to the disgust or revulsion at that which is considered to be repugnant. Because of the constant changes in public attitudes about what is obscene, some civil libertarians have concluded that it is impossible to assign a universally meaningful definition of such terms as "obscenity" and "pornography." Therefore, these civil libertarians assume that any legislation which includes such terms is *ipso facto* unconstitutionally vague. Many legal authorities must envy Justice Porter Stewart's sharp eye for unconstitutional hard-core pornography or obscenity: "I know it when I see it," he claimed in a 1964 case.

In the absence of Stewart's infallible vision, lawmakers and jurists have proposed obscene materials to include "that form of immorality which has relation to sexual impurity and has a tendency to excite lustful thoughts," or contradictorily, "that sort of treatment of sexual matters in such a vulgar and indecent way so that it tends to arouse a feeling of disgust and revulsion," or "materials calculated to corrupt and debauch the minds and morals of average people" or will "offend the common conscience of the community" or "having a substantial tendency to deprave or corrupt the readers by inciting lascivious thoughts or arousing lustful desire."

Although civil libertarians claim that it is impossible to define these matters objectively, conservatives have continually claimed that some authors or artists are actually the enemies of civilized society and their obscene works can do great harm. Society has a right to censor their works in order to protect itself against their pernicious influence. State legislatures have legitimate police authority to protect public morals. As Lord Patrick Devlin wrote:

> * * * a sense of right and wrong is necessary for the life of a community. It is not necessary that their appreciation of right and wrong, tested in the light of one set or another of those abstract propositions about which men forever dispute, should be correct. * * * What the lawmaker has to ascertain is not the true belief but the common belief.[20]

20. Lord Patrick Devlin, *The Enforcement of Morals* (New York: Oxford University Press, 1965), p. 94.

Conservatives on this question are willing to offer an elaborate definition of "obscenity" to protect public morals and the "life of a community." Harry M. Clor, a conservative political analyst, offers such a definition to include the following:

> An obscene book, story magazine, motion picture, or play is one which tends predominantly to
>
> 1. Arouse lust or appeal to prurient interest.
>
> 2. Arouse sexual passion in connection with scenes of extreme violence, cruelty or brutality.
>
> 3. Visually portray in detail, or graphically describe in lurid detail, the violent physical destruction, torture, or dismemberment of a human being, provided that this is done to exploit morbid or shameful interest in these matters and not for genuine scientific, educational, or artistic purposes.
>
> 4. Visually portray, or graphically describe, in lurid physical detail, the death or dead body of a human being provided this is done to exploit morbid or shameful interest in these matters and not for genuine scientific, educational, or artistic purposes.[21]

Although Clor's position on what constitutes "obscenity" or unprotected First Amendment expression is one of the clearest attempts to articulate a restrictive view of certain forms of expression, it does contain a number of difficulties. How, for example, is one to determine whether a given book, story, or play tends to do any of the above things predominantly? Is a work to be judged by the subject matter of some of its pages, most of its pages, all of its pages? Or is it to be judged by the effect it has in society as a whole? Who is to say what a "genuine" scientific, educational, or artistic purpose is—the national community or a panel of experts from the local community? A judge? A jury? Finally, how can one distinguish those works that are predominantly devoted to "impersonal or degrading" or "dehumanizing" lust from those that are not?

The Supreme Court first faced these questions in the case of *Roth v. United States*, 354 U.S. 476 (1957). In this case Justice William Brennan spoke for the Court and developed what has become known as "the prurient interest" standard—"whether to the average person, applying contemporary community standards, the dominant theme of the material taken as a whole appeals to a prurient interest." (At p. 489). Material of this kind is not a kind of speech that is constitutionally protected. Sex and obscenity however, are not synonymous. Sex, the Court stated, is "a great and mysterious motive force in human life, has indisputably been a subject of absorbing interest to mankind through the ages; it is one of the vital problems of human interest and public concern." (At p. 487). Portrayal of sex in art and literature is entitled to constitutional protection unless it violates the "prurient interest" standard.

21. Harry M. Clor, *Obscenity and Public Morality* (Chicago: University of Chicago Press, 1969), p. 245.

In the *Roth* case, Justices Black and Douglas argued that so-called obscene material deserves the same kind of protection that is provided to other types of expression and may be suppressed only upon clear evidence that a particular publication has "an impact that the government can control." Justice Douglas' dissenting opinion expressed confidence that, if free to choose, most people will reject noxious literature. He further commented that:

> * * * if the First Amendment guarantee of freedom of speech and press is to mean anything in this field, it must allow protests even against the moral code that the standard of the day sets for the community. (At p. 513).

What emerged from *Roth* and subsequent decisions was a three-part test indicating that for material to be constitutionally obscene and thus not entitled to any constitutional protection, it must be established that:

(1) the dominant theme of the material taken as a whole appeals to a prurient interest in sex;

(2) the material is patently offensive because it affronts contemporary community standards relating to the description or representation of sexual matters;

(3) the material is utterly without redeeming social value.

In 1966 the Court seemed to be willing to restrict its support for obscenity regulation by stating in the so-called *Fanny Hill* case (technically known as *A Book Named "John Cleland's Memoirs of a Woman of Pleasure" v. Massachusetts*, 383 U.S. 413) that a book must fail *all* of the three Roth tests before it can be regarded as obscene. The trial court admitted that *Fanny Hill* has a "modicum of social value," and therefore the Supreme Court concluded that it could not be considered obscene.

It is to the contemporary Burger Court that we must look for the present posture on obscenity. Perhaps no other civil liberties area demonstrates better the Burger Court's willingness to modify a previous Warren Court policy. In 1973, Chief Justice Burger handed down several decisions altering the standards relating to obscenity. The doctrinal case, *Miller v. California*, 413 U.S. 15 (1973), placed additional authority in the hands of state regulators. The decision was split 5–4. Chief Justice Burger wrote the opinion of the Court changing the basic framework set up by Justice Brennan in both the *Roth* and *Fanny Hill* cases. In *Miller* the Court softened the three-part test by rejecting the "utterly without redeeming social value" test in favor of asking whether the material "taken as a whole, lacks serious literary, artistic, political, or scientific value." Chief Justice Burger for the majority also emphasized that states may use contemporary community standards, not national standards, in determining what is obscene. As in *Roth*, the Court again concluded that material, whether composed of words or pictures, had to fail all three tests to be considered legally obscene.

MILLER v. CALIFORNIA

Supreme Court of the United States, 1973.
413 U.S. 15, 93 S.Ct. 2607, 37 L.Ed.2d 419.

Mr. Chief Justice BURGER delivered the opinion of the Court.

This is one of a group of "obscenity-pornography" cases being reviewed by the Court in a re-examination of standards enunciated in earlier cases involving what Mr. Justice Harlan called "the intractable obscenity problem."

Appellant conducted a mass mailing campaign to advertise the sale of illustrated books, euphemistically called "adult" material. After a jury trial, he was convicted of violating California Penal Code § 311.2(a), a misdemeanor, by knowingly distributing obscene matter, and the Appellate Department, Superior Court of California, County of Orange, summarily affirmed the judgment without opinion. Appellant's conviction was specifically based on his conduct in causing five unsolicited advertising brochures to be sent through the mail in an envelope addressed to a restaurant in Newport Beach, California. The envelope was opened by the manager of the restraurant and his mother. They had not requested the brochures; they complained to the police.

The brochures advertise four books entitled "Intercourse," "Man-Woman," "Sex Orgies Illustrated," and "An Illustrated History of Pornography," and a film entitled "Marital Intercourse." While the brochures contain some descriptive printed material, primarily they consist of pictures and drawings very explicitly depicting men and women in groups of two or more engaging in a variety of sexual activities, with genitals often prominently displayed.

* * *

II

This much has been categorically settled by the Court, that obscene material is unprotected by the First Amendment.
* * *

We acknowledge, however, the inherent dangers of undertaking to regulate any form of expression. State statutes designed to regulate obscene materials must be carefully limited. As a result, we now confine the permissible scope of such regulation to works which depict or describe sexual conduct. That conduct must be specifically defined by the applicable state law, as written or authoritatively construed. A state offense must also be limited to works which, taken as a whole, appeal to the prurient interest in sex, which portray sexual conduct in a patently offensive way, and which, taken as a whole, do not have serious literary, artistic, political, or scientific value.

The basic guidelines for the trier of fact must be: (a) whether "the average person, applying contemporary community standards" would find that the work, taken as a whole, appeals to the prurient interest; (b) whether the work depicts or describes, in a patently offensive way, sexual conduct specifically defined by the applicable state law; and (c) whether the work, taken as a whole, lacks serious literary, artistic, political, or scientific value. We do not adopt as a constitutional standard the "*utterly* without redeeming social value" test of *Memoirs v. Massachusetts*; that concept has never commanded the adherence of more than three Justices at one time. If a state law that regulates obscene material is thus limited, as written or construed, the First Amendment values applicable to the States through the Fourteenth Amendment are adequately protected by the ultimate power of appellate courts to conduct an independent review of constitutional claims when necessary.

We emphasize that it is not our function to propose regulatory schemes for the States. That must await their concrete legislative efforts. It is possible, however, to give a few plain examples of what a state statute could define for regulation under part (b) of the standard announced in this opinion, *supra:*

(a) Patently offensive representations or descriptions of ultimate sexual acts, normal or perverted, actual or simulated.

(b) Patently offensive representations or descriptions of masturbation, excretory functions, and lewd exhibition of the genitals.

Sex and nudity may not be exploited without limit by films or pictures exhibited or sold in places of public accommodation any more than live sex and nudity can be exhibited or sold without limit in such public places. At a minimum, prurient, patently offensive depiction or description of sexual conduct must have serious literary, artistic, political, or scientific value to merit First Amendment protection. For example, medical books for the education of physicians and related personnel necessarily use graphic illustrations and descriptions of human anatomy. In resolving the inevitably sensitive questions of fact and law, we must continue to rely on the jury system, accompanied by the safeguards that judges, rules of evidence, presumption of innocence, and other protective features provide, as we do with rape, murder, and a host of other offenses against society and its individual members.[9]

Mr. Justice BRENNAN, * * * has abandoned his former position and now maintains that no formulation of this Court, the Congress, or the States can adequately distinguish obscene material unprotected by the First Amendment from protected expression, *Paris Adult Theatre I v. Slaton,* (BRENNAN, J., dissenting). Paradoxically, Mr. Justice BRENNAN indicates that suppression of unprotected obscene material is permissible to avoid exposure to unconsenting adults, as in this case, and to juveniles, although he gives no indication of how the division between protected and nonprotected materials may be drawn with greater precision for these purposes than for regulation of commercial exposure to consenting adults only. Nor does he indicate where in the Constitution he finds the authority to distinguish between a willing "adult" one month past the state law age of majority and a willing "juvenile" one month younger.

Under the holdings announced today, no one will be subject to prosecution for the sale or exposure of obscene materials unless these materials depict or describe patently offensive "hard core" sexual conduct specifically defined by the regulating state law, as written or construed. We are satisfied that these specific prerequisites will provide fair notice to a dealer in such materials that his public and commercial activities may bring prosecution. If the inability to define regulated materials with ultimate, god-like precision altogether removes the power of the States or the Congress to regulate, then "hard core" pornography may be exposed without limit to the juvenile, the passerby, and the consenting adult alike, as, indeed, Mr. Justice DOUGLAS contends. * * * In this belief, however, Mr. Justice DOUGLAS now stands alone.

9. The mere fact juries may reach different conclusions as to the same material does not mean that constitutional rights are abridged. As this Court observed in *Roth v. United States,* "it is common experience that different juries may reach different results under any criminal statute. That is one of the consequences we accept under our jury system."

Mr. Justice BRENNAN also emphasizes "institutional stress" in justification of his change of view. Noting that "[t]he number of obscenity cases on our docket gives ample testimony to the burden that has been placed upon this Court," he quite rightly remarks that the examination of contested materials "is hardly a source of edification to the members of this Court." *Paris Adult Theatre I v. Slaton.* * * *

It is certainly true that the absence, since *Roth* of a single majority view of this Court as to proper standards for testing obscenity has placed a strain on both state and federal courts. But today, for the first time since *Roth* was decided in 1957, a majority of this Court has agreed on concrete guidelines to isolate "hard core" pornography from expression protected by the First Amendment.

* * *

III

Under a National Constitution, fundamental First Amendment limitations on the powers of the States do not vary from community to community, but this does not mean that there are, or should or can be, fixed, uniform national standards of precisely what appeals to the "prurient interest" or is "patently offensive." These are essentially questions of fact, and our Nation is simply too big and too diverse for this Court to reasonably expect that such standards could be articulated for all 50 States in a single formulation, even assuming the prerequisite consensus exists. When triers of fact are asked to decide whether "the average person, applying contemporary community standards" would consider certain materials "prurient," it would be unrealistic to require that the answer be based on some abstract formulation. The adversary system, with lay jurors as the usual ultimate factfinders in criminal prosecutions, has historically permitted triers of fact to draw on the standards of their community, guided always by limiting instructions on the law. To require a State to structure obscenity proceedings around evidence of a *national* "community standard" would be an exercise in futility.

* * *

We conclude that neither the State's alleged failure to offer evidence of "national standards," nor the trial court's charge that the jury consider state community standards, were constitutional errors. * * *

It is neither realistic nor constitutionally sound to read the First Amendment as requiring that the people of Maine or Mississippi accept public depiction of conduct found tolerable in Las Vegas, or New York City.[13] * * * People in different States vary in their tastes and attitudes, and this diversity is not to be strangled by the absolutism of imposed uniformity. * * *

We hold that the requirement that the jury evaluate the materials with reference to "contemporary standards of the State of California" serves this protective purpose and is constitutionally adequate.

IV

The dissenting Justices sound the alarm of repression. But, in our view, to equate the free and robust exchange of ideas and political debate with commercial exploitation of obscene material de-

13. In *Jacobellis v. Ohio* (1964), two Justices argued that application of "local" community standards would run the risk of preventing dissemination of materials in some places because sellers would be unwilling to risk criminal conviction by testing variations in standards from place to place. The use of "national" standards, however, necessarily implies that materials found tolerable in some places, but not under the "national" criteria, will nevertheless be unavailable where they are acceptable. Thus, in terms of danger to free expression, the potential for suppression seems at least as great in the application of a single nationwide standard as in allowing distribution in accordance with local tastes, * * *

means the grand conception of the First Amendment and its high purposes in the historic struggle for freedom. * * *

There is no evidence, empirical or historical, that the stern 19th century American censorship of public distribution and display of material relating to sex, in any way limited or affected expression of serious literary, artistic, political, or scientific ideas. On the contrary, it is beyond any question that the era following Thomas Jefferson to Theodore Roosevelt was an "extraordinarily vigorous period," not just in economics and politics, but in *belles lettres* and in "the outlying fields of social and political philosophies." We do not see the harsh hand of censorship of ideas—good or bad, sound or unsound—and "repression" of political liberty lurking in every state regulation of commercial exploitation of human interest in sex. * * *

* * * One can concede that the "sexual revolution" of recent years may have had useful byproducts in striking layers of prudery from a subject long irrationally kept from needed ventilation. But it does not follow that no regulation of patently offensive "hard core" materials is needed or permissible; civilized people do not allow unregulated access to heroin because it is a derivative of medicinal morphine.

In sum, we (a) reaffirm the *Roth* holding that obscene material is not protected by the First Amendment; (b) hold that such material can be regulated by the States, subject to the specific safeguards enunciated above, without a showing that the material is *"utterly* without redeeming social value"; and (c) hold that obscenity is to be determined by applying "contemporary community standards," not "national standards." The judgment of the Appellate Department of the Superior Court, Orange County, California, is vacated and the case remanded to that court for further proceedings not inconsistent with the First Amendment standards established by this opinion.

Vacated and remanded.

Mr. Justice DOUGLAS, dissenting.

I

Today we leave open the way for California to send a man to prison for distributing brochures that advertise books and a movie under freshly written standards defining obscenity which until today's decision were never the part of any law.

The Court has worked hard to define obscenity and concededly has failed. * * *

* * *

Today the Court retreats from the earlier formulations of the constitutional test and undertakes to make new definitions. This effort, like the earlier ones, is earnest and well intentioned. The difficulty is that we do not deal with constitutional terms, since "obscenity" is not mentioned in the Constitution or Bill of Rights. And the First Amendment makes no such exception from "the press" which it undertakes to protect nor, as I have said on other occasions, is an exception necessarily implied, for there was no recognized exception to the free press at the time the Bill of Rights was adopted which treated "obscene" publications differently from other types of papers, magazines, and books. So there are no constitutional guidelines for deciding what is and what is not "obscene." The Court is at large because we deal with tastes and standards of literature. What shocks me may be sustenance for my neighbor. What causes one person to boil up in rage over one pamphlet or movie may reflect only his neurosis, not shared by others. We deal here with a regime of censorship which, if adopted, should be done by constitutional amendment after full debate by the people.

Obscenity cases usually generate tremendous emotional outbursts. They have no business being in the courts. If a constitutional amendment authorized censorship, the censor would probably be an administrative agency. Then criminal prosecutions could follow as, if, and when publishers defied the censor and sold their literature. Under that regime a publisher would know when he was on dangerous ground. Under the present regime—whether the old standards or the new ones are used—the criminal law becomes a trap. A brand new test would put a publisher behind bars under a new law improvised by the courts after the publication. * * *

* * *

III

While the right to know is the corollary of the right to speak or publish, no one can be forced by government to listen to disclosure that he finds offensive. There is no "captive audience" problem in these obscenity cases. No one is being compelled to look or to listen. Those who enter newsstands or bookstalls may be offended by what they see. But they are not compelled by the State to frequent those places; and it is only state or governmental action against which the First Amendment, applicable to the States by virtue of the Fourteenth, raises a ban.

The idea that the First Amendment permits government to ban publications that are "offensive" to some people puts an ominous gloss on freedom of the press. That test would make it possible to ban any paper or any journal or magazine in some benighted place. The First Amendment was designed "to invite dispute," to induce "a condition of unrest," to "create dissatisfaction with conditions as they are," and even to stir "people to anger." *Terminiello v. Chicago.* The idea that the First Amendment permits punishment for ideas that are "offensive" to the particular judge or jury sitting in judgment is astounding. No greater lev-

eler of speech or literature has ever been designed. To give the power to the censor, as we do today, is to make a sharp and radical break with the traditions of a free society. The First Amendment was not fashioned as a vehicle for dispensing tranquilizers to the people. Its prime function was to keep debate open to "offensive" as well as to "staid" people. The tendency throughout history has been to subdue the individual and to exalt the power of government. The use of the standard "offensive" gives authority to government that cuts the very vitals out of the First Amendment. As is intimated by the Court's opinion, the materials before us may be garbage. But so is much of what is said in political campaigns, in the daily press, on TV, or over the radio. By reason of the First Amendment—and solely because of it—speakers and publishers have not been threatened or subdued because their thoughts and ideas may be "offensive" to some.

If there are to be restraints on what is obscene, then a constitutional amendment should be the way of achieving the end. There are societies where religion and mathematics are the only free segments. It would be a dark day for America if that were our destiny. But the people can make it such if they choose to write obscenity into the Constitution and define it.

We deal with highly emotional, not rational, questions. To many the Song of Solomon is obscene. I do not think we, the judges, were ever given the constitutional power to make definitions of obscenity. If it is to be defined, let the people debate and decide by a constitutional amendment what they want to ban as obscene and what standards they want the legislatures and the courts to apply. Perhaps the people will decide that the path towards a mature, integrated society requires that all ideas competing for acceptance must have no censor. Perhaps they will decide otherwise. Whatever the choice, the courts will have some guidelines. Now we have none except our own predilections.

Mr. Justice BRENNAN, with whom Mr. Justice STEWART and Mr. Justice MARSHALL join, dissenting.

In my dissent in *Paris Adult Theatre I v. Slaton,* decided this date, I noted that I had no occasion to consider the extent of state power to regulate the distribution of sexually oriented material to juveniles or the offensive exposure of such material to unconsenting adults. * * * I need not now decide whether a statute might be drawn to impose, within the requirements of the First Amendment, criminal penalties for the precise conduct at issue here. For it is clear that under my dissent in *Paris Adult Theatre I*, the statute under which the prosecution was brought is unconstitutionally overbroad, and therefore invalid on its face. * * *

NOTES AND QUESTIONS

1. Justice Brennan wrote the original *Roth* and *Fanny Hill* decisions. But with the passage of time and the continuing difficulty the Supreme Court experienced with obscenity cases, he backed away from the standards he proposed in those cases. The rationale for his change of views is contained in his dissent in a companion case to *Miller, Paris Adult Theatre I v. Slaton,* 413 U.S. 49 (1973). In *Paris* the Court decided that so long as states adhere to the *Miller* principles, they may constitutionally ban the showing of obscene films in commercial theatres to consenting adults. Justice Brennan dissented from this decision, noting that "I am convinced that the approach initiated 16 years ago in (*Roth*), and culminating in the Court's decision today, cannot bring stability to this area of the law without jeopardizing fundamental First Amendment values, and I have concluded that the time has come to make a significant departure from that approach." (At pp. 73–74).

Justice Brennan placed the cause of the problem squarely on the vagueness of the so-called "tests" developed by the Court. The meaning of concepts such as "prurient interest," "patent offensiveness," and so on:

necessarily varies with the experience, outlook, and even idiosyncracies of the person defining them. Although we have assumed that obscenity does exist and that we "know it when (we) see it," * * * we are manifestly unable to describe it in advance except by reference to concepts so elusive that they fail to distinguish clearly between protected and unprotected speech. (At p. 84).

Consequently, Justice Brennan concluded that he would rule that states may only prohibit obscene materials from being viewed by unconsenting adults and juveniles. Of course, as Chief Justice Burger points out in *Miller,* the ambiguity of deciding what is "obscene" remains. But the volume of cases would necessarily diminish.

Which of the positions on obscenity as expressed in these cases most reflects your own?

2. In a footnote to his dissent, Justice Brennan quotes this passage from the President's Commission on Obscenity and Pornography:

"In sum, empirical research designed to clarify the question has found no evidence to date that exposure to explicit sexual materials plays a significant role in the causation of delinquent or criminal behavior among youth or adults. The Commission cannot conclude that exposure to erotic materials is a factor in the causation of sex crime or sex delinquency." (*Report of the Commission on Obscenity and Pornography* 27, 1970). (At p. 108, footnote 26).

Justice Brennan goes on to quote from the *Report* that

"(on) the positive side, explicit sexual materials are sought as a source of entertainment and information by substantial numbers of American adults. At times, these materials also appear to serve to increase and facilitate constructive communication about sexual matters within marriage." (*Id.*)

Does the report of this research change your views on the issue of obscenity? How much weight should be accorded to it?

3. The question of the permissible restraints by local authorities on movie theatres that show films containing nudity still plagues the contemporary Court. In *Erznoznik v. Jacksonville*, 422 U.S. 205 (1975), the Court by a 6–3 vote decided that a city ordinance cannot prevent a drive-in threatre from showing films containing nudity where the movie screen is visible from a public place. The Court claimed that the city ordinance impermissibly discriminates against movies solely on the basis of their content, and is unnecessarily broad in proscribing on-screen nudity. Given the fact that these movies could be seen outside of drive-in property, do you think there are any other valid interests or considerations that the Court should have weighed in making this ruling?

4. In *Miller*, the majority permits the statewide "community" to be the basis for applying the "prurient interest" section. One year after *Miller* the Court in *Jenkins v. Georgia*, 418 U.S. 153 (1974), claimed that no precise geographic area is dictated by constitutional law. Rather the juror in applying the community standards of the "average person in the contemporary community" may draw on knowledge of the community from which she comes. The Court seemed to be accepting a local standard with its great variations in taste and attitudes, but still asserting that the local jury does not "have unbridled discretion in determining what is 'patently offensive.'" (At p. 160).

In 1978, the Court again refined the community standard, indicating in *Pinkus v. United States*, 496 U.S. 293, that juries may not consider the possible reactions of children in applying the community standard to what is obscene. However, juries may consider the views of "sensitive" adults as well as the special interests of deviant and sexual groups. In short, "community" is, except for children, to be broadly construed.

5. Broadcasting media has traditionally been more subject to government regulation than print media. Among the reasons advanced for tighter restrictions are the intrusion of radios and television into the privacy of the home, the ease with which children come into contact with broadcasting, and the limitations the broadcasting spectrum places on the number of stations. Consequently the chief regulatory agency, the Federal Communications Commission, monitors broadcasting activities with special care on behalf of the general public.

The Supreme Court has often upheld the FCC's regulatory power over the "electronic media." For example, in *Red Lion Broadcasting Co. v. F. C. C.,* 395 U.S. 367 (1969), the Court ruled that broadcasters must give free time to those whom they criticize. As already noted, the Court decided the reverse for the print media in *Miami Herald Pub. Co. v. Tornillo,* 418 U.S. 241 (1974).

A more recent case involves an FCC ruling against the use of "indecent" language on a New York radio station. The station had aired a 12 minute monologue by humorist George Carlin entitled "Filthy Words." During the monologue, Carlin sought to satarize contemporary attitudes toward four-letter words by repeating them over and over in various contexts. He began the monologue by referring to the words as those "you couldn't say on the public airwaves, the ones you definitely wouldn't say, ever." Carlin was more prophetic than he realized. In *F. C. C. v. Pacifica Foundation,* 98 S.Ct. 3026 (1978), the Court upheld the FCC's disapproval of the monologue. The FCC claimed to be acting pursuant to a federal law, 18 U.S.C.A. § 1464, which forbids the use of "any obscene, indecent, or profane language by means of radio communication." The FCC admitted the words weren't constitutionally obscene but argued that they were "patently offensive."

The Court of Appeals for the D.C. Circuit had ruled against the FCC in a 2–1 decision. The Supreme Court, with Justice Stevens writing for the five-man majority, reversed. Justice Stevens agreed that the words used were "speech" under the First Amendment and that they are entitled to constitutional protection, though dependent on the situation. Here, much like the erotic but not unconstitutionally obscene movies in *Young v. American Mini Theatres,* 427 U.S. 50 (1976), discussed *supra,* p. 98, the use of the words in the broadcasting context put them outside the boundaries of the First Amendment. Citing the pervasive presence of broadcasting media in American lives and the need to protect children, Justice Stevens concluded that "We simply hold that when the Commission finds that a pig has entered the parlor, the exercise of its regulatory power does not depend on proof that the pig is obscene." (At p. 3041).

The four dissenters assailed the willingness of the majority to rule that speech which is not unconstitutionally obscene under prior precedents can nevertheless be prohibited. Justice Brennan argued that the sensibilities of the Justices do not reflect the diversity of contemporary American society: "Today's decision will * * * have its greatest impact on broadcasters desiring to reach, and listening audiences composed of, persons who do not share the Court's view as to which words or expressions are acceptable and who, for a variety of reasons, including a conscious desire to flout majoritarian conventions, express themselves using words that may be regarded as offensive by those from different socio-economic backgrounds." (At p. 3054). He pointed out that words by Shakespeare and Chaucer, even the Bible, could be similarly banned under the majority's rationale. He disputed the argument that the limited availability of broadcasting space justifies greater regulation, citing appeals court Chief Judge David Bazelon's comment that "Although scarcity has justified *increasing* the diversity of speakers and speech, it has never been held to justify censorship." (At p. 3051, footnote 4; emphasis in original).

Justice Brennan also noted that those who find the words offensive can turn off the broadcast and pointed out that some parents might find the monologue to be a beneficial educational experience for their children.

Justice Stewart in his dissent argued that the constitutional issue could have been avoided altogether by reading "indecent" to mean the same thing as "obscene" and thus confining FCC sanctions to previous Court precedents.

How would you rule on the monologue? Should the electronic media be more stringently regulated by the government than the print media?

B. Standards of Good Taste in the Public Educational Setting

There are really two issues involved in issues of obscenity in the public educational setting. First, one must consider how to reach a decision that certain expression is obscene, and secondly, one must consider whether students should be punished for using obscenity and if so, how regulation and punishment is to be implemented—through a system of prior restraints or through subsequent discipline. While prior restraints pertain primarily to printed material, there is the additional consideration of the use of prior restraints to screen campus speakers and films.

The doctrinal case presented below involves the distribution of allegedly obscene materials at a public college.

PAPISH v. BOARD OF CURATORS OF THE UNIV. OF MO.

Supreme Court of the United States, 1973.
410 U.S. 667, 93 S.Ct. 1197, 35 L.Ed.2d 618.

Per Curiam.

Petitioner, a graduate student in the University of Missouri School of Journalism, was expelled for distributing on campus a newspaper "containing forms of indecent speech" in violation of a bylaw of the Board of Curators. The newspaper, the Free Press Underground, had been sold on this state university campus for more than four years pursuant to an authorization obtained from the University Business Office. The particular newspaper issue in question was found to be unacceptable for two reasons. First, on the front cover the publishers had reproduced a political cartoon previously printed in another newspaper depicting policemen raping the Statue of Liberty and the Goddess of Justice. The caption under the cartoon read: " * * * With Liberty and Justice for All." Secondly, the issue contained an article entitled "M———f——— Acquitted," which discussed the trial and acquittal on an assault charge of a New York City youth who was a member of an organization known as "Up Against the Wall, M———f———."

Following a hearing, the Student Conduct Committee found that petitioner had violated Par. B of Art. V of the General Standards of Student Conduct which requires students "to observe generally accepted standards of conduct" and specifically prohibits "indecent conduct or speech." [2] Her expulsion, after affirmance first by the Chancellor of the University and then by its Board of Curators, was made effective in the middle of the spring semester. Although she was then permitted to remain on campus until the end of the semester, she was not given credit for the one course in which she made a passing grade.

After exhausting her administrative review alternatives within the University, petitioner brought an action for declaratory and injunctive relief * * * in the United States District Court for the Western District of Missouri. She claimed that her expulsion was improperly premised on activities protected by the First Amendment. The District Court denied relief, and the Court of Appeals affirmed, one judge dissenting. Rehearing *en banc* was denied by an equally divided vote of all the judges in the Eighth Circuit.

The District Court's opinion rests, in part, on the conclusion that the banned

issue of the newspaper was obscene. The Court of Appeals found it unnecessary to decide that question. Instead, assuming that the newspaper was not obscene and that its distribution in the community at large would be protected by the First Amendment, the court held that on a university campus "freedom of expression" could properly be "subordinated to other interests such as, for example, the conventions of decency in the use and display of language and pictures." The court concluded that "[t]he Constitution does not compel the University * * * [to allow] such publications as the one in litigation to be publicly sold or distributed on its open campus." * * *

* * * We think * * * that the mere dissemination of ideas—no matter how offensive to good taste—on a state university campus may not be shut off in the name alone of "conventions of decency." Other recent precedents of this Court make it equally clear that neither the political cartoon nor the headline story involved in this case can be labeled as constitutionally obscene or otherwise unprotected. There is language in the opinions below which suggests that the University's action here could be viewed as an exercise of its legitimate authority to enforce reasonable regulations as to the time, place, and manner of speech and its dissemination. While we have repeatedly approved such regulatory authority, the facts set forth in the opinions below

2. In pertinent part, the bylaw states:

"Students enrolling in the University assume an obligation and are expected by the University to conduct themselves in a manner compatible with the University's functions and missions as an educational institution. For that purpose students are required to observe generally accepted standards of conduct. * * * [I]ndecent conduct or speech * * * are examples of conduct which would contravene this standard. * * * "

Miss Papish, a 32-year-old graduate student, was admitted to the graduate school of the University in September 1963. Five and one-half years later, when the episode under

consideration occurred, she was still pursuing her graduate degree. She was on "academic probation" because of "prolonged submarginal academic progress," and since November 1, 1967, she also had been on disciplinary probation for disseminating Students for a Democratic Society literature found at a university hearing to have contained "pornographic, indecent and obscene words." This dissemination had occurred at a time when the University was host to high school seniors and their parents. But disenchantment with Miss Papish's performance, understandable as it may have been, is no justification for denial of constitutional rights.

show clearly that petitioner was expelled because of the disapproved *content* of the newspaper rather than the time, place, or manner of its distribution.[6]

Since the First Amendment leaves no room for the operation of a dual standard in the academic community with respect to the content of speech, and because the state University's action here cannot be justified as a nondiscriminatory application of reasonable rules governing conduct, the judgments of the courts below must be reversed. Accordingly the petition for a writ of certiorari is granted, the case is remanded to the District Court, and that court is instructed to order the University to restore to petitioner any course credits she earned for the semester in question and, unless she is barred from reinstatement for valid academic reasons, to reinstate her as a student in the graduate program.

Reversed and remanded.

Mr. Chief Justice BURGER, dissenting.

I join the dissent of Justice REHNQUIST which follows and add a few observations.

* * *

In theory, at least, a university is not merely an arena for the discussion of ideas by students and faculty; it is also an institution where individuals learn to express themselves in acceptable, civil terms. We provide that environment to the end that students may learn the self-

restraint necessary to the functioning of a civilized society and understand the need for those external restraints to which we must all submit if group existence is to be tolerable.

I find it curious—even bizarre * * * to say that a state university is impotent to deal with conduct such as that of the petitioner. Students are, of course, free to criticize the university, its faculty, or the Government in vigorous, or even harsh, terms. But it is not unreasonable or violative of the Constitution to subject to disciplinary action those individuals who distribute publications which are at the same time obscene and infantile. To preclude a state university or college from regulating the distribution of such obscene materials does not protect the values inherent in the First Amendment; rather, it demeans those values. The anomaly of the Court's holding today is suggested by its use of the now familiar "code" abbreviation for the petitioner's foul language.

The judgment of the Court of Appeals was eminently correct. It should be affirmed.

Mr. Justice REHNQUIST, with whom The CHIEF JUSTICE and Mr. Justice BLACKMUN join, dissenting.

* * *

I

Petitioner Papish has for many years been a graduate student at the University of Missouri. Judge Stephenson, writing

---

6. It is true, as Mr. Justice REHNQUIST'S dissent indicates, that the District Court emphasized that the newspaper was distributed near the University's memorial tower and concluded that petitioner was engaged in "pandering." The opinion makes clear, however, that the reference to "pandering" was addressed to the content of the newspaper and to the organization on the front page of the cartoon and the headline, rather than to the manner in which the newspaper was disseminated. As the Court of Appeals opinion states, "[t]he facts are not in dispute." The charge against petitioner was quite unrelated to either the place or manner of distribution.

The Dean's charge stated that the "forms of speech" contained in the newspaper were "improper on the University campus." Moreover, the majority below quoted without disapproval petitioner's verified affidavit stating that "no disruption of the University's functions occurred in connection with the distribution." Likewise, both the dissenting opinion in the Court of Appeals and the District Court opinion refer to this same uncontroverted fact. Thus, in the absence of any disruption of campus order or interference with the rights of others, the sole issue was whether a state university could proscribe this form of expression.

for the Court of Appeals in this case, summarized her record in these words:

"Miss Papish's academic record reveals that she was in no rush to complete the requirements for her graduate degree in Journalism. She possesses a 1958 academic degree from the University of Connecticut; she was admitted to graduate school at the University of Missouri in September in 1963; and although she attended school through the fall, winter, and summer semesters, she was, after 6 years of work, making little, if any, significant progress toward the achievement of her stated academic objective. At the time of her dismissal, Miss Papish was enrolled in a one-hour course entitled 'Research Journalism' and in a three-hour course entitled 'Ceramics 4.' In the semester immediately preceding her dismissal, she was enrolled only in 'Ceramics 3.' "

Whatever may have been her lack of ability or motivation in the academic area, petitioner had been active on other fronts. In the words of the Court of Appeals:

"3. On November 1, 1967, the Faculty Committee on Student Conduct, after notice of charges and a hearing, placed Miss Papish on disciplinary probation for the remainder of her student status at the University. The basis for her probation was her violation of the general standard of student conduct. * * * This action arose out of events which took place on October 14, 1967 at a time when the University was hosting high school seniors and their parents for the purpose of acquainting them with its educational programs and other aspects of campus life. She specifically was charged, *inter alia*, with openly distributing, on University grounds, without the permission of appropriate University personnel, two non-University publications of the Students for Democratic Society (SDS). It was alleged in the notice of charges, and apparently established at the ensuing hearing, that one of these publications, the *New Left Notes*, contained 'pornographic, indecent and obscene words, "f———," "bull s———," and "sh—s." ' The notice of charges also recites that the other publication, *The CIA at College: Into Twilight and Back*, contained 'a pornographic and indecent picture depicting two rats apparently fornicating on its cover. * * *'

"4. Some two weeks prior to the incident causing her dismissal, Miss Papish was placed on academic probation because of prolonged submarginal academic progress. It was a condition of this probation that she pursue satisfactory work on her thesis, and that such work be evidenced by the completion and presentation of several completed chapters to her thesis advisor by the end of the semester. By letter dated January 31, 1969, Miss Papish was notified that her failure to comply with this special condition within the time specified would result in the termination of her candidacy for a graduate degree."

It was in the light of this background that respondents finally expelled petitioner for the incident described in the Court's opinion. The Court fails to note, however, two findings made by the District Court with respect to the circumstances under which petitioner hawked her newspaper near the memorial tower of the University:

"The Memorial Tower is the central unit of integrated structures dedicated to the memory of those students who died in the Armed Services in World Wars I and II. Other adjacent units include the Student Union and a Non-Sectarian chapel for prayer and meditation. Through the Memorial Arch pass parents of students, guests of the University, students, including many persons under 18 years of age and high school students."

"The plaintiff knowingly and intentionally participated in distributing the publication to provoke a confrontation with the authorities by pandering the publication with crude, puerile, vulgar obscenities."

II

I continue to adhere to the dissenting views expressed in *Rosenfeld v. New Jersey,* (1972), that the public use of the word "M———f———" is "lewd and obscene" as those terms were used by the Court in *Chaplinsky v. New Hampshire,* 315 U.S. 568 (1942). There the Court said:

"There are certain well-defined and narrowly limited classes of speech, the prevention and punishment of which have never been thought to raise any Constitutional problem. These include the lewd and obscene, the profane, the libelous, and the insulting or 'fighting' words—those which by their very utterance inflict injury or tend to incite an immediate breach of the peace. It has been well observed that such utterances are no essential part of any exposition of ideas, and are of such slight social value as a step to truth that any benefit that may be derived from them is clearly outweighed by the social interest in order and morality."

* * * A state university is an establishment for the purpose of educating the State's young people, supported by the tax revenues of the State's citizens. The notion that the officials lawfully charged with the governance of the university have so little control over the environment for which they are responsible that they may not prevent the public distribution of a newspaper on campus which contained the language described in the Court's opinion is quite unacceptable to me, and I would suspect would have been equally unacceptable to the Framers of the First Amendment. This is indeed a case where the observation of a unanimous Court in *Chaplinsky* that "such utterances are no essential part of any exposition of ideas, and are of such slight social value as a step to truth that any benefit that may be derived from them is clearly outweighed by the social interest in order and morality" applies with compelling force.

III

The Court cautions that "disenchantment with Miss Papish's performance, understandable as it may have been, is no justification for denial of constitutional rights." * * * There is reason to think that the "disenchantment" of which the Court speaks may, after this decision, become widespread among taxpayers and legislators. The system of tax-supported public universities which has grown up in this country is one of its truly great accomplishments; if they are to continue to grow and thrive to serve an expanding population, they must have something more than the grudging support of taxpayers and legislators. But one can scarcely blame the latter if, told by the Court that their only function is to supply tax money for the operation of the university, the "disenchantment" may reach such a point that they doubt the game is worth the candle.

NOTES AND QUESTIONS

1. The recent Court has tended to be supportive of public use of language and symbols that are considered vulgar and offensive except with regard to broadcasting and movies. In *Cohen v. California,* 403 U.S. 15 (1971), the Court voided the conviction of a young man who had been convicted of breach of the peace because he displayed on his jacket the

words "fuck the draft." The Court overturned his conviction stating that the display of such words were protected under the First Amendment, particularly when they are used to protest against a war policy (the Vietnam War). Justice John Harlan indicated that words have an "emotive" as well as a "cognitive" (thought) function and suggested that the emotive impact "may often be the more important element of the overall message sought to be communicated." (At p. 26). Most of the other contemporary "vulgarisms" have also been cleared by the Court of charges of being offensive, thereby, in effect, undermining the ruling in *Chaplinsky v. New York.* Obviously, the dissents in *Papish* indicate that not all Justices agree with these trends.

In *Papish* the words expressed are judged on the basis of a previous case, *Rosenfeld v. New Jersey,* not to be obscene. Nor are they considered profanity or "fighting words" under the ruling in *Chaplinsky.* Do you agree with the court of appeals and with the dissenters that even if the newspaper is not obscene and could be distributed in society at large with impunity, "campus 'freedom of expression' could properly be 'subordinated to other interests such as, for example, the conventions of decency in the use and display of languages and pictures.' " ? If you were to take this position, would you require a more precisely drawn institutional rule than the one involved in this case? Would you permit prior restraints to screen out inappropriate expression as suggested in *Eisner* or only utilize subsequent punishment?

2. How much control might an educational institution have over a campus radio or television station which it operates? Suppose Ms. Papish had read the literature she was circulating on campus over the air on the campus radio station. Would the University of Missouri be on firmer grounds for suspending her?

3. Would you apply the *Papish* decision to other educational settings such as the high school, junior high school, elementary school? If not, how would you define what is "obscene?" Would you use the same tests from *Miller* or devise new tests more appropriate for the educational setting? For example, would you judge obscenity issues by *student* standards rather than those set for the community-at-large? Would such standards be more stringent or more lenient than the ones employed by the community at large?

Right to Read Defense Comm. v. School Committee of the City of Chelsea, 454 F.Supp. 703 (D.Mass.1978), involves an attempt by a school board to use the local community standards test from *Miller* to remove an anthology of writings by adolescents from the school library. Many in the community, including parents and school board members, objected to a poem in the anthology written by a 15 year old New York City high school student. The poem was entitled "The City to a Young Girl" and was filled with street language.

Prior to trial, however, the board abandoned the community standard argument, apparently because while the poem was objectionable, it did not fall into the obscene category. The school board relied on its statutory control over curriculum to justify removal of the book.

The court observed that while the school board could control the purchasing of books for the library—indeed even decide whether to have a library at all—it does not have the power to remove books merely because some people find them offensive.

> * * * compelling policy considerations argue against any public authority having such an unreviewable power of censorship. There is more at issue here than the poem * * *. If this work may be removed by a committee hostile to its language and theme, then the precedent is set for removal of any other work. The prospect of successive school [boards] "sanitizing" the school library of views divergent from their own is alarming, whether they do it book by book or one page at a time. (At p. 714; material in brackets added).

The district court agreed with the Sixth Circuit in *Minarcini v. Strongsville City School District, supra,* at p. 161, that the school library is a "mighty resource" in the marketplace of ideas and concluded that "the most effective antidote to the poison of mindless orthodoxy is ready access to a broad sweep of ideas and philosophies." (At p. 715).

Suppose the school board refused to authorize the purchase of certain books for the library not for financial reasons or overcrowding of library shelves but because they consider the book "filthy and not fit for young minds." Same result?

4. Like obscenity, defamatory utterances are generally beyond the protection afforded by the Constitution. But where public officials are the targets, the statements must do more than hold the plaintiff up to public hatred, contempt, or ridicule, as we saw in *New York Times v. Sullivan* (1964). Since public officials are so likely to be the targets of criticism and debate, to recover damages, plaintiffs must show that not only was the utterance untrue, it was motivated by "actual malice," that is, intentional and reckless disregard for truth.

In the educational setting, school officials are frequently criticized in strong language. Recall that even Chief Justice Burger noted in his *Papish* dissent that "Students are, of course, free to criticize the university, its faculty, or the Government in vigorous, or even harsh, terms." Thus, courts are usually unsympathetic to restrictions or sanctions placed on expression in the educational environment where school officials bear the brunt of criticism.

How far does this go? Should the *New York Times* rule apply to all educators as public officials? Does the nature of the particular educational setting involved play a role in what is permissible and what isn't? For example, should junior high students have the same latitude in criticism of educational officials as college students? At what point do student utterances aimed specifically at school officials go beyond the protections of the First/Fourteenth Amendments?

5. Generally, the developing law suggests at least some support for the following types of regulations governing student expression within the educational setting:

1. Reasonable time, place, and manner rules which are content-neutral and do not shut off entirely the channels of communication;

2. A system of prior restraints, provided guidelines are developed and promulgated to expedite the review process and offer some opportunity of appeal;

3. Regulations against the use of obscene, libelous, or profane material.

Obviously, the legality of these approaches may be heavily influenced by the facts of a particular situation, the level of schooling involved (collegiate, secondary, and so on), and relevant statutory and case law.

With these generalities and caveats in mind, and drawing upon the cases discussed in this and earlier sections, which of the following actions by public educational officials or statements of educational policy do you think violate protected student rights of expression?

a. Disciplining a student who during his address at a high school assembly calls the school principal a "son-of-a-bitch." The remark triggers a flurry of laughter and hoots.

b. Disciplining a student for the same utterance as in (a), only this time the utterance is made in informal conversation on school grounds and is overheard by other students and school officials.

c. Disciplining a student for calling a school official "a stupid prick" at a local drive-in where other students overheard the remark. Any difference if the student was an 8th grader rather than a high school junior?

d. Disciplining a high school student for burning two white rats to death as part of an art exhibit. Any difference if the setting is a public art college?

e. College policy requiring prior review of student art before it is put on public display (1) around the campus, (2) in the office of admissions, (3) in a classroom, (4) in the library. Same result in the high school setting?

f. College officials request a preview of a student play before it is allowed to be presented on the campus because nudity is allegedly practiced throughout the play and the sex act is allegedly featured in two scenes. Would it make any difference if the play were open only to the campus community? If the tests from *Miller* are used, how should "community" be defined?

g. High school policy requiring that all speakers invited on campus by student organizations must be approved by educational officials. Same result in the collegiate setting?

h. College officials request an opportunity to review a decision by the student government to invite the president of the American Nazi Party to the campus for a speech because many of the Jewish students have made threats to disrupt the presentation.

i.   Refusal of college officials to allow a "wet T-shirt" contest to be held in the campus student union. Suppose the officials prohibited the contest anywhere on campus?

j.   College officials discipline a student for displaying a pumpkin in the window of his dorm room with the work "FUCK" carved out and highlighted by a lighted candle the night of Halloween.

V. THE DEVELOPMENT OF RIGHTS OF ASSEMBLY AND ASSOCIATION

The rights of expression would, of course, be empty rights if persons could not come together to communicate. Thus, the First Amendment's guarantee of the right of assembly is an important right and has been carried over to apply to the states as well through the Fourteenth Amendment. Though not mentioned in the First Amendment, the right of association is considered implicit in the right to assemble and has also been carried over to apply to the states through the Fourteenth Amendment. Likewise, the right to petition the government for redress of grievances is an important right in both the federal and state arenas. Both of the cases excerpted in this section are recent U. S. Supreme Court decisions and thus are particularly significant.

A. The Right to Assemble

Just how far the right of assembly goes within the public educational setting is the subject of the first case included in this section. It is important to note at the outset that where assembly and petition rights are involved, regulations of time, place, and manner are particularly apt to be challenged, since the latter are primarily designed to regulate the former. In *Grayned v. Rockford,* Richard Grayned was convicted for participating in a demonstration in front of a public high school during school hours. Grayned and about 200 others resorted to picketing after the principal took no action on their demands for greater involvement by blacks in school affairs. Grayned's brother and twin sister were then enrolled in the school. The facts surrounding the arrests were contradictory. Police reported a noisy, unruly crowd, which was disturbing instruction. Those arrested claimed the demonstration was peaceful. Grayned, along with 39 others, was tried and convicted of violating two Rockford ordinances, one banning picketing and the other excessive noise. He challenged both ordinances as invalid on their face but did not urge that, as applied to him, the ordinances punished constitutionally protected activity. The Illinois Supreme Court upheld both ordinances. The U. S. Supreme Court granted certiorari.

GRAYNED v. ROCKFORD

Supreme Court of the United States, 1972.
408 U.S. 104, 92 S.Ct. 2294, 33 L.Ed.2d 222.

Mr. Justice MARSHALL delivered the opinion of the Court.

* * *

I

At the time of appellant's arrest and conviction, Rockford's antipicketing ordinance provided that

"A person commits disorderly conduct when he knowingly:

* * *

"(i) Pickets or demonstrates on a public way within 150 feet of any primary or secondary school building while the school is in session and one-half hour before the school is in session and one-half hour after the school session has been concluded, provided that this subsection does not prohibit the peaceful picketing of any school involved in a labor dispute. * * *"

This ordinance is identical to the Chicago disorderly conduct ordinance we have today considered in *Police Department of Chicago v. Mosley.* For the reasons given in *Mosley,* we agree with dissenting Justice Schaefer below, and hold that (the antipicketing ordinance) violates the Equal Protection Clause of the Fourteenth Amendment. Appellant's conviction under this invalid ordinance must be reversed.

II

The antinoise ordinance reads, in pertinent part, as follows:

"[N]o person, while on public or private grounds adjacent to any building in which a school or any class thereof is in session, shall willfully make or assist in the making of any noise or diversion which disturbs or tends to disturb the peace or good order of such school session or class thereof.
* * *"

Appellant claims that, on its face, this ordinance is both vague and overbroad, and therefore unconstitutional. We conclude, however, that the ordinance suffers from neither of these related infirmities.

A.   Vagueness

* * *

Although the question is close, we conclude that the antinoise ordinance is not impermissibly vague. The court below rejected appellant's arguments "that proscribed conduct was not sufficiently specified and that police were given too broad a discretion in determining whether conduct was proscribed." Although it referred to other, similar statutes it had recently construed and upheld, the court below did not elaborate on the meaning of the antinoise ordinance. In this situation, as Mr. Justice Frankfurter put it, we must "extrapolate its allowable meaning." Here, we are "relegated * * * to the words of the ordinance itself," to the interpretations the court below has given to analogous statutes, and, perhaps to some degree, to the interpretation of the statute given by those charged with enforcing it. "Extrapolation," of course, is a delicate task, for it is not within our power to construe and narrow state laws.

With that warning, we find no unconstitutional vagueness in the antinoise ordinance. Condemned to the use of words, we can never expect mathematical certainty from our language. The words of the Rockford ordinance are marked by "flexibility and reasonable breadth, rather than meticulous specificity," but we think it is clear what the ordinance as a whole prohibits. Designed, according to its preamble, "for the protection of Schools," the ordinance forbids deliberately noisy or diversionary activity that disrupts or is about to disrupt normal school activities. It forbids this willful activity at fixed times—when school is in session—and at a sufficiently fixed place —"adjacent" to the school. Were we left with just the words of the ordinance, we might be troubled by the imprecision of the phrase "tends to disturb." * * *

Although the prohibited quantum of disturbance is not specified in the ordinance, it is apparent from the statute's announced purpose that the measure is whether normal school activity has been or is about to be disrupted. We do not have here a vague, general "breach of the peace" ordinance, but a statute written specifically for the school context, where the prohibited disturbances are easily measured by their impact on the normal activities of the school. Given this "particular context," the ordinance gives "fair notice to those to whom [it] is directed." * * *

* * *

B. Overbreadth

* * * Specifically, appellant contents that the Rockford ordinance unduly interferes with First and Fourteenth Amendment rights to picket on a public sidewalk near a school. We disagree. * * *

Clearly, government has no power to restrict such activity because of its message. Our cases make equally clear, however, that reasonable "time, place and manner" regulations may be necessary to further significant governmental interests, and are permitted. For example, two parades cannot march on the same street simultaneously, and government may allow only one. A demonstration or parade on a large street during rush hour might put an intolerable burden on the essential flow of traffic, and for that reason could be prohibited. If overampli-

fied loudspeakers assault the citizenry, government may turn them down. Subject to such reasonable regulation, however, peaceful demonstrations in public places are protected by the First Amendment. Of course, where demonstrations turn violent, they lose their protected quality as expression under the First Amendment.

* * * The crucial question is whether the manner of expression is basically incompatible with the normal activity of a particular place at a particular time. * * *

* * * we do not think that Rockford's ordinance is an unconstitutional regulation of activity around a school. Our touchstone is *Tinker v. Des Moines School District,* in which we considered the question of how to accommodate First Amendment rights with the "special characteristics of the school environment." * * *

Just as *Tinker* made clear that school property may not be declared off limits for expressive activity by students, we think it clear that the public sidewalk adjacent to school grounds may not be declared off limits for expressive activity by members of the public. But in each case, expressive activity may be prohibited if it "materially disrupts classwork or involves substantial disorder or invasion of the rights of others."

* * *

Rockford's antinoise ordinance goes no further than *Tinker* says a municipality may go to prevent interference with its schools. It is narrowly tailored to further Rockford's compelling interest in having an undisrupted school session conducive to the students' learning, and does not unnecessarily interfere with First Amendment rights. Far from having an impermissibly broad prophylactic ordinance, Rockford punishes only conduct which disrupts or is about to disrupt normal school activities. That decision is made, as it should be, on an individualized basis, given the particular fact situation. Peaceful picketing which does not interfere with the ordinary functioning of the school is permitted. And the ordinance gives no license to punish anyone because of what he is saying.

We recognize that the ordinance prohibits some picketing that is neither violent nor physically obstructive. Noisy demonstrations that disrupt or are incompatible with normal school activities are obviously within the ordinance's reach. Such expressive conduct may be constitutionally protected at other places or other times, but next to a school while classes are in session, it may be prohibited.[45] The antinoise ordinance imposes no such restriction on expressive activity before or after the school session, while the student/faculty "audience" enters and leaves the school.

* * *

Rockford's modest restriction on some peaceful picketing represents a considered and specific legislative judgment that some kinds of expressive activity should be restricted at a particular time and place, here in order to protect the schools. Such a reasonable regulation is not inconsistent with the First and Fourteenth Amendments. The antinoise ordinance is not invalid on its face.[50]

The judgment is affirmed in part and reversed in part.

* * *

Mr. Justice DOUGLAS, dissenting in part.

While I join Part I of the Court's opinion, I would also reverse the appellant's conviction under the antinoise ordinance.

* * *

Appellant was one of 200 people picketing a school and carrying signs pro-

moting a black cause—"Black cheerleaders to cheer too," "Black history with black teachers," "We want our rights," and the like. Appellant, however, did not himself carry a picket sign. There was no evidence that he yelled or made any noise whatsoever. Indeed, the evidence reveals that appellant simply marched quietly and on one occasion raised his arm in the "power to the people" salute.

The pickets were mostly students; but they included former students, parents of students, and concerned citizens. They had made proposals to the school board on their demands and were turned down. Hence the picketing. The picketing was mostly by black students who were counseled and advised by a faculty member of the school. The school contained 1,800 students. Those counseling the students advised they must be quiet, walk hand in hand, no whispering, no talking.

Twenty-five policemen were stationed nearby. There was noise but most of it was produced by the police who used loudspeakers to explain the local ordinance and to announce that arrests might be made. The picketing did not stop, and some 40 demonstrators, including appellant, were arrested.

The picketing lasted 20 to 30 minutes and some students went to the windows of the classrooms to observe it. It is not clear how many there were. The picketing was, however, orderly or, as one officer testified, "very orderly." There was no violence. And appellant made no noise whatever.

* * *

The school where the present picketing occurred was the center of a racial

45. Different considerations, of course, apply in different circumstances. For example, restrictions appropriate to a single-building high school during class hours would be inappropriate in many open areas on a college campus, just as an assembly that is permitted outside a dormi-

tory would be inappropriate in the middle of a mathematics class.

50. It is possible, of course, that there will be unconstitutional applications; but that is not a matter which presently concerns us.

conflict. Most of the pickets were indeed students in the school. The dispute doubtless disturbed the school; and the blaring of the loudspeakers of the police was certainly a "noise or diversion" in the meaning of the ordinance. But there was no evidence that appellant was noisy or boisterous or rowdy. He walked quietly and in an orderly manner. As I read this record, the disruptive force loosed at this school was an issue dealing with race—an issue that is preeminently one for solution by First Amendment means.* That is all that was done here; and the entire picketing, including appellant's part in it, was done in the best First Amendment tradition.

NOTES AND QUESTIONS

1. Both *Grayned v. Rockford* and the next case, *Healy v. James,* were decided in June of 1972, a time when educational administrators and the general public were increasingly concerned about student discipline and racial tensions within all sectors of education. The Court indicated in *Healy* that it was not unaware of the recent period of student disruption.

In *Grayned* the majority concludes that the antipicketing ordinance is unconstitutional based on reasoning in *Police Dept. of Chicago v. Mosley,* 408 U.S. 92, decided during the same term. There the Court declared a Chicago anti-picketing ordinance unconstitutional because in exempting a certain type of picketing—peaceful labor picketing—the ordinance violated the Equal Protection Clause of the Fourteenth Amendment. The Court acknowledged, however, that the ordinance also intruded on protected "expressive conduct" and thus was not a content-neutral time, place, and manner regulation. Said Justice Marshall for the majority:

> * * * There is an "equality of status in the field of ideas," and government must afford all points of view an equal opportunity to be heard. Once a forum is opened up to assembly or speaking by some groups, government may not prohibit others from assembling or speaking on the basis of what they intend to say. Selective exclusions from a public forum may not be based on content alone, and may not be justified by reference to content alone.
>
> * * *
>
> In this case, the ordinance itself describes impermissible picketing not in terms of time, place, and manner, but in terms of subject matter. The regulation "thus slip[s] from the neutrality of time, place, and circumstance into a concern about content." (at pp. 96 and 99)

* The majority asserts that "appellant's sole claim * * * is that he was convicted under facially unconstitutional ordinances" and that there is, therefore, no occasion to consider whether his activities were protected by the First Amendment. Appellant argues, however, that the ordinance is overly broad in that it punishes constitutionally protected activity. * * * If the ordinance applies to appellant's activities and if appellant's activities are constitutionally protected, then the ordinance is overly broad and, thus, unconstitutional. There is no merit, therefore, to the Court's suggestion that the question whether "appellant's particular behavior was protected by the First Amendment," is not presented.

Mosley alleged that the ordinance prevented his peaceful picketing at a Chicago high school, while carrying a sign reading "Jones High School practices black discrimination. Jones High School has a black quota."

In *Grayned* the Court upholds the antinoise statute. Are you as troubled as Justice Douglas that appellant was one of many arrested with no attempt to ascertain the specific degree of his guilt? In rejecting Justice Douglas' claims, is the majority supporting dragnet arrests or indirectly criticizing Grayned for not raising the issue of an unconstitutional application of an otherwise valid statute? If Grayned had narrowed his claim to his own individual situation and not attempted a broad challenge to the constitutionality of the statute, would the outcome likely have been different?

2. In upholding the antinoise statute, Justice Marshall dismisses appellant's argument that the statute is unconstitutionally vague "though the question is close." Had the statute been a federal rather than a state law, the ruling may have been different. However, since it is a state law and since the Supreme Court of Illinois had had previous occasion to interpret the meaning of "tending to disturb the peace" as a situation where there is "imminent threat of violence," the Court feels constrained to give the statute a constitutional reading. Do you agree that "the ordinance gives 'fair notice to those to whom (it) is directed' "?

3. Justice Marshall also dismisses appellant's claim that the ordinance is overbroad in prohibiting constitutionally-protected conduct under the First/Fourteenth Amendments. In rejecting the argument, Justice Marshall notes that the ordinance does not constitute a blanket prohibition on picketing. In what way is it not? Rather the ordinance constitutes a reasonable time, place, manner regulation on peaceful demonstrations. In deciding these issues, Justice Marshall suggests that the overbreadth test for time, place, and manner regulations ought to be "whether the manner of expression is basically incompatible with the normal activity of a particular place at a particular time." Does this test help you decide the validity of any of the school rules listed on page 130, following *Soglin v. Kauffman*?

B. The Right of Association

Healy v. James involves the efforts of a local chapter of the 1960s activist group, Students for a Democratic Society (SDS), to gain recognition as a campus organization at Central Connecticut State College. Pursuant to campus procedures, the students filed a request for official recognition with the Student Affairs Committee. While satisfied with the clarity and legitimacy of the petitioning group's announced objectives, the Committee expressed concern about the relationship of the local organization to the National SDS, which was known to have advocated and engaged in illegal and sometimes violent activity. However, by a vote of six-to-two, the Committee eventually recommended to the college president, Dr. James, that the local chapter be recognized as a student organization at CCSC. At the same time, the Committee noted that if the group violated campus rules, immediate suspension be considered.

Dr. James rejected the Committee's recommendations. He considered the organization's philosophy to be in direct conflict with the College's commitment to academic freedom. As a result of the denial of recognition, the students filed a suit in federal court, claiming denial of the rights of expression and association. The federal district court ordered a rehearing to clarify ambiguities surrounding the president's decision. After the hearing, which was conducted by the dean of student affairs, President James again denied recognition for substantially the same reasons as before. When the case returned to the courtroom, the district court dismissed the action. By a two-to-one vote, the Court of Appeals for the Second Circuit affirmed the lower court's decision. The U. S. Supreme Court unanimously reversed the judgment and remanded the case for reconsideration.

HEALY v. JAMES

Supreme Court of the United States, 1972.
408 U.S. 169, 92 S.Ct. 2338, 33 L.Ed.2d 266.

Mr. Justice POWELL delivered the opinion of the Court.

* * *

II

* * *

Among the rights protected by the First Amendment is the right of individuals to associate to further their personal beliefs. While the freedom of association is not explicitly set out in the Amendment, it has long been held to be implicit in the freedoms of speech, assembly, and petition. There can be no doubt that denial of official recognition, without justification, to college organizations burdens or abridges that associational right. The primary impediment to free association flowing from nonrecognition is the denial of use of campus facilities for meetings and other appropriate purposes. The practical effect of nonrecognition was demonstrated in this case when, several days after the President's decision was announced, petitioners were not allowed to hold a meeting in the campus coffee shop because they were not an approved group.

Petitioners' associational interests also were circumscribed by the denial of the use of campus bulletin boards and the school newspaper. If an organization is to remain a viable entity in a campus community in which new students enter on a regular basis, it must possess the means of communicating with these students. Moreover, the organization's ability to participate in the intellectual give and take of campus debate, and to pursue its stated purposes, is limited by denial of access to the customary media for communicating with the administration, faculty members, and other students. Such impediments cannot be viewed as insubstantial.

Respondents and the courts below appear to have taken the view that denial of official recognition in this case abridged no constitutional rights. The District Court concluded that

"President James' discretionary action in denying this application cannot be legitimately magnified and distorted into a constitutionally cognizable interference with the personal ideas or beliefs of any segment of the college students; neither does his action deter in any material way the individual advocacy of their personal beliefs; nor can his action be reasonably construed to be an invasion of, or having a chilling effect on academic freedom."

In that court's view all that was denied petitioners was the "administrative seal of official college respectability." A majority of the Court of Appeals agreed that petitioners had been denied only the "college's stamp of approval." Respondents take that same position here, arguing that petitioners still may meet as a group off campus, that they still may distribute written material off campus, and that they still may meet together informally on campus—as individuals, but not as CCSC–SDS.

We do not agree with the characterization by the courts below of the consequences of nonrecognition. We may concede, as did Mr. Justice Harlan in his opinion for a unanimous Court in *NAACP v. Alabama ex rel. Patterson,* that the administration "has taken no direct action * * * to restrict the rights of [petitioners] to associate freely * * *." But the Constitution's protection is not limited to direct interference with fundamental rights. The requirement in *Patterson* that the NAACP disclose its membership lists was found to be an impermissible, though indirect, infringement of the members' associational rights. Likewise, in this case, the group's possible ability to exist outside the campus community does not ameliorate significantly the disabilities imposed by the President's action. * * *

The opinions below also assumed that petitioners had the burden of showing entitlement to recognition by the College. * * * But apart from any particular issue, once petitioners had filed an application in conformity with the requirements, the burden was upon the College administration to justify its decision of

rejection. It is to be remembered that the effect of the College's denial of recognition was a form of prior restraint, denying to petitioners' organization the range of associational activities described above. While a college has a legitimate interest in preventing disruption on the campus, which under circumstances requiring the safeguarding of that interest may justify such restraint, a "heavy burden" rests on the college to demonstrate the appropriateness of that action.

III

These fundamental errors—discounting the existence of a cognizable First Amendment interest and misplacing the burden of proof—require that the judgments below be reversed. But we are unable to conclude that no basis exists upon which nonrecognition might be appropriate. * * * Four possible justifications for nonrecognition, all closely related, might be derived from the record and his statements. Three of those grounds are inadequate to substantiate his decision: a fourth, however, has merit.

A

* * * Despite assurances from petitioners and their counsel that the local group was in fact independent of the National organization, it is evident that President James was significantly influenced by his apprehension that there was a connection. Aware of the fact that some SDS chapters had been associated with disruptive and violent campus activity, he apparently considered that affiliation itself was sufficient justification for denying recognition.

Although this precise issue has not come before the Court heretofore, the Court has consistently disapproved governmental action imposing criminal sanctions or denying rights and privileges solely because of a citizen's association with an unpopular organization. * * * The government has the burden of establishing a knowing affiliation with an organization possessing unlawful aims and goals, and a specific intent to further those illegal aims.

Students for a Democratic Society, as conceded by the College and the lower courts, is loosely organized, having various factions and promoting a number of diverse social and political views, only some of which call for unlawful action. Not only did petitioners proclaim their complete independence from this organization, but they also indicated that they shared only some of the beliefs its leaders have expressed. On this record it is clear that the relationship was not an adequate ground for the denial of recognition.

B

* * *

The mere disagreement of the President with the group's philosophy affords no reason to deny it recognition. As repugnant as these views may have been, especially to one with President James' responsibility, the mere expression of them would not justify the denial of First Amendment rights. Whether petitioners did in fact advocate a philosophy of "destruction" thus becomes immaterial. The College, acting here as the instrumentality of the State, may not restrict speech or association simply because it finds the views expressed by any group to be abhorrent. * * *

C

As the litigation progressed in the District Court, a third rationale for President James' decision—beyond the questions of

affiliation and philosophy—began to emerge. His second statement, issued after the court-ordered hearing, indicates that he based rejection on a conclusion that this particular group would be a "disruptive influence at CCSC." * * *

If this reason, directed at the organization's activities rather than its philosophy, were factually supported by the record, this Court's prior decisions would provide a basis for considering the propriety of nonrecognition. * * *

The record, however, offers no substantial basis for that conclusion. * * *

D

* * * The College's Statement of Rights, Freedoms, and Responsibilities of Students contains * * * an explicit statement with respect to campus disruption. The regulation, carefully differentiating between advocacy and action, is a reasonable one, and petitioners have not questioned it directly. Yet their statements raise considerable question whether they intend to abide by the prohibitions contained therein.[22] * * * the critical line for First Amendment purposes must be drawn between advocacy, which is entitled to full protection, and action, which is not. Petitioners may, if they so choose, preach the propriety of amending or even doing away with any or all campus regulations. They may not, however, undertake to flout these rules. * * * Just as in the community at large, reasonable regulations with respect to the time, the place, and the manner in which student groups conduct

---

22. The Court of Appeals found that petitioners "failed candidly to respond to inquiries whether they would resort to violence and disruption on the CCSC campus, including interruption of classes." While petitioners' statements may be read as intimating a rejection of reasonable regulations in advance, there is in fact substantial ambiguity on this point. The questions asked by members of the Student Affairs Committee do not appear to have

been propounded with any clear distinction in mind between that which the petitioners might advocate and the conduct in which they might engage. Nor did the Student Affairs Committee attempt to obtain a clarification of the petitioners' ambiguous answers by asking specifically whether the group was willing to abide by the Student Bill of Rights governing all campus organizations.

* * *

their speech-related activities must be respected. A college administration may impose a requirement, such as may have been imposed in this case, that a group seeking official recognition affirm in advance its willingness to adhere to reasonable campus law. Such a requirement does not impose an impermissible condition on the students' associational rights. Their freedom to speak out, to assemble, or to petition for changes in school rules is in no sense infringed. It merely constitutes an agreement to conform with reasonable standards respecting conduct. This is a minimal requirement, in the interest of the entire academic community, of any group seeking the privilege of official recognition.

Petitioners have not challenged in this litigation the procedural or substantive aspects of the College's requirements governing applications for official recognition. * * * Assuming the existence of a valid rule, * * * we do conclude that the benefits of participation in the internal life of the college community may be denied to any group that reserves the right to violate any valid campus rules with which it disagrees.[24]

IV

We think the above discussion establishes the appropriate framework for consideration of petitioners' request for campus recognition. Because respondents failed to accord due recognition to First Amendment principles, the judgments below approving respondents' denial of recognition must be reversed. Since we cannot conclude from this record that petitioners were willing to abide by reasonable campus rules and regulations, we order the case remanded for reconsideration. We note, in so holding, that the wide latitude accorded by the Constitu-

tion to the freedoms of expression and association is not without its costs in terms of the risk to the maintenance of civility and an ordered society. Indeed, this latitude often has resulted, on the campus and elsewhere, in the infringement of the rights of others. Though we deplore the tendency of some to abuse the very constitutional privileges they invoke, and although the infringement of rights of others certainly should not be tolerated, we reaffirm this Court's dedication to the principles of the Bill of Rights upon which our vigorous and free society is founded.

Reversed and remanded.

Mr. Chief Justice BURGER, concurring.

I am in agreement with what is said in the Court's opinion and I join in it. I do so because I read the basis of the remand as recognizing that student organizations seeking the privilege of official campus recognition must be willing to abide by valid rules of the institution applicable to all such organizations. This is a reasonable condition insofar as it calls for the disavowal of resort to force, disruption, and interference with the rights of others.

The District Judge was troubled by the lack of a comprehensive procedural scheme that would inform students of the steps to be taken to secure recognized standing, and by the lack of articulated criteria to be used in evaluating eligibility for recognition. It was for this reason, as I read the record, that he remanded the matter to the college for a factual inquiry and for a more orderly processing in a *de novo* hearing within the college administrative structure. It is within that structure and within the academic com-

---

24. In addition to the College administration's broad rulemaking power to assure that the traditional academic atmosphere is safeguarded, it may also impose sanctions on those who violate the rules. We find, for instance, that the Student Af-

fairs Committee's admonition to petitioners in this case suggests one permissible practice—recognition, once accorded, may be withdrawn or suspended if petitioners fail to respect campus law.

munity that problems such as these should be resolved. The courts, state or federal, should be a last resort. Part of the educational experience of every college student should be an experience in responsible self-government and this must be a joint enterprise of students and faculty. It should not be imposed unilaterally from above, nor can the terms of the relationship be dictated by students. Here, in spite of the wisdom of the District Court in sending the case back to the college, the issue identified by the Court's opinion today was not adequately addressed in the hearing.

* * *

Against this background, the action of the Court in remanding on this issue is appropriate.

Mr. Justice DOUGLAS.

While I join the opinion of the Court, I add a few words.

* * * the status quo of the college or university is the governing body (trustees or overseers), administrative officers, who include caretakers, and the police, and the faculty. Those groups have well-defined or vaguely inferred values to perpetuate. The customary technique has been to conceive of the minds of students as receptacles for the information which the faculty have garnered over the years. Education is commonly thought of as the process of filling the receptacles with what the faculty in its wisdom deems fit and proper.

Many, inside and out of faculty circles, realize that one of the main problems of faculty members is their own re-education or re-orientation. Some have narrow specialties that are hardly relevant to modern times. History has passed others by, leaving them interesting relics of a bygone day. More often than not they represent those who withered under the pressures of McCarthyism or other forces of conformity and represent but a timid replica of those who once brought distinction to the ideal of academic freedom.

The confrontation between them and the oncoming students has often been upsetting. The problem is not one of choosing sides. Students—who, by reason of the Twenty-sixth Amendment, become eligible to vote when 18 years of age—are adults who are members of the college or university community. Their interests and concerns are often quite different from those of the faculty. They often have values, views, and ideologies that are at war with the ones which the college has traditionally espoused or indoctrinated. When they ask for change, they, the students, speak in the tradition of Jefferson and Madison and the First Amendment.

The First Amendment does not authorize violence. But it does authorize advocacy, group activities, and espousal of change.

The present case is minuscule in the events of the 60's and 70's. But the fact that it has to come here for ultimate resolution indicates the sickness of our academic world, measured by First Amendment standards. Students as well as faculty are entitled to credentials in their search for truth. If we are to become an integrated, adult society, rather than a stubborn status quo opposed to change, students and faculties should have communal interests in which each age learns from the other. Without ferment of one kind or another, a college or university (like a federal agency or other human institution) becomes a useless appendage to a society which traditionally has reflected the spirit of rebellion (appendix to Justice Douglas' opinion deleted).

Mr. Justice REHNQUIST, concurring in the result.

While I do not subscribe to some of the language in the Court's opinion, I concur in the result that it reaches. As I understand the Court's holding, the case is sent back for reconsideration because respondents may not have made it sufficiently clear to petitioners that the decision as to recognition would be critically influenced by petitoners' willingness to agree in advance to abide by reasonable regulations promulgated by the college.

I find the implication clear from the Court's opinion that the constitutional limitations on the government's acting as administrator of a college differ from the limitations on the government's acting as sovereign to enforce its criminal laws.

* * *

* * *

Prior cases dealing with First Amendment rights are not fungible goods, and I think the doctrine of these cases suggests two important distinctions. The government as employer or school administrator may impose upon employees and students reasonable regulations that would be impermissible if imposed by the government upon all citizens. And there can be a constitutional distinction between the infliction of criminal punishment, on the one hand, and the imposition of milder administrative or disciplinary sanctions, on the other, even though the same First Amendment interest is implicated by each.

Because some of the language used by the Court tends to obscure these distinctions, which I believe to be important, I concur only in the result.

NOTES AND QUESTIONS

1. Note that the Supreme Court rejects the view expressed by both lower courts that only the "administrative seal of official college respectability" has been denied the students. Previous rulings of the Court had established that even indirect restriction of fundamental rights is beyond state power in the absence of convincing reasons. Justice Powell asserts that denial of recognition constitutes "a form of prior restraint" which demands a "heavy burden" of justification from the college. Thus, while the Court has not directly ruled on prior restraints in the educational setting, there appears to be a presumption against their validity, at least at the collegiate level.

Though the Supreme Court has not directly ruled on the associational rights of public high school students, the *Healy* decision coupled with its reliance on *Tinker v. Des Moines School Dist.,* suggest a similar approach. Lower courts in recent years have been increasingly supportive of high school student associational rights. For example, in *Dixon v. Beresh,* 361 F.Supp. 253 (E.D.Mich.1973), the court ruled that where there is no evidence of disorder, to deny recognition to student groups because they advocate controversial ideas or take one side of an issue "is patently unconstitutional." (At p. 254). The court relied on *Tinker* and on several press cases, including *Eisner v. Stamford Bd.* discussed earlier in this chapter.

2. Note the contrast in values about the educational environment evident in the opinions of Justices Douglas and Rehnquist, both of whom concur with the majority decision. Which most nearly corresponds with your own?

3. Does the *Healy* decision eliminate entirely any discretion by campus officials in extending recognition to student organizations which

request it? For example, should administrative discretion be greater where the student group desiring recognition is primarily social rather than political? Can the latter make the same claim to First Amendment freedoms? Consider the following hypothetical case.

The SFN Movement v. Oceanside State Univ.

A number of students on the Oceanside campus had engaged in nude bathing at the several "swimsuit optional" beaches along the nearby coast. State law permits public nudity at the discretion and under the regulation of local governmental units. Some students, along with two vocal faculty members of the Sociology Department, regard nudity as a way of life, the true liberated environment. "Clothes," said one faculty member, "are defense mechanisms. They are the most tangible evidence of the many communication barriers we establish against open communication and human understanding."

Twenty-five students met recently on the Oceanside campus to form a Students For Nudity (SFN) organization at Oceanside State. In order to be recognized as an official student organization on the campus, organizations aspiring to this status have to follow the procedures outlined in the *Student Handbook*. Members of SFN filed the necessary information, including the designation of the two sociology faculty members as advisors to the organization.

Shortly after completing all the necessary filing procedures, the students were notified by the dean of students that the purpose of the organization—to practice and promote nudity as a way of life at Oceanside State University—was not appropriate to the mission of the institution and the organizational petition was therefore rejected. The students appealed the decision to the president of the university.

What arguments would each side make? If you were the campus president, what decision would you reach? Same decision if the setting were a public high school?

4. Are recognized student organizations independent agencies or extensions of the state? To what extent can they be regulated by the educational institution? Aside from college newspapers, which seem to draw some independent status from the constitutional right to freedom of the press, it would appear that recognized student organizations including student government do not become independent by virtue of institutional recognition or by virtue of receipt of student mandatory fees, which may make the organization financially independent. A recent state supreme court decision to this effect is *Good v. Associated Students of the Univ. of Wash.*, 542 P.2d 762 (Washington, 1975). In *Good,* several students asserted that required membership in ASUW coupled with a mandatory student activity fee denied them their rights under the First Amendment and the state constitution. The students claimed that they have a constitutional right *not* to associate with any group, and they pointed out that by the terms of their enrollment, they were forced to join an organization whose programs and views they did not support.

The Washington State Supreme Court first found that ASUW was an agency of the state and therefore eligible to receive mandatory student activity fees.

> We believe that the range of powers given to the board is sufficiently wide to encompass their decision to provide student activities and services through a separate nonprofit corporation, so long as that entity is in essence an agency of the university and subject to ultimate control by the board. This view is buttressed by the fact that the legislature is well aware of the corporate nature of the ASUW. (At p. 764).

As to the students' assertions that their associational rights were infringed, the court stated that the university could not mandate membership of a student in the ASUW:

> * * * we have no hesitancy in holding that the state, through the university, may not compel membership in an association such as ASUW, which purports to represent *all* the students at the university including these plaintiffs. That association expends funds for political and economic causes to which the dissenters object and promotes and espouses political, social, and economic philosophies which the dissenters find repugnant to their own views. There is no room in the First Amendment for such absolute compulsory support, allocation and representation. We recognize that First Amendment rights are not absolute, but the university presents no arguments or facts to justify any exception, narrow as it would have to be, which might exist if a compelling state interest were presented. (At p. 768; emphasis in original).

At the same time, the Washington Supreme Court acknowledged that a mandatory student fee program for proper university activities would not infringe on any constitutional rights.

> Dissenting students should not have the right to veto every event, speech or program with which they disagree. On the other hand, the ASUW is not totally unchecked in its use of these fees mandatorily extracted from students. * * * it cannot become the vehicle for the promotion of one particular viewpoint, political, social, economic, or religious. (At p. 769).

Thus, it is the duty of the university to oversee ASUW activities and expenditures to this end. The high court remanded the case to determine if the university had been derelict in its duties in this respect. Note the difficult tradeoff facing both ASUW and the university with regard to this ruling. On the one hand, ASUW is the official representative of the student body and presumably speaks with an independent voice; on the other hand ASUW exists and functions under the auspices of the university. Too much regulation is likely to jeopardize the status of ASUW in the eyes of the students. Too little may subject both ASUW and university officials to court suits. Furthermore, whatever regulation is employed must not infringe on the constitutional rights of student government leaders.

5. In 1977 the U. S. Supreme Court decided a case involving the constitutionality of the agency shop in public employment. An agency shop is a form of union security agreement whereby all who are in a collective bargaining unit must pay to the union a service fee as a condition of employment equal to union membership dues, even though some may not hold membership in the union. Agency shops have much in common with mandatory student activity fees and raise similar issues involving rights of expression and association. In *Abood v. Detroit Bd. of Educ.*, 431 U.S. 209 (1977), the Court upheld the constitutionality of agency shops even though employees "may very well have ideological objections to a wide variety of activities undertaken by the union * * *." (At p. 222). However, where the fees were used for purposes other than collective bargaining, e. g., political lobbying, taking sides in social controversies, and so on, employees are entitled to refunds since compulsory payment would violate their First/Fourteenth Amendment rights of expression and association. How might this ruling have an impact on compulsory membership in student organizations and on mandatory student activity fee programs?

6. Increasingly, the courts have been confronted with suits by homosexual groups demanding the right to function as campus student organizations. That the matter is fraught with controversy is well demonstrated by *Gay Lib v. University of Missouri*, 416 F.Supp. 1350 (W.D.Mo.1976), rev'd, 558 F.2d 848 (8th Cir. 1977). In *Gay Lib* the district court had ruled against recognition of the Gay Lib organization based on testimony by psychiatrists that formal recognition would tend to perpetuate or expand homosexual behavior in violation of the state's sodomy law. In 1976 the U. S. Supreme Court upheld the validity of a sodomy statute of the State of Virginia similar to Missouri's. Said the district court,

> * * * the First Amendment does not require that the University sanction and permit the free association of individuals as a student campus organization where, as the Court now finds from the evidence, that association is likely to incite, promote, and result in acts contrary to and in violation of the sodomy statute of the State of Missouri. The matters of Gay Lib, or for that matter any of those on the school campus who desire to do so, are free to express within the law their beliefs and views of homosexuality and of the Missouri Criminal Statutes on that subject. But it is a far different thing to show a right under the First Amendment to receive official school recognition of Gay Lib with all of the associational conditions that are likely to result therefrom. (At p. 1370).

The Eighth Circuit Court of Appeals in a 2–1 ruling reversed the lower court decision, primarily because no testimony had sufficiently linked the group to illegal acts. Noting that censorship in an academic environment is "hardly the recognition of a healthy democratic society," the Court rejected the testimony of the medical experts as merely speculative. "Even accepting the opinions of defendants' experts at face value, we find it insufficient to justify a governmental prior restraint on the right of a group of students to associate for the purposes avowed in their statement * * *." (At p. 854). Once again, it appears clear that absent illegal *conduct* or a clear intention actually to engage in illegal conduct, the presumption is that recognition cannot be denied. In 1978 the U. S. Supreme Court declined to review the court of appeals' decision. Thus for seven midwestern states under the jurisdiction of the Eighth Circuit Court of Appeals, public postsecondary educational institutions cannot refuse to recognize student homosexual organizations based on their theme alone. Should the ruling be applied to secondary schools as well? To junior high schools? Might the rationale advanced by the school in *Trachtman v. Anker* (see p. 169, *supra*) be successfully employed in support of non-recognition in these educational settings? In his dissenting opinion in *Gay Lib v. University of Missouri,* Circuit Judge Regan argued that campus officials not only relied on expert advice in denying recognition to Gay Lib but also acted out of an obligation to other students: " * * * state university officials have a responsibility * * * to *all* students on campus, and that responsibility encompasses a right to protect latent or potential homosexuals from becoming overt homosexual students." (At p. 859; emphasis in original).

7. Once an organization is recognized, to what extent can educational officials accord it different treatment from other organizations? A case arising at the University of New Hampshire in 1973 raised this question in relation to the sponsorship of a campus dance by the Gay Students Organization. The governor of the state, Meldrim Thompson, Jr., became so incensed over the matter that he wrote an open letter to the University Board of Trustees stating that "indecency and moral filth will no longer be allowed on our campuses" and warning that if "firm, fair, and positive action to rid your campuses of socially abhorrent activities" were not undertaken, he would "stand solidly against the expenditure of one more cent of taxpayers' money for your institution." He added, "I am not interested in legalistic hairsplitting that begs these important issues." *Gay Students Organization v. Bonner,* 367 F.Supp. 1088 (1974) at p. 1092.

Faced with this ultimatum, the president of the university, Thomas N. Bonner, denied to GSO the right to schedule social functions, though other organizational rights were not impaired. GSO brought suit, citing *Healy v. James.*

The university maintained that *Healy* excluded associational rights for purely social functions, such as the dance. From your reading of *Healy,* was the university correct? The district court ruled that the group's associational rights under *Healy* had been abridged. The Federal Court of Appeals for the First Circuit went even farther by noting that the university restriction had also invaded GSO's " 'more traditional First Amendment rights.' "

> * * * The GSO was created, as its Statement of Purpose attests, to promote the free exchange of ideas among homosexuals and between homosexuals and heterosexuals, and to educate the public about bisexuality and homosexuality. GSO claims that social events in which discussion and exchange of ideas can take place in an informal atmosphere can play an important part in this communication. It would seem that these communicative oppor-

tunities are even more important for it than political teas, coffees, and dinners are for political candidates and parties, who have much wider access to the media, being more highly organized and socially accepted. And beyond the specific communications at such events is the basic "message" GSO seeks to convey—that homosexuals exist, that they feel repressed by existing laws and attitudes, that they wish to emerge from their isolation, and that public understanding of their attitudes and problems is desirable for society. 509 F.2d 652 (1974) at p. 661.

University concerns about "grandstanding," possible breach of the peace ordinances, and deviate sexual activity were rejected as irrelevant or speculative.

At the same time, the court of appeals was sensitive to the clash of deeply felt values inherent in the case, to the precarious position of the university caught between the conflicting demands of students and the larger community whose taxes it needs, and to the difficult role of the court.

The underlying question, usually not articulated, is whether, whatever may be Supreme Court precedent in the First Amendment area, group activity promoting values so far beyond the pale of the wider community's values is also beyond the boundaries of the First Amendment, at least to the extent that university facilities may not be used by the group to flaunt its credo. If visceral reactions suggest an affirmative answer, the next task for judges is to devise a standard which, while damping down the First Amendment on a university campus, is generally applicable and free from the dangers of arbitrariness. At this point troubles arise. How are the deeply felt values of the community to be identified? On an issue such as permissive abortion, the wider community may well be divided among those believing in "the right to life", those believing in "the right to control over one's body", and those who do not feel deeply either way. Assuming that "community-wide values" could be confidently identified, and that a university could limit the associational activity of groups challenging those values, such an approach would apply also to socialists, conscientious objectors, vivisectionists, those favoring more oil refineries. As to each group, there are sectors of the community to whom its values are anathema. Or, if values be limited to morals, the barrier would reach those attracted to pre-marital sex, atheism, the consumption of alcoholic beverages, esoteric heterosexual activity, violence on television, or dirty books. This is not to suggest that a university is powerless to proscribe either harmful activity or incitement of illegal activity, but it is to say that we are unable to devise a tolerable standard exempting this case at the threshold from general First Amendment precedents. (At p. 658).

Do you believe the court of appeals took the only principled position in deciding this case? How else might the court have rendered a judgment without relying on its own value position on the issue of homosexuality? What is wrong with deciding the case on a strictly moral basis? Might the court have *forced* the state to maintain its appropriations so that the university would not have to suffer for observing constitutional requirements? Should courts consider taking such action when confronting potentially divisive issues?

Elsewhere in his opinion, Chief Judge Coffin for the 1st Circuit commented that "a university may have some latitude in regulating organizations such as fraternities and sororities which are purely social." (At p. 659). Can you see a distinction? Does *Healy* stand for this proposition?

8. These cases demonstrate a troublesome issue which we have seen before: there appears to be no constitutional requirement that public educational institutions have a recognition policy for student organizations. But once one is instituted, educational officials may exercise discretion only within narrow limits. Do you think *Healy* and its progeny might result in the curtailment of recognition policies at some institutions? If this occurred, what recourse might students have? Could they assert a constitutional right to a recognition policy for student organizations? Any more or less so than for access to outside speakers? Extracurricular activities such as a school newspaper? A mandatory student fee policy? Parades and dances on campus? On-campus solicitation? Why might courts be reluctant to require educational institutions to provide these activities? What distinguishes these activities from the rights of students as seen in *Tinker, Papish, Grayned* and related cases?

VI. SUMMARY

This has been a long chapter. A good deal of material has been explored, beginning with some general remarks about the nature of freedom and the standards of decision making used by members of the Supreme Court in deciding First Amendment issues. Judicial decision making about rights of expression in the political and social setting is a complex and controversial process. Judicial involvement in student freedom of expression matters is complicated by an additional variable, the orientation of the judge to the educational environment. Below, this critical variable has been added to the figure introduced at the start of the chapter to illustrate all of the influences impinging on the judge confronted with a student First Amendment case. Notice how judicial support for student rights can be both positively and negatively influenced by the orientation of the judge to the educational environment. Review some of the cases contained in this chapter and see if you can determine to what extent the court's orientation to the educational setting influenced the decision.

Figure 3–3: Judicial Support for Student Freedom of Expression

DIRECTION OF INFLUENCE

INFLUENCING VARIABLES		Promoting	Retarding	Uncertain
	Value Position on Individual and Government	Support for Social Pluralism	Support for Societal Order	
	Value Position on Freedom	Negative Freedom Some Form of Positive Freedom	Freedom as Necessity (conservative interpretation)	
	Approach to First Amendment	Absolute-Literalist Preferred Position	Balancing Bad Tendency	Time, Place, Manner Clear and Present Danger
	Orientation to Role of Court	Activism	Restraintism	Neutrality
	Orientation to Educational Environment	Youth Entitled to Rights Non-Deferral to Educational Professionals View Educational Mission as: —Marketplace of Ideas —Promote Student Self-Development	Youth Not Entitled to Rights Deferral to Educational Professionals View Educational Mission as: —Inculcate Social Values —Promote Respect for Authority	Role of Social Science Research Rulings of Other Courts Situational Factors: —Type of School —Level of Schooling —Facts of Case

[B9657]

The last twenty years have been a turbulent period in the history of civil liberties in this nation, witnessing major shifts on the speech-action distinction culminating in the *Brandenburg* case, which was an attempt to liberalize the forms of advocacy within the political system. The Supreme Court has struggled to define what constitutes "symbolic speech" in the political and social setting, yet used a symbolic speech case to extend rights of expression to students. Although the freedom of the press has been frequently upheld for students and non-students alike, there exists the unresolved problem of what interests justify some form of prior restraint. In the important area of obscenity regulation, the Supreme Court has been moving toward a decentralized "community" standard with all of its consequent problems. Finally, rights of assembly and association have been regarded as important in the educational world as in society-at-large.

There is by no means a ready consensus on judicial resolution of any of these areas. Nor is there a consensus about using judicial decisions in the political and social setting as precedent for rulings about student rights. Most courts seek to protect student rights, yet at the same time to take into account the dangers of judicial intervention in those educational matters where judicial expertise is limited. The problem, of course, is to differentiate those areas where courts should take an activist approach from those where courts should defer to the educational or political process. Considering the discussion so far, in what areas would you prefer the judiciary play an activist role? In what areas a restraintist role? In future chapters we will return to these questions, for they are basic to the construction of a philosophy about the role of courts in resolving issues of constitutional rights.

Chapter Four

"The First Amendment has erected a wall between church and state. That wall must be kept high and impregnable."

Justice Hugo Black
Everson v. Board of Educ., 1947

"RELIGIOUS FREEDOM"

Issues that relate to the problems of church and state have aroused controversy among the pious and impious alike. The most important source of religious freedom is the First Amendment's provision that "Congress shall make no law respecting an establishment of religion, or prohibiting the free exercise thereof * * *." In effect, these First Amendment provisions include two separate but related issues that will be explored in this chapter: what role should the government play regarding religious and religiously-affiliated organizations (the Establishment Clause) and how much freedom should the government permit in the name of religion (the Free Exercise Clause)?

Taken together, these provisions have meant different things to different people, as the following three examples reveal. In the nineteenth and early twentieth centuries, a Christian consensus prevailed in American society. That consensus was succinctly expressed in 1851 by U. S. Supreme Court Justice Joseph Story:

> Now there will probably be found few persons in this or any other Christian country, who would deliberately contend that it was unreasonable, or unjust to foster and encourage the Christian religion generally, as a matter of sound policy, as well as of revealed truth.[1]

For Justice Story, the Christian religion must be the source of the American public purpose. Without this religious source, our society would not only be ungodly but also without a moral bond of unity.

During the mid-twentieth century, a greater emphasis on religious pluralism and tolerance developed. Professor Leo Pfeffer, a strong advocate of both political and religious pluralism, claims that separation of church and state on the one hand and religious freedom for all on the other were conceived as a unitary principle by the Founders of the Republic. As Pfeffer has noted, "Notwithstanding occasional instances of apparent conflict, separation guarantees freedom, and freedom requires separation." Pfeffer goes on to point out that experiences in other countries illustrate that "religious freedom is most secure where church and state are separated, and least secure where church and state are united."[2] For Pfeffer, "com-

1. Joseph Story, *Commentaries on the Constitution* (Boston: Little, Brown, 1851), Vol. II, at p. 592.

2. Leo Pfeffer, *Church, State, and Freedom* Rev.Ed. (Boston: Beacon Press, 1967), at p. 727.

plete separation of church and state is best for church and best for state, and secures freedom for both." [3]

During the early 1960s, Dr. Timothy Leary of Harvard University was performing experiments on the effects of ingesting LSD. Leary was particularly intrigued by the religious images prison inmates used in describing an LSD experience. Leary rapidly became an advocate of using LSD so that it might help him understand why his prison subjects talked so frequently about "heaven and hell" or "seeing God" or "being born again" after using the drug.[4] By the late 1960s Leary claimed the right to use LSD as an integral part of his religious freedom and the ritual of his church, the League for Spiritual Discovery.

Note how very different these views about the religion clauses are. For Justice Story freedom of religion means the freedom to foster Christianity. For Professor Pfeffer freedom of religion means the freedom from state coercion of religious belief and the importance of religious diversity in a free society. For Dr. Timothy Leary it means the right to use such ritualistic practices as the ingestion of LSD if one is to effectively express one's spiritual needs. These three competing images reveal a continuing controversy as to what constitutes "religion", what are legitimate forms of religious expression, and what the role of the government should be with respect to the religion clauses.

Most of the cases involving the Establishment Clause and many involving the Free Exercise Clause have involved public and private educational institutions. This is not surprising, given the natural ties most Americans have historically seen uniting family, church, and school. The first federal act to aid education, the 1787 Northwest Ordinance, stated that "Religion, morality, and knowledge being essential to good government and the happiness of mankind, schools and the means of education shall forever be encouraged." For many years such practices as Bible reading, prayer, and the observance of religious events through assemblies, plays, and religiously-oriented curricula were part of public school operation. These components of the program were thought to assist in good moral development, just as patriotic exercises were considered good preparation for citizenship. It wasn't until comparatively recently that these practices and others like them were challenged.

A review of recently decided cases will show that challenges to school policy based on the religion clauses continue. Efforts to accommodate the religious character of our society in the public schools or through aid to non-public educational institutions inevitably trigger suits based on the Establishment Clause, while compulsory school attendance, curriculum requirements, and the like prompt challenges based on the Free Exercise Clause. This chapter focuses first on the Establishment Clause.

---

3. *Id.*, at p. 728.

4. See Milton R. Konvitz, *Religious Liberty and Conscience: A Constitutional Inquiry* (New York: Viking Press, 1969), at pp. 62–68.

I. GOVERNMENT AND THE ESTABLISHMENT OF RELIGION

Great numbers of colonists coming to America sought refuge from religious persecution experienced elsewhere. Most sought escape from the Anglican church establishment in England. This was particularly the case with the Puritans and Congregationalists of New England and the Quakers of Pennsylvania.

It is important to recall as well that many other colonists were persecuted for their religious beliefs in colonial America. Baptists and New England Presbyterians found themselves protesting alliances between the colonial governors and the powerful local Anglicans and Congregationalists. The major American constitutional value of the separation of church and state grew out of this purely American religious conflict. Many religious groups during the revolutionary era simply contended that one could not protest unjust British exercise of religious power while some Americans exercised power on similar grounds over other Americans. A consensus was eventually formed during the years immediately preceding the writing of the Constitution to the effect that only liberty of conscience for all religions would provide genuine freedom for any one religion. This meant strict separation of church and state.

Even though many of the colonists became great supporters of the church-state separation principle, one should remember that the phrase itself is not found in the Constitution. The historic nature of that separation is a major part of the continuing public and constitutional controversy over religion in America. John Cotton, the great supporter of Puritanism, was a supporter of an established church in America. Roger Williams, the pious clergyman, was totally opposed to a state-supported church. Thomas Jefferson advocated strict separation between church and state. Speaking to a group of Baptists in Danbury, Connecticut, in 1802, Jefferson argued pointedly that the First Amendment erected "a wall of separation between Church and State." [5] The nation continues to debate the meaning of Jefferson's "wall" metaphor, which finds its way into the early cases dealing with the Establishment Clause.

The First Amendment begins with the statement, "Congress shall make no law respecting an establishment of religion * * *." Since the statement appears so prominently in the Amendment, it points out citizen opposition to a national church as found in many of the countries from which the colonists had come. Most authorities also agree that, given the diversity of religions in America, the prohibition was meant to keep government from preferring one religion over another by preventing Congress from advancing the cause of any religion. This seems apparent from the adjective "an" appearing before "establishment."

In effect, the First Amendment appears to erect Thomas Jefferson's "wall of separation" between church and the federal government. Once the Establishment Clause was carried over to apply to the states through the word "liberty" of the Fourteenth Amendment in the *Everson* case,

---

5. Cited in Ellis Sandoz, *Conceived in Liberty: American Individual Rights Today* (North Scituate, Mass.: Duxbury Press, 1978), at p. 121.

which is excerpted below, that same prohibition applied to state and local governments. For reasons already discussed, it applies as well to public educational officials.

The problem with the wall of separation concept, however, is that such a strict interpretation would thwart the intention of the Free Exercise Clause. By being hostile to religious activity, the government may intrude on the right of individuals to practice their religion. Such might be the case, for example, if the government eliminated tax exemptions for churches and religious schools and, as a result, many close. On the other hand, by acccommodating religious beliefs or by fostering one belief over another, government may violate the Establishment Clause, as, for example, when a school district employs members of the clergy to teach religion in the schools or requires that only the Biblical view of Creation be taught in science courses. In short, the two religion clauses are in a state of dynamic tension. That tension is well demonstrated by the early cases involving the Establishment Clause.

A. Background: A Wall of Separation Versus Government Neutrality

The first case in which the U. S. Supreme Court interpreted the Establishment Clause as applied to the educational setting was *Everson v. Board of Educ.*, 330 U.S. 1 (1947). This is the famous "wall of separation" case. Since curriculum challenges figure so prominently in the Establishment Clause cases, the second case included in this section is *Epperson v. Arkansas*, 393 U.S. 97 (1968), which struck down the practice of teaching only the Biblical view of the origin of man.

EVERSON v. BOARD OF EDUC.

Supreme Court of the United States, 1947.
330 U.S. 1, 67 S.Ct. 504, 91 L.Ed. 711.

Mr. Justice BLACK delivered the opinion of the Court.

A New Jersey statute authorizes its local school districts to make rules and contracts for the transportation of children to and from schools.[1] The appellee, a township board of education, acting pursuant to this statute authorized reimbursement to parents of money expended by them for the bus transportation of their children on regular busses operated by the public transportation system. Part of this money was for the payment of transportation of some children in the community to Catholic parochial schools. These church schools give their students, in addition to secular education, regular religious instruction conforming to the religious tenets and modes of worship of the Catholic Faith. The superintendent of these schools is a Catholic priest.

---

1. "Whenever in any district there are children living remote from any schoolhouse, the board of education of the district may make rules and contracts for the transportation of such children to and from school, including the transportation of school children to and from school other than a public school, except such school as is operated for profit in whole or in part.
"When any school district provides any transportation for public school children to and from school, transportation from any point in such established school route to any other point in such established school route shall be supplied to school children residing in such school district in going to and from school other than a public school, except such school as is operated for profit in whole or in part."

The appellant, in his capacity as a district taxpayer, filed suit in a State court challenging the right of the Board to reimburse parents of parochial school students. He contended that the statute and the resolution passed pursuant to it violated both the State and the Federal Constitutions. That court held that the legislature was without power to authorize such payment under the State constitution. The New Jersey Court of Errors and Appeals reversed, holding that neither the statute nor the resolution passed pursuant to it was in conflict with the State constitution or the provisions of the Federal Constitution in issue. The case is here on appeal. * * *

* * *

Since there has been no attack on the statute on the ground that a part of its language excludes children attending private schools operated for profit from enjoying state payment for their transportation, we need not consider this exclusionary language; it has no relevancy to any constitutional question here presented.[2]

* * *

* * *

* * * The New Jersey statute is challenged as a "law respecting an establishment of religion." The First Amendment, as made applicable to the states by the Fourteenth, commands that a state "shall make no law respecting an establishment of religion, or prohibiting the free exercise thereof." These words of the First Amendment reflected in the minds of early Americans a vivid mental picture of conditions and practices which they fervently wished to stamp out in order to preserve liberty for themselves and for their posterity. Doubtless their goal

has not been entirely reached; but so far has the Nation moved toward it that the expression "law respecting an establishment of religion," probably does not so vividly remind present-day Americans of the evils, fears, and political problems that caused that expression to be written into our Bill of Rights. Whether this New Jersey law is one respecting the "establishment of religion" requires an understanding of the meaning of that language, particularly with respect to the imposition of taxes. Once again, therefore, it is not inappropriate briefly to review the background and environment of the period in which that constitutional language was fashioned and adopted.

[Historical Review]

* * *

The "establishment of religion" clause of the First Amendment means at least this: Neither a state nor the Federal Government can set up a church. Neither can pass laws which aid one religion, aid all religions, or prefer one religion over another. Neither can force nor influence a person to go to or to remain away from church against his will or force him to profess a belief or disbelief in any religion. No person can be punished for entertaining or professing religious beliefs or disbeliefs, for church attendance or non-attendance. No tax in any amount, large or small, can be levied to support any religious activities or institutions, whatever they may be called, or whatever form they may adopt to teach or practice religion. Neither a state nor the Federal Government can, openly or secretly, participate in the affairs of any religious organizations or groups and vice

---

2. * * * Although the township resolution authorized reimbursement only for parents of public and Catholic school pupils, appellant does not allege, nor is there anything in the record which would offer the slightest support to an allegation, that there were any children in the township who attended or would have attended, but for want of transportation, any but public and Catholic schools. It will be appropriate to consider the exclusion of students of private schools operated for profit when and if it is proved to have occurred, is made the basis of a suit by one in a position to challenge it, and New Jersey's highest court has ruled adversely to the challenger. * * *

versa. In the words of Jefferson, the clause against establishment of religion by law was intended to erect "a wall of separation between Church and State."

We must consider the New Jersey statute in accordance with the foregoing limitations imposed by the First Amendment. But we must not strike that state statute down if it is within the state's constitutional power even though it approaches the verge of that power. New Jersey cannot consistently with the "establishment of religion" clause of the First Amendment contribute tax-raised funds to the support of an institution which teaches the tenets and faith of any church. On the other hand, other language of the amendment commands that New Jersey cannot hamper its citizens in the free exercise of their own religion. Consequently, it cannot exclude individual Catholics, Lutherans, Mohammedans, Baptists, Jews, Methodists, Non-believers, Presbyterians, or the members of any other faith, *because of their faith, or lack of it,* from receiving the benefits of public welfare legislation. While we do not mean to intimate that a state could not provide transportation only to children attending public schools, we must be careful, in protecting the citizens of New Jersey against state-established churches, to be sure that we do not inadvertently prohibit New Jersey from extending its general State law benefits to all its citizens without regard to their religious belief.

Measured by these standards, we cannot say that the First Amendment prohibits New Jersey from spending tax-raised funds to pay the bus fares of parochial school pupils as a part of a general program under which it pays the fares of pupils attending public and other schools. It is undoubtedly true that children are helped to get to church schools. There is even a possibility that some of the children might not be sent to the church schools if the parents were compelled to pay their children's bus fares out of their own pockets when transportation to a public school would have been paid for by the State. The same possibility exists where the state requires a local transit company to provide reduced fares to school children including those attending parochial schools, or where a municipally owned transportation system undertakes to carry all school children free of charge. Moreover, state-paid policemen, detailed to protect children going to and from church schools from the very real hazards of traffic, would serve much the same purpose and accomplish much the same result as state provisions intended to guarantee free transportation of a kind which the state deems to be best for the school children's welfare. And parents might refuse to risk their children to the serious danger of traffic accidents going to and from parochial schools, the approaches to which were not protected by policemen. Similarly, parents might be reluctant to permit their children to attend schools which the state had cut off from such general government services as ordinary police and fire protection, connections for sewage disposal, public highways and sidewalks. Of course, cutting off church schools from these services, so separate and so indisputably marked off from the religious function, would make it far more difficult for the schools to operate. But such is obviously not the purpose of the First Amendment. That Amendment requires the state to be a neutral in its relations with groups of religious believers and non-believers; it does not require the state to be their adversary. State power is no more to be used so as to handicap religions, than it is to favor them.

This Court has said that parents may, in the discharge of their duty under state compulsory education laws, send their children to a religious rather than a public school if the school meets the secular educational requirements which the state has power to impose. See Pierce v. Society of Sisters. It appears that these parochial schools meet New Jersey's requirements. The State contributes no money to the schools. It does not support them. Its legislation, as applied, does no more than provide a general program to help parents get their children, regardless of their religion, safely and expeditiously to and from accredited schools.

The First Amendment has erected a wall between church and state. That wall must be kept high and impregnable. We could not approve the slightest breach. New Jersey has not breached it here.

Affirmed.

Mr. Justice JACKSON, dissenting.

I find myself, contrary to first impressions, unable to join in this decision. I have a sympathy, though it is not ideological, with Catholic citizens who are compelled by law to pay taxes for public schools, and also feel constrained by conscience and discipline to support other schools for their own children. * * * The Court's opinion marshals every argument in favor of state aid and puts the case in its most favorable light, but much of its reasoning confirms my conclusions that there are no good grounds upon which to support the present legislation. In fact, the undertones of the opinion, advocating complete and uncompromising separation of Church from State, seem utterly discordant with its conclusion yielding support to their commingling in educational matters. The case which irresistibly comes to mind as the most fitting precedent is that of Julia, who, according to Byron's reports, "whispering 'I will ne'er consent,'—consented."

I.

The Court sustains this legislation by assuming two deviations from the facts of this particular case; first, it assumes a state of facts the record does not support, and secondly, it refuses to consider facts which are inescapable on the record.

The Court concludes that this "legislation, as applied, does no more than provide a general program to help parents get their children, regardless of their religion, safely and expeditiously to and from accredited schools," and it draws a comparison between "state provisions intended to guarantee free transportation" for school children with services such as police and fire protection, and implies that we are here dealing with "laws authorizing new types of public services * * *" This hypothesis permeates the opinion. The facts will not bear that construction.

The Township of Ewing is not furnishing transportation to the children in any form; it is not operating school busses itself or contracting for their operation; and it is not performing any public service of any kind with this taxpayer's money. All school children are left to ride as ordinary paying passengers on the regular busses operated by the public transportation system. What the Township does, and what the taxpayer complains of, is at stated intervals to reimburse parents for the fares paid, provided the children attend either public schools or Catholic Church schools. This expenditure of tax funds has no possible effect on the child's safety or expedition in transit. As passengers on the public busses they travel as fast and no faster, and are as safe and no safer, since their parents are reimbursed as before.

In addition to thus assuming a type of service that does not exist, the Court also insists that we must close our eyes to a discrimination which does exist. The resolution which authorizes disbursement of this taxpayer's money limits reimbursement to those who attend public schools and Catholic schools. That is the way the Act is applied to this taxpayer.

* * *

If we are to decide this case on the facts before us, our question is simply this: Is it constitutional to tax this complainant to pay the cost of carrying pupils to Church schools of one specified denomination?

II.

* * *

The function of the Church school is a subject on which this record is meager. It shows only that the schools are under superintendence of a priest and that "religion is taught as part of the curriculum." But we know that such schools are parochial only in name—they, in fact, represent a world-wide and age-old policy of the Roman Catholic Church. * * *

It is no exaggeration to say that the whole historic conflict in temporal policy between the Catholic Church and non-Catholics comes to a focus in their respective school policies. The Roman Catholic Church, counseled by experience in many ages and many lands and with all sorts and conditions of men, takes what, from the viewpoint of its own progress and the success of its mission, is a wise estimate of the importance of education to religion. It does not leave the individual to pick up religion by chance. It relies on early and indelible indoctrination in the faith and order of the Church by the word and example of persons consecrated to the task.

[Our public school] * * * is organized on the premise that secular education can be isolated from all religious teaching so that the school can inculcate all needed temporal knowledge and also maintain a strict and lofty neutrality as to religion. The assumption is that after the individual has been instructed in worldly wisdom he will be better fitted to choose his religion. * * *

I should be surprised if any Catholic would deny that the parochial school is a vital, if not the most vital, part of the Roman Catholic Church. If put to the choice, that venerable institution, I should expect, would forego its whole service for mature persons before it would give up education of the young, and it would be a wise choice. Its growth and cohesion, discipline and loyalty, spring from its schools. Catholic education is the rock on which the whole structure rests, and to render tax aid to its Church school is indistinguishable to me from rendering the same aid to the Church itself.

III.

It is of no importance in this situation whether the beneficiary of this expenditure of tax-raised funds is primarily the parochial school and incidentally the pupil, or whether the aid is directly bestowed on the pupil with indirect benefits to the school. The state cannot maintain a Church and it can no more tax its citizens to furnish free carriage to those who attend a Church. The prohibition against establishment of religion cannot be circumvented by a subsidy, bonus or reimbursement of expense to individuals for receiving religious instruction and indoctrination.

* * *

It seems to me that the basic fallacy in the Court's reasoning, which accounts for its failure to apply the principles it avows, is in ignoring the essentially religious test by which beneficiaries of this expenditure are selected. A policeman protects a Catholic, of course—but not because he is a Catholic; it is because he is a man and a member of our society. The fireman protects the Church school —but not because it is a Church school; it is because it is property, part of the assets of our society. Neither the fireman nor the policeman has to ask before he renders aid "Is this man or building identified with the Catholic Church." But before these school authorities draw a check to reimburse for a student's fare they must ask just that question, and if the school is a Catholic one they may render aid because it is such, while if it is of any other faith or is run for profit, the help must be withheld. To consider the converse of the Court's reasoning will best disclose its fallacy. That there is no parallel between police and fire protection and this plan of reimbursement is apparent from the incongruity of the limitation of this Act if applied to police and fire service. Could we sustain an Act that said police shall protect pupils on the way to or from public schools and Catholic schools but not while going to and coming from other schools, and firemen shall extinguish a blaze in public or Catholic school buildings but shall not put out a blaze in Protestant Church schools or private schools operated for profit? That is the true analogy to the case we have before us and I should think it pretty plain that such a scheme would not be valid.

* * *

Mr. Justice FRANKFURTER joins in this opinion.

Mr. Justice RUTLEDGE, with whom Mr. Justice FRANKFURTER, Mr. Justice JACKSON and Mr. Justice BURTON agree, dissenting.

* * *

"Well aware that Almighty God hath created the mind free; * * * that to compel a man to furnish contributions of money for the propagation of opinions which he disbelieves, is sinful and tyrannical; * * *

"We, the General Assembly, do enact, That no man shall be compelled to frequent or support any religious worship, place, or ministry whatsoever, nor shall be enforced, restrained, molested, or burthened in his body or goods, nor shall otherwise suffer on account of his religious opinions or belief. * * * " 1

I cannot believe that the great author of those words, or the men who made

them law, could have joined in this decision. Neither so high nor so impregnable today as yesterday is the wall raised between church and state by Virginia's great statute of religious freedom and the First Amendment, now made applicable to all the states by the Fourteenth. * * *

* * *

Does New Jersey's action furnish support for religion by use of the taxing power? Certainly it does, if the test remains undiluted as Jefferson and Madison made it, that money taken by taxation from one is not to be used or given to support another's religious training or belief, or indeed one's own. * * *

* * * Here parents pay money to sent their children to parochial schools and funds raised by taxation are used to reimburse them. This not only helps the children to get to school and the parents to send them. It aids them in a substantial way to get the very thing which they are sent to the particular school to secure, namely, religious training and teaching.

* * *

New Jersey's action therefore exactly fits the type of exaction and the kind of evil at which Madison and Jefferson struck. Under the test they framed it cannot be said that the cost of transportation is no part of the cost of education or of the religious instruction given. That it is a substantial and a necessary element is shown most plainly by the continuing and increasing demand for the state to assume it. Nor is there pretense that it relates only to the secular instruction given in religious schools or that any attempt is or could be made toward allocating proportional shares as between the secular and the religious instruction. It is precisely because the instruction is religious and relates to a particular faith, whether one or another, that parents send their children to religious schools under the Pierce doctrine. And the very purpose

---

1. "A Bill for Establishing Religious Freedom," enacted by the General Assembly of Virginia, January 19, 1786.

of the state's contribution is to defray the cost of conveying the pupil to the place where he will receive not simply secular, but also and primarily religious teaching and guidance.

Yet this very admixture is what was disestablished when the First Amendment forbade "an establishment of religion." Commingling the religious with the secular teaching does not divest the whole of its religious permeation and emphasis or make them of minor part, if proportion were material. Indeed, on any other view, the constitutional prohibition always could be brought to naught by adding a modicum of the secular.

* * *

* * * transportation, where it is needed, is as essential to education as any other element. Its cost is as much a part of the total expense, except at times in amount, as the cost of textbooks, of school lunches, of athletic equipment, of writing and other materials; indeed of all other posing the total burden. * * *

* * *

For me, therefore the feat is impossible to select so indispensable an item from the composite of total costs, and characterize it as not aiding, contributing to, promoting or sustaining the propagation of beliefs which it is the very end of all to bring about. * * * Payment of transportation is no more, nor is it any the less essential to education, whether religious or secular, than payment for tuitions, for teachers' salaries, for buildings, equipment and necessary materials. Nor is it any the less directly related, in a school giving religious instruction, to the primary religious objective all those essential items of cost are intended to achieve. No rational line can be drawn between payment for such larger, but not more necessary, items and payment for transportation. The only line that can be so drawn is one between more dollars and less. Certainly in this realm such a

line can be no valid constitutional measure.

* * *

[Our constitutional policy] * * * does not deny the value or the necessity for religious training, teaching or observance. Rather it secures their free exercise. But to that end it does deny that the state can undertake or sustain them in any form or degree. For this reason the sphere of religious activity, as distinguished from the secular intellectual liberties, has been given the twofold protection and, as the state cannot forbid, neither can it perform or aid in performing the religious function. The dual prohibition makes that function altogether private. It cannot be made a public one by legislative act. * * *

* * *

That policy necessarily entails hardship upon persons who forego the right to educational advantages the state can supply in order to secure others it is precluded from giving. Indeed this may hamper the parent and the child forced by conscience to that choice. But it does not make the state unneutral to withhold what the Constitution forbids it to give. On the contrary it is only by observing the prohibition rigidly that the state can maintain its neutrality and avoid partisanship in the dissensions inevitable when sect opposes sect over demands for public moneys to further religious education, teaching or training in any form or degree, directly or indirectly. * * *

The problem then cannot be cast in terms of legal discrimination or its absence. This would be true, even though the state in giving aid should treat all religious instruction alike. Thus, if the present statute and its application were shown to apply equally to all religious schools of whatever faith, yet in the light of our tradition it could not stand. For then the adherent of one creed still would pay for the support of another, the childless taxpayer with others more fortunate. Then too there would seem to be no bar to making appropriations for transportation and other expenses of children attending public or other secular schools, after hours in separate places and classes for their exclusively religious instruction. The person who embraces no creed also would be forced to pay for teaching what he does not believe. Again, it was the furnishing of "contri-butions of money for the propagation of opinions which he disbelieves" that the fathers outlawed. That consequence and effect are not removed by multiplying to all-inclusiveness the sects for which support is exacted. The Constitution requires, not comprehensive identification of state with religion, but complete separation.

* * *

NOTES AND QUESTIONS

1. Note that Justice Black confines his majority opinion to the relatively narrow grounds on which the taxpayer challenged the payment of funds. He specifically refuses to consider the exclusion of profit-making private schools from the terms of the statute. He also sets aside consideration of whether other religious groups besides Catholics are able to receive tranportation repayments. These larger questions, however, play a prominent role in the dissents, particularly the one by Justice Jackson. The different approaches illustrate how judges view the role of the judiciary. (Recall our discussion of judicial activism, neutralism, and self-restraint.)

Justice Black argues that the wall of separation "must be kept high and impregnable." Yet in the end he approves the transportation reimbursement program as part of a general program designed to get children safely to and from public and state-approved parochial schools. Such a program, he maintains, is basically *neutral* toward religion; failure to provide the transportation "would make it far more difficult for the schools to operate." He cautions that the First Amendment "does not require the state to be their adversary." If the state were to refuse such payments, would the state still be neutral or would the state now be denying the free exercise of religion to the Catholic children and parents?

Justice Jackson makes a point of noting that the township does not operate school buses. Thus, the payments are not in the form of a public service like police and fire protection. Safety is not a factor since, presumably, if the state did not underwrite the transportation cost, many parents would still use public transportation. Does his argument undermine those of the majority on this point? What about his comments regarding the nature of the parochial schools? Does the fact that these schools are approved by the state as alternatives to the public schools acknowledge that they perform some secular service? As schools, are these institutions less religious in character than churches? Assuming schools perform a greater public function than churches, should they be entitled to greater state assistance? How does Justice Rutledge counter this theory?

Having read the opinions in this narrowly decided (5–4) and important case, which most nearly reflects your own? What values weigh most heavily in your decision?

Note that while the Court permitted state reimbursement of bus transportation for students attending sectarian schools, it did not *require* states to provide such service. Even assuming a state wished to provide such a program, its constitution may prohibit it. Thus, for example, the State of Washington Supreme Court ruled two years after *Everson* that a state statute providing transportation to students attending sectarian schools, as well as to those attending public schools, was unconstitutional under the state constitution. *Visser v. Nooksack Valley School Dist.*, 207 P.2d 198 (Washington, 1949). A clause in that document provided that no money or property shall be appropriated for the support of any religious establishment. The plaintiffs, who had sued a local school board for funds pursuant to the statute, relied on *Everson* in support of their claims. The Washington court, however, noted that *Everson* pertained only to the First Amendment and had no bearing on the state constitution. The high state court then declined to follow the *Everson* rationale in construing the state constitutional provision.

2. A year later in *McCollum v. Board of Educ.*, 333 U.S. 203, Justice Black for the majority invalidated a release time program whereby religious instruction was given to students on a voluntary basis in the public schools. The Court concluded that the use of public school classrooms to conduct the program during school hours was an impermissible advancement of religion since it provided "sectarian groups an invaluable aid in that it helps to provide pupils for their religious classes through use of the state's compulsory public school machinery." (At p. 212).

However, four years later in *Zorach v. Clauson*, 343 U.S. 306, the Court sanctioned a New York program that allowed students interested in religious instruction to leave school early so that they could receive religious instruction at off-campus centers. Wrote Justice Douglas for the majority,

> [w]e are a religious people whose institutions presuppose a Supreme Being. We guarantee the freedom to worship as one chooses. We make room for as wide a variety of beliefs and creeds as the spiritual needs of man deem necessary. We sponsor an attitude on the part of government that shows no partiality to any one group and that lets each flourish according to the zeal of its adherents and the appeal of its dogma. When the state encourages religious instruction or cooperates with religious authorities by adjusting the schedule of public events to sectarian needs, it follows the best of our traditions. For it then respects the religious nature of our people and accommodates the public service to their spiritual needs. (At pp. 313–314).

The students had to have written consent from their parents. Periodically, the churches notified the schools of those who did not show up for the religious instruction. Justice Black wrote the *McCollum* decision but dissented in *Zorach*. Can you see any fundamental differences in these two cases? From the standpoint of the student who chooses not to partake of religious instruction, is the state accommodation of religious interests any less onerous in one case than the other? Which is most in line with the reasoning in *Everson*?

3. *Everson* answered the question about underwriting the cost of bus transportation for students attending religious schools. What about state programs providing books to students in these schools? This was the issue in *Board of Educ. v. Allen*, 392 U.S. 236 (1968). In this case the Court upheld a New York statute requiring local school districts to lend textbooks without charge to all children in grades seven through twelve enrolled in both public and nonpublic state-approved schools. A local school board challenged the law because it included parochial school children among those eligible for the textbook loans.

In this case both Justices Black and Douglas dissented, along with Justice Fortas. Justice Black asserted that books could be easily distinguished from bus fares. Do you agree? Justice Black saw this law the result of strong lobbying efforts by religious groups and predicted that the Court would soon be seeing laws passed to provide funds to religious schools to purchase property on which to build schools, to construct the schools themselves, and pay the teachers' salaries. He concluded that "The First Amendment's prohibition against governmental establishment of religion was written on the assumption that state aid to religion and religious schools generates discord, disharmony, hatred, and strife among our people, and that any government that supplies such aids is to that extent a tyranny." (At p. 254). Justice Black blamed the majority decision in *Allen* for setting in motion such a parade of horribles; to what extent might his own decision in *Everson* be responsible?

Justice White for the majority noted that the law was designed to benefit all school children, regardless of the school they attend. The law thus has a secular purpose. Since the books are only loaned to the children and since only state-approved books are involved, the program is designed to benefit only the secular component of the education provided by religious schools. Noting the value of nonpublic education "in raising national levels of knowledge, competence, and experience," Justice White concluded that "we cannot agree with appellants either that all teaching in a sectarian school is religious or that the processes of secular and religious training are so intertwined that secular textbooks furnished to students by the public are in fact instrumental in the teaching of religion." (At p. 248).

Justice Douglas, however, found the textbook loan program less pristine. He noted that the statute empowers parochial school personnel initially to select the texts they wish to have loaned, with the school board passing on the acceptability of the requests. "Can there be the slightest doubt," he asked, "that the head of the parochial school will select the book or books that best promote its sectarian creed?" If the school board should resist approving the books requested, "then the battle line between church and state will have been drawn and the contest will be on to keep the school board independent or to put it under church domination and control." (At p. 256).

In his dissent Justice Fortas stressed the different treatment accorded nonpublic schools. "This statute calls for furnishing special, separate, and particular books, specifically, separately, and particularly chosen by

religious sects or their representatives for use in their sectarian schools."
(At p. 271).

Based on the views expressed in *Allen*, is this decision a logical extension of the *Everson* case or rather a significant departure? Can the line
between permissible and impermissible aid to religious schools be easily
drawn after *Allen*? Any more so than after *Everson*?

4. The "wall of separation" approach is most evident where purely
religious activities involving the public schools are involved. Two cases
stand out in this area, both very unpopular with the general public when
announced. Much of that unpopularity continues. In *Engel v. Vitale*, 370
U.S. 421 (1962), Justice Black for the majority overturned a theoretically
non-denominational prayer prepared by the State Board of Regents for
use in New York State public schools. The prayer read: "Almighty
God, we acknowledge our dependence upon Thee, and we beg Thy blessings
upon us, our parents, our teachers, and our Country." The prayer, concluded Justice Black, even though denominationally neutral, was contrary
to the thrust of the Establishment Clause. " * * * (W)e think that
the constitutional prohibition against laws respecting an establishment of
religion must at least mean that in this country it is no part of the business
of government to compose official prayers for any group of the American
people to recite as a part of the religious program carried on by government." (At p. 425).

Do you think it would make any difference if the prayer were voluntary? The New York Court of Appeals concluded that it would, agreeing with the trial court that the prayer was constitutional as long as the
Board of Education set up some procedure whereby those who objected
to reciting the prayer could be excused. Justice Black, however, disagreed,
stating that the Establishment Clause is violated whether or not coercion
is present, since the government-sponsored prayer exerts "an indirect
coercive" force on religious minorities and nonbelievers.

Justice Stewart in dissent argued that the decision ignored the spir-
itual traditions and heritage of the the country. He questioned the im-
plications of the decision for such government-sponsored activities as the
opening of the House and Senate sessions with prayer, the printing of
"In God We Trust" on coins, the payment of the salaries of the official
Chaplains of Congress and the military, and the singing of stanzas of "The
Star-Spangled Banner." He pointed out that even the sessions of the
Supreme Court open with the words, "God save the United States and this
Honorable Court." Does *Engel* imply that these activities constitute an
impermissible government assistance to religion? In a footnote Justice
Black responded:

> There is of course nothing in the decision reached here that is
> inconsistent with the fact that school children and others are of-
> ficially encouraged to express love for our country by reciting
> historical documents such as the Declaration of Independence
> which contain references to the Deity or by singing officially
> espoused anthems which include the composer's professions of
> faith in a Supreme Being, or with the fact that there are many

manifestations in our public life of belief in God. Such patriotic or ceremonial occasions bear no true resemblance to the unquestioned religious exercise that the State of New York has sponsored in this instance. (Footnote 21 at p. 435).

Can you see the distinction? It was less clear to Justice Stewart, who used a footnote himself to counter with the question, "is the Court suggesting that the Constitution permits judges and Congressmen and Presidents to join in prayer, but prohibits school children from doing so?" (Footnote 19 at p. 450).

5.   One year later in *School Dist. of Abington v. Schempp*, 374 U.S. 203, the Court held that state laws and practices requiring selection and reading of passages from the Holy Bible and recitation of the Lord's Prayer were unconstitutional for reasons similar to those advanced in *Engel*. But in this case Justice Clark for the majority sought to articulate the criteria for judging Establishment cases. The government must be neutral, he maintained, and in order to determine if government is neutral, two questions must be asked:

1.   What is the purpose of the challenged law?

2.   What is the primary effect of the law?

If the purpose or the primary effect is to aid or inhibit religion, the government is not neutral. Thus, to be constitutional under the Establishment Clause, "there must be a secular legislative purpose and a primary effect that neither advances nor inhibits religion." (At p. 222). Justice Clark added that the Free Exercise Clause

> withdraws from legislative power, state and federal, the exertion of any restraint on the free exercise of religion. Its purpose is to secure religious liberty in the individual by prohibiting any invasions thereof by civil authority. Hence it is necessary in a free exercise case for one to show the coercive effect of the enactment as it operates against him in the practice of his religion. The distinction between the two clauses is apparent—a violation of the Free Exercise Clause is predicated on coercion while the Establishment Clause violation need not be so attended. (At pp. 222 and 223).

Justice Clark then applied the Establishment criteria to previous cases, reconfirming all the decisions. Would you agree insofar as the cases above are concerned?

In a long concurring opinion Justice Brennan explored at length the history of the two religion clauses and concluded that "not every involvement of religion in public life is unconstitutional." He explored a number of situations involving the two religion clauses, noting that certain types of cases raise no constitutional questions. He cited, as one example, government provision of chaplains and places of worship for prisoners and military personnel. Refusal to accommodate the need of these persons to express their religious beliefs, he wrote, would constitute government hostility to religion, not neutrality. He also noted that there are numerous activities which may have been religious in origin but which nave ceased to have religious meaning, such as the patriotic exercises described by Justice Stewart in his *Engel* dissent. These cases raise no serious constitutional question under the Establishment Clause.

Justice Stewart, again in dissent, was concerned about the infringement the *School Dist. of Abington v. Schempp* decision would have on free exercise rights. "(T)here is involved in these cases a substantial free exercise claim on the part of those who affirmatively desire to have their children's school day open with the reading of passages from the Bible." (At p. 312). For Justice Stewart the critical factor under the Establishment Clause is the element of coercion. "In the absence of coercion upon those who do not wish to participate—because they hold less strong beliefs, other beliefs, or no beliefs at all—such provisions cannot, in my view, be held to represent the type of support of religion barred by the Establishment Clause." (At p. 316). Would you agree that if exemptions for those who do not wish to participate are provided, no element of coercion exists? If you are one of three third grade students out of thirty to leave the classroom every day when Bible-reading is to be conducted, would you feel any degree of government coercion? Should the Court rule differently depending upon the age and grade level of the students involved?

Despite the fact that Justice Clark pointed out that the *Schempp* decision did not jeopardize the study of religion including the Bible when part of a secular curricular program, much of the criticism of the Court's decision assumed that it did. Numerous constitutional amendments were proposed immediately after the decision and for some time thereafter to restore Bible reading and other religious exercises to the public school curriculum. None has been successful. Efforts in this direction continue today, albeit on a diminished scale.

6. Consider the following hypothetical case:

HYPOTHETICAL: *The Case of the Bells*

It was the first week of December at West Thumper State College. Snow was on the ground and the holiday spirit seemed to settle on the village of West Thumper and the college. Students hurried to and from classes in the crisp, cold air, hardly noticing any change in college routine.

But Sam Goldstein, an Orthodox Jew, noticed. So did Ima Atheist, who vigorously opposes all religions. They knew, along with several others on the campus, that the chimes signalling the passing of the hours at West Thumper were playing different songs at noon. Usually the chimes strike the noon hour, then for ten minutes play the school song, or, on special occasions, a patriotic melody, school "fight" song, or semi-classical music.

But today the chimes were playing Christmas carols. Sam and Ima listened at opposite sides of the campus as the chimes rang out "Silent Night," "Oh Little Town of Bethlehem," and similar Christian carols. Non-Christian and secular carols were not included as part of the program. Sam and Ima objected. They both hurried to the administration building, determined to make their views known.

The dean of students could hardly believe anyone at West Thumper could be opposed to Christmas carols. He questioned Sam and Ima about their opposition. Sam and Ima, who arrived at the same time in the dean's office, argued that the college as a state institution should not proselytize the Christian faith. Ima added, "The college shouldn't be in the business of pushing religion—any religion. I think it is even illegal."

The dean listened to the two, then said, shaking his head, "But Dr. Smith has played those same carols at noon for the college for almost forty years at Christmas." He added, "This is a revered tradition at West Thumper."

But Sam and Ima were adamant. "Times have changed," they said. The dean, realizing that higher authority would have to decide the matter, asked Sam and Ima to see the college president.

The president listened briefly to Sam and Ima. Then, noticing the time, said, "I have an appointment across campus. Please return tomorrow and be prepared to present your views in depth." He also asked the college's legal counsel to be present to present the institution's side.

Based on previous discussion and cases, what arguments would you make for each side? If you were to decide this hypothetical case what decision would you reach?

EPPERSON v. STATE OF ARKANSAS

Supreme Court of the United States, 1968.
393 U.S. 97, 89 S.Ct. 266, 21 L.Ed.2d 228.

Mr. Justice FORTAS delivered the opinion of the Court.

I.

This appeal challenges the constitutionality of the "anti-evolution" statute which the State of Arkansas adopted in 1928 to prohibit the teaching in its public schools and universities of the theory that man evolved from other species of life. The statute was a product of the upsurge of "fundamentalist" religious fervor of the twenties. The Arkansas statute was an adaption of the famous Tennessee "monkey law" which that State adopted in 1925. The constitutionality of the Tennessee law was upheld by the Tennessee Supreme Court in the celebrated *Scopes* case in 1927.

The Arkansas law makes it unlawful for a teacher in any state-supported school or university "to teach the theory or doctrine that mankind ascended or descended from a lower order of animals," or "to adopt or use in any such institution a textbook that teaches" this theory. Violation is a misdemeanor and subjects the violator to dismissal from his position.

The present case concerns the teaching of biology in a high school in Little Rock. According to the testimony, until the events here in litigation, the official textbook furnished for the high school biology course did not have a section on the Darwinian Theory. Then, for the academic year 1965–1966, the school administration, on recommendation of the teachers of biology in the school system, adopted and prescribed a textbook which contained a chapter setting forth "the theory about the origin * * * of man from a lower form of animal."

Susan Epperson, a young woman who graduated from Arkansas' school system and then obtained her master's degree in zoology at the University of Illinois, was employed by the Little Rock school system in the fall of 1964 to teach 10th grade biology at Central High School. At the start of the next academic year, 1965, she was confronted by the new textbook (which one surmises from the record was not unwelcome to her). She faced at least a literal dilemma because she was supposed to use the new textbook for classroom instruction and presumably to teach the statutorily condemned chapter; but to do so would be a criminal offense and subject her to dismissal.

She instituted the present action in the Chancery Court of the State, seeking a declaration that the Arkansas statute is void and enjoining the State and the defendant officials of the Little Rock school system from dismissing her for violation of the statute's provisions. * * *

* * * [The Chancery Court] held that the challenged statute is unconstitutional because, in violation of the First Amendment, it "tends to hinder the quest for knowledge, restrict the freedom to learn, and restrain the freedom to teach." * * *

On appeal, the Supreme Court of Arkansas reversed. * * * It sustained the statute as an exercise of the State's power to specify the curriculum in public schools. It did not address itself to the competing constitutional considerations.

* * * Only Arkansas and Mississippi have such "anti-evolution" or "monkey" laws on their books. There is no record of any prosecutions in Arkansas under its statute. It is possible that the statute is presently more of a curiosity than a vital fact of life in these States. Nevertheless, the present case was brought, the appeal as of right is properly here, and it is our duty to decide the issues presented.

II.

At the outset, it is urged upon us that the challenged statute is vague and uncertain and therefore within the condemnation of the Due Process Clause of the Fourteenth Amendment. The contention that the Act is vague and uncertain is supported by language in the brief opinion of Arkansas' Supreme Court. That court, perhaps reflecting the discomfort which the statute's quixotic prohibition necessarily engenders in the modern mind, stated that it "expresses no opinion" as to whether the Act prohibits "explanation" of the theory of evolution or merely forbids "teaching that the theory is true." Regardless of this uncertainty, the court held that the statute is constitutional.

On the other hand, counsel for the State, in oral argument in this Court, candidly stated that, despite the State Supreme Court's equivocation, Arkansas would interpret the statute "to mean that to make a student aware of the theory * * * just to teach that there was such a theory" would be grounds for dismissal and for prosecution under the statute; and he said "that the Supreme Court of Arkansas' opinion should be interpreted in that manner." He said: "If Mrs. Epperson would tell her students that 'Here is Darwin's theory, that man ascended or descended from a lower form of being,' then I think she would be under this statute liable for prosecution."

In any event, we do not rest our decision upon the asserted vagueness of the statute. On either interpretation of its language, Arkansas' statute cannot stand. It is of no moment whether the law is deemed to prohibit mention of Darwin's theory, or to forbid any or all of the infinite varieties of communication embraced within the term "teaching." Under either interpretation, the law must be stricken because of its conflict with the constitutional prohibition of state laws respecting an establishment of religion or prohibiting the free exercise thereof. The overriding fact is that Arkansas' law selects from the body of knowledge a particular segment which it proscribes for the sole reason that it is deemed to conflict with a particular religious doctrine; that is, with a particular interpretation of the Book of Genesis by a particular religious group.

* * *

* * * The State's undoubted right to prescribe the curriculum for its public schools does not carry with it the right to prohibit, on pain of criminal penalty, the teaching of a scientific theory or doctrine where that prohibition is based upon reasons that violate the First Amendment. It is much too late to argue that the State may impose upon the teachers in its schools any conditions that it chooses, however restrictive they may be of constitutional guarantees.

In the present case, there can be no doubt that Arkansas has sought to prevent its teachers from discussing the theory of evolution because it is contrary to the belief of some that the Book of Genesis must be the exclusive source of doctrine as to the origin of man. No suggestion has been made that Arkansas' law may be justified by considerations of state policy other than the religious views of some of its citizens. It is clear that fundamentalist sectarian conviction was and is the law's reason for existence. * * *

Arkansas' law cannot be defended as an act of religious neutrality. Arkansas did not seek to exercise from the curricula of its schools and universities all discussion of the origin of man. The law's effort was confined to an attempt to blot out a particular theory because of its supposed conflict with the Biblical account, literally read. Plainly, the law is contrary to the mandate of the First, and in violation of the Fourteenth Amendment to the Constitution.

The judgment of the Supreme Court of Arkansas is reversed.

Reversed.

Mr. Justice BLACK, concurring.

I am by no means sure that this case presents a genuinely justiciable case or controversy. Although * * * the statute alleged to be unconstitutional was passed by the voters of Arkansas in 1928, we are informed that there has never been even a single attempt by the State to enforce it. And the pallid, unenthusiastic, even apologetic defense of the Act presented by the State in this Court indicates that the State would make no attempt to enforce the law should it remain on the books for the next century. Now, nearly 40 years after the law has slumbered on the books as though dead, a teacher alleging fear that the State might arouse from its lethargy and try to punish her has asked for a declaratory judgment holding the law unconstitutional. She was subsequently joined by a parent who alleged his interest in seeing that his two then school-age sons "be informed of all scientific theories and hypotheses * * *." But whether this Arkansas teacher is still a teacher, fearful of punishment under the Act, we do not know. It may be as has been published in the daily press, that she has long since given up her job as a teacher and moved to a distant city, thereby escaping the dangers she had imagined might befall her under this lifeless Arkansas Act. And there is not one iota of concrete evidence to show that the parent-intervenor's sons have not been or will not be taught about evolution. The textbook adopted for use in biology classes in Little Rock includes an entire chapter dealing with evolution. There is no evidence that this chapter is not being freely taught in the schools that use the textbook and no evidence that the intervenor's sons, who were 15 and 17 years old when this suit was brought three years ago, are still in high school or yet to take biology. Unfortunately, however, the State's languid interest in the case has not prompted it to keep this Court informed concerning facts that might easily justify dismissal of this alleged lawsuit as moot or as lacking the qualities of a genuine case or controversy.

Notwithstanding my own doubts as to whether the case presents a justiciable controversy, the Court brushes aside these doubts and leaps headlong into the middle of the very broad problems involved in federal intrusion into state powers to decide what subjects and schoolbooks it may wish to use in teaching state pupils. While I hesitate to enter into the consideration and decision of such sensitive state-federal relationships, I reluctantly acquiesce. But agreeing to consider this as a genuine case or controversy, I cannot agree to thrust the Federal Government's long arm the least bit further into state school curriculums than decision of this particular case requires. * * *

It is plain that a state law prohibiting all teaching of human development or biology is constitutionally quite different from a law that compels a teacher to teach as true only one theory of a given doctrine. It would be difficult to make a First Amendment case out of a state law eliminating the subject of higher mathematics, or astronomy, or biology from its curriculum. And, for all the Supreme Court of Arkansas has said, this particular Act may prohibit that and nothing else. This Court, however, treats the Arkansas Act as though it made it a misdemeanor to teach or to use a book that teaches that evolution is true. But it is not for this Court to arrogate to itself the power to determine the scope of Arkansas statutes. Since the highest court of Arkansas has deliberately refused to give its statute that meaning, we should not presume to do so.

It seems to me that in this situation the statute is too vague for us to strike it down on any ground but that: vagueness.

Under this statute as construed by the Arkansas Supreme Court, a teacher cannot know whether he is forbidden to mention Darwin's theory at all or only free to discuss it as long as he refrains from contending that it is true. It is an established rule that a statute which leaves an ordinary man so doubtful about its meaning that he cannot know when he has violated it denies him the first essential of due process. Holding the statute too vague to enforce would not only follow long-standing constitutional precedents but it would avoid having this Court take unto itself the duty of a State's highest court to interpret and mark the boundaries of the State's laws. And, more important, it would not place this Court in the unenviable position of violating the principle of leaving the States absolutely free to choose their own curriculums for their own schools so long as their action does not palpably conflict with a clear constitutional command.

The Court, not content to strike down this Arkansas Act on the unchallengeable ground of its plain vagueness, chooses rather to invalidate it as a violation of the Establishment of Religion Clause of the First Amendment. I would not decide this case on such a sweeping ground for the following reasons, among others:

1. In the first place I find it difficult to agree with the Court's statement that "there can be no doubt that Arkansas has sought to prevent its teachers from discussing the theory of evolution because it is contrary to the belief of some that the Book of Genesis must be the exclusive source of doctrine as to the origin of man." It may be instead that the people's motive was merely that it would be best to remove this controversial subject from its schools; there is no reason I can imagine why a State is without power to withdraw from its curriculum any subject deemed too emotional and controversial for its public schools. And this Court has consistently held that it is not

for us to invalidate a statute because of our views that the "motives" behind its passage were improper; it is simply too difficult to determine what those motives were.

2. A second question that arises for me is whether this Court's decision forbidding a State to exclude the subject of evolution from its schools infringes the religious freedom of those who consider evolution an anti-religious doctrine. If the theory is considered anti-religious, as the Court indicates, how can the State be bound by the Federal Constitution to permit its teachers to advocate such an "anti-religious" doctrine to schoolchildren? The very cases cited by the Court as supporting its conclusion that the State must be neutral, not favoring one religious or anti-religious view over another. The Darwinian theory is said to challenge the Bible's story of creation; so too have some of those who believe in the Bible, along with many others, challenged the Darwinian theory. Since there is no indication that the literal biblical doctrine of the origin of man is included in the curriculum of Arkansas schools, does not the removal of the subject of evolution leave the State in a neutral position toward these supposedly competing religious and anti-religious doctrines? Unless this Court is prepared simply to write off as pure nonsense the views of those who consider evolution an anti-religious doctrine, then this issue presents problems under the Establishment Clause far more troublesome than are discussed in the Court's opinion.

3. I am also not ready to hold that a person hired to teach school children takes with him into the classroom a constitutional right to teach sociological, economic, political, or religious subjects that the school's managers do not want discussed. * * * I question whether it is absolutely certain, as the Court's opinion indicates, that "academic freedom" permits a teacher to breach his contractual agreement to teach only the subjects designated by the school authorities who hired him.

Certainly the Darwinian theory, precisely like the Genesis story of the creation of man, is not above challenge. In fact the Darwinian theory has not merely been criticized by religionists but by scientists, and perhaps no scientist would be willing to take an oath and swear that everything announced in the Darwinian theory is unquestionably true. The Court, it seems to me, makes a serious mistake in bypassing the plain, unconstitutional vagueness of this statute in order to reach out and decide this troublesome, to me, First Amendment question. However wise this Court may be or may become hereafter, it is doubtful that, sitting in Washington, it can successfully supervise and censor the curriculum of every public school in every hamlet and city in the United States. I doubt that our wisdom is so nearly infallible.

I would either strike down the Arkansas Act as too vague to enforce, or remand to the State Supreme Court for clarification of its holding and opinion.

Mr. Justice HARLAN, concurring.

* * *

Mr. Justice STEWART, concurring in the result.

The States are most assuredly free "to choose their own curriculums for their own schools." A State is entirely free, for example, to decide that the only foreign language to be taught in its public school system shall be Spanish. But would a State be constitutionally free to punish a teacher for letting his students know that other languages are also spoken in the world? I think not.

It is one thing for a State to determine that "the subject of higher mathematics, or astronomy, or biology" shall or shall not be included in its public school curriculum. It is quite another thing for a State to make it a criminal offense for a public school teacher so much as to mention the very existence of an entire system of respected human thought. That kind of criminal law, I think, would clearly impinge upon the guarantees of free communication contained in the First Amendment, and made applicable to the States by the Fourteenth.

The Arkansas Supreme Court has said that the statute before us may or may not be just such a law. The result, as Mr.

Justice BLACK points out, is that "a teacher cannot know whether he is forbidden to mention Darwin's theory at all." Since I believe that no State could constitutionally forbid a teacher "to mention Darwin's theory at all," and since Arkansas may, or may not, have done just that, I conclude that the statute before us is so vague as to be invalid under the Fourteenth Amendment.

NOTES AND QUESTIONS

1. This case is important as much for what it holds as for what it does *not* hold. Note that all Justices agree that the state has control of school curriculum and thus can remove subjects from study as long as the removal is not for unconstitutional reasons. Justice Black is particularly reluctant to interfere with the state's control of its schools, preferring to apply the vagueness doctrine to the statute rather than read into it a desire by the state to promote the Biblical view of creation. Are his arguments convincing?

Recall our discussion in earlier chapters about parental and student desire to influence curriculum decision making. *Epperson* makes it clear that such challenges are unlikely to be successful except where a specific constitutional right is infringed. While parents and students have had some success based on freedoms of speech and press in thwarting school board control of such open forums as the library and school newspapers, courts have not supported similar challenges to school board control of school curriculum. Challenges to such control are far more likely to be successful if they are directly based on the Establishment and/or Free Exercise Clauses. These clauses furnish courts with a manageable standard for becoming involved in curriculum disputes. As a recent study concluded,

> * * * By relying on the historical principle of separation of church and state, courts can intervene in curriculum decisions without having to make the difficult assessments of educational value required by a free speech analysis or the equally difficult determinations concerning the importance and sincerity of individuals' religious beliefs required by a free exercise analysis. The establishment clause protects society against the imposition of a state religion. The remedy for its breach is a complete prohibition of the offending practice.[6]

2. *Epperson* has been followed by a steady parade of cases in the lower federal courts based on the Establishment Clause. For example, in *Daniels v. Waters,* 515 F.2d 485 (6th Cir. 1975), a Tennessee statute which

---

6. Project "Education and the Law: State Interests and Individual Rights," 74 *Mich.* L.Rev. 1373, June, 1976, at p. 1431. (Hereafter cited as Michigan *Project.)*

required the teaching of the Biblical version of creation whenever the theory of evolution was discussed and further required non-Biblical versions of evolution to be identified as "theories" and not "scientific fact" (all "occult" or "satanical beliefs" of human origin were prohibited) was struck down as an infringement on the Establishment Clause. Said the court,

> The result of this legislation is a clearly defined preferential position for the Biblical version of creation as opposed to any account of the development of man based on scientific research and reasoning. For a state to seek to enforce such a preference by law is to seek to accomplish the very establishment of religion which the First Amendment to the Constitution of the United States squarely forbids. (At p. 489).

In 1978 the Fifth Circuit Court of Appeals *en banc* ruled in *Meltzer v. Board of Public Instruction of Orange City*, 577 F.2d 311, that Bible reading as part of morning devotional or inspirational services in the public school setting is unconstitutional. However, the court divided equally on the issue of whether the lower court had correctly refused to rule on the constitutionality of the school board's guidelines for the distribution of religious literature at designated locations in the school and on the issue of whether a Florida state statute which requires teachers to inculcate Christian virtues in their classrooms presents a "live case or controversy." The district court, in an unreported decision, ruled that since the school had agreed to place in the library religious literature which outside groups wish to make available to students, the matter was settled. The lower court also ruled that since the "Christian virtue" statute is unlikely to be enforced and is also subject to a variety of interpretations, no judicial intervention was warranted. The equally divided vote by the court of appeals had the effect of upholding the district court's rulings on these two issues. In 1979, the U. S. Supreme Court denied certiorari with only Justices Brennan and Marshall dissenting.

If school policy is silent on the teaching of evolution from the Biblical viewpoint but a teacher of biology always includes mention of it when discussing the origin of man, would disgruntled parents and students have cause against the school board? Against the teacher? Should the teacher have constitutional protection under the First/Fourteenth Amendments to teach the course in this manner? Suppose a public university professor were the subject of a similar complaint. Any reason to treat the professor differently? In *Lynch v. Indiana State Univ. Bd. of Trustees*, 378 N.E.2d 900 (Ind.1978), an Indiana court of appeals upheld the dismissal of a math professor who read from the Bible at the beginning of his classes. The fact that the professor allowed students to leave during the reading was not deemed sufficient to protect the students from an unconstitutional advancement of religion. The professor argued that denying him the right to read from the Bible unconstitutionally thwarted his religious freedom. How might this argument be countered? We will review freedom of religion issues later in the chapter.

If a school board requires a variety of views, both religious and secular, to be presented in teaching the evolution of man, is the school being neutral under the Establishment Clause? Should the Establishment Clause take precedence over professional opinions about pedagogy? If only secular views of evolution are allowed, might a student or parent accuse the state of fostering a "religion of secularism" as Justice Black suggests? Of atheism? Would either be likely to be successfully challenged under the Establishment Clause?

B. The Contemporary Struggle Over Parochiaid: Extending the Pupil Benefit Theory

Parochiaid is defined as any form of direct or indirect aid for parochial and other nonpublic educational institutions, primarily at the elementary and secondary level. Since the 1960s nonpublic schools, most of which are religiously affiliated (see Figure 4–1), have had greater reason to seek government assistance as costs have risen, particularly for personnel. Personnel costs typically account for 75–85 percent of a school budget. In many Catholic schools, lay faculty have replaced religious faculty, who worked for far less compensation. The union movement in the public sector has also contributed to a rise in personnel costs in the nonpublic schools, as the nonpublic institutions struggle to compete for quality faculty members. At some nonpublic schools, chiefly Catholic, faculty unions have been formed to seek increases in faculty salaries and benefits.

Figure 4–1: Affiliation of American Nonpublic Educational Institutions (1976)

A. Elementary-Secondary	Number of Institutions		Percent of Total U.S. School Enrollment
Total Nonpublic Institutions	14,755		9.3%
Independent		2,206	
Church-Related		12.549	
Catholic			8,986
Protestant			2,679
Jewish			265
Other			619

B. Postsecondary	Number of Institutions		Percent of Total U.S. College Enrollment
Total Nonpublic Institutions	1,608		21%
Independent	823		
Church-Related	785		
Catholic		242	
Protestant		504	
Jewish		24	
Other		15	

Source: Correspondence with National Center for Educational Statistics, U. S. Office of Education, Washington, D.C.   [B9661]

In higher education the situation is much the same. (Note: in higher education, the percentage of nonpublic colleges and universities which are religiously affiliated is much lower. See Figure 4–1.) Inflation, rising energy costs, the need to build and maintain modern facilities, the costs of complying with new government regulation—these and other factors have worked to increase costs tremendously in recent years. Some institutions have been forced to close their doors.

At the same time, both the nonpublic and public schools and colleges look forward to decreasing applicant pools of traditional-age students. Since the 1970s the National Center for Educational Statistics has reported a steady decline in total enrollment in elementary and secondary schools. By the early 1980s the total elementary and secondary schools is expected to fall to approximately 45 million students, down from a peak of 51 million in 1970. As these students move on to postsecondary education, smaller enrollments will be evident in many of these institutions. In New York State, for example, full-time enrollment in degree-granting public and non-public colleges and universities is expected to decline from a peak of over 1 million students in 1977 to 875,000 students by 1990.[7]

Despite enrollment declines, economic problems coupled with increasing disenchantment with the public schools have focused more attention on legislative programs to aid the nonpublic sector. In a 1974 Gallup poll, 52 percent of the nation's adults favored a constitutional amendment to permit the government to provide financial aid to church-related nonpublic schools. Opposition to the proposal dropped from 44 to 35 percent between 1970 and 1974. In 1977 the prestigious Carnegie Commission on Higher Education called for increased government support for nonpublic postsecondary education.[8]

Underlying these proposals is a belief in the value of healthy diversity in education. Many believe that effectiveness of our educational system is enhanced by the presence of a vibrant nonpublic sector to provide competition to the public sector and to offer alternatives to students. Essential to this view, of course, is the assumption that nonpublic and public educational institutions are really different.

To the extent such difference is religiously-based, government assistance programs run headlong into the Establishment Clause. To avoid establishment problems, proponents of aid to religious schools and colleges have insisted that the money is designed to benefit students, building on the pupil benefit theory first advanced in *Everson*. In the face of continued judicial resistance, ingenious programs have been designed to meet court approval. As described below, few have been successful. Is a constitutional amendment the only answer? Keep this question in mind as we review recent attempts to provide government assistance to nonpublic educational institutions.

7. *The Regents Tentative Statewide Plan for the Development of Postsecondary Education*, State Education Department, Albany, N. Y., 1976, Table 5, p. 25.

8. *The States and Private Higher Education: Problems and Policies in a New Era* (San Francisco: Jossey-Bass, 1977).

(1) The Direct Aid Cases

The first important case of the 1970s to deal with increased government assistance to nonpublic elementary and secondary schools is *Lemon v. Kurtzman*, 403 U.S. 602 (1971) [9] Lemon invalidated two state statutes providing state aid to church-related elementary and secondary schools. The Pennsylvania statute passed in 1968 provided reimbursement for the cost of teacher's salaries, textbooks, and instructional material—all used for specifically secular purposes. Schools desiring reimbursement kept separate accounting systems subject to state audit. Some 1100 nonpublic elementary and secondary schools with a student population of over 500,000 students participated in the program. More than 96 percent of the schools were Roman Catholic. The Rhode Island statute, enacted in 1969, authorized state payment of salary supplements to teachers of secular subjects in nonpublic elementary schools. Teachers receiving such supplements had to be teaching in a nonpublic school at which the average per-pupil expenditure on secular education was less than the average in the state public schools. To comply with this requirement and to administer the supplement program, eligible schools had to submit financial data. Some 250 teachers, all employed in parochial schools, applied for benefits prior to the Court decision.

Writing for the majority, Chief Justice Warren Burger noted that both legislatures "have * * * sought to create statutory restrictions designed to guarantee the separation between secular and religious educational functions and to ensure that state financial aid supports only the former." (At p. 613). But using a new test derived from a case upholding tax exemptions for churches, he invalidated both statutes because they impermissibly entangled government with religious affairs. The so-called "excessive entanglement" test was put forward in *Walz v. Tax Comm.*, 397 U.S. 664 (1970). In that case, Chief Justice Burger wrote:

> Granting tax exemptions to churches necessarily operates to afford an indirect economic benefit and also gives rise to some, but yet a lesser, involvement than taxing them. In analyzing either alternative the questions are whether the involvement is excessive, and whether it is a continuing one calling for official and continuing surveillance leading to an impermissible degree of entanglement. (At pp. 674–675).

In *Walz* he concluded that entanglement would be more excessive if the churches were taxed. Tax exemptions, he stated, represent a "kind of benevolent neutrality toward churches and religious exercise generally * * *." (At pp. 676–677).

But in *Lemon* the opposite was true. Insofar as the Rhode Island program was concerned, Chief Justice Burger concluded that in order to be assured that the secular and the religious were not comingled,

> A comprehensive, discriminatory, and continuing state surveillance will inevitably be required to ensure that * * * restric-

---

9. Two other cases, *Earley v. DiCenso* and *Robinson v. DiCenso* were consolidated with *Lemon* and decided in the same opinion.

tions are obeyed and the First Amendment otherwise respected. Unlike a book, a teacher cannot be inspected once so as to determine the extent and intent of his or her personal beliefs and subjective acceptance of the limitations imposed by the First Amendment. These prophylactic contacts will involve excessive and enduring entanglement between state and church. (At p. 619).

Likewise, the teacher compensation system of the Pennsylvania statute involved excessive entanglement of the state with religion. In addition the Chief Justice noted that it involved direct subsidies to religious schools, unlike *Everson* and *Allen*, where the assistance went to parents and students. Direct subsidies invite surveillance and thus promote "an intimate and continuing relationship between church and state." (At p. 622).

Lemon gave the Chief Justice further opportunity to expand on the nuances of the entanglement test announced in *Walz*. He stated that political divisiveness is an off-shoot of the entanglement test and would be inevitable under statutes like those of Rhode Island and Pennsylvania.

> * * * In a community where such a large number of pupils are served by church-related schools, it can be assumed that state assistance will entail considerable political activity. Partisans of parochial schools, understandably concerned with rising costs and sincerely dedicated to both the religious and secular educational missions of their schools, will inevitably champion this cause and promote political action to achieve their goals. Those who oppose state aid, whether for constitutional, religious, or fiscal reasons, will inevitably respond and employ all of the usual political campaign techniques to prevail. Candidates will be forced to declare and voters to choose. It would be unrealistic to ignore the fact that many people confronted with issues of this kind will find their votes aligned with their faith.

> Ordinarily political debate and division, however vigorous or even partisan, are normal and healthy manifestations of our democratic system of government, but political division along religious lines was one of the principal evils against which the First Amendment was intended to protect. The potential divisiveness of such conflict is a threat to the normal political process. To have States or communities divide on the issues presented by state aid to parochial schools would tend to confuse and obscure other issues of great urgency. We have an expanding array of vexing issues, local, and national, domestic and international, to debate and divide on. It conflicts with our whole history and tradition to permit questions of the Religion Clauses to assume such importance in our legislatures and in our elections that they could divert attention from the myriad issues and problems that confront every level of government. (At pp. 622–623).

Chief Justice Burger noted a finding of the lower court in the Rhode Island case that the parochial school system's " 'monumental and deepening financial crisis' " would " 'inescapably' " require larger annual appropriations. He assumed the same situation would occur in Pennsylvania.

The problem with the entanglement test is that it appears to be at cross-purposes with the earlier secular legislative purpose and primary effect tests. For example, if the institutions are pervasively religious, then the state must take special precautions to see that aid is used only for secular ends. But it is these very precautions that may undermine the statute under the entanglement test. This appears to have been the case with the Rhode Island and Pennsylvania statutes in *Lemon*.

In a companion case to *Lemon* involving construction grants to religiously affiliated colleges and universities, the Supreme Court came to the opposite conclusion, upholding the state aid plan. Part of the rationale for the different treatment in *Tilton v. Richardson,* 403 U.S. 672 (1971) relates to the Court's conception of the nature of postsecondary educational institutions and students, and partly to concern for the Free Exercise Clause. Recall that the Court is concerned lest a too strict reading of the Establishment Clause deny persons their right to religious freedom.

TILTON v. RICHARDSON

Supreme Court of the United States, 1971.
403 U.S. 672, 91 S.Ct. 2091, 29 L.Ed.2d 790.

Mr. Chief Justice BURGER announced the judgment of the Court and an opinion in which Mr. Justice HARLAN, Mr. Justice STEWART and Mr. Justice BLACKMUN join.

The Higher Education Facilities Act was passed in 1963 in response to a strong nationwide demand for the expansion of college and university facilities to meet the sharply rising number of young people demanding higher education. The Act authorizes federal grants and loans to "institutions of higher education" for the construction of a wide variety of "academic facilities." But § 751(a)(2) expressly excludes

"any facility used or to be used for sectarian instruction or as a place for religious worship, or * * * any facility which * * * is used or to be used primarily in connection with any part of the program of a school or department of divinity * * *."

The Act is administered by the United States Commissioner of Education. He advises colleges and universities applying

for funds that under the Act no part of the project may be used for sectarian instruction, religious worship, or the programs of a divinity school. The Commissioner requires applicants to provide assurances that these restrictions will be respected. The United States retains a 20-year interest in any facility constructed with Title I funds. If, during this period, the recipient violates the statutory conditions, the United States is entitled to recover an amount equal to the proportion of its present value that the federal grant bore to the original cost of the facility. During the 20-year period, the statutory restrictions are enforced by the Office of Education primarily by way of on-site inspections.

Appellants are citizens and taxpayers of the United States and residents of Connecticut. They brought this suit for injunctive relief against the officials who administer the Act. Four church-related colleges and universities in Connecticut receiving federal construction grants under Title I were also named as defendants. Federal funds were used for five projects at these four institutions: (1) a library building at Sacred Heart University; (2) a music, drama, and arts building at Annhurst College; (3) a science building at Fairfield University; (4) a library building at Fairfield; and (5) a language laboratory at Albertus Magnus College. * * * The District Court ruled that Title I authorized grants to church-related colleges and universities. It also sustained the constitutionality of the Act, finding that it had neither the purpose nor the effect of promoting religion. * * *

* * *

Every analysis must begin with the candid acknowledgment that there is no single constitutional caliper that can be used to measure the precise degree to which these three factors are present or absent. Instead, our analysis in this area must begin with a consideration of the cumulative criteria developed over many years and applying to a wide range of governmental action challenged as violative of the Establishment Clause.

There are always risks in treating criteria discussed by the Court from time to time as "tests" in any limiting sense of that term. Constitutional adjudication does not lend itself to the absolutes of the physical sciences or mathematics. The standards should rather be viewed as guidelines with which to identify instances in which the objectives of the Religion Clauses have been impaired. And, as we have noted in Lemon v. Kurtzman and Earley v. DiCenso, candor compels the acknowledgment that we can only dimly perceive the boundaries of permissible government activity in this sensitive area of constitutional adjudication.

Against this background we consider four questions: First, does the Act reflect a secular legislative purpose? Second, is the primary effect of the Act to advance or inhibit religion? Third, does the administration of the Act foster an excessive government entanglement with religion? Fourth, does the implementation of the Act inhibit the free exercise of religion?

The stated legislative purpose appears in the preamble where Congress found and declared that

"the security and welfare of the United States require that this and future generations of American youth be assured ample opportunity for the fullest development of their intellectual capacities, and that this opportunity will be jeopardized unless the Nation's colleges and universities are encouraged and assisted in their efforts to accommodate rapidly growing numbers of youth who aspire to a higher education."

This expresses a legitimate secular objective entirely appropriate for governmental action.

The simplistic argument that every form of financial aid to church-sponsored activity violates the Religion Clauses was rejected long ago in Bradfield v. Roberts, 175 U.S. 291 (1899). There a federal construction grant to a hospital operated by a religious order was upheld. Here the Act is challenged on the ground that its primary effect is to aid the religious purposes of church-related colleges and universities. Construction grants surely aid these institutions in the sense that the construction of buildings will asssist them to perform their various functions. But bus transportation, textbooks, and tax exemptions all gave aid in the sense that religious bodies would otherwise have been forced to find other sources from which to finance these services. Yet all of these forms of governmental assistance have been upheld.

* * * The crucial question is not whether some benefit accrues to a religious institution as a consequence of the legislative program, but whether its principal or primary effect advances religion.

* * *

The Act itself was carefully drafted to ensure that the federally subsidized facilities would be devoted to the secular and not the religious function of the recipient institutions. It authorizes grants and loans only for academic facilities that will be used for defined secular purposes and expressly prohibits their use for religious instruction, training, or worship. These restrictions have been enforced in the Act's actual administration, and the record shows that some church-related institutions have been required to disgorge benefits for failure to obey them.

Finally, this record fully supports the findings of the District Court that none of the four church-related institutions in this case has violated the statutory restrictions. The institutions presented evidence that there had been no religious services or worship in the federally financed facilities, that there are no religious symbols or plaques in or on them, and that they had been used solely for nonreligious purposes. On this record, therefore, these buildings are indistinguishable from a typical state university facility. Appellants presented no evidence to the contrary.

Appellants instead rely on the argument that government may not subsidize any activities of an institution of higher learning that in some of its programs teaches religious doctrines. This argument rests on *Everson* where the majority stated that the Establishment Clause barred any "tax * * * levied to support any religious * * * institutions * * * whatever form they may adopt to teach or practice religion." In *Allen*, however, it was recognized that the Court had fashioned criteria under which an analysis of a statute's purpose and effect was determinative as to whether religion was being advanced by government action.

Under this concept appellants' position depends on the validity of the proposition that religion so permeates the secular education provided by church-related colleges and universities that their religious

and secular educational functions are in fact inseparable. The argument that government grants would thus inevitably advance religion did not escape the notice of Congress. It was carefully and thoughtfully debated, but was found unpersuasive. It was also considered by this Court in *Allen*. There the Court refused to assume that religiosity in parochial elementary and secondary schools necessarily permeates the secular education that they provide.

This record, similarly, provides no basis for any such assumption here. Two of the five federally financed buildings involved in this case are libraries. The District Court found that no classes had been conducted in either of these facilities and that no restrictions were imposed by the institutions on the books that they acquired. There is no evidence to the contrary. The third building was a language laboratory at Albertus Magnus College. The evidence showed that this facility was used solely to assist students with their pronunciation in modern foreign languages—a use which would seem peculiarly unrelated and unadaptable to religious indoctrination. Federal grants were also used to build a science building at Fairfield University and a music, drama, and arts building at Annhurst College.

There is no evidence that religion seeps into the use of any of these facilities. Indeed, the parties stipulated in the District Court that courses at these institutions are taught according to the academic requirements intrinsic to the subject matter and the individual teacher's concept of professional standards. Although appellants introduced several institutional documents that stated certain religious restrictions on what could be taught, other evidence showed that these restrictions were not in fact enforced and that the schools were characterized by an atmosphere of academic freedom rather than religious indoctrination. All four institutions, for example, subscribe to the 1940 Statement of Principles on Academic Freedom and Tenure endorsed by the American Association of University Professors and the Association of American Colleges.

Rather than focus on the four defendant colleges and universities involved in this case, however, appellants seek to shift our attention to a "composite profile" that they have constructed of the "typical sectarian" institution of higher education. We are told that such a "composite" institution imposes religious restrictions on admissions, requires attendance at religious activities, compels obedience to the doctrines and dogmas of the faith, requires instruction in theology and doctrine, and does everything it can to propagate a particular religion. Perhaps some church-related schools fit the pattern that appellants describe. Indeed, some colleges have been declared ineligible for aid by the authorities that administer the Act. But appellants do not contend that these four institutions fall within this category. Individual projects can be properly evaluated if and when challenges arise with respect to particular recipients and some evidence is then presented to show that the institution does in fact possess these characteristics. We cannot, however, strike down an Act of Congress on the basis of a hypothetical "profile."

Although we reject appellants' broad constitutional arguments we do perceive an aspect in which the statute's enforcement provisions are inadequate to ensure that the impact of the federal aid will not advance religion. * * *

* * *

Under § 754(b)(2), * * * a recipient institution's obligation not to use the facility for sectarian instruction or religious worship would appear to expire at the end of 20 years. We note, for example, that an institution applying for a federal grant is only required to provide

assurances that the facility will not be used for sectarian instruction or religious worship "during at least the period of the Federal interest therein (as defined in section 754 of this title)."

Limiting the prohibition for religious use of the structure to 20 years obviously opens the facility to use for any purpose at the end of that period. It cannot be assumed that a substantial structure has no value after that period and hence the unrestricted use of a valuable property is in effect a contribution of some value to a religious body. Congress did not base the 20-year provision on any contrary conclusion. If, at the end of 20 years, the building is, for example, converted into a chapel or otherwise used to promote religious interests, the original federal grant will in part have the effect of advancing religion.

To this extent the Act therefore trespasses on the Religion Clauses. * * *

This circumstance does not require us to invalidate the entire Act, however. * * *

* * *

We next turn to the question of whether excessive entanglements characterize the relationship between government and church under the Act. * * *

* * *

There are generally significant differences between the religious aspects of church-related institutions of higher learning and parochial elementary and secondary schools. The "affirmative if not dominant policy" of the instruction in pre-college church schools is "to assure future adherents to a particular faith by having control of their total education at an early age." There is substance to the contention that college students are less impressionable and less susceptible to religious indoctrination. Common observation would seem to support that view, and Congress may well have entertained it. The skepticism of the college student is not an inconsiderable barrier to any attempt or tendency to subvert the congressional objectives and limitations. Furthermore, by their very nature, college and postgraduate courses tend to limit the opportunities for sectarian influence by virtue of their own internal disciplines. Many church-related colleges and universities are characterized by a high degree of academic freedom and seek to evoke free and critical responses from their students.

The record here would not support a conclusion that any of these four institutions departed from this general pattern. All four schools are governed by Catholic religious organizations, and the faculties and student bodies at each are predominantly Catholic. Nevertheless, the evidence shows that non-Catholics were admitted as students and given faculty appointments. Not one of these four institutions requires its students to attend religious services. Although all four schools require their students to take theology courses, the parties stipulated that these courses are taught according to the academic requirements of the subject matter and the teacher's concept of professional standards. The parties also stipulated that the courses covered a range of human religious experiences and are not limited to courses about the Roman Catholic religion. The schools introduced evidence that they made no attempt to indoctrinate students or to proselytize. Indeed, some of the required theology courses at Albertus Magnus and Sacred Heart are taught by rabbis. Finally, as we have noted, these four schools subscribe to a well-established set of principles of academic freedom, and nothing in this record shows that these principles are not in fact followed. In short, the evidence shows institutions with admittedly religious functions but whose predominant higher education mission is to provide their students with a secular education.

Since religious indoctrination is not a substantial purpose or activity of these church-related colleges and universities, there is less likelihood than in primary and secondary schools that religion will permeate the area of secular education. This reduces the risk that government aid will in fact serve to support religious activities. Correspondingly, the necessity for intensive government surveillance is diminished and the resulting entanglements between government and religion lessened. Such inspection as may be necessary to ascertain that the facilities are devoted to secular education is minimal and indeed hardly more than the inspections that States impose over all private schools within the reach of compulsory education laws.

The entanglement between church and state is also lessened here by the nonideological character of the aid that the Government provides. * * *

Finally, government entanglements with religion are reduced by the circumstance that * * * the Government aid here is a one-time, single-purpose construction grant. There are no continuing financial relationships or dependencies, no annual audits, and no government analysis of an institution's expenditures on secular as distinguished from religious activities. Inspection as to use is a minimal contact.

No one of these three factors standing alone is necessarily controlling; cumulatively all of them shape a narrow and limited relationship with government which involves fewer and less significant contacts than the two state schemes before us in *Lemon* and *DiCenso*. The relationship therefore has less potential for realizing the substantive evils against which the Religion Clauses were intended to protect.

We think that cumulatively these three factors also substantially lessen the potential for divisive religious fragmentation in the political arena. This conclusion is admittedly difficult to document, but neither have appellants pointed to any continuing religious aggravation on this matter in the political processes. Possibly this can be explained by the character and diversity of the recipient colleges and universities and the absence of any intimate continuing relationship or dependency between government and religiously affiliated institutions. The potential for divisiveness inherent in the essentially local problems of primary and secondary schools is significantly less with respect to a college or university whose student constituency is not local but diverse and widely dispersed.

Finally, we must consider whether the implementation of the Act inhibits the free exercise of religion in violation of the First Amendment. Appellants claim that the Free Exercise Clause is violated because they are compelled to pay taxes, the proceeds of which in part finance grants under the Act. Appellants, however, are unable to identify any coercion directed at the practice or exercise of their religious beliefs. Their share of the cost of the grants under the Act is not fundamentally distinguishable from the impact of the tax exemption sustained in *Walz* or the provision of textbooks upheld in *Allen*.

We conclude that the Act does not violate the Religion Clauses of the First Amendment except that part of § 754(b)(2) providing a 20-year limitation on the religious use restrictions contained in § 751(a)(2). We remand to the District Court with directions to enter a judgment consistent with this opinion.

Vacated and remanded.

Mr. Justice DOUGLAS, with whom Mr. Justice BLACK and Mr. Justice MARSHALL concur, dissenting in part.

*   *   *

The public purpose in secular education is, to be sure, furthered by the [federal] program. Yet the sectarian purpose is aided by making the parochial school system viable. The purpose is to increase "student enrollment" and the students obviously aimed at are those of the particular faith now financed by taxpayers' money. Parochial schools are not beamed at agnostics, atheists, or those of a competing sect. The more sophisticated institutions may admit minorities; but the dominant religious character is not changed.

The reversion of the facility to the parochial school at the end of 20 years is an outright grant, measurable by the present discounted worth of the facility. A gift of taxpayers' funds in that amount would plainly be unconstitutional. The Court properly bars it even though disguised in the form of a reversionary interest.

But the invalidation of this one clause cannot cure the constitutional infirmities of the statute as a whole. The Federal Government is giving religious schools a block grant to build certain facilities. The fact that money is given once at the beginning of a program rather than apportioned annually as in *Lemon* and *DiCenso* is without constitutional significance. * * * The plurality's distinction is in effect that small violations of the First Amendment over a period of years are unconstitutional (see *Lemon* and *DiCenso*) while a huge violation occurring only once is *de minimis*. I cannot agree with such sophistry.

* * * The facilities financed by taxpayers' funds are not to be used for "sectarian" purposes. Religious teaching and secular teaching are so enmeshed in parochial schools that only the strictest supervision and surveillance would insure compliance with the condition. Parochial schools may require religious exercises, even in the classroom. A parochial school operates on one budget. Money not spent for one purpose becomes available for other purposes. Thus the fact that there are no religious observances in

ʳfederally financed facilities is not controlling because required religious observances will take place in other buildings.

* * *

* * * (s)urveillance creates an entanglement of government and religion which the First Amendment was designed to avoid. Yet after today's decision there will be a requirement of surveillance which will last for the useful life of the building * * *. The price of the subsidy under the Act is violation of the Free Exercise Clause. Could a course in the History of Methodism be taught in a federally financed building? Would a religiously slanted version of the Reformation or Quebec politics under Duplessis be permissible? How can the Government know what is taught in the federally financed building without a continuous auditing of class-

room instruction? Yet both the Free Exercise Clause and academic freedom are violated when the Government agent must be present to determine whether the course content is satisfactory.

* * *

Much is made of the need for public aid to church schools in light of their pressing fiscal problems. * * *

The mounting wealth of the churches makes ironic their incessant demands on the public treasury. * * *

* * *

I dissent not because of any lack of respect for parochial schools but out of a feeling of despair that the respect which through history has been accorded the First Amendment is this day lost.

* * *

NOTES AND QUESTIONS

1. Justice White's concurring and dissenting opinion in *Lemon* contained comments relative to *Tilton*. He questioned why the Court should reach an opposite conclusion in *Tilton*. "Surely the notion that college students are more mature and resistant to indoctrination is a make-weight, for in *Tilton* there is careful note of the federal condition on funding and the enforcement mechanism available." (At p. 688). Would you agree? Do you think that college students are less likely to be influenced by religious doctrine than younger students? Should the Court require extensive social science evidence before making such an assumption? Or is common sense enough?

Justice White also noted that the Court seemed more inclined to trust college teachers in religious institutions not to stray from government guidelines than secondary school teachers. He questioned such an assumption in light of the fact that "within five years the majority of teachers in Rhode Island parochial schools will be lay persons, many of them non-Catholic." Should this make a difference? To the extent that religious schools in Rhode Island become more public through such changes, should they be more eligible for aid? According to one commentator, history shows that one of the concerns behind the Establishment Clause was a fear that state-assisted religious organizations would lose their vitality and stray from their own doctrinal beliefs in the hopes of securing additional dollars.[10] There is evidence in at least one state with a policy of strong

10. See J. L. Underwood, "Permissible Entanglement Under the Establishment Clause," 25 *Emory L. Journal* 17, Winter 1976, at pp. 29–34.

support for nonpublic education that state aid does influence religious institutions to "desectarianize." [11]   If such a tendency does occur, to what extent has government interfered with religious freedom by furthering a secularization of nonpublic religious schools through such aid programs? Or have the institutions themselves changed their mission?   Would the latter raise Establishment or Free Exercise Clause questions?   To what extent are religiously-affiliated educational institutions really different from their independent or public counterparts in the first place?   (You may wish to review some of the social science research described in Chapter One on this point.)   If there is little difference or if differences are extinguished proportionate to aid received, should courts require nonpublic institutions to recognize student constitutional rights in the same manner as public educational institutions?   (See the "public function" theory described in Chapter Two.)

2.   Note that in *Tilton* Chief Justice Burger highlights the Free Exercise Clause as an independent fourth test.   Note also that the political divisiveness test, though not given independent status, is discussed.   While the secular legislative purpose test, the primary effect test, and the excessive entanglement test all have been accorded independent status, the free exercise and political divisiveness tests are sometimes given independent status and sometimes assumed to be part of the other three, dependent in part on the nature of the case and in part on the Justice writing the opinion.   In any event, in *Tilton* Justice Burger acknowledges that the "tests" are hardly objective.   He refers to them as "guidelines."

3.   The Chief Justice cites an old case *Bradfield v. Roberts,* 175 U.S. 291 (1899) in support of the proposition that not every form of financial aid to church-sponsored activity is unconstitutional under the Establishment Clause.   On the other hand, Justice Douglas in dissent notes that the federal grant program has the indirect effect of making the religious colleges "viable."   But what about the transportation reimbursement program in *Everson,* a 5–4 decision in which Justice Douglas was in the majority?   In his dissent in *Walz,* Justice Douglas admitted that he had grave doubts about his position in *Everson.*   Of course, the counter to the Douglas view of *no* aid to religious schools and colleges is that such a position tends to place government against the free exercise of religion, assuming that attendance at a religious educational institution is part of the exercise of one's religion.

4.   In a 1976 case, *Roemer v. Board of Public Works of Md.,* 426 U.S. 736, the Supreme Court in a 5–4 decision upheld a Maryland program of grants to nonpublic colleges.   The noncategorical grants, the size of which are based on nonreligious student enrollment, can only be used for nonsectarian purposes.   Of the 18 institutions eligible for the funds, five were church-related.

Opponents argued that the aid program differed from the one-time-only construction grants of *Tilton v. Richardson,* since the Maryland program is continuous.   It thus serves to advance religion and also to excess-

11.   See Robert O. Berdahl, "The Politics of State Aid" in David W. Breneman and Chester E. Finn, (Ed) *Public Policy and*   *Private Higher Education* (Washington, D. C.: The Brookings Institution, 1978), at p. 335.

ively entangle government with religious affairs through continuing surveillance.

The majority split in ruling on the grant program. Joining Justice Blackmun, who wrote the opinion for the Court, were Chief Justice Burger and Justice Powell. Blackmun relied on *Hunt v. McNair*, 413 U.S. 734 (1973), a case upholding a state finance program enabling nonpublic colleges to secure revenue from the sale of tax-free bonds to underwrite construction costs, to uphold the Maryland scheme. As in *Hunt*, Blackmun applied the *Tilton* tests. He found that the grant program had a secular purpose since all nonpublic education was entitled to benefits and did not impermissibly advance religion since the religious institutions "are not pervasively sectarian." He acknowledged that mandatory religion courses are taught at the institutions by Roman Catholic clerics but considered these courses a supplement to the regular liberal arts program. Similarly, the fact that some classes begin with prayer was insufficient to alter the finding of the district court. Besides, he noted, the aid could only be used for nonsectarian purposes.

Insofar as excessive entanglement was concerned, Justice Blackmun agreed with the district court that the procedure for requesting funds and filing audits on an annual basis did not excessively involve the state in the affairs of the religious colleges. As in *Tilton,* political divisiveness was not an issue since only postsecondary institutions receive aid, most of them non-religious. He acknowledged, however, the delicacy of applying the entanglement test in this case.

> There is no exact science in gauging the entanglement of church and state. The wording of the test, which speaks of "*excessive* entanglement," itself makes that clear. The relevant factors we have identified are to be considered "cumulatively" in judging the degree of entanglement. *Tilton v. Richardson.* They may cut different ways, as certainly they do here. In reaching the conclusion that it did, the District Court gave dominant importance to the character of the aided institutions and to its finding that they are capable of separating secular and religious functions. For the reasons stated above, we cannot say that the emphasis was misplaced, or the finding erroneous. (At pp. 766–767).

Justice White wrote a separate concurring view, joined in by Justice Rehnquist, in which he emphasized his continuing opposition to the excessive entanglement test. "I see no reason to indulge in the redundant exercise of evaluating the same facts and findings under a different label." (At p. 769). Do you see the excessive entanglement test as redundant?

Justices Brennan, Marshall, Stewart, and Stevens dissented. Justice Brennan concluded that the grant program did advance religion and was thus the kind of general subsidy program the Establishment Clause was meant to prevent. Justice Stewart wrote that since the theology courses are not taught as academic disciplines but rather as a means of providing religious experiences to the students, the grant program serves to advance religion. He pointed out that in *Tilton,* the institutions made no attempt to inculcate the religious beliefs of the affiliated church.

In his dissent, Justice Stevens pointed out "the pernicious tendency of a state subsidy to tempt religious schools to compromise their religious mission without wholly abandoning it." (At p. 775). (During oral argument, counsel for the appellant taxpayers pointed out that one of the five colleges had agreed to curtail some sectarian practices in order to get money.)

Do you find the decision in *Roemer* easy to reconcile with *Tilton*? Do you think the Court should heavily rely on the findings of the lower court as preferred by Justice Blackmun or should make an independent judgment? Which of the views expressed by the Justices most nearly corresponds to your own regarding government assistance to nonpublic postsecondary educational institutions?

5. Title 7 of the 1964 Civil Rights Act as amended by the Equal Employment Opportunity Act of 1972 granted religiously affiliated institutions an exemption from its prohibition against religious discrimination in employment. Thus, such institutions could legally prefer persons of a certain faith in hiring practices. If a religious organization claimed the exemption on religious grounds, has it automatically declared itself ineligible for state aid under the Establishment Clause? Is it consistent public policy, in other words, to allow a religious institution to discriminate in employment on religious grounds and still be eligible for state and federal funds? Any more so than in the area of student rights? Might the religious character of the institution make a difference, e. g., a secondary school, seminary, or church-related college? If aid were denied because educational institutions take advantage of religious exemptions, what choices do these institutions face? Do you think a convincing public policy case can be made for religiously-affiliated educational institutions to "have their cake and eat it too" in this respect?

(2) The Indirect Aid Cases

After *Lemon* state legislative efforts were increasingly focused on ways to provide *indirect* aid to these institutions by channeling asistance through parents and students. The rationale advanced was that the state was not aiding the schools but rather providing benefits to parents and students. This has come to be known as "the pupil benefit theory," which really made its first appearance in *Everson v. Board of Educ.,* the 1947 "wall of separation" case. It was part of the rationale for New York State's statute struck down in *Committee for Public Educ. v. Nyquist,* 413 U.S. 756 (1973). The law signed in 1972 established three types of financial aid programs for nonpublic elementary and secondary schools. The first type involved direct grants from the state to the schools for maintenance and repair of school facilities. The purpose of the maintenance and repair program was to ensure the health, safety, and welfare of the students. Only schools serving low-income families were targeted for this type of assistance. Eligible schools were required to submit an audited statement of their expenses for maintenance and repairs and were then reimbursed through the grants.

The second type of aid was of the indirect variety, as was the third type. The second type was a tuition grant program designed to provide low income parents with tuition grants of $50 for each grade school child and $100 for each high school child enrolled. Participating parents were required to submit a receipted tuition bill. The third type of aid was in the form of a tax benefit program for those ineligible under the tuition grant program. Parents with adjusted gross incomes less than $9000 could subtract up to $1000 for each of as many as three dependents enrolled in nonpublic schools. As income rose, the tuition credits declined, ceasing completely for those with incomes over $25,000. The amount of the deduction was not related to the actual cost of attending the nonpublic schools.

In New York State about 20 percent of the state's elementary and secondary school population attends nonpublic schools, 85 percent of which are religiously affiliated, mostly with the Catholic Church. Nearly all of the 250 schools entitled to the maintenance and repair grants under the statute were Roman Catholic.

In striking down the statute in *Nyquist,* Justice Powell for the majority concluded that the maintenance and repair program had the primary effect of aiding religion. He distinguished *Everson v. Board of Educ.* and *Board of Educ. v. Allen* since neither involved direct money grants to religious schools. Nor did *Tilton v. Richardson* apply, since in that case the construction grants went to colleges and universities, not elementary and secondary schools.

Both the tuition reimbursement and tax credit programs also failed the primary effect test, which now takes on the connotation of having "some" effect. It made no difference that this aid went to parents rather than to the schools. He noted that,

> if the grants are offered as an incentive to parents to send their children to sectarian schools by making unrestricted cash payments to them, the Establishment Clause is violated whether or not the actual dollars given eventually find their way into the sectarian institutions. Whether the grant is labeled a reimbursement, a reward, or a subsidy, its substantive impact is still the same. (At p. 786).

Justice Powell was unsympathetic to the state's claim that it was promoting the free exercise of religion. By asserting such a purpose, he explained, the state was not remaining neutral but actually advancing religion contrary to the Establishment Clause. (Note again the dynamic tension between these two constitutional provisions.) Nor was he persuaded that the tax exemptions allowed in *Walz* were similar. Tax exemptions, he pointed out, have been universally approved in the country both before and after the adoption of the First Amendment. The New York tax relief plan, however, was innovative and not based on precedent. More significantly for constitutional purposes, the tax exemptions in *Walz* minimized government entanglement with religion, while the New York plan "would tend to increase rather than limit the involvement between Church and State." (At p. 793). Finally, the tax exemption in *Walz* applied to a variety of institutions, not just the religious. He noted that the parties in *Nyquist* agreed that "tax reductions authorized by this law flow primarily to the parents of children attending sectarian, nonpublic schools." (At p. 794).

Once again, the majority called attention to the problem of political divisiveness such aid programs tend to engender, calling it " 'a warning signal' not to be ignored." (At p. 798).

Chief Justice Burger and Justices White and Rehnquist dissented from the majority opinion with regard to the tuition grant and tax relief portions of the statute, viewing them as little different from the type of aid upheld in *Everson* and *Allen*.

After *Nyquist* many commentators wondered what types of targeted aid beyond bus reimbursement (*Everson*) and textbook loan programs (*Allen*) could be upheld. In particular, much concern was focused on voucher plans. Did *Nyquist* sound the death knell for *all* types of indirect aid? In 1977, Senators Moynihan and Packwood proposed a federal tuition tax credit plan which they asserted was quite different from the type struck down in *Nyquist*. Unlike the New York plan in that case, the Moynihan-Packwood proposal would have provided tax credits to anyone having to pay tuition, whether in public or non-public schools or colleges.* By lumping the two types of beneficiaries together to create a broad class receiving benefits from the bill, the sponsors maintained that the proposal was constitutional. Are they right? Is the government really promoting the establishment of religion contrary to the intent of the Establishment Clause by providing police and fire protection, transportation services, and the like to religiously-affiliated schools and colleges if these services are provided to other types of public and nonpublic institutions as well? A recent federal district court decision in Minnesota accepts this rationale in upholding that state's law permitting parents of students attending public or nonpublic schools to claim up to $700 per year in income tax exemptions for expenses for tuition, textbooks, and transportation per child. In a 2 to 1 decision in *Minnesota Civil Liberties Union v. Roemer*, 452 F.Supp. 1316 (D.C.Minn.1978), Chief Judge Devitt admitted that the tuition component of the law was "particularly troublesome," but went on to uphold the statute as "analogous to the long recognized practice of tax deductible contributions to religious and charitable causes by federal and state governments" upheld in *Walz v. Tax. Comm.* (At p. 1322). He distinguished the statute from the New York law struck down in *Nyquist* since, unlike the New York plan, tax relief was directed to both the parents of students attending public school and nonpublic school. He also noted that the law had gone unchallenged since its enactment in 1955.

In dissent, Judge Alsop observed that separation of church and state was a principle much older than the statute and that, regardless of its longevity, the Minnesota law "does aid religious institutions by providing an economic benefit to religious schools * * *." (At p. 1323). Although tax relief conceivably could be claimed by the parents of children attending public schools, Judge Alsop noted that the number of taxpayers required to pay such tuition is so limited that this feature broadens the scope of the Minnesota law "only imperceptively" beyond that of the New

---

* In May, 1979, the Court in a 6 to 3 decision affirmed without opinion lower court decisions striking down a New Jersey tax credit scheme which was limited to the parents of nonpublic school students. The case was Byrne v. Public Funds for Public Education, —— U.S. ——. The lower courts relied heavily on *Nyquist*.

York statute. If you were to decide this case, would you opt for the "secularization of services" approach of *Walz v. Tax Comm.* to uphold the law or rely on *Board of Educ. v. Nyquist* to strike it down as an impermissible advancement of religion? Is there any way judicial neutralists could decide this issue without jeopardizing their approach to judging?

In *Americans United for Separation of Church and State v. Rogers,* 429 U.S. 1029 (1976), the Supreme Court refused to rule on a four-year old Missouri tuition aid scheme which opponents said unconstitutionally benefits religious colleges. The Missouri Supreme Court ruling thus was left standing. That court concluded that the tuition grants, which ranged up to $900 per student, are constitutional, even though the law does not specifically limit the grants to secular use. According to the attorney for the appellant taxpayers, "This is the only case ever upheld where a state can give money to students without specific restrictions that it can't be used for sectarian purposes." He noted that "all they have to do is give the money to the student. The school then can spend it on anything it wants to." [12] In October, 1977, the Supreme Court routinely affirmed two lower federal court decisions upholding the constitutionality of similar tuition assistance programs in two other states.

Do you find it anomalous that a tuition aid scheme can be upheld if it applies to postsecondary education but not if it benefits elementary and secondary schools? Do you see the Court's changing its mind about *Nyquist* if a federal tax credit plan is passed including all public and nonpublic educational institutions at all levels?

Litigation over indirect aid plans at the elementary and secondary level continues. In *Meek v. Pittenger,* 421 U.S. 349 (1975), the Court ruled on four Pennsylvania parochiaid programs. The programs provided for the loan of textbooks, instructional materials, instructional equipment, and auxiliary services to religiously affiliated schools. In this legislation Pennsylvania had tried to meet the objections of earlier cases. Thus, the instructional equipment (projection equipment, recording equipment, and laboratory equipment) and materials (books, periodicals, globes, photographs, and the like) were *loans,* not grants as in *Lemon.* The auxiliary services (guidance, counseling, diagnostic testing, and so on) were to be provided by public school personnel. In Pennsylvania 25 percent of the students attend nonpublic schools (96 percent of which are sectarian), and the legislature hoped to provide all nonpublic institutions with these educational benefits.

In *Meek* the Supreme Court upheld the textbook part, relying on *Allen.* However, the other programs were rejected. Unlike the textbooks, the instructional materials and equipment were directly loaned to nonpublic schools and thus failed the primary effect test as an unconstitutional advancement of religion. The auxiliary services provision was also struck down because in order for auxiliary personnel to remain ideologically neutral "the state would have to impose limitations on the activities of auxiliary personnel and then engage in some form of continuing surveillance to

---

12. As quoted in *Higher Education Daily,* December 14, 1976, at p. 2.

ensure that those restrictions were being followed." (At p. 372). It made no difference that the auxiliary personnel were employees of the public school systems; the danger of fostering an impermissible advancement of religion remained.

The *Meek* decision revealed that the Court itself was divided on the question of indirect aid to nonpublic elementary and secondary schools. The opinions disclosed a three-way split. Justices Brennan, Douglas, and Marshall would have struck down all of the elements of the program. Chief Justice Burger, who had dissented from the majority view on the tuition and tax relief portions of the New York program in *Nyquist*, would have sustained all elements. He was joined by Justices Rehnquist and White. The middle group of Justices Stewart, Blackmun, and Powell supported only the textbook provision. Thus six of the nine Justices agreed that other than the textbook loan program, the Pennsylvania legislation was unconstitutional. Interestingly, three Justices would have overruled *Allen*, including Justice Brennan, who originally supported the ruling.

Some commentators concluded on the basis of *Meek* that no type of aid beyond bus transportation, textbook loans, and general health and safety measures such as police and fire protection could pass muster. Thus one commentator flatly stated that *"Meek* signals the end of the use of 'tests' to determine the legitimacy of any program of aid to children attending religious primary or secondary schools."[13] Still, Justice Stewart, who wrote the majority opinion, did acknowledge for himself and Justices Blackmun and Powell that diagnostic testing services and testing to protect the health of nonpublic school youngsters were acceptable, though not severable from the rest of the Pennsylvania program. Given the willingness of Justices Burger, White, and Rehnquist to support this type of parochiaid, the door was thus open to at least some expansion of aid to the nonpublic sector. In 1977 the Court, with Justice Stevens now replacing retiring Justice Douglas, had occasion to rule once again on the issue.

Wolman v. Walter, 433 U.S. 229 (1977), involves a taxpayer challenge to an Ohio law enacted after the *Meek* decision. The statute, capitalizing on the lessons to be learned from *Meek*, sought to provide a variety of services to nonpublic school students as well as their public school counterparts. Included were books, instructional materials and equipment, standardized testing and scoring, diagnostic services, therapeutic services, and field trip transportation. The law explicitly provided that services were to be used only for secular purposes. At the time, more than 96 percent of the nonpublic school students in Ohio attended sectarian schools, and more than 92 percent attended Catholic schools. The federal district court ruled that the statute was constitutional.

13. J. E. Nowak, "The Supreme Court, the Religion Clauses and the Nationalization of Education," 70 *Northwestern Univ.L. Rev.* 883, 1976, at pp. 891–892.

WOLMAN v. WALTER

Supreme Court of the United States, 1977.
433 U.S. 229, 97 S.Ct. 2593, 53 L.Ed.2d 714.

Mr Justice BLACKMUN delivered the opinion of the Court (Parts I, V, VI, VII, and VIII), together with an opinion (Parts II, III, and IV), in which The Chief Justice, Mr. Justice STEWART, and Mr. Justice POWELL joined.

* * *

II

The mode of analysis for Establishment Clause questions is defined by the three-part test that has emerged from the Court's decisions. In order to pass muster, a statute must have a secular legislative purpose, must have a principal or primary effect that neither advances nor inhibits religion, and must not foster an excessive government entanglement with religion.

In the present case we have no difficulty with the first prong of this three-part test. We are satisfied that the challenged statute reflects Ohio's legitimate interest in protecting the health of its youth and in providing a fertile educational environment for all the school children of the State. As is usual in our cases, the analytical difficulty has to do with the effect and entanglement criteria.

* * *

III

Textbooks

* * *

This system for the loan of textbooks to individual students bears a striking resemblance to the systems approved in *Board of Education v. Allen,* and in *Meek v. Pittenger,* * * *

* * * Accordingly, we conclude that § 3317.06(A) is constitutional.

IV

Testing and Scoring

Section 3317.06 authorizes expenditure of funds

"(J) To supply for use by pupils attending nonpublic schools within the district such standardized tests and scoring services as are in use in the public schools of the state."

These tests "are used to measure the progress of students in secular subjects." Nonpublic school personnel are not involved in either the drafting or scoring of the tests. The statute does not authorize any payment to nonpublic school personnel for the costs of administering the tests.

In *Levitt v. Committee for Public Education,* 413 U.S. 472, (1973), this Court invalidated a New York statutory scheme for reimbursement of church-sponsored schools for the expenses of teacher-prepared testing. The reasoning behind that decision was straight-forward. The system was held unconstitutional because "no means are available, to assure that internally prepared tests are free of religious instruction."

* * * The State may require that schools that are utilized to fulfill the State's compulsory education requirement meet certain standards of instruction, and may examine both teachers and pupils to ensure that the State's legitimate interest is being fulfilled.

* * * Under the section at issue, the State provides both the schools and the school district with the means of ensuring that the minimum standards are met. The nonpublic school does not control the content of the test or its result. This serves to prevent the use of the test as a part of religious teaching, and thus avoids that kind of direct aid to religion found present in *Levitt*. Similarly, the inability of the school to control the test eliminates the need for the supervision that gives rise to excessive entanglement. We therefore agree with the District Court's conclusion that § 3317.06(J) is constitutional.

V

Diagnostic Services

Section 3317.06 authorizes expenditures of funds

"(D) To provide speech and hearing diagnostic services to pupils attending nonpublic schools within the district. Such service shall be provided in the nonpublic school attended by the pupil receiving the service.

* * *

"(F) To provide diagnostic psychological services to pupils attending nonpublic schools within the district. Such services shall be provided in the school attended by the pupil receiving the service."

It will be observed that these speech and hearing and psychological diagnostic services are to be provided within the nonpublic school. It is stipulated, however, that the personnel (with the exception of physicians) who perform the services are employees of the local board of education; that physicians may be hired on a contract basis; that the purpose of these services is to determine the pupil's deficiency or need of assistance; and that treatment of any defect so found would take place off the nonpublic school premises.

Appellants assert that the funding of these services is constitutionally impermissible. They argue that the speech and hearing staff might engage in unrestricted conversation with the pupil and, on occasion, might fail to separate religious instruction from secular responsibilities.

They further assert that the communication between the psychological diagnostician and the pupil will provide an impermissible opportunity for the intrusion of religious influence.

The District Court found these dangers so insubstantial as not to render the statute unconstitutional. We agree. This Court's decisions contain a common thread to the effect that the provision of health services to all school children—public and nonpublic—does not have the primary effect of aiding religion.
* * *

* * * The Court in *Meek* explicitly stated that the provision of diagnostic speech and hearing services by Pennsylvania seemed "to fall within that class of general welfare services for children that may be provided by the State regardless of the incidental benefit that accrues to church-related schools." The provision of such services was invalidated only because it was found unseverable from the unconstitutional portions of the statute.

* * *

We conclude that providing diagnostic services on the nonpublic school premises will not create an impermissible risk of the fostering of ideological views. It follows that there is no need for excessive surveillance, and there will not be impermissible entanglement. We therefore hold that §§ 3317.06(D) and (F) are constitutional.

VI

Therapeutic Services

Sections 3317.06(G), (H), (I), and (K) authorize expenditures of funds for certain therapeutic, guidance, and remedial services for students who have been identified as having a need for specialized attention. Personnel providing the services must be employees of the local board of education or under contract with the State Department of Health. The services are to be performed only in public schools, in public centers, or in mobile units located off the nonpublic school premises. * * *

Appellants concede that the provision of remedial, therapeutic, and guidance services in public schools, public centers, or mobile units is constitutional if both public and nonpublic school students are served simultaneously. Their challenge is limited to the situation where a facility is used to service only nonpublic school students. They argue that any program that isolates the sectarian pupils is impermissible because the public employee providing the service might tailor his approach to reflect and reinforce the ideological view of the sectarian school attended by the children. Such action by the employee, it is claimed, renders direct aid to the sectarian institution. Appellants express particular concern over mobile units because they perceive a danger that such a unit might operate merely as an annex of the school or schools it services.

* * *

We recognize that, unlike the diagnostician, the therapist may establish a relationship with the pupil in which there might be opportunities to transmit ideological views. In *Meek* the Court acknowledged the danger that publicly employed personnel who provide services analogous to those at issue here might transmit religious instruction and advance religious beliefs in their activities. But, * * * the Court emphasized that this danger arose from the fact that the services were performed in the pervasively sectarian atmosphere of the church-related school. * * *

The fact that a unit on a neutral site on occasion may serve only sectarian pupils does not provoke the same concerns that troubled the Court in *Meek*. The influence on a therapist's behavior that is exerted by the fact that he serves a sectarian pupil is qualitatively different from the influence of the pervasive atmosphere of a religious institution. The dangers perceived in *Meek* arose from the nature of the institution, not from the nature of the pupils.

Accordingly, we hold that providing therapeutic and remedial services at a neutral site off the premises of the nonpublic schools will not have the impermissible effect of advancing religion. Neither will there be any excessive entanglement arising from supervision of public employees to insure that they maintain a neutral stance. It can hardly be said that the supervision of public employees performing public functions on public property creates an excessive entanglement between church and state. Sections 3317.06(G), (H), (I), and (K) are constitutional.

VII

Instructional Materials and Equipment

Sections 3317.06(B) and (C) authorize expenditures of funds for the purchase and loan to pupils or their parents upon individual request of instructional materials and instructional equipment of the kind in use in the public schools within the district and which is "incapable of diversion to religious use." Section 3717.06 also provides that the materials and equipment may be stored on the premises of a nonpublic school and that publicly hired personnel who administer the lending program may perform their services upon the nonpublic school premises when necessary "for efficient implementation of the lending program."

* * *

Appellees seek to avoid *Meek* by emphasizing that it involved a program of direct loans to nonpublic schools. In contrast, the material and equipment at issue under the Ohio statute are loaned to the pupil or his parent. In our view, however, it would exalt form over substance if this distinction were found to justify a result different from that in *Meek*. * * *

* * *

If a grant in cash to parents is impermissible [as in *Nyquist*], we fail to see how a grant in kind of goods furthering the religious enterprise can fare any better.[17] Accordingly, we hold §§ 3317.-06(B) and (C) to be unconstitutional.[18]

VIII

Field Trips

Section 3317.06 also authorizes expenditures of funds:

"(L) To provide such field trip transportation and services to nonpublic school students as are provided to public school students in the district. School districts may contract with commercial transportation companies for such transportation service if school district busses are unavailable."

There is no restriction on the timing of field trips; the only restriction on number lies in the parallel the statute draws to field trips provided to public school students in the district. * * * The choice of destination * * * will be made by the nonpublic school teacher from a wide range of locations.

* * * The field trips are an integral part of the educational experience, and where the teacher works within and for a sectarian institution, an unacceptable risk of fostering or religion is an inevitable byproduct. * * * Funding of field trips, therefore, must be treated as was the funding of maps and charts in *Meek v. Pittenger*, the funding of buildings and tuition in *Committee for Public Education v. Nyquist*, and the funding of teacher-prepared tests in *Levitt v. Committee for Public Education;* it must be declared an impermissible direct aid to sectarian education. * * *

IX

In summary, we hold constitutional those portions of the Ohio statute authorizing the State to provide nonpublic school pupils with books, standardized testing and scoring, diagnostic services, and therapeutic and remedial services. We hold unconstitutional those portions relating to instructional materials and equipment and field trip services.

The judgment of the District Court is therefore affirmed in part and reversed in part.

It is so ordered.

The CHIEF JUSTICE dissents from Parts VII and VIII of the Court's opinion. (Justices WHITE and REHNQUIST joined the Chief Justice in his dissent.)

17. In many respects, *Nyquist* was a more difficult case than the present one. First, it was at least arguable in *Nyquist* that the tuition grant did not end up in the hands of the religious schools since the parent was free to spend the grant money as he chose. No similar argument could be made here since the parties have stipulated expressly that material and equipment must be used to supplement courses. Second, since the grant in *Nyquist* was limited to 50% of tuition, it was arguable that the grant should be seen as supporting only the secular part of the church-school enterprise. An argument of that kind also could not be made here, for *Meek* makes clear that the material and equipment are inextricably connected with the church-related school's religious function.

18. There is, as there was in *Meek*, a tension between this result and *Board of Edu-* *cation v. Allen.* *Allen* was premised on the view that the educational content of textbooks is something that can be ascertained in advance and cannot be diverted to sectarian uses. * * *

Board of Education v. Allen has remained law, and we now follow as a matter of *stare decisis* the principle that restriction of textbooks to those provided the public schools is sufficient to ensure that the books will not be used for religious purposes. In more recent cases, however, we have declined to extend that presumption of neutrality to other items in the lower school setting. It has been argued that the Court should extend *Allen* to cover all items similar to textbooks. When faced, however, with a choice between extension of the unique presumption created in *Allen* and continued adherence to the principles announced in our subsequent cases, we choose the latter course.

Mr. Justice BRENNAN, concurring and dissenting.

* * *

* * * The Court holds that Ohio has managed * * * to fashion a statute that avoids an effect or entanglement condemned by the Establishment Clause. But "The [First] Amendment nullifies sophisticated as well as simple-minded * * *" attempts to avoid its prohibitions, and, in any event, ingenuity in draftsmanship cannot obscure the fact that this subsidy to sectarian schools amounts to $88,800,000 (less now the sums appropriated to finance §§ 3317.-06(B) and (C) which today are invalidated) just for the initial biennium. The Court nowhere evaluates this factor in determining the compatibility of the statute with the Establishment Clause, * * *. Its evaluation, * * * compels in my view the conclusion that a divisive political potential of unusual magnitude inheres in the Ohio program. This suffices without more to require the conclusion that the Ohio statute in its entirety offends the First Amendment's prohibition against laws "respecting an establishment of religion."

Mr. Justice MARSHALL, concurring and dissenting.

I join Parts I, V, VII, and VIII of the Court's opinion. For the reasons stated below, however, I am unable to join the remainder of the Court's opinion or its judgment upholding the constitutionality of §§ 3317.06(A), (G), (H), (I), (J), and (K).

The Court upholds the textbook loan provision, § 3317.06(A), on the precedent of *Board of Education v. Allen*. It also recognizes, however, that there is "a tension" between *Allen* and the reasoning of the Court in *Meek v.*

Pittenger. I would resolve that tension by overruling *Allen*. I am now convinced that *Allen* is largely responsible for reducing the "high and impregnable" wall between church and state erected by the First Amendment, to "a blurred, indistinct, and variable barrier," incapable of performing its vital functions of protecting both church and state.

* * *

By overruling *Allen*, we would free ourselves to draw a line between acceptable and unacceptable forms of aid that would be both capable of consistent application and responsive to the concerns discussed above. That line, I believe, should be placed between general welfare programs that serve children in sectarian schools because the schools happen to be a convenient place to reach the programs' target populations and programs of educational assistance. General welfare programs, in contrast to programs of educational assistance, do not provide "[s]ubstantial aid to the educational function" of schools,[5] whether secular or sectarian, and therefore do not provide the kind of assistance to the religious mission of sectarian schools we found impermissible in *Meek*. Moreover, because general welfare programs do not assist the sectarian functions of denominational schools, there is no reason to expect that political disputes over the merits of those programs will divide the public along religious lines.

* * *

The Court upholds paragraphs (H), (I), and (K), which it groups with paragraph (G), under the rubric of "therapeutic services." I cannot agree that the services authorized by these three paragraphs should be treated like the psychological services provided by paragraph (G). Paragraph (H) authorizes the pro-

---

5. To some extent, of course, any program that improves the general well-being of a student may assist his education. The distinction is between programs that help the school educate a student and welfare programs that may have the effect of making a student more receptive to being educated.

vision of guidance and counseling services. The parties stipulated that the functions to be performed by the guidance and counseling personnel would include assisting students in "developing meaningful educational and career goals," and "Planning school programs of study." In addition, these personnel will discuss with parents "their children's a) educational progress and needs, b) course selections, c) educational and vocational opportunities and plans, and d) study skills." The counselors will also collect and organize information for use by parents, teachers, and students. This description makes clear that paragraph (H) authorizes services that would directly support the educational programs of sectarian schools. It is, therefore, in violation of the First Amendment.

Paragraphs (I) and (K) provide remedial services and programs for disabled children. The stipulation of the parties indicates that these paragraphs will fund specialized teachers who will both provide instruction themselves and create instructional plans for use in the students' regular classrooms. These "therapeutic services" are clearly intended to aid the sectarian schools to improve the performance of their students in the classroom. I would not treat them as if they were programs of physical or psychological therapy.

Finally, the Court upholds paragraph (J), which provides standardized tests and scoring services, on the ground that these tests are clearly nonideological and that the State has an interest in assuring that the education received by sectarian school students meets minimum standards. I do not question the legitimacy of this interest, and if Ohio required students to obtain specified scores on certain tests before being promoted or graduated, I would agree that it could administer those tests to sectarian school students to ensure that its standards were being met. The record indicates, however, only that

the tests "are used to measure the progress of students in secular subjects." It contains no indication that the measurements are taken to assure compliance with state standards rather than for internal administrative purposes of the schools. To the extent that the testing is done to serve the purposes of the sectarian schools rather than the State, I would hold that its provision by the State violates the First Amendment.

Mr. Justice POWELL, concurring in part and dissenting in part.

Our decisions in this troubling area draw lines that often must seem arbitrary. No doubt we could achieve greater analytical tidiness if we were to accept the broadest implications of the observation in *Meek v. Pittenger*, that "[s]ubstantial aid to the educational function of [sectarian] schools * * * necessarily results in aid to the sectarian enterprise as a whole." If we took that course, it would become impossible to sustain state aid of any kind—even if the aid is wholly secular in character and is supplied to the pupils rather than the institutions. *Meek* itself would have to be overruled, along with *Board of Education v. Allen,* and even perhaps *Everson v. Board of Education.* The persistent desire of a number of States to find proper means of helping sectarian education to survive would be doomed. This Court has not yet thought that such a harsh result is required by the Establishment Clause. Certainly few would consider it in the public interest. Parochial schools, quite apart from their sectarian purpose, have provided an educational alternative for millions of young Americans; they often afford wholesome competition with our public schools; and in some States they relieve substantially the tax burden incident to the operation of public schools. The State has, moreover, a legitimate interest in facilitating education of the highest quality for all children within its boundaries, whatever school their parents have chosen for them.

It is important to keep these issues in perspective. At this point in the 20th century we are quite far removed from the dangers that prompted the Framers to include the Establishment Clause in the Bill of Rights. The risk of significant religious or denominational control over our democratic processes—or even of deep political division along religious lines—is remote, and when viewed against the positive contributions of sectarian schools, any such risk seems entirely tolerable in light of the continuing oversight of this Court. Our decisions have sought to establish principles that preserve the cherished safeguard of the Establishment Clause without resort to blind absolutism. If this endeavor means a loss of some analytical tidiness, then that too is entirely tolerable. Most of the Court's decision today follows in this tradition, and I join Parts I through VI of its opinion.

With respect to Part VII, I concur only in the judgment. I am not persuaded, nor did *Meek* hold, that all loans of secular instructional material and equipment "inescapably [have] the primary effect of providing a direct and substantial advancement of the sectarian enterprise." If that were the case, then *Meek* surely would have overruled *Allen*. Instead the Court reaffirmed *Allen*, thereby necessarily holding that at least some such loans of materials helpful in the educational process are permissible—so long as the aid is incapable of diversion to religious uses, and so long as the materials are lent to the individual students or their parents and not to the sectarian institutions. Here the statute is expressly limited to materials incapable of diversion. Therefore the relevant question is whether the materials are such that they are "furnished for the use of *individual* students and at their request."

The Ohio statute includes some materials such as wall maps, charts and other classroom paraphernalia for which the concept of a loan to individuals is a transparent fiction. A loan of these items is indistinguishable from forbidden "direct aid" to the sectarian institution itself, * * *. Since the provision makes no attempt to separate these instructional materials from others meaningfully lent to individuals, I agree with the Court that it cannot be sustained under our precedents. But I would find no constitutional defect in a properly limited provision lending to the individuals themselves only appropriate instructional materials and equipment similar to that customarily used in public schools.

I dissent as to Part VIII, concerning field trip transportation. The Court writes as though the statute funded the salary of the teacher who takes the students on the outing. In fact only the bus and driver are provided for the limited purpose of physical movement between the school and the secular destination of the field trip. As I find this aid indistinguishable in principle from that upheld in *Everson, supra*, I would sustain the District Court's judgment approving this part of the Ohio statute.

Mr. Justice STEVENS, concurring in part and dissenting in part.

The distinction between the religious and secular is a fundamental one. To quote from Clarence Darrow's argument in the *Scopes* case:

> "The realm of religion * * * is where knowlege leaves off, and where faith begins, and it never has needed the arm of the State for support, and wherever it has received it, it has harmed both the public and the religion that it would pretend to serve."

The line drawn by the Establishment Clause of the First Amendment must also have a fundamental character. It should not differentiate between direct and indirect subsidies, or between instructional materials like globes and maps on the one hand and instructional materials like textbooks on the other. For that reason, rather than the three-part test described in Part II of the Court's opinion. I would adhere to the test enunciated for the Court by Mr. Justice Black:

> "No tax in any amount, large or small, can be levied to support any religious activities or institutions, whatever they may be called, or whatever form they may adopt to teach or practice religion." *Everson v. Board of Education.*

Under that test, a state subsidy of sectarian schools is invalid regardless of the form it takes. The financing of buildings, field trips, instructional materials, educational tests, and school books are all equally invalid. For all give aid to the school's educational mission, which at heart is religious.[3] On the other hand, I am not prepared to exclude the possibility that some parts of the statute before us may be administered in a constitutional manner. The State can plainly provide public health services to children attending nonpublic schools. The diagnostic and therapeutic services described in Parts V and VI of the Court's opinion may fall into this category. Although I have some misgivings on this point, I am not prepared to hold this part of the statute invalid on its face.

This Court's efforts to improve on the *Everson* test have not proved successful. "Corrosive precedents" have left us without firm principles on which to decide these cases. As this case demonstrates, the States have been encouraged to search for new ways of achieving forbidden ends. What should be a "high and impregnable" wall between church and state, has been reduced to a "blurred, indistinct, and variable barrier." The result has been, as Clarence Darrow predicted, harm to "both the public and the religion that [this aid] would pretend to serve." [7]

Accordingly, I dissent from Parts II, III and IV of the Court's opinion.

---

3. It is the sectarian school itself, not the legislation, that is "entangled" with religion:

> "The very purpose of many of those schools is to provide an integrated secular and religious education; the teaching process is, to a large extent, devoted to the inculcation of religious values and belief. Substantial aid to the educational function of such schools, accordingly, necessarily results in aid to the sectarian school enterprise as a whole. '[T]he secular education those schools provide goes hand in hand with the religious mission that is the only reason for the schools' existence. Within the institution, the two are inextricably intertwined.'"

7. In *Roemer v. Maryland Public Works Board*, I spoke of "the pernicious tendency of a state subsidy to tempt religious schools to compromise their religious mission without wholly abandoning it." This case presents an apt illustration. To qualify for aid, sectarian schools must relinquish their religious exclusivity. As the District Court noted, the statute provides aid "to pupils attending only those nonpublic schools whose admission policies make no distinction as to * * * creed * * * of either its pupils or of its teachers." Similarly, sectarian schools will be under pressure to avoid textbooks which present a religious perspective on secular subjects, so as to obtain the free textbooks provided by the State.

NOTES AND QUESTIONS

1. In *Wolman* the Ohio legislature sought to take advantage of Justice Stewart's suggestion in *Meek v. Pittenger* that some forms of parochiaid might be constitutional if such legislation were tailored to the *Meek* opinion. Obviously, the effort was worth it. Note how the *Wolman* lineup of Justices changes from that of *Meek*, though in quite consistent fashion. In this 5–4 decision, Stewart is again in the majority, as are Blackmun and Powell. They uphold all but the instructional materials and equipment and the field trip provisions of the Ohio statute. The most permissive of the Justices in these cases, Chief Justice Burger, Justice White, and Justice Rehnquist, would uphold all of the provisions, a position consistent with their dissents in *Meek*. Of the opposite view is Justice Brennan, who would strike down all of them. Justice Marshall agrees that only the diagnostic service provision is constitutional, and Justice Stevens agrees that only the diagnostic service and therapeutic service provisions are constitutional. The swing-men, then, appear to be Justices Stewart, Blackmun, and Powell, and, to a lesser extent, Justice Stevens. As long as the Court is balanced in this fashion, the outcome of Establishment cases can probably be effectively predicted. Reconsider the constitutionality of tax credit plans. What decision would you think the Court might make in these matters? (Review the lineup of the Justices in *Nyquist* and *Meek,* as well as Justice Blackmun's comment in *Wolman* about channeling instructional materials and equipment on a loan basis to parents and students rather than schools.)

2. Does the fact that some 90 percent of nonpublic schools are religiously-affiliated probably preclude the adoption of a voucher plan for low-income students? How might a voucher plan be implemented in a way to assure constitutionality? Some commentators have recently pressed the argument that a voucher plan not only provides low-income students with greater educational opportunity, it also increases their right to religious freedom. The same is true of tax credit and tuition refund-type programs. Stated slightly differently, this argument could mean that if government *doesn't* provide these kinds of benefits, it is infringing on the Free Exercise Clause. (Some say the present system of compulsory elementary and secondary schooling intrudes on the rights of parents and students to First Amendment freedoms as well as by monopolizing the educational process.) Is this a viable argument or merely a restatement of the incompatibility of the two religion clauses? We will have occasion to consider this again below.

3. In these cases there is much discussion about the potential evils of political divisiveness over parochiaid programs. One commentator has asserted that the Supreme Court's decisions made in part to avoid such political divisiveness have really contributed to it. Consider the following:

> * * * political conflict may well increase political division along religious lines. As inner city school performance continues to decrease, one would expect increased pressure on government to aid private schools so that the residents of the city have an alternative to the public school system. However, it will be in the inter-

est of those who favor religiously oriented education to oppose such aid if it is not provided on an equal basis to parochial schools. Those who favor parochial schools will perceive that aid to non-religious private schools directly threatens their existence by offering an alternative to the public school system which the state has placed in an economically preferred position to their schools. This would leave religious schools at a dual disadvantage in the market place. Public schools would have the benefit of the highest governmental subsidy, while private nonreligious schools would have less subsidy but greater responsiveness to parents and teachers. The religiously oriented schools would be the only ones where the students or their families are required to bear the full cost of operating the school. Those who favor the continued existence of parochial schools would find it beneficial to oppose aid to both the public schools and nonreligious private schools. Thus, one may expect to see new forms of political division along religious lines due to the majority's ban on aid to parochial schools.[14]

But isn't this a different type of political divisiveness from that engendered by parochiaid?

4. The Establishment cases raise two fundamental questions. First, does the Establishment Clause strike down anything which has the effect of making religion more viable or does it prohibit only the direct advancement of religion? If the latter, how direct must the linkage be? And secondly, is there a difference between aiding a church and aiding a religiously-affiliated educational institution? If so, at what level of education is this difference most apparent?

Review the decisions of the major Establishment Clause cases as outlined in Figure 4–2. Utilizing the cases and the tests the Justices have articulated in reaching their decisions, how would you decide the following hypothetical situations? If you had only your own ideas about the Establishment Clause to go on, would your decisions be different?

14. Nowak, *Id.*, at pp. 907–908.

Figure 4–2: Chronological Chart: Major Establishment Clause Decisions, 1947–1978

Supreme Court Cases	Decision	Comment
Everson v. Board of Educ., 1947	Upheld bus transportation reimbursement for parochial school children as public welfare legislation.	States the "wall of separation" theory; concludes that public welfare legislation does not create a breach.
McCollum v. Board of Educ., 1948	Struck down a release time program involving use of public school classrooms by sectarian groups.	Sectarian influence within the school breaches the wall of separation.
Zorach v. Clauson, 1952	Upheld a release time program where students leave the public school premises.	The recent "excessive entanglement" test may jeopardize this decision.
Engel v. Vitale, 1962	Struck down the reading of a non-denominational school prayer prepared by state officials.	Sectarian influence within the school breaches the wall of separation.
Abington School District v. Schempp, 1963	Struck down laws requiring reading of Biblical passages in public schools.	Same as above, also introduces the secular legislative purpose and primary effect tests.
Board of Education v. Allen, 1968	Upheld the loan of secular texts to nonpublic school students.	Controversial decision, some Justices urge it be overruled.
Epperson v. State of Arkansas, 1968	Struck down a statute prohibiting the teaching of evolution in the public schools.	Sectarian influence within the school breaches the wall of separation.
Walz v. Tax Commissioners, 1970	Upheld tax exemptions for churches.	Introduces the third test, excessive entanglement of state with church.
Lemon v. Kurtzman, 1971	Struck down reimbursement to nonpublic schools for teachers' salaries, texts, and instructional materials.	Indicates that direct monetary aid to schools breaches the wall of separation.
Tilton v. Ricardson, 1971	Upheld one-time construction grants for nonpublic colleges and universities.	Introduces the view that college students are less susceptible to religious indoctrination.
Committee for Public Education v. Nyquist, 1973	Struck down direct reimbursement for maintenance and repairs of nonpublic schools and indirect use of tuition grants and tax benefits to parents.	Indirect schemes to aid the parent breaches wall of separation since the money flows to nonpublic school.
Meek v. Pittenger, 1975	Upheld a textbook loan program based on Allen but struck down loans of instructional equipment to nonpublic schools and auxiliary services by public school personnel in nonpublic schools.	Like the grants in Lemon, nonmonetary loans to nonpublic schools advances religion.
Roemer v. Board of Public Works, 1976	Upheld direct noncategorical grants to be used for non-sectarian purposes at nonpublic colleges and universities.	An extension of Tilton; clearly illustrates different treatment for postsecondary education.
Wolman v. Walter, 1977	Upheld text book loan program, standardized testing, diagnotic service, and counseling program for nonpublic schools. Struck down instructional equipment loan program to parents and field trip transportation program.	Upholds several nonmonetary pupil benefit programs carefully tailored to avoid advancing religion.

a. A voluntary prayer program for elementary school students during free periods in a public school.

b. A mandatory silent meditation program at the start of the school day in a public elementary school after attendance is taken in homeroom.

c. Same program as in (b) above for high school seniors.

d. Catholic student asserts that denial of space to worship in a public college violates his free exercise rights and demands that the institution furnish a room where Mass can be held.

e. Any difference in (d) above if the college is largely residential and located 50 miles from the nearest Catholic church?

f. Catholic taxpayer demands relief from paying taxes to support the public schools, which they do not use, preferring to send their children to parochial schools.

g. Atheist taxpayer demands a refund of that portion of his taxes being utilized to underwrite the cost of furnishing bus service and textbooks to students attending denominational schools.

h. Suspension of classes at a public college for the two Jewish holidays of Rosh Hashanah and Yom Kippur.

i. A challenge to the invocation and benediction at commencement ceremonies at a public high school.

j. Holding commencement ceremonies at a public college in a Catholic church.

k. Would it make any difference in (j) above if the church had the only large meeting area in the immediate vicinity of the college?

l. A state program providing driver education to students attending religious schools.

Note that some of these situations could raise either Establishment or Free Exercise issues or both. Can government ever truly be neutral? We will explore some of these situations in greater depth in the next section. You may wish, therefore, to reconsider some of your responses later.

II. GOVERNMENT AND THE FREE EXERCISE OF RELIGION

What is a church? Can any group of people legally constitute themselves into a church, formulate sanctioned ritual, and appoint clergy? Can the state decide that one group is a legitimate church and another is not? How is a "religious belief" to be defined? Can a proper distinction be made between religious belief (expression) and religious ritual (action)?

The Supreme Court's attempt to define freedom of religious belief, ritual, education, and proselytizing should be viewed as a specific application of freedom of speech. Freedom to speak and freedom to exercise one's religious beliefs provide the constitutional foundation for intellectual freedom. This section examines two specific areas of religious freedom with which the Supreme Court has dealt, namely, the kinds of expression which are considered "religious" and the degree to which one can constitutionally engage in religiously compelled ritual or conduct. Since the free exercise cases involving the political and social setting are so closely interrelated with those involving education, our discussion will not distinguish between them.

A.　What Constitutes Religious Belief?

Consider the interesting case of *Malnak v. Maharishi Mahesh Yogi,* 440 F.Supp. 1284 (D.C.N.J.1977), involving an elective course in Transcendental Meditation at five New Jersey public high schools. Plaintiffs argued that TM is a religion and that as such, offering it in the public schools is an infringement on the Establishment Clause. Defendants contended that TM is a philosophy, not a religion. As a philosophy, the school board can include it pursuant to its power to determine the nature of the curriculum.

How should the issue be resolved? In the nineteenth century, courts would probably have concluded that TM is not a religion. A survey of the cases of that period illustrates that "religion" for purposes of the Establishment Clause and the Free Exercise Clause referred to "theistic notions respecting divinity, morality, and worship　*　*　*　recognized as legitimate and protected only insofar as it was generally accepted as 'civilized' by Western standards." [15] Viewed in this way Transcendental Meditation could be taught in the public schools since the Establishment Clause would not be implicated. Nor would the Free Exercise Clause be infringed if government prohibited the practice of TM.

The growing diversity of religious belief and practice in the country since the turn of the century has necessitated a broader view of "religion" in order to extend Free Exercise Clause protection. A good illustration of the Supreme Court's evolving approach are the conscientious objector cases involving the military draft. The Selective Service Act of 1917 granted exemptions from combat service to conscientious objectors affiliated with a "well-recognized religious sect or organization (then) organized and existing　*　*　*　where　*　*　*　creed or principles forbid its members to participate in war in any form　*　*　*." In *The Selective Service Cases,* 245 U.S. 366 (1918), the Supreme Court upheld the provisions of this act against constitutional attack as an establishment of religion.

In 1965 the Supreme Court first came to terms with whether a belief in God is essential for religious conscientious objection under a 1940 statute as amended in 1948. The Universal Military Training and Service Act provided exemptions for anyone who "by reason of religious training or belief is conscientiously opposed to participation in war in any form." In 1948, Congress defined "religious training or belief" to mean "an individual's belief in relation to a Supreme Being involving duties superior to those arising from any human relation, but　*　*　*　not (including) essentially political, sociological, or philosophical views or a merely personal moral code." An exemption for humanistically motivated conscientious objection to war was apparently excluded. Daniel Seeger sought exemption as a conscientious objector during the Vietnam War. He admitted

15.　Laurence H. Tribe, *American Constitutional Law* (Mineola, N. Y.: The Foundation Press, 1977), at p. 826.

his skepticism about the existence of God. However, he did acknowledge a " 'belief in and devotion to goodness and virtue for their own sakes, and a religious faith in a purely ethical creed.' " (At p. 166). The Court in *United States v. Seeger*, 380 U.S. 163 (1965), avoided an explicit definition of "religious training and belief" but held that Seeger's claim to exemption as a conscientious objector was valid because he was not presenting a "merely personal code." Justice Clark for the majority concluded that "We think it clear that the beliefs which prompted his objection occupy the same place in his life as the belief in a traditional deity holds in the lives of his friends, the Quakers." (At p. 187). The Court did require that a claim to exemption as a conscientious objector had to be based on ethical grounds which transcend the individual's own desires for himself. Congress acknowledged the *Seeger* decision by deleting the reference to a Supreme Being in a 1967 amendment to the statute. However, the religious bases for exemption remained.

Toward the end of the Vietnam War five years later, the Supreme Court applied the rationale of the *Seeger* decision to a conscientious objector who denied even more explicitly that his views on war were "religious" in the conventional sense of the term. In *Welsh v. United States*, 398 U.S. 333 (1970), Welsh refused to be drafted because he claimed that " 'the taking of a life—anyone's life—to be morally wrong.' " (At p. 343). In an apparent effort to avoid facing the issue of whether exemptions for religious reasons constitute an unconstitutional advancement of religion under the Establishment Clause, Justice Black in a plurality opinion interpreted the selective service statute as amended in 1967 to apply to Welsh's nontheistic views. Justice Harlan in a concurring opinion indicated his preference for ruling that the statute's restrictions to religious beliefs violated the Establishment Clause.

While both the *Seeger* and *Welsh* cases involve Congressional statutes and not the words of the First Amendment directly, the opinions clearly indicate a preference by the Justices for a broad view of what is "religion." These decisions serve to limit the precedential value of earlier decisions such as *Hamilton v. Regents of the Univ. of Cal.*, 293 U.S. 245 (1934). There a state university dismissed members of a religious denomination for their refusal to participate in military science courses. The Court held that the curricular requirement itself did not conflict with the students' free exercise of their religion.

Returning to the Transcendental Meditation case, we find the district court relying on the broad view advanced in *Seeger* to rule that inclusion of TM in the school curriculum is an unconstitutional advancement of religion under the Establishment Clause since more than the stress-reducing properties of the technique were being taught. The court noted that some 70 percent of class time was devoted not to exercises but to discussion of the contents of the textbook entitled *Science of Creative Intelligence for Secondary Education: First Year Course*. After carefully examining the text, the court characterized it as a religious treatise:

> The textbook clearly teaches and assumes that there exists and has existed eternally an unmanifested or uncreated field of

life which is unbounded or infinite. This field of life is present everywhere, both within and without everything in the universe; * * *. * * * Contact with this field of being bestows upon individuals the ability to choose between right and wrong spontaneously, without regard to moral codes and laws. Manifestly, the textbook describes some sort of ultimate reality which in its various forms is given the name "god" in common usage. (At p. 1320).

Whether called "a supreme being, God, the ultimate reality, creative intelligence," the conceptions used in the text, stated the court, are religious in nature. As the court noted, "although the precise conceptions or definitions of the ultimate reality or supreme being will differ from religion to religion, the religious nature of the concept is incontrovertible." (At p. 1322).

Such a broad interpretation of religion raises disturbing questions where Establishment Clause issues are involved. As here, a broad reading of "religion" for Free Exercise purposes if carried over to the Establishment Clause may prevent the government from involvement with many worthwhile humanistic endeavors. Some commentators thus believe "religion" should be interpreted two ways: broadly for Free Exercise purposes but narrowly under the Establishment Clause.[16] Such interpretations would provide the greatest latitude to accommodating individual beliefs.

NOTES AND QUESTIONS

1. In *Sapp v. Renfroe,* 372 F.Supp. 1193 (N.D.Ga.1974), Tim Sapp, a high school student in the Decatur, Georgia, school system challenged the constitutionality of a mandatory ROTC military training course for tenth graders. He complained that the requirement violated his personal belief system. Exemptions under Decatur High School policy were extended only for the physically disabled and for those who objected on religious grounds. The district court upheld the school policy, noting the secular value of the course.

> * * * the Court notes * * * that the program serves a valid educational purpose and bears a rational connection to the fulfillment of the state school system's position of *parens patriae* by teaching students discipline, leadership, personal hygiene and first aid. The additional topics of military science, military organization, firearms safety and marksmanship also serve valid educational goals and do not violate Sapp's First Amendment freedom. (At p. 1196).

The court took note of the Sixth Circuit Court of Appeals' decision in *Spence v. Bailey,* 465 F.2d 797 (6th Cir. 1972). There the circuit court, relying on *Seeger,* held a high school's mandatory ROTC requirement violative of the First Amendment's guarantee of religious freedom. But the Georgia court distinguished *Spence* by noting that Tim Sapp's views

16. Tribe, *Id.,* pp. 827–828.

were not religiously based. In light of *Welsh,* should the decision have been the other way? Or does the *Hamilton* case provide sufficient support for the district court's ruling in favor of the Decatur course requirement? Sapp appealed but the case was declared moot since he had graduated from high school. 511 F.2d 172 (5th Cir. 1975).

2. Although the Supreme Court in *Welsh* interpreted the Selective Service Act to grant exemption to persons with strong and sincere moral and ethical beliefs against all war and that their consciences need not be religiously-based, it later refused to grant this exemption to *particular* wars as many opponents of the Vietnam War wished. *Gillette v. United States,* 401 U.S. 437 (1971). Would it have been inconsistent with *Welsh* to decide the reverse?

B.   Where Does Belief End and Unconstitutional Practice Begin?

The Supreme Court has never permitted the government to punish individuals for pure religious *belief* that is not directly accompanied by action. The problem exists when a person's religious belief compels action that runs contrary to the law. Although the Court has generally indicated that an individual cannot be forced to express particular religious tenets or to profess public affirmations that are contrary to one's religious beliefs, the Court has been embroiled in controversy when this principle has been applied in practice.

(1) The Flag Salute Cases

An early illustration of this controversy involves the Jehovah's Witnesses' refusal to participate in compulsory flag salute exercises in the public schools. The Witnesses instruct their children that saluting the flag constitutes worship of a "graven image," contrary to biblical teaching. For the Witnesses, compulsory flag salute requires a breach of conscience which is contrary to the Free Exercise Clause. This conflict of conscience was presented to the Supreme Court in *Minersville School Dist. v. Gobitis,* 310 U.S. 586 (1940). The Court decided with one dissenter that the expulsion of Lilian and William Gobitis from public schools for refusing to salute the flag was valid.

Justice Frankfurter wrote the majority opinion in the *Gobitis* case. He contended that the Court was not involved in the question of whether it was appropriate to require dissenting school children to salute the flag; the Court was deciding, rather, only that it was *constitutional* to do so. For Frankfurter the question was whether this compulsory flag salute was a wise use of legislative authority. His response was that it was an issue that should be decided "in the forum of public opinion and before legislative assemblies * * *." (At p. 600). Frankfurter claimed that this particular legislation requiring compulsory flag salute was " * * * of general scope not directed against doctrinal loyalties of particular sects." (At p. 594). The implication of Justice Frankfurter's opinion was that the state had a constitutional right to compel all school children to salute the flag. The only question that may properly be asked is whether a school board had reasons for thinking that the compulsory salute to the flag would help to realize legitimate educational ends. Frankfurter, as a judicial self-restraintist, could not deny that the school board might properly hold such a view. The inculcation of patriotism through participation in the flag salute ceremony was a valid governmental policy that the states could establish despite the religious objections of some persons; there should be no "exceptional immunity" to those with religious scruples.

Justice Stone was the sole dissenter. Stone took the position that the "very essence of * * * liberty * * * is the freedom of the individual from compulsion as to what he shall think and what he shall say, at least where the compulsion is to bear false witness to his religion." (At p. 604). The violation of religious beliefs in the interest of promoting national unity was in Stone's view an impermissible means to a legitimate end.

After the *Gobitis* case, many additional local school boards established compulsory flag salute regulations, which were clearly intolerant of those persons who refused to participate in the exercise. With the entrance of the United States into World War II in 1941, the increased intensity of patriotic activities undoubtedly contributed to the proliferation of such school policies. The *Gobitis* decision itself certainly encouraged some school boards to establish compulsory flag salute exercises. The decision produced great legal debate as well as unleashed a wave of persecution against the Jehovah Witnesses.

Three years later the *Gobitis* case was overruled by the Supreme Court in *West Virginia State Bd. of Educ. v. Barnette.*

WEST VIRGINIA STATE BD. OF EDUC. v. BARNETTE

Supreme Court of the United States, 1943.
319 U.S. 624, 63 S.Ct. 1178, 87 L.Ed. 1628.

Mr. Justice JACKSON delivered the opinion of the Court.

* * *

The Board of Education on January 9, 1942, adopted a resolution containing recitals taken largely from the Court's Gobitis opinion and ordering that the salute to the flag become "a regular part of the program of activities in the public schools," that all teachers and pupils "shall be required to participate in the salute honoring the Nation represented by the Flag; provided, however, that refusal to salute the Flag be regarded as an Act of insubordination, and shall be dealt with accordingly."

The resolution originally required the "commonly accepted salute to the Flag" which it defined. Objections to the salute as "being too much like Hitler's" were raised by the Parent and Teachers Association, the Boy and Girl Scouts, the Red Cross and the Federation of Women's Clubs. Some modification appears to have been made in deference to these objections, but no concession was made to Jehovah's Witnesses.[4] What is now re-

---

4. They have offered in lieu of participating in the flag salute ceremony "periodically and publicly" to give the following pledge:

"I have pledged my unqualified allegiance and devotion to Jehovah, the Almighty God, and to His Kingdom, for which Jesus commands all Christians to pray.

"I respect the flag of the United States and acknowledge it as a symbol of freedom and justice to all.

"I pledge allegiance and obedience to all the laws of the United States that are consistent with God's law, as set forth in the Bible."

quired is the "stiff-arm" salute, the saluter to keep the right hand raised with palm turned up while the following is repeated: "I pledge allegiance to the Flag of the United States of America and to the Republic for which it stands; one Nation, indivisible, with liberty and justice for all."

Failure to conform is "insubordination" dealt with by expulsion. Readmission is denied by statute until compliance. Meanwhile the expelled child is "unlawfully absent" and may be proceeded against as a delinquent. His parents or guardians are liable to prosecution, and if convicted are subject to fine not exceeding $50 and jail term not exceeding thirty days.

Appellees, citizens of the United States and of West Virginia, brought suit in the United States District Court for themselves and others similarly situated asking its injunction to restrain enforcement of these laws and regulations against Jehovah's Witnesses. The Witnesses are an unincorporated body teaching that the obligation imposed by law of God is superior to that of laws enacted by temporal government. Their religious beliefs include a literal version of Exodus, Chapter 20, verses 4 and 5, which says: "Thou shalt not make unto thee any graven image, or any likeness of anything that is in heaven above, or that is in the earth beneath, or that is in the water under the earth; thou shalt not bow down thyself to them nor serve them." They consider that the flag is an "image" within this command. For this reason they refuse to salute it.

Children of this faith have been expelled from school and are threatened with exclusion for no other cause. Officials threaten to send them to reformatories maintained for criminally inclined juveniles. Parents of such children have been prosecuted and are threatened with prosecutions for causing delinquency.

* * *

There is no doubt that, in connection with the pledges, the flag salute is a form of utterance. Symbolism is a primitive but effective way of communicating ideas. The use of an emblem or flag to symbolize some system, idea, institution, or personality, is a short cut from mind to mind. Causes and nations, political parties, lodges and ecclesiastical groups seek to knit the loyalty of their followings to a flag or banner, a color or design. * * *

* * * Here it is the State that employs a flag as a symbol of adherence to government as presently organized. It requires the individual to communicate by word and sign his acceptance of the political ideas it thus bespeaks. Objection to this form of communication when coerced is an old one, well known to the framers of the Bill of Rights.

It is also to be noted that the compulsory flag salute and pledge requires affirmation of a belief and an attitude of mind. It is not clear whether the regulation contemplates that pupils forego any contrary convictions of their own and become unwilling converts to the prescribed ceremony or whether it will be acceptable if they simulate assent by words without belief and by a gesture barren of meaning. It is now a commonplace that censorship or suppression of expression of opinion is tolerated by our Constitution only when the expression presents a clear and present danger of action of a kind the State is empowered to prevent and punish. It would seem that involuntary affirmation could be commanded only on even more immediate and urgent grounds than silence. But here the power of compulsion is invoked without any allegation that remaining passive during a flag salute ritual creates a clear and present danger that would justify an effort even to muffle expression. To sustain the compulsory flag salute we are required to say that a Bill of Rights which guards the individual's right to speak his own mind, left it open to public authorities to compel him to utter what is not in his mind.

Whether the First Amendment to the Constitution will permit officials to order observance of ritual of this nature does not depend upon whether as a voluntary exercise we would think it to be good, bad or merely innocuous. * * *

Nor does the issue as we see it turn on one's possession of particular religious views or the sincerity with which they are held. While religion supplies appellees' motive for enduring the discomforts of making the issue in this case, many citizens who do not share these religious views hold such a compulsory rite to infringe constitutional liberty of the individual. * * *

* * * The question which underlies the flag salute controversy is whether such a ceremony so touching matters of opinion and political attitude may be imposed upon the individual by official authority under powers committed to any political organization under our Constitution. We examine rather than assume existence of this power and, against this broader definition of issues in this case, re-examine specific grounds assigned for the Gobitis decision.

* * *

National unity as an end which officials may foster by persuasion and example is not in question. The problem is whether under our Constitution compulsion as here employed is a permissible means for its achievement.

Struggles to coerce uniformity of sentiment in support of some end thought essential to their time and country have been waged by many good as well as by evil men. Nationalism is a relatively recent phenomenon but at other times and places the ends have been racial or territorial security, support of a dynasty or regime, and particular plans for saving souls. As first and moderate methods to attain unity have failed, those bent on its accomplishment must resort to an every-increasing severity. As governmental pressure toward unity becomes greater, so strife becomes more bitter as to whose unity it shall be. Probably no deeper division of our people could proceed from any provocation than from finding it necessary to choose what doctrine and whose program public educational officials shall compel youth to unite in embracing. Ultimate futility of such attempts to compel coherence is the lesson of every such effort from the Roman drive to stamp out Christianity as a disturber of its pagan unity, the Inquisition, as a means to religious and dynastic unity, the Siberian exiles as a means to Russian unity, down to the fast failing efforts of our present totalitarian enemies. Those who begin coercive elimination of dissent soon find themselves exterminating dissenters. Compulsory unification of opinion achieves only the unanimity of the graveyard.

It seems trite but necessary to say that the First Amendment to our Constitution was designed to avoid these ends by avoiding these beginnings. There is no mysticism in the American concept of the State or of the nature or origin of its authority. We set up government by consent of the governed, and the Bill of Rights denies those in power any legal opportunity to coerce that consent. Authority here is to be controlled by public opinion, not public opinion by authority.

The case is made difficult not because the principles of its decision are obscure but because the flag involved is our own. Nevertheless, we apply the limitations of the Constitution with no fear that freedom to be intellectually and spiritually diverse or even contrary will disintegrate the social organization. To believe that patriotism will not flourish if patriotic ceremonies are voluntary and spontaneous instead of a compulsory routine is to make an unflattering estimate of the appeal of our institutions to free minds. We can have intellectual individualism and the rich cultural diversities that we owe to exceptional minds only at the price of occasional eccentricity and abnormal attitudes. When they are so harmless to others or to the State as those we deal with here, the price is not too great. But freedom to differ is not limited to things that do not matter much. That would be a mere shadow of freedom. The test of its substance is the right to differ as to things that touch the heart of the existing order.

If there is any fixed star in our constitutional constellation, it is that no official, high or petty, can prescribe what shall be orthodox in politics, nationalism, religion, or other matters of opinion or force citizens to confess by word or act their faith therein. If there are any circumstances which permit an exception, they do not now occur to us.

We think the action of the local authorities in compelling the flag salute and pledge transcends constitutional limitations on their power and invades the sphere of intellect and spirit which it is the purpose the First Amendment to our Constitution to reserve from all official control.

The decision of this Court in Minersville School District v. Gobitis and the holdings of those few per curiam decisions which preceded and foreshadowed it are overruled, and the judgment enjoining enforcement of the West Virginia Regulation is affirmed.

Affirmed.

Mr. Justice ROBERTS and Mr. Justice REED adhere to the views expressed by the Court in Minersville School District v. Gobitis, * * *.

Mr. Justice BLACK and Mr. Justice DOUGLAS, concurring.

We are substantially in agreement with the opinion just read, but since we originally joined with the Court in the Gobitis case, it is appropriate that we make a brief statement of reasons for our change of view.

Reluctance to make the Federal Constitution a rigid bar against state regulation of conduct thought inimical to the public welfare was the controlling influence which moved us to consent to the Gobitis decision. Long reflection convinced us that although the principle is sound, its application in the particular case was wrong. We believe that the statute before us fails to accord full scope to the freedom of religion secured to the appellees by the First and Fourteenth Amendments.

* * *

Words uttered under coercion are proof of loyalty to nothing but self-interest. Love of country must spring from willing hearts and free minds, inspired by a fair administration of wise laws enacted by the people's elected representatives within the bounds of express constitutional prohibitions. These laws must, to be consistent with the First Amendment, permit the widest toleration of conflicting viewpoints consistent with a society of free men.

Neither our domestic tranquillity in peace nor our martial effort in war depend on compelling little children to participate in a ceremony which ends in nothing for them but a fear of spiritual condemnation. If, as we think, their fears are groundless, time and reason are the proper antidotes for their errors. The ceremonial, when enforced against conscientious objectors, more likely to defeat than to serve its high purpose, is a handy implement for disguised religious persecution. As such, it is inconsistent with our Constitution's plan and purpose.

Mr. Justice MURPHY, concurring.

* * *

Mr. Justice FRANKFURTER, dissenting.

* * *

Under our constitutional system the legislature is charged solely with civil concerns of society. If the avowed or intrinsic legislative purpose is either to promote or to discourage some religious community or creed, it is clearly within the constitutional restrictions imposed on legislatures and cannot stand. But it by no means follows that legislative power is wanting whenever a general non-discriminatory civil regulation in fact touches conscientious scruples or religious beliefs of an individual or a group.

* * *

* * *

When dealing with religious scruples we are dealing with an almost numberless variety of doctrines and beliefs entertained with equal sincerity by the particular groups for which they satisfy man's needs in his relation to the mysteries of the universe. * * *

* * *

That which to the majority may seem essential for the welfare of the state may offend the consciences of a minority. But, so long as no inroads are made upon the actual exercise of religion by the minority, to deny the political power of the majority to enact laws concerned with civil matters, simply because they may offend the consciences of a minority, really means that the consciences of a minority are more sacred and more enshrined in the Constitution than the consciences of a majority.

* * *

Saluting the flag suppresses no belief nor curbs it. Children and their parents may believe what they please, avow their belief and practice it. It is not even remotely suggested that the requirement for saluting the flag involves the slightest restriction against the fullest opportunity on the part both of the children and of their parents to disavow as publicly as they choose to do so the meaning that others attach to the gesture of salute. All channels of affirmative free expression are open to both children and parents. Had we before us any act of the state putting the slightest curbs upon such free expression, I should not lag behind any member of this Court in striking down such an invasion of the right to freedom of thought and freedom of speech protected by the Constitution.

I am fortified in my view of this case by the history of the flag salute controversy in this Court. Five times has the precise question now before us been adjudicated. Four times the Court unanimously found that the requirement of such a school exercise was not beyond the powers of the states. Indeed in the first three cases to come before the Court the constitutional claim now sustained was deemed so clearly unmeritorious that this Court dismissed the appeals for want of a substantial federal question. * * *

What may be even more significant than this uniform recognition of state authority is the fact that every Justice— thirteen in all—who has hitherto participated in judging this matter has at one or more times found no constitutional infirmity in what is now condemned. Only the two Justices sitting for the first time on this matter have not heretofore found this legislation inoffensive to the "liberty" guaranteed by the Constitution. And among the Justices, who sustained this measure were outstanding judicial leaders in the zealous enforcement of constitutional safeguards of civil liberties—men like Chief Justice Hughes, Mr. Justice Brandeis, and Mr. Justice Cardozo, to mention only those no longer on the Court.

One's conception of the Constitution cannot be severed from one's conception of a judge's function in applying it. The Court has no reason for existence if it merely reflects the pressures of the day. Our system is built on the faith that men set apart for this special function, freed from the influences of immediacy and form the deflections of worldly ambition, will become able to take a view of longer range than the period of responsibility entrusted to Congress and legislatures. We are dealing with matters as to which legislators and voters have conflicting views. Are we as judges to impose our strong convictions on where wisdom lies? That which three years ago had seemed to five successive Courts to lie within permissible areas of legislation is now outlawed by the deciding shift of opinion of two Justices. What reason is there to believe that they or their successors may not have another view a few years hence?

* * *

* * *

NOTES AND QUESTIONS

1. Whose rights are involved in this case? Does the majority opinion adequately distinguish between the rights of the parents who brought the case and the rights of their children? Is this case more appropriately one of parental rights than student rights? Or is it both?

2. What exactly does the majority hold? Note Justice Jackson's statement that,

> Nor does the issue as we see it turn on one's possession of particular religious views or the sincerity with which they are held. While religion supplies appellees' motive for enduring the discomforts of making the issue in this case, many citizens who do not share these religious views hold such a compulsory rite to infringe constitutional liberty of the individual.

This case coupled with *Pierce v. Society of the Sisters of the Holy Names of Jesus and Mary*, 268 U.S. 510 (1925), and the remaining case in this chapter have convinced some critics of the American public schooling system that there is sufficient freedom of thought implicit in the First/Fourteenth Amendments to undermine compulsory schooling and the control of school boards over curriculum content. They thus read *Barnette* more broadly to apply to all students, not just those with particular religious beliefs, and to academic instruction, not just patriotic exercises. As one commentator has noted,

> The logical conclusion (of the *Barnette* decision) is too evident: any compulsion in education is necessarily unconstitutional. Public or national fellowship is an end which the state may foster and encourage—even in education—but always by "persuasion and example," never by force.[17] (Material in brackets added).

Another commentator elaborates on the nature of the unconstitutional force compulsory schooling is said to exert:

> The state provides a "free" public education to all children of appropriate age and qualifications through its system of public schools. But the state may not condition the provision of this education—whether it be a right or a privilege—upon the sacrifice by parents of their First Amendment rights. Yet this is

_____

17. Peter J. Riga *"Yoder* and Free Exercise," 6 *J.Law and Educ.*, 449, October, 1977, at p. 454.

precisely the effect of a school system that requires a child to attend a school controlled by a majority of the public in order to receive a "free" education.　The public school will represent and attempt to inculcate values that a particular family may find abhorrent to its own basic beliefs and way of life.　The family is then faced with the choice of (1) abandoning its beliefs in order to gain the benefit of a state-subsidized education, or (2) forfeiting the proffered government benefit in order to preserve the family belief structure from government interference.[18]

These arguments, of course, are often made by those who advocate an end to compulsory schooling, the adoption of a voucher system, or substitution of home education.　Note that the constitutional basis is not the Free Exercise Clause but the whole of the First Amendment. Do you think Justice Jackson's majority opinion in *Barnette* carries such an implication?　Reconsider the purposes of compulsory schooling as you reflect on the implications of *Barnette*.　Could R. Freeman Butts' views about the mission of American elementary and secondary schools as expressed in Chapter One be realized other than through compulsory schooling?

Others have read *Barnette* much more restrictively.　Note the following:

> *　*　*　In the curriculum indoctrination situation, for example, courts must assess educational policies and values to determine a violation and fashion a remedy.　It would be difficult, however, to determine when exposure has become indoctrination or when a balanced presentation of ideas has occurred. Such determinations require an understanding of subtle interactions and relationships in the educational system, including the manner in which various subjects, ideas, and techniques influence students.　Clearly, courts do not possess the level of expertise necessary to make such judgments.　In *Barnette,* on the other hand, the parents attacked the required observance of a ritual, which was merely an adjunct to the content of the curriculum.　In that case, the determination of unconstitutionality was based primarily upon a judgment of good citizenship, which the Court felt uniquely competent to make.　Thus, the court's lack of competence in educational matters was less important.

> There are, moreover, several problems with the proposed remedy for curriculum indoctrination.　Separate programs for dissenting children could create detrimental divisiveness, which has been a continuing concern of the courts in religion cases and was further reiterated in *Barnette.*　Further, the efficiency of school operations and the quality of education might be seriously impaired by a complex system of exemptions and special classes.

> Thus, while the right to be free from interference with thought appears to have been given a sound theoretical founda-

18.　Stephen Aarons, "The Separation of School and State: *Pierce* Reconsidered," 46 *Harvard Ed.Rev.*, 76, Feb., 1976, at p. 100.

tion in *Barnette,* the courts' relative inexpertise in the field of education and the practical difficulties of formulating a remedy are likely to prevent them from recognizing such a claim, thereby leaving intact the school boards' pervasive control of curriculum.[19]

Which view most nearly approximates your own? To date, courts have usually limited *Barnette* to flag salute situations. In addition, those protesting such compulsion have usually had to show how a specific Constitutional right is infringed. Challenges to compulsory school laws have generally failed. For example, in *Scoma v. Chicago Bd. of Educ.,* 391 F.Supp. 452 (N.D.Ill.1974), the parents sought to argue the broad interpretation of their rights under the First/Fourteenth Amendments in opposition to compulsory schooling. The court rejected their expansive view, noting that "Aside from claims based on the exercise of religion clause, compulsory attendance statutes have generally been regarded as valid." (At p. 461).

3. In a part of the *Barnette* opinion not included in the excerpt, the *Hamilton v. Board of Regents of the Univ. of California* case is distinguished because attendance at the state university was optional whereas in *Barnette* it was not, and also because the state has the power to raise a militia and impose service duties therein upon its citizens. But in his dissent Justice Frankfurter maintains that since both the military training requirement in *Hamilton* and the flag salute in *Barnette* treat all religions the same, "I find it impossible, so far as constitutional power is concerned, to differentiate what was sanctioned in the *Hamilton* case from what was nullified in this case." (At p. 657). How persuasive is this assertion?

4. Recent issues involving the flag salute relate primarily to the system of exemptions provided those students who do not wish to participate for religious or political reasons. Thus, for example, in *Goetz v. Ansell,* 477 F.2d 636 (2d Cir. 1973), the court upheld the right of a high school student to remain quietly seated during the flag salute and in doing so struck down a school board regulation requiring those who did not want to participate in the ceremony to leave the classroom or remain standing in silence. Since standing is part of the flag salute ceremony, the court reasoned that requiring the student to stand violated his convictions. Leaving the classroom was also objectionable because it smacked of punishment. The court concluded that as long as the student did not engage in disruptive activities, remaining seated during the flag salute could be permitted.

5. *Gobitis* and *Barnette* provide ample illustration that judicial decision making is not always made without an awareness of the times. In *Barnette* Justices Douglas and Black reconsider their decision made three years earlier to follow the majority in *Gobitis.* By 1943, the midpoint of World War II, it was apparent that the flag salute, which had not been part of the American school scene prior to the war years, bore an uncomfortable similarity to the Nazi salute. Rather than continu-

---

19. Michigan *Project, supra,* at pp. 1446–1447.

ing to look at the issue as one of legislative authority, Justices Douglas and Black now view it as one of individual rights.

Justice Frankfurter's opinion for the Court in *Gobitis* and his adherence to it in his dissent in *Barnette* reflect in part his belief in judicial restraint. But other factors may well have been involved. As a Jew and as a loyal American, Frankfurter found Adolph Hitler abhorrent. *Gobitis* was decided shortly after the German conquest of Czechoslovakia, Poland, Finland, Denmark, and Norway. Frankfurter assembled his opinion in the case while the Nazi march continued across Luxembourg, Holland, and Belgium. His correspondence during this period shows that these events had a profound influence on him. Richard Danzig of the Stanford Law School contends that they prompted the Justice to frame the issue in terms of legislative authority and not individual rights. According to Danzig, framing the question in this way enabled Frankfurter to "inflate" the original issue involving the action of a single school district to one involving the moral right of legislatures to determine, in the words Frankfurter used in the case, "the appropriateness of various means to evoke that unifying sentiment without which there can ultimately be no liberties, civil or religious." [20] Only in this way could the government shake Americans from their isolationism and make them aware of what was occurring in Europe.

The context within which *Gobitis* and *Barnette* were decided illustrate that "the times" or "what is in the air" may well have a significant impact on judicial opinion. Such contextual effects can influence the phrasing of the issue, the selection of a particular interpretation, and ultimately the decision of the judge. It is thus important to consider the context within which judicial decision making goes on. As you read the remainder of the cases in this book, consider to what extent contextual effects may have influenced the judicial outcomes.

(2) The Mormon and Old Order Amish Cases

The most difficult issues in the area of free exercise of religion concern the belief plus action aspects of practicing a religion wherein certain actions compelled or encouraged by a person's religion clash with otherwise legitimate governmental action. Three issues involving polygamy, LSD, and religiously-motivated educational practices have proved troublesome in this respect.

The first major case was *Reynolds v. United States*, 98 U.S. 145 (1878). The case arose in the later 1870s over the Mormon practice of multiple marriages or polygamy. The United States Congress passed a law prohibiting polygamy. The issue posed by Congress' action was whether the law violated the Free Exercise Clause. Chief Justice Morrison R. Waite, speaking for the Court, claimed that there is a clear distinction between religious beliefs on the one hand and actions stemming from those beliefs on the other. Waite argued that Mormons could hold the belief that God permits men to have many wives, but they had no constitutional

---

20. Richard Danzig, "How Questions Begot Answers in Felix Frankfurter's First Flag Salute Opinion," 1977 *Sup.Ct.Rev.* 257, 1977, at p. 261.

right to *act out* their beliefs because to do so violates social duty and public order. The Chief Justice claimed that under the Free Exercise Clause,

> Congress was deprived of all legislative power over mere opinion, but was left free to reach actions which were in violation of social duties or subversive of good order. * * * Laws are made for the government of actions, and while they cannot interfere with mere religious beliefs and opinions, they may with practices. Suppose one believed that human sacrifices were a necessary part of religious worship; would it be seriously contended that the civil government under which he lived could not interfere to prevent a sacrifice? (At pp. 164 & 166).

For Waite and a majority of the Court, prohibition against polygamy (or human sacrifice) was a valid governmental policy enacted for secular purposes. This conservative emphasis on "social duty" and public order was the standard used in the case against the Mormons, or to put it in Chief Justice Waite's words, "Polygamy has always been odious among the northern and western nations of Europe * * *." (At p. 164). Although very few legal advocates today would use Waite's reasoning or exact wording, we still are faced with controversy over whether religious conscience provides a defense to the exercise of valid governmental authority.

The first major decision to extend the protection of the Free Exercise Clause to religiously-motivated behavior was *Sherbert v. Verner*, 374 U.S. 398 (1963). There the Court ruled that it was unconstitutional for a state to deny unemployment benefits to a person who refuses to accept available work on Saturday because of her religious beliefs. This case is also important because the majority opinion by Justice Brennan spoke in terms of a "compelling state interest" to justify infringement upon the exercise of an individual's religion:

> We must next consider whether some compelling state interest enforced in the eligibility provisions of the South Carolina statute justifies the substantial infringement of appellant's First Amendment right. It is basic that no showing merely of a rational relationship to some colorable state interest would suffice * * *. (At p. 406).

Finding none, the Court struck down the welfare restriction. Interestingly, Justice Brennan asserted that a Sunday closing law upheld by the Court two years earlier in *Braunfeld v. Brown*, 366 U.S. 599 (1961), met such a compelling state test by having a "uniform day of rest" for all workers. Three Justices in *Sherbert* disagreed, pointing out that the state criminal law against Sunday retail sales had the effect of forcing the plaintiff, Abraham Braunfeld, to choose between his business and his religion, and thus was clearly an unconstitutional interference with religious freedom. To date, *Braunfeld* has not been overruled. Why did Justice Brennan not simply overrule *Braunfeld*, since it clearly appears to run counter to the standards he set forth in *Sherbert*?

About one hundred years after the *Reynolds* decision and one year after the *Sherbert* decision, the California Supreme Court used the compelling interest approach to strike down a state ban on the use of the narcotic peyote by Navajo Indians in their religious ceremonies. As a sacrificial symbol peyote is considered an integral part of the religion of the Native American Church. The hallucinatory properties are believed to allow participants to experience the Deity. In 1962 a group of Navajo Indians were arrested in California for using peyote in their religious ceremony, the only occasion the drug can be used, according to church doctrine. They were convicted of the crime of possessing peyote, and they appealed to the California Supreme Court. The prosecution's argument was based on the *Reynolds* decision: laws against narcotics and their use could not be disobeyed on the grounds of individual religious conscience. In *People v. Woody*, 394 P.2d 813 (1964), the California Supreme Court held that the state law could not be interpreted to prohibit religious ceremonial use of peyote. The California Court claimed that the state may limit religious practices only when it shows a "compelling state interest," citing the *Sherbert* decision. The court claimed that the ceremonial use of peyote constitutes slight danger to the state and its enforcement of narcotic laws. In this case the balancing of interests and values favored religious conscience. Justice Matthew Tobriner speaking for the court made the following observation.

> In a mass society, which presses at every point toward conformity, the protection of self-expression, however unique, of the individual and the group becomes ever more important. The varying current of the subcultures that flow into the mainstream of our national life gives it depth and beauty. We preserve a greater value than an ancient tradition when we protect the rights of Indians who honestly practiced an old religion in using peyote one night at a meeting in a desert hogan near Needles, California. (At pp. 821–822).

The issue of psychedelics and the free exercise of religion was also involved in one of the most widely publicized cases of the 1960s involving Dr. Timothy Leary's conviction by a district court for illegal trafficking in marijuana. Leary claimed membership in a Hindu sect that considers the use of marijuana essential to meditation and spiritual illumination. The lower court and the Court of Appeals for the Fifth Circuit rejected Leary's contention, agreeing that trafficking in the drug posed a substantial threat to public safety and order. Dr. Leary's attempt to use the *Woody* decision on his behalf was rejected. Leary eventually appealed to the U. S. Supreme Court and was granted certiorari. The Court reversed the conviction. The reversal, however, was based on technical due process grounds and not on the free exercise issue. *Leary v. United States*, 395 U.S. 6 (1969).

Taken together, these decisions demonstrate considerable difference of opinion on what is protected under the Free Exercise Clause and what is not. At this stage in our constitutional history, we can conclude that religiously compelled conduct is not free from regulation. The "compelling state interest" standard does, as we have seen, provide judges with considerably more discretion in their attempt to balance the values of religious conscience against public order. But, of course, there is nothing requiring judges to give religion a "preferred position" over the Tenth Amendment powers of the state, or prohibiting them from reaching dissimilar outcomes when using this approach.

Our final excerpted case in this chapter, *Wisconsin v. Yoder*, brings together our discussion of the definition to be accorded to "religion" in the First Amendment and our discussion of the somewhat hazy distinction between religious belief and religious action. *Wisconsin v. Yoder* involves the refusal of Old Order Amish parents to abide by Wisconsin's compulsory school law.

WISCONSIN v. YODER

Supreme Court of the United States, 1972.
406 U.S. 205, 92 S.Ct. 1526, 32 L.Ed.2d 15.

Mr. Chief Justice BURGER delivered the opinion of the Court.

* * *

Respondents Jonas Yoder and Wallace Miller are members of the Old Order Amish religion, and respondent Adin Yutzy is a member of the Conservative Amish Mennonite Church. They and their families are residents of Green County, Wisconsin. Wisconsin's compulsory school-attendance law required them to cause their children to attend public or private school until reaching age 16 but the respondents declined to send their children, ages 14 and 15, to public school after they complete the eighth grade. The children were not enrolled in any private school, or within any recognized exception to the compulsory-attendance law, and they are con-

ceded to be subject to the Wisconsin statute.

On complaint of the school district administrator for the public schools, respondents were charged, tried, and convicted of violating the compulsory-attendance law in Green County Court and were fined the sum of $5 each.[3] Respondents defended on the ground that the application of the compulsory-attendance law violated their rights under the First and Fourteenth Amendments. The trial testimony showed that respondents believed, in accordance with the tenets of Old Order Amish communities generally, that their children's attendance at high school, public or private, was contrary to the Amish religion and way of life. They believed that by sending their children to high school, they would not only expose themselves to the danger of the

3. Prior to trial, the attorney for respondents wrote the State Superintendent of Public Instruction in an effort to explore the possibilities for a compromise settlement. Among other possibilities, he suggested that perhaps the State Superintendent could administratively determine that the Amish could satisfy the compulsory-attendance law by establishing their own vocational training plan similar to one that has been established in Pennsylvania. Under the Pennsylvaia plan, Amish children of high school age are required to attend an Amish vocational school for three hours a week, during which time they are taught

such subjects as English, mathematics, health, and social studies by an Amish teacher. For the balance of the week, the children perform farm and household duties under parental supervision, and keep a journal of their daily activities. The major portion of the curriculum is home projects in agriculture and homemaking.
* * *

The Superintendent rejected this proposal on the ground that it would not afford Amish children "substantially equivalent education" to that offered in the schools of the area.

censure of the church community, but, as found by the county court, also endanger their own salvation and that of their children. * * *

* * *

Formal high school education beyond the eighth grade is contrary to Amish beliefs, not only because it places Amish children in an environment hostile to Amish beliefs with increasing emphasis on competition in class work and sports and with pressure to conform to the styles, manners, and ways of the peer group, but also because it takes them away from their community, physically and emotionally, during the crucial and formative adolescent period of life. During this period, the children must acquire Amish attitudes favoring manual work and self-reliance and the specific skills needed to perform the adult role of an Amish farmer or housewife. They must learn to enjoy physical labor. Once a child has learned basic reading, writing, and elementary mathematics, these traits, skills, and attitudes admittedly fall within the category of those best learned through example and "doing" rather than in a classroom. And, at this time in life, the Amish child must also grow in his faith and his relationship to the Amish community if he is to be prepared to accept the heavy obligations imposed by adult baptism. In short, high school attendance with teachers who are not of the Amish faith—and may even be hostile to it—interposes a serious barrier to the integration of the Amish child into the Amish religious community. * * *

The Amish do not object to elementary education through the first eight grades as a general proposition because they agree that their children must have basic skills in the "three R's" in order to read the Bible, to be good farmers and citizens, and to be able to deal with non-Amish people when necessary in the course of daily affairs. They view such a basic

education as acceptable because it does not significantly expose their children to worldly values or interfere with their development in the Amish community during the crucial adolescent period. * * *

* * *

* * * The Wisconsin Circuit Court affirmed the convictions. The Wisconsin Supreme Court, however, sustained respondents' claim under the Free Exercise Clause of the First Amendment and reversed the convictions. A majority of the court was of the opinion that the State had failed to make an adequate showing that its interest in "establishing and maintaining an educational system overrides the defendants' right to the free exercise of their religion."

There is no doubt as to the power of a State, having a high responsibility for education of its citizens, to impose reasonable regulations for the control and duration of basic education. Providing public schools ranks at the very apex of the function of a State. Yet even this paramount responsibility was, in *Pierce,* made to yield to the right of parents to provide an equivalent education in a privately operated system. * * * Thus, a State's interest in universal education, however highly we rank it, is not totally free from a balancing process when it impinges on fundamental rights and interests, such as those specifically protected by the Free Exercise Clause of the First Amendment, and the traditional interest of parents with respect to the religious upbringing of their children so long as they, in the words of *Pierce,* "prepare [them] for additional obligations."

* * *

* * * A way of life, however virtuous and admirable, may not be interposed as a barrier to reasonable state regulation of education if it is based on purely secular considerations; to have the protection of the Religion Clauses, the claims must be rooted in religious belief.

Although a determination of what is a "religious" belief or practice entitled to constitutional protection may present a most delicate question, the very concept of ordered liberty precludes allowing every person to make his own standards on matters of conduct in which society as a whole has important interests. Thus, if the Amish asserted their claims because of their subjective evaluation and rejection of the contemporary secular values accepted by the majority, much as Thoreau rejected the social values of his time and isolated himself at Walden Pond, their claims would not rest on a religious basis. Thoreau's choice was philosophical and personal rather than religious, and such belief does not rise to the demands of the Religion Clauses.

Giving no weight to such secular considerations, however, we see that the record in this case abundantly supports the claim that the traditional way of life of the Amish is not merely a matter of personal preference, but one of deep religious conviction, shared by an organized group, and intimately related to daily living. That the Old Order Amish daily life and religious practice stem from their faith is shown by the fact that it is in response to their literal interpretation of the Biblical injunction from the Epistle of Paul to the Romans, "be not conformed to this world * * *." This command is fundamental to the Amish faith. Moreover, for the Old Order Amish, religion is not simply a matter of theocratic belief. As the expert witnesses explained, the Old Order Amish religion pervades and determines virtually their entire way of life, regulating it with the detail of the Talmudic diet through the strictly enforced rules of the church community.

The record shows that the respondents' religious beliefs and attitude toward life, family, and home have remained constant —perhaps some would say static—in a period of unparalleled progress in human knowledge generally and great changes in education. The respondents freely concede, and indeed assert as an article of faith, that their religious beliefs and what we would today call "life style" have not altered in fundamentals for centuries. Their way of life in a church-oriented community, separated from the outside world and "worldly" influences, their attachment to nature and the soil, is a way inherently simple and uncomplicated, albeit difficult to preserve against the pressure to conform. Their rejection of telephones, automobiles, radios, and television, their mode of dress, of speech, their habits of manual work do indeed set them apart from much of contemporary society; these customs are both symbolic and practical.

As the society around the Amish has become more populous, urban, industrialized, and complex, particularly in this century, government regulation of human affairs has correspondingly become more detailed and pervasive. The Amish mode of life has thus come into conflict increasingly with requirements of contemporary society exerting a hydraulic insistence on conformity to majoritarian standards. So long as compulsory education laws were confined to eight grades of elementary basic education imparted in a nearby rural schoolhouse, with a large proportion of students of the Amish faith, the Old Order Amish had little basis to fear that school attendance would expose their children to the worldly influence they reject. But modern compulsory secondary education in rural areas is now largely carried on in a consolidated school, often remote from the student's home and alien to his daily home life. As the record so strongly shows, the values and programs of the modern secondary school are in sharp conflict with the fundamental mode of life mandated by the Amish religion; modern laws requiring compulsory secondary education have accordingly engendered great concern and conflict. The conclusion is inescapable that secondary schooling, by exposing Amish children to worldly influences in terms of attitudes, goals, and values contrary to beliefs, and by substantially interfering with the religious development of the Amish child and his integration into the way of life of the Amish faith community at the crucial adolescent stage of development, contravenes the basic religious tenets and practice of the Amish faith, both as to the parent and the child.

The impact of the compulsory-attendance law on respondents' practice of the Amish religion is not only severe, but inescapable, for the Wisconsin law affirmatively compels them, under threat of criminal sanction, to perform acts undeniably at odds with fundamental tenets of their religious beliefs. * * * As the record shows, compulsory school attendance to age 16 for Amish children carries with it a very real threat of undermining the Amish community and religious practice as they exist today; they must either abandon belief and be assimilated into society at large, or be forced to migrate to some other and more tolerant region.

* * *

Wisconsin concedes that under the Religion Clauses religious beliefs are absolutely free from the State's control, but it argues that "actions," even though religiously grounded, are outside the protection of the First Amendment. * * * It is true that activities of individuals, even when religiously based, are often subject to regulation by the States in the exercise of their undoubted power to promote the health, safety, and general welfare, or the Federal Government in the exercise of its delegated powers. But to agree that religiously grounded conduct must often be subject to the broad police power of the State is not to deny that there are areas of conduct protected by the Free Exercise Clause of the First Amendment and thus beyond the power of the State to control, even under regula-

tions of general applicability. This case, therefore, does not become easier because respondents were convicted for their "actions" in refusing to send their children to the public high school; in this context belief and action cannot be neatly confined in logic-tight compartments.

* * *

The State advances two primary arguments in support of its system of compulsory education. It notes, as Thomas Jefferson pointed out early in our history, that some degree of education is necessary to prepare citizens to participate effectively and intelligently in our open political system if we are to preserve freedom and independence. Further, education prepares individuals to be self-reliant and self-sufficient participants in society. We accept these propositions.

However, the evidence adduced by the Amish in this case is persuasively to the effect that an additional one or two years of formal high school for Amish children in place of their long-established program of informal vocational education would do little to serve those interests. Respondents' experts testified at trial, without challenge, that the value of all education must be assessed in terms of its capacity to prepare the child for life. It is one thing to say that compulsory education for a year or two beyond the eighth grade may be necessary when its goal is the preparation of the child for life in modern society as the majority live, but it is quite another if the goal of education be viewed as the preparation of the child for life in the separated agrarian community that is the keystone of the Amish faith.

The State attacks respondents' position as one fostering "ignorance" from which the child must be protected by the State. No one can question the State's duty to protect children from ignorance but this argument does not square with the facts disclosed in the record. Whatever their idiosyncrasies as seen by the majority, this record strongly shows that the Amish community has been a highly successful social unit within our society, even if apart from the conventional "mainstream." Its members are productive and very law-abiding members of society; they reject public welfare in any of its usual modern forms. The Congress itself recognized their self-sufficiency by authorizing exemption of such groups as the Amish from the obligation to pay social security taxes. * * *

* * *

The State, however, supports its interest in providing an additional one or two years of compulsory high school education to Amish children because of the possibility that some such children will choose to leave the Amish community, and that if this occurs they will be ill-equipped for life. The State argues that if Amish children leave their church they should not be in the position of making their way in the world without the education available in the one or two additional years the State requires. However, on this record, that argument is highly speculative. There is no specific evidence of the loss of Amish adherents by attrition, nor is there any showing that upon leaving the Amish community Amish children, with their practical agricultural training and habits of industry and self-reliance, would become burdens on society because of educational shortcomings. * * *

There is nothing in this record to suggest that the Amish qualities of reliability, self-reliance, and dedication to work would fail to find ready markets in today's society. * * *

* * *

The requirement for compulsory education beyond the eighth grade is a relatively recent development in our history.

Less than 60 years ago, the educational requirements of almost all of the States were satisfied by completion of the elementary grades, at least where the child was regularly and lawfully employed.[15]

* * *

* * * The origins of the requirement for school attendance to age 16, an age falling after the completion of elementary school but before completion of high school, are not entirely clear. But to some extent such laws reflected the movement to prohibit most child labor under age 16 that culminated in the provisions of the Federal Fair Labor Standards Act of 1938. * * *

The requirement of compulsory schooling to age 16 must therefore be viewed as aimed not merely at providing educational opportunities for children, but as an alternative to the equally undesirable consequence of unhealthful child labor displacing adult workers, or, on the other hand, forced idleness. The two kinds of statutes—compulsory school attendance and child labor laws—tend to keep children of certain ages off the labor market and in school; this regimen in turn provides opportunity to prepare for a livelihood of a higher order than that which children could pursue without education and protects their health in adolescence.

In these terms, Wisconsin's interest in compelling the school attendance of Amish children to age 16 emerges as somewhat less substantial than requiring such attendance for children generally. * * *

* * *

Contrary to the suggestion of the dissenting opinion of Mr. Justice DOUGLAS, our holding today in no degree depends on the assertion of the religious interest of the child as contrasted with that

---

15. * * * Even today, an eighth grade education fully satisfies the educational requirements of at least six States. A number of other States have flexible provi-

sions permitting children aged 14 or having completed the eighth grade to be excused from school in order to engage in lawful employment. * * *

of the parents. It is the parents who are subject to prosecution here for failing to cause their children to attend school, and it is their right of free exercise, not that of their children, that must determine Wisconsin's power to impose criminal penalties on the parent. The dissent argues that a child who expresses a desire to attend public high school in conflict with the wishes of his parents should not be prevented from doing so. There is no reason for the Court to consider that point since it is not an issue in the case. The children are not parties to this litigation. The State has at no point tried this case on the theory that respondents were preventing their children from attending school against their expressed desires, and indeed the record is to the contrary.[21]

* * *

* * *

For the reasons stated we hold, with the Supreme Court of Wisconsin, that the First and Fourteenth Amendments prevent the State from compelling respondents to cause their children to attend formal high school to age 16. Our disposition of this case, however, in no way alters our recognition of the obvious fact that courts are not school boards or legislatures, and are ill-equipped to determine the "necessity" of discrete aspects of a State's program of compulsory education. This should suggest that courts must move with great circumspection in performing the sensitive and delicate task of weighing a State's legitimate social concern when faced with religious claims for exemption from generally applicable educational requirements. It cannot be overemphasized that we are not dealing with a way of life and mode of education by a group claiming to have recently discovered some "progressive" or more enlightened process for rearing children for modern life.

Aided by a history of three centuries as an identifiable religious sect and a long history as a successful and self-sufficient segment of American society, the Amish in this case have convincingly demonstrated the sincerity of their religious beliefs, the interrelationship of belief with their mode of life, the vital role that belief and daily conduct play in the continued survival of Old Order Amish communities and their religious organization, and the hazards presented by the State's enforcement of a statute generally valid as to others. * * * In light of this convincing showing, one that probably few other religious groups or sects could make, and weighing the minimal difference between what the State would require and what the Amish already accept, it was incumbent on the State to show with more particularity how its admittedly strong interest in compulsory education would be adversely affected by granting an exemption to the Amish.

Nothing we hold is intended to undermine the general applicability of the State's compulsory school-attendance statutes or to limit the power of the State to promulgate reasonable standards that, while not impairing the free exercise of religion, provide for continuing agricultural vocational education under parental and church guidance by the Old Order Amish or others similarly situated. The States have had a long history of amicable and effective relationships with church-sponsored schools, and there is no basis for assuming that, in this related context, reasonable standards cannot be established concerning the content of the continuing vocational education of Amish children under parental guidance, provided always that state regulations are not

21. The only relevant testimony in the record is to the effect that the wishes of the one child who testified corresponded with those of her parents. Testimony of Frieda Yoder, to the effect that her personal re-

ligious beliefs guided her decision to discontinue school attendance after the eighth grade. The other children were not called by either side.

inconsistent with what we have said in this opinion.

Affirmed.

Mr. Justice POWELL and Mr. Justice REHNQUIST took no part in the consideration or decision of this case.

Mr. Justice STEWART, with whom Mr. Justice BRENNAN joins, concurring.

* * *

Mr. Justice WHITE, with whom Mr. Justice BRENNAN and Mr. Justice STEWART join, concurring.

* * *

This would be a very different case for me if respondents' claim were that their religion forbade their children from attending any school at any time and from complying in any way with the educational standards set by the State. Since the Amish children are permitted to acquire the basic tools of literacy to survive in modern society by attending grades one through eight and since the deviation from the State's compulsory-education law is relatively slight, I conclude that respondents' claim must prevail, largely because "religious freedom—the freedom to believe and to practice strange and, it may be, foreign creeds—has classically been one of the highest values of our society."

The importance of the state interest asserted here cannot be denigrated, however * * *.

Pierce v. Society of Sisters, lends no support to the contention that parents may replace state educational requirements with their own idiosyncratic views of what knowledge a child needs to be a productive and happy member of society; * * *. In the present case, the State is not concerned with the maintenance of an educational system as an end in itself, it is rather attempting to nurture and develop the human potential of its children, whether Amish or non-Amish: to expand their knowledge, broaden their sensibilities, kindle their imagination, foster a spirit of free inquiry, and increase their human understanding and tolerance. It is possible that most Amish children will wish to continue living the rural life of their parents, in which case their training at home will adequately equip them for their future role. Others, however, may wish to become nuclear physicists, ballet dancers, computer programmers, or historians, and for these occupations, formal training will be necessary. There is evidence in the record that many children desert the Amish faith when they come of age.[3] A State has a legitimate interest not only in seeking to develop the latent talents of its children but also in seeking to prepare them for the life style that they may later choose, or at least to provide them with an option other than the life they have led in the past. In the circumstances of this case, although the question is close, I am unable to say that the State has demonstrated that Amish children who leave school in the eighth grade will be intellectually stultified or unable to acquire new academic skills later. The statutory minimum school attendance age set by the State is, after all, only 16.

* * *

Mr. Justice DOUGLAS, dissenting in part.

I agree with the Court that the religious scruples of the Amish are opposed to the education of their children beyond the grade schools, yet I disagree with the Court's conclusion that the matter is

---

3. Dr. Hostetler testified that though there was a gradual increase in the total number of Old Order Amish in the United States over the past 50 years, "at the same time the Amish have also lost members [of] their church" and that the turnover rate was such that "probably two-thirds [of the present Amish] have been assimilated non-Amish people." Justice Heffernan, dissenting below, opined that "[l]arge numbers of young people voluntarily leave the Amish community each year and are thereafter forced to make their way in the world."

within the dispensation of parents alone. The Court's analysis assumes that the only interests at stake in the case are those of the Amish parents on the one hand, and those of the State on the other. The difficulty with this approach is that, despite the Court's claim, the parents are seeking to vindicate not only their own free exercise claims, but also those of their high-school-age children.

* * *

* * * If the parents in this case are allowed a religious exemption, the inevitable effect is to impose the parents' notions of religious duty upon their children. Where the child is mature enough to express potentially conflicting desires, it would be an invasion of the child's rights to permit such an imposition without canvassing his views. * * * As the child has no other effective forum, it is in this litigation that his rights should be considered. And, if an Amish child desires to attend high school, and is mature enough to have that desire respected, the State may well be able to override the parents' religiously motivated objections.

Religion is an individual experience. It is not necessary, nor even appropriate, for every Amish child to express his views on the subject in a prosecution of a single adult. Crucial, however, are the views of the child whose parent is the subject of the suit. Frieda Yoder has in fact testified that her own religious views are opposed to high-school education. I therefore join the judgment of the Court as to respondent Jonas Yoder. But Frieda Yoder's views may not be those of Vernon Yutzy or Barbara Miller. I must dissent, therefore, as to respondents Adin Yutzy and Wallace Miller as their motion to dismiss also raised the question of their children's religious liberty.

* * *

It is the future of the student, not the future of the parents, that is imperiled by today's decision. If a parent keeps his child out of school beyond the grade school, then the child will be forever barred from entry into the new and amazing world of diversity that we have today. The child may decide that that is the preferred course, or he may rebel. It is the student's judgment, not his parents', that is essential if we are to give full meaning to what we have said about the Bill of Rights and of the right of students to be masters of their own destiny.[3] If he is harnessed to the Amish way of life by those in authority over him and if his education is truncated, his entire life may be stunted and deformed. The child, therefore, should be given an opportunity to be heard before the State gives the exemption which we honor today.

* * *

I think the emphasis of the Court on the "law and order" record of this Amish group of people is quite irrelevant. A religion is a religion irrespective of what the misdemeanor or felony records of its members might be. * * * Amish, whether with a high or low criminal record, certainly qualify by all historic standards as a religion within the meaning of the First Amendment.

* * *

3. The court below brushed aside the students' interests with the offhand comment that "[w]hen a child reaches the age of judgment, he can choose for himself his religion." But there is nothing in this record to indicate that the moral and intellectual judgment demanded of the student by the question in this case is beyond his capacity. Children far younger than the 14- and 15-year-olds involved here are regularly permitted to testify in custody and other proceedings. Indeed, the failure to call the affected child in a custody hearing is often reversible error. Moreover, there is substantial agreement among child psychologists and sociologists that the moral and intellectual maturity of the 14-year-old approaches that of the adult. The maturity of Amish youth, who identify with and assume adult roles from early childhood, is certainly not less than that of children in the general population.

NOTES AND QUESTIONS

1. Do you believe this case was rightly decided? What does it tell you about the views of the Justices concerning the rationale of public education? Are they correct in playing down the socialization function of high school? Note Chief Justice Burger's suggestion that a major reason for compulsory education beyond the eighth grade is to keep students out of the job market. Note also that Justice White in his concurring opinion emphasizes that "This would be a very different case for me if respondents' claim were that their religion forbade their children from attending any school at any time * * *."

2. Note Justice Douglas' concern for the rights of students. Do you agree with him that their interests were subordinated to those of the parents and the state in this case? Suppose a child urgently needs medical attention but the parents refuse because of their religious beliefs. Where these cases have arisen, courts generally decide in favor of the state and against the parents. As noted earlier in *Prince v. Massachusetts*, 321 U.S. 158 (1944), the Supreme Court ruled in favor of the state over the objections of the parents, even though the objections were grounded in both parental rights and religious freedom. There the Court upheld the application of a state statute against a nine year old girl's selling of religious material on a public street corner in accord with her and her mother's religious beliefs. The Court declared that the "family itself is not beyond regulation in the public interest, as against a claim of religious liberty," and further noted that "The State's authority over children's activities is broader than over like actions of adults." (At pp. 166 and 168).

The outcome, however, is not always certain. For example, in *In re Green*, 292 A.2d 387 (Penn., 1972), state officials sought to have a badly crippled 17 year old boy declared a "neglected child" under state law and a guardian appointed. State doctors had recommended a spinal fusion to prevent the boy's becoming an invalid. The mother agreed to the surgery, provided no blood transfusions would be used. As a Jehovah's Witness, the mother believed the Bible proscribes blood transfusions. The Supreme Court of Pennsylvania sided with the mother, concluding that since the child's life was not endangered, the state's interest did not outweigh the importance of the religious beliefs of the parents. But the court did remand the case to the lower court to ascertain the boy's views on the matter, agreeing with Justice Douglas in *Yoder* that in a case of this sort, the views of the child should be heard. Three of the seven judges in *Green* would have decided in favor of the state, based on *Prince v. Massachusetts*. They disagreed that sending the case back to ascertain the child's view would be of value.

> We are herein dealing with a young boy who has been crippled most of his life, consequently, he has been under the direct control and guidance of his parents for that time. To now presume that he could make an independent decision as to what is best for his welfare and health is not reasonable. Moreover, the mandate of the Court presents this youth with a most painful choice between the wishes of his parents and their religious convictions on

the one hand, and his chances for a normal, healthy life on the other. We should not confront him with this dilemma. (At p. 395).

Should the child make the final decision in this case? Should the children in *Yoder*? Could they really express an independent view? To what extent would their views be likely to reflect those of their parents? Would it have been better for the Court to endorse the compromise proposed by the Amish and rejected by the state superintendent to the effect that a separate public school be established for Amish children? One commentator believes the Court should try to steer a middle course between parent rights and state rights in the interest of preserving an open forum for children.[21] Would you agree that this approach to the rights of children has merit? For what ages and grade levels?

3. *Yoder* demonstrates quite clearly that the Free Exercise Clause will not be used very often to strike down legitimate expressions of state authority in educational matters. Note in particular how much stress Chief Justice Burger places on the uniqueness of the Old Order Amish religion and his assertion that few other religious groups or sects could make such a strong case against the compulsory school law. Note also in the last paragraph of his opinion that he acknowledges the power of the state "to promulgate reasonable regulations" in lieu of compulsory schooling for this particular religious sect.

It is clear then that the Establishment Clause is more likely to be successful when used to strike down school programs and policies favorable to religion than the Free Exercise Clause is likely to be successful in mandating exemptions for religious or philosophically based reasons.

The contemporary cases illustrate how reluctant courts are to use the Free Exercise Clause to strike down governmental educational policies and programs. For example, in *Cornwall v. State Bd. of Educ.*, 314 F.Supp. 340 (D.C.Md.1969), aff'd 428 F.2d 471 (4th Cir.), *cert. denied* 400 U.S. 942 (1970), Maryland taxpayer-parents sought to prevent the implementation of a sex education program in the Baltimore County Public Schools. The plaintiffs claimed the program violates their rights under the First/Fourteenth Amendments to control the sex education of their children and their right to free exercise of their religion. The parents also asserted the program will establish religious concepts in the schools contrary to the Establishment Clause. The district court flatly rejected all their arguments, noting that the sex education program could be viewed as a legitimate public health measure and was well within the power of state school officials to institute. On appeal to the Fourth Circuit Court of Appeals, the district court decision was affirmed in a brief *per curiam* opinion. The U. S. Supreme Court refused to hear the case.

In *Brusca v. State of Mo. ex rel State Bd. of Educ.*, 332 F.Supp. 275 (E.D.Mo.1971), a decision the U. S. Supreme Court affirmed without opin-

21. Robert A. Burt, "Developing Constitutional Rights of, In, and For Children," 39 *Law and Contemp.Prob.* 118, 1975, at p. 130. In this connection, review the comments by Edward Ladd in Chapter One about "stairstepping" student rights. See p. 12.

ion in 1972, parents of school age children asserted the unconstitutionality of provisions of the Missouri constitution and implementing statutes which set up and finance public schools but prohibit aid directly or indirectly to religious schools. The plaintiffs argued that the provisions deny them free exercise of their religion, while compelling them to support public schools to which they are opposed. So as to avoid the entanglement problem of *Lemon v. Kurtzman* and later cases, the parents demanded relief in the form of tuition grants. The federal district court reiterated the view that while the state cannot prohibit a parent from sending his or her children to a religious affiliated or independent school under the *Pierce v. Society of Sisters* ruling, the state is not compelled to finance a child's nonpublic school education. In fact, legislation with such an intent would not have a purely secular purpose but would act to advance the cause of religion. The court noted that the Free Exercise Clause is written in terms of what the government cannot do to the individual, not in terms of what the individual can get from the government. Nor were the provisions of the Missouri legislation necessarily hostile to religion or to those wishing to send their children to sectarian schools. The court noted that

> Other taxpayers—e. g., bachelors, childless couples, corporations —pay taxes for the support of schools and receive no more benefit from such tax payments than do the parent-plaintiffs who forego sending their children to free public schools. (At p. 279).

What key assumption about sectarian schools must necessarily be made in order for the court to reach this decision? Why should bachelors, childless couples, corporations, and parents who send their children to nonpublic schools have to pay taxes to support the free public school system?

In *Davis v. Page*, 385 F.Supp. 395 (D.C.N.H.1974), the district court denied claims by Apostolic Lutherans that the use of audio-visual equipment in elementary school classrooms violated their religious beliefs. The court emphasized that the state has an interest in providing "uniform education for all its youngsters" and that "it is impossible for the state to provide an educational program which is totally acceptable to all religious faiths." (At p. 405). To attempt to do so "would create a stratified school structure, where division and derision would flourish." (Id.) However, the court did agree that excusing the children from participating in non-educational activities where audio-visual equipment is used does not violate the Establishment Clause and represents an agreeable accommodation with the plaintiffs' religious beliefs under the Free Exercise Clause.

Not all cases, however, are won by state officials. In *State v. Whisner*, 351 N.E.2d 750 (1976), the Ohio Supreme Court departed from the usual pattern in striking down state efforts to regulate a nonpublic religious school. The Ohio Board of Education exercised its powers under a state statute to set minimum standards for the Tabernacle Christian School, a new institution subscribing to a "born again" fundamentalist sect. When unsuccessful in securing compliance, state officials ordered the parents arrested for sending their children to a nonchartered institution in violation of state law. The Ohio Supreme Court ruled that the minimum standards were so comprehensive as to violate both the parents' right to freedom of religion and their right to control the upbringing of their children. The court implied that less comprehensive standards would be permissible, thus forcing the state to develop two sets of standards—one for public and one for nonpublic schools—or to abandon efforts to regulate the latter. *Whisner* is important as an extension of *Yoder* in preferring the interests of the parent over those of the state. If *Whisner* is followed in other jurisdictions, it will broaden the use of religious freedom and parental rights to challenge the actions of public school officials.

The tension between the Free Exercise and Establishment Clauses is well illustrated by a 1975 Delaware Supreme Court ruling involving the University of Delaware. In *Keegan v. University of Del.,* 349 A.2d 14 (Del. 1975), the court ruled that the university's ban against organized prayer in dormitory common rooms violates the students' right to pursue their religious freedom. To accommodate the students does not serve to place the university in the position of promoting an establishment of religion, ruled the court, since only adult students are involved and since the common rooms were utilized for a variety of purposes. Compare this ruling with the earlier U. S. Supreme Court decisions pertaining to prayers in public elementary and secondary schools. Are the distinguishing features sufficiently evident to justify the contrary Delaware ruling? In 1976, the U. S. Supreme Court refused to grant certiorari in the *Keegan* case.

In *Johnson v. Huntington Beach Union High School Dist.,* 137 Cal.Rptr. 43 (California 1977), a California court of appeal affirmed a lower court decision upholding a school district's refusal to recognize a student bible club as a school organization. Would the decision have been the same if the students wished to rent school facilities for use during non-school hours?

4. It should be evident by now that it is by no means a simple task for the state to be neutral with regard to religion. Too much accommodation of religious beliefs will prompt charges of unconstitutional advancement of religion contrary to the Establishment Clause; too little will prompt charges of unconstitutionally restricting the free exercise of religion contrary to the Free Exercise Clause. Based on your reading of the Free Exercise Clause and your view of the state interest in public education, how would you decide the following hypothetical situations? (You may wish as well to review your responses to the hypotheticals advanced at the end of the previous section on the Establishment Clause as well).

    a. Parents (but not their 5th grade child) object on religious grounds to passages describing various scientific views about the formation of the earth in a public school science book.

    b. Same situation as in (a), only here the child is a senior in high school.

    c. Students at a public college assert that the on-campus residency requirement violates their religious beliefs. The students are not part of any established church; their religion is unique to them and asserts the importance of communal living.

d. Suppose in (c) above, the students are affiliated with an established religion which commands communal living in a nonpublic setting.

e. A student who is a member of the school glee club objects to the singing of a particular song and wishes to remain seated during its singing.

f. Public high school does not serve kosher lunches. Jewish parents and students object. Suppose at one time the school accommodated Catholics by serving fish to all students on Friday. Would it make any difference if over half the student body is Jewish?

g. Catholic parents seek to have books their religion considers sacrilegious removed from the school library.

h. Atheist parents seek to force school officials to include books on atheism in the high school library because the inclusion of such books promotes critical inquiry and open-mindedness. They argue that the failure to include such books amounts to unconstitutional censorship of a free speech forum.

i. Suppose in (h) above religious parents ban together to prevent school officials from adding the books to the library, claiming violation of their Free Exercise rights.

j. Suppose in (i) above the religious parents argue that complying with the atheist parents' wishes amounts to unconstitutional government support of a religious establishment, since no religious books are now included in the library.

k. Challenge by parents on philosophical grounds to a compulsory school flu immunization program. Suppose the parents effectively point out that the shots are only partially effective and that some students are actually made ill by them.

l. Eleven year old girl is the subject of much derision and abuse in public school because of her extensive facial disfigurement. School officials including the school psychiatrist believe that the girl will suffer lasting emotional trauma unless plastic surgery is undertaken very soon. Parents refuse because of a philosophical belief against doctors. The girl is too confused to express a clear viewpoint. Public health officials and school officials seek court action to have the child declared a "neglected child" under a state statute and have the court appoint a guardian.

5. Consider the following hypothetical case.

HYPOTHETICAL: *Athletes v. Minnefornia State Univ.*

Several weeks prior to the football game between Minnefornia State University and Billy Claxton College, a fundamentalist Baptist institution, several players on the Minnefornia team decided to take some action to protest what they regard as racially discriminatory policies of the Baptist college. Included among the six dissident players were four Black students.

After considerable deliberation, the six football players decided that the best way to publicize their opposition would be to wear black armbands during the game with Claxton College. They also decided to write a joint letter to the university newspaper and to the town papers announcing what they intended to do and why.

After reading the story the coach confronted the six, asking if they really intended to wear the black armbands. They said they did. They remained steadfast in their determination, despite pleadings from the coach, who reminded them of the coaching rule prohibiting participation by students in their role as football players in protests or demonstrations. The rule did not apply to athletes in their capacity as students away from the practice and playing field. The football players said they thought the rule was unfair and probably illegal. But the coach insisted the contrary, pointing out that as football players, the students were agents of the university and any demonstration they might mount would have grave legal consequences. He emphasized that he had no alternative but to enforce the rule and suspend the six from the team.

The six football players sued the coach and the university for violating their rights.

Based on previous discussion and cases, what arguments would you make for each side? Note that both free expression cases from the previous chapter and the religion cases in this chapter are implicated in this hypothetical situation. If you were to decide the outcome, what decision would you reach?

III. SUMMARY

Complexities surrounding religious freedoms result primarily from the built-in tensions between the Establishment Clause and the Free Exercise Clause of the First Amendment as they have been interpreted by the U. S. Supreme Court. Given that *stare decisis* prevents any drastic reworking of past interpretations, the tensions are bound to characterize religious disputes for some time to come.

Nevertheless, the cases do illustrate that some kinds of government assistance to religious institutions are likely to be upheld and some kinds of religious expression are likely to be protected. Based on the decisions to date and the three basic Establishment Clause "tests" the Court has developed, it appears the Supreme Court will be more inclined to allow state aid to religiously-affiliated elementary and secondary schools under the following conditions (*Everson* and *Allen* are notable exceptions):

    a. Government funds are not transferred directly to the religiously-sponsored schools.

        (1) When dollars are not involved, government is less inclined to exercise inspection powers.

        (2) There may be less political divisiveness when dollars aren't involved.

        (3) When government tax money isn't involved, no one will be forced to subsidize the belief of another.

    (4) Where dollars aren't involved, religious institutions are less likely to forsake their beliefs for more government aid.

b. The aid is designed to provide a social service enjoyed by nonreligious institutions as well.

c. Assistance programs do not involve placing state personnel in religious institutions and minimize continuous contact with the religiously-affiliated institution.

d. Government inspection is likely to occur only in remote and extreme instances.

Insofar as religiously-affiliated postsecondary educational institutions are concerned, the Supreme Court appears to be more inclined to allow state aid programs under either of these conditions:

a. The educational institutions are not permeated with religion and there are prohibitions on the use of aid for religious activity.

b. The aid goes directly to students.

We should be aware of the fact, however, that much controversy surrounds the Establishment Clause, as contemporary concern over educational vouchers, tuition refunds, and tax credit plans indicate. There appears to be no easy way to draw the line between what is and what is not allowed.

Free exercise issues are easier to resolve because the Free Exercise Clause in combination with the First Amendment's protection of speech provides strong support for freedom of religious expression. However, where *actions* are part of religious expression, courts are more circumspect, as the *Reynolds* and *Yoder* decisions attest.

Once again, judicial resolution of student/parent disputes based on the religion clauses are dependent in part on judicial notions about the meaning of these constitutional provisions and in part on other variables. (Review Figure 3–3 in the previous chapter.)

Chapter Five

"The history of liberty has largely been the history of observance of procedural safeguards."

Justice Felix Frankfurter
McNabb v. U. S. (1943)

" * * * we decline to ignore the historic judgment of educators and thereby formalize the academic dismissal process by requiring a hearing."

Justice William Rehnquist
Board of Curators v. Horowitz, 1978

"RIGHTS OF THE ACCUSED"

Our political and social system assumes that persons accused of breaking rules should not be treated arbitrarily. For justice to be done, similar treatment must be accorded to persons similarly situated. For example, if an accused person is by law to be accorded the right to legal counsel, then anyone in the category of an accused ought to be entitled to that right.

The Anglo-American concept of justice assumes as well that legal procedures must award fair compensation to victims and punish people in ways appropriate to their unlawful acts. The operative principle is one of "fairness." Justice also demands within our tradition that the government does not violate the law in the process of enforcing it. It recognizes that every accused person (defendant) has rights.

The term that crystalizes these ideas of consistency, fairness, and government observance of rights of the defendant is *due process of law.* We assume that without due process of law, no government can establish justice. In specific situations, however, neither "justice" nor "due process of law" are terms easily applied, as the following sections make clear.

I. WHAT IS JUSTICE?

A. Justice as Following the Rules

This approach to "justice" is most familiar. A judge is just, a school board decision is just, or a jury is just when they follow the set of rules or procedures that are set down by a constitution, a charter, a statute, or set of bylaws. "Justice", then, is following the rules.

Proceduralists place great value on the establishment of "neutral principles of law" which can be applied to all persons in like manner. They are uneasy about judicial discretion. For the proceduralists, "justice" is following the set of carefully circumscribed rules of the legal game. This adherence to rules is the essence of legal fairness.

B. Justice as Social Order

Many Americans claim that although the freedoms contained in the Bill of Rights are of great importance, these rights are only possible within a framework of order and stability. Thus many view justice as emphasizing strong laws and vigorous enforcement against those who tamper with domestic tranquility. Under this view, a just society is one that places a heavy legal burden on the criminal elements rather than those who are authorized to enforce the law. "Bringing criminals to justice" is an apt characterization of this view.

C. Justice as Social Welfare

Some advocates claim that justice in society is more than following the rules; justice must be concerned with the content and application of those rules which most crucially affect human welfare. According to John Stuart Mill, the great English liberal political philosopher, all persons are deemed to have a right to equal treatment before the law except when some social expediency requires the reverse.

The "justice as social welfare" advocates, then, do not consider procedural regularity as sacrosanct. If those in authority can demonstrate that a particular law is socially useful, then exceptions to equal treatment may have to be made. For example, it may be necessary for the state to provide attorneys for the defense of indigent defendants in the interest of fair treatment, even though, as a general rule, defendants are responsible for securing their own attorneys.

D. Justice as Egalitarianism

Radicals who criticize the fundamental social order claim that for "justice" to be a reality, all persons must be treated identically. Respect for human beings must be based only on humanitarian concerns. The poorest worker and the manager of a corporation share in a common humanity and each deserves an identical vote, courtroom treatment, education, medical care, and income. The rich have no greater claim to societal services than the poor. Thus, for egalitarianism to be a reality, the rich need to be "leveled down" and the poor "leveled up."

Radicals contend that the only way for such a leveling process to occur is for there to be a major transformation of the economic system in the direction of economic equality. Only in this way can all persons be treated with human dignity and a cooperative community emerge. "Justice" in these terms can only be realized when goods and services such as legal assistance are distributed according to human need rather than in terms of wealth, status, or intelligence.

II. DUE PROCESS IN THE POLITICAL AND SOCIAL SETTING

Given the various approaches to justice, there is a great deal of value conflict about what constitutes fairness. The key constitutional means to achieve "justice" however it is defined are found in the Due Process Clauses of the Fifth and Fourteenth Amendments. The Fifth Amendment, which pertains to the federal government, and the Fourteenth Amendment, which pertains to states, both provide that the government may not deprive persons of "life, liberty, or property, without due process of law." Much of the legal and political debate about achieving justice through due process of law surrounds which of two ways due process is defined: substantively or procedurally. *Substantive due process* means that the content (or substance) of the laws and actions of public officials must be fair. Substantive due process thus invites judges to reconsider the decisions of others. Those who consider justice to mean social welfare are most likely to subscribe to substantive due process. The complexities of substantive due process were first noted in Chapter Three with respect to the fairness of public school and college rules. Rules which are vague or overbroad are less likely to be upheld where constitutionally protected interests are involved. In order to determine vagueness and overbreadth, courts must look to the content of the rules in question.

Procedural due process means that laws or rules must be administered in a fair manner, that is, according to predetermined procedures such as notice of charges and a hearing. Those who consider justice as adherence to pre-announced rules are most likely to subscribe to procedural due process. Substantive due process focuses on *what* the law states and on the *outcomes* of its application; procedural due process focuses on *how* it is implemented.

A. Due Process of Law and the Supreme Court

The question of what process is due Americans under the Constitution is not answered by the phrase itself. No phrase in the Constitution is more vague and sweeping than "due process of law." Explicating the meaning of this phrase has been one of the Supreme Court's greatest burdens. Some critics have accused the Court of straying far afield from the intent of the Framers of the two due process clauses in trying to give meaning to the concept. A contemporary critic of the Court, Harvard Law Professor Raoul Berger, contends, for example, that the concept of due process of law historically means simply having access to the courts.[1]

But the Court has not been inclined to view due process so narrowly. The Justices have always claimed that there must be procedural fairness in government activities. As Justice Felix Frankfurter asserted, "The history of liberty has largely been the history of observance of procedural safeguards."[2] For Justice Black, who viewed justice as meaning adherence to procedures, due process of law had only one meaning: strict adherence to the specific rights outlined in the Bill of Rights, particularly the Fifth and Sixth Amendments. And, contrary to Raoul Berger's reading of history, Justice Black believed that the authors of the Fourteenth Amendment Due Process Clause intended to secure those same procedural protections for defendants in state actions.

But most of the other Justices in the Supreme Court have been more flexible in their views, embracing a concept of justice more closely associated with the social welfare view. As Justice Frankfurter has stated:

Due process of law, as a historic and generative principle, precludes defining, and thereby confining, these standards of con-

---

1. Berger asserts that history demonstrates that "due process was *not* a catchall for all the other safeguards the Bill of Rights provided to a defendant; it had a special and limited function: to insure through service of proper, that is 'due,' process that a defendant would be given a chance

to answer [in court]." Raoul Berger, *Government by Judiciary* (Cambridge, Mass.: Harvard Univ. Press, 1977), at p. 199. (Emphasis in original; material in brackets added.)

2. *McNabb v. U. S.*, 318 U.S. 332 (1943), at p. 347.

duct more precisely than to say that convictions cannot be brought about by methods that offend a "sense of justice." [3]

One is left with the subjective intuitions of what offends a "sense" of justice and thus necessarily must enter the thicket of substantive due process where the values of the judges play a major role in deciding what is or is not due process. In 1952, the Supreme Court held that a man could not be convicted on the basis of evidence obtained by holding him down and pumping his stomach. In that case, *Rochin v. California,* 342 U.S. 165 (1952), the Supreme Court ruled that Rochin had been denied due process because the stomach pumping offended the general concepts of "civilized conduct," "a sense of justice," and "the community's sense of fair play and decency." By contrast, in later cases the Court claimed that it was not a denial of due process to take blood samples from suspected drunk drivers.

Nevertheless, if we seek to discern the Court's position on due process by noting trends during the past quarter of a century, we can conclude that the Due Process Clauses of the Fifth and Fourteenth Amendments have generally been interpreted to institute greater procedural restraints on government. Frequently, the Court has come to the rescue of individuals or groups who would have suffered because of some defect in the formalities of a proceeding. Thus, while not abandoning substantive due process, the Court has been more actively involved in securing procedural protections for the accused in the interest of justice.

B. The Supreme Court Protects the Accused Adult

The common law principle which the American colonists took with them from England required the government to assume that people were innocent until proven guilty. In practice, this has meant that a person has a right to certain protections both when he is a suspect and after criminal charges have been formally filed. During the past quarter century, particularly during the years Earl Warren served as Chief Justice, the Supreme Court has literally revolutionized the criminal justice process by establishing specific rights for the accused. A discussion of some of these revolutionary protections in the political and social setting follows.

(1) Prelude to Prosecution: Policing the Police

Police have always viewed pretrial confessions as essential to effective crime control. Police organizations have contended that about 80 percent of all felony convictions result largely from such confessions.[4] The Supreme Court has indicated that there must exist legal guarantees protecting the suspect against attempts to extract confessions.

In the early 1960s, the Supreme Court began to spell out these guarantees. A key 1964 case involved Danny Escobedo, who was arrested by Chicago police on suspicion of murder. Danny was questioned at length by the police at the same time his attorney was seeking permission to advise his client. Escobedo requested counsel, but his request was not granted. In the course of the interrogation he made some incriminating statements.

---

3. *Rochin v. California,* 342 U.S. 165 (1952), at p. 173.

4. Ed Cray, *The Big Blue Line* (New York: Coward-McCann, 1967), at p. 70.

The Supreme Court reversed his conviction in *Escobedo v. Illinois,* 378 U.S. 478 (1964), holding that counsel must be available through all the stages of a focused investigation. In overturning Escobedo's conviction, the five-man majority required that the Sixth Amendment right to counsel as applied to the states through the Fourteenth Amendment apply to all criminal investigations by state police authorities. The case establishes a general judicial distrust of confessions.

The thrust of the *Escobedo* decision was to require the adversary system, traditionally restricted to the trial stage, to be hauled back to the earlier stages of the criminal investigation. Justice Arthur Goldberg, speaking for the slim majority, made it clear that a person must be permitted to consult with a lawyer as soon as a police investigation makes him a prime suspect. Justice Goldberg presented the majority's specific holding in the following terms:

> We hold, therefore, that where, as here, the investigation is no longer a general inquiry into an unsolved crime but has begun to focus on a particular suspect, the suspect has been taken into police custody, the police carry out a process of interrogations that lends itself to eliciting incriminating statements, the suspect has requested and has been denied an opportunity to consult with his lawyer, and the police have not effectively warned him of his absolute constitutional right to remain silent, the accused has been denied the "Assistance of Counsel" in violation of the Sixth Amendment to the Constitution as "made obligatory upon the States by the Fourteenth Amendment," and that no statement elicited by the police during the interrogation may be used against him at a criminal trial. (At pp. 490–491).

In the 1966 case of *Miranda v. Arizona,* 384 U.S. 436, the Supreme Court expanded the *Escobedo* precedent by deciding that a confession could not be admitted as evidence unless the suspect was explicitly informed of his constitutional right to remain silent and to obtain legal counsel. On March 13, 1963, Ernesto Miranda was arrested by the Phoenix police, taken to the local station, and placed in a lineup for identification by a woman who had been robbed. The woman picked out Miranda. An eighteen-year-old girl who had recently been raped also identified Miranda as her assailant. Miranda was then taken to an interrogation room and questioned. His interrogators did not indicate that he had a right to an attorney; there was some disagreement whether they had told him that statements he made would be used against him in court.

After two hours of interrogation, Miranda confessed in writing to both crimes. He was tried separately by juries, but with the same judge. At the rape trial, Miranda's defense attorney objected when the prosecution introduced the confession into evidence, stating that "the Supreme Court of the United States says a man is entitled to an attorney at the time of his arrest." The judge admitted the confession into evidence over the lawyer's objections. The jurors found Miranda guilty in both trials, and the judge sentenced him to between forty and fifty-five years in prison on the two convictions.

Miranda's lawyer appealed the convictions to the Arizona Supreme Court, which treated the two convictions as companion cases. In April, 1965, the Arizona court held the confession was admissible because, under the Escobedo rule, "the suspect must have requested and been denied the opportunity to consult with his lawyer," and Miranda had not directly asked for counsel. Miranda and his lawyer asked the United States Supreme Court to review the case. The Court agreed to hear the case along with three others that sought to extend the scope and application of the Escobedo rule. Chief Justice Warren noted that *Escobedo* had been interpreted in various ways and had come to "varying conclusions". The Court now agreed to explore some of the problems raised and "to give concrete guidelines for law enforcement agencies and courts to follow." The Supreme Court in another slim five-to-four majority, reversed Miranda's conviction. The Chief Justice wrote the opinion of the Court laying out some very concrete guidelines. There were several concurring and dissenting opinions. Only Justice Harlan's dissent is excerpted here.

MIRANDA v. ARIZONA

Supreme Court of the United States, 1966.
384 U.S. 436, 86 S.Ct. 1602, 16 L.Ed.2d 694.

Mr. Chief Justice WARREN delivered the opinion of the Court.

The cases before us raise questions which go to the roots of our concepts of American criminal jurisprudence: the restraints society must observe consistent with the Federal Constitution in prosecuting individuals for crime. More specifically, we deal with the admissibility of statements obtained from an individual who is subjected to custodial police interrogation and the necessity for procedures which assure that the individual is accorded his privilege under the Fifth Amendment to the Constitution not to be compelled to incriminate himself.

* * *

We start here, as we did in *Escobedo*, with the premise that our holding is not an innovation in our jurisprudence, but is an application of principles long recognized and applied in other settings. We have undertaken a thorough re-examination of the *Escobedo* decision and the principles it announced, and we reaffirm it. That case was but an explication of basic rights that are enshrined in our Constitution—that "No person * * * shall be compelled in any criminal case to be a witness against himself," and that "the accused shall * * * have the Assistance of Counsel"—rights which were put in jeopardy in that case through official overbearing. These precious rights were fixed in our Constitution only after centuries of persecution and struggle. And in the words of Chief Justice Marshall, they were secured "for ages to come, and * * * designed to approach immortality as nearly as human institutions can approach it."

* * *

I.

The constitutional issue we decide in each of these cases is the admissibility of statements obtained from a defendant questioned while in custody or otherwise deprived of his freedom of action in any significant way. In each, the defendant was questioned by police officers, detectives, or a prosecuting attorney in a room in which he was cut off from the outside world. In none of these cases was the defendant given a full and effective warning of his rights at the outset of the interrogation process. In all the cases, the questioning elicited oral admissions, and in three of them, signed statements as well which were admitted at their trials. They all thus share salient features—incommunicado interrogation of individuals in a police-dominated atmosphere, resulting in self-incriminating statements without full warnings of constitutional rights.

An understanding of the nature and setting of this in-custody interrogation is essential to our decisions today. The difficulty in depicting what transpires at such interrogations stems from the fact that in this country they have largely taken place incommunicado. From extensive factual studies undertaken in the early 1930's including the famous Wickersham Report to Congress by a Presidential Commission, it is clear that police violence and the "third degree" flourished at that time. In a series of cases decided by this Court long after these studies, the police resorted to physical brutality—beating, hanging, whipping—and to sustained and protracted questioning incommunicado in order to extort confessions. The Commission on Civil Rights in 1961 found much evidence to indicate that "some policemen still resort to physical force to obtain confessions." The use of physical brutality and violence is not, unfortunately, relegated to the past or to any part of the country. * * *

* * *

* * * the modern practice of in-custody interrogation is psychologically rather than physically oriented. * * * Interrogation still takes place in privacy. Privacy results in secrecy and this in turn results in a gap in our knowledge as to what in fact goes on in the interrogation rooms. A valuable source of information about present police practices, however, may be found in various police manuals and texts which document procedures employed with success in the past, and

which recommend various other effective tactics.

[A review of manuals and texts follows.]

* * *

From these representative samples of interrogation techniques, the setting prescribed by the manuals and observed in practice becomes, clear. In essence, it is this: To be alone with the subject is essential to prevent distraction and to deprive him of any outside support. The aura of confidence in his guilt undermines his will to resist. He merely confirms the preconceived story the police seek to have him describe. Patience and persistence, at times relentless questioning, are employed. To obtain a confession, the interrogator must "patiently maneuver himself or his quarry into a position from which the desired objective may be attained." When normal procedures fail to produce the needed result, the police may resort to deceptive stratagems such as giving false legal advice. It is important to keep the subject off balance, for example, by trading on his insecurity about himself or his surroundings. The police then persuade, trick, or cajole him out of exercising his constitutional rights.

Even without employing brutality, the "third degree" or the specific stratagems described above, the very fact of custodial interrogation exacts a heavy toll on individual liberty and trades on the weakness of individuals.

* * *

In these cases, we might not find the defendants' statements to have been involuntary in traditional terms. Our concern for adequate safeguards to protect precious Fifth Amendment rights is, of course, not lessened in the slightest. In each of the cases, the defendant was thrust into an unfamiliar atmosphere and run through menacing police interrogation procedures. The potentiality for compulsion is forcefully apparent, for example, in *Miranda*, where the indigent Mexican defendant was a seriously disturbed individual with pronounced sexual fantasies, and in *Stewart*, in which the defendant was an indigent Los Angeles Negro who had dropped out of school in the sixth grade. To be sure, the records do not evince overt physical coercion or patent psychological ploys. The fact remains that in none of these cases did the officers undertake to afford appropriate safeguards at the outset of the interrogation to insure that the statements were truly the product of free choice.

It is obvious that such an interrogation environment is created for no purpose other than to subjugate the individual to the will of his examiner. This atmosphere carries its own badge of intimidation. To be sure, this is not physical intimidation, but it is equally destructive of human dignity. The current practice of incommunicado interrogation is at odds with one of our Nation's most cherished principles—that the individual may not be compelled to incriminate himself. Unless adequate protective devices are employed to dispel the compulsion inherent in custodial surroundings, no statement obtained from the defendant can truly be the product of his free choice.

* * *

III.

Today, * * *, there can be no doubt that the Fifth Amendment privilege is available outside of criminal court proceedings and serves to protect persons in all settings in which their freedom of action is curtailed in any significant way from being compelled to incriminate themselves. We have concluded that without proper safeguards the process of in-custody interrogation of persons suspected or accused of crime contains inherently compelling pressures which work to undermine the individual's will to resist and to compel him to speak where he would not otherwise do so freely. In order to combat these pressures and to per-

mit a full opportunity to exercise the privilege against self-incrimination, the accused must be adequately and effectively apprised of his rights and the exercise of those rights must be fully honored.

* * *

At the outset, if a person in custody is to be subjected to interrogation, he must first be informed in clear and unequivocal terms that he has the right to remain silent. For those unaware of the privilege, the warning is needed simply to make them aware of it—the threshold requirement for an intelligent decision as to its exercise. More important, such a warning is an absolute prerequisite in overcoming the inherent pressures of the interrogation atmosphere. It is not just the subnormal or woefully ignorant who succumb to an interrogator's imprecations, whether implied or expressly stated, that the interrogation will continue until a confession is obtained or that silence in the face of accusation is itself damning and will bode ill when presented to a jury. Further, the warning will show the individual that his interrogators are prepared to recognize his privilege should he choose to exercise it.

* * *

The warning of the right to remain silent must be accompanied by the explanation that anything said can and will be used against the individual in court. This warning is needed in order to make him aware not only of the privilege, but also of the consequences of forgoing it. It is only through an awareness of these consequences that there can be any assurance of real understanding and intelligent exercise of the privilege. Moreover, this warning may serve to make the individual more acutely aware that he is faced with a phase of the adversary system—that he is not in the presence of persons acting solely in his interest.

* * *

* * * we hold that an individual held for interrogation must be clearly in-

formed that he has the right to consult with a lawyer and to have the lawyer with him during interrogation under the system for protecting the privilege we delineate today. As with the warnings of the right to remain silent and that anything stated can be used in evidence against him, this warning is an absolute prerequisite to interrogation. No amount of circumstantial evidence that the person may have been aware of this right will suffice to stand in its stead. Only through such a warning is there ascertainable assurance that the accused was aware of this right.

If an individual indicates that he wishes the assistance of counsel before any interrogation occurs, the authorities cannot rationally ignore or deny his request on the basis that the individual does not have or cannot afford a retained attorney. The financial ability of the individual has no relationship to the scope of the rights involved here. The privilege against self-incrimination secured by the Constitution applies to all individuals. The need for counsel in order to protect the privilege exists for the indigent as well as the affluent. In fact, were we to limit these constitutional rights to those who can retain an attorney, our decisions today would be of little significance. The cases before us as well as the vast majority of confession cases with which we have dealt in the past involve those unable to retain counsel. While authorities are not required to relieve the accused of his poverty, they have the obligation not to take advantage of indigence in the administration of justice. * * *

In order fully to apprise a person interrogated of the extent of his rights under this system then, it is necessary to warn him not only that he has the right to consult with an attorney, but also that if he is indigent a lawyer will be appointed to represent him. Without this additional warning, the admonition of the right to consult with counsel would often

be understood as meaning only that he can consult with a lawyer if he has one or has the funds to obtain one. The warning of a right to counsel would be hollow if not couched in terms that would convey to the indigent—the person most often subjected to interrogation —the knowledge that he too has a right to have counsel present. As with the warnings of the right to remain silent and of the general right to counsel, only by effective and express explanation to the indigent of this right can there be assurance that he was truly in a position to exercise it.

Once warnings have been given, the subsequent procedure is clear. If the individual indicates in any manner, at any time prior to or during questioning, that he wishes to remain silent, the interrogation must cease. At this point he has shown that he intends to exercise his Fifth Amendment privilege; any statement taken after the person invokes his privilege cannot be other than the product of compulsion, subtle or otherwise. Without the right to cut off questioning, the setting of in-custody interrogation operates on the individual to overcome free choice in producing a statement after the privilege has been once invoked. If the individual states that he wants an attorney, the interrogation must cease until an attorney is present. At that time, the individual must have an opportunity to confer with the attorney and to have him present during any subsequent questioning. If the individual cannot obtain an attorney and he indicates that he wants one before speaking to police, they must respect his decision to remain silent.

* * *

Our decision is not intended to hamper the traditional function of police officers in investigating crime. When an individual is in custody on probable cause, the police may, of course, seek out evidence in the field to be used at trial against him. Such investigation may include inquiry of persons not under restraint. General on-the-scene questioning as to facts surrounding a crime or other general questioning of citizens in the fact-finding process is not affected by our holding. It is an act of responsible citizenship for individuals to give whatever information they may have to aid in law enforcement. In such situations the compelling atmosphere inherent in the process of in-custody interrogation is not necessarily present.

In dealing with statements obtained through interrogation, we do not purport to find all confessions inadmissible. Confessions remain a proper element in law enforcement. Any statement given freely and voluntarily without any compelling influences is, of course, admissible in evidence. The fundamental import of the privilege while an individual is in custody is not whether he is allowed to talk to the police without the benefit of warnings and counsel, but whether he can be interrogated. There is no requirement that police stop a person who enters a police station and states that he wishes to confess to a crime, or a person who calls the police to offer a confession or any other statement he desires to make. Volunteered statements of any kind are not barred by the Fifth Amendment and their admissibility is not affected by our holding today.

To summarize, we hold that when an individual is taken into custody or otherwise deprived of his freedom by the authorities in any significant way and is subjected to questioning, the privilege against self-incrimination is jeopardized. Procedural safeguards must be employed to protect the privilege, and unless other fully effective means are adopted to notify the person of his right of silence and to assure that the exercise of the right will be scrupulously honored, the following measures are required. He must be warned prior to any questioning that he has the right to remain silent, that anything he says can be used against him in a court of law, that he has the right to the presence of an attorney, and that if he cannot afford an attorney one will be appointed for him prior to any questioning if he so desires. Opportunity to exercise these rights must be afforded to him throughout the interrogation after such warnings have been given, and such opportunity afforded him, the individual may knowingly and intelligently waive these rights and agree to answer questions or make a statement. But unless and until such warnings and waiver are demonstrated by the prosecution at trial, no evidence obtained as a result of interrogation can be used against him.

IV.

* * *

In announcing these principles, we are not unmindful of the burdens which law enforcement officials must bear, often under trying circumstances. We also fully recognize the obligation of all citizens to aid in enforcing the criminal laws. This Court, while protecting individual rights, has always given ample latitude to law enforcement agencies in the legitimate exercise of their duties. The limits we have placed on the interrogation process should not constitute an undue interference with a proper system of law enforcement. As we have noted, our decision does not in any way preclude police from carrying out their traditional investigatory functions. Although confessions may play an important role in some convictions, the cases before us present graphic examples of the overstatement of the "need" for confessions. In each case authorities conducted interrogations ranging up to five days in duration despite the presence, through standard investigating practices, of considerable evidence against each defendant. * * *

Mr. Justice CLARK, dissenting and concurring.

* * *

Mr. Justice HARLAN, whom Mr. Justice STEWART and Mr. Justice WHITE join, dissenting.

* * * The new rules are not designed to guard against police brutality or other unmistakably banned forms of coercion. Those who use third-degree tactics and deny them in court are equally able and destined to lie as skillfully about warnings and waivers. Rather, the thrust of the new rules is to negate all pressures, to reinforce the nervous or ignorant suspect, and ultimately to discourage any confession at all. * * *

To incorporate this notion into the Constitution requires a strained reading of history and precedent and a disregard of the very pragmatic concerns that alone may on occasion justify such strains. I believe that reasoned examination will show that the Due Process Clauses provide an adequate tool for coping with confessions and that, even if the Fifth Amendment privilege against self-incrimination be invoked, its precedents taken as a whole do not sustain the present rules. Viewed as a choice based on pure policy, these new rules prove to be a highly debatable, if not one-sided, appraisal of the competing interests, imposed over widespread objection, at the very time when judicial restraint is most called for by the circumstances.

* * *

There are several relevant lessons to be drawn from * * * constitutional history. The first is that with over 25 years of precedent the Court has developed an elaborate, sophisticated, and sensitive approach to admissibility of confessions. It is "judicial" in its treatment of one case at a time, * * * flexible in its ability to respond to the endless mutations of fact presented, and ever more familiar to the lower courts. Of course, strict certainty is not obtained in this developing process, but this is often so with constitutional principles, and disagreement is usually confined to that borderland of close cases where it matters least.

The second point is that in practice and from time to time in principle, the Court has given ample recognition to society's interest in suspect questioning as an instrument of law enforcement. * * *

* * *

The Court's opening contention, that the Fifth Amendment governs police station confessions, is perhaps not an impermissible extension of the law but it has little to commend itself in the present circumstances. Historically, the privilege against self-incrimination did not bear at all on the use of extra-legal confessions, for which distinct standards evolved: * * * Even those who would readily enlarge the privilege must concede some linguistic difficulties since the Fifth Amendment in terms proscribes only compelling any person "in any criminal case to be a witness against himself." * * * It then emerges from a discussion of *Escobedo* that the Fifth Amendment requires for an admissible confession that it be given by one distinctly aware of his right not to speak and shielded from "the compelling atmosphere" of interrogation. From these key premises, the Court finally develops the safeguards of warning, counsel, and so forth. I do not believe these premises are sustained by precedents under the Fifth Amendment.

* * *

A closing word must be said about the Assistance of Counsel Clause of the Sixth Amendment, which is never expressly relied on by the Court but whose judicial precedents turn out to be linchpins of the confession rules announced today. * * * While the Court finds no pertinent difference between judicial proceedings and police interrogation, I believe the differences are so vast as to disqualify wholly the Sixth Amendment precedents as suitable analogies in the present cases.

* * *

Examined as an expression of public policy, the Court's new regime proves so dubious that there can be no due compensation for its weakness in constitutional law.

Without at all subscribing to the generally black picture of police conduct painted by the Court, I think it must be frankly recognized at the outset that police questioning allowable under due process precedents may inherently entail some pressure on the suspect and may seek advantage in his ignorance or weaknesses. The atmosphere and questioning techniques, proper and fair though they be, can in themselves exert a tug on the suspect to confess, and in this light "[t]o speak of any confessions of crime made after arrest as being 'voluntary' or 'uncoerced' is somewhat inaccurate, although traditional. A confession is wholly and incontestably voluntary only if a guilty person gives himself up to the law and becomes his own accuser." Until today, the role of the Constitution has been only to sift out *undue* pressure, not to assure spontaneous confessions.

* * *

What the Court largely ignores is that its rules impair, if they will not eventually serve wholly to frustrate, an instrument of law enforcement that has long and quite reasonably been thought worth the price paid for it. There can be little doubt that the Court's new code would markedly decrease the number of confessions. To warn the suspect that he may remain silent and remind him that his confession may be used in court are minor obstructions. To require also an express waiver by the suspect and an end to questioning whenever he demurs must heavily handicap questioning. And to suggest or provide counsel for the suspect simply invites the end of the interrogation.

How much harm this decision will inflict on law enforcement cannot fairly be predicted with accuracy. Evidence on the role of confessions is notoriously incomplete * * *. We do know that some crimes cannot be solved without confessions, that ample expert testimony attests to their importance in crime control, and that the Court is taking a real risk with society's welfare in imposing its new regime on the country. The social costs of crime are too great to call the new rules anything but a hazardous experimentation.

* * *

* * * it may make the analysis more graphic to consider the actual facts of one of the four cases reversed by the Court. *Miranda v. Arizona* serves best, being neither the hardest nor easiest of the four under the Court's standards.

On March 3, 1963, an 18-year-old girl was kidnapped and forcibly raped near Phoenix, Arizona. Ten days later, on the morning of March 13, petitioner Miranda was arrested and taken to the police station. At this time Miranda was 23 years old, indigent, and educated to the extent of completing half the ninth grade. He had "an emotional illness" of the schizophrenic type, according to the doctor who eventually examined him; the doctor's report also stated that Miranda was "alert and oriented as to time, place, and person," intelligent within normal limits, competent to stand trial, and sane within the legal definition. At the police station, the victim picked Miranda out of a lineup, and two officers then took him into a separate room to interrogate him, starting about 11:30 a. m. Though at first denying his guilt, within a short time Miranda gave a detailed oral confession and then wrote out in his own hand and signed a brief statement admitting and describing the crime. All this was accomplished in two hours or less without any force, threats or promises and—I will assume this though the record is uncertain,—without any effective warnings at all.

Miranda's oral and written confessions are now held inadmissible under the Court's new rules. One is entitled to feel astonished that the Constitution can be read to produce this result. These confessions were obtained during brief, day-time questioning conducted by two officers and unmarked by any of the traditional indicia of coercion. They assured a conviction for a brutal and unsettling crime, for which the police had and quite possibly could obtain little evidence other than the victim's identifications, evidence which is frequently unreliable. There was, in sum, a legitimate purpose, no perceptible unfairness, and certainly little risk of injustice in the interrogation. Yet the resulting confessions, and the responsible course of police practice they represent, are to be sacrificed to the Court's own finespun conception of fairness which I seriously doubt is shared by many thinking citizens in this country.

*   *   *

Mr. Justice WHITE, with whom Mr. Justice HARLAN and Mr. Justice STEWART join, dissenting.

*   *   *

NOTES AND QUESTIONS

1. The *Miranda* decision insists that the accused be told that an attorney will be provided for him free if he cannot afford to hire one. A 1972 decision required that an attorney be made available to anyone threatened with even a single day in jail.[5] The *Miranda* decision and its progeny have been attacked on the grounds that the Court is protecting the guilty and restricting police too severely. The arguments in its defense center on the protection the individual suspect receives from painful police coercion and on the stimulus these decisions provide for more thorough and scrupulous police investigation. The strongest argument given in defense of the right to remain silent and have legal counsel is that it helps prevent the conviction of innocent persons.

2. When Miranda was retried, it was not possible, of course, for the prosecutors to use his original confession as part of their case against him. However, Miranda had also confessed his crime to his common law wife, who told police. Based on this and other evidence, Miranda was reconvicted for a term of from 20 to 30 years in prison.

It is important to realize that reversals of convictions as in *Miranda* because of procedural errors do not automatically result in setting criminals free. They are likely to be tried again. Nor does retrial violate the double jeopardy provision of the Fifth Amendment. The double jeopardy clause ("nor shall any person be subject for the same offense to be twice put in jeopardy of life or limb") prevents trying the same person twice for the same crime. Thus, if a person is found not guilty of a particular offense, the government cannot retry the person on a lesser charge for the same act. Nor may the government retry a person found guilty of a particular offense a second time on a greater charge. However, the double jeopardy clause, which in 1969 in *Benton v. Maryland*, 395 U.S. 784, was applied to the states through the Fourteenth Amendment, does not prohibit the retrying of a person where there were procedural errors, nor does it prohibit trying an accused person in both federal and state courts for the same offense. Despite considerable criticism in recent years, the presumption first

5.   *Argersinger v. Hamlin*, 407 U.S. 25 (1972).

announced in *United States v. Lanza*, 260 U.S. 377 (1922)—that the federal system of government establishes two general jurisdictions, one state and one federal, and that an accused can break the laws of both through a single act—remains valid. The Court has also ruled that a single crime may result in multiple violations of the law, each of which may be tried separately. *Gore v. U. S.*, 357 U.S. 386 (1958). For example, an act which injures several persons may constitute a crime against each. However, if a jury has acquitted a person of committing a crime against one victim in a multi-victim situation, the Supreme Court has ruled that the government cannot retry the person with regard to the other victims using essentially the same facts. *Ashe v. Swenson*, 397 U.S. 436 (1970).

3. The late Professor Herbert Packer in his book, *The Limits of the Criminal Sanction*, suggests that there are two approaches to the criminal process within the United States: the Crime Control Model and the Due Process Model. These approaches view the goals and procedures of the criminal justice system in very different ways. Packer contrasts the Crime Control Model with the Due Process Model as follows:

> The value system that underlies the Crime Control Model is based on the proposition that the repression of criminal conduct is by far the most important function to be performed by the criminal process * * *. * * * In order to achieve this high purpose, the Crime Control Model requires that primary attention be paid to the efficiency with which the criminal process operates to screen suspects, determine guilt, and secure appropriate dispositions of persons convicted of crime.
>
> * * *
>
> * * * The image that comes to mind is an assembly-line conveyor belt down which moves an endless stream of cases, never stopping, carrying the cases to workers who stand at fixed stations and who perform on each case as it comes by the same small but essential operation that brings it one step closer to being a finished product, or, to exchange the metaphor for the reality, a closed file. * * *
>
> * * *
>
> * * * If the Crime Control Model resembles an assembly line, the Due Process Model looks very much like an obstacle course its successive stages is designed to present formidable impediments to carrying the accused any further along the process. * * *
>
> * * *
>
> * * * The Due Process Model insists on the prevention and elimination of mistakes to the extent possible.[6]

These two models stress very different values. The Crime Control Model stresses the need for speed and efficiency in the interest of societal security, while the Due Process Model stresses the need to jealously guard the rights of the accused. The first thus corresponds with the view of

---

6. Herbert L. Packer, *The Limits of the Criminal Sanction* (Stanford, Calif.: Stanford University Press, 1968), at pp. 158–164.

justice as social order, while the second relates more to viewing justice as adherence to set procedures. As the opinions in *Miranda* demonstrate, much debate has arisen over whether the Court should be "activist" in support of the effectiveness of law enforcement authorities. Of the two approaches, which most nearly corresponds to your own views?

4. Since the *Miranda* ruling, there have been many decisions elaborating on its themes. For example, in *Orozco v. Texas*, 394 U.S. 324 (1969), the Court extended the *Miranda* safeguards to apply to questioning of a suspect in custody outside the police station, even in bed in his own home. By the 1970s it became clear that the Burger Court would not extend the *Miranda* ruling. In fact, several decisions were handed down limiting the scope of *Miranda*. For example, in *Oregon v. Hass*, 420 U.S. 714 (1975), the Court with all four Nixon appointees in the majority concluded that statements made by a suspect after he has been warned of his rights but before his lawyer appears can be used to impeach his trial testimony. Still, in 1977 the Court rejected, though narrowly, a clear opportunity to overrule *Miranda* in a case involving a murder suspect who during a long car ride provided incriminating statements to police after he had received the *Miranda* warnings. In response to leading statements by one of the officers, the suspect led police to the body of a girl he had murdered. His lawyer was not present in the car. The Court in *Brewer v. Williams*, 430 U.S. 387, avoided the *Miranda* issue, ruling that the evidence was inadmissible because the right to counsel had been violated. Chief Justice Burger wrote a strong dissent claiming that the majority was punishing the public for the mistakes of law enforcement officers and questioning the need for a new trial when the suspect was clearly guilty.

(2) Protecting the Accused: A Fair Trial

The Sixth Amendment to the Constitution establishes a number of impressive rights of a defendant in a criminal case. Trials must be speedy. Trials must also be public since secret trials are less apt to be fair. Defendants possess the right to be confronted with the witnesses against them. The defendant also has the right to have compulsory process for obtaining witnesses in his favor by having courts issue subpoenas requiring people to give testimony. Finally, the defendant has the extremely important procedural right to professional legal advice. In *Gideon v. Wainwright*, 372 U. S. 335 (1965), the court firmly established the right of individuals accused of a federal or state crime to have counsel for their defense. In *Gideon*, the Supreme Court overturned the Florida conviction of Clarence Gideon, who, as an indigent defendant, was unable to afford legal counsel. None had been appointed by the Florida court for him, even though he requested it. Gideon conducted his own defense at his trial as best he could. Like most states at that time, Florida had assigned counsel for people unable to afford their own lawyer only in cases involving the death penalty.

This highly dramatic case of Clarence Gideon, who appealed directly to the Supreme Court by laboriously printing his appeal in pencil from his jail cell, firmly established the right to counsel in all criminal cases even if the government has to appoint counsel at its own expense. However, this case did not clearly spell out at what point in the criminal justice process counsel must be available. In the later *Escobedo* and *Miranda* cases, the Supreme Court established the right to counsel as soon as a police investigation makes a person a prime suspect.

By the mid-1970s, it became clear that the Burger Court would not expand the precedents in criminal proceedings set by the Warren Court, and in fact would work to limit their application. With the addition of more conservative and restraintist Justices, the Court ruled in *Kirby v. Illinois*, 406 U.S. 682 (1972), that a person who has not been formally accused of a crime has no right to have counsel during a pre-indictment identification session at a police station. In 1974, the Court further refused to extend the Warren Court precedents in a six-to-three decision holding that the right to counsel does not extend to prisoners facing disciplinary hearings though other procedural safeguards do except in unusual circumstances. *Wolff v. McDonnell,* 418 U.S. 539.

But the basic precedents set in the 1960s still stand.

Professor Herbert Packer has summarized well the present perspective which has become the legal foundation of procedural due process:

> * * * there is the assumption that there are limits to the powers of government to investigate and apprehend persons suspected of committing crimes. * * * a degree of scrutiny and control must be exercised with respect to the activities of law enforcement officers * * *.
>
> * * *
>
> * * * (There is also) the notion that the alleged criminal is not merely an object to be acted upon but an independent entity in the process who may, if he so desires, force the operators of the process to demonstrate to an independent authority (judge and jury) that he is guilty of the charges against him.[7]

The Supreme Court has, in effect, spelled out through a number of recent precedents what constitutes fairness and "a sense of justice" within our constitutional polity. Many liberals have applauded the Warren Court for its protection of the accused, while criticizing the Burger Court for failing to extend these precedents. Conservatives were outraged by what they considered to be the Warren Court's coddling of criminals, while more pleased with the approach of the Burger Court. Radicals claim that justice, like medical care, is a commodity to be sold to the highest bidder. Rights of the accused are generally available in a real sense only to those who can pay for them. Quality legal service costs money, which is unequally distributed in a capitalist society. The poor are faced with the full array of talent and resources available to the prosecutor's office. To depend upon an inexperienced or harried court-appointed lawyer, say these critics, is to be virtually helpless in the criminal justice process. While there are a handful of attorneys who have dedicated their professional lives to the defense of the poor and helpless and who have been willing to assume the financial hardship of such a life, they remain but a mere handful, unable to alter the unequal justice of the overall system. Radicals contend that until the emptiness of these procedural rights for the disadvantaged are clearly perceived, justice as they envision it will never be achieved.

7. *Id.,* at pp. 156–157.

C. The Supreme Court Protects the Juvenile Offender

Traditionally, special courts have been established for juveniles whereby the state can protect youthful offenders from the adversary process. Juvenile hearings have therefore been considered civil, not criminal proceedings. The practice has been that children are not entitled to the constitutional rights of adult defendants in criminal cases such as bail, indictment, public trial, immunity against self-incrimination, and counsel. By the late 1960s, the Warren Court had severely scrutinized procedures in adult criminal trials. The standards followed in juvenile courts were bound to receive similar scrutiny.

In 1967 the Supreme Court ruled that the Due Process Clause of the Fourteenth Amendment applies to proceedings in state juvenile courts to adjudge a juvenile delinquent. In *In re Gault*, 387 U.S. 1, a fifteen-year-old boy, Gerald Gault, had been charged in an Arizona juvenile proceeding with making indecent statements in a phone call to a neighbor. No notice of arrest had been given to Gerald's parents, who were away when he was taken into custody, nor were they informed of the specific charges filed with the court. The accuser was not present at Gerald's first hearing, and no record was made. At a second hearing, conflicting testimony was given and a probation officer's referral report was filed with the court, but no copy was made available to the parents or Gerald. Again, the accusor was not present and no record was made. At the end of this process, Gerald was committed to a state institution as a juvenile delinquent until he reached 21 years of age. Arizona law did not provide for appeal.

One would have assumed that the juvenile court system would have prevented such a bizarre situation from occurring. But the discretion originally considered the only means to prevent juveniles from the harshness of adult criminal procedure appears to have been prostituted in *Gault* in the hands of those less committed to the idealism of the social reformers who set the system up. *Gault* illustrates very well the tension between allowing decision makers the discretion to fit the system to the needs of those subject to it and providing unchanging procedural safeguards to protect persons from an abuse of that discretion. At issue is where the balance should be struck: how much procedural due process is due?

After the decision of the juvenile court, Gerald Gault's parents filed a writ of habeas corpus with the Arizona Supreme Court. At the habeas corpus proceeding, the witnesses had trouble agreeing on what had transpired at the two hearings before the juvenile court judge, since there were no records. The juvenile court judge in cross-examination could not spell out how he had found Gerald Gault delinquent:

"Q. All right. Now, Judge, would you tell me under what section of the law or tell me under what section of—of the code you found the boy delinquent?

"A. Well, there is a—I think it amounts to disturbing the peace. I can't give you the section, but I can tell you the law, that when one person uses lewd language in the presence of another person, that it can amount to—and I consider that when a person makes it over the phone, that it is considered in the presence,

I might be wrong, that is one section. The other section upon which I consider the boy delinquent is Section 8–201, Subsection (d), habitually involved in immoral matters." (Footnote 5, *In re Gault*, 387 U.S. 1 at p. 8).

The Arizona high court refused to issue the writ. The U. S. Supreme Court reversed the judgment. Justice Abe Fortas presented the position of the majority that while juvenile courts exist to "rehabilitate" juveniles rather than punish them for their crimes, it is not valid for juvenile courts to ignore rules requiring fair procedures.

IN RE GAULT

Supreme Court of the United States, 1967.
387 U.S. 1, 87 S.Ct. 1428, 18 L.Ed.2d 527.

Mr. Justice FORTAS delivered the opinion of the Court.

* * *

From the inception of the juvenile court system, wide differences have been tolerated—indeed insisted upon—between the procedural rights accorded to adults and those of juveniles. In practically all jurisdictions, there are rights granted to adults which are withheld from juveniles. In addition to the specific problems involved in the present case, for example, it has been held that the juvenile is not entitled to bail, to indictment by grand jury, to a public trial or to trial by jury. It is frequent practice that rules governing the arrest and interrogation of adults by the police are not observed in the case of juveniles.

* * *

The early reformers were appalled by adult procedures and penalties, and by the fact that children could be given long prison sentences and mixed in jails with hardened criminals. They were profoundly convinced that society's duty to the child could not be confined by the concept of justice alone. They believed that society's role was not to ascertain whether the child was "guilty" or "innocent," but "What is he, how has he become what he is, and what had best be done in his interest and in the interest of the state to save him from a downward career." The child—essentially good, as they saw it—was to be made "to feel that he is the object of [the state's] care and solicitude," not that he was under arrest or on trial. The rules of criminal procedure were therefore altogether inapplicable. The apparent rigidities, technicalities, and harshness which they observed in both substantive and procedural criminal law were therefore to be discarded. The idea of crime and punishment was to be abandoned.

These results were to be achieved, * * * by insisting that the proceedings were not adversary, but that the state was proceeding as *parens patriae*. The right of the state, as *parens patriae*, to deny to the child procedural rights available to his elders was elaborated by the assertion that a child, unlike an adult, has a right "not to liberty but to custody." He can be made to attorn to his parents, to go to school, etc. If his parents default in effectively performing their custodial functions—that is, if the child is "delinquent"—the state may intervene. In doing so, it does not deprive the child of any rights, because he has none. It merely provides the "custody" to which the child is entitled. On this basis, proceedings involving juveniles were described as "civil" not "criminal" and therefore not subject to the requirements which restrict the state when it seeks to deprive a person of his liberty.

* * *

Failure to observe the fundamental requirements of due process has resulted in instances, which might have been avoided, of unfairness to individuals and inadequate or inaccurate findings of fact and unfortunate prescriptions of remedy. * * *

It is claimed that juveniles obtain benefits from the special procedures applicable to them which more than offset the disadvantages of denial of the substance of normal due process. * * * the observance of due process standards, intelligently and not ruthlessly administered, will not compel the States to abandon or displace any of the substantive benefits of the juvenile process. But it is important, we think, that the claimed benefits of the juvenile process should be candidly appraised. * * *

Certainly, * * * the high crime rates among juveniles * * * could not lead us to conclude that the absence of constitutional protections reduces crime, or that the juvenile system, functioning free of constitutional inhibitions as it has largely done, is effective to reduce crime or rehabilitate offenders. We do not mean by this to denigrate the juvenile court process or to suggest that there are not aspects of the juvenile system relating to offenders which are valuable. But the features of the juvenile system which its proponents have asserted are of unique benefit will not be impaired by constitutional domestication. For example, the commendable principles relating to the processing and treatment of juveniles separately from adults are in no way involved or affected by the procedural issues under discussion. Further, we are told that one of the important benefits of the special juvenile court procedures is that they avoid classifying the juvenile as a "criminal." The juvenile offender is now classed as a "delinquent." There is, of course, no reason why this should not continue. It is disconcerting, however, that this term has come to involve only slightly less stigma than the term "criminal" applied to adults. It is also emphasized that in practically all jurisdictions, statutes provide that an adjudication of the child as a delinquent shall not operate as a civil disability or disqualify him for civil service appointment. There is no reason why the application of due process requirements should interfere with such provisions.

* * *

* * * While due process requirements will, in some instances, introduce a degree of order and regularity to Juvenile Court proceedings to determine delinquency, and in contested cases will introduce some elements of the adversary system, nothing will require that the conception of the kindly juvenile judge be replaced by its opposite, nor do we here rule upon the question whether ordinary due process requirements must be observed with respect to hearings to determine the disposition of the delinquent child.

* * *

* * * Under our Constitution, the condition of being a boy does not justify a kangaroo court. The traditional ideas of Juvenile Court procedure, indeed, contemplated that time would be available and care would be used to establish precisely what the juvenile did and why he did it—was it a prank of adolescence or a brutal act threatening serious consequences to himself or society unless corrected? Under traditional notions, one would assume that in a case like that of Gerald Gault, where the juvenile appears to have a home, a working mother and father, and an older brother, the Juvenile Judge would have made a careful inquiry and judgment as to the possibility that the boy could be disciplined and dealt with at

home, despite his previous transgressions. Indeed, so far as appears in the record before us, except for some conversation with Gerald about his school work and his "wanting to go to * * * Grand Canyon with his father," the points to which the judge directed his attention were little different from those that would be involved in determining any charge of violation of a penal statute. The essential difference between Gerald's case and a normal criminal case is that safeguards available to adults were discarded in Gerald's case. The summary procedure as well as the long commitment was possible because Gerald was 15 years of age instead of over 18.

If Gerald had been over 18, he would not have been subject to Juvenile Court proceedings. For the particular offense immediately involved, the maximum punishment would have been a fine of $5 to $50, or imprisonment in jail for not more than two months. Instead, he was committed to custody for a maximum of six years. If he had been over 18 and had committed an offense to which such a sentence might apply, he would have been entitled to substantial rights under the Constitution of the United States as well as under Arizona's laws and constitution. The United States Constitution would guarantee him rights and protections with respect to arrest, search and seizure, and pretrial interrogation. It would assure him of specific notice of the charges and adequate time to decide his course of action and to prepare his defense. He would be entitled to clear advice that he could be represented by counsel, and, at least if a felony were involved, the State would be required to provide counsel if his parents were unable to afford it. If the court acted on the basis of his confession, careful procedures would be required to assure its voluntariness. If the case went to trial, confrontation and opportunity for cross-examination would be guaranteed. So wide a gulf between the State's treatment

of the adult and of the child requires a bridge sturdier than mere verbiage, and reasons more persuasive than cliché can provide.

* * *

We now turn to the specific issues which are presented to us in the present case.

* * *

* * * Due process of law requires * * * notice which would be deemed constitutionally adequate in a civil or criminal proceeding. It does not allow a hearing to be held in which a youth's freedom and his parents' right to his custody are at stake without giving them timely notice, in advance of the hearing, of the specific issues that they must meet. * * *

* * *

We conclude that the Due Process Clause of the Fourteenth Amendment requires that in respect of proceedings to determine delinquency which may result in commitment to an institution in which the juvenile's freedom is curtailed, the child and his parents must be notified of the child's right to be represented by counsel retained by them, or if they are unable to afford counsel, that counsel will be appointed to represent the child.

* * *

We conclude that the constitutional privilege against self-incrimination is applicable in the case of juveniles as it is with respect to adults. We appreciate that special problems may arise with respect to waiver of the privilege by or on behalf of children, and that there may well be some differences in technique—but not in principle—depending upon the age of the child and the presence and competence of parents. The participation of counsel will, of course, assist the police, Juvenile Courts and appellate tribunals in administering the privilege. If counsel was not present for some permissible reason when an admission was obtained, the greatest care must be taken to assure that the admission was voluntary, in the sense not only that it was not coerced or suggested, but also that it was not the product of ignorance of rights or of adolescent fantasy, fright or despair.

* * *

This Court has not held that a State is required by the Federal Constitution "to provide appellate courts or a right to appellate review at all." In view of the fact that we must reverse the Supreme Court of Arizona's affirmance of the dismissal of the writ of habeas corpus for other reasons, we need not rule on this question in the present case or upon the failure to provide a transcript or recording of the hearings—or, indeed, the failure of the Juvenile Judge to state the grounds for his conclusion. * * *

For the reasons stated, the judgment of the Supreme Court of Arizona is reversed and the cause remanded for further proceedings not inconsistent with this opinion.

It is so ordered.

Mr. Justice BLACK, concurring.

* * *

Where a person, infant or adult, can be seized by the State, charged, and convicted for violating a state criminal law, and then ordered by the State to be confined for six years, I think the Constitution requires that he be tried in accordance with the guarantees of all the provisions of the Bill of Rights made applicable to the States by the Fourteenth Amendment. Undoubtedly this would be true of an adult defendant, and it would be a plain denial of equal protection of the laws—an invidious discrimination—to hold that others subject to heavier punishments could, because they are children, be denied these same constitutional safeguards. I consequently agree with the Court that the Arizona law as applied here denied to the parents and their son the right of notice, right to counsel, right against self-incrimination,

and right to confront the witnesses against young Gault. Appellants are entitled to these rights, not because "fairness, impartiality and orderliness—in short, the essentials of due process"—require them and not because they are "the procedural rules which have been fashioned from the generality of due process," but because they are specifically and unequivocally granted by provisions of the Fifth and Sixth Amendments which the Fourteenth Amendment makes applicable to the States.

* * *

Mr. Justice WHITE, concurring.

* * *

Mr. Justice HARLAN, concurring in part and dissenting in part.

* * *

The proper issue here is however, not whether the State may constitutionally treat juvenile offenders through a system of specialized courts, but whether the proceedings in Arizona's juvenile courts include procedural guarantees which satisfy the requirements of the Fourteenth Amendment. Among the first premises of our constitutional system is the obligation to conduct any proceeding in which an individual may be deprived of liberty or property in a fashion consistent with the "traditions and conscience of our people." The importance of these procedural guarantees is doubly intensified here. First, many of the problems with which Arizona is concerned are among those traditionally confined to the processes of criminal justice; their disposition necessarily affects in the most direct and substantial manner the liberty of individual citizens. Quite obviously, systems of specialized penal justice might permit erosion, or even evasion, of the limitations placed by the Constitution upon state criminal proceedings. Second, we must recognize that the character and consequences of many juvenile court proceedings have in fact closely resembled those of ordinary criminal trials. Nothing before us suggests that juvenile courts were intended as a device to escape constitutional constraints, but I entirely agree with the Court that we are nonetheless obliged to examine with circumspection the procedural guarantees the State has provided.

* * *

It is well settled that the Court must give the widest deference to legislative judgments that concern the character and urgency of the problems with which the State is confronted. Legislatures are, as this Court has often acknowledged, the "main guardian" of the public interest, and, within their constitutional competence, their understanding of that interest must be accepted as "well-nigh" conclusive. This principle does not, however, reach all the questions essential to the resolution of this case. The legislative judgments at issue here embrace assessments of the necessity and wisdom of procedural guarantees; these are questions which the Constitution has entrusted at least in part to courts, and upon which courts have been understood to possess particular competence. The fundamental issue here is, therefore, in what measure and fashion the Court must defer to legislative determinations which encompass constitutional issues of procedural protection.

* * *

* * * only three procedural requirements should, in my opinion, now be deemed required of state juvenile courts by the Due Process Clause of the Fourteenth Amendment: first, timely notice must be provided to parents and children of the nature and terms of any juvenile court proceeding in which a determination affecting their rights or interests may be made; second, unequivocal and timely notice must be given that counsel may appear in any such proceeding in behalf of the child and its parents, and that in cases in which the child may be confined in an institution, counsel may, in circumstances of in-

digency, be appointed for them; and third, the court must maintain a written record, or its equivalent, adequate to permit effective review on appeal or in collateral proceedings. These requirements would guarantee to juveniles the tools with which their rights could be fully vindicated, and yet permit the States to pursue without unnecessary hindrance the purposes which they believe imperative in this field. Further, their imposition now would later permit more intelligent assessment of the Necessity under the Fourteenth Amendment of additional requirements, by creating suitable records from which the character and deficiencies of juvenile proceedings could be accurately judged. * * *

The Court has consistently made plain that adequate and timely notice is the fulcrum of due process, whatever the purposes of the proceeding. Notice is ordinarily the prerequisite to effective assertion of any constitutional or other rights; without it, vindication of those rights must be essentially fortuitous. So fundamental a protection can neither be spared here nor left to the "favor or grace" of state authorities.

Provision of counsel and of a record, like adequate notice, would permit the juvenile to assert very much more effectively his rights and defenses, both in the juvenile proceedings and upon direct or collateral review. * * * The facts of this case illustrate poignantly the difficulties of review without either an adequate record or the participation of counsel in the proceeding's initial stages. At the same time, these requirements should not cause any substantial modification in the character of juvenile court proceedings. * * *

* * *

* * * Gerald Gault and his parents were not provided adequate notice of the terms and purposes of the proceedings in which he was adjudged delinquent; they were not advised of their rights to be represented by counsel; and no record in any form was maintained of the proceedings. It follows, for the reasons given in this opinion, that Gerald Gault was deprived of his liberty without due process of law, and I therefore concur in the judgment of the Court.

Mr. Justice STEWART, dissenting.

The Court today uses an obscure Arizona case as a vehicle to impose upon thousands of juvenile courts throughout the Nation restrictions that the Constitution made applicable to adversary criminal trials. I believe the Court's decision is wholly unsound as a matter of constitutional law, and sadly unwise as a matter of judicial policy.

Juvenile proceedings are not criminal trials. They are not civil trials. They are simply not adversary proceedings. Whether treating with a delinquent child, a neglected child, a defective child, or a dependent child, a juvenile proceeding's whole purpose and mission is the very opposite of the mission and purpose of a prosecution in a criminal court. The object of the one is correction of a condition. The object of the other is conviction and punishment for a criminal act.

* * *

I possess neither the specialized experience nor the expert knowledge to predict with any certainty where may lie the brightest hope for progress in dealing with the serious problems of juvenile delinquency. But I am certain that the answer does not lie in the Court's opinion in this case, which serves to convert a juvenile proceeding into a criminal prosecution.

* * *

* * * The Supreme Court of Arizona found that the parents of Gerald Gault "knew of their right to counsel, to subpoena and cross examine witnesses, of the right to confront the witnesses against Gerald and the possible consequences of a finding of delinquency." It further found that "Mrs. Gault knew the exact nature of the charge against Gerald from the day he was taken to the detention home." And, * * * no issue of compulsory self-incrimination is presented by this case.

I would dismiss the appeal.

NOTES AND QUESTIONS

1. Note that the Court refused to rule whether there is a right to a transcript of the hearing or a right of appeal. Are these essential for due process to be accorded youthful offenders or are the procedures mandated by the Court adequate to assure fairness? Justice Harlan in his concurring and dissenting opinion considers the right to a record of the proceedings to be essential.

2. The range of views expressed by the Justices in this case illustrates the differences of opinion about due process as a means to assure that justice is done. This case is particularly relevant to our discussion about the rights of students. How much procedural due process is required in the educational setting to assure that justice is done? As we will see, the same concerns about treading on the prerogatives of professionals are expressed in cases involving students, particularly where wholly academic decisions are in dispute.

Note in *Gault* that Justice Black appears to take a position regarding the rights of children at variance with his dissent in *Tinker v. Des Moines School Dist.* (Chapter Three) where he refused to endorse the majority's extension of First/Fourteenth Amendment rights of expression to students in the public educational setting. What accounts for the difference? Note also Justice Stewart's dissent. In perhaps the most controversial case involving extension of due process rights to students, *Goss v. Lopez,* which we will review shortly, Justice Stewart sided with the majority in favor of extension.

3. The Court considered it necessary, after *Gault,* to reaffirm that juvenile court proceedings are not criminal prosecutions. Therefore, the due process standard that is required is "fundamental fairness" and not a complete incorporation of all Bill of Rights protections required in state criminal trials. In the companion cases, *McKeiver v. Pennsylvania* and *In re Burris,* 403 U.S. 528 (1971), the Court concluded that many procedural requirements accorded to adults such as a jury trial are not available to juveniles. The state retains an interest in protecting the juvenile against the stigma of criminality, and consequently the juvenile proceeding should not be viewed as fully adversarial. Would you concur with this view? Should students involved in serious disciplinary disputes be treated any differently?

In two later cases, however, the Court borrowed from the criminal trial model to add two important procedural safeguards to juvenile hearings. In *In re Winship,* 397 U.S. 358 (1970), the Court held that the commonly used preponderance of the evidence test in civil trials is not sufficient in juvenile hearings. Proof beyond a reasonable doubt is required. Justice Brennan for the majority noted that "civil labels and good intentions do not themselves obviate the need for criminal due process safeguards in juvenile courts * * *." At p. 368). In 1975 the Court unanimously decided in *Breed v. Jones,* 421 U.S. 519, that a juvenile's constitutional protection against being tried twice for the same offense (double jeopardy clause of the Fifth Amendment) is violated by a trial as an adult after a juvenile court has concluded that the juvenile has broken the law. Should similar procedural requirements be applied to long term suspension and expulsion proceedings involving students?

D. Due Process of Law in Public and Private Organizations

In modern American society, public administrative agencies and personnel have considerable authority to take action in many areas of life including health and welfare. Given the extensive powers of administrative agencies, Congress in 1946 passed the Administrative Procedure Act, 5 U.S.C.A. § 1361 which sought to standardize the procedural protections that must be observed in federal actions affecting persons and property. Such requirements as notice, hearing, and general fairness of procedure must be provided. Like juvenile hearing procedures, administrative agency procedures have not established all of the protections that must apply in an adult court proceeding.

In 1970 the Supreme Court ruled in a far-reaching case, *Goldberg v. Kelly,* 397 U.S. 254 (1970), that state welfare payments could not be cut off without an evidentiary hearing, during which the welfare recipient would be permitted to make an oral presentation, cross-examine adverse witnesses before an impartial arbiter, and be represented by counsel. In this 5–3 decision, Justice William Brennan argued that once a state makes welfare available to the needy, the welfare recipient must be guaranteed basic procedural due process protections under the Fourteenth Amendment Due Process Clause before termination of benefits. The majority claimed that to deny persons public aid while they wait for the court system to vindicate their rights would deprive eligible persons of the very necessities of life. The Court thus found sufficient entitlement in the Fourteenth Amendment "property" provision to require a prior hearing to determine the basis for termination and give the welfare recipient an opportunity to mount a defense. Later, the Court extended the *Goldberg* principle to government employment and to public education, as described below.

The Court has also held in a long line of cases that when the government seeks to restrain an individual's freedom to exercise specific constitutional rights or punish a person for doing so, a prior hearing is required. This is not to say that sanctions cannot be levied. It is to say that before doing so, the government must prove that there are valid reasons for taking action. And the best way to make this determination is to afford the individual an opportunity to challenge the evidence against him and present evidence in his favor. As the Court noted in *Hurtado v. California*, 110 U.S. 516 (1884), due process is designed to protect "those fundamental principles of liberty and justice which lie at the base of all our civil and political institutions * * *." (At p. 535).

Wisconsin v. Constantineau, 400 U.S. 433 (1971), does for *non-specific* liberty interests inherent in the word "liberty" of the Fourteenth Amendment what *Goldberg v. Kelly* does for property interests. There the Supreme Court ruled that it is unconstitutional for government officials to post the names of habitual drunkards in retail liquor outlets without according those whose names are subject to posting to a prior hearing. Said Justice Douglas for the majority, "Where a person's good name, reputation, honor, or integrity is at stake because of what the government is doing to him, notice and an opportunity to be heard are essential." (At p. 437). Exactly what these non-specific liberty interests are and when they come into play remains the subject of considerable dispute. Chapter Eight explores this issue in some detail.

Rights of due process have been hard won in public organizations. To what extent ought they to be available in the private corporate sector? Professor David W. Ewing of the Harvard Business School argues that few Americans enjoy the same guarantees of free speech, privacy, and due process of law during working hours that they are entitled to as citizens. Employee satisfaction and morale as well as organizational effectiveness suffer as a result. Is it consistent and wise, he asks, for our society to tolerate the exclusion of these rights from corporate and bureaucratic life?

> A great many of these companies and agencies are despotic in the harshest sense of that word. In speeches and publications we may criticize the governments of small nations in Africa and Latin America for their rejection of rights. But the gross national products of some of those nations are no larger than the multi-billion-

dollar sales volumes of some U. S. corporations. Is it consistent to criticize one group but not the other? [8]

For employee rights to be a reality, Ewing suggests a voluntary corporate effort to provide employees with "bills of rights" and the opportunity to challenge higher level decision making through grievance mechanisms, ombudsmen, and arbitrators. Voluntary efforts failing, he would have courts extend protection to aggrieved workers, or, better yet, have legislatures pass new laws guaranteeing employee rights in the workplace. In his quest for "industrial justice," Ewing necessarily faces some of the same legal problems explored in Chapter Two related to extending rights to students in nonpublic educational institutions. (See especially the section entitled "Theories of Expansion," pp. 77ff).

III. DUE PROCESS IN THE EDUCATIONAL SETTING

Goldberg v. Kelly concluded that minimum due process protections must be accorded to welfare recipients because of the important interests at stake. In two highly significant cases in 1974, the Supreme Court extended due process rights to tenured teachers at public educational institutions on reasoning similar to *Goldberg*. In *Board of Regents v. Roth,* 408 U.S. 564, Justice Stewart concluded that due process procedures apply when a person "has a legitimate claim of entitlement" to a government-provided benefit. Property rights, he went on, "are created and their dimensions defined by existing rules or understandings that stem from an independent source such as state law—rules or understandings that secure certain benefits and that support claims of entitlement to those benefits." (At p. 577). A teacher tenure rule or law creates a property interest since it confers upon the holder an expectation that employment will be continued. Before terminating such a property right, the government must provide the teacher with an opportunity to challenge the proposed action. Hence, as with the welfare recipient in *Goldberg,* tenured teachers are entitled to procedural due process. However, because nontenured teachers have no expectation of continued employment, they do not have due process rights.[*] Do students have sufficient entitlement to their education to be entitled to due process rights? This section explores some of the main issues underlying this question.

A. Outlining the Main Issues

The expansion of governmental influences in the lives of the individual in our society coupled with distrust of the benevolence of public officials has triggered a drive on many fronts for greater protection from unrea-

---

8. David W. Ewing, *Freedom Inside the Organization: Bringing Civil Liberties to the Worker* (New York: E. P. Dutton, 1977), at p. 229.

* In the companion case of *Perry v. Sindermann*, 408 U.S. 593 (1972), the Court concluded that if a teacher could show that even though no explicit tenure policy existed at a public educational institution, a *de facto* tenure system was in fact in place,

then due process procedures would be required. Justice Stewart for the majority noted:
   * * * Proof of such a property interest would not, of course, entitle him to reinstatement. But such proof would obligate * * * officials to grant a hearing at his request, where he could be informed of the grounds for his nonretention and challenge their sufficiency. (At p. 603).

sonable and arbitrary government action. *Miranda, In re Gault,* and particularly *Goldberg* and *Roth* are manifestations of this trend. Given the time students spend in educational institutions, it is natural that the debate over the applicability of due process to settings outside of the courtroom include them.

(1) Arguments For and Against Due Process in Public Education

Arguments for the application of due process rights for students center on the need to assure students and their parents that school officials act fairly when making decisions on their behalf. As the late Harvard Law Professor Zechariah Chafee wrote many years ago regarding educators in general:

> It is easy to understand how educational authorities believe that they will secure efficiency and desired standards through the possession of absolute powers. However, an institution which professes to prepare youth for life in a democracy might easily give them an example of fair play when it is conducting its own affairs.[9]

Students, it is asserted, have Fourteenth Amendment property interests in their education. The fact that students are compelled to attend school until a certain age sets up a statutory entitlement to an education, much as welfare recipients are entitled to the benefits set aside for them. Similarly, since the credentialling effect of schooling is directly related to acceptance into the job market, students, it is said, have an important stake in completing their education. Others argue that school is essential for training young persons to live effectively in a democratic society. As the Supreme Court asserted in the landmark desegregation case, *Brown v. Board of Educ. of Topeka,* 347 U.S. 483 (1954):

> Today, education is perhaps the most important function of state and local governments. Compulsory school attendance laws and the great expenditures for education both demonstrate our recognition of the importance of education to our democratic society. * * * It is the very foundation of good citizenship. Today it is a principal instrument in awakening the child to cultural values, in preparing him for later professional training, and in helping him to adjust normally to his environment. In these days, it is doubtful that any child may reasonably be expected to succeed in life if he is denied the opportunity of an education. (At p. 493).

If the school treats the student unfairly, argues William G. Buss, the student "will tend to learn that 'democracy implies respect for the elementary rights of men,' or that it does not, depending on whether his 'government'—the school—treats him and his classmates fairly or unfairly."[10]

Student liberty interests, it is argued, also require due process protection. In order for school officials to meet their burden of proof in seeking

---

9. Zechariah Chafee, "The Internal Affairs of Associations Not for Profit," 43 *Harvard L.Rev.* 993, 1930, at p. 1027.

10. William G. Buss, "Procedural Due Process for School Discipline: Probing the Constitutional Outline," 119 *U. of Pa.L.Rev.* 547, February, 1971, at p. 549.

to restrict student rights, it is asserted that an opportunity must be provided to students to enable them to explain themselves and present evidence on their behalf before discipline is imposed. Whether specific constitutional rights are involved or non-specific liberty interests such as the right to a good reputation, proponents of due process argue that it is essential that school authorities act fairly, for what is once done may never be undone.

Opponents of the extension of due process to the educational environment, however, argue that school officials must have an unfettered right to discipline students to maintain an ordered environment conducive to learning. It has become altogether clear that disorder has become a major problem throughout the American educational system. Daily reports of student violence abound. A recent survey conducted by the National School Boards Association revealed that 75 percent of the school districts surveyed reported nonattendance as the most serious problem, followed by violations of school regulations, assaults, abuse of teachers, theft, vandalism, and class disruption.[11] Some commentators have noted that a student is safer in the streets than in the schools.

Mandating due process requirements before school officials can impose discipline, it is argued, will exacerbate an already serious problem by tieing the hands of school officials and preventing effective action. Furthermore, it is alleged that the high cost involved in meeting whatever due process requirements are imposed will result in the shift of resources away from the institutional program. One critic of court-backed student due process regulations has pointed out that legal requirements themselves have a built-in cost:

> What is nearly always ignored is that the cost in resources of a constitutional rule is not measured alone in what it demands of the state to achieve compliance. A second cost comes when, once having complied, and believing a simpler proceeding will work better, the state is not free to change.[12]

Court-backed due process requirements thus constitute a bar to the development of other dispute settlement devices better suited to the needs of the educational environment.

Others assert that discipline is an educational device designed to teach students to recognize authority and practice self-restraint. To the extent rigid legal requirements hamper or curtail the administration of student discipline, a valuable learning experience is sacrificed to meaningless bureaucratic ritual. Superimposing the due process requirements of the criminal courts upon the traditional operation of the educational institution, it is said, will also undermine the relationship of respect and trust between student and teacher and thus get in the way of successful teaching, learning, and counseling.

In short, court involvement on the side of the student undermines the authority and expertise of the educator to establish procedures tailored to

---

11. Ad Hoc Committee on Discipline, *Report: Discipline in Our Big City Schools* (Washington, D. C.: NSBA, 1977), at p. 6.

12. J. Harvie Wilkinson, "*Goss v. Lopez*: The Supreme Court as School Superintendent" 1975 *Sup.Ct.Rev.* 25, 1975, at p. 61 (footnote 180).

the needs of the educational setting and thus works in the long run to the disadvantage of the student.

(2) Due Process: How Much and When?

Assuming the student is entitled to constitutionally required due process under the Fourteenth Amendment Due Process Clause or comparable state constitutional provision, what process is due the student and at what point in time? As the Supreme Court itself has noted:

> "Due process" is an elusive concept. Its exact boundaries are undefinable, and its content varies according to specific factual contexts. * * * as a generalization, it can be said that due process embodies the differing rules of fair play, which through the years, have become associated with differing types of proceedings. Whether the Constitution requires that a particular right obtain in a specific proceeding depends upon a complexity of factors. The nature of the alleged right involved, the nature of the proceeding, and the possible burden on that proceeding, are all considerations which must be taken into account.[13]

Typical of the approach most courts have followed until recently is the decision in *Woods v. Simpson,* 126 A. 882 (Maryland, 1924). There the Court of Appeals of Maryland refused to reconsider the female student's claim that the University of Maryland denied her due process by refusing to enroll her after she declined to answer questions regarding the planting of a newspaper story, later judged to be false. The story alleged that men officials of the university had been making "objectionable suggestions to girl students, and otherwise exhibiting a wrong moral attitude toward them." (At p. 882). Said the court:

> The maintenance of discipline, the upkeep of the necessary tone and standards of behavior in a body of students in a college, is, of course, a task committed to its faculty and officers; not to the courts. It is a task which demands special experience, and is often one of much delicacy, especially in dealing with girl students; and the officers must, of necessity, be left untrammeled in handling the problems which arise, as their judgment and discretion may dictate, looking to the ends to be accomplished. Only in extraordinary situations can a court of law ever be called upon to step in between students and the officers in charge of them. When it is made clear that an action with respect to a student has been, not an honest exercise of discretion, looking to the proper ends, but beyond the limits of that discretion, or arising from some motive extraneous to the purposes committed to that discretion, the courts may be called upon for relief. In such case the officials have, as it is sometimes stated, acted arbitrarily, or abused their discretion; and the courts may be required to remedy that. (At p. 883).

13. *Hannah v. Larche,* 363 U.S. 420 (1960), at p. 442.

While courts have never abandoned this substantive due process approach when asked to review decisions made by educational officials, they more recently have been willing to impose procedural due process requirements on student disciplinary decision making. If decisions are made pursuant to preestablished and announced procedures, it is assumed the actual outcomes are more likely to be fair and reasonable. The question, however, is again how much and when.

Procedural due process can be as all-encompassing as that required in adult criminal trials. Protections include those listed in the Bill of Rights, particularly the Fifth and Sixth Amendments, supplemented by court rulings as in *Miranda v. Arizona* and by statutory protections. Or procedural due process can have some of the same features as criminal trials but without others such as a jury, complex rules of evidence, and standards of proof. This was the type of procedure prescribed in *Goldberg v. Kelly*. A third option would involve only the rudiments of procedural due process. As one commentator suggests, such skeletal due process would contemplate "only the barest rudiments: advance notice of the charges, a statement of the evidence backing them up, some chance to present one's own side of the story, and perhaps a brief statement of the reasons for adverse action." [14]

At what point are any of these due the student? What type of procedures should pertain to minor infractions of the rules? To major infractions? Should due process apply only to disciplinary actions or decisions based entirely on academic grounds?

For those who view justice as social welfare, requiring an approach tailored to individual circumstances, there is in addition the underlying question whether procedural due process by itself will really insure basic fairness. As a matter of principle, should judges not only mandate procedural safeguards but also conduct a thorough substantive review of the proceedings? Should courts routinely accept the findings of educators or, when in doubt, make an independent determination of the facts? To what extent do courts possess both the time and resources to undertake such efforts? Do judges possess sufficient expertise to modify or override the decisions of professional educators? These are difficult questions to answer and the responses courts have made to date have not always pleased educators, students, or the general public.

(3) At What Age and in What Institutions?

Since most students attending colleges and universities are legally considered adults, they are clearly entitled to whatever due process procedures have been established. At the opposite end of the scale are elementary school students. Should they be entitled to similar procedural safeguards? One commentator has suggested the following approach.

> Whenever a choice is appropriate to ensure an efficient and orderly proceeding, the parent should tend to direct the exercise of procedural rights when the accused student is in the primary grades, and the student should tend to be in control by the time

14. Wilkinson, *supra*, at p. 40.

he is in high school. In between, control should gradually shift to the student. Whenever evidence of a conflict of interests arises, both parent and student should be afforded independent procedural safeguards.[15]

It is unclear, however, how such a sliding scale would operate for those "in between." As noted in the first chapter, there are some advantages to setting arbitrary age classifications.

Should nonpublic educational institutions be required to observe student due process rights and, if so, to what extent? For reasons already advanced, public educational institutions are covered by the terms of the Fourteenth Amendment to the U. S. Constitution. But nonpublic institutions are not. Are students attending the latter any less entitled to due process?

Because of the similarity between public and nonpublic educational institutions in the functions they perform and because of the important stake students in both types of institutions have in continued enrollment, courts have increasingly held the nonpublic institution to standards of "fundamental fairness." However, courts have at the same time been reluctant to consider nonpublic institutions the equivalent of the public just because they receive public funds and perform similar educational activities. See, for example, *Grossner v. Trustees of Columbia Univ.*, 287 F.Supp. 535 (S.D.N.Y.1968). As noted in Chapter Two, contract law appears to be the preferred approach for courts to use in extending rights to nonpublic school students. Public school students are also beneficiaries of this approach. While it is true that some nonpublic institutions may write into handbooks or other documents a disavowal of any implied or expressed obligation to provide due process, courts are less likely to uphold them. As one source notes, "Just as automobile warranty disclaimers have been held void in view of the importance of and need for the defense of the consumer, provisions of this kind might be denied effect because of the interest in and occasion for the protection of the student." [16] Federal and state laws mandating consumer protection for students and threatening non-complying institutions with loss of funding and/or accreditation serve as a further stimulus to fair treatment.

On the other hand, courts are usually not inclined to prescribe detailed procedural due process requirements on nonpublic institutions. The standard of review for nonpublic institutions generally remains the same as the old standard suggested for public institutions in *Woods v. Simpson*: only wholly arbitrary action by school administrators may be ground for court review. However, if the institution has established detailed procedures and then deviates from those procedures in a way the court determines to be significant, a review of internal decision may be forthcoming. For example, in *Kwiatkowski v. Ithaca College*, 368 N.Y.S.2d 973 (New York, 1975), a state court ruled that Ithaca College, a nonpublic institution, had to accord the student a second appeal hearing since, contrary to its own rules, the college failed to accord him the same rights on appeal as those

---

15. Buss, *supra*, at p. 589.

16. Note, "Developments in the Law—Academic Freedom," 81 *Harv.L.Rev.* 1045, 1968, at p. 1147.

permitted during the initial hearing. Some have suggested that decisions like this could be avoided if the procedures for serious disciplinary actions are not spelled out but set forth only generally. Whether ambiguous procedures would conform to a court's conception of fundamental fairness, however, is open to question, given the varying legal conceptions of what that concept entails.

B. Due Process and Disciplinary Disputes in Public Education

It is in the public sector where the most extensive court involvement on behalf of student due process rights has occurred. The following section presents two doctrinal cases setting forth procedural due process requirements to be followed in student disciplinary actions in public schools and colleges. As will be evident, courts have gone beyond the "fundamental fairness" standard to hold that students do have specific constitutional procedural due process rights prior to serious disciplinary action in the public educational setting.

DIXON v. ALABAMA STATE BD. OF EDUC.

United States Court of Appeals, Fifth Circuit, 1961.
294 F.2d 150.

RIVES, Circuit Judge.

The question presented * * *, is whether due process requires notice and some opportunity for hearing before students at a tax-supported college are expelled for misconduct. We answer that question in the affirmative.

The misconduct for which the students were expelled has never been definitely specified. Defendant Trenholm, the President of the College, testified that he did not know why the plaintiffs and three additional students were expelled and twenty other students were placed on probation. The notice of expulsion [2] which Dr. Trenholm mailed to each of the plaintiffs assigned no specific ground for expulsion, but referred in general

2. Letter from Alabama State College, Montgomery, Alabama, dated March 4, 1960, signed by H. Councill Trenholm, President:

"Dear Sir:

"This communication is the official notification of your expulsion from Alabama State College as of the end of the 1960 Winter Quarter.

"As reported through the various news media, The State Board of Education considered this problem of Alabama State College at its meeting on this past Wednesday afternoon. You were one of the students involved in this expulsion-directive by the State Board of Education. I was directed to proceed accordingly.

"On Friday of last week, I had made the recommendation that any subsequently-confirmed action would not be effective until the close of this 1960 Winter Quarter so that each student could thus have the opportunity to take this quarter's examinations and to qualify for as much OH–Pt credit as possible for the 1960 Winter Quarter.

"The State Board of Education, * * * includes the following in its regulations * * *:

"'Pupils may be expelled from any of the Colleges:

"'a. For willful disobedience to the rules and regulations established for the conduct of the schools.

"'b. For willful and continued neglect of studies and continued failure to maintain the standards of efficiency required by the rules and regulations.

"'c. For Conduct Prejudicial to the School and for Conduct Unbecoming a Student or Future Teacher in Schools of Alabama, for Insubordination and Insurrection, or for Inciting Other Pupils to Like Conduct.

"'d. For any conduct involving moral turpitude.'"

In the notice received by each of the students paragraph "c," just quoted, was capitalized.

terms to "this problem of Alabama State College."

The acts of the students considered by the State Board of Education before it ordered their expulsion are described in the opinion of the district court * * * from which we quote in the margin.[3]

As shown by the findings of the district court, * * * the only demonstration which the evidence showed that *all* of the expelled students took part in was that in the lunch grill located in the basement of the Montgomery County Courthouse. The other demonstrations were found to be attended "by several if not all of the plaintiffs." We have carefully read and studied the record, and agree with the district court that the evidence does not affirmatively show that *all* of the plaintiffs were present at any but the one demonstration.

Only one member of the State Board of Education assigned the demonstration attended by all of the plaintiffs as the sole basis for his vote to expel them. Mr. Harry Ayers testified:

"Q. Mr. Ayers, did you vote to expel these negro students because they went to the Court House and asked to be served at the white lunch counter? A. No, I voted because they violated a law of Alabama.

"Q. What law of Alabama had they violated? A. That separating of the races in public places of that kind.

"Q. And the fact that they went up there and requested service, by violating the Alabama law, then you voted to have them expelled? A. Yes.

"Q. And that is your reason why you voted? A. That is the reason."

3. "On the 25th day of February, 1960, the six plaintiffs in this case were students in good standing at the Alabama State College for Negroes in Montgomery, Alabama * * * On this date, approximately twenty-nine Negro students, including these six plaintiffs, according to a prearranged plan, entered as a group a publicly owned lunch grill located in the basement of the county courthouse in Montgomery, Alabama, and asked to be served. Service was refused; the lunchroom was closed; the Negroes refused to leave; police authorities were summoned; and the Negroes were ordered outside where they remained in the corridor of the courthouse for approximately one hour. On the same day, John Patterson, as Governor of the State of Alabama and as chairman of the State Board of Education, conferred with Dr. Trenholm, a Negro educator and president of the Alabama State College, concerning this activity on the part of some of the students. Dr. Trenholm was advised by the Governor that the incident should be investigated, and that if he were in the president's position he would consider expulsion and/or other appropriate disciplinary action. On February 26, 1960, several hundred Negro students from the Alabama State College, including several if not all of these plaintiffs, staged a mass attendance at a trial being held in the Montgomery County Courthouse, involving the perjury prosecution of a fellow student. After the trial these

students filed two by two from the courthouse and marched through the city approximately two miles back to the college. On February 27, 1960, several hundred Negro students from this school, including several if not all of the plaintiffs in this case, staged mass demonstrations in Montgomery and Tuskegee, Alabama. On this same date, Dr. Trenholm advised all of the student body that these demonstrations and meetings were disrupting the orderly conduct of the business at the college and were affecting the work of other students, as well as work of the participating students. Dr. Trenholm personally warned plaintiffs Bernard Lee, Joseph Peterson and Elroy Embry, to cease these disruptive demonstrations immediately, and advised the members of the student body at the Alabama State College to behave themselves and return to their classes. * * *

"On or about March 1, 1960, approximately six hundred students of the Alabama State College engaged in hymn singing and speech making on the steps of the State Capitol. Plaintiff Bernard Lee addressed students at this demonstration, and the demonstration was attended by several if not all of the plaintiffs. Plaintiff Bernard Lee at this time called on the students to strike and boycott the college if any students were expelled because of these demonstrations."

The most elaborate grounds for expulsion were assigned in the testimony of Governor Patterson:

"Q. There is an allegation in the complaint, Governor, that—I believe it is paragraph six, the defendants' action of expulsion was taken without regard to any valid rule or regulation concerning student conduct and merely retaliated against, punished, and sought to intimidate plaintiffs for having lawfully sought service in a publicly owned lunch room with service; is that statement true or false?

"A. Well, that is not true; the action taken by the State Board of Education was—was taken to prevent—to prevent incidents happening by students at the College that would bring—bring discredit upon—upon the School and be prejudicial to the School, and the State—as I said before, the State Board of Education took—considered at the time it expelled these students several incidents, one at the Court House at the lunch room demonstration, the one the next day at the trial of this student, the marching on the steps of the State Capitol, and also this rally held at the church, where—where it was reported that—that statements were made against the administration of the School. In addition to that, the—the feeling going around in the community here due to—due to the reports of these incidents of the students, by the students, and due to reports of incidents occurring involving violence in other States, which happened prior to these things starting here in Alabama, all of these things were discussed by the State Board of Education prior to the taking of the action that they did on March 2 and as I was present and acting as Chairman, as a member of the Board, I voted to expel these students and to put these others on probation because I felt that that was what was in the best interest of the College.

And the—I felt that the action should be—should be prompt and immediate, because if something—something had not been done, in my opinion, it would have resulted in violence and disorder, and that we wanted to prevent, and we felt that we had a duty to the—to the —to the parents of the students and to the State to require that the students behave themselves while they are attending a State College, and that is (sic) the reasons why we took the action that we did. That is all."

Superintendent of Education Stewart testified that he voted for expulsion because the students had broken rules and regulations pertaining to all of the State institutions, and, when required to be more specific, testified:

"The Court: What rule had been broken is the question, that justified the expulsion insofar as he is concerned?
"A. I think demonstrations without the consent of the president of an institution."

The testimony of other members of the Board assigned somewhat varying and differing grounds and reasons for their votes to expel the plaintiffs.

The district court found the general nature of the proceedings before the State Board of Education, the action of the Board, and the official notice of expulsion given to the students as follows:

"Investigations into this conduct were made by Dr. Trenholm, as president of the Alabama State College, the Director of Public Safety for the State of Alabama under directions of the Governor, and by the investigative staff of the Attorney General for the State of Alabama.

"On or about March 2, 1960, the State Board of Education met and received reports from the Governor of the State of Alabama, which reports embodied the investigations that had been made and which reports identified these six plaintiffs, together with several others, as the 'ring leaders' for the group of students that had been participating in the above-recited activities. During this meeting, Dr. Trenholm, in his capacity as president of the college reported to the assembled members of the State Board of Education that the action of these students in demonstrating on the college campus and in certain downtown areas was having a disruptive influence on the work of the other students at the college and upon the orderly operation of the college in general. Dr. Trenholm further reported to the Board that, in his opinion, he as president of the college could not control future disruptions and demonstrations. There were twenty-nine of the Negro students identified as the core of the organization that was responsible for these demonstrations. This group of twenty-nine included these six plaintiffs. After hearing these reports and recommendations and upon the recommendation of the Governor as chairman of the Board, the Board voted unanimously, expelling nine students, including these six plaintiffs, and placing twenty students on probation. This action was taken by Dr. Trenholm as president of the college, acting pursuant to the instructions of the State Board of Education. Each of these plaintiffs, together with the other students expelled, was officially notified of his expulsion on March 4th or 5th, 1960. No formal charges were placed against these students and no hearing was granted any of them prior to their expulsion."

The evidence clearly shows that the question for decision does not concern the sufficiency of the notice or the adequacy of the hearing, but is whether the students had a right to any notice or hearing whatever before being expelled.[4] * * * After careful study and con-

---

4. The plaintiff Dixon testified:

"Q. Now on that day—from February 25 until the date that you received your letter of expulsion, which you have already identified, will you tell the Court whether any person at the College gave you any official notice that your conduct was unbecoming as a student of Alabama State College? A. No.

"Q. Did the president or any other person at the College arrange for any type of hearing where you had an opportunity to present your side prior to the time you were expelled? A. No.

"Q. Your answer was no? A. No."

The testimony of Governor Patterson, Chairman of the State Board of Education, was in accord:

"Q. Did the State Board of Education, prior to the time it expelled the plaintiffs, give them an opportunity to appear either before the College or before the Board in order to present their sides of this pic—of this incident? A. No, other than receiving the report from Dr. Trenholm about it.

"Q. Did the Board direct Dr. Trenholm to give the students formal notice of why they were expelled? A. No, the

Board—the Board passed a resolution instructing Dr. Trenholm to expel the students and put twenty on probation, and Dr. Trenholm carried that out."

State Superintendent of Education Stewart testified:

"Q. Were these students given any type of hearing, or were formal charges filed against them before they were expelled? A. They were—Dr. Trenholm expelled the students; they weren't given any hearing.

"Q. No hearing? A. I don't think they would be given a hearing in any of our schools in this State; if they couldn't behave themselves, I think they should go home.

"Q. Do you—were they warned at all prior to expulsion? A. Not as I know of; I can't answer that question. Dr. Trenholm was in the meeting, and that afternoon after the Board meeting, he was given the—the decision, and he was the one who took action.

"Q. When the State Board of Education expels a student, is there any possibility of appeal or any opportunity for him to present his side of the story? A. I never have heard of it."

sideration, we find ourselves unable to agree with the conclusion of the district court that no notice or opportunity for any kind of hearing was required before these students were expelled.

It is true, as the district court said, that " * * * there is no statute or rule that requires formal charges and/or a hearing * * *," but the evidence is without dispute that the usual practice at Alabama State College had been to give a hearing and opportunity to offer defenses before expelling a student. Defendant Trenholm, the College President, testified:

"Q. The essence of the question was, will you relate to the Court the usual steps that are taken when a student's conduct has developed to the point where it is necessary for the administration to punish him for that conduct?

"A. We normally would have conference with the student and notify him that he was being asked to withdraw, and we would indicate why he was being asked to withdraw. That would be applicable to academic reasons, academic deficiency, as well as to any conduct difficulty.

"Q. And at this hearing ordinarily that you would set, then the student would have a right to offer whatever defense he may have to the charges that have been brought against him?

"A. Yes."

Whenever a governmental body acts so as to injure an individual, the Constitution requires that the act be consonant with due process of law. The minimum procedural requirements necessary to satisfy due process depend upon the circumstances and the interests of the parties involved. * * *

It is not enough to say, as did the district court in the present case, "The right to attend a public college or university is not in and of itself a constitutional right." That argument was emphatically answered by the Supreme Court in the Cafeteria and Restaurant Workers Union case, when it said * * * 'One may not have a constitutional right to go to Bagdad, but the Government may not prohibit one from going there unless by means consonant with due process of law.' " As in that case, so here, it is necessary to consider "the nature both of the private interest which has been impaired and the governmental power which has been exercised."

The appellees urge upon us that under a provision of the Board of Education's regulations the appellants waived any right to notice and a hearing before being expelled for misconduct.

"Attendance at any college is on the basis of a mutual decision of the student's parents and of the college. Attendance at a particular college is voluntary and is different from attendance at a public school where the pupil may be required to attend a particular school which is located in the neighborhood or district in which the pupil's family may live. Just as a student may choose to withdraw from a particular college at any time for any personally-determined reason, the college may also at any time decline to continue to accept responsibility for the supervision and service to any student with whom the relationship becomes unpleasant and difficult."

We do not read this provision to clearly indicate an intent on the part of the student to waive notice and a hearing before expulsion. If, however, we should so assume, it nonetheless remains true that the State cannot condition the granting of even a privilege upon the renunciation of the constitutional right to procedural due process. * * *

The precise nature of the private interest involved in this case is the right to remain at a public institution of higher learning in which the plaintiffs were students in good standing. It requires no argument to demonstrate that education is vital and indeed, basic to civilized society. Without sufficient education the plaintiffs would not be able to earn an adequate livelihood, to enjoy life to the fullest, or to fulfill as completely as possible the duties and responsibilities of good citizens.

There was no offer to prove that other colleges are open to the plaintiffs. If so, the plaintiffs would nonetheless be injured by the interruption of their course of studies in mid-term. It is most unlikely that a public college would accept a student expelled from another public college of the same state. Indeed, expulsion may well prejudice the student in completing his education at any other institution. Surely no one can question that the right to remain at the college in which the plaintiffs were students in good standing is an interest of extremely great value.

Turning then to the nature of the governmental power to expel the plaintiffs, it must be conceded, as was held by the district court, that that power is not unlimited and cannot be arbitrarily exercised. Admittedly, there must be some reasonable and constitutional ground for expulsion or the courts would have a duty to require reinstatement. The possibility of arbitrary action is not excluded by the existence of reasonable regulations. There may be arbitrary application of the rule to the facts of a particular case. Indeed, that result is well nigh inevitable when the Board hears only one side of the issue. In the disciplining of college students there are no considerations of immediate danger to the public, or of peril to the national security, which should prevent the Board from exercising at least the fundamental principles of fairness by giving the accused students notice of the charges and an opportunity to be heard in their own defense. Indeed, the example set by the Board in failing so to do, if not corrected by the courts, can well break the spirits of the expelled students and of others familiar with the injustice, and do inestimable harm to their education.

* * *

* * * We are confident that precedent as well as a most fundamental constitutional principle support our holding that due process requires notice and some opportunity for hearing before a student at a tax-supported college is expelled for misconduct.

For the guidance of the parties in the event of further proceedings, we state our views on the nature of the notice and hearing required by due process prior to expulsion from a state college or university. They should, we think, comply with the following standards. The notice should contain a statement of the specific charges and grounds which, if proven, would justify expulsion under the regulations of the Board of Education. The nature of the hearing should vary depending upon the circumstances of the particular case. The case before us requires something more than an informal interview with an administrative authority of the college. By its nature, a charge of misconduct, as opposed to a failure to meet the scholastic standards of the college, depends upon a collection of the facts concerning the charged misconduct, easily colored by the point of view of the witnesses. In such circumstances, a hearing which gives the Board or the administrative authorities of the college an opportunity to hear both sides in considerable detail is best suited to protect the rights of all involved. This is not to imply that a full-dress judicial hearing, with the right to cross-examine witnesses, is required. Such a hearing, with the attending publicity and disturbance of college activities, might be detrimental to the college's educational atmosphere and impractical to carry out. Nevertheless, the rudiments of an adversary proceeding may be preserved without encroaching upon the interests of the college. In the instant case, the student should be given the names of the witnesses against him and an oral or written report on the facts to which each witness testifies. He should also be given the opportunity to present to the Board, or at least to an administrative official of the college, his own defense against the charges and to produce either oral testimony or written affidavits of witnesses in his behalf. If the hearing is not before the Board directly, the results and findings of the hearing should be presented in a report open to the student's inspection. If these rudimentary elements of fair play are followed in a case of misconduct of this particular type, we feel that the requirements of due process of law will have been fulfilled.

The judgment of the district court is reversed and the cause is remanded for further proceedings consistent with this opinion.

Reversed and remanded.

CAMERON, Circuit Judge (dissenting).

The opinion of the district court in this case is so lucid, literate and moderate that I cannot forego expressing surprise that my brethren of the majority can find fault with it. In this dissent I shall try to avoid repeating what the lower court has so well said and to confine myself to an effort to refute the holdings of the majority where they do attack and reject the lower court's opinion.

A good place to start is the quotation made by the majority from the recent case of Cafeteria and Restaurant Workers Union v. McElroy wherein the discussion is made of one's right to "go to Bagdad." I would add to the language quoted by the majority from that case the sentences which follow it:

"It is the petitioner's claim that due process in this case required that Rachel Brawner be advised of the specific grounds for her exclusion and be accorded a hearing at which she might refute them. We are satisfied, however, that under the circumstances of this case such a procedure was not constitutionally required.

"The Fifth Amendment does not require a trial-type hearing in every conceivable case of government impairment of private interests. ' * * * The very nature of due process negates any concept of inflexible procedures universally applicable to every imaginable situation. * * * "Due process," unlike some legal rules, is not a technical conception with a fixed content unrelated to time, place and circumstances.' It is 'compounded of history, reason, the past course of decisions * * *'

"As these and other cases make clear, consideration of what procedure due process may require under any given set of circumstances must begin with a determination of the *precise nature of the government function involved as well as of the private interest that has been affected by governmental action.* Where it has been possible to characterize that private interest (perhaps in over-simplification) as a mere privilege subject to the Executive's plenary power, it has traditionally been held that notice and hearing are not constitutionally required. * * * "
[Emphasis added.]

The failure of the majority to follow the reasoning of McElroy results, in my opinion, from a basic failure to understand the nature and mission of schools. The problem presented is *sui generis.*

Everyone who has dealt with schools knows that it is necessary to make many rules governing the conduct of those who attend them, which do not reach the concept of criminalty but which are designed to regulate the relationship between school management and the student based upon practical and ethical considerations which the courts know very little about and with which they are not equipped to deal. To extend the injunctive power of federal courts to the problems of day to day dealings between school authority and student discipline and morale is to add to the now crushing responsibilities of federal functionaries, the necessity of qualifying as a Gargantuan aggregation of wet nurses or baby sitters. I do not believe that a balanced consideration of the problem with which we are dealing contemplates any such extreme attitude. Indeed, I think that the majority has had to adopt the minority view of the courts in order to reach the determination it has here announced.

* * *

Before [appellants] were notified of their expulsion they had issued public statements admitting everything which was the basis of their expulsion, and had disclosed everything they could have brought forward in any hearing which might have been given them before they were notified that their conduct required their separation from connection with the college. * * *

We are trying here the actions of State officials, which actions we are bound to invest with every presumption of fairness and correctness. Certainly the Board had before it a responsible and credible showing which justified their finding that these appellants were guilty of wilful disobedience of the rules and directives of the head of the college they were attending and of conduct prejudicial to the school and unbecoming a student or future teacher in the schools of Alabama, as well as of insubordination and insurrection and inciting other peoples to like conduct. It is undisputed that the Board made a leisurely and careful investigation and passed its judgment in entire good faith. The State of Alabama had no statute and the school had no rule or regulation requiring any other hearing than that which was had, and the Board was entirely justified in declining "to continue to accept responsibility for the supervision and service to any student with whom the relationship becomes unpleasant and difficult." It is worth noting, too, that

President Trenholm, testifying as a witness for appellants, stated that the rules of the school had been in effect more than thirty years; and that there was no requirement in them for notice or hearing and that prior practices did not include such as a precedent.

It is undisputed that failure to act as the Board did act would have resulted in a complete disruption of discipline and probable breaking up of a school whose history ran back many years, and whose president had held the position for thirty-five years. If he and the School Board had done less, they would, in my opinion, have been recreant to their duties. The moderate action they took did bring order out of chaos and enable the school to continue operation.

I do not feel that we are called upon here to volunteer our ideas of procedure in separating students from state colleges and universities. I think each college should make its own rules and should apply them to the facts of the case before it, and that the function of a court would be to test their validity if challenged in a proper court proceeding.

* * *

Certainly I think that the filing of charges, the disclosure of names of proposed witnesses, and such procedures as the majority discusses are wholly unrealistic and impractical and would result in a major blow to our institutions of learning. Every attempt at discipline would probably lead to a *cause célébre,* in connection with which federal functionaries would be rushed in to investigate whether a federal law had been violated. * * *

I think, moreover, that, in these troublous times, those in positions of responsibility in the federal government should bear in mind that the maintenance of the safety, health and morals of the people is committed under our system of government to the states. * * *

I dissent.

NOTES AND QUESTIONS

1. Viewing the facts, is there any doubt about the involvement of the plaintiffs in the demonstrations and their awareness of how this was upsetting college officials? If the students were obviously guilty, then why should notice and a hearing be required? Should notice and a hearing be required in *every* instance where long-term suspension or expulsion is involved or only where reasonable doubt exists about the guilt of accused students?

2. Note the institutional rule the students were charged with violating. Might they have also successfully challenged the rule as overbroad?

3. Note the dictum on what due process is required. Despite the widespread acceptance of the *Dixon* ruling in both federal and state courts (the Supreme Court denied certiorari in the case) judges are not in agreement as to how much process the accused student is due. There is general agreement that notice and a hearing are fundamental procedural requirements in serious disciplinary actions at public institutions and that where such procedural due process is provided, judges will be most reluctant to reconsider the fairness of disciplinary action. But an infinite variety of variables can affect this general position. For example, how serious must the threatened disciplinary action be? How clearly must the rules be written and how effectively must they be communicated to the student? Can the official who brings disciplinary charges against a student also be a member of the hearing board? Should the accused student have the right to have an attorney present or would the assistance of a fellow student or teacher be preferable? Must the right to an appeal be provided? Can a student be punished on campus for violating a state law off campus?

These questions are not easily answered. One way to begin, however, is to focus on major components thought to be part of procedural due process as developed in the political and social setting and then decide what is most appropriate for schools and colleges as special purpose institutions. The following list sets forth these components roughly in chronological order:

a. Notice of the charge.

b. An opportunity to know evidence supporting the charge.

c. Assistance of counsel.

d. Appearance before an unbiased tribunal.

e. Opportunity to present a defense and call witnesses.

f. Opportunity for cross-examination.

g. The making of a record of the action.

h. A decision based only on the evidence presented.

i. Opportunity for appeal and/or judicial review.

While there are others, these factors, many of which are constitutionally required in criminal prosecutions (see the Fifth and Sixth Amendments) provide an operational definition of procedural due process. Note that many questions remain. For example, how far in advance of the hearing must notice be given? Should notice be written? How detailed should the notice be? Should the evidence supporting the charge be included in the notice or made available later? Such questions can be raised *ad infinitum* for each of the components. Judge Rives in *Dixon* suggests further that the exact nature of the hearing will depend on the circumstances of a particular case.

Clearly, the administration of discipline in schools and colleges would be brought to a standstill if a prolonged and expensive procedure coupled with court review were necessary every time public educational authorities seek to enforce institutional rules in the interest of an ordered educational environment. Further, the adversary nature of such a prolonged process would likely undermine the spirit of cooperation between student and teacher considered an important ingredient of the educational process. While courts have followed *Goldberg* in requiring some type of due process where important interests are affected by government action, they have been reluctant to impose criminal law procedure on public administrative hearings, including student disciplinary hearings in schools and colleges. One distinguished jurist has noted that,

> The required degree of procedural safeguards varies *directly* with the importance of the private interest affected and the need for * * * the particular safeguard * * * and *inversely* with the burden * * * of affording it. (Emphasis added) [17]

Thus, the more serious the consequences of the proposed action, the more procedural safeguards may be required, consonant with the ability of the organization to provide them and continue to function effectively.

What this has meant in practice is the development of a kind of "common law" governing serious student discipline problems in public institutions, i. e., those which could result in long-term suspension or expulsion, building on the precedent set in *Dixon*. Some of the more significant cases denoting boundary lines are the following.*

a. **Institutional Rules:** *Soglin v. Kauffman,* 418 F.2d 163 (7th Cir. 1969), held that institutional rules must be narrowly drawn and effectively promulgated to be valid. In *Soglin* a rule against "misconduct" afforded "no safeguard against the imposition of disciplinary proceedings overreaching permissible limits and penalizing activities which are free from any taint of impropriety." (At p. 168). [See "Regulating Student Expression" in Chapter Three for a discussion of the construction of valid institutional rules.]

b. **Notice of Charges:** the prevailing rule is that students must be provided with a written notice of the charges in sufficient time before the

---

17. Henry J. Friendly, "Some Kind of Hearing," 123 *Univ. of Pa.L.Rev.* 1267, 1975, at 1278.

* Some states have statutes or policies developed by administrative agencies, e. g., the state education department, which describe the procedures to be followed in student disciplinary proceedings. To determine what procedures should be followed in a given situation, the requirements, if any, of relevant statutes and policies should be ascertained first. The next step is to consider relevant state and federal case law.

hearing to prepare a defense.[18] Some courts have held that where high school age or younger students are involved, their parents should also receive notice of the charges. As the court in *Sullivan v. Houston Independent School Dist.,* 307 F.Supp. 1328 (S.D.Tex.1969), concluded in striking down summary dismissal of students who produced and distributed an underground newspaper critical of school officials:

> Parents or guardians have legal obligations to children of high school age and common sense dictates that they should be included in any disciplinary action against their children which could result in severe punishment. Indeed it may be even more crucial that proper written notice of charges be provided to parents for often they do not know what transpired at school. When severe discipline is contemplated—either expulsion or suspension for a substantial time—the student and his parents should be given ample time before the hearing to examine the charges, prepare a defense, and gather evidence and witnesses. (At p. 1343).

While there are exceptions, most courts suggest that the notice inform the student when and where the hearing will be held, disclose what the nature of the evidence is and provide the student with a list of procedural rights or refer her to an appropriate section of the student handbook. If the student is to be permitted knowing waiver of the right to a formal hearing in favor of informal proceedings, it should occur at this stage.

c. **Hearing:** Virtually all courts have held that student disciplinary hearings are civil administrative reviews and not criminal trials. Thus, a full-blown adversary proceeding complete with jury trial is not required. The hearing is designed to give each side a fair and ample opportunity to present the facts.

The prevailing view with regard to the need for an *impartial tribunal* is stated by Circuit Judge Roney in *Jenkins v. Louisiana State Bd. of Educ.,* 506 F.2d 992 (5th Cir. 1975): "There is no question but that a student charged with misconduct has a right to an impartial tribunal." (At p. 1003). But the court added that it would not disqualify members of a hearing body "solely because they are employees of the college or because they might have participated in an initial investigation of the incident which necessitates the hearing." *(Id.)* In *Jenkins,* six students at Grambling College, a Louisiana state institution, were appealing a lower court decision refusing to enjoin their suspensions for their involvement in a campus disruption. The circuit court sustained all but one of the suspensions. In *Winnick v. Manning,* 460 F.2d 545 (2nd Cir. 1972), the court suggested that a tribunal composed of students and faculty would be preferable to a single hearing officer who happened to be the associate dean of students. However, the court refused to overturn a decision against the student on this ground alone. And in *Pride v. Howard Univ.,* 384 A.2d 31 (D.C.1978), the District of Columbia Court of Appeals ruled that the university, considered a nonpublic institution, did not break its contract with the student

---

18. Note: Since student disciplinary actions are not considered criminal in nature, *Miranda* warnings are not required when a student is being charged with a rule violation.

when two of the eight members of the judiciary board did not show up for a hearing on misconduct. A quorum of the members, said the court, is sufficient to sustain a vote of suspension. From these decisions, it is clear that most courts place the burden on the student of showing that the decision maker was biased or unfair. (Query: Many assume student affairs administrative personnel are advocates of student interests. Would there be an advantage to offering a student a choice of having her case decided by either the dean of students or by an independent tribunal in lieu of a formal hearing?)

The impartiality of the hearing tribunal was also an important issue in a recent U. S. Supreme Court case involving public school teachers. Before striking teachers can be disciplined, the school board must accord them a hearing. But if the board is a party to the dispute, can it be impartial? In *Hortonville School Dist. v. Hortonville Educ. Ass'n*, 426 U.S. 482 (1976), the Supreme Court upheld the right of local school boards to impose sanctions on striking teachers, including dismissal. More had to be shown, wrote Chief Justice Burger, than that the board was " 'involved' " in the events preceding the strike to overcome the traditional power of boards over their employees.

Most courts have supported a *private hearing* rather than one which is public, in deference to the interests of the accused. The 1974 Family Educational Rights and Privacy Act (Buckley Amendment) suggests such hearings must be closed if the results are in any way to become part of a student's academic record. In a 1976 case involving disciplinary hearings at the University of Florida, a Florida district court of appeals ruled against two newspapers, one of them the campus student press, which sought to have the hearings open to the public in accord with the state's open meetings law. The court based its ruling in *Marston v. Gainsville Sun Publishing Co.*, 341 So.2d 783 (Fla.1976), in part on Florida law pertaining to confidentiality of records and in part on the Buckley Amendment. It should be pointed out that students may waive their rights under the applicable provisions of the Buckley Amendment. If a student wishes a public hearing, should the institution be able to keep it closed as part of a general institutional approach to campus discipline?

Courts disagree on the *right to counsel*. A case often considered as significant as the *Dixon* case, *Esteban v. Central Missouri State College*, 277 F.Supp. 649 (W.D.Mo.1967), 290 F.Supp. 622 (1968), appr'd 415 F.2d 1077 (8th Cir. 1969) *cert. denied* 398 U.S. 965 (1970), held that plaintiff students were entitled to have counsel to advise them at the hearing, though the attorneys could not question witnesses. That case is important because Justice Blackmun, then a circuit judge, wrote the opinion upholding the decision of the district court. However, the complex factual situation in *Esteban* may have accounted in large measure for the procedures specified by the district court. Some courts have held that right to counsel will vary, depending upon the factual situation in individual cases. Thus, in *French v. Bashful*, 303 F.Supp. 1333 (E.D.La.1969), the court agreed that where the institution benefits from legal counsel, so too may the student. In *French* the prosecution was conducted by a senior law student. The court ordered a rehearing.

In *Gabrilowitz v. Newman,* 582 F.2d 100 (1st Cir. 1978), the First Circuit Court of Appeals affirmed an unreported district court ruling that the University of Rhode Island must allow a student charged with a serious criminal offense in both criminal court and on-campus proceedings to have legal counsel represent him at the campus hearing. The university permitted accused students to have an advisor from the university community present at the hearing but did not allow employment of an outside attorney. The student in this case was charged with violent assault with intent to rape. Steven Gabrilowitz asserted need for an attorney so as not to jeopardize his criminal trial by statements he might make at the campus hearing. If he were to remain silent at the campus hearing, he might well be subject to expulsion. The court noted that "all that appellee asks is that he be allowed the advice of counsel when he throws his college degree into the balance against a possible loss of liberty." (At p. 105). The presence of counsel, the court concluded, would offer him assistance in deciding what and how much to say. And since the conversations between attorney and client are privileged, the attorney could not be called to testify at a later criminal trial, unlike the informal advisor provided under university rules. The appeals court noted that the case was unique in that criminal charges were pending and that the right to counsel under these circumstances was to be limited. The attorney could only advise his client, not play an active role in the campus proceeding.

Judge Campbell dissented from the ruling, pointing out that the majority had opened the door to requiring counsel in almost every situation:

> Most conduct of a serious enough nature to merit disciplinary action will involve at least colorable misdemeanors, if not felonies, and a student very well might contend that the fact that criminal charges may be brought, even if they are not pending, requires the presence of counsel at his hearing. (At p. 107).

Would you agree that the narrow scope of the ruling will prove to be difficult to maintain? If attorneys were permitted by law to play a non-directed role in all college or school disciplinary hearings, would the essentially non-adversary character of these deliberations be undermined? At what point would you draw the line?

A review of the cases will show that quite often in situations involving expulsion, educational officials either on their own or pursuant to state statute have allowed students to have attorneys. At the pre-collegiate level, the need for counsel may be greater, given compulsory attendance, the importance of a high school diploma, and the relative immaturity of younger students. In any case, while courts have by no means mandated it, more and more educational institutions are allowing students to be represented by legal counsel.

Virtually all courts allow students an opportunity for *presentation of a defense* as inherent in procedural due process. There is less consensus on the *right to cross-examination.* Many courts have held that cross-examination is not essential to school disciplinary proceedings, while others such as in *Esteban* have ruled that it is. It would appear that where there is a discrepancy in the facts, cross-examination may be the only effective means of eliciting the truth. Such was the court's conclusion in *DeJesus v. Penberthy*, 344 F.Supp. 70 (D.Conn.1972). There the Board of Education concluded that one student, Jose DeJesus, had hit another student despite conflicting statements read to the Board (the students did not appear before the Board). DeJesus was expelled for the remainder of the school year. The district court stated that while cross-examination is not essential in every instance,

> In these circumstances cross-examination would certainly have been a preferable way of aiding in resolution of the dispute. * * * In a case such as this, involving expulsion, the accusing testimony should normally be taken in the presence of the plaintiff and subject to cross-examination. However, if upon a convincing showing to the Board by the school authorities, the Board determines that confrontation and even cross-examination will inhibit rather than advance the search for truth, the Board may hear the witnesses (or some of them) out of presence of the accused student, and, in extreme cases, omit cross-examination by the accused student or his representative. Responsibility for probing the accusing testimony will then rest with the Board. If testimony is taken in the absence of the accused student, he must be furnished with a summary of the testimony he was not permitted to hear. (At p. 76).

Freedom from self-incrimination is not considered essential by many courts, since hearings in the educational setting are not criminal in nature.* As the court stated in *Buttny v. Smiley*, 281 F.Supp. 280 (D.Colo. 1968), "We know of no legal authority that requires university officials to advise a student involved in disciplinary proceedings of his right to remain silent * * *." (At p. 287). As noted below, the self-incrimination issue raises significant problems where students are subject to off-campus criminal proceedings for the same offense.

Most courts as in *Esteban* ask that student guilt or innocence be determined by *substantial evidence*, thus eschewing the "beyond reasonable doubt" standard of criminal trials. But not all courts agree. In *Smyth v. Lubbers*, 398 F.Supp. 777 (W.D.Mich.1975), two students at Grand Valley State College in Allendale, Michigan, were found guilty of possession of marijuana in their dormitory room by an All College Judiciary. The students were suspended. One of the grounds for their suit was that the college failed to accord them due process of law. The court concluded that since the consequences for the students were so serious, "substantial evidence" as a basis for a guilty decision was inadequate. Said the court, "* * * given the nature of the charges and the serious consequences of conviction, the court believes the higher standard of 'clear and convincing evidence' may be required. The 'clear and convincing evidence' standard is well below the criminal standard * * *." (At p. 799).

Finally, there is general agreement that students are entitled to a *written report* stating the findings of the tribunal and the reason for the

---

* Note that *In re Gault* mandates this right in juvenile court proceedings. Would you extend it to student long-term suspension and expulsion hearings?

imposition of the sanction. Many courts also allow either side to make a *transcript or recording of the proceeding* at their own expense. Why do you think a full transcript might be important to have? What happens in its absence?

d. **Appeal:** If the hearing is not held before the highest administrative officials, most courts agree that the *right of appeal* to the highest administrative official or board is an important procedural safeguard. As we have seen, courts are reluctant to become involved in challenges to institutional disciplinary actions where administrative remedies have not been exhausted. *Becker v. Oswald*, 360 F.Supp. 1131 (M.D.Pa.1973), states the prevailing view: " * * * failure to exhaust state administrative remedies bars a civil rights suit for injunctive relief unless the remedies are inadequate or resort to them would be futile." (At p. 1133). In *Becker*, a student at Pennsylvania State University charged with unlawful possession of controlled substances was dismissed from the university following a disciplinary hearing. He began a suit based on the Civil Rights Act, 42 U.S.C.A. § 1983,* for violation of his due process rights because he claimed the hearing was inadequate and the evidence insufficient to support the University Hearing Board's decision. However, Becker did not exercise his right to appeal the decision to the University Appeals Board.

e. **Off-Campus Judicial Proceedings:** Courts have uniformly held that there is no *double-jeopardy* violation if a student who violates both school regulations and statutory laws by the same offense is subject to two different hearings, one administrative (school) and one criminal (off campus). Courts view the proceedings as taking place in two different settings. Nor is a student's self-incrimination rights necessarily violated by appearing before a campus disciplinary board prior to a trial on the same charges in criminal court. In *Nzuve v. Castleton State College,* 335 A.2d 321 (Vermont, 1975) Stephen Nzuve complained that a campus hearing on charges of illegal burglary, attempted rape, and simple assault in a college dormitory would prejudice his pending criminal case on the same charges. Nzuve claimed that if he elected to testify at the campus hearing, the statements he would make could be used against him in the criminal case and prematurely disclose his defenses to the prosecution. The Supreme Court of Vermont, relying on an earlier California case, rejected his argument:

> Educational institutions have both a need and a right to formulate their own standards and to enforce them; such enforcement is only coincidentally related to criminal charges and the defense

---

* Most states also have an administrative procedure act which allows an appeal to a state court from a final administrative decision, e. g., student expulsion decision. However, since federal law 42 U.S.C.A. § 1983 provides for federal civil suits against persons who, acting under color of state law, deprive others of their civil rights, most challenges to the action of public educational officials are filed in federal courts. This statute was enacted under Congress' power to enforce the Fourteenth Amendment. We will study it and related federal judicial procedure in the next chapter. Since 1983 suits provide the plaintiff with an independent legal recourse, they often trigger evidentiary trials before federal district courts. This is particularly true where the record from the administrative hearing is incomplete and/or the parties cannot agree on a common rendition of the facts. Thus, 1983 actions can amount to more than a review of decisions made at the administrative hearing.

against them. To hold otherwise would, in our view, lead logically to the conclusion that civil remedies must, as a matter of law, wait for determination until related criminal charges are disposed of. By parallel, the owner of stolen property could not obtain damages or its recovery until criminal prosecution had been completed. Similarly, in the instant case, the complaining witness could not have redress for the assault on her, if proven, until the pending criminal charges had run their long course of trial and appeal. Nor would it be at all unusual for the temporary relief here sought to enable the plaintiff to complete his education, thus effectively completing an "end run" around the disciplinary rules and procedures of the college. (At p. 325).

The court therefore balanced the needs of the educational institution against those of the student, striking the balance for the former. The court did note, however, that it was not *requiring* the campus hearing to take place prior to the criminal case. Thus, it would seem appropriate that where campus hearings can easily be postponed pending the outcome of a criminal case on the same charge, the interests of the student and the interests of the institution would both be effectively served.

It is not considered contrary to fundamental fairness to discipline a student for conduct occurring *solely* off campus, if the rules stipulate that off-campus conduct may be grounds for disciplinary action. In *Krasnow v. Virginia Polytechnic Institute*, 551 F.2d 591 (4th Cir. 1977), the Fourth Circuit Court of Appeals affirmed a lower court dismissal of an action by university students seeking an injunction against the university's rule against the unlawful use or possession of drugs by students, whether or not on university property. Said the court, "The university clearly has the prerogative to determine that any unlawful possession of drugs or criminal conduct on the part of students is detrimental to the university." (At p. 592). It noted further that no "irrebuttable presumption" against the student would be set up by such a rule, since the student continues to retain procedural due process rights in a campus hearing held on off-campus conduct. Thus a school or college hearing board cannot assume *a priori* that the student should be disciplined for off-campus acts but only *if* the act would be detrimental to the educational institution. The linkage between the off-campus and on-campus harm must be clear.

4. It should be clear from all of the above that due process in the public educational setting does not require a specific and rigid procedure in every situation. Flexibility is allowed, even to the point of upholding minor deviations from announced procedures. In *Winnick v. Manning,* cited above, plaintiff Winnick complained that because his case was not heard by the Student Conduct Committee (it had disbanded at the end of the year) but instead by the associate dean of students, he was denied due process. The court concluded:

> * * * we are not inclined to hold that every deviation from a university's regulations constitutes a deprivation of due process. Here the alleged deviations did not rise to constitutional proportions and did not constitute in themselves a denial of due process.

Furthermore, the alleged deviations were minor ones and did not affect the fundamental fairness of the hearing. Under all of the circumstances, we do not believe appellant was deprived of due process. (At p. 550).

However, there are limits beyond which flexibility will not be tolerated. For example, in *Escobar v. State Univ. of N. Y. College at Old Westbury*, 427 F.Supp. 850 (E.D.N.Y.1977), the district court refused to allow the president of the institution to impose a different punishment from that imposed by the Judicial Council contrary to college rules:

> * * * not every deviation from a university's regulations constitutes a deprivation of due process. But where, as here, an offending student has been formally charged under the college's disciplinary code, has been subjected to a hearing, has been officially sentenced, and has commenced compliance with that sentence, it is a denial of due process of law for the chief administrative officer to step in, conduct his own *in camera* [private] review of the student's record, and impose a different punishment without complying with any of the procedures which have been formally established for the college. (At p. 858; material in brackets added).

As long as courts straddle the procedural-substantive due process fence by requiring some key elements of procedural due process but reserving the right to review the decision process in the interest of "fundamental fairness," discrepancies among courts, both federal and state, are bound to arise. The only way, therefore, to know what the law is in a given area is to review relevant statutes and the decisions of courts having jurisdiction for that area.

At the same time, educational institutions themselves have been moving rapidly to comply with the law and, in many cases, to go well beyond it in the interest of protecting students. A 1976 survey of 155 public and nonpublic colleges and universities in the United States conducted by the Southern College Personnel Association revealed that 81 percent of the respondents (109) allow representation by outside counsel, 98 percent allow cross-examination of witnesses, 99 percent allow the accused student to remain silent (presumably without prejudice for doing so), and fully 100 percent provide for the right to an appeal.[19]

5. Circumstances dictate that some aspects of procedural due process are more important than others. For example, where the outcome turns on the testimony of two witnesses whose testimony is directly contradictory, cross-examination may be the only way to establish the truth. Or where a board of education is openly hostile to students, an ad hoc reviewing agency may be essential to accord the student fundamental fairness. One commentator suggests that the written record is vitally important:

> As a protective device for the student's interests, the record is both the least and the most important single safeguard. If the

19. Report on Follow-Up Survey of ACLU Research on Academic Freedom, Summer, 1976. Results were mailed to participating institutions in August, 1976, by the Southern College Personnel Association.

other * * * safeguards are granted, the student has most likely received a fair hearing; if he did not receive a fair hearing, nothing would be more likely to reveal the deficiency to the reviewing court than an adequate record. With an adequate record, the court might be able to determine the effect of a hearing with no counsel or right to cross-examine before an improperly interested or biased tribunal. The presumption would certainly be that due process was denied under these conditions, but the court might determine from the record that the student did receive a fair hearing.[20]

Viewing the features of procedural due process outlined in Question #3 above, which do you think are most important? Under what circumstances? How would you rule on the following hypotheticals? (Assume only public institutions are involved.)

a. College student receives notice of charges against him by telephone the morning of the hearing. He protests both at the hearing and after its conclusion that he could not present an adequate defense. He eventually sues for reinstatement based on violation of his due process rights.

b. College student protests that she was asked questions at the hearing about an incident occurring after she received notice of the charges against her. The chairman of the disciplinary panel disregards her protest and the committee recommends punishment based partly on the original charge and partly on her responses regarding the later infraction. The president of the college upholds the decision to suspend the student. The student sues college officials for violating her due process rights.

c. High school discipline committee concludes that on the basis of a prior record of numerous minor infractions, an eleventh grade student caught rifling another student's locker should be expelled. The student protests the decision on the ground that the other infractions should have no bearing on the outcome of the present case. A committee of the school board upholds the expulsion. The student and his parents sue the school board for violating his due process rights.

d. A high school student accused of attacking another student refuses to appear before an all-faculty discipline committee because no students are included as members. The committee concludes that the student is guilty, based on the evidence, and recommends a suspension for the remainder of the semester. The school board upholds the action. The student and his parents sue school officials for violating his due process rights.

e. Sixth grade student who incessantly talks in class even after repeated warnings from the teacher is asked to stay after school to wash the blackboards. The student demands a hearing. School officials refuse to honor the request. The student and his parents sue school officials for violating his due process rights.

20. Buss, *supra*, at p. 640.

f. A college student charged with possession of marijuana on campus is told by the chairman of the discipline committee that he must answer the questions posed to him by members of the committee; failure to do so will result in a finding of guilty. In return, the chairman promises that the hearing, the deliberations, and the decision will be kept strictly confidential. The student is found guilty and suspended for a semester. The only student member of the committee, who also was the only one voting not guilty, later breaches the confidence by describing the deliberations. The dean of students refuses to overturn the original finding or order a new hearing, since the breached information involved truths about the student and the deliberations. The campus president upholds the dean. The suspended student sues campus officials for violating his due process rights.

g. High school freshman is accused of indecent behavior for wearing a blouse without a bra. She demands a hearing at which she intends to mount an affirmative defense by challenging the decency rule as vague and overbroad. Her request is denied, and she is suspended until she conforms to the rule. Student and her parents sue school officials for reinstatement on due process grounds.

h. High school student body president is accused of disrupting a P.T.A. meeting by releasing a dozen pidgeons into the auditorium. He demands a public hearing before the student body, pointing to the "public trial" provision of the Sixth Amendment. School officials refuse, stating that all disciplinary hearings are private in order to provide an appropriate atmosphere and to protect the reputational rights of the accused. The student leader refuses to attend the hearing and is found guilty *in absentia* based on the evidence presented. He is suspended for the balance of the semester, a decision upheld by the school board. Student and his parents sue school officials on due process grounds.

i. Seventh grade student at a junior high school is caught by school officials selling drugs to other students in a public park across from the school. The student and his parents attend a hearing before the school principal, dean, and one faculty member. The parents point out that the school rules contain no references to "selling drugs." The principal responds that while the rules do not specifically include mention of drugs, the sale of drugs is illegal in the state. He points out in addition that the rules do include the sentence "Conduct off campus which adversely affects the suitability of the student as a member of the school may be subject to appropriate disciplinary action." Based on evidence produced at the hearing, the student is expelled. The school board upholds the action. The parents sue school officials for violating the due process rights of their child.

GOSS v. LOPEZ

Supreme Court of the United States, 1975.
419 U.S. 565, 95 S.Ct. 729, 42 L.Ed.2d 725.

Mr. Justice WHITE delivered the opinion of the Court.

*   *   *

I

Ohio law, Rev.Code § 3313.64, provides for free education to all children between the ages of six and 21. Section 3313.66 of the Code empowers the principal of an Ohio public school to suspend a pupil for misconduct for up to 10 days or to expel him. In either case, he must notify the student's parents within 24 hours and state the reasons for his action. A pupil who is expelled, or his parents, may appeal the decision to the Board of Education and in connection therewith shall be permitted to be heard at the board meeting. The board may reinstate the pupil following the hearing. No similar procedure is provided in § 3313.66 or any other provision of state law for a suspended student. Aside from a regulation tracking the statute, at the time of the imposition of the suspensions in this case the CPSS [Columbus Public School System] had not itself issued any written procedure applicable to suspensions. Nor, so far as the record reflects, had any of the individual high schools involved in this case. Each, however, had formally or informally described the conduct for which suspension could be imposed.

The nine named appellees, each of whom alleged that he or she had been suspended from public high school in Columbus for up to 10 days without a hearing pursuant to § 3313.66, filed an action against the Columbus Board of Education and various administrators of the CPSS under 42 U.S.C. § 1983. The complaint sought a declaration that § 3313.66 was unconstitutional in that it permitted public school administrators to deprive plaintiffs of their rights to an education without a hearing of any kind, in violation of the procedural due process component of the Fourteenth Amendment. It also sought to enjoin the public school officials from issuing future suspensions pursuant to § 3313.66 and to require them to remove references to the past suspensions from the records of the students in question.

The proof below established that the suspensions in question arose out of a period of widespread student unrest in the CPSS during February and March of 1971. Six of the named plaintiffs, Rudolph Sutton, Tyrone Washington, Susan Cooper, Deborah Fox, Clarence Byars and Bruce Harris, were students at the Marion-Franklin High School and were each suspended for 10 days on account of disruptive or disobedient conduct committed in the presence of the school administrator who ordered the suspension. One of these, Tyrone Washington, was among a group of students demonstrating in the school auditorium while a class was being conducted there. He was ordered by the school principal to leave, refused to do so and was suspended. Rudolph Sutton, in the presence of the principal, physically attacked a police officer who awas attempting to remove Tyrone Washington from the auditorium. He was immediately suspended. The other four Marion-Franklin students were suspended for similar conduct. None was given a hearing to determine the operative facts underlying the suspension, but each, together with his or her parents, was offered the opportunity to attend a conference, subsequent to the effective date of the suspension, to discuss the student's future.

Two named plaintiffs, Dwight Lopez and Betty Crome, were students at the Central High School and McGuffey Junior High School, respectively. The former was suspended in connection with a disturbance in the lunchroom which involved some physical damage to school property. Lopez testified that at least 75 other students were suspended from his school on the same day. He also testified below that he was not a party to the destructive conduct but was instead an innocent bystander. Because no one from the school testified with regard to this incident, there is no evidence in the record indicating the official basis for concluding otherwise. Lopez never had a hearing.

Betty Crome was present at a demonstration at a high school different from the one she was attending. There she was arrested together with others, taken to the police station, and released without being formally charged. Before she went to school on the following day, she was notified that she had been suspended for a 10-day period. Because no one from the school testified with respect to this incident, the record does not disclose how the McGuffey Junior High School principal went about making the decision to suspend Betty Crome nor does it disclose on what information the decision was based. It is clear from the record that no hearing was ever held.

There was no testimony with respect to the suspension of the ninth named plaintiff, Carl Smith. The school files were also silent as to his suspension, although as to some, but not all, of the other named plaintiffs the files contained either direct references to their suspensions or copies of letters sent to their parents advising them of the suspension.

On the basis of this evidence, the three-judge court declared that plaintiffs were denied due process of law because they were "suspended without hearing prior to suspension or within a reasonable time thereafter," and that, § 3316.66 Ohio Rev.Code and regulations issued pursuant thereto were unconstitutional in permitting such suspensions. It was ordered that all references to plaintiffs' suspensions be removed from school files.

Although not imposing upon the Ohio school administrators any particular disciplinary procedures and leaving them "free to adopt regulations providing for fair procedures which are consonant with the educational goals of their schools and reflective of the characteristics of their school and locality," the District Court declared that there were "minimum requirements of notice and hearing prior to suspension, except in emergency situations." * * *

The defendant school administrators have appealed the three-judge court's decision. * * * We affirm.

II

* * *

Although Ohio may not be constitutionally obligated to establish and maintain a public school system, it has nevertheless done so and has required its children to attend. * * * The authority possessed by the State to prescribe and enforce standards of conduct in its schools, although concededly very broad, must be exercised consistently with constitutional safeguards. Among other things, the State is constrained to recognize a student's legitimate entitlement to a public education as a property interest which is protected by the Due Process Clause and which may not be taken away for misconduct without adherence to the minimum procedures required by that clause.

The Due Process Clause also forbids arbitrary deprivations of liberty. "Where a person's good name, reputation, honor, or integrity is at stake because of what the government is doing to him," the minimal requirements of the clause must be satisfied. School authorities here suspended appellees from school for periods of up to 10 days based on charges of misconduct. If sustained and recorded, those charges could seriously damage the students' standing with their fellow pupils and their teachers as well as interfere with later opportunities for higher education and employment. * * *

Appellants proceed to argue that even if there is a right to a public education protected by the Due Process Clause generally, the clause comes into play only when the State subjects a student to a "severe detriment or grievous loss." The loss of 10 days, it is said, is neither severe nor grievous and the Due Process Clause is therefore of no relevance. * * * The Court's view has been that as long as a property deprivation is not *de minimis*, its gravity is irrelevant to the question whether account must be taken of the Due Process Clause. A 10-day suspension from school is not *de minimis* in our view and may not be imposed in complete disregard of the Due Process Clause.

A short suspension is of course a far milder deprivation than expulsion. But, "education is perhaps the most important function of state and local governments." and the total exclusion from the educational process for more than a trivial period, and certainly if the suspension is for 10 days, is a serious event in the life of the suspended child. Neither the property interest in educational benefits temporarily denied nor the liberty interest in reputation, which is also implicated, is so insubstantial that suspensions may constitutionally be imposed by any procedure the school chooses, no matter how arbitrary.

III

* * *

* * * The student's interest is to avoid unfair or mistaken exclusion from the educational process, with all of its unfortunate consequences. The Due Process Clause will not shield him from suspensions properly imposed, but it disserves both his interest and the in-

terest of the State if his suspension is in fact unwarranted. The concern would be mostly academic if the disciplinary process were a totally accurate, unerring process, never mistaken and never unfair. Unfortunately, that is not the case, and no one suggests that it is. Disciplinarians, although proceeding in utmost good faith, frequently act on the reports and advice of others; and the controlling facts and the nature of the conduct under challenge are often disputed. The risk of error is not at all trivial, and it should be guarded against if that may be done without prohibitive cost or interference with the educational process.

The difficulty is that our schools are vast and complex. Some modicum of discipline and order is essential if the educational function is to be performed. Events calling for discipline are frequent occurrences and sometimes require immediate, effective action. Suspension is considered not only to be a necessary tool to maintain order but a valuable educational device. The prospect of imposing elaborate hearing requirements in every suspension case is viewed with great concern, and many school authorities may well prefer the untrammeled power to act unilaterally, unhampered by rules about notice and hearing. But it would be a strange disciplinary system in an educational institution if no communication was sought by the disciplinarian with the student in an effort to inform him of his defalcation and to let him tell his side of the story in order to make sure that an injustice is not done. * * *

We do not believe that school authorities must be totally free from notice and hearing requirements if their schools are to operate with acceptable efficiency. Students facing temporary suspension have interests qualifying for protection of the Due Process Clause, and due process requires, in connection with a suspension of 10 days or less, that the student be given oral or written notice of the charges against him and, if he denies them, an explanation of the evidence the authorities have and an opportunity to present his side of the story. The clause requires at least these rudimentary precautions against unfair or mistaken findings of misconduct and arbitrary exclusion from school.[10]

There need be no delay between the time "notice" is given and the time of the hearing. In the great majority of cases the disciplinarian may informally discuss the alleged misconduct with the student minutes after it has occurred. We hold only that, in being given an opportunity to explain his version of the facts at this discussion, the student first be told what he is accused of doing and what the basis of the accusation is. Lower courts which have addressed the question of the *nature* of the procedures required in short suspension cases have reached the same conclusion. Since the hearing may occur almost immediately following the misconduct, it follows that as a general rule notice and hearing should precede removal of the student from school. We agree with the District Court, however, that there are recurring situations in which prior notice and hearing cannot be insisted upon. Students whose presence poses a continuing danger to persons or property or an ongoing threat of disrupting the academic process may be immediately removed from school. In such cases, the necessary notice and rudimentary hearing should follow as soon as practicable, as the District Court indicated.

In holding as we do, we do not believe that we have imposed procedures on school disciplinarians which are inappro-

priate in a classroom setting. Instead we have imposed requirements which are, if anything, less than a fair-minded school principal would impose upon himself in order to avoid unfair suspensions. Indeed, according to the testimony of the principal of Marion-Franklin High School, that school had an informal procedure, remarkably similar to that which we now require, applicable to suspensions generally but which was not followed in this case. Similarly, according to the most recent memorandum applicable to the entire CPSS, school principals in the CPSS are now required by local rule to provide at least as much as the constitutional minimum which we have described.

We stop short of construing the Due Process Clause to require, countrywide, that hearings in connection with short suspensions must afford the student the opportunity to secure counsel, to confront and cross-examine witnesses supporting the charge or to call his own witnesses to verify his version of the incident. Brief disciplinary suspensions are almost countless. To impose in each such case even truncated trial type procedures might well overwhelm administrative facilities in many places and, by diverting resources, cost more than it would save in educational effectiveness. Moreover, further formalizing the suspension process and escalating its formality and adversary nature may not only make it too costly as a regular disciplinary tool but also destroy its effectiveness as part of the teaching process.

On the other hand, requiring effective notice and informal hearing permitting the student to give his version of the

---

10. Appellants point to the fact that some process is provided under Ohio law by way of judicial review. Appellants do not cite any case in which this general administrative review statute has been used to appeal from a disciplinary decision by a school official. If it be assumed that it could be so used, it is for two reasons insufficient to save inadequate procedures at the school level. First * * * the

decision by the school—even if made upon inadequate procedures—is entitled to weight in the court proceeding. Second, without a demonstration to the contrary, we must assume that delay will attend any proceeding, that the suspension will not be stayed pending hearing, and that the student meanwhile will irreparably lose his educational benefits.

events will provide a meaningful hedge against erroneous action. At least the disciplinarian will be alerted to the existence of disputes about facts and arguments about cause and effect. He may then determine himself to summon the accuser, permit cross-examination and allow the student to present his own witnesses. In more difficult cases, he may permit counsel. In any event, his discretion will be more informed and we think the risk of error substantially reduced.

Requiring that there be at least an informal give-and-take between student and disciplinarian, preferably prior to the suspension, will add little to the factfinding function where the disciplinarian has himself witnessed the conduct forming the basis for the charge. But things are not always as they seem to be, and the student will at least have the opportunity to characterize his conduct and put it in what he deems the proper context.

We should also make it clear that we have addressed ourselves solely to the short suspension, not exceeding 10 days. Longer suspensions or expulsions for the remainder of the school term, or permanently, may require more formal procedures. Nor do we put aside the possibility that in unusual situations, although involving only a short suspension, something more than the rudimentary procedures will be required.

IV

The District Court found each of the suspensions involved here to have occurred without a hearing, either before or after the suspension, and that each suspension was therefore invalid and the statute unconstitutional insofar as it permits such suspensions without notice or hearing. Accordingly, the judgment is affirmed.

Mr. Justice POWELL with whom The CHIEF JUSTICE, Mr. Justice BLACKMUN, and Mr. Justice REHNQUIST join, dissenting.

I

* * *

The Ohio suspension statute allows no serious or significant infringement of education. It authorizes only a maximum suspension of eight school days, less than 5% of the normal 180-day school year. Absences of such limited duration will rarely affect a pupil's opportunity to learn or his scholastic performance. Indeed, the record in this case reflects no educational injury to appellees. Each completed the semester in which the suspension occurred and performed at least as well as he or she had in previous years. Despite the Court's unsupported speculation that a suspended student could be "seriously damaged" there is no factual showing of any such damage to appellees.

The Court also relies on a perceived deprivation of "liberty" resulting from any suspension, arguing—again without factual support in the record pertaining to these appellees—that a suspension harms a student's reputation. * * *

II

In prior decisions, this Court has explicitly recognized that school authorities must have broad discretionary authority in the daily operation of public schools. This includes wide latitude with respect to maintaining discipline and good order. * * *

* * *

The Court today turns it back on these precedents. * * *

Moreover, the Court ignores the experience of mankind, as well as the long history of our law, recognizing that there *are* differences which must be accommodated in determining the rights and duties of children as compared with those of adults. Examples of this distinction abound in our law: in contracts, in torts, in criminal law and procedure, in criminal sanctions and rehabilitation, and in the right to vote and to hold office. Until today, and except in the special context of the First Amendment issue in *Tinker*, the educational rights of children and teenagers in the elementary and secondary schools have not been analogized to the rights of adults or to those accorded college students. Even with respect to the First Amendment, the rights of children have not been regarded as "coextensive with those of adults."

A

* * *

The State's interest, broadly put, is in the proper functioning of its public school system for the benefit of *all* pupils and the public generally. Few rulings would interfere more extensively in the daily functioning of schools than subjecting routine discipline to the formalities and judicial oversight of due process. Suspensions are one of the traditional means—ranging from keeping a student after class to permanent expulsion—used to maintain discipline in the schools. It is common knowledge that maintaining order and reasonable decorum in school buildings and classrooms is a major educational problem, and one which has increased significantly in magnitude in recent years. Often the teacher, in protecting the rights of other children to an education (if not his or their safety), is compelled to rely on the power to suspend.

The facts set forth in the margin[10] leave little room for doubt as to the magnitude of the disciplinary problem in the public schools, or as to the extent of reliance upon the right to suspend. They also demonstrate that if hearings were required for a substantial percentage of short-term suspensions, school authorities would have time to do little else.

B

The State's generalized interest in maintaining an orderly school system is not incompatible with the individual interest of the student. Education in any meaningful sense includes the inculcation of an understanding in each pupil of the necessity of rules and obedience thereto. This understanding is no less important than learning to read and write. One who does not comprehend the meaning and necessity of discipline is handicapped not merely in his education but throughout his subsequent life. In an age when the home and church play a diminishing role in shaping the character and value judgments of the young, a heavier responsibility falls upon the schools. When an immature student merits censure for his conduct, he is rendered a disservice if appropriate sanctions are not applied or if procedures for their application are so formalized as to invite a challenge to the teacher's authority—an invitation which rebellious or even merely spirited teenagers are likely to accept.

The lesson of discipline is not merely a matter of the student's self-interest in the shaping of his own character and personality; it provides an early understanding of the relevance to the social compact of respect for the rights of others. The classroom is the laboratory in which this lesson of life is best learned. * * *

* * *

C

One of the more disturbing aspects of today's decision is its indiscriminate reliance upon the judiciary, and the adversary process, as the means of resolving many of the most routine problems arising in the classroom. In mandating due process procedures the Court misapprehends the reality of the normal teacher-pupil relationship. There is an ongoing relationship, one in which the teacher must occupy many roles—educator, adviser, friend and, at times, parent-

---

10. An *amicus* brief filed by the Children's Defense Fund states that *at least 10%* of the junior and senior high school students in the States sampled were suspended *one or more* times in the 1972–1973 school year. -* * *

* * *

substitute.[12] It is rarely adversary in nature except with respect to the chronically disruptive or insubordinate pupil whom the teacher must be free to discipline without frustrating formalities.

The Ohio statute, providing as it does for due notice both to parents and the Board, is compatible with the teacher-pupil relationship and the informal resolution of mistaken disciplinary action. We have relied for generations upon the experience, good faith and dedication of those who staff our public schools, and the nonadversary means of airing grievances that always have been available to pupils and their parents. One would have thought before today's opinion that this informal method of resolving differences was more compatible with the interests of all concerned than resort to any constitutionalized procedure, however blandly it may be defined by the Court.

D

*   *   *

Nor does the Court's due process "hearing" appear to provide significantly more protection than that already available. The Court holds only that the principal must listen to the student's "version of the events," either before suspension or thereafter—depending upon the circumstances. Such a truncated "hearing" is likely to be considerably less meaningful than the opportunities for correcting mistakes already available to students and parents. Indeed, in this case all of the students and parents were offered an opportunity to attend a conference with school officials.

*   *   *

III

No one can foresee the ultimate frontiers of the new "thicket" the Court now enters. Today's ruling appears to sweep within the protected interest in education a multitude of discretionary decisions in the educational process. Teachers and other school authorities are required to make many decisions that may have serious consequences for the pupil. They must decide, for example, how to grade the student's work, whether a student passes or fails a course, whether he is to be promoted, whether he is required to take certain subjects, whether he may be excluded from interscholastic athletics or other extracurricular activities, whether he may be removed from one school and sent to another, whether he may be bused long distances when available schools are nearby, and whether he should be placed in a "general," "vocational," or "college-preparatory" track.

In these and many similar situations claims of impairment of one's educational entitlement identical in principle to those before the Court today can be asserted with equal or greater justification. Likewise, in many of these situations, the pupil can advance the same types of speculative and subjective injury given critical weight in this case. The District Court, relying upon generalized opinion evidence, concluded that a suspended student may suffer psychological injury in one or more of the ways set forth in the margin below. The Court appears to adopt this rationale.

It hardly need be said that if a student, as a result of a day's suspension, suffers "a blow" to his "self esteem," "feels powerless," views "teachers with resentment," or feels "stigmatized by his teachers," identical psychological harms will flow from many other routine and necessary school decisions. The student who is given a failing grade, who is not promoted, who is excluded from certain extracurricular activities, who is assigned to

---

12. The role of the teacher in our society historically has been an honored and respected one, rooted in the experience of decades that has left for most of us warm memories of our teachers, especially those of the formative years of primary and secondary education.

a school reserved for children of less than average ability, or who is placed in the "vocational" rather than the "college preparatory" track, is unlikely to suffer any less psychological injury than if he were suspended for a day for a relatively minor infraction.[19]

If, as seems apparent, the Court will now require due process procedures whenever such routine school decisions are challenged, the impact upon public education will be serious indeed. The discretion and judgment of federal courts across the land often will be substituted for that of the 50-state legislatures, the 14,000 school boards and the 2,000,000 teachers who heretofore have been responsible for the administration of the American public school system. If the Court perceives a rational and analytically sound distinction between the discretionary decision by school authorities to suspend a pupil for a brief period, and the types of discretionary school decisions described above, it would be prudent to articulate it in today's opinion. Otherwise, the federal courts should prepare themselves for a vast new role in society.

* * *

NOTES AND QUESTIONS

1. One commentator has suggested that *Goss* represents an attempt by the Supreme Court to deal with the "second generation" problems resulting from the desegregation of public schools. Since school disruption is often the result of black-white confrontation as in *Goss*, and since black students are frequently those subject to discipline, again as in *Goss* (all the defendants in *Goss* were black), the informal notice and hearing requirements mandated by the decision were designed to alleviate what many might consider continued discrimination against black students. "The silent expectation of *Goss* is that a hearing, however abbreviated, may help relieve racial tensions by enhancing the appearance of evenhanded discipline, by reducing the number of arbitrary or mistaken suspensions of minority students, and perhaps by encouraging communication between school officials and suspected student troublemakers and malcontents."[21]

2. There were many unanswered questions stemming from the majority decision, partly attributable to some of the vague phrases contained in the opinion. For example, what are the operational meanings of "suspension," "as soon as practicable," "unusual situations," "emergency situations"? Even the term "hearing" is vaguely defined. Suppose a dispute arose between a suspended student and a high school principal as to whether the *Goss* requirements had been met prior to the suspension. Who

19. There is, no doubt, a school of modern psychological or psychiatric persuasion than maintains that *any* discipline of the young is detrimental. Whatever one may think of the wisdom of this unproved theory, it hardly affords dependable support for a *constitutional* decision. Moreover, even the theory's proponents would concede that the magnitude of injury depends primarily upon the individual child or teenager. A classroom reprimand by the teacher may be more traumatic to the shy, timid introvert than expulsion would be to the aggressive, rebellious extrovert. In my view we tend to lose our sense of perspective and proportion in a case of this kind. For the average, normal child—the vast majority—suspension for a few days is simply *not* a detriment; it is a commonplace occurrence, with some 10% of all students being suspended; it leaves no scars; affects no reputations; indeed, it often may be viewed by the young as a badge of some distinction and a welcome holiday.

21. Wilkinson, *supra*, at p. 32.

should be believed? What procedures might prevent such a dispute from occurring?

Note that with this decision, a student could conceivably be entitled to *two* hearings, one for a temporary suspension and another, more formal hearing for resolution of a major dispute where long-term suspension or expulsion might be likely. For the second hearing, the majority suggests that more elaborate procedural safeguards may be necessary, such as right to counsel and to cross-examination.

3. Consider the "property interest" argument of the majority. Would a senior be entitled to more procedural due process than a freshman because of the greater time and effort spent toward graduation? Also note references in the dissent to the differences between the rights of adults and children. If this line of reasoning were projected, elementary school children would have fewer due process rights for temporary suspensions than high school and college students. Yet, according to a recent study by the National School Boards Association, discipline problems are concentrated in junior high schools and the early grades of high school.[22] From your reading of the majority decision, do you think the majority intended to have their ruling apply to junior high school and elementary school students as well as those in higher grades? To their parents?

Consider the "liberty interest" argument asserted by the majority. Rather than a denial of liberty under the Fourteenth Amendment Due Process Clause, could a suspension be a "badge of some distinction" as suggested by Justice Powell in the final footnote of the dissent? Truancy is considered one of the most prevalent discipline problems in school.

Justice Powell is often regarded as the "education expert" on the Supreme Court since he served for many years as chairman of the Richmond, Virginia, public school board. He was also a member of the State of Virginia Board of Education during the turbulent 1960s. Should this experience give his views more credibility than those of the other Justices? Note his fears that due process claims will now be made over a "multitude of discretionary decisions" made in the educational process. Do the situations he lists have the potential effect of depriving students of more property and liberty interests than temporary suspensions? If so, should due process rights be applied to them as well?

Consider the liberty and/or property interests involved in the following hypothetical situations. Based on your reading of the majority decision, decide whether (1) the student harm is *de minimus* and no hearing is necessary, (2) an informal procedure similar to *Goss* is required, or (3) a more formal procedure is required. In the case of the formal procedure, what components would you consider essential? (Assume only public educational institutions are involved below.)

    a.   Teacher hears an obscenity directed to her while she is writing on the blackboard in a tenth grade algebra class. She turns to see Jimmie red-faced and smiling. He blurts out, "I didn't do nothin'!"

22. *Discipline in Our Big City Schools, supra.*

The teacher suspends Jimmie from her classroom for the remainder of the week.

b. Suspension of a ninth grade student for 20 days after the student committed the same offense for the third time. On each of the other occasions, the student was suspended for three days.

c. Removal of an eighth grade student from an advanced curricular track to a slower one.

d. Involuntary transfer of a high school student to a high school equivalency class meeting at night and composed mostly of working adults.

e. Three-day suspension of an eleventh grade student after she was caught stealing money from a teacher's purse. Assume only three days are left before the end of school for the year; final exams are scheduled on these days with make-up allowed only for *bona fide* medical excuses.

f. Immediate suspension of several students seen fleeing the scene of a fire in a janitor's closet at a high school. The students were observed laughing loudly and inadvertently dropping a book of matches as they ran.

g. A high school sophomore who has been suspended for a semester demands to be readmitted, claiming that he has been rehabilitated and no longer is prone to physical violence.

h. Twenty-five students hold a demonstration outside the college administration building. College officials ask them to leave. They refuse, and administrators decide to discipline them.

i. Principal learns that a student has brought a firearm into the high school contrary to school rules. The principal sends a note to the student's homeroom teacher informing the student to leave the school immediately.

j. Teacher orders a student to clean blackboards after school for two hours.

k. Tenth grade student is placed on probation for smoking cigarettes in the men's room during recess.

l. Decision to use behavior modification drugs for a hyperactive child. The parents object.

At some point one must decide where lines are to be drawn separating those situations where no procedural due process is required from those where some type of due process is required. One possibility is to require due process procedures only when specific constitutional or statutory rights such as freedom of speech are involved or when physical separation from school or college is likely. Another might be when students who have been suspended for long periods of time demand readmission. Would you support these propositions?

Some courts have found a sufficient liberty and/or property interest in an extracurricular activity to warrant a hearing when continued enjoyment is denied for disciplinary reasons. Thus, in *Warren v. National*

Ass'n of Secondary School Principals, 375 F.Supp. 1043 (N.D.Tex.1974), the court ruled that a student could not be suspended from the National Honor Society without a fair and impartial hearing since important liberty interests (the student's reputation) were involved. In *Behagen v. Intercollegiate Conference of Faculty Representatives*, 346 F.Supp. 602 (D.Minn. 1972), the court concluded that student athletes have a sufficient property interest in intercollegiate athletics to warrant their being accorded notice and a hearing prior to prolonged suspension by a state-related intercollegiate conference.

Representative of the cases deciding in the opposite direction is *Parish v. National Collegiate Athletic Ass'n*, 361 F.Supp. 1220 (W.D.La.1973), *aff'd* 506 F.2d 1028 (5th Cir. 1975). There, the court concluded that while the National Collegiate Athletic Association is sufficiently state-related to be covered by the terms of the Fourteenth Amendment, student-athletes do not have sufficient property interests in interscholastic athletic competition to warrant due process procedures prior to declaration of ineligibility. In accord is a recent state case, *National Collegiate Athletic Ass'n v. Gillard*, 352 So.2d 1072 (Miss., 1977). In *Gillard* the Supreme Court of Mississippi, citing numerous federal and state cases, concluded that "The basic decision of the case * * * is the simple statement that Gillard's 'right' to engage in intercollegiate football is not a 'property' right that falls within the due process clause of either section 14 of the Mississippi Constitution or the Fourteenth Amendment to the United States Constitution." (At p. 1081). However, while there may be no right to engage in extracurricular activities such as amateur athletics, the opportunity to do so cannot be extended to some but denied to others unfairly. Challenges to denial of extracurricular privileges thus have raised equal protection questions, a matter to be explored in the next chapter.

It should also be pointed out that state and federal statutes as well as institutional policies may stipulate certain due process procedures. Thus, for example, the 1974 Family Educational Rights and Privacy Act contains elaborate provisions outlining procedures to be followed in allowing students or their parents to review their educational records and to mount complaints. Decisions like *NCAA v. Gillard* have prompted a call for legislation to extend due process rights to students involved in disputes between interscholastic organizations and their institutional members.[23]

4. Not only will the contours of due process be determined by the interest affected, so too might the identity of the student be an influential factor. For example, handicapped students may be entitled to more due process because of their limited capacity to look out for their own interests. Consider the case of the child who is judged to be sufficiently mentally retarded or emotionally disturbed to warrant removal from a normal classroom and placement in a special program. Some courts have recognized the need for more formal due process safeguards in this situation. *Pennsylvania Ass'n for Retarded Children v. Pennsylvania*, 343 F.Supp 279 (E.D.Pa.1972) and *Mills v. Board of Educ.*, 348 F.Supp. 866 (D.D.C.

---

23. For a discussion of due process issues involving the NCAA, see G. A. Martin, Jr., "Due Process and Its Future Within the NCAA," 10 *Conn.L.Rev.* 290, Winter, 1978.

1972). Similarly, children who may need drug treatment in the educational setting for such behavioral problems as hyperactivity may warrant more formal due process proceedings prior to the administering of the drug.

Since 1977 the rights of handicapped students have been significantly broadened by effective enforcement of federal legislation, most notably Section 504 of the Rehabilitation Act of 1973, 29 U.S.C.A. § 794, and the Education for All Handicapped Children Act, 20 U.S.C.A. § 1401. These laws and their implementing regulations apply to institutions receiving federal funds directly or indirectly and are designed to advance the interests of the approximately 8 million disabled children and 28 million handicapped adults in the country. Included in the regulations are extensive due process requirements.

5. What role has social science research played in the *Goss* decision? Do you think Justice Powell downgraded the findings of the researchers or treated them more realistically than the majority? In later correspondence with the authors, the attorney for the school expressed the view that the *amici curiae* briefs filed in support of the student's case "bombarded" the Supreme Court "with statistics and examples totally unrelated to the actual record which was before the case." While several footnotes reflected some of these statistics, the attorney concluded that overall, "I am not at all convinced that any one of those organizations had any real impact on the final outcome." Based on your reading of the majority opinion, would you agree?

6. The *Goss* decision was greeted by a good deal of criticism and uncertainty in the educational community, much of which continues. Many commentators predicted the decision would cause administrators to forego the use of suspension as a disciplinary device because of the threat of legal challenge. One authority described the hazards confronting the administrators contemplating suspending a student as follows:

> If the student denies the accusation, the procedural problem becomes more complicated. The student's denial creates two additional duties for school authorities. They must give the student both "an explanation of the evidence the authorities have" and "an opportunity to present his side of the story." The "explanation of the evidence" is not clearly defined in the opinion. In many instances the identification of the witness(es) by the disciplinarian places the witness (teacher, staff member or student) in serious danger of retaliation from either the accused or his or her friends. Few schools are staffed to provide "protection" to witnesses during or after school hours, and it is not a simple matter to balance "constitutional rights" of an accused student with the potentially serious consequences to other members of the school community. Until the Court clarifies the extent and nature of the duty to explain the evidence, disciplinarians face tough decisions when challenged by the accused student who demands to know "who says I did this or that?" [24]

24. William R. Hazard, "*Goss* and *Wood*: More and Better Due Process Required," in R. J. Anson and Peter J. Kuriloff, *Professional Discretion and Liability Under Goss and Wood* (Washington, D. C.: Capitol Publications, 1975), pp. 75–76.

At the same time we have already noted the public's desire for more, not less, discipline in the nation's schools.

A second view has been that the ruling will degenerate into a ritualized process devoid of substance or meaning. Many believe *Miranda* has had this effect on law enforcement in society at large. Yet note that in one sense the ruling does leave ample opportunity for the assertion of professional discretion. As the Court's majority opinion itself points out,

> At least the disciplinarian will be alerted to the existence of disputes about facts and arguments about cause and effect. He may then determine himself to summon the accuser, permit cross-examination, and allow the student to present his own witnesses. In more difficult cases, he may permit counsel. In any event, his discretion will be more informed and we think the risk of error substantially reduced.

Also note that unlike *Miranda*, the ambiguity of *Goss* makes ritualizing the due process procedures difficult. At the very least, the ruling presents administrators with the need to develop specific policy statements, since the Court did not spell them out. Furthermore, an insensitive application of the Court's ruling could invite further legal challenges and perhaps further judicial inroads into the exercise of professional discretion.

A third view is that in the long run *Goss* will have limited impact because it will be ignored. School officials in some districts have also been slow to implement other rulings. For example, in the case of the 1969 landmark *Tinker v. Des Moines School Dist.* decision, one survey showed that nearly one-fourth of Texas school districts ignored the ruling three years later.[25] The Court's emphasis on the informality of the required due process procedures in *Goss* coupled with the ambiguity of what exactly is required could invite a casual response.

One factor, however, may make it difficult to ignore the *Goss* ruling. In a companion case, *Wood v. Strickland*, 420 U.S. 308, the Supreme Court ruled that officials including school board members could be personally liable for damages if they violate a student's constitutional rights. The key passage of the *Wood* ruling is as follows:

> * * * in the specific context of school discipline, we hold that a school board member is not immune from liability for damages under § 1983 if he knew or reasonably should have known that the action he took within his sphere of official responsibility would violate the constitutional rights of the student affected, * * *. (At p. 322).

Such liability holds even if the violation is done without malice but only through ignorance or oversight. Said the Court:

> The official himself must be acting sincerely and with a belief that he is doing right, but an act violating a student's constitutional rights can be no more justified by ignorance or disregard

---

25. Mark G. Yudof, "Student Discipline in Texas Schools," 3 *J.Law & Educ.* 221, April 1974, at p. 231.

of settled, indisputable law on the part of one entrusted with suspension of students' daily lives than by the presence of actual malice. (At p. 321).

Thus, if suspension is to be used as a discipline device, school officials have special reason to pay attention to the Court's ruling.

In *Carey v. Piphus*, 435 U.S. 247 (1978), the Supreme Court in an 8–0 decision elaborated on the *Wood* ruling by concluding that students who are suspended from elementary and secondary schools without procedural due process are entitled only to nominal damages (in this case, $1) unless proof is introduced to show actual injuries justifying larger, compensatory amounts. In *Carey* the students sought $5000 in damages for the illegal suspensions. In an important footnote, however, Justice Powell, who wrote the opinion, noted that "This is not to say that exemplary or punitive damages might not be awarded in a proper case under § 1983 with the specific purpose of determining or punishing violations of constitutional rights." (At p. 257; fn. 11). The Court also noted that the defendants in 1983 suits face potential liability for attorneys' fees under the Civil Rights Attorneys' Fees Awards Act of 1976, 42 U.S.C.A. 1988. Since attorneys' fees can be strikingly large, this federal law provides, in Justice Powell's words, "additional—and by no means inconsequential—assurance that agents of the State will not deliberately ignore due process rights." (*Id.*) Thus, while students will experience no windfalls from *Wood*, administrators may suffer substantial monetary penalties for denials of student due process rights even absent proof of actual student injuries.

Another 1978 case, *Monell v. New York City Dept. of Social Services*, 436 U.S. 658 (1978), may have additional significant consequences for school boards in the context of student due process rights, for it held that § 1983 actions are not limited to "persons" only but may also include government entities as well. By overruling an earlier decision, *Monroe v. Pape*, 365 U.S. 167 (1961), to the contrary, the Court opened an avenue for plaintiffs to recover damages from the government itself when governmental agents abrogate constitutional rights. Since governmental units have greater resources than individual employees, this ruling is noteworthy. It remains to be seen whether governmental agencies such as school boards can protect themselves from suit through state "sovereign immunity" acts. However, the ruling may be somewhat less significant in the educational setting, for the Supreme Court has assumed jurisdiction of § 1983 cases against school boards in the past despite *Pape*, though most of these cases were confined to school desegregation issues and included school board members and school officials as defendants along with the boards themselves.

7. The ambiguity of the *Goss* ruling and Justice White's parting remark regarding the possible need for more formal procedures for long term suspensions and expulsions constitute an invitation to further litigation. Whether such litigation will result in judicial inroads in educational decision making is unclear. The decision was a 5–4 decision, with a particularly outspoken dissent written by the generally acknowledged educational expert on the court, Justice Lewis F. Powell. The *Wood* decision was

similarly a 5–4 decision, with the same Justices dissenting. Both decisions are thus not good indicators of future Supreme Court trends.

A year after *Goss*, the Court ruled in another five-to-four decision that a publicly-employed policeman who is classified as a permanent employee can be dismissed without a hearing if none is required under state law or by contractual agreement. Nor was the policeman's reputation damaged when the reasons advanced for his discharge turned out to be false. Justice Stevens for the majority in *Bishop v. Wood*, 426 U.S. 341 (1976), concluded that since the city ordinance under which the policeman was fired did not provide a hearing, none was required. Nor was his reputation damaged, since the reasons for his discharge were never made public. The dissenters argued that as a permanent employee, the policeman had a property interest in his job and had a right to notice and a hearing under the Due Process Clause. Critics of the Court's decision pointed out the anomaly inherent in the fact that students are entitled to due process before suspension from school but policemen have no such right when dismissed from their jobs. Many saw *Bishop* as a retreat from *Goldberg v. Kelly, Board of Regents v. Roth, Wisconsin v. Constantineau, Goss*, and similar cases and feared the property and liberty interest arguments were rapidly losing their strength.

Further refinement of the liberty interest argument in the educational setting appeared in early 1977 when the High Court ruled that a marginal nontenured teacher who was not rehired partly because of the exercise of freedom of speech is not entitled to reinstatement.* As we noted in *Mt. Healthy School Dist. v. Doyle*, 429 U.S. 274 (1977), in Chapter Three, Justice Rehnquist for a unanimous Court ruled that a candidate for tenure ought not to be able to prevent his employer from fairly assessing the candidate's record and reaching a decision not to continue the appointment simply by engaging in constitutionally protected activity. The proper approach in situations where nontenured teachers can show that free speech activity played a substantial role in the decision of nonrenewal, according to Justice Rehnquist, is for the school to demonstrate "by a preponderance of the evidence that it would have reached the same decision * * * even in the absence of the protected conduct." (At p. 287). One commentator pointed out the "chilling effect" the ruling could have on the exercise of free speech:

> * * * [I]f (a teacher) is like most teachers and has a few mistakes in his file, he had better be wary of writing that letter, delivering that speech, or placing that call. Because, as I read *Mt. Healthy*, school boards are now permitted to consider constitutionally protected behavior as "the straw that broke the camel's

---

* Since nontenured teachers have no property rights except in unusual situations under the *Perry v. Sindermann* and *Board of Regents v. Roth*, rulings, the school board could have refused to renew the teacher's contract without providing any reasons whatsoever. However, the superintendent did set forth the reasons in a letter. One of the reasons referred to an episode involving the teacher and a local radio station.

back" in determining whether to renew the contracts of nonten-ured teachers.[26]

Student rights to due process also appeared to weaken in 1977, for the Court struck a blow *for* disciplinarians by ruling in another 5–4 decision that corporal punishment in the public schools without any due process safeguards does not violate student constitutional rights. Thus, the trend of Supreme Court rulings in the due process area is unclear, though lower courts, of course, will continue to determine the future of much of the law within their jurisdictions. At this point it is safe to say that a balance between educational and legal interpretations of the suspension process has not been reached.

8. HYPOTHETICAL: *Parents v. School Officials of Westward High School*

As the dean of students at Westward Public High School entered the deserted hallway on May 20th, he was startled to observe Ann Senior standing outside a teacher's office. She appeared engrossed in reading what looked like a letter. The dean quickly drew alongside Ann. He was surprised to see the typed heading on the piece of paper—"Answer Key to Senior Comprehensive Mathematics Examination." The dean yanked the sheet from Ann's grasp. He told the startled student to follow him to his office.

Once they entered the office, the dean gave Ann a chance to explain. He added that in light of her poor academic record in mathematics, her explanation "had better be good." Ann, obviously flustered, said she had wanted to leave a note for the teacher but could find no pencil on the desk. Rather than open the desk, she took what appeared to her to be a blank piece of paper off the top of the desk with her out of the office in hopes of finding a pencil elsewhere, writing her note, and then returning the written message to the teacher's desk. When she left the office in search of a pencil, Ann said she happened to turn the sheet over and noticed that it was not blank but "had writing on it." It was indeed the answer sheet to the comprehensive exam she was scheduled to take the next day.

When Ann finished, the dean told her she was temporarily suspended, effective immediately, pending a full hearing on the matter. She began to protest, but the dean refused to listen to her further. He left the office. Ann missed her math exam and her biology exam. She was not able to secure the dean's permission to take these two remaining tests.

The School Judicial Committee (SJC), chaired by an English teacher who also happened to have a law degree, consisted of four teachers and one student. The Committee provided Ann with timely notice and a hearing. At the hearing, the SJC questioned the dean and the mathematics teacher. The latter said he could not say definitely whether he had placed the answer key in or on his desk while he left to get his mail. The SJC also allowed Ann to give her views and question the other witnesses. After private deliberations, the SJC announced its decision. Based on the testimony it heard and Ann's poor record in mathematics, the Committee found "sub-

---

26. Thomas J. Flygare "Supreme Court clarifies First Amendment Rights of Teach-ers," 58 *Phi Delta Kappan* 645, April, 1977, at p. 646.

stantial evidence" that Ann had really intended to find out the answers to the examination. It recommended that she be placed on probation and repeat the last semester of her math program over the summer. Since she had scored a zero on her biology exam (students are notified that make-ups can be scheduled only for *bona fide* medical excuses), she failed the course and would have to repeat it during the summer as well. The principal of the school, the superintendent, and the school board upheld the SJC's recommendations.

Ann's parents filed a 1983 lawsuit on her behalf against school officials, alleging that she was denied due process of law.

———

Based on previous discussion and cases, what arguments would you make for each side? If you were to decide this hypothetical case, what decision would you reach?

C. Corporal Punishment: Cruel and Unusual Punishment and a Violation of Due Process?

Corporal punishment as a means of enforcing discipline in the public schools dates back to the colonial period. *In loco parentis* provided the early rationale for allowing educators to use corporal punishment; the traditional admonition of "spare the rod and spoil the child" prevailed both in the home and in the educational setting.

In more modern times, corporal punishment has become increasingly disfavored as a discipline tool in public schools. Part of the reason relates to the decline of *in loco parentis* and the corresponding concern with student rights. The growing influence of psychology in the educational setting also has been a factor. Counseling and guidance, coupled with nonphysical punishment, has become the accepted way to deal with deviant behavior in the majority of cases. Still, the use of physical punishment continues to command support, particularly among more authoritarian and conservative educators and parents. Contemporary concern about the absence of discipline in schools gave corporal punishment a new lease on life, though many expected the lease to be brief as legal challenges mounted.

At the time of the 1977 Supreme Court decision about the issue of corporal punishment in the schools, 21 states specifically authorized the moderate use of corporal punishment. Only two states prohibited corporal punishment. The remainder apparently relied on the common law of reasonableness in allowing school authorities to use corporal punishment to keep order in the educational environment. Excessive force, however, in virtually all states subjected school authorities to possible civil and criminal liability.

Challenges to corporal punishment have come from two general areas. First, the use of physical punishment against students was alleged to be in violation of the Eighth Amendment's ban against cruel and unusual punishments. And secondly, the administration of punishment without complying with prior procedural due process was said to violate the Fourteenth Amendment Due Process Clause.

Before examining the recent Supreme Court decision on corporal punishment in the educational setting, let us briefly review how the Supreme Court has treated the Eighth Amendment ban against cruel and unusual punishments in the political and social setting.

(1) Cruel and Unusual Punishments: What is "Cruel" and "Unusual"?

The Constitution includes many clauses aimed at protecting the criminal suspect and defendant; yet it includes only one provision for the person who is convicted, namely the Eighth Amendment prohibition against "cruel and unusual punishments." Although the courts have never explicitly defined what kinds of punishments are "cruel and unusual", their decisions have recently indicated a position that the severity of sentences should be related to the seriousness of the crime.

A major question that confronts the U. S. Supreme Court on this issue is, how do judges decide whether a penalty is "cruel" or "unusual"? Should they be guided by their personal intuitions? Should they base their decisions on public opinion or the "spirit" of the times? Mr. Justice Frankfurter expressed his particular approach to the judges' quandary in a case that dealt with the Louisiana sentencing of convicted murdered Willie Francis to die in the electric chair. The switch was thrown and the mechanism malfunctioned. Francis was returned to his cell while the mechanism was fixed. In the duration, the Justices were asked to intervene and declare a second trip to the executioner as "cruel and unusual" punishment. In his concurring opinion, Frankfurter spoke in the following terms:

> * * * I cannot rid myself of the conviction that were I to hold that Louisiana would transgress [the Constitution by carrying out] * * * the death sentence, I would be enforcing my private view rather than that consensus of society's opinion which * * * is the standard enjoined by the Constitution.[27]

The Frankfurter approach raises, of course, the question of how this consensus is derived. Frankfurter's position seems to be one of social and/or cultural conscience. For Frankfurter, the double electrocution order would not violate or shock the conscience of Americans. Therefore, he placed his personal convictions aside, supplied the fifth vote needed to support the double electrocution order, and deferred to the state of Louisiana. The four dissenters objected to death-by-installment, concerning themselves more with Willie Francis than the national conscience.

The points raised by Frankfurter continue to plague the contemporary Court as it has tried to develop a position on whether the death penalty constitutes "cruel and unusual punishment." It was not until 1972 that the Court met the issue directly. In *Furman v. Georgia*, 408 U.S. 238 (1972), the Justices in a 5–to–4 *per curiam* decision ruled that the death penalty was cruel and unusual in the three death penalty cases before them. It is important to note that only two Justices argued that capital punishment in

27. *Louisiana ex rel. Francis v. Resweber,* 329 U.S. 459 (1947) at p. 471; material in brackets added.

every case should be abolished. The other three Justices in the majority claimed that in a system where, out of all the perpetrators of serious crime, only a "random few" are given the death penalty, there is a denial of equal protection because they are "capriciously selected."

Given the very slim majority and the reasoning of the three Justices in the majority, many states rapidly passed new laws making the death penalty mandatory for *specific* crimes. Specifying the crimes that would receive the death penalty, it was thought, might satisfy the concerns of the three Justices who were concerned with the randomness and capriciousness of previous death penalty sentences.

On July 2, 1976, the Supreme Court ruled that the death penalty was not inherently cruel and unusual. Justice Stewart speaking for a new majority in the seven-to-two decision in *Gregg v. Georgia*, 428 U.S. 153 (1976), based his decision on "society's endorsement of the death penalty" as demonstrated by the specific laws passed by 35 state legislatures. Therefore, Stewart claimed that "a heavy burden rests on those who would attack the judgment of the representatives of the people." (At p. 175). The new capital punishment law in Georgia satisfied the *Furman* objectives by providing specific guidelines and not permitting the "capriciousness" of juries. There, the law provided a two-part proceeding, the first to determine the guilt of the accused and the second to decide on the type of punishment. On the same day as the *Gregg* decision the Court ruled in *Woodson v. North Carolina*, 428 U.S. 280 (1976), and *Roberts v. Louisiana*, 428 U.S. 325 (1976), that mandatory death penalty laws are unconstitutional because, unlike the two-stage process, they do not provide for fair consideration of the individual defendant and of the individual crime. The Court thus retained the right to evaluate whether statutes provide the necessary specific guidelines that must prevent capriciousness in the death penalty sentencing process.

The *Gregg* decision does not lay this intensely controversial issue to rest. A future Court may well reject the arguments of "society's endorsement" and the deference to state legislatures that provide specific guidelines, and may instead rule that the death penalty is inherently arbitrary and capricious because of its very finality.

NOTES AND QUESTIONS

1. The *Gregg* decision countered the argument that "evolving standards of decency" have rendered capital punishment morally unacceptable by citing recent legislation which, the court said, indicates that many if not most Americans find the death penalty "appropriate and necessary" in some cases. If, indeed, most Americans hold this pro-death penalty position, does this mean that the Supreme Court should merely reflect popular opinion or should it proceed to define what many consider higher standards of justice, decency, and human rights?

2. If it could be shown that the death penalty has a deterrent effect against the high incidence of crime, does that justify its imposition? If strong corporal punishment has a deterrent effect against student behavior problems, does that justify its imposition?

3. In *Coker v. Georgia*, 433 U.S. 584 (1977), the Court ruled that the imposition of the death penalty for rape is invalid since the penalty is grossly disproportionate to the offense. An important factor in this decision is the fact that the crime of rape does not involve the loss of life and thus is not one of the most serious criminal offenses to which capital punishment can apply. Would you agree?

(2) Corporal Punishment in Public Educational Institutions

The Court squarely confronted the corporal punishment issue insofar as it pertains to public elementary and secondary schools in *Ingraham v. Wright* (1977). There, two students, James Ingraham and Roosevelt Andrews, both junior high school students in Dade County, Florida, through their parents challenged the paddling they had received at Drew Junior High School. Willie J. Wright was the principal of the school. Because Ingraham was slow to leave the stage of the school auditorium when asked to do so by a teacher, he was subjected to more than 20 swats with a paddle measuring two feet in length, four inches wide, and one-half inch thick. Jim Ingraham never consented to the paddling; it required two school officials to hold him down while Wright spanked him on the buttocks with the paddle. The paddling was severe enough to produce a bruise requiring medical attention and keeping him out of school for eleven days. Andrews was paddled nearly a dozen times for various minor infractions during his first year at Drew, and at one point suffered sufficient damage to his arm to render it useless for a week. Sixteen students testified at the district court hearing against the harsh system of discipline at Drew. Their testimony clearly demonstrated that the punishment Ingraham and Andrews received was not atypical. One student, for example, testified that he refused to take a whipping because he hadn't done anything wrong.

A.   * * * I told him, I say, "Mr. Barnes, I didn't do nothing; that's why I refuse not to take a whipping."

Q.   What did he do?

A.   So he told me, say, "You are going to take this one." I said, "Mr. Barnes, I didn't do nothing. I'm not taking no whipping." So I was leaning over the table and I said, "I'm not taking a whipping," and I was hit across the head with the board. He was hitting me across the head with the board, and my back and everything.

Q.   He was whipping you where?

A.   Across the head, with the board, he was hitting me all across the head and on the back. I was begging him for mercy to stop and he wouldn't listen. So he had some chairs in there and I was falling in the chairs as he was hitting me with the board. Then after a while he took off his belt and then started to hit me with the belt and hit me with the buckle part, and tears was coming out of me." (Transcripts at pp. 594–95).

The petitioners challenged the paddling and the statutory authorization for it as being cruel and unusual punishment under the Eighth Amendment as applied to the states through the Fourteenth Amendment, and also a violation of procedural due process. A third question related to whether severe corporal punishment is so arbitrary and unrelated to any legitimate educational purpose and thus *per se* a violation of the Due Process Clause was not addressed by the Supreme Court. Statutory authority for the administering of corporal punishment in the Florida school system is found in Florida Statute 232.27 (1961), which prohibits only "degrading or unduly severe" types of physical sanctions by the principal or teacher in charge of the school. A local school board policy then in effect spelled out directions and limitations, including administering punishment in the presence of another adult. The policy cautioned against (but did not prevent) the administering of corporal punishment to students under psychological or medical treatment. It also warned about the possibility of personal liability in the case of physical injury.

The federal district court accepted the students' testimony but found no constitutional basis for relief. A panel of the Fifth Circuit Court of Appeals reversed, ruling the paddling to be a cruel and unusual punishment and a violation of procedural due process. But upon a rehearing before the full panel of judges for the Fifth Circuit, the panel's conclusions were rejected and the lower court's decision affirmed. The Supreme Court granted certiorari on the cruel and unusual punishment and procedural due process issues.

INGRAHAM v. WRIGHT

Supreme Court of the United States, 1977.
430 U.S. 651, 97 S.Ct. 1401, 51 L.Ed.2d 711.

Mr. Justice POWELL delivered the opinion of the Court.

*   *   *

III

The Eighth Amendment provides, "Excessive bail shall not be required, nor excessive fines imposed, nor cruel and unusual punishments inflicted." Bail, fines and punishment traditionally have been associated with the criminal process, and by subjecting the three to parallel limitations the text of the Amendment suggests an intention to limit the power of those entrusted with the criminal law function of government. An examination of the history of the Amendment and the decisions of this Court construing the proscription against cruel and unusual punishment confirms that it was designed to protect those convicted of crimes. We adhere to this longstanding limitation and hold that the Eighth Amendment

does not apply to the paddling of children as a means of maintaining discipline in public schools.

*   *   *

[Subsections A and B describing the history of the Eighth Amendment have been deleted.]

C

Petitioners acknowledge that the original design of the Cruel and Unusual Punishments Clause was to limit criminal punishments, but urge nonetheless that the prohibition should be extended to ban the paddling of schoolchildren. Observing that the Framers of the Eighth Amendment could not have envisioned our present system of public and compulsory education, with its opportunities for noncriminal punishments, petitioners contend that extension of the prohibition against cruel punishments is necessary lest we afford greater protection to criminals than to schoolchildren. It would be anomalous, they say, if schoolchildren could be beaten without constitutional redress, while hardened criminals suffering the same beatings at the hands of their jailors might have a valid claim under the Eighth Amendment. Whatever force this logic may have in other settings, we find it an inadequate basis for wrenching the Eighth Amendment from its historical context and extending it to traditional disciplinary practices in the public schools.

The prisoner and the schoolchild stand in wholly different circumstances, separated by the harsh facts of criminal conviction and incarceration. The prisoner's conviction entitles the State to classify him as a "criminal," and his incarceration deprives him of the freedom "to be with family and friends and to form the other enduring attachments of normal life." Prison brutality, as the Court of Appeals observed in this case, is "part of the total punishment to which the individual is subjected for his crime and, as such, is a proper subject for Eighth Amendment scrutiny." * * *

The schoolchild has little need for the protection of the Eighth Amendment. Though attendance may not always be voluntary, the public school remains an open institution. Except perhaps when very young, the child is not physically restrained from leaving school during school hours; and at the end of the school day, the child is invariably free to return home. Even while at school, the child brings with him the support of family and friends and is rarely apart from teachers and other pupils who may witness and protest any instances of mistreatment.

The openness of the public school and its supervision by the community afford significant safeguards against the kinds of abuses from which the Eighth Amendment protects the prisoner. In virtually every community where corporal punishment is permitted in the schools, these safeguards are reinforced by the legal constraints of the common law. Public school teachers and administrators are privileged at common law to inflict only such corporal punishment as is reasonably necessary for the proper education and discipline of the child; any punishment going beyond the privilege may result in both civil and criminal liability. As long as the schools are open to public scrutiny, there is no reason to believe that the common law constraints will not effectively remedy and deter excesses such as those alleged in this case.

We conclude that when public school teachers or administrators impose disciplinary corporal punishment, the Eighth Amendment is inapplicable. The pertinent constitutional question is whether the imposition is consonant with the requirements of due process.

IV

* * * we find that corporal punishment in public school implicates a constitutionally protected liberty interest, but we hold that the traditional common law remedies are fully adequate to afford due process.

A

* * *

The Due Process Clause of the Fifth Amendment, later incorporated into the Fourteenth, was intended to give Americans at least the protection against governmental power that they had enjoyed as Englishmen against the power of the Crown. The liberty preserved from deprivation without due process included the right "generally to enjoy those privileges long recognized at common law as essential to the orderly pursuit of happiness by free men." Among the historic liberties so protected was a right to be free from and to obtain judicial relief, for unjustified intrusions on personal security.

While the contours of this historic liberty interest in the context of our federal system of government have not been defined precisely, they always have been thought to encompass freedom from bodily restraint and punishment. It is fundamental that the state cannot hold and physically punish an individual except in accordance with due process of law.

This constitutionally protected liberty interest is at stake in this case. There is, of course a *de minimis* level of imposition with which the Constitution is not concerned. But at least where school authorities, acting under color of state law, deliberately decide to punish a child for misconduct by restraining the child and inflicting appreciable physical pain, we hold that Fourteenth Amendment liberty interests are implicated.[43]

B

"[T]he question remains what process is due." Were it not for the common law privilege permitting teachers to inflict reasonable corporal punishment on children in their care, and the availability of the traditional remedies for abuse, the case for requiring advance procedural safeguards would be strong indeed. But here we deal with a punishment—paddling—within that tradition, and the question is whether the common law

remedies are adequate to afford due process. * * *

* * *

1

* * *

We turn now to a consideration of the safeguards that are available under applicable Florida law.

2

Florida has continued to recognize, and indeed has strengthened by statute, the common law right of a child not to be subjected to excessive corporal punishment in school. Under Florida law the teacher and principal of the school decide in the first instance whether corporal punishment is reasonably necessary under the circumstances in order to discipline a child who has misbehaved. But they must exercise prudence and restraint. For Florida has preserved the traditional judicial proceedings for determining whether the punishment was justified. If the punishment inflicted is later found to have been excessive—not reasonably believed at the time to be necessary for the child's discipline or training—the school authorities inflicting it may be held liable in damages to the child and, if malice is shown, they may be subject to criminal penalties.[45]

* * *

---

43. Unlike *Goss v. Lopez*, this case does not involve the state-created property interest in public education. The purpose of corporal punishment is to correct a child's behavior without interrupting his education. That corporal punishment may, in a rare case, have the unintended effect of temporarily removing a child from school affords no basis for concluding that the practice itself deprives students of property protected by the Fourteenth Amendment.

* * *

45. * * * Both the District Court, and the Court of Appeals, expressed the view that the common law tort remedy was available to the petitioners in this case. And petitioners conceded in this Court that a teacher who inflicts excessive punishment on a

child may be held both civilly and criminally liable under Florida law.

In view of the statutory adoption of the common law rule, and the unanimity of the parties and the courts below, the doubts expressed in Mr. Justice White's dissenting opinion as to the availability of tort remedies in Florida can only be viewed as chimerical. The dissent makes much of the fact that no Florida court has ever "recognized" a damage remedy for unreasonable corporal punishment. But the absence of reported Florida decisions hardly suggests that no remedy is available. Rather, it merely confirms the common-sense judgment that excessive corporal punishment is exceedingly rare in the public schools.

* * * Teachers and school authorities are unlikely to inflict corporal punishment unnecessarily or excessively when a possible consequence of doing so is the institution of civil or criminal proceedings against them.[46]

It still may be argued, of course, that the child's liberty interest would be better protected if the common law remedies were supplemented by the administrative safeguards of prior notice and a hearing. We have found frequently that some kind of prior hearing is necessary to guard against arbitrary impositions on interests protected by the Fourteeenth Amendment. But where the State has preserved what "has always been the law of the land," the case for administrative safeguards is significantly less compelling.[47]

* * *

3

But even if the need for advance procedural safeguards were clear, the question would remain whether the incremental benefit could justify the cost. Acceptance of petitioners' claims would work a transformation in the law governing corporal punishment in Florida and most other States. Given the impracticability of formulating a rule of procedural due process that varies with the severity of the particular imposition, the prior hearing petitioners seek would have to precede *any* paddling, however moderate or trivial.

Such a universal constitutional requirement would significantly burden the use of corporal punishment as a disciplinary measure. Hearings—even informal hearings—require time, personnel, and a diversion of attention from normal school pursuits. School authorities may well choose to abandon corporal punishment rather than incur the burdens of complying with the procedural requirements. Teachers, properly concerned with maintaining authority in the classroom, may well prefer to rely on other disciplinary measures—which they may view as less effective—rather than confront the possible disruption that prior notice and a hearing may entail.[50] Paradoxically, such an alteration of disciplinary policy is most likely to occur in the ordinary case where the contemplated punishment is well within the common law privilege.[51]

---

46. The low incidence of abuse, and the availability of established judicial remedies in the event of abuse, distinguish this case from *Goss v. Lopez*. The Ohio law struck down in *Goss* provided for suspensions from public school of up to 10 days without "any written procedure applicable to suspensions." Although Ohio law provided generally for administrative review, the Court assumed that the short suspensions would not be stayed pending review, with the result that the review proceeding could serve neither a deterrent nor a remedial function. In these circumstances, the Court held the law authorizing suspensions unconstitutional for failure to require "that there be at least an informal give-and-take between [the] student and disciplinarian, preferably prior to the suspension * * *." The subsequent civil and criminal proceedings available in this case may be viewed as affording substantially greater protection to the child than the informal conference mandated by *Goss*.

* * *

47. * * *

* * * We have no occasion in this case, to decide whether or under what circumstances corporal punishment of a public school child may give rise to an independent federal cause of action to vindicate substantive rights under the Due Process Clause.

* * *

50. If a prior hearing, with the inevitable attendant publicity within the school, resulted in rejection of the teacher's recommendation, the consequent impairment of the teacher's ability to maintain discipline in the classroom would not be insubstantial.

51. The effect of interposing prior procedural safeguards may well be to make the punishment more severe by increasing the anxiety of the child. For this reason, the school authorities in Dade County found it desirable that the punishment be inflicted as soon as possible after the infraction.

Elimination or curtailment of corporal punishment would be welcomed by many as a societal advance. But when such a policy choice may result from this Court's determination of an asserted right to due process, rather than from the normal processes of community debate and legislative action, the societal costs cannot be dismissed as insubstantial. We are reviewing here a legislative judgment, rooted in history and reaffirmed in the laws of many States, that corporal punishment serves important educational interests. This judgment must be viewed in light of the disciplinary problems common-place in the schools. Assessment of the need for, and the appropriate means of maintaining, school discipline is committed generally to the discretion of school authorities subject to state law. * * *

"At some point the benefit of an additional safeguard to the individual affected * * * and to society in terms of increased assurance that the action is just, may be outweighed by the cost." We think that point has been reached in this case. In view of the low incidence of abuse, the openness of our schools, and the common law safeguards that already exist, the risk of error that may result in violation of a schoolchild's substantive rights can only be regarded as minimal. Imposing additional administrative safeguards as a constitutional requirement might reduce that risk marginally, but would also entail a significant intrusion into an area of primary educational re-

sponsibility. We conclude that the Due Process Clause does not require notice and a hearing prior to the imposition of corporal punishment in the public schools, as that practice is authorized and limited by the common law.[55]

* * *

Affirmed.

Mr. Justice WHITE, with whom Mr. Justice BRENNAN, Mr. Justice MARSHALL, and Mr. Justice STEVENS join, dissenting.

* * *

I

A

The Eighth Amendment places a flat prohibition against the infliction of "cruel and unusual punishments." This reflects a societal judgment that there are some punishments that are so barbaric and inhumane that we will not permit them to be imposed on anyone, no matter how opprobrious the offense. If there are some punishments that are so barbaric that they may not be imposed for the commission of crimes, designated by our social system as the most thoroughly reprehensible acts an individual can commit, then *a fortiori*, similar punishments may not be imposed on persons for less culpable acts, such as breaches of school discipline. Thus, if it is constitutionally impermissible to cut off someone's ear for the commission of murder, it must be unconstitutional to cut off a child's ear

---

55. Mr. Justice WHITE's dissenting opinion offers no manageable standards for determining what process is due in any particular case. The dissent apparently would require, as a general rule, only "an informal give-and-take between student and disciplinarian." But the dissent would depart from these "minimal procedures"— requiring even witnesses, counsel, and cross-examination—in cases where the punishment reaches some undefined level of severity. School authorities are left to guess at the degree of punishment that will require more than an "informal give-and-take" and at the additional process that may be constitutionally required. The impracticability of such an approach is self-

evident, and illustrates the hazards of ignoring the traditional solution of the common law.

We agree with the dissent that the *Goss* procedures will often be, "if anything, less than a fair-minded principal would impose upon himself." But before this Court invokes the Constitution to impose a procedural requirement, it should be reasonably certain that the effect will be to afford protection appropriate to the constitutional interests at stake. The dissenting opinion's reading of the Constitution suggests no such beneficial result and, indeed, invites a lowering of existing constitutional standards.

for being late to class. Although there were no ears cut off in this case, the record reveals beatings so severe that if they were inflicted on a hardened criminal for the commission of a serious crime, they might not pass constitutional muster.

Nevertheless, the majority holds that the Eighth Amendment "was designed to protect [only] those convicted of crimes," relying on a vague and inconclusive recitation of the history of the Amendment. Yet the constitutional prohibition is against cruel and unusual *punishments*; nowhere is that prohibition limited or modified by the language of the Constitution. Certainly the fact that the Framers did not choose to insert the word "criminal" into the language of the Eighth Amendment is strong evidence that the Amendment was designed to prohibit all inhumane or barbaric punishments, no matter what the nature of the offense for which the punishment is imposed.

* * *

C

In fact, as the Court recognizes, the Eighth Amendment has never been confined to criminal punishments.[4] Never-

theless, the majority adheres to its view that any protections afforded by the Eighth Amendment must have something to do with criminals, and it would therefore confine any exceptions to its general rule that only criminal punishments are covered by the Eighth Amendment to abuses inflicted on prisoners. Thus, if a prisoner is beaten mercilessly for a breach of discipline, he is entitled to the protection of the Eighth Amendment, while a school child who commits the same breach of discipline and is similarly beaten is simply not covered.

The purported explanation of this anomaly is the assertion that school children have no need for the Eighth Amendment. We are told that schools are open institutions, subject to constant public scrutiny; that school children have adequate remedies under state law,[5] and that prisoners suffer the social stigma of being labeled as criminals. How any of these policy considerations got into the Constitution is difficult to discern, for the Court has never considered any of these factors in determining the scope of the Eighth Amendment.

The essence of the majority's argument is that school children do not need

---

4. In *Estelle v. Gamble*, 429 U.S. 97 (1976), a case decided this Term, the Court held that "deliberate indifference to the medical needs of prisoners" by prison officials constitutes cruel and unusual punishment prohibited by the Eighth Amendment. Such deliberate indifference to a prisoner's medical needs clearly is not punishment inflicted for the commission of a crime; it is merely misconduct by a prison official. Similarly, the Eighth Circuit has held that whipping a prisoner with a strap in order to maintain discipline is prohibited by the Eighth Amendment. *Jackson v. Bishop*, 404 F.2d 571 (CA8 1968) (Blackmun, J.). See also *Knecht v. Gillman*, 488 F.2d 1136 (CA8 1973) (injection of vomit-inducing drugs as part of aversion therapy held to be cruel and unusual); *Vann v. Scott*, 467 F.2d 1235 (CA7 1972) (Stevens, J.). (Eighth Amendment protects runaway children against cruel and inhumane treatment, regardless

of whether such treatment is labeled "rehabilitation" or "punishment").

5. By finding that bodily punishment invades a constitutionally protected liberty interest within the meaning of the Due Process Clause, the majority suggests that the Clause might also afford a remedy for excessive spanking independently of the Eighth Amendment. If this were the case, the Court's present thesis would have little practical significance. * * *

Petitioners in this case did raise the substantive due process issue in their petition for certiorari, but consideration of that question was foreclosed by our limited grant of certiorari. If it is probable that school children would be entitled to protection under some theory of substantive due process, the Court should not now affirm the judgment below, but should amend the grant of certiorari and set this case for reargument.

Eighth Amendment protection because corporal punishment is less subject to abuse in the public schools than it is in the prison system. However, it cannot be reasonably suggested that just because cruel and unusual punishments may occur less frequently under public scrutiny, they will not occur at all. The mere fact that a public flogging or a public execution would be available for all to see would not render the punishment constitutional if it were otherwise impermissible. Similarly, the majority would not suggest that a prisoner who is placed in a minimum security prison and permitted to go home to his family on the weekends should be any less entitled to Eighth Amendment protections than his counterpart in a maximum security prison. In short, if a punishment is so barbaric and inhumane that it goes beyond the tolerance of a civilized society, its openness to public scrutiny should have nothing to do with its constitutional validity.

Nor is it an adequate answer that school children may have other state and constitutional remedies available to them. Even assuming that the remedies available to public school students are adequate under Florida law, the availability of state remedies has never been determinative of the coverage or of the protections afforded by the Eighth Amendment. The reason is obvious. The fact that a person may have a state-law cause of action against a public official who tortures him with a thumb screw for the commission of an antisocial act has nothing to do with the fact that such official conduct is cruel and unusual punishment prohibited by the Eighth Amendment. * * *

D

* * *

The issue presented in this phase of the case is limited to whether corporal punishment in public schools can *ever* be prohibited by the Eighth Amendment. I am therefore not suggesting that spanking in the public schools is in every instance prohibited by the Eighth Amendment. My own view is that it is not. I only take issue with the extreme view of the majority that corporal punishment in public schools, no matter how barbaric, inhumane, or severe, is never limited by the Eighth Amendment. Where corporal punishment becomes so severe as to be unacceptable in a civilized society, I can see no reason that it should become any more acceptable just because it is inflicted on children in the public schools.

II

The majority concedes that corporal punishment in the public schools implicates an interest protected by the Due Process Clause—the liberty interest of the student to be free from "bodily restraint and punishment" involving "appreciable physical pain" inflicted by persons acting under color of state law. The question remaining, as the majority recognizes, is what process is due.

The reason that the Constitution requires a State to provide "due process of law" when it punishes an individual for misconduct is to protect the individual from erroneous or mistaken punishment that the State would not have inflicted had it found the facts in a more reliable way. In *Goss v. Lopez*, the Court applied this principle to the school disciplinary process, holding that a student must be given an informal opportunity to be heard before he is finally suspended from public school. * * *

The Court now holds that these "rudimentary precautions against unfair or mistaken findings of misconduct," are not required if the student is punished with "appreciable physical pain" rather than with a suspension, even though both punishments deprive the student of a constitutionally protected interest. Although the respondent school authorities provide absolutely *no* process to the student before the punishment is finally inflicted, the majority concludes that the student is nonetheless given due process because he can later sue the teacher and recover damages if the punishment was "excessive."

This tort action is utterly inadequate to protect against erroneous infliction of punishment for two reasons. First, under Florida law, a student punished for an act he did not commit cannot recover damages from a teacher "proceeding in utmost good faith * * * on the reports and advice of others,"; the student has no remedy at all for punishment imposed on the basis of mistaken facts, at least as long as the punishment was reasonable from the point of view of the disciplinarian, uninformed by any prior hearing.[11] The "traditional common law remedies" on which the majority relies, thus do nothing to protect the student from the danger that concerned the Court in *Goss*—the risk of reasonable, good faith mistake in the school disciplinary process.

Second, and more important, even if the student could sue for good faith error in the infliction of punishment, the lawsuit occurs after the punishment has been finally imposed. The infliction of physical pain is final and irreparable; it cannot be undone in a subsequent proceeding. There is every reason to require, as

the Court did in *Goss*, a few minutes of "informal give-and-take between student and disciplinarian" as a "meaningful hedge" against the erroneous infliction of irreparable injury.

*　*　*

The majority emphasizes, as did the dissenters in *Goss*, that even the "rudimentary precautions" required by that decision would impose some burden on the school disciplinary process. But those costs are no greater if the student is paddled rather than suspended; the risk of error in the punishment is no smaller; and the fear of "a significant intrusion" into the disciplinary process is just as exaggerated. The disciplinarian need only take a few minutes to give the student "notice of the charges against him and, if he denies them, an explanation of the evidence the authorities have and an opportunity to present his side of the story." In this context the Constitution requires, "if anything, less than a fair-minded principal would impose upon himself" in order to avoid injustice.[18]

I would reverse the judgment below.

Mr. Justice STEVENS, dissenting.

*　*　*

NOTES AND QUESTIONS

1. Do you find Justice Powell's arguments on the due process issue convincing in light of the Court's prior decision in *Goss v. Lopez?* Note that in a footnote Justice Powell acknowledges that in *Goss* the Court was concerned that the review process would take place *after* the suspension and thus "could serve neither a deterrent nor a remedial function." Here, he maintains that "The subsequent civil and criminal proceedings available

11.　　　　*　*　*
*　*　* the majority does not cite a single case decided under Florida law that recognizes a student's right to sue a school official to recover damages for excessive punishment, *　*　*

*　*　*

18. My view here expressed that the minimal procedures of *Goss* are required for any corporal punishment implicating the

student's liberty interest is of course not meant to imply that this minimum would be constitutionally sufficient no matter how severe the punishment inflicted. The Court made this reservation explicit in *Goss* by suggesting that more elaborate procedures such as witnesses, counsel, and cross-examination might well be required for suspensions longer than the 10-day maximum involved in that case. A similar caveat is appropriate here.

in this case may be viewed as affording substantially greater protection to the child than the informal conference mandated by *Goss*." Is this convincing? Compare the arguments of the four dissenters.

2. Note the shift of one Justice in this case from the lineup in *Goss* resulted in a different orientation of the Court to student due process rights. Justice Stewart here joined the Nixon appointees (Chief Justice Burger and Justices Blackmun, Powell, and Rehnquist), whereas in *Goss* he sided with the other Justices. The retirement of Justice Douglas and subsequent appointment of Justice Stevens made no difference in the outcome, since the position of the two in *Goss* and *Ingraham* is consistent. Both cases are 5–4 decisions. Of the two, which do you think is the more likely candidate to be overruled in the future in order to make the approach of the Court to student disciplinary due process issues more consistent? Which would you prefer be overruled?

Note also that *Ingraham* involves junior high school students. If the same situation in *Ingraham* were to occur in a community college, would the result be the same? Or might the age of the student coupled with the absence of a compulsory attendance rule suggest a different result? What about a senior in high school?

3. The Court declines to consider a third issue, namely, whether severe corporal punishment upon public school students is arbitrary and capricious, and unrelated to any legitimate educational purpose. Later, in a footnote, Justice Powell states that the Court is not considering in this case whether there might be an independent federal cause of action to vindicate substantive rights under the Due Process Clause. Note Justice White's reference to these statements in footnote five.

It would appear that the Court was unwilling or unable to resolve the substantive due process issue in *Ingraham*, leaving it for a future determination. As we will note in Chapter Eight, the Court has been very reluctant to strike down legislative policy or actions on substantive due process grounds. However, the Court has used this concept recently to invalidate laws restricting access of married persons to contraceptives and the right of women to abortions. Note that the substantive due process claim here is phrased in terms of "severe" corporal punishment, not corporal punishment *per se*. Thus, had the Court taken up the substantive due process claim and agreed with it, it remains uncertain whether all corporal punishment would have been outlawed.

4. The Court suggests that available remedies to students and parents are adequate.[28] These remedies include civil and criminal law provisions similar to those in Florida. Will the *Ingraham* decision result in a plethora of suits against educators? This is an interesting question. The emerging law of "educational malpractice" is creating new worries among both public and nonpublic educators. Student suits are being brought on civil (and,

---

28. This assertion has prompted some critics to conclude that the Burger Court is moving away from an inclination to intervene on behalf of students. See, for example, the charges expressed in Irene Rosenberg, "*Ingraham v. Wright*: The Supreme Court's Whipping Boy," 78 *Columbia L.Rev.* 75, January, 1978, to the effect that the Burger Court is resurrecting the states rights doctrine at the expense of students' federal constitutional rights. At pp. 95ff.

where malice is evident, on criminal) grounds against school officials for alleged violations of legal duties. The civil suits are most frequently based on the law of torts, that body of law which provides redress for wrongful physical or emotional injury caused by one person to another, or on the law of contracts, that body of law providing redress for breach of legal duties agreed upon by the parties. Unlike constitutional law, the law of torts and of contracts applies to both the public and nonpublic sectors. For example, in *Zumbrun v. Univ. of Southern Calif.*, 25 Cal.App.3d 1, 101 Cal.Rptr. 499 (1972), the California Court of Appeal for the Second District asserted that "The basic legal relation between a student and a private university or college is contractual in nature" and agreed that a student has a right to a determination whether a portion of her tuition should be refunded when a professor failed to give all the lectures and the final examination for a course in which she was enrolled. (At pp. 504–505). In *Eden v. Board of Trustees of State Univ.*, 374 N.Y.S.2d 686 (New York, 1975), a state appeals court ruled that under New York law, students have a contractual right to enroll in an educational program to which they have been admitted and for which there is insufficient evidence of financial exigency to justify cancellation. The students had been notified that the program in podiatric medicine at the State University at Stony Brook was being terminated because of a fiscal crisis. They brought suit on contractual grounds. And in *Hoffman v. Board of Educ. of New York City*, Index No. 12593/71 Supreme Court of New York, Queens Cty., a jury awarded $750,000 to a student who had been misclassified as mentally retarded through most of his schooling experience. The award has been appealed.

However, the doctrine of "sovereign immunity"—governments cannot be sued without their consent—may provide protection from such suits to many public officials in states where the doctrine has not been waived. Note the interesting reversal over constitutional law: nonpublic educational institutions may be more affected by these nonconstitutional suits than public institutions.[29]

5. Some found the *Ingraham* decision particularly surprising since only two years before the Court had affirmed the ruling of a lower court sanctioning corporal punishment for public school children provided due process procedures are observed. That case, *Baker v. Owen*, 395 F.Supp. 294 (M.D.N.C.1975), aff'd 423 U.S. 907 (1975), involved the paddling of a sixth grade pupil over the objections of both the child and the child's mother. The district court ruled that the punishment did not violate the Fourteenth Amendment liberty right of the mother to control the upbringing of the child. But since the child has a liberty interest in avoiding corporal punishment, prior due process procedures are required. Interestingly the court noted that " * * * the legal system, once quite tolerant of physical punishment in many contexts, has become less so." (At p. 301).

29. For more information about the student consumer movement, see Michael A. Liethen, "Institutional Liabilities," in *Students* *and Their Institutions* (Washington, D. C.: American Council on Education, 1978).

Basing its conclusion on *Goss v. Lopez,* the district court stipulated the following procedural requirements must be accorded the student in advance of the administration of corporal punishment:

    a.   Corporal punishment "may never be used unless the student was informed beforehand that specific misbehavior could occasion its use, and, subject to this exception, it should never be employed as a first line of punishment for misbehavior."

    b.   "Second, a teacher or principal must punish corporally in the presence of a second school official * * * who must be informed beforehand and in the student's presence of the reasons for the punishment."

    c.   Thirdly, the person who administered the punishment "must provide the child's parent, upon request, a written explanation of his reasons and the name of the second official who was present." (At pp. 302–303).

The plaintiffs did not assert that the punishment was cruel and unusual under the Eighth Amendment. In fact, the court concluded that the paddling in this instance was not cruel and unusual.

Only the district court's decision that state corporal punishment law is not unconstitutional was appealed to the Supreme Court.[30] Thus, the latter's affirmance did not involve the procedural due process ruling in *Baker.* This being the case, *Ingraham* is the only expression of the Supreme Court's views regarding procedural due process in the administering of corporal punishment.

In *Baker* doctors testified that the sixth grader who suffered the punishment "is an abnormally frail and sensitive child to whom such a paddling could be more emotionally or psychologically damaging than to the normal child * * *." (At p. 303). The court, however, said the teacher didn't know this condition existed. *Baker* thus follows a traditional line of cases holding that if a student is supersensitive physically or emotionally to corporal punishment, the parents or the student must make the fact known to the school for there to be a remedy against future damaging punishment. A competing legal approach places greater responsibility on the educator to find this out.

Would the procedures the court outlined protect the teacher from civil or criminal suits when the administered punishment injures the child? Are the procedures adequate from the standpoint of the child? In light of *Ingraham,* does *Baker* have any continuing validity? Do you think parents should be able to prevent the use of corporal punishment on their children? The interest of the state in maintaining discipline within schools appears to rule out this option.

    6.   The outcry which greeted the *Ingraham* decision was reminiscent of reaction to the recent capital punishment decisions. The close division of the Court added to the reaction. A *New York Times* editorial suggested that each member of the errant majority "deserves at least five whacks." Columnist Carl Rowan wrote, "By all the rules of simple justice and com-

---

30. *Id.,* at p. 103.

mon sense, I know I am right in saying we do not need to heap teacher violence on top of student violence in our schools." [31]

Other commentators noted that since a majority of both the general public and teachers favor paddling, public opinion figured heavily in the Court's decision, particularly in light of criticisms which met the earlier *Goss v. Lopez* ruling. Might the failure to date of social science to demonstrate a workable solution to problems of school discipline have also played a role in the decision?

But there were many who voiced support for *Ingraham*. Various spokesmen for the nation's teachers and school administrators spoke out in favor of the decision, noting that student violence, which has grown to major proportions in many schools, now has a counter force. Interestingly, the National Education Association, the largest organization of teachers, supported the students in *Ingraham,* while its rival, the American Federation of Teachers, supported the school officials. What is your view?

7. Justice Powell concludes that "where school authorities, acting under color of state law, deliberately decide to punish a child for misconduct by restraining the child and inflicting appreciable physical pain, we hold that the Fourteenth Amendment liberty interests are implicated." Are liberty interests also involved when a student is *verbally* chastized? Is ridicule and derision as potentially damaging as physical punishment? Should administrative safeguards such as prior notice and a hearing be required?

One commentator notes that emotional distress continues to be one of the most unprotected interests in the law of torts.[32] Usually, a school official's conduct has to be intentional or outrageous for a student to recover damages under applicable statutes. Often, evidence of actual severe injury has to be shown as well. Why do you suppose the standards to recover are set so high where verbal chastisement is concerned?

D.   Due Process and Academic Disputes

What right should students have to due process in disputes involving academic matters such as grades, ability grouping, grade promotion, and dismissal? No area of educational operation illustrates the hesitancy of judicial involvement in internal school and college operation as much as disputes over academic decisions. One of the reasons is the relative infrequency of factual disputes, thus undercutting much of the rationale for procedural due process. Judges are left with involvement for substantive due process reasons: was the decision fundamentally fair? To make such a determination, judges fear that they will end up substituting their views for those of educators, a task for which judges have neither the skill nor the time.

Nevertheless, the impact of adverse academic decisions on students is surely no less than disciplinary action. As one commentator notes, "It seems a strange system, indeed, in which a junior high school student must

---

31. *Chicago Daily News*, May 30, 1977.

32. George E. Stevens, "Verbal Chastisement in Elementary and Secondary Schools:

A Suggestion," 6 *J.Law & Educ.* 319, July, 1977.

be granted notice and hearing prior to disciplinary suspension of no more than ten days, while medical or doctoral students can be dismissed from school permanently without any of the protections of the due process clause coming into play.[33]

The problem is to decide if due process protections should apply at all and if so, in what situations. It need not be an all-or-nothing proposition. Some have tried to minimize judicial involvement by suggesting that because of the absence of factual disputes in most academic decisions, due process should only apply when academic dismissal is likely. Thus, a student who receives a failing grade or is not promoted from one grade to another would not be entitled to due process rights or judicial review except in egregious circumstances. Of course, the institutions themselves may establish due process procedures for these situations; the point is that the courts would not mandate that they be required. Nor would students whose applications to public educational institutions such as law schools are rejected be entitled to due process rights. As one jurist has pointed out, " * * * I would draw a distinction between cases in which government is seeking to take action against the citizen from those in which it is simply denying a citizen's request."[34] Some have suggested that whatever is developed not apply to elementary and secondary students because their loss is less onerous and because the state often has an obligation under compulsory school laws to continue their education in some fashion.

These exercises in line-drawing do help to minimize legal intrusions into traditional academic judgmental areas. But at the same time, they exclude many students who believe they have been wronged. A student who disputes placement in a vocational high school track, whose application to medical school is summarily rejected, or who is not promoted to a higher grade for reasons of "immaturity" takes little comfort in knowing that these lines have been drawn in the interest of harmonizing judicial involvement with the exercise of professional judgment. Once again, there are no easy answers.

Somewhat reluctantly, courts in the 1960s first began to consider student complaints over academic decision making. In the early cases, the courts limited their review to seeing that decisions involving student academic dismissal at public colleges were made fairly. The first case in this section, *Connelly v. University of Vermont and State Agricultural College,* 244 F.Supp. 156 (D.Vt.1965) is the most often cited. Like the early decisions involving student expulsions from public educational institutions, *Connelly* limits judicial involvement to seeing that student dismissals are not arbitrary or capricious under the Fourteenth Amendment Due Process Clause and places the burden on the student of proving the contrary. Unlike the later disciplinary cases we have reviewed, courts almost uniformly have been reluctant to impose procedural due process requirements on academic decision making. Thus *Dixon v. Alabama State Board* and its progeny have no parallel where academic disputes are concerned.

33. R. Lawrence Dessem, "Student Due Process Rights in Academic Dismissals from the Public Schools," 5 *J.Law and Educ.* 277, July, 1976, at p. 285.

34. Friendly, *supra,* at p. 1295.

The pattern began to change somewhat, however, in the 1970s, particularly after *Goss v. Lopez*. Some courts began to suggest that student Fourteenth Amendment liberty and property interests in their educational experience at public institutions warranted procedural due process as a constitutional necessity prior to dismissal for unsatisfactory performance. To date, almost all of the decisions have involved postsecondary students. *Greenhill v. Bailey,* 519 F.2d 5 (8th Cir. 1975), is the leading case. There the appeals court reversed the lower court by holding that because Greenhill's medical school had seriously damaged his reputation (a liberty interest) in dismissing him for academic reasons, the school had to provide him with notice and a hearing. Because of the inadequacy of Greenhill's prior academic record, he had not been recommended by a promotions committee for senior class status at the University of Iowa College of Medicine. Appeals were to no avail. The assistant dean of the College of Medicine informed the Liaison Committee on Medical Education of the Association of American Medical Colleges that Greenhill had been dismissed for poor academic standing and added that the apparent reason was "lack of intellectual ability or insufficient preparation." It was the action of the assistant dean which disturbed the appeals court. Relying on *Goss*, the court held that "the action by the school in denigrating Greenhill's intellectual ability, as distinguished from his performance, deprived him of a significant interest in liberty, for it admittedly 'imposed on him a stigma or other disability that foreclose(s) his freedom to take advantage of other * * * opportunities.'" (At p. 8). The court ruled that he was entitled to notice of the "charges" against him and a hearing "to permit him to clear his name." The court noted that Greenhill had never been notified that lack of intellectual ability was one of the reasons for his dismissal, nor had he been told that the action against him would be reported to the Association of American Medical Colleges.

The same liberty and property argument was used by Charlotte Horowitz against the University of Missouri-Kansas City Medical School. She was dismissed in 1973, shortly before her graduation, on the grounds that she lacked personal hygiene and did not relate well to patients and colleagues. Ms. Horowitz had received high scores in the admissions tests and academically was near the top of her class. The district court dismissed her case, but the Court of Appeals for the Eighth Circuit, the same court which rendered the *Greenhill* decision, reversed the decision on grounds similar to those they advanced in *Greenhill*. The case went to the U. S. Supreme Court, which overturned the appeals court decision in 1978. The case, *Board of Curators of the Univ. of Missouri v. Charlotte Horowitz,* is the second excerpted in this section.

As you read the cases and ponder the notes and questions, consider whether due process procedures in your view ought to be included in any of the three following instances and, if so, what process you think is due.

a. A second year law student at a public university is notified at the end of the year that his grades do not warrant his continued enrollment. So far the student has spent $10,000, including residency costs and tuition. This does not include deferred income, since had he been employed, he would likely have made over $12,000 in this period. The student is informed of his status by mail. Included with the letter is a copy of the law school's academic policy statement. The statement is distributed to all freshmen annually, is included in the law school bulletin, and is posted in the law school building. The student protests.

b. All students at a public college must maintain a 1.8 (out of a possible 4.0) overall grade point average to continue to be enrolled. Failure to do so means being placed on academic probation. If the GPA is not raised to a 2.0 at the end of the following semester, the student is automatically dismissed. All students are informed of the grading policy.

A student receives a 1.8 GPA during the first semester and a 1.7 during the second. For her to continue, she must receive at least a 1.85 during the third semester. Illness causes her to miss three weeks of classes during this time; the student, however, does not request a leave of absence. Rather than withdraw and lose her money (refunds are given only through the first two weeks of the semester), she continues. She receives only a 1.5 GPA for her third semester, thus falling below the minimum for the three semesters. The student is automatically dismissed. She protests.

c. A student at a public high school continues to have academic trouble, barely passing from term to term. After two years of such mediocre performance, the student's teachers recommend to the principal that the student be transferred to a public vocational high school located some distance from the student's home. The principal concurs in the recommendation, and the student's parents are notified that a transfer will take place at the start of the student's junior year. Both parents and the student object and request a hearing. No hearing is granted, since the transfer policy indicates that hearings are only necessary for disciplinary, not administrative, transfers. The student and his parents protest.

CONNELLY v. THE UNIV. OF VERMONT AND STATE AGRICULTURAL COLLEGE

United States District Court for the District of Vermont, 1965.
244 F.Supp. 156.

GIBSON, District Judge.

* * *

The substance of the plaintiff's complaint is as follows: He is a third year student at the defendant's College of Medicine, and during the months of March through June of 1964, he was enrolled in a 12-week course in pediatrics-obstetrics. He states that due to illness he missed a portion of the course from May 11 to June 7, 1964, that he made up this lost time from July 1 to July 16, 1964, and that he believes his grades prior to his illness were 82 and 87 in the pediatrics and obstetrics parts of the

course respectively. He further states that on July 17, 1964 he was advised that he had failed the pediatrics-obstetrics course and could not advance to his fourth year by reason of having failed 25 per cent or more of the major courses of his third year, this under a rule of the College of Medicine. The plaintiff then petitioned the College's Committee on Advancement for permission to repeat his third year's work. His petition was denied and he was subsequently dismissed from school. He alleges that his teacher during the period from July 1 to July 16, 1964 decided early in that period "that he would not give plaintiff a passing grade in said pediatrics-obstetrics course regardless of his prior work in the Spring and regardless of the quality of his work in said make up period." The plaintiff alleges that his work was of passing quality, and that his dismissal was wrongful, improper, arbitrary, summary and unjust. He prays that it be rescinded by the mandate of this Court.

* * *

The important question presented here is whether plaintiff's allegation that his instructor in the make up period from July 1 to July 16, 1964 failed him without proper attention to the quality of his work and on the basis of a decision made prior to the completion by plaintiff of his pediatrics-obstetrics course, states a cause of action * * *. This Court is of the opinion that it does to a limited extent.

Where a medical student has been dismissed for a failure to attain a proper standard of scholarship, two questions may be involved; the first is, was the student in fact delinquent in his studies or unfit for the practice of medicine? The second question is, were the school authorities motivated by malice or bad faith in dismissing the student, or did they act arbitrarily or capriciously? In general, the first question is not a matter for judicial review. However, a student dismissal motivated by bad faith, arbitrariness or capriciousness may be actionable.

* * *

The effect of [prior] decisions is to give the school authorities absolute discretion in determining whether a student has been delinquent in his studies, and to place the burden on the student of showing that his dismissal was motivated by arbitrariness, capriciousness or bad faith. The reason for this rule is that in matters of scholarship, the school authorities are uniquely qualified by training and experience to judge the qualifications of a student, and efficiency of instruction depends in no small degree upon the school faculty's freedom from interference from other noneducational tribunals. It is only when the school authorities abuse this discretion that a court may interfere with their decision to dismiss a student.

* * *

The rule of judicial nonintervention in scholastic affairs is particularly applicable in the case of a medical school. A medical school must be the judge of the qualifications of its students to be granted a degree; Courts are not supposed to be learned in medicine and are not qualified to pass opinion as to the attainments of a student in medicine. In the instant case, the plaintiff Connelly alleges on information and belief

* * * that, on the basis of his work in the Pediatrics-Obstetrics course during the Spring of 1964 and the continued 16 day make up period in July, 1964, he either received, or, in the alternative, should have received a passing grade therein and that his work in said course was comparable to and in many instances superior to the work of other students who received a passing grade in that course.

Whether the plaintiff should or should not have received a passing grade for the period in question is a matter wholly within the jurisdiction of the school authorities, who alone are qualified to make such a determination. The subject matter of this count of the complaint is not a subject for judicial review and this count of the complaint fails to state any claim for which relief can be granted.

However, to the extent that the plaintiff has alleged his dismissal was for reasons other than the quality of his work, or in bad faith, he has stated a cause of action. He has alleged

* * * that the agent of defendant's College of Medicine who taught plaintiff from July 1 to July 16, 1964 decided early in said period that he would not give plaintiff a passing grade in said Pediatrics-Obstetrics course regardless of his prior work in the Spring and regardless of the quality of his work in said make up period.

The plaintiff has also alleged that the action of defendant in dismissing him was "summary and arbitrary." The allegation that the plaintiff was failed by an instructor who had made up his mind to fail him before he completed the course is equivalent, in this Court's opinion, to an allegation of bad faith, arbitrariness, and capriciousness on the part of the said instructor, and if proven, this Court would be justified in affording the plaintiff appropriate relief.

* * *

It should be emphasized that this Court will not pass on the issue of whether the plaintiff should have passed or failed his pediatrics-obstetrics course, or whether he is qualified to practice medicine. This must and can only be determined by an appropriate department or committee of the defendant's College of Medicine. Therefore, should the plaintiff prevail on the issue of whether the defendant acted arbitrarily, capriciously or in bad faith, this Court will then order the defendant University to give the plaintiff a fair and impartial hearing on his dismissal order.

ORDER

Therefore it is ordered that the motions of defendant to dismiss and for Summary Judgment under Rule 56, F.R. C.P. be and hereby are denied. The case is to be set for hearing on the limited issue of whether the defendant University acted arbitrarily, capriciously, or in bad faith in dismissing the plaintiff.

NOTES AND QUESTIONS

1. Note that the burden is placed on the student to show that the academic dismissal was arbitrary or capricious. If the student can show the court that it was, then the court will order the university to grant the student a fair hearing. Obviously, few students will be able to prove such an allegation. This is the primary reason for the desire to impose prior procedural due process requirements on public educational officials.

2. Later cases generally followed the *Connelly* rule, though there were refinements. *Woody v. Burns*, 188 So.2d 56 (Florida, 1966), involved a student who disclosed during registration that he had dropped a required course the previous semester, contrary to the wishes of his advisor. He had obtained the signature of another faculty member on his class assignment card. Woody's case was heard by the Faculty Discipline Committee, which found him guilty of "conduct unbecoming a University of Florida student in which he did knowingly cause a university record to be altered against the stated wishes of his Department Head." Woody was placed on disciplinary probation for the remainder of his undergraduate life at the institution. When he petitioned to register late for classes in the College of Architecture and Fine Arts, his petition was summarily denied. Woody protested, asserting that the department in effect expelled him from the College of Architecture and Fine Arts without notice and a hearing. The College of Architecture and Fine Arts countered that Woody's failure to take the required course constituted a defiance of the college requirements and resulted in his disqualifying himself from further attendance.

The appeals court ruled in favor of Woody, concluding that the department decision against him constituted disciplinary action, since the faculty committee from his department circumvented the disciplinary committee and imposed its own penalty on non-academic grounds. Thus, while the discipline committee had decided that Woody could continue as a student on probation, the department action precluded his doing so without offering him an opportunity to present his case.

The *Woody* decision is important because it requires institutions and academic departments to distinguish between academic and non-academic dismissals; it also suggests that institutions and academic departments develop a coordinated approach to these matters. As one commentator has cautioned,

> An institution does not have to conduct a hearing for every student dismissed for academic infraction. However, the machinery to meet the obligations of due process should be established and identified in anticipation of the rare situation in which arbitrary treatment is charged by the student.[35]

But others warn that the more detailed and explicit academic procedures are, the more likely institutional officials will have created a property interest requiring procedural safeguards. As one writer has noted,

> Those school districts that try to spell out standards for grades and promotions, for assignment to particular tracks or schools, have simultaneously engendered a legitimate reliance and hence a property interest on the part of students within their jurisdiction.[36]

In other words, like the compulsory school law, once a state creates a property interest, it cannot take away that right without procedural due process.

Of equal significance in this respect is the growing tendency of courts to hold both public and nonpublic institutions liable under contract law where policy statements are not followed. In *Lyons v. Salve Regina College,* 422 F.Supp. 1354 (D.R.I.1976), *rev'd* 565 F.2d 200 (1st Cir. 1977), Sheila Lyons, had received As and Bs in most of her classes, but she received a failure in one course after missing several sessions when she accompanied a sick friend to the hospital. The instructor, Lyons contended, had assured her that an incomplete would be the only result of her absence. However, she received an F. Lyons took the matter to the Grade Appeals Committee, pursuant to college regulations.

The Grade Appeals Committee recommended two-to-one that the failed course be converted to an incomplete, but the associate dean of the college overruled the recommendation, and the student was dropped from the nursing program. The lower court based its decision on the fact that the evidence indicated the decision of the hearing committee was final

---

35. William Toombs and Elaine DiBiase, "College Rules and Court Decisions: Notes on Student Dismissal" 2 *J.Coll. & Univ.L.* 355, Summer, 1975, at p. 365.

36. Wilkinson, *supra,* at p. 49.

unless appealed, and thus the dean was bound by the recommendation. The Court of Appeals for the First Circuit, however, took a different view and reversed the decision. Said Judge Caffrey for the court:

> There is nothing in the instant record to indicate that a student at Salve Regina College had any rational basis for believing the word 'recommendation' meant anything other than its normal, everyday meaning. * * * Nothing in the student manual suggests that a recommendation by the Committee could reasonably be thought to be anything more than an expression of the Committee's opinion * * *. (At pp. 202–203).

In 1978, the Supreme Court refused to review the decision by the appeals court.

In *Steinberg v. Chicago Medical School,* 371 N.E.2d 634 (1977), the Illinois Supreme Court ruled that a private university accepting an application fee has a contractual obligation to evaluate the student applicant on the basis of announced criteria. Since in this case the $15 application fee and its acceptance pursuant to a brochure describing the criteria on which applications would be judged constituted a contract and since the institution apparently evaluated the applications according to the monetary contributions made on behalf of those accepting admission, a legitimate cause of action existed. The question arises, however, how a rejected applicant can discover whether such criteria were in fact applied in situations where there is no advance indication of how decisions are reached. Should students have to resort to court suits or should institutions be required to offer every student who complains a hearing? The burdens the latter approach would impose on institutions such as medical schools which are heavily oversubscribed is obvious.

The student consumer movement suggests that the contract approach may be vigorously pursued in the future to challenge academic decisions in all sorts of educational institutions, particularly since other avenues seem closed off. Students are apt to charge that contractual provisions were not followed and/or that institutional action was arbitrary and capricious. So far, most courts have remanded these cases to determine if the student can prove the charges, rather than deciding for the student. Nevertheless, the student does gain a hearing, and this may be of significant importance, particularly at nonpublic institutions.

3. Later cases also addressed the question of the *criteria* used by educators in making academic decisions. For example, is a provision in an academic policy statement indicating that a student may be dismissed not only for academic failure but also for deficiencies in other areas valid? In *Wong v. Regents of the Univ. of California,* 93 Cal.Rptr. 502 (California, 1971), a California appeals court ruled that such a provision in a medical school manual was not unconstitutionally vague. Wong had been dismissed after his third year (which he had repeated) at the University of California Medical School. He contended in part that the phrase, "Students may be placed on probation or made subject to dismissal not only for scholastic deficiencies but also for deficiencies in other qualifications for these professions" was unconstitutionally vague. The court disagreed, noting that

"It would appear that there are many tests of medical student proficiency in addition to the successful passing of written course examinations." (At p. 832). Wong's appeal to the California Supreme Court was denied. A similar decision was reached in a 1974 federal district court case, *Depperman v. University of Ky.*, 371 F.Supp. 73 (E.D.Ky.1974), regarding a medical school policy statement that indicated "Any student may be denied permission to continue enrollment in the College of Medicine if, in the opinion of the Faculty Council, his knowledge, character, or mental or physical fitness cast grave doubts upon his potential capabilities as a physician."

In a 1977 Montana case, *Johnson v. Sullivan,* 571 P.2d 798, the Montana State Supreme Court ruled that the University of Montana Law School's system of computing cumulative grade point averages which takes into account a failing grade even if a student later passes the course does not violate students' due process rights. The suit was brought by Sandra Johnson, who failed out of law school in 1975. She claimed that had her second grade in the repeated constitutional law course been used without averaging in the earlier failure as was the practice elsewhere in the university, she could have continued her legal education. The law school dean testified that since a repeater, having taken the course before, would have a competitive edge on other students, the law school faculty concluded that averaging the two grades together would more accurately reflect a student's ability. Additionally, the law school noted the heavy responsibility placed on it to certify student competency, given the fact that the state's diploma privilege entitles a law graduate to be admitted to practice without taking the bar examination.

4. Cheating is usually considered a disciplinary, not an academic, matter. Thus notice and a hearing, at the minimum, are required at public educational institutions. Nevertheless, there are difficulties separating the disciplinary from the academic. For example, should a student who is expelled from a public community college because of a failure to submit a physical examination report, failure to report prior attendance at a hospital school of nursing and submit a transcript, and failure to attend classes on a regular basis be entitled to notice and a hearing? The federal district court in *Brookins v. Bonnell,* 362 F.Supp. 379 (E.D.Pa.1973), responded in the affirmative. The court initially commented that:

> This case is not the traditional disciplinary situation where a student violates the law or a school regulation by actively engaging in prohibited activities. Plaintiff has allegedly failed to act and comply with school regulations for admission and class attendance by passively ignoring these regulations. These alleged failures do not constitute misconduct in the sense that plaintiff is subject to disciplinary procedures. They do constitute misconduct in the sense that plaintiff was required to do something. (At p. 383).

Noting that factual discrepancies were clearly evident, the court concluded that a hearing should be afforded the student in this case.

Once a student has been formally admitted and satisfactorily completed a full semester of classes, justice would seem to require that the student be afforded a fair opportunity to establish that he had fully met the entrance requirements, or, if not, that there existed countervailing considerations (such as some fault on the part of the College) that would preclude dismissal. (At p. 384).

In *McDonald v. Trustees of the Univ. of Illinois,* 375 F.Supp. 95 (N.D. Ill.E.D.1974), aff'd, 503 F.2d 105 (7th Cir. 1974) three medical students were charged with cheating on an examination. The students were given an extensive evidentiary hearing before the College of Medicine Committee on Student Discipline. The College Committee found each guilty and recommended expulsion with the possibility of a readmission if they passed a similar examination a year hence. The students were expelled. They challenged the action, arguing that the evidence against them was circumstantial and did not meet the "substantial evidence" rule commonly used by courts in reviewing school disciplinary actions involving student rights of expression. The court asserted that the cheating case was different in that constitutionally protected behavior was not involved.

Their offense was unique to the academic community. The charges against them were heard by a tribunal composed of teachers and fellow students, peculiarly suited to hear the charge and weigh the evidence submitted in support of them. (At p. 104).

The court concluded that the "substantial evidence" criterion need not be present in the case. It was enough that there was "some evidence" to justify the expulsions. The court was unwilling to substitute its judgment for that of the primary fact finders but noted that "a state court sitting in review of its own state's educational institutions" might fashion a stricter standard of review.

5. The use of standardized and nonstandardized tests to determine student placement and promotion in the educational system has come under increasing challenge in recent years. Most of the challenges have arisen under the Equal Protection Clause in connection with race and sex discrimination, a topic to be discussed in Chapter Seven. Some commentators, however, believe that courts will increasingly be asked to rule on the use of tests under the Due Process Clause.[37] For example, as noted earlier, several cases have held that the parents of handicapped students are entitled to due process rights regarding the exclusion of their children from the public schools. Likewise, some courts are inclined to extend procedural guarantees to the parents of children who, based on test results, are subject to placement in special education classes. See, for example, *Cuyahoga County Ass'n for Retarded Children and Adults v. Essex,* 411 F.Supp. 46 (N.D.Ohio 1976), where the court directed that procedural safeguards be extended to situations involving placement of children in special education classes in Ohio. The Education for All Handicapped Children Act of 1975, 20 U.S.C.A. § 1401, which requires that all handicapped children are entitled to a free public education designed to meet their special needs, has served to bolster this line of cases.

---

37. See, for example, Paul L. Tractenberg and Elaine Jacoba "Pupil Testing: A Legal View" 59 *Phi Delta Kappan* 249, December, 1977.

More troublesome are the cases where tests are used to place normal children in curricular tracks or determine pupil promotion from one grade to another. Courts to date have by and large stayed out of these cases except where ethnic, racial, or sex discrimination issues may be involved. Nevertheless, as one commentator notes, court involvement has been extensive enough to suggest that educators "must exercise greater care and sensitivity in evaluating the educational potential and needs of students and in acting upon those evaluations" lest the courts "impose such a requirement." [38]

BOARD OF CURATORS OF THE UNIV. OF MO. v. CHARLOTTE HOROWITZ

Supreme Court of the United States, 1978.
435 U.S. 78, 98 S.Ct. 948, 55 L.Ed.2d 124.

Mr. Justice REHNQUIST delivered the opinion of the Court.

* * *

I

Respondent was admitted with advanced standing to the Medical School in the fall of 1971. During the final years of a student's education at the school, the student is required to pursue in "rotational units" academic and clinical studies pertaining to various medical disciplines such as Obstetrics-Gynecology, Pediatrics, and Surgery. Each student's academic performance at the School is evaluated on a periodic basis by the Council on Evaluation, a body composed of both faculty and students, which can recommend various actions including probation and dismissal. The recommendations of the Council are reviewed by the Coordinating Committee, a body composed solely of faculty members and must ultimately be approved by the Dean. Students are not typically allowed to appear before either the Council or the Coordinating Committee on the occasion of their review of the student's academic performance.

In the spring of respondent's first year of study, several faculty members expressed dissatisfaction with her clinical performance during a pediatrics rotation.

The faculty members noted that respondent's "performance was below that of her peers in all clinical patient-oriented settings," that she was erratic in her attendance at clinical sessions, and that she lacked a critical concern for personal hygiene. Upon the recommendation of the Council on Evaluation, respondent was advanced to her second and final year on a probationary basis.

Faculty dissatisfaction with respondent's clinical performance continued during the following year. For example, respondent's docent, or faculty adviser, rated her clinical skills as "unsatisfactory." In the middle of the year, the Council again reviewed respondent's academic progress and concluded that respondent should not be considered for graduation in June of that year; furthermore, the Council recommended that, absent "radical improvement," respondent be dropped from the School.

Respondent was permitted to take a set of oral and practical examinations as an "appeal" of the decision not to permit her to graduate. Pursuant to this "appeal," respondent spent a substantial portion of time with seven practicing physicians in the area who enjoyed a good reputation among their peers. The physi-

38. Tractenberg, *Id.*, at p. 253.

cians were asked to recommend whether respondent should be allowed to graduate on schedule and, if not, whether she should be dropped immediately or allowed to remain on probation. Only two of the doctors recommended that respondent be graduated on schedule. Of the other five, two recommended that she be immediately dropped from the school. The remaining three recommended that she not be allowed to graduate in May and be continued on probation pending further reports on her clinical progress. Upon receipt of these recommendations, the Council on Evaluation reaffirmed its prior position.

The Council met again in mid-May to consider whether respondent 'should be allowed to remain in school beyond June of that year. Noting that the report on respondent's recent surgery rotation rated her performance as "low-satisfactory," the Council unanimously recommended that "barring receipt of any reports that Miss Horowitz has improved radically, [she] not be allowed to re-enroll in the * * * School of Medicine." The Council delayed making its recommendation official until receiving reports on other rotations; when a report on respondent's emergency rotation also turned out to be negative, the Council unanimously reaffirmed its recommendation that respondent be dropped from the School. The Coordinating Committee and the Dean approved the recommendation and notified respondent, who appealed the decision in writing to the University's Provost for Health Sciences. The Provost sustained the School's actions after reviewing the record compiled during the earlier proceedings.

II

A

To be entitled to the procedural protections of the Fourteenth Amendment, respondent must in a case such as this demonstrate that her dismissal from the School deprived her of either a "liberty" or a "property" interest. Respondent has never alleged that she was deprived of a property interest. Because property interests are creatures of state law respondent would have been required to show at trial that her seat at the Medical School was a "property" interest recognized by Missouri state law. Instead, respondent argued that her dismissal deprived her of "liberty" by substantially impairing her opportunities to continue her medical education or to return to employment in a medically related field.

* * *

B

We need not decide, however, whether respondent's dismissal deprived her of a liberty interest in pursuing a medical career. Nor need we decide whether respondent's dismissal infringed any other interest constitutionally protected against deprivation without procedural due process. Assuming the existence of a liberty or property interest, respondent has been awarded at least as much due process as the Fourteenth Amendment requires. The School fully informed respondent of the faculty's dissatisfaction with her clinical progress and the danger that this posed to timely graduation and continued enrollment. The ultimate decision to dismiss respondent was careful and deliberate. These procedures were sufficient under the Due Process Clause of the Fourteenth Amendment. * * *

In *Goss v. Lopez* we held that due process requires, in connection with the suspension of a student from public school for disciplinary reasons, "that the student be given oral or written notice of the charges against him and, if he denies them, an explanation of the evidence the authorities have and an opportunity to present his side of the story." The Court of Appeals apparently read *Goss* as requiring some type of formal hearing at which respondent could defend her academic ability and performance. * * *

Since the issue first arose 50 years ago, state and lower federal courts have recognized that there are distinct differences between decisions to suspend or dismiss a student for disciplinary purposes and similar actions taken for academic reasons which may call for hearings in connection with the former but not the latter. * * *

* * *

Academic evaluations of a student, in contrast to disciplinary determinations, bear little resemblance to the judicial and administrative factfinding proceedings to which we have traditionally attached a full hearing requirement. In *Goss*, the school's decision to suspend the students rested on factual conclusions that the individual students had participated in demonstrations that had disrupted classes, attacked a police officer, or caused physical damage to school property. The requirement of a hearing, where the student could present his side of the factual issue, could under such circumstances "provide a meaningful hedge against erroneous action." The decision to dismiss respondent, by comparison, rested on the academic judgment of school officials that she did not have the necessary clinical ability to perform adequately as a medical doctor and was making insufficient progress toward that goal. Such a judgment is by its nature more subjective and evaluative than the typical factual questions presented in the average disciplinary decision. Like the decision of an individual professor as to the proper grade for a student in his course, the determination whether to dismiss a student for academic reasons requires an expert evaluation of cumulative information and is not readily adapted to the procedural tools of judicial or administrative decisionmaking.

Under such circumstances, we decline to ignore the historic judgment of educators and thereby formalize the academic dismissal process by requiring a hearing. The educational process is not by nature adversarial; instead it centers around a continuing relationship between faculty and students, "one in which the teacher must occupy many roles—educator, adviser, friend, and, at times, parent-substitute." This is especially true as one advances through the varying regimes of the educational system, and the instruction becomes both more individualized and more specialized. In *Goss*, this Court concluded that the value of some form of hearing in a disciplinary context outweighs any resulting harm to the academic environment. Influencing this conclusion was clearly the belief that disciplinary proceedings, in which the teacher must decide whether to punish a student for disruptive or insubordinate behavior, may automatically bring an adversarial flavor to the normal student-teacher relationship. The same conclusion does not follow in the academic context. We decline to further enlarge the judicial presence in the academic community and thereby risk deterioration of many beneficial aspects of the faculty-student relationship. * * *

III

In reversing the District Court on procedural due process grounds, the Court of Appeals expressly failed to "reach the substantive due process ground advanced by Horowitz." Respondent urges that we remand the cause to the Court of Appeals for consideration of this additional claim. In this regard, a number of lower courts have implied in dictum that academic dismissals from state institutions can be enjoined if "shown to be clearly arbitrary or capricious." Even assuming that the courts can review under such a standard an academic decision of a public educational institution, we agree with the District Court that no showing of arbitrariness or capriciousness has been made in this case. * * *

The judgment of the Court of Appeals is therefore reversed.

Mr. Justice POWELL, concurring.

*   *   *

Mr. Justice WHITE, concurring in part and concurring in the judgment.

*   *   *

The Court * * * assumes the existence of a protected interest, proceeds to classify respondent's expulsion as an "academic dismissal" and concludes that no hearing of any kind or any opportunity to respond is required in connection with such an action. Because I disagree with this conclusion, I feel constrained to say so and to concur only in the judgment.

As I see it, assuming a protected interest, respondent was at the minimum entitled to be informed of the reasons for her dismissal and to an opportunity personally to state her side of the story. Of course, she had all this, and more. I also suspect that expelled graduate or college students normally have the opportunity to talk with their expellers and that this sort of minimum requirement will impose no burden that is not already being shouldered and discharged by responsible institutions.

Mr. Justice MARSHALL, concurring in part and dissenting in part.

I agree with the Court that, "[a]ssuming the existence of a liberty or property interest, respondent has been awarded at least as much due process as the Fourteenth Amendment requires." I cannot join the Court's opinion, however, because it contains dictum suggesting that respondent was entitled to even less procedural protection than she received. I also differ from the Court in its assumption that characterization of the reasons for a dismissal as "academic" or "disciplinary" is relevant to resolution of the question of what procedures are required by the Due Process Clause. Finally, I disagree with the Court's decision not to remand to the Court of Appeals for consideration of respondent's substantive due process claim.

*   *   *

II

* * * According to our prior decisions, * * * three factors are of principal relevance in determining what process is due:

> "First, the private interest that will be affected by the official action; second, the risk of an erroneous deprivation of such interest through the procedures used, and the probable value, if any, of additional or substitute procedural safeguards; and finally, the Government's interest, including the function involved and the fiscal and administrative burdens that the additional or substitute procedural requirement would entail."

As the Court recognizes, the "private interest" involved here is a weighty one: "the deprivation to which respondent was subjected—dismissal from a graduate medical school—was more severe than the 10-day suspension to which the high school students were subjected in *Goss*." One example of the loss suffered by respondent is contained in the stipulation of facts: respondent had a job offer from the psychiatry department of another university to begin work in September 1973; the offer was contingent on her receiving the M. D. degree. * * *

Neither of the other two factors * * * justifies moving from a high level to the lower level of protection involved in *Goss*. There was at least some risk of error inherent in the evidence on which the dean relied in his meetings with and letters to respondent; * * *

Nor can it be said that the university had any greater interest in summary proceedings here than did the school in *Goss*. * * * Under these circumstances—with respondent having much more at stake than did the students in *Goss*, the administration at best having no more at stake, and the meetings between respondent and the dean leaving some possibility of erroneous dismissal —I believe that respondent was entitled to more procedural protection than is provided by "informal give-and-take" before the school could dismiss her.

The contours of the additional procedural protection to which respondent was entitled need not be defined in terms of the traditional adversarial system so familiar to lawyers and judges.

* * * In establishing the procedure under which respondent was evaluated separately by seven physicians who had had little or no previous contact with her, it appears that the medical school placed emphasis on obtaining "a fair and neutral and impartial assessment." In order to evaluate respondent, each of the seven physicians spent approximately one half-day observing her as she performed various clinical duties and then submitted a report on her performance to the dean. It is difficult to imagine a better procedure for determining whether the school's allegations against respondent had any substance to them. * * * I therefore believe that the appeal procedure utilized by respondent, together with her earlier notices from and meetings with the dean, provided respondent with as much procedural protection as the Due Process Clause requires.

III

The * * * resolution of this case under our traditional approach does not turn on whether the dismissal of respondent is characterized as one for "academic" or "disciplinary" reasons. In my view, the effort to apply such labels does little to advance the due process inquiry, as is indicated by examination of the facts of this case.

The minutes of the meeting at which it was first decided that respondent should not graduate contain the following:

"This issue is *not one of academic achievement*, but of performance, relationship to people and ability to communicate."

By the customary measures of academic progress, moreover, no deficiency was apparent at the time that the authorities decided respondent could not graduate; prior to this time, according to the stipulation of facts, respondent had received "credit" and "satisfactory grades" in all of her courses, including clinical courses.

It may nevertheless be true, as the Court implies, that the school decided that respondent's inadequacies in such areas as personal hygiene, peer and patient relations, and timeliness would impair her ability to be "a good medical doctor." Whether these inadequacies can be termed "pure academic reasons," as the Court calls them, is ultimately an irrelevant question, and one placing an undue emphasis on words rather than functional considerations. The relevant point is that respondent was dismissed largely because of her conduct, just as the students in *Goss* were suspended because of their conduct.

* * *

* * * a talismanic reliance on labels should not be a substitute for sensitive consideration of the procedures required by due process. When the facts disputed are of a type susceptible to determination by third parties, as the allegations about respondent plainly were, there is no more reason to deny all procedural protection to one who will suffer a serious loss than there was in *Goss v. Lopez*, and indeed there may be good reason to provide even more protection, * * *. A court's characterization of the reasons for a student's dismissal adds nothing to the effort to find procedures that are fair to the student and the school and that promote the elusive goal of determining the truth in a manner consistent with both individual dignity and society's limited resources.

IV

While I agree with the Court that respondent received adequate procedural due process, I cannot join the Court's judgment because it is based on resolution of an issue never reached by the Court of Appeals. That court, taking a properly limited view of its role in constitutional cases, refused to offer dictum on respondent's substantive due process claim when it decided the case on procedural due process grounds.   *   *   *

I would reverse the judgment of the Court of Appeals and remand for further proceedings.

Mr. Justice BLACKMUN, with whom Mr. Justice BRENNAN joins, concurring in part and dissenting in part.

*   *   *

NOTES AND QUESTIONS

1. A critical question surrounding the majority opinion is whether the five Justices believe *any* kind of due process procedure is *ever* required in student academic disputes at public institutions. Note that the majority opinion does not stop with noting that Ms. Horowitz had sufficient due process prior to dismissal but goes on to suggest that academic decision making "is not readily adapted to the procedural tools of judicial or administrative decisionmaking." Justice Rehnquist emphasizes that the Court refuses to "further enlarge the judicial presence in the academic community;" he even is reluctant to endorse the arbitrary and capricious standard used by lower courts.

It is this aspect of the decision which most troubles both Justices White and Marshall. Justice Rehnquist acknowledges in a footnote (not excerpted) that the harm Ms. Horowitz suffered was more substantial than the 10-day suspension in *Goss*, but states that "the severity of the deprivation is only one of several factors that must be weighed in deciding the exact due process owed."

Also troubling Justice Marshall is what he sees as the similarity between *Goss* and *Horowitz*: the fact that conduct or conduct-related behavior in both cases resulted in sanctions against the students. The majority, however, notes in another footnote (not excerpted) that personal hygiene and timeliness are academic criteria not readily adapted to fact-finding procedures. In his concurring opinion, Justice Powell specifically addressed Justice Marshall's concern by stating that "It is well to bear in mind that respondent was attending a medical school where competence in clinicial courses is as much a prerequisite to graduation as satisfactory grades in other courses." Thus, the exercise of skills and techniques in actual practice in the *Horowitz* case is quite different from the personal misbehavior of the students in *Goss*.

In their brief concurring and dissenting opinion, Justices Blackmun and Brennan refuse to take sides, through they agree with Justice Marshall that a remand on the substantive due process issue would be appropriate.

Horowitz thus finds at least two Justices, and possibly as many as four, advocating an extension of the *Goss*-type informal due process procedures to academic disputes.

2. Equally interesting is the majority's handling of *Greenhill v. Bailey*. In a footnote (not excerpted), the majority simply state the *Greenhill* holding, noting that "in the court's (The *Greenhill* court) opinion"

the communication of Greenhill's dismissal to the Liaison Committee of the Association of American Medical Colleges removed the case from the typical academic dismissal situation and implicated a liberty interest, thus necessitating greater procedural safeguards. Justice Rehnquist clearly put distance between the Supreme Court and the *Greenhill* decision by refusing to endorse it. How the Supreme Court stands on the liberty interest argument is thus unclear.

In a part of the opinion not excerpted, Justice Rehnquist notes that in *Bishop v. Wood*, 426 U.S. 341 (1976), the Court ruled that the dismissal of a policeman without a hearing created no liberty interest problem. But in that opinion, the Supreme Court stated that since the reasons for the decision were not made public, "it cannot properly form the basis for a claim that petitioner's interest in his 'good name, honor, or integrity' was thereby impaired." (At p. 348).

3. The implications of the *Horowitz* decision were clear enough to the attorneys for Ms. Horowitz. The attorney who represented her said the decision gives medical educators "carte blanche in their dealings with students." He said the court's characterization of her dismissal as based on academic performance and not her appearance and sex * paves the way for calling any deficiency "academic" and thus avoiding due process requirements for disciplinary decisions.[39]

Justice Marshall expressed similar concerns about labeling, noting in a footnote (not excerpted) that "The Court's reliance on labels * * * may give those school administrators who are reluctant to accord due process to their students an excuse for not doing so." Do you agree?

4. In a case contemporary to that of *Horowitz, Ross v. Pennsylvania State Univ.*, 445 F.Supp. 147 (M.Pa.1978), the district court concluded that Ross had a property interest in his education since he had a reasonable expectation that if he performed satisfactorily and paid required fees, he would receive the degree he sought. Ross was a masters degree candidate in ceramic sciences. Characterizing the relationship between Ross and Penn State as contractual, the court concluded that the relationship was sufficient to support a property interest. And that interest, in turn, was sufficient to require a hearing where the decision to terminate the student as in Ross' case was based in part on motivation and attitude, and not strictly on academic achievement. A hearing would allow the student an opportunity to explain any reason for his poor scholarship. The court specifically *excluded* the situation where termination is based exclusively on failure to achieve a certain grade point average because "no purpose in a hearing would be served." Do you agree?

The U. S. Court of Appeals for the Tenth Circuit came to a similar conclusion in a 1975 case, *Gaspar v. Bruton*, 513 F.2d 843. There a practi-

---

* One of Ms. Horowitz's supporters stated in a *New York Times* article that Ms. Horowitz had unquestionable academic achievements but she is "a bright New York Jewish woman who didn't conform to the accepted image of how a doctor should look and act." Nadine Brozan, "Woman's Ouster by Medical School Reaches Supreme Court," *New York Times*, November 7, 1977, at p. 48. © by the *New York Times* Company. Reprinted by permission.

39. *Higher Education Daily*, March 7, 1978, p. 5.

cal nurse student had been dismissed from a public vocational-technical school for deficiencies in her clinical work. She filed suit, alleging that her dismissal deprived her of due process rights under the Fourteenth Amendment. The Tenth Circuit, relying on *Goss*, concluded that "school authorities, in order to satisfy Due Process prior to termination or suspension of a student for deficiencies in meeting minimum academic performance, need only advise the student with respect to such deficiencies in any form. All that is required is that the student be made aware prior to termination of his failure or impending failure to meet those standards." (At p. 851). The circuit court affirmed the lower court decision that Gaspar's constitutional rights had not been violated in that she had been informed of her academic status prior to dismissal. In *Horowitz* Justice Rehnquist referred twice to *Gaspar* but did not discuss the case or indicate whether the Supreme Court endorsed its reasoning.

Note that the attorneys for Charlotte Horowitz did not make a property argument but chose instead to focus on the liberty interest. Would the results have been different had they chosen to follow the *Ross* approach? After the *Horowitz* decision, do either of these cases still have precedential value or are they in effect mooted?

5.   HYPOTHETICAL: *The Case of Susan Student*

Susan Student is a first semester senior at Minnefornia State College, majoring in secondary education. Minnefornia State has a regulation which states "all secondary education majors must take a required sequence of four (4) courses in education and must receive a minimum of 2.0 GPA in each course before being eligible to undertake a student teaching assignment."

Susan has received the minimum 2.0 GPA in each of the first three courses. She is now completing the fourth course of the required sequence. The instructor did not hand out a syllabus for the course. School policy recommends a syllabus, but one is not required.

Susan didn't enjoy her fourth course. She found the subject-matter repetitive and the instructor hard to follow. Being reticent by nature, Susan didn't often participate in class discussion, though the instructor occasionally said class participation was welcomed and emphasized the point by stating "assertive personalities make the best teachers because they can control a class better." Susan took a passive role in the course, though her rate of attendance was high and she faithfully completed all the reading material.

On the final exam, Susan scored a C+ (2.5), but she nevertheless received a D (1.0) in the course. Startled and angered by her course grade, she confronted the instructor. He said that he counted class participation as "an important factor, one of several, in figuring a final grade." He added, "I guess class participation might be something like 30 percent of the grade, though my grading system is largely subjective." He added, "I really question whether you are ready for student teaching, Susan. Maybe you should find another career goal."

Furious with what she regarded as an entirely unfair grading system and unprofessional behavior by the teacher, she went to the chairperson of the Educational Department. The Education Department had no formal policy to review student complaints about grades. The chairperson agreed to set up an ad hoc committee of himself and two faculty members from the department to review the matter. After reviewing Susan's file and listening to her complaint, the committee backed the instructor. Both the vice president for academic affairs and the campus president endorsed the committee's action.

Susan decided, with the encouragement of fellow students, to take her case to court. "It was a kangeroo court," she said. "I had no due process rights at all. In fact, they even reviewed my whole record before letting me talk with them. I think this was totally uncalled for."

———

Susan and the college have stipulated that no sex discrimination issue is involved. Based on previous discussion and cases, what arguments would you make for each side? If you were to decide this hypothetical case, what decision would you reach?

IV. SUMMARY

This chapter once again illustrates the complexity involved in judicial resolution of disputes involving students. To help the reader sort out the variables impinging on judicial decision-making in this context, the figure from Chapter Three is in part reintroduced on the following page. In place of factors related to the concept of freedom and to interpreting the First Amendment we have inserted variables related to defining justice and interpreting the Fourteenth Amendment Due Process Clause. As before, we caution that this figure is not a predictive device but is to be used as a means of outlining those factors which relate to the involvement of the judiciary in the educational environment—here in the interest of student due process rights.

In this chapter various ways the concept of justice can be defined were first described. Many in our society conceive of justice as a means of preserving order, while others view justice as "fair treatment" of the accused. Under the later interpretation, what is fair treatment will vary, dependent upon the characteristics of the accused and situational circumstances. Generally, conservatives are aligned with the justice-as-order viewpoint, while liberals are more inclined to embrace justice as social welfare.

Due process, the legal means to justice in American society, is a nebulous concept susceptible to any number of operational definitions. Generally, courts have in recent years been more inclined to define due process as synonymous with specific procedure, leaving substantive issues to the original decision maker. The high-water mark for procedural due process for the accused in the political and social setting was *Miranda v. Arizona* in 1966; since then, the Supreme Court has shifted more towards the Crime Control Model. The 1960s also saw the far-reaching decisions of *In re Gault* and *Goldberg v. Kelly,* which extended procedural protection to the juvenile court process and to public administrative processes involving the termination of welfare benefits. Since then, some retreat has been evident.

Figure 5–1: Judicial Support for Student
Due Process Rights

DIRECTION OF INFLUENCE

		Promoting	Retarding	Uncertain
INFLUENCING VARIABLES	Value Position on Individual and Government	Support for Rights of the Accused	Support for Societal Order	
	Value Position on Justice	Procedural Justice Justice as Social Welfare Justice as Egalitarianism	Justice as Social Order	
	Approach to Due Process	Procedural Due Process		Substantive Due Process
	Orientation to Role of Court	Activism	Restraintism	Neutrality
	Orientation to Educational Environment	Youth Entitled to Rights Non-Deferral to Educational Professionals View Educational Mission as Training-Ground for Democracy	Youth Not Entitled to Rights Deferral to Educational Professionals View Educational Mission as: —Inculcating Respect for Authority	Role of Social Science Research Rulings of Other Courts Situational Factors: —Type of School —Level of Schooling —Facts of Case

[B9655]

In the public educational setting, courts have also been active in extending procedural due process protections to students, beginning with the landmark case of *Dixon v. Alabama State Board* in 1961. The high-water mark paralleling *Miranda* and *Goldberg* was *Goss v. Lopez* in 1975, when the Supreme Court concluded that students are entitled to informal due process procedures prior to temporary suspensions. We have chosen this case for an intensive examination in the next chapter of how our legal system operates.

Since *Goss,* however, both the growing concern for order in the educational environment and increasing court awareness of the uniqueness of schools and colleges as special-purpose institutions appear to have curtailed further judicial involvement on the side of the student. Thus, in 1977 the Supreme Court upheld corporal punishment in public schools without any procedural due process safeguards and in 1978 refused to extend procedural due process protections to students threatened with academic dismissal.

Despite the contemporary judicial emphasis in both the political and social setting and the educational setting on procedure, courts have always reserved the right to involve themselves where decisions by public officials are arbitrary or unreasonable. Substantive due process is thus not dead. As one commentator has noted, "The quest for justice is ultimately substantive as well as procedural, responsive to the entitlements that underlie relationships as well as to the quality of the relationships themselves." [40]

In education, the role of substantive due process is significant, since courts are reluctant to impose procedures on decision-making by professionals, particularly where wholly academic concerns are involved. Students hoping for judicial involvement on their side in academic disputes have the burden of proving to the satisfaction of judges that the decisions were arbitrary or capricious.

In the view of most judges, then, justice for students is closely related to the nature and purpose of educational institutions; for this reason, judicial involvement on the side of the accused student has been more restricted than for the accused in the political and social setting.

---

40. David L. Kirp, "Proceduralism and Bureaucracy: Due Process in the School Set-   ting" 280 *Stan.L.Rev.* 841, May, 1976, at p. 875.

Chapter Six

"GOSS v. LOPEZ:

"ANATOMY OF A STUDENT RIGHTS CASE" *

Goss v. Lopez, a doctrinal student rights decision included in the previous chapter, has been selected to illustrate how a civil case is processed through the court system. *Goss* is an interesting case partly because of the facts involved and partly because of the arguments advanced by both sides. The 1975 Supreme Court's five-to-four decision was—and remains—controversial. *Goss* is also significant in that it represents the high water mark to date for legal involvement in student due process matters.

The case began in February, 1971, during student disturbances at several Columbus, Ohio, public schools and culminated in the Supreme Court decision in 1975. A chart outlining the sequence of events during this five year period will be presented later in the chapter to help the reader follow the development of the case. While a number of students eventually brought suits against school officials, we will concentrate only on the principal plaintiff, Dwight Lopez.**

I. THE GRIEVANCE

A. Events Leading to the Law Suit

The dispute involving Dwight Lopez arose over a cancellation by school officials of black student use of the school auditorium during Black History Week. Some of the black students responded by vandalizing the school cafeteria. In light of these disturbances and concurrent black-white confrontations in the community, the principal of Central High School, Mr. Calvin Park, suspended classes. Other schools, like Central High School, were also affected by racial tensions during this period, and similar situations developed, resulting in school disruptions and student suspensions. This gave rise to the joint suit by Dwight's parents and the parents of the other students. When Mr. Park announced on February 26th that classes were suspended, Dwight, like the other students, left school. That same day, Mr. Park telephoned Dwight to notify him that he was being suspended from school indefinitely. Dwight was not told why he was suspended. The follow-up letter below confirmed in writing what Mr. Park had said by telephone.

---

* Note: The principal attorneys who argued this case—Denis Murphy and Peter Roos for plaintiffs, and Thomas Bustin for defendants—assisted in the preparation of this chapter. Much of the case record was provided by the Harvard Center for Law and Education.

** Originally, two suits were brought by two groups of students. Both suits were similar. Only the one described in this chapter was actually litigated.

CENTRAL HIGH SCHOOL

75 Washington Boulevard, Columbus, Ohio 43215

February 26, 1971

Mr. and Mrs. Manuel Lopez
831 Franklin Ave.
Columbus, Ohio

Dear Mr. and Mrs. Lopez:

We have had a continued problem in school for several days and today a group of students disrupted our complete school program.

Dwight was in the group and we need to have a personal conference with you and Dwight to determine what the problems may be.

Please keep him at home until a conference can be arranged. This will take some time. We will be communicating with you.

Respectfully,

CALVIN PARK
Principal

On March 1 Dwight's parents were advised to appear at a special Board of Education meeting on March 8th, and on March 5 they were notified that an appointment had been set for them with the Director of Pupil Personnel for the Columbus school system, Mr. H. M. Williams, also for March 8th.

Dwight and his mother went to the Board of Education offices on the 8th, but were prevented from entering the building by demonstrations at the door. Later that same day Mrs. Lopez and her daughter, Mrs. Alma Robinson, called the Office of Pupil Personnel but were unable to talk with school officials. Mrs. Robinson wrote a letter on March 22nd to the School Board. On March 25th the following reply was received from Mr. Williams.

March 24, 1971

Mrs. Eileen Lopez
1112 Miller Avenue
Columbus, Ohio 43206

Dear Mrs. Lopez:

I have received a letter from your daughter, Mrs. Alma Robinson, pertaining to your son, Dwight. She was inquiring as to the status of Dwight and his returning to school in Columbus.

As you no doubt recall, I had scheduled an appointment with you and Dwight on March 8, 1971 at 8:30 a. m. The purpose of this conference was to discuss various possibilities relating to Dwight's future educational plans.

This appointment was not kept nor did I receive from you a request to set up another conference. Since Dwight is 19 years of age and is no longer of compulsory school age, I thought that possibly you had made other plans for Dwight.

In regards to Dwight's placement in a Columbus School, permission is granted for him to enroll in Adult Day School, 272 S. Nelson Road, immediately. Waiver of fees is being recommended.

Sincerely,

H. M. WILLIAMS, *Director*
Pupil Personnel

While Dwight had not requested a transfer, he did not return to Central High School. A year later Dwight finished high school by attending night classes at Columbus Adult Night School. At no time had he been advised of the specific reasons for his prior suspension, and no hearing into the matter had ever been conducted by Central High School.

NOTES AND QUESTIONS

1. Do you think the letter of February 26 adequately informs Dwight why he was being suspended?

2. What point is Mr. Williams making in his comment about Dwight's age in the letter of March 24th?

3. How strong a case does Dwight have? Can you foresee the issues which will eventually be highlighted by the attorneys?

B. Pre-Trial Clash of Interests: The Plaintiffs' Side

Dwight and his mother were not the only ones distressed by events occurring in the Columbus City Schools. The Columbus Branch of the NAACP had the names of others who believed they were being unfairly disciplined by school officials. Eventually officials at the local branch of the NAACP asked parents and students to come to their offices for a conference. They also asked I. W. Barkan, a Columbus attorney who had frequently represented the NAACP, to get some lawyers together to listen to the students' complaints. Mr. I. W. Barkan of that firm asked Denis J. Murphy, a partner in a firm with offices in the same building as Mr. Barkan, to go to a meeting at the offices of the NAACP. Mr. Murphy had a background in civil rights litigation since he had represented the Housing Opportunity Center of Metropolitan Columbus, a fair housing agency funded under the federal Model Cities program.

The lawyers interviewed the parents and students several days after most of the suspensions had been meted out. Mr. Murphy invited Ken Curtin, then a lawyer employed by the Legal Aid Society of Columbus, to assist in the case. Mr. Curtin had successfully litigated public school issues involving freedom of speech and continuing education for pregnant students in the federal district court, and Mr. Murphy knew of his continuing interest in students rights.

After affidavits had been taken from the students and parents describing their side of the dispute, Mr. Murphy and Mr. Curtin discussed strategy. They had reservations about challenging the action of school officials because they believed suspensions without a prior hearing for a minimal period were probably constitutionally permissible during periods of emergency. They were concerned that the court might conclude that the school officials were justified in their actions. On the other hand, the affidavits pointed out how seriously the suspensions had affected the students. One of the students said she was arrested on her way home from school as she walked past another school where a disturbance was taking place. She was taken to juvenile detention home but soon released. When her mother called the school to determine her daughter's status, she was advised that her daughter had been arrested on her way home from school. She was also told that her daughter had been suspended from school.

Because of their commitment to justice and to the black community, the two attorneys resolved to go ahead with a challenge to the suspensions, even though they admitted in correspondence with the authors that "factually, the case was not the best." They selected Dwight Lopez for the lead plaintiff, partly because he made an articulate witness and partly because they felt the case might become a landmark decision and they "liked the sound of Lopez in the title."

Their first task was to determine the legal authority for the actions of the school administrators. They found that the grant of authority to suspend students from the public schools was contained in Section 3313.66 of the Ohio Revised Code. That section read as follows:

"§ 3313.66 Suspension or expulsion.

The superintendent of schools of a city or exempted village, the executive head of a local school district, or the principal of a public school may suspend a pupil from school for not more than ten days. Such superintendent or executive head may expel a pupil from school. Such superintendent, executive head, or principal shall within twenty-four hours after the time of expulsion or suspension, notify the parent or guardian of the child, and the clerk of the board of education in writing of such expulsion or suspension including the reasons therefor. The pupil or the parent, or guardian, or custodian of a pupil so expelled may appeal such action to the board of education at any meeting of the board and shall be permitted to be heard against the expulsion. At the request of the pupil, or his parent, guardian, custodian, or attorney, the board may hold the hearing in executive session but may act upon the expulsion only at a public meeting. The board may, by a majority vote of its full membership, reinstate such pupil. No pupil shall be suspended or expelled from any school beyond the current semester."

In accordance with this statute the Administrative Guide of the Columbus Public Schools outlined the policy of the District with respect to student discipline. Section 1010 of the Administrative Guide read:

ADMINISTRATIVE GUIDE

Section 1010—DISCIPLINE OF PUPILS

1010.01—Disciplinary measures shall be reasonable and appropriate to the nature of the misbehavior of the offending pupil and in accordance with the holdings of Ohio courts of law.

1010.02—Although no statute makes a specific mention of corporal punishment, Ohio courts have held that a teacher or principal may administer such punishment. In the Columbus Public Schools, corporal punishment may be used as a last resort and after all other means of punishment have proved ineffectual. Corporal punishment must be administered in the presence of at least one adult witness.

1010.03—Under no circumstances shall punishment be cruel or excessive or administered from malice or passion.

1010.04—Pupils may be suspended or expelled from school in accordance with the provisions of Section 3313.66 of the Revised Code.

Note that Section 1010.04 conveys the right to suspend or expel pupils in accord with the state law. The following section of the Columbus Schools Policy Statement on Discipline, a local document based on 1010.04, placed final responsibility on the principal for maintaining and administering a system of school discipline.

The principal, by virtue of his position of authority, shall keynote the approach to good discipline in his school. In this vital area of school affairs, he and his staff shall work cooperatively on problems of behavior. The administrator may deem it best to use forms of punishment not available to the teacher, such as corporal punishment or suspension. The final decision on the appropriate form of punishment to be employed rests with the administrator, since such responsibility has been delegated to him by the Board of Education.

After further investigation, the attorneys concluded that there was no evidence that the school had acted contrary to school policy or to state law. In fact the laws granted a good deal of leeway to school officials. They concluded that this leeway could operate to deprive students of their constitutional rights of due process under the Fourteenth Amendment to the Constitution. It was this approach which they decided to take in this case.

(1) Researching the Law

The basis for suit would be an old but revered federal law, 42 U.S.C.A. § 1983. This statute is derived from a law passed after the Civil War as part of Congress' efforts to enforce the terms of the Fourteenth Amendment by providing a civil remedy for wrongs committed by state officials. Note that the Thirteenth, Fourteenth, and Fifteenth Amendments have final sections giving Congress the power to enforce the substantive provisions by "appropriate legislation." The federal law referred to here is an example of the use of that section. The law can be found in 42 U.S.C.A. § 1983. The provision reads as follows:

§ 1983. Civil action for deprivation of rights

Every person who, under color of any statute, ordinance, regulation, custom, or usage, of any State or Territory, subjects, or causes to be subjected, any citizen of the United States or other person within the jurisdiction thereof to the deprivation of any rights, privileges, or immunities secured by the Constitution and laws, shall be liable to the party injured in an action at law, suit in equity, or other proper proceeding for redress.

While the law is certainly short enough, this provision has been repeatedly interpreted over the years such that the commentary and referenced cases in the commercially produced annotated versions of the United States Code run into the hundreds of pages. The lawyer using this statute must, of course, be familiar with relevant holdings relating to his or her particular situation.

Using legal treatises and encyclopedias, law review articles, the federal and state reporters, and other tools of legal research,[1] the lawyer investigates the development of the law as it pertains to his case. With this task completed, the lawyer is ready to decide the next step. One possibility, of course, is to attempt settlement outside of court. The attorneys, for example, could have inquired whether school officials would be willing to reinstate Dwight, remove any penalties against him, and change the suspension policy. Since the matter involved a number of students and a state law, the matter was largely beyond the power of the school officials to resolve, assuming they would have consented to modify their actions and procedures. The attorneys would then decide whether to take legal action against the school policy and the supportive state law or to drop the case altogether.

Suits under 42 U.S.C.A. § 1983 are particularly important because they challenge the actions of state officials acting under color of state law. They thus raise a "federal question" under Article III, Section 2 of the United States Constitution and are appropriately a subject of federal judicial power.

Under its power to control the functioning of lower federal courts in accord with the provisions of Article III, Section 2, Congress has provided that federal district courts shall hear disputes under 42 U.S.C.A. § 1983. This declaration is found in another statute, 28 U.S.C.A. § 1343(3).

At the time the *Goss v. Lopez* suit was brought, Congress stipulated that because of their importance, cases like *Goss* which demand an injunction against further enforcement of a state statute required a hearing before a three-judge district court. This stipulation was found in 28 U.S.C.A. § 2281 (this section has since been repealed). According to § 2281, a three-judge court is necessary for securing both temporary and permanent injunctions against continued enforcement of state statutes. Other sections cited in § 2281 describe the composition and procedures of the three-judge district court, and outline the power of these tribunals to issue "declaratory judgments" to determine what the correct reading of the law is. Three-judge federal courts also have the power to provide remedies in addition to declaratory judgments where warranted.

Finally, Rule 23(a) of the Federal Rules of Civil Procedures provides for class action suits whereby the original plaintiff or plaintiffs may sue

---

1. See Appendix C for an outline of the rudiments of legal research.

on behalf of the entire group of others suffering the same problem. This eliminates the time lag and inconvenience inherent in a case-by-case approach.

(2) Filing the Complaint

Having thoroughly researched the law pertaining to the suspensions and to relevant legal procedure, Mr. Curtin and Mr. Murphy, with Mr. Barkan as trial counsel,* formally notified the court and the school officials of their intention to sue by filing a "complaint." The complaint must be filed with the court and "served" upon the defendants so that they can be informed of the action against them and prepare counter-action. The complaint sets forth the plaintiff's claim and asserts the jurisdiction of the court to hear the claim. The rules pertaining to drawing up the complaint and seeing that it is served on the defendants are complex. All we need to note here is that the complaint is not a legal treatise or "brief" complete with cited cases and statutes. Rather, it is a legal document setting forth the plaintiff's claim. The accompanying memorandum of law, however, lends necessary supporting legal weight to the complaint.

Reprinted below are relevant parts of the complaint filed on March 31, 1971, by plaintiffs' attorneys. We have omitted the list of named plaintiffs and defendants, concentrating only on the principal plaintiff, Dwight Lopez, and the principal defendant, Herbert Williams, and later, Norval Goss.

IN THE UNITED STATES DISTRICT COURT
FOR THE SOUTHERN DISTRICT OF OHIO
EASTERN DIVISION

CIVIL ACTION NO. 71–67

Mrs. Eileen Lopez,
parent and next friend
of Dwight A. Lopez, a minor
1112 Melter Avenue
Columbus, Ohio 43206

and * * *

on behalf of themselves and all
others similarly situated

vs. *Plaintiffs,*

Herbert M. Williams, individually
and as Director of the Department
of Pupil Personnel of the
Columbus Public Schools
270 East State Street
Columbus, Ohio 43215
and * * *

Defendants.

* A designation formally required by local federal court rules.

Complaint

1.   This is an action for injunctive and declaratory relief authorized by Title 42 U.S.C. Section 1983 to secure rights, privileges and immunities established by the First and Fourteenth Amendment to the Constitution of the United States.

Jurisdiction

2.   The jurisdiction of this Court is invoked under Title 28 U.S.C. Section 1343(3) providing for original jurisdiction of this Court in suits authorized by Title 42 U.S.C. Section 1983 and under Title 28 U.S.C. Sections 2201 and 2202 relating to declaratory judgments.

3.   Plaintiffs respectfully request that a three-judge Court be convened pursuant to Title 28 U.S.C. Section 2281 in that plaintiffs seek to enjoin the enforcement of State Statute by an officer of the State on the grounds that said statute and its implementation violate the Constitution of the United States.

Class Action

4.   Plaintiffs bring this action on their own behalf and on behalf of all other students residing in the City of Columbus who are similarly situated and affected by the policy and usage complained of herein.   The members of the class on whose behalf plaintiffs sue are so numerous as to make it impracticable to bring them all individually before this Court. There are common questions of law and fact involved and plaintiffs' claim is typical of the claim of the entire class.   Plaintiffs fairly and adequately represent and will protect the interest of the class.   Defendants have acted on grounds generally applicable to plaintiffs' class.   The questions of law and fact common to the members of the class predominate over any questions affecting only individual members and a class action is superior to other available methods for the fair and efficient adjudication of the controversy.

*   *   *

Claim of Dwight Lopez

11.   Mrs. Eileen Lopez is the parent and natural guardian of Dwight Lopez, a minor, 19 years of age on whose behalf she has filed suit.   Dwight Lopez is in the 12th grade at Central High School.

12.   Lopez was suspended without prior hearing on the 26th of February by defendant Calvin Park, principal of Central High School.   Lopez was advised of the suspension in writing by a letter mailed to him and received February 27, 1971.   No return date was fixed in his suspension.   On March 1, 1971 Mr. and Mrs. Lopez were advised that they would have to appear at the Board of Education before Dwight Lopez could return to school.

13.   On March 5, 1971 the School Board acting through defendant Herbert M. Williams delivered a letter to Mr. and Mrs. Lopez advising them to appear March 8, 1971 at 8:30 A.M.   Because of a demonstration being conducted at the Board of Education offices that morning neither Dwight

or Mr. and Mrs. Lopez appeared at the Board as scheduled. No new date has been fixed for appearance before the Board. Dwight Lopez has not been advised of the complete and specific reasons for his suspension, and no hearing has been held concerning being readmitted to Central High School, and he is being denied an opportunity to continue his education there.

14. Following March 8, 1971 Mrs. Lopez called the School Board on several occasions, as did her daughter, Alma Robinson, but no new date was set for hearing. Mrs. Robinson thereafter wrote to the School Board on March 22, 1971 and by letter dated March 25, 1971 received March 26, 1971 from defendant, H. M. Williams, Mrs. Lopez was advised that since Dwight had missed his appointment March 8, 1971 and had made no attempt to make a new appointment, he was granted permission to report to the adult day school at Nelson Road.

15. To the date of the filing of this Complaint no hearing has ever been held in Dwight Lopez's case and he has not been advised in writing the reason for his suspension or expulsion from the regular day school of Central High School.

* * *

38. Defendants have acted pursuant to Section 3313.66 of the Ohio Revised Code, the Administrative Guide of the Columbus Public Schools, and the Policy Statement in Discipline of the Columbus Public Schools none of which provides any standards for the exercise of school administrator's disciplinary authority or fair proceedings through which a student has an opportunity to challenge the proposed disciplinary measure.

39. On information and belief, there are no other school rules or regulations relied upon by defendants as authorized aforesaid disciplinary actions.

40. Under color of State law Defendants have acted intentionally, deliberately, and knowingly in violation of the First and Fourteenth Amendments to the Constitution of the United States and Title 42 U.S.C. Section 1983, rendering defendants liable to plaintiffs in law and equity.

Cause of Action

41. Section 3313.66 of the Ohio Revised Code, Section 1010.04 of the Administrative Guide of the Columbus Public Schools, and the Columbus Policy Statement in Discipline provide no ascertainable standards of conduct for violation of which high school students may be suspended and expelled. Said statute, Administrative Guide, and Policy Statement are unconstitutional because their vagueness and overbreadth deprive students of rights secured under the First and Fourteenth Amendments to the Constitution of the United States.

42. Section 3313.66 of the Ohio Revised Code, Section 1010.04 of the Administrative Guide of the Columbus Public Schools, and the Columbus Policy Statement in Discipline authorize the suspension and expulsion of high school students without prior notice and a hearing with such minimal rights as a written statement of the reasons for the proposed discipline,

the right to cross-examination, the right to pre-hearing discovery procedure, the right to submit relevant evidence and the right to be represented by counsel. Said statute, Administrative Guide, and Policy Statement are unconstitutional because their lack of procedural safeguards deprives students of rights secured under the Fourteenth Amendments to the Constitution of the United States.

43. In the instant case defendants have effected suspensions, expulsions, and involuntary transfers of students without prior hearings which comport with minimal standards of due process. Defendants actions have been arbitrary, unequal and discriminatory in violation of plaintiffs rights secured by the First and Fourteenth Amendments to the Constitution of the United States.

Prayer for Relief

44. Wherefore, plaintiffs respectfully pray that this Court:

(1) Assume jurisdiction of this cause and convene a three-judge district Court to determine the controversy pursuant to Title 28 U.S.C. Section 2281.

(2) Enter a preliminary and a final order pursuant to Title 28 U.S.C. Sections 2201 and 2202 and Rule 57 of the Federal Rules of Civil Procedure declaring that Section 3313.66 of the Ohio Revised Code is unconstitutional.

(3) Enter a preliminary and a final order pursuant to Title 28 U.S.C. Sections 2201 and 2202 and Rule 57 of the Federal Rules of Civil Procedure declaring that the Administrative Guide and the Policy Statement on Discipline of the Columbus Public Schools insofar as they relate to suspensions and expulsions are unconstitutional.

(4) Issue a preliminary and a permanent injunction restraining the defendant, their successors in office, agents and employees from further enforcement of the unconstitutional provisions of their discipline policy and Section 3313.66 of the Ohio Revised Code.

(5) Issue a preliminary and a permanent injunction ordering that plaintiffs' school records be expunged of any notation of the aforementioned suspensions and that plaintiffs be allowed to make up any school work or tests occurring during their absence from school.

(6) Maintain jurisdiction of this cause until such time as defendants establish a hearing procedure in conformity with the requirements of the Fourteenth Amendment to the Constitution of the United States.

(7) Award plaintiffs their costs and disbursements incurred herein together with such further alternative relief as may seem just and equitable.

* * *

The accompanying memorandum of law presented plaintiffs' arguments and supporting cases, both of which are reasserted frequently later in the case. They are not excerpted here. It is sufficient at this point to note that the memorandum argued why a three-judge court is appropriate;

why a class action should be maintained; and specifically how the Ohio law, school policy, and the action of school officials violated plaintiffs' rights. A supplementary memorandum was later filed to add more recent judicial developments to the original memorandum.

NOTES AND QUESTIONS

1. The following opening section of the Columbus Policy Statement on Discipline set forth the philosophy of the Columbus Public Schools regarding discipline:

> The belief that the Columbus Public School System has a responsibility to teach proper behavior patterns is based on the following premises:
>
> 1. The school must provide educational opportunities so every child may achieve to his fullest potential and become a contributing citizen in a democracy.
>
> 2. The child is a social being and as such must learn to recognize that certain types of behavior are necessary in a democratic society. Disciplined behavior is a basic need of such a society.
>
> 3. Discipline is a developmental need of each pupil. There is a feeling of security if limits are known to pupils and they live within appropriate limits.
>
> 4. Discipline has two major purposes: 1) securing a classroom atmosphere conducive to maximum educational achievement; 2) helping each pupil develop self control.
>
> 5. The development of an educational environment conducive to learning and individual self control is delegated to the school by society as its agency for perpetuating and improving the democratic way of life. Thus good discipline is a legitimate task and assigned responsibility of the school.

A later section outlined the responsibilities of students.

Interestingly, this emphasis on "discipline as a learning experience" was never employed by the defendants directly; much later in the case, an association of Ohio School officials strongly asserted this argument in a brief submitted to the U. S. Supreme Court. As we shall see, some members of the Supreme Court subsequently endorsed it.

2. From your reading of the statute, Section 1010.04 of the Administrative Guide, and the Columbus Policy Statement, do you think the state and school policy on the handling of suspensions was adequate? If not, how would you change it?

3. Note that as a minor, Dwight does not have the right to sue in the federal courts. Though the courts have yet to rule definitively on the matter, there seems to be no procedural problem if a child who does not have parental approval wishes to litigate. Federal practice provides that the "(c)ourt shall appoint a guardian * * * for an infant or incompetent person not otherwise represented in an action or shall make such other order as it deems proper for the protection of the infant or incompetent

person." Section 17(c) of the Federal Rules of Civil Procedure. This section is usually broadly construed so that if a child and his parents are in disagreement about going to court over a non-frivolous matter, the judge will usually appoint a special representative for the child.

4.   Shortly after the filing of *Goss v. Lopez*, the three-judge court procedure came under attack. The three-judge mechanism was set up to handle particularly important federal question issues involving individual rights, governmental processes, and general welfare. As originally established, the three-judge court was convened by the chief judge of the circuit and usually consisted of one circuit court judge and two district judges. Appeal from a three-judge court goes directly to the U. S. Supreme Court. Congress established the three-judge court mechanism to curb the power of the single judge in making decisions with far-reaching consequences.

Criticism has focused on the *ad hoc* nature of the three-judge court. They bypass the federal courts of appeal, thus adding to the already heavy workload of the U. S. Supreme Court, and the records are often devoid of the refined analysis and research of appellate-level legal arguments. Furthermore, the Supreme Court Justices may feel particularly compelled to review appeals from three-judge decisions carefully to provide the appellant with an adequate opportunity for appeal.

In August of 1976, Section 2281 was abolished. Other changes were instituted to provide for three-judge courts only "when otherwise required by an Act of Congress, or when an action is filed challenging the constitutionality of the apportionment of Congressional districts or the apportionment of any statewide body." The jurisdiction of three-judge courts has thus been substantially curtailed.

C.   Pre-Trial Clash of Interests: The Defendants' Side

When the complaint was filed with the court, the document was simultaneously served on the defendants. The attorneys * for the defendant school officials first reviewed the complaint and talked with those specifically named as defendants to ascertain the merits, if any, of the plaintiffs' case. Had the defense attorneys concluded on the basis of their investigations that the case was hopeless, the defense costs prohibitive, and the outlook for success dim, they would have probably advised school officials to settle.

In this instance, however, the matter was more serious than a single suspension. Here the plaintiffs had instituted a class action suit alleging the unconstitutionality of the defendants' actions as well as the policies and state law under which they were operating. Consequently, the attorneys for the defendants resolved to fight the suit rather than attempt settlement.

(1)   Filing the Motion to Dismiss

The first action was to file a "motion" with the court urging that the case be dismissed for want of a substantial claim of constitutional dimen-

---

* The Columbus City Attorney, who is an
elected official, and his staff represented
the Columbus School Board.

sions. A "motion" is a formal request to the court asking it to consider the action the motion proposes. In ruling on a motion, a court is resolving questions of law, not fact. There are many types of motions, and they require a detailed knowledge of legal procedure. In this case the motion to dismiss was filed on April 19, 1971, and served on the plaintiffs. It is reported below.

IN THE UNITED STATES DISTRICT COURT
FOR THE SOUTHERN DISTRICT OF OHIO
EASTERN DIVISION
(Title omitted in printing)
Civil Action 71–67

Motion to Dismiss

Now come defendants and move this Honorable Court for an order dismissing plaintiffs' complaint for the reasons that:

1.   The complaint in its present form does not allege facts upon which relief can be granted under Title 42, U.S.C.A., Section 1983.

2.   The Court lacks jurisdiction to grant plaintiffs' request for a declaratory judgment under Title 28, U.S.C.A., Sections 2201 and 2202, for the reason that the complaint and facts recited therein fail to disclose the presence of a justiciable case or controversy with respect to the constitutional validity of Section 3313.66 of the Ohio Revised Code in that the facts recited do not demonstrate that the statute directly applies to these plaintiffs, or that their interests are adversely affected by the operation of the statute.

JOHN C. YOUNG,
City Attorney

WILLIAM J. MELVIN
Chief Trial Attorney, of counsel

THOMAS A. BUSTIN
Senior Assistant City Attorney
Trial Attorney
Attorneys for Defendants

Accompanying the motion to dismiss was a memorandum in support of the motion. Since, like the plaintiffs' memorandum of law, the defendants' memorandum advanced arguments and supporting cases repeated later, they are not excerpted here. It is sufficient once again to summarize the contents of the memorandum. In it the defendants argued that the weight of precedent shows that courts rarely interfere with reasonable discretion exercised by school officials, that the plaintiffs' claim of specific constitutional infringement is unclear, and that there is no requirement for a structured due process proceeding in school suspension cases; therefore, the request for a three-judge court is improper under the law.

On the same date the defendants also filed a memorandum specifically against the plaintiffs' motion that a temporary restraining order be issued by the three-judge panel to reinstate the students and prohibit school officials from acting under the Ohio statute (see the prayer for relief section of the complaint above). In this memorandum the defendants further developed their position that less-than-ten day suspensions were reasonable and asserted that the entire matter was not appropriate for federal legal involvement. Once again, the memoradum is not excerpted here because the same arguments will be advanced later.

NOTES AND QUESTIONS

1. Considering what you know about this case, do you think the defendants' attorneys made a wise decision in deciding not to advise their clients to settle out of court?

2. The defendants pointed out in their memorandum in support of the motion to dismiss that in the absence of a sharply defined constitutional right, the only requirement imposed upon the school board or school officials is that they act in a "reasonable fashion." From what you know so far, does this characterization fit the circumstances of Dwight Lopez's case?

(2) The Court Refuses to Rule on the Motion to Dismiss

On September 27, 1971, the district judge having reviewed the materials submitted thus far, notified the Cheif Judge of the United States Court of Appeals for the Sixth Circuit that a three-judge court should be appointed to hear the case.

In his short opinion accompanying the notification and certificate, Judge Kinneary described the case, noting that the plaintiffs had established sufficient cause for a three-judge court to be established in accordance with Title 28 U.S.C.A. § 2281 and related provisions.

On October 4, Chief Judge Phillips of the Sixth Circuit Court of Appeals responded by appointing the special tribunal. Serving on the court would be Judge Kinneary and Judge Carl B. Rubin of the District Court, and Appellate Judge John W. Peck from the Sixth Circuit. Copies of all the materials filed thus far in the case were sent to all three judges, and counsel for both parties were notified of Chief Judge Phillips' action.

On March 30, 1972, Judge Kinneary, who would be the chief judge for the three-judge court, met with Mr. Barkan, Mr. Murphy, and Mr. Curtin, and with Mr. Bustin, the counsel for the defendants. He advised the attorneys that he would not consider and dispose of the defendants' motion to dismiss the complaint until more information could be provided. Judge Kinneary asked counsel for the defendants to prepare an "answer" to the complaint on or before April 10 so that the issues could be more sharply focused. And he also suggested that the lawyers consider filing stipulations of fact whereby both sides could agree on a common rendition of factual matters and that each side file a memorandum of law, i. e., legal brief, arguing the points of law involved in the case. The attorneys agreed that the three-judge court could decide the case on this basis, and thus there would be no need for a trial. As we shall see, however, a trial was eventually necessary. Judge Kinneary ended the session by setting tentative dates for submission of the stipulations of fact and the memorandum of law.

Figure 6–1 lists the chronology of events in *Goss*. It should be consulted frequently throughout the chapter to keep developments in the case in perspective.

Figure 6–I: Chronology of Events: Goss v. Lopez, 419 U.S. 565 (1975)

1971	1972	1973	1974	1975
1. February 26: School disturbances occur; Dwight suspended.	1. March 30: Memorandum to File by Judge Kinneary.	1. January 26: Stipulation of Parties filed.	1. January 7: Appellees' Jurisdictional Statement filed.	1. January 22: Supreme Court decision announced.
2. February 26: Letter informs Dwight of suspension.	2. April 7: Answer filed by Defendants.	2. May 25: Defendants file Motion to Strike Stipulations as Three-Judge Court asserts need for Evidentiary Hearing.	2. January 22: Appellees' Motion to Affirm filed.	
3. March 1: Mrs. Lopez advised of Board of Education meeting.	3. June 1: Defendants' Memorandum of Law filed per Judge Kinneary's directions.	2a. June 5: Three-Judge Court issues Guideline for Hearing.	3. February 19: Supreme Court notes Probable Jurisdiction and requests filing of briefs.	
4. March 5: Mrs. Lopez scheduled to meet with Mr. Williams.	4. June 2: Plaintiffs' Memorandum of Law filed per Judge Kinneary's directions.	3. July 12: Plaintiffs file Trial Brief.	4. April 19: Appellants' Brief filed.	
5. March 8: Board of Education meeting; Mrs. Lopez tries to meet with Mr. Williams.	5. October 10: Stipulations of Fact filed.	4. July 13: Defendants file Trial Brief.	5. May 29: Appellees' Brief filed.	
6. March 24: Dwight transferred to Adult Day School; Mr. Williams replies to Mrs. Lopez.	6. October 18: Defendants' Final Brief filed.	5. July 13: Pre-Trial deposition of John Ellis and Phillip Fulton.	6. May–June: Amici Curiae Briefs filed.	
7. March 31: Complaint filed by Plaintiffs.	7. October 20: Plaintiffs' Final Brief filed.	6. July 16: Oral hearing before Judge Kinneary.	7. October 4: Appellants' Reply Brief filed.	
8. April 19: Defendants' Motion to Dismiss and Memorandum Contra Three-Judge Court filed.		7. July 17: Defendants' Motion to Dismiss; Plaintiffs file Reply shortly thereafter.	8. October 16: Oral Argument before the Supreme Court.	
9. September 27: District Judge Kinneary upholds Plaintiffs' request for Three-Judge Court.		8. August 31: Plaintiffs file Amended Complaint.		
10. October 4: Chief Judge Phillips designates members of Three-Judge Court.		9. September 12: Defendants' Answer on Behalf of Substituted Parties.		
		10. September 12: Opinion and Order of Three-Judge District Court.		
		11. September 17: Judgment of Three-Judge Court.		
		12. November 9: Defendants' Notice of Appeal to U. S. Supreme Court.		
		13. November 28: Request for Certification of Record to Supreme Court.		
		14. December 19: Record Certified to Supreme Court.		

[B9662]

NOTES AND QUESTIONS

1.   A motion to dismiss is typically decided as a pure question of law as applied to the complaint. Do you concur that Judge Kinneary needed information in addition to the complaint before he could decide how to rule on the motion to dismiss?

2.   The growing desire to process cases without the expensive and time-consuming trial stage is evident in *Goss v. Lopez*. Judge Kinneary and the lawyers seem confident at this point that the court can issue a ruling without a trial. They also are optimistic that both sides can agree on the facts, with disagreement confined to legal issues to be argued in the memoranda of law. Note that Judge Kinneary takes a leading role in speeding resolution of the case. Some judges, probably a majority given today's crowded court calendars, believe they should take a leading role in settlement talks. Thus the pre-trial conference has become a standard part of adjudication. It is not surprising that except for those cases raising substantial constitutional issues, the majority of civil cases are settled before trial. Courts are in reality the last resort for the resolution of disputes.

3.   Suppose the defendants had agreed to reinstate Dwight Lopez. Would you be willing to settle on this basis? Did the case really involve Dwight Lopez, or was he merely a symbol of a larger cause?

4.   Note that the plaintiffs' attorneys had requested a temporary restraining order in their complaint. Judge Kinneary never set it down for hearing, probably because most of the students were back in school by the time the judge decided a three-judge court would be necessary to decide the constitutional issues raised by the case. The passage of time would also prompt the plaintiffs' attorneys to question whether they should have requested a three-judge court hearing. As Denis Murphy later commented in correspondence with the authors, "the U. S. Supreme Court personnel had changed so drastically we thought that with a three-judge court's finding the statute unconstitutional, there was every likelihood that the Supreme Court would not summarily affirm but accept it for argument and render a decision that would be adverse to the interest we were seeking to protect." The narrowness of the Supreme Court decision suggests Mr. Murphy was very nearly right. Alternatively, the plaintiffs' attorneys could have had a regular hearing before the district court. In this case, the appeal would have had to go up on the normal route to the Sixth Circuit Court of Appeals and then to the U. S. Supreme Court. But Mr. Murphy rejected this route. "Our feeling was that there was less likelihood that the Supreme Court would take the case or it would have gotten that far under those circumstances." Thus, the alternative route probably had less chance of establishing a definitive constitutional right for all public school students.

5.   Shortly after the case was filed, Mr. Murphy and Mr. Curtin requested that the Harvard Center for Law and Education, a non-profit legal research and legal aid center, assist in the case. The Harvard Center is one of approximately ten centers funded then through the federal Office of Economic Opportunity (OEO) and now by the Legal Services Corpora-

tion to assist local legal service programs with litigation that is either novel or especially complex. Educational issues were and are the specialty of the Center. Mr. Curtin was familiar with its activities. The Harvard Center was able to become actively involved through liaison with the Legal Aid Society of Columbus, where Mr. Curtin was employed. Initially, Mr. Eric Van Loon of the Center assisted during the early stages. Later, Mr. Peter Roos, who had joined the Center in December of 1972, became involved in the case. Given Mr. Roos' specialization in educational law, he became the principal attorney for the plaintiffs. He argued the case both before the trial court and the U. S. Supreme Court. The Harvard Center paid the minimal trial costs and the costs of the appeal. None of the attorneys received any legal fees from the plaintiffs for their services.

(3) Preparing the Answer

As Judge Kinneary had requested, counsel for defendants filed their answer to the plaintiffs' complaint on April 7, 1972. Up to this time counsel for the defendants had relied on pointing out the weaknesses in the underlying legal theory of the plaintiffs as seen in the complaint. In his motions thus far in the case, Mr. Bustin argued that the defendants hadn't done anything wrong for which the law would hold them accountable. In technical terms, the defendants "demurred," that is, sought to show that even if the plaintiffs' facts were correct, they still had not stated a claim recognizable by a federal court.

This is one of several strategies available to the defense. As we shall see, Mr. Bustin never abandoned this initial strategy, frequently pointing out in later briefs that the defendants stood by their original motion to dismiss. A defense attorney normally does not want the record to reflect that a motion to dismiss has been abandoned, since if the case is appealed, the option remains available to the appellate court to overrule the lower court on the original motion to dismiss. This strategy is known as "making an appellate record."

Since Judge Kinneary decided not to rule on the dismissal motion at this time, Mr. Bustin had to meet the assertions of the plaintiffs directly. He did so in the answer reprinted in the part below. (Again, material unrelated to the principle plaintiff, Dwight Lopez, has been deleted.)

IN THE UNITED STATES DISTRICT COURT

FOR THE SOUTHERN DISTRICT OF OHIO

EASTERN DIVISION

Filed Apr. 7, 1972

(Title omitted in Printing)

Civil Action No. 71–67

ANSWER

First Defense

1. Defendants without abandoning the motion to dismiss they filed on April 19, 1971, file the following as their answer, as requested by the Court.

2. Defendants admit that the action is denominated an action for declaratory and injunctive relief as alleged in paragraph one of the complaint and that the jurisdiction of this Court is invoked as alleged in paragraph two of the complaint, but deny that the facts alleged warrant the assertion of such jurisdiction.

3. Defendants admit that a three judge Court has been convened to hear the instant case.

4. By way of further answer, defendants deny the allegations contained in paragraph four of the complaint.

5. Defendants admit that Herbert Williams was Director of Pupil Personnel at the time the complaint was filed but aver that he has since retired and been replaced by Norval Goss; admit that Calvin Park was principal of Central High School; * * * admit that Harold H. Eibling was Superintendent of Schools of the Columbus Public School system at the time of filing of the complaint, but aver that he has since retired and has been replaced by John Ellis and admit that the Columbus Board of Education manages the Columbus Public School system.

6. Defendants by way of further answer admit that Dwight Lopez, age nineteen (19) was suspended from Central High School on February 26, 1971, admit that a letter dated February 26, 1971 was forwarded to the parents of Dwight Lopez, which letter advised his parents that Dwight had been suspended for being involved in a school disruption and requested that a conference be arranged with his parents. Defendants further admit that a letter was sent to Dwight's parents advising them to appear March 8, 1971, at 8:30 A.M. for a conference but that the parents did not appear and defendants communicated by phone with Mrs. Lopez and were informed by Mrs. Lopez that they were organizing. Defendants deny that Dwight Lopez is being denied an opportunity to continue his education, deny the allegation that he has not been given a reason or reasons for his suspension, and aver that several attempts were made to set up a conference with Dwight's parents relating to his suspension without success. Defendants admit that Dwight Lopez was transferred to Adult Day High School on March 24, 1971; further aver that he is presently attending the school and deny for want of knowledge all other allegations contained in paragraph fourteen of the complaint.

* * *

15. Defendants by way of further answer admit that the provisions of Section 3313.66, Revised Code, proscribes the procedural conduct of defendants, and deny each and every other allegation contained in the Complaint.

Second Defense

16. Defendants aver that the complaint in its present form fails to state a claim cognizable under Title 42, Section 1983, fails to state a claim demonstrating that a specific Constitutional right possessed by any of the plaintiffs had been violated; that the provisions of Section 3313.66, Revised Code, are procedural in nature and do not proscribe or prescribe conduct on the part of plaintiffs, acting as a limitation on the inherent power possessed by defendants, and that given the conduct on the part of

plaintiffs as alleged herein, the temporary action taken by defendants was not arbitrary or unreasonable and fully comported with the due process requirements of the 14th Amendment to the United States Constitution.

Third Defense

17.   Defendants aver that plaintiffs had adequate administrative remedies available to them to review the temporary suspensions, and an appeal by way of Chapter 2506 of the Revised Code which in light of the facts presented in this case should have been exhausted prior to bringing an action under Title 42, Section 1983.

Wherefore, the defendants and each of them demand judgment dismissing the Complaint, with costs.

* * *

NOTES AND QUESTIONS

1.   Note that Mr. Bustin reiterated the position previously asserted, that is, the facts do not warrant convening a three-judge court nor instituting a class-action suit.

2.   Note that Norval Goss has replaced Herbert Williams as Director of Pupil Personnel for the Columbus School District. When the case was first filed, the abbreviated case name was *Lopez v. Williams*. Later it became *Lopez v. Goss*. At the appeal stage the order was reversed. Note also that since Lopez was only one of the plaintiffs and Williams/Goss only one of the defendants, the name of the case quite properly should be listed *Lopez et al. v. Williams et al.* (In the complaint and at various other stages of the case, all the names were spelled out).

3.   Do you find any difference in the defendants' rendition of the facts involving Dwight Lopez from that stated in plaintiffs' complaint?

4.   In the section labeled "Third Defense," the defendants state that "an appeal (of the suspension and transfer) by way of Chapter 2506 of the Revised Code should have been exhausted prior to bringing an action under Title 42, Section 1983." This section of the Ohio Statutes provides that a decision of state and local agencies such as the school board are appealable to the Common Pleas Court. And from there, cases are appealable to the Court of Appeals and the Ohio Supreme Court. Thus, defendants assert the plaintiff students already have ready avenues of appeal within the Ohio judicial system. How might the plaintiffs have responded? Does this case really involve seeking relief for the individual students? Why was a federal court chosen over a state court?

5.   Do you think the answer has helped sharpen the issues in this case? Review the complaint, *supra,* and then state the issue or issues as you see them.

II. PRE–TRIAL BRIEFS AND STIPULATIONS

The essence of the case is first spelled out in the memoranda of law filed according to Judge Kinneary's instructions in early June of 1972. Below we present key excerpts from the brief of the plaintiffs filed on June 2, and the brief of the defendants filed on June 1. We have retained case citations (but not page references) in this one instance to illustrate the important role of legal precedent in legal briefs. This is particularly true where constitutional issues are involved, since attorneys know that courts are reluctant to exercise judicial review over state and federal legislation. When a constitutional issue surfaces, courts usually seek ways of deciding cases other than overturning the work of legislative bodies. As we shall see, the defendants repeatedly argue that this is a case wholly lacking in weighty constitutional issues. See if you agree as you read these excerpts. Also ask yourself whether the precedents cited by the attorneys really do support the points they are trying to make.

A. Plaintiffs' Brief

IN THE UNITED STATES DISTRICT COURT
FOR THE SOUTHERN DISTRICT OF OHIO
EASTERN DIVISION

Eileen Lopez, *et al.*,
    Plaintiffs,
    –vs–
Herbert M. Williams, *et al.*,
    Defendants.

Civil Action No. 71–67

BRIEF OF PLAINTIFFS
Statement of the Case

This is a class action in which student plaintiffs, on behalf of all public school students in Columbus, challenge the constitutionality of Section 3313.66 of the Ohio Revised Code, Section 1010.04 of the Administrative Guide of the Columbus Public Schools, and the Columbus Public School Policy Statement on Discipline. * * *

The statute, administrative guide, and policy statement are challenged because they authorize suspensions or expulsions of high school students, sometimes as long as a semester, without providing the minimal due process safeguards of notice and a prior hearing. They are also challenged because they allow public officials to stigmatize students without due process of law. They are also challenged as being vague and overbroad because they provide no ascertainable standards of conduct for violation of which students may be suspended or expelled.

I. PUBLIC SCHOOL OFFICIALS MAY NOT DENY STUDENTS AN EDUCATION, AN IMPORTANT PUBLIC RIGHT, WITHOUT DUE PROCESS OF LAW.

A. *The right of young citizens to attend free public schools is a fundamental liberty protected by the statutes of Ohio and the Fourteenth Amendment to the Constitution.* Ohio recognizes the value of education by making school attendance compulsory for all citizens between the ages of six and eighteen. The law further requires parents to send their children to school, and makes it a criminal offense for parents to fail to do so.

Under the Constitution, "liberty" has traditionally included the right to education. In an early education case, *Meyer v. Nebraska,* 262 U.S. 390, 399 (1923), Mr. Justice McReynolds, defined the right as follows:

> * * * Without doubt, it denotes not merely freedom from bodily restraint, but also the right of the individual to contract to engage in any of the common occupations of life, *to acquire useful knowledge,* * * * and, generally, to enjoy those privileges long recognized at common law as essential to the orderly pursuit of happiness by free men. (Emphasis added by plaintiffs).

The holding of *Brown v. Board of Educ.,* now almost two decades old, stated the importance of education more broadly, and explained its vital role in the functioning of a democracy:

> Today, education is perhaps the most important function of state and local governments. Compulsory school attendance laws and the great expenditures for education both demonstrate our recognition of the importance of education to our democratic society. It is required in the performance of our most basic public responsibilities, even service in the armed forces. It is the very foundation of good citizenship. Today it is a principal instrument in awakening the child to cultural values, in preparing him for later professional training, and in helping him to adjust normally to his environment. In these days, it is doubtful that any child may reasonably be expected to succeed in life if he is denied the opportunity of an education. Such an opportunity, where the state has undertaken to provide it, is a right which must be made available to all on equal terms.

347 U.S. 483, 493 (1954). The Court again affirmed this holding only two weeks ago in *State of Wisconsin v. Yoder,* (S.Ct. May 15, 1972) 40 U.S.L.W. 4476, 4481–83 (May 16, 1972) (Burger, C. J.) ("Providing public schools ranks at the very apex of the function of a State" at 4478)

* * *

B. *Because of education's importance, its denial, even for a short period of time, constitutes irreparable harm.* In *Dixon v. Alabama State Bd. of Educ.,* a leading case in student due process rights, the Fifth Circuit spoke broadly of the harm that ensues from a denial of education:

> Without sufficient education the plaintiffs would not be able to earn an adequate livelihood, to enjoy life to the fullest, or to fulfill as completely as possible the duties and responsibilities of good citizens. 294 F.2d 150, 157 (5th Cir. 1961).

The National Advisory Committee on Civil Disorders spoke similarly, at length, about the special hardship such a denial works on the children of low-income families: their opportunities to learn, to make a living, and to engage in the common occupations will be drastically curtailed for the rest of their lives. *Report of the National Advisory Committee on Civil Disorders,* pp. 424–56 (1968).

The economic plight of students above the compulsory attendance age who do not return to school after a long suspension or expulsion, or who do not complete their high school education for any other reason, has also been judicially recognized.

* * *

Here in Ohio, only last year, Judge Young described the irreparable injury to a high school student under the very statute challenged in this action:

> * * * There is more to public school attendance than purely academic credits, and cutting a pupil off from the society and companionship of his peers for an indefinite length of time is not only an injury, but it is one which in the nature of things cannot be repaired, particularly for a student in his last year of regular high school attendance. His remaining days as a senior student are limited, and those taken away can never be given back. *Lawton v. Nightingale,* No. C 70–343 (N.D.Ohio Jan. 15, 1971) (Slip opinion at 3–4).

* * *

C. *Public officials may not withhold an important public good from citizens, especially where the deprivation produces substantial harm, without Due Process of Law.*

Students retain the full panoply of citizenship rights during the time they are in school. The Supreme Court stated firmly in *Shelton v. Tucker,* 364 U.S. 479, 487 (1960), that "The vigilant protection of constitutional freedoms is nowhere more vital than in the community of American Schools". Any remaining doubt about this question was resolved emphatically three years ago in *Tinker v. Des Moines Independent Community School Dist.,* 393 U.S. 503 (1969). * * *

The Supreme Court has repeatedly affirmed during the past two decades that the denial of a government benefit, or government action to the detriment of an individual, requires a due process hearing. The Supreme Court has required a prior hearing before public assistant benefits can be taken from a beneficiary (*Goldberg v. Kelly,* 397 U.S. 254 (1970)); before prejudgment garnishment (*Sniadach v. Family Finance,* 395 U.S. 337 (1969)); before eviction from public housing (*Thorpe v. Housing Authority of the City of Durham,* 433 F.2d 998 (4th Cir. 1970)); before deprivation of parenthood (*Armstrong v. Mauzo,* 380 U.S. 545 (1954)); before deprivation of the right to take a bar examination (*Schware v. Board of Bar Examiners,* 353 U.S. 232 (1957)); before dismissal from government employment (*Slochover v. Board of Higher Educ.,* 350 U.S. 551 (1956)); and before a citizen's car and driver's licenses could be taken from him (*Bell v. Burson,* 91 S.Ct. 1586 (1971)).

D. *Students may not be excluded from public education without Due Process of Law.*

Allowing short-term summary suspensions from school is like allowing a welfare cut-off or a garnishment or a license suspension three (or 15) days before a hearing. The language in *Goldberg, Sniadach* and *Bell* left no room for such concessions. Moreover, suspensions from school can be vastly more damaging than the temporary suspension of welfare or wage payments. The welfare recipient in *Goldberg* could have claimed payments retroactively at the hearing which was scheduled to take place after the cut-off. The employee in *Sniadach*, faced with a garnishment order freezing only $31.59 in wages, could expect to enjoy the free use of this money after prevailing at trial. Yet, the court ordered a prior hearing in both cases. A more serious loss faces the suspended student. There is no such thing as a temporary postponement of schooling. Suspension inevitably involved a permanent denial of access to education for the days missed; they cannot be recouped.

The principle that students may not be excluded from school for a substantial period of time without a prior hearing has been judicially well-established for more than a decade.

* * *

The portions of Section 3313.66 which authorize superintendents, executive heads, and principals to suspend pupils from school for up to ten days, without notice or a prior hearing, * * * violate many courts' interpretations of the United States Constitution, although there is less judicial unanimity on this point. Multiple or consecutive short-term suspensions are frequently aggregated, as in this case, so that the "short-term suspensions" really constitute exclusion from school for a substantial period of time. In these instances, they are as unconstitutionally defective as long-term suspensions or expulsions without due process of law.

A number of courts have faced the issue more squarely, however, and have held that suspensions for ten days or three days, or even two days, constituted a severe enough deprivation of the right of education to require a *prior* due process hearing. Applying the schoolhouse analogue of the clear and present danger test, a Wisconsin Court, for example, ruled that:

> Unless the element of danger to persons or property is present, suspension should not occur without specification of charges, notice of hearing, and hearing. *Stricklin v. Regents of the Univ. of Wisconsin,* 297 F.Supp. 416, 420 (W.D.Wisc.1969).

* * *

II. PUBLIC SCHOOL OFFICIALS, AS AGENTS OF THE STATE, MAY NOT STIGMATIZE STUDENTS WITHOUT DUE PROCESS OF LAW.

An independent ground for requiring a hearing prior to suspension or expulsion from school is that the exclusion represents a "badge of disgrace" to many people.

* * *

A school suspension represents a decision by school authorities that a student is a problem child, or undesirable, or, * * * an "outcast". * * * It was a Federal District Court, in fact, which stated:

> Suspension is a particularly humiliating punishment evoking images of the public penitent of medieval Christendom and colonial Massachusetts, the outlaw of the American West, and the ostracized citizen of classical Athens. Suspension is an officially-

sanctioned judgment that a student be for some period removed beyond that pale. *Sullivan v. Houston Independent School Dist.* 333 F.Supp. 1140, 1172 (S.D.Tex.1971).

This Court should void the statutes and regulations challenged in this action because they authorize public officials to stigmatize certain citizens without due process of law.

III. THE CHALLENGED STATUTE AND REGULATION ARE UN-CONSTITUTIONALLY VAGUE AND OVERBROAD BECAUSE THEY PROVIDE NO ASCERTAINABLE STANDARD FOR AC-CEPTABLE CONDUCT.

* * *

Plaintiffs here have been suspended from school for a prolonged period of time for failing, in the words of the Columbus Public Schools Policy Statement on Discipline, to "behave in such way that they will bring credit to themselves and their school." This standard is no less vague or overbroad than * * * the suspensions for "misconduct" which the Seventh Circuit, per Judge Cummings, voided for vagueness. *Soglin v. Kauffman,* 418 F.2d 163 (1969). The rules challenged here suffer the same constitutional infirmities.

* * *

NOTES AND QUESTIONS

1. The first section of the plaintiffs' brief asserts that education is a fundamental right which cannot be denied, "even for a short period of time," without "causing irreparable harm." Do you agree with this assertion? From your own experience, would you say that a short term suspension from school would create "irreparable harm"?

2. Plaintiffs' attorneys also assert that suspension from school is a "badge of disgrace." Do you view suspension this way? Might students in the late 1960s? Is the "badge of disgrace" argument a sound one? What do you think might bolster this line of attack? Could social science research help?

3. From your perspective, which of the arguments of the plaintiffs seem to be particularly persuasive? Which are less so? What kind of information do you think is necessary to bolster the weak parts of the brief? Would a trial help produce the desired information?

B. Defendants' Brief

IN THE UNITED STATES DISTRICT COURT
FOR THE SOUTHERN DISTRICT OF OHIO
EASTERN DIVISION

Eileen Lopez, etc., Plaintiffs, vs. Herbert M. Williams, et al., Defendants	Civil Action No. 71–67

Brief of Defendants

While it has not been settled or determined what the evidence will be in this case, defendants submit that on the pleadings filed this Court can determine as a matter of law that Section 3313.66, Revised Code, does not violate the due process clause of the 14th Amendment to the United States Constitution.

From the pleadings it is clear that the central issue before this Court is the validity of Section 3313.66, Revised Code. Further, that section is being tested in the light of a series of suspensions received by the plaintiffs. No expulsions are involved in this case. * * *

Since defendants have filed a motion to dismiss in this case and that motion remains pending, defendants will not restate the arguments made in support of that motion in this brief. Defendants fully rely on that motion and the arguments and authorities cited in support.

It is defendants' belief that when this case is viewed critically, the argument can be made and supported that the instant case presents a situation in which Federal jurisdiction should not have been assumed. In this connection this Court's attention is directed to the case of *Farrell v. Joel*, 437 F.2d 160 (1971) which was a case involving a ten day suspension from a high school. The plaintiff in that case claimed that she had not been afforded procedural due process. Therein the Court in discussing that contention pointed out as follows * * *:

> "However, the inquiry does not end with this assumption; it only begins. Due process does not invariably require the procedural safeguards accorded in criminal proceedings. Rather, 'the very nature of due process negates any concept of inflexible procedures universally applicable to every imaginable situation.' Cafeteria and Restaurant Workers, Local 423, *AFL–CIO v. McElroy*, 367 U.S. 886 (1961). See *Hannah v. Larche*, 363 U.S. 420 (1960). ('Due process' is an elusive concept. Its exact boundaries are undefinable, and its content varies according to specific factual contexts.') *We believe that in these school discipline cases the nature of the sanction affects the validity of the procedure used in imposing it.*" (Emphasis added by defendants)

* * *

The statute * * * which is under attack, by its terms proscribes the conduct of those school officials charged with administering the schools on a day to day basis. Broken down, the statute by its terms provides the following:

(1) A limitation is placed upon the inherent disciplinary power possessed by administrators in that a student may not be suspended for a period exceeding ten days.

(2) It provides that an administrator may expel a student; however, the student is given a right of appeal and hearing before the school board.

(3) It provides that the administrator is to notify the parent or guardian and the clerk of the board within twenty-four hours of the suspension or expulsion of the fact of such action and the reasons.

(4) It provides that a suspension or expulsion may not extend beyond a current semester.

It is defendants' position that the statute, as a direct limitation on disciplinary sanctions, is not vague and in the area of suspension does not permit a serious sanction. Further, a statute which curtails an administrator's power of suspension to the point of permitting only a discretionary ten day suspension cannot be said to be so broad in its scope as to impinge upon fundamental rights possessed by a high school student. Particularly is this conclusion appropriate when the relationship of the student to the high school is viewed in the light of the school's comprehensive authority to prescribe and control conduct in the school on a day to day basis. A search of the Ohio cases will disclose no case where a challenge has been made to the statute in State courts, although it is suggested that a procedure or remedy is available in State court wherein an aggrieved party could challenge the statute, and any action by an administrator felt to be arbitrary.

* * *

In addition to the *Farrell* case, * * * which involved a ten day suspension * * * this Court's attention is directed to the case of *Baker v. Downey City Board of Education*, 307 F.Supp. 517 (1969) which involved a ten day suspension. Therein the Court * * * in discussing the due process argument reasoned:

"Plaintiffs further contend that their rights to procedural due process required that they be given specifications of charges, notice of hearing, and a hearing, prior to the suspensions.

"Judge Moore, in *Madera v. Board of Educ.*, 386 F.2d 778, 789 (1967), states:

'*Law and order in the classroom should be the responsibility of our respective educational systems. The courts should not usurp this function and turn disciplinary problems, involving suspension, into criminal adversary proceedings, which they definitely are not.*'

* * *

"*Due process is not a fixed, or inflexible procedure which must be accorded in every situation. It varies with the circumstances involved.* In the instant case, the school officials were charged with the conduct of the educational program *and if the temporary suspension of a high school student could not be accomplished without first preparing specifications of charges, giving notice of hearing, and holding a hearing, or any combination of these procedures, the discipline and ordered conduct of the educational atmosphere required by good educational standards, would be difficult to maintain.* * * * (Emphasis added by defendants)

* * *

In the context and posture of the case presently before this Court, even considering only the pleadings it can be said that the suspensions arose out of school disruptions of one form or another. This is the pattern which runs throughout the case. If as the cases seem to indicate a distinction is to be drawn between discipline administered in a high school and that administered in a college, if administrators are to be accorded wide latitude in administering the schools on a day to day basis and if the type of sanction involved is critical in a resolution of due process considerations, then, the conclusion is supportable that Section 3313.66, Revised Code is not violative of the due process clause to the United States Constitution. * * * Further, they do not allege, nor can they, that resort to State court would not have provided them with relief from alleged wrongs, if they exist. What these plaintiffs really seek is to fasten upon local school authorities the same due process requirements found necessary in a criminal proceeding. Discipline in a high school involving nothing more than a possible suspension not exceeding ten days does not pose a serious due process question unless this Court is ready to conclude that due process is a fixed and inflexible procedure applicable to every situation. Defendants submit that any one of the plaintiffs, if he or she felt the school administrator acted arbitrarily could have had that action reviewed pursuant to Section 2506.01, Revised Code. That should have been accomplished before coming to Federal Court.

The present case does not, when viewed critically, provide a situation in which jurisdiction should have been invoked. No serious claim is made that anyone of the plaintiffs has been or will in the future be effectively denied their right to an education through a suspension ranging from five to ten days. In fact, careful scrutiny of the facts elicited, or to be elicited, would demonstrate the opposite. Further, the limited sanction of a ten day suspension which the school administrators may apply as a disciplinary procedure is not so serious a sanction in the context of a high school setting that it can only be applied after providing a statement of charges, notice of hearing and hearing. *Tillman v. Dade County School Bd.*, 327 F. Supp. 930 (1971), and *Madera, supra*, 386 F.2d 778. The section is constitutional on its face, does not violate the due process clause, and plaintiffs plead no set of facts such as warrants the assertion of Section 1983 jurisdiction in this case.

* * *

NOTES AND QUESTIONS

1. What is a "fundamental right?" Aside from specific constitutional provisions, what examples can you give of fundamental rights? Is the right to an education a fundamental right?

2. Note that the defendants are forced into the somewhat uncomfortable position of asserting that a ten-day suspension or less does not affect either fundamental student interests or result in irreparable harm. In effect, the defendant school officials *downplay* the importance of each day of formal schooling, while the plaintiff students *emphasize* the importance of school attendance!

3. Do you think the defendants sufficiently demonstrated that high school students are treated differently from college students insofar as procedural due process is concerned? How might the plaintiffs counter this assertion?

4. Refer back to Section 3313.66 of the Ohio Revised Code and then compare the assertions of the plaintiffs and of the defendants with respect to the vagueness issue. Who has the stronger position?

5. In light of the facts in this case as we know them thus far, which side do you believe has made the stronger argument?

6. Do you think the three-judge court should decide the case on the basis of the briefs or do you think a trial is necessary?

C. Stipulations of Fact

On October 10, 1972, both sides submitted the stipulations of fact requested by the judge. Since there was no dramatic change from the facts as we know them, the stipulations are not reprinted here.

The filing of the stipulations prompted the defendants to submit a final brief to the court in which they argued that the case was not a proper one for a class action. They had not included this point in their first brief. In their final brief, filed on October 18, 1972, the defendants also pointed out additional cases supporting their view that high school officials have a right to maintain a system of discipline in schools, that no tangible right of the plaintiffs had been infringed and thus the plaintiffs would have the court strike down the Ohio statute in the abstract, and that the court should either dismiss the case or uphold the constitutionality of the challenged statute. It is interesting to note that the defendants concentrated more on the factual aspects of the case in the supplement than in their first brief. Note for example, this passage:

> With respect to each of the plaintiffs named in the stipulations of fact, a notice was forwarded to the plaintiff or the parents of plaintiff, notifying them of the suspension. * * * Specifically, there is a total absence of any evidence such as would demonstrate that these plaintiffs' right to obtain an education or right to complete their education was in any way abridged by the suspensions handed out or by the operation of Section 3313.66, Revised Code. Further, there is no showing by way of evidence that the specific suspensions or the operation of Section 3313.66, Revised Code, either operated or operates in such a manner as to deprive them of the complete and full benefits of a public school education.

Shortly after the filing of the defendants' supplemental brief, the plaintiffs filed a reply to defendants' final brief. In the reply, plaintiffs attempted to counter the additional arguments of the defendants by asserting that there were no cases treating high school students differently from college students and that the cases cited by the defendants pointed this out. Plaintiffs also repeated that very real interests of the students were adversely affected by the suspensions, citing the long suspension of Dwight Lopez and his transfer to another school as an example. They also sought in the following excerpt to counter the defendants' claim to have offered to meet with the parents of the children.

> The Defendants in their final brief indicate that the school district in each instance sent out notices to the parents informing them of the suspensions. Further, they indicate that attempts were made in several instances to have informal meetings with the parents of the Plaintiffs. Presumably, this is offered to show that the district has a constitutionally permissible procedure to deal with suspensions. This information clearly shows that such is *not* the case.

> Although the Supreme Court has indicated that the nature of a hearing will vary with the situation, several rather clear requirements must universally be met. First, "the fundamental requisite of Due Process of Law is the opportunity to be heard". Secondly, the hearing must be "at a meaningful time and in a meaningful manner". Thirdly, as stated in *Goldberg v. Kelley*

> > "In almost every setting where important decisions turn on question of Fact, Due Process requires an opportunity to confront and cross-examine adverse witnesses"

> and, as further stated in *Goldberg,*

> > "of course an impartial decision maker is essential".

NOTES AND QUESTIONS

1. Notice how the issues are slowly being narrowed as a result of the exchange of briefs and stipulations of fact. As indicated previously, the American legal system seeks to eliminate as much of the element of "surprise" as possible in civil proceedings before the trial. "Trial by ambush" so characteristic of early courtroom dramas on television has now largely been eliminated by the "discovery" process. In 1938 the Federal Rules of Civil Procedure provided for full disclosure of the facts by both sides prior to trial. Most of the states have adopted these same measures to apply to their civil proceedings. Through the tools of discovery (e. g., depositions, interrogatories, production of documents), the essential facts emerge for both sides to consider. Oftentimes, as in this case, pre-trial procedures are important means of seeking to eliminate a hearing altogether.

2. What the plaintiffs have asked for is *more* procedural due process for students *earlier* in discipline cases. Do you think the specific procedures outlined by the plaintiffs above are appropriate to less-than-ten day suspensions? Might they be impossible to administer in a situation such as that which occurred at Central High School? Plaintiffs admit that in situations where a "clear and present danger" exists, school officials might be exempt from having to comply with such procedures, though the burden of proof will rest on them.

3. Have the supplemental briefs changed your mind about which side presented the stronger argument? Do you think a hearing is still required?

D. Filing of Trial Briefs

On January 26, 1973, counsel for both parties stipulated that the case could be determined on its merits, the motion, pleadings, stipulations, exhibits, and briefs which had been filed. But on May 25 the three-judge court informed both sides that it could not decide the case, that further stipulations would not help, and that the only recourse was a full evidentiary hearing. Defendants thereupon requested that all prior stipulations of fact be removed and that the plaintiffs be required to prove the allegations in their complaint.

On June 5 the three-judge court issued to both parties a memorandum entitled "Guideline for Hearing." The guideline set forth the expectations the judges had for the hearing and is worth reprinting because it provides insight for the first time into their thinking. As you read the memorandum, ponder why the judges were unable to decide the case without a hearing.

Memorandum—Guideline for Hearing

The parameters of a student's due process right to notice and hearing in cases of suspension are determined in large part by the event which gives rise to the suspension. The type of notice, how it is given, and when it is given is dependent upon the gravity of the threat to proper school discipline and atmosphere. Similarly, the minimum requisites of a due process hearing are a function of the gravity of the alleged disciplinary breach and the severity of the proposed sanction.

In all cases, the school authorities must accord their students due process of law. But school authorities are permitted wide latitude in devising methods and procedures which meet the individual requirements of their schools and school systems and the minimum requirements of due process of law.

Plaintiffs have the burden of proving that they were denied due process of law when they were suspended from the Columbus Public School System. Their burden is to establish the facts surrounding their suspensions.

These facts would include the date of suspension, the reason for the suspension, the length of suspension, and the procedures, or absence of procedures, followed by the school board and imposing the suspensions.

In defense of the suit, the Columbus School Board may, if it chooses, present evidence demonstrating that they accorded the suspended students due process of law. These facts might include the circumstances existing in the school prior to the time of the imposition of the suspension, the alleged activities in which each of the suspended students engaged, the notice, if any, given to the students to desist from the disruptive behavior, the notice of suspension to the student and the facts surrounding their removal from the school premises, notice given to the parents of the suspension, content of meetings held between administrators, parent and student, and all of the facts surrounding any hearing type meetings held between the administrator, parent and student.

––––––

Trial briefs were prepared by both parties and submitted to the court in July. Since the legal arguments were similar to those contained in the pre-trial briefs previously submitted, they are not excerpted here. There are, however, a few additional arguments presented by each side which should be noted in passing.

The plaintiffs presented a brief arguing that a suspension, regardless of length, requires that notice be given the student, that the student be able to present evidence and confront opposing witnesses, and that there be an impartial trier of facts. The Ohio law and related Columbus School policies did not provide any of these. The plaintiffs tried to show that the weight of Supreme Court cases, the "most thoughtful" of lower court cases, the serious psychological and educational harm a suspension can cause (a point they intended to bring out in the hearing), and the need for uniformity—all necessitate such a hearing. The plaintiffs suggested a recent district court decision *Vail v. Board of Educ. of Portsmouth School Dist.*, 354 F.Supp. 592 (D.C.N.H.1973), as the appropriate model. The *Vail* court held that:

> "due process requires at least an informal administrative consultation with a student *before any* suspension is imposed so that the student can know why he is being disciplined and so that the student can have the opportunity to persuade the school official that the suspension is not justified, e. g., that this is a situation of mistaken identity or that there is some other compelling reason not to take action." (emphasis added by plaintiffs).

The plaintiffs continued in their brief:

> The court further proceeded to require that a more complete hearing had to be given in the event that a suspension was to exceed five days. * * * It should be emphasized in light of the facts that will be before this court that the "informal administrative consultation" referred to in *Vail* is a consultation designed to elicit the truth, i. e., identity and culpability. Contrasted with this is the apparent practice in Columbus under 3313.66 of holding a conference to merely inform a student of the fact of suspension.

The *Vail* decision, argued the plaintiffs, was part of a trend to accord students more due process rights. The Ohio statute, they asserted, was woefully deficient in safeguarding student interests, as well as being unconstitutionally vague and overbroad.

In their conclusion the plaintiffs requested the court, among other things, to "order the Columbus School District to come forward with a student code within a reasonable number of days, which code provides for the opportunity of hearings prior to suspension, expulsion or disciplinary transfer (excepting extraordinary circumstances)". Such a code should consist of the three elements of procedural due process advanced in their brief.

The defendants argued once again that no clear constitutional right was involved in the case, and that the Supreme Court had ruled repeatedly that in the absence of such a right, no specific procedural due process rights under the Fourteenth Amendment are necessary. They focused particularly on one recent Supreme Court decision decided several months earlier in 1973, *San Antonio v. Rodriguez,* a case discussed in the next chapter. The defendants quoted this passage from the case:

> "Education, of course, is not among the rights afforded explicit protection under our Federal Constitution. Nor do we find any basis for saying it is implicitly so protected. As we have said, the undisputed importance of education will not alone cause this Court to depart from the usual standards of reviewing a State's social and economic legislation."

Nor had Ohio created such a right through its statutes, argued the defendants.

> * * * in examining the Ohio Constitutional provisions regarding public schools and laws enacted pursuant to the Constitution we find no provision that grants to Ohio children an unrestricted right to attend school. A basic right of liberty or property is not sharply implicated in the instant litigation, and until such a right is directly and sharply implicated no Federal question is presented and no civil right cognizable under Section 1983 is involved.

Perhaps the biggest surprise came late in the brief when the defendants revealed that on July 10, 1973, the Columbus School system had enacted new pupil guidelines to be followed by all principals in the system. Included in the guidelines were "most of the things that the plaintiffs had requested be initiated * * *." Specifically, defendants noted the new guidelines provided for:

1. An enumeration of the grounds for suspension; and

2. A conference with the pupil for the purpose of eliciting facts surrounding the alleged offense prior to the suspension of the pupil; and

3. An opportunity for the pupil to submit evidence on his behalf with respect to the alleged offense; and

4. Subsequent to the suspension, the pupil and the parent or guardian are given an opportunity to confer with the principal, at the earliest possible time, to again review the offense which gave rise to the suspension; and

5. If the suspension was subsequently found to be erroneous, all references to such suspension are to be expunged from the pupils' records.

As a result, concluded the defendants, "this case is moot."

NOTES AND QUESTIONS

1. Which of the briefs do you think presented the stronger argument? Do you think the *San Antonio* Supreme Court decision outweighed the importance of *Vail v. Board of Educ.,* which plaintiffs highlighted? We will see how plaintiffs handled *San Antonio* later.

Note that in preparing trial briefs, the plaintiffs' principle attorney, now Peter Roos, had to make some difficult decisions concerning strategy. In correspondence with the authors, Mr. Roos admitted,

> I went through some agonizing periods trying to determine whether to fight the ten-day suspension law on the grounds that it was too long to permit without due process; or whether to go all the way and say that any suspension for more than a trivial period of time required due process. No case before *Goss* had said that any suspension must be preceded by a hearing. I decided to take the latter approach notwithstanding the lack of specific precedent, due to the belief that the Court would perceive our request to *reduce* the number of days allowable without a hearing as a request to substitute the Court's judgment for that of the Ohio Legislature.

Since courts are extremely reluctant to function as legislatures, Mr. Roos had reason to be concerned.

2. What about the new procedures implemented in the Columbus school system in July? Did they effectively render the case moot? Which of the claims of the plaintiffs still stood, if any? Why do you suppose the defendants decided to institute these new procedures at this particular time?

3. If you were the counsel for the plaintiffs, how would you respond to the defendants' brief?

III. THE HEARING AND THE DECISION OF THE DISTRICT COURT

A. Pre-Trial Depositions

At the same time the briefs were filed, the pre-hearing depositions were conducted. A "deposition" is testimony taken outside of court but pursuant to specific guidelines established by the court. Attorneys regularly take depositions as a means of discovery relating to the other side's case. Such testimony is recorded by a court stenographer and has the same value as testimony taken in open court. In this case the plaintiff sought depositions from John Ellis, Superintendent of the Columbus Public Schools, and from Mr. Phillip Fulton, principal of one of the high schools where suspensions had occurred. Mr. Fulton's testimony provided a comprehensive review of the facts surrounding the disturbances at his school; interestingly, he was called as a witness by the plaintiffs. As noted above, the defense chose not to dispute the facts as presented in the case, preferring instead to focus on issues of law and policy, and thus took no depositions.

The depositions of Dr. Ellis provides interesting background information and is excerpted in part here. What did Dr. Ellis say that shed new light on this case? Note that Mr. Peter Roos, attorney from the Harvard Center for Law and Education, functioned as trial attorney for the plaintiffs, while Mr. Crawford handled the case for the defendants.

*   *   *

Q.   *   *   *

Now, you state that each school has its own regulations; is that a correct statement of what you said?   A.   Virtually each school does.   There may be one or two.   We have some very small schools that would not have a particularly extensive list of rules and regulations.

Q.   Okay.   Is there any essential place that these rules and regulations promulgated by the schools can be obtained?   A.   The various school rules that exist are not catalogued or organized in any single central place at the present time.

Q.   Do you have any knowledge concerning the methods that these rules are conveyed to the pupils?   Is there any standard procedure for conveying the rules that we are now talking about to the pupils?   A.   The typical methods would be school assemblies, announcements on the P.A. system, school handbooks, school bulletins, memos sent to parents, council meetings.   These would vary from one school to another, but in many schools all procedures would be used.

Q.   But the central administration does not have a procedure for insuring that these are distributed to each of the students?   A.   That is correct.

Q.   With respect to the regulations dealing with suspensions, it is mentioned that a notice is to be sent out within twenty-four hours; is that not correct?   A.   A letter to the parent.

Q.   A letter to the parent or guardian?   A.   A letter to the parent or guardian that should be preceded by a phone call possibly, but the first written document would be the letter.

Q.   Is there—strike that.

Would it be fair to say that the letters, in terms of their detail and what not, would vary as they are sent out?   I mean, is there any standard format concerning the amount of detail that is contained in such a letter? A.   The amount of detail would have to be determined by the principal, because the incidents would vary.   The length of explanation would vary.

Q.   Now, the letter that I am referring to—this is Exhibit 2, Section A4.   There is mention of a carbon copy of the letter to Pupil Personnel.   Do you know if that—for how long that letter remains in the child's file?   A. No.

Q.   You don't know how long?

Mr. Bustin: I want to object.

Mr. Roos: Let me back up a second.

By Mr. Roos:

Q.   With respect to what happens to that letter when it arrives at Pupil Personnel, if you know?   A.   No, I don't know.

Q.   Is there a file maintained in the schools on each individual child? A.   Yes.

Q.   What sort of things go into that file?   A.   We had basic biographical information showing name, address, birth dates, parents, their residence.   We also have a health record that would include the immunizations a student would receive and any medical admonitions that we should follow in the event that the student might be diabetic or have epilepsy. We would also include in the file basic scholastic information, such as the grades received and also such factors as attendance and honors earned. Later in the secondary schools, we have such things as a request to send transcripts to college and the various procedures relating to insuring that students receive an application and are handled expeditiously when they request such a transcript to be made. In summary, it is a fairly comprehensive description of basic information.

Oh, I omitted in my earlier discussion the dates enrolled in the school if the student is new to the district, scholastic record that he had previous— at the previous school and any other pertinent information that would be forwarded in that. It could include medical information.

Q. Would correspondence to the family or guardians of the pupil be in the file? A. This would vary from school to school. In most cases correspondence, if it were of a significant nature, would be included. A simple note to the parent would not necessarily be included.

Q. Would a letter concerning a suspension or expulsion be in a file? A. In most cases I would think that it would be.

Q. I am referring now to, I think, high school students. What uses are made of the files? A. The files are for the professional use of the teaching and administrative personnel of the school.

Q. Now, you mentioned that they are used in responding to college requests for transcripts and things of this sort. Is that a correct statement of what you said? A. Yes. We would indicate when transcripts were sent.

Q. Do you respond to requests from employers, the military, and others concerning—let me rephrase the question. Do you receive requests from employers and others concerning a given student? A. We sometimes receive requests for verification of graduation or things of that nature.

Q. Do you receive requests for recommendations from employers? A. You mean written formal requests?

Q. Written or oral—any sort of requests from employers. A. That could happen occasionally. More frequently we receive notification of employment possibilities which are passed out to the guidance counselors and others. So students who are interested may apply.

Q. Concerning a student who may have graduated or who may have left the system and are out in the job market or elsewhere, do you ever receive requests for information concerning them—recommendations, transcripts, or what not? A. I do not personally receive any such requests or have not. Whether an individual principal may, would be a question that you should refer to a principal.

Q. I see. In your experience as a principal and as a school administrator, do you know if those sorts of requests are made in general? A. Requests do come from time to time in school systems. In our response to such requests, we confine any information released to very basic items such as, they graduated, something of that nature.

Q. Now, concerning college recommendations. My recollection of applying for college is that colleges do ask for recommendations. Is that not so, more than just mere requests for transcripts? A. The college process places a heavy responsibility on the student to identify persons within the school system whom he would like to have write references for him to colleges. The process, therefore, is that the student takes whatever application form the college wishes and hands or sends it to someone he chooses to write a recommendation.

* * *

DIRECT EXAMINATION

By Mr. Crawford:

Q. Doctor, before you were asked to review what has been marked as Exhibit 1 and 2—Plaintiff's Exhibit 1 and 2—you referred to those exhibits as being directives from a popular school administrative body to principals in the school system. If a principal does not follow those directives, would that not following of the directive be an authorized or unauthorized act? A. It would be unauthorized. The principals are obligated to follow all the rules and regulations of the Board of Education and the administrative regulations of the central office.

Q. Also, you were asked to make reference to the files that were being obtained by this school system for each pupil. Reference was made to the information required by employers, military, colleges, from those files. Could you state what part of the files would be available to the persons outside of the school system? A. We attempt to preserve the integrity of the individual whenever we discuss the record. What he has accomplished in school, basic information such as the grades received, attendance, entrance and leaving dates would be information that we would convey. It would be highly unusual if we would discuss whether a student was suspended or an item falling into that category. Increasingly we are constantly aware that they do have their rights. We must be. We want to give careful consideration so that we do not violate their rights.

Q. Is there a master card—let's say—that would follow a student throughout the school system—a central document? Would there be more than one document that would be considered as a master record? A. Master records would be more appropriate. We have an informational file in which various documents can be placed in them. For the most part, the basic information is contained on a single four sided document that is inserted into the folder.

Q. So if a letter was inserted in the folder, would that letter be part of that master card you were referring to? A. The letter would not be on the card, but could be in the folder.

Q. When an employer or college or military or any other authorized person requests information and the Columbus School System makes a request for data on a pupil, from what documents is this data to be obtained? A. From Exhibit 7 or all the exhibits I previously discussed.

* * *

Q. Is there a policy in the Columbus School System about the documents that are to be used to give information to persons requesting it? A. I don't think we have that in writing.

Q. What is the policy? A. The policy is to release only information that would be considered standard information, such as the attendance, grades, test scores.

Q. Doctor, in my last question, you mentioned—A. If you would hold it a minute, I would like to refer to the specific section in the administrative guide that gives instructions on that question. * * * Section 1016.03 of the Administrative Guide states that information contained in all official school records, including the permanent record data listed, Section 1016.01 of this Guide is confidential and shall be available only to employees of the Board, parents and guardians, law enforcement officials, and such other individuals as principals of each school may designate.

* * *

Mr. Crawford: I have nothing further.

RECROSS EXAMINATION

By Mr. Roos:

Q. Doctor Ellis, I don't have all of those exhibits in front of me, but if my recollection is correct, there was ample room for comments at various places; is that a correct statement? A. That is a correct statement. Although, if you would attend a committee discussion, you would sometimes think that we could never provide enough room for comments.

Q. You could never provide enough room for comments? In those places, it certainly is not inconceivable that mention of a suspension or expulsion or transfer could appear; would that not be so? A. That could be so.

Q. Okay. One of the cards apparently is released commonly, or the information is released commonly is information concerning attendance; is that correct? A. That could be released, yes.

Q. If a child were suspended or expelled, would he not—how would that appear on his attendance card? A. As absent.

Q. Now, where in this cumulative record, assuming that the child is still in the school, the Columbus School System—let's say hypothetically a senior at Marion-Franklin. Where would that card—that cumulative card folder—be kept? A. At the school.

Q. And would it be kept with any other documents, or is it physically separate from all other documents? A. It would be kept separate from other documents for convenience of insuring that the cumulative records were all in the same place.

Q. I see. If a child were transferred from one school to another, that would be reflected in one of the exhibits? That is in the cumulative record folder; is it not? A. Yes.

Q. Is there any reflection whether the transfer was voluntary or involuntary? A. I am not certain if we formally indicate whether it is voluntary or involuntary.

Q. But it might appear?   A.   I don't know.

NOTES AND QUESTIONS

1.   What was the purpose behind Mr. Roos' questions relating to the development and dissemination of schools' rules? How might these questions relate to the plaintiffs' case? How might they relate to the new procedures announced by the defendants?

2.   Why did Mr. Roos ask so many questions about the contents of a student's file and the release of the information in it? How might the answers Dr. Ellis gave be used by the plaintiffs to support their case?

3.   On direct examination, Mr. Crawford got Dr. Ellis to state that if local school principals deviate from the policies established by the central office, they are acting without authorization. Did this response demolish the point Mr. Roos had in mind on the development and dissemination of school rules? Or only partly so? Should Mr. Crawford have asked Dr. Ellis about school policy on releasing information from a student's folder, as he did?

4.   Note that as the deposition proceeds, the scope of questioning narrows. At a trial, recross and redirect examination must be confined to previous testimony and not be used to introduce new lines of inquiry. Dependent upon court rules, that is not necessarily true in a discovery deposition. In a discovery proceeding where the procedure is relatively informal, redirect or recross examination might proceed because the attorney simply forgot to ask a question earlier. Further, usually where one party is cross-examining the other party, no direct examination of that party by his own counsel takes place. In Dr. Ellis's case, Mr. Crawford probably decided to conduct direct examination so as to minimize or avoid entirely having Dr. Ellis appear at the time of the trial. There are other reasons also why an attorney might wish to examine his own client; one reason might be only to make the client feel better about things that were left unsaid in a procedure that is a little foreign to him.

5.   The 1974 Family Educational Rights and Privacy Act (Buckley Amendment) has dramatically changed student record-keeping in the nation's schools and colleges in the interest of safeguarding student rights of privacy. This legislation provides comprehensive protection to student educational records and also provides the student or parent with access to them. Most educational records are covered; not included are records privately maintained by institutional personnel for their own use, documents maintained for law enforcement purposes, employment records, and files maintained by medical personnel. In the case of medical records, however, the student can designate a physician or other professional to review the records on his or her behalf.

The Buckley Amendment also requires educational institutions to establish procedures for notifying students (or parents of those not over the age of 18 and financially independent) of records maintained, the methods for reviewing and copying them, and procedures under the Act for challenging school records.

While most educational institutions are covered by the Buckley Amendment, the sanctions (termination of federal funding) may have little or no influence on those nonpublic educational institutions which receive no direct or indirect federal aid.

B.   The District Court Proceedings

Below we present excerpts from the evidentiary hearing before the district court. In the United States civil actions are heard in courts which have the combined powers of law and equity. A civil action is classified as one "at law" or "in equity" depending on the relief sought. If only money damages are sought, then the court acts as a law court. A jury is provided if either plaintiff or defendant wants one. If something other than monetary relief is sought, such as an injunction or, as in this case, expungement of student records, then the court acts as a court of equity. There is no jury in equity cases and rules of evidence are not applied as strictly. *Goss v. Lopez* was heard before a three-judge federal district court sitting as a court in equity.

Frequently, the term "hearing" is used to describe the nature of the proceedings in civil actions. "Hearing" is a very broad term and encompasses both trial-like proceedings and those where only issues are presented and debated, as, for example, before an appellate court. The three-judge proceeding in *Goss v. Lopez* is best labeled a "trial" or "evidentiary hearing". Later, when the attorneys appear before the U. S. Supreme Court, the proceeding is better known as an "oral argument" or "appellate hearing."

We will begin with the testimony of the principle plaintiff, Dwight Lopez, and conclude with the testimony of Dr. Herbert Rie, an expert called by the plaintiffs.

(1)   Testimony of Dwight Lopez

IN THE UNITED STATES DISTRICT COURT
SOUTHERN DISTRICT OF OHIO
EASTERN DIVISION

Civil Action 71–67

(Title Omitted in Printing)

PROCEEDING

Before the Honorable Joseph P. Kinneary, Chief Judge, sitting at Columbus, Ohio, July 16, 1973.

DWIGHT LOPEZ,

called as a witness on behalf of the plaintiff, having been first duly sworn, testified as follows:

DIRECT EXAMINATION

By Mr. Roos:

Q.   Please state your name.   A.   Dwight Lopez.

Q. Mr. Lopez were you attending Central High School on Friday, February 26, 1971? A. Yes, I was.

Q. On that date were you suspended from Central High School in Columbus? A. Yes, I was.

Q. Who suspended you? A. Mr. Parks, the principal.

Q. How did you find out that you were suspended? A. When I got home, there was a call to my house from Mr. Parks. When I was at home, there was a call to my house from Mr. Parks, stating that I was suspended.

Q. You were at home rather than at school? A. Yes, sir.

Q. Why were you at home? A. School was dismissed that day.

Q. Did Mr. Parks tell you personally that you were suspended? A. He did not.

Q. He told you on the telephone? A. Yes.

Q. At the time that he called you, did he tell you of the reasons for your suspension? A. No, he did not.

Q. Did you do anything that day at the school?

The Court: What day are you referring to?

Mr. Roos: February 26th.

The Court: Is that the last day you were in school, Mr. Lopez? A. Yes, sir.

The Court: You may proceed. Did you go the full school day on that day? A. No, sir, school was let out around 10:30, 11:00 o'clock, sir.

The Court: The whole student body was dismissed at that time?

The Witness: Yes, sir.

The Court: You with them?

The Witness: Yes, sir.

The Court: All right. You may proceed.

By Mr. Roos:

Q. On February 26th, did you do anything that violated any rules, to your knowledge, rules of the school or other rules? A. No.

Q. How many other students on that day were suspended, to your knowledge? A. To my knowledge, at least—well, a few that I know, 75 that I know personally but there were more.

Q. At any time prior to receiving the call from Mr. Parks, did you have an opportunity to tell your side of the story? A. No.

The Court: Why don't you ask him if there was a hearing conducted in connection with the suspension.

Q. (By Mr. Roos) At any time prior to the suspension by Mr. Parks, were you given a hearing to tell your side of the story? A. No.

Q. What was the first thing in writing which you received? A. I received a letter the next day after I was suspended from the school stating that I was suspended.

Q. Is that letter dated February 26? A. Yes, it was.

Mr. Roos: Your Honor, that is Exhibit 1A. It was agreed between plaintiffs and defendants that I would not have to identify it otherwise.

The Court: Fine. You may proceed.

By Mr. Roos:

Q. You received this after you had been suspended; is that correct? A. Yes.

Q. Did you receive a further letter dated March 1 from the school authorities? A. Yes, I did.

Q. That is Exhibit 1B, Your Honor.

Q. Were you already under suspension when you received this letter? A. Yes, I was.

Q. Did you receive a letter dated March 5 setting an appointment at Pupil Personnel for March 8th? A. Yes, I did.

Q. That is 1C, Your Honor.

Were you under suspension at the time you received this letter? A. Yes, I was.

Q. At the time you received this letter, had you been out of school approximately a week? A. Yes.

Q. Prior to March 8, 1971, did you have any opportunity to meet with any school officials? A. No, I did not.

Q. Did you keep the March 8th appointment? A. No, I did not.

Q. Can you explain why not? A. There was a rally at the Board of Education and we could not get in, my mother and sisters and I.

Q. Prior to March 24th, did you have any correspondence, either orally or in writing, from anybody at the school department, either at Central or anyone in the Columbus School System, did you have any correspondence whatsoever? A. No, I did not.

Q. Between March 8th and March 24th did you have reason to believe that you were suspended from school? A. Yes, there was—Well, at the rally they had at the Board of Education, the Board reinstated the students that were suspended, and they were to return to school. I did return to school that following afternoon.

The Court: On what date was that, the following afternoon, March the 9th?

The Witness: It was the day that I had the appointment set up for the Pupil Personnel, sir.

The Court: That was March the 8th?

Mr. Roos: March the 8th, Your Honor.

The Witness: The students were to be reinstated but I went to school and they would not open the doors. All the doors were locked. I did knock or pound on the door and one teacher did come. I believe it was the gym teacher, men's gym teacher, and he wouldn't let us in. We told him that we were reinstated and he said that the school had no prior knowledge to us being reinstated and refused to open the door.

By Mr. Roos:

Q. During the period between March 8th and March 24th, did you and/or your family, members of your family, attempt to contact the school officials concerning your suspension? A. Yes. My sister wrote a letter and she called. My mother called, but as far as we could get was the secretary and she kept telling us that the guy, the head of Pupil Personnel, either wasn't in or he was busy, so that's as far as we could ever get.

Q. Were any of your calls returned? A. No, they weren't returned.

Q. On March 24th did you receive a letter transferring you to another school in the Columbus system? A. Yes, I did.

Q. Had you requested this transfer? A. No, I did not.

Q. Were you given any hearing prior to the transfer? A. No, there wasn't.

Q. Did this transfer result in any difficulty to you? A. Yes, the difficulty would be when my mother and I went down to Adult Day School, that is to the school I was transferred to, the principal of Adult Day School did have the impression that I was definitely a trouble maker, he stated I would not be able to take any courses that I wasn't making a B average.

Mr. Bustin: Your Honor, I am going to object to what somebody else is saying. It is heresay.

Mr. Roos: Your Honor, it's not being offered—

The Court: Overruled. Go ahead.

A. Any subject I wasn't making at least a B average or above, I would not be able to take in Adult Day School. His attitude was bad, so I didn't go to Adult Day School. Instead I just didn't go.

By Mr. Roos:

Q. You ultimately did get into another school though; is that correct? A. Yes, I did.

Q. When you did get in, did you have difficulty making up the work that you had missed during the time you had been out of school? A. Yes, I never did catch up fully to what I did miss and the change from one way of teaching to another made it a little worse than what I had already had.

Mr. Roos: Your Honor, the letter of March 24th is Exhibit 1D.

Nothing further of this witness.

The Court: You may cross-examine, Mr. Bustin.

CROSS–EXAMINATION

By Mr. Bustin:

Q. Mr. Lopez, how old were you at the time that you were suspended? A. I was 19.

Q. Nineteen years of age? A. Yes.

The Court: What year of school were you in at that time? A. My senior year, sir.

Q. What was taking place at the school at the time that the whole school was dismissed? A. There was a student disruption.

Q. Did the Pupil Personnel Department make any attempt to set up a meeting with you on or about March 5th? A. Yes, there was. I did have —Well, I can't remember the exact date, but there was an appointment set up because I did receive a letter saying there was an appointment.

Q. Did you keep it? A. No, I did not.

Q. What was the nature of that communication that you received on March the 5th? Who did you receive it from?

The Court: Was it addressed to you or your parents? A. It was addressed to my parents.

The Court: What did it say? Did it request that you and your parents meet with the school officials? A. Yes, sir, that's the way it was.

The Court: Did it set up a date for meeting with them? A. Yes.

The Court: What was the date? A. March the 8th.

The Court: All right.

By Mr. Bustin:

Q. When you appeared at the Pupil Personnel Department on March 8—Let's say first: Did you appear there on March 8th? A. Yes, I did appear.

Q. Were your parents with you? A. Yes, she was, my mother.

Q. Your mother was with you? A. Yes.

Q. I believe your testimony is you did not keep that appointment? A. It was impossible for me to keep the appointment. They had the doors blocked with people, and I could not get in.

Q. Did you try to get in? A. Yes, sir. Yes, there was an attempt to get in.

Q. I didn't hear you. A. Yes, we did try to get in.

Q. Did try to get in. Who was blocking the door? A. The people in the rally, the people, several hundreds of people.

Q. Hundreds of people. Mr. Lopez, I take it you have graduated from Columbus Public Schools? A. Yes, I have.

Q. What date did you graduate, do you know? A. I graduated June 10th of last year.

The Court: Of 1972? A. Yes, sir.

The Court: Does that mean there was a year's delay in your graduation? A. Well, sir, I was in night school and you can only take four subjects a night and each subject is half a credit.

The Court: When you did not go to the school to which you were ordered to go, after you were suspended from Central High School, wasn't it—A. Yes, sir.

The Court:—did you then decide to go to night school? A. Yes, sir, that's when I decided to go to night school.

The Court: How old were you then? A. Eighteen. Ninteen, sir.

The Court: Nineteen? A. Yes, sir.

The Court: So, at that age, did you have a choice as to where you would go to school? A. I don't understand, sir.

The Court: Maybe you can inform me, Mr. Bustin. I think the compulsory age is 18; isn't it?

Mr. Bustin: That's right, Your Honor.

The Court: When an individual is 19, can they choose where to go if they are, let's say, academically eligible?

Mr. Bustin: The answer to that question is normally yes, the individual who is over the compulsory age would have a choice.

The Court: Then would you agree that this witness at the age of 19, when he chose not to go to the school to which he was ordered transferred, and instead chose to go to night school, had the right to do that?

Mr. Bustin: I would agree with that.

The Court: So, after you left Central High School, Dwight, you started to night school; is that correct? A. Yes, sir.

The Court: In relation to the 25th of March of 1971, when did you start to night school? A. I started night school in September the same year, sir.

The Court: So, you didn't go back to school either in the day or the night after you were suspended from Central High School and until you started to night school the following September? A. No, sir, I couldn't get in because the semester had—

The Court: My question to you is: After you were suspended from Central High School on February the 26th of 1971, you did not go to school any place until the following September; is that correct? A. Yes, sir.

The Court: Go ahead.

By Mr. Bustin:

Q. Mr. Lopez, where did you go to school during the 68–69 school year? A. It was in the vicinity of Salem, Philadelphia, Comer Heights, Pennsylvania, just outside of Philadelphia.

Mr. Bustin: Did you attend any school here in Columbus during that year. A. Well, I went there one full year. I can't remember.

Q. Do you know, Mr. Lopez, at the time you were suspended, how many credits you had earned in school? Say this was your senior year. Do you know how many credits you had earned at that time? A. No, I don't.

Mr. Bustin: That's all the questions I have.

The Court: Do you have any further questions, Mr. Roos?

Mr. Ross: Just one further question, Your Honor.

The Court: All right.

REDIRECT EXAMINATION

By Mr. Roos:

Q. Mr Lopez, to your knowledge were there many people attending Columbus school, or in your personal knowledge, who were 19 years of age? A. Yes, there was.

Mr. Roos: Thank you. No further questions, Your Honor.

The Court: Dwight, when you received a notice of suspension, did it say how long you were suspended? A. No, it didn't say.

The Court: Did anyone ever tell you either verbally or in writing why you were suspended? A. No, sir.

The Court: Are you sure? A. Yes, sir, I am sure.

The Court: You stated a few moments ago that on the 26th of February, 1971, there was a student disruption at Central High School; is that correct? A. Yes, sir.

The Court: What was the nature of that disruption? What happened there, Dwight? A. It started during Black History Week. The students wanted to put on their own black history show and they requested the use of the auditorium, and the request was granted; but, when they found out who the speakers were, or would be, they refused. That led to tension. A few weeks later—

The Court: Let's come up then to the 26th of February. You were in school that day; weren't you? A. Yes, sir.

The Court: You said there was a student disruption. What was the nature of the student disruption? Who did what? A. Two students were shot that night, two black students.

The Court: Were shot? A. Yes, by white students from another school.

The Court: During the day? A. No, it was—

The Court: I am talking about, Dwight, during the school day of February the 26th. You stated on your direct examination that there was a student disruption at the school that day. I am trying to find out from you if you know, and I assume that you know because you said there was a student disruption there, what was the nature of that disruption? Who did what? A. The students overthrew tables.

The Court: Where were the tables? A. In the lunch room, and broke a few windows, and that's all that I could see that was done.

The Court: Did you take part in that disruption? A. No, sir, I was in class. I had what they called free study in the lunch room at the time. The students came in the lunch room and started overthrowing the tables, and I and a few more friends of mine, we walked out. We just walked out.

The Court: You are saying now, and you are under oath, that you took no part in that student disruption on February 26th? A. That's right, sir. I didn't have anything to do with it at all.

The Court: Did you ever receive a letter from the school authorities telling you why you were suspended? A. No, sir, I never got a letter saying why I was suspended; just that I was suspended, and that was it.

The Court: Did anyone tell you on February 26th to leave the premises of the school? How did you know you were suspended? A. The school was let out early that day.

The Court: Did you leave with all the other students? A. Yes, sir.

The Court: You weren't asked to leave before or anything like that; you were not singled out by any of the school administrators and told to leave; were you? A. No, sir.

The Court: You left with the rest of the students? A. Yes, sir.

The Court: You didn't go back to school the next day; did you? A. No, sir.

The Court: Why not? A. The next day, well that happened on a Friday, the next day was Saturday, sir.

The Court: You didn't go back the next Monday; did you? A. No, sir.

The Court: Why didn't you go back? A. The Friday that I was suspended, I received a call.

The Court: Wait. Were you suspended—You left with all the other students on Friday; didn't you? A. Yes, sir.

The Court: Because the whole student body was let out about 10:30 in the morning? A. Yes, sir.

The Court: After you left the premises of the school, how did you find out that you were not to return to school the following Monday? A. The principal called my house that Friday that I was suspended.

The Court: That Friday? A. Yes, and stated that I was suspended.

The Court: Did he tell your mother or did he tell you? A. He told my mother I was suspended.

Q. You weren't there? A. I was there standing next—I answered the phone and he asked to speak to my mother.

The Court: He told your mother that you were suspended from school and you were not to return to school on the following Monday; is that correct? A. Yes, sir.

The Court: Did he give your mother any reason why you were suspended? A. No, sir.

The Court: Later on you received a letter either on the 5th or the 6th of March telling you to come to the Education Building on the 8th of March; is that correct? A. Yes, sir.

The Court: You didn't get into this meeting that you were supposed to have on the 8th of March; did you? A. No, sir.

The Court: Did you ever go back with your mother or anyone else on the 9th or the 10th or the 11th or 12th of March? Did you ever make an attempt to go back there? A. We called for another appointment but they wouldn't speak to us, sir.

The Court: You found out nothing until the 25th of March; is that right? A. Yes, sir.

The Court: And on the 25th of March you got a letter saying that you were transferred to another school; is that correct? A. Yes, sir.

The Court: Does anyone have any further questions of this witness?

Mr. Bustin: May I ask another question, Your Honor?

The Court: Yes.

RECROSS–EXAMINATION

By Mr. Bustin:

Q. Mr. Lopez, have you ever seen a letter of February 26, 1971, directed to your parents? A. Yes, sir.

Q. Does that letter not say that there had been a disruption at school in which a group of students was involved, and does it not say that Dwight was in the group? A. I can't remember. I wasn't in the group.

Q. I will hand you what has been marked as Plaintiff Exhibit 1A. Have you ever seen that letter? A. I don't remember seeing it. My mother received it. It was written to her.

Q. Are you saying that your mother never went over that letter with you, or that you could have seen it and don't remember? A. I can't remember. I may have seen it. I don't know. I can't remember.

The Court: You may step down from the witness stand. Your testimony is finished now.

Do you want to ask another question?

Mr. Bustin: No, Your Honor.

The Court: Call your next witness, Mr. Murphy.

* * *

NOTES AND QUESTIONS

1. What new information did the testimony of Dwight Lopez produce? Is the fact that the Board of Education reinstated the suspended students at the March 8th rally of any significance? Note that Dwight denies having any contact with school officials from the start of his suspension on February 26 until March 24th, when he was notified of his transfer to Adult Day School. Recall as well that he testified he could not get into the Board of Education building for his March 8th meeting and that when he then went to Central High School, he could not gain admittance. Correspondence with Mr. Calvin Park, then principal of Central, reveals a slightly different recall of events:

At the time of his appointment at the Pupil Personnel Office at the Board of Education, Dwight Lopez came to my office and insisted that he be permitted to reenter classes at Central High. I told him he was to report to the Pupil Personnel Office at the Board of Education, as indicated in his letter, and whatever decision they made there concerning school attendance I would accept. I verified by telephone, while Dwight was with me, that he was expected at the Pupil Personnel Office. I'm confident that had Dwight made himself known at the Pupil Personnel Office he would have been heard and assisted in planning for his continued school participation.

As Dwight Lopez was older than the compulsory school age he did not have to comply with the requests for conferences. However, I urged the Pupil Personnel Office to make a school assignment for Mr. Lopez. Due to his age he was assigned to evening school, a program primarily for adults.

Sometime later Dwight Lopez came to me for assistance to enroll in evening school. We were able to accomplish this and I am glad to report that Dwight eventually graduated.

Had this testimony been introduced, would it have made any difference in Dwight Lopez's case?

2. Suppose Dwight had actually been a "trouble maker," as the principal of the Adult Day School apparently believed. Should this information be allowed into the hearing? Which side would it help? Note that here Dwight testified that the principal of the Adult Day School *considered* him a trouble-maker. Can you see the strategy of Dwight's lawyers in wanting such information presented? Mr. Bustin objected on the grounds of hearsay to Dwight's testimony, but was overruled.

The rules of evidence are complex and require many hours of study to master. Generally testimony which is "hearsay," that is, statements which do not stem directly from the knowledge of the witness but constitute "second hand" information are excluded. So too is testimony which could mislead the jury or is irrelevant to the proceeding. Under present Federal Rules of Evidence, "hearsay" is defined as a "statement, other than one made by the declarant while testifying at the trial or hearing, offered in evidence to prove the truth of the matter asserted." It is the second-hand aspect of hearsay testimony that makes it objectionable. Thus, someone might be permitted to testify about what somebody else said if it is only offered as proof that the person said it, rather than for the truth of the matter asserted *per se*.

The rules of evidence also restrict the kinds of questions attorneys can ask witnesses. For example, on direct examination, attorneys can generally not "lead" their witnesses by suggesting the correct answer, e. g., "You were able to overhear the conversation, weren't you?" Also excluded in most circumstances are questions which try to draw a conclusion from the witness. Lawyers, not witnesses, make conclusions in their opening and final arguments. On cross-examination, as anyone who has watched some of the more realistic courtroom portrayals on television and in the movies can tell, the attorney has more freedom to question the witness. Leading questions, for example, are permitted because the attorney desires not to prompt the witness but attack the accuracy or veracity of previous statements.

There are numerous exceptions, however, to rules of evidence, and so, as here, testimony which appears to fall into one or the other of the excluded categories is allowed despite objections from opposing attorneys. It should be pointed out that rules of evidence are not applied as strictly in a case trial before a judge as before a jury. What is required in each instance is a delicate balancing of interests by the judge, who alone is responsible for the fairness of the hearing.

3. What was the significance of all the questions about Dwight's age? Did Mr. Roos on re-direct examination effectively counter the points made by Mr. Bustin?

4. Note that Judge Kinneary plays a major role in the hearing by asking numerous questions of his own. Where, as here, the case is tried before a judge, the judge's activist role may have entirely different implications than would be the case in a jury trial. Why might this be the case in our adversary system of justice? Do you think Judge Kinneary's questions were helpful in this case? In what way?

(2) Testimony of Norval Goss

NORVAL GOSS,

called as a witness on behalf of the defendants, having been first duly sworn, testified as follows:

DIRECT EXAMINATION

By Mr. Bustin:

Q. Do you want to state your name, please? A. My name is Norval Goss.

Q. What is your position with the schools? A. I am the Director of Pupil Personnel.

Q. Can you describe that briefly, what that means? A. That involves keeping records of students attendance, enrollment, personnel records, cumulative files.

Q. For the record, Your Honor, on plaintiff's list of exhibits, this is listed as Exhibit 14.

Mr. Goss, I will hand you what has been marked as Defendant's Exhibit A and ask you to identify that. A. This is a bulletin which has been sent from my office to principals concerning suspension of students. The date is July the tenth, 1973.

Q. Is the procedure now in force in the Columbus Public Schools? A. Yes, it is.

Q. Mr. Goss, have you had occasion to examine the cumulative records of the particular students which are involved in this litigation? A. Yes, I have.

Q. Have you examined those records in light of their point hours throughout the years? A. Yes.

Q. Mr. Goss, I will hand you what has been marked as Defendant Exhibit B and ask you to identify that. A. This is a sheet listing the number of credits earned during each year and the point average during each year of the students involved. It also gives, with the exception of Betty Crome who has not yet graduated, it gives their high school career.

Q. Is that compilation based upon the cumulative records which are listed on plaintiff exhibit? A. Yes, it is. From the cumulative records, I prepared it personally.

Q. Mr. Goss has your department of pupil personnel at any time since March or April of 1971 received any requests from other schools or employers for information concerning the suspension of these particular children? A. I would not be able to say that because the request would go to the individual school rather than to our department.

Q. It goes to the principal? A. Right.

Q. How many credits does it take in the Columbus Public School System to graduate? A. It takes 17.

Q. Mr. Goss, for clarification on Defendant Exhibit B, I notice under Dwight Lopez that for the year 68–69 a figure of two tenths is shown. What does that represent? A. That means that Dwight Lopez passed physical education only that year, the only subject that he passed, was two tenths of a credit in physical education.

Mr. Bustin: I think that's all the questions I have, Your Honor.

CROSS–EXAMINATION

By Mr. Roos:

Q. Mr. Goss, for how long have you been in the Columbus School System? A. Eighteen years.

Q. Could you describe doing what? A. I started as a teacher, taught for three years; entered an administrative training program for a year; served as assistant principal of several different buildings. For the last three school years I have been in the Department of Pupil Personnel, the last two years as director of that department. The year, previous to that assisting the director of that department.

Q. In your experience in the Columbus School System, recognizing that you are now in pupil personnel, what was the effect on a student with respect to work missed during the time that they were suspended? Did a student receive a zero for work missed? A. Yes.

Q. This would have an effect ultimately on the grades that a student received; would it not? A. It could have. In these cases it doesn't appear to have.

Q. That's uncertain. You say it doesn't appear? A. It doesn't appear to have. I can't say for sure.

Q. But a zero would have an effect? Zero certainly is not a 50 or 100? A. That's right.

Mr. Bustin: Your Honor, I am going to object. I think this is beyond our direct examination; argumentative.

The Court: I will agree to that.

Mr. Roos: Your Honor, I would like to call this witness as plaintiffs' witness.

The Court: You may go ahead. It's beyond the scope of the direct examination, Mr. Roos, but I am not going to let you call this witness in your own case now, because you should have made that decision before.

I will let you continue your examination along the lines of what harm it will do, even though I consider it beyond the scope of the direct examination.

Mr. Roos: But you are not allowing me to call this witness as the plaintiffs' witness?

The Court: No, I am not.

By Mr. Roos:

Q. In your experience in the school system, are there other harms that can result from being out of school as a suspended student? A. Well, I am not a psychologist and I could not comment as the psychologist has commented. I would have to say that any absence from school can, of course, have negative effects, and that would include suspension from school.

Q. Educational effects, I would gather, is what you are primarily talking about? A. They can have, not necessarily.

Q. But a zero automatically would have a negative effect, would it not? A. It obviously has a negative effect on that.

Q. Mr. Goss, you mentioned that new rules have been adopted concerning suspensions and expulsions; is that correct? A. This is essentially a statement of the procedures that have been in effect for a number of years.

The Court: Just give him a responsive answer. A. Yes, I am sorry. Yes.

Q. These are defendants Exhibit 14? A. Yes.

Q. Could you tell us the procedure that was utilized in adopting these rules? A. Now, is this the rules, July 10, 1973?

Q. That is correct, the July the 10th rules. A. Mr. Dumaree, who is the deputy superintendent of schools, and is responsible for administration of all the buildings, felt that it was very desirable for us to have a firmly written procedure of what we have always done.

We have relied in the past upon 3313.66 as giving the principal the authority to suspend a student, and we have not felt that it was specifically necessary for us to have a specific statement of this. Mr. Dumaree felt that we should. He asked me to draft a copy of this.

After several draftings, revisions, consultation with various people in the school system and outside the school system, input from Dr. Ellis, the superintendent, and clearance by a committee of principals, this document was the final product.

Q. Was this document approved by the Board? A. No, this document was not and documents of this type are not normally approved by the Board of Education.

Q. It could be amended without the Board also; is that correct? A. Yes.

Q. In developing procedures, you rely primarily on 3313.66 of the Ohio Statute? A. That is—

The Court: I think this witness has stated that everyone in the educational system, all principals, relied on 3313.66 as the authority to suspend * * *

Mr. Roos: Nothing further of this witness, Your Honor.

The Court: Mr. Bustin, do you have any further questions?

Mr. Bustin: No, Your Honor. I have no further questions of this witness.

By the Court:

Q. Mr. Goss, may I assume that since this procedure for suspension, which went out from you to all principals on July 10, 1973, may I assume that you are prepared to explain this procedure? A. Yes, sir.

Q. Let's go down to the paragraph or the part of the first page which is designated as suspension procedures. For the sake of my question, let us assume that a pupil at Central High School has engaged in an activity which interfered with the orderly functioning of the school, and a teacher brings that to the attention of the principal.

Let's go on with that language. "Whenever an incident occurs that may lead to a suspension, the principal or assistant principal shall investigate the nature of the alleged offense before commencing suspension procedures."

Tell us what that means? What does he do? What do you contemplate that a principal or an assistant principal would do in the investigation?

A. I think what it means is that they would look into the circumstances that have happened, give the student—call the student in, ask the teacher, ask the student what the situation has been, and get their sides of the story, so to speak.

Q. No. We are not up to that yet. This procedure enjoins upon the principal or the assistant principal the duty of investigating the alleged offense before commencing suspension procedures. What does that mean? What does he do? What do you contemplate that a principal or an assistant principal would do under that language? A. I am not sure exactly what you mean.

Q. Let me repeat it to you, Mr. Goss. For the sake of my question, we will assume that a student at the Central High School has been reported by his teacher. Let's say his home room teacher, if there is such a thing today, has been reported by his home room teacher as engaging in an activity which threatens or interferes with the orderly functioning of the school and the teacher comes to the principal's office and says so and so did this.

What does the principal, or what is the principal obliged to do under the language of the first sentence there? A. It is our intention that the principal should talk with the student too, rather than just taking.—

Q. He is supposed to investigate it before he talks to the student; isn't he? A. No, that's part of the investigation.

Q. All right. Do you contemplate that you call the student into his office? A. Yes.

Q. What happens then? A. He would ask the student what had happened too.

Q. Let's assume even that the person who makes the complaint against the student is present, do you contemplate that that person would be present while the student is being questioned? A. That would be at the discretion of the principal.

Q. So, the teacher that reported it may be there or may not be there depending upon the discretion of the principal; is that it? A. Yes.

Q. Let's assume that the teacher is not there. What do you contemplate the principal would say to the student? A. As I say, he would ask the student what had happened so that he might present his side of the story, so to speak.

Q. Does a principal make any charge against the student at that point? A. Probably. He would say, your home room teacher has said that you did such and such; what do you say?

Q. Suppose the student denies it happens. A. Well, this becomes a matter of the judgment—

Q. You are at a hearing stage, but your language there, if you will look at your plan, in the second sentence, "Unless the pupil is unavailable or unwilling to discuss the incident with the principal * * *"

Now, mind you, you are investigating the alleged misbehavior by the student. This investigation shall include a discussion with the pupil so that the pupil may be given an opportunity to be heard with respect to the alleged offense.

Are you at the hearing stage or are you at the investigative stage at that point?

A. I am not sure that we had enough legal consideration to make—

Q. What you are saying to the Court is that you don't know whether you are at the investigative stage or the hearing? A. Investigative and hearing in my terms would be very closely intermingled.

Q. Let's assume that you are in a hearing stage then. So far, this is what's happened: The teacher came to you and reported an incident to the principal, and the principal hears the story from the teacher and the principal calls the student into his office.

The teacher may or may not be there, and the student is confronted with this complaint made by his teacher, and he is given an opportunity to explain it or deny it, or admit it; is that correct, at that point?

A. Essentially, yes, I suppose.

Q. Let's assume that after the principal has had the complaint from the teacher and he has had the story or the defense or the explanation from the pupil, the principal decides to suspend the pupil. At that point do you contemplate under these rules that you have sent out to all the principals that the principal would be acting then under Section 3313.66? A. Yes.

Q. They may suspend up to, is it ten days? A. Up to ten days.

Q. These rules or these guidelines or these suspension procedures that you have published provide that if the principal determines that grounds for suspension do exist, he then suspends the pupil; doesn't he? A. Yes.

Q. What does he say to the pupil? A. He is instructed to tell the pupil the reason for the suspension and the term, the length of the suspension.

Q. This also provides that the principal shall notify the pupil of the exact reason and the length of the suspension. Does he do that verbally or in writing? A. Probably both.

Q. What do you mean probably? A. The student is there—If the student is there, he would inform him that you are suspended for such and such an offense.

Q. And further informs the pupil that the suspension means that he must stay out, must stay—Next he must notify the parent or guardian of the suspension by phone, if possible, and explain the reason and the length of the suspension. Does that contemplate that the parent or the guardian may not get a written notice of the suspension and the reasons for the suspension? A. No. If they contact them by phone, they would also get a letter.

Q. They would also get a letter? A. But they will attempt to notify them by phone because it is quicker.

Q. In the case of the ordinary suspension, is the pupil ordered off the property immediately? A. Again, it would depend upon whether the principal has been able to get in touch with the parents on the phone and tell them that the student is suspended, and is coming home, or they should come and get them.

Q. Under this plan, Mr. Goss, do you contemplate that the pupil will have the opportunity, except for his own statements, to the principal, to call any witnesses in his own defense? A. That would be the judgment of the principal.

Q. That's up to the principal and not the student; is that it? A. That's right.

The Court: That's all. You may step down.

NOTES AND QUESTIONS

1. Mr. Goss testified as a witness, in fact, the only witness, for the defense. Do you think the attorneys for the defendants should have presented more witnesses? How might additional testimony about the facts in the case have strengthened the defendants' arguments?

In correspondence with the authors, Mr. Calvin Park, principal of Central High School, elaborated on the suspension incident as follows:

> The disturbance at school that brought about the suspension of Dwight Lopez and others was a well organized and pre-planned refusal of many students to attend class. After listening to their complaints I asked them to return to class and follow their schedules so that school could continue in a normal fashion. Some students chose to run through the halls and throw the school into a chaotic situation. I finally had to dismiss school for the day.

> Many students had been identified as members of the dissident group while I was meeting with them. To ascertain with certainty whether or not the individuals had returned to class or continued with the disruption I requested teachers to check their record of class attendance and verify the presence or absence of the students in question. Dwight Lopez was one of the students that did not return to class. The students that had ignored the request to return to class were notified by letter of a time to return to school with their parents for a conference to clarify the problem.

Should Mr. Park have been called to testify? Might his testimony have helped bolster the defendant's case? In later correspondence with the authors, Mr. Bustin reaffirmed this strategy of presenting only one witness to testify about the factual situation. He noted that

> It was our position at the outset that the Federal Constitution and specifically the Fourteenth Amendment did not apply to the situation posed by the Ohio Statutes involved in the litigation. That being the case, there was really no additional state of facts such as would alter the situation. Either the Fourteenth Amendment applied to the statute or it did not.

Review the briefs filed by the defendants and note their arguments that no property or liberty right under the Fourteenth Amendment is involved. Mr. Bustin added,

> * * * having argued the case before the Supreme Court and based upon the questions which were asked, I remain convinced that the case essentially from start to finish always involved a question of law. The main focus of the Court's questions did not center around the fact situation but centered around the law and policy which would not only govern that situation but all situations in general.

He concluded that the position eventually put forward by the four dissenters when the U. S. Supreme Court ruled on the case was "essentially a reproduction" of the defendants' arguments of law.

The U. S. Supreme Court, of course, is not a trial court. The Justices must rely on the facts already presented in the case at the trial stage. Recall Mr. Murphy's concern at the outset that the circumstances surrounding the suspensions might in the eyes of the court have justified the school officials' actions. Do you think the counsel for the defendants may have focused too much on questions of law to the neglect of the particular factual circumstances surrounding the suspensions? Would their case have been stronger had they played up the turmoil occurring in and out of the schools at the time?

2. Mr. Goss was asked to describe Dwight's academic record. Did his answer help or hurt Dwight? Should Dwight's academic record make any difference? Suppose Dwight had a history of poor grades, frequent minor disciplinary actions, and peripheral involvement in school disruption. Would such a record change your views about whether school officials had acted fairly in suspending him? Suppose under these circumstances school officials said they were suspending Dwight as a precautionary measure, even though he had not been involved in the lunchroom fracas. Should information about a student's prior academic record and behavior be allowed into the hearing?

3. Do you think Mr. Roos' cross-examination of Mr. Goss was effective? What did his answers add to the plaintiffs' case, if anything?

4. Judge Kinneary also questioned Mr. Goss about the recently-instituted new suspension procedures. Was the resulting testimony more helpful to one side than the other?

(3) Testimony of Herbert Rie

HERBERT E. RIE,

called as a witness on behalf of the plaintiffs, having been first duly sworn, testified as follows:

DIRECT EXAMINATION

By Mr. Roos:

Q. Mr. Rie, will you please state your full name for the record? A. Herbert E. Rie.

Q. Could you tell the Court what your present position is? A. Yes, I am chief psychologist at Children's Hospital here in Columbus. I am Professor in the Ohio State University Departments of Pediatrics and Psychology.

Q. In the course of your experience as a psychologist, have you had experience in dealing with children? A. Yes, I deal almost exclusively with children and have for the last 15 years.

Q. In your experience as a psychologist, have you had dealings with children who have been excluded from schools, suspended, expelled, or otherwise? A. Yes.

Q. For how long have you had such sorts of dealings? A. Throughout that 15-year period to which I referred.

Q. During the course of your experience, have you had an opportunity to observe psychological effects of exclusion from school? A. Yes, I have.

Q. Could you tell this Court the sorts of things that you have observed? A. Yes.

Mr. Bustin: Your Honor, for the record we make the same objection we did to the previous psychologist's testimony as to relevance, and I believe this is cumulative of this.

The Court: Go ahead.

A. My observations over the years have been that the effects of a child being excluded from school are essentially negative, though I would want to put my specific observations in the context that one cannot, of course, speak unequivocally about the adaptation of all individuals to a given circumstance.

There are going to be exceptions and hence it's almost impossible to predict before hand whether all children are going to respond in a given way. The majority, however, in my opinion, respond to a greater or lesser degree in the way that I would like to describe:

First: There is in many cases an impact upon the child's feelings regarding himself. It tends to be a blow to his self esteem; and

Secondly: It tends to generate feelings of relative powerlessness and helplessness in the child.

It tends further to affect his attitudes toward the school or toward the school system or towards specific school personnel such that he is inclined, following such an episode, to view the school system with greater resentment, suspicion and fear.

It is likely to affect the child further in that certain incidental learning occurs, not intended. It occurs unwittingly. That is by being excluded from school, on the occasion of a problem, there invariably is a problem or suspected problem, the child learns with this termination of communication and interaction that this is the preferred mode of contending with problems, namely that one interposes space and time between those individuals who have encountered the problem between them.

Secondly: It confirms for him that on the occasion of a problem between an individual and an adult in authority over him, in this case the school teacher or the school personnel in his particular school, that given the termination of communication and the exclusion of the child, there can be, for him, little explanation, little understanding, little confirmation of what has actually occurred, what it is that he has done for which he is being excluded in explicit terms, and hence the likelihood that his own inferences unchecked by any communication with those who have imposed this particular management upon him without the opportunity to check in a sense the reality of his own inferences. These are very often in children who are in trouble likely to be far more devastating than perhaps was intended.

There is furthermore in our experience, particularly if there have been repeated exclusions from school, the probability of the child being stigmatized and treated prejudicially thereafter.

We have a great deal of evidence both with respect to positive expectations on the part of a school system concerning a child, or in this instance negative, that individuals dealing with the school child are likely to contend with him consistent with those expectations and thereby, on the basis of this prior knowledge and expectations, to alter their modes of dealing with them.

In this instance, expecting him in a sense to be a so-called trouble maker, and dealing with him on the basis not of verifiable pre-characteristics of the child but rather on the basis of the past record of his having been expelled.

Finally, and lastly—

Q. May I interject at this point? A. Yes.

The Court: No. Would you mind letting the doctor conclude finally, because I will have a couple questions.

Mr. Roos: Fine.

The Court: Go ahead.

A. I wanted to add as a supplement in a sense to what I have said already what I would regard as a number of possible, what I suppose I would call second order effects:

They may or may not occur. They occur in some cases.

Given the circumstances I have referred to thus far, the child is identified as one of the consequences, as the problem, and there is therefore often, not invariably but often, failure to seek the other conditions which interacted with the child to lead to his exclusion from school.

That is if one has identified the problem, one has acted upon it, there is, of course, little need logically to do anything else.

There is then the consequent failure in some cases to seek help for the child if he needs it, because the problem has ostensibly been dealt with, and furthermore the feelings engendered by his behavior that has led to the exclusion are not conducive to sympathetic concern for the child.

There may be general disapproval of the child as a consequence of his expulsion by his family, by neighbors, by acquaintances who then regard him with further suspicion, with expectations that indeed he is going to be a trouble maker, and the child in that sense may be further alienated from resources than he is already.

Finally: It seems to me there is, in many cases, the child's inability to maintain himself academically and the feelings attendant upon that, particularly if the exclusion is prolonged, or if there are frequent exclusions from school.

By The Court:

Q. Doctor, you frequently used the term the child in the testimony you have just given. Does the term the child include students through the high school years, that is through what we know as the ninth, tenth, and eleventh grades? A. As I am using it, it does, though at the different levels, the different kinds of multiple reactions I have spoken of would generally be experienced in differing degrees.

Q. Doctor, you may or may not know that in Ohio a suspension may not be for more than ten days. Assuming that a suspension from school is for ten days or less, are all of the statements you have made equally valid to this period of ten days? A. Yes, sir, in the context within which

I placed them initially that the reaction will vary from child to child and will surely be dependent upon the frequence of any such exclusion for any given child.

The Court: Go ahead.

By Mr. Roos:

Q. With respect to a child who views himself as innocent and who is not given an opportunity to contest his innocence, would the effects you described be greater or lesser, and to what extent?

Mr. Bustin: Objection, Your Honor.

The Court: I will overrule your objection, but I think I know how the doctor is going to answer that question.

A. I would say that the effects upon a child who has in this sense been unjustly excluded from school might be different, that is with respect to the particular reactions the child has. I have listed a variety of potential reactions.

The child who is in your sense unjustly excluded from school is not as likely to have a blow to his self esteem given what he knows of his own behavior and status as the child with whom that isn't the case. He is far more likely however to react with resentment against the system which has treated him as he would view it, I assume, unjustly.

The Court: Doctor, that's equally true in any other system in life; isn't it?

A. Surely.

The Court: You may proceed.

Mr. Roos: No further questions of this witness, Your Honor.

CROSS–EXAMINATION

By Mr. Bustin:

Q. Doctor, have you had an opportunity to actually examine the respective plaintiffs, children in this particular case? A. I have not.

Q. Have you looked or examined or studied their school records? A. I don't know the plaintiffs.

Q. You don't know at all? A. I do not.

The Court: Let me say, doctor, there are five plaintiffs here.

A. Let me say then, in response to your question, that since our psychology staff at the hospital sees some 1300 children per year, it is conceivable that someone on my staff or I perhaps even have indeed seen one of these plaintiffs, but not in connection with this particular action and not in preparation for it.

Q. I take it by your testimony then you have not examined their school records, their cumulative records? A. I have not.

Q. Have you talked to any of the school officials at any of the schools involved, Marion Franklin, Central, McGuffey? A. Not about this particular action or the behavior which brings the students here, no. We communicate with the students constantly and, of course, have communications with these particular schools you have mentioned regarding many students and many problems, but again not regarding this particular action.

Mr. Bustin: No further questions, Your Honor.

Mr. Roos: Nothing further of this witness.

By The Court:

Q. Dr. Rie, over the broad range of pupils, whether they are in the primary grades or the secondary grades, who are subjected to a suspension under Ohio Law, do you have any opinion as to whether or not the effects are generally harmful?

Now, I have in mind, of course, the qualification that you made before you started your testimony, but what I sincerely want to know from you is whether or not the disciplinary measure of suspension of a pupil from a primary or a secondary school in Ohio is generally harmful?

A. I would say that generally it is. Modified, however, again by the provision simply that it need not be devastating; that there are few events in the lives of children, single events, which are "so-called traumatic."

* * *

It is difficult indeed to find anything that would be beneficial in this kind of action save in one instance, in that instance in which the school child, and I mean the full age range of school, kindergarten through high school, in which the child finds the school situation for whatever reason so tense, so anxiety provoking, so disorganizing in a sense for him that he cannot adapt to it in a useful way that's acceptable.

Under those circumstances of extreme tension, it may be helpful to the child to separate him from that environment temporarily for his own relief; however, as in most instances, children and adults as well react under crisis far better if they have an opportunity to know what the circumstances are, if they are given the chance to predict what is going to ensue, and hence even in that instance from a psychologic prospective, it would be preferable with prior communication about the intent of the action.

Q. Is that your professional way of saying, doctor, that when a student, we will say, at the high school level is charged with an infraction of the rules or some other activity which threatens the orderly functioning of the class in which he is located, that it is far better to give that person an explanation of what he did and give him an opportunity to defend himself, so to speak? A. I would certainly think so. Again, there are exceptions, of course, to most everything. As I said, one can generalize, but human beings, and if there is an occasion of extreme emergency, obviously one must act immediately. In the instance of a suicide attempt or presumed suicide attempt, anticipated suicide attempt. I am choosing that explicitly not as a school problem but as a psychological problem. One doesn't wait. One obviously intervenes.

Q. You have to act under, shall we say, the necessity of the expediency of the circumstances? That is to say, if a student, a pretty well-grown, 16-year old boy gets up and strikes a female teacher, he should be removed immediately; is that correct? A. Surely.

* * *

NOTES AND QUESTIONS

1. Dr. Rie was one of several expert witnesses the plaintiffs placed on the stand. Opinion testimony from an expert may be rendered on ultimate issues in a case, unlike opinion testimony from lay witnesses. Before recent changes in the Federal Rules of Evidence, a lay witness could not testify that someone seemed angry. The witness could only describe the physical manifestations of those conditions. On the other hand, an expert witness may give scientific or technical opinions based on his specialized knowledge. Therefore, an expert witness has to be first qualified as an expert before he is allowed to render his opinion. That is the reason why it is necessary to go into the expert's background.

Presently, under Federal Rules of Evidence, a lay witness can give conclusionary evidence but only (a) if it is rationally based on the perception of the witness and (b) is helpful to a clear understanding of his testimony or determination of a fact in issue. Expert witnesses, on the other hand, continue to have far greater leeway in presenting conclusionary testimony.

Does Dr. Rie's testimony change your views about the "badge of disgrace" argument advanced by the plaintiffs in their pleadings?

2. Mr. Bustin objected to Dr. Rie's testimony on grounds of relevance. Has he made a good point?

3. How much of the decision in this case should be based on the social science findings presented by Dr. Rie and others? Consider the views of one distinguished jurist: "The court's constitutional adjudications are based on positive law that is embodied in the Constitution and decisions rather than on the most recent published social science study." [2] Interestingly, plaintiffs' attorneys revealed in correspondence with the authors that they had first contacted a nationally known expert to testify on behalf of their clients. The expert, a personal friend of one of the attorneys, refused to testify because of a personal belief that strict discipline is necessary in the educational setting and unfettered suspensions are one means to this end.

4. Assuming no other testimony was presented, how would you decide *Goss v. Lopez* at the conclusion of the hearing?

C. Post-Hearing Motions

On July 17, 1973, defendants filed a motion to dismiss the case, asserting that at the close of plaintiffs' evidence, they had not established that protected right had been infringed and that they had not established that the Ohio law was unconstitutional. In a supporting memorandum the defendants pointed out that the suspensions arose from a period of stress and disruption. They asserted that the "compilation of the school work by each of the individual plaintiffs will not support a conclusion that any of these particular plaintiffs sustained any harm" as a result of the suspensions. In the case of Dwight Lopez, the memorandum noted that he

2. William E. Doyle, "Can Social Science Data Be Used in Judicial Decisionmaking?" 6 *J.Law and Educ.* 13, January, 1977. Judge Doyle serves on the U. S. Court of Appeal, Tenth Circuit.

had earned only two-tenths of a credit for the 1968–69 school year, and thus, "if Mr. Lopez had any delay in graduating, it was due solely to the fact that he earned so few credits." The testimony of the school psychologists, argued the defendants, was irrelevant to establishing any harm suffered by the named plaintiffs. Thus, the memorandum asked the court to dismiss the case.

Shortly thereafter, attorneys for the plaintiffs filed a "reply" in which they sought to counter arguments made by the defendants in their preliminary trial brief and their motion to dismiss. They first squarely confronted *San Antonio v. Rodriguez*, the 1973 Supreme Court case which had stated that education is not a fundamental interest. Said the plaintiffs,

> To leap from the *Rodriguez* holding that education is not a "fundamental interest" to the point that *no* process is due when one is deprived of an education is a momentous *non sequitur*. The *Rodriguez* Court was merely exploring the fundamentality of education in order to determine what standard to apply in making an equal protection inquiry. Whether education is fundamental for equal protection analysis has no bearing on whether the deprivation of education can be accomplished without any due process.

The plaintiffs thus argued that *San Antonio* was irrelevant to this case, since *San Antonio* concerned the Fourteenth Amendment Equal Protection Clause and not the Due Process Clause. They also quoted from another recent Supreme Court case, *Board of Regents v. Roth*, 408 U.S. 564 (1972), showing that whenever a governmental entity stigmatizes a person or injures "a person's good name or reputation," due process must be provided. It makes no difference, argued the plaintiffs, whether education is the context within which the stigma occurred or not.

The plaintiffs went on to assert that no legislature can deprive a person of protected rights and that judicial scrutiny of legislative action is proper in this case. They disagreed that the students had not suffered harm, pointing out several ways in which harm had occurred either through problems of readjustment to school or through permanent notations on school records. They also pointed out that since this was a class action suit, "Harms, unsuffered by the named plaintiffs, are likely to occur to other members of the class." Finally, the plaintiffs argued that neither the old system nor the new system for suspension procedures provided "meaningful safeguards."

On August 31, 1973, the plaintiffs filed an amended complaint consisting only of name changes which had occurred since the original complaint had been filed. On September 12 the defendants filed an answer on behalf of substituted parties which included name changes as well as the addition of several sections outlining new lines of defense. These new arguments had been developed during the pleadings and the hearing. Since they have been noted earlier, they are not discussed here.

NOTES AND QUESTIONS

1. Note the arguments of the plaintiffs about *San Antonio v. Rodriguez*. The Equal Protection Clause is quite different from the Due Process Clause, as noted in the next chapter. Cases involving it, therefore, may not be applicable to due process issues.

2. Based on the latest round of motions, which side do you think should win? Have you changed your mind at all during the development of this case?

D. The District Court Decision

On September 12, 1973, the decision of the district court was announced. Reprinted below is the judgment of the court (372 F.Supp. 1279).

UNITED STATES DISTRICT COURT
SOUTHERN DISTRICT OF OHIO
EASTERN DIVISION

EILEEN LOPEZ, et al.,
      Plaintiffs

vs   Civil Action 71–67

HERBERT M. WILLIAMS, et al.,
      Defendants

JUDGMENT

This action came on for hearing before the Court, the Honorable John W. Peck, Judge, United States Court of Appeals for the Sixth Circuit; the Honorable Joseph P. Kinneary, Chief Judge, United States District Court; and the Honorable Carl B. Rubin, United States District Judge, and the issues having been duly heard and a decision having been duly rendered;

IT IS ORDERED AND ADJUDGED that plaintiffs were denied due process of law because they were suspended without adequate hearing. It is further concluded that the statute and regulation challenged are not unconstitutionally vague and overbroad.

The Court Declares that Section 3313.66, Ohio Revised Code and the regulations adopted by the Columbus Public Schools pursuant thereto which were in force at the time of plaintiffs' suspensions are unconstitutional, in that they provide for suspension from the Columbus Public Schools without first affording the student due process of law.

It is Ordered that the defendants delete all reference to the suspensions and disciplinary transfers of plaintiffs from the records of the Columbus Public Schools.

IT IS FURTHER ORDERED that the plaintiffs recover of defendants their costs of action.

Dated at Columbus, Ohio, this 17th day of September, 1973.

_____
                                Clerk of Court

In a lengthy opinion, Chief Judge Kinneary, (writing for all three judges) discussed the reasons for the court's decision with respect to both findings of fact and conclusions of law. His statements about the facts in the case summarize much of what has already been reviewed. He noted that issues of fact were not contested by the parties and proceeded rather quickly to discuss the court's legal opinion.

Judge Kinneary concluded that the class action suit was properly maintained and that the court had jurisdiction of the case. He disagreed that the new guidelines for suspension had mooted the case because "the new guidelines have no impact upon the constitutional claims of the named plaintiffs or of any member of the class they represent who was suspended prior to July 10, 1973."

Judge Kinneary also disagreed with the defendants that the plaintiffs should have first exhausted state remedies before bringing their case to a federal court, noting that "The Civil Rights Act of 1871 was intended by Congress to provide a federal remedy for the deprivation of constitutional rights which was supplementary to state remedies."

In his section on procedural due process, the Judge offered commentary on each of the major contested issues in the case. Excerpts from his opinion follow.

LOPEZ v. WILLIAMS

United States District Court for the Southern District of Ohio, 1973
372 F.Supp. 1279.

OPINION

KINNEARY, Chief District Judge.

This matter is before the Court on plaintiffs' motion for judgment on the pleadings under the provisions of Rule 12(c) of the Federal Rules of Civil Procedure.

This is an action for injunctive and declaratory relief arising out of the suspension of the nine plaintiffs from Columbus Public School System in February and March, 1971.

* * *

The Supreme Court has not resolved the question of whether a student's statutory right to an education is a liberty which is protected by due process of law. The Supreme Court has frequently referred to the importance of education in the American system of government.

* * *

The Supreme Court's holding (in *San Antonio v. Rodriguez*) that the right to an education is not explicitly or implicitly guaranteed by the Constitution does not affect the determination of whether it is a liberty or property which cannot be interfered with by the State without the protection of due procedural safeguards.

* * * interests included within the concepts of liberty and property are often rights created by the State which have no Constitutional status.

The question presented is whether the State created right to an education is a protected liberty under the Fourteenth Amendment's due process clause.

* * *

Considering the importance of education in our society today, the Court HOLDS that the State created entitlement to an education is a liberty protected by the due process clause of the Fourteenth Amendment.

The Court now turns to the more difficult question of what process is due a student before the State may deprive him of his right to an education by imposing a suspension not to exceed 10 days.

*   *   *

Due process is not a straitjacket imposed by the Courts upon educators. The minimum requirements of notice and a hearing prior to suspension, except in emergency situations, does not require inflexible procedures. Courts must be mindful not to require educators to follow specific or particular procedural frameworks. Due process is satisfied if the procedures are "reasonably calculated to be fair to the student and lead to a reliable determination of the factual issues involved." *   *   *

The Fourteenth Amendment due process requirement of notice in a hearing are "nothing more than fair play." If school administrators follow procedures which result in a fair factual determination made after notice and an opportunity to defend against the charges of misconduct, then no matter how informal the procedure, the student has been accorded the minimum requirements of the due process clause of the Fourteenth Amendment of the Constitution of the United States.

The decisions which have dealt with the subject in the composite provide that at a minimum procedural fairness requires:

1. Immediate removal of a student whose conduct disrupts the academic atmosphere of the school, endangers fellow students, teachers or school officials, or damages property.

2. Immediate written notice to the student and parents of the reason(s) for the removal from school and the proposed suspen-

sion should be given within 24 hours.

3. Not later than 72 hours after the actual removal of the student from school, the student and his parents must be given an opportunity to be present at a hearing before a school administrator who will determine if a suspension should be imposed.

Such hearing, which is not a judicial proceeding, must provide at a minimum

(a) Statements in support of the charge(s) against the student upon which the hearing is conducted.

(b) Statements by the student and others in defense of the charge(s) and/or in mitigations or explanation of his conduct.

(c) The administrator is not required to permit the presence of counsel or follow any prescribed judicial rules in conducting the hearing.

(d) The administrator should, within 24 hours advise the student and his parents by letter of his decision and the reasons therefor.

School administrators are free to adopt regulations providing for fair suspension procedures which are consonant with the educational goals of their schools and reflective of the characteristics of their school and locality. There is no one way to insure fairness in the suspension process. The choice of the best procedure for a particular school system should be left to the school officials charged with the administration of that school system.

In the present case plaintiffs were not accorded a hearing. The conference required by school regulations following suspension was not a fact-finding hearing, but rehabilitative in nature. None of the named plaintiffs were in fact afforded even this conference. There is no evidence in the record that any of the plaintiffs voluntarily relinquished their right to a hearing.

The Court HOLDS that plaintiffs were not accorded due process of law, in that they were suspended without hearing prior to suspension or within a reasonable time thereafter.

The Court ORDERS that references to the suspensions of plaintiffs or members of their class be removed from all records of the Columbus Public Schools.

Plaintiffs contend that the disciplinary regulations under which they were suspended are void because they are unconstitutionally vague and overbroad.

* * * Plaintiffs have failed to prove that their conduct at the time of their suspensions was entitled to First Amendment protection. On the contrary, the evidence establishes that the various school administrators acted to restore order and discipline in their schools. In such circumstances, the actions of school administrators do not contravene the First Amendment.

* * *

NOTES AND QUESTIONS

1. Do you agree with the decision of the three-judge court?

2. In correspondence with the authors, Denis Murphy, one of the attorneys for the plaintiffs, revealed that he was surprised Judge Kinneary in the end wrote the opinion. During the course of one of the pre-trial sessions, Judge Kinneary turned to Mr. Murphy and, according to the latter, said "The next thing you know, Denis, parents will have to get court permission to spank their kids." At another point in a pre-trial conference, Judge Kinneary appeared concerned about where to draw the line for procedural due process in the academic setting. Apparently, the Judge resolved his reservations prior to writing the opinion.

3. Specifically, how would Judge Kinneary's due process proscriptions change the Columbus school procedures under which Dwight was suspended? How would they change the procedures implemented in July of 1973? Note that his due process composite relates to the student whose conduct warrants "immediate removal" from school. Under these circumstances, a hearing must be provided within three days to determine whether a suspension should be imposed. The judge's comment does not appear to relate to non-emergency situations where student suspension is being contemplated. The composite advanced by Judge Kinneary was the source of considerable confusion later on about what the federal court had in fact ruled.

4. Review the complaint filed in 1971. How successful were the plaintiffs? If you were Dwight, would you feel the effort was worth it? If you were plaintiffs' attorneys? Note that the complaint, like most, uses a shotgun approach. As Denis Murphy pointed out,

> you state a claim on every aspect you think might come up in the case, even though some of the claims made may not be as worthwhile pursuing as others. There was disagreement among counsel,

for example, with respect to the questions that arose as a result of the arguments concerning overbreadth and vagueness.

5. If you were asked to advise defendants' attorneys whether or not to appeal, what advice would you give? What would be the arguments you would advise counsel to present on appeal?

IV. THE APPELLATE PROCESS

Our legal system provides for avenues of appeal in both criminal and civil cases at the state and federal level. The appellate structure is outlined in Chapter Two. It is commonly said that the trial judge tries the case and the appellate judge tries the trial judge. In a way this is true, for appellate courts do not retry cases; instead they review the entire record of materials related to the case, read briefs submitted by opposing attorneys, and listen to oral arguments by the attorneys in order to decide whether fairness was provided and the law applied correctly at the trial court level. Courts of appeal deal essentially with the law, not factual issues. In deciding cases, appellate courts follow rules of law set forth in earlier cases—the doctrine of *stare decisis*. All appellate court opinions are found in law libraries and provide the basis for legal research. It is from appellate courts that new precedents are occasionally set as judges apply the law to new and unique situations. We will see in this case that the defendants argued the three-judge trial court made errors in interpreting the law.

A. Appellants' Notice of Appeal

Since this case involved the judgment of a three-judge federal court on a constitutional issue, the avenue of appeal led directly to the Supreme Court. Had the ruling been by a single judge, the appeal would have first gone to the Sixth Circuit Court of Appeals. It has already been noted that Congress has curtailed much of the jurisdiction of three-judge courts.

On November 9, 1973, the attorneys for the defendants filed a notice of appeal to the Supreme Court of the United States.

Section 28 U.S.C.A. § 1253 provides for direct appeals to the Supreme Court.

In support of their notice, the appellants (note that now the name of the case reverses, with the defendants becoming the initiators of the action) filed a jurisdictional statement in which they sought to argue why the Supreme Court should reverse the lower court decision. In their statement the appellants presented three questions for review:

The questions presented by this appeal are:

1. Where the United States Supreme Court has concluded that the importance of education alone will not elevate education to the status of a fundamental right guaranteed either explictly or implicitly by the Federal Constitution and where the lower court has recognized that education is not a property right, may a district court hold that

education is a liberty protected by the Federal Constitution solely on the basis that it is important?

2. Is a statute, providing for a temporary limited suspension by a principal of a local school, which has not been determined to result in condemning students to suffer grievous loss subject to the procedural protections required by the Due Process Clause of the Fourteenth Amendment to the United States Constitution?

3. Can a State create a liberty which is recognized as being subject to protection by the Fourteenth Amendment of the United States Constitution?

With respect to the first issue, the appellants pointed out that the three-judge district court "put itself squarely in conflict with this Court's opinion in *San Antonio v. Rodriguez.*" The lower court, argued the appellants, "not finding any other protected right implicated, not finding education is a property right, concludes in a vacuum that the importance of education makes it a liberty protected by the Federal Constitution." Such a conclusion, argued the appellants, "is historically incorrect and will not withstand scrutiny."

The appellants also noted that according to the district court, secondary school officials could suspend students up to three days without a hearing. Yet the ten-day suspension permitted by the state statute was ruled unconstitutional. Such a conclusion was unwarranted, argued the appellants, and an "intrusion into a legitimate State activity, namely local school management."

As to the second and third questions, the appellants noted that "This Court has never held that a State may create a liberty" and reiterated the three-versus ten-day dichotomy they saw the lower court advancing, questioning whether any "grievous loss" could result from a suspension of *either* duration.

If the true test today, as promulgated by this Court, is one of not only determining whether or not the interest is one within the concepts of liberty or property set out in the language of the Fourteenth Amendment, but also one of determining to what extent a person is condemned to suffer grievous loss of that interest, then the lower court did not apply the test. If a sharply defined fundamental interest is not grievously implicated, how can it be concluded that a period of ten days or seven days is sufficient to place the entire statute, on its face, in direct conflict with the Due Process Clause of the Fourteenth Amendment?

The lower court, argued the appellants, simply ignored the decisions of other federal courts and imposed rigid due process procedure on school officials detrimental to the operation of educational institutions. Such a ruling constituted an unwarranted invasion in state and local affairs.

The appellants concluded by urging that the district court decision be reversed.

If education and control of the classroom in the high school setting are to remain primarily a matter of local control, then a real need exists to resolve the questions surrounding discipline which continue to occur. The Due Process Clause should not be used or become a weapon to venerate form over real substance. The relationship between education and the students who participate in the system is a matter of state concern and state law. No deference was shown to that principle in this case. If the power of a principal to suspend a student is to be further restricted from ten days to three days, such action should rest with the body that created the system, namely the State Legislature.

The interest of the state in its educational system and discipline within that system has not become so inferior to the interest of a student that it can be concluded that a restrictive statute such as section 3313.66 of the Ohio Revised Code is unconstitutional on its face. The Federal Constitution does not command such finite scrutiny of legislative discretion.

The decision of the lower court should be reversed.

NOTES AND QUESTIONS

1. Note that the appellants state the questions in the most favorable fashion to their case. Which of the arguments presented by appellants seems most convincing?

2. Review Judge Kinneary's opinion. Do you believe the appellants have understood his comments about three- versus ten-day suspensions correctly?

3. Do you think a "grievous loss" should be required in every instance for due process procedures to be required? Where should the line most properly be drawn for the application and non-application of the Due Process Clause?

B. The Appellees' Response

The appellees responded by filing a motion to affirm the judgment of the district court. The motion to affirm is commonly filed in response to a jurisdictional statement. It is through this device that appellees sought to get the Court to affirm the judgment without full briefing and argument.

They contended in support of their motion that "the questions presented are so insubstantial" as to require no other Supreme Court action than to affirm the lower court ruling. The appellees first contended that the appellants had misunderstood the district court's opinion with regard to the three- versus ten-day suspension issue.

     *   *   *   contrary to assertions by Appellants the District Court did not rule that a three (3) day suspension is constitutionally permissible while a ten (10) day suspension (without a prior hearing) is unconstitutional. The Court did rule rather that a prior hearing is always required except when there are extraordinary circumstances. When extraordinary circumstances exist, a

student may be suspended without a prior hearing but must be given a subsequent hearing within three days of the exclusion. This holding and this perspective merely places school suspensions into the mainstream of this Court's Due Process decisions, * * *.

The appellees also asserted that the district court had not imposed a rigid due process system on school officials but rather had indicated that "procedures could be informal so long as an inquiry into the correctness of the suspension was made."

Once again the appellees tried to show that the Court's ruling in the *San Antonio v. Rodriguez* case was decided on grounds substantially different from the instant case and thus was not controlling on the issue of whether or not education is a fundamental right entitled to constitutional protection. In any case, the compulsory school law had created a right to an education, argued the appellees, regardless of what one called it under the 14th Amendment.

> Thus whether one characterizes education as "liberty" as the lower Court did, or as "property" it is clear that education in Ohio is a protected interest. Under this Court's holdings, followed by the District Court, the State cannot deprive a citizen of a protected interest without Due Process of law. Yet this is precisely what was done to the Appellees in the instant case and what the District Court's ruling redresses. Such is clearly correct, perfectly consistent with *Rodriguez*, and requires no reconsideration by this High Court.

The appellees went on to argue that the Supreme Court had in a long line of cases required state officials to provide due process procedures when a liberty or property interest is endangered. A "grievous loss" need not be a prerequisite.

> Analysis of the three cases cited by the Appellants indicates that the phrase has been a rare tool used only sparingly by this Court in a few limited situations in which a violation of liberty was thought to be in doubt. There is no such doubt in the present case. It is unquestioned that a whole class of school children were completely excluded from their right to education for definite periods of time.

Even if some element of loss is required to invoke procedural protections, "the record provides substantial unrefuted evidence of such." The appellees concluded that the present case fit in with the trend toward requiring an informal hearing prior to suspension except in an emergency.

> The Court below went out of its way to indicate that a hearing could be informal, so long as it was reasonably designed to elicit the truth. In so ruling the lower Court merely was applying this Court's ample precedent that a hearing must precede the deprivation of a liberty by the State. Full scale argument is surely not needed to confirm the correctness of this rather limited ruling. This Court should summarily affirm the decision below.

NOTES AND QUESTIONS

1. Which of the arguments presented by appellees seems most convincing?

2. Could the continued emphasis on the "informality" of the required hearing weaken the entire case the appellees have tried to present from the beginning? Why do you suppose the appellees were playing down the significance of the district court decision?

3. Based on the arguments presented in the jurisdictional statement and the reply, which side made the stronger arguments? Do you think the Supreme Court should 1) reverse the lower court decision, 2) affirm the lower court decision, 3) hold a hearing on the matter?

C. The Filing of Briefs

On November 28, 1973, the appellants requested a certification of record pursuant to Rule 12 of the U. S. Supreme Court Rules. The official records of the case were certified to the Supreme Court on December 19th. On February 19, 1974, the Supreme Court notified the parties of probable jurisdiction of the case and requested the filing of briefs on the merits of the case.

Appellants began their brief by repeating the three questions presented in their jurisdictional statement and reviewing the basic facts of the case. Quite simply, said the appellants,

> The state creates a system of public education and as a part of the system establishes a system of internal student discipline. The system is created by the state to serve its purposes of protection and perpetuation. Discipline and order are an integral part of, and necessarily essential to, the internal management of the system.

In no way, argued the appellants, was a constitutional right involved. In fact, "In terms of the historical analysis of education as an individual pursuit, attendance or participation in the State educational system can be viewed as a limitation upon one's liberty rather than creating a new right of liberty." Thus, to the extent there may be a liberty to pursue education as suggested in earlier cases, such a liberty refers to individual educational pursuits carried on *outside* of the public schools. The district court was thus incorrect in assuming compulsory attendance in public schools creates a new right of liberty. This is so because the purpose of public education is to serve the state and "not solely or basically for the purpose of furthering the interests of the individual." Interestingly, the appellants cited several liberal and radical authorities to support their view about schools including Christopher Jencks, Daniel P. Moynihan, and, in their reply brief, Ivan Illich.

Even if the Court should decide that such a right had been created by the state, asserted the appellants, no serious harm was suffered by any student. No racial discrimination was involved, nor had a substantive constitutional right been infringed. In fact, appellants argued that not only had the students graduated or moved to the next grade on time, some had actually advanced ahead of time and had achieved at a higher level *after* the suspensions. Repeating many of the same arguments and supporting cases advanced in their previous filings, the appellants emphasized how the Supreme Court's own rulings supported their case. They concluded that the three-judge district court had usurped the functions of the state legislature and urged that the ruling be reversed.

The appellees, having lost the battle for a summary Supreme Court affirmation of the lower court decision, launched their case before the Supreme Court with a lengthy brief on the merits. They began by pointing out that the real issue was whether or not *any* hearing should be accorded students threatened with a temporary suspension. They admitted that some of the suspensions "might fit within an 'emergency' exception to the prior hearing rule," but went on to note that even in these situations, no subsequent hearing was offered or held. "Surely in an emergency situation when nerves might be on edge, and the chance for mistaken or capricious action is heightened, the need for procedural protections is that much greater."

Like the appellants, attorneys for the appellees repeated most of their earlier arguments and tried to show how recent Supreme Court rulings supported their case, e. g., *Board of Regents v. Roth*. Confronting the appellants' arguments about the limitation public schooling poses on the students' liberty, the appellees asserted that "this argument falls of its own weight." Not only would such a line of reasoning result in a reversal of *Tinker v. Des Moines School Dist.*, it simply conflicted with the cases and represented "a dangerous inroad on an important protected interest which has long been granted special constitutional protection by this Court." Here, Ohio has created a constitutional right under the 14th Amendment to a public education and such a right cannot be denied without a minimum guarantee of due process. Once again, the appellees noted that *San Antonio* dealt with the Equal Protection Clause and was thus irrelevant to the case.

Appellees also repeated their arguments that the students had been harmed sufficiently for a prior hearing to be necessary, citing both the loss of education during the suspension and the testimony of Dr. Herbert Rie. The attorneys argued that suspension could limit both college and employment possibilities, citing a survey they had conducted in preparation for the brief which showed that four of twelve Ohio colleges expressly asked for suspension data on undergraduate application forms. Only a prior hearing could prevent such harm, argued the appellees, because if an error had been made, there is no way to adequately compensate a student *after* the suspension. The damage has been done. "For a child to be declared innocent of wrongdoing after having been irreparably excluded from school for a period of time would inevitably appear to be administrative double-talk. The potential psychological fall-out would seem to be far from speculative."

Finally, the appellees tackled the history of unsupportive lower court rulings by confronting them directly.

The lower court decisions, insofar as they provide guidance for this Court, present an irrefutable argument for a prior hearing rule. These cases, by their very inconclusiveness and judicial arbitrariness show the unworkability of a conceptual framework that attempts to measure harm and to place such measurement into a formula for determining whether a prior hearing is required. The decision by the lower court in the present case in its reliance upon this Court's precedents presents a stark contrast to the judicial uncertainty found in many other decisions.

They also noted that the American Association of School Administrators had recently resolved that suspensions and expulsions should not be utilized unless " 'the health and safety of other students or personnel in all schools is jeopardized.' "

In their reply brief, appellants sought to counter the thrust of appellees' arguments by emphasizing that public schooling is primarily for the benefit of the state, not the student. The language in prior Supreme Court decisions, reiterated the appellants, refers to "education" broadly defined to mean the general right to acquire knowledge, not attend public schools. Appellants continued to play down the importance of public schooling, referring to school attendance at one point as "the occupation of a school building." Thus, Supreme Court cases mandating hearings before terminating other types of public benefits such as welfare payments are not appropriate to the instant case. Furthermore, argued the appellants, the insistence of appellees for "an almost wooden preoccupation with the need for a hearing within the framework of academic discipline" would result in "engrafting upon the present system what is tantamount to an adversary relationship　*　*　*."

> The concept of education which is portrayed in the briefs submitted by appellees and their friends is one which reduces a very complex pursuit to a question of class attendance and booklearning. Education, the pursuit of knowledge and corresponding personality growth, involves much more. Particularly is this conclusion true in the primary and secondary school area. Concepts of citizenship, respect for authority, self discipline and responsibility are very much a part of the fabric of the pursuit of knowledge. It is a mistake to equate academic discipline with the assessment of criminal responsibility. It is an even greater mistake to insist, in substance, that a teacher or principal should be more concerned with the assessment of culpability than with the personality entrusted to his care.

NOTES AND QUESTIONS

1. Note the interesting argument the appellants made about the proper definition of "education" in order to accommodate language in prior Supreme Court cases such as *Pierce v. Society of the Sisters of the Holy Names of Jesus and Mary.* Do you suppose they developed this line of reasoning because the primary case supporting their view that schooling is not a constitutional right, *San Antonio v. Rodriguez*, concerned the Equal

Protection Clause and not the Due Process Clause? Do you think it helped their case to play down the importance of public schooling to the point where they referred to school attendance as occupying a building? Once again, note that the appellant school officials quite ironically endorse the views of those liberal and radical educational commentators who assert that schooling has a very limited impact on the student.

Do you find anything disturbing about appellants' insistence on the limited value of schooling on the one hand and their comments about the danger of instituting an adversary system in the schooling process on the other? Compare their comments on the first point with the passage from their reply brief on the dangers of an adversary process.

2. Which of the arguments presented by appellants do you think was the strongest? Might they have strengthened their case by pointing to the circumstances surrounding the school suspensions? Should they have emphasized the new procedures implemented in July of 1973?

3. The appellees also made some shifts of emphasis in their appeal briefs. They strengthened their position that *any* suspension for more than a trivial period requires due process. They had first made this assertion in their brief submitted to the three-judge court, citing the *Vail* decision. After the decision, they strengthened this argument to highlight the need for a new policy decision regarding short suspensions. As Mr. Roos noted in correspondence with the authors, " * * * it must be realized that the Supreme Court, much more than any other court is making policy and not merely following precedent. Thus policy arguments and considerations play a much larger role."

They also decided to place more emphasis on the "property" interest the students had in their education and less on the "liberty" interest previously argued (compare, for example, the memorandum of law they filed with Judge Kinneary). This shift was partly attributable to the Supreme Court ruling in *San Antonio v. Rodriguez* that education is not a fundamental right. While *San Antonio* concerned the Equal Protection Clause and not the Due Process Clause, the Court had nevertheless gone on record in opposition to education as a liberty interest. However, in a recent due process case, *Board of Educ. v. Roth*, 408 U.S. 564 (1972), the Supreme Court had supported the concept of property right.

> To have a property interest in a benefit, a person clearly must have more than an abstract need or desire for it. He must have more than a unilateral expectation of it. He must, instead, have a legitimate claim of entitlement to it. It is a purpose of the ancient institution of property to protect those claims upon which people rely in their daily lives, reliance that must not be arbitrarily undermined. It is a purpose of the constitutional right to a hearing to provide an opportunity for a person to vindicate those claims. (At p. 577).

Property rights, said the Court, can be created by law. If so, then the person threatened with deprivation has a "legitimate claim of entitlement" sufficient to warrant a hearing under the 14th Amendment Due Process Clause. Since Ohio had undertaken to provide public schooling, it had created a property interest, argued the appellees, sufficient to warrant a hearing. This shift of emphasis from "liberty" to "property," said Peter Roos later, "turned out to be the correct decision."

However, Mr. Roos admitted in correspondence with the authors that the appellees made an incorrect decision in not developing strategy to combat a line of argument advanced in an *amici curiae* brief by the Buckeye Association and several other associations of Ohio school administrators. This brief, the only one submitted to the Supreme Court in support of appellants, strongly endorsed short-term disciplinary suspensions as an educational experience.

> The use of such suspensions is a part of education. It is vital both to the maintenance of an orderly process of education for all who are in attendance in public schools and to the development of a sense of discipline and control in individual students. The importance of this tool is indicated by the following figures: in the Cincinnati School District in the school year 1972–73, there were 4,054 short-term suspensions out of a total student enrollment of 81,007; in the Akron City School District in the school year 1972–73, there were 7,352 short-term suspensions out of a total enrollment of 57,000 students; and in the Cleveland City School District in the school year 1972–73, there were 14,598 short-term suspensions out of a total enrollment of 142,053. These figures make absolutely clear that a constitutional requirement of a hearing prior to the short-term suspension of every student would render this basic tool unavailable. The time of administrators, teachers, and students consumed in hearings in this number of cases would be obviously enormous.

> The importance of the student suspension device to this educational process in Ohio is related to the fact that Ohio's compulsory attendance law applied to students between the ages of 6 and 18 years. This is the longest period required by any state. States where there are fewer older students and different disciplinary problems may well find that the Ohio procedure is unnecessary, unsuitable or even undesirable. It is the position of Amici Curiae that such judgments are best left to the administrators, legislators and ultimately to the people of the various states. Only through a flexible process whereby individual states are allowed to utilize a variety of educational tools can the goal of an improved educational process be attained.

In their response to the Buckeye Association brief, appellees did not comment on these particular assertions. Mr. Roos later acknowledged that the failure to counter the "suspension-is-educational" claims of the Association was a mistake. "While I do not believe that such is the case and while literature probably could have been marshalled, time constraints led me to let that assertion sit." From a logistical standpoint, Mr. Calvin Park, principal of Central High School, appears to share some of Mr. Roos' concerns about the value of suspensions. In correspondence with the authors, Mr. Park noted that:

> My experience with suspension has been that very seldom could I get parents to come to school for a conference. We had to go to the home and then often parents were not available.

> It was not unusual for parents to state that they had no control over the student in question. However when I offered the services of school personnel to assist them if they cared to declare the child incorrigible at court, not once did any parent follow through in that direction.

4. Compare the arguments of the appellants with those of the appellees regarding the actual harm suffered by the students. Which appears stronger?

5. If you were to rule on the appeal at this point, what decision would you reach and why?

D. Oral Argument Before the Supreme Court

At 1:15 P.M. on Wednesday, October 16, 1974, Thomas Bustin representing the appellants and Peter Roos representing the appellees appeared before the United States Supreme Court to present their oral arguments. Mr. Bustin was first to appear before the Court, all of whose members were in attendance. Mr. Bustin began with a review of the facts in the case and briefed the Court on the main thrust of appellants' arguments.

(1) Appellants' Oral Argument

As is customary, the Justices frequently interrupted with questions and comments, which often ranged far beyond the issue presented in the briefs. Questions began early in Mr. Bustin's presentation. It is possible to identify the questioners only if their names become part of the conversation, which is transcribed from a tape recording by a court reporter. From the *Goss v. Lopez* transcript, it appears Chief Justice Warren Burger played a major role in the questioning of both attorneys, particularly the appellants.

Much of the initial questioning focused on the matter of jurisdiction. Members of the Court asked whether the district court had issued an injunction in the case. In order for the Supreme Court to have jurisdiction of the case, an injunction had to have been issued by the three-judge court. When one of the Justices pointed out that the three-judge court had ordered an expungement of the records of the suspended students, the matter appeared to be settled.

In his opening comments, Mr. Bustin again construed the district court opinion to require due process procedures only for suspensions over three days in length. No such requirements, he asserted, were mandated for shorter suspensions. Much of the later questioning focused on this point.

Then the Justice's questions shifted to the purpose of the school records. Mr. Bustin admitted that information recorded on the records could be released to outsiders, including employers and colleges, though

school policy was against such disclosure. The Justices asked how binding the "policy" was.

* * *

Q. * * * Is there anything you can point to in writing that says
that this material will not be made available at any time?

MR. BUSTIN: No, Your Honor, not in the posture of the record as
it appears before this Court.

However, I fail to see the significance of the record showing the three-
day suspension, if you will. We view the three-day suspension as being
part and parcel of the education process. It is really no different when the
school official is looking at that particular person's record, if you will, and
they see on that record the fact that the person has flunked mathematics.
I think that the college or employer looking at that particular record is
going to be as much influenced by the grade that that individual received
in mathematics, for example, as he is by—

Q. What experience do you have in evaluating school records?

MR. BUSTIN: I have no individual experience.

Q. I did not think so.

* * *

[The questioning then shifted back to the three-day suspension issue,
with considerable attention directed to the Ohio statute. The Court found
the law confusing. One Justice called the statute "odd." In the course of
their questions, the justices posed far-ranging and difficult hypothetical
situations for Mr. Bustin.]

* * *

Q. Would it be correct or incorrect to say that the difference between the three-judge federal court and the Ohio statute is the difference
between ten days and three days on this suspension?

MR. BUSTIN: They seem to be going off, as I view it—the only way
I can view it is a difference between three and ten days, they seem to make
three days okay and the period of ten days as violating due process.

Q. Would you make the same argument if it were a hundred?

MR. BUSTIN: Were a hundred?

Q. A hundred days. A hundred-day suspension.

MR. BUSTIN: Under my analysis, this particular case, as I have set
forth in my brief, while expulsion is not involved in this case, I would
have to say that a right of liberty of property would not be involved where
the person—

Q. But it would be in the expulsion?

MR. BUSTIN: No, Your Honor, I do not believe so.

Q. And so it would not have been involved in a hundred days either?

MR. BUSTIN: No, Your Honor.

Q. You feel that you have to take that position?

MR. BUSTIN: I feel that the position, in light of the *Roth* case, for
example, and also the *Cafeteria Workers* case follows, that the student who

is removed from the process, and you used for a hundred days, is in no worse position than the non-tenure teacher who is only told that he is non-renewed. Where the district does not say to every other district in Ohio, for example, "Don't bother with this child" or closes every door to him, then I see the student in your hundred-day situation being in much the same posture.

Q. On your basis then, I gather, it just would not be a question of a pre-suspension hearing; it would be a hearing at all. You would think that he could be terminated or expelled for a hundred or a thousand days without any hearing at any time, before or after.

MR. BUSTIN: As I analyze the Constitution in this sense, I believe that I would have to answer yes to that.

Q. Yes, and what if you are wrong about that, that there has to be a hearing at some time?

MR. BUSTIN: Then it seems to me that—

Q. What about this case then?

MR. BUSTIN: It seems to me that we are down to a net posture of drawing lines, and it is really a question of where will we stop, and I can come back to my situation of do we go to a hearing process with the person who is receiving a grade or something of that similar nature.

Q. If you were trying to defend a 100-day statute, you would have some additional problems of showing that that did not totally disrupt the students' school progress for that year, would you not? I am now talking about practical problems, whether they are constitutional or not. This is another question.

MR. BUSTIN: Yes, I might have—

Q. Suspension for a hundred days is certainly going to pretty well cut him out for the school year unless some substitute teaching is provided; is that not so?

MR. BUSTIN: Yes.

Q. The difference between ten days and three days is merely a matter of judgment in drawing the line?

MR. BUSTIN: I believe it fits into the doctrine that inculcating self-discipline and respect for authority is part and parcel of the process. I think a legislature that does this, as it has done here with this statute—

Q. You seem to make an argument along these lines negatively by pointing out, as I recall it, that all of these students did just as well or better after they came back to school. Is that correct? Did I read your brief correctly?

MR. BUSTIN: Yes, as I read the record and have analyzed the record, I believe that the record does not disclose the particular suspensions involved in this case really had any effect on the outcome of their proceeding through the process.

* * *

[A short time later, Mr. Bustin appeared to have trouble pointing out why the school district was opposed to providing due process procedures for student suspensions of longer than three days. But one member of the Court suggested a rationale, which Mr. Bustin subsequently endorsed.]

* * *

Q. And the seven days is so important to you, and I am asking why.

MR. BUSTIN: I think it is important to the system and the relationship that the district tries to establish in that system. And it is important that the—

Q. But specifically why is the seven days so necessary in order to maintain discipline?

MR. BUSTIN: Specifically because I think—

Q. You like it.

MR. BUSTIN: Pardon?

Q. You like it.

MR. BUSTIN: Not because I like it. I think it is because the legislature wants to have the principal in his relationship with the student have a broad range of authority here, limited authority, to protect not only the individual but the entire school district.

Q. What about five days? And you know where I am going to end up, nine.

MR. BUSTIN: I think it is this type of line drawing that you are engaging in that gets us into this type of problem. I think that is a line that should be drawn by the legislative body if they still have any kind of discretionary authority.

Q. Mr. Bustin, in a number of the states they have statutes which limit the right to strike except after ten days notice. They call it colloquially at least a cooling-off period. Would it be your view that there is some cooling-off process involved in the ten days that would not be provided in a three-day period, or at least that that was the judgment of the legislature?

MR. BUSTIN: You could look at it from the face of this record and say that in a sense, because here the principal, as portrayed in the testimony of Principal Fulton, when he handed out these suspensions, was trying to restore order so that the vast bulk of students could get on with the process of day-to-day learning. So, I think you could characterize it in a sense as a cooling-off period. And also from this sense—the principal tries to, during this period—and it is portrayed in his testimony also— meet with the student and his parents and discuss the student's entire school record, with the emphasis on trying to find out what the student's problem is and how they can get that student progressing again. So, in that sense, you could characterize it as a cooling-off period.

* * *

[Shortly before the end of Mr. Bustin's presentation, one member of the Court wondered out loud whether the district court indeed had set a three-day time limit, but the issue was not pursued.

The questioning of Mr. Bustin ended with a request for information about the revised school discipline policy announced in July, 1973, shortly before the district court hearing. Mr. Bustin responded that the district court "sluffed them off in a footnote."]

NOTES AND QUESTIONS

1. Note how extensively the Justices' questions ranged outside of the relatively narrow issues presented to them in the briefs. They are inclined to be quite impatient with responses they consider irrelevant or erroneous. Thus, when Mr. Bustin began to speculate about how school records are likely to be evaluated by outsiders, he never got an opportunity to finish his statement.

2. Perhaps the most difficult part of an attorney's presentation before the Supreme Court is the request to respond to hypothetical situations. Questions of this type enable the Justices to stray far beyond the record presented to them in the briefs and probe the implications of some of the policy considerations underlying the case. At the same time, the questions pose a great challenge to the attorney, who may be appearing before the Supreme Court for the first time, as were both of these attorneys. How well do you think Mr. Bustin did in responding to the questions about where due process lines should be drawn? Did he have to state that a suspension of up to 100 days does not require due process? Note the statute in question only spoke in terms of ten days.

3. How do you explain Mr. Bustin's apparent oversight of *Dixon v. Alabama State Board* in his assertion that the Constitution requires no due process procedures even in the event of expulsion? Does *Dixon* apply to this case or can it be distinguished?

4. How significant do you think the "cooling-off" argument is in support of Mr. Bustin's position? Do you think the attorneys for appellants should have presented this argument in their briefs? Was it a "missed opportunity?"

5. One of the highlights of any lawyer's career is an opportunity to argue a case before the U. S. Supreme Court. The Foundation of the Federal Bar Association publication, *Equal Justice Under Law,* describes what it is like to be present when the Court is in session.

"Opening formalities link the current day to the past. The Marshal or Deputy Marshal acts as Crier. A few minutes before 10 a. m., Crier and Clerk, formally dressed in cutaways, go to their desks below the ends of the high bench. Pencils, pens, papers, and briefs are waiting at each Justice's place.

"At their tables, attorneys glance over notes or confer softly. A young man may fidget slightly, smoothing hair that falls to his collar, while a veteran checks his watch. Seconds will count, for today each counsel has only 30 minutes—unless he or she has a very unusual case.

"Meanwhile, the Justices themselves, summoned by buzzer, have gathered in their conference room. Each shakes hands with all the others, even if they were chatting a few minutes earlier. Chief Justice Fuller instituted this unvarying custom as a sign that 'harmony of aims if not of views is the Court's guiding principle.' Then they don their black robes and assemble behind the red velvet draperies.

"Promptly at 10 the Crier brings down his gavel. Everyone rises instantly as he intones: "The Honorable, the Chief Justice and the Associate Justices of the Supreme Court of the United States!"

"Even on routine days these moments never lose their drama. It rises to throat-drying intensity on occasions when great issues are in the balance.

"Simultaneously, as the Crier speaks, the nine Justices stride through openings in the curtains and move to their places. The Crier chants his call for silence: 'Oyez! Oyez!! Oyez!!!' From the centuries that Anglo-Norman or 'law French' was the language of English courts, the word for 'Hear ye!' survives.

"Steady-voiced, the Crier continues: 'All persons having business before the Honorable, the Supreme Court of the United States, are admonished to draw near and give their attention, for the Court is now sitting. God save the United States and this Honorable Court!'

"The gavel falls again. The Justices and all others take their seats.
* * *

* * *

"Though muted by the occasion, individuality shows clearly as the Justices begin their work. Usually, as the first item of business, the Court admits attorneys to its bar. Then, if an opinion is ready for release, the Chief Justice calls for it, and its author announces it. A dissenter may speak for those Justices who disagree: ' * * * we think the Court muddies the waters further * * * we would affirm the judgment below * * *.'

* * *

"Argument is easier for all to follow since the Justices approved a change in the shape of their bench. 'I remember when I used to argue cases here,' a senior lawyer recalls. 'I would get two questions at once, from opposite ends of the bench—the Justices couldn't see or hear each other.' In 1972, at the suggestion of the Chief Justice, the bench was altered to its present shape, with two wings each set at an 18-degree angle, a form that has been widely used in American courts since the mid-1950's.

"Even the technical cases can stir alert attention as the lawyer begins—'Mr. Chief Justice, and may it please the Court * * *'—and develops his theme—' * * * insurance companies are entitled to justice like anybody else. * * *' The questions start. * * *

* * *

"An attorney used to this Court may take an unwelcome idea in stride: 'Possibly, your Honor, but I would suggest. * * *' Or suavely field a question on what Congress intended in a statute: ' * * * the Congress does many things that I wonder at. * * *'

* * *

"With veiled ruefulness a lawyer remarks, 'I see my time is running short'; or the Chief Justice may offer a gentle reminder, 'Counsel, you are now using up your rebuttal time.' Or the other way around: 'We have taken much of your time with our questions; we will give you six more minutes.'

"When a red light glows on the lectern, the Chief Justice says, 'Thank you, Mr. Smith. The case is submitted.'" [3]

On the day of oral argument in *Goss v. Lopez*, Mr. Roos moved the admission to the Supreme Court bar of Mr. Murphy and Mr. Curtin. Mr. Roos had previously been admitted to the Supreme Court bar, though he had not addressed the Court. Later, Mr. Bustin and Mr. Roos, in turn, addressed the Justices from a long single desk in the middle of which is a podium. On each side of the podium are quill pens. All participants are free to take the pens with them when their argument is concluded. Since addressing the United States Supreme Court is a rare opportunity, the quill pens take on special significance, much like the other traditions of the Court which unfortunately do not lend themselves to such tangible remembrances.

(2) Appellees' Oral Argument

Mr. Roos began his presentation by clarifying the three-day issue which had so concerned the Court during Mr. Bustin's oral argument.

MR. ROOS: Mr. Chief Justice, and may it please the Court:

I think that a misunderstanding of the lower court's opinion has developed in the questioning of Mr. Bustin. I think that a close reading of that opinion would show that what the court did was say that a prior hearing is required whenever there is a suspension, except when there is an emergency situation. And when there is an emergency situation, the school district can suspend a student for up to 72 hours but must provide a subsequent hearing.

This was the position that was urged by us at the lower court, and we believe that this is the gist of the decision of the lower court, and this in fact is the common accommodation in plans that are voluntarily adopted.

Q. In other words, you do not read the opinion to say that a suspension without a hearing for three days is constitutionally valid?

MR. ROOS: That is correct, Your Honor. The court did not engage in the line drawing that seemed to appear in Mr. Bustin's argument. It was really rather a prior hearing as required, but there may be circumstances when there is intense disruption of the school or when the student is a danger to himself or to others, that would justify doing away with the prior hearing. But in that instance, a hearing must be provided within 72 hours thereafter.

Q. But that means that the discretion in the first instance rests with the principal under this opinion for 72 hours.

MR. ROOS: That is correct, Your Honor.

Q. What if we decided to slice it a little differently and say six days, not ten days as the statute prescribed, not three as the District Court, but six? Do you think there would be any basis for that?

MR. ROOS: Your Honor, as I understand the lower court's opinion— and this would be certainly the position that we would urge—it is not say-

3. From: *Equal Justice Under Law* © 1975, at pp. 127–133. Reprinted, courtesy of   The Foundation of the Federal Bar Association.

ing that a principal has absolute discretion to suspend a student for three days. What it is saying is that there may be emergency situations which may justify doing away with the prior hearing. It is not saying that a principal has an absolute carte blanche to throw a kid out.

Q. Who is going to determine that, when, and with what consequences?

MR. ROOS: Your Honor, obviously there has to be great reliance upon the good faith of school administrators. At some point or other, it does boil down to that. * * *

* * *

[This explanation appeared to satisfy the members of the Court, for the questioning did not return to the three-day issue.

The Court again focused on the July, 1973, revised discipline policy of the school district, wondering if it would have been sufficient to satisfy appellees.]

Q. Mr. Roos, if the procedures, guidelines, whatever they called it, pages 25 to 29, effective—as I understand it, or so it says here, at least— July 10, 1973, had been operative at the time this case arose, would you be here?

MR. ROOS: I think we would, Your Honor.

Your Honor, excuse me, there was testimony by the chief witness for the district, Mr. Goss, as to how they functioned. That testimony, Your Honor, starts at 164 and runs to 171. It does cover more than how those newly adopted procedures do operate. But there is testimony concerning—

Q. And the gist of it is?

MR. ROOS: The gist of it is, Your Honor—they really did not know what they meant—and the gist of it is that they were leaving everything up to the principal to determine whether there would be any sort of meaningful protection.

* * *

[After some further discussion, members of the Court asked Mr. Roos the kind of "line-drawing" questions they had asked Mr. Bustin, only this time concentrating on suspensions *less than* one day.]

Q. Mr. Roos, I am not quite clear yet as to your position. Do I understand you to say that any suspension, however brief, requires a prior hearing absent an emergency?

MR. ROOS: That is correct, Your Honor.

Q. So, the principal, for example, could not send a student home for the last hour of a day if the student had misbehaved or had been disruptive?

MR. ROOS: Your Honor, a severance from the school for the rest of the day might be something different from—it might be in the nature, in fact, of a cooling-off period. We would assume that that would be what it would be, so that it might be something different from a severance for several days.

Q. In my day it used to work the other way. You had to stay a little longer in school, stay after school.

Q. Mr. Roos, slicing that day up, you say a suspension for one hour without any notice and for any reason is appropriate.

Obviously then my next question, and I do not want to, as it will be two hours, three hours, until we get your point.

MR. ROOS: Your Honor, it is generally our position that a severance from the school system, putting a child out of the school system as opposed to punishments that might happen internally within the school system or the one-hour, two-hour, end-of-the-day sort of thing, something that is as final and as abrupt as saying, "You shall not come back tomorrow or for ten days," has the potential for creating serious disruptions in the educational progress of the student and also has some of the stigmatizing consequences that were alluded to before.

There certainly is some area of line drawing, and I cannot deny that, Your Honor. But I think that the key is severance. I think that the key is severance, Your Honor.

[Members of the Court asked about the impact of children's age on their entitlement to due process.]

Q. Mr. Roos, under your submission, is the age of the child or the grade of the pupil relevant in any situation? Or, putting it differently, as I recall, the ages of these appellees range from 13 to 19. Does the age make any difference? Does it make any difference whether one is a senior in high school or, say, a sixth grader?

MR. ROOS: In terms of the right to a prior hearing or the right to a hearing, Your Honor?

Q. Yes.

MR. ROOS: I don't think so. A child who is in elementary school is just as needful of the protection as is the child who is in high school. And we were talking about severance from the school system. As a practical matter, Your Honor, I have had quite a good deal of experience in analyzing statistics and what not on suspensions and expulsions. As a practical matter, they very rarely occur at the elementary school level. It is primarily at the junior high and high school level. But they could occur and under our analysis there would be no particular reason that we could think of for distinguishing between an elementary school system and a high school system.

Q. May I ask you this: Is it your view that or does the record support the view that a one-day suspension of a sixth grade child would adversely affect the performance of that child in that grade?

MR. ROOS: Your Honor, the record does support that it could adversely affect a child.

Q. Is that somebody's speculation, or is there any demonstration of it?

MR. ROOS: There is ample, uncontroverted testimony of the sorts of harms that can and do occur in a suspension.

Q. For one day?

MR. ROOS: Any suspension, Your Honor. I would draw this Court's attention especially to the testimony of Dr. Rie, * * *.

The harms that he describes and which are uncontroverted all could occur or are substantially likely to occur to any child, irrespective of age and irrespective of length.

It is true clearly that the longer an exclusion, the likelihood of harm or the magnitude of the harm may increase. We would not argue that that is not the case. But we do argue and argue forcefully that even a short-term suspension can have stigmatizing consequences, can have educational consequences, and what not.

* * *

[Finally, the Court asked Mr. Roos to distinguish between police arrests and suspensions from school.]

MR. ROOS: Arrest. I know that this Court has mentioned arrest. There is no reason whatsoever for not holding a prior hearing in a school suspension case. In an arrest situation, where an emergency may occur, there is obviously need for quick action.

Q. Very often people are arrested in situations where there is no emergency.

MR. ROOS: That is so, Your Honor.

Q. Sometimes with a warrant and sometimes without. Usually with a warrant. There is no notice in advance, is there?

MR. ROOS: I suppose that often is the case, Your Honor. But we would submit that there is no reason whatsoever, there is no reason ad-vanced by our opponents and there is no reason that we can conjure up for not holding some form of protection to insure that the sorts of alarms that we have set out in our brief and which are well documented in the record will not occur.

Thereupon, the questioning of Mr. Roos ceased and Chief Justice Burger announced that the case was submitted. The time was 2:09 P.M.; oral argument had lasted almost one hour.

NOTES AND QUESTIONS

1. Compared to Mr. Bustin, how did Mr. Roos fare with the Court? Which attorney in your view was more effective in oral argument? Were there any new points made which would cause you to reconsider your view about the correctness of the district court decision? When Peter Roos was preparing his oral argument before the Supreme Court, members of the Lopez team met the day prior to the hearing in the offices of the Lawyers Committee for Civil Rights in Washington, D. C. The Lawyers Committee had assembled a number of experts on student rights matters to review likely questions from members of the Supreme Court. As Mr. Murphy recalls, "The preparation was such that they predicted in incredible detail questions Peter was eventually asked from the bench on the date of the argument."

2. Note the comments by Mr. Roos about the application to suspensions of *less* than one day. Is his position clear to you? Do you agree?

3. Note also Mr. Roos' comments about the relevancy of *age* to the due process issue. In the case of an elementary school youngster, should the due process proceeding involve only the student or the parents as well?

Based on what we have learned about social science research, would you agree with Mr. Roos that "There is ample, uncontroverted testimony of the sorts of harms that can and do occur in suspension?" Does the age and class rank of the student make any difference? That is, would a third grader be apt to suffer more or less harm than a high school senior? Can social science tell us?

4. Do you think Mr. Roos makes a convincing distinction between police arrest and school suspension as they involve the absence or presence of procedural due process? Neither the Court nor Mr. Roos referred to the *Miranda* ruling; does it provide a comparable procedural due process protection to persons under arrest?

5. With the conclusion of oral argument, the case rested with the Court. The following excerpt from an earlier edition of *Equal Justice Under Law*, describes the process the Court members follow in deciding the cases before them. .

"The Court follows a schedule of two weeks of Monday-through-Thursday argument, then two weeks of recess for writing opinions and studying petitions for review. On Fridays after argument, the argued cases come before the Justices in their secluded conference room. Here the procedure follows the same pattern as action on petitions, but with much more extended discussion.

"Several days after discussion ends and a vote is taken, an opinion is assigned for writing. If the Chief Justice has voted with the majority, he makes the assignment. If not, the senior Justice of the majority assigns the opinion. The dissenters agree among themselves who shall set down their viewpoint. Even without an assignment, a Justice may write his own opinion, concurring or dissenting.

"Law clerks working for the Justices comb every possible source for useful material. These young men come to the Court as honor graduates of the leading law schools, usually upon the recommendation of a dean or professor.

"Appointment as a law clerk is regarded as a great stride toward success in a demanding profession. The roster of those who have served the Justices is long and distinguished.

* * *

"Writing an opinion means long, lonely hours of hard work for most Justices. * * *

"When the author of an opinion feels he has an 'unanswerable document,' he sends it to the print shop, which operates under rigid security restrictions on the Supreme Court's ground floor. From conference decision to final draft, the Court's findings are carefully guarded. All parties to a case have a right to learn the decision at the same time, from an official announcement. Moreover, a leak might upset the stock market and even the economy of the country.

"Often, after receiving proofs from the print shop, the author finds that his work has only begun. He may revise his draft several times before he circulates copies to his eight brethren.

"Then he waits to learn whether those who voted with him still agree, and what they say about his proposed opinion. As Justice Brennan once put it, 'often some who voted with him at conference will advise that they reserve final judgment pending circulation of the dissent. It is common experience that dissents change votes, even enough votes to become the majority.'

"Constantly the Justices exchange comments, in memoranda or at the lunch table. To discuss ideas and wording in complete privacy, they use a special telephone 'opinion line' that does not go through the switchboard. A Justice may revise his draft as many as ten times before it wins final approval as the opinion of the Court.

"Once all corrections and revisions are in hand, a master proof goes back to the shop for printing. On the day of their release, final copies go to the Clerk of the Court for safekeeping. Several dozen copies also go to the Court's press officer * * * who also puts them under lock and key.

"In Court, the author of the majority opinion announces the decision; * * * Authors of concurrences and dissents follow suit.

"As soon as a decision is announced, the Clerk slips a copy of the opinion into a pneumatic tube that whisks it to the ground-floor press room. There the press officer hands out copies to waiting reporters.

"At six desks before the bench in the Courtroom are other men and women from the wire services and major newspapers. They hurry the news by pneumatic tube to colleagues huddled with Teletype machines and telephones in tiny cubicles directly under the bench.

"Thus, within minutes the world gets the news of Supreme Court decisions that have been months in the making. * * * " [4]

E. Reactions to the Decision

In the last chapter we reviewed some administrative concerns about the *Goss* ruling, which is excerpted there. (You may wish to review it at this point.) Insofar as school life in general is concerned, the reactions to the ruling have been of two general types. There were some who predicted *Goss* would contribute to deterioration of relationships between students and their teachers and administrators. One commentator, for example, concluded that the Supreme Court had inadvisably intruded into the internal affairs of educational institutions.

For more than any other reason, *Goss v. Lopez* is bad law because of the mold into which it promises to cast and harden the relationships between students and school authorities in the future. The mold, of course, is the pre-form of due process, or those spe-

---

4. *Equal Justice Under Law*, Id., 1965 Ed., at pp. 138–141.

cific minimum procedures announced by the Supreme Court. * * * Students will get THE PROCEDURE, neither more nor less, and relationships between students and school authorities will be cast in the form of constitutional confrontation.[5]

Of course, if the Court's decision is ignored or administrators simply cease to use suspensions, then such an adversary relationship will be less likely to occur. There is some evidence that alternatives to suspension are being increasingly used.[6]

The second reaction is more positive. Like the attorneys for the plaintiffs, many believe that respect for our system of government can best be engendered when school officials themselves practice fair play in school operation. *Goss* is thus viewed as a step in that direction. Furthermore, it is important to note that the Court did recognize suspension as "not only a necessary tool to maintain order but a valuable educational device." Thus, the Court may have created a new opportunity for educators to turn a potential suspension into a valuable educational experience. In a face-to-face encounter with a student threatened with suspension, the school administrator may find what could at first be an unpleasant experience turning into a valuable counseling and guidance opportunity.

What about the reactions of the parties to the suit? A number of commentators have pointed out that plaintiffs' attorneys really fell far short of getting what they intended when the suit was originally brought. We asked plaintiffs' attorneys to comment on this observation. Speaking for Mr. Curtin and himself, Mr. Murphy replied as follows:

> We disagree completely. Although we firmly believed that Fourteenth Amendment Rights should be extended to children in public schools and that poor and black students were disproportionately penalized by school discipline procedures, we felt that our chances of success in the district court were extremely limited by the context of racial violence and by lack of Supreme Court precedent in this area. When the case was scheduled for hearing in the Supreme Court we thought our substantial victory in Ohio would be transformed into a national instruction to the legal community to stop cluttering up court dockets with litigation intruding upon the "necessary discretion" traditionally granted to local school authorities. Instead, the doors have been opened a little wider and district judges so inclined now have a precedent to rely on. We sought constitutional protection for the right to a public education and we won!!

5. Arthur A. Kola, "Hard Choices in School Discipline and the Hardening of the Due Process Mold" in Anson and Kuriloff, p. 36. *Professional Discretion and Liability under Goss and Wood* (Washington, D.C.: Capitol Publications, 1975).

6. According to a recent article in the *New York Times*, in-school suspension programs with strong counseling overtones, alternative schools, and compulsory classes in basic skills are three increasingly utilized approaches. "Schools Developing Alternatives to Student Suspensions," *NYT*, Wednesday, May 18, 1977.

Mr. Roos added,

> While many child advocates hoped for a ruling which would have required such procedural hurdles as to effectively stop school officials from suspending students, this was never recognized by the attorneys as a realistic hope. In fact, what we got went beyond the ruling of *any* court that had previously considered the issue. The opinion requires a genuine search for the truth by school officials and absent such a search we believe *Goss* has been violated. Viewed in this light the case must be seen as a substantial step forward.

Norval Goss, who continued as the Director of Pupil Personnel, maintains the decision had little impact at all in the Columbus School System.

> We were all amazed at how little impact this case had on the local scene. There was much more publicity nationally than there was here in Columbus. It was necessary for me to expunge the records of the students involved. We also revised our policy concerning suspensions, but in most ways there was little noticeable impact on our school system.

One of the reasons, of course, was the new student suspension procedures his office put into effect in July of 1973. In addition, by the time the case came before the Supreme Court, Congress had passed the Family Educational Rights and Privacy Act (Buckley Amendment), designed to eliminate many abuses of student record keeping in the nation's schools.

> Mr. Murphy recalls that the local coverage of the decision in Columbus was one-sided on behalf of the Columbus School System. "The Columbus School System had chosen to take the case to the Supreme Court and it lost, but from what was reported it was hard to perceive that, in fact the Columbus School System lost the case."

Insofar as winning or losing is concerned, Norval Goss certainly agrees with Mr. Murphy's assessment.

> I personally feel we may have "lost the battle but won the war." It is very clear to us that the principal *does* have the right to suspend a student.

The difficulty for Mr. Murphy is that *Goss,* like any procedural due process case, "does not get to the ultimate injustice which is not the process but the imposition of a penalty." If administrators make a mistake, they "would simply do it all over again and the result would be the same."

The *Goss* ruling prompted the Ohio legislature to modify the statute pertaining to suspension and expulsion in the public schools. Relevant sections of the new statute read as follows.

§ 3313.66   Suspension or expulsion.

(A) The superintendent of schools of a city, exempted village, or local school district, or the principal of a public school may suspend a pupil from school for not more than ten school days. No pupil shall be suspended unless prior to the suspension such superintendent or principal:

(1) Gives the pupil written notice of the intention to suspend him and the reasons for the intended suspension; and

(2) Provides the pupil an opportunity to appear at an informal hearing before the principal, assistant principal, superintendent, or superintendent's designee and challenge the reason for the intended suspension or otherwise to explain his actions.

* * *

(C) If a pupil's presence poses a continuing danger to persons or property or an ongoing threat of disrupting the academic process taking place either within a classroom or elsewhere on the school premises, the superintendent, or a principal, or assistant principal may remove a pupil from curricular or extracurricular activities or from the school premises, and a teacher may remove a pupil from curricular or extracurricular activities under his supervision, without the notice and hearing requirements * * *. As soon as practicable after making such a removal, the teacher shall submit in writing to the principal the reasons for such removal.

If a pupil is removed under this division from a curricular or extracurricular activity or from the school premises, written notice of the hearing and of the reason for the removal shall be given to the pupil as soon as practicable prior to the hearing, which shall be held within seventy-two hours from the time the initial removal is ordered. * * * The individual who ordered, caused, or requested the removal to be made shall be present at the hearing.

* * *

[§ 3313.66.1]   § 3313.661

On or before September 1, 1976, each board of education shall adopt a code regarding suspension, expulsion, and removal specifying the types of misconduct for which a pupil may be suspended, expelled, or removed, and a copy of the code shall be posted in a central location in the school and made available to pupils upon request. Thereafter, no pupil shall be suspended, expelled, or removed except in accordance with the code adopted by the board of education of the school district in which the pupil attends school.

Thus, while the debate continues on about the effectiveness of the ruling, changes in the way in which public school students are disciplined have occurred. To this extent, *Goss* has set a new national precedent in the operation of public educational institutions.

At the least, it seems that the Goss ruling coupled with the *Wood v. Strickland* ruling will result in better training of educational administrators in educational law. The exercise of administrative discretion has to be conditioned with the knowledge that there are both educational and legal consequences to administrative action. This awareness, plus the promulgation of more precise school rules and guidelines for students, may very well be the most significant impact of the case.

NOTES AND QUESTIONS

1. From your experience in educational institutions, how would you characterize the *Goss v. Lopez* decision? Do you regard it as a significant contribution to student rights?

2. Is Mr. Murphy suggesting that the Court should have flatly outlawed *all* suspensions? Or is he suggesting that courts in general should be less concerned with procedures and more with substance? One commentator suggests that the decision has not been well received because it assumes a view about the functioning of schools which is by no means shared by many parents and by many in the educational community. The *Goss* decision, notes David Kirp,

> implies the desirability of colloquy and exchange of information, rather than a one-way communication of values. It indicates that there may be valid perceptions of injustice to be gleaned from students. Most importantly, it treats the educational value of interchanges between schools and disciplinarians as of greater moment than allegiance to hierarchy.[7]

If courts were to be less concerned with due process procedure and more with substance, would they be more or less likely to be charged with meddling in educational affairs? Do judges have the qualifications and the experience to be effective in determining substantive matters of school operation and discipline?

We are thus confronted again with a basic issue we investigated first in Chapter One. Who should make decisions about student rights and what standards should guide those decisions?

7. David L. Kirp, "Due Process in Schools," 28 *Stanford L.Rev.* 841 (May 1, 1976), p. 851.

" *   *   *   when a State's distribution of benefits or imposition of
burdens hinges on the color of a person's skin or ancestry, that
individual is entitled to a demonstration that the challenged classification is necessary to promote a substantial State interest."

> Justice Lewis F. Powell, Jr.
> *University of California Regents v. Bakke,*
> 1978

"RIGHTS OF EQUAL PROTECTION"

Equality has become one of the major moral standards to which societies aspire. The passion for equality inherent in the simple phrase "all
men are created equal" tends to be universalistic and has exerted an extraordinary impact over social life. To state that persons are "equal,"
however, raises a host of vexing issues which foster a continuing debate
as to what it means to be human and what rights a human being should
be guaranteed.

Individuals as they develop from birth become different, some stronger and some more talented. The fact of actual inequality of strength and
intellect seems incontrovertible. If persons are not actually equal, then
how can the notion of equality make sense? Equality, like freedom and
justice, is a concept that belongs to the sphere of values. It is used as a
moral standard in that people believe it ought in some sense to exist. And
this is so despite the obvious ways in which persons differ in strength,
talent, and intellect. In essence, the assertion that persons are equal is a
moral claim that in fundamental ways, regardless of their differences,
all persons deserve to be treated in a particular way. Nevertheless, a
basic question about equality does come to mind. If people differ in such
characteristics as physical strength, intelligence, wealth, education, sex,
race, religion, and so on, are all these differences to be considered irrelevant to the way people are treated or are some characteristics relevant and
others irrelevant? This question forms the basis of one of the great debates of contemporary politics, law, and education. The major value
positions that have been articulated about equality are briefly explored
below.

I.   EQUALITY: THE TROUBLING IDEAL

A.   Equality of Legal Treatment

Many of the founders of our constitutional government were ardent
proponents of a natural rights philosophy which claimed that all persons
possess "equal" rights to "life, liberty and the pursuit of happiness." This
has come to mean that all persons deserve *equality before the law.* From
this perspective, no exceptions to the rules or regulations of society should
be permitted unless all who qualify for the exemption are given it. In

American society, some exemptions are not considered permissible under any circumstances. For example, legislatures cannot exclude racial minorities from the enjoyment of civil rights.

Yet, equality before the law may itself imply the existence of basic inequalities, since laws bear more heavily on some than on others. For example, while all persons may be required to pay sales taxes according to fixed percentages, the law does not say that their income levels must be identical. Large families with little income may actually pay more in sales taxes than small families with large incomes. Equality before the law does not entail a moral belief in social or economic equality. Those who advocate equality of legal treatment as their primary political or legal value may advocate equal *access* to public education, but not the right to receive equal grades or job placement. Since individual freedom is also an important value to proponents of equality of legal treatment, they are not inclined to compromise reliance on individual initiative by an expansive view of equality. Equality of legal treatment, then, can be viewed as the most conservative of the interpretations of equality.

B. Equality of Opportunity

This formulation of equality argues that government must provide every person with the *opportunity* to obtain the benefits of life that her talents permit her to achieve. This approach to equality places great importance on the provision of minimal resources so that a person has a chance to compete in an environment of scarce resources.

Both the advocates of equality of legal treatment and equality of opportunity claim that human life is a competitive race where not all can be winners. But they do differ on one important point. The advocates of equality of legal treatment claim that all have an equal right, in effect, to run the race or play the game, with some relative winners and some relative losers because of different abilities and stations in life. The advocates of equality of opportunity claim that not only should everyone have a right to run the race but that the government has a duty to provide certain minimal resources to the disadvantaged so that people start at the same starting line and have a real chance to run the competitive gauntlet. Those who support this second view argue that if government does not provide certain positive resources, the talented who also happen to be poor or members of a heretofore disenfranchised group may not have any real chance to compete. Equality of opportunity is thus a more liberal view of the nature of equality, though it can be considered less so where inequalities among groups of people stem from prior illegal acts of state discrimination. In the latter case, the remedies of equality of opportunity are designed to place the victims of such discrimination in the position they would have been in, save for the discriminatory treatment. A prime example are the school segregation cases to be discussed later in the chapter.

C. Equality of Result

Equality of result is clearly the most radical or egalitarian view. From this perspective, persons possess some basic needs in common such as good nutrition, an hospitable environment, a quality education, and so on. All persons must have these basic needs fulfilled in equal fashion regardless of talent, background, or influence. The fulfillment of basic human needs should not be part of a competitive process; the resources of society must be equally distributed. All persons deserve to have these needs met simply because they are human beings. Whatever inequalities of condition such as wealth or status which actually exist in a society can be permitted to exist (if at all) only *after* basic needs are met. Those who advocate a moderate form of this position claim that some may be heavily taxed by the government so that all may be provided minimal levels of well-being. The difference between those who take this moderate approach and those who subscribe to equality of opportunity is really a matter of degree. Thus, the former may argue for a heavily graduated income tax to "level down" the rich and "level up" the poor, while the latter may be satisfied with a less extreme taxation program, provided the benefits are distributed to the needy in the form of social welfare. Those who advocate a more radical variation of equality of result claim that only a socialist society offering complete social and economic equality can liberate mankind from the yoke of competition and conflict. This radical view of equality necessarily suggests a restricted view of individual freedom since, at the extremes, an inverse relationship exists between equality and freedom—the more of one there is, the less of the other. In this way, equality and freedom are values which to some degree are in a state of dynamic tension.

II. DEVELOPMENT OF THE FOURTEENTH AMENDMENT EQUAL PROTECTION CLAUSE

Most laws classify, that is, they attempt to draw lines between and among groups of people in distributing economic and social benefits or establishing rules of order. Some examples include:

(a) Welfare laws see that benefits go to the needy, not to those who are well off.

(b) Compulsory schools laws are usually applied to children, not adults.

(c) University admissions committees distinguish between students on the basis of past performance and academic potential.

Depending upon one's view of equality, not every form of discrimination is thought to be unwarranted. The problem posed for constitutional law is deciding the grounds on which differential treatment and procedures should be tolerated. Making this determination may be easy. For example, if the records of a court show that black defendants always receive more severe sentences than whites do for the same type of criminal offenses, most Americans would view the unequal treatment to be unjustified. On the other hand, most Americans are not disturbed that very young children are denied the right to marry, for age, unlike race, is often considered a relevant reason for unequal treatment. A more difficult cases involves the validity of quota systems which provide special slots for minority applicants to professional schools. Again, depending upon one's view of equality, some may view this as unfair "reverse discrimination" against white competitors, while others may view a quota system as just compensation for previous unfair discrimination. The problem of quotas highlights the difficulty involved in formulating explicit criteria to use in deciding what constitutes proper and improper forms of classification.

The constitutional basis for deciding issues of equality is found in the Equal Protection Clause of the Fourteenth Amendment, which requires that no state shall "deny to any person within its jurisdiction the equal protection of the laws." The original purpose of this clause was to eliminate state discrimination against blacks. While the intention of the post-Civil War framers was to grant equal status under the law to former slaves, the wording of the Amendment itself does not restrict its application to any particular group. In order to extend to persons equal protection under federal laws, the Supreme Court has read into the Due Process Clause of the Fifth Amendment principles of equality that are, for all practical purposes, identical to those applied to the states in the Fourteenth Amendment.

In order to prove a violation of the Equal Protection Clause, two requirements must be satisfied. First, there must be some form of state action. The clause was created to prevent governmental discrimination; it was not intended to stop discriminatory practices by private individuals. The second requirement is that some form of unwarranted discrimination must be proven. When both factors are present, then a violation of the Equal Protection Clause may have occurred.

A. "Old" Equal Protection and the Rational Test

Since there are many competing interest groups involved in the political process, legislators usually must arrange compromises in order to get laws enacted. Even where compromises are not necessary, the scope of legislation cannot be drawn with mathematical exactness. The result is that some groups may be exempted from coverage, even though one might assume they would be covered. For example, a state legislature might impose a 50-miles per hour speed limit on state highways but exempt buses or certain other vehicles from the law.

Traditionally, courts have not demanded a close fit between the classification established by the laws and the legislative purpose in passing them. The assumption under the "old" equal protection has been that political and administrative realities make exactness impossible; some persons may not be covered by a law, while others in many respects similarly situated will be covered. All the courts have demanded when a law has been challenged as a violation of the Equal Protection Clause is that the relationship between the classification system or "line-drawing" of the law and the legislative purpose in making the law be rational and reasonable. The presumption is that since the legislatures make laws, legislators are in the best position to know who should and who should not be covered. In addition, legislatures are more accountable than courts to the public, so that changes in the laws can be made in response to shifting public opinion. Again and again in their opinions, judges assert that courts are not legislatures and cannot undertake remedial tasks better left to the political process.

Because of the tendency of courts to allow legislators a good deal of flexibility in drawing up laws, challenges to state legislation under old equal protection have been relatively few and unsuccessful. Such remains the case for most economic and social legislation today.

A recent and classic example of the traditional approach emerged in the case of *Dandridge v. Williams,* 397 U.S. 471 (1970). The case concerned a challenge to Maryland's administrative regulation which placed a limit of $250 a month on Aid to Families With Dependent Children (AFDC) grants, without concern for the size of the family. The challengers claimed that the regulation discriminated against larger families and was in violation of the Equal Protection Clause. The Court in a 5 to 3 decision rejected the argument. Justice Stewart, speaking for the Court, ruled that since Maryland's classification of welfare recipients has some reasonable basis, it does not offend the Constitution even though it results in some inequality.

> In the area of economics and social welfare, a State does not violate the Equal Protection Clause merely because the classifications made by its laws are imperfect. If the classification has "some reasonable basis," it does not offend the Constitution simply because the classification "is not made with mathematical nicety or because in practice it results in some inequality." "The problems of government are practical ones and may justify, if they do not require, rough accommodations—illogical, it may be, and unscientific." "A statutory discrimination will not be set aside if any state of facts reasonably may be conceived to justify it."
>
> * * *
>
> Under this long-established meaning of the Equal Protection Clause, it is clear that the Maryland maximum grant regulation is constitutionally valid. * * *
>
> * * * the Equal Protection Clause does not require that a State must choose between attacking every aspect of a problem or not attacking the problem at all. It is enough that the State's action be rationally based and free from invidious discrimination. The regulation before us meets that test. (At pp. 485–487).

The Court held that Maryland's reasons for limiting the aid—to encourage gainful employment, to allocate scarce resources to deal with the needs of as many families as possible, and to encourage an equitable balance between welfare families and those supported by gainful employment—were rational and reasonable.

While the rule of applying the rational test to social and economic legislation is simple enough to state, it is far less clear exactly what falls into these categories. Thus, there is often considerable disagreement whether the rational test of old equal protection is warranted or should be replaced by the more sensitive approach of "new" equal protection.

B. "New" Equal Protection and the Compelling State Purpose Test

Only in a few select instances does the Supreme Court apply more than a rational test to state and federal legislation under the Equal Protection Clause. In these instances the Court looks carefully at the challenged act (applies "strict scrutiny") to see if the government can show a *compelling purpose* for its action. "New" equal protection is used only in cases involving "suspect classifications" and cases involving "fundamental rights." Without becoming overly specific, "suspect classifications" are classifications based primarily on race, and "fundamental rights" are specific constitutional guarantees such as freedom of speech and press and certain other less specific rights considered to be "fundamental." When equal protection violations in these two types of cases are alleged to have occurred, then the compelling state purpose test is likely to be employed.

The compelling state purpose test is vastly more strict than the rational approach, and few laws survive such a challenge. In order to meet the more rigorous compelling state purpose test, the government must show a very great need to legislate and enjoys little presumption that its classification is valid. Wherever possible, therefore, those challenging state laws on equal protection grounds hope to challenge them on the basis of new rather than old equal protection. This means they must show that the law in question falls into either the suspect classification or fundamental rights category, a task that is not always easy.

Why the Supreme Court has opted for this stricter view of equal protection in some cases is the subject of considerable debate. Some believe a majority of the members of the Warren Court, which introduced new equal protection, were embued with a different view of equality from their predecessors—one closer to equality of opportunity or a moderate form of equality of result. From these perspectives, the Equal Protection Clause can be read to require the government to take positive action to eliminate gross disparities between groups of people. Others view the Court's adoption of new equal protection as the manifestation of a power drive in competition with the other branches of government. As you read the cases involving new equal protection and the critical commentary directed at these decisions, consider what the likely motivation for the heightened judicial involvement is and whether or not it is justified. Consider as well where the dividing line between old and new equal protection should be drawn.

(1) *Suspect Classifications and Race*

The first area receiving strict scrutiny under new equal protection were classifications based on race. Considering the historical roots of the Fourteenth Amendment, concern about classifications based on race is not surprising.

The roots of the American dilemma on the racial issue go deep into history: to introduction of slavery in Virginia in 1619, to the liberation of blacks from slavery, to the Reconstruction period which really did not make them free. With the final withdrawal of Federal troops from the South after the Civil War, came "Jim Crow" laws—the systematic legal segregation of the races in the South. "Jim Crow" laws legalized segregation of schools, trains, prisons, even water fountains. Segregation became a way of life in the South and was carried over by custom to most of the North.

It was inevitable that exploited blacks would seek help from the Supreme Court, hoping for a color-blind application of the Constitution. This was not to be the case. The Supreme Court in the *Civil Rights Cases*, 109 U.S. 3 (1883), declared two provisions of the Civil Rights Acts of 1875 unconstitutional. These federal laws had outlawed discrimination in places of public accommodation and had imposed penalties directly on private persons maintaining such places even if the state was not involved. The provisions were struck down because the Court pointed out that the 14th Amendment applies to the actions of states, not private individuals.

A more decisive set-back for integrationists occurred in the seminal case of *Plessy v. Ferguson*, 163 U.S. 537 (1896). The Court upheld the criminal conviction of Homer Plessy, a man of "one-eight African blood," for violation of the segregation rules of Louisiana's Railroad Accommodation Law. The Court sanctioned legal segregation in the following terms:

> We consider the underlying fallacy of the plaintiff's argument to consist in the assumption that the enforced separation of the two races stamps the colored race with the badge of inferiority. If this be so, it is not by reason of anything found in the act, but solely because the colored race choses to put that construction upon it. * * * The argument also assumes that social prejudices may be overcome by legislation, and that equal rights cannot be secured to the negro except by an enforced commingling of the two races. We cannot accept this proposition. * * * Legislation is powerless to eradicate racial instincts * * *. If one race be inferior to the other socially, the Constitution of the United States cannot put them upon the same plane. (At pp. 551–552).

In his dissent, Justice Harlan argued that the ruling was contrary to the manifest tenor of the Constitution:

> * * * in the view of the Constitution, in the eye of the law, there is no caste here. Our Constitution is color-blind, and neither knows nor tolerates classes among citizens. (At p. 559)

He criticized the Court for sanctioning the right of the state to condition the enjoyment of civil rights on the basis of race, and he predicted that the ruling would come to be regarded as pernicious as any the Court had rendered.

> We boast of the freedom enjoyed by our people above all other peoples. But it is difficult to reconcile that boast with a state of the law which, practically, puts the brand of servitude and degradation upon a large class of our fellow-citizens, our equals before the law. The thin disguise of "equal" accommodations for passengers in railroad coaches will not mislead any one, nor atone for the wrong this day done. (At p. 562).

Plessy maintained that separation implied inferiority only in the minds of black people, for such facilities were not inherently unequal. Later the Court began its inquiry into whether separate facilities in a given situation were in fact equal. The Court found that subsidizing out-of-state higher education for blacks circumvents the requirement that states provide equal facilities within the state; [1] that segregated law schools are unequal because such intangibles as faculty and reputation, community standing, and prestige are lacking; [2] and that segregated instruction within an integrated graduate school inhibits effective study and student discussion by black people and is therefore unequal.[3]

These decisions set the stage for the 1954 landmark *Brown* ruling. The *Brown* case, which extended these principles to all of public education, remains one of the most important cases in American constitutional history.

The National Association for the Advancement of Colored People (NAACP) was the primary interest group involved in seeking redress from the Supreme Court in the area of "separate but equal" educational facilities. It began its strategies with law and professional schools in the 1930s and 1940s because the strategists thought the members of the Court, all of them lawyers, would be sympathetic to the law student's need for intellectual and social interaction.

The NAACP's successes in these suits led in the early 1950s to suits against segregated elementary, junior, and senior high schools. Black parents in several southern states sued their local school boards, charging a denial of equal protection because their children were not obtaining the same education as white children. The NAACP demonstrated an important shift in strategy in these suits. The goal was still equal treatment for blacks and whites. However, now the lawyers for the black parents no longer emphasized the inevitable inequality of separate facilities. Instead they wanted to demonstrate that even if a black school *had* equal facilities, the Equal Protection Clause was still violated because any separation of the races in the classroom reduces the quality of the learning process and is inherently unequal.

The master strategist who led these many suits to the Supreme Court was the black attorney, Thurgood Marshall, later to be appointed a Justice on the Supreme Court. Marshall was also to argue the case before the Supreme Court. The distinguished lawyer, John W. Davis, led groups of attorneys supporting the respective school boards. The battle between these two men was one of the most tension-ridden the Court has experienced. The marble corridors were jammed. The Ku Klux Klan threatened military reprisals if the Court should rule in favor of the blacks. South Carolina's Governor, James I. Byrnes, threatened to dissolve the public school system by an amendment to the state constitution.

In his oral argument, Davis relied heavily on the *Plessy* case as the controlling precedent on issue of separate but equal facilities. Marshall

1. *Missouri ex rel. Gaines v. Canada*, 305 U.S. 337 (1938).

2. *Sweatt v. Painter*, 339 U.S. 629 (1950).

3. *McLaurin v. Oklahoma State Regents*, 339 U.S. 637 (1950).

relied on the testimony of sociologists and psychologists. He sought to demonstrate that separate facilities have a "detrimental" effect upon black children because such facilities produce a sense of inferiority which deeply affects the motivation to learn. Segregation, therefore, has a tendency to retard the educational and mental development of black children. Marshall also pointed to a number of precedents that viewed purely racial distinctions as "odious and insidious." Marshall consistently argued that state-imposed segregation must end; it harms black children, placing them beyond the pale of respectability. On May 17, 1954, the Chief Justice spoke for a unanimous Court: "We conclude that in the field of public education the doctrine of 'separate but equal' has no place."

BROWN v. BOARD OF EDUC.

Supreme Court of the United States, 1954.
347 U.S. 483, 74 S.Ct. 686, 98 L.Ed. 873.

Mr. Chief Justice WARREN delivered the opinion of the Court.

These cases come to us from the States of Kansas, South Carolina, Virginia, and Delaware. They are premised on different facts and different local conditions, but a common legal question justifies their consideration together in this consolidated opinion.

In each of the cases, minors of the Negro race, through their legal representatives, seek the aid of the courts in obtaining admission to the public schools of their community on a nonsegregated basis. In each instance, they have been denied admission to schools attended by white children under laws requiring or permitting segregation according to race. This segregation was alleged to deprive the plaintiffs of the equal protection of the laws under the Fourteenth Amendment. In each of the cases * * * (the Court relied on) the so-called "separate but equal" doctrine announced by this Court in Plessy v. Ferguson * * *.

* * *

The plaintiffs contend that segregated public schools are not "equal" and cannot be made "equal," and that hence they are deprived of the equal protection of the laws. Because of the obvious importance of the question presented, the Court took jurisdiction. Argument was heard in the 1952 Term, and reargument was heard this Term on certain questions propounded by the Court.

Reargument was largely devoted to the circumstances surrounding the adoption of the Fourteenth Amendment in 1868. It covered exhaustively consideration of the Amendment in Congress, ratification by the states, then existing practices in racial segregation, and the views of proponents and opponents of the Amendment. This discussion and our own investigation convince us that, although these sources cast some light, it is not enough to resolve the problem with which we are faced. At best, they are inconclusive. The most avid proponents of the post-War Amendments undoubtedly intended them to remove all legal distinctions among "all persons born or naturalized in the United States." Their opponents, just as certainly, were antagonistic to both the letter and the spirit of the Amendments and wished them to have the most limited effect. What others in Congress and the state legislatures had in mind cannot be determined with any degree of certainty.

An additional reason for the inconclusive nature of the Amendment's history, with respect to segregated schools, is the status of public education at that time. In the South, the movement toward free common schools, supported by general taxation, had not yet taken hold. Education of white children was largely in the hands of private groups. Education of Negroes was almost nonexistent, and practically all of the race were illiterate. In fact, any education of Negroes was forbidden by law in some states. Today, in contrast, many Negroes have achieved outstanding success in the arts and sciences as well as in the business and professional world. It is true that public school education at the time of the Amendment had advanced further in the North, but the effect of the Amendment on Northern States was generally ignored in the congressional debates. Even in the North, the conditions of public education did not approximate those existing today. The curriculum was usually rudimentary; ungraded schools were common in rural areas; the school term was but three months a year in many states; and compulsory school attendance was virtually unknown. As a consequence, it is not surprising that there should be so little in the history of the Fourteenth Amendment relating to its intended effect on public education.

* * *

* * * Here * * * there are findings below that the Negro and white schools involved have been equalized, or are being equalized, with respect to buildings, curricula, qualifications and salaries of teachers, and other "tangible" factors. Our decision, therefore, cannot turn on merely a comparison of these tangible factors in the Negro and white schools involved in each of the cases. We must look instead to the effect of segregation itself on public education.

In approaching this problem, we cannot turn the clock back to 1868 when the Amendment was adopted, or even to 1896 when Plessy v. Ferguson was writ-

ten. We must consider public education in the light of its full development and its present place in American life throughout the Nation. Only in this way can it be determined if segregation in public schools deprives these plaintiffs of the equal protection of the laws.

Today, education is perhaps the most important function of state and local governments. Compulsory school attendance laws and the great expenditures for education both demonstrate our recognition of the importance of education to our democratic society. It is required in the performance of our most basic public responsibilities, even service in the armed forces. It is the very foundation of good citizenship. Today it is a principal instrument in awakening the child to cultural values, in preparing him for later professional training, and in helping him to adjust normally to his environment. In these days, it is doubtful that any child may reasonably be expected to succeed in life if he is denied the opportunity of an education. Such an opportunity, where the state has undertaken to provide it, is a right which must be made available to all on equal terms.

We come then to the question presented: Does segregation of children in public schools solely on the basis of race, even though the physical facilities and other "tangible" factors may be equal, deprive the children of the minority group of equal educational opportunities? We believe that it does.

* * * To separate [Negroes] * * * from others of similar age and qualifications solely because of their race generates a feeling of inferiority as to their status in the community that may affect their hearts and minds in a way unlikely ever to be undone. The effect of this separation on their educational opportunities was well stated by a finding in the Kansas case by a court which nevertheless felt compelled to rule against the Negro plaintiffs:

"Segregation of white and colored children in public schools has a detrimental effect upon the colored children. The impact is greater when it has the sanction of the law; for the policy of separating the races is usually interpreted as denoting the inferiority of the negro group. A sense of inferiority affects the motivation of a child to learn. Segregation with the sanction of law, therefore, has a tendency to [retard] the educational and mental development of Negro children and to deprive them of some of the benefits they would receive in a racial[ly] integrated school system."

Whatever may have been the extent of psychological knowledge at the time of Plessy v. Ferguson, this finding is amply supported by modern authority.[11] Any language in Plessy v. Ferguson contrary to this finding is rejected.

We conclude that in the field of public education the doctrine of "separate but equal" has no place. Separate educational facilities are inherently unequal. Therefore, we hold that the plaintiffs

and others similarly situated for whom the actions have been brought are, by reason of the segregation complained of, deprived of the equal protection of the laws guaranteed by the Fourteenth Amendment. This disposition makes unnecessary any discussion whether such segregation also violates the Due Process Clause of the Fourteenth Amendment.

Because these are class actions, because of the wide applicability of this decision, and because of the great variety of local conditions, the formulation of decrees in these cases presents problems of considerable complexity. On reargument, the consideration of appropriate relief was necessarily subordinated to the primary question—the constitutionality of segregation in public education. We have now announced that such segregation is a denial of the equal protection of the laws. In order that we may have the full assistance of the parties in formulating decrees, the cases will be restored to the docket, and the parties are requested to present further argument   *   *   *.
*   *   *

It is so ordered.

NOTES AND QUESTIONS

1.   Note that having decided the segregation of schools constitutes a violation of the Equal Protection Clause, Chief Justice Warren does not take up the question of segregation under the Due Process Clause. In the instance of segregation in the District of Columbia school system, however, the task could not be avoided since the Fifth Amendment, which applies only to the federal government, does not contain an equal protection provision. Why couldn't the Chief Justice simply include the District of Columbia under the Fourteenth Amendment Equal Protection Clause?

11. K. B. Clark, Effect of Prejudice and Discrimination on Personality Development (Midcentury White House Conference on Children and Youth, 1950); Witmer and Kotinsky, Personality in the Making (1952), c. VI; Deutscher and Chein, The Psychological Effects of Enforced Segregation: A Survey of Social Science Opinion, 26 J.Psychol. 259 (1948); Chein,

What are the Psychological Effects of Segregation Under Conditions of Equal Facilities?, 3 Int.J.Opinion and Attitude Res. 229 (1949); Brameld, Educational Costs, in Discrimination and National Welfare (MacIver, ed., 1949), 44–48; Frazier, The Negro in the United States (1949), 674–681. And see generally Myrdal, An American Dilemma (1944).

In *Bolling v. Sharpe,* 347 U.S. 497 (1954), decided the same day as *Brown,* the Chief Justice again speaking for a unanimous Court ruled that the "life, liberty, or property without due process" provision of the Fifth Amendment prohibits racially segregated schooling in the District of Columbia.

> The Fifth Amendment, which is applicable in the District of Columbia, does not contain an equal protection clause as does the Fourteenth Amendment which applies only to the states. But the concepts of equal protection and due process, both stemming from our American ideal of fairness, are not mutually exclusive. The "equal protection of the laws" is a more explicit safeguard of prohibited unfairness than "due process of law," and, therefore, we do not imply that the two are always interchangeable phrases. But, as this Court has recognized, discrimination may be so unjustifiable as to be violative of due process.

* * *

> In view of our decision that the Constitution prohibits the states from maintaining racially segregated public schools, it would be unthinkable that the same Constitution would impose a lesser duty on the Federal Government. We hold that racial segregation in the public schools of the District of Columbia is a denial of the due process of law guaranteed by the Fifth Amendment to the Constitution. (At pp. 499–500).

2. Note the discussion of the purpose of the Fourteenth Amendment. One contemporary critic of judicial activism accuses the Court in the *Brown* decision of straying far from the original meaning behind the Amendment:

> The * * * segregation decisions go beyond the assumption of powers "not warranted" by the Constitution; they represent the arrogation of powers that the framers plainly *excluded.* The Court, it is safe to say, has flouted the will of the framers and substituted an interpretation in flat contradiction of the original design: to leave * * * segregation * * * to State governance. * * * When Chief Justice Warren asserted that "we cannot turn back the clock to 1868," he in fact rejected the framers' intention as irrelevant. On that premise the entire Constitution merely has such relevance as the Court chooses to give it, and the Court is truly a "continuing constitutional convention," constantly engaged in revising the Constitution * * *. Such conduct impels me to conclude that the Justices are (sic) become a law unto themselves.[4] (Emphasis in original).

What do you think about this criticism? Would it have been preferable to wait until a constitutional amendment could have been adopted outlawing school segregation? Is it likely such an amendment could easily

---

4. Raoul Berger, *Government by Judiciary* (Cambridge, Mass.: Harvard University Press, 1977), at p. 408.

have been passed? Is it possible the framers kept the Fourteenth Amendment's wording rather vague so that it could be adapted by later courts to changing times? Should the Court act to update the Constitution to modern times?

3. How important was the social science evidence to the outcome of *Brown*? The debate over the role and the quality of the social science evidence discussed in *Brown* has never ceased.[5] Footnote 11 in *Brown* sets forth the social science data relied on by the Court. Briefly, the documents and testimony introduced into the case included a study of the opinions of social scientists about the effect of segregation on black children, a review of scientific evidence about the role of the environment in human development, and a research report by Professor Kenneth B. Clark on the self-perceptions of black children. Virtually all the evidence showed that a segregated environment has deep psychological consequences for black children and produces guilt feelings in white children. The so-called "doll test" conducted by Professor Clark, a black psychologist, was particularly poignant. The experiment involved the use of two dolls, completely alike except that one was black and one white. School children were asked to pick the doll they found most attractive, the one they would like to play with, the doll that looked "bad" and so on. They were also asked to identify the white and "colored" doll to be sure they were aware of the difference. The results showed that the children were well aware of the difference and that they preferred the white dolls.

The survey of the attitudes of social scientists about the effects of segregation has been severely criticized on several grounds, the chief of which are: that *opinions* do not constitute adequate evidence, that whatever research supported the views of the respondents was not specifically revealed, and that no tests of statistical significance were reported.[6] How might the doll test used by Dr. Clark be criticized as it relates to *de jure* school segregation?

Given the criticisms of this research and of social science research in general as discussed in Chapter One, was *Brown* wrongly decided? Or do the rights of citizens depend upon something other than social science research? If so, what? Professor Mark Yudof suggests that ethical principles form the basis for the *Brown* decision:

> Basic ethical principles assert the truth of facts that cannot be proven; in other words, barring the most extraordinary advances in learning, even the most scientific among us must rely upon rather unscientific interpretations of historical experience. Indeed because ethical principles are not necessarily dependent on

5. See, for example, Edmond Cahn, "Jurisprudence," 30 *New York Univ.L.Rev.* 150, 1955; Jack Greenberg, "Social Scientists Take the Stand," 54 *Mich.L.Rev.* 953, 1956; Herbert Garfinkel, "Social Science Evidence and the School Desegregation Cases," 21 *J.Pol.* 37, 1959; Kenneth B. Clark, "The Desegregation Cases: Criticism of the Social Scientist's Role, 5 *Vill.L.Rev.* 224, 1959; Ernest Van den Haag, "Social Science Testimony in the Desegregation Cases—A Reply to Professor Kenneth Clark," 6 *Vill.L.Rev.* 69, 1960; and Frank Goodman, "De Facto School Segregation: A Constitutional and Empirical Analysis," (Part IV) 50 *Calif.L.Rev.* 275, 1972.

6. Steven I. Miller and Jack Kavanagh "Empirical Evidence," 4 *J.Law & Educ.* 159, January, 1975.

empirical verification, they can operate as standards that relieve courts of the obligation to reweigh social science data in every case. * * * The [desegregation] cases can be explained only by reference to such principles. * * * An affirmation by the state that whites are superior to blacks is ethically unacceptable, regardless of any particular harm that may result: it simply does not comport with widely shared notions as to how a just society should function.[7]

Is the Supreme Court best able to ascertain and assert these principles? Can they be implied from constitutional provisions or are they found elsewhere? What about Professor Berger's concern that such an approach turns the Court into a " 'continuing constitutional convention' "?

In assessing the impact of the *Brown* decision, Professors Kirp and Yudof point out that had the Court chosen to reaffirm the 1896 *Plessy* ruling, the blow to racial equality and the civil rights movement in general would have been overwhelming, reaching well beyond the courts into the legislative, education, and political arenas. "Too often judges and lawyers ignore a fundamental truth that is obvious to laymen and politicians: regardless of the formal rules of constitutional adjudication, a judicial declaration that a state law is constitutional is likely to enshrine it as the recommended solution of a difficult question of public policy." [8]

4. Chief Justice Warren was able to present a unanimous front in the *Brown* case. This undoubtedly helped to blunt the virulent Southern attacks of the decision. However, the problem of implementing the decision was about to begin. In *Brown v. Bd. of Educ.*, 349 U.S. 294 (1955) (known frequently as *Brown II*), the Court dealt with the extremely difficult problem of enforcement of its 1954 decision. This case and subsequent desegregation cases will be discussed in detail later in the chapter.

Brown was followed by a host of decisions outlawing all types of public segregation: *Mayor of Baltimore v. Dawson,* 350 U.S. 877 (1955), beaches; *Gayle v. Browder,* 352 U.S. 903 (1956), buses; *Holmes v. Atlanta,* 350 U.S. 879 (1955), golf courses; *New Orleans City Park Improvement Ass'n v. Detiege,* 358 U.S. 54 (1958), parks; *Lee v. Washington,* 390 U.S. 333 (1968), prison facilities. These and similar decisions usually took the form of *per curiam* orders, based on *Brown.*

The Court also carefully reviewed the administration of laws which may appear neutral on their face but in application have a discriminatory effect. Thus, in *Reitman v. Mulkey,* 387 U.S. 369 (1967), the Court invalidated a California constitutional amendment which prohibited the state from interfering with the right of property owners to sell or rent their property. The amendment had the effect not only of repealing existing laws against private racial discrimination * but also of placing the state

---

7. Mark G. Yudof, "Equal Educational Opportunity and the Courts," 51 *Tex.L.Rev.* 411, 1973, at pp. 446–447.

8. David L. Kirp and Mark G. Yudof, *Educational Policy and the Law* (San Francisco: McCutchan Publishing Co., 1974), at p. 319.

* Recall that under the Tenth Amendment reserved powers provision of the U. S. Constitution, states have sufficient police powers to pass regulatory laws applying to private persons and organizations, including nonpublic schools.

in a position of sanctioning racial discrimination. The Court concluded that such state involvement with invidious discrimination could not be condoned. Similarly, in *Hunter v. Erickson,* 393 U.S. 385 (1969), the Court overturned a city charter amendment limiting the city council's right to pass anti-discrimination ordinances without approval of a majority of the city's voters. And in *Hernandez v. Texas,* 347 U.S. 475 (1954), the Court overturned the conviction of a Mexican-American who claimed that his racial group were being systematically excluded from jury service.

Both *Reitman* and *Hunter* have been severely criticized since they imply state action when none is clearly evident. How firmly they stand as precedents may be open to question, though the Court may well continue to be particularly sensitive to classifications which directly or indirectly are drawn along racial lines.

A more complex remedial problem arose in the 1960s. Equality of opportunity advocates often assert that if the legacy of pervasive class discrimination by law is to be eradicated, compensatory programs must be implemented on behalf of those who have suffered the discrimination. Under the rubric of "affirmative action," a number of programs were implemented voluntarily or at governmental insistence in both public and private employment and in education to increase the representation of blacks and other minorities, and later, women. Employment or admissions policies which require a specific percentage or quota of persons be selected from designated minority groups are often criticized by advocates of equality of legal treatment, who believe the cause of integration is not well served by policies that discriminate in reverse. Consequently, they argue that equal protection of the laws demands a "color-blind" or neutral approach. While the controversy over quotas in employment continues, the *Bakke* case discussed later in this chapter curtailed the use of quotas in admissions programs at public educational institutions. In time, *Bakke* may become as significant a precedent as *Brown.*

5. The shift to integration raised an interesting dilemma for those public institutions which were segregated and wished to remain so. Could all-black schools in a black community continue to operate? Self-enforced segregation would appear to have some constitutional backing in the First Amendment right to assemble and to associate. Many were concerned that the Court would find state action in almost every organizational entity, including private clubs. But in *Moose Lodge v. Irvis,* 407 U.S. 163 (1972), the Court refused to extend the *Brown* principle to private clubs with state liquor licenses. The issue of self-enforced separation in the educational context is more complex and will be dealt with in more detail later in the chapter.

6. While not using the terms associated with new equal protection, *Brown* is really the first new equal protection case. In the companion case of *Bolling v. Sharpe,* Chief Justice Warren noted that "classifications based solely upon race must be scrutinized with particular care, since they are contrary to our traditions and hence constitutionally suspect." (At p. 499). Later, the explicit use of the compelling state purpose test in association with classifications based on race emerged. For example, in *Loving v. Vir-*

ginia, 388 U.S. 1 (1967), the Court overturned a state miscegenation statute which prohibited interracial marriages and punished violators as felons. Speaking for a unanimous Court, Chief Justice Warren wrote:

> At the very least, the Equal Protection Clause demands that racial classifications, especially suspect in criminal statutes, be subjected to the "most rigid scrutiny," and if they are ever to be upheld, they must be shown to be necessary to the accomplishment of some permissible state objective, independent of the racial discrimination which it was the object of the Fourteenth Amendment to eliminate. (At p. 11).

(2) Other Suspect Classifications

Racial groups, while suffering the most from pervasive prejudice and resulting discrimination, are not alone in finding little hope for redress from the political process. As Justice Stone noted in 1937, special attention may be required for "discrete and insular minorities * * * [whose] condition * * * tends seriously to curtail the operation of those political processes ordinarily to be relied upon to protect minorities * * *." [9]

In recent years strict scrutiny has been sought for legislative classifications pertaining to national origin, alienage, gender, age, illegitimacy, handicapped persons, homosexuals, and the poor, to cite the most prominent. To date the Court has extended suspect classification status with its corresponding strict scrutiny review only to national origin,[10] illegitimacy,[11] and alienage,[12] though the Court has wavered somewhat in recent decisions involving illegitimacy. At least part of the reason for the Court's reluctance to broaden the suspect classification category is reflected in this observation from Justice Rehnquist: "It would hardly take extraordinary ingenuity for a lawyer to find 'insular and discrete' minorities at every turn in the road." [13]

The difficulty of separating classifications into two categories, one almost always permissible and one almost always not, has led some members of the Court to adopt intermediate levels of review—what has become known as the "sliding scale." Classifications relating to sex frequently appear to fall into this intermediate category. The sliding scale, however, has the disadvantage of making a murky decision process even more so.

Gender and poverty/wealth classifications represent two complex issues, both of which are closely related to educational institutions. The remainder of this section focuses on the former; later parts of this chapter will review poverty/wealth classifications as related to the financing of schools and will again review gender-based classifications specifically related to the educational context.

Beliefs in the inferior status of women are at least as old as written history. English common law, whose traditions were quite important in

---

9. *United States v. Carolene Products Co.,* 304 U.S. 144 (1937), at p. 153 (footnote 4).

10. *Oyama v. California,* 332 U.S. 633 (1948).

11. *Levy v. Louisiana,* 391 U.S. 68 (1967).

12. *Graham v. Richardson,* 403 U.S. 365 (1971).

13. Dissenting in *Sugarman v. Dougall,* 413 U.S. 634 (1973), at p. 657.

the development of this nation, prohibited women from owning property or entering into contracts with other parties. The Founders of the Republic simply assumed that voting rights would not include women. Thomas Jefferson, for example, believed that " 'Were our state a pure democracy there would still be excluded from our deliberations　*　*　*　women, who, to prevent deprivation of morals and ambiguity of issues, should not mix promiscuously in gatherings of men.' " Jefferson added, " 'The appointment of a woman to office is an innovation for which the public is not prepared, nor am I.' " [14]

By the nineteenth century, women began to gain some attention from legislatures. In 1839, Mississippi enacted a law granting women the right to sue or be sued without involving their husbands and the right to make contracts. They could manage their own property, have jobs without their husband's consent, and keep what they earned! Many other states took Mississippi's lead and established their own statutes.

Unfortunately for the burgeoning women's rights movement, the Supreme Court was not as progressive. In 1875, the Court held that denial of voting rights to women was not unconstitutional.[15] It was not until the Twenty-First Amendment to the Constitution, ratified in 1920, that the barriers to women's voting rights were finally removed.

The Court also upheld state laws that restricted the occupational opportunities to women. In 1873 the Court sustained an Illinois law that prevented women from being lawyers. Justice Bradley, concurring in the decision, wrote:

> Man is, or should be, woman's protector and defender. The natural and proper timidity and delicacy which belongs to the female sex evidently unfits it for many of the occupations of civil life.
> *　*　*
>
> 　*　*　* The paramount destiny and mission of woman are to fulfill the noble and benign offices of wife and mother. This is the law of the Creator.[16]

Interestingly, the early cases tended to rely on religious reasons for excluding women from activities other than those related to being a wife and mother, while more recent decisions cite physiological and psychological reasons, often with reference to social science research and economic statistics.

More recently, in 1948 the Supreme Court upheld a Michigan law prohibiting women from being hired as bartenders unless related to a male owner of the bar.[17] The majority of the Court specifically claimed that all women could be excluded from the bartending profession, deferring to the legislature's reasonable judgment that there are moral and social problems inherent in female bartending.

---

14. As cited in Martin Gruberg, *Women in American Politics* (Oshkosh, Wisc.: Academic Press, 1968), at p. 4.

15. *Minor v. Happersett*, 88 U.S. (21 Wall.) 162 (1875).

16. *Bradwell v. Illinois*, 83 U.S. 130 (1873), at p. 141.

17. *Goesaert v. Cleary*, 335 U.S. 464 (1948).

It should be pointed out that such protective legislation for women was not always sanctioned by the Court. During the industrialization of America, conservative Justices often struck down social legislation such as maximum hour and minimum wage legislation for women and children in the interest of protecting a purported "liberty of contract." Thus, for example, in *Adkins v. Children's Hospital*, 261 U.S. 525 (1923), the Court overturned a minimum wage law in the District of Columbia. Speaking for the majority, Justice Sutherland noted that the law was "simply and exclusively a price-fixing law, confined to adult women * * *, who are legally as capable of contracting for themselves as men." (At p. 554). Later, after continuing publicity about the exploitation of women and children in the sweatshops of industrial America and in the face of continued efforts by legislatures to prevent such abuses, the Court overturned the *Adkins* decision and upheld a State of Washington minimum wage law for women and children in *West Coast Hotel v. Parrish,* 300 U.S. 379 (1937). Chief Justice Hughes rhetorically asked:

> What can be closer to the public interest than the health of women and their protection from unscrupulous and overreaching employers? And if the protection of women is a legitimate end of the exercise of the state power, how can it be said that the requirement of the payment of a minimum wage fairly fixed in order to meet the very necessities of existence is not an admissible means to that end? (At p. 398).

The *West Coast* decision set the pattern for the Court's subsequent application of the supportive rational test to social legislation. Ironically, the *Adkins* approach which was most unpopular when it was announced, may now be realizing a rebirth.

Without question, the 1960s and 1970s brought women victories at two levels: the Courts began to strike down a host of restrictive laws as denials of equal protection, and Congress passed laws aimed at combatting discrimination by private individuals on the basis of sex, beginning with Title VII of the Civil Rights Act of 1964, which outlawed sex discrimination in employment. In *Reed v. Reed,* 404 U.S. 71 (1971), the Court unanimously declared that an Idaho statute which gave preference to males to administer a decedent's estate was unconstitutional, holding that a difference in sex must " 'be reasonable, not arbitrary, and must rest upon some ground of difference having a fair and substantial relation to the object of the legislation * * *.' " (At p. 76, quoting *Royster Guano Co. v. Virginia,* 253 U.S. 412 (1920)) The "fair and substantial" phrase has been utilized to separate *Reed* from the earlier cases. The decision became a landmark in women's rights; it was the first to invalidate a statute on grounds of sexual discrimination. It gave some feminists a hope that the equality of the sexes could be achieved through judicial interpretation of the Fourteenth Amendment Equal Protection Clause.

The *Reed* decision is significant partly because of its break with past precedents and partly because the Court did not specifically apply the strict scrutiny-compelling state purpose test to reach its decision. While the Court purported to rely on old equal protection, commentators suggested that at least some of the Justices were ready to apply suspect classification status to women—despite the fact that women do not constitute a minority group in America. The suspicion turned out to be correct. In *Frontiero v. Richardson,* 411 U.S. 677 (1973), the Court clearly stated that sex discrimination merited careful review. However, only a plurality of the Court, not a majority, opted for treating sex as a suspect classification.

The case involved Mrs. Sharron Frontiero, an Air Force Lieutenant who claimed that a Congressional statute denied her equal protection of the laws by awarding servicemen housing allowances and medical care benefits for their wives regardless of dependency upon the husband, but authorizing benefits for female members of the military *only* if the latter could demonstrate that they supported their husbands. The American Civil Liberties Union, in an *amicus curiae* brief, argued that sexual classifications such as the one involved in this case were suspect and should be viewed as presumptively invalid. The ACLU claimed that:

> "Legislative discrimination grounded on sex, for purposes unrelated to any biological difference between the sexes, ranks with legislative discrimination based on race, another congenital, unalterable trait of birth, and merits no greater judicial deference. The time is ripe now for this Court to repudiate the premise that, with minimal justification, the legislature may draw "a sharp line between the sexes," just as this Court has repudiated once settled law that differential treatment of the races is constitutionally permissible." [18]

The Supreme Court now had the opportunity to go beyond the *Reed* case to hold sexual classifications as inherently suspect and presumptively invalid under the Equal Protection Clause. The Court, in an eight to one decision, declared the Congressional fringe benefit scheme unconstitutional. However, only four justices held that sexual classifications were inherently suspect. Three other justices, though concurring in the decision, rejected the application of new equal protection to gender-based classifications. Justice Stewart concurred with the decision but used the *Reed* precedent as the basis for his reasoning. Justice Rehnquist was the sole dissenter.

---

18. Cited in Richard Cortner, *The Supreme Court and Civil Rights Policy* (Palo Alto, Calif.: Mayfield Publishing Co., 1975), at p. 204.

FRONTIERO v. RICHARDSON

Supreme Court of the United States, 1973.
411 U.S. 677, 93 S.Ct. 1764, 36 L.Ed.2d 583.

Mr. Justice BRENNAN announced the judgment of the Court in an opinion in which Mr. Justice DOUGLAS, Mr. Justice WHITE, and Mr. Justice MARSHALL join.

*   *   *

I

*   *   *

Appellant Sharron Frontiero, a lieutenant in the United States Air Force, sought increased quarters allowances, and housing and medical benefits for her husband, appellant Joseph Frontiero, on the ground that he was her "dependent." Although such benefits would automatically have been granted with respect to the wife of a male member of the uniformed services, appellant's application was denied because she failed to demonstrate that her husband was dependent on her for more than one-half of his support. Appellants then commenced this suit, contending that, by making this distinction, the statutes unreasonably discriminate on the basis of sex in violation of the Due Process Clause of the Fifth Amendment. In essence, appellants asserted that the discriminatory impact of the statutes is twofold: first, as a procedural matter, a female member is required to demonstrate her spouse's dependency, while no such burden is imposed upon male members; and, second, as a substantive matter, a male member who does not provide more than one-half of his wife's support receives benefits, while a similarly situated female member is denied such benefits. Appellants therefore sought a permanent injunction against the continued enforcement of these statutes and an order directing the appellees to provide Lieutenant Frontiero with the same housing and medical bene-

fits that a similarly situated male member would receive.

*   *   *

II

At the outset, appellants contend that classifications based upon sex, like classifications based upon race, alienage, and national origin, are inherently suspect and must therefore be subjected to close judicial scrutiny. We agree and, indeed, find at least implicit support for such an approach in our unanimous decision only last Term in Reed v. Reed.

*   *   *

There can be no doubt that our Nation has had a long and unfortunate history of sex discrimination. Traditionally, such discrimination was rationalized by an attitude of "romantic paternalism" which, in practical effect, put women, not on a pedestal, but in a cage. *   *   *

*   *   * (O)ur statute books gradually became laden with gross, sterotyped distinctions between the sexes and, indeed, throughout much of the 19th century the position of women in our society was, in many respects, comparable to that of blacks under the pre-Civil War slave codes. Neither slaves nor women could hold office, serve on juries, or bring suit in their own names, and married women traditionally were denied the legal capacity to hold or convey property or to serve as legal guardians of their own children. And although blacks were guaranteed the right to vote in 1870, women were denied even that right—which is itself "preservative of other basic civil and political rights"—until adoption of the Nineteenth Amendment half a century later.

It is true, of course, that the position of women in America has improved markedly in recent decades. Nevertheless, it can hardly be doubted that, in part because of the high visibility of the sex characteristic, women still face pervasive, although at times more subtle, discrimination in our educational institutions, in the job market and, perhaps most conspicuously, in the political arena.[17]

* * *

Moreover, since sex, like race and national origin, is an immutable characteristic determined solely by the accident of birth, the imposition of special disabilities upon the members of a particular sex because of their sex would seem to violate "the basic concept of our system that legal burdens should bear some relationship to individual responsibility * * *." And what differentiates sex from such nonsuspect statuses as intelligence or physical disability, and aligns it with the recognized suspect criteria, is that the sex characteristic frequently bears no relation to ability to perform or contribute to society. As a result, statutory distinctions between the sexes often have the effect of inviduously relegating the entire class of females to inferior legal status without regard to the actual capabilities of its individual members.

* * *

With these considerations in mind, we can only conclude that classifications based upon sex, like classifications based upon race, alienage, or national origin, are inherently suspect, and must therefore be subjected to strict judicial scrutiny. Applying the analysis mandated by that stricter standard of review, it is clear that the statutory scheme now before us is constitutionally invalid.

III

The sole basis of the classification established in the challenged statutes is the sex of the individuals involved. * * * a female member of the uniformed services seeking to obtain housing and medical benefits for her spouse must prove his dependency in fact, whereas no such burden is imposed upon male members. In addition, the statutes operate so as to deny benefits to a female member, such as appellant Sharron Frontiero, who provides less than one-half of her spouse's support, while at the same time granting such benefits to a male member who likewise provides less than one-half of his spouse's support. Thus, to this extent at least, it may fairly be said that these statutes command "dissimilar treatment for men and women who are * * * similarly situated."

Moreover, the Government concedes that the differential treatment accorded men and women under these statutes serves no purpose other than mere "administrative convenience." In essence, the Government maintains that, as an empirical matter, wives in our society frequently are dependent upon their husbands, while husbands rarely are dependent upon their wives. Thus, the Government argues that Congress might reasonably have concluded that it would be both cheaper and easier simply conclusively to presume that wives of male members are financially dependent upon their husbands, while burdening female members with the task of establishing dependency in fact.

The Government offers no concrete evidence, however, tending to support its view that such differential treatment in fact saves the Government any money.

---

17. It is true, of course, that when viewed in the abstract, women do not constitute a small and powerless minority. Nevertheless, in part because of past discrimination, women are vastly underrepresented in this Nation's decisionmaking councils. There has never been a female President, nor a female member of this Court. Not a single woman presently sits in the United States Senate, and only 14 women hold seats in the House of Representatives. And, as appellants point out, this underrepresentation is present throughout all levels of our State and Federal Government.

In order to satisfy the demands of strict judicial scrutiny, the Government must demonstrate, for example, that it is actually cheaper to grant increased benefits with respect to *all* male members, than it is to determine which male members are in fact entitled to such benefits and to grant increased benefits only to those members whose wives actually meet the dependency requirement. Here, however, there is substantial evidence that, if put to the test, many of the wives of male members would fail to qualify for benefits. And in light of the fact that the dependency determination with respect to the husbands of female members is presently made solely on the basis of affidavits rather than through the more costly hearing process, the Government's explanation of the statutory scheme is, to say the least, questionable.

In any case, our prior decisions make clear that, although efficacious administration of governmental programs is not without some importance, "the Constitution recognizes higher values than speed and efficiency." And when we enter the realm of "strict judicial scrutiny," there can be no doubt that "administrative convenience" is not a shibboleth, the mere recitation of which dictates constitutionality. On the contrary, any statutory scheme which draws a sharp line between the sexes, *solely* for the purpose of achieving administrative convenience, necessarily commands "dissimilar treatment for men and women who are * * * similarly situated," and therefore involves the "very kind of arbitrary legislative choice forbidden by the [Constitution] * * *." We therefore conclude that, by according differential treatment to male and female members of the uniformed services for the sole purpose of achieving administrative convenience, the challenged statutes violate the Due Process Clause of the Fifth Amendment insofar as they require a female member to prove the dependency of her husband.

Reversed.

Mr. Justice STEWART concurs in the judgment, agreeing that the statutes before us work an invidious discrimination in violation of the Constitution. Reed v. Reed.

Mr. Justice REHNQUIST dissents * * *

Mr. Justice POWELL, with whom The CHIEF JUSTICE and Mr. Justice BLACKMUN join, concurring in the judgment.

I agree that the challenged statutes constitute an unconstitutional discrimination against servicewomen in violation of the Due Process Clause of the Fifth Amendment, but I cannot join the opinion of Mr. Justice BRENNAN * * *. It is unnecessary for the Court in this case to characterize sex as a suspect classification, with all of the far-reaching implications of such a holding. Reed v. Reed, which abundantly supports our decision today, did not add sex to the narrowly limited group of classifications which are inherently suspect. In my view, we can and should decide this case on the authority of *Reed* and reserve for the future any expansion of its rationale.

There is another, and I find compelling, reason for deferring a general categorizing of sex classifications as invoking the strictest test of judicial scrutiny. The Equal Rights Amendment, which if adopted will resolve the substance of this precise question, has been approved by the Congress and submitted for ratification by the States. If this Amendment is duly adopted, it will represent the will of the people accomplished in the manner prescribed by the Constitution. By acting prematurely and unnecessarily, as I view it, the Court has assumed a decisional responsibility at the very time when state legislatures, functioning within the traditional democractic process, are debating the proposed Amendment. It seems to me that this reaching out to pre-empt by judicial action a major political deci-sion which is currently in process of resolution does not reflect appropriate respect for duly prescribed legislative processes.

* * *

NOTES AND QUESTIONS

1. Note that the Fifth Amendment Due Process Clause again carries an equal protection implication for the federal government as in *Bolling v. Sharpe.*

2. Following *Reed* and *Frontiero,* the Court continued to note its concern for gender-based classifications, though never explicitly endorsing suspect classification status. For example, in *Stanton v. Stanton,* 421 U.S. 7 (1975), the Court by a vote of 8–1 found a Utah statute providing for parental support for sons until 21 but only for daughters until 18 to be irrational. In *Cleveland Bd. of Educ. v. LaFleur,* 414 U.S. 632 (1974), the Court disapproved mandatory school board rules requiring pregnant teachers to take unpaid maternity leaves for periods of several months before and after childbirth. In this case the majority relied on the Due Process Clause rather than the Equal Protection Clause to strike down the policies as unduly restrictive of the fundamental liberty to marriage and procreation. (Chapter Eight reviews the use of the Due Process Clause to invalidate legislation restrictive of fundamental rights.) The Court, purporting to employ a rational approach, carefully reviewed the justification for the policies—to protect the health of the mother and unborn child and to be assured that students have a physically capable instructor in the classroom—and found them inadequate. Justice Stewart for the majority concluded that "The rules contain an irrebuttable presumption of physical incompetency, and that presumption applies even when the medical evidence as to an individual's physical status might be wholly to the contrary." (At p. 644). Justice Powell, concurring in the result, disapproved this "irrebuttable presumption" analysis, preferring to rely on the Equal Protection Clause. Whichever clause is used, the Court did appear to be openly sensitive to the needs of women. In *Turner v. Department of Employment Security,* 423 U.S. 44 (1975), the Court relied on *LaFleur* to invalidate a state statute making pregnant women ineligible for unemployment benefits during the last three months of pregnancy and the six weeks following delivery. The Court ruled the statute constitutes an irrebuttable presumption noting that a "more individualized means" must be utilized in denying unemployment benefits.

In *Craig v. Boren,* 429 U.S. 190 (1976), the Court by a vote of 7–2 invalidated an Oklahoma protective statute under the Equal Protection Clause which allowed women to buy 3.2 beer at 18 but restricted men until 21. While not specifically mentioning strict scrutiny, the majority found that despite an array of statistics purporting to show a high correlation between gender and alcohol-related traffic accidents, the state hadn't proven that "the gender-based difference be substantially related to achievement of the statutory objective." (At p. 204). In his concurring opinion, Justice Powell used a footnote to admit that while he disfavored a "middle-tiered" approach between the rational and compelling state purpose approaches, "candor compels the recognition that the relatively deferential 'rational basis' standard of review normally applied takes on a sharper focus when we address a gender-based classification. So much is clear from our recent cases." (Unnumbered footnote; at p. 211).

In 1978 the Justices left standing a decision by the Court of Appeals for the First Circuit that a New Hampshire statutory rape law was unconstitutional because it punished men but not women. Though the Supreme Court's action had no national legal precedent, it did suggest that in the future, men-only statutory rape laws may not survive Supreme Court review.

3. While gender-based classifications thus appear to trigger a more-than-rational-but-less-than-strict scrutiny by the Court, not all such classifications have been struck down. For example in *Kahn v. Shevin,* 416 U.S. 351 (1974), five Justices upheld a Florida statute which exempted $500 worth of property from taxation for widows but not for widowers on the grounds that a disproportionate economic burden existed for the widow. Justice Douglas relied on *Reed v. Reed* to uphold the Florida legislature's desire of "cushioning the financial impact of spousal loss upon the sex for which that loss imposes a disproportionately heavy burden." (At p. 355). And in *General Electric Co. v. Gilbert,* 429 U.S. 125 (1976), the Court upheld the right of GE to deny disability benefits to women for pregnancies under a company disability plan. Justice Rehnquist ruled for the majority that the failure to cover pregnancy-related disabilities does not constitute sex discrimination under the Civil Rights Act of 1964, despite Equal Employment Opportunity Commission guidelines to the contrary. Professor Laurence Tribe of the Harvard Law School concludes that the *Gilbert* case and an earlier case similar to it "evidence a degree of judicial blindness to the extreme importance for women of being able to combine the roles of employees and child bearers if they choose." Tribe contends that:

> Women will not enjoy truly *equal* rights in the labor market until it is recognized that their health care needs are indeed different from men's and that insurance coverage for absences incurred during pregnancy and childbirth may be needed if women are in fact to be placed in positions of equal opportunity.[19] (Emphasis in original)

Tribe contrasted the situation to race discrimination, noting how astonishing it would be if the Court were to uphold a statute excluding sickle-cell anemia from state disability insurance coverage.

19. Laurence H. Tribe, *American Constitutional Law* (Mineola, N. Y.: Foundation Press, 1978), at pp. 1072–1073. Of what significance is it that the Supreme Court is composed of all male members? Advocates of women's rights make a point of noting that women hold fewer than 2 percent of all federal judgeships and only about 4 percent of judgeships on state courts of general jurisdiction.

These recent decisions have provided added stimulus to proponents of the Equal Rights Amendment (ERA). In 1972, forty-nine years after it was first introduced, a constitutional amendment guaranteeing equal rights for women and men was passed by Congress and submitted to the States for ratification. Its language is simple: "Equality of rights under the law shall not be denied or abridged by the United States or by any state on account of sex." Proponents of the ERA look upon it as a necessary psychological step in granting new dignity to women under the law.

(3) Fundamental Rights

The second category of new equal protection involves classifications relating to the exercise of fundamental rights. Fundamental rights include those specifically mentioned in the Constitution, e. g., speech, press, association, as well as other rights which the Supreme Court has decided are intimately related to specific Constitutional rights and are thus "fundamental," e. g., marriage, personal privacy, access to the courts, interstate travel. Equal protection challenges are likely to be advanced when classifications deny fundamental rights altogether such as occurs under durational residency requirements or when classifications make it harder for some to enjoy these rights than others, for example, a poll tax on voting.

The first fundamental rights case involving a clear enunciation of new equal protection is *Shapiro v. Thompson*, 394 U.S. 618 (1969), involving the denial of welfare benefits to individuals who have lived in an area less than one year. Interestingly, the Court did not consider the right involved to be a right to welfare but rather the right to interstate travel. Based on earlier precedents which established that the right to travel is implicit in the Constitution, the Court ruled that a federal or state one-year residency requirement has the effect of denying the exercise of this fundamental right. Justice Brennan for the Court acknowledged that a residency requirement is an effective device for limiting the influx of poor families, but he claimed such a state purpose was not compelling:

> We recognize that a State has a valid interest in preserving the fiscal integrity of its programs. It may legitimately attempt to limit its expenditures, whether for public assistance, public education, or any other program. But a State may not accomplish such a purpose by invidious distinctions between classes of its citizens. (At p. 633).

After examining the operation of the challenged residency requirements in two states and the District of Columbia, Justice Brennan questioned whether the programs could even pass a rational test under old equal protection:

> * * * a classification of welfare applicants according to whether they have lived in the state for one year would seem irrational and unconstitutional. But, of course, the traditional criteria do not apply in these cases. Since the classification here touches on the fundamental right of interstate movement, its constitutionality must be judged by the stricter standard of whether it promotes a *compelling* state interest. Under this standard,

the waiting-period requirement clearly violates the Equal Protection Clause. (Emphasis in original; at p. 638).

The fundamental rights-strict scrutiny approach has not been without its detractors. Justice Harlan in *Shapiro* noted in his dissent:

> Virtually every state statute affects important rights.   *   *   * to extend the "compelling interest" rule to all cases in which such rights are affected would go far toward making this Court a "super-legislature." (At p. 661).

Justice Harlan also objected to the fundamental right concept, stating "I must reiterate that I know of nothing which entitles this Court to pick out particular human activities, characterize them as 'fundamental,' and give them added protection under an unusually stringent equal protection test." (At p. 662).

The fundamental rights branch of the new equal protection has been utilized to strike down such restrictive legislation or policies as residency requirements for voting,[20] the denial of speech rights to some but not others,[21] the restriction of voting rights in school board elections to parents of school children and property owners,[22] and the denial of a stenographic transcript of criminal trial proceedings where necessary for an effective appeal.[23]

C. Growth of Legislation and Federal Enforcement

The 1954 *Brown* decision related exclusively to the provisions of the 14th Amendment. After some delay, Congress joined the Court in seeking to eradicate racial and other forms of discrimination through extensive legislation. The first major piece of legislation was the 1964 Civil Rights Act, which prohibited racial or ethnic discrimination in federally-assisted programs and activities. This legislation empowered the Department of Health, Education, and Welfare to develop guidelines for school desegregation and enforce them through threatened termination of federal aid.[24]

The 1964 Act was followed by a host of other laws designed to eliminate discrimination against race, ethnicity, sex, age, and the handicapped in a variety of contexts. Major legislation now in effect which affects students is outlined in Figure 7–1.

20. *Dunn v. Blumstein*, 405 U.S. 330 (1972).

21. *Police Dept. of Chicago v. Mosley*, 408 U.S. 92 (1972).

22. *Kramer v. Union Free School District No. 15*, 395 U.S. 621 (1969).

23. *Griffin v. Illinois*, 351 U.S. 12 (1956).

24. For a discussion of the complex relationships between the judiciary and administrative agencies pursuing the same goals, see Note, "The Courts, HEW, and Southern School Desegregation," 77 *Yale L.Journal* 321 (1967).

Figure 7–1: Major Federal Civil Rights Statutes and Executive Orders Affecting Students

STATUTES/EXECUTIVE ORDERS	PURPOSE
Civil Rights Act of 1866 * 42 U.S.C. Sec. 1981	Prohibits racial discrimination in making and enforcing contracts.
Civil Rights Act of 1871 42 U.S.C. Sec. 1983	Prohibits denial of constitutional and statutory rights by public officials.
Civil Rights Act of 1971 42 U.S.C. Sec. 1985(3)	Prohibits conspiracies by public officials to deprive persons of rights of equality guaranteed by the federal government.
Civil Rights Act of 1964, Title IV 42 U.S.C. Sec. 2000c. As amended in 1972	Prohibits discrimination based on race, color, religion, sex, or national origin in public schools and colleges.
Civil Rights Act of 1964, Title VI 42 U.S.C. Sec. 2000d	Prohibits discrimination on basis of race, color, or national origin in any federally assisted program or activity.
Civil Rights Act of 1964, Title VII * 42 U.S.C. Sec. 2000e. As amended by the Equal Employment Opportunity Act of 1972	Prohibits discrimination on basis of race, color, national origin, religion, and sex in areas of public and private employment, including education. Establishes the Equal Employment Opportunity Commission (EEOC) to enforce its terms.
Federal Executive Order 11246 of 1965 Amended by Executive Order 11375 of 1967	Prohibits discrimination on basis of race, sex, color, religion, or national origin by federal contractors and requires those with over $50,000 in federal contracts to file affirmative action plans with HEW.
Education Amendments of 1972, Title IX 20 U.S.C. Sec. 1681	Prohibits discrimination on the basis of sex against students and employees at educational institutions receiving federal assistance. Exempts single-sex institutions or those with contrary religious beliefs and certain other single-sex organizations, e. g., Boy Scouts.
Vietnam Era Veterans' Readjustment Assistance Act of 1972 38 U.S.C. Sec. 2012. As amended in 1974	Requires government contractors to take affirmative action in employment of Vietnam veterans where government contracts involve $10,000 or more.
Rehabilitation Act of 1973 29 U.S.C. Sec. 794 (Sec. 504 of the Rehabilitation Act of 1973). As amended in 1974	Prohibits discrimination against persons with physical, mental, or psychological disabilities in federally assisted programs and activities. Also requires affirmative action to bring the handicapped into the mainstream of American life.

* The Supreme Court ruled in 1976 that these acts provide relief to whites as well as blacks and other minorities. *McDonald v. Sante Fe Trail Transportation Co.*, 427 U.S. 273 (1976).

Figure 7–1: Major Federal Civil Rights Statutes and Executive Orders Affecting Students—Continued

STATUTES/EXECUTIVE ORDERS	PURPOSE
Equal Educational Opportunities Act of 1974 .... 20 U.S.C. Sec. 1701	Amends the Elementary and Secondary Education Act of 1965 by stating that all children enrolled in public schools are entitled to equal educational opportunity without regard to race, color, sex, or national origin.
Education for All Handicapped Children Act of 1975 .... 20 U.S.C. Sec. 1401	Requires that all handicapped children have a free public education designed to meet their unique needs.
Age Discrimination Act of 1975 .... 42 U.S.C. Sec. 6101	Prohibits unreasonable discrimination based on age in federally-assisted programs or activities.
Civil Rights Attorney's Fees Award Act of 1976 .... 42 U.S.C. Sec. 1988	Provides that courts may allow prevailing party in equal rights suit reasonable attorneys fees as part of the cost.

Some legislation went beyond the elimination of discrimination and mandated that affirmative action be taken to advance the cause of certain groups. Prime examples include the Rehabilitation Act of 1973 pertaining to the handicapped and the Vietnam Era Veteran's Readjustment Assistance Act of 1974. Both are designed to bring their respective groups into the mainstream of American life. In particular, the affirmative action thrust of contemporary state and federal legislation has provoked considerable controversy.

While beyond the scope of this book, the reader should be aware that most court suits today involving equal protection are statutorily-based. The escalating number of equal rights cases relates partly to the prevalence of discrimination in society and partly to the complexity of the federal regulations which are promulgated and enforced by the appropriate governmental agency responsible for implementing particular laws. On more than one occasion, Congressmen have accused federal bureaucrats of exceeding Congress' intention, as well as the meaning of the Equal Protection Clause, in the zeal to implement civil rights laws. Title IX of the 1972 Education Amendments and § 504 of the 1973 Rehabilitation Act are two recently enacted laws which have generated seemingly endless controversy and litigation. In the case of Title IX, HEW spent two years of deliberation before final regulations were issued on June 4, 1975. In the process, the agency received some 10,000 comments about the law and its application. These comments reflected a substantial diversity of views from a wide spectrum of citizens, a fact which led one commentator to note that "Exactly how far institutions must go in bringing about equality in education is left unclear by the Title IX regulations * * *." [24] Similarly, § 504 of the Rehabilitation Act of 1973 has produced protracted negotiations and, in some cases, legal battles over such matters as whether the act applies to overweight students (Oral Roberts University's weight reduction policy was the target of a complaint filed with HEW in 1977), whether the nature of a person's disability can be a factor in admissions decision making (the federal Court of Appeals for the Fourth Circuit has ruled that it cannot be),[25] and whether institutions must provide special services for the handicapped such as interpreters for deaf students. Section 504 has also aroused considerable concern, as has Title IX, about costs incurred in modifying educational facilities to comply with the law. One study conducted by the Association of Physical Plant Administrators has estimated that it would cost the nation's colleges and universities one billion dollars to comply with Section 504.[26] Fiscal concerns have prompted a number of educators to call for shifting some of the cost-burden to the government.

One illustration will suffice here to show how difficult the equal rights enforcement process is. In 1969 a coalition of civil rights groups complained to HEW that 10 states, including North Carolina, had not desegregated their public higher education systems. The following year a suit was started by the NAACP Legal Defense Fund against HEW, accusing the agency of insufficient enforcement of Title VI of the 1964 Civil Rights Act in these states. In 1973, U.S. District Court Judge John H. Pratt ruled in favor of the civil rights groups. *Adams v. Richardson*, 356 F.Supp. 92 (D.C.D.C.1973). He ordered HEW to commence enforcement proceedings against the ten states with respect to both elementary/secondary school districts and postsecondary institutions not in compliance with Title VI. The Court of Appeals for the District of Columbia affirmed the district court's order, but allowed extensions on deadlines for filing of desegregation plans for the public higher education systems, since HEW hadn't developed guidelines for state-wide systems of education in relation to Title VI. *Adams v. Richardson*, 480 F.2d 1159 (D.C.Cir. 1973).

After protracted negotiations, HEW secured and accepted desegregation plans for higher educational systems in eight of the states, referring Louisiana and Mississippi to the Department of Justice for litigation based on their failures to comply. In 1976 the NAACP again petitioned the district court for relief, claiming that HEW had accepted ineffective desegregation plans in these states. In 1977 Judge Pratt ruled that HEW had indeed accepted plans which did not meet the guidelines HEW had developed in response to Judge Pratt's earlier ruling. The plans did not contain specific commitments for desegregating student bodies and faculties, for eliminating program duplication at black and white colleges, and for enhancing black institutions long disadvantaged by discriminatory treatment. Noting that HEW itself agreed the plans were ineffective and noting that the public higher educational systems in these states con-

24. Mark A. Kadzielski "Title IX of the Education Amendments of 1972: Change or Continuity?" 6 *J.Law & Educ.* 183, April, 1977, at p. 196.

25. *Davis v. Southeastern Community College,* 574 F.2d 1158 (4th Cir. 1978).

26. *Higher Education Daily,* May 23, 1978, at p. 2.

tinued to receive federal aid, Judge Pratt ordered HEW to submit further guidelines to six of the states (the other four were either involved in litigation over the issue or then negotiating with HEW) and to require the submission of revised plans within a specific time frame.

By March of 1978 desegregation plans under the revised guidelines were accepted in five of the six states. North Carolina's plan was rejected, and HEW began proceedings to terminate federal funding to higher education in that state. But on May 12, 1978, agreement was finally reached between Joseph A. Califano, HEW Secretary, and William C. Friday, President of the University of North Carolina.[27] Attorneys for NAACP's Legal Defense Fund were unhappy with the agreement, however, and future challenges to the plan and its implementation in future years seemed likely.

Civil rights groups on several occasions have complained about the lackadaisical attitude of HEW and other agencies charged with enforcing the civil rights laws. For example, in 1975 a coalition of 57 civil rights and women's groups called on then HEW Secretary David Matthews to correct the "shocking inexcusable failure and refusal of the department to carry out its legal obligations."[28] Yet, the process of enforcement is difficult, given the staggering workload facing enforcement agencies,* the virtually limitless variety of situations arising under the regulations, and the tendency of many institutions to "play out the string" through protracted court proceedings. It should also be pointed out that HEW, as an executive department, is not immune to the politics of the incumbent President. Thus, during the Nixon-Ford Administrations, its leadership was less motivated to take the lead in vigorous enforcement of the civil rights laws than under the Johnson Administration, when much of the legislation was passed.

III. OLD EQUAL PROTECTION AND STUDENTS

A. The Financing of Public Schools

As originally conceived, American public elementary and secondary schools were both locally controlled and financed. But with industrialization and the resulting shift of much of the population to urban areas, differences in taxable resources of local communities began to yield great variance in local spending for education. Efforts were made at the state level to equalize the expenditures by various "add-on" funding programs. But even with additional funds, true equalization was rarely achieved.

It was this situation which faced the Court in *San Antonio v. Rodriguez*, 411 U.S. 1 (1973). In the late 1940s Texas reviewed its school

27. For a revealing account of how final agreement was reached, see Lorenzo Middleton "How the U. S. and N. C. Reached Accord," *The Chronicle of Higher Education*, May 22, 1978.

28. Cheryl Fields "57 Rights Groups Hit HEW on Anti-Bias Enforcement," *Id.*, December 22, 1975.

* HEW's Office of Civil Rights has statutory responsibility as of 1978 for enforcing Title VI of the 1964 Civil Rights Act, which covers 16,000 public school districts nearly 3000 colleges and universities, and some 30,000 health and social science agencies; Section 504 of the Rehabilitation Act, which applies to these same institutions, and Title IX of the Education Amendments of 1972, which applies to public and nonpublic educational institutions receiving federal funds. HEW is also charged with responsibility for enforcing several other nondiscrimination statutes.

finance system and, finding great inequities, established the Minimum Foundation School Program (MFSP). This program, involving both local and state contributions to a special fund, was aimed at contributing money to local districts for teacher salaries, operating expenses, and transportation costs. Eighty percent of the funding came from the state with the remaining from local districts on an ability-to-pay basis. Thus, each local district had to levy a property tax to support its contribution, and at the time of the suit, each district imposed such a tax to yield funds in excess of its mandatory contributions to the Foundation Program. The excess went to support local schools.

In operation the revised financing system helped to correct inequities but did not erase interdistrict differences. Thus in 1967–68 Edgewood Independent School District, serving a predominant Mexican-American community in the core-city sector of San Antonio, contributed $26 per pupil above its MFSP contribution at a property tax rate of $1.05 per $100 of valuation. The MFSP added $222 per pupil, and with an additional $108 from federal funds, Edgewood had a total of $356 per pupil to spend. By contrast, Alamo Heights Independent School District, serving an affluent white residential community in San Antonio, contributed $333 per pupil above its MFSP contribution at a property tax rate of 85¢ per $100 of valuation. The MFSP added $225 per pupil with an additional $36 from federal funds for a total of $594 per pupil. Similar interdistrict differences occurred elsewhere in Texas and, indeed, throughout the nation.

Plaintiffs argued that the Texas financing system violated the Equal Protection Clause by discriminating unfairly against the poor. In order to make their case, plaintiffs tried to show that wealth is a suspect classification and that education is a fundamental interest, thus requiring a compelling state purpose in maintaining this type of school financing, a purpose Texas agreed it could not meet. Texas, on the other hand, argued that its system was rational under old equal protection and did, though imperfectly, work to reduce disparities among districts. For example, Alamo Heights derived almost 13 times as much money from local taxes as Edgewood did in 1967–68; the MFSP program reduced the ratio to approximately two-to-one.

The federal district court concluded that Texas could meet neither a compelling state purpose test nor a rational state purpose test in maintaining its school finance system. The case was appealed to the Supreme Court.

SAN ANTONIO INDEPENDENT SCHOOL DIST. v. RODRIGUEZ

Supreme Court of the United States, 1973.
411 U.S. 1, 93 S.Ct. 1278, 36 L.Ed.2d 16.

Mr. Justice POWELL delivered the opinion of the Court.

*   *   *

II

A

The wealth discrimination discovered by the District Court in this case, and by several other courts that have recently struck down school-financing laws in other States, is quite unlike any of the forms of wealth discrimination heretofore reviewed by this Court. Rather than focusing on the unique features of the alleged discrimination, the courts in these cases have virtually assumed their findings of a suspect classification through a simplistic process of analysis: since, under the traditional systems of financing public schools, some poorer people receive less expensive educations than other more affluent people, these systems discriminate on the basis of wealth. This approach largely ignores the hard threshold questions, including whether it makes a difference for purposes of consideration under the Constitution that the class of disadvantaged "poor" cannot be identified or defined in customary equal protection terms, and whether the relative—rather than absolute—nature of the asserted deprivation is of significant consequence. Before a State's laws and the justifications for the classifications they create are subjected to strict judicial scrutiny, we think these threshold considerations must be analyzed more closely than they were in the court below.

The case comes to us with no definitive description of the classifying facts or delineation of the disfavored class. Examination of the District Court's opinion and of appellees' complaint, briefs, and contentions at oral argument suggests, however, at least three ways in which the discrimination claimed here might be described. The Texas system of school financing might be regarded as discriminating (1) against "poor" persons whose incomes fall below some identifiable level of poverty or who might be characterized as functionally "indigent," or (2) against those who are relatively poorer than others, or (3) against all those who, irrespective of their personal incomes, happen to reside in relatively poorer school districts. Our task must be to ascertain whether, in fact, the Texas system has been shown to discriminate on any of these possible bases and, if so, whether the resulting classification may be regarded as suspect.

The precedents of this Court provide the proper starting point. The individuals, or groups of individuals, who constituted the class discriminated against in our prior cases shared two distinguishing characteristics: because of their impecunity they were completely unable to pay for some desired benefit, and as a consequence, they sustained an absolute deprivation of a meaningful opportunity to enjoy that benefit. *   *   *

*   *   *

Only appellees' first possible basis for describing the class disadvantaged by the Texas school-financing system—discrimination against a class of definably "poor" persons—might arguably meet the criteria established in these prior cases. Even a cursory examination, however, demonstrates that neither of the two distinguishing characteristics of wealth classifications can be found here. First, in support of their charge that the system discriminates against the "poor," appellees have made no effort to demonstrate that it operates to the peculiar disadvantage of any class fairly definable as indigent, or as composed of persons whose incomes are beneath any designated poverty level. Indeed, there is reason to believe that the poorest families are not necessarily clustered in the poorest property districts.

* * *

Second, neither appellees nor the District Court addressed the fact that, unlike each of the foregoing cases, lack of personal resources has not occasioned an absolute deprivation of the desired benefit. The argument here is not that the children in districts having relatively low assessable property values are receiving no public education; rather, it is that they are receiving a poorer quality education than that available to children in districts having more assessable wealth. Apart from the unsettled and disputed question whether the quality of education may be determined by the amount of money expended for it, a sufficient answer to appellees' argument is that, at least where wealth is involved, the Equal Protection Clause does not require absolute equality or precisely equal advantages. Nor indeed, in view of the infinite variables affecting the educational process, can any system assure equal quality of education except in the most relative sense. Texas asserts that the Minimum Foundation Program provides an "adequate" education for all children in the State. By providing 12 years of free public-school education, and by assuring teachers, books, transportation, and operating funds, the Texas Legislature has endeavored to "guarantee, for the welfare of the state as a whole, that all people shall have at least an adequate program of education. This is what is meant by 'A Minimum Foundation Program of Education.' " * * *

* * *

We thus conclude that the Texas system does not operate to the peculiar disadvantage of any suspect class. But in recognition of the fact that this Court has never heretofore held that wealth discrimination alone provides an adequate basis for invoking strict scrutiny, appellees have not relied solely on this contention. They also assert that the State's system impermissibly interferes with the exercise of a "fundamental" right and that accordingly the prior decisions of this Court require the application of the strict standard of judicial review. It is this question—whether education is a fundamental right, in the sense that it is among the rights and liberties protected by the Constitution—which has so consumed the attention of courts and commentators in recent years.

* * *

B

* * *

Education, of course, is not among the rights afforded explicit protection under our Federal Constitution. Nor do we find any basis for saying it is implicitly so protected. * * * the undisputed importance of education will not alone cause this Court to depart from the usual standard for reviewing a State's social and economic legislation. It is appellees' contention, however, that education is distinguishable from other services and benefits provided by the State because it bears a peculiarly close relationship to other rights and liberties accorded protection under the Constitution. Specifically, they insist that education is itself a fundamental personal right because it is essential to the effective exercise of First Amendment freedoms and to intelligent utilization of the right to vote. * * *

* * *

Even if it were conceded that some identifiable quantum of education is a constitutionally protected prerequisite to the meaningful exercise of either right, we have no indication that the present levels of educational expenditures in Texas provide an education that falls short.

Whatever merit appellees' argument might have if a State's financing system occasioned an absolute denial of educational opportunities to any of its children, that argument provides no basis for finding an interference with fundamental rights where only relative differences in spending levels are involved and where —as is true in the present case—no charge fairly could be made that the system fails to provide each child with an opportunity to acquire the basic minimal skills necessary for the enjoyment of the rights of speech and of full participation in the political process.

* * *

* * * Education, perhaps even more than welfare assistance, presents a myriad of "intractable economic, social, and even philosophical problems." * * *

* * * On even the most basic questions in this area the scholars and educational experts are divided. Indeed, one of the major sources of controversy concerns the extent to which there is a demonstrable correlation between educational expenditures and the quality of education—an assumed correlation underlying virtually every legal conclusion drawn by the District Court in this case. Related to the questioned relationship between cost and quality is the equally unsettled controversy as to the proper goals of a system of public education. And the question regarding the most effective relationship between state boards of education and local school boards, in terms of their respective responsibilities and degrees of control, is now undergoing searching re-examination. The ultimate wisdom as to these and related problems of education is not likely to be divined for all time even by the scholars who now so earnestly debate the issues. In such circumstances, the judiciary is well advised to refrain from imposing on the States inflexible constitutional restraints that could circumscribe or handicap the continued research and experimentation

so vital to finding even partial solutions to educational problems and to keeping abreast of ever-changing conditions.

* * *

The foregoing considerations buttress our conclusion that Texas' system of public school finance is an inappropriate candidate for strict judicial scrutiny. These same considerations are relevant to the determination whether that system, with its conceded imperfections, nevertheless bears some rational relationship to a legitimate state purpose. It is to this question that we next turn our attention.

III

* * *

Appellees do not question the propriety of Texas' dedication to local control of education. To the contrary, they attack the school-financing system precisely because, in their view, it does not provide the same level of local control and fiscal flexibility in all districts. Appellees suggest that local control could be preserved and promoted under other financing systems that resulted in more equality in educational expenditures. While it is no doubt true that reliance on local property taxation for school revenues provides less freedom of choice with respect to expenditures for some districts than for others, the existence of "some inequality" in the manner in which the State's rationale is achieved is not alone a sufficient basis for striking down the entire system.
* * *

Appellees further urge that the Texas system is unconstitutionally arbitrary because it allows the availability of local taxable resources to turn on "happenstance." They see no justification for a system that allows, as they contend, the quality of education to fluctuate on the basis of the fortuitous positioning of the boundary lines of political subdivisions and the location of valuable commercial and industrial property. But any scheme of local taxation—indeed the very existence of identifiable local governmental units—requires the establishment of jurisdictional boundaries that are inevitably arbitrary. It is equally inevitable that some localities are going to be blessed with more taxable assets than others.

* * *

Moreover, if local taxation for local expenditures were an unconstitutional method of providing for education then it might be an equally impermissible means of providing other necessary services customarily financed largely from local property taxes, including local police and fire protection, public health and hospitals, and public utility facilities of various kinds. We perceive no justification for such a severe denigration of local property taxation and control as would follow from appellees' contentions. It has simply never been within the constitutional prerogative of this Court to nullify statewide measures for financing public services merely because the burdens or benefits thereof fall unevenly depending upon the relative wealth of the political subdivisions in which citizens live.

* * * to the extent that the Texas system of school financing results in unequal expenditures between children who happen to reside in different districts, we cannot say that such disparities are the product of a system that is so irrational as to be invidiously discriminatory. Texas has acknowledgedged its shortcomings and has persistently endeavored—not without some success—to ameliorate the differences in levels of expenditures without sacrificing the benefits of local participation. The Texas plan is not the result of hurried, ill-conceived legislation. It certainly is not the product of purposeful discrimination against any group or class. On the contrary, it is rooted in decades of experience in Texas and elsewhere, and in major part is the product of responsible studies by qualified people. * * * One also must remember

that the system here challenged is not peculiar to Texas or to any other State. In its essential characteristics, the Texas plan for financing public education reflects what many educators for a half century have thought was an enlightened approach to a problem for which there is no perfect solution. We are unwilling to assume for ourselves a level of wisdom superior to that of legislators, scholars, and educational authorities in 50 States, especially where the alternatives proposed are only recently conceived and nowhere yet tested. The constitutional standard under the Equal Protection Clause is whether the challenged state action rationally furthers a legitimate state purpose or interest. We hold that the Texas plan abundantly satisfies this standard.

IV

* * *

* * * The consideration and initiation of fundamental reforms with respect to state taxation and education are matters reserved for the legislative processes of the various States, and we do no violence to the values of federalism and separation of powers by staying our hand. We hardly need add that this Court's action today is not to be viewed as placing its judicial imprimatur on the status quo. The need is apparent for reform in tax systems which may well have relied too long and too heavily on the local property tax. And certainly innovative thinking as to public education, its methods, and its funding is necessary to assure both a higher level of quality and greater uniformity of opportunity. These matters merit the continued attention of the scholars who already have contributed much by their challenges. But the ultimate solutions must come from the lawmakers and from the democratic pressures of those who elect them.

Reversed.

Mr. Justice STEWART, concurring.

* * *

Mr. Justice BRENNAN, dissenting.

* * *

Mr. Justice WHITE, with whom Mr. Justice DOUGLAS and Mr. Justice BRENNAN join, dissenting.

* * *

* * * this case would be quite different if it were true that the Texas system, while insuring minimum educational expenditures in every district through state funding, extended a meaningful option to all local districts to increase their per-pupil expenditures and so to improve their children's education to the extent that increased funding would achieve that goal. The system would then arguably provide a rational and sensible method of achieving the stated aim of preserving an area for local initiative and decision.

The difficulty with the Texas system, however, is that it provides a meaningful option to Alamo Heights and like school districts but almost none to Edgewood and those other districts with a low per-pupil real estate tax base. In these latter districts, no matter how desirous parents are of supporting their schools with greater revenues, it is impossible to do so through the use of the real estate property tax. In these districts, the Texas system utterly fails to extend a realistic choice to parents because the property tax, which is the only revenue-raising mechanism extended to school districts, is practically and legally unavailable. That this is the situation may be readily demonstrated.

* * *

* * * It is evident from statistics in the record that show that, applying an equalized tax rate of 85¢ per $100 assessed valuation, Alamo Heights was able to provide approximately $330 per pupil in local revenues over and above the Local Fund Assignment. In Edgewood, on the other hand, with an equalized tax rate of $1.05 per $100 of assessed valuation, $26 per pupil was raised beyond the Local Fund Assignment. * * *

In order to equal the highest yield in any other Bexar County district, Alamo Heights would be required to tax at the rate of 68¢ per $100 of assessed valuation. Edgewood would be required to tax at the prohibitive rate of $5.76 per $100. But state law places a $1.50 per $100 ceiling on the maintenance tax rate, a limit that would surely be reached long before Edgewood attained an equal yield. Edgewood is thus precluded in law, as well as in fact, from achieving a yield even close to that of some other districts.

* * *

* * * If the State aims at maximizing local initiative and local choice, by permitting school districts to resort to the real property tax if they choose to do so, it utterly fails in achieving its purpose in districts with property tax bases so low that there is little if any opportunity for interested parents, rich or poor, to augment school district revenues. Requiring the State to establish only that unequal treatment is in furtherance of a permissible goal, without also requiring the State to show that the means chosen to effectuate that goal are rationally related to its achievement, makes equal protection analysis no more than an empty gesture.[6]

---

6. The State of Texas appears to concede that the choice of whether or not to go beyond the state-provided minimum "is easier for some districts than for others. Those districts with large amounts of taxable property can produce more revenue at a lower tax rate and will provide their children with a more expensive education." The State nevertheless insists that districts have a choice and that the people in each district have exercised that choice by providing some real property tax money over and above the minimum funds guaranteed by the State. Like the majority, however, the State fails to explain why the Equal Protection Clause is not violated, or how its goal of providing local government with realistic choices as

In my view, the parents and children in Edgewood, and in like districts, suffer from an invidious discrimination violative of the Equal Protection Clause.

* * *

Mr. Justice MARSHALL, with whom Mr. Justice DOUGLAS concurs, dissenting.

* * *

I

* * *

B

* * * appellants reject the suggestion that the quality of education in any particular district is determined by money—beyond some minimal level of funding which they believe to be assured every Texas district by the Minimum Foundation School Program. * * *

In my view, though, even an unadorned restatement of this contention is sufficient to reveal its absurdity. * * *

* * * It is an inescapable fact that if one district has more funds available per pupil than another district, the former will have greater choice in educational planning than will the latter. In this regard, I believe the question of discrimination in educational quality must be deemed to be an objective one that looks to what the State provides its children, not to what the children are able to do with what they receive. That a child forced to attend an underfunded school with poorer physical facilities, less experienced teachers, larger classes, and a narrower range of courses than a school with substantially more funds—and thus with greater choice in educational planning—may nevertheless excel is to the credit of the child, not the State.

Indeed, who can ever measure for such a child the opportunities lost and the tal-

ents wasted for want of a broader, more enriched education? Discrimination in the opportunity to learn that is afforded a child must be our standard.

* * * Likewise, it is difficult to believe that if the children of Texas had a free choice, they would choose to be educated in districts with fewer resources, and hence with more antiquated plants, less experienced teachers, and a less diversified curriculum. In fact, if financing variations are so insignificant to educational quality, it is difficult to understand why a number of our country's wealthiest school districts, which have no legal obligation to argue in support of the constitutionality of the Texas legislation, have nevertheless zealously pursued its cause before this Court.

* * *

* * * the majority's apparent reliance upon the adequacy of the educational opportunity assured by the Texas Minimum Foundation School Program seems fundamentally inconsistent with its own recognition that educational authorities are unable to agree upon what makes for educational quality * * *. If, as the majority stresses, such authorities are uncertain as to the impact of various levels of funding on educational quality, I fail to see where it finds the expertise to divine that the particular levels of funding provided by the Program assure an adequate educational opportunity—much less an education substantially equivalent in quality to that which a higher level of funding might provide. * * *

* * *

C

Despite the evident discriminatory effect of the Texas financing scheme, both the appellants and the majority raise sub-

---

to how much money should be expended on education is implemented, where the system makes it much more difficult for some than for others to provide additional educational funds and where, as a prac-

tical and legal matter, it is impossible for some districts to provide the educational budgets that other districts can make available from real property tax revenues.

stantial questions concerning the precise character of the disadvantagd class in this case. The District Court concluded that the Texas financing scheme draws "distinction between groups of citizens depending upon the wealth of the district in which they live" and thus creates a disadvantaged class composed of persons living in property-poor districts. In light of the data introduced before the District Court, the conclusion that the school children of property-poor districts constitute a sufficient class for our purposes seems indisputable to me.

* * *

II

* * *

A

* * * The Court apparently seeks to establish today that equal protection cases fall into one of two neat categories which dictate the appropriate standard of review—strict scrutiny or mere rationality. But this Court's decisions in the field of equal protection defy such easy categorization. A principled reading of what this Court has done reveals that it has applied a spectrum of standards in reviewing discrimination allegedly violative of the Equal Protection Clause. This spectrum clearly comprehends variations in the degree of care with which the Court will scrutinize particular classifications, depending, I believe, on the constitutional and societal importance of the interest adversely affected and the recognized invidiousness of the basis upon which the particular classification is drawn.
* * *

I therefore cannot accept the majority's labored efforts to demonstrate that fundamental interests, which call for strict scrutiny of the challenged classification, encompass only established rights which we are somehow bound to recognize from the text of the Constitution itself.
* * *

I would like to know where the Constitution guarantees the right to procreate, Skinner v. Oklahoma ex rel. Williamson, 316 U.S. 535 (1942), or the right to vote in state elections, e. g., Reynolds v. Sims, 377 U.S. 533 (1964), or the right to an appeal from a criminal conviction, e. g., Griffin v. Illinois, 351 U.S. 12, (1956). These are instances in which, due to the importance of the interests at stake, the Court has displayed a strong concern with the existence of discriminatory state treatment. But the Court has never said or indicated that these are interests which independently enjoy full-blown constitutional protection.

* * *

* * * Although not all fundamental interests are constitutionally guaranteed, the determination of which interests are fundamental should be firmly rooted in the text of the Constitution. The task in every case should be to determine the extent to which constitutionally guaranteed rights are dependent on interests not mentioned in the Constitution. As the nexus between the specific constitutional guarantee and the nonconstitutional interest draws closer, the nonconstitutional interest becomes more fundamental and the degree of judicial scrutiny applied when the interest is infringed on a discriminatory basis must be adjusted accordingly. Thus, it cannot be denied that interests such as procreation, the exercise of the state franchise, and access to criminal appellate processes are not fully guaranteed to the citizen by our Constitution. But these interests have nonetheless been afforded special judicial consideration in the face of discrimination because they are, to some extent, interrelated with constitutional guarantees. * * *

* * *

A similar process of analysis with respect to the invidiousness of the basis on which a particular classification is drawn has also influenced the Court as to the appropriate degree of scrutiny to be accorded any particular case. The highly suspect character of classifications based on race, nationality, or alienage is well established. * * * In the context of economic interests, we find that discriminatory state action is almost always sustained, for such interests are generally far removed from constitutional guarantees. * * *

* * * the majority today attempts to force this case into the same category for purposes of equal protection analysis as decisions involving discrimination affecting commercial interests. By so doing, the majority singles this case out for analytic treatment at odds with what seems to me to be the clear trend of recent decisions in this Court, and thereby ignores the constitutional importance of the interest at stake and the invidiousness of the particular classification, factors that call for far more than the lenient scrutiny of the Texas financing scheme which the majority pursues. * * *

B

* * *

The special concern of this Court with the educational process of our country is a matter of common knowledge. * * *

* * *

Education directly affects the ability of a child to exercise his First Amendment rights, both as a source and as a receiver of information and ideas, whatever interests he may pursue in life. * * *

* * * Education serves the essential function of instilling in our young an understanding of and appreciation for the principles and operation of our governmental processes. Education may instill the interest and provide the tools necessary for political discourse and debate. Indeed, it has frequently been suggested that education is the dominant factor affecting political consciousness and participation. * * *

* * * The factors just considered, including the relationship between education and the social and political interests enshrined within the Constitution, compel us to recognize the fundamentality of education and to scrutinize with appropriate care the bases for state discrimination affecting equality of educational opportunity in Texas' school districts—a conclusion which is only strengthened when we consider the character of the classification in this case.

C

* * *

* * * The means for financing public education in Texas are selected and specified by the State. It is the State that has created local school districts, and tied educational funding to the local property tax and thereby to local district wealth. At the same time, governmentally imposed land use controls have undoubtedly encouraged and rigidified natural trends in the allocation of particular areas for residential or commercial use, and thus determined each district's amount of taxable property wealth. In short, this case, in contrast to the Court's previous wealth discrimination decisions, can only be seen as "unusual in the extent to which governmental action *is* the cause of the wealth classifications."

In the final analysis, then, the invidious characteristics of the group wealth classification present in this case merely serve to emphasize the need for careful judicial scrutiny of the State's justifications for the resulting interdistrict discrimination in the educational opportunity afforded to the schoolchildren of Texas.

D

The nature of our inquiry into the justifications for state discrimination is essentially the same in all equal protection cases: We must consider the substantiality of the state interests sought to be served, and we must scrutinize the reasonableness of the means by which the State has sought to advance its interests. Differences in the application of this test are, in my view, a function of the constitutional importance of the interests at stake and the invidiousness of the particular classification. * * *

Thus, when interests of constitutional importance are at stake, the Court does not stand ready to credit the State's classification with any conceivable legitimate purpose, but demands a clear showing that there are legitimate state interests which the classification was in fact intended to serve. * * *

The only justification offered by appellants to sustain the discrimination in educational opportunity caused by the Texas financing scheme is local educational control. * * *

* * *

* * * even if we accept Texas' general dedication to local control in educational matters, it is difficult to find any evidence of such dedication with respect to fiscal matters. It ignores reality to suggest—as the Court does—that the local property tax element of the Texas financing scheme reflects a conscious legislative effort to provide school districts with local fiscal control. If Texas had a system truly dedicated to local fiscal control, one would expect the quality of the educational opportunity provided in each district to vary with the decision of the voters in that district as to the level of sacrifice they wish to make for public education. In fact, the Texas scheme produces precisely the opposite result. Local school districts cannot choose to have the best education in the State by imposing the highest tax rate. Instead, the quality of the educational opportunity offered by any particular district is largely determined by the amount of taxable property located in the district—a factor over which local voters can exercise no control.

* * *

* * * If for the sake of local education control, this Court is to sustain interdistrict discrimination in the educational opportunity afforded Texas school children, it should require that the State present something more than the mere sham now before us.

* * *

NOTES AND QUESTIONS

1. Note the different treatment Justices Powell and Marshall give to defining the type of poverty/wealth discrimination present in the case. Justice Powell sets forth two conditions which he claims the Court has always asked with respect to discrimination against the poor: 1) the class of poor persons must be completely unable to pay for some desired benefit and 2) the class must sustain absolute deprivation of that benefit. Some commentators have questioned whether this is indeed an accurate reading of the Court's poverty cases.[29] Since the poor in this case are not centered in one community but reside in both rich and poor districts and since no one has suffered absolute deprivation given the Minimum Foundation School Program, the criteria are not met. Justice Marshall views the poor as being those persons residing in property-poor school districts.

What about Justice Powell's concern that finding local taxation unconstitutional in this instance would result in similar challenges to other

29. See, for example, Tribe, *supra*, at p. 1124.

social programs dependent on local taxes, e. g., police and fire protection, public health, and so on? Can education be distinguished sufficiently to avoid opening a Pandora's box of similar challenges? Or should the state be forced to equalize all such services?

Some commentators have suggested that the majority chose this case to call a halt to continued extensions of previous Warren Court precedents involving poverty/wealth as a suspect classification. In previous cases, particularly those involving access to the political process for racial minorities and to the judicial process for indigent criminals, the Court had been inclined to apply strict scrutiny to wealth discrimination. Thus, for example, the Warren Court struck down the poll tax in *Harper v. Virginia Bd. of Elections,* 383 U.S. 663 (1966), since "Wealth, like race, creed, or color, is not germane to one's ability to participate intelligently in the electoral process". (At p. 688). And in *Douglas v. California,* 372 U.S. 353 (1963), the Court struck down a state policy of providing indigent appellants with counsel for their first appeal only if the appellate court agreed it would be useful. The Court asserted that " * * * there can be no equal justice where the kind of an appeal a man enjoys 'depends on the amount of money he has.' " (At p. 355). The Burger Court put considerable distance between these essentially egalitarian decisions of the Warren Court era in *San Antonio* by tightening the criteria for poverty to be a suspect classification, thus adding to the precedent set in a 1971 case, *James v. Valtierra,* 402 U.S. 137, in which the Court refused to strike down an amendment to the California constitution providing that no low-rent housing projects could be developed or promoted by the state until approved by a majority of voters at a community election. (Compare with *Reitman v. Mulkey* and *Hunter v. Erickson, supra,* pages 513–514.) In *James,* Justice Black for the majority refused to acknowledge that a wealth classification was involved and refused to extend the *Hunter* precedent to a wealth classification. Justice Marshall in dissent pointed out that:

> It is far too late in the day to contend that the Fourteenth Amendment prohibits only racial discriminations; and to me, singling out the poor to bear a burden not placed on any other class of citizens tramples the values the Fourteenth Amendment was designed to protect. (At p. 145).

The majority in *San Antonio* spoke in terms of *minimum access,* not equal results, and showed particular concern for deference to the legislature in spending finite resources for seemingly infinite and intractable social problems. *San Antonio* and its progeny demonstrate that poverty/wealth classifications remain closer to old equal protection than to the new.

One concern which troubles many authorities in the poverty law field is the overlap between poverty and race. To what extent is a racially-based classification really masquerading as a classification based on relative degrees of wealth? For example, in *Village of Arlington Heights v. Metropolitan Housing Development Corp.,* 429 U.S. 252 (1977), a nonprofit real estate developer sought to build a low income housing project in Arlington

Heights, a wealthy suburb outside Chicago. He was unable to get local governmental officials to change the zoning classification from single-family to multi-family. The developer sued, charging race discrimination. The Court rejected the argument, noting that proof of racially discriminatory motives had not been proven, even though the classification would have a greater impact on racial minorities than other groups. The Court ruled the classification to be a legitimate governmental attempt to preserve land values and maintain the Village's zoning plan. A critical question this case raises for plaintiffs, of course, is securing the necessary proof to show a racially discriminatory purpose or motivation. The showing of a disproportionate *impact* on racial groups is not enough. This same theme now runs through contemporary decisions on ending school segregation in the North and is the focus of attention in affirmative action cases involving employment, topics to be discussed in greater depth below.

2. Note that while the majority disagrees that education is a fundamental right, Justice Powell does suggest that there may be a constitutional right to a *certain amount* of state-financed education. Thus, his qualifying statement—"Even if it were conceded that some identifiable quantum of education is a constitutionally protected prerequisite * * * "—may have great significance, particularly where students may be totally excluded from the educational process at an early age or are provided with an inferior education. But of what nature is the "quantum" of education? Is the quantum defined in terms of the acquisition of facts and skills— the academic aspect of education? Or is it defined in terms of pupil interaction—the melting pot or socialization aspect of education? As noted later, these different interpretations have great influence in Court-sanctioned remedies for past *de jure* school desegregation.

Suppose a student were suspended for a year because of repeated infractions of school rules. Would the school district have to provide the student with an alternative educational experience during his suspension? One commentator argues in the affirmative, noting that "The bottom line must be that no matter how disruptive or irritating a child's behavior, s(he) still has a right to education." [30] But note that the majority in *San Antonio* talks in terms of "some" identifiable quantum. If by "some" the Supreme Court means that education is fundamental only during a limited span of years, then the right to an education would vary with the age of a student unless a state chose to provide more than the minimum. At what grade level should education be considered fundamental?

Suppose a state refused to renew its welfare program. Could the Equal Protection Clause be utilized in this situation, even though there is no state action as it has been traditionally understood under the Fourteenth Amendment? Might there be constitutional protection for a minimum amount of state-financed welfare? If we assume that the Equal Protection Clause does require the government to take affirmative action to see that a certain minimum of education, welfare, and other benefits are provided every person, what view of equality is being advanced?

30. Merle McClung, "The Problem of the Due Process Exclusion: Do Schools Have a Continuing Responsibility to Educate Children With Behavior Problems?" 3 *J. Law and Educ.* 489, October, 1974, at p. 527.

Equality of legal treatment? Equality of opportunity? Equality of result? Would you support the "minimum guarantee" approach?[31]

What role does the social science evidence introduced into the case play in this determination? Even though correlations between expenditures and quality education are conflicting, does Justice Marshall find a convincing way around the ambiguity of the research in his reference to the determination of the property-rich districts to hold on to their higher expenditures? To the majority's implicit acknowledgement that minimum levels of education can be ascertained? Or does the confusion about the impact of formal education on the learner justify the majority's conclusion that education presents too many " 'intractable economic, social, and even philosophical problems' " to warrant being accorded fundamental status? Recall Professor Yudof's comment above regarding the relationship of ethical principles to judicial decision making.

3. Justice White points out that by restricting the upper limit a local district may tax itself, the state makes it impossible for some districts to provide higher educational budgets. Thus, the state has guaranteed the continuance of inequality by its own actions, a clear violation of the Equal Protection Clause. Why do you suppose the state maintains such a restriction? In a footnote (not excerpted), Justice Powell points out that appellees never relied on this argument and thus "the constitutionality of that statutory provision is not before us and must await litigation in a case which is properly presented." *

4. Justice Marshall's dissent offers extensive commentary on old and new equal protection, concluding that there really are not just two standards but a spectrum of standards evident in the Court's prior decisions. He would prefer the Court to acknowledge its variable standards by deciding equal protection cases on the basis of the relationship of rights and classifications to specific constitutional provisions. Applying his approach to questions of fundamental interests, he states that "As the nexus between the specific constitutional guarantee and the nonconstitutional interest draws closer, the nonconstitutional interest becomes more fundamental" and consequently the Court's scrutiny becomes more strict. He cites the example of the Court's usually sustaining state discrimination where economic interests are involved, and accuses the majority of forcing this case into a similar mold. What significance is it that the word "property" appears in the Fourteenth Amendment? According to Justice Marshall's approach, should economic interests actually be entitled to *greater,* not lesser, support by the Court? Indeed, during the late 19th and early 20th cen-

---

31. The concept of minimum protection is more completely described in Frank L. Michelman, "Foreword: On Protecting the Poor Through the Fourteenth Amendment," 83 *Harv.L.Rev.* 7, November, 1969.

* In *Hargrave v. Kirk*, 313 F.Supp. 944 (M. D.Fla.1970), the district court held that a Florida statute restricting the upper limit a county could tax itself for education was a violation of the Equal Protection Clause. However, the decision was later vacated and remanded by the Supreme Court. *Askew v. Hargrave*, 401 U.S. 476 (1971). In its *per curiam* decision, the Court noted that the matter was under consideration in the state court on state constitutional grounds and thus was premature for judgment by federal courts. The Court also noted that the overall effect of a state financing system on a particular city must be considered in ruling on a particular aspect of it, such as a restriction on county taxing power.

turies, the Court elevated property and related interests to almost sancti-
fied status, striking down most state regulatory legislation as a violation
of due process (the Equal Protection Clause was rarely used at this time).
Would Justice Marshall's variable approach help rationalize the Court's
equal protection decision making? Or would it make what many now consider a largely subjective process even more so—and hence variable?

   5. It was estimated in the case that it would require Texas to double
its expenditures to bring all schools in the state up to the level of expenditure in the wealthiest districts. Might this fact coupled with the fear of
starting a flood of suits against local support for other social services have
been of major influence in the majority's decision?

   6. As a result of *San Antonio,* those protesting unequal financing of
schools resorted to state constitutions to challenge existing state finance
systems. Nearly all the states list education as a fundamental interest in
their constitutions. To date such suits have been successful in a growing
number of states including California,[32] New Jersey,[33] and Connecticut.[34]
As a result of these suits, state legislatures have had to revise their school
finance systems. The resulting redistribution of funds may result in a shift
of dollars away from wealthy districts. One commentator has suggested
that this redistribution, often called "district power equalizing," will benefit the nonpublic sector:

> Equalizing school finance will create a vacuum as the high quality,
> well-supported public schools erode. In turn, independent schools
> of high quality * * * will have substantial numbers of new
> clients, willing and able to pay.[35]

   A more serious form of attrition from the nation's schools—"white
flight" resulting from desegregation—will be discussed in the next section.

B. Other Applications of Old Equal Protection

   Aside from classifications based on race, alienage, or national origin;
classifications relating to specific constitutional rights or certain other
rights considered fundamental;* and classifications affected by statutes **
or state constitutions, the old equal protection applies to most school and
college classifications. For example, at the elementary and secondary level, courts usually defer to local school boards on assignments of students
to schools. (It is important to note that in the absence of a state constitutional or a statutory provision, there is no right to attend a neighborhood
school.)

   In postsecondary education, a number of issues involving old equal
protection have surfaced. Differential tuition charges to out-of-state students have long been the practice in much of postsecondary education. The

---

32. *Serrano v. Priest,* 487 P.2d 1241 (1971).

33. *Robinson v. Cahill,* 303 A.2d 273 (1973).

34. *Horton v. Meskill,* 332 A.2d 113 (1974).

35. Stanton Leggett "How Will Equalizing
School Finance Affect Your School?" *Independent School,* May, 1977, at p. 24.

* To be discussed later in the chapter.

** For example, classifications relating to
student records are affected by the Family
Educational Rights and Privacy Act (Buckley Amendment) and those relating to sex
are influenced by Title IX of the Educational Amendments of 1972.

rationale advanced in defense of this policy is that low in-state tuition is intended to benefit state taxpayers and their families. Thus, out-of-state residents are usually required to establish domicile in the state and, after a limited time, are granted lower tuition assessments. In *Starns v. Malkerson,* 326 F.Supp. 234 (D.C.Minn. 4th Div. 1970), a Minnesota district court ruled against a challenge to Minnesota's one-year residential requirement for in-state tuition. Plaintiffs had tried to show that the requirement unconstitutionally restricted their fundamental right to travel and could therefore not meet a compelling state purpose test under new equal protection. Judge Lord for the three-judge court disagreed that the residency requirement substantially affected the right to travel, noting the large number of out-of-state students in attendance at the University of Minnesota. He concluded that no fundamental right was involved in the case. Plaintiffs further challenged the state's "irrebuttable presumption" against establishing residency in less than a year's time. Both had married husbands who had obtained employment in the state; therefore, they argued that even though they had not resided in the state for a full year, they clearly had taken up state residence. Judge Lord refused to find the irrebuttable presumption irrational under old equal protection, nor did he conclude that the purpose of the policy did not serve a valid state purpose. He agreed with defendants that the one-year waiting period "is a rational attempt by the State to achieve partial cost equalization between those who have and those who have not recently contributed to the State's economy through employment, tax payments and expenditures therein." (At p. 240). The U. S. Supreme Court affirmed the decision without opinion in 1971.

Another challenge to out-of-state tuition payments reached the Supreme Court in 1973. In *Vlandis v. Kline,* 412 U.S. 441, the Court ruled against a Connecticut policy which prevented out-of-state students from *ever* changing their residence status, no matter what evidence they might have introduced. The Court found the irrebuttable presumption a violation of due process but distinguished *Malkerson* since the Minnesota durational residency requirement allowed students to qualify for lower tuition payments after one year of residency. In 1978 the Supreme Court turned down an opportunity to rule again on out-of-state tuition charges, remanding a case involving non-immigrant aliens (children of diplomats) to the Maryland Court of Appeals for a determination if such persons under state law can ever become residents of the state. *Elkins v. Moreno,* 435 U.S. 647 (1978).

Another application of old equal protection relates to on-campus residency requirements for certain classes of students, such as freshmen and sophomores. Where such regulations are based on a "living and learning" concept and not solely to increase institutional revenues, they have generally been upheld. The prevailing view is well illustrated in Chief Judge Dawkins' observations in *Pratz v. Louisiana Polytechnic Institute,* 316 F. Supp. 872 (W.D.La.1970):

> If sound educational policies * * * dictate that the educational
> mission of the State is best carried out by providing for the great
> majority of student citizens of each State adequate housing and
> eating facilities at a cost which can be afforded by all students

seeking entrance into a particular university, then we do not think it our place to decree otherwise. (At p. 885)

In *Schare v. State Univ. of New York at Stony Brook,* 437 F.Supp. 969 (E.D.N.Y.1977), a New York district court upheld a university regulation requiring all students living on-campus who do not buy meal plans to pay $25 per semester fee for use of cooking facilities in the dorms. Finding no suspect classification and no fundamental right involved, the court concluded that "It does not seem unreasonable to assume that students eating at least five meals a week in the cafeteria will use dormitory cooking facilities less than students not on such a plan, and, therefore, it does not seem unreasonable to charge the heavy users twenty-five dollars a semester." (At p. 971). Do you think this is a fair decision? How would you react to a student complaint that charging her $25 without assurance that she in fact uses the cooking facilities amounts to an "irrebuttable presumption" and thus violates her right to due process of law?

Finally, in *Benner v. Oswald,* 444 F.Supp. 545 (M.D.Pa.1978), a Pennsylvania district court ruled that Penn State University's method of selecting its Board of Trustees members, which provides for participation by agricultural and industrial societies and by university alumni but not by undergraduate students, does not violate the Equal Protection Clause. Four undergraduates had charged that their relationship to the institution entitled them to participate in Board elections. They cited the Supreme Court voting case precedents in which the Court had utilized new equal protection to strike down state restrictions on voting. The court found that in fact the selection process is not an "election" in the ordinary sense; rather it is limited to the respective constituencies and bears more of a resemblance "to selection of the board members of a private organization." (At p. 561). Thus, the voting cases decided by the U. S. Supreme Court are not applicable. Further, the court found a rational basis for the scheme in that Penn State has had a historic commitment to agricultural and technical goals and that continued representation of these interests on the Board serves a valid purpose. Likewise, the court agreed that the university has a valid interest in having alumni representation on the Board. While the court questioned Penn State's contention that undergraduates should not be represented, Judge Muir concluded:

> The Court cannot say that it is wholly irrational for Penn State to attempt to choose the members of its Board of Trustees from persons who have a generalized interest in the University's affairs and who would, in Penn State's opinion, be able to maintain their objectivity towards substantially all of the university's actions. Therefore, Penn State's actions do not violate the equal protection clause of the United States Constitution. (At p. 562)

The district court decision was affirmed by the Third Circuit Court of Appeals in early 1979.

These few examples suggest that reasonable rules which treat groups and classes of students differently will not raise substantial equal protection issues unless the rules can be proven to be irrational, are applied in an irrational way, or affect a suspect classification or fundamental right.

IV. NEW EQUAL PROTECTION AND STUDENTS

A. Race as a Suspect Classification

Since *Brown v. Board of Educ.*, the path toward desegregation of the nation's educational system has been marked by numerous pitfalls and obstacles, not all of them foreseen or surmountable. This section is divided into three parts, roughly corresponding to what appear to be major legal demarcations, to describe the developing equal protection law as applied to school desegregation. Each of the three parts contains a leading case. Only U. S. Supreme Court cases are discussed for reasons of space, though the reader should be aware that there are many decisions on school desegregation made by the lower courts.

It is important to note that even a cursory review of the available literature will reveal the voluminous amount of writing since 1954 in the suspect classification area, most particularly racial discrimination in education. The subject's complexity is reflected in numerous commentaries from authorities in political science, education, and law. Only the major developments are described in the limited space in this section. At the risk of sacrificing readability, we have tried to compensate for necessary brevity by including more frequent references than in previous chapters to some of the many sources which are available. We hasten to assure the reader, however, that a careful reading of the footnotes is not necessary to an understanding of the text.

(1) De Jure Segregation

The 1954 *Brown* decision did not address the question of suitable relief for the plaintiffs. The Court requested further argument on this matter and announced its decision in 1955 in *Brown v. Board of Educ.*, 349 U.S. 294, commonly referred to as *Brown II*. Based on the arguments presented and the views of the attorneys-general of the affected states, the Court concluded that the federal district courts which originally heard the cases were best able to fashion appropriate remedies. The Justices remanded the principle cases to those courts. Chief Justice Warren, who again wrote the unanimous opinion, did not set any hard-and-fast deadlines for desegregation of the previously segregated schooling systems. Instead, he used phrases such as "prompt and reasonable start," "at the earliest practicable date," and "with all deliberate speed." The Court has subsequently been criticized for not being firmer, for little progress toward desegregation was made by the eleven southern states practicing segregation during the succeeding decade. However, considering that the other branches of government had yet to take a stand against segregation and considering the obvious hostility of much of the population in the affected areas toward the decision, the Court probably had little practical choice but to adopt a go-slow posture. One commentator on the role of the Court in this period has noted that the Court specifically refrained from adopting an activist posture, leaving these matters to those political and educational authorities charged with operating educational institutions.

* * * the Court, having announced its principle, and having required a measure of initial compliance, resumed its posture of passive receptiveness to the complaints of litigants * * *. The Court placed itself in position to engage in a continuing colloquy with the political institutions, leaving it to them to tell the Court what expedients of accommodation and compromise they deemed necessary.[36]

Regardless of the reasons for the Court's retreat to a passive posture, the Court did not change its pattern during the next decade in the face of southern resistance to lower court efforts to achieve desegregation. But there were several notable exceptions. One such exception occurred in 1958 when the school board and superintendent in Little Rock, Arkansas, sought postponement of their desegregation plan for Central High School in light of continuing opposition by the governor and the state legislature. The petitioners complained that it was impossible to integrate the school when the legislature eliminated compulsory attendance, when the governor dispatched the National Guard to place the school off-limits to blacks, and when unruly crowds threatened the safety of school children. The integration of nine black children was accomplished during this period only after a federal injunction enjoined Governor Orval Faubus from obstructing integration and the President of the United States dispatched federal troops to Little Rock to quell disturbances. The petitioners feared that these events made operating Central High School on an integrated basis impossible.

In *Cooper v. Aaron,* 358 U.S. 1 (1958), a unanimous Court, while sympathetic to the problems of the school officials, refused to allow a postponement. The opinion, signed by all the Justices, asserted that "the constitutional rights of children not to be discriminated against in school admission on grounds of race or color * * * can neither be nullified openly and directly by state legislators or state executive or judicial officers, nor nullified indirectly by them through evasive schemes for segregation whether attempted 'ingeniously or ingenuously.' " (At p. 17). The opinion pointed out that the three new Justices who had been appointed since *Brown* joined in the decision. The opinion also pointedly referred to past judicial principles in refuting the claim of the governor and legislature that they were not bound by the *Brown* decision.

The reluctance of many federal district court judges to implement the *Brown* decision coupled with such delaying tactics as ignoring the *Brown* decision, closing public schools, transforming public institutions into nonpublic, developing ingenious pupil assignment plans, and the like, resulted in very little integration during the decade following *Brown*. It has been estimated that in 1964, only 2 percent of black students in the 11 southern states affected by *Brown* were attending school with whites.[37]

By 1964 the events in the South, particularly the violence, which was being dramatically recorded on film for television news programs, solidified

---

36. Alexander Bickel, *The Least Dangerous Branch.* (New York: Bobbs-Merrill, 1962), at p. 254.

37. Casper Weinberger "Some Thoughts on the 20th Anniversary of *Brown v. Board of Educ.,* 4 *J.Law & Educ.* 33, January, 1975, at p. 33.

public opinion in the North and helped prod a reluctant Congress to action. The 1964 Civil Rights Act, which empowered the Department of Health, Education, and Welfare to cut off federal funds from those school districts refusing to integrate and also placed the power of the U. S. Attorney General's office at the disposal of private citizens faced with racial discrimination in public schooling, significantly quickened the pace of integration.[38] President Lyndon B. Johnson issued Executive Order No. 11247 in September, 1965, specifically ordering the Attorney General to coordinate federal enforcement. With these two actions, the three branches of the federal government were aligned in their opposition to continued *de jure* school segregation.

Beginning in 1964 the Court became more actively involved in implementing its 1954 mandate. In *Griffin v. Prince Edward County*, 377 U.S. 218, the Court was confronted with a plan in one of the Virginia counties involved in the original *Brown* decision to frustrate school integration by closing the public schools and granting funds to white children to attend nonpublic schools. Justice Black for the Court, himself a southerner, noted that public schools in all other Virginia counties were open and functioning. He concluded that the Prince Edward County school closing was

> for one reason, and one reason only: to ensure, through measures taken by the county and the State, that white and colored children * * * would not, under any circumstances, go to the same school. Whatever nonracial grounds might support a State's allowing a county to abandon public schools, the object must be a constitutional one, and grounds of race and opposition to desegregation do not qualify as constitutional. (At p. 231).

Justice Black noted that from 1959 to 1963 the black school children were without formal education entirely. Claiming that there has been "too much deliberation and not enough speed" in enforcing the *Brown* mandate in Prince Edward County, he directed the federal district court to take such action as necessary to "guarantee that these petitioners will get the kind of education that is given in the State's public schools." (At pp. 229 and 234).

One interesting sidelight of the *Griffin* case is the question whether a state could legally shut down its school system. Justice Black avoided this issue since only the Prince Edward County schools in Virginia had been closed. Under the circumstances he held that the federal court has the authority to reopen the public schools in that county. Justices Clark and Harlan disagreed with this aspect of the opinion. Whether a county or a state could close its schools entirely on nonracial grounds without violating the Equal Protection Clause remains unclear, though *San Antonio* appears to cast doubt on the prospect as noted above.

The role of the Supreme Court in implementing the *Brown* mandate increased in the late 1960s. In 1968 the Court dealt a blow to the use of freedom of choice plans whereby students could choose the school they wish

---

38. For a discussion of the role of HEW's Office of Education, which was charged with administering the 1964 Act, see Gary Orfield, *The Reconstruction of Southern Education* (N. Y.: Wiley-Interscience, 1969).

to attend. Earlier, the Court had ruled out transfer plans allowing students subject to rezoning to transfer from a school in which they were a racial minority to one in which they would be in the majority.[39] The 1968 case, *Green v. County School Bd.*, 391 U.S. 430, is particularly important because the Court picked up the thread of *Brown II* and again addressed the question of appropriate remedies to eradicate *de jure* school segregation.

The *Green* Case involved the New Kent County school district, a small rural district in eastern Virginia. About sixty percent of the 1300 pupils were black and attended a combined elementary and secondary school at one end of the district. The white children attended a similar school at the other end of the district. The population of the county was scattered, so that the school buses traveled overlapping routes in transporting pupils to their respective schools. After a delay caused by continuing state opposition to *Brown* and *Brown II*, the school board in 1965 adopted a freedom of choice plan in order to remain eligible for federal financial aid.*

Justice Brennan, writing the unanimous opinion for the Court, noted that *Brown II* stipulated that school boards were "clearly charged with the affirmative duty to take whatever steps might be necessary to convert to a unitary system in which racial discrimination would be eliminated root and branch." (At pp. 437–438). Observing that the dual system in New Kent County had persisted for ten years beyond *Brown II,* Justice Brennan stated that only a remedy to disestablish the dual system "that promises realistically to work, and promises realistically to work *now*" would be acceptable. (At p. 439). The freedom of choice plan, while not *per se* unconstitutional, was not by itself acceptable.

> The New Kent School Board's "freedom-of-choice plan" cannot be accepted as sufficient to "effectuate a transition" to a unitary system. In three years of operation not a single white child has chosen to attend Watkins school and although 115 Negro children enrolled in New Kent school in 1967 * * *, 85 percent of the Negro children in the system still attend the all-Negro Watkins school. (At p. 471).

The school board, Justice Brennan concluded, had to develop a new plan to effectuate a system where there would be no black school and no white school, "but just schools." He suggested the use of zoning and school consolidation as two possibilities to make this possible.

Green is important because it demands more than a color-blind approach to eliminating *de jure* segregation. School districts had to take *affirmative action* to integrate educational institutions. Results, not appearances, were what counted. Critics accused the Court of going beyond the dictates of *Brown II* by insisting not just in an end to *de jure* school

---

39. *Goss v. Board of Educ.*, 373 U.S. 683 (1963).

* As noted earlier, HEW guidelines were developed in 1965 to implement the terms of the 1964 Civil Rights Act, which authorized the termination of federal funding to those schools not in compliance with *Brown v. Board of Educ.* One of the guidelines allowed the use of freedom of choice plans so long as they proved effective in eradicting segregation.

segregation but in the obligation of school authorities previously operating segregated schools to create truly integrated institutions.*

In several cases from 1968 to 1970, the Court reemphasized its "at once" requirement in *Green,* though several Justices disagreed as to actual time implications. It was not until 1971 that the Court considered the implications of the *Green* holding for large southern metropolitan school districts with a history of *de jure* segregation. *Swann v. Charlotte-Mecklenburg Bd. of Educ.,* 402 U.S. 1 (1971) represents the high tide of Court involvement in sanctioning a variety of remedies to eradicate *de jure* school segregation. The case arose over disputes between the federal district court and school officials to develop a plan to desegregate the Charlotte-Mecklenburg school system encompassing Charlotte, North Carolina, and surrounding Mecklenburg County. The system then consisted of 84,000 pupils, 71 percent of whom were white, and 107 schools. Most of the blacks attended school in Charlotte with some 14,000 concentrated in 21 virtually all-black schools.

The district court determined that the school board had acted to maintain a segregated system and ordered the school board to develop a plan for both faculty and student desegregation. After finding the school board's efforts unacceptable, the court appointed an educational expert to draft a desegregation plan. The expert's plan, like the plan the school board eventually submitted, proposed to desegregate the high schools by establishing attendance zones shaped much like wedges of a pie extending into the suburbs. Junior high schools were also rezoned, and in addition, the expert recommended creation of satellite schools in outlying areas to be grouped where necessary with all-black inner city schools so that all schools would be desegregated. Elementary schools were to be desegregated not only by rezoning as the school board proposed but also by pairing and grouping of certain inner city and suburban schools. Substantial busing would be necessary to carry out the plan.

The district court accepted the expert's plan, but the Court of Appeals for the Fourth Circuit disapproved the desegregation of the elementary school and remanded the case. After further deliberations, the district court directed that the expert's plan remain in effect, and the school board reluctantly acquiesced. The case reached the Supreme Court on the issue of the appropriateness of the district court's remedy.

---

* These cases have served to obfuscate relevant terminology. As applied to the South, "desegregation" now takes on the connotation of "integration." Caution should be exercised in using equal protection terminology as applied to *de jure* and *de facto* settings, so that intended meanings are, in fact, conveyed.

SWANN v. CHARLOTTE–MECKLENBURG BD. OF EDUC.

Supreme Court of the United States, 1971.
402 U.S. 1, 91 S.Ct. 1267, 28 L.Ed.2d 554.

Mr. Chief Justice BURGER delivered the opinion of the Court.

* * *

Over the 16 years since *Brown II,* many difficulties were encountered in implementation of the basic constitutional requirement that the State not discriminate between public school children on the basis of their race. Nothing in our national experience prior to 1955 prepared anyone for dealing with changes and adjustments of the magnitude and complexity encountered since then.
* * *

* * *

The problems encountered by the district courts and courts of appeals make plain that we should now try to amplify guidelines, however incomplete and imperfect, for the assistance of school authorities and courts.[5] * * *

If school authorities fail in their affirmative obligations under * * * (*Brown* and subsequent rulings), judicial authority may be invoked. * * *

* * *

In seeking to define even in broad and general terms how far this remedial power extends it is important to remember that judicial powers may be exercised only on the basis of a constitutional violation. Remedial judicial authority does not put judges automatically in the shoes of school authorities whose powers are plenary. Judicial authority enters only when local authority defaults.

School authorities are traditionally charged with broad power to formulate and implement educational policy and might well conclude, for example, that in

order to prepare students to live in a pluralistic society each school should have a prescribed ratio of Negro to white students reflecting the proportion for the district as a whole. To do this as an educational policy is within the broad discretionary powers of school authorities; absent a finding of a constitutional violation, however, that would not be within the authority of a federal court.
* * * In default by the school authorities of their obligation to proffer acceptable remedies, a district court has broad power to fashion a remedy that will assure a unitary school system.

* * *

We turn now to the problem of defining with more particularity the responsibilities of school authorities in desegregating a state-enforced dual school system in light of the Equal Protection Clause. Although the several related cases before us are primarily concerned with problems of student assignment, it may be helpful to begin with a brief discusson of other aspects of the process.

* * * Independent of student assignment, where it is possible to identify a "white school" or a "Negro school" simply by reference to the racial composition of teachers and staff, the quality of school buildings and equipment, or the organization of sports activities, a prima facie case of violation of substantive constitutional rights under the Equal Protection Clause is shown.

When a system has been dual in these respects, the first remedial responsibility of school authorities is to eliminate invid-

---

5. The necessity for this is suggested by the situation in the Fifth Circuit where 166 appeals in school desegregation cases were heard between December 2, 1969, and September 24, 1970. * * *

ious racial distinctions. With respect to such matters as transportation, supporting personnel, and extracurricular activities, no more than this may be necessary. Similar corrective action must be taken with regard to the maintenance of buildings and the distribution of equipment. In these areas, normal administrative practice should produce schools of like quality, facilities, and staffs. Something more must be said, however, as to faculty assignment and new school construction.

In the companion *Davis* case, the Mobile school board has argued that the Constitution requires that teachers be assigned on a "color blind" basis. It also argues that the Constitution prohibits district courts from using their equity power to order assignment of teachers to achieve a particular degree of faculty desegregation. We reject that contention.

* * *

The construction of new schools and the closing of old ones are two of the most important functions of local school authorities and also two of the most complex. * * * Over the long run, the consequences of the choices will be far reaching. People gravitate toward school facilities, just as schools are located in response to the needs of people. * * *

* * * In addition to the classic pattern of building schools specifically intended for Negro or white students, school authorities have sometimes, since Brown, closed schools which appeared likely to become racially mixed through changes in neighborhood residential patterns. This was sometimes accompanied by building new schools in the areas of white suburban expansion farthest from Negro population centers in order to maintain the separation of the races with a minimum departure from the formal principles of "neighborhood zoning." Such a policy does more than simply influence the short-run composition of the student body of a new school. It may well promote segregated residential patterns which, when combined with "neighborhood zoning," further lock the school system into the mold of separation of the races. * * *

* * * In devising remedies where legally imposed segregation has been established, it is the responsibility of local authorities and district courts to see to it that future school construction and abandonment are not used and do not serve to perpetuate or re-establish the dual system. When necessary, district courts should retain jurisdiction to assure that these responsibilities are carried out.

The central issue in this case is that of student assignment, and there are essentially four problem areas:

* * *

(1) *Racial Balances or Racial Quotas.*

* * *

We are concerned in these cases with the elimination of the discrimination inherent in the dual school systems, not with myriad factors of human existence which can cause discrimination in a multitude of ways on racial, religious, or ethnic grounds. * * * We do not reach in this case the question whether a showing that school segregation is a consequence of other types of state action, without any discriminatory action by the school authorities, is a constitutional violation requiring remedial action by a school desegregation decree. This case does not present that question and we therefore do not decide it.

* * *

In this case it is urged that the District Court has imposed a racial balance requirement of 71%–29% on individual schools. * * *

* * * If we were to read the holding of the District Court to require, as a matter of substantive constitutional right, any particular degree of racial balance or mixing, that approach would be disapproved and we would be obliged to reverse. The constitutional command to desegregate schools does not mean that every school in every community must always reflect the racial composition of the school system as a whole.

*   *   *

We see *   *   * that the use made of mathematical ratios was no more than a starting point in the process of shaping a remedy, rather than an inflexible requirement. From that starting point the District Court proceeded to frame a decree that was within its discretionary powers, as an equitable remedy for the particular circumstances.[9] *   *   *

(2) *One-race Schools.*

*   *   *

*   *   * the existence of some small number of one-race, or virtually one-race, schools within a district is not in and of itself the mark of a system that still practices segregation by law. The district judge or school authorities should make every effort to achieve the greatest possible degree of actual desegregation and will thus necessarily be concerned with the elimination of one-race schools. *   *   * but in a system with a history of segregation the need for remedial criteria of sufficient specificity to assure a school authority's compliance with its constitutional duty warrants a presumption against schools that are substantially disproportionate in their racial composition. Where the school authority's proposed plan for conversion from a dual to a unitary system contemplates the continued existence of some schools that are all or predominately of one race, they have the burden of showing that such school assignments are genuinely nondiscriminatory. The court should scrutinize such schools, and the burden upon the school

authorities will be to satisfy the court that their racial composition is not the result of present or past discriminatory action on their part.

An optional majority-to-minority transfer provision has long been recognized as a useful part of every desegregation plan. Provision for optional transfer of those in the majority racial group of a particular school to other schools where they will be in the minority is an indispensable remedy for those students willing to transfer to other schools in order to lessen the impact on them of the state-imposed stigma of segregation. In order to be effective, such a transfer arrangement must grant the transferring student free transportation and space must be made available in the school to which he desires to move. *   *   *

(3) *Remedial Altering of Attendance Zones.*

The maps submitted in these cases graphically demonstrate that one of the principal tools employed by school planners and by courts to break up the dual school system has been a frank—and sometimes drastic—gerrymandering of school districts and attendance zones. An additional step was pairing, "clustering," or "grouping" of schools with attendance assignments made deliberately to accomplish the transfer of Negro students out of formerly segregated Negro schools and transfer of white students to formerly all-Negro schools. More often than not, these zones are neither compact nor contiguous; indeed they may be on opposite ends of the city. As an interim corrective measure, this cannot be said to be beyond the broad remedial powers of a court.

---

9. In its August 3, 1970, memorandum holding that the District Court plan was "reasonable" under the standard laid down by the Fourth Circuit on appeal, the District Court explained the approach taken as follows:

"This court has not ruled, and does not rule that 'racial balance' is required un-

der the Constitution; nor that all black schools in all cities are unlawful; nor that all school boards must bus children or violate the Constitution; *nor that the particular order entered in this case would be correct in other circumstances not before this court.*" (Emphasis in original.)

Absent a constitutional violation there would be no basis for judicially ordering assignment of students on a racial basis. All things being equal, with no history of discrimination, it might well be desirable to assign pupils to schools nearest their homes. But all things are not equal in a system that has been deliberately constructed and maintained to enforce racial segregation. The remedy for such segregation may be administratively awkward, inconvenient, and even bizarre in some situations and may impose burdens on some; but all awkwardness and inconvenience cannot be avoided in the interim period when remedial adjustments are being made to eliminate the dual school systems.

* * * "Racially neutral" assignment plans proposed by school authorities to a district court may be inadequate; such plans may fail to counteract the continuing effects of past school segregation resulting from discriminatory location of school sites or distortion of school size in order to achieve or maintain an artificial racial separation. When school authorities present a district court with a "loaded game board," affirmative action in the form of remedial altering of attendance zones is proper to achieve truly nondiscriminatory assignments. In short, an assignment plan is not acceptable simply because it appears to be neutral.

* * *

We hold that the pairing and grouping of noncontiguous school zones is a permissible tool and such action is to be considered in light of the objectives sought. * * * Maps do not tell the whole story since noncontiguous school zones may be more accessible to each other in terms of the critical travel time, because of traffic patterns and good highways, than schools geographically closer together. Conditions in different localities will vary so widely that no rigid rules can be laid down to govern all situations.

(4) *Transportation of Students.*

* * * No rigid guidelines as to student transportation can be given for application to the infinite variety of problems presented in thousands of situations. Bus transportation has been an integral part of the public education system for years, and was perhaps the single most important factor in the transition from the one-room schoolhouse to the consolidated school. * * *

* * * The District Court's conclusion that assignment of children to the school nearest their home serving their grade would not produce an effective dismantling of the dual system is supported by the record.

* * *

The decree provided that the buses used to implement the plan would operate on direct routes. Students would be picked up at schools near their homes and transported to the schools they were to attend. The trips for elementary school pupils average about seven miles and the District Court found that they would take "not over 35 minutes at the most." This system compares favorably with the transportation plan previously operated in Charlotte under which each day 23,600 students on all grade levels were transported an average of 15 miles one way for an average trip requiring over an hour. In these circumstances, we find no basis for holding that the local school authorities may not be required to employ bus transportation as one tool of school desegregation. Desegregation plans cannot be limited to the walk-in school.

An objection to transportation of students may have validity when the time or distance of travel is so great as to either risk the health of the children or significantly impinge on the educational process. District courts must weigh the soundness of any transportation plan in light of what is said in subdivisions (1), (2), and (3) above. * * *

* * * On the facts of this case, we are unable to conclude that the order of the District Court is not reasonable, feasible and workable. * * *

At some point, these school authorities and others like them should have achieved full compliance with this Court's decision in *Brown I.* * * *

It does not follow that the communities served by such systems will remain demographically stable, for in a growing, mobile society, few will do so. Neither school authorities nor district courts are constitutionally required to make year-by-year adjustments of the racial composition of student bodies once the affirmative duty to desegregate has been accomplished and racial discrimination through official action is eliminated from the system. This does not mean that federal courts are without power to deal with future problems; but in the absence of a showing that either the school authorities or some other agency of the State has deliberately attempted to fix or alter demographic patterns to affect the racial composition of the schools, further intervention by a district court should not be necessary.

For the reasons herein set forth, the judgment of the Court of Appeals is affirmed as to those parts in which it affirmed the judgment of the District Court. The order of the District Court, dated August 7, 1970, is also affirmed.

It is so ordered.

NOTES AND QUESTIONS

1. There are several caveats expressed in Chief Justice Burger's opinion which are to become significant in later decisions. Note his reference to the many factors which can bring about a segregated school system and his disclaimer that the Court is making judgments about any of them except the actions of school officials. Note also his assertion that where there is no evidence of past discrimination by school authorities, judicially-ordered re-assignment of students on a racial basis may be inappropriate. Finally, note his comment that once full compliance with *Brown I* is achieved, continued court-ordered year-by-year adjustments to changed conditions is not required. These caveats provide some insight into the thinking of at least some of the Justices and suggest that there would arise situations where they would not be as supportive of court-ordered desegregation.

2. There were several companion cases to *Swann*, one of which is cited in the *Swann* opinion. In one of the companion cases, *North Carolina Bd. of Educ. v. Swann*, 402 U.S. 43 (1971), Chief Justice Burger struck down a portion of a statute known as the North Carolina Anti-Busing Law because it interfered with the affirmative duty of school officials to remedy past discrimination:

> The legislation before us flatly forbids assignment of any student on account of race or for the purpose of creating a racial balance or ratio in the schools. The prohibition is absolute, and it would inescapably operate to obstruct the remedies granted by the District Court in the *Swann* case. But more important the statute exploits an apparently neutral form to control school assignment plans by directing that they be "color blind"; that requirement, against the background of segregation, would render illusory the promise of Brown v. Board of Education. Just as

the race of students must be considered in determining whether a constitutional violation has occurred, so also must race be considered in formulating a remedy. To forbid, at this stage, all assignments made on the basis of race would deprive school authorities of the one tool absolutely essential to fulfillment of their constitutional obligation to eliminate existing dual school systems. (At p. 46.)

In the companion cases, the Chief Justice, again speaking for a unanimous Court, makes it clear that where dual school systems exist because of past action by school authorities, a racially-neutral, "color-blind," approach will not pass muster. And yet, wasn't that the goal of *Brown I*? Does the Fourteenth Amendment Equal Protection Clause compel that schools be integrated even against the wishes of those attending them? At what point is a school system "unitary"? Note the reliance of the Court on racial balance "as a starting point."

3. The extensive remedial action mandated by *Swann* is predicated on the assumption that past pervasive *de jure* discrimination by public officials caused the neighborhood, and hence school segregation, which then existed in Charlotte-Mecklenburg. But a number of commentators have pointed out that this assumption is much too simplistic. Mark Yudof, Professor of Law at the University of Texas, has noted that "There is no evidence that segregated schools materially influenced racial isolation by neighborhood in southern communities." [40] Need there be empirical evidence or is common sense enough? Yudof goes on to assert that "Where the whole structure of society reflects the inferior status assigned to blacks, it is difficult to say that any particular practice or institution caused segregated neighborhoods." [41] Given these circumstances, then, ought the burden of proving the *lack* of relationship between past *de jure* segregation and continuing segregated schooling be placed on school officials before the remedial requirements discussed in *Swann* be imposed. Would such an approach ever constitute a realistic option for the school board, given the likelihood that *de jure* school policies played some role, however small, in influencing residential patterns, e. g., site selection and construction, zoning and busing patterns, assignment of teachers, and the like? Should courts tailor their degree of remediation to the actual effects of illegal *de jure* segregation? These disturbing questions begin to attract the concern of some members of the Court when cases involving northern school segregation arise, as the next section points out.

4. Inherent in the *Swann* approach is reliance on busing to accomplish court-mandated school integration. Of all the remedial tools available to courts and school officials, busing has been the most criticized. Antipathy to court-ordered busing has not been limited to white families. As Professor Archibald Cox has observed, "There must be many parents in the inner cities who share very similar misgivings about the government's 'pushing their children around' by assigning them to the so-called 'better' neighborhoods." [42] Over the years, polls taken of the general public and

40. Mark G. Yudof "Equal Educational Opportunity and the Courts," 51 *Tex.L.Rev.* 411, 1973, at p. 452.

41. *Id.*

42. Archibald Cox, *The Role of the Supreme Court in American Government* (New York: Oxford University Press, 1976), at p. 87.

also of school officials show high percentages opposed to court-ordered busing. For example, in 1972, some 70 percent of the public said they opposed busing for integration purposes in a *New York Times*-CBS survey.[43] The combination of student radicalism, black rioting, and more aggressive efforts by courts and administrative agencies to desegregate schools contributed to the strong anti-busing attitude which became particularly pronounced by the 1972 federal elections. Since schools have been busing children for some time,* it would seem that much of the opposition is not to busing *per se* but to where some of the buses will go. The busing issue appears to be mainly a symbol of deeper emotions related to the concept of school integration itself.

As already noted, the Court maintained in *Swann* that the amount of busing required for integrating the schools would not differ substantially from that previously required to maintain segregation. The United States Commission on Civil Rights pointed out several years after *Swann* that despite the general impression that busing plans involve considerable increases in both money and travel time, the converse is generally true.[44]

In any case, the years immediately following the *Swann* decision saw a number of proposals for congressional curbs on school busing, including one introduced by the Nixon Administration in 1972. A watered-down version of the proposal providing a moratorium on busing became law late that year. But because of its vague wording, the measure did not impede courts from issuing busing orders. In 1974 the Nixon Administration succeeded in getting a stronger measure written into law. The anti-busing provisions became part of the Education Amendments of 1974, 88 Stat. 484. Among other provisions which speak against racial balance and in favor of the neighborhood school is one which prevents federal courts and administrative agencies from ordering "the implementation of a plan that would require the transportation of any student to a school other than the school closest to his place of residence." (Sec. 215a of Pub.L. 93–380). The provision thus also restrains the remedial power of HEW, whose leadership then was controlled by the Republican Administration, opponents of vigorous enforcement of the 1964 Civil Rights Act. However, the law would not apply in situations where more extensive busing is required to secure the rights of victims of *de jure* school segregation. The 1964 Act contains an introductory passage which states that the provisions "are not intended to modify or diminish the authority of the courts of the United States to enforce fully the Fifth and Fourteenth Amendments." Thus the prime effect is to emphasize that busing is to be used only as a last resort and then to be carefully tailored to what is necessary to eliminate illegal school segregation.

In June, 1976, the Ford Administration proposed new anti-busing measures designed to make busing a "last resort" and used only in areas

---

43. Gary Orfield, *Must We Bus?* (Washington, D. C.: The Brookings Institution, 1978), at p. 113.

* Over half the children in public elementary and secondary schools currently ride buses to school. Orfield, *Id.*, at p. 128.

44. *Public Knowledge and Busing Opposition: An Interpretation of a New National Survey* (Washington, D. C.: U. S. Commission on Civil Rights, 1973).

where *de jure* segregation was proven to exist.   The proposal also placed curbs on the time school busing could be used as a remedy.   The proposal did not get out of committee.

Busing was not a major issue in the election campaigns of 1976 and sentiment against court-ordered busing declined in Congress.   No major anti-busing measures were introduced in Congress in 1977.   Court-ordered busing has become a less volatile political issue, though public opposition continues.[45]

The constitutionality of these measures has not been tested to date. There are a number of legal scholars who question whether Congress has the power to interfere with the historic authority of the federal courts "to say what the law is."   As noted above, the Supreme Court ruled in *North Carolina Bd. of Educ. v. Swann* that the state's anti-busing law was unconstitutional.   The issue is more complicated at the federal level, however, because Congress has the power under section five of the Fourteenth Amendment to pass enabling legislation to enforce the terms of section one, and also has substantial power in Article III to control the jurisdiction of the federal courts.   The uncertainty surrounding the effectiveness of legislation in this context has led some to believe that only a constitutional amendment could effectively curtail judicial use of busing as a remedy to *de jure* school segregation.

5.   Behind the busing issue lurks a deeper question: Does busing of school children to achieve integration result in favorable consequences for the students?   Among social scientists, this question appears to be as volatile as the whole concept of busing is to much of the general public.   The evidence to date has been mixed.   The Coleman Report discussed in Chapter One revealed that socio-economic factors are most related to school achievement; the mixture of black and white students in a school has little impact.   The first full-fledged analysis was reported in 1972.   David L. Armor, then a sociologist at Harvard, concluded from his research on seven busing programs in northern cities that "busing is *not* an effective policy instrument for raising the achievement of black students or for increasing interracial harmony."[46]   The following year a group of social scientists led by fellow Harvard professor Thomas F. Pettigrew offered a stinging critique of Armor's research, questioning the validity of the data, the standards used to gather it, and Armor's conclusions.   Pettigrew and associates noted that Armor had left out a number of studies showing positive results on student attitude and achievement when black and white students are bused to the same school and asserted that his one-year time span criterion was too short to make sweeping conclusions.   They also maintained that the issue is far more complex than Armor would have one believe:

We believe it to be unrealistic to expect any type of educational innovation to close most of the racial differential in achievement

---

45.   For a detailed discussion of the political battles over court-ordered busing, see Orfield, *Must We Bus? supra*, chapter 8 "The President, Congress, and Antibusing Politics."

46.   David Armor "The Evidence on Busing: Research Report," 28 *The Public Interest* 90, Summer, 1972, at p. 115.

while gross racial disparities, especially economic ones, remain in American society. Furthermore, we know of no social scientists who ever claimed school desegregation alone could close most of the differential. We are pleased to note the many instances where effective desegregation has apparently benefitted the achievement of both black and white children * * *.[47]

Since the appearance of the Armor-Pettigrew articles, which taken together well illustrate once again the ambiguities surrounding social science research, many articles, reports, and books have appeared on the busing topic. A recent review of the available evidence concludes that "Though it is possible to state with some confidence that desegregation does not hurt students and though we are beginning to understand the complexity of the process, it is not possible to describe the positive educational effects accurately." [48] Much of the difficulty centers on the methodological problems associated with studying the outcomes of education. A second factor is the difficulty inherent in conducting research on human beings outside of the laboratory. Nevertheless, some research has been reported which suggests that an integrated environment may be the most beneficial educational climate. The National Assessment of Education Progress, which measures educational trends nationwide, reported in 1976 that blacks performed best in schools with large white majorities.[49] And a recent study by Robert L. Crain and Rita E. Mahard reported substantial educational gains when desegregation has existed since first grade.[50]

If the research on busing were to show that court-ordered integration was not initially having a positive influence on student achievement, should courts call a halt to integration-by-busing? Can courts rely on social science research to this extent? Even if the research were irrefutable, might there be other reasons for requiring an integrated educational system? Consider the case of the speaker whose right to speak in public is upheld over the objections of his irate listeners. Can this analogy be applied to desegregating school systems?

6. Interestingly, the Court split 5–4 during the same year *Swann* was decided in holding that the city of Jackson, Mississippi, had not acted discriminatorily in closing its public swimming pools after they had been ordered desegregated. The city had desegregated most of its public facilities in line with the *per curiam* rulings following *Brown*. However, the city decided to close the pools rather than operate them on a desegregated basis. In *Palmer v. Thompson*, 403 U.S. 217 (1971), Justice Black for the majority affirmed the lower court ruling that the city was justified in closing the pools to preserve order and because the pools could not be operated economically on an integrated basis. Justice Black stated that there was no "affirmative duty" to operate swimming pools, nor was there precedent on which to conclude that closing the pools was an act of state-endorsed segregation, even if there was some evidence to believe the city

---

47. Thomas F. Pettigrew, et al., "Busing: A Review of 'The Evidence,'" 30 *The Public Interest* 88, Winter, 1973, at p. 99.

48. Orfield, *Must We Bus? supra*, at p. 125.

49. *Id.*, at p. 126.

50. *Id.* Robert Crain and Rita Mahard, "Desegregation and Black Achievement" 42 *J. of Law & Contemp.Prob.* ——, 1979.

had acted out of opposition to integration. He refused to use the public school cases, principally *Griffin v. Prince Edward County,* as precedent. *Griffin,* decided in 1964, held that the county could not close its schools to avoid court-ordered integration.

The dissenters viewed the city's purported reasons as a guise for unconstitutional racism and asserted that the judiciary had a right to scrutinize the motives of public officials for their official acts. They would have used the school cases as precedents for ordering the swimming pools to be reopened.

Palmer is interesting because it raises the issue whether courts can consider the *motives* of public officials.[51] Under old equal protection, the federal courts usually do not question motives in ascertaining the rationality of legislative action, looking only at the effects. But *Griffin* suggests a different approach where racial classifications are concerned. Justice Black wrote the *Griffin* opinion in which he noted that the closing was "for one reason, and one reason only," to avoid integrating the schools.

Should courts seek to scrutinize the motives of public officials in suspect classification areas? Was *Palmer* wrongly decided? The issue becomes more significant where the line between the effects of *de jure* and *de facto* segregation in education is difficult to draw.

7.   In 1972 the Supreme Court had an opportunity to decide the circumstances under which public officials could carve a new school district out of a larger district then in the process of integrating. In *Wright v. Council of City of Emporia,* 407 U.S. 451 (1972), the Court concluded in a 5–4 decision that the federal district court had been correct in enjoining the city of Emporia, Virginia, from setting up a separate school system even though as a city, it had this prerogative under state law. From the facts of the case, Justice Stewart for the majority concluded that the effect of the creation of a new district at this time would be to frustrate the achievement of a unitary school system. He emphasized that the district court had properly focused on the *effect* of the proposed action, not on the motivation or purpose behind it.

The four Nixon appointees dissented. Speaking for the four, Chief Justice Burger noted that even with the new district, both Emporia and Greenville county districts would have a majority of black students. The facts of the case, he maintained, showed primarily that city officials wanted more control over their schools, in part to upgrade educational programs. He disputed the majority's contention that the effect of the new district would be to impede desegregation. And he spoke out against racial balancing:

> It can be no more said that racial balance is the norm to be sought, than it can be said that mere racial imbalance was the condition requiring a judicial remedy. * * * Obsession with * * * minor statistical differences reflects the gravely mistaken view

51. See Paul Brest, *"Palmer v. Thompson:* An Approach to the Problem of Unconstitutional Legislative Motive," 1971 *Sup. Ct.Rev.* 98, 1971. Professor Brest notes that the record clearly indicated the clo-sure was racially motivated and argues that courts should refrain from blanket refusals to inquire into legislative and administrative motivation.

that a plan providing more consistent racial ratios is somehow more unitary than one which tolerates a lack of racial balance. (At pp. 473–474).

But what is "the norm to be sought?" How should a unitary school system be defined? The elusive answers in part account for the differing views in this case.

In the companion case, *United States v. Scotland Neck City Bd. of Educ.*, 407 U.S. 484 (1972), all nine Justices agreed that the North Carolina state law enacted to allow Scotland Neck, a town of 3000 persons, to create a separate school district within a long-standing county school system would have the effect of undermining desegregation. According to Justice Stewart, " * * * the disparity in the racial composition of the Scotland Neck schools and the schools remaining in * * * the * * * County system would be 'substantial' by any standard of measurement." (At p. 490). Chief Justice Burger's brief concurring opinion noted that the facts warranted a conclusion different from that in *Emporia*. While he spoke neither of racial balance nor of unconstitutional motives, it appears that the imbalance which would have been engendered by the proposed new district confirmed his suspicion that the move was intended to avoid school integration. Is it possible in your view to decide these cases by considering only the actions of public officials apart from their intentions? If so, why do the results differ from the *Palmer* decision? Justice Stewart, who wrote for the Court in both *Emporia* and *Scotland Neck*, was among the majority in *Palmer v. Thompson*. Is he consistent in his approach to the issues in these cases? Might the fact that in both *Emporia* and *Scotland Neck*, the school districts were in the midst of desegregating explain Justice Stewart's positions in these cases?

8. In *Runyon v. McCrary*, 427 U.S. 160 (1976), the Court in a 7–2 decision ruled that a federal law, 42 U.S.C.A. § 1981, originally part of an 1866 statute, prohibits commercially-operated nonpublic schools which advertise for students from discriminating on the basis of race. 42 U.S. C.A. § 1981 states that:

"All persons within the jurisdiction of the United States shall have the same right in every State and Territory to make and enforce contracts, to sue, be parties, give evidence, and to the full and equal benefit of all laws and proceedings for the security of persons and property as is enjoyed by white citizens, and shall be subject to like punishment, pains, penalties, taxes, licenses, and exactions of every kind, and to no other."

Justice Stewart for the majority noted that the Court had held in *Jones v. Alfred H. Mayer Co.*, 392 U.S. 409 (1968), that another statute, 42 U.S.C.A. § 1982, drawn from the same section of the 1866 Act prohibited private racial discrimination in the sale or rental of real and personal property. Like § 1982, Justice Stewart stated that § 1981 is not limited to state action since the 1866 statute was based on the Thirteenth Amendment to the Constitution, not the Fourteenth. He stated that applying the statute to the schools did not interfere with protected rights of free association and privacy, or a parent's right to direct the education of children.   Justice Stewart was careful to note that the Court was not making any decision with regard to private social clubs or similar organizations, to nonpublic schools with single-sex student bodies, to sectarian schools, or to sectarian schools which may practice racial discrimination on religious grounds.   The decision, however, did have signficance for the many so-called "freedom schools" set up in the South to avoid court-ordered public school integration.*

Justices White and Rehnquist dissented.   Writing for both, Justice White asserted that 42 U.S.C.A. § 1981 was never intended to reach beyond discriminations imposed by state law and compel the making of contracts by unwilling parties.

> What is conferred by 42 U.S.C.A. § 1981 is the *right*—which was enjoyed by whites—"to make contracts" with other willing parties and to "enforce" those contracts in court.   Section 1981 would thus invalidate any state statute or court-made rule of law which would have the effect of disabling Negroes or any other class of persons from making contracts or enforcing contractual obligations or otherwise giving less weight to their obligations than is given to contractual obligations running to whites.   The statute by its terms does not require any private individual or institution to enter into a contract or perform any other act under any circumstances; and it consequently fails to supply a cause of action by respondent students against petitioner schools based on the latter's racially motivated decision not to contract with them.   (At pp. 194–195).

Justice Stevens, however, in his concurring opinion pointed out that even if *Jones v. Alfred H. Mayer* represented a significant break with the original intention of the framers of the law, the *Jones* interpretation "surely accords with the prevailing sense of justice today."   (At p. 191).   Thus he joined the majority in "the interest of stability and orderly development of the law."   (At p. 190).   Which of the two positions would you follow?

Considering that applicants will still have to pass entrance tests to the schools affected by the decision and considering that 90 percent of the nonpublic schools in the country did not practice racial discrimination prior to the decision,* how significant is *Runyon* likely to be in terms of increasing integration in the nonpublic sector?   Where does its chief significance lie?

In 1975 the Internal Revenue Service modified its procedures on tax exemptions to prohibit nonpublic educational institutions with racially discriminatory admissions policies from obtaining federal income tax exemption.   At least one court action has been started to eliminate tax exemp-

---

* Nonpublic enrollments have fallen in every part of the country in recent years except in the Southeast. In that region, it has been estimated that over 25 percent of all pupils attend a nonpublic school—far above the national average of less than 10 percent.

* The Council for American Private Education (CAPE) representing 13,500 schools enrolling 90 percent of all nonpublic school students filed a brief on the side of the black parents in *Runyon*.

tions for those nonpublic schools which have only a token black enrollment. How successful would such suits likely be? Would you support these efforts?

In 1978 the Supreme Court refused to review an appeals court ruling involving a nonpublic school which for sectarian reasons refused admission to blacks. In *Brown v. Dade Christian Schools, Inc.,* 556 F.2d 310 (5th Cir. 1977), the federal court of appeals was presented with a most difficult confrontation between two principles: the right of blacks to make contracts as supported in *Runyon* and the freedom of religion. Since both are considered fundamental, which should yield? Sitting *en banc,* the judges evidenced significant differences in resolving the issue. In his plurality opinion, Judge Hill agreed with the district court's view that the segregation policy at the Baptist school was not religiously based. He noted that it had been recently instituted, could be changed by majority vote of church members, and was not central to church doctrine. Judge Goldberg concurred in the result but asserted that some members of the church may hold such religious beliefs and argued that the views of the congregation must be considered. He thus moved beyond the issue of defining religion to balance the free exercise claim of some members of the congregation with the right of blacks to make contracts. Finding the segregation policy to be a minor part of the religion since church doctrine speaks against intermarriage, not comingling, Judge Goldberg struck the balance on the side of the right to contract. The dissenters agreed with Judge Goldberg on the religion issue in light of the broad definition given "religion" in *United States v. Seeger,* 380 U.S. 163 (1965) (See Chapter Four, p. 277ff) but would have remanded the case back to the district judge for a balancing of religious freedom against the right of blacks to make contracts.

It is clear that *Dade Christian Schools* provides little guidance to resolving disputes between religious and contractual rights since a sincere religious belief was ruled not to be at stake.[52] The decision, however, does suggest a two-step approach to resolving such a conflict: (1) is the segregative policy a central tenet of the religion and (2) does its exercise outweigh the compelling governmental interest in eliminating racial discrimination? Assuming a sincere religious belief is at stake, how would you strike the balance?

9. Recall that Chief Justice Burger in *Swann* suggested that continued court-ordered year-by-year adjustments to changed conditions after compliance in the establishment of a unitary school system is not required. In *Pasadena City Bd. of Educ. v. Spangler,* 427 U.S. 424 (1976), the Court ruled that a federal district judge had exceeded his powers in ordering that a 1970 plan constructed to eliminate schools with a majority of minority students be perpetuated in the face of population shifts. Justice Rehnquist for the majority emphasized that the Pasadena system had achieved full compliance with the judge's 1970 order and that there was no showing that post-1971 changes resulted from the actions of school officials. The changes, he maintained, appeared to be the result of random changes in residential patterns.

---

52. For a brief discussion of this interesting case, see Note, "Sectarian School Asserts Its Religious Beliefs: Have the Courts Narrowed the Constitutional Right to Free Exercise of Religion?" 32 *U.Miami L.Rev.* 709, June, 1978.

10. School desegregation involves many issues, of course, aside from desegregating the student bodies. For example, the Supreme Court has ruled that students are entitled to integrated faculties, *Rogers v. Paul,* 382 U.S. 198 (1965), and has approved federal courts' ordering compensatory programs in communications skills and other services as part of a school desegregation decree, *Milliken v. Bradley II,* 433 U.S. 267 (1977).

Considerable litigation has involved student discipline in racially tense schools. For example, in *Tillman v. Dade County School Bd.,* 327 F.Supp. 930 (S.D.Fla.1971), suspended high school students challenged the suspension of 93 students, 87 of whom were blacks. The district court agreed that "when figures speak courts listen," but rejected the complaint. The facts showed that school officials had taken photographs to identify the students and since black students had been confined to the campus while white students were kept off school grounds, blacks were more easily identified. The court concluded that the fact that more blacks were thus identified than whites "was nothing more than a fortuitous circumstance, a result of their physical location" and did not support the charge of unlawful racial discrimination. Do you agree?[53]

In *Tate v. Board of Educ.,* 453 F.2d 975 (8th Cir. 1972), the court of appeals ruled that a demonstration without material disruption except for the walkout of 29 black high school students during the playing of "Dixie" was not protected by the First/Fourteenth Amendment.

In *Larry P. v. Riles,* 343 F.Supp. 1306 (N.D.Cal.1972), to be reviewed in greater depth later in the chapter, the court upheld a racial discrimination challenge to the use of IQ tests in pupil placement.

Unfortunately, space prevents more than a cursory review of many of these issues. However, the reader should realize that extensive "second-stage" litigation has been generated after desegregation decrees are implemented. Many of these incidents, of course, never reach the courts but continue to demand considerable attention from school officials.

(2) De Facto Segregation

Two years after *Swann,* the Supreme Court confronted the first school desegregation case involving the North. School segregation in northern cities is commonplace. In 1972 over 70 percent of all black students in the North and West attended predominately black schools.[54] By contrast, largely due to the efforts by all branches of the federal government after 1964, integrated schooling had become a reality in the South ten years later. As recently as 1968, 68 percent of all black students were in total isolation in the South. But by 1974, the figure had dropped to 8.7 percent.[55]

The first northern case, *Keyes v. School Dist. No. I,* 413 U.S. 189 (1973), involved the city-wide Denver school district, which then served nearly 100,000 pupils in 119 schools. The school system had never been

---

53. For greater exploration of discipline involving black students in public schools, see Mark G. Yudof "Suspension and Expulsion of Black Students from the Public Schools: Academic Capital Punishment and the Constitution," 39 *Law & Contemp. Prob.* 374, 1975.

54. Orfield, *Must We Bus? supra,* at p. 57.

55. "Title VI of the Civil Rights Act of 1964—Ten Years Later," Office of HEW, July, 1974, at p. 3.

operated under a constitutional or statutory provision mandating or permitting segregation. But petitioners had been successful in convincing the federal district court that school officials through gerrymandering of attendance zones, assignment of teachers, use of mobile classroom units, transportation programs, and the like had engaged in deliberate racial segregation in one section of the district involving seven schools. The petitioners then sought to show that because school officials had engaged in discrimination in one portion of the district, they had a responsibility to desegregate the entire system, including the heavily segregated schools in the inner city. The Court of Appeals for the Tenth Circuit rejected this contention. Justice Brennan for the majority remanded the case to the district court to determine whether district-wide desegregation was required. In so doing, he set forth guidelines which placed considerable burden upon school officials. Assuming the absence of a systematic program of segregation which would justify a district-wide remedial plan similar to that in *Swann*, Justice Brennan maintained that the fact that discriminatory action took place in one part of a district would nevertheless justify a remedial plan for the entire district unless school officials could prove that they had not engaged in intentional segregation elsewhere and that racial concentration in schools was the result of geographic location:

> * * * we hold that a finding of intentionally segregative school board actions in a meaningful portion of a school system, as in this case, creates a presumption that other segregated schooling within the system is not adventitious. It establishes, in other words, a prima facie case of unlawful segregative design on the part of school authorities, and shifts to those authorities the burden of proving that other segregated schools within the system are not also the result of intentionally segregative actions. This is true even if it is determined that different areas of the school district should be viewed independently of each other because, even in that situation, there is high probability that where school authorities have effectuated an intentionally segregative policy in a meaningful portion of the school system, similar impermissible considerations have motivated their actions in other areas of the system. (At p. 208).

Justice Brennan emphasized that it would not be enough for school officials to rely on a logical, racially neutral explanation for their actions, such as conforming to residential patterns in parts of the city. "Their burden is to adduce proof sufficient to support a finding that segregative intent was not among the factors that motivated their action." (At p. 210). He cautioned that the Court was not deciding whether neighborhood school policy by itself would justify racial or ethnic concentrations.

> It is enough that we hold that the mere assertion of such a policy is not dispositive where, as in this case, the school authorities have been found to have practiced *de jure* segregation in a meaningful portion of the school system by techniques that indicate that the "neighborhood school" concept has not been maintained free of manipulation. (At p. 212).

Note that Justice Brennan speaks of "segregative intent." In asserting that judges can look behind actions and consider the intentions of public officials under the circumstances present in *Keyes,* his comments appear to run counter to the assertions of Justice Black in *Palmer v. Thompson,* the swimming pool closure case, and Justice Stewart in *Wright v. City of Emporia,* the case involving the formation of a new school district, Justice Powell in his concurring and dissenting opinion picked up on this theme, pointing out that the Court appeared to be applying different standards to northern and southern school segregation. In the South the history of *de jure* segregation made the illegality of school board actions easy to discern; but in the North, the absence of pervasive segregation laws and policies made this determination much harder. To fit the North into the *de jure* model, Justice Powell claimed the majority resorted to looking for "segregative intent." This is made particularly difficult, he said, because the Court has not made clear "what suffices to establish the requisite 'segregative intent' for initial constitutional violation." (At p. 233).

To avoid the appearance of applying two different standards and in the process having to deal with "slippery" issues such as intent or purpose "especially when related to hundreds of decisions made by school authorities under varying conditions over many years," Justice Powell urged that the *de jure/de facto* approach be abandoned in favor of a uniform rule to be applied nationally.

> I would hold, quite simply, that where segregated public schools exist within a school district to a substantial degree, there is a *prima facie* case that the duly constituted public authorities * * * are sufficiently responsible to warrant imposing upon them a nationally applicable burden to demonstrate they nevertheless are operating a genuinely integrated school system. (At p. 224).

The right to be enforced, said Justice Powell, is the right under the Equal Protection Clause to attend integrated schools. But this right does not go so far as to require racial balance in schools. If school officials can show that appropriate steps have been taken within a neighborhood school concept to integrate faculties, to assure equal facilities, to drawing up attendance zones and opening/closing schools with integration in mind, then predominately black or white schools legally may continue to exist, since the socio-economic factors behind the existence of such schools are beyond the control of school officials. Justice Powell strongly endorsed the neighborhood school system and also spoke out strongly against forced busing, labelling busing "the single most disruptive element in education today * * *." (At p. 253).

Justice Rehnquist in his dissent maintained that the *Brown* decision was intended only to end the practice of dual school systems in the South. The "affirmative duty to integrate" of *Green v. County School Bd.,* not envisioned in *Brown,* was meant to apply only to pervasive school segregation in the South. Justice Rehnquist dissented from its application to the North. He also decried the majority's adding "to this potpourri a confusing enunciation of evidentiary rules in order to make it more likely that the trial court will on remand reach the result which the Court apparently wants it to reach." (At p. 265). On remand, the district court concluded that the evidence indicated that the Denver district was in fact a dual system. Writing for the court, Judge Doyle stated that "Under the (Supreme) Court's definition it cannot be argued that within a unified school district such as that at bar there can exist conscious and knowing segregation in one area and innocent segregation in another." *Keyes v. School Dist. No. I*, 368 F.Supp. 207, at p. 210 (D.C.Colo.1973). The Court of Appeals for the Tenth Circuit affirmed the decision in 1975. 521 F.2d 465.

Keyes is an interesting decision for several reasons. Its discussion of "affirmative action-to-integrate" in a northern context foreshadows the benchmark case of *Regents of the Univ. of California v. Bakke* involving so-called "reverse discrimination" in medical school admission decision making. This case forms the basis for the next section. *Keyes* also is important because it includes Mexican-Americans with blacks as a discriminated class in the educational setting. The Denver school system at the time was 20 percent Mexican-American and only 14 percent black. Citing its prior decision in *Hernandez v. Texas,* 347 U.S. 475 (1954), that Mexican-Americans constitute an identifiable class for Fourteenth Amendment suspect classification purposes, Justice Brennan also referred to a number of studies describing the history of discrimination against Mexican-Americans. Some commentators, however, have questioned the inclusion of Mexican-Americans, citing the historical context of the Fourteenth Amendment.

Finally, the case raises the interesting question as to what racial mix constitutes a segregated school. Justice Brennan noted that the lower court concluded that a concentration of 70 to 75 percent of either blacks or Mexican-Americans places schools in the inferior, hence segregated, category. But Justice Brennan noted that there are a number of factors which must be taken into consideration aside from the racial makeup of the student body in making this determination. Does a heavy preponderance of an identifiable racial minority *ipso facto* classify a school as segregated? As inferior? Educational authorities, particularly those favoring community control of schools, are in disagreement as to the answers. In part, the dilemma goes back to how "education" is defined: the acquisition of facts and skills or the opportunity to socialize with a diverse group of peers.

One issue which *Keyes* did not resolve is the nature and extent of remedies in northern desegregation cases. While Justices Brennan and Powell differed in their approach to determining illegal segregation in the North, a more substantial difference related to remedial action. Justice Powell's strong endorsement of the neighborhood school concept and his disapproval of forced busing suggest a policy of judicial restraint in approving court-mandated remedies.

The remedy issue came squarely before the Court in the highly significant *Milliken v. Bradley* case excerpted below. In *Milliken* the district court found that Detroit school officials had acted to maintain a segregated school system in the city of Detroit through the drawing of attendance zones, the transportation of black students, and the building of schools. The court also found that the state of Michigan had acted to reinforce the segregation by providing less transportation money for Detroit schools, by delaying a school board plan for developing high quality "magnet schools" in segregated areas, and by generally concurring in the past actions of the Detroit school board. The district court went so far as to suggest a conspiracy by federal, state, and local officials in reinforcing segregation in the Detroit schools. At the time, the Detroit system consisted of 319 schools with an enrollment of 276,000 students. Surrounding the Detroit system were 85 suburban districts with an enrollment of some 750,000 students.

The district court found that if it accepted any desegregation proposal limited only to the Detroit district, the result would be a virtual all-black system (racial balance in the Detroit system would produce schools 64 percent black). Noting that such a remedy would not achieve desegregation and would further stimulate white flight to the suburbs, the district court turned toward an interdistrict, metropolitan remedy involving the 85 suburban school districts. A panel established by the court proposed that 53 of these districts be joined with Detroit to form 15 clusters, each containing part of the Detroit system and 2 or more suburban districts. The district court approved the plan and ordered Detroit to secure at least 295 buses of effectuate desegregation on this basis, with the cost to be charged to the state. The Court of Appeals for the Sixth Circuit substantially affirmed the district court decision. As Chief Justice Burger's decision makes clear, the Supreme Court refused to accept the interdistrict remedial plan.

MILLIKEN v. BRADLEY

Supreme Court of the United States, 1974.
418 U.S. 717, 94 S.Ct. 3112, 41 L.Ed.2d 1069.

Mr. Chief Justice BURGER delivered the opinion of the Court.

* * *

Viewing the record as a whole, it seems clear that the District Court and the Court of Appeals shifted the primary focus from a Detroit remedy to the metropolitan area only because of their conclusion that total desegregation of Detroit would not produce the racial balance which they perceived as desirable. Both courts proceeded on an assumption that the Detroit schools could not be truly desegregated—in their view of what constituted desegregation—unless the racial composition of the student body of each school substantially reflected the racial composition of the population of the metropolitan area as a whole. The metropolitan area was then defined as Detroit plus 53 of the outlying school districts. * * * The clear import of * * * language from *Swann* is that desegregation, in the sense of dismantling a dual school system, does not require any particular racial balance in each "school, grade or classroom." [19]

19. Disparity in the racial composition of pupils within a single district may well constitute a "signal" to a district court at the outset, leading to inquiry into the causes accounting for a pronounced racial identifiability of schools within one school system. * * * However, the use of significant racial imbalance in schools within an autonomous school district as a signal which operates simply to shift the burden of proof, is a very different matter from equating racial imbalance with a constitutional violation calling for a remedy. * * *

Here the District Court's approach to what constituted "actual desegregation" raises the fundamental question, not presented in *Swann*, as to the circumstances in which a federal court may order desegregation relief that embraces more than a single school district. The court's analytical starting point was its conclusion that school district lines are no more than arbitrary lines on a map drawn "for political convenience." Boundary lines may be bridged where there has been a constitutional violation calling for interdistrict relief, but the notion that school district lines may be casually ignored or treated as a mere administrative convenience is contrary to the history of public education in our country. No single tradition in public education is more deeply rooted than local control over the operation of schools; local autonomy has long been thought essential both to the maintenance of community concern and support for public schools and to quality of the educational process. * * *

The Michigan educational structure involved in this case, in common with most States, provides for a large measure of local control, and a review of the scope and character of these local powers indicates the extent to which the interdistrict remedy approved by the two courts could disrupt and alter the structure of public education in Michigan. The metropolitan remedy would require, in effect, consolidation of 54 independent school districts historically administered as separate units into a vast new super school district. Entirely apart from the logistical and other serious problems attending large-scale transportation of students, the consolidation would give rise to an array of other problems in financing and operating this new school system. Some of the more obvious questions would be: What would be the status and authority of the present popularly elected school boards? Would the children of Detroit be within the jurisdiction and operating control of a school board elected by the parents and residents of other districts? What board or boards would levy taxes for school operations in these 54 districts constituting the consolidated metropolitan area? What provisions could be made for assuring substantial equality in tax levies among the 54 districts, if this were deemed requisite? What provisions would be made for financing? Would the validity of long-term bonds be jeopardized unless approved by all of the component districts as well as the State? What body would determine that portion of the curricula now left to the discretion of local school boards? Who would establish attendance zones, purchase school equipment, locate and construct new schools, and indeed attend to all the myriad day-to-day decisions that are necessary to school operations affecting potentially more than three-quarters of a million pupils?

It may be suggested that all of these vital operational problems are yet to be resolved by the District Court, * * *. But it is obvious from the scope of the interdistrict remedy itself that absent a complete restructuring of the laws of Michigan relating to school districts the District Court will become first, a *de facto* "legislative authority" to resolve these complex questions, and then the "school superintendent" for the entire area. This is a task which few, if any, judges are qualified to perform and one which would deprive the people of control of schools through their elected representatives.

* * *

* * * Before the boundaries of separate and autonomous school districts may be set aside by consolidating the separate units for remedial purposes or by imposing a cross-district remedy, it must first be shown that there has been a constitutional violation within one district that produces a significant segregative effect in another district. Specifically, it must be shown that racially discriminatory acts of the state or local school districts, or

of a single school district have been a substantial cause of interdistrict segregation. Thus an interdistrict remedy might be in order where the racially discriminatory acts of one or more school districts caused racial segregation in an adjacent district, or where district lines have been deliberately drawn on the basis of race. In such circumstances an interdistrict remedy would be appropriate to eliminate the interdistrict segregation directly caused by the constitutional violation. * * *

The record before us, * * * contains evidence of *de jure* segregated conditions only in the Detroit schools; indeed, that was the theory on which the litigation was initially based and on which the District Court took evidence. With no showing of significant violation by the 53 outlying school districts and no evidence of any interdistrict violation or effect, the court went beyond the original theory of the case as framed by the pleadings and mandated a metropolitan area remedy. To approve the remedy ordered by the court would impose on the outlying districts, not shown to have committed any constitutional violation, a wholly impermissible remedy based on a standard not hinted at in *Brown I* and *II* or any holding of this Court.

In dissent, Mr. Justice WHITE and Mr. Justice MARSHALL undertake to demonstrate that agencies having statewide authority participated in maintaining the dual school system found to exist in Detroit. They are apparently of the view that once such participation is shown, the District Court should have a relatively free hand to reconstruct school districts outside of Detroit in fashioning relief. Our assumption, *arguendo*, that state agencies did participate in the maintenance of the Detroit system, should make it clear that it is not on this point that we part company. The difference

between us arises instead from established doctrine laid down by our cases. *Brown,* * * *, *Green,* * * *, *Swann,* * * *, *Scotland Neck,* * * * and *Emporia,* * * *, each addressed the issue of constitutional wrong in terms of an established geographic and administrative school system populated by both Negro and white children. In such a context, terms such as "unitary" and "dual" system, and "racially identifiable schools," have meaning, and the necessary federal authority to remedy the constitutional wrong is firmly established. But the remedy is necessarily designed, as all remedies are, to restore the victims of discriminatory conduct to the position they would have occupied in the absence of such conduct. Disparate treatment of white and Negro students occurred within the Detroit school system, and not elsewhere, and on this record the remedy must be limited to that system.

The constitutional right of the Negro respondents residing in Detroit is to attend a unitary school system in that district. Unless petitioners drew the district lines in a discriminatory fashion, or arranged for white students residing in the Detroit district to attend schools in Oakland and Macomb Counties, they were under no constitutional duty to make provisions for Negro students to do so. The view of the dissenters, that the existence of a dual system in *Detroit* can be made the basis for a decree requiring cross-district transportation of pupils, cannot be supported on the grounds that it represents merely the devising of a suitably flexible remedy for the violation of rights already established by our prior decisions. It can be supported only by drastic expansion of the constitutional right itself, an expansion without any support in either constitutional principle or precedent.[22]

22.   The suggestion in the dissent of Mr. Justice MARSHALL that schools which have a majority of Negro students are not "desegregated," whatever the racial makeup of the school district's population and how-

ever neutrally the district lines have been drawn and administered, finds no support in our prior cases. * * *
The dissents also seem to attach importance to the metropolitan character of Detroit

We recognize that the six-volume record presently under consideration contains language and some specific incidental findings thought by the District Court to afford a basis for interdistrict relief. However, these comparatively isolated findings and brief comments concern only one possible interdistrict violation and are found in the context of a proceeding that, as the District Court conceded, included no proof of segregation practiced by any of the 85 suburban school districts surrounding Detroit.

*   *   *

*   *   *

We conclude that the relief ordered by the District Court and affirmed by the Court of Appeals was based upon an erroneous standard and was unsupported by record evidence that acts of the outlying districts effected the discrimination found to exist in the schools of Detroit. Accordingly, the judgment of the Court of Appeals is reversed and the case is remanded for further proceedings consistent with this opinion leading to prompt formulation of a decree directed to eliminating the segregation found to exist in Detroit city schools, a remedy which has been delayed since 1970.

Reversed and remanded.

Mr. Justice STEWART, concurring.

*   *   *

Mr. Justice DOUGLAS, dissenting.

*   *   *

Mr. Justice WHITE, with whom Mr. Justice DOUGLAS, Mr. Justice BRENNAN, and Mr. Justice MARSHALL join, dissenting.

*   *   *

Regretfully, and for several reasons, I can join neither the Court's judgment nor its opinion. The core of my disagreement is that deliberate acts of segregation

and their consequences will go unremedied, not because a remedy would be infeasible or unreasonable in terms of the usual criteria governing school desegregation cases, but because an effective remedy would cause what the Court considers to be undue administrative inconvenience to the State. The result is that the State of Michigan, the entity at which the Fourteenth Amendment is directed, has successfully insulated itself from its duty to provide effective desegregation remedies by vesting sufficient power over its public schools in its local school districts. If this is the case in Michigan, it will be the case in most States.

*   *   *

Despite the fact that a metropolitan remedy, if the findings of the District Court accepted by the Court of Appeals are to be credited, would more effectively desegregate the Detroit schools, would prevent resegregation, and would be easier and more feasible from many standpoints, the Court fashions out of whole cloth an arbitrary rule that remedies for constitutional violations occurring in a single Michigan school district must stop at the school district line. Apparently, no matter how much less burdensome or more effective and efficient in many respects, such as transportation, the metropolitan plan might be, the school district line may not be crossed. Otherwise, it seems, there would be too much disruption of the Michigan scheme for managing its educational system, too much confusion, and too much administrative burden.

*   *   *

I am surprised that the Court, sitting at this distance from the State of Michigan, claims better insight than the Court of Appeals and the District Court as to whether an interdistrict remedy for equal protection violations practiced by the

---

and neighboring school districts. But the constitutional principles applicable in school desegregation cases cannot vary in accordance with the size or population dis-

persal of the particular city, county, or school district as compared with neighboring areas.

State of Michigan would involve undue difficulties for the State in the management of its public schools. * * *

I am even more mystified as to how the Court can ignore the legal reality that the constitutional violations, even if occurring locally, were committed by governmental entities for which the State is responsible and that it is the State that must respond to the command of the Fourteenth Amendment. * * *

* * *

The Court draws the remedial line at the Detroit school district boundary, even though the Fourteenth Amendment is addressed to the State and even though the *State* denies equal protection of the laws when its public agencies, acting in its behalf, invidiously discriminate. * * * I cannot understand, nor does the majority satisfactorily explain, why a federal court may not order an appropriate interdistrict remedy, if this is necessary or more effective to accomplish this constitutionally mandated task. * * * In this case, both the right and the State's Fourteenth Amendment violation have concededly been fully established, and there is no acceptable reason for permitting the party responsible for the constitutional violation to contain the remedial powers of the federal court within administrative boundaries over which the transgressor itself has plenary power.

The unwavering decisions of this Court over the past 20 years support the assumption of the Court of Appeals that the District Court's remedial power does not cease at the school district line. * * *

* * *

* * * There are indeed limitations on the equity powers of the federal judiciary, * * *. Until now the Court has * * * looked to practical considerations in effectuating a desegregation decree, such as excessive distance, transportation time, and hazards to the safety of the schoolchildren involved in a proposed plan. That these broad principles have developed in the context of dual school systems compelled or authorized by state statute * * * does not lessen their current applicability to dual systems found to exist in other contexts, like that in Detroit, where intentional school segregation does not stem from the compulsion of state law, but from deliberate individual actions of local and state school authorities directed at a particular school system. The majority properly does not suggest that the duty to eradicate completely the resulting dual system in the latter context is any less than in the former. But its reason for incapacitating the remedial authority of the federal judiciary in the presence of school district perimeters in the latter context is not readily apparent.

The result reached by the Court certainly cannot be supported by the theory that the configuration of local governmental units is immune from alteration when necessary to redress constitutional violations. In addition to the well-established principles already noted, the Court has elsewhere required the public bodies of a State to restructure the State's political subdivisions to remedy infringements of the constitutional rights of certain members of its populace, notably in the reapportionment cases. * * *

Nor does the Court's conclusion follow from the talismanic invocation of the desirability of local control over education. * * * If restructuring is required to meet constitutional requirements, local authority may simply be redefined in terms of whatever configuration is adopted, with the parents of the children attending schools in the newly demarcated district or attendance zone continuing their participation in the policy management of the schools with which they are concerned most directly. The majority's suggestion that judges should not attempt to grapple with the administrative problems attendant on a reorganization of school attendance patterns is wholly without foundation. It is precisely this sort of task which the district courts have been properly exercising to vindicate the constitutional rights of Negro students since *Brown I* * * *.

* * *

* * * Confining the remedy to the boundaries of the Detroit district is quite unrelated either to the goal of achieving maximum desegregation or to those intensely practical considerations, such as the extent and expense of transportation, that have imposed limits on remedies in cases such as this. The Court's remedy, in the end, is essentially arbitrary and will leave serious violations of the Constitution substantially unremedied.

* * *

Mr. Justice MARSHALL, with whom Mr. Justice DOUGLAS, Mr. Justice BRENNAN, and Mr. Justice WHITE join, dissenting.

* * *

The great irony of the Court's opinion and, in my view, its most serious analytical flaw may be gleaned from its concluding sentence, in which the Court remands for "prompt formulation of a decree directed to eliminating the segregation found to exist in Detroit city schools, a remedy which has been delayed since 1970." The majority, however, seems to have forgotten the District Court's explicit finding that a Detroit-only decree, the only remedy permitted under today's decision, "would not accomplish desegregation."

Nowhere in the Court's opinion does the majority confront, let alone respond to, the District Court's conclusion that a remedy limited to the city of Detroit would not effectively desegregate the Detroit city schools. * * *

* * *

The Court * * * misstates the basis for the District Court's order by suggesting that since the only segregation proved at trial was within the Detroit school system, any relief which extended beyond the jurisdiction of the Detroit Board of Education would be inappropriate because it would impose a remedy on outlying districts "not shown to have committed any constitutional violation." The essential foundation of interdistrict relief in this case was not to correct conditions within outlying districts * * *. Instead, interdistrict relief was seen as a necessary part of any meaningful effort by the State of Michigan to remedy the state-caused segregation within the city of Detroit.

Rather than consider the propriety of interdistrict relief * * * the Court has conjured up a largely fictional account of what the District Court was attempting to accomplish. With all due respect, the Court, in my view, does a great disservice to the District Judge who labored long and hard with this complex litigation by accusing him of changing horses in midstream and shifting the focus of this case from the pursuit of a remedy for the condition of segregation within the Detroit school system to some unprincipled attempt to impose his own philosophy of racial balance on the entire Detroit metropolitan area. * * *

* * *

We held in *Swann* * * * that where *de jure* segregation is shown, school authorities must make "every effort to achieve the greatest possible degree of actual desegregation." * * * If these words have any meaning at all, surely it is that school authorities must, to the extent possible, take all practicable steps to ensure that Negro and white children in fact go to school together. This is, in the final analysis, what desegregation of the public schools is all about.

* * *

Under a Detroit-only decree, Detroit's schools will clearly remain racially identifiable in comparison with neighboring schools in the metropolitan community.

Schools with 65% and more Negro students will stand in sharp and obvious contrast to schools in neighboring districts with less than 2% Negro enrollment. Negro students will continue to perceive their schools as segregated educational facilities and this perception will only be increased when whites react to a Detroit-only decree by fleeing to the suburbs to avoid integration. School district lines, however innocently drawn, will surely be perceived as fences to separate the races when, under a Detroit-only decree, white parents withdraw their children from the Detroit city schools and move to the suburbs in order to continue them in all-white schools. The message of this action will not escape the Negro children in the city of Detroit. It will be of scant significance to Negro children who have for years been confined by *de jure* acts of segregation to a growing core of all-Negro schools surrounded by a ring of all-white schools that the new dividing line between the races is the school district boundary.

Nor can it be said that the State is free from any responsibility for the disparity between the racial makeup of Detroit and its surrounding suburbs. The State's creation, through *de jure* acts of segregation, of a growing core of all-Negro schools inevitably acted as a magnet to attract Negroes to the areas served by such schools and to deter them from settling either in other areas of the city or in the suburbs. By the same token, the growing core of all-Negro schools inevitably helped drive whites to other areas of the city or to the suburbs. * * *

The State must also bear part of the blame for the white flight to the suburbs which would be forthcoming from a Detroit-only decree and would render such a remedy ineffective. Having created a system where whites and Negroes were intentionally kept apart so that they could not become accustomed to learning together, the State is responsible for the fact that many whites will react to the dismantling of that segregated system by attempting to flee to the suburbs. Indeed, by limiting the District Court to a Detroit-only remedy and allowing that flight to the suburbs to succeed, the Court today allows the State to profit from its own wrong and to perpetuate for years to come the separation of the races it achieved in the past by purposeful state action.

The majority asserts, however, that involvement of outlying districts would do violence to the accepted principle that "the nature of the violation determines the scope of the remedy." Not only is the majority's attempt to find in this single phrase the answer to the complex and difficult questions presented in this case hopelessly simplistic, but more important, the Court reads these words in a manner which perverts their obvious meaning. The nature of a violation determines the scope of the remedy simply because the function of any remedy is to cure the violation to which it is addressed. In school segregation cases, as in other equitable causes, a remedy which effectively cures the violation is what is required. * * * To read this principle as barring a district court from imposing the only effective remedy for past segregation and remitting the court to a patently ineffective alternative is, in my view, to turn a simple commonsense rule into a cruel and meaningless paradox. * * *

Nor should it be of any significance that the suburban school districts were not shown to have themselves taken any direct action to promote segregation of the races. Given the State's broad powers over local school districts, it was well within the State's powers to require those districts surrounding the Detroit school district to participate in a metropolitan remedy. * * *

* * *

Desegregation is not and was never expected to be an easy task. Racial attitudes ingrained in our Nation's childhood and adolescence are not quickly thrown aside in its middle years. But just as the inconvenience of some cannot be allowed to stand in the way of the rights of others, so public opposition, no matter how strident, cannot be permitted to divert this Court from the enforcement of the constitutional principles at issue in this case. Today's holding, I fear, is more a reflection of a perceived public mood that we have gone far enough in enforcing the Constitution's guarantee of equal justice than it is the product of neutral principles of law. In the short run, it may seem to be the easier course to allow our great metropolitan areas to be divided up each into two cities—one white, the other black—but it is a course, I predict, our people will ultimately regret. I dissent.

NOTES AND QUESTIONS

1. The *Milliken* decision is particularly effective in pointing out the horns of the remedial dilemma. On the one hand, desegregation remedies are judged constitutional only where those school districts involved have practiced segregation or suffered the effects of it. On the other hand, confinement of the remedies to only those districts may result in little substantial change in the racial composition of the schools. The right of students to attend integrated schools is thus frustrated. But is this the constitutional right? Note that Chief Justice Burger in a footnote rejects Justice Marshall's assertion that schools with a majority of blacks are not desegregated. How would Chief Judge Burger state the constitutional right of the Detroit students?

Justice White in his dissent places a good deal of emphasis on the role of the state in the Detroit situation. Since the state had concurred in the efforts to keep the Detroit schools segregated and since the Fourteenth Amendment speaks in terms of states, Justice White concludes that an interdistrict remedy is clearly warranted. Do you agree? What about the value of neighborhood schools? Or is the importance of the neighborhood school policy overrated? One source notes that fewer than half of all children in elementary school in the nation and about a quarter of high school students attend a school within a mile of the home.[56] A recent study of state statutory power over local schools by the National Lawyers' Committee for Civil Rights Under Law revealed that, while there is considerable variation, the typical state has extensive state guidelines with few options for the local school. In reviewing the implications of the data, Professor Frederick M. Wirt concludes that the notion of local control "does not portray the reality of modern public education."[57] What are the implications of this information for the *Milliken* decision? Should the Court hesitate to embrace the neighborhood school concept before reviewing social science research? Or does the Court mean something else in subscribing to the neighborhood school concept?

2. Justice Marshall predicted that the *Milliken* decision would stimulate whites to flee the Detroit schools for the suburbs. Another commentator has suggested that in other cities where enclaves of whites remain,

---

56. Orfield, *Must We Bus? supra*, at p. 129.

57. Frederick M. Wirt, "What State Laws Say About Local Control," 59 *Phi Delta Kappan* 517, April, 1978, at p. 520.

civil rights groups will be reluctant to bring suits for fear of driving out the few remaining whites.[58] White flight, of course, is not solely a result of court-ordered school desegregation. Population changes in the nation's largest cities show that the movement of whites to the suburbs has occurred for many years before school desegregation became a major issue. For example, in the 1960s Detroit's white population dropped 29 percent while its black population grew 37 percent. By 1970 blacks comprised 44 percent of the population. Nevertheless, school desegregation may be a new stimulus to changing demographic patterns. The complexity of the subject, however, has made it difficult for social science researchers to arrive at a consensus regarding the extent of its influence.

University of Chicago Professor James S. Coleman presented findings in 1975 that tended to show a greater loss of whites occurs when central city schools are desegregated, particularly if the schools have large percentages of blacks and the surrounding suburbs are mostly white.[59] The loss, however, is limited largely to the first year of desegregation and is relatively small, increasing white exodus 5 to 10 percent over a 10 year period. According to Coleman, desegregation of central city schools may consequently result in more actual segregation *between* school districts, just as Justice Marshall feared in *Milliken.*

Coleman's study was subsequently severely criticized by a variety of researchers.[60] This extensive critique coupled with the inability of other researchers to replicate Coleman's original study has undermined much of the significance of the study. More recent studies have pointed out the complexity of the factors that relate to family movement from one residential area to another and have suggested that generalizations based on available research are unwarranted.[61]

3.   If white flight coupled with other socio-economic factors does result in the re-segregation of school districts like Detroit, is a metropolitan approach as suggested by the dissenters in *Milliken* the only answer? James Coleman admitted that his research on white flight did point to metropolitanism as one solution. However, Coleman rejected this option because it involved extensive busing and denied parents and children the option of attending neighborhood schools. Instead, he suggested the courts concern themselves with segregated residential housing.

Obviously, housing does influence school-going patterns. In 1976 the Supreme Court ruled unanimously in *Hills v. Gautreaux,* 425 U.S. 284 (1976), that a metropolitan plan to remedy housing discrimination could be instituted in Chicago. Justice Stewart for the Court distinguished *Milliken* by noting that the U. S. Department of Housing and Urban Develop-

---

58.   Cox, *supra*, at p. 83.

59.   James S. Coleman, Sara D. Kelly, and John Moore *Trends in School Segregation,* 1968–73 (Washington, D. C.: Urban Institute, 1975). A shorter description of the research findings is contained in J. S. Coleman "Racial Segregation in the Schools: New Research with New Policy Implications" 57 *Phi Delta Kappan* 75, October, 1975.

60.   For a summary of much of the criticism, see Robert L. Green and Thomas F. Pettigrew "Urban Desegregation and White Flight: A Response to Coleman," 57 *Phi Delta Kappan* 399, February, 1976.

61.   See, for example, Robert G. Wegmann "White Flight and School Resegregation: Some Hypotheses," 58 *Phi Delta Kappan* 389, January, 1977.

ment (HUD), unlike the Detroit suburban school districts, had violated constitutional and statutory prohibitions against racial discrimination in selecting housing sites in the Chicago housing market. The market, by HUD's own regulations, was not confined just to Chicago city limits. Nor would the metropolitan remedy undermine local government in the same manner as a metropolitan school desegregation plan in Detroit.

> In contrast to the desegregation order in (*Milliken*), a metropolitan relief order directed to HUD would not consolidate or in any way restructure local government units. The remedial decree would neither force suburban governments to submit public housing proposals to HUD nor displace the rights and powers accorded local government entities under federal or state housing statutes or existing land-use laws. (At pp. 305–306).

The significance of this case for education appears limited, given the distinguishing features of the HUD operation and the fact that local governments must consent to HUD involvement in their housing markets. But *Gautreaux* does suggest that federal influence may be necessary to effectuate metropolitan remedies. Would you favor a federal law which forced suburban communities to accept low income housing? Would such an approach to desegregation be more likely to work than court-mandated school desegregation? Would further federal action be required, such as providing jobs and social services for low-income families? What would be the major objections to this kind of governmental action?

4.   Note that *Milliken* appears to have no impact on remedial action *within* single districts to eliminate *de jure* school segregation. But note also that the Chief Justice suggests judicial remedies should be limited to what will "restore the victims of discriminatory conduct to the position they would have occupied in the absence of such conduct." Since any number of factors could have contributed to segregation in a single district, how can the degree of school board involvement be ascertained? Should the courts try to tailor the remedies to the degree of school board causation? Or, given the pervasive racial discrimination which has characterized much of American life, should the courts through their remedial powers seek to foster an integrated environment where, in the words of Justice Marshall, "Negro and white children in fact go to school together"? [62]

Clearly, *Milliken* raises serious questions about the role of the courts in the operation of the nation's schooling system and society in general. Harvard Law Professor Archibald Cox offers this commentary:

> It is plain that in undertaking to wipe out the consequences of past violations of the Fourteenth Amendment in public school education, the federal courts have taken on altogether novel and overwhelming tasks in the name of "constitutional adjudication" that subject the institution to strains never before experienced.

62.   For a discussion of this complex issue in relation to the *Keyes-Milliken-Gautreaux-Brinkman* decisions, see Stephen B. Kanner, "From Denver to Dayton: The Development of a Theory of Equal Protection Remedies," 72 *Northwestern L.Rev.* 382, July-August, 1977.

One novel aspect is the affirmative character of the remedies judicially prescribed. Second, the necessary components of any programme of integrated education in a large city appear to commit the courts to constant executive or administrative supervision of the organization, employment practices, curriculum, and extra-curricular activities * * *. Third, desegregation decrees have all the qualities of social legislation. They pertain to the future. They are mandatory, they govern millions of people. They re-order people's lives in a way that benefits some and disappoints others in order to achieve social objectives.[63]

Should courts be activist in mandating integration in education? Are they the only hope for racial minorities? What are the dangers of such an activist role? As Professor Cox points out:

The courts cannot possibly go it alone. At the very minimum the community's professional educators must co-operate. Even that will hardly do if the political community withholds its support and the people are recalcitrant. The danger is not inconsiderable because these quasi-legislative decrees cannot be said, like true legislation, to have the legitimacy which flows from the processes of democratic self-government.[64]

5. If you were the district court judge faced with Chief Justice Burger's call for a "prompt formulation of a decree directed to eliminating the segregation found to exist in Detroit city schools, a remedy which has been delayed since 1970," how would you proceed?

In the early summer of 1977, The Supreme Court was again confronted with the Detroit desegregation case, *Milliken v. Bradley*, 433 U.S. 267 (*Milliken II*). In an unanimous ruling, the Court upheld the district court's order requiring Detroit school officials to provide compensatory and remedial educational programs for schoolchildren and requiring the state to bear part of the costs. Specifically ordered in this case had been a remedial reading and communications skills program, in-service training of teachers, a new nondiscriminatory testing program, and expanded counseling and career guidance services. Writing again for the majority, Chief Justice Burger affirmed that federal courts have sufficient equitable power to remedy not only unconstitutional assignment of pupils in a previously segregated system but also "other inequalities built into a dual system founded on racial discrimination." (At p. 283). The Chief Justice noted:

Children who have been thus educationally and culturally set apart from the larger community will inevitably acquire habits of speech, conduct, and attitudes reflecting their cultural isolation. They are likely to acquire speech habits, for example, which vary from the environment in which they must ultimately function and compete, if they are to enter and be a part of that community. This is not peculiar to race; in this setting, it can affect any children who, as a group, are isolated by force of law from the mainstream.

63. Cox, *supra*, at pp. 86–87.   64. *Id.*, at p. 88.

Pupil assignment alone does not automatically remedy the impact of previous, unlawful educational isolation; the consequences linger and can be dealt with only by independent measures. (At p. 287).

To what extent do you believe the upholding of these remedial programs constitutes a sufficient remedy for previous *de jure* segregation in Detroit? Are they likely to be more or less effective than the original district court plan involving the joining of the 53 largely white suburban school districts with the Detroit district? Interestingly, by the time *Milliken II* reached the Supreme Court, the percentage of black students in the Detroit system had increased to 71.5 percent compared with 64 percent in 1974.

On the same day *Milliken II* was decided, the Court delivered another unanimous decision (Justice Marshall did not participate) involving desegregation plans in Dayton, Ohio. *Dayton Bd. of Educ. v. Brinkman*, 433 U.S. 406 (1977). While specifically reaffirming *Keyes,* the Court rejected the extensive Dayton system-wide busing plan ordered by the district court at the behest of the Court of Appeals for the Sixth Circuit as "entirely out of proportion to the constitutional violations found by the District Court * * *." (At p. 418). But the rejection was based primarily on the confusing and ambiguous record in the case and on the tangled involvement of the district court and court of appeals. Speaking for the Court, Justice Rehnquist remanded the case to the district court for more specific findings and, if necessary, the taking of additional evidence.

Dayton is important because it reaffirms that the remedy must be tailored to the unconstitutional acts and that to impose a system-wide remedy such as cross-town busing, there must be a clear factual record demonstrating violations. Justice Rehnquist spelled out what the Justices had in mind in these terms:

> The duty of both the District Court and the Court of Appeals in a case such as this, where mandatory segregation by law of the races in the schools has long since ceased, is to first determine whether there was any action in the conduct of the business of the school board which was intended to, and did in fact, discriminate against minority pupils, teachers, or staff. * * * If such violations are found, the District Court in the first instance, subject to review by the Court of Appeals, must determine how much incremental segregative effect these violations had on the racial distribution of the Dayton school population as presently constituted, when that distribution is compared to what it would have been in the absence of such constitutional violations. The remedy must be designed to redress that difference, and only if there has been a systemwide impact may there be a systemwide remedy. (At p. 420).

Some civil rights groups had feared the Court might use the *Dayton* case to strike down system-wide busing under any circumstances or overrule earlier cases such as *Swann* and *Keyes*. This did not happen.

Nevertheless, the "incremental segregative effect" requirement posed heavy burdens on those challenging racial segregation in schools and served notice in unmistakable terms that the Court would not allow the federal judiciary unfettered discretion in reconstituting the nation's school districts in the interest of racial integration. Shortly after the *Dayton* decision, the Court remanded cases involving desegregation in Omaha and Milwaukee on grounds similar to *Dayton*.

Figure 7–2 below will assist the reader to keep the major Supreme Court school desegregation decisions from 1954 to 1978 in perspective.

Figure 7–2:

Major School Desegregation Decisions, 1954–1978

Supreme Court Cases	Decision	Significance
Brown v. Board of Educ., 1954 (Brown I)	Public educational facilities which are racially segregated are inherently discriminatory even if equal.	Overruled the "separate but equal" doctrine of Plessy v. Ferguson, 1896, and began the movement to end de jure segregation in the public sector.
Brown v. Board of Educ., 1955 (Brown II)	Remanded Brown I cases to lower federal courts, which were charged with fashioning remedies "with all deliberate speed."	Removed the Supreme Court from direct involvement with fashioning remedies.
Griffin v. Prince Edward Cty., 1964	Ordered public schools which had been closed to avoid desegregation to be reopened.	Beginning of increased Supreme Court involvement in implementing its Brown I mandate.
Green v. County School Bd., 1968	Outlawed freedom of choice plans which do not result in integrated schools.	Demands more than a color-blind approach in areas of previous de jure segregation in the interest of establishing unitary school systems in which discrimination is eliminated "root and branch."
Swann v. Charlotte-Mecklenburg Board of Educ., 1971	Approved a variety of court-ordered remedies including cross-town busing to achieve school integration.	High tide of Supreme Court support for remedies designed to achieve integration in former de jure segregated school systems.
Wright v. Emporia, 1972	5–4 decision enjoining the creation of a new school district out of a larger one.	Emphasized that the effect, not the intent behind it, would be to frustrate integration. Pattern of unanimous school desegregation rulings ends.
Keyes v. School District No. I, 1973	Burden of proof placed on school officials to show that intentional discrimination in one section of a school district has not been repeated elsewhere in the district.	First northern desegregation case. Majority now speaks in terms of "segregative intent." Justice Powell suggests de facto/de jure distinction be abandoned.
Milliken v. Bradley, 1974 (Milliken I)	5–4 decision limiting remedies to the school district(s) where de jure segregation previously occurred.	Limits court efforts to eliminate one-race school systems in the North and West.
Runyan v. McCrary, 1976	Used a 1866 civil rights law to prohibit racial discrimination by most nonpublic schools.	Dampened efforts to start "white academies" but raised questions about bona fide exemptions and meaningful enforcement.

Figure 7-2:

Major School Desegregation Decisions, 1954–1978—Continued

Supreme Court Cases	Decision	Significance
Pasadena City Bd. v. Spangler, 1976	Struck down court efforts to enforce periodic adjustments to original desegregation plan.	Demographic changes occurring after a desegregation order is in place are beyond judicial remedial powers.
Milliken v. Bradley, 1977 (Milliken II)	Unanimous ruling approving extensive court-ordered remedies in areas previously intentionally segregated.	Clarifies questions raised about continued Supreme Court endorsement of Swann.
Dayton Bd. of Educ. v. Brinkman, 1977	Rejects system-wide busing plan because of confusing facts in the case.	Reaffirms that remedies must be carefully tailored to unconstitutional acts. Demands proof of the necessity for extensive remedies such as cross-town busing.

[B9659]

6. Some communities have called for decentralization of school systems. The community control movement has been centered in urban areas where large, impersonal school systems are most apt to exist. The leading experiment in community control is New York City. In order to assure greater representation of that city's numerous ethnic and racial groups in the schools, the New York City system was divided into thirty community districts by state law in 1969. Each district was governed by a community school board composed of elected nonprofessionals. Because of continuing strife between central office administrators and community district leaders, opposition of the teacher union, voter apathy, and other problems, the decentralization experiment was not a total success.

To what extent is community control compatible with integration? Can a particular ethnic or racial community legally control its own schools when the result is perpetuation of one-race institutions? The answers are unclear, in large part because of the ambiguity surrounding the issue of "purpose or intent" in creating such schools. In *Keyes*, Justice Brennan left this issue for future resolution, as we have seen, noting simply that:

> We have no occasion to consider in this case whether a "neighborhood school policy" of itself will justify racial or ethnic concentrations in the absence of a finding that school authorities have committed acts constituting *de jure* segregation. (At p. 212).

The problem is particularly complex because several purposes may be involved in a decentralization program, making it difficult to assess whether segregative intent is involved or not. For many black leaders, the community school movement is a particularly troublesome issue. How might Justice Marshall respond to the issue, in light of his opinions?

In higher education, the nation's black colleges have a legal obligation, like their white counterparts, to integrate. Recently, some black college officials have expressed concern that the influx of white students may undermine the heritage of racial pride which has served as the backbone of these institutions in the past. For example, the president of

Florida A & M University noted in 1978 that the image of his institution as an all-black institution "is the single most important thing that Florida A & M has that is marketable." [65] While acknowledging that his institution has begun to integrate, the chief executive added that "I think we deserve to have Florida A & M remain a predominantly black institution."

How would you resolve the dilemma between compulsion to integrate and desire to maintain a separatist existence in the nation's educational system?[66]

7. Consider the following hypothetical case:

Blacktown Independent School System consists of 16,000 students, five elementary schools, three junior high schools, and two high schools. Seventy percent of Blacktown students are black. The white students are not scattered through the school system but rather concentrated in two of the elementary schools, one of the junior high schools, and one of the high schools. A majority of Blacktown school officials are white.

Fairfax Independent School System is located in the town of Fairfax, about twenty miles from Blacktown. The two towns are the only population concentrations for a radius of fifty miles. The Fairfax school system consists of 25,000 students, six elementary schools, three junior high schools, and three high schools. Ninety percent of Fairfax students are white. The remaining ten percent minority enrollment is concentrated in one elementary school, one junior high school, and one high school—all located in one general section of town.

De jure segregation has been practiced for many years by Blacktown school officials in a state which has never had a state policy of segregation. In many instances, the white students are bused past all-black schools near their homes to their assigned institutions. Fairfax school officials have not engaged in similar segregative actions. State education officials have known about Blacktown segregative actions and have helped enforce them by approving disproportionate awards of state funds to various schools in the system. It has been suggested that the state has also helped sustain the *status quo* in Fairfax by lax enforcement statewide of fair employment and housing laws.

The parents of several Blacktown school children have filed suit in federal court against continued practice of school segregation and demand effective remedies for past injustices.

———

Based on previous discussion and cases, what arguments would you make for the parents? As a federal judge, what decision would you reach concerning appropriate remedies? As an educator, would you respond differently?

65. As quoted in Lorenzo Middleton, "Challenges for A Proud Black University," *The Chronicle of Higher Education*, November 27, 1978, at p. 8.

66. For an interesting discussion of how pluralism can be achieved within an integrated framework, see Note, "Cultural Pluralism," 13 *Harvard Civil Rights/Civil Liberties Rev.* 133, Winter, 1978.

(3) Affirmative Action Programs

An affirmative action policy which in addition to making special efforts to seek out previously excluded persons and to encourage their applications for jobs, education, and so on, actually redistributes resources, services, or opportunities from previously advantaged groups to previously disadvantaged groups, is often labeled "benign" discrimination. Beginning in the 1960s, affirmative action and preferential treatment programs were increasingly utilized, going well beyond equal treatment under the law to direct that compensation be given to those groups who have suffered past discrimination.

During the 1970s the judiciary was faced with attempts to apply the Equal Protection Clause to prohibit so-called "reverse discrimination." In *DeFunis v. Odegaard*, 416 U.S. 312 (1974), the Supreme Court was asked to decide whether an affirmative action program used by the University of Washington Law School was in violation of the Equal Protection Clause. The law school had established procedures which gave special consideration to black, Chicano, American Indian, and Filipino applicants. DeFunis, a white male, had been denied admission. He claimed that he was the victim of "reverse discrimination" because his qualifications were superior to many of those minority candidates who had been given special treatment. The university admitted that DeFunis' grades and Law School Aptitude Test scores were superior to those of some 36 minority students who had been admitted. The university, though, justified its rules by arguing that other factors beyond scores and grades could be used in admissions decision making. One such factor was the expansion of legal education to minorities whose past access to law school had been negligible.

A Washington state trial court disagreed with the university and ordered DeFunis' admission to the University of Washington Law School in 1971. The state supreme court reversed that ruling, agreeing with the university that it had met a compelling state interest test under new equal protection in maintaining the special admissions program, even though the law school itself may never have practiced racial discrimination in the past. DeFunis took the matter to the U. S. Supreme Court. Justice Douglas issued an order suspending the enforcement of the Washington court's decision until the High Court could resolve the issue. Pending disposition of the appeal, DeFunis was permitted to attend the law school. By the time the Court considered the case in 1974, DeFunis was close to completing his studies.

The Court voted 5–4 to refuse to decide the *DeFunis* case. The Court held that since DeFunis would complete his degree by the end of the 1974 spring semester, there was no longer a live case and controversy. The case was declared moot. In its *per curiam* decision, the Court admitted, however, that this constitutional issue would more than likely soon be before it again. Only Justice Douglas wrote an opinion on the merits, arguing that preferential treatment on the basis of race, benign or otherwise, violates the Equal Protection Clause, though acknowledging that individual characteristics including background could be taken into consideration. He also questioned whether the law school aptitude test discriminated against blacks and urged the case be remanded for a new trial partly to explore this issue.

Three years later, Allan Bakke, a white applicant to the University of California Medical School at Davis, asked the Court to rule on the constitutionality of the medical school's policy of maintaining a quota of sixteen minority candidates and the preferential treatment accorded them. In 1973 Bakke applied to 13 medical schools, including the medical school of the University of California at Davis, and was denied admission to all. The Davis Medical School, which opened in 1968, had instituted a special admissions program in 1973. Unlike its regular admissions program, the special program did not automatically reject applicants with GPAs below 2.5 on a scale of 4.0. Rather, those who checked economically and/or educationally disadvantaged on the application form and thus were eligible for special admissions were reviewed even if they had GPAs which would have automatically excluded them under the regular program. On the basis of interviews as well as scores and grades, the special admissions committee determined the strongest applicants and advanced their recommendations for admission to the general admissions committee. The candidates were never compared with the regular group. They were admitted on a rolling basis until the 16 places reserved for the special admissions group out of 100 in the freshman class were filled. From 1971 to 1974 the special program produced 63 minority students (21 blacks, 30 Mexican-Americans, and 12 Asians). No disadvantaged whites were admitted under the program. (In 1974 the criteria were changed so that only disadvantaged minority applicants could be considered under the special program.) By contrast, the regular program produced 44 minority students (1 black, 6 Mexican Americans, and 37 Asians).

Bakke made a strong showing in 1973, scoring 468 out of a possible 500 points in the rating scale used by the admissions committee. However, no one with a point total below 470 was admitted through the regular admissions program; in addition, Bakke had applied late. Bakke wrote a letter of protest to the medical school, pointing out his belief that the special admissions program operated as a racial quota. After he was rejected a second time, he filed suit, noting that applicants with lower grades, scores, and ratings than his were admitted both years through the special program, for which he was not eligible. He claimed the special admissions program thus discriminated against him contrary to Title VI of the 1964 Civil Rights Act, which prohibits discrimination on the basis of race, color, or national origin in federally assisted programs and activities; contrary to the Equal Protection Clause of the Fourteenth Amendment; and contrary to the California constitution.

The trial court agreed with Bakke but refused to order his admission, stating he had failed to prove he would have been admitted save for the special program. Both Bakke and the university appealed. The California Supreme Court in a 6–1 decision upheld the trial court, applying strict scrutiny to the medical school special admissions program since a racial classification was involved. The University of California argued the program met a strict scrutiny test. The California Supreme Court agreed that the institution had compelling purposes to seek to enroll more applicants from minority groups but asserted there are other ways to accomplish this goal without conflicting with the Fourteenth Amendment Equal Protection Clause. In effect, the court ordered the medical school to adopt a racially neutral or "colorblind" admissions procedure. The court did not rule with regard to either the Title VI or the California constitution claims. The university was ordered to admit Bakke to the Davis Medical School.

The University of California appealed the California Supreme Court decision to the U. S. Supreme Court in 1977 . Certainly the decision in *Regents of the Univ. of Cal. v. Bakke,* 438 U.S. 265 (1978), is one in which definitions of equality in the Fourteenth Amendment play a crucial role. Some feared the decision would give constitutional legitimacy to affirmative action programs and preferential treatment for minorities, while others feared an end to these programs in education and possibly in employment as well. Professor Archibald Cox, speaking for the University of California in oral argument, claimed that affirmative action and preferential treatment programs for minorities are the only effective means of increasing the extremely small number of minority doctors. Cox argued that a racially conscious test for admission which sets aside certain places for qualified minority applicants thus serves a legitimate goal. Bakke's lawyer argued that even if such programs are effective instruments in making society less dominated by racial inequalities, they are still unconstitutional because they violate the rights of those like Allan Bakke who lose out as a result.

The Supreme Court's 5–4 decision, excerpted below, steered a very narrow course between opposing views in the case. The Court affirmed the lower-court order admitting Bakke to medical school. Justice Powell, speaking for the majority in this section of the decision, claimed that quotas based entirely on race in situations where no previous discrimination has been found are illegal. However, Justice Powell then sided with four other Justices to decide 5–4 that a university admissions committee can consider race as one factor in admissions decision making. While regarded in many quarters as a masterpiece in judicial statesmanship, critics wondered how significant a precedent the decision represents, given that one person, Justice Powell, provided the necessary linkage to tie the diverse views together.

UNIVERSITY OF CAL. REGENTS v. BAKKE

Supreme Court of the United States, 1978.
438 U.S. 265, 98 S.Ct. 2733, 57 L.Ed.2d 750.

Mr. Justice POWELL announced the judgment of the Court.

* * *

For the reasons stated in the following opinion, I believe that so much of the judgment of the California court as holds petitioner's special admissions program unlawful and directs that respondent be admitted to the Medical School must be affirmed. For the reasons expressed in a separate opinion, my Brothers The CHIEF JUSTICE, Mr. Justice STEWART, Mr. Justice REHNQUIST, and Mr. Justice STEVENS concur in this judgment.

I also conclude for the reasons stated in the following opinion that the portion of the court's judgment enjoining petitioner from according any consideration to race in its admissions process must be reversed. For reasons expressed in separate opinions, my Brothers Mr. Justice

BRENNAN, Mr. Justice WHITE, Mr. Justice MARSHALL, and Mr. Justice BLACKMUN concur in this judgment.

Affirmed in part and reversed in part.

* * *

II

In this Court the parties neither briefed nor argued the applicability of Title VI of the Civil Rights Act of 1964. Rather, as had the California court, they focused exclusively upon the validity of the special admissions program under the Equal Protection Clause. Because it was possible, however, that a decision on Title VI might obviate resort to constitutional interpretation, we requested supplementary briefing on the statutory issue.

* * *

* * * Examination of the voluminous legislative history of Title VI reveals a congressional intent to halt federal funding of entities that violate a prohibition of racial discrimination similar to that of the Constitution. Although isolated statements of various legislators, taken out of context, can be marshalled in support of the proposition that [the act] enacted a purely colorblind scheme, without regard to the reach of the Equal Protection Clause, these comments must be read against the background of both the problem that Congress was addressing and the broader view of the statute that emerges from a full examination of the legislative debates.

* * *

In view of the clear legislative intent, Title VI must be held to proscribe only those racial classifications that would violate the Equal Protection Clause or the Fifth Amendment.

III

A

* * *

En route to [the] crucial battle over the scope of judicial review, the parties fight a sharp preliminary action over the proper characterization of the special admissions program. Petitioner prefers to view it as establishing a "goal" of minority representation in the medical school. Respondent, echoing the courts below, labels it a racial quota.

This semantic distinction is beside the point: the special admissions program is undeniably a classification based on race and ethnic background. To the extent that there existed a pool of at least minimally qualified minority applicants to fill the 16 special admissions seats, white applicants could compete only for 84 seats in the entering class, rather than the 100 open to minority applicants. Whether this limitation is described as a quota or a goal, it is a line drawn on the basis of race and ethnic status.

* * * The guarantee of equal protection cannot mean one thing when applied to one individual and something else when applied to a person of another color. If both are not accorded the same protection, then it is not equal.

* * *

* * * Racial and ethnic distinctions of any sort are inherently suspect and thus call for the most exacting judicial examination.

B

* * *

Petitioner urges us to adopt for the first time a more restrictive view of the Equal Protection Clause and hold that discrimination against members of the white "majority" cannot be suspect if its purpose can be characterized as "benign." The clock of our liberties, however, cannot be turned back to 1868. It is far too late to argue that the guarantee of equal protection to *all* persons permits the recognition of special wards entitled to a degree of protection greater than that accorded others. * * *

* * * The concepts of "majority" and "minority" necessarily reflect temporary arrangements and political judgments. * * * the white "majority" itself is composed of various minority groups, most of which can lay claim to a history of prior discrimination at the hands of the state and private individuals. Not all of these groups can receive preferential treatment and corresponding judicial tolerance of distinctions drawn in terms of race and nationality, for then the only "majority" left would be a new minority of White Anglo-Saxon Protestants. There is no principled basis for deciding which groups would merit "heightened judicial solicitude" and which would not.[36] Courts would be asked to evaluate the extent of the prejudice and consequent harm suffered by various minority groups. Those whose societal injury is thought to exceed some arbitrary level of tolerability then would be entitled to preferential classifications at the expense of individuals belonging to other groups. Those classifications would be free from exacting judicial scrutiny. As these preferences began to have their desired effect, and the consequences of past discrimination were undone, new judicial rankings would be necessary. The kind of variable sociological and political analysis necessary to produce such rankings simply does not lie within the judicial competence—even if they otherwise were politically feasible and socially desirable.

* * *

C

Petitioner contends that on several occasions this Court has approved preferential classifications without applying the most exacting scrutiny. Most of the cases upon which petitioner relies are drawn from three areas: school desegregation, employment discrimination, and sex discrimination. Each of the cases cited presented a situation materially different from the facts of this case.

The school desegregation cases are inapposite. Each involved remedies for clearly determined constitutional violations. Racial classifications thus were designed as remedies for the vindication of constitutional entitlement. Moreover, the scope of the remedies was not permitted to exceed the extent of the violations. Here, there was no judicial determination of constitutional violation as a predicate for the formulation of a remedial classification.

---

36. As I am in agreement with the view that race may be taken into account as a factor in an admissions program, I agree with my Brothers BRENNAN, WHITE, MARSHALL, and BLACKMUN that the portion of the judgment that would proscribe all consideration of race must be reversed. But I disagree with much that is said in their opinion.

They would require as a justification for a program such as petitioner's, only two findings: (i) that there has been some form of discrimination against the preferred minority groups "by society at large," (it being conceded that petitioner had no history of discrimination), and (ii) that "there is reason to believe" that the disparate impact sought to be rectified by the program is the "product" of such discrimination * * *.

The breadth of this hypothesis is unprecedented in our constitutional system. The first step is easily taken. No one denies the regrettable fact that there has been societal discrimination in this country against various racial and ethnic groups. The second step, however, involves a speculative leap: but for this discrimination by society at large, Bakke "would have failed to qualify for admission" because Negro applicants—nothing is said about Asians—would have made better scores. Not one word in the record supports this conclusion, and the plurality offers no standard for courts to use in applying such a presumption of causation to other racial or ethnic classifications. This failure is a grave one, since if it may be concluded *on this record* that each of the minority groups preferred by the petitioner's special program is entitled to the benefit of the presumption, it would seem difficult to determine that any of the dozens of minority groups that have suffered "societal discrimination" cannot also claim it, in any area of social intercourse.

The employment discrimination cases also do not advance petitioner's cause. For example, in *Franks v. Bowman Transportation Co.,* 424 U.S. 747 (1975), we approved a retroactive award of seniority to a class of Negro truck drivers who had been the victims of discrimination—not just by society at large, but by the respondent in that case. While this relief imposed some burdens on other employees, it was held necessary " 'to make [the victims] whole for injuries suffered on account of unlawful employment discrimination.' " The courts of appeals have fashioned various types of racial preferences as remedies for constitutional or statutory violations resulting in identified, race-based injuries to individuals held entitled to the preference. Such preferences also have been upheld where a legislative or administrative body charged with the responsibility made determinations of past discrimination by the industries affected, and fashioned remedies deemed appropriate to rectify the discrimination. But we have never approved preferential classifications in the absence of proven constitutional or statutory violations.

Nor is petitioner's view as to the applicable standard supported by the fact that gender-based classifications are not subjected to this level of scrutiny. Gender-based distinctions are less likely to create the analytical and practical problems present in preferential programs premised on racial or ethnic criteria. * * * More importantly, the perception of racial classifications as inherently odious stems from a lengthy and tragic history that gender-based classifications do not share. In sum, the Court has never viewed such classification as inherently suspect or as comparable to racial or ethnic classifications for the purpose of equal-protection analysis.

* * *

In this case, * * * there has been no determination by the legislature or a responsible administrative agency that the University engaged in a discriminatory practice requiring remedial efforts. Moreover, the operation of petitioner's special admissions program is quite different from the remedial measures approved in [other] cases. It prefers the designated minority groups at the expense of other individuals who are totally foreclosed from competition for the 16 special admissions seats in every medical school class. Because of that foreclosure, some individuals are excluded from enjoyment of a state-provided benefit—admission to the medical school—they otherwise would receive. When a classification denies an individual opportunities or benefits enjoyed by others solely because of his race or ethnic background, it must be regarded as suspect.

IV

We have held that in "order to justify the use of a suspect classification, a State must show that its purpose or interest is both constitutionally permissible and substantial, and that its use of the classification is 'necessary * * * to the accomplishment' of its purpose or the safeguarding of its interest."

* * * The special admissions program purports to serve the purposes of: (i) "reducing the historic deficit of traditionally disfavored minorities in medical schools and the medical profession,"; (ii) countering the effects of societal discrimination; [43] (iii) increasing the

* * *

43. Racial classifications in admissions conceivably could serve a fifth purpose, one which petitioner does not articulate: fair appraisal of each individual's academic promise in the light of some cultural bias in grading or testing procedures. To the

extent that race and ethnic background were considered only to the extent of curing established inaccuracies in predicting academic performance, it might be argued that there is no "preference" at all. Nothing in this record, however, suggests either that any of the quantitative factors con-

number of physicians who will practice in communities currently underserved; and (iv) obtaining the educational benefits that flow from an ethnically diverse student body. It is necessary to decide which, if any, of these purposes is substantial enough to support the use of a suspect classification.

A

If petitioner's purpose is to assure within its student body some specified percentage of a particular group merely because of its race or ethnic origin, such a preferential purpose must be rejected not as insubstantial but as facially invalid. Preferring members of any one group for no reason other than race or ethnic origin is discrimination for its own sake. This the Constitution forbids.

B

The State certainly has a legitimate and substantial interest in ameliorating, or eliminating where feasible, the disabling effects of identified discrimination. * * *

We have never approved a classification that aids persons perceived as members of relatively victimized groups at the expense of other innocent individuals in the absence of judicial, legislative, or administrative findings of constitutional or statutory violations. * * *

Petitioner does not purport to have made, and is in no position to make, such findings. Its broad mission is education, not the formulation of any legislative policy or the adjudication of particular claims of illegality. * * *

Hence, the purpose of helping certain groups whom the faculty of the Davis Medical School perceived as victims of "societal discrimination" does not justify a classification that imposes disadvantages upon persons like respondent, who bear no responsibility for whatever harm the beneficiaries of the special admissions program are thought to have suffered. To hold otherwise would be to convert a remedy heretofore reserved for violations of legal rights into a privilege that all institutions throughout the Nation could grant at their pleasure to whatever groups are perceived as victims of societal discrimination. That is a step we have never approved.

C

Petitioner identifies, as another purpose of its program, improving the delivery of health care services to communities currently underserved. It may be assumed that in some situations a State's interest in facilitating the health care of its citizens is sufficiently compelling to support the use of a suspect classification. But there is virtually no evidence in the record indicating that petitioner's special admissions program is either needed or geared to promote that goal. * * *

D

The fourth goal asserted by petitioner is the attainment of a diverse student body. This clearly is a constitutionally permissible goal for an institution of higher education. Academic freedom, though not a specifically enumerated constitutional right, long has been viewed as a special concern of the First Amendment. The freedom of a university to make its own judgments as to education includes the selection of its student body. * * *

* * *

Ethnic diversity, however, is only one element in a range of factors a university properly may consider in attaining the goal of a heterogeneous student body. Although a university must have wide dis-

sidered by the Medical School were culturally biased or that petitioner's special admissions program was formulated to correct for any such biases. Furthermore, if race or ethnic background were used solely to arrive at an unbiased prediction of academic success, the reservation of fixed numbers of seats would be inexplicable.

cretion in making the sensitive judgments as to who should be admitted, constitutional limitations protecting individual rights may not be disregarded. Respondent urges—and the courts below have held—that petitioner's dual admissions program is a racial classification that impermissibly infringes his rights under the Fourteenth Amendment. As the interest of diversity is compelling in the context of a university's admissions program, the questions remains whether the program's racial classification is necessary to promote this interest.

V

A

It may be assumed that the reservation of a specified number of seats in each class for individuals from the preferred ethnic groups would contribute to the attainment of considerable ethnic diversity in the student body. But petitioner's argument that this is the only effective means of serving the interest of diversity is seriously flawed. In a most fundamental sense the argument misconceives the nature of the state interest that would justify consideration of race or ethnic background. It is not an interest in simple ethnic diversity, in which a specified percentage of the student body is in effect guaranteed to be members of selected ethnic groups, with the remaining percentage an undifferentiated aggregation of students. The diversity that furthers a compelling state interest encompasses a far broader array of qualifications and characteristics of which racial or ethnic origin is but a single though important element. Petitioner's special admissions program, focused *solely* on ethnic diversity, would hinder rather than further attainment of genuine diversity.

* * *

The experience of other university admissions programs, which take race into account in achieving the educational diversity valued by the First Amendment, demonstrates that the assignment of a fixed number of places to a minority group is not a necessary means toward that end. * * * (Discussion of the Harvard University admissions program follows.)

* * *

In such an admissions program, race or ethnic background may be deemed a "plus" in a particular applicant's file, yet it does not insulate the individual from comparison with all other candidates for the available seats. The file of a particular black applicant may be examined for his potential contribution to diversity without the factor of race being decisive when compared, for example, with that of an applicant identified as an Italian-American if the latter is thought to exhibit qualities more likely to promote beneficial educational pluralism. Such qualities could include exceptional personal talents, unique work or service experience, leadership potential, maturity, demonstrated compassion, a history of overcoming disadvantage, ability to communicate with the poor, or other qualifications deemed important. In short, an admissions program operated in this way is flexible enough to consider all pertinent elements of diversity in light of the particular qualifications of each applicant, and to place them on the same footing for consideration, although not necessarily according them the same weight. Indeed, the weight attributed to a particular quality may vary from year to year depending upon the "mix" both of the student body and the applicants for the incoming class.

This kind of program treats each applicant as an individual in the admissions process. The applicant who loses out on the last available seat to another candidate receiving a "plus" on the basis of ethnic background will not have been foreclosed from all consideration for that seat simply because he was not the right color or had the wrong surname. It would mean only that his combined qualifications, which may have included similar non-objective factors, did not outweigh those of the other applicant. His qualifications would have been weighed fairly and competitively, and he would have no basis to complain of unequal treatment under the Fourteenth Amendment.

It has been suggested that an admissions program which considers race only as one factor is simply a subtle and more sophisticated—but no less effective—means of according racial preference than the Davis program. A facial intent to discriminate, however, is evident in petitioner's preference program and not denied in this case. No such facial infirmity exists in an admissions program where race or ethnic background is simply one element—to be weighed fairly against other elements—in the selection process. * * * And a Court would not assume that a university, professing to employ a facially nondiscriminatory admissions policy, would operate it as a cover for the functional equivalent of a quota system. In short, good faith would be presumed in the absence of a showing to the contrary in the manner permitted by our cases.

B

* * *

The fatal flaw in petitioner's preferential program is its disregard of individual rights as guaranteed by the Fourteenth Amendment. Such rights are not absolute. But when a State's distribution of benefits or imposition of burdens hinges on the color of a person's skin or ancestry, that individual is entitled to a demonstration that the challenged classification is necesary to promote a substantial state interest. Petitioner has failed to carry this burden. For this reason, that portion of the California court's judgment holding petitioner's special admissions program invalid under the Fourteenth Amendment must be affirmed.

C

In enjoining petitioner from ever considering the race of any applicant, however, the courts below failed to recognize that the State has a substantial interest that legitimately may be served by a properly devised admissions program involving the competitive consideration of race and ethnic origin. For this reason, so much of the California court's judgment as enjoins petitioner from any consideration of the race of any applicant must be reversed.

VI

With respect to respondent's entitlement to an injunction directing his admission to the Medical School, petitioner has conceded that it could not carry its burden of proving that, but for the existence of its unlawful special admissions program, respondent still would not have been admitted. Hence, respondent is entitled to the injunction, and that portion of the judgment must be affirmed.

(Appendix outlining Harvard University's admissions program is deleted.)

Opinion of Mr. Justice BRENNAN, Mr. Justice WHITE, Mr. Justice MARSHALL, and Mr. Justice BLACKMUN, concurring in the judgment in part and dissenting.

* * *

I

(Justice Brennan reviews the history of discrimination against blacks since slavery.)

* * *

Against this background, claims that law must be "colorblind" or that the datum of race is no longer relevant to public policy must be seen as aspiration rather than as description of reality. * * * Yet we cannot—and as we shall demonstrate, need not under our

Constitution or Title VI, which merely extends the constraints of the Fourteenth Amendment to private parties who receive federal funds—let color blindness become myopia which masks the reality that many "created equal" have been treated within our lifetimes as inferior both by the law and by their fellow citizens.

II

The threshold question we must decide is whether Title VI of the Civil Rights Act of 1964 bars recipients of federal funds from giving preferential consideration to disadvantaged members of racial minorities as part of a program designed to enable such individuals to surmount the obstacles imposed by racial discrimination. * * *

In our view, Title VI prohibits only those uses of racial criteria that would violate the Fourteenth Amendment if employed by a State or its agencies; it does not bar the preferential treatment of racial minorities as a means of remedying past societal discrimination to the extent that such action is consistent with the Fourteenth Amendment. * * *

(Detailed review of the statutory history of Title VI follows.)

III

A

The assertion of human equality is closely associated with the proposition that differences in color or creed, birth or status, are neither significant nor relevant to the way in which persons should be treated. Nonetheless, the position that * * * "[o]ur Constitution is colorblind," has never been adopted by this Court as the proper meaning of the Equal Protection Clause. Indeed, we have expressly rejected this proposition on a number of occasions.

Our cases have always implied that an "overriding statutory purpose," could be found that would justify racial classifications. * * *

We conclude, therefore, that racial classifications are not *per se* invalid under the Fourteenth Amendment. Accordingly, we turn to the problem of articulating what our role should be in reviewing state action that expressly classifies by race.

B

* * *

Unquestionably we have held that a government practice or statute which restricts "fundamental rights" or which contains "suspect classifications" is to be subjected to "strict scrutiny" and can be justified only if it furthers a compelling government purpose and, even then, only if no less restrictive alternative is available. But no fundamental right is involved here. Nor do whites as a class have any of the "'traditional indicia of suspectness: the class is not saddled with such disabilities, or subjected to such a history of purposeful unequal treatment, or relegated to such a position of political powerlessness as to command extraordinary protection from the majoritarian political process."

* * *

On the other hand, the fact that this case does not fit neatly into our prior analytic framework for race cases does not mean that it should be analyzed by applying the very loose rational-basis standard of review that is the very least that is always applied in equal protection cases. * * * Instead, a number of considerations—developed in gender discrimination cases but which carry even more force when applied to racial classifications—lead us to conclude that racial classifications designed to further remedial purposes " 'must serve important governmental objectives and must be substantially related to achievement of those objectives.' " [35]

First, race, like, "gender-based classifications too often [has] been inexcusably utilized to stereotype and stigmatize politically powerless segments of society." * * *

Second, race, like gender and illegitimacy, is an immutable characteristic which its possessors are powerless to escape or set aside. * * *

* * *

In sum, because of the significant risk that racial classifications established for ostensibly benign purposes can be misused, causing effects not unlike those created by invidious classifications, it is inappropriate to inquire only whether there is any conceivable basis that might sustain such a classification. Instead, to justify such a classification an important and articulated purpose for its use must be shown. In addition, any statute must be stricken that stigmatizes any group or that singles out those least well represented in the political process to bear the brunt of a benign program. Thus our review under the Fourteenth Amendment should be strict—not " 'strict' in theory and fatal in fact," because it is stigma that causes fatality—but strict and searching nonetheless.

IV

Davis' articulated purpose of remedying the effects of past societal discrimination is, under our cases, sufficiently important to justify the use of race-conscious admissions programs where there is a sound basis for concluding that minority underrepresentation is substantial and chronic, and that the handicap of past discrimination is impeding access of minorities to the medical school.

A

* * *

* * * the presence or absence of past discrimination by universities or employers is largely irrelevant to resolving respondent's constitutional claims. The claims of those burdened by the race-conscious actions of a university or employer who has never been adjudged in violation of an antidiscrimination law are not any more or less entitled to deference than the claims of the burdened nonminority workers in *Franks v. Bowman*, 424 U.S. 747 (1976), in which the employer had violated Title VII, for in each case the employees are innocent of past discrimination. And, although it might be argued that, where an employer has violated an antidiscrimination law, the expectations of nonminority workers are them-

---

35. We disagree with our Brother POWELL's suggestion that the presence of "rival groups who can claim that they, too, are entitled to preferential treatment" distinguishes the gender cases or is relevant to the question of scope of judicial review of race classifications. We are not asked to determine whether groups other than those favored by the Davis program should similarly be favored. All we are asked to do is to pronounce the constitutionality of what Davis has done.

But, were we asked to decide whether any given rival group—German-Americans for example—must constitutionally be accorded preferential treatment, we do have a "principled basis" for deciding this question, one that is well-established in our cases: The Davis program expressly sets out four classes which receive preferred status. The program clearly distinguishes

whites, but one cannot reason from this to a conclusion that German-Americans, as a national group, are singled out for invidious treatment. And even if the Davis program had a differential impact on German-Americans, they would have no constitutional claim unless they could prove that Davis intended invidiously to discriminate against German-Americans. If this could not be shown, then "the principle that calls for the closest scrutiny of distinctions in laws denying fundamental rights * * * is inapplicable," and the only question is whether it was rational for Davis to conclude that the groups it preferred had a greater claim to compensation than the groups it excluded. Thus, claims of rival groups, although they may create thorny political problems, create relatively simple problems for the courts.

selves products of discrimination and hence "tainted," and therefore more easily upset, the same argument can be made with respect to respondent. If it was reasonable to conclude—as we hold that it was—that the failure of minorities to qualify for admission at Davis under regular procedures was due principally to the effects of past discrimination, then there is a reasonable likelihood that, but for pervasive racial discrimination, respondent would have failed to qualify for admission even in the absence of Davis' special admissions program.

Thus, our cases under Title VII of the Civil Rights Act have held that, in order to achieve minority participation in previously segregated areas of public life, Congress may require or authorize preferential treatment for those likely disadvantaged by societal racial discrimination. Such legislation has been sustained even without a requirement of findings of intentional racial discrimination by those required or authorized to accord preferential treatment, or a case-by-case determination that those to be benefited suffered from racial discrimination. These decisions compel the conclusion that States also may adopt race-conscious programs designed to overcome substantial, chronic minority underrepresentation where there is reason to believe that the evil addressed is a product of past racial discrimination.[42]

B

Properly construed, therefore, our prior cases unequivocally show that a state government may adopt race-conscious programs if the purpose of such programs is to remove the disparate racial impact its actions might otherwise have and if there is reason to believe that the disparate impact is itself the product of past discrimination, whether its own or that of society at large. There is no question that Davis' program is valid under this test.

Certainly, on the basis of the undisputed factual submissions before this Court, Davis had a sound basis for believing that the problem of underrepresentation of minorities was substantial and chronic and that the problem was attributable to handicaps imposed on minority applicants by past and present racial discrimination. * * *

(Discussion of the underrepresentation of minorities in the medical profession follows.)

* * *

---

42. We do not understand Mr. Justice POWELL to disagree that providing a remedy for past racial prejudice can constitute a compelling purpose sufficient to meet strict scrutiny. Yet, because petitioner is a university, he would not allow it to exercise such power in the absence of "judicial, legislative, or administrative findings of constitutional or statutory violations." While we agree that reversal in this case would follow *a fortiori* had Davis been guilty of invidious racial discrimination or if a federal statute mandated that universities refrain from applying any admissions policy that had a disparate and unjustified racial impact, we do not think it of constitutional significance that Davis has not been so adjudged.

Generally, the manner in which a State chooses to delegate governmental functions is for it to decide. Control over the University is to be found not in the legislature, but rather in the Regents who have been vested with full legislative (including policymaking), administrative, and adjudicative powers by the citizens of California.

Because the Regents can exercise plenary legislative and administrative power, it elevates form over substance to insist that Davis could not use race-conscious remedial programs until it had been adjudged in violation of the Constitution or an antidiscrimination statute. For, if the Equal Protection Clause required such a violation as a predicate, the Regents could simply have promulgated a regulation prohibiting disparate treatment not justified by the need to admit only qualified students, and could have declared Davis to have been in violation of such a regulation on the basis of the exclusionary effect of the admissions policy applied during the first two years of its operation.

* * *

C

The second prong of our test—whether the Davis program stigmatizes any discrete group or individual and whether race is reasonably used in light of the program's objectives—is clearly satisfied by the Davis program.

It is not even claimed that Davis' program in any way operates to stigmatize or single out any discrete and insular, or even any identifiable, nonminority group. Nor will harm comparable to that imposed upon racial minorities by exclusion or separation on grounds of race be the likely result of the program. It does not, for example, establish an exclusive preserve for minority students apart from and exclusive of whites. Rather, its purpose is to overcome the effects of segregation by bringing the races together. True, whites are excluded from participation in the special admissions program, but this fact only operates to reduce the number of whites to be admitted in the regular admissions program in order to permit admission of a reasonable percentage—less than their proportion of the California population—of otherwise underrepresented qualified minority applicants.

Nor was Bakke in any sense stamped as inferior by the Medical School's rejection of him. Indeed, it is conceded by all that he satisfied those criteria regarded by the School as generally relevant to academic performance better than most of the minority members who were admitted. Moreover, there is absolutely no basis for concluding that Bakke's rejection as a result of Davis' use of racial preference will affect him throughout his life in the same way as the segregation of the Negro school children in *Brown I* would have affected them. Unlike discrimination against racial minorities, the use of racial preferences for remedial purposes does not inflict a pervasive injury upon individual whites in the sense that wherever they go or whatever they

do there is a significant likelihood that they will be treated as second-class citizens because of their color. This distinction does not mean that the exclusion of a white resulting from the preferential use of race is not sufficiently serious to require justification; but it does mean that the injury inflicted by such a policy is not distinguishable from disadvantages caused by a wide range of government actions, none of which has ever been thought impermissible for that reason alone.

In addition, there is simply no evidence that the Davis program discriminates intentionally or unintentionally against any minority group which it purports to benefit. The program does not establish a quota in the invidious sense of a ceiling on the number of minority applicants to be admitted. Nor can the program reasonably be regarded as stigmatizing the program's beneficiaries or their race as inferior. The Davis program does not simply advance less qualified applicants; rather, it compensates applicants, whom it is uncontested are fully qualified to study medicine, for educational disadvantage which it was reasonable to conclude was a product of state-fostered discrimination. Once admitted, these students must satisfy the same degree requirements as regularly admitted students; they are taught by the same faculty in the same classes; and their performance is evaluated by the same standards by which regularly admitted students are judged. Under these circumstances, their performance and degrees must be regarded equally with the regularly admitted students with whom they compete for standing.   *   *   *

D

We disagree with the lower courts' conclusion that the Davis program's use of race was unreasonable in light of its objectives. First, as petitioner argues, there are no practical means by which it could achieve its ends in the foreseeable future without the use of race-conscious measures. With respect to any factor (such as poverty or family educational background) that may be used as a substitute for race as an indicator of past discrimination, whites greatly outnumber racial minorities simply because whites make up a far larger percentage of the total population and therefore far outnumber minorities in absolute terms at every socio-economic level. * * * Moreover, while race is positively correlated with differences in GPA and MCAT scores, economic disadvantage is not. Thus, it appears that economically disadvantaged whites do not score less well than economically advantaged whites, while economically advantaged blacks score less well than do disadvantaged whites. These statistics graphically illustrate that the University's purpose to integrate its classes by compensating for past discrimination could not be achieved by a general preference for the economically disadvantaged or the children of parents of limited education unless such groups were to make up the entire class.

Second, the Davis admissions program does not simply equate minority status with disadvantage. Rather, Davis considers on an individual basis each applicant's personal history to determine whether he or she has likely been disadvantaged by racial discrimination. The record makes clear that only minority applicants likely to have been isolated from the mainstream of American life are considered in the special program; other minority applicants are eligible only through the regular admissions program. * * *

E

Finally, Davis' special admissions program cannot be said to violate the Constitution simply because it has set aside a predetermined number of places for qualified minority applicants rather than using minority status as a positive factor to be considered in evaluating the applications of disadvantaged minority applicants. For purposes of constitutional adjudication, there is no difference between the two approaches. In any admissions program which accords special consideration to disadvantaged racial minorities, a determination of the degree of preference to be given is unavoidable, and any given preference that results in the exclusion of a white candidate is no more or less constitutionally acceptable than a program such as that at Davis. Furthermore, the extent of the preference inevitably depends on how many minority applicants the particular school is seeking to admit in any particular year so long as the number of qualified minority applicants exceeds that number. There is no sensible, and certainly no constitutional, distinction between, for example, adding a set number of points to the admissions rating of disadvantaged minority applicants as an expression of the preference with the expectation that this will result in the admission of an approximately determined nunber of qualified minority applicants and setting a fixed number of places for such applicants as was done here.

The "Harvard" program, as those employing it readily concede, openly and successfully employs a racial criterion for the purpose of ensuring that some of the scarce places in institutions of higher education are allocated to disadvantaged minority students. That the Harvard approach does not also make public the extent of the preference and the precise workings of the system while the Davis program employs a specific, openly stated number, does not condemn the latter plan for purposes of Fourteenth Amendment adjudication. It may be that the Harvard plan is more acceptable to the public than is the Davis "quota." If it is, any State, including California, is free to adopt it in preference to a less acceptable alternative, just as it is generally free, as far as the Constitution is concerned, to abjure granting any racial preferences in its admissions program. But there is no basis for preferring a particular preference program simply because in achieving the same goals that the Davis Medical School is pursuing, it proceeds in a manner that is not immediately apparent to the public.

IV

Accordingly, we would reverse the judgment of the Supreme Court of California holding the Medical School's special admissions program unconstitutional and directing respondent's admission, as well as that portion of the judgment enjoining the Medical School from according any consideration to race in the admissions process.

Separate opinion of Mr. Justice WHITE.

* * *

Mr. Justice MARSHALL.

* * *

The position of the Negro today in America is the tragic but inevitable consequence of centuries of unequal treatment. Measured by any benchmark of comfort or achievement, meaningful equality remains a distant dream for the Negro. * * * At every point from birth to death the impact of the past is reflected in the still disfavored position of the Negro.

In light of the sorry history of discrimination and its devastating impact on the lives of Negroes, bringing the Negro into the mainstream of American life should be a state interest of the highest order. To fail to do so is to ensure that America will forever remain a divided society.

* * *

While I applaud the judgment of the Court that a university may consider race in its admissions process, it is more than a little ironic that, after several hundred years of class-based discrimination against Negroes, the Court is unwilling to hold that a class-based remedy for that discrimination is permissible. In declining

to so hold, today's judgment ignores the fact that for several hundred years Negroes have been discriminated against, not as individuals, but rather solely because of the color of their skins. It is unnecessary in 20th century America to have individual Negroes demonstrate that they have been victims of racial discrimination; the racism of our society has been so pervasive that none, regardless of wealth or position, has managed to escape its impact. The experience of Negroes in America has been different in kind, not just in degree, from that of other ethnic groups. It is not merely the history of slavery alone but also that a whole people were marked as inferior by the law. And that mark has endured. The dream of America as the great melting pot has not been realized for the Negro; because of his skin color he never even made it into the pot.

* * *

It is because of a legacy of unequal treatment that we now must permit the institutions of this society to give consideration to race in making decisions about who will hold the positions of influence, affluence and prestige in America. For far too long, the doors to those positions have been shut to Negroes. If we are ever to become a fully integrated society, one in which the color of a person's skin will not determine the opportunities available to him or her, we must be willing to take steps to open those doors. I do not believe that anyone can truly look into America's past and still find that a remedy for the effects of that past is impermissible.

It has been said that this case involves only the individual, Bakke, and this University. I doubt, however, that there is a computer capable of determining the number of persons and institutions that may be affected by the decision in this case. For example, we are told by the Attorney General of the United States that at least 27 federal agencies have adopted regulations requiring recipients of federal funds to take *"affirmative action* to overcome the effects of conditions which resulted in limiting participation * * * by persons of a particular race, color, or national origin." * * * I cannot even guess the number of state and local governments that have set up affirmative action programs, which may be affected by today's decision.

I fear that we have come full circle. After the Civil War our government started several "affirmative action" programs. This Court in the *Civil Rights Cases* and *Plessy v. Ferguson* destroyed the movement toward complete equality. For almost a century no action was taken, and this nonaction was with the tacit approval of the courts. Then we had *Brown v. Board of Education* and the Civil Rights Acts of Congress, followed by numerous affirmative action programs. *Now*, we have this Court again stepping in, this time to stop affirmative action programs of the type used by the University of California.

Mr. Justice BLACKMUN.

* * *

It is somewhat ironic to have us so deeply disturbed over a program where race is an element of consciousness, and yet to be aware of the fact, as we are, that institutions of higher learning, albeit more on the undergraduate than the graduate level, have given conceded preferences up to a point to those possessed of athletic skills, to the children of alumni, to the affluent who may bestow their largess on the institutions, and to those having connections with celebrities, the famous, and the powerful.

* * *

I am not convinced, as Mr. Justice POWELL seems to be, that the difference between the Davis program and the one employed by Harvard is very profound or constitutionally significant. The line between the two is a thin and indistinct one. In each, subjective application is at work. Because of my conviction that admission programs are primarily for the educators, I am willing to accept the representation that the Harvard program is one where good faith in its administration is practiced as well as professed. I agree that such a program, where race or ethnic background is only one of many factors, is a program better formulated than Davis' two-track system. The cynical, of course, may say that under a program such as Harvard's one may accomplish covertly what Davis concedes it does openly. I need not go that far, for despite its two-track aspect, the Davis program, for me, is within constitutional bounds, though perhaps barely so. * * *

It is worth noting, perhaps, that governmental preference has not been a stranger to our legal life. We see it in veterans' preferences. We see it in the aid-to-the-handicapped programs. We see it in the progressive income tax. We see it in the Indian programs. We may excuse some of these on the ground that they have specific constitutional protection or, as with Indians, that those benefited are wards of the Government. Nevertheless, these preferences exist and may not be ignored. * * *

* * * In order to get beyond racism, we must first take account of race. There is no other way. And in order to treat some persons equally, we must treat them differently. We cannot—we dare not—let the Equal Protection Clause perpetrate racial supremacy.

So the ultimate question as it was at the beginning of this litigation, is: Among the qualified, how does one choose?

Mr. Justice STEVENS, with whom The CHIEF JUSTICE, Mr. Justice STEWART, and Mr. Justice REHNQUIST join, concurring in the judgment in part and dissenting in part.

* * *

* * * Whether the judgment of the state court is affirmed or reversed, in whole or in part, there is no outstanding injunction forbidding any consideration of racial criteria in processing applications.

It is therefore perfectly clear that the question whether race can ever be used as a factor in an admissions decision is not an issue in this case, and that discussion of that issue is inappropriate.

Both petitioner and respondent have asked us to determine the legality of the University's special admissions program by reference to the Constitution. Our settled practice, however, is to avoid the decision of a constitutional issue if a case can be fairly decided on a statutory ground. * * * Since, * * *, a dispositive statutory claim was raised at the very inception of this case, and squarely decided in the portion of the trial court judgment affirmed by the California Supreme Court, it is our plain duty to confront it. * * *

* * * The University, through its special admissions policy, excluded Bakke from participation in its program of medical education because of his race. The University also acknowledges that it was, and still is, receiving federal financial assistance [under Title VI]. The plain language of the statute therefore requires affirmance of the judgment below. A different result cannot be justified unless that language misstates the actual intent of the Congress that enacted the statute or the statute is not enforceable in a private action. Neither conclusion is warranted.

(Detailed review of the statutory history of Title VI follows.)

* * *

As with other provisions of the Civil Rights Act, Congress' expression of its policy to end racial discrimination may independently proscribe conduct that the Constitution does not. However, we need not decide the congruence—or lack of congruence—of the controlling statute and the Constitution since the meaning of the Title VI ban on exclusion is crystal clear: Race cannot be the basis of excluding anyone from participation in a federally funded program.

* * *

* * * It is therefore our duty to affirm the judgment ordering Bakke admitted to the University.

Accordingly, I concur in the Court's judgment insofar as it affirms the judgment of the Supreme Court of California. To the extent that it purports to do anything else, I respectfully dissent.

NOTES AND QUESTIONS

1. What did the Supreme Court actually decide? Justice Brennan asserts in a section of his concurring and dissenting opinion not excerpted here that:

> The difficulty of the issue presented—whether Government may use race-conscious programs to redress the continuing effects of past discrimination—and the mature consideration which each of our Brethren has brought to it have resulted in many opinions, no single one speaking for the Court. But this should not and must not mask the central meaning of today's opinions: Government may take race into account when it acts not to demean or insult any racial group, but to remedy disadvantages cast on minorities by past racial prejudice, at least when appropriate find-

ings have been made by judicial, legislative, or administrative bodies with competence to act in this area.

Justice Stevens counters with this comment in a footnote which is also not excerpted:

> Four Members of the Court have undertaken to announce the legal and constitutional effect of this Court's judgment. * * * It is hardly necessary to state that only a majority can speak for the Court or determine what is the "central meaning" of any judgment of the Court.

But hasn't a majority of five in effect supported Justice Brennan's assertion?

Because four members choose to rely on Title VI, thus expressing no view regarding the Equal Protection Clause, and because Justice Powell carefully qualifies his support for the use of racially-related criteria in medical school admissions, it is unclear how significant a precedent *Bakke* may prove to be for other types of affirmative action and preferential treatment programs. Professor Paul Freund of Harvard Law School told *Time* magazine that "the very fact it is somewhat fuzzy leaves room for development and on the whole that's a good thing." [67] Would you agree?

A number of cases were awaiting decision by the Supreme Court and lower courts prior to the *Bakke* decision. Some involved education, while a number of others related to employment. Included in the education category was *Cannon v. University of Chicago,* 559 F.2d 1077 (7th Cir. 1977), a case involving a woman who claimed under Title IX that she had been denied admission to the University of Chicago Medical School, a private institution, because of her sex. Title IX prohibits sex discrimination in federally-supported programs. At issue was whether she has a private right to sue under Title IX or must allow her case to be handled by HEW. Justice Powell in *Bakke* refused to consider this issue as it relates to Title VI, as well as the related question of whether a private person has to exhaust administrative remedies prior to suing. Justices Brennan, Marshall, and Blackmun concurred, while the four Justices represented by Justice Stevens went beyond this position to suggest that a private right of action does exist. Only Justice White disagreed. In May, 1979, the Court decided the *Cannon* case by holding that Title IX, as well as Title VI, confer private rights of action. Speaking for the majority, Justice Stevens rejected the university's fears of burdensome litigation by disappointed applicants as unsubstantiated and speculative. The university had argued that the threat of individual court suits might intimidate admissions committees. Justices Powell, White, and Blackmun dissented in the case.

In the employment area, a number of issues loom before the Court. For example, Title VII of the 1964 Civil Rights Act forbids discrimination in public and private employment on the basis of race, ethnic origin or religion, while Executive Order 11246 requires federal contractors to set up affirmative action plans. These plans must not discriminate against any applicant because of race, color, religion, sex, or national origin. Enforcement of Title VII frequently results in consent decrees in lieu of court ac-

---

67. *Time,* July 10, 1978, at p. 7.

tion whereby violaters agree to set up preferential programs involving quotas and timetables. To what extent will *Bakke* limit such programs? A case in point is *EEOC v. American Telephone & Telegraph Co.*, 556 F.2d 167 (3rd Cir. 1977). AT&T agreed to goals and timetables after extensive prodding by the Justice Department and the Equal Employment Opportunity Commission, which found the company guilty of practicing both sex and race discrimination. The employee union, however, challenged the plan as "reverse discrimination," claiming it would compromise the seniority rights of its members. Shortly after *Bakke*, the Justices without recorded dissent refused to review the court of appeals ruling upholding the consent decree, thus lending support to the view expressed by Justice Brennan regarding the "central meaning" of *Bakke*.

Suppose AT&T had undertaken the affirmative action-preferential plan voluntarily? In December, 1978, the Court agreed to hear a controversial case involving a voluntary affirmative action program at Kaiser Aluminum and Chemical Corporation. Brian Weber, an employee at Kaiser's Gramercy, Louisiana, plant filed suit in 1974 charging that the Kaiser affirmative action program, which was voluntarily included in a union contract, violated Title VII by reserving spaces for blacks. Kaiser agreed to reserve 50 percent of the openings in the Gramercy plant training program until the number of black skilled craftsmen in the plant reached 39 percent, the percent of minority population in the Gramercy area. At the time, only 5 percent of the skilled craftsmen in the plant were black. In *Weber v. Kaiser Aluminum & Chemical Corp.*, 415 F.Supp. 761 (E.D.La.1976), *aff'd* 563 F.2d 216 (5th Cir. 1977), both the district court and the Fifth Circuit Court of Appeals ruled in favor of Weber. Both noted that Kaiser had never been found guilty of discrimination against blacks and concluded that under these circumstances, no person could be discriminated against under Title VII even if in the interest of a national social policy. In light of *Bakke*, how might the Supreme Court rule in this case?

Interestingly, the same day the Supreme Court announced it would hear the *Weber* case, the Equal Employment Opportunity Commission (EEOC) announced new guidelines to take effect in January, 1979, under Title VII designed to assist employers develop affirmative action programs on their own without waiting until a grievance is filed. The new guidelines stated that an employer would not be violating Title VII by:

1. Conducting a self-analysis of his existing employment system;

2. Asserting a reasonable basis for concluding that affirmative action is appropriate (based on EEOC criteria);

3. Taking voluntary affirmative action, including race, sex, and national origin hiring goals and timetables, to overcome the effects of past or present discriminatory practices.

The guidelines clearly imply that employers are obligated by law and encouraged by EEOC to eliminate barriers to equal employment opportunity without awaiting investigative action by a government agency. In return, EEOC planned to issue an opinion protecting employers from reverse discrimination charges. If the new guidelines had been in effect at the time of the *Weber* suit and EEOC had issued an opinion asserting no reasonable cause for finding Kaiser guilty of reverse discrimination, would the Supreme Court's ruling likely be the same?

There are, of course, numerous other complaints which have surfaced over the implementation of and even the constitutionality of the federal statutory programs outlined in Figure 7–I, as well as similar state programs and those voluntarily instituted by public and private organizations. Some of the hypothetical cases included below are based on these complaints. *Bakke* appears to assure that litigation is likely to accelerate dramatically in the future.

2.   In an unexcerpted portion of their concurring and dissenting opinions, Justices Brennan and Stevens engage in a protracted discussion of the legislative history of Title VI designed to prove that the statute does or does not allow voluntary racial preference by organizations receiving federal funding.   Justice Powell concurs with Justice Brennan and those members of the Court joining in the latter's views that Title VI does not mandate a colorblind approach.   In a lengthy footnote Justice Brennan accuses Justice Stevens of giving "undue weight to a few isolated passages among the thousands of pages of the legislative history of Title VI."   Presumably, during legislative debate those supporting the enactment of the original bill occasionally understated its import, while opponents stated the reverse.   Under these circumstances, is there any way one can ever be certain of the meaning of the words?   Note again the definitive role the U. S. Supreme Court (and, where state laws are concerned, the highest state court) plays in statutory construction.

3.   Justice Powell maintains that there is no significant distinction between the terms "quota" and "goal" as applied to the special admissions program at the Davis Medical School.   Archibald Cox, the attorney for the University of California, however, maintained in oral argument before the Court that the difference is real.   Unlike exclusionary quotas, the special admissions program did not set arbitrary limits: "Certainly it was not a quota in the older sense of an arbitrary limit put on the number of members of a nonpopular group who would be admitted to an institution which was looking down its nose at them."   Rather, Cox labeled the program a "goal," noting that other minority applicants were admitted through the regular admissions program.   Thus, Cox would label an *exclusionary* program a "quota" and an *inclusionary* program a "goal."   He had more difficulty, however, assigning a label to the complement of 84 students admitted under the regular admissions program.   In response to questions from Justice Stevens, he stated that he would not label it a quota.   But neither was it a goal in the same sense as the special admissions target figure of 16, since non-disadvantaged minorities were ineligible for the special program.   Would it be accurate to refer to the 84 figure as a quota, but one which carries no racial stigma?

Since Bakke brought his lawsuit, the quota approach to admissions has virtually disappeared from America's campuses.[68]   In their place are

---

68. Lorenzo Middleton, "Those Vanishing Quotas," *The Chronicle of Higher Education,* July 10, 1978, at p. 8.

programs similar to Harvard's, which include race as one factor in admissions. Quotas have always been unpopular with Americans, regardless of the rationale for their use. For example, a Gallop Poll taken in 1977 showed 83 percent of those sampled believed ability should be the determining factor in getting jobs and places in college. Of nonwhites included in the poll, 64 percent endorsed this view. The antipathy toward racial preference is reflected in an unexcerpted footnote by Justice Powell where he notes that "Fairness in individual competition for opportunities, especially those provided by the State, is a widely cherished American ethic."

The Harvard admissions program cited approvingly by Justice Powell avoids selecting only those most qualified by virtue of grades and scores, since if these were the only criteria, "Harvard College would lose a great deal of its vitality and intellectual excellence." [69] Thus, in addition to selecting a group of students for their intellectual achievement and potential, the Harvard admissions staff looks for students with diverse backgrounds and experiences. Included are students from disadvantaged economic, racial, and ethnic groups. In practice, then, race is a factor which may tip the balance in favor of a particular applicant. Harvard officials are concerned about numbers as well, for a token complement of black students would neither contribute real diversity to the student body nor provide a supportive environment for minority students. Since both the Harvard program and the Davis admissions program are concerned with numbers of minority applicants, to what extent are they really different? In this regard, compare Justice Powell's comments with those of Justice Blackmun.

Will the Harvard approach to admitting minority applicants effectively serve to increase the numbers of racial minorities in the nation's professional schools? Two factors may be determinative: the numbers of minorities included in the pool of applicants at a particular institution and the criteria used to decide who gets admitted. One result of *Bakke* is that admissions officers must work harder to get minorities to apply, since no longer can they guarantee that a certain number of places will be set aside for minorities. All applicants must be evaluated together in a single pool. While race is one factor which still can be used in the selection process, its relative weight will remain uncertain. Too much weight could result in reverse discrimination challenges by non-minority applicants who are rejected; too little weight will likely decrease the number of minority students being admitted, since presumably greater emphasis would be given to test scores and grades. A study commissioned by the Law School Admissions Council in 1976 showed that a colorblind admissions policy would have resulted in the rejection of more than 70 percent of the minority students then enrolled at 129 law schools.[70] The study also revealed that the great preponderance of persons in the law school applicant population with low income backgrounds are not members of a minority group. And a 1978 study by the Association of American Medical Colleges revealed that prior to the *Bakke* decision, minority recruit-

69. Appendix to the *amicus curiae* brief submitted by Columbia University, Harvard University, Stanford University, and the University of Pennsylvania.

70. *Learning and the Law* (Chicago: American Bar Association, Spring, 1977).

ment in the nation's medical, colleges had reached a standstill with no progress reported in increasing minority representation since 1975.[71] Much of the impact of *Bakke* will thus be determined by the policies and practices employed by the institutions themselves and their "gatekeepers," the admissions officers.

4.   At the 1977 Davis Medical School graduation ceremonies for the class Allan Bakke couldn't enter, the recipient of the senior-class award as the most likely to succeed was one of the 16 minority-group students admitted under the special admissions program. Of the 16 admitted in 1973, only one dropped out of the program. The others completed their program about on a par with the regular students.

The issue of entrance standards is part of a larger debate about the nature and use of aptitude and achievement tests. To what extent do such tests actually measure what they purport to measure and to what extent are they related to job performance? At the time of the *Bakke* case, the California State Assembly's postsecondary education subcommittee charged that the admissions criteria used at the nine campuses of the University of California were ineffective and, worse, discriminatory. The subcommittee stated that while the heavy use of quantifiable information such as grades and test scores predicts well for first year graduate school performance, such objective data does not assess an individual's effectiveness as a professional. Similar concerns have been expressed by a number of commentators about the Law School Aptitude Test, state bar examinations, the Graduate Record Examination, and similar screening devices.

Quantifiable data provide a means for educators to determine student needs and to assess student competencies. But used alone, tests are challengeable on a number of grounds. Since only certain kinds of behavior can be adapted to a testing format, other behaviors which may be relevant are left out. Potential intelligence (aptitude or ability) and operant intelligence (achievement) are difficult to distinguish from each other. And both are related as well to a complex and little understood mix of individual physiological characteristics, genetic influences, and environmental conditions.[72] Thus, an aptitude or achievement score on a particular test may reveal more about a person's lifestyle than about her intellectual capabilities.

Experience shows that minorities usually perform below the level of white students on most aptitude tests. For example, studies consistently show that blacks score 15 points lower on I.Q. tests than whites.[73] Likewise, the minority students at the Davis Medical School performed lower than the white applicants. Justice Brennan concludes that "the failure of minorities to qualify for admission at Davis under regular procedures

71.   Robert L. Jacobson "No Progress in Recruiting Minority Medical Students," *The Chronicle of Higher Education*, October 2, 1978, at p. 6.

72.   For a discussion of educational testing and related legal concerns, see Thomas E. Shea "An Educational Perspective of the Legality of Intelligence Testing and Ability Grouping," 6 *J.Law & Educ.* 137, April, 1977, and Paul L. Tractenberg and Elaine Jacoby "Pupil Testing: A Legal View," 59 *Phi Delta Kappan* 249, December, 1977.

73.   Shea, *Id.*, at pp. 156–157.

was due principally to the effects of past discrimination   *   *   *." In a footnote not excerpted here, Justice Powell questions why Asians were included in the special admissions program, given the substantial numbers admitted through the regular program. Are they properly classified as a minority in this case?

Most, but not all, research in this highly controversial area supports Justice Brennan's conclusion that cultural deprivation, not genetic factors, are largely responsible for the lower performance levels of minority groups.[74] If true, to what extent does it follow that institutions which have never overtly discriminated have the same obligation to give preferential treatment to minorities as those that have? Is this a moral or legal obligation?

A number of equal protection suits have been aimed at the use of aptitude and achievement tests which serve to separate students into different groups.[75] Since blacks and other minorities traditionally score lower, they often end up predominately in one group. While courts have been reluctant to apply strict scrutiny under new equal protection to the use of testing devices, they have generally required educators to offer proof of the validity of challenged tests as a defense against charges of illegal intraschool segregation. Thus, for example, in *Larry P. v. Riles,* 343 F. Supp. 1306 (N.D.Cal.1972), the federal district court issued a preliminary injunction restraining the San Francisco Unified School District from using IQ tests to classify students into special classes for the educable mentally retarded. The court noted that while black students constituted 28.5 percent of all students in the district, 66 percent of all students in the special classes were black. This imbalance coupled with the heavy reliance of school officials on IQ tests was sufficient in the judgment of the court to shift the burden of proof to the school district. Finding inadequate justification offered by the school district, the district court issued the injunction. The court noted that some school systems have abandoned the IQ test altogether in favor of achievement tests and teacher evaluations. Is this move any more educationally defensible? Legally defensible?

Larry P. v. Riles is one of a number of cases where lower federal courts have disallowed the use of tests that produce discriminatory results. While the U. S. Supreme Court to date has not decided a case involving educational testing, the Court has ruled with respect to the use of tests in employment. In *Washington v. Davis,* 426 U.S. 229 (1976), the Court held

---

74. See, for example, citations in Shea, *Id.* For a background discussion, see Jerome Kagan, "The IQ Puzzle: What Are We Measuring?" 14 *Inequality in Educ.* 5, July, 1973; and Arthur Jensen, "The Differences are Real," Berkeley Rice, "The High Cost of Thinking the Unthinkable," and Theodosius Dobzhansky, "Differences Are Not Deficits" in 7 *Psychology Today* 79, December, 1973. See Cheryl Fields, "Heredity and Environment, But Not Race, Found to Influence Intelligence," in *The Chronicle of Higher Education,* September 12, 1977, for a discussion of more recent research.

75. For a general background discussion, see David L. Kirp, "Student Classification, Public Policy, and the Courts" in *The Rights of Children* (Cambridge, Mass.: Harvard Educ. Review, 1974). A longer and heavily footnoted version of this article appeared under the title "Schools as Sorters: The Constitutional and Policy Implications of Student Classification," 121 *Univ. of Penn.L.Rev.* 705, April, 1973.

that a civil service test of verbal skills which blacks fail more often than whites is nevertheless valid unless it can be shown that the use of the test is motivated by racial bias or that the test has no rational relationship to job performance. In *Davis,* black applicants who failed the test challenged its use as a screening device for the police officer training program. The Court in a 7–2 decision noted that the test is widely used in the federal civil service and that the police department had made substantial efforts to recruit minorities. The Court also found that test results correlated with police training course completion rates. Justice White for the majority noted that:

> Disproportionate impact is not irrelevant, but it is not the sole touchstone of an invidious racial discrimination forbidden by the Constitution. Standing alone, it does not trigger the rule that racial classifications are to be subjected to the strictest scrutiny and are justifiable only by the weightiest of considerations. (At p. 242).

Shortly after its decision in *Washington v. Davis,* the Court declined to hear a constitutional challenge brought by blacks against the Georgia bar examination, which blacks fail more often than whites. *Tyler v. Vickery,* 426 U.S. 940 (1976).

In cases alleging violations of Title VII of the 1964 Civil Rights Act forbidding discrimination in public and private employment, the Court applies a tougher set of standards in accord with the act and its regulations drawn up by the implementing agency, the Equal Employment Opportunity Commission. Under Title VII, a showing of racially differential impact is sufficient to shift the burden to the employer to show the challenged test to be an adequate measure of job performance. Unlike the *Davis* case where Title VII was not involved, the added burden of showing *intent to discriminate* is not necessary. Thus, in the leading case, *Griggs v. Duke Power Co.,* 401 U.S. 424 (1971), the Court ruled in an 8–0 decision (Justice Brennan did not participate) that under Title VII, educational requirements such as a high school diploma or intelligence tests such as the I.Q. test which operate to exclude blacks cannot be upheld unless the employer can show such devices are directly related to job performance. The burden of proof is thus thrust upon the employer. Even with the added burden upon the employer, the cases demonstrate that Title VII will not always result in the rejection of the employer screening device. Thus, in 1978 the Court affirmed a lower court ruling that a state's use of the National Teacher Examination, which has a disproportionate impact on blacks, is a rational means to certify public school teachers under the Fourteenth Amendment. Justices White and Brennan dissented, basing their objection in part on *Griggs. National Educ. Ass'n v. South Carolina,* 434 U.S. 1026 (1978). The lower court determined that a state study showing that the test correlates with teacher training programs was sufficiently trustworthy to sustain South Carolina's burden under Title VII of the 1964 Civil Rights Act.

In the absence of legislation, why do you suppose the Court is reluctant to apply strict scrutiny under new equal protection to testing devices which disproportionately affect minorities? Should it? Should

Congress extend Title VII to admissions and graduation decision making in education?

5. Based on the *Bakke* decision and the other cases involving race as a suspect classification included above, how would you decide the following hypothetical situations?

a. A Jewish student who is rejected by a state university medical school contests the decision not to consider him a disadvantaged student. He claims the fact he was raised by immigrant parents who spoke only Yiddish at home should have qualified him for the institution's voluntary special admissions program, which gives preferential treatment to an unspecified number of minorities.

b. A university president at a public institution denies a group of blind students recognition as a campus organization because the organization would discriminate against sighted persons. The bylaws require the officers and a majority of voting members to be blind. Denial of recognition means no office space, no funds from student fees, and no publicity. The blind students sue campus officials for violating their rights of association. Do campus officials have a defense under the Equal Protection Clause? Under any of the statutes listed in Figure 7–I? Could a school or college legally have a rule forbidding this type of discrimination?

c. Several white students sue a public university which allows its student government to appoint two minority students, two women, and two men to the student court. The students claim a violation of Title VI of the 1964 Civil Rights Act and of the Fourteenth Amendment Equal Protection Clause. Any difference if the public university at one time was a white-only institution pursuant to a state segregation law?

d. A private institution sets aside 50 percent of its scholarship funds for minority applicants. White students who demonstrate financial need claim the policy violates the Fourteenth Amendment Equal Protection Clause. Any difference if the students base their case on Title VI of the 1964 Civil Rights Act?

e. Black students who are rejected at a formerly all-black public college protest the fact that favoritism is given to white students in the admissions process. They cite the Fourteenth Amendment Equal Protection Clause and Title VI of the 1974 Civil Rights Act in support of their contention that the college must employ a colorblind admissions policy.

f. A formerly all-female public university includes a statement in its recruitment literature that males will be given special preference in the admissions process. Several female applicants who are rejected with higher scores and grades than some males who are admitted sue the university, claiming a violation of the Fourteenth Amendment Equal Protection Clause. Any difference if they base their suit on Title IX of the 1972 Education Amendments?

g. The parents of several black students who failed a state-mandated English competency test required for high school graduation sue public school officials claiming the test has a disproportionate impact on black students and is thus unconstitutional under the Fourteenth Amendment Equal Protection Clause. Part of their suit alleges that the schools in which their children have been enrolled have not prepared the children for the competency test, primarily because the schools were underfinanced in relation to wealthier suburban institutions.

h. State statute provides that school boards are to consider race as one factor in building, consolidating, and closing schools in the interest of promoting integrated communities.

6. Consider the following hypothetical case:

White v. Board of Governors of Minnefornia State Univ., et al

The Black Student Movement (BSM), a recognized student organization at Minnefornia State University, receives an allocation of funds from mandatory student activity fees collected by the university and operates under the supervision of the Student Government Association (SGA). As a recognized student organization, BSM must comply with all university rules and regulations.

At the inception of the organization in 1967, membership in the BSM was restricted to black students. In 1974, because of a policy decision by the university's Board of Governors, BSM added one sentence to its membership policy statement to the effect that any student regardless of race could become a member if his or her views, in the opinion of BSM members, were consistent with the goals of the organization. At the time of this action, all members were black. BSM has never had a white student as a member.

Lilly White, a dedicated and outspoken integrationist, applied in 1975 for membership in BSM. She was informed that BSM "is an organization that recognizes the distinctly different cultural and historical evolution of the black community vis-a-vis that of the broader society." The goals of BSM, she was told, are:

1. to strive for unity among all BSM members;
2. to offer outlets such as concerts and plays for expressing black ideas and culture;
3. to provide BSM members with continuous contact with the surrounding black community.

Claiming that Lilly could never appreciate the cultural and historical heritage of black people, BSM refused her application for membership. Lilly protested the decision, noting that she has dedicated her life to ending the divisiveness of separatist policies and is committed to insuring equal opportunity for all people regardless of race, color, or creed. She accused BSM of promoting a segregationist posture and also accused the Student Government Association and the Board of Governors of condoning a segregationist organization on campus.

After exhausting administrative remedies open to her at Minnefornia without success, Lilly brought suit against the BSM, the Student Government Association, and the Board of Governors of Minnefornia State University, claiming a violation of the Fourteenth Amendment Equal Protection Clause and Title VI of the 1964 Civil Rights Act.

Based on previous discussion and cases, what arguments would you make for each side? If you were to decide this hypothetical case, what decision would you reach?

B. Sex as a Suspect Classification

Susan Vorchheimer graduated with honors from a junior high school in Philadelphia. She applied to Central High School, a public school in the city for males, and was rejected because of her sex. Philadelphia has a unique system of four types of senior high schools: academic, comprehensive, technical, and magnet. There are only two schools in the academic category, Central High School for Boys and Philadelphia High School for Girls. Attendance at these two high schools is voluntary and is based on competitive examinations. At the time of the suit, only 7 percent of Philadelphia students qualified for admission to the two schools. Both were organized in the nineteenth century and both have a long tradition of academic excellence and college placement. The two schools are substantially equal in quality, and both have an enrollment of about 2000 students with a faculty numbering over 100. Comprehensive high schools, one of which Susan eventually attended pending disposition of her case by the district court, are coeducational and have slightly lower admission standards than the two academic high schools.

Susan visited both Girls High and Central High. She disliked the atmosphere at the former: "I just didn't like the impression it gave me. I didn't think I would be able to go there for three years and not be harmed in any way by it." She chose Central High School. When she was refused admission because of her sex, Susan brought a class action against the Philadelphia School District. After a trial, the district court granted an injunction, ordering that she and other qualified female students be admitted to Central High School. The Court of Appeals for the Third Circuit was confronted with two issues: Do the sex-segregated academic high schools in Philadelphia violate federal statutes against sex discrimination and/or do they violate the Equal Protection Clause of the Fourteenth Amendment?

VORCHHEIMER v. SCHOOL DIST. OF PHILADELPHIA

United States Court of Appeals, Third Circuit, 1976.
532 F.2d 880.

Joseph F. WEIS, Jr., Circuit Judge.

* * *

In 1972 Congress provided that the benefits of educational programs funded through federal monies should be available to all persons without discrimination based on sex. The statute applies, however, to only specified types of educational institutions and excludes from its cov-

erage the admission policies of secondary school.[4] * * *

* * *

* * * In an early part of [the Equal Educational Opportunities Act of 1974] Congress finds that maintenance of dual school systems in which students are assigned solely on the basis of sex denies equal protection. Despite that poli-

---

4. Moreover, there is a specific exclusion of the admissions policies of public colleges

which traditionally enrolled only students of one sex.

cy pronouncement, however, the statute does not prohibit the states from segregating schools on the basis of sex although there is a specific proscription on segregation based on race, color or national origin. Insofar, then, that the Equal Educational Opportunities Act of 1974 might have application to established single-sex schools, the legislation is at best ambiguous.

* * *

The Act's policy declaration is that children are entitled to "equal educational opportunity" without regard to race, color, or sex. The finding of the district court discloses no inequality in opportunity for education between Central and Girls High Schools. We cannot, therefore, find that language applicable here.

* * *

We conclude the legislation is so equivocal that it cannot control the issue in this case. * * *

Finding no Congressional enactments which authoritatively address the problem, we must consider the constitutional issues which provided the impetus for issuance of the injunction.

The district court reviewed the line of recent cases dealing with sex discrimination * * *. As a result of that analysis, the district judge reasoned that, while the Supreme Court has not held sex to be a suspect classification, a stricter standard than the rational relationship test applies and is denominated "fair and substantial relationship."

In each of the cases cited, however, there was an actual deprivation or loss of a benefit to a female which could not be obtained elsewhere. * * *

In each instance where a statute was struck down, the rights of the respective sexes conflicted, and those of the female were found to be inadequate. None of the cases was concerned with a situation in which equal opportunity was extended to each sex or in which the restriction applied to both. And, significantly, none occurred in an educational setting.

The nature of the discrimination which the plaintiff alleges must be examined with care. She does not allege a deprivation of an education equal to that which the school board makes available to boys. Nor does she claim an exclusion from an academic school because of a quota system, or more stringent scholastic admission standards. Moreover, enrollment at the single-sex schools is applicable only to high schools and is voluntary, not mandatory. The plaintiff has difficulty in establishing discrimination in the school board's policy. If there are benefits or detriments inherent in the system, they fall on both sexes in equal measure.

* * * Race is a suspect classification under the Constitution, but the Supreme Court has declined to so characterize gender. We are committed to the concept that there is no fundamental difference between races and therefore, in justice, there can be no dissimilar treatment. But there are differences between the sexes which may, in limited circumstances, justify disparity in law. * * *

Equal educational opportunities should be available to both sexes in any intellectual field. However, the special emotional problems of the adolescent years are matters of human experience and have led some educational experts to opt for one-sex high schools. While this policy has limited acceptance on its merits, it does have its basis in a theory of equal benefit and not discriminatory denial.

* * *

The record does contain sufficient evidence to establish that a legitimate educational policy may be served by utilizing single-sex high schools. The primary aim of any school system must be to furnish an education of as high a quality as is feasible. Measures which would allow innovation in methods and techniques to achieve that goal have a high degree of relevance. Thus, given the objective of a quality education and a controverted, but respected theory that adolescents may study more effectively in single-sex schools, the policy of the school board here does bear a substantial relationship.

We need not decide whether this case requires application of the rational or substantial relationship tests because, using either, the result is the same. * * *

* * *

We are not unsympathetic with her desire to have an expanded freedom of choice, but its cost should not be overlooked. If she were to prevail, then all public single-sex schools would have to be abolished. The absence of these schools would stifle the ability of the local school board to continue with a respected educational methodology. It follows too that those students and parents who prefer an education in a public, single-sex school would be denied their freedom of choice. The existence of private schools is no more an answer to those people than it is to the plaintiff.

It is not for us to pass upon the wisdom of segregating boys and girls in high school. We are concerned not with the desirability of the practice but only its constitutionality. Once that threshold has been passed, it is the school board's responsibility to determine the best methods of accomplishing its mission.

The judgment of the district court will be reversed.

GIBBONS, Circuit Judge (dissenting).

* * * No doubt had the issue in this case been presented to the Court at any time from 1896 to 1954, a "separate but equal" analysis would have carried the day. I was under the distinct impression, however, that "separate but equal" analysis, especially in the field of public education, passed from the fourteenth amendment jurisprudential scene over

twenty years ago. The majority opinion, in establishing a twentieth-century sexual equivalent to the *Plessy* decision, reminds us that the doctrine can and will be invoked to support sexual discrimination in the same manner that it supported racial discrimination prior to *Brown*.

* * *

On August 21, 1974, Congress passed a series of amendments to the Elementary and Secondary Education Act of 1965. One of these amendments was the Equal Educational Opportunities Act of 1974 (hereinafter E.E.O.A.). Section 202 (a)(1) of this Act declared it to be the public policy of the United States that "all children enrolled in public schools are entitled to equal educational opportunity without regard to race, color, sex, or national origin." Had Congress stopped there one could argue, as the majority does, that a policy of "equal educational opportunity" does not preclude a "separate but equal" analysis, at least outside the racial context. But Congress went further. Relying specifically on the legislative authority conferred by § 5 of the fourteenth amendment, it made a series of legislative findings in § 203, the most important of which for the purpose of this appeal was that:

> (1) the maintenance of dual school systems in which students are assigned to schools solely on the basis of * * * sex * * * denies those students the equal protection of the laws guaranteed by the fourteenth amendment.

We are thus confronted with an explicit legislative finding that the maintenance of a dual school system on the basis of sex violates the equal protection clause. Philadelphia operates such a system in its senior academic high schools. We need look no further than this legislative finding in order to find a violation * * *. But Congress was not content, as the majority suggests, merely to assert broad legislative findings that might later prove to be inconsistent with or unrelated to its specific statutory scheme, for it defined in § 204 of the amendment a number of unlawful practices based on its findings.

* * *

* * * The statutory language of the E.E.O.A. convinces me that Congress did not inadvertently add the word "sex" to the list of prohibited bases for assigning public school students, but included it in those subsections with the express objective of abolishing single-sex public schools.

Rather than discuss the statutory language of the E.E.O.A., the majority engages in an extensive analysis of what Congress did not say or do in enacting that statute. Focusing on what it alleges to be congressional silence on the issue of school assignment on the basis of sex during the hearings and debates on the E.E.O.A., the majority finds an ambiguity in the statute and concludes that "a realistic and, in our view, inescapable interpretation is that Congress deliberately chose not to act and to leave open the question of single-sex schools." This is certainly a novel use of legislative history, or more precisely, of legislative nonhistory as a tool for statutory construction. The majority argues that Congress spoke clearly in 1972 when it did not enact legislation prohibiting single-sex schools and that the silence of the ninety-second Congress should control this court's interpretation of the words the ninety-third Congress used in enacting the E.E.O.A. in 1974. Congressional silence, especially that of a different Congress, I submit, can never be used to supersede the otherwise clear language of a statute.

* * *

Unlike the majority, I find it particularly difficult to say on the basis of the record in this case that the exclusion of females from Central bears a fair and substantial relationship to any of the Philadelphia School Board's legitimate objectives. Admittedly coeducation at the senior high school level has its supporters and its critics. The majority is also undoubtedly correct in suggesting that a legitimate educational policy may be served by utilizing single-sex high schools. But certainly that observation does not satisfy the substantial relationship test. Some showing must be made that a single-sex academic high school policy advances the Board's objectives in a manner consistent with the requirements of the Equal Protection Clause.

The Board, as the district court emphasized, did not present sufficient evidence that coeducation has an adverse effect upon a student's academic achievement. Indeed, the Board could not seriously assert that argument in view of its policy of assigning the vast majority of its students to coeducational schools. Presumably any detrimental impact on a student's scholastic achievement attributable to coeducation would be as evident in Philadelphia's coeducational comprehensive schools which offer college preparatory courses as the Board suggests it would be in its exclusively academic high schools. Thus, the Board's single-sex policy reflects a choice among educational techniques but not necessarily one substantially related to its stated educational objectives. One of those objectives, in fact, is to provide "educational options to students and their parents." The implementation of the Board's policy excluding females from Central actually precludes achievement of this objective because there is no option of a coeducational academic senior high school.

Because I agree with the district court that the Board has not made the required showing of a substantial relationship between its single-sex academic high school policy and its stated educational objectives, I would affirm the decision below even if I were willing to ignore the pertinent provisions of the E.E.O.A.

NOTES AND QUESTIONS

1. In April of 1977 the U. S. Supreme Court affirmed the court of appeals decision in a *per curiam* decision by an equally divided Court. Justice Rehnquist did not participate in the decision. Thus divided, the affirmance has no precedential value. It only records the fact that the lower court's decision stands.

2. Note the varying treatments of statutory interpretation in this case. The majority places much stock in the exemption in the Education Amendments of 1972 granted to single-sex institutions and carries this fact over to the 1974 Equal Educational Opportunities Act, which they note is primarily related to busing and school integration. In a footnote not excerpted, Judge Weis refers to a statement by Justice Brennan to the effect that statements of legislative purposes need not be taken at face value in equal protection cases when a review of statutory history demonstrates that the asserted purpose could not have been the goal of the legislation. Thus the majority rejects the literal interpretation dissenting Judge Gibbons gives to the 1974 Act. Should judges look behind "plain language" to ascertain legislative intentions? Or, assuming the majority is correct in inferring that Congress really didn't mean what it said in the 1974 Act, would it be preferable to accept the literal interpretation and let Congress then amend the law? Which would be more responsible judging?

In 1976 Congress amended Title IX of the 1972 Education Amendments on sex discrimination (which exempted single-sex schools from coverage) to exclude Boys State and Girls State, father-son and mother-daughter activities, and beauty pageants. Does this give further credence to the view of the majority about what Congress had in mind in drawing up the 1974 Act?

3. Judge Gibbons faults school officials for not presenting evidence that coeducational learning is harmful in support of its sex-segregated high schools. Actually, school officials did present evidence showing that some educators subscribe to the value of single-sex education. They also produced an expert witness who described his belief, based on studies of New Zealand's sex-segregated schools, that students in these institutions are more academically oriented and spend more time doing homework. Another witness testified that a higher percentage of persons listed in *Who's Who of American Women* attended single-sex schools. What do you think about this research? How influential is it, in your view? Why did Judge Gibbons choose to ignore it?

Susan Vorchheimer, on the other hand, argued that attending Girls High would cause her psychological or other injury. One commentator has viewed the harms of single-sex education in these terms:

> * * * it is apparent * * * that all-girl schools like Girls High have played a role in cultivating the attitudes and behavior of women that have kept the great majority from achieving professional prominence and positions of power, regardless of ability. In other words, the touted educational equivalency of

Girls and Central is meaningless unless the students of both schools are inculcated with the same career objectives and attitudes toward professional achievement. In a society in which many still insist there is a vast chasm between the proper roles of men and women, the only way that it can be assured that intellectually superior girls like Susan Vorchheimer will be exposed to the career perspectives and personal values instilled in the boys at Central is to allow them admission to that school. These possible differences between Girls and Central in the presentation and inculcation of values may be the undefined type of harm that Vorchheimer feared and which prompted her to attend a co-educational comprehensive school rather than an all-girl academic school.[76]

Would it have helped Susan's case if she had marshalled social science research findings supportive of the coeducational environment? How influential was social science evidence in this case? How influential could it have been?

4. Dormitory regulations which treat men and women differently are likely to be subjected to more than a rational purpose scrutiny under the Equal Protection Clause since classifications based on sex are involved. For example, in *Texas Woman's Univ. v. Chayklintaste*, 521 S.W.2d 949 (Texas, 1975), a Texas appellate court ruled that the institution, which had begun to admit men, could not under the Fourteenth Amendment Equal Protection Clause and the Texas constitution allow men to live off campus while requiring women to live in university housing.

Having provided housing facilities for women, it is unconstitutionally discriminating against its male students when it does not provide substantially equivalent and equal housing facilities for men. And, as a necessary corollary, it is unconstitutionally discriminating against its female students when it permits male students to live in off-campus private housing facilities, but by its parietal rule denies its female students the same right or privilege. (At p. 951).

Texas Woman's University subsequently changed the regulation to require all undergraduates except in certain situations to live on campus. The Texas Supreme Court upheld the revised rule, 530 S.W.2d 927 (Texas, 1975), and also agreed that the regulation was a rational age discrimination (the rule applied only to students under 23 years of age) based on university evidence of a "live and learn" policy.

Other rulings against different treatment of male and female students as a denial of equal protection include the use of higher test scores for girls than boys because of a desire to maintain a 50–50 ratio between male and female students in a public high school for the academically talented,[77] and the exclusion of females from non-contact male-oriented athletic pro-

76. Note, "Single-Sex Schools: The Last Bastion of 'Separate But Equal,'" 1977 *Duke L. Journal* 259, March, 1977, at p. 272.

77. *Berkelman v. San Francisco Unified School Dist.*, 501 F.2d 1264 (9th Cir. 1974).

grams such as tennis and cross-country skiing.[78] While participation in athletic programs has not uniformly been considered a fundamental right, courts have generally concluded that under the Equal Protection Clause educational institutions must advance rational reasons to deny participation to some students while extending it to others. Such reasons were not present in *Brenden* but were considered present in *Bucha v. Illinois High School Ass'n*, 351 F.Supp. 69 (N.D.Ill.1972), upholding differential treatment of girls' and boys' competitive athletic contests in Illinois:

> [Historical separation of the sexes in competitive athletics coupled with physical and psychological differences between the sexes] * * * lend substantial credence to the fears expressed by women coaches and athletes in defendants' affidavits that unrestricted athletic competition between the sexes would consistently lead to male domination of interscholastic sports and actually result in a decrease in female participation in such events. This court finds that such opinions have a rational basis in fact and are a constitutionally sufficient reason for prohibiting athletic interscholastic competition between boys and girls in Illinois. (At p. 75; material in brackets added).

In *Bucha*, the court followed the prevailing view in rejecting the association's argument that it, as a private organization, is not subject to suit. Courts have consistently found athletic associations so entwined with public educational institutions as to constitute state action under the Fourteenth Amendment.

The fact that sex is not considered the equivalent of race as a suspect classification under the Equal Protection Clause is clearly illustrated by those cases such as *Vorchheimer* and *Bucha* which refuse to rule against separate treatment for male and female students. Other cases in this category include an unsuccessful challenge to the exclusion of gynecological care and pap tests from a university student health plan,[79] dormitory curfews for women,[80] "split-court" basketball rules for a girl's high school league,[81] and to a requirement that men, but not women, participate in the Corps of Cadets at a military college.[82]

More recently, state and federal legislation, particularly Title IX of the 1972 Education Amendments, have been relied on to secure equal treatment for both sexes. Suits based on Title IX are much more likely to be successful, given the specific intentions of the federal act as spelled out by the accompanying comprehensive—and complex—regulations. These regulations extend the protection of the act to any part of the educational institution receiving federal funds, as well as to agencies which

78. *Brenden v. Independent School Dist.*, 477 F.2d 1292 (8th Cir. 1973).

79. *Bond v. Virginia Polytechnic Institute and State Univ.*, 381 F.Supp. 1023 (W.D. Va.1974).

80. *Robinson v. Board of Regents of Eastern Kentucky Univ.*, 475 F.2d 707 (6th Cir. 1973), *cert. denied*, 416 U.S. 982 (1974).

81. *Cape v. Tennessee Secondary School Athletic Ass'n*, 563 F.2d 793 (6th Cir. 1977).

82. *Williams v. Owen*, 245 S.E.2d 638 (Ga. 1978).

receive substantial assistance from the recipient institution. The regulations contain specific rules forbidding sex discrimination in a variety of contexts including financial aid, admissions (single sex institutions are exempted), courses (except sex education or physical education), student employment, and extracurricular activities (except competitive skill and contact sports). Discrimination on account of marital or parental status is also barred.

5. Other inequalities have also been the subject of court suits. Court actions have been brought and won against discrimination involving the physically or mentally handicapped,[83] discrimination against married students,[84] the exclusion of unmarried pregnant girls from school,[85] unjustifiable age discrimination,[86] and the exclusion of the children of illegal aliens from school.[87] In virtually all of the successful cases, the classification plan was considered clearly unreasonable or irrational. For example, in *Doe v. Plyler*, which involved the children of illegal aliens,[88] the district court concluded:

> * * * in this case the bulk of defendants' evidence was directed at proving what none tried to dispute, that Mexican immigration into the United States has caused grave overcrowding in the border school districts, which has been compounded by the poverty of the parents of the Mexican children and their special needs (bilingual education, free lunch, free breakfast, and free clothing). Excluding illegal immigrant children because of these problems is both irrational, because the undocumented children as a class are basically indistinguishable from the legally resident alien children in terms of their needs, and ineffectual, because the dominant problem remains unsolved. (At p. 589).

The district judge went on to suggest that the state's system of financing schools, approved in *San Antonio v. Rodriguez*, was beginning to weaken, forcing unfair decisions to be made:

> Texas' present method of financing public education by relying heavily upon the property wealth within a school district has

83. E. g., *Pennsylvania Ass'n for Retarded Children v. Pennsylvania*, 334 F.Supp. 1257 (E.D.Pa.1971), *aff'd* 343 F.Supp. 279 (1972) (three judge court), approving a consent agreement between the parties making free public education available to handicapped students.

84. E. g., *Hollon v. Mathis Ind. School Dist.*, 358 F.Supp. 1269 (S.D.Tex.1973), vacated for mootness, 491 F.2d 92 (5th Cir. 1974), granting a temporary restraining order to prohibit male married student's exclusion from interscholastic athletics.

85. E. g., *Ordway v. Hargraves*, 323 F.Supp. 1155 (D.Mass.1977), holding that there was no evidence presented to warrant excluding an unmarried, pregnant girl from high school and thus denied her the right to an education. The Equal Protection Clause was not specifically mentioned in this case.

86. E. g., *Purdie v. Univ. of Utah*, 584 P.2d 831 (Utah, 1978), involving the rejection of a 51 year old female applicant for a graduate program. The Utah Supreme Court found the age discrimination irrational under the Equal Protection Clause and the Utah constitution.

87. E. g., *Doe v. Plyler*, 458 F.Supp. 569 (E.D.Tex.1978), ruling that the exclusion of children of alien parents illegally residing in the state from school was irrational. The decision was limited to one school district in the state.

88. For a discussion of the issues involved in the exclusion of the children of illegal aliens from school, see R. F. Kare and F. Velarde-Munoz, "Undocumented Aliens and the Constitution: Limitations on State Action Denying Undocumented Children Access to Public Education," 5 *Hastings Const.L.Quarterly* 461, Winter, 1978.

apparently begun to strain at the seams. The state, as well as the children attending threadbare schools, now finds the contemporary policy unsupportable. This court expresses no opinion as to how the State of Texas might readjust its public school financing scheme in order to respond to the stark inequalities of educational opportunity between children in the border and metropolitan school districts * * *. The court can, however, invalidate state efforts that fail to demonstrate a rational basis and that make scapegoats of a defenseless group, chosen in an arbitrary, or even invidious manner. (At p. 590).

Suspect classification has rarely been invoked in these cases, though some courts appear to be exercising a more searching scrutiny than under the traditional rational test of old equal protection.

In addition, state and federal statutes have broadened the equal protection rights of some students, chiefly the handicapped.[89] (See figure 7–I). Public Law 94–142, the Education for All Handicapped Children Act, has been an important stimulant, for example, to the rediscovery of the benefits of "mainstreaming" students with special problems and/or needs through the regular classroom program.

6. Some commentators have suggested that the new equal protection be applied to children. Young people, as noted throughout this book, are frequently not allowed to make decisions for themselves. Even the Supreme Court largely ignored the interests of the children in the 1925 *Pierce* case, which established the right of nonpublic schools to exist, and in the 1972 *Yoder* case, which involved the claim of Old Order Amish to be free from compulsory schooling. To provide greater representation to children, a semi-suspect classification, according to one authority, could take the form of a "rule that all age-based lines, and all governmental allocations of responsibility or opportunity dependent on the circumstances of youth, are 'semi-suspect' in the limited sense that there must be an opportunity, absent strong justification for denying it, for a child to *rebut* any implied or asserted age-based incapacity."[90]

Another commentator has advocated that student status be considered a suspect classification.

> * * * students possess many of the characteristics of a "discrete and insular" minority. They are a class saddled with disabilities; they have suffered a history of purposeful unequal treatment based on tenacious assumptions of inequality; as long as they are minors, they possess an unalterable trait over which they have no control and for which they are not responsible. Realistically, they cannot resort to the political process to seek redress of their grievances.[91]

89. For a background discussion on the handicapped, see Joan Alschuler, "Education for the Handicapped," 7 *J.Law & Educ.* 523, October, 1978.

90. Tribe, *supra,* at p. 1080. For further development of Tribe's thesis, see Tribe, "Childhood, Suspect Classifications, and Conclusive Presumptions: Three Linked Riddles," 39 *Law and Contemp.Prob.* 8, 1975.

91. Leon Letwin "After *Goss v. Lopez:* Student Status as Suspect Classification?" 29 *Stanford L.Rev.* 627, April, 1977, at p. 659.

If students were considered a suspect classification as a class, then the burden of proof under equal protection would shift to school officials. As Letwin notes, the question then becomes, "Why should students *not* be accorded the same constitutional rights as others?"

If a factual case can be made that students' incompetence to exercise certain constitutional rights creates intolerable risks to themselves or to others, restriction may be warranted. The presumptive starting point, however, should be rejection of any such claim. The burden should lie where it generally does when constitutional rights are at stake: on the party seeking to curtail those rights. Experience suggests that often the state can present nothing more to overcome such a presumption than the bare assertion that curtailment is necessary.[92]

A number of questions arises under these suggestions. How might they affect compulsory schooling laws? Age-of-majority statutes? Driver licensing? If student status is considered suspect, would strict scrutiny be applied only to students below the age-of-majority? Or to all students, regardless of age? What would happen to age-based discriminations within the school setting? For example, if a student objects to a school rule limiting participation on the student newspaper to juniors and seniors, what standards of proof would the school have to bear? Should Letwin's proposal be extended to academic matters such as a requirement that all seniors must take senior English or college freshmen must take the history of western civilization? Is either Tribe's or Letwin's proposal realistic?

7. Based on the cases read and discussed in this chapter, how would you decide the following hypothetical situations using only the Equal Protection Clause (assume all the institutions involved are public)?

a. Student body president is suspended for two semesters for possession of marijuana. Normally, similar violations of college rules result in suspension for only one semester. The dean of students states she decided on the harsher punishment because of the student's position of leadership. The campus president backed the dean. Student protests on equal protection grounds.

b. Male student wears a dress to high school, which, if worn by a female student, would conform to the institutional dress code. The student is suspended until he changes into clothes traditionally worn by males. The student protests on equal protection grounds.

c. A male college student is denied the opportunity to attend an all-female college which has a nationally-recognized program in women's studies. The student asserts that there are no comparable programs at other public higher educational institutions in the state. He brings suit against the institution on equal protection grounds.

8. Consider the following hypothetical case:

The Case of Susan Student

West Thumper State College has a rule prohibiting discrimination on the basis of race, national origin, sex, religion, and handicapped status by

---

92. *Id.*, at p. 643.

any member or organization affiliated with the institution. The rule applies to recognized student organizations. Violations are to be handled through normal campus adjudicatory machinery; a special *ad hoc* procedure can be implemented as well by the campus affirmative action officer. Students bringing charges must choose one or the other mechanisms. Appeal of decisions involving discrimination charges are heard directly by the college president.

Susan Student had worked hard as a member of the editorial board of the college paper. As one of five assistant editors, Susan had major responsibility for putting out the weekly edition of the *West Thumper Ramrod*. She completed her assignments on time and was generally regarded as a very competent journalist.

At West Thumper, the editor of the student newspaper is selected annually from among the members of the editorial board. In May the incumbent editor meets with the newly-elected student body president to make the selection. A faculty member from the Department of Journalism sits in on these sessions, but at the invitation of the students, since the paper is student-funded. The *Ramrod* is not formally a part of any department, though most journalism students work on the paper. Indeed, it is recognized as the best way for these students to get job-related experience. The paper owns its own equipment but occupies its space on campus free of charge. Susan's sole ambition is to become editor of the college paper.

This year, Susan, a junior at the college, fully expected to get the appointment. Indeed, she had worked especially hard, putting out a special student election edition of the paper. The special issue was widely regarded as one of the best issues of the *Ramrod* in recent years. In addition to supervising the publication of the election issue, Susan had written the editorial describing the preferences of the editorial board. She and the editor disagreed on the choice to recommend for student body president, but three of the members of the board backed Susan's views about the desirability of electing a female student. She was given the assignment of writing the editorial. As it turned out, the editor's choice, a male student, won the election.

Two days after the incumbent editor and newly-elected student body president met, the choice for next year's editor was announced. It was not Susan. She was furious. Susan confronted the incumbent editor, demanding an explanation. He said, "We discussed it, Susan, and we decided on John because we believe him better qualified and more objective in his reporting." He added, "Besides, it didn't help for you to back the wrong horse in the election."

Susan, obviously upset by the turn of events, charged that the decision was a blatant example of sex discrimination. She told the editor that she intended to take the matter to the Judicial Committee.

The Judicial Committee, composed of two appointed male faculty members and three elected male students, after hearing both sides of the dispute, unanimously refused to overturn the choice of the newspaper editor. The Committee agreed that it should not interfere in a matter so closely related to freedom of the press and so inconclusive with regard to the sex discrimination charge. Susan appealed to the campus president.

———

Based on previous discussion and cases, what arguments would you make for each side? If you were to decide this hypothetical case, what decision would you reach and why?

C. The Limited Range of Fundamental Rights

Violations of specific constitutional rights such as freedom of speech or press automatically require strong state justification, as the discussions in Chapters Three and Four point out. Since these rights already have independent constitutional backing, the strict scrutiny approach of new equal protection furnishes an additional protection against their transgression.

The strict scrutiny of new equal protection is also applied to situations where rights not specifically mentioned in the Constitution but considered "fundamental" are involved. What constitutes such a right is subject, of course, to Supreme Court interpretation. As noted earlier in this chapter, the Court has ruled that interstate travel falls into the fundamental category, while the right to education, at least in the context of unequal school financing, does not. The right to privacy will be discussed in the next chapter.

Other rights considered fundamental include the right to vote. Under the Twenty-Sixth Amendment to the Constitution, the right to vote in state and federal elections may not be denied because the voter is eighteen years old or older. While states can impose other voter qualifications in the interest of preserving the integrity of the election process, the Supreme Court has decided in numerous cases that restrictions will be closely scrutinized. Where restrictions have the effect of granting the right to vote to some but not to others and thus raising an equal protection issue, the Court applies the strict scrutiny approach and demands a compelling state justification for the different treatment.

To what extent can states treat students differently from other voters in setting voter qualifications? For example, should a college town with a population of 5000 be able to impose additional voter qualifications on the 4000 students in residence at a nearby college? Do town officials have reason to believe students with little stake in the community may determine the outcome of local elections and referenda? Is this a valid concern under the Equal Protection Clause? One commentator asserts that "such special requirements operate with the same basic purpose and effect as exclusions based on race, sex, or occupation," adding that:

> The exclusion of students would appear to be particularly inequitable in view of the fact that they are regarded by the Census Bureau as residents of their college towns and are therefore taken into account in determining the legislative representation and federal aid to which these communities are entitled.[93]

93. Kenneth J. Guido, Jr. "Student Voting and Residency Qualifications: The After-math of the Twenty-Sixth Amendment," 47 New York Univ.L.Rev. 32, 1972, at p. 58.

Since the Supreme Court ruled in *Dunn v. Blumstein,* 405 U.S. 330 (1972) that one year in-state and three month in-county residence requirements do not satisfy a compelling state interest in determining voter qualifications, challenges to student residency requirements have mounted. It is important to note that the Court did not rule out residency requirements entirely. The Justices noted that states have the power to require that voters be *bona fide* residents of the relevant political community. But such requirements must be "appropriately defined and uniformly applied." (At p. 343). A residency requirement of 30 days, suggested the majority, would be adequate to undertake administrative tasks designed to prevent fraud. While the states thus can impose some means to ascertain voting qualifications, the options are limited.

Voter qualification issues involving students have arisen in many localities. Representative of a recent case is *Paulson v. Forest City Community School Dist.,* 238 N.W.2d 344 (Iowa, 1976). There, taxpayers and voters in the school district brought an action against election officials, contesting a referendum in which students voted on the issuance of school bonds. As it turned out, the voting was sufficiently close that if 140 or more students attending nearby Waldorf College voted affirmatively and if they were not qualified to vote, the bond proposition failed. The Supreme Court of Iowa affirmed the lower court's decision that under state law the students were qualified to vote, even though their hometowns may have been outside the district. The court ruled that state law allows persons to "declare" their home and that since the students had declared the college to be their place of residence, they were qualified to vote in the referendum. The court refused to take up the taxpayers' argument that even if qualified to vote in local elections, the students were not qualified to vote in referenda. The taxpayers claimed a compelling state interest is present in a small community with a large nearby college to prevent students from overwhelming the local residents and saddling them with debts. The court concluded that this is a matter for the legislature and indicated no opinion "on the constitutionality of a statute differentiating voter qualifications for candidate and referenda elections." (At pp. 350–351). Do you think such a state restriction would meet a compelling state interest test?

New equal protection challenges have also been leveled at restrictions placed by school officials on married students. Following the Supreme Court's assertion that marriage is a fundamental right,[94] virtually all contemporary state and federal courts apply the strict scrutiny test to such restrictions, and in most instances, the requisite compelling state interest requirement has been lacking. Characteristic of the cases is *Bell v. Lone Oak Independent School Dist.,* 507 S.W.2d 636 (Tex.1974). There, the Court of Civil Appeals of Texas, Texarkana, ruled that a school board

---

94. The two leading cases are *Skinner v. Oklahoma,* 316 U.S. 535 (1942), involving an equal protection challenge to a state law providing for sterilization of habitual criminals, and *Loving v. Virginia,* 388 U.S. 1 (1967), involving due process and equal protection challenges to a state anti-miscegenation statute. In *Skinner,* Justice Douglas noted that "Marriage and pro-creation are fundamental to the very existence and survival of the race." (At p. 541). And in *Loving,* Chief Justice Warren observed that "The freedom to marry has long been recognized as one of the vital personal rights essential to the orderly pursuit of happiness by free men." (At p. 12).

regulation prohibiting married high school students from participating in extracurricular activities violated the Equal Protection Clause of the Fourteenth Amendment. Noting that the state had sanctioned the marriage ceremony by statute, the court observed that "It * * * seems illogical to say that a school district can make a rule punishing a student for entering into a status authorized and sanctioned by the laws of this state." (At p. 638). The court noted that the burden of proof was upon school officials to show that its rule should be upheld as a necessary restraint to promote a compelling state purpose and concluded that no such proof was forthcoming. While the cases show school officials attempting to justify restrictions on married students by reference to a number of potential problems, few convincing statistics have been introduced. Perhaps the more recent rulings striking down differential treatment of married students will, as a byproduct, furnish school authorities with an opportunity to produce more convincing evidence.

V. SUMMARY

In recent decades, the Supreme Court in concert with the lower federal courts and with state courts has made impressive attempts to assure that equality of legal treatment becomes a reality in American society. Beginning with *Brown,* the Court has taken decisive steps to eradicate *de jure* race and ethnic discrimination, and has whittled away at more obvious forms of sex discrimination.

But to many, equality of legal treatment is not enough. They maintain that legal equality is an empty formalism if the resources in society are distributed in such a way as to give substantial power to some groups at the expense of others. This contradiction between formal rights and actual conditions is reflected in the sarcastic observation made some years ago by Anatole France, the former French leader, that the law in all its majesty forbids rich as well as poor to sleep under bridges on rainy nights, to beg in the streets, and to steal bread.

Expressing a sensitivity to gross inequalities in the racial context, the Supreme Court in more recent cases has upheld efforts to eliminate the heritage of past *de jure* discrimination in the interest of equality of opportunity. *Swann, Milliken II,* and even the *Bakke* decision, ambiguous as it is, are testimonials to at least some concern for remedial action to compensate for past injustices. Congress and many of the states have also taken up the cause of bringing a variety of heretofore excluded groups into the mainstream of society.

In making decisions about the meaning of equal protection, courts cannot avoid considering the meaning of equality itself. Where educational institutions are concerned, other considerations are important as well. Figure 7–3 outlines the major variables impinging on judicial involvement in student equal protection issues.

Figure 7–3: Judicial Support for Student Equal Protection Rights

DIRECTION OF INFLUENCE

INFLUENCING VARIABLES	Promoting	Retarding	Uncertain
Value Position on Government and Distribution of Resources	Support for Expanding Opportunity to the Disadvantaged	Support for Individual Competition and Merit	
Value Position on Equality	Equality of Opportunity Equality of Result *		Equality of Legal Treatment (colorblind)
Approach to Equal Protection Clause	New Equal Protection —Fundamental Rights —Suspect Classifications	Old Equal Protection	
Orientation to Role of Court	Activism	Restraintism	Neutrality
Orientation to Educational Environment	Youth Entitled to Rights Non-Deferral to Educational Professionals View Education as a Fundamental Right View Student Status as a Suspect Classification *	Youth Not Entitled to Rights Deferral to Educational Professionals View Education as a Non-fundamental Right View Student Status as a Non-suspect Classification	Role of Social Science Research Rulings of Other Courts Situational Factors —Facts of Case, e. g., *de jure* versus *de facto* segregation

* No present advocates on Supreme Court.

[B9992]

In the political and social setting as well as in the educational, equal protection issues raise important questions about the role of courts. How activist should they be in applying the Equal Protection Clause to non-racial discriminations? How activist should judges be in seeking to bring about a more equitable distribution of resources? When faced with legislative inaction, many people, particularly those belonging to disfavored groups, look to the courts for relief from social injustice. But judicial history shows that courts become involved in equal protection challenges only in the grosser instances of discrimination. To keep the Equal Protection Clause manageable, the Supreme Court has refused to become involved in *de facto* discrimination, racial or otherwise. The *Milliken I* and *San Antonio* decisions are apt testimony to judicial restraint. Overuse of equal protection places the judge in the same line-drawing role as the legislator. Aside from race discrimination and certain other forms of discrimination which have prompted the development of more searching judicial inquiry, individual and group political action at the local and national level remains the primary avenue to establish the reordering of societal priorities ideological groups urge for creating what they regard as the humane society.

Part III

EMERGING RIGHTS AND A RECONSIDERATION

Chapter Eight

"This Court has occasionally pushed beyond established constitutional contours to protect the vulnerable and to further basic human values."

Justice Thurgood Marshall
Wyman v. James, 1971

"EMERGING RIGHTS OF PRIVACY"

The most often quoted definition of the "right to privacy" is simply "the right to be let alone." Although few in a society which places great importance on individualism would deny the importance of "the right to be let alone," there is also an awareness of society's "need to know" in certain situations. The ongoing conflict between personal privacy and efforts to intrude upon that privacy manifests itself in several ways.

Privacy issues are apt to arise in the course of criminal investigations. The growing use of computerized information systems and electronic surveillance have increased traditional fears of encroaching government and organized crime. Yet efforts to control the use of these technological tools through security checks and covert investigations threaten to intrude upon personal privacy. Advocates of crime prevention assert that no person is an island in our increasingly complex and interdependent society. If this were so, criminal investigation could not be conducted.

Privacy issues also arise in disputes over the enforcement of social mores. Society has no legitimate interest, say privacy advocates, in interfering with intimate personal relationships. Private social interaction is considered essential for maximizing individual growth and satisfaction. Nor does society have any right to assert control over such personal matters as grooming, sterilization, abortion, drug use, and the right to die. It is inaccurate to classify some of these activities as crimes, say privacy advocates, since there are no victims. Following the ancient adage that "every man's home is his castle," privacy advocates also note that privacy has a "place-oriented" dimension, which protects the activities one pursues in a particular place from public scrutiny and regulation. Others note that society has a legitimate interest in preventing behavior which threatens moral decay and eventual social breakdown. Therefore, privacy must yield when it serves to cloak anti-social behavior.

Finally, privacy issues for many individuals—most certainly students —are involved in the enforcement of rules in the organizational setting. Businesses and educational institutions often assert the need to maintain conduct and personal appearance standards which many employees and students find objectionable.

Until recently, it was common practice to invade rather than guarantee privacy. The origins of the right to privacy are relatively recent by legal standards. Before 1890, no British or American court had decided a case expressly on the invasion of such a right. In 1890, two lawyers, Samuel D. Warren and Louis D. Brandeis co-authored an article on privacy for the *Harvard Law Review,* which was to have great legal implications for debates about privacy.[1] Warren and Brandeis wrote that the common law "secures to each individual the right of determining, ordinarily, to what extent his thoughts, sentiments, and emotions shall be communicated to others." The concept of privacy that Warren and Brandeis defined was narrowly based, having mostly to do with the use of personal information by prying newspaper columnists.

While there is no "right" to privacy specifically mentioned in either the main body of the Constitution or the Bill of Rights, some constitutional scholars and judges have argued that a right to privacy is nevertheless inferred in our Constitution. The First Amendment prohibits government scrutiny of political expression and association; and thus, is said to protect associational privacy. The Third Amendment prohibits the practice of invading private homes for the quartering of troops and thus is said to protect privacy of the home. The Fourth Amendment prevents unreasonable searches and seizures and thus is said to protect privacy of the person. The Fifth Amendment prohibits the government from compelling persons to make revelations which could be used to incriminate them in court, and thus is said to protect privacy of information. Also relevant is the Ninth Amendment, which states that particular rights in the Constitution should not be taken to "deny or disparage others retained by the people." Some persons claim that privacy is such a right. Finally, the Fourteenth Amendment provision against deprivation of liberty has been relied on to secure a right to privacy in actions involving states and local municipalities.

The present reality in American law is that the concept of a constitutional general right to privacy is still amorphous. The Supreme Court has so far refused to hold that the Constitution contains a comprehensive or absolute right to privacy, defined broadly as "the right to be let alone." However, the Court has made a number of important decisions in that direction. As Professor Alan Westin points out in *Data Banks in a Free Society,* "In the course of protecting some explicitly stated Constitutional rights, the Supreme Court has given protection over the past decades to many important 'components' of the rights to privacy." [2]

Rights of privacy can, of course, be conferred by statute. In fact, in *Katz v. United States,* 389 U.S. 347, a 1967 Supreme Court decision excerpted below, Justice Stewart for the majority observed that "the protection of a person's *general* right to privacy—his right to be let alone by other people—is * * * left largely to the law of the individual states." (At pp. 350–351; emphasis in original). Federal statutes can also secure privacy rights. A prime example is the 1974 Family Educational Rights and Privacy Act (FERPA), to be discussed later. Rights of privacy can emanate from institutional rules as well. Thus, some businesses and edu-

---

1. Samuel D. Warren and Louis D. Brandeis, "The Right of Privacy", 4 *Harv.L.Rev.* 193, 1890, at p. 198.

2. Alan F. Westin and Michael A. Baker, *Data Banks in a Free Society* (New York: Quadrangle Books, 1972), at p. 18.

cational organizations specifically provide employees and students with privacy rights in such areas as clothing lockers and dormitory rooms.

The tension between individual privacy and social inquiry underlies all the aspects of privacy to be discussed in this chapter. The chapter has been divided into two parts. The first part explores issues related to search and seizure, and the second focuses on personal rights of privacy as reflected in judicial decision making about such matters as contraceptives, abortions, sexual preferences, hair length, and student records. Throughout, the evolving law in the political and social setting is compared and contrasted with legal developments in the educational setting. It will become apparent that judicial sensitivity to age differences, and to purported differences between society-at-large and educational institutions, plays a major role in shaping the case law in this sensitive area.

I. SEARCHES AND SEIZURES

No area of the common law has been repeated more often than the expression "a man's home is his castle." Yet, the Founding Fathers were quite aware that police authorities must have the capacity to obtain evidence related to a crime. But they were opposed to the infamous "writs of assistance" the British used to rummage at will through possessions of suspected smugglers. The Framers decided to make such capricious searches and seizures unconstitutional by adoption of the Fourth Amendment. The Fourth Amendment states, "The right of the people to be secure in their persons, houses, papers, and effects, against unreasonable searches and seizures, shall not be violated, and no Warrants shall issue, but upon probable cause, supported by Oath or affirmation, and particularly describing the place to be searched, and the persons or things to be seized." But what is an "unreasonable" search and seizure? Does the absence of a semi-colon after the word "violated" mean that only searches conducted pursuant to a warrant are reasonable? Or are there some searches which can be considered reasonable even if no warrant is issued? Does the Amendment restrict only public officials or private persons as well? Are wiretapping and other forms of electronic surveillance covered by the Amendment or only tangible objects? What is "probable cause" for the issuing of a search warrant? The Supreme Court has had to deal with these questions in its efforts to apply the Fourth Amendment to specific situations.

A. Searches and Seizures in the Political and Social Setting

The Supreme Court has ruled that for a search to be "reasonable" under the Fourth Amendment, a search warrant is generally required and is to be issued upon a showing of probable cause. However, search warrants are not required when there is probable cause coupled with exigent circumstances that make securing a warrant impracticable.[3] For example, a warrant could not be profitably secured when the police are running after a jewel thief. The Court has also countenanced police actions to obtain a blood sample without a warrant from an arrested person to show that the

---

3. *Coolidge v. New Hampshire*, 403 U.S. 443 (1971).

person was driving a car while intoxicated.[4]   In such situations search warrants are not required, because medical detection would be impossible if time were taken to obtain one.   Other instances where the Supreme Court has ruled that search warrants are not necessary include a street detention and weapons search of a person upon reasonable suspicion that a crime may be about to begin,[5] a full search of a person incident to a lawful arrest,[6] an inventory search of an automobile impounded for parking violations,[7] and searches of suspicious letters from abroad by customs inspectors.[8]   While the exceptions to the warrant process are limited, they encompass many of the searches which are conducted and are a source of continual litigation.

Search warrants require a showing of "probable cause."   The Supreme Court has concluded that probable cause must be more substantial than a police investigator's impulsive suspicions.   On the other hand, "probable cause" is not intended to mean "evidence to convict," which would be far too restrictive.   The Court has claimed that the correct test is whether a reasonable person, given sufficient information to render an independent, neutral judgment would reach the common sense conclusion that a warrant should be issued.   The Court has further ruled that a "neutral and detached magistrate" must issue the warrant.   As Justice Jackson noted, "When the right of privacy must reasonably yield to the right to search is, as a rule, to be decided by a judicial officer, not by a policeman or government enforcement agent." [9]

In 1921 the Court ruled that since the Fourth Amendment was intended to deter unlawful government action in harmony with the other provisions of the Bill of Rights, searches by private persons are not restricted by the Amendment and evidence so obtained cannot be excluded from legal proceedings.[10]   This decision has significance for the nonpublic educational sector.

Just a few decades ago, police officers consistently and with impunity ignored the Fourth Amendment.   Searches were frequently conducted without obtaining warrants from the courts even when one could easily have been obtained.   General searches or so-called "fishing expeditions" were not unknown.   In 1914 the Supreme Court began a fifty year process of enforcing the Fourth Amendment.   In *Weeks v. United States,* 232 U.S. 383 (1914), the Court ruled that in order to guarantee the enforcement of the Fourth Amendment in criminal prosecutions in federal courts, all evidence obtained by a federal officer in violation of the Fourth Amendment would be excluded.   In 1949 a defendant in a state criminal case asked the Supreme Court to make this so-called exclusionary rule apply to state criminal prosecutions as well.   More than two-thirds of the states

4. *Schmerber v. California,* 384 U.S. 757 (1966).

5. *Terry v. Ohio,* 392 U.S. 1 (1968).

6. *United States v. Robinson,* 414 U.S. 218 (1973).

7. *South Dakota v. Opperman,* 428 U.S. 364 (1976).

8. *United States v. Ramsey,* 431 U.S. 607 (1977).

9. *Johnson v. United States,* 333 U.S. 10 (1948), at p. 14.

10. *Burdeau v. McDowell,* 256 U.S. 465 (1921).

opposed such an extension, arguing that police authorities rarely engaged in illegal searches. The Court ruled in *Wolf v. Colorado*, 338 U.S. 25 (1949), that the Fourteenth Amendment Due Process Clause did not prohibit the admission of evidence obtained by unreasonable search or seizure in a state court trial, even though unreasonable searches and seizures could not be conducted by state officials. Twelve years later, the Warren Court overruled the *Wolf* holding. In *Mapp v. Ohio*, 367 U.S. 643 (1961), the Court claimed that the Fourth Amendment would have little effectiveness without the exclusionary rule. The *Mapp* ruling stands with the 1966 *Miranda v. Arizona* ruling as one of the most important milestones in legally circumscribing local police conduct. It is important to note, however, that many searches and seizures continue to be conducted without a valid search warrant when one ought to be required under the law. In fact, some social science research studies demonstrate that the exclusionary rule has not been an effective deterrent to state and local police, many of whom have pursued their business pretty much as usual.[11]

The most critical problem in the search and seizure area involves wiretapping and various forms of eavesdropping. Experts in the field are persuaded that vast numbers of wiretaps continue to be placed almost routinely. Justice William O. Douglas once stated that he was "morally certain" that the sacrosanct Conference Room of the Supreme Court itself had been bugged. The Court experienced its first confrontation with wiretapping and the Fourth Amendment in *Olmstead v. United States*, 277 U.S. 438 (1928). In a close 5 to 4 decision, the Court held that wiretapping did not violate Fourth Amendment protection against unreasonable searches and seizures, since nothing *tangible* was seized during a wiretapping. Furthermore, the wiretapping was done *outside* the living quarters of the victim. In effect, the Court's position in the *Olmstead* case was that:

> There was no searching. There was no seizure. The evidence was secured by the use of the sense of hearing and that only. There was no entry of the houses or offices of the defendants.

In dissent, Justice Brandeis made the following prophetic statement:

> Subtler and more far-reaching means of invading privacy have become available to the Government. Discovery and invention have made it possible for the Government by means far more effective than stretching upon the rack, to obtain disclosure in court of what is whispered in the closet. * * * Advances in the psychic and related sciences may bring means of exploring unexpressed beliefs, thoughts, and emotions. * * * Can it be that the Constitution affords no protection against such invasions of individual security? (At pp. 473–474).

However, in 1934, Congress did ban the interception of private communication by third parties. Electronic surveillance performed without

11. See, for example, the discussion in Note, "Trends in Legal Commentary on the Exclusionary Rule," 65 *J. of Criminal Law and Criminology*, 373, 1974, at p. 382ff.

However, as this book goes to press, advance information on two statistical studies—one by the General Accounting Office and one by the U.S. Law Enforcement Assistance Administration—suggest that the exclusionary rule is much more effective than previously believed.

the use of telephone cables was not affected by the statute. Therefore "bugging" was valid under the *Olmstead* rule if no physical area was invaded when placing the bug. The *Olmstead* doctrine was the rule of law until the 1960s. By the late 1960s it became clear to a majority of the members of the Warren Court that some controls would have to be placed on the use of sophisticated surveillance techniques by governmental agencies. In the *Katz* decision below, the Court abandoned the doctrine that the Fourth Amendment forbids only physical invasions and seizures developed in *Olmstead* and replaced it with the individual's right to privacy. The Court asserted that the Fourth Amendment "protects people, not places." What a person seeks to preserve as private, even in an area accessible to the public, may be constitutionally protected.

Katz had been convicted of transmitting betting information in violation of a federal statute. The critical evidence against him was a series of voice recordings made from a number of his telephone conversations. The evidence had been obtained by an eavesdropping device attached to the outside of a public phone booth from which he made calls on betting information. The F.B.I. was careful to record only the voice of Katz. The court of appeals rejected Katz's attempt to exclude the recordings, claiming that there was no violation of the Fourth Amendment because there was no physical entrance by the F.B.I. into the area that was occupied by him. Katz appealed to the Supreme Court. The Supreme Court overturned the conviction and with it the doctrine that the Fourth Amendment could only be applied to situations of physical intrusion.

KATZ v. UNITED STATES

Supreme Court of the United States, 1967.
389 U.S. 347, 88 S.Ct. 507, 19 L.Ed.2d 576.

Mr. Justice STEWART delivered the opinion of the Court.

*   *   *

The petitioner has phrased [the] questions as follows:

"A. Whether a public telephone booth is a constitutionally protected area so that evidence obtained by attaching an electronic listening recording device to the top of such a booth is obtained in violation of the right to privacy of the user of the booth.

"B. Whether physical penetration of a constitutionally protected area is necessary before a search and seizure can be said to be violative of the Fourth Amendment to the United States Constitution."

We decline to adopt this formulation of the issues. In the first place the correct solution of Fourth Amendment problems is not necessarily promoted by in-

cantation of the phrase "constitutionally protected area." Secondly, the Fourth Amendment cannot be translated into a general constitutional "right to privacy." That Amendment protects individual privacy against certain kinds of governmental intrusion, but its protections go further, and often have nothing to do with privacy at all. Other provisions of the Constitution protect personal privacy from other forms of governmental invasion. But the protection of a person's *general* right to privacy—his right to be let alone by other people—is, like the protection of his property and of his very life, left largely to the law of the individual States.

*   *   * the parties have attached great significance to the characterization of the telephone booth from which the petitioner placed his calls. The petitioner has strenuously argued that the booth was a "constitutionally protected area." The Government has maintained with equal vigor that it was not. But this effort to decide whether or not a given "area," viewed in the abstract, is "constitutionally protected" deflects attention from the problem presented by this case. For the Fourth Amendment protects people, not places. What a person knowingly exposes to the public, even in his own home or office, is not a subject of Fourth Amendment protection. But what he seeks to preserve as private, even in an area accessible to the public, may be constitutionally protected. * * *

The Government stresses the fact that the telephone booth from which the petitioner made his calls was constructed partly of glass, so that he was as visible after he entered it as he would have been if he had remained outside. But what he sought to exclude when he entered the booth was not the intruding eye—it was the uninvited ear. He did not shed his right to do so simply because he made his calls from a place where he might be seen. No less than an individual in a business office, in a friend's apartment, or in a taxicab, a person in a telephone booth may rely upon the protection of the Fourth Amendment. One who occupies it, shuts the door behind him, and pays the toll that permits him to place a call is surely entitled to assume that the words he utters into the mouthpiece will not be broadcast to the world. To read the Constitution more narrowly is to ignore the vital role that the public telephone has come to play in private communication.

The Government contends, however, that the activities of its agents in this case should not be tested by Fourth Amendment requirements, for the surveillance technique they employed involved no physical penetration of the telephone booth from which the petitioner placed his calls. It is true that the absence of such penetration was at one time thought to foreclose further Fourth Amendment

inquiry, Olmstead v. United States, 277 U.S. 438; Goldman v. United States, 316 U.S. 129, for that Amendment was thought to limit only searches and seizures of tangible property. * * * Thus, although a closely divided Court supposed in *Olmstead* that surveillance without any trespass and without the seizure of any material object fell outside the ambit of the Constitution, we have since departed from the narrow view on which that decision rested. * * * Once * * * it is recognized that the Fourth Amendment protects people—and not simply "areas"—against unreasonable searches and seizures it becomes clear that the reach of that Amendment cannot turn upon the presence or absence of a physical intrusion into any given enclosure.

* * *

The question remaining for decision, then, is whether the search and seizure conducted in this case complied with constitutional standards. * * *

* * *

It is apparent that the agents in this case acted with restraint. Yet the inescapable fact is that this restraint was imposed by the agents themselves, not by a judicial officer. They were not required, before commencing the search, to present their estimate of probable cause for detached scrutiny by a neutral magistrate. They were not compelled, during the conduct of the search itself, to observe precise limits established in advance by a specific court order. Nor were they directed, after the search had been completed, to notify the authorizing magistrate in detail of all that had been seized. In the absence of such safeguards, this Court has never sustained a search upon the sole ground that officers reasonably expected to find evidence of a particular crime and voluntarily confined their activities to the least intrusive means consistent with that end. * * *

"Over and again this Court has emphasized that the mandate of the

[Fourth] Amendment requires adherence to judicial processes," and that searches conducted outside the judicial process, without prior approval by judge or magistrate, are *per se* unreasonable under the Fourth Amendment—subject only to a few specifically established and well-delineated exceptions.

It is difficult to imagine how any of those exceptions could ever apply to the sort of search and seizure involved in this case. Even electronic surveillance substantially contemporaneous with an individual's arrest could hardly be deemed an "incident" of that arrest. Nor could the use of electronic surveillance without prior authorization be justified on grounds of "hot pursuit." And, of course, the very nature of electronic surveillance precludes its use pursuant to the suspect's consent.

The Government does not question these basic principles. Rather, it urges the creation of a new exception to cover this case. It argues that surveillance of a telephone booth should be exempted from the usual requirement of advance authorization by a magistrate upon a showing of probable cause. We cannot agree. * * * These considerations do not vanish when the search in question is transferred from the setting of a home, an office, or a hotel room to that of a telephone booth. Wherever a man may be, he is entitled to know that he will remain free from unreasonable searches and seizures. The government agents here ignored "the procedure of antecedent justification * * * that is central to the Fourth Amendment," a procedure that we hold to be a constitutional precondition of the kind of electronic surveillance involved in this case. Because the surveillance here failed to meet that condition, and because it led to the petitioner's conviction, the judgment must be reversed.

It is so ordered.

Judgment reversed.

Mr. Justice MARSHALL took no part in the consideration or decision of this case.

Mr. Justice DOUGLAS, with whom Mr. Justice BRENNAN joins, concurring.

While I join the opinion of the Court, I feel compelled to reply to the separate concurring opinion of my Brother WHITE, which I view as a wholly unwarranted green light for the Executive Branch to resort to electronic eavesdropping without a warrant in cases which the Executive Branch itself labels "national security" matters.

Neither the President nor the Attorney General is a magistrate. In matters where they believe national security may be involved they are not detached, disinterested, and neutral as a court or magistrate must be. Under the separation of powers created by the Constitution, the Executive Branch is not supposed to be neutral and disinterested. Rather it should vigorously investigate and prevent breaches of national security and prosecute those who violate the pertinent federal laws. The President and Attorney General are properly interested parties, cast in the role of adversary, in national security cases. They may even be the intended victims of subversive action. Since spies and saboteurs are as entitled to the protection of the Fourth Amendment as suspected gamblers like petitioner, I cannot agree that where spies and saboteurs are involved adequate protection of Fourth Amendment rights is assured when the President and Attorney General assume both the position of adversary-and-prosecutor and disinterested, neutral magistrate.

* * *

Mr. Justice HARLAN, concurring.

* * *

Mr. Justice WHITE, concurring.

I agree that the official surveillance of petitioner's telephone conversations in a public booth must be subjected to the test of reasonableness under the Fourth Amendment and that on the record now before us the particular surveillance undertaken was unreasonable absent a warrant properly authorizing it. This application of the Fourth Amendment need not interfere with legitimate needs of law enforcement.**

In joining the Court's opinion, I note the Court's acknowledgment that there are circumstances in which it is reasonable to search without a warrant. In this connection, * * * the Court points out that today's decision does not reach national security cases. Wiretapping to protect the security of the Nation has been authorized by successive Presidents. * * * We should not require the warrant procedure and the magistrate's judgment if the President of the United States or his chief legal officer, the Attorney General, has considered the requirements of national security and authorized electronic surveillance as reasonable.

Mr. Justice BLACK, dissenting.

While I realize that an argument based on the meaning of words lacks the scope, and no doubt the appeal, of broad policy discussions and philosophical discourses on such nebulous subjects as privacy, for me the language of the Amendment is the crucial place to look in construing a written document such as our Con-stitution. The Fourth Amendment says that

"The right of the people to be secure in their persons, houses, papers, and effects, against unreasonable searches and seizures, shall not be violated, and no Warrants shall issue, but upon probable cause, supported by Oath or affirmation, and particularly describing the place to be searched, and the persons or things to be seized."

The first clause protects "persons, houses, papers, and effects, against unreasonable searches and seizures * * *." These words connote the idea of tangible things with size, form, and weight, things capable of being searched, seized, or both. The second clause of the Amendment still further establishes its Framers' purpose to limit its protection to tangible things by providing that no warrants shall issue but those "particularly describing the place to be searched, and the persons or things to be seized." A conversation overheard by eavesdropping, whether by plain snooping or wiretapping, is not tangible and, under the normally accepted meanings of the words, can neither be searched nor seized. In addition the language of the second clause indicates that the Amendment refers not only to something tangible so it can be seized but to something already in existence so it can be described. Yet the Court's interpretation would have the Amendment apply to overhearing future conversations

---

** In previous cases, which are undisturbed by today's decision, the Court has upheld, as reasonable under the Fourth Amendment, admission at trial of evidence obtained (1) by an undercover police agent to whom a defendant speaks without knowledge that he is in the employ of the police, Hoffa v. United States, 385 U.S. 293 (1966); (2) by a recording device hidden on the person of such an informant, Lopez v. United States, 373 U.S. 427 (1963); Osborn v. United States, 385 U.S. 323 (1966); and (3) by a policeman listening to the secret micro-wave transmissions of an agent conversing with the defendant in another location, On Lee v. United States, 343 U.S. 747 (1952). When one man speaks to another he takes all the risks ordinarily in-herent in so doing, including the risk that the man to whom he speaks will make public what he has heard. The Fourth Amendment does not protect against unreliable (or law-abiding) associates. It is but a logical and reasonable extension of this principle that a man take the risk that his hearer, free to memorize what he hears for later verbatim repetitions, is instead recording it or transmitting it to another. The present case deals with an entirely different situation, for as the Court emphasizes the petitioner "sought to exclude * * * the uninvited ear," and spoke under circumstances in which a reasonable person would assume that uninvited ears were not listening.

which by their very nature are nonexistent until they take place. How can one "describe" a future conversation, and, if one cannot, how can a magistrate issue a warrant to eavesdrop one in the future? It is argued that information showing what is expected to be said is sufficient to limit the boundaries of what later can be admitted into evidence; but does such general information really meet the specific language of the Amendment which says "particularly describing"? Rather than using language in a completely artificial way, I must conclude that the Fourth Amendment simply does not apply to eavesdropping.

* * *

* * * In interpreting the Bill of Rights, I willingly go as far as a liberal construction of the language takes me, but I simply cannot in good conscience give a meaning to words which they have never before been thought to have and which they certainly do not have in common ordinary usage. I will not distort the words of the Amendment in order to "keep the Constitution up to date" or "to bring it into harmony with the times." It was never meant that this Court have such power, which in effect would make us a continuously functioning constitutional convention.

* * *

NOTES AND QUESTIONS

1. Note that Justice Black's literal reading of the Fourth Amendment prevents him from extending its protections to searches involving electronic devices. How would Justice Black be likely to respond to the contention that his view locks the Constitution into a historical period considerably different from the present?

2. In 1971 the Court by a vote of 6 to 3 (Justices Douglas, Harlan, and Marshall dissented) held that it was not unconstitutional for an electronic device to be voluntarily carried without a warrant by an informer for purposes of overhearing conversations between the informer and another person. *United States v. White,* 401 U.S. 745. Justice White, who wrote the opinion, supports similar situations in the interest of law enforcement in his *Katz* footnote. Justice Douglas was moved in his dissent in the *White* case to question:

> * * * must everyone live in fear that every word he speaks may be transmitted or recorded and later repeated to the entire world? I can imagine nothing that has a more chilling effect on people speaking their minds and expressing their veiws on important matters. The advocates of that regime should spend some time in totalitarian countries and learn first-hand the kind of regime they are creating here. (At pp. 764–765).

How do you view Justice White's assertions in the *Katz* footnote, many of which were repeated in *U. S. v. White?*

3. In 1968 a majority of the members of Congress reacted against the *Katz* decision by including a provision in the Omnibus Crime Control and Safe Streets Act permitting limited use of wiretapping and eavesdropping devices in the investigation of a variety of federal crimes. The requirements for a permissible wiretap or "bug" included the following: it had to be detailed and particularized, conditions for its use had to be detailed and carefully circumscribed, the applications had to be signed by the

Attorney General or an assistant Attorney General specially designated by the former for this purpose, and a warrant had to be obtained from a federal judge granting permission for such surveillance. In cases of emergency investigations of organized crime and national security matters, a law enforcement officer could employ the listening devices for a maximum of 48 hours without a warrant.

In 1974 the Supreme Court had an opportunity to interpret certain sections of the 1968 Act. Attorney General John Mitchell allowed one of his executive assistants to sign applications for wiretaps. The Court held such a procedure illegal in *United States v. Giordano,* 416 U.S. 505 (1974). Under the statute only the Attorney General or his statutory designee may authorize an application for a wiretap warrant.

On the issue of national security problems, Attorney General Mitchell claimed the unlimited power to eavesdrop on domestic groups suspected of subversion. In fact, the White House ordered wiretaps on thirteen government officials and four newspersons in their effort to plug leaks of foreign policy information. In 1972 this issue was confronted in *United States v. United States Dist. Court,* 407 U.S. 297 (1972). The Supreme Court held unanimously that so far as domestic security measures were concerned, the requirements of prior judicial warrant procedures must be implemented.

4. Automobile searches have proven particularly troublesome to the courts. Not only are automobiles obviously different from places such as houses and apartments, they are also frequently used in crimes. In 1978 the Supreme Court ruled that passengers in an automobile do not have standing to challenge the legality of an automobile search unless they can show a legitimate privacy interest. *Rakas v. Illinois,* 99 S.Ct. 421 (1978). In *Rakas* the police stopped a car suspected to have been used in a robbery. After asking the occupants to get out, they searched the car's interior, finding a sawed-off rifle under the front seat and rifle shells in the glove compartment. Petitioner-passengers sought to show that the warrantless search was illegal, since it violated the "plain view" doctrine announced in *Harris v. United States,* 390 U.S. 234 (1968). In *Harris* the Court held that "objects falling in the plain view of an officer who has a right to be in the position to have that view are subject to seizure and may be introduced as evidence." (At p. 236). The "plain view" doctrine is designed to eliminate rummaging at will in search of unlawful items. Since neither the rifle nor the shells were in plain view, the petitioners sought to have them excluded as evidence in their trial.

The five-man majority pointed out that the Court has always treated automobile searches differently from other kinds of searches. In his opinion for the Court, Justice Rehnquist initially observed that:

> Each time the exclusionary rule is applied it exacts a substantial social cost for the vindication of Fourth Amendment rights. Relevant and reliable evidence is kept from the trier of fact and the search for truth is deflected. Since our cases generally have held that one whose Fourth Amendment rights are violated may successfully suppress evidence obtained in the course of an illegal

search and seizure, misgivings as to the benefit of enlarging the class of persons who may invoke that rule are properly considered when deciding whether to expand standing to assert Fourth Amendment violations. (At 427).

In this instance, he noted that since the passengers did not own the automobile and refused to say they owned the rifle and the shells (why did they refuse?), their Fourth Amendment rights were not affected. The four dissenters disagreed, calling the Court's decision contrary to case precedent, the logic of the Fourth Amendment, and common sense. Justice White for the dissenters pointed out that ownership had never been a determining factor in searches, citing the *Katz* ruling:

> Katz had no possessory interest in the public telephone booth, at least no more than petitioners had in their friend's car; Katz was simply legitimately present. And the decision in *Katz* was based not on property rights but on the theory that it was essential to securing "conditions favorable to the pursuit of happiness" that the expectation of privacy in question be recognized. (At p. 442).

Justice White predicted that the *Rakas* ruling would make it "open season" on automobiles:

> This decision invites police to engage in patently unreasonable searches every time an automobile contains more than one occupant. Should something be found, only the owner of the vehicle, or of the item, will have standing to seek suppression, and the evidence will presumably be usable against the other occupants. (At p. 443).

In the educational context, to what extent might the *Rakas* ruling have relevance for searches of property which students do not own, e. g., lockers, dorm rooms? Note that *Rakas* involved an automobile search, not a search of a dwelling. Justice Rehnquist pointed out:

> It is unnecessary for us to decide here whether the same expectations of privacy are warranted in a car as would be justified in a dwelling place in analogous circumstances. (At p. 433).

But the Justice added:

> But here petitioners' claim is one which would fail even in an analogous situation in a dwelling place since they made no showing that they had any legitimate expectation of privacy in the glove compartment or area under the seat of the car in which they were merely passengers. (Id.).

What is required to show a "legitimate expectation of privacy" aside from ownership of the premises? How much of *Katz's* assertion that the Fourth Amendment "protects people, not places" remains? It is to the highly sensitive—and controversial—topic of student protection against unreasonable searches and seizures to which we now turn.

B. Searches and Seizures in the Educational Setting

The preceding discussion demonstrates that the Fourth Amendment permits searches by authorized government officials in the following situations: (1) pursuant to a valid arrest, (2) probable cause exists and exigent circumstances rule out obtaining a search warrant, and (3) probable cause exists and a search warrant has been issued. Persons may also knowingly consent to being searched. As a deterrent to invalid searches, the Supreme Court has ruled that evidence obtained other than in these ways must be excluded from trial.

The situation in the educational setting is somewhat different. While the Supreme Court has not yet ruled that the Fourth Amendment applies to students, lower courts have tended to infer from the 1969 *Tinker v. Des Moines* decision and from *Katz v. United States,* or have found inherent in the Fourteenth Amendment liberty provision, some degree of privacy which follows the student into the public school. Since neither the Fourth nor the Fourteenth Amendments apply to private persons and educational institutions, students in the nonpublic sector do not have the same protection. However, when law enforcement officials become involved in searches at nonpublic schools, Fourth Amendment protections apply.

The problem facing the courts is not whether students at public institutions have rights of privacy *per se* but rather deciding at what point and in what situations students are entitled to expect freedom from governmental intrusion. Is a student entitled to Fourth Amendment protections when school officials conduct searches on school premises? If only internal school disciplinary sanctions are involved, do Fourth Amendment protections apply? Does the nature of the search make a difference, i. e., student lockers, student dormitory rooms, student possessions, the student himself? Can evidence secured by school officials without a warrant be legally introduced into an off-campus judicial proceeding?

There are difficult questions, and the courts have not always answered them in similar ways. Because most of the decisions to date involve lower federal and state courts whose jurisdictional scope is limited, the case law in this area is extremely localized. Generally, state courts handle most of the search cases involving elementary and secondary schools, and tend to favor school officials. Federal courts are more involved in college and university search and seizure cases, and tend to favor the student. A major reason for the different treatment is the serious discipline problem plagueing many elementary and secondary schools; another is that the majority of all college students are now legally adults.

A key issue for all students is whether the fruits of a search can be introduced into a criminal or juvenile proceeding. A typical situation involves a tip to educational officials that drugs may be found in a particular student's locker or dorm room. The officials search unannounced and find the drugs. The evidence is turned over to the police, who then process the student through the judicial system. The student seeks to suppress the evidence, arguing that the search was illegal. Most of the cases involving searches and seizures revolve around this critical issue. Students and their parents argue that the use of evidence seized pursuant to lesser standards of Fourth Amendment protection on campus constitutes a violation of the Fourth Amendment, the Fifth Amendment provision against self-incrimination, or the general constitutional right of privacy (discussed in the next section). As in other civil actions claiming violation of constitutional rights, the federal Civil Rights Act of 1871, 42 U.S.C.A. § 1983, furnishes the basis for suit. On some occasions, students and parents use state tort law or criminal law provisions to bring an action against educational officials.

Obviously, the student wants protection from unannounced searches and from the use in both internal and off-campus disciplinary proceedings of the evidence obtained from them. Educational officials, on the other hand, seek to prevent their institutions from becoming sanctuaries for illegal activities. Most searches involve drugs and weapons, and in most instances, these items are uncovered. They argue that they have a legal obligation to students, parents, and teachers to see that the educational environment is safe and is conducive to teaching and learning. Some educators also feel particularly obligated to protect immature and impressionable youngsters from potentially self-destructive behavior. In order to carry out these responsibilities, educational officials ask either that they be exempt from the Fourth Amendment, or that a lower standard of cause exist for in-school searches, and warrants not be required. It is asserted that having to comply with a warrant requirement would bring outside law enforcement officers into schools and colleges, and jeopardize internal disciplinary procedures. Indeed, many violations are never reported to the police but handled as matters of internal discipline.

To date, most courts allow school officials in the interest of maintaining an orderly educational environment to conduct a warrantless search of a student's locker, person, and property within the elementary and secondary school upon "reasonable suspicion" (not probable cause) that illegal materials are present. Most courts do not require that a student's permission be obtained, and usually allow the fruits of such a search to be turned over to the police for use in an off-campus criminal trial or juvenile proceeding. Some courts, however, carefully review the matter of reasonableness when an unconsented search of an elementary or secondary school student's person is involved. For example, in *Bellnier v. Lund,* 438 F.Supp. 47 (N.D.N.Y.1977), a strip search of an entire fifth grade class was instituted to find $3 one student reported missing. The search turned up nothing. Nor was a search of student desks, books, and coats any more fruitful. After two hours, the searching ended. The money was never found. The children through their parents filed a 42 U.S.C.A. § 1983 lawsuit against the teachers and administrators who were involved in the search, contending it violated their Fourth Amendment rights. The court agreed, noting that while a lesser standard than "probable cause" is necessary to uphold the search as reasonable, the circumstances did not justify a strip search. Judge Munson observed:

> It is entirely possible that there was reasonable suspicion, and even probable cause, based upon the facts, to believe that *some-one* in the classroom has possession of the stolen money. There were no facts, however, which allowed the officials to particularize with respect to which students might possess the money,

something which has time and again, with exceptions not relevant to this case, been found to be necessary to a reasonable search under the Fourth Amendment. (At p. 54; emphasis in original).

It was the general nature of the student search which most concerned Judge Munson; no effort was made to particularize the person and place to be searched. The judge went on to note that as applied to a particular student "reasonable" is a function of the child's age, the child's history and record in school, the seriousness and prevalence of the problem to which the search is directed, and the exigency requiring an immediate warrantless search.

While the search was ruled illegal in *Bellnier v. Lund,* plaintiff students could not recover damages because the school defendants had acted in good faith. The court specifically noted that the holding of *Wood v. Strickland,* a 1975 Supreme Court decision (see Chapter Five, at p. 369ff), would not be applied because the law of student searches is so unsettled.

When school officials conduct warrantless searches without police involvement, some courts theorize that the searchers are acting as private persons *in loco parentis* and are not subject to the Fourth Amendment.[12] It should be pointed out, however, that the *in loco parentis* doctrine is rapidly losing its vitality in the search context in many jurisdictions. Other courts conclude that even though school officials are public officials, the Fourth Amendment standards are sufficiently relaxed in the school setting to allow warrantless searches on reasonable suspicion and the use of evidence from the search in both on- and off-campus judicial proceedings.[13]

While educational officials appear to have a good deal of leeway in conducting warrantless searches of student lockers, the students themselves, and student belongings in the elementary and secondary setting, that same leeway is apt to be circumscribed in searches of college students. In higher education, warrants are more apt to be required, and evidence obtained without a warrant is less likely to be allowed into an off-campus judicial proceeding.

When law enforcement officials take an active part in student searches regardless of the age and grade level of the students, normal Fourth Amendment search requirements are increasingly being required and any evidence obtained without complying with Fourth Amendment procedures will usually be excluded from off-campus judicial proceedings.

The following two cases illustrate the emerging rights of student privacy as it pertains to searches in the educational setting. The first is a Louisiana Supreme Court ruling representing the farthest position to date any court has taken in applying Fourth Amendment protections to students in the elementary and secondary school setting. The second case involves dormitory searches in higher education and is significant in distinguishing between searches for internal disciplinary purposes and searches where off-campus judicial action is contemplated.

---

12. See, for example, *Mercer v. State,* 450 S.W.2d 715 (Tex., 1970).

13. See, for example, *People v. Singletary,* 333 (N.E.2d 369 (N.Y., 1975).

STATE v. MORA

Supreme Court of Louisiana, 1975.
307 So.2d 317.

BARHAM, Justice.

Relator was convicted of possession of marijuana, a violation of La.R.S. 40:966C, and was sentenced to six months' imprisonment in the parish jail. We granted certiorari upon relator's application to review the trial court's denial of a motion to suppress the marijuana which formed the basis of the prosecution and a motion to suppress a confession. We find merit in relator's arguments alleging error in the trial court's ruling on his motion to suppress the marijuana and we therefore pretermit consideration of relator's other complaint.

At the time that the marijuana was seized, relator was a seventeen-year-old high school senior who was participating in a physical education class at the school he attended. Each participant changed from street clothes to gym clothes before joining in the class activities and, in accordance with a customary practice, placed his wallet and other valuables in an individual small canvas bag provided for that purpose. Once the small valuables bags were filled, they were all placed in a large duffel bag which was locked for safekeeping in the instructor's office for the duration of the class.

On the day of the search and seizure, relator obtained his small valuables bag from the instructor. The instructor testified at the hearing on the motion to suppress that the relator turned his back while filling the canvas bag, that his actions were furtive, and that he experienced some difficulty in placing his wallet, which appeared to be bulky, into the small canvas bag. Once the small valuables bag had been placed in the duffel bag, the instructor locked the duffel bag in his office. The instructor further testified that after reflecting on relator's furtive actions and considering them in light of his knowledge that some of relator's companions were narcotics users and that there was talk of the use of drugs by different student groups, he decided to inspect the contents of relator's wallet. When he opened the wallet, he found a plastic bag which contained a leafy green substance. Believing the substance to be marijuana, he summoned the school principal. The principal concurred in the instructor's belief and notified the juvenile authorities, to whom the marijuana was ultimately released. Relator's prosecution ensued and the motion to suppress the marijuana was heard and denied.

The Fourth Amendment to the United States Constitution and Article I, § 7 of the Louisiana Constitution of 1921 (in effect at the time of the search in question) safeguard persons from unreasonable searches conducted without a warrant. However, the applicability of these constitutional prohibitions against unreasonable searches and the exclusionary rule is limited to cases where the seizure is effected by governmental agencies. Concomitantly, the fruits of searches and seizures conducted by private persons are not subject to exclusion. Therefore, before we can decide the constitutionality of the search itself, we must initially determine whether the instructor and the school principal who effected the search and seizure were functioning as private persons, exempt from the stricture of the constitutional provisions, or as governmental agents, subject to those provisions.

Principals and instructors, like others employed by the State through its school boards, are responsible for public education in this State and are charged with the responsibility of implementing the policies of the State in this respect. * * * Because of the function of these school officials and their strict accountability to the State, we must conclude that these school officials, insofar as they are discharging their duties by enforcing State policies and regulations, are within the purview of the Fourth Amendment's prohibition; therefore, their students must be accorded their constitutional right to be free from warrantless searches and seizures.

We must now consider whether the search and seizure effected by these State officials violated the constitutional stricture against unreasonable searches and seizures and whether suppression of the seized marijuana was consequently mandated under *Mapp*.

"The general rule is that a search conducted without a warrant is per se unconstitutional * * *." However, it is possible for a search without a warrant to be constitutional, if and only if it falls within one of those categories recognized as "specifically established and well-delineated exceptions" to the warrant requirement.   Two examples of such exceptions are searches incident to a lawful arrest and certain automobile searches.

We hold that a search on school grounds of a student's personal effects by a school official who suspects the presence or possession of some unlawful substance is not a "specifically established and well-delineated" exception to the warrant requirement and that the fruits of such a search may not be used by the State prosecutorial agency as the basis for criminal proceedings.

For the reasons assigned, the relator's motion to suppress is maintained and his conviction and sentence are reversed.

SUMMERS, J., dissents and assigns reasons.

SANDERS, C. J., and MARCUS, J., dissent for reasons assigned by SUMMERS, J.

SUMMERS, Justice (dissenting).

*   *   *

Decisions of this Court are not rendered in a vacuum.   I believe it to be widely accepted that school authorities are impressed with the obligation to maintain discipline over the students committed to their charge.   Common experience requires a recognition that when large numbers of teenagers are gathered together in such an environment, their inexperience and lack of mature judgment will often create hazards to those in the group.   Parents who surrender their children to schools in order that they may continue to develop intellectually and socially have a right to expect certain safeguards.   The   school   environment presents "special characteristics" which must determine the light in which constitutional principles are applied.

It is particularly during the high school years of their children when parents are justifiably concerned that they not be unduly subjected to antisocial behavior, especially the illegal use of dangerous drugs.   The inquisitive nature, daring, and susceptibility to suggestion of high school students increases the danger in this sensitive area.   These conditions require that school authorities investigate any charge or reasonable suspicion that a student is using or possessing narcotics. Appropriate steps must be taken if the evidence substantiates the charge or suspicion.   Unattended by vigilant school authorities imposing proper discipline and restraint, the use of drugs could proliferate like wildfire.

*   *   *

Not only in Louisiana but generally throughout the Nation, a school teacher stands in the place of a parent to his students.   He may exercise such authority and control, restraint and correction as may be reasonably necessary to enable him to perform his duties as teacher and accomplish the purposes of education. And his power and duty extend beyond the teaching and preservation of order and discipline to matters affecting the morals, health and safety of the students. * * *

Government interest both national and state in requiring that the traditional tests of reasonableness be applied to searches and seizures is to be balanced against the compelling interest of the state in preserving the doctrine of in loco parentis in the school communities of the land; the public necessity and the fundamental social concept the doctrine represents antedating the Fourth Amendment demand its preservation. To reconcile these divergent interests and preserve the essential merits of each, in the narrowly defined area of the school community, a standard of reasonable suspicion rather than the traditional probable cause to justify a search is warranted by the "distinct relationship" between the high school official and the student. * * *

In applying these principles to the facts of this case, I am satisfied that the coach who made the initial intrusion into defendant's privacy by opening his valuables bag had a reasonable suspicion to believe that the valuables bag contained prohibited dangerous drugs.

Not only is the search justified by this rational and reasonable suspicion, but the circumstances imposed upon the coach the duty to proceed as he did under his obligation in loco parentis, not only to correct the breach of discipline but to protect the student body as a whole from the unwholesome drug traffic threatening the school.

There is, moreover, an element of consent to this search which arises from the in loco parentis status and authority the parent delegates to teachers when he sends his children to school. No one would say the parent could not make such a search, and, logically, the parent consents that this authority is transferred to and vested in the teacher. For the teacher to fail to carry out the corresponding responsibility would itself amount to malfeasance. Also to be considered in justification of this search is the fact that defendant surrendered possession of his wallet containing the marijuana to Scott the coach and with it the implied consent to inspect.

The search and seizure satisfied constitutional requirements.

* * *

NOTES AND QUESTIONS

1. The decision was appealed to the U. S. Supreme Court, which remanded the case back to the Louisiana tribunal to ascertain whether a federal or a state right was involved, or both. On remand, the Louisiana Supreme Court stated that the search violated both the Fourth Amendment and a provision of the state constitution, and that under Louisiana law, school officials are considered governmental agents. 330 So.2d 900 (1976). The dissenters disagreed that either the state constitution or a state law was involved and argued that the U. S. Supreme Court should take the case.[14] If the Court had done so, how do you think they would have ruled?

14. Note that where state law is involved, the U. S. Supreme Court usually defers to the interpretation given constitutional and statutory provisions by the highest state court. Thus the dissenters argued that the majority sought to shield the decision from review by the U. S. Supreme Court.

What would you want them to rule? One dissenter, Justice Summers, pointed out that the justice who had written the original *Mora* decision was no longer on the court and that the author of the remand opinion had not participated in the case. Excluding him, Justice Summers pointed out that the state court was evenly divided. In December of 1976, the U. S. Supreme Court let the Louisiana high court decision stand by refusing *certiorari* in the case. The *Mora* decision, of course, pertains only to Louisiana.

2. Until a 1967 case, it was often assumed that routine inspections of homes and offices could be carried out without obtaining search warrants. However, in *Camara v. Municipal Court,* 387 U.S. 523 (1967), the Supreme Court ruled that municipal fire, health, and housing inspection programs require search warrants in nonemergency situations where consent is not granted.

Suppose a school principal uses his master key to conduct a general administrative search of all student lockers when school is not in session. Is such a search reasonable? In *State v. Stein*, 456 P.2d 1 (Kansas, 1969), the Supreme Court of Kansas ruled that the right of inspection of student lockers "is inherent in the authority vested in school administrators and that the same must be retained and exercised in the management of our schools if their educational functions are to be maintained and the welfare of the student bodies preserved." (At p. 3). Do you agree? Should the evidence found in a general inspection of all lockers be used against a particular student in a school disciplinary hearing? In a juvenile hearing off campus? The purpose of the search may be a determining factor. For example, a general administrative search of student lockers at the end of the semester for overdue books would probably raise no legal issue, particularly if students are notified at the start of the school year that such searches are routinely conducted. Such searches are really no different from searches of airline passengers prior to boarding a plane. In the latter case, governmental interest in protecting airline passengers from hyjackings justifies the incursion into an individual's right of privacy. Such searches are thus *per se* reasonable. But suppose in the course of a search for overdue library books, school officials come across a weapon or cache of illegal drugs. May these items be used against a student both on and off campus? The answer is yes, given the U. S. Supreme Court's "plain view" decision (see p. 634, *supra*). However, if the purpose of the search is solely to cooperate with the police by uncovering evidence to be used in a criminal prosecution or juvenile proceeding, the evidence may be excluded because Fourth Amendment requirements are not being met.

3. The relationship between police officers and school officials when joined in a student search is particularly complex. When police officers come to a school and ask for assistance from school officials, can the latter transfer their authority to the former? One commentator has noted that " * * * when the sole purpose of the search is to find evidence of a crime, the school administrator is a law enforcement officer, whatever his

formal title." [15]   Generally as noted above, where it can be demonstrated that a search is part of a criminal investigation or seeks evidence to be used exclusively in a criminal case, Fourth Amendment requirements of probable cause and a search warrant where procurable will be held to apply, whether school officials act alone, act in concert with the police, or offer no resistance to a police request to search. The problem is one of proof. Were school officials acting as law enforcement officers or were they seeking to protect the school community by ferreting out contraband? In the latter instance the evidence turned up in a warrantless search where reasonable cause is present usually can be turned over to the police for use in an off-campus action against the student. The issue becomes particularly difficult where the motivation for the search encompasses both purposes—find evidence for use in a criminal investigation and also protect the school community. And in the elementary and secondary setting, to date, the courts have favored the interests of school officials over those of students, thus allowing even illegally seized evidence to be introduced into off-campus criminal trials and juvenile hearings.

4.   While courts generally allow the use of evidence obtained by school officials to be introduced in off-campus judicial proceedings, the rationale is not altogether clear. If the school officials are presumed to be acting as private persons, should the evidence so obtained be admitted? Might not law enforcement officers seek to enlist the assistance of school authorities to conduct searches which the police cannot conduct because probable cause is lacking? If the *in loco parentis* theory is used to justify such measures, as Justice Summers asserts in his *Mora* dissent, does it really apply? Would a parent be likely to turn evidence obtained from his child over to the police?

5.   Respond to each of the following by answering where applicable: (1) Were there adequate grounds for the search, (2) in which would you require a search warrant, and (3) in which would you apply the exclusionary rule if the inculpatory evidence obtained from the search were turned over to police officers.

    a.   As the principal approaches, a student quickly stands and places something in his pocket. The principal asks that he empty his pockets or be subject to disciplinary action for disobeying. The student refuses, and the principal uses force to disclose the pocket contents, which turn out to be car keys and a cigarette lighter. Suppose the student and his parents sue the school officials for damages under a state tort law pertaining to assault. Does the student have a case?

    b.   Suppose in (a) above the student refused to empty his pocket and the principal then calls the police, who extract a package of marijuana. No warrant is obtained. The student is taken to

---

15.   William G. Buss, "Searches of Students By School Officials in Public Schools," 20 *Inequality in Education* 5, 1975, at p. 7.

juvenile court and also is required to appear before the school disciplinary committee.

c. School officials, based on a rumor that a female student is selling pills on campus, bring the girl to the principal's office. Despite her objections, the student is searched by the dean of girls. Drugs are found in her purse and among her clothes. The police are called, and the student is taken to juvenile hall.

d. Several times a semester, the school principal conducts a general search of all student lockers, seeking to uncover stolen school property and unauthorized possessions such as weapons and drugs. There is a notice in the student handbook that the school reserves the right to conduct such searches. Students found to have stolen or unauthorized possessions are subject to school discipline and may be turned over to police as well.

e. Suppose in (d) above the student handbook is silent on the subject of locker searches. Any difference in your response?

f. Police enter the school and request that the principal open a certain student's locker.

g. Briefcases and bookbags are routinely searched as students leave the library.

h. A school custodian finds a purse in the school cafeteria. In an attempt to locate the owner, he opens the purse looking for identification and finds a bottle of illegal amphetamines. He turns the purse and its contents over to school officials, who contact the police.

6. In light of the shifting currents of search and seizure law, several commentators have suggested that educational officials follow certain procedures to protect student rights of privacy.[16] Major recommendations include:

a. Where searches of jointly-controlled property such as lockers and carrels are contemplated, students should be made aware that such property is subject to periodic inspections and that unauthorized material "in plain view" is subject to confiscation. However, indiscriminate "fishing expeditions" should not be conducted.

b. Students should be informed that school officials may require them to reveal the contents of their pockets, purses, bookbags, etc., where there are reasonable grounds to believe that the student is in possession of unlawful items.

c. When there are reasonable grounds for searching a student or his property, school officials should first seek to obtain a search

16. See for example Robert E. Phay and George T. Rogister, Jr., "Searches of Students and the Fourth Amendment," 5 J. *Law and Educ.* 57, January, 1976, at pp. 72–73.

warrant. If circumstances make doing so impossible or impracticable, school officials should try to obtain the student's consent and have the student present when the search is conducted.

d. A witness should be present when a search is being carried out.

e. If a major reason for the search is to obtain criminal evidence, school officials should inform law enforcement officers and, if time permits, allow them to conduct the search.

f. If police officials request permission to search a student or his property, school officials should require them to obtain a search warrant unless the search falls into one of the exceptions to Fourth Amendment requirements.

Would you accept these safeguards? Would you modify them or add to them? Why might it be important that procedural safeguards involving searches and seizures be followed for internal disciplinary action where long term suspension or expulsion are likely outcomes?

PIAZZOLA v. WATKINS

United States District Court, M.D.Alabama, N.D., 1970.
316 F.Supp. 624.

JOHNSON, Chief Judge.

The petitioners were indicted by a grand jury of Pike County, Alabama, for the offense of illegal possession of marijuana. After pleas of not guilty were interposed, trials were had, and petitioner Piazzola was convicted on April 25, 1968 and petitioner Marinshaw on April 26, 1968. The convictions were affirmed by the Alabama Court of Criminal Appeals. The matter is presented to this Court upon a habeas corpus petition filed April 24, 1970. The basis for the petition is that the convictions violate the Fourth Amendment to the Constitution of the United States. * * *

                    * * *

On the morning of February 28, 1968, the Dean of Men of Troy State University was called to the office of the Chief of Police of Troy, Alabama, to discuss "the drug problem" at the University. Two State narcotic agents and two student informers from Troy State University were also present. Later on that same day, the Dean of Men was called to the city police station for another meeting; at this time he was informed by the officers that they had sufficient evidence that marijuana was in the dormitory rooms of certain Troy State students and that they desired the cooperation of University officials in searching these rooms. The police officers were advised by the Dean of Men that they would receive the full cooperation of the University officials in searching for the marijuana. The informers, whose identities have not yet been disclosed, provided the police officers with names of students whose rooms were to be searched. Still later on that same day (which was during the week of final examinations at the University and was to be followed by a week-long holiday) the law enforcement officers, accompanied by some of the University officials, searched six or seven dormitory rooms located in two separate residence halls. The rooms of both Piazzola and Marinshaw were searched without search warrants and without their consent. Present during the search of the room occupied by Marinshaw were two State narcotic agents, the University security officer, and a counselor of the residence hall where Marinshaw's room was located. Piazzola's room was searched twice. Present during the first search were two State narcotic agents and a University official; no evidence was found at this time. The second search of Piazzola's room, which disclosed the incriminating evidence, was conducted solely by the State and city police officials.

At the time of the seizure the University had in effect the following regulation:

> The college reserves the right to enter rooms for inspection purposes. If the administration deems it necessary, the room may be searched and the occupant required to open his personal baggage and any other personal material which is sealed.

Each of the petitioners was familiar with this regulation. After the search of the petitioners' rooms and the discovery of the marijuana, they were arrested, and the State criminal prosecutions and convictions ensued. The basic question presented is whether the evidence that formed the basis for the petitioners' convictions and present incarceration was obtained as a result of an unreasonable search and seizure within the meaning of the Fourth Amendment to the Constitution of the United States. As justification for the search and seizure, the respondents rely almost entirely upon this Court's opinion in Moore v. Student Affairs Committee of Troy State University, 284 F.Supp. 725 (M.D.Ala.). The Moore case involved judicial review of the constitutional validity of University administrative proceedings which resulted in the suspension of Gary Moore from Troy University. The suspension in the Moore case was based upon a search of Moore's dormitory room by University officials and the discovery of marijuana in his room. In Moore, this Court emphasized:

> A student naturally has the right to be free of unreasonable searches and seizures, and a tax-supported public college may not compel a "waiver" of that right as a condition precedent to admission.

Upon the facts presented in Moore, this Court held that the University regulation authorizing the search of dormitory rooms was a reasonable exercise of University supervisory duties,   * * *. After making a finding that the regulation was "facially reasonable", this Court further held that the regulation was reasonably applied and stated:

> The regulation was reasonably applied in this case. The constitutional boundary line between the right of the school authorities to search and the right of a dormitory student to privacy must be based on a reasonable belief on the part of the college authorities that a student is using a dormitory room for a purpose which is illegal or which would otherwise seriously interfere with campus discipline. Upon this submission, it is clear that such a belief existed in this case.

> This standard of "reasonable cause to believe" to justify a search by college administrators—even where the sole purpose is to seek evidence of suspected violations of law—is lower than the constitutionally protected criminal law standard of "probable cause." This is true because of the special necessities of the student-college relationship and because college disciplinary proceedings are not criminal proceedings in the constitutional sense.

* * *

It is settled law that the Fourth Amendment does not prohibit reasonable searches when the search is conducted by a superior charged with a responsibility of maintaining discipline and order or of maintaining security. A student who lives in a dormitory on campus which he "rents" from the school waives objection to any reasonable searches conducted pursuant to reasonable and necessary regulations such as this one. [Footnotes omitted.]

This court does not find *Moore* applicable in the case *sub judice.* Here, the search was instigated and in the main executed by State police and narcotic bureau officials. The only part the University officials played in the search of the petitioners' dormitory rooms was at the request of and under the direction of the State law enforcement officers. Under such circumstances the State of Alabama, upon the petitioners' motion to suppress, had the burden of showing probable cause for the search of petitioners' rooms. The standard of "reasonable cause to believe" laid down by this Court in *Moore* as a justification for a search by college officials that resulted in school disciplinary proceedings cannot be the justification for a search by a police officer for the sole purpose of gathering evidence for criminal prosecutions. * * *

No * * * evidence was offered by the State in justification of the search, except * * * that the officers "had information," that they believed that information, and that, implied by the testimony, there were some unnamed informers whose information or credibility as informers was never discussed.

The State's evidence on the question of probable cause failed completely. Under the circumstances that existed in this case, in order to establish probable cause the State police officers must give the underlying facts or circumstances upon which they base their conclusions. Furthermore, when officers contend that they searched upon information from an informer, they must show that the informer was reliable, and the evidence must also reflect some

factual basis for the informant's conclusions.

The State argues, in support of its warrantless search, that the petitioners consented to the search indirectly by reason of the University regulation. This argument cannot stand. As stated earlier, this was not a University initiated search for University purposes, but rather a police initiated search for criminal prosecution purposes. The fact that the University officials agreed to the search gives it no validity. As this Court emphasized in *Moore*, students and their college share a special relationship, which gives to the college certain special rights including the right to enter into and inspect the rooms of its students under certain situations. However, the fact that the college has this right—for a restricted purpose—does not mean that the college may exercise the right by admitting a third party. * * *

* * *

Since there was no warrant, no probable cause for searching without a warrant, and no waiver or consent, the search of petitioners' dormitory rooms by State law enforcement officers, including narcotic agents and Troy city police officers, on February 28, 1968, was in violation of the petitioners' rights as guaranteed by the Fourth Amendment to the Constitution of the United States. It follows that the convictions of the petitioners, having been based solely upon the fruits of such search, are likewise illegal and cannot stand. Accordingly, it is the

Order, judgment and decree of this Court that the conviction of Frank Piazzola on April 25, 1968, and the conviction of Terrance Marinshaw on April 26, 1968, both in the Circuit Court of Pike County, Alabama, which convictions form the basis for the present incarceration of each, be and each of said convictions is hereby set aside. It is further

Ordered that Frank Piazzola and Terrance Marinshaw be released immediately by the State authorities now holding them in custody pursuant to said convictions.

NOTES AND QUESTIONS

1. Note the distinction the court makes between searches conducted by university officials for internal disciplinary purposes and searches involving outside law enforcement officers. Note also the refusal of the court to give any weight to the fact that university officials consented to the police search. The search was ruled illegal, and the evidence obtained could not be used to convict the students. Thus they were released from custody. The decision was affirmed by the Fifth Circuit Court of Appeals in 1971. 442 F.2d 284.

2. Suppose the search had been carried out solely by university officials acting upon reasonable cause to believe that illegal drugs were being used in Piazzola's room. Under the *Moore* decision by this same district court, evidence so obtained could be introduced in internal disciplinary proceedings. But two important decisions from different federal jurisdictions take different approaches to this same issue and reveal in the process the lack of consensus among judges about on-campus searches and their relationship to internal disciplinary proceedings.

In *Smyth v. Lubbers,* 398 F.Supp. 777 (1975), the U. S. District Court for the Western District of Michigan ruled that "reasonable cause" was an insufficient standard for a valid search by college officials even though only an internal disciplinary hearing was involved. Noting that the imposition of penalties, such as long term suspension, has a severe impact on a student and noting that resort to internal university proceedings would not necessarily shield the student from the intrusion of civil authorities, Chief Judge Fox concluded that the "probable cause" standard from the political and social setting must be required.

> The only possible justification for requiring less than probable cause for a search of an adult student's lodging whether with or without a warrant, is that the student's privacy is somehow less than that of other adults; or that the College's interest in enforcing laws and regulations is somehow greater than that of the community. * * * these contentions [are] rejected. (At p. 791; material in brackets added)

He also emphasized that university officials should obtain a warrant unless circumstances make it impractical to do so. As an alternative to going to civil authorities for a warrant, the judge suggested a procedure whereby the campus judicial committee would be empowered to issue warrants internal to the institution, though he admitted this might be too sensitive a matter for on-campus agencies to handle. The judge went on to apply the exclusionary rule to evidence illegally seized in order to "preserve the integrity and thus the legitimacy of the College as the maker and enforcer of regulations." (At p. 794).

Chief Judge Fox's decision with respect to the exclusionary rule served as the point of departure for the judge in *Morale v. Grigel,* 422 F.Supp. 988 (D.N.H.1976). In that case the judge concluded that even though the search of a student's room was illegal under the Fourth Amendment, the evidence against the student could nevertheless be used against him in campus judicial proceedings.   This was so because the exclusionary rule has been specifically limited to criminal actions.   Campus judicial proceedings are considered civil, not criminal, proceedings.   The judge concluded that "the Supreme Court has intentionally left students basically remediless in the federal courts for violation of their Fourth Amendment rights."   (At p. 1001).   Thus the product of the illegal search, a marijuana pipe and some marijuana seeds, were legally used to suspend Morale from school.

Morale v. Grigel is also an interesting case because the court appeared to take a different tact in discussing the legality of college searches.   Rather than saddle campus officials with the same requirements imposed on law enforcement personnel as in *Smyth,* the court concluded that the public institution involved in the case, the New Hampshire Technical Institute, should limit the *scope* of its searches to matters which "furthers its functioning as an educational institution."

> The search must further an interest that is separate and distinct from that served by New Hampshire's criminal law.   * * *   intensive searches of rooms for stolen goods serve no legitimate interest of the Institute.   (At p. 998).

Searches for stolen goods (in this case, another student's stereo) should be left to off campus law enforcement officials.   Do you agree that a college has no "legitimate interest" in conducting searches for stolen goods?   In addition to a showing of reasonable (or probable) cause for a search, should the college or university have to show that stealing on campus disrupts or disturbs the operation of its academic functions?   Should those matters which do not directly relate to academics be automatically turned over to the police?   The fact that the Institute's room check and search policies had not been written down, and had been by custom limited to room checks for health and safety reasons, may have been a factor in the decision.   So, too, may have been the judge's repeated assertion that students should not be shielded from criminal law enforcement authorities.

> A college cannot, in this day and age, protect students under the aegis of *in loco parentis* authority from the rigors of society's rules and laws, just as it cannot, under the same aegis, deprive students of their constitutional rights.   (At p. 997).

But may there not be valid reasons for preferring campus disciplinary procedures over the criminal justice system?

Of the three approaches presented in *Moore, Smyth,* and *Morale,* which would you prefer (a) as a student (b) as an educator?   Would you apply the same preference to the elementary-secondary level?   Note that while there does seem to be a difference in court treatment of searches in elementary and secondary schools, not all judges adhere to this dichotomy. Thus cases from the college level often are used as precedents for rulings in the elementary-secondary level and vice-versa.

A U. S. Supreme Court decision from the political and social setting may have precedential value for educational searches.   *Wyman v. James,*

400 U.S. 309 (1971), involved the issue whether a beneficiary of Aid to Families with Dependent Children (AFDC) may refuse a warrantless visit by a caseworker without risking loss of benefits. The lower court ruled against the search. The Supreme Court reversed, Justice Blackmun pointing out that welfare inspections are not "searches" in the Fourth Amendment sense. Even if such a search has some of the same characteristics, a caseworker visit without a warrant is not "unreasonable". Justice Blackmun distinguished the *Camara v. Municipal Court* ruling, *supra*, p. 642, noting that here no criminal prosecution was involved. The only consequence in *Wyman* was the loss of AFDC benefits. What relevance, if any, might *Wyman* have for educational searches involving only on-campus disciplinary proceedings?

3. In *People v. Lanthier*, 488 P.2d 625 (1971), the Supreme Court of California denied a motion to suppress evidence gathered by officials at a private university pursuant to a warrantless search and turned over to the police, who subsequently prosecuted the student for possession of marijuana. In *Lanthier* a supervisor of maintenance services was called to find the source of a malodorous smell in the university library. Using his pass key, the supervisor opened library lockers until he found the source of the odor, a briefcase containing 38 packets of what he suspected was marijuana. University officials called the police to help them identify the substance which gave off the odor. It was indeed marijuana. Without securing a warrant because of the pressures of time, the police stationed themselves near the locker where the packets were found. Defendant was arrested when he returned to reclaim the briefcase. Given the desire to remove the source of the odor which was causing complaints in the library and given the reasonable efforts to identify the substance, the California court ruled that the evidence was obtained pursuant to a legal search and therefore was admissible. Does the ruling in this case square with *Piazzola?*

II. THE RIGHT TO PERSONAL PRIVACY

During the mid-1960s the Supreme Court introduced the concept of privacy outside of the search and seizure context and affirmed the observation of many constitutional scholars that constitutional law develops to meet the new demands of society. The new demands came from growing fears of government invasion of privacy in human relationships. Sexual privacy became an issue of "emerging rights." An important factor in highlighting this clash of interests was the emergence of a more permissive sexual attitude in society. The case that was to give the Court the opportunity to elevate personal privacy to the status of a constitutional right was *Griswold v. Connecticut*, 381 U.S. 479 (1965). Shortly thereafter, the Court extended the concept of privacy to abortions in *Roe v. Wade,* 410 U.S. 113 (1973), perhaps the most controversial decision of the Burger Court.

During this same period, privacy became an issue in the educational setting. Dress codes at the secondary educational level, particularly those provisions relating to male hair length, and the efforts of educational officials at all levels to combat widespread use of drugs, most notably marijuana, generated a great number of lawsuits. Teachers as well were more apt to challenge what they believed to be unwarranted infringement on their lifestyles. Abuses of student records led both to court challenges and the passage of the Family Educational Rights and Privacy Act (Buckley Amendment) in 1974.

This part of the chapter leads off with a discussion of the *Griswold* case, then focuses on issues of privacy in the educational setting. Included in the latter is a federal district court case, *Merriken v. Cressman,* 364 F.Supp. 913 (E.D.Pa.1973), which involves a test used to uncover potential drug abusers in the Norristown, Pennsylvania, public schools. The second section continues the discussion of personal privacy in terms of sex-related behavior, focusing on *Roe v. Wade* and issues of morality in the educational setting. The third section briefly reviews the statutory setting as related to privacy.

A.   The Constitutional Right to Privacy

(1) Penumbras, Emanations, and the Griswold Case

Griswold v. Connecticut addressed the constitutionality of a Connecticut statute prohibiting the use of any drug, medicinal article, or instrument for the purpose of preventing conception. In effect, the statute made it a crime to use contraceptive devices punishable by not less than a $50 fine and/or sixty days to one year in jail. The law had been on the books since 1879.

Estelle Griswold, the Executive Director of the Planned Parenthood League of Connecticut and the League's medical director, a licensed physician and a professor at Yale Medical School, were found guilty of violating an accessory statute which provided that any person who counsels another to commit any offense may be prosecuted as if he were the principal offender. At a birth clinic sponsored by Planned Parenthood, both defendants had given married persons information and advice on the ways to prevent conception. They were fined one hundred dollars. Their appeal to higher Connecticut courts failed, and they appealed to the U. S. Supreme Court.

In the *Griswold* decision the Court split 7 to 2 with Justice Douglas speaking for the majority. For Douglas, the statute was invalid because it had a direct impact on the personal, private relationship between married persons. Although the Constitution is silent about privacy, the Court concluded that there exists a right of privacy inherent in several discrete clauses of the Bill of Rights. These provisions produce penumbras * within which there exists a constitutionally protected "zone of personal privacy." The state, wrote Douglas, cannot enter this domain any more than it can abridge freedom of speech.

Despite assertions to the contrary, the majority's position suggested that the Court would become more activist in identifying fundamental

---

* Webster's defines "penumbra" as "a shadow cast (as in an eclipse) where the light is partly but not wholly cut off by the intervening body: a space of partial illumination between the perfect shadow on all sides and the full light. * * *" *Webster's Third New International Dictionary* (Springfield, Mass.: Merriam, 1961).

rights beyond those specifically stated in the Constitution. This, in turn, suggested that the Court would carefully review the substance of challenged state and federal legislation to see that such rights are not infringed. Justice Black's dissent is a classic statement of the opposing viewpoint. The fact that Justices Douglas and Black, generally regarded as the most liberal members of the Warren Court, are on opposite sides in this case is an apt illustration of how values about the proper role of courts can influence judicial decision making. (See Chapter Two, p. 33ff).

GRISWOLD v. STATE OF CONNECTICUT

Supreme Court of the United States, 1965.
381 U.S. 479, 85 S.Ct. 1678, 14 L.Ed.2d 510.

Mr. Justice DOUGLAS delivered the opinion of the Court.

* * *

We think that appellants have standing to raise the constitutional rights of the married people with whom they had a professional relationship. * * *

Certainly the accessory should have standing to assert that the offense which he is charged with assisting is not, or cannot constitutionally be a crime.

* * *

Coming to the merits, we are met with a wide range of questions that implicate the Due Process Clause of the Fourteenth Amendment. Overtones of some arguments suggest that Lochner v. State of New York, 198 U.S. 45, should be our guide. But we decline that invitation as we did in West Coast Hotel Co. v. Parrish, 300 U.S. 379. We do not sit as a super-legislature to determine the wisdom, need, and propriety of laws that touch economic problems, business affairs, or social conditions. This law, however, operates directly on an intimate relation of husband and wife and their physician's role in one aspect of that relation.

The association of people is not mentioned in the Constitution nor in the Bill of Rights. The right to educate a child in a school of the parents' choice— whether public or private or parochial—

is also not mentioned. Nor is the right to study any particular subject or any foreign language. Yet the First Amendment has been construed to include certain of those rights.

By Pierce v. Society of Sisters, * * * the right to educate one's children as one chooses is made applicable to the States by the force of the First and Fourteenth Amendments. By Meyer v. State of Nebraska, * * * the same dignity is given the right to study the German language in a private school. In other words, the State may not, consistently with the spirit of the First Amendment, contract the spectrum of available knowledge. The right of freedom of speech and press includes not only the right to utter or to print, but the right to distribute, the right to receive, the right to read and freedom of inquiry, freedom of thought, and freedom to teach—indeed the freedom of the entire university community.

Without those peripheral rights the specific rights would be less secure. And so we reaffirm the principle of the Pierce and the Meyer cases.

In NAACP v. State of Alabama, 357 U.S. 449, we protected the "freedom to associate and privacy in one's associations," noting that freedom of association was a peripheral First Amendment right. Disclosure of membership lists of a constitutionally valid association, we held, was invalid "as entailing the likelihood of a substantial restraint upon the exercise by petitioner's members of their right to freedom of association." In other words, the First Amendment has a penumbra where privacy is protected from governmental intrusion. In like context, we have protected forms of "association" that are not political in the customary sense but pertain to the social, legal, and economic benefit of the members. NAACP v. Button, 371 U.S. 415. In Schware v. Board of Bar Examiners, 353 U.S. 232, we held it not permissible to bar a lawyer from practice, because he had once been a member of the Communist Party. The man's "association with that Party" was not shown to be "anything more than a political faith in a political party" and was not action of a kind proving bad moral character.

Those cases involved more than the "right of assembly"—a right that extends to all irrespective of their race or ideology. De Jonge v. State of Oregon, 299 U.S. 353. The right of "association," like the right of belief, West Virginia State Board of Education v. Barnette, 319 U.S. 624, is more than the right to attend a meeting; it includes the right to express one's attitudes or philosophies by membership in a group or by affiliation with it or by other lawful means. Association in that context is a form of expression of opinion; and while it is not expressly included in the First Amendment its existence is necessary in making the express guarantees fully meaningful.

The foregoing cases suggest that specific guarantees in the Bill of Rights have penumbras, formed by emanations from those guarantees that help give them life and substance. Various guarantees create zones of privacy. The right of association contained in the penumbra of the First Amendment is one, as we have seen. The Third Amendment in its prohibition against the quartering of soldiers "in any house" in time of peace without the consent of the owner is another facet of that privacy. The Fourth Amendment explicitly affirms the "right of the people to be secure in their persons, houses, papers, and effects, against unreasonable searches and seizures." The Fifth Amendment in its Self-Incrimination Clause enables the citizen to create a zone of privacy which government may not force him to surrender to his detriment. The Ninth Amendment provides: "The enumeration in the Constitution, of certain rights, shall not be construed to deny or disparage others retained by the people."

The Fourth and Fifth Amendments were described in Boyd v. United States, 116 U.S. 616, as protection against all governmental invasions "of the sanctity of a man's home and the privacies of life." We recently referred in Mapp v. Ohio, 367 U.S. 643, to the Fourth Amendment as creating a "right to privacy, no less important than any other right carefully and particularly reserved to the people."

* * * These cases bear witness that the right of privacy which presses for recognition here is a legitimate one.

The present case, then, concerns a relationship lying within the zone of privacy created by several fundamental constitutional guarantees. And it concerns a law which, in forbidding the *use* of contraceptives rather than regulating their manufacture or sale, seeks to achieve its goals by means having a maximum destructive impact upon that relationship. Such a law cannot stand in light of the familiar principle, so often applied by this Court, that a "governmental purpose to control or prevent activities constitutionally subject to state regulation may not be achieved by means which sweep unnecessarily broadly and thereby invade the area of protected freedoms." Would we allow the police to search the sacred precincts of marital bedrooms for telltale signs of the use of contraceptives? The very idea is repulsive to the notions of privacy surrounding the marriage relationship.

We deal with a right of privacy older than the Bill of Rights—older than our political parties, older than our school system. Marriage is a coming together for better or for worse, hopefully enduring, and intimate to the degree of being sacred. It is an association that promotes a way of life, not causes; a harmony in living, not political faiths; a bilateral loyalty, not commercial or social projects. Yet it is an association for as noble a purpose as any involved in our prior decisions.

Reversed.

Mr. Justice GOLDBERG, whom The CHIEF JUSTICE and Mr. Justice BRENNAN join, concurring.

* * *

* * * In reaching the conclusion that the right of marital privacy is protected, as being within the protected penumbra of specific guarantees of the Bill of Rights, the Court refers to the Ninth Amendment, I add these words to emphasize the relevance of that Amendment to the Court's holding.

* * *

The Ninth Amendment reads, "The enumeration in the Constitution, of certain rights, shall not be construed to deny or disparage others retained by the people." The Amendment is almost entirely the work of James Madison. It was introduced in Congress by him and passed the House and Senate with little or no debate and virtually no change in language. It was proffered to quiet expressed fears that a bill of specifically enumerated rights could not be sufficiently broad to cover all essential rights and that the specific mention of certain rights would be interpreted as a denial that others were protected.

* * *

While this Court has had little occasion to interpret the Ninth Amendment,

"[i]t cannot be presumed that any clause in the constitution is intended to be without effect." * * * To hold that a right so basic and fundamental and so deep-rooted in our society as the right of privacy in marriage may be infringed because that right is not guaranteed in so many words by the first eight amendments to the Constitution is to ignore the Ninth Amendment and to give it no effect whatsoever. * * *

* * * While the Ninth Amendment—and indeed the entire Bill of Rights—originally concerned restrictions upon *federal* power, the subsequently enacted Fourteenth Amendment prohibits the States as well from abridging fundamental personal liberties. And, the Ninth Amendment, in indicating that not all such liberties are specifically mentioned in the first eight amendments, is surely relevant in showing the existence of other fundamental personal rights, now protected from state, as well as federal, infringement. * * *

* * *

Mr. Justice HARLAN, concurring in the judgment.

* * *

In my view, the proper constitutional inquiry in this case is whether this Connecticut statute infringes the Due Process Clause of the Fourteenth Amendment because the enactment violates basic values "implicit in the concept of ordered liberty," Palko v. State of Connecticut, 302 U.S. 319. While the relevant inquiry may be aided by resort to one or more of the provisions of the Bill of Rights, it is not dependent on them or any of their radiations. The Due Process Clause of the Fourteenth Amendment stands, in my opinion, on its own bottom.

* * *

Mr. Justice WHITE, concurring in the judgment. * * *

Mr. Justice BLACK, with whom Mr. Justice STEWART joins, dissenting.

*   *   *

The Court talks about a constitutional "right of privacy" as though there is some constitutional provision or provisions forbidding any law ever to be passed which might abridge the "privacy" of individuals. But there is not. There are, of course, guarantees in a certain specific constitutional provisions which are designed in part to protect privacy at certain times and places with respect to certain activities. Such, for example, is the Fourth Amendment's guarantee against "unreasonable searches and seizures."

*   *   *

*   *   * "Privacy" is a broad, abstract and ambiguous concept which can easily be shrunken in meaning but which can also, on the other hand, easily be interpreted as a constitutional ban against many things other than searches and seizures. *   *   * I like my privacy as well as the next one, but I am nevertheless compelled to admit that government has a right to invade it unless prohibited by some specific constitutional provision. For these reasons I cannot agree with the Court's judgment and the reasons it gives for holding this Connecticut law unconstitutional.

*   *   *

My Brother GOLDBERG has adopted the recent discovery that the Ninth Amendment as well as the Due Process Clause can be used by this Court as authority to strike down all state legislation which this Court thinks violates "fundamental principles of liberty and justice," or is contrary to the "traditions and [collective] conscience of our people." He also states, without proof satisfactory to me, that in making decisions on this basis judges will not consider "their personal and private notions." One may ask how they can avoid considering them. Our Court certainly has no machinery with which to take a Gallup Poll. And

the scientific miracles of this age have not yet produced a gadget which the Court can use to determine what traditions are rooted in the "[collective] conscience of our people." Moreover, one would certainly have to look far beyond the language of the Ninth Amendment to find that the Framers vested in this Court any such awesome veto powers over lawmaking, either by the States or by the Congress. Nor does anything in the history of the Amendment offer any support for such a shocking doctrine. The whole history of the adoption of the Constitution and Bill of Rights points the other way, and the very material quoted by my Brother GOLDBERG shows that the Ninth Amendment was intended to protect against the idea that "by enumerating particular exceptions to the grant of power" to the Federal Government, "those rights which were not singled out, were intended to be assigned into the hands of the General Government [the United States], and were consequently insecure." That Amendment was passed, not to broaden the powers of this Court or any other department of "the General Government," but, as every student of history knows, to assure the people that the Constitution in all its provisions was intended to limit the Federal Government to the powers granted expressly or by necessary implication. If any broad, unlimited power to hold laws unconstitutional because they offend what this Court conceives to be the "[collective] conscience of our people" is vested in this Court by the Ninth Amendment, the Fourteenth Amendment, or any other provision of the Constitution, it was not given by the Framers, but rather has been bestowed on the Court by the Court. This fact is perhaps responsible for the peculiar phenomenon that for a period of a century and a half no serious suggestion was ever made that the Ninth Amendment, enacted to protect state powers against federal invasion, could be used as a weapon of federal power to prevent state legislatures from passing laws they consider appropriate to govern local affairs. Use of any such broad, unbounded judicial authority would make of this Court's members a day-to-day constitutional convention.

I repeat so as not to be misunderstood that this Court does have power, which it should exercise, to hold laws unconstitutional where they are forbidden by the Federal Constitution. My point is that there is no provision of the Constitution which either expressly or impliedly vests power in this Court to sit as a supervisory agency over acts of duly constituted legislative bodies and set aside their laws because of the Court's belief that the legislative policies adopted are unreasonable, unwise, arbitrary, capricious or irrational. The adoption of such a loose, flexible, uncontrolled standard for holding laws unconstitutional, if ever it is finally achieved, will amount to a great unconstitutional shift of power to the courts which I believe and am constrained to say will be bad for the courts and worse for the country. Subjecting federal and state laws to such an unrestrained and unrestrainable judicial control as to the wisdom of legislative enactments would, I fear, jeopardize the separation of governmental powers that the Framers set up and at the same time threaten to take away much of the power of States to govern themselves which the Constitution plainly intended them to have.

I realize that many good and able men have eloquently spoken and written, sometimes in rhapsodical strains, about the duty of this Court to keep the Con-

stitution in tune with the times. The idea is that the Constitution must be changed from time to time and that this Court is charged with a duty to make those changes. For myself, I must with all deference reject that philosophy. The Constitution makers knew the need for change and provided for it. Amendments suggested by the people's elected representatives can be submitted to the people or their selected agents for ratification. That method of change was good for our Fathers, and being somewhat old-fashioned I must add it is good enough for me. And so, I cannot rely on the Due Process Clause or the Ninth Amendment or any mysterious and uncertain natural law concept as a reason for striking down this state law. The Due Process Clause with an "arbitrary and capricious" or "shocking to the conscience" formula was liberally used by this Court to strike down economic legislation in the early decades of this centruy, threatening, many people thought, the tranquility and stability of the Nation. See, e. g., Lochner v. State of New York. That formula, based on subjective considerations of "natural justice," is no less dangerous when used to enforce this Court's views about personal rights than those about economic rights. I had thought that we had laid that formula, as a means for striking down state legislation, to rest once and for all in cases like West Coast Hotel Co. v. Parrish, * * *.

* * *

Mr. Justice STEWART, whom Mr. Justice BLACK joins, dissenting.

* * *

NOTES AND QUESTIONS

1. *Griswold* is important because in the process of sanctioning privacy as a constitutional entitlement in the context of the use of contraceptives by married persons, the Justices engage in a far-ranging discussion about sources of rights which are not listed in the Constitution but are given constitutional status by the Supreme Court. It will be helpful at this point to review some of the points made elsewhere in this book about constitutional rights. As noted in Chapter Three, there is general

consensus among the members of the Supreme Court today that the *specific* rights listed in the Bill of Rights (sometimes referred to as "contextually demonstrable" rights) such as freedom of religion and speech carry preferred status over federal and state regulation.   Specific rights are channeled through the "liberty" provision of the Fourteenth Amendment Due Process Clause to protect persons in the state setting.   Since the Constitution applies only to federal and state governments, instrumentalities, and officials, similar protection is not available from the Constitution to persons in the private sector.

Disagreement exists among the Justices, however, about the source and nature of *non-specific* constitutional rights such as parental rights, marriage, travel, and privacy.   Some, most notably Justice Douglas, say that these rights can be inferred from emanations seen in the penumbra of specific rights.   Thus, freedom of association is derived from freedom of speech and assembly, the right to silence from the freedom of speech, and so on.   Others such as former Justice Goldberg suggest that non-specific rights are derived from the Ninth Amendment.   Still others rely on the word "liberty" in the Fourteenth Amendment.   This is Justice Harlan's view as expressed in his concurring opinion in *Griswold*.   However, exclusive reliance on the liberty provision of the Fourteenth Amendment creates a problem for situations involving federal invasions of rights, since the Fourteenth Amendment applies only to states and subunits thereof.

Clearly, the most expansive view would be to suggest that non-specific rights are derived from a combination of specific constitutional provisions, the Ninth Amendment, *and* the "liberty" and "property" provisions of the Fourteenth Amendment.   Justice Douglas comes closest to this interpretation in *Griswold*.   At the opposite end of the spectrum is Justice Black, who would limit constitutional protection to those specific rights listed in the Bill of Rights.   Which of these views is to be preferred?   Given that different Justices value things differently, what are the implications of the expansive view for the legal concept of *stare decisis?*   For the political system?

2.   Note Justice Douglas' reference to *Lochner v. New York*, a 1905 decision in which the Court threw out a New York law regulating hours and working conditions in the baking industry.   In that case Justice Peckham for the Court ruled that the right to make a contract "is part of the liberty of the individual protected by the Fourteenth Amendment * * *" (At p. 53).   In many similar cases until the end of the 1930s, the Justices, many of whom had been corporate attorneys, used "liberty of contract" to strike down similar economic and social legislation designed to correct such evils as child labor, impure food, and exploitation of women.   The refusal of the Court to defer to legislatures during this period and its strong protection for liberty of contract has come to be known as *substantive due process*.   This concept meant that the Court would scrutinize the *substance* of legislation very carefully to be sure there was no infringement on protected economic rights.

By the late 1930s more liberal Justices (from the non-economic civil liberties standpoint) abandoned substantive due process in favor of deference to the political arena when economic and social matters were involved. Only when legislation affected specific constitutional rights was the Court activist in its defense of the individual. In *Griswold,* Justice Douglas maintains a steadfast refusal to follow *Lochner,* asserting that "We do not sit as a super-legislature * * *." Is he convincing?

Interestingly, today the women's rights movement seeks to return to the *Lochner* era by having most of the laws enacted to protect women from exploitation in the labor market struck down. They seek to do so, however, largely on equal protection grounds. Do you think the Court should return to a vigorous defense of contractual rights as a Fourteenth Amendment liberty interest? Can you explain the decline of the right to contract and the rise of the right to privacy as a constitutionally protected right? If privacy is in the penumbra of the Bill of Rights, what other rights might be lurking there? Does all of this lend credence to Justice Black's comment that the expansive view would have the Court sit as a "day-to-day continuous constitutional convention" engaged in reinterpreting the Constitution? How viable is the alternative Justice Black suggests?

3. Justice Douglas' opinion put great stress on the right to marital privacy. Does the opinion, then, simply uphold a right to privacy restricted to the intimacy of married couples, or does his phrasing in the opinion create an open-ended right to whatever content the Supreme Court might choose to give it? In 1972 the Court extended its *Griswold* precedent in *Eisenstadt v. Baird,* 405 U.S. 438. Justice Brennan speaking for the Court claimed that it is unconstitutional to try to forbid the dissemination of birth control information and devices to unmarried persons. For Justice Brennan, the right to privacy, if it is to be meaningful, must guarantee the right of the individual, married or single, to be free from unwarranted governmental interference in relationships that so fundamentally affect a person's decision whether to bear or beget a child. It is interesting to note that the Court's opinion was based on the Equal Protection Clause. Why might the Court have been reluctant to use the same rationale advanced in *Griswold?*

4. Does the right to privacy cover personal grooming? This issue emerged in a 1976 case, *Kelley v. Johnson,* 425 U.S. 238. In that case, the Court ruled in a 6 to 2 decision (Justice Stevens did not participate) that police regulations prescribing the style and length of hair, sideburns, and mustaches of policemen are not unduly restrictive of the policeman's right to choose his hairstyle. Weighing the interest of the police department and the interest of the policeman, Justice Rehnquist for the majority struck the balance for the former. Both through a desire to make police officers readily recognizable to the general public and to foster an *esprit de corps* within the police force, the department had demonstrated sufficient justification to regulate grooming styles. Justice Marshall, joined by Justice Brennan, dissented, noting that:

> An individual's personal appearance may reflect, sustain, and nourish his personality and may well be used as a means of expressing his attitude and lifestyle. In taking control over a citizen's personal appearance, the Government forces him to sacrifice

substantial elements of his integrity and identity as well. (At pp. 250–251).

The opinion by Justice Rehnquist distinguished grooming rights from the privacy rights asserted in *Griswold,* and assumed, but did not hold, that these rights are part of a general Fourteenth Amendment right to liberty. *Kelley* indicated that the Court would not prefer every asserted right of privacy over reasonable government regulation. While there might be a personal right of grooming, it would not be as preferred as, for example, the First Amendment's guarantee of freedom of speech.

(2) Applying Griswold to the Educational Setting

Merriken v. Cressman involves the administering of a testing program designed to identify potential drug abusers among eighth graders in Norristown, Pennsylvania. The test, called the Critical Period of Intervention (CPI), purported to identify behavioral patterns similar to users of marijuana, LSD, barbiturate, or amphetamine through questionnaire responses. Students were asked questions about their backgrounds and family life, and were also asked to identify others in the class who got into fights or quarrels, made unusual or inappropriate remarks, or had to be coaxed or forced to work with other students. Once identified, potential student drug abusers were to be assigned to peer groups for behavior modification or were to be referred to outside specialists.

Plaintiffs, a student in the eighth grade at Stewart Junior High School and his mother, objected to the test as an infringement on their constitutional right to privacy. After the suit was instituted, the school district modified its procedures so that parental consent was necessary for students to participate in the CPI program, though parents could not see the actual test. Child psychiatrists testified at the hearing that the testing program posed several dangers, including the possibility that students labelled as potential drug abusers may actually decide to act the part. They also pointed out that some children may be singled out for unpleasant treatment from other students for refusing to take the test (Michael Merriken was accused of being a drug user because his mother refused to let him take the test). Testimony from school officials showed that while confidentiality would be stressed, it could not be guaranteed.

MERRIKEN v. CRESSMAN

United States District Court, E.D. Pennsylvania, 1973.
364 F.Supp. 913.

OPINION and ORDER

John Morgan DAVIS, District Judge.

* * *

The main thrust of the Plaintiffs' argument that the CPI Program is an involuntary invasion of constitutionally protected rights, is the violation of the right to privacy. They base their argument mainly on Griswold v. Connecticut, in which the Supreme Court ruled that inherent in the first nine Amendments to the Constitution is a right to privacy which is binding on the States as well. In a more recent case, the Supreme Court re-emphasized its position on the right of privacy in Roe v. Wade, * * *

* * * The CPI Program questionnaire asks whether the student's family is "very close, somewhat close, not too close, or not close at all." * * * In addition, the student is asked to answer questions of such intimate things of his parents as to whether they "hugged and kissed him good-night when he was small" * * *; whether they told him how "much they loved him or her" * * *; whether the parents "seemed to know that the student's needs or wants are" * * *; and whether the student "feels that he is loved by his parents" * * *.

The above questions are samples which represent the highly personal nature of the entire questionnaire. These questions go directly to an individual's family relationship and his rearing. There probably is no more private a relationship, excepting marriage, which the Constitution safeguards than that between parent and child. This Court can look upon any invasion of that relationship as a direct violation of one's Constitutional right to privacy.

The fact that the students are juveniles does not in any way invalidate their right to assert their Constitutional right to privacy. * * * This Court would add that the right to privacy is on an equal or possibly more elevated pedestal than some other individual Constitutional rights and should be treated with as much deference as free speech. * * *

* * * In the case at Bar, the children are never given the opportunity to consent to invasion of their privacy; only the opportunity to refuse to consent by returning a blank questionnaire. Whether this procedure is Constitutional is questionable, but the Court does not have to face that issue because the facts presented show that the parents could not have been properly informed about the CPI Program and as a result could not have given informed consent for their children to take the CPI test.

* * *

The facts * * * show that the letters to the parents were "selling devices" aimed at gaining consent without giving negative information that would make the parents completely aware of "the relevant circumstances and likely consequences" of the Program. Mr. Streit, the man who conceived the CPI Program, admitted that the letter to the parents gave only one side of the test picture. There were no statements to the parents concerning the self-fulfilling prophecy, scapegoating of those children who opted not to participate or the ultimate use of the data as it would affect their children and law authorities who might find it necessary to use that information to learn more about the drug situation in the local community.

* * *

The actual testing of the students and the results gained are suspect. All that the Program does state is that it will identify patterns similar to marijuana, LSD, barbiturate or amphetamine users. There is no reference to the use of drugs and there are no statements as to what constitutes abuse. The study nowhere defines what is a potential drug abuser and is vague in the relationship of its background analysis to the intended results.

There is a statement concerning the confidentiality of the test during its administration and during the immediate evaluation period that is comprehensive and well explained, but the credibility of the confidentiality of this Program breaks down when the potential drug abusers are reported to the school superintendent. The school will then attempt remediation by the use of teachers, guidance counselors and others, who have had little training in the area of psychological therapy in either individual or group therapy sessions. The ultimate use of this information, although possibly gained with a great deal of scientific success, is the most serious problem that faces the

Court. How many children would be labeled as potential drug abusers who in actuality are not, and would be subjected to the problem of group therapy sessions conducted by inexperienced individuals?

Strict confidentiality is not maintained after evaluation and there are many opportunities for a child to suffer insurmountable harm from a labeling such as "drug abuser" at an age when the cruelty of other children is at an extreme. * * *

When a program talks about labeling someone as a particular type and such a label could remain with him for the remainder of his life, the margin of error must be almost nil. The preliminary statistics and other evidence indicate there will be errors in identification. * * *

The Court, in balancing the right of an individual to privacy and the right of the Government to invade that privacy for the sake of public interest, strikes the balance in favor of the individual in the circumstances shown in this case. * * *

* * *

* * * As the Program now stands the individual loses more than society can gain in its fight against drugs. The Court will enjoin this Program as it fails to meet Constitutional standards.

* * *

NOTES AND QUESTIONS

1. Aside from Fourth Amendment considerations, most courts are inclined to accord students some measure of privacy in the public educational setting. As *Merriken* points out, the task facing courts is to balance "the right of the individual to privacy and the right of the Government to invade that privacy for the sake of the public interest." Do you believe Judge Davis struck the balance correctly?

2. Issues of privacy have been most litigated in the context of grooming codes, particularly those pertaining to male hair length. *Kelley v. Johnson,* discussed in the Notes following *Griswold,* considered the issue as related to the public employment of policemen. The *Kelley* ruling engendered considerable speculation about possible rights of teachers and other school employees in this respect. So far the Supreme Court has refused to hear a case dealing either with teacher or student alleged rights of privacy as applied to personal grooming. Insofar as teachers are concerned, a 1974 decision by the Seventh Circuit Court of Appeals may be highly significant. In *Miller v. School Dist. No. 167,* 495 F.2d 658, then Judge John Paul Stevens, later to become Justice Stevens, ruled against the right of a teacher to wear a beard and long sideburns contrary to school regulations. Judge Stevens noted that "the impairment of the individual's interest in selecting his own life style which results from the employment decision of one local school board is much less significant than the deprivations of liberty which have been condemned in other cases." (At p. 665). In this instance the school board had valid reason to prescribe faculty grooming requirements, given its responsibility to prevent adverse impact on the educational process. Judge Stevens added that students "have a valid interest in not being compelled to associate with persons they or their parents consider objectionable," and consequently look to the school board for protection. (At p. 667).

It should be pointed out that where specific constitutional rights (those actually listed in the Constitution) are implicated in objections to state-imposed grooming codes, some courts are more inclined to intervene. Thus, in *Teterud v. Gillman*, 385 F.Supp. 153 (S.D.Iowa 1974), aff'd 522 F.2d 357 (8th Cir. 1975), the court upheld the right of an American Indian inmate to wear long hair since it was judged to be an integral part of his religion. In *Braxton v. Board of Public Instruction*, 303 F.Supp. 958 (M.D.Fla.1969), the court upheld the right of a black school teacher to wear a goatee since it was "an appropriate expression of his heritage, culture, and racial pride." However, the *Braxton* holding is questionable in light of the Equal Protection Clause. Should blacks be exempted from grooming codes, but not whites?

Students, of course, are not employees. Thus, cases involving teachers have limited applicability. To date, the federal circuits are evenly divided on whether students have a constitutional right to wear their hair in the manner they choose. Those circuits which have ruled against students assert either that hair length is not a constitutional right and thus can be regulated at will [17] or that it does have at least some constitutional protection but, as in *Miller* above, is outweighed by the interests of educational authorities.[18]

Where courts have found such a constitutional right to exist, they are unclear as to exactly what the source of this right is, some preferring the First Amendment or other provision of the Bill of Rights and some looking to the "liberty" provision of the Fourteenth Amendment. Some courts have utilized the Equal Protection Clause to strike down hair length regulations which apply only to boys or which apply only to a specific category of students such as those participating in athletics or band. For example, in *Crews v. Cloncs,* 432 F.2d 1259 (7th Cir. 1970), the federal court of appeals rejected the health and safety arguments of the school principal, noting that long-haired girls participated safely in physical education, science lab, and industrial art classes. So far, the "new equal protection" approach, demanding a compelling state purpose, has not been used since sex is not considered a suspect classification (see Chapter Seven, p. 609ff), nor personal grooming a fundamental right (see Chapter Seven p. 620ff). Thus a rational purpose is sufficient under the Equal Protection Clause, though school officials have found it difficult to convince some courts that there is any rational reason for male hair length regulations.

More recently, advocates of personal grooming rights have looked to federal and state civil rights legislation to bolster their case. Thus, Title

---

17. See, for example, *Karr v. Schmidt,* 460 F.2d 609 (5th Cir. 1972). However, in *Lansdale v. Tyler Junior College,* 470 F.2d 659 (5th Cir. 1972), the same court struck down a hair length regulation in a state junior college as irrational and unrelated to any legitimate college interest. This led one commentator to note that "Apparently, high school students in the southern United States are handed a new constitutional right along with their diploma at commencement." Comment, "Long Hair and The Law: A Look At Constitutional and Title VII Challenges to Public and Private Regulations of Male Grooming" 24 *Kansas L.Rev.* 143, 1975, at p. 155.

18. In *Farrell v. Smith,* 310 F.Supp. 732 (D. Me.1970), the federal district court ruled that, while hair length is a fundamental right, the state vocational school had a compelling interest to regulate hair length because long-haired students might adversely affect other students' employment opportunities. Since the federal appeals court for this circuit had ruled earlier that personal grooming is a fundamental right under the liberty provision of the Fourteenth Amendment, *Richards v. Thurston,* 424 F. 2d 1281 (1st Cir. 1970), the district court could not avoid confronting the preferred status of personal grooming.

VII of the 1964 Civil Rights Act has been utilized in the employment context to fight employer grooming codes, for the most part unsuccessfully. In light of federal and state legislation against sex discrimination, some attorneys have advised educational officials to abandon all appearance regulations beyond those reasonably related to modesty and safety.

With the decline of student radicalism in the 1970s and with the question settled, albeit inconsistently in much of the country, litigation over personal grooming has fallen off. Nevertheless, the disturbing questions raised by the hair length cases continue. How would you respond to the following:

   a.   Is there in your view a constitutional right to wear one's hair as one wishes? If so, where is this right found?

   b.   If there is such a right, is it to be on an equal footing with specific constitutional rights such as freedom of religion and thus preferred over government regulation, or is this right less fundamental and entitled only to "some" constitutional protection?

   c.   In the context of public education, should educational authorities have the power to prescribe teacher grooming codes? Student grooming codes?

   d.   If grooming codes treat men and women differently, is there a violation of the Equal Protection Clause?

   3.   Note that school officials may have a difficult balancing act where issues of privacy run headlong into the rights of others. In *Trachtman v. Anker,* 563 F.2d 512 (2nd Cir. 1977), a case discussed in Chapter Three, school officials sought to ban a survey of student sexual habits and acts proposed by the editor of the high school newspaper, who then intended to publish the results. The student editor asserted the ban infringed upon his constitutional rights of expression. School officials maintained the survey would infringe upon the privacy rights of other students. The lower court ruled in part against the school, allowing the survey to be administered to juniors and seniors but not younger students. The court of appeals reversed the lower court, concluding that school officials have a duty "to protect the students committed to their care, who are compelled by law to attend school, from peer contacts and pressures which may result in emotional disturbance to some of those students whose responses are sought." (At p. 519).

   Tarasoff v. The Regents of the Univ. of Calif., 551 P.2d 334 (Calif.1976) presents a question related to the right of privacy, namely, to what extent is confidentiality between doctor and patient inviolate? *Tarasoff* involved a lover's quarrel between two students at the University of California at Berkeley. The situation confronted health officials at the institution with a difficult choice. They could maintain confidentiality with the male student, who said he intended to kill his girl friend, or they could break the confidentiality and warn the intended victim. They chose the former. Two months later the patient murdered the girl. Her parents sued the doctors and the university. The California Supreme Court ruled that a psychotherapist whose patients threaten the lives of others has a legal obligation to warn the prospective victim, even though doing so may breach doctor-patient confidentiality:

> When a therapist determines, or pursuant to the standards of his profession should determine, that his patient presents a serious danger of violence to another, he incurs an obligation to use reasonable care to protect the intended victim against such danger. (At p. 340).

The American Psychiatric Association and several California associations protested the ruling on the grounds that it would undermine the doctor-patient relationship. The court countered, however, with the observation that "The protective privilege ends where the public peril begins." (At p. 347).

4. Student privacy issues in the collegiate setting frequently arise in terms of on-campus residency requirements. Residency requirements and related rules, sometimes referred to as parietal regulations, are most often challenged as infringements on students' First/Fourteenth Amendment right of association, an invasion of the students' privacy, or an unreasonable classification in violation of the Equal Protection Clause. Equal protection issues concerning residency requirements are discussed in Chapter Seven. Generally, courts uphold residency requirements as long as they are at least in part related to the educational function of the institution and no unusual circumstances are present. A recent case in point is *Prostrollo v. University of S. D.*, 369 F.Supp. 778 (D.C.S.D.1974), *rev'd* 507 F.2d 775 (8th Cir. 1974). There, the lower court found no evidence of any enrichment of student life as a result of living in campus housing and concluded that the sole reason for the requirement was to pay off bonded indebtedness. The appeals court reversed, noting that a "live and learn" policy was part of the rationale for the freshman and sophomore student residency requirement and insofar as the privacy issue was concerned, concluded that "The interest in living precisely where one chooses is not fundamental within our constitutional scheme." (At p. 781). Nor did the residency requirement interfere with the freedom of association:

> Freedom of association has been recognized as a fundamental right, but even fundamental rights are not so absolute as to be protected from all incidental effects of otherwise legitimate legislation. (At p. 781).

The court refused to regard either privacy or association as preferred over reasonable government regulation. Should courts (1) accept assertions of a live and learn policy from educational officials, (2) demand objective evidence of student benefits, or (3) make an independent investigation? Which would be most compatible with the nature of the judiciary?

In *Futrell v. Ahrens*, 540 P.2d 214 (N.M.1975), students at New Mexico State University brought suit to enjoin enforcement of parietal rules prohibiting visitation of the opposite sex in dorm rooms. The students alleged that the rules were unreasonable and infringed on their rights of association and privacy. The New Mexico Supreme Court concluded that the right to association "has never been construed as an absolute right of association between a man and woman at any and all places and times." (At p. 216). Insofar as privacy is concerned, the court simply found *Griswold* and related cases inapplicable. The decision of the lower court upholding the regulation was affirmed.

5. Is it an invasion of privacy for police officers, posing as students, to enroll in an university and engage in the covert recording of class discussions and private meetings, compiling police dossiers, and filing intelligence reports—all in the interest of preventing crime even though no specific illegal activity or acts are under investigation? This was the issue facing the California Supreme Court in *White v. Davis*, 533 P.2d 222 (1975). The California court unanimously concluded that such large-scale surveillance activity by the Los Angeles Police Department amounted to a *per se* violation of both freedom of expression and association provisions of the state and federal Constitutions, and also of a privacy provision which had been recently added to the California constitution. The California high court ruled that the lower court had dismissed the case in error; it was remanded for trial. Justice Tobriner for the court pointed out that since protected rights were involved, the police department would have to advance compelling reasons for such surveillance to be sustained. He pointed out that "Given the delicate nature of academic freedom, we visualize a substantial probability that this alleged covert police surveillance will chill the exercise of First Amendment rights." (At p. 224).

The opinion is particularly noteworthy for its discussion of and reliance upon the privacy provision of the California constitution. Justice Tobriner stated the moving force behind voter adoption of the new provision in November, 1972, was "a more focused privacy concern, relating to the accelerating encroachment on personal freedom and security caused by increased surveillance and data collection-activity in contemporary society." (At p. 233). The activities of the Los Angeles Police Department, the justice concluded, "state a *prima facie* violation of the state constitutional right of privacy." (At p. 234).

Another interesting case related to the same issue is *Menard v. Saxbe,* 498 F.2d 1017 (D.C.Cir. 1974). It involves a nineteen-year old college student who was arrested during the summer while working in Los Angeles. Menard had been waiting until the early hours of the morning in a park for a friend. When the friend failed to appear at the appointed time, Menard left the park bench to find out the time. After he returned to the bench, he was approached by two police officers who questioned him relative to reports of a prowler. They also confronted Menard with a wallet they had found near the park bench. Menard said he knew nothing about the prowler or the wallet, a statement corroborated by his friend who finally appeared. Despite continued protestations, Menard was arrested, booked, and fingerprinted. He remained in police custody for two days, then was released. No charges were ever filed. Nevertheless, the police retained a file on the incident, as did the F.B.I. to whom his fingerprints had been sent for checking. After repeated attempts to have the matter expunged from F.B.I. files, Menard resorted to the courts, alleging the violation of numerous rights including privacy. The lower court ruled that while expungement would not be ordered, the F.B.I. could not release the information about Menard from its criminal files to anyone other than law enforcement personnel and federal agencies should he seek employment with them.   328 F.Supp. 718 (D.C.D.C.1971).   The decision was based on statutory provisions related to the F.B.I., not on Menard's constitutional claims.   The federal court of appeals also did not reach the constitutional issues, concluding that under federal law the F.B.I. had no authority to retain Menard's arrest record in its criminal files once it was informed by the California police that a detention, not an arrest, had taken place.   However, the court did note that the federal agency could keep Menard's fingerprints in a neutral non-criminal file, "provided there is no reference of any kind to indicate that the prints originated in a source for criminal files."   (At p. 1090).

A similar incident occurred a few years later when Newark high school student Lori Paton wrote a letter to the Socialist Labor Party but inadvertently addressed it to the Socialist Workers Party.   Her letter requested information for a social studies class.   The F.B.I., which was monitoring mail addressed to the Socialist Workers Party, sent an agent to investigate the matter.   When nothing turned up, the incident was dropped from further investigation;   however, a reference remained in the F.B.I. files. Lori Paton, through her father and her social studies teacher, sued to have her file expunged, claiming violation of numerous constitutional rights and a federal statute relating to tampering with the mail.   Since the investigation had been reported in the school newspaper and in local and national media, Lori also sued for $65,000 damages, alleging her reputational rights had been tarnished.   The federal district court agreed to have her file, which was labeled "Subversive Matter—Socialist Workers Party," expunged but refused to award damages.   *Paton v. LaPrade*, 382 F.Supp. 1118 (D.C.N.J.1974).   The Third Circuit Court of Appeals reversed the judgment and remanded the case back to the district court for further proceedings.   524 F.2d 862 (3rd Cir. 1975).

B.   Sexual Practices and the Constitution

One of the most persistent social and political issues this nation has faced is the moral and legal problems of abortions.   The debate over the morality of abortion has centered on two areas: the right of a woman to use her body as she chooses and the question of the fetus' status as a human being.   Pro-abortion advocates often argue that the decision to abort is a matter of personal conscience and choice, and that state intervention would violate the pregnant woman's right to privacy.   They also point out that childbirth may deprive a woman of the life style she prefers and force her to accept a radically different future against her will. She (or society) might have to shoulder a financial burden of giving birth to the child and caring for it;   she might have to abandon her educational and career plans.   The woman should be permitted, then, to reach her own private decision to terminate or not to terminate her pregnancy.   Antiabortionists respond by stating that the unborn child's right to life is more fundamental and more compelling than the mother's right of privacy.   The mother has a responsibility and an obligation to nurture the potential life developing within her. Any inconveniences surrounding a pregnancy and child's birth does not justify aborting that life.

These arguments about the right to use one's body as one chooses and the fetus' right to life were weighed by the Supreme Court in *Roe v. Wade,* 410 U.S. 113 (1973), excerpts of which follow. In *Roe* a pregnant single woman, suing under the fictitious name of Jane Roe, challenged the constitutionality of the Texas criminal abortion laws. According to the Texas Penal code, the performance of an abortion, except to save the life of the mother, constituted a crime that was punishable by a prison sentence of two to five years. At the time of the *Roe* case, abortion legislation varied widely from state to state. Roe instituted an action in the U. S. District Court for the Northern District of Texas, seeking a declaratory judgment that the Texas statute was unconstitutional. The three-judge court held that the Texas criminal abortion statutes were void because they were unconstitutionally overbroad and vague. The appeal was taken by all the parties to the U. S. Supreme Court.

The Court carefully weighed the interests involved, then ruled in part for the mother and in part for the state. Justice Harry Blackmun wrote the opinion of the Court with concurrence of six other Justices. The Court, as Justice Blackmun elaborates below, based its decision on the constitutional right of privacy. Justice Blackmun argued that the states must leave the question of abortion to the sole discretion of the pregnant woman and her physician during the first trimester (three months) of pregnancy. During the second trimester, the state may regulate the procedures by which an abortion takes place provided these regulations reasonably relate to the health of the mother. Since the state has a compelling interest in protecting the potentiality of human life after "viability"—when the fetus presumably has the capability of living outside the mother's womb—the state may regulate and even prohibit abortions during the third trimester except when it is necessary to preserve the mother's life or health. The *Roe* decision resolved the major legal issue involved in the abortion issue, but it did not resolve, and in fact stimulated, controversy surrounding the underlying moral and political questions.

ROE v. WADE

Supreme Court of the United States, 1973.
410 U.S. 113, 93 S.Ct. 705, 35 L.Ed.2d 147.

Mr. Justice BLACKMUN delivered the opinion of the Court.

*   *   *

We forthwith acknowledge our awareness of the sensitive and emotional nature of the abortion controversy, of the vigorous opposing views, even among physicians, and of the deep and seemingly absolute convictions that the subject inspires. One's philosophy, one's experiences, one's exposure to the raw edges of human existence, one's religious training, one's attitudes toward life and family and their values, and the moral standards one establishes and seeks to observe, are all likely to influence and to color one's thinking and conclusions about abortion.

In addition, population growth, pollution, poverty, and racial overtones tend to complicate and not to simplify the problem.

Our task, of course, is to resolve the issue by constitutional measurement, free of emotion and of predilection. We seek earnestly to do this, and, because we do, we have inquired into, and in this opinion place some emphasis upon, medical and medical-legal history and what that history reveals about man's attitudes toward the abortion procedure over the centuries. * * *

The Texas statutes that concern us * * * make it a crime to "procure an abortion," as therein defined, or to attempt one, except with respect to "an abortion procured or attempted by medical advice for the purpose of saving the life of the mother." Similar statutes are in existence in a majority of the States.

* * *

The principal thrust of appellant's attack on the Texas statutes is that they improperly invade a right, said to be possessed by the pregnant woman, to choose to terminate her pregnancy. Appellant would discover this right in the concept of personal "liberty" embodied in the Fourteenth Amendment's Due Process Clause; or in personal, marital, familial, and sexual privacy said to be protected by the Bill of Rights or its penumbras, see Griswold v. Connecticut, * * *. * * *

* * *

Three reasons have been advanced to explain historically the enactment of criminal abortion laws in the 19th century and to justify their continued existence.

It has been argued occasionally that these laws were the product of a Victorian social concern to discourage illicit sexual conduct. Texas, however, does not advance this justification in the present case, and it appears that no court or commentator has taken the argument seriously. * * *

A second reason is concerned with abortion as a medical procedure. When most criminal abortion laws were first enacted, the procedure was a hazardous one for the woman. This was particularly true prior to the development of antisepsis. * * *

Modern medical techniques have altered this situation. Appellants and various *amici* refer to medical data indicating that abortion in early pregnancy, that is, prior to the end of the first trimester, although not without its risk, is now relatively safe. Mortality rates for women undergoing early abortions, where the procedure is legal, appear to be as low as or lower than the rates for normal childbirth. Consequently, any interest of the State in protecting the woman from an inherently hazardous procedure, except when it would be equally dangerous for her to forgo it, has largely disappeared. Of course, important state interests in the areas of health and medical standards do remain. The State has a legitimate interest in seeing to it that abortion, like any other medical procedure, is performed under circumstances that insure maximum safety for the patient. This interest obviously extends at least to the performing physician and his staff, to the facilities involved, to the availability of aftercare, and to adequate provision for any complication or emergency that might arise. The prevalence of high mortality rates at illegal "abortion mills" strengthens, rather than weakens, the State's interest in regulating the conditions under which abortions are performed. Moreover, the risk to the woman increases as her pregnancy continues. Thus, the State retains a definite interest in protecting the woman's own health and safety when an abortion is proposed at a late stage of pregnancy.

The third reason is the State's interest —some phrase it in terms of duty—in protecting prenatal life. Some of the argument for this justification rests on the theory that a new human life is present from the moment of conception. The State's interest and general obligation to protect life then extends, it is argued, to prenatal life. Only when the life of the pregnant mother herself is at stake, balanced against the life she carries within her, should the interest of the embryo or fetus not prevail. Logically, of course, a legitimate state interest in this area need not stand or fall on acceptance of the belief that life begins at conception or at some other point prior to live birth. In assessing the State's interest, recognition may be given to the less rigid claim that as long as at least *potential* life is involved, the State may assert interests beyond the protection of the pregnant woman alone.

* * *

It is with these interests, and the weight to be attached to them, that this case is concerned.

The Constitution does not explicitly mention any right of privacy. In a line of decisions, however, * * * the Court has recognized that a right of personal privacy, or a guarantee of certain areas or zones of privacy, does exist under the Constitution. * * *

This right of privacy, whether it be founded in the Fourteenth Amendment's concept of personal liberty and restrictions upon state action, as we feel it is, or, as the District Court determined, in the Ninth Amendment's reservation of rights to the people, is broad enough to encompass a woman's decision whether or not to terminate her pregnancy. The detriment that the State would impose upon the pregnant woman by denying this choice altogether is apparent. Specific and direct harm medically diagnosable even in early pregnancy may be involved. Maternity, or additional offspring, may force upon the woman a distressful life and future. Psychological harm may be imminent. Mental and

physical health may be taxed by child care. There is also the distress, for all concerned, associated with the unwanted child, and there is the problem of bringing a child into a family already unable, psychologically and otherwise, to care for it. In other cases, as in this one, the additional difficulties and continuing stigma of unwed motherhood may be involved. All these are factors the woman and her responsible physician necessarily will consider in consultation.

* * * As noted above, a State may properly assert important interests in safeguarding health, in maintaining medical standards, and in protecting potential life. At some point in pregnancy, these respective interests become sufficiently compelling to sustain regulation of the factors that govern the abortion decision. The privacy right involved, therefore, cannot be said to be absolute. In fact, it is not clear to us that the claim asserted by some *amici* that one has an unlimited right to do with one's body as one pleases bears a close relationship to the right of privacy previously articulated in the Court's decisions. The Court has refused to recognize an unlimited right of this kind in the past. Jacobson v. Massachusetts, 197 U.S. 11 (1905) (vaccination); Buck v. Bell, 274 U.S. 200 (1927) (sterilization).

* * *

The appellee and certain *amici* argue that the fetus is a "person" within the language and meaning of the Fourteenth Amendment. * * *

The Constitution does not define "person" in so many words. * * *

* * * But in nearly all these instances, the use of the word is such that it has application only postnatally. None indicates, with any assurance, that it has any possible prenatal application.[54]

54. When Texas urges that a fetus is entitled to Fourteenth Amendment protection as a person, it faces a dilemma. Neither in Texas nor in any other State are all abortions prohibited. Despite broad proscription, an exception always exists. The exception contained in Art. 1196, for an abortion procured or attempted by medical advice for the purpose of saving the life of the mother, is typical. But if the fetus

* * *

Texas urges that, apart from the Fourteenth Amendment, life begins at conception and is present throughout pregnancy, and that, therefore, the State has a compelling interest in protecting that life from and after conception. We need not resolve the difficult question of when life begins. When those trained in the respective disciplines of medicine, philosophy, and theology are unable to arrive at any consensus, the judiciary, at this point in the development of man's knowledge, is not in a position to speculate as to the answer.

* * *

With respect to the State's important and legitimate interest in the health of the mother, the "compelling" point, in the light of present medical knowledge, is at approximately the end of the first trimester. This is so because of the now-established medical fact, * * * that until the end of the first trimester mortality in abortion may be less than mortality in normal childbirth. It follows that, from and after this point, a State may regulate the abortion procedure to the extent that the regulation reasonably relates to the preservation and protection of maternal health. Examples of permissible state regulation in this area are requirements as to the qualifications of the person who is to perform the abortion; as to the licensure of that person; as to the facility in which the procedure is to be performed, that is, whether it must be a hospital or may be a clinic or some other place of less-than-hospital status; as to the licensing of the facility; and the like.

This means, on the other hand, that, for the period of pregnancy prior to this

"compelling" point, the attending physician, in consultation with his patient, is free to determine, without regulation by the State, that, in his medical judgment, the patient's pregnancy should be terminated. If that decision is reached, the judgment may be effectuated by an abortion free of interference by the State.

With respect to the State's important and legitimate interest in potential life, the "compelling" point is at viability. This is so because the fetus then presumably has the capability of meaningful life outside the mother's womb. State regulation protective of fetal life after viability thus has both logical and biological justifications. If the State is interested in protecting fetal life after viability, it may go so far as to proscribe abortion during that period, except when it is necessary to preserve the life or health of the mother.

Measured against these standards, Art. 1196 of the Texas Penal Code, in restricting legal abortions to those "procured or attempted by medical advice for the purpose of saving the life of the mother," sweeps too broadly. The statute makes no distinction between abortions performed early in pregnancy and those performed later, and it limits to a single reason, "saving" the mother's life, the legal justification for the procedure. The statute, therefore, cannot survive the constitutional attack made upon it here.

* * *

To summarize and to repeat:

1. A state criminal abortion statute of the current Texas type, that excepts from criminality only a *life-saving* procedure on behalf of the mother, without

---

is a person who is not to be deprived of life without due process of law, and if the mother's condition is the sole determinant, does not the Texas exception appear to be out of line with the Amendment's command?

There are other inconsistencies between Fourteenth Amendment status and the typical abortion statute. It has already been pointed out that in Texas the woman

is not a principal or an accomplice with respect to an abortion upon her. If the fetus is a person, why is the woman not a principal or an accomplice? Further, the penalty for criminal abortion specified by Art. 1195 is significantly less than the maximum penalty for murder prescribed by Art. 1257 of the Texas Penal Code. If the fetus is a person, may the penalties be different?

regard to pregnancy stage and without recognition of the other interests involved, is violative of the Due Process Clause of the Fourteenth Amendment.

(a) For the stage prior to approximately the end of the first trimester, the abortion decision and its effectuation must be left to the medical judgment of the pregnant woman's attending physician.

(b) For the stage subsequent to approximately the end of the first trimester, the State, in promoting its interest in the health of the mother, may, if it chooses, regulate the abortion procedure in ways that are reasonably related to maternal health.

(c) For the stage subsequent to viability, the State in promoting its interest in the potentiality of human life may, if it chooses, regulate, and even proscribe, abortion except where it is necessary, in appropriate medical judgment, for the preservation of the life or health of the mother.

2. The State may define the term "physician," as it has been employed in the preceding paragraphs of this Part XI of this opinion, to mean only a physician currently licensed by the State, and may proscribe any abortion by a person who is not a physician as so defined.

*   *   *

It is so ordered.

Affirmed in part and reversed in part.

Mr. Justice STEWART, concurring.

In 1963, this Court, in Ferguson v. Skrupa, 372 U.S. 726, purported to sound the death knell for the doctrine of substantive due process, a doctrine under which many state laws had in the past been held to violate the Fourteenth Amendment. As Mr. Justice Black's opinion for the Court in *Skrupa* put it: "We have returned to the original constitutional proposition that courts do not substitute their social and economic be-

liefs for the judgment of legislative bodies, who are elected to pass laws."

Barely two years later, in Griswold v. Connecticut the Court held a Connecticut birth control law unconstitutional. In view of what had been so recently said in *Skrupa*, the Court's opinion in *Griswold* understandably did its best to avoid reliance on the Due Process Clause of the Fourteenth Amendment as the ground for decision. Yet, the Connecticut law did not violate any provision of the Bill of Rights, nor any other specific provision of the Constitution. So it was clear to me then, and it is equally clear to me now, that the *Griswold* decision can be rationally understood only as a holding that the Connecticut statute substantively invaded the "liberty" that is protected by the Due Process Clause of the Fourteenth Amendment. As so understood, *Griswold* stands as one in a long line of pre-*Skrupa* cases decided under the doctrine of substantive due process, and I now accept it as such.

*   *   *

Mr. Justice REHNQUIST, dissenting.

*   *   *

*   *   * I have difficulty in concluding, as the Court does, that the right of "privacy" is involved in this case. Texas, by the statute here challenged, bars the performance of a medical abortion by a licensed physician on a plaintiff such as Roe. A transaction resulting in an operation such as this is not "private" in the ordinary usage of that word. Nor is the "privacy" that the Court finds here even a distant relative of the freedom from searches and seizures protected by the Fourth Amendment to the Constitution, which the Court has referred to as embodying a right to privacy.

If the Court means by the term "privacy" no more than that the claim of a person to be free from unwanted state regulation of consensual transactions may be a form of "liberty" protected by the Fourteenth Amendment, there is no doubt that similar claims have been upheld in our earlier decisions on the basis of that liberty. I agree with the statement of Mr. Justice STEWART in his concurring opinion that the "liberty," against deprivation of which without due process the Fourteenth Amendment protects, embraces more than the rights found in the Bill of Rights. But that liberty is not guaranteed absolutely against deprivation, only against deprivation without due process of law. The test traditionally applied in the area of social and economic legislation is whether or not a law such as that challenged has a rational relation to a valid state objective. Williamson v. Lee Optical Co., 348 U.S. 483 (1955). The Due Process Clause of the Fourteenth Amendment undoubtedly does place a limit, albeit a broad one, on legislative power to enact laws such as this. If the Texas statute were to prohibit an abortion even where the mother's life is in jeopardy, I have little doubt that such a statute would lack a rational relation to a valid state objective under the test stated in *Williamson*. But the Court's sweeping invalidation of any restrictions on abortion during the first trimester is impossible to justify under that standard, and the conscious weighing of competing factors that the Court's opinion apparently substitutes for the established test is far more appropriate to a legislative judgment than to a judicial one.

* * *

* * * As in *Lochner* and similar cases applying substantive due process standards to economic and social welfare legislation, the adoption of the compelling state interest standard will inevitably require this Court to examine the legislative policies and pass on the wisdom of these policies in the very process of deciding whether a particular state interest put forward may or may not be "compelling." The decision here to break pregnancy into three distinct terms and to outline the permissible restrictions the State may impose in each one, for example, partakes more of judicial legislation than it does of a determination of the intent of the drafters of the Fourteenth Amendment.

The fact that a majority of the States reflecting, after all the majority sentiment in those States, have had restrictions on abortions for at least a century is a strong indication, it seems to me, that the asserted right to an abortion is not "so rooted in the traditions and conscience of our people as to be ranked as fundamental." Even today, when society's views on abortion are changing, the very existence of the debate is evidence that the "right" to an abortion is not so universally accepted as the appellant would have us believe.

To reach its result, the Court necessarily has had to find within the Scope of the Fourteenth Amendment a right that was apparently completely unknown to the drafters of the Amendment. * * *

* * *

NOTES AND QUESTIONS

1. In the companion case *Doe v. Bolton*, 410 U.S. 179 (1973), the Court invalidated parts of the Georgia abortion law, which had been enacted in 1968 and patterned after the American Law Institute's Model Penal Code. About one-fourth of the states had enacted similar statutes. The portions struck down primarily related to procedural requirements in addition to the stipulation that an abortion must be based upon the "best clinical judgment" of a licensed physician.

Since 1973 the Court has had several opportunities to elaborate on the principles expressed in *Roe*. In *Planned Parenthood of Mo. v. Danforth,*

v. Doe, 432 U.S. 464; *Poelker v. Doe,* 432 U.S. 519. Justices Brennan, Marshall, and Blackmun dissented, pointing out the implications of the decisions for impoverished pregnant women.

Given the narrowness of some of these decisions and given the intense reaction generated by them, it is clear that litigation will continue in this sensitive area for some time. Prime candidates for early appearances before the Supreme Court are state efforts to regulate access of minors to contraceptives, to require some form of written consent before minors can have abortions, and to restrict access of pregnant women to abortion clinics. It should also be noted that like the school prayer decisions discussed in Chapter Four, the abortion rulings have generated calls for constitutional amendments to overturn them.

2. As stated in the Notes following *Griswold,* the derivation of non-specific constitutional rights from provisions in the Bill of Rights or the liberty and property provisions of the Fourteenth Amendment is a highly controversial process with significant ramifications for the rule of the Supreme Court, Congress, and the state legislatures. Another dimension of this same process relates to the "weight" to be assigned these non-specific rights. For example, is privacy to be considered a *preferred* right like freedom of speech, demanding that the state show a compelling reason to regulate or restrict it? Or is privacy to be assigned a less significant weight? We noted in *Kelley v. Johnson* (the 1976 policeman's hair length case) that while Justice Rehnquist for the majority considered personal grooming rights a liberty interest derived from the liberty provision of the Fourteenth Amendment, he accorded it relatively modest significance. Thus, the police department's grooming regulations did not have to meet a compelling test to be upheld. Similarly, the right of the parent to control the upbringing of his or her children is a recognized constitutional right but it does not rise to the preferred status of freedom of speech. Thus compulsory schooling laws are routinely preferred to parental rights, but freedom of speech follows the student into the school.

In *Roe* the privacy-related right of the woman to an abortion is regarded by the majority as sufficiently preferred to demand a compelling state reason to interfere with it. At different points in the woman's pregnancy, however, the interests of the state in safeguarding the health of the mother and the life of the child do become compelling and outweigh the mother's right to an abortion. If medical evidence is conflicting, how can Justice Blackmun know exactly where the state's interest becomes compelling? How does he know that the privacy right encompasses abortions and that it is to be given "preferred" constitutional status? Note Justice Rehnquist's dissent in which he asserts that "The decision here to break pregnancy into three distinct terms and to outline the permissible restrictions the State may impose in each one * * * partakes more of judicial legislation than it does of a determination of the intent of the drafters of the Fourteenth Amendment." Has the Court in *Roe* indeed become a "super-legislature"?

The problem of identifying and assigning weights to constitutional rights was addressed in a thoughtful comment by Justice Douglas in his concurring opinion in the companion case to *Roe, Doe v. Bolton.* After a brief comment in the significance of the Ninth Amendment, Justice Douglas suggested three categories of constitutional rights, ranging from those with absolute protection to those with something less than absolute protection:

> The Ninth Amendment obviously does not create federally enforceable rights. It merely says, "The enumeration in the Constitution of certain rights, shall not be construed to deny or disparage others retained by the people." But a catalogue of these rights includes customary, traditional and time-honored rights, amenities, privileges, and immunities that come within the sweep of "The Blessings of Liberty" mentioned in the preamble to the Constitution. Many of them, in my view, come within the meaning of the term "liberty" as used in the Fourteenth Amendment.
>
> *First is the autonomous control over the development and expression of one's intellect, interests, tastes, and personality.*
>
> These rights are protected by the First Amendment and, in my view, they are absolute, permitting of no exceptions. * * *
>
> *Second is freedom of choice in the basic decisions of one's life respecting marriage, divorce, procreation, contraception, and the education and upbringing of children* * * *.
>
> These rights, unlike those protected by the First Amendment, are subject to some control by the police power. Thus, the Fourth Amendment speaks only of "unreasonable searches and seizures" and of "probable cause." These rights are "fundamental," and we have held that in order to support legislative action the statute must be narrowly and precisely drawn and that a "compelling state interest" must be shown in support of the limitation. * * *
>
> *Third is the freedom to care for one's health and person, freedom from bodily restraint or compulsion, freedom to walk, stroll, or loaf.*
>
> These rights, though fundamental, are likewise subject to regulation on a showing of "compelling state interest." * * * (At pp. 211–213).

Is Justice Douglas' classification helpful? Or has he "opened the floodgates" of constitutional protection to all sorts of behavior, turning the Court into a super-legislature and the Constitution into a catchall document whose meaning varies with the value systems of the Justices?

By way of articulating your own approach to this complex and sensitive issue, consider which of the items below you would consider fundamental constitutional rights with preferred status over any form of governmental regulation. Which would you consider less fundamental but still constitutionally protected? (Locate where in the Constitution you think these fundamental rights are found.) Which would you consider not to be constitutional rights at all?

   a. speech

   b. nudity

    c. trial by jury

    d. hair length

    e. homosexual behavior

    f. driving a car

    g. marijuana smoking

    h. suicide

    j. welfare

    k. education

    l. employment

    m. consumption of alcohol

Aside from a few cases like *Griswold* and *Roe,* the Court has generally narrowly interpreted constitutional provisions to avoid an open-ended approach to constitutional rights. Thus, in recent cases, it has accorded either minimal or no constitutional status to education, employment, hair length, sexual preferences, or welfare. The likelihood that nudity, hair length, driving a car, marijuana smoking, suicide, or consumption of alcohol will ever achieve fundamental constitutional status through Court interpretation is questionable. One must therefore depend on Congress and state legislatures to confer rights in these areas commensurate with the wishes and conomic resources of the electorate.

3.   Should homosexual activity be included under the privacy umbrella of protected rights? In *Doe v. Commonwealth's Attorney for the City of Richmond,* 403 F.Supp. 1199 (E.D.Va.1975), the district court in a 2 to 1 decision distinguished *Griswold,* noting that the ruling related to sexual activity incident to marriage, while homosexuality "is obviously no portion of marriage, home, or family life." (At p. 1202). Since no fundamental right to privacy was involved, the state need not prove a compelling reason for the law. "It is enough for upholding the legislation to establish that the conduct is likely to end in a contribution to moral delinquency." (*Id.*) Since the statute "has ancestry going back to Judaic and Christian law," the majority considered it to be rational and appropriate. Judge Merhige dissented:

> A mature individual's choice of an adult sexual partner, in the privacy of his or her own home, would appear to me to be a decision of the utmost private and intimate concern. Private consensual sex acts between adults are matters in which the state has no legitimate interest. (At p. 1203).

Using the *Eisenstadt v. Baird* decision, *supra,* as evidence, the dissenting judge asserted that the Supreme Court had not confined *Griswold* to sexual matters between married persons. He also noted that the state "made no tender of any evidence which even impliedly demonstrated that homosexuality causes society any significant harm." (At p. 1205). In 1976 the Supreme Court affirmed the district court's decision, with Justices Brennan, Marshall, and Stevens on record as voting to hear the case. Just how much precedential value the affirmation has is open to question, given the controversy surrounding opinionless summary judgments by the Supreme Court. (See Chapter Two, p. 32).

4. "Immorality" is apt to be an important factor in many teacher dismissals at the elementary and secondary level, given the freer life styles of the present and continuing hostility from many elements of the community who view the teacher as an authority figure and role model in the classroom. Courts often agree with school officials that a teacher's moral behavior is a significant factor in teacher employment.[19] The critical test is whether deviant behavior is likely to have a negative impact on students and the school. For example, in *Sullivan v. Meade City Independent School Dist.*, 387 F.Supp. 1237 (D.C.S.D.1975), the district court affirmed dismissal of an unmarried teacher who was living with her boyfriend. The smallness of the community, the fact that the living arrangement was well known in and out of the school, and that 140 persons had signed a petition protesting the teacher's conduct convinced both school officials and the court that the teacher's out-of-school conduct was having a detrimental impact upon the students she was teaching: "It would seem reasonable for the school board to conclude that controversy between the plaintiff and the parents and the community members of this locale would make it difficult for Miss Sullivan to maintain the proper educational setting in her classroom." (At p. 1247).

A federal district court in Delaware recently reached the opposite conclusion with regard to a college administrator who became pregnant out of wedlock. In *Lewis v. Delaware State College*, 455 F.Supp. 239 (D.C. Del.1978), the court issued a preliminary injunction ordering the reinstatement of Bessie Lewis as Director of Residence Halls for Women. The college president had argued that the birth of an illegitimate child violated the institution's "unwritten moral standards," particularly in light of the counseling responsibilities of the women's residence hall director. However, the court noted that plaintiff's counseling responsibilities were minimal. The court concluded that the plaintiff had been denied both procedural and substantive due process, as well as her right to personal privacy. Relying on the abortion cases, the court noted that where the right to bear a child is involved, the state "must establish a compelling state interest for their decision not to renew the plaintiff's contract." (At p. 249). Since Bessie Lewis had little counseling responsibilities, since others on the college staff had had illegitimate children, and since the students were of adult age, the court concluded that the state could not meet this burden. The court cautioned, however, that under other circumstances, the decision to bear an illegitimate child may well be grounds for dismissal from government employment.

The problem is that despite considerable effort, courts have had a difficult time articulating the *criteria* to be used in ascertaining when teacher sex-related behavior is constitutionally protected and when it so intrudes upon the educational setting that it loses protection. The complexity and sensitivity of the issues in this area are well illustrated by court

19. For a review of cases involving teacher morality from the vantage point of the mid-1970s, see Samuel N. Francis and Charles E. Stacey "Law and the Sensual Teacher," 58 *Phi Delta Kappan* 98, October, 1977.

treatment of homosexual teachers. By the late 1970s courts were divided on upholding the right of homosexual teachers to continue to hold their jobs. Against a backdrop of increasing hostility toward homosexuality in the educational setting, the U.S. Supreme Court in 1978 let stand two state court decisions holding that teachers can be dismissed for being homosexuals.[20]

5. In recent years student privacy issues related to sex have been given some court attention. At the elementary and secondary level, sex education courses have frequently been challenged by parents, usually unsuccessfully, given the general reluctance of courts to interfere with the school board's plenary control over curriculum issues where specific constitutional rights are not being infringed. (See Chapter Two, p. 60ff). As noted in the previous chapter, the Equal Protection Clause has frequently been used to strike down discriminatory treatment accorded married students and unmarried pregnant girls. In general, proof of adverse effects on the school is necessary before action can be taken by school officials against either category of student. However, in *Houston v. Prosser,* 361 F.Supp. 295 (N.C.Ga.1973), the district court found no equal protection flaw in a plan by the Decatur, Georgia, school system requiring a student who becomes a parent to attend night school. After finding no fundamental right was infringed, the court concluded that it was rational for the school system to exclude young parents from regular school session: "Because of their precociousness, it is conceivable that their presence in a regular daytime school could result in a disruption thereof." (At p. 299). It apparently did not trouble the court that no actual disruption had occurred. Should this have been a determinative factor? Nevertheless, the court found the school plan illegal because it unjustifiably charged tuition to night school students but not to day school students. The tuition policy kept the plaintiff, a fifteen year old girl in 9th grade, from attending school altogether.

In higher education, the most frequent source of litigation involves the associational rights of gay students, a topic discussed in some detail in Chapter Three. Here again, absent material disruption, the prevailing view is that educational officials cannot prevent gay students from exercising First Amendment rights of expression and association.

In connection with student privacy rights, consider the following hypothetical.

John and Mary v. Officials of State Univ.

John and Mary, two freshmen at State University, met at an orientation dance and soon became close friends. Because neither had a car and because of the freshmen residency requirement, John and Mary found their activities mostly revolving around the campus, its classes, and functions. As time went by, the two decided to live together. Neither seriously considered marriage at this point in their relationship. Both were 19 years of age. The age of majority in Minnefornia is 18. (State University permits

---

20. *Gaylord v. Tacoma School Dist.*, 559 P.
2d 1340 (Wash., 1977). *Crish v. Board of
Educ.*, 366 A.2d 1337 (N.J., 1977).

married students to live off campus since they have no housing for married students).

While John and Mary knew they couldn't live together officially in the dorms, they thought they could work out an arrangement with their respective roommates allowing them to spend a few nights in John's room and a few nights in Mary's room every week. John talked the matter over with his roommate, Steve, who agreed "to think it over." Steve, however, frankly told John that he had no other place to sleep; besides, said Steve, "I have my books and things here; I don't want to have to carry them back and forth every week from some other place on campus." He added, "And I definitely don't want to move in with Mary's roommate!" Steve did consent, however, to allowing John and Mary to use the room for three days the following week when he would be attending his sister's wedding in another state.

After the second night in John's room, the pair were issued a warning by the resident assistant for the dormitory. Noting that cohabitation was contrary to dorm rules, the RA said that if the two stayed together in John's room, he would have to report them to the dean. Later, John's comment to Mary was, "Oh, he's just jealous. He never liked me very much anyway." But John and Mary did think the matter over very carefully. After much discussion, they decided to risk staying together once more, since John's roommate would return the next day.

The RA made a point of checking on the room that night and, finding them together, brought them to the dean. Eventually, John and Mary were denied freshmen residency on campus for their conduct after a hearing. This meant that they could not continue as students at State University, since all freshment must live on campus.

Feeling outraged at the university's action, John and Mary instituted a suit against the institution based on the following:

1. The residency requirement is unconstitutional because it infringes on student privacy rights.

2. The rule against cohabitation is unconstitutional for the same reason.

3. The punishment was disproportionate to the offense and thus a denial of due process.

They asked for reinstatement and further requested that all mention of the incident be deleted from their records.

———

What arguments would you make for John and Mary? What arguments for the university? If you were to decide this case, what decision would you reach and why? If a court were to decide it, what would be the likely outcome?

C. Legislation and Privacy Rights

Many political and legal advocates claim that the present case-by-case development of a right to privacy has been too slow to keep pace with speeding technological advances and too dependent upon what individual judges make of such amorphous concepts as the "inherent right to privacy." These advocates claim that for privacy or the "right to be let alone" to take hold in our society, there must be statutory protection of specific areas of privacy. The statutory approach would, it is claimed, in combination with case law help nationalize the right of privacy in a variety of contexts. The general concerns of these advocates include:

1. More attention must be paid not only to the citizen's right of access about data concerning him, but also to the avoidance of all unnecessary sharing of data stored in the filing systems and data banks of business, government, and educational institutions.

2. More attention must be given to the dangers of gathering personal or group information, however service-oriented the original intention of the organization. A new sense that the organization has no right to inquire into certain areas of one's life needs to be defined and fostered.

Those who take the statutory approach claim that if the nation does not continue scrupulously to guard the important areas of privacy of information and the citizen's right of access to data banks, we could become a totally controlled and administered society. The remainder of this chapter will discuss some of the major statutes developed to protect the individual from uncontrolled data collection and disbursement in the political, social, and educational environments, as well as assure a general right to privacy.

Recent federal and state statutes have made some headway in providing specific protection of privacy. At the federal level, the Freedom of Information Act, 5 U.S.C.A. § 552, was enacted by Congress in 1966 to make documents of executive departments and agencies generally available to the public. In 1974 the Act was strengthened by passage of the Federal Privacy Act, 5 U.S.C.A. § 552a, which directly related to bureaucratic snooping and was a clear response against the growing tendency of government to compile an endless stream of data and use it against the individual. The bugging practices of the Nixon Administration as revealed in the Senate Watergate hearings were a prime stimulus to this legislation. The Act states that "in order to protect the privacy of individuals identified in information systems maintained by Federal Agencies, it is necessary and proper for Congress to regulate the collection, maintenance, use, and dissemination of information by * * * [Federal] agencies." The Act's purpose is to establish safeguards for the individual against the invasion of privacy which "* * * is a personal and fundamental right protected by the Constitution of the United States * * *". These objectives are to be achieved "by requiring Federal agencies, except as otherwise provided by law, to (1) permit an individual to determine what records pertaining to him are collected, maintained, used or disseminated by such agencies; (2) permit an individual to prevent records pertaining to him obtained by such agencies for a particular purpose from being used or made available for another purpose without his consent; (3) permit an individual to gain access to information pertaining to him in Federal agency records, to have a copy made of all or any portion thereof, and to correct or amend such records." In addition, federal agencies are subject to civil suit for damages incurred as a consequence of intentional action which violates any of the individual's rights that are stipulated in the Act. The federal agencies must make a "reasonable" effort to guarantee the accuracy and completeness of the records. Those areas that are specifically not subject to the requirements of the Act include: investigatory information compiled for purposes of law enforcement records maintained by the Central Intelligence Agency, information dealing with the physical protection of the President, and testing materials that are used solely to assess the qualifications of individuals who are being considered for appointment or promotion in federal service.

In 1975 Congress passed the Government in the Sunshine Act, 5 U.S. C.A. § 552b, designed to remove some of the secrecy from governmental affairs by requiring the meetings of executive departments and agencies to be open to the public except in certain specific situations. At the state level, some states have adopted so-called "sunshine" laws similar to the 1975 federal measure. Others have sought legislative and constitutional protection for personal privacy. As noted earlier in this chapter, California passed a new constitutional amendment in 1972 after spirited political debate about the wisdom of including the term "privacy" in the constitution. The new provision states that "All people are by nature free and independent, and have certain inalienable rights, among which are those of enjoying and defending life and liberty; acquiring, possessing, and protecting property; and pursuing and obtaining safety, and happiness, and privacy." Many critics claim that the amendment is worded so generally that it is impossible to apply. Could the use of the term "privacy" in a constitution affect court decisions which must balance the individual's interest in privacy against the interests of the public's health, safety, and welfare? While an affirmative answer is probably in order, elevating privacy to constitutional status thrusts the courts even more into the uncomfortable task of applying an imprecise term to specific situations.

As far as students are concerned, the most important piece of legislation to date is the 1974 Family Educational Rights and Privacy Amendment (FERPA), commonly known as the Buckley Amendment, 20 U.S.C.A. § 1232g. The Buckley Amendment applies to most educational institutions in the country and is intended to protect the privacy rights of parents and students by providing rights related to the keeping of student records. Until the child is 18 years of age or attends college, parents exercise the rights on behalf of their children. Abuse of student records had become commonplace prior to the passage of the law.[21] Much of the abuse was done unknowingly, yet the damage in terms of college rejections, lost employment opportunities, and tainted reputations was great. The Buckley Amendment seeks to eliminate such abuse by giving parents and students access to their records and the opportunity to challenge inaccurate, misleading, or inappropriate information contained in them. The measure also limits the educational institutions' disclosure of data to third parties without consent of the parents or student. In addition, each institution is

21. See Merle McClung, "Student Records: The Family Educational Rights and Privacy Act of 1974," 22 *Inequality in Education* 5, July, 1977.

to develop a policy statement outlining the rights guaranteed by the act and setting forth the institutional procedures under which the rights can be exercised. The institutional penalty for noncompliance is loss of federal funding.

Just how effective the law is in safeguarding student privacy rights is still a matter of conjecture and debate, since final regulations pertaining to the legislation were not in place until 1976. Some institutions are still unclear whether the law pertains to them and in what way. A few remain ignorant of its passage altogether. Students at the high school and collegiate level have often found the law a hindrance to their efforts to secure confidential references for college admissions and employment. To provide for confidentiality, complex waiver systems have been developed at some educational institutions. The law's complexity coupled with the problems it poses for confidentiality has unfortunately led older students to believe the Buckley Amendment is designed not to protect students but rather to saddle them with more bureaucratic red tape.

Another federal statute, 20 U.S.C.A. § 1232h, provides parents and guardians with the right to inspect material used in connection with any federally-sponsored research or experimental program designed to improve teaching in the nation's schools. A second section was added to that statute in 1978 to prohibit the use of psychiatric or psychological examinations which invade students' privacy in connection with this research. Note the close resemblance the amendment bears to Judge Davis' opinion in Merriken v. Cressman, p. 654, supra.

(b) No student shall be required, as part of any applicable program, to submit to psychiatric examination, testing, or treatment, or psychological examination, testing, or treatment, in which the primary purpose is to reveal information concerning:

(1) political affiliations;

(2) mental and psychological problems potentially embarrassing to the student or his family;

(3) sex behavior and attitudes;

(4) illegal, anti-social, self-incriminating and demeaning behavior;

(5) critical appraisals of other individuals with whom respondents have close family relationships;

(6) legally recognized privileged and analogous relationships, such as those of lawyers, physicians, and ministers; or

(7) income (other than that required by law to determine eligibility for participation in a program or for receiving financial assistance under such program), without the prior consent of the student (if the student is an adult or emancipated minor), or in the case of unemancipated minor, without the prior written consent of the parent.

Whether state laws and institutional rules will follow the precedent set in *Merriken* and in this federal statute to broaden the privacy rights of students and teachers remains to be seen.

III. SUMMARY

The right to privacy is a very broad concept which oftentimes conflicts with society's right to know in the interest of public security. The Fourth Amendment has provided the greatest amount of privacy to individuals in the context of governmental searches and seizures. Because of the special nature of public schools and colleges, searches conducted by educational officials are less likely to run afoul of the Fourth Amendment as applied to the states through the Fourteenth Amendment, though its protections become greater for both public and nonpublic students when outside law enforcement officers are involved in or conduct a student search. To date, the Supreme Court has not heard a case involving the Fourth Amendment and student searches.

The right of privacy has also been extended to matters incident to marriage. In the process of enveloping marriage and childbearing in a cloak of privacy in *Griswold v. Connecticut* (1965) and *Roe v. Wade* (1973), respectively, the Supreme Court triggered a continuing controversy about the constitutional source of privacy in a context unrelated to searches and seizures. As noted in the Notes following these two cases, *Griswold* and *Roe* have prompted questions about what other rights may be inferred from the provisions of the Constitution. So far, the Court has been reluctant to broaden the right to privacy to matters unrelated to marriage and abortion. Thus, students have found limited judicial support for a right to personal grooming and to freedom from parietal rules. Teachers have also found little judicial support for personal grooming rights. In and out of the educational environment, homosexuality has generally won little constitutional support.

Recent legislative activity suggests that greater protection to privacy may be forthcoming outside of the judicial arena. Thus, all citizens are now protected from unauthorized surveillance and data collection by federal agencies. Some localities have passed laws protecting the rights of homosexuals. And the Buckley Amendment has provided parents and students with rights related to the keeping of student records.

Judicial and legislative attempts to seriously grapple with the complexity of the various components of privacy and the statutory efforts to provide citizen protection against unwarranted surveillance, data collection, and persecution reveal a willingness of our legal and political institutions to respond to the changed conditions of today's society. At the same time, they underscore the continuing tension between the rights of the individual and the responsibilities of those who govern society and manage its educational institutions.

" * * * a society so riven that the spirit of moderation is gone, no court *can* save; * * * a society where that spirit flourishes, no court *need* save; * * * in a society which evades its responsibility by thrusting upon the courts the nurture of that spirit, that spirit in the end will perish. What is the spirit of moderation? It is * * * in a word * * * faith in the sacredness of the individual."

> Judge Learned Hand
> "The Contribution of an Independent Judiciary"

"RECONSIDERING THE BASIC ISSUES"

The purpose of this brief concluding chapter is to review some of the major concerns addressed in the book's two introductory chapters, drawing upon the cases and discussions from Part II. The chapter concludes with a look toward the future.

I. DEFINING FREEDOM, JUSTICE, AND EQUALITY: THE ROLE OF THE JUDICIARY

A. Conceptions About Rights

Conceptions about freedom, justice, and equality ultimately relate to the views one has about the nature of the individual and the purpose of government. Some believe the individual to be inherently good and argue that the best government is one which intrudes as little as possible on the individual's growth and development. Others believe that the individual rarely acts benevolently and therefore government must have sufficient authority to assure peace and security. Between these two poles lie a variety of views, colored to a certain extent by philosophical and theological beliefs, as well as by experience and the results of scientific research.

In Chapter One we noted briefly the ideological positions each of the three dominant groups in American society—liberals, conservatives, and radicals—take regarding the character of individual rights and the purpose of educational institutions. It is not possible to say at present which view is most nearly correct. Too little is known about the process of human development. But it is possible to say that all three groups by virtue of their common American cultural experience are committed to living within a constitutional framework where decisions about fundamental rights and the legitimacy of governmental power are ultimately resolved by an independent judiciary. The criteria guiding the judges are set forth in the United States Constitution, with the ideals of the Declaration of Independence furnishing the theoretical backdrop.

B. The Role of the Judiciary

In resolving issues of constitutional rights, judges are influenced by an array of factors, just as are social scientists. Recall Henry M. Levin's comments in Chapter One that researchers cannot escape the influence of their own socialization. So it is with judges, who bring preconceived notions and propensities with them to the bench. No more than other decision makers can judges ever be truly objective and infallible. Yet, as Alexander Hamilton observed, an independent judiciary remains the best means, all things considered, for preserving the democratic tradition and securing the rights of individuals:

> This independence of the judges is * * * requisite to guard the Constitution and the rights of individuals from the effects of those ill humors, which the arts of designing men, or the influence of particular conjunctures, sometimes disseminate among the people themselves, and which, though they speedily give place to better information, and more deliberate reflection, have a tendency, in the meantime, to occasion dangerous innovations in the government, and serious oppressions of the minor party in the community. * * *
>
> * * *
>
> But it is not with a view to infractions of the Constitution only, that the independence of judges may be an essential safeguard against the effects of occasional ill humors in the society. These sometimes extend no farther than to the injury of the private rights of particular classes of citizens, by unjust and partial laws.[1]

But while the judiciary is the most effective forum for the resolution of many disputes, there are some issues which do not lend themselves to judicial resolution. The Constitution furnishes little guidance for determining at what point judges should defer to legislators, school boards, parents, or others who also claim the prerogative to decide. As we noted in Chapter Two, judges themselves have different views on the role of the judiciary, some preferring an activist role, others embracing judicial self-restraint, and still others opting for a neutralist approach.

For federal judges, and particularly for the Justices on the Supreme Court, the role of the judiciary, the least democratic and weakest branch of government, is a central concern. Justice Robert H. Jackson once questioned, "Must we first maintain a system of free political government to assure a free judiciary, or can we rely on an aggressive, activist judiciary to guarantee free government?"[2] He concluded that "the attitude of a society and of its organized political forces, rather than its legal machinery, is the controlling force in the character of free institutions."[3] In short, there are limits to the effective assertion of judicial power.

As important as the contributions of the courts have been in promoting the principles and ideals by which a constitutional democracy must be guided, there are dangers in permitting the courts to become the primary instruments for defending freedom of expression, the rights of the

1. Alexander Hamilton, "The Judiciary Department" (Federalist Paper No. 78), *The Federalist* (New York: Modern Library, 1937), at pp. 508–509.

2. Robert H. Jackson, *The Supreme Court and the American System of Government* (New York: Harper and Row, 1955), at p. 81.

3. *Id.*

accused, equality, and personal privacy. It should not be forgotten that basic responsibility for the enforcement of constitutional rights rests in the political, social, and educational arenas. It is there that workable programs must be designed to protect the individual from the capricious and unfair actions of others. As Archibald Cox has observed of the Supreme Court:

> The Court must know us better than we know ourselves. Its opinions may * * * sometimes be the voice of the spirit, reminding us of our better selves. * * * But while the opinions of the Court can help to shape our national understanding of ourselves, the roots of its decisions must be already in the nation. The aspirations voiced by the Court must be those the community is willing not only to avow but in the end to live by. The legitimacy of the great constitutional decisions rests upon the accuracy of the Court's perceptions of this kind of common will and upon the Court's ability, by expressing its perceptions, ultimately to command a consensus.[4]

The judiciary has been relatively successful in its activist role in defense of civil liberties because the legal values it has enunciated have been in general accord with the ethical and religious sentiments of the majority of society. The concurrence of legal values with ethical and religious sentiments allows the Supreme Court to serve at times as the national conscience. However, it is questionable whether the nation is well served when political representatives avoid painful responsibilities by letting the judiciary assume the full burden of securing constitutional rights. It has been largely in default of action by our political representatives, our professional educators, and many of our religious and cultural institutions that the judicial branch has found it necessary to enter specific areas and assume certain tasks which it is sometimes felt ill-equipped to handle. As became evident in the course of the discussion in Chapter Seven, the school finance and recent desegregation decisions serve as cases-in-point. In *San Antonio v. Rodriguez* and *Milliken v. Bradley,* 1973 and 1974 rulings, respectively, the majority on the Court became increasingly vocal in pointing out the limitations of courts to design and implement broad remedial programs. Large-scale social change, they maintain, is better left to legislatures. The danger of judicial noninvolvement, however, is that other decision makers will not be capable of acting effectively, thereby perpetuating the situation which gave rise to the complaint. Wrongs go unrighted, leaving the courts open to charges of evading their constitutional responsibilities.

The role of the federal judiciary is further complicated by the need to maintain the pre-eminence of the U. S. Constitution on the one hand and by increasing pressure to respond to issues undreamed of by the Founding Fathers nearly 200 years ago on the other. Our discussion of privacy issues in Chapter Eight highlights this dilemma. Electronic surveillance, contraception, abortion, homosexuality, euthanasia are a few of the grow-

---

4. Archibald Cox, *The Role of the Supreme Court in American Government* (N. Y.: Oxford University Press, 1976), at pp. 117–118.

ing number of privacy issues coming before the courts. How should judges rule with regard to them? At what point does involvement threaten to convert courts into "continuous constitutional conventions", rewriting the provisions of the Constitution in accord with the predilections of the judges?

It is clear from our study that the role of the judiciary and the process of judging are exceedingly complex and sensitive matters. They must be considered when calling upon the courts to intervene on behalf of securing individual rights and liberties.

II. COURTS AND STUDENTS

The sensitive and complex nature of constitutional decision making is highlighted in considering the rights of students and faculty members. Schools and colleges are special-purpose institutions whose clients have traditionally had few rights. Parents control their children outside of educational institutions, and educational officials exercised similar authority *in loco parentis* and by virtue of their professional role over students. The latter have also had broad powers over the behavior of school employees. Educational institutions have always been characterized by a low-degree of technology and high dependence on professionalism. Despite conflicting research findings on the actual impact of the educational process on the learner, the importance of formal education in our society is unquestioned. Schools and colleges remain the focus of public attention and the topic of endless debate and controversy.

Given these factors, courts have long hesitated to become involved in the internal affairs of educational institutions, leaving decision making by and large to state legislatures and public or private boards of trustees. Beginning in the late 1960s, however, courts became increasingly involved in disputes involving both students and teachers. The growing length of time students spend in school, the lowering of the age of majority in many states, the drive for equality by disenfranchised groups including students, the extension of the Fourteenth Amendment state action principle to social service organizations, the abuses of *in loco parentis*—these and other factors served to convince judges that, in the words of Justice Fortas in *Tinker v. Des Moines School Dist.* (1969) "It can hardly be argued that either students or teachers shed their constitutional rights to freedom of speech or expression at the schoolhouse gate."

A. The Developing Constitutional Framework

As revealed in Part II, the consequence has been the development of a body of constitutional law applying specifically to students. Since faculty members are employees, they are entitled to somewhat less constitutional protection within the public educational setting. Briefly, the announced opinions of the U. S. Supreme Court indicate that:

1. Students at public educational institutions have a constitutional right to freedom of expression so long as the educational process is not materially disrupted or the rights of others substantially infringed. *Tinker v. Des Moines School Dist.* (1969); *Papish v. Board of Curators* (1973).

2. College students at public educational institutions have a constitutional right to associate. *Healy v. James* (1972).

3. Nonpublic educational institutions, including those religiously affiliated, have a constitutional right to exist, and parents have the right to send their children to them in lieu of public schooling. *Pierce v. Society of Sisters* (1925). (While this case and those listed in Number 4 below involve the rights of parents, they indirectly affect the rights of students and so are included here.)

4. Public educational institutions cannot force students to profess a belief and must remain neutral with regard to religious matters. *West Virginia v. Barnette* (1943); *Engel v. Vitale* (1962); *Abington Township v. Schempp* (1963); *Epperson v. Arkansas* (1968).

5. Students at public educational institutions have Fourteenth Amendment property interests which warrant informal due process procedures before a temporary suspension is imposed and warrant more formal procedures prior to long term suspension or expulsion. *Goss v. Lopez* (1975).

6. Students have a right to be free from state-maintained school segregation on racial grounds and from racial discrimination in admissions decision making at all educational institutions. *Brown v. Board of Educ.* (1954) and later cases; *Runyan v. McCrary* (1976); *University of California Regents v. Bakke* (1978).

Faced with an infinite variety of factual disputes, state courts and lower federal courts have drawn upon these precedents and others from the political and social setting, as well as upon the provisions of state constitutions, to apply the law to specific situations. The result has been the growth of a second-stage of legal principles which augment and refine the pronouncements of the Supreme Court. Thus, for example, students in most jurisdictions have at least some entitlement to freedom of the press, while students in many parts of the country have a constitutional right to personal grooming. In some states, state supreme courts have ruled that students and their parents have a state constitutional right to substantially equal school financing. Because student constitutional law is heavily influenced by the rulings of state courts and lower federal courts, it is important to review the decisions of these tribunals to ascertain what the law is in a given region.

B. A Look to the Future

Despite recent gains, students do not enjoy the full sweep of adult constitutional rights. In part, this reflects the fact that most students are children; as the Supreme Court has made clear on a number of occasions, children are not entitled to the same constitutional rights as adults. And in part it also reflects the continuing reluctance of many courts to become involved in the internal affairs of public and nonpublic educational institutions. Thus in most jurisdictions, a number of student-related interests have not to date achieved federal constitutional backing. Included are freedom from compulsory school laws, procedural due process prior to academic dismissal, and the right to a sexually-integrated education.

The Supreme Court has rejected claims of a constitutional right to education, to procedural due process prior to the imposition of corporal punishment, and to equalized educational finance. The Court has not yet heard a case involving student entitlement to Fourth Amendment protection from unreasonable searches and seizures.

In many of these areas, of course, nothing precludes legislatures, state education agencies, school boards, and boards of trustees from extending such rights to students. Indeed, many public and private schools and colleges have gone well beyond the legal minimum in providing students and faculty members with civil rights protections. Thus, for example, a state may decide to eliminate all *de facto* school segregation or assure all students of rudimentary due process in disputes over academically-related issues.

A number of commentators continue to argue that courts should minimize their involvement lest judicially-imposed requirements thwart the purpose and functioning of educational institutions and intrude upon the Tenth Amendment plenary power of states over education. The same argument is made regarding nonpublic educational institutions and the Fourteenth Amendment property rights of non-public school operators. The problem with these assertions is that often educational officials, like our political representatives, are reluctant to correct abuses which oppress the lives of persons subject to their authority. Undoubtedly public schools and colleges are better places for students and teachers as a result of those doctrinal judicial rulings securing constitutional protection for student and faculty rights of expression and association, for the right to be free of state-imposed religious indoctrination, for fair play in the imposition of discipline, and for the end to odious *de jure* racial segregation.

At the same time, the fact that courts have had to make these rulings raises questions about the relationship between the internal affairs of complex organizations and the judiciary. The question posed by Justice Jackson above has much relevance to the educational setting. Are we asking too much of our judicial system in utilizing litigation as a decision-making tool to effect change over the operation of social organizations such as the school and college? Are there more appropriate ways to obtain relief from the burdens of *de facto* segregation, unequal school finance, inflexible compulsory school laws, oppressive behavioral rules and curricular requirements, unfair academic decision making? The same question posed for society-at-large can be posed for those in educational institutions: to what extent is the propensity to litigate an indication of the unwillingness or inability of other governance bodies and officials to wrestle with complex problems?

APPENDICES

Appendix A. Briefing Cases

The mere reading of a case is not very enlightening. It is important to have some idea of what to look for in the case, and to acquire the knack of reading between the lines of the opinions. In addition, the student should consider why the case is important; its political, social, and economic background; the implications of the ruling; and the probable reactions of various groups to it.

Students are strongly advised to outline or "brief" case decisions prior to class discussion. Case briefs will be valuable in highlighting the importance of assigned cases and will provide a ready reference to them. Obviously, no one else's case analysis will be as valuable to you as your own.

Every brief should contain the following elements:

Identification of Case

1. Name of Case
2. Citation (for possible later reference to complete official text)
3. Date decided

Analysis of Case

4. Background and Facts (about three lines)
5. Issues (no more than two or three issues per case in one line each; include "yes" or "no" answers after each issue)
6. Decision of the Court (one line)
7. Majority Opinion or reasons for the Decision (about three to six lines)
8. Any Dissenting or Concurring Opinions (two or three lines each)
9. Comment: leave blank space for comments related to Notes following the case, to class discussion, etc. (You may wish to place comments on the case in another set of class notes or on a separate sheet opposite your case brief. Some prefer to use special notebook paper with an extra-wide left margin for briefing cases. With this type of paper, commentary about the case is best placed in the margin opposite relevant key points in the brief.)

In the brief below, each of these elements is indicated by the numerals above.

(1, 2, 3) *Pierce v. Society of Sisters*, 268 U.S. 510 (1925)

(4) *Background and Facts*: The Society of Sisters operates academies as an Oregon Corporation, organized in 1880. The schools are Catholic and generate income. The Oregon Compulsory Education Act of 1922, which goes into effect in 1926, has already caused a decrease in enrollment and income because it compels

parents to send their children to public schools. The law has had a similar impact on Hill Military Academy, a private proprietary (for profit) school incorporated in 1908. The lower court issued a restraining order preventing appellants from enforcing the Oregon law.

(5) *Issue*: Whether a state law requiring all children to attend public school deprives those operating a nonpublic school of their property without due process of law under the 14th Amendment.

(6) *Decision*: Yes. Lower court ruling sustained.

(7) *Opinion*: Mr. J. McReynolds. The state can, of course, "reasonably" regulate all schools. However, this right does not extend to destroying appellees' schools and their property interest in operating schools. Such state action is in violation of the Due Process Clause of the 14th Amendment. There are no "peculiar circumstances" which justify such a sweeping education attendance law.

Additionally, the law interferes with the right of parents to control the upbringing of their children.

(8) *No Dissenting or Concurring Opinions*

(9) *Comment*: The case is decided on economic grounds (property interest of nonpublic school operators) and not on the freedom of choice of parents or children. However, the court in dictum does discuss the right of the parents to exert control over the education of their children. From this dictum comes the modern importance of this case to both parents and nonpublic educational institutions.

Issues of a case should always be stated as questions which can be answered by "yes" or "no". Unless you can do this, you do not understand the case. Issues should be stated only to cover what was actually decided in the case. In other words, narrowly. But the reader should always consider whether the opinion implies a broader issue or issues. Ponder the implications for future legal challenges.

In summarizing the opinion, outline the main points or subsidiary questions in the judge's argument which are used to reach the answer the court gives to each issue. Your summary may be very concise or quite detailed. This is a matter for individual choice, and the length of the "opinion" section of your brief will also vary with the importance and complexity of the case you are briefing. But, in general, *remember that a brief should be brief*. Most of the space in a brief is taken up by the summary of reasoning contained in the opinions. Be sure to include all the opinions, and in your personal comments it is valuable to include a statement indicating which of the opinions you think is most valid.

At the end of a section or prior to a midterm or final, consider making an index to your briefs to be placed at the front of the notebook containing them. (A loose-leaf notebook is best because the pages can be inserted and removed with ease.) The index should be in the same order as the case briefs appear in your notebook and should consist of the name and date of the case, plus the *holding* of the court, i. e., the rule of law stated by the court to answer the issues the case presents. A holding should never be more than two or three sentences long. In constructing a holding, try to include the following:

1. The branch of government involved, if any, e. g., state legislature.

2. The provision of the Constitution involved, if any, e. g., the Due Process Clause of the 14th Amendment.

3. The subject under discussion, e. g., compulsory public school attendance law.

4. The outcome of the court's discussion (answer to the issue), e. g., a compulsory public school attendance law denies the right of persons to operate a nonpublic school.

Thus in *Pierce v. Society of Sisters,* a respectable holding would be:

A state may not pass a compulsory public school attendance law because such a law violates the property rights of persons under the Due Process Clause of the Fourteenth Amendment to operate nonpublic schools.

An index of holdings preceding accumulated case briefs will provide ready access to the broad spectrum of legal decisions covered in the course. If you need to consult the briefs, you can turn to them quickly. An index of your making is also probably the best way to become familiar with the cases you have briefed and is thus most profitably constructed just prior to a test or examination.

If you are unsure about the quality of your briefs or find you are spending an inordinate amount of time briefing cases, see the instructor. In general, it should take you no more than 20 minutes to brief an edited case after you have read it carefully, underlying significant passages as you read.

Appendix B.   Researching the Law

A. CASE REPORTS

All federal appellate and most district court decisions and opinions are formally reported in their entirety in volumes available in any law school and some university libraries. Supreme Court decisions may be found in the United States Reports (or, before 1874, the reports issued under the names of the various court reporters). Somewhat more useful at times are the two privately published sets of Supreme Court reports, one of which is entitled the Supreme Court Reporter and is published by West Publishing Company. A published set of reports for the lower federal courts is also available from West; it has gone under various titles but at present is published as two sets, Federal Reporter (2nd series) for decisions of the federal courts of appeal, and the Federal Supplement for the district courts. There are reports for the appellate decisions of the state courts, published separately for each state; in addition, West Publishing Company puts out regional volumes which include the appellate decisions of the state courts in various regions of the country.

There is a uniform system of citing both federal and state cases so that any reader may find them easily. It consists of the name of the case, the volume number, the name of the volume, page, and date—in that order. Consequently, *Pierce v. Society of Sisters* in Chapter Two is cited: *Pierce v. Society of Sisters*, 268 U.S. 510 (1925). Abbreviations appearing in federal case citations are these: "U.S." means United States Reports; "S.Ct.," Supreme Court Reporter; "L.Ed.," Lawyers' Edition. "F.2d." stands for Federal Reporter (2nd series), while "F.Supp." means Federal Supplement. The volumes containing state cases also have a system of abbreviations.

In a case citation, the name appearing to the left is the initiator of the suit or "plaintiff" and the name appearing to the right is the "defendant." On appeal to a higher court as in *Pierce,* the name to the left is the initiator of the appeal or "appellant," while the name appearing to the right is the "appellee." (On petitions of certiorari to the United States Supreme Court, the appellant is called the "petitioner" and the appellee is called the "respondent.") Frequently, the order of the names will reverse on appeal, since if the plaintiff wins at the trial court level, the defendant may seek a review of the decision in a higher court and thus becomes the initiator of the action.

It should be noted that in a case system of law the case reports are the basic materials of study. No study of law is complete if the student is not acquainted with case materials and how to use them. In researching the law, the student is cautioned to use the original reports if possible because they are not edited and because they include all the concurring and dissenting opinions, which casebooks sometimes leave out or greatly condense.

B. OTHER STUDY MATERIALS

Cases give the raw material. Perspective, however, can best be obtained by reading secondary source materials. A general treatment of law and law-related topics can be found in treatises and textbooks, such as the one you are reading. In addition, there are hundreds of books published on various phases of law, some of which are included in our chapter reference and bibliographical sections. Current materials may also be found in law reviews published by the country's law schools, political science journals, educational periodicals, and similar scholarly and popular publications. In order to use them, however, one must be familiar with the indexes. Law reviews are separately indexed in the *Index to Legal Periodicals* and the *Law Review Digest*. Political science journals are indexed primarily in the *Public Affairs Information Service* index; education materials are indexed in the *Education Index* and the *Current Index to Journals in Education*; popular publications are indexed in *Readers' Guide*. The *New York Times* and its index are also valuable for current reports.

There are legal encyclopedias which include analyses of legal topics and include key cases. One such encyclopedia is *Corpus Juris Secundum* published by West Publishing Company. *C.J.S.* represents a re-statement of the entire body of American law based upon all reported cases since 1658. West also publishes comprehensive digests of all published cases for single states, groups of neighboring states, single courts or court systems such as the federal courts, and all courts of law in the country.

These are a few of the more detailed legal resources available to practicing attorneys and students of the law. Legal research is complex, and it is beyond our scope to include a lengthy discussion of it here. A brief reference section appears below for the benefit of those who may wish to make full use of a legal reference section or law library.

C. SELECTED SOURCES IN LEGAL RESEARCH

1. Pamphlets issued by the lawbook publishers themselves, such as *West's Law Finder*. These pamphlets can be obtained usually free of charge and are available for use at most law school libraries. They serve as a useful guide to the legal volumes issued by the respective publishers.

2. Morris L. Cohen, *Legal Research in a Nutshell*, 3rd Ed. (St. Paul, Minn.: West Publishing Company, 1978).

3. Myron J. Jacobstein and Roy M. Merskey, *Fundamentals of Legal Research* (Mineola, N. Y.: Foundation Press, Inc., 1977). A comprehensive source.

4. Miles O. Price and Harry Bitner, *Effective Legal Research: A Practical Manual of Law Books and Their Uses* 3rd Ed. (Boston: Little, Brown, 1969). A comprehensive source.

Appendix C.   United States Constitution

We the People of the United States, in Order to form a more perfect Union, establish Justice, insure domestic Tranquility, provide for the common defence, promote the general Welfare, and secure the Blessings of Liberty to ourselves and our Posterity, do ordain and establish this Constitution for the United States of America.

ARTICLE I

Section 1.   All legislative Powers herein granted shall be vested in a Congress of the United States, which shall consist of a Senate and House of Representatives.

Section 2.   [1]   The House of Representatives shall be composed of Members chosen every second Year by the People of the several States, and the Electors in each State shall have the Qualifications requisite for Electors of the most numerous Branch of the State Legislature.

[2]   No Person shall be a Representative who shall not have attained to the Age of twenty five Years, and been seven Years a Citizen of the United States, and who shall not, when elected, be an Inhabitant of that State in which he shall be chosen.

[3]   Representatives and direct Taxes shall be apportioned among the several States which may be included within this Union, according to their respective Numbers, which shall be determined by adding to the whole Number of free Persons, including those bound to Service for a Term of Years, and excluding Indians not taxed, three fifths of all other Persons. The actual Enumeration shall be made within three Years after the first Meeting of the Congress of the United States, and within every subsequent Term of ten Years, in such Manner as they shall by Law direct.   The Number of Representatives shall not exceed one for every thirty Thousand, but each State shall have at Least one Representative; and until such enumeration shall be made, the State of New Hampshire shall be entitled to chuse three, Massachusetts eight, Rhode Island and Providence Plantations one, Connecticut five, New York six, New Jersey four, Pennsylvania eight, Delaware one, Maryland six, Virginia ten, North Carolina five, South Carolina five, and Georgia three.

[4]   When vacancies happen in the Representation from any State, the Executive Authority thereof shall issue Writs of Election to fill such Vacancies.

[5]   The House of Representatives shall chuse their Speaker and other Officers; and shall have the sole Power of Impeachment.

Section 3. [1] The Senate of the United States shall be composed of two Senators from each State, chosen by the Legislature thereof, for six Years; and each Senator shall have one Vote.

[2] Immediately after they shall be assembled in Consequence of the first Election, they shall be divided as equally as may be into three Classes. The Seats of the Senators of the first Class shall be vacated at the Expiration of the Second Year, of the second Class at the Expiration of the fourth Year, and of the third Class at the Expiration of the sixth Year, so that one third may be chosen every second Year; and if Vacancies happen by Resignation, or otherwise, during the Recess of the Legislature of any State, the Executive thereof may make temporary Appointments until the next Meeting of the Legislature, which shall then fill such Vacancies.

[3] No Person shall be a Senator who shall not have attained to the Age of thirty Years, and been nine Years a Citizen of the United States, and who shall not, when elected, be an Inhabitant of that State for which he shall be chosen.

[4] The Vice President of the United States shall be President of the Senate, but shall have no Vote, unless they be equally divided.

[5] The Senate shall chuse their other Officers, and also a President pro tempore, in the Absence of the Vice President, or when he shall exercise the Office of President of the United States.

[6] The Senate shall have the sole Power to try all Impeachments. When sitting for that Purpose, they shall be on Oath or Affirmation. When the President of the United States is tried, the Chief Justice shall preside: And no Person shall be convicted without the Concurrence of two thirds of the Members present.

[7] Judgment in Cases of Impeachment shall not extend further than to removal from Office, and disqualification to hold and enjoy any Office of honor, Trust, or Profit under the United States: but the Party convicted shall nevertheless be liable and subject to Indictment, Trial, Judgment, and Punishment, according to Law.

Section 4. [1] The Times, Places and Manner of holding Elections for Senators and Representatives, shall be prescribed in each State by the Legislature thereof; but the Congress may at any time by Law make or alter such Regulations, except as to the Places of chusing Senators.

[2] The Congress shall assemble at least once in every Year, and such Meeting shall be on the first Monday in December, unless they shall by Law appoint a different Day.

Section 5. [1] Each House shall be the Judge of the Elections, Returns, and Qualifications of its own Members, and a Majority of each shall constitute a Quorum to do Business; but a smaller Number may adjourn from day to day, and may be authorized to compel the Attendance of absent Members, in such Manner, and under such Penalties as each House may provide.

[2]   Each House may determine the Rules of its Proceedings, punish its Members for disorderly Behavior, and, with the Concurrence of two thirds, expel a Member.

[3]   Each House shall keep a Journal of its Proceedings, and from time to time publish the same, excepting such Parts as may in their Judgment require Secrecy; and the Yeas and Nays of the Members of either House on any question shall, at the Desire of one fifth of those Present, be entered on the Journal.

[4]   Neither House, during the Session of Congress, shall, without the Consent of the other, adjourn for more than three days, nor to any other Place than that in which the two Houses shall be sitting.

Section 6.   [1]   The Senators and Representatives shall receive a Compensation for their Services, to be ascertained by Law, and paid out of the Treasury of the United States.   They shall in all Cases, except Treason, Felony and Breach of the Peace, be privileged from Arrest during their Attendance at the Session of their respective Houses, and in going to and returning from the same; and for any Speech or Debate in either House, they shall not be questioned in any other Place.

[2]   No Senator or Representative shall, during the Time for which he was elected, be appointed to any civil Office under the Authority of the United States, which shall have been created, or the Emoluments whereof shall have been increased during such time; and no Person holding any Office under the United States, shall be a Member of either House during his Continuance in Office.

Section 7.   [1]   All Bills for raising Revenue shall originate in the House of Representatives; but the Senate may propose or concur with Amendments as on other Bills.

[2]   Every Bill which shall have passed the House of Representatives and the Senate, shall, before it become a Law, be presented to the President of the United States; If he approve he shall sign it, but if not he shall return it, with his Objections to the House in which it shall have originated, who shall enter the Objections at large on their Journal, and proceed to reconsider it.   If after such Reconsideration two thirds of that House shall agree to pass the Bill, it shall be sent together with the Objections, to the other House, by which it shall likewise be reconsidered, and if approved by two thirds of that House, it shall become a Law.   But in all such Cases the Votes of both Houses shall be determined by yeas and Nays, and the Names of the Persons voting for and against the Bill shall be entered on the Journal of each House respectively.   If any Bill shall not be returned by the President within ten Days (Sundays excepted) after it shall have been presented to him, the Same shall be a Law, in like Manner as if he had signed it, unless the Congress by their Adjournment prevent its Return in which Case it shall not be a Law.

[3]   Every Order, Resolution, or Vote, to Which the Concurrence of the Senate and House of Representatives may be necessary (except on a question of Adjournment) shall be presented to the President of the United

States; and before the Same shall take Effect, shall be approved by him, or being disapproved by him, shall be repassed by two thirds of the Senate and House of Representatives, according to the Rules and Limitations prescribed in the Case of a Bill.

Section 8.   [1]   The Congress shall have Power To lay and collect Taxes, Duties, Imposts and Excises, to pay the Debts and provide for the common Defence and general Welfare of the United States; but all Duties, Imposts and Excises shall be uniform throughout the United States;

[2]   To borrow money on the credit of the United States;

[3]   To regulate Commerce with foreign Nations, and among the several States, and with the Indian Tribes;

[4]   To establish an uniform Rule of Naturalization, and uniform Laws on the subject of Bankruptcies throughout the United States;

[5]   To coin Money, regulate the Value thereof, and of foreign Coin, and fix the Standard of Weights and Measures;

[6]   To provide for the Punishment of counterfeiting the Securities and current Coin of the United States;

[7]   To Establish Post Offices and Post Roads;

[8]   To promote the Progress of Science and useful Arts, by securing for limited Times to Authors and Inventors the exclusive Right to their respective Writings and Discoveries;

[9]   To constitute Tribunals inferior to the supreme Court;

[10]   To define and punish Piracies and Felonies committed on the high Seas, and Offenses against the Law of Nations:

[11]   To declare War, grant Letters of Marque and Reprisal, and make Rules concerning Captures on Land and Water;

[12]   To raise and support Armies, but no Appropriation of Money to that Use shall be for a longer Term than two Years;

[13]   To provide and maintain a Navy;

[14]   To make Rules for the Government and Regulation of the land and naval Forces;

[15]   To provide for calling forth the Militia to execute the Laws of the Union, suppress Insurrections and repel Invasions;

[16]   To provide for organizing, arming, and disciplining, the Militia, and for governing such Part of them as may be employed in the Service of the United States, reserving to the States respectively, the Appointment of the Officers, and the Authority of training the Militia according to the discipline prescribed by Congress;

[17]   To exercise exclusive Legislation in all Cases whatsoever, over such District (not exceeding ten Miles square) as may, by Cession of particular States, and the Acceptance of Congress, become the Seat of the Government of the United States, and to exercise like Authority over all Places purchased by the Consent of the Legislature of the State in which the Same

shall be, for the Erection of Forts, Magazines, Arsenals, dock-Yards, and other needful Buildings;—And

[18]   To make all Laws which shall be necessary and proper for carrying into Execution the foregoing Powers, and all other Powers vested by this Constitution in the Government of the United States, or in any Department or Officer thereof.

Section 9.   [1]   The Migration or Importation of Such Persons as any of the States now existing shall think proper to admit, shall not be prohibited by the Congress prior to the Year one thousand eight hundred and eight, but a Tax or duty may be imposed on such Importation, not exceeding ten dollars for each Person.

[2]   The privilege of the Writ of Habeas Corpus shall not be suspended, unless when in Cases of Rebellion or Invasion the public Safety may require it.

[3]   No Bill of Attainder or ex post facto Law shall be passed.

[4]   No Capitation, or other direct, Tax shall be laid, unless in Proportion to the Census or Enumeration herein before directed to be taken.

[5]   No Tax or Duty shall be laid on Articles exported from any State.

[6]   No Preference shall be given by any Regulation of Commerce or Revenue to the Ports of one State over those of another: nor shall Vessels bound to, or from, one State be obliged to enter, clear, or pay Duties in another.

[7]   No money shall be drawn from the Treasury, but in Consequence of Appropriations made by Law; and a regular Statement and Account of the Receipts and Expenditures of all public Money shall be published from time to time.

[8]   No Title of Nobility shall be granted by the United States: And no Person holding any Office of Profit or Trust under them, shall, without the Consent of the Congress, accept of any present, Emolument, Office, or Title, of any kind whatever, from any King, Prince, or foreign State.

Section 10.   [1]   No State shall enter into any Treaty, Alliance, or Confederation; grant Letters of Marque and Reprisal; coin Money; emit Bills of Credit; make any Thing but gold and silver Coin a Tender in Payment of Debts; pass any Bill of Attainder, ex post facto Law, or Law impairing the Obligation of Contracts, or grant any Title of Nobility.

[2]   No State shall, without the Consent of the Congress, lay any Imposts or Duties on Imports or Exports, except what may be absolutely necessary for executing it's inspection Laws: and the net Produce of all Duties and Imposts, laid by any State on Imports or Exports, shall be for the Use of the Treasury of the United States; and all such Laws shall be subject to the Revision and Controul of the Congress.

[3]   No State shall, without the Consent of Congress, lay any Duty of Tonnage, keep Troops, or Ships of War in time of Peace, enter into any Agreement or Compact with another State, or with a foreign Power, or engage in War, unless actually invaded, or in such imminent Danger as will not admit of delay.

ARTICLE II

Section 1. [1] The executive Power shall be vested in a President of the United States of America. He shall hold his Office during the Term of four Years, and, together with the Vice President, chosen for the same Term, be elected, as follows:

[2] Each State shall appoint, in such Manner as the Legislature thereof may direct, a Number of Electors, equal to the whole Number of Senators and Representatives to which the State may be entitled in the Congress; but no Senator or Representative, or Person holding an Office of Trust or Profit under the United States, shall be appointed an Elector.

[3] The Electors shall meet in their respective States, and vote by Ballot for two Persons, of whom one at least shall not be an Inhabitant of the same State with themselves. And they shall make a List of all the Persons voted for, and of the Number of Votes for each; which List they shall sign and certify, and transmit sealed to the Seat of the Government of the United States, directed to the President of the Senate. The President of the Senate shall, in the Presence of the Senate and House of Representatives, open all the Certificates, and the Votes shall then be counted. The Person having the greatest Number of Votes shall be the President, if such Number be a Majority of the whole Number of Electors appointed; and if there be more than one who have such Majority, and have an equal Number of Votes, then the House of Representatives shall immediately chuse by Ballot one of them for President; and if no Person have a Majority, then from the five highest on the List the said House shall in like Manner chuse the President. But in chusing the President, the Votes shall be taken by States the Representation from each State having one Vote; A quorum for this Purpose shall consist of a Member or Members from two thirds of the States, and a Majority of all the States shall be necessary to a Choice. In every Case, after the Choice of the President, the Person having the greater Number of Votes of the Electors shall be the Vice President. But if there should remain two or more who have equal Votes, the Senate shall chuse from them by Ballot the Vice President.

[4] The Congress may determine the Time of chusing the Electors, and the Day on which they shall give their Votes; which Day shall be the same throughout the United States.

[5] No person except a natural born Citizen, or a Citizen of the United States, at the time of the Adoption of this Constitution, shall be eligible to the Office of President; neither shall any Person be eligible to that Office who shall not have attained to the Age of thirty five Years, and been fourteen Years a Resident within the United States.

[6] In case of the removal of the President from Office, or of his Death, Resignation or Inability to discharge the Powers and Duties of the said Office, the Same shall devolve on the Vice President, and the Congress may by Law provide for the Case of Removal, Death, Resignation or Inability, both of the President and Vice President, declaring what Officer shall then act as President, and such Officer shall act accordingly, until the Disability be removed, or a President shall be elected.

[7]   The President shall, at stated Times, receive for his Services, a Compensation, which shall neither be increased nor diminished during the Period for which he shall have been elected, and he shall not receive within that Period any other Emolument from the United States, or any of them.

[8]   Before he enter on the Execution of his Office, he shall take the following Oath or Affirmation: "I do solemnly swear (or affirm) that I will faithfully execute the Office of President of the United States, and will to the best of my Ability, preserve, protect and defend the Constitution of the United States."

Section 2.   [1]   The President shall be Commander in Chief of the Army and Navy of the United States, and of the militia of the several States, when called into the actual Service of the United States; he may require the Opinion, in writing, of the principal Officer in each of the Executive Departments, upon any Subject relating to the Duties of their respective Offices, and he shall have Power to grant Reprieves and Pardons for Offenses against the United States, except in Cases of Impeachment.

[2]   He shall have Power, by and with the Advice and Consent of the Senate to make Treaties, provided two thirds of the Senators present concur; and he shall nominate, and by and with the Advice and Consent of the Senate, shall appoint Ambassadors, other public Ministers and Consuls, Judges of the supreme Court, and all other Officers of the United States, whose Appointments are not herein otherwise provided for, and which shall be established by Law; but the Congress may by Law vest the Appointment of such inferior Officers, as they think proper, in the President alone, in the Courts of Law, or in the Heads of Departments.

[3]   The President shall have Power to fill up all Vacancies that may happen during the Recess of the Senate, by granting Commissions which shall expire at the End of their next Session.

Section 3.   He shall from time to time give to the Congress Information of the State of the Union, and recommend to their Consideration such Measures as he shall judge necessary and expedient; he may, on extraordinary Occasions, convene both Houses, or either of them, and in Case of Disagreement between them, with Respect to the Time of Adjournment, he may adjourn them to such Time as he shall think proper; he shall receive Ambassadors and other public Ministers; he shall take Care that the Laws be faithfully executed, and shall Commission all the Officers of the United States.

Section 4.   The President, Vice President and all civil Officers of the United States, shall be removed from Office on Impeachment for, and Conviction of, Treason, Bribery, or other high Crimes and Misdemeanors.

ARTICLE III

Section 1.   The judicial Power of the United States, shall be vested in one supreme Court, and in such inferior Courts as the Congress may from time to time ordain and establish.   The Judges, both of the supreme and inferior Courts, shall hold their Offices during good Behaviour, and shall, at stated Times, receive for their Services a Compensation, which shall not be diminished during their Continuance in Office.

Section 2. [1] The judicial Power shall extend to all Cases, in Law and Equity, arising under this Constitution, the Laws of the United States, and Treaties made, or which shall be made, under their Authority;—to all Cases affecting Ambassadors, other public Ministers and Consuls;—to all Cases of admiralty and maritime Jurisdiction;—to Controversies to which the United States shall be a Party;—to Controversies between two or more States;—between a State and Citizens of another State;—between Citizens of different States;—between Citizens of the same State claiming Lands under the Grants of different States, and between a State, or the Citizens thereof, and foreign States, Citizens or Subjects.

[2] In all Cases affecting Ambassadors, other public Ministers and Consuls, and those in which a State shall be a Party, the supreme Court shall have original Jurisdiction. In all the other Cases before mentioned, the supreme Court shall have appellate Jurisdiction, both as to Law and Fact, with such Exceptions, and under such Regulations as the Congress shall make.

[3] The trial of all Crimes, except in Cases of Impeachment, shall be by Jury; and such Trial shall be held in the State where the said Crimes shall have been committed; but when not committed within any State, the Trial shall be at such Place or Places as the Congress may by Law have directed.

Section 3. [1] Treason against the United States, shall consist only in levying War against them, or, in adhering to their Enemies, giving them Aid and Comfort. No Person shall be convicted of Treason unless on the Testimony of two Witnesses to the same overt Act, or on Confession in open Court.

[2] The Congress shall have Power to declare the Punishment of Treason, but no Attainder of Treason shall work Corruption of Blood, or Forfeiture except during the Life of the Person attainted.

ARTICLE IV

Section 1. Full Faith and Credit shall be given in each State to the public Acts, Records, and judicial Proceedings of every other State. And the Congress may by general Laws prescribe the Manner in which such Acts, Records and Proceedings shall be proved, and the Effect thereof.

Section 2. [1] The Citizens of each State shall be entitled to all Privileges and Immunities of Citizens in the several States.

[2] A Person charged in any State with Treason, Felony, or other Crime, who shall flee from Justice, and be found in another State, shall on demand of the executive Authority of the State from which he fled, be delivered up, to be removed to the State having Jurisdiction of the Crime.

[3] No Person held to Service or Labour in one State, under the Laws thereof, escaping into another, shall, in Consequence of any Law or Regula-

tion therein, be discharged from such Service or Labour, but shall be delivered up on Claim of the Party to whom such Service or Labour may be due.

Section 3. [1] New States may be admitted by the Congress into this Union; but no new State shall be formed or erected within the Jurisdiction of any other State; nor any State be formed by the Junction of two or more States, or Parts of States, without the Consent of the Legislatures of the States concerned as well as of the Congress.

[2] The Congress shall have Power to dispose of and make all needful Rules and Regulations respecting the Territory or other Property belonging to the United States; and nothing in this Constitution shall be so construed as to Prejudice any Claims of the United States, or of any particular State.

Section 4. The United States shall guarantee to every State in this Union a Republican Form of Government, and shall protect each of them against Invasion; and on Application of the Legislature, or of the Executive (when the Legislature cannot be convened) against domestic Violence.

ARTICLE V

The Congress, whenever two thirds of both Houses shall deem it necessary, shall propose Amendments to this Constitution, or, on the Application of the Legislatures of two thirds of the several States, shall call a Convention for proposing Amendments, which, in either Case, shall be valid to all Intents and Purposes, as part of this Constitution, when ratified by the Legislatures of three fourths of the several States, or by Conventions in three fourths thereof, as the one or the other Mode of Ratification may be proposed by the Congress; Provided that no Amendment which may be made prior to the Year One thousand eight hundred and eight shall in any Manner affect the first and fourth Clauses in the Ninth Section of the first Article; and that no State, without its Consent, shall be deprived of its equal Suffrage in the Senate.

ARTICLE VI

[1] All Debts contracted and Engagements entered into, before the Adoption of this Constitution shall be as valid against the United States under this Constitution, as under the Confederation.

[2] This Constitution, and the Laws of the United States which shall be made in Pursuance thereof; and all Treaties made, or which shall be made, under the Authority of the United States, shall be the supreme Law of the Land; and the Judges in every State shall be bound thereby, any Thing in the Constitution or Laws of any State to the Contrary notwithstanding.

[3] The Senators and Representatives before mentioned, and the Members of the several State Legislatures, and all executive and judicial Officers, both of the United States and of the several States, shall be bound by Oath or Affirmation, to support this Constitution; but no religious Test shall ever be required as a Qualification to any Office or public Trust under the United States.

Article VII

The Ratification of the Conventions of nine States shall be sufficient for the Establishment of this Constitution between the States so ratifying the Same.

ARTICLES IN ADDITION TO, AND AMENDMENT OF, THE CONSTITUTION OF THE UNITED STATES OF AMERICA, PROPOSED BY CONGRESS, AND RATIFIED BY THE LEGISLATURES OF THE SEVERAL STATES PURSUANT TO THE FIFTH ARTICLE OF THE ORIGINAL CONSTITUTION.

Amendment I [1791]

Congress shall make no law respecting an establishment of religion, or prohibiting the free exercise thereof; or abridging the freedom of speech, or of the press; or the right of the people peaceably to assemble, and to petition the Government for a redress of grievances.

Amendment II [1791]

A well regulated Militia, being necessary to the security of a free State, the right of the people to keep and bear Arms, shall not be infringed.

Amendment III [1791]

No Soldier shall, in time of peace be quartered in any house, without the consent of the Owner, nor in time of war, but in a manner to be prescribed by law.

Amendment IV [1791]

The right of the people to be secure in their persons, houses, papers, and effects, against unreasonable searches and seizures, shall not be violated, and no Warrants shall issue, but upon probable cause, supported by Oath or affirmation, and particularly describing the place to be searched, and the persons or things to be seized.

Amendment V [1791]

No person shall be held to answer for a capital, or otherwise infamous crime, unless on a presentment or indictment of a Grand Jury, except in cases arising in the land or naval forces, or in the Militia, when in actual service in time of War or public danger; nor shall any person be subject for the same offence to be twice put in jeopardy of life or limb; nor shall be compelled in any criminal case to be a witness against himself, nor be deprived of life, liberty, or property, without due process of law; nor shall private property be taken for public use, without just compensation.

AMENDMENT VI [1791]

In all criminal prosecutions, the accused shall enjoy the right to a speedy and public trial, by an impartial jury of the State and district wherein the crime shall have been committed, which district shall have been previously ascertained by law, and to be informed of the nature and cause of the accusation; to be confronted with the witnesses against him; to have compulsory process for obtaining witnesses in his favor, and to have the Assistance of Counsel for his defence.

AMENDMENT VII [1791]

In Suits at common law, where the value in controversy shall exceed twenty dollars, the right of trial by jury shall be preserved, and no fact tried by jury, shall be otherwise re-examined in any Court of the United States, than according to the rules of the common law.

AMENDMENT VIII [1791]

Excessive bail shall not be required, nor excessive fines imposed, nor cruel and unusual punishments inflicted.

AMENDMENT IX [1791]

The enumeration in the Constitution, of certain rights, shall not be construed to deny or disparage others retained by the people.

AMENDMENT X [1791]

The powers not delegated to the United States by the Constitution, nor prohibited by it to the States, are reserved to the States respectively, or to the people.

AMENDMENT XI [1798]

The Judicial power of the United States shall not be construed to extend to any suit in law or equity, commenced or prosecuted against one of the United States by Citizens of another State, or by Citizens or Subjects of any Foreign State.

AMENDMENT XII [1804]

The Electors shall meet in their respective states and vote by ballot for President and Vice-President, one of whom, at least, shall not be an inhabitant of the same state with themselves; they shall name in their ballots the person voted for as President, and in distinct ballots the person voted for as Vice-President, and they shall make distinct lists of all persons voted for as President, and of all persons voted for as Vice-President, and of the number of votes for each, which lists they shall sign and certify, and transmit sealed to the seat of the government of the United States, directed to the President of the Senate;—The President of the Senate shall, in the presence of the Senate and House of Representatives, open all the certificates and the votes shall then be counted;—The person having the greatest number of votes for President, shall be the President, if such number be a majority of the whole number of Electors appointed; and if no person have such majority, then from the persons having the highest numbers not exceeding three on the list of those voted for as President, the House of Representatives shall choose immediately, by ballot, the President. But in choosing the President, the votes shall be taken by states, the representation from each state having one vote; a quorum for this purpose shall consist of a member or members from two-thirds of the states, and a majority of all the states shall be necessary to a choice. And if the House of Representatives shall not choose a President whenever the right of choice shall devolve upon them before the fourth day of March next following, then the Vice-President shall act as President, as in the case of the death or other constitutional disability of the President.—The person having the greatest number of votes as Vice-President, shall be the Vice-President, if such number be a majority of the whole number of Electors appointed, and if no person have a majority, then from the two highest numbers on the list, the Senate shall choose the Vice-President; a quorum for the purpose shall consist of two-thirds of the whole number of Senators, and a majority of the whole number shall be necessary to a choice. But no person constitutionally ineligible to the office of President shall be eligible to that of Vice-President of the United States.

Amendment XIII [1865]

Section 1. Neither slavery nor involuntary servitude, except as a punishment for crime whereof the party shall have been duly convicted, shall exist within the United States, or any place subject to their jurisdiction.

Section 2. Congress shall have power to enforce this article by appropriate legislation.

Amendment XIV [1868]

Section 1. All persons born or naturalized in the United States, and subject to the jurisdiction thereof, are citizens of the United States and of the State wherein they reside. No State shall make. or enforce any law which shall abridge the privileges or immunities of citizens of the United States; nor shall any State deprive any person of life, liberty, or property, without due process of law; nor deny to any person within its jurisdiction the equal protection of the laws.

Section 2.　Representatives shall be apportioned among the several States according to their respective numbers, counting the whole number of persons in each State, excluding Indians not taxed.　But when the right to vote at any election for the choice of electors for President and Vice President of the United States, Representatives in Congress, the Executive and Judicial officers of a State, or the members of the Legislature thereof, is denied to any of the male inhabitants of such State, being twenty-one years of age, and citizens of the United States, or in any way abridged, except for participation in rebellion, or other crime, the basis of representation therein shall be reduced in the proportion which the number of such male citizens shall bear to the whole number of male citizens twenty-one years of age in such State.

Section 3.　No person shall be a Senator or Representative in Congress, or elector of President and Vice President, or hold any office, civil or military, under the United States, or under any State, who having previously taken an oath, as a member of Congress, or as an officer of the United States, or as a member of any State legislature, or as an executive or judicial officer of any State, to support the Constitution of the United States, shall have engaged in insurrection or rebellion against the same, or given aid or comfort to the enemies thereof.　But Congress may by a vote of two-thirds of each House, remove such disability.

Section 4.　The validity of the public debt of the United States, authorized by law, including debts incurred for payment of pensions and bounties for services in suppressing insurrection or rebellion, shall not be questioned.　But neither the United States nor any State shall assume or pay any debt or obligation incurred in aid of insurrection or rebellion against the United States, or any claim for the loss or emancipation of any slave; but all such debts, obligations and claims shall be held illegal and void.

Section 5.　The Congress shall have power to enforce, by appropriate legislation, the provisions of this article.

Amendment XV [1870]

Section 1.　The right of citizens of the United States to vote shall not be denied or abridged by the United States or by any State on account of race, color, or previous condition of servitude.

Section 2.　The Congress shall have power to enforce this article by appropriate legislation.

Amendment XVI [1913]

The Congress shall have power to lay and collect taxes on incomes, from whatever source derived, without apportionment among the several States, and without regard to any census or enumeration.

Amendment XVII [1913]

[1]   The Senate of the United States shall be composed of two Senators from each State, elected by the people thereof, for six years; and each Senator shall have one vote.   The electors in each State shall have the qualifications requisite for electors of the most numerous branch of the State legislatures.

[2]   When vacancies happen in the representation of any State in the Senate, the executive authority of such State shall issue writs of election to fill such vacancies: *Provided,* That the legislature of any State may empower the executive thereof to make temporary appointments until the people fill the vacancies by election as the legislature may direct.

[3]   This amendment shall not be so construed as to affect the election or term of any Senator chosen before it becomes valid as part of the Constitution.

Amendment XVIII [1919]

Section 1.   After one year from the ratification of this article the manufacture, sale, or transportation of intoxicating liquors within, the importation thereof into, or the exportation thereof from the United States and all territory subject to the jurisdiction thereof for beverage purposes is hereby prohibited.

Section 2.   The Congress and the several States shall have concurrent power to enforce this article by appropriate legislation.

Section 3.   This article shall be inoperative unless it shall have been ratified as an amendment to the Constitution by the legislatures of the several States, as provided in the Constitution, within seven years from the date of the submission hereof to the States by the Congress.

Amendment XIX [1920]

[1]   The right of citizens of the United States to vote shall not be denied or abridged by the United States or by any State on account of sex.

[2]   Congress shall have power to enforce this article by appropriate legislation.

Amendment XX [1933]

Section 1.   The terms of the President and Vice President shall end at noon on the 20th day of January, and the terms of Senators and Representatives at noon on the 3d day of January, of the years in which such terms would have ended if this article had not been ratified; and the terms of their successors shall then begin.

Section 2. The Congress shall assemble at least once in every year, and such meeting shall begin at noon on the 3d day of January, unless they shall by law appoint a different day.

Section 3. If, at the time fixed for the beginning of the term of the President, the President elect shall have died, the Vice President elect shall become President. If the President shall not have been chosen before the time fixed for the beginning of his term, or if the President elect shall have failed to qualify, then the Vice President elect shall act as President until a President shall have qualified; and the Congress may by law provide for the case wherein neither a President elect nor a Vice President elect shall have qualified, declaring who shall then act as President, or the manner in which one who is to act shall be selected, and such person shall act accordingly until a President or Vice President shall have qualified.

Section 4. The Congress may by law provide for the case of the death of any of the persons from whom the House of Representatives may choose a President whenever the right of choice shall have devolved upon them, and for the case of the death of any of the persons from whom the Senate may choose a Vice President whenever the right of choice shall have devolved upon them.

Section 5. Sections 1 and 2 shall take effect on the 15th day of October following the ratification of this article.

Section 6. This article shall be inoperative unless it shall have been ratified as an amendment to the Constitution by the legislatures of three-fourths of the several States within seven years from the date of its submission.

AMENDMENT XXI [1933]

Section 1. The eighteenth article of amendment to the Constitution of the United States is hereby repealed.

Section 2. The transportation or importation into any State, Territory, or possession of the United States for delivery or use therein of intoxicating liquors, in violation of the laws thereof, is hereby prohibited.

Section 3. This article shall be inoperative unless it shall have been ratified as an amendment to the Constitution by conventions in the several States, as provided in the Constitution, within seven years from the date of the submission hereof to the States by the Congress.

AMENDMENT XXII [1951]

Section 1. No person shall be elected to the office of the President more than twice, and no person who has held the office of President, or acted as President, for more than two years of a term to which some other person was elected President shall be elected to the office of President more than once. But this Article shall not apply to any person holding the office of President when this Article was proposed by the Congress, and shall not prevent any person who may be holding the office of President, or acting as President, during the term within which this Article becomes operative from holding the office of President or acting as President during the remainder of such term.

Section 2.   This article shall be inoperative unless it shall have been ratified as an amendment to the Constitution by the legislatures of three-fourths of the several States within seven years from the date of its submission to the States by the Congress.

AMENDMENT XXIII [1961]

Section 1.   The District constituting the seat of Government of the United States shall appoint in such manner as the Congress may direct:

A number of electors of President and Vice President equal to the whole number of Senators and Representatives in Congress to which the District would be entitled if it were a State, but in no event more than the least populous state; they shall be in addition to those appointed by the states, but they shall be considered, for the purposes of the election of President and Vice President, to be electors appointed by a state; and they shall meet in the District and perform such duties as provided by the twelfth article of amendment.

Section 2.   The Congress shall have power to enforce this article by appropriate legislation.

AMENDMENT XXIV [1964]

Section 1.   The right of citizens of the United States to vote in any primary or other election for President or Vice President, for electors for President or Vice President, or for Senator or Representative in Congress, shall not be denied or abridged by the United States, or any State by reason of failure to pay any poll tax or other tax.

Section 2.   The Congress shall have power to enforce this article by appropriate legislation.

AMENDMENT XXV [1967]

Section 1.   In case of the removal of the President from office or of his death or resignation, the Vice President shall become President.

Section 2.   Whenever there is a vacancy in the office of the Vice President, the President shall nominate a Vice President who shall take office upon confirmation by a majority vote of both Houses of Congress.

Section 3.   Whenever the President transmits to the President pro tempore of the Senate and the Speaker of the House of Representatives his written declaration that he is unable to discharge the powers and duties of his office, and until he transmits to them a written declaration to the contrary, such powers and duties shall be discharged by the Vice President as Acting President.

Section 4.   Whenever the Vice President and a majority of either the principal officers of the executive departments or of such other body as Congress may by law provide, transmit to the President pro tempore of the Senate and the Speaker of the House of Representatives their written declaration that the President is unable to discharge the powers and duties of his office, the Vice President shall immediately assume the powers and duties of the office as Acting President.

Thereafter, when the President transmits to the President pro tempore of the Senate and the Speaker of the House of Representatives his written declaration that no inability exists, he shall resume the powers and duties of his office unless the Vice President and a majority of either the principal officers of the executive department or of such other body as Congress may by law provide, transmit within four days to the President pro tempore of the Senate and the Speaker of the House of Representatives their written declaration and the President is unable to discharge the powers and duties of his office.   Thereupon Congress shall decide the issue, assembling within forty-eight hours for that purpose if not in session.   If the Congress, within twenty-one days after receipt of the latter written declaration, or, if Congress is not in session, within twenty-one days after Congress is required to assemble, determines by two-thirds vote of both Houses that the President is unable to discharge the powers and duties of his office, the Vice President shall continue to discharge the same as Acting President; otherwise, the President shall resume the powers and duties of his office.

AMENDMENT XXVI [1971]

Section 1.   The right of citizens of the United States, who are eighteen years of age or older, to vote shall not be denied or abridged by the United States or by any State on account of age.

Section 2.   The Congress shall have power to enforce this article by appropriate legislation.

Appendix D. Legal Terminology

The following terms and their definitions are designed to facilitate the reading of this text. Taken together, they do not, of course, constitute a comprehensive list of legal terminology. For other terms not included in this list, readers are advised to consult either *Black's Law Dictionary,* an exhaustive collection available at law libraries and most college and university libraries, or Daniel Oran's *Law Dictionary for Non-Lawyers,* a more compact source especially geared to the needs of the non-lawyer. Both are published by West Publishing Company. The definitions below are based on those given in both of these dictionaries. In each instance, only the most common meaning or meanings as they relate to the topics discussed in *Constitutional Rights and Student Life* are provided.

A fortiori: With stronger reason, as in if it is true that a twenty-one year old is an adult, then, *a fortiori,* a twenty-five year old person is an adult.

A priori: Presumptively valid; what follows must be naturally deduced from what went before.

Adversary system: System of law in America, where the truth is thought to be best revealed through a clash of interests in the courtroom between opposite sides to a dispute.

Affidavit: A written statement sworn to before a person officially permitted by law to administer an oath.

Amicus curiae: "Friend of the court"; a person or organization allowed to appear in a lawsuit, usually to file arguments in the form of a brief supporting one side or the other, even though not party to the dispute.

Answer: The first pleading by the defendant in a lawsuit. This statement sets forth the defendant's responses to the charges contained in the plaintiff's "complaint."

Appeal: Asking a higher court to review the actions of a lower court in order to correct mistakes or injustice. "An appeal" is the process whereby such a request is made.

Beyond a reasonable doubt: The level of proof required to convict a person of a crime. This is the highest level of proof required in any type of trial. Compare with *by a fair preponderance of the evidence,* the level of proof in civil cases.

Blackstone: An influential treatise on the law of England, written in the eighteenth century. Full title is *Blackstone's Commentaries on the Common Law.* Since the American system of law is largely based on the English system, Blackstone is frequently consulted and cited in case law.

Brief: A written summary or condensed statement of a case. Also a written statement prepared by one side in a lawsuit to explain its case to the judge.

By a fair preponderance of the evidence: The level of proof required in a civil case. This level is lower than that required in criminal cases. See *beyond a reasonable doubt*.

Cause of action: Facts sufficient to support a valid lawsuit.

Certiorari: A request for review of a lower court decision, which the higher court can refuse.

Circumstantial evidence: Evidence which indirectly proves a main fact in question. Such evidence is open to doubt, since it is inferential, e. g., a student seen in the vicinity of the locker room at the time of a theft is the thief.

Civil case: Every lawsuit other than a criminal proceeding. Most civil cases involve a lawsuit brought by one person against another and usually concern money damages.

Class action: A lawsuit brought by one person on behalf of himself or herself and all other persons in the same situation.

Code: A collection of laws.

Compelling state interest: A reason for a public law, rule, policy, or action that is strong enough to justify limiting a person's constitutional or federal statutory rights. Judges who regard individual constitutional rights as occupying a "preferred position" among other constitutional provisions (such as the right of states to pass laws) utilize this standard in deciding conflicts between laws/rules and individual rights. In effect, it requires the government to show a valid purpose in the regulation and the absence of alternative ways to accomplish this purpose other than by limiting individual rights.

Compensatory damages: Damages which relate to the actual loss suffered by a plaintiff, as opposed to *punitive damages*.

Complaint: The first main paper filed in a civil lawsuit. It includes, among other things, a statement of the wrong or harm done to the plaintiff by the defendant and a request for specific help from the court. The defendant responds to the complaint by filing an "answer".

Constitution: Fundamental principles of governance. Constitutions may be written (United States) or unwritten (England). As the basic law of the country, most other laws are drawn from the provisions of the constitution and must yield when in conflict with it. Constitutions serve to limit opportunities for governmental abuse of power.

Contract: An agreement that affects the legal relationship between two or more persons. To be a contract, an agreement must involve: at least one promise, consideration (i. e., something of value promised or given), persons legally capable of making binding agreements, and a reasonable amount of agreement between the persons as to what the contract means.

Contract of adhesion: A contract in which all the bargaining power and therefore the contractual terms are unfairly on one side.

Criminal case: Cases involving crimes against the laws of the state; unlike civil cases, the state is the prosecuting party.

De facto: In fact; actual; a situation that exists in fact whether or not it is lawful. *De facto* segregation is that which exists regardless of the law or the actions of civil authorities. See *de jure*.

Defendant (appellee): The person against whom a legal action is brought. This legal action may be civil or criminal. At the appeal stage, the party against whom an appeal is taken is known as the appellee. Usually, the appellee is the winner in the lower court.

De jure: Of right; legitimate; lawful, whether or not in actual fact. *De jure* segregation is that which is sanctioned by law. See *de facto*.

De minimus: Small, unimportant; not worthy of concern.

De novo: New; completely new from the start; for example: a trial *de novo* is a completely new trial ordered by the trial judge or by an appeals court.

Declaratory judgment: A judicial action that states the rights of the parties or answers a legal question without awarding any damages or ordering that anything be done. A person may ask a court for a declaratory judgment only if there is a real, not theoretical, problem that involves real legal consequences.

Defamation: Injuring a person's character or reputation by false or malicious statements. This includes both *libel* and *slander*. See these terms.

Dictum: A digression; a discussion of side points or unrelated points. Short for *obiter dictum*; plural is *dicta*.

Disclaimer: The refusal to accept certain types of responsibility. For example, a college catalogue may disclaim any responsibility for guaranteeing that the courses contained therein will actually be offered since courses, programs, and instructors are likely to change without notice.

En banc: The full panel of judges assigned to a court sit to hear a case.

Equity: Fairness; the name of a type of court originating in England to handle legal problems when the existing laws did not cover some situations in which a person's rights were violated by another person. In the United States, civil courts have both the powers of law and equity. If only money is represented in a case, the court is acting as a law court and will give only monetary relief. The court provides a jury if the parties want one, and it enters a judgment in favor of either the plaintiff or defendant. If something other than money is requested—injunction, declaratory judgment, specific performance of a contractual agreement, etc.—then the court takes jurisdiction in equity and will grant a decree ordering acts to be done or not done. There is no jury in an equity case. Actions at law and suits in equity involve civil cases, not criminal.

Estoppel: Being stopped from proving something (even if true) in court because of something said before that shows the opposite (even if false).

Ex parte: With only one side present; an *ex parte* judicial proceeding involves only one party without notice to, or contestation by, any person adversely affected.

Ex rel: On behalf of; when a case is titled *State ex rel. Doe v. Roe*, it means that the state is bringing a lawsuit against Roe on behalf of Doe.

Expunge: Blot out. For example, a court order requesting that a student's record be expunged of any references to disciplinary action during such and such a time period means that the references are to be "wiped off the books."

Fiduciary: A relationship between persons in which one person acts for another in a position of trust.

Hearing: An oral proceeding before a court or quasi-judicial tribunal. Hearings which describe a process to ascertain facts and provide evidence are labeled "trial-like hearings" or, simply, "trials." Hearings which relate to a presentation of ideas as distinguished from facts and evidence are known as "arguments." The former occur in trial courts and the latter occur in appellate courts. The terms "trial," "trial-type hearing," "quasi-judicial hearing," "evidentiary hearing," and "adjudicatory hearing" are all used by courts and have overlapping meanings. See *trial*.

Hearsay: Second-hand evidence; facts not in the personal knowledge of the witness, but a repetition of what others said that is used to prove the truth of what those others said.

Holding: The rule of law in a case; that part of the judge's written opinion that applies the law to the facts of the case and about which can be said "the case means no more and no less than this." A holding is the opposite of *dictum*.

In camera: "In chambers"; in a judge's private office; a hearing in court with all spectators excluded.

In loco parentis: In place of the parent; acting as a parent with respect to the care, supervision, and discipline of a child.

In re: In the matter of; this is a prefix to the name of a case often used when a child is involved. For example, *"In re Mary Smith"* might be the title of a child neglect proceeding even though it is really against the parents.

Infra: Later in the article or book. For example, *infra*, p. 236, means to turn to that page, which is further on. Opposite of *supra*.

Informed consent: A person's agreement to allow something to happen (such as surgery) that is based on a full disclosure of facts needed to make the decision intelligently.

Injunction: A court order requiring someone to do something or refrain from taking some action.

Inter alia: Among other things, usually used when what is being mentioned is only part of what there is; for example, "We found in the box, *inter alia*, a book."

Ipse dixit: A statement that depends for its persuasiveness on the authority of the person who said it.

Ipso facto: By the fact itself; by the mere fact that.

Judicial review: The power of a court to declare a statute unconstitutional; also the power to interpret the meaning of laws.

Jurisdiction: Right of a court to hear a case; also the geographical area within which a court has the right and power to operate. Original jurisdiction means that the court will be the first to hear the case; appellate jurisdiction means that the court reviews cases on appeal from lower court rulings.

Jus tertii: The right of a third party not involved in a lawsuit to property that is involved in the suit.

Justiciable: Proper for a court to decide. For example, a justiciable controversy in a real dispute that a court may handle.

Law: Basic rules of order as pronounced by a government. Common law refers to laws originating in custom or practice. Statute law are laws passed by legislatures and recorded in public documents. Case law are the pronouncements of courts.

Libel: Written defamation; published false and malicious written statements that injure a person's reputation.

Mandamus: A writ issued by a court commanding that some official duty be performed. This was the writ William Marbury requested of the U. S. Supreme Court in the famous case of *Marbury v. Madison* (1803).

Material: Important; going to the heart of the matter; for example, a material fact is one necessary to reach a just decision.

Misrepresentation: A false statement; if knowingly done, misrepresentation may be illegal and result in punishment.

Moot: Abstract; for the sake of argument; not a real case involving a real dispute.

Motion: A request made by a lawyer that a judge take certain action, such as dismissing a case. Motions are an intimate part of legal procedure and come in many forms.

Pander: To solicit for purposes of prostitution.

Parens patriae: The historical right of all governments to take care of persons under their jurisdiction, particularly minors and incapacitated persons.

Per curiam: An unsigned decision and opinion of a court, as distinguished from one signed by a judge.

Plaintiff: The person who brings a lawsuit against another person. At the appeal stage, the person bringing the appeal is called the "appellant" and is usually the one losing in the lower court action.

Pleading: The process of making formal, written statements of each side of a case. First the plaintiff submits a paper with facts and claims; then the defendant submits a paper with facts and counterclaims; then the plaintiff responds; and so on until all issues and questions are clearly posed for a trial.

Political question: A question that the courts will not decide because it concerns a decision more properly made by another branch of government such as the legislature.

Precedent: A court decision on a question of law that gives authority or direction on how to decide a similar question of law in a later case with similar facts. Ruling by precedent is usually conveyed through the term *stare decisis*.

Prima facie: Clear on the face of it; presumably, a fact that will be considered to be true unless disproved by contrary evidence. For example, a *prima facie* case is a case that will win unless the other side comes forward with evidence to dispute it.

Punitive damages: Money awarded to a person by a court that is over and above the damages actually sustained. Punitive damages are designed to serve as a deterrent to similar acts in the future.

Quasi-judicial: The case-deciding function of an administrative agency.

Remand: To send back; for example, a higher court may send a case back to the lower court, asking that certain action be taken.

Res judicata: A thing decided. Thus, if a court decides a case, the matter is settled and no new lawsuit on the same subject may be brought by the persons involved.

Scienter: Knowingly; with guilty knowledge.

Seriatim: One by one.

Sine qua non: A thing or condition that is indispensable.

Slander: Oral defamation; the speaking of false and malicious words that injure another person's reputation, business, or property rights.

Sovereign immunity: The government's freedom from being sued for money damages without its consent.

Standing: A person's right to bring a lawsuit because he or she is directly affected by the issues raised.

Stare decisis: "Let the decision stand"; a legal rule that when a court has decided a case by applying a legal principle to a set of facts, that court should stick by that principle and apply it to all later cases with clearly similar facts unless there is a good, strong reason not to. This rule helps promote fairness and reliability in judicial decision-making and is inherent in the American legal system. See *precedent*.

Sui generis: Unique; one of a kind.

Supra: Earlier in an article or book. For example, *supra*, p. 11, means to turn to that page which appeared earlier. Opposite of *infra*.

Tort: A civil wrong done by one person to another. For an act to be a tort, there must be: a legal duty owed by one person to another, a breach of that duty, and harm done as a direct result of the action. Examples of torts are negligence, battery, and libel—all of them remedied by resort to legal action.

Trial: A process occurring in a court whereby opposing parties present evidence, subject to cross-examination and rebuttal, pertaining to the matter in dispute. See *hearing*.

Ultra vires: Going beyond the specifically delegated authority to act; for example, a school board which is by law restricted from punishing students for behavior occurring wholly off-campus acts *ultra vires* in punishing a student for behavior observed at a private weekend party.

ANNOTATED BIBLIOGRAPHY

For reasons of space, the following annotated bibliography offers no more than a sampling of the many sources which relate to the topics discussed in this book. But it will provide a starting place for those who wish to know more. With a few exceptions, those sources which are already cited in the chapters are not listed. The emphasis here has been placed on including a range of both traditional and newer sources which are readily available at most college and law school libraries.

General Sources

Archibald Cox, *The Role of the Supreme Court in American Government* (New York: Oxford Univ. Press, 1976). An excellent, nontechnical overview of the role of the U. S. Supreme Court. In some 100 pages, Cox reviews the involvement of the Court in such areas as disputes between the branches of government, disputes over individual rights, and disputes about equal protection of the laws. Throughout, he ponders the proper role of the Court in our governmental system.

Learned Hand, *The Bill of Rights* (Cambridge: Harvard University Press, 1958). A famous jurist's defense of judicial modesty and the limits of judicial expertise.

Journal of Law and Education. This quarterly journal covers many law-related educational topics. Included is a case summary section which highlights recent court decisions covering all sectors of education and all types of cases, including those involving students and teachers.

Richard Funston, *A Vital National Seminar: The Supreme Court in American Political Life* (Palo Alto, Calif.: Mayfield Publishing Co., 1978). A discussion of how Court decisions mirror the climate of the times.

Project, "Education and the Law: State Interests and Individual Rights," 74 *Mich.L.Rev.* 1373, June, 1976. A lengthy and comprehensive legal review of state interests and student, teacher, and parent rights as related to the educational setting.

Bernard Schwartz, *The Great Rights of Mankind: A History of the American Bill of Rights* (New York: Oxford University Press, 1977). A lucid history of the major problems and interpretations of human rights in America from the English backgrounds to the present.

Laurence H. Tribe, *American Constitutional Law* (Mineola, N. Y.: Foundations Press, 1978). A comprehensive treatise on the development of constitutional law to the present. This massive work is directed more to the advanced student, to scholars, and to legal practitioners. See also Harold W. Chase and Craig R. Ducat, *Constitutional Interpretation* (St. Paul, Minn.: West Publishing Co., 1974), a classroom text covering most of the same topics.

Chapter One

Howard R. Bowen, *Investment in Learning: The Individual and Social Value of American Higher Education* (San Francisco: Jossey-Bass, 1977). A Carnegie Commission report on the impact of postsecondary education on the learner and society. This exhaustive study looks at the consequences of formal education from many perspectives including cognition, moral development, economic productivity, and the whole person.

Lawrence A. Cremin, *Traditions of American Education* (New York: Basic Books, 1977). A readable account of the evolvement of the American educational system by a leading educational historian. This book focuses on the broad range of educational activities both in and out of the formal school throughout American history and advocates public policy positions regarding the future care and education of young children.

John E. Coons and Stephen D. Sugarman, "Family Choice in Education: A Model State System for Vouchers", 59 *Calif.L.Rev.* 321, March, 1971. A lengthy and detailed discussion of inadequacies in public education, followed by a proposal for a model voucher law to be called the Family Choice in Education Act.

Kenneth M. Dolbeare and Patricia Dolbeare, *American Ideologies: The Competing Beliefs of the 1970s*, 3rd Ed. (Chicago: Rand, McNally Publishing Co., 1976). A comprehensive discussion of liberal, conservative, and radical positions in American politics.

Robert B. Fowler and Jeffrey R. Orenstein, *Contemporary Issues in Political Theory* (New York: John Wiley, 1977). An extensive discussion of the major approaches to the issues of freedom, equality, and justice.

Russell Kirk, *A Program for Conservatives* (Chicago: H. Regnery Co., 1954). A good statement of the classic conservative position on the need for educated elites and reliance upon tradition.

Michael Parenti, *Power and the Powerless* (New York: St. Martin's Press, 1978). A detailed radical critique of American liberal institutions and orthodoxy.

The Rights of Children (Cambridge, Mass.: Harvard Educ. Review, 1974). A collection of essays devoted to exploring the topic from several different perspectives. Contributors are leading commentators and researchers in the field. Another excellent source is volume 39, No. 3, of *Law and Contemporary Problems,* 1975, which contains a similar series of articles on the rights of children.

Arthur M. Schlessinger, Jr., *The Crisis of Confidence: Ideas, Power and Violence in America* (Boston: Houghton, Mifflin, 1969). A staunch defence of liberal principles, against the challenges of the 1960s and 1970s.

David B. Tyack, *The One Best System* (Cambridge, Mass.: Harvard University Press, 1974). A detailed and sensitive account from an interdisciplinary perspective of the American urban public schooling system. Includes substantial commentary on reform movements, past and present.

Chapter Two

Stephen Aarons, "Is Educating Your Own Child A Crime?" *Saturday Rev.*, November 25, 1978. A case study of a lengthy legal struggle between a Massachusetts couple and public school officials over home education; presents an interesting real-life parallel to the hypothetical situation in this chapter involving the Smith family.

Stephen T. Early, Jr., *Constitutional Courts of the U. S.* (Totowa, N. J.: Littlefield, Adams and Co., 1977). A comprehensive handbook describing the federal judicial system. This non-technical paperback will serve as a valuable resource for students and teachers alike.

Martin P. Golding, *Philosophy of Law* (Englewood Cliffs, N. J.: Prentice-Hall, 1975). A brief introduction to the major problems and approaches to law.

Mary-Michelle U. Hirschoff, "Parents and the Public School Curriculum: Is There a Right to Have One's Child Excused From Objectionable Instruction?", 50 *So.Calif.L.Rev.* 871, July, 1977. A detailed discussion of the issue, concluding that parents should have the right to excuse their children from instruction which conflicts with the parental value system since the *Pierce v. Society of Sisters* decision coupled with rulings related to religious exemptions do not afford meaningful choice for most parents.

Otto F. Kraushaar, *American Nonpublic Schools* (Baltimore: The Johns Hopkins Univ. Press, 1972). The leading comprehensive source on the development of and contemporary nature of American nonpublic schools. Includes some chapters on debated issues of public aid and state regulation.

Walter F. Murphy and C. Herman Pritchett (Eds.), *Courts, Judges and Politics: An Introduction to the Judicial Process* (New York: Random House, 1974). A comprehensive text on judicial organization, judicial power, methods of judicial decision-making, and judicial impact. Also included are some of the best articles and excerpts from books in the field.

David W. Rohde and Harold J. Spaeth, *Supreme Court Decision Making* (San Francisco: W. H. Freeman and Co., 1976). An empirical discussion of the norms, values, and procedures that are influential within the Supreme Court's internal decision-making process.

William T. Schantz, *The American Legal Environment* (St. Paul, Minn.: West Publishing Co., 1976). A fine legal textbook for the non-law student. Provides extensive commentary and illustrative cases on the nature and kinds of law, the composition of the American political system, the types of legal actions (civil, equity, criminal), and the variety of cases (juvenile, antitrust, divorce, torts, etc.).

Stephen L. Wasby, *The Supreme Court in the Federal Judicial System* (New York: Holt, Rinehart and Winston, 1978). An up-to-date discussion of the Supreme Court as a major policy maker in the political system.

Frederick M. Wirt and Michael W. Kirst, *The Political Web of American Schools* (Boston: Little, Brown, 1972). A thorough examination of the political aspects of American education. One of the few books combining the political science perspective with the educational.

Chapter Three

Harry M. Clor (Ed.), *Censorship and Freedom of Expression* (Chicago: Rand McNally, 1971). A good collection of diverse positions on the issue of obscenity and censorship.

Craig R. Ducat, *Modes of Constitutional Interpretation* (St. Paul, Minn.: West Publishing Co., 1978). A useful critical discussion of absolutism, the balancing of interests, and the preferred freedoms approaches to constitutional interpretation in the First Amendment area.

Thomas I. Emerson, David Haber, and Norman Dorsen, *Political and Civil Rights in the United States,* 3rd Ed. (Boston: Little, Brown, 1967). Vol. I. A comprehensive discussion of major First Amendment problem areas.

Leon Letwin, "Administrative Censorship of the Independent Student Press—Demise of the Double Standard?" 28 *So.Carolina L.Rev.* 565, March, 1977. An interesting and spirited account of the Fourth Circuit Court of Appeals' difficulty in sustaining student punishment under prior restraint systems despite that circuit's endorsement of such systems. The article concludes that prior restraints are as unworkable in the educational sector as they are in society at large.

Sheldon H. Nahmod, "First Amendment Protection for Learning and Teaching: The Scope of Judicial Review," 18 *Wayne L.Rev.* 1479, Summer, 1972. Very thorough review of the issues and problems involved in judicial First Amendment decision-making pertaining to educational matters.

Lisa Newall, "A Right of Access to Student Newspapers at Public Universities", 4 *J.Coll. & Univ.L.* 209, Spring, 1977. A thorough review of the cases and the perplexing issues they raise, particularly with regard to the extent to which campus newspapers are public forums.

Note, "Public School as Public Forum," 54 *Texas L.Rev.* 90, December, 1975. A detailed and technical analysis of the public forum approach to free speech issues. Points out that the public forum analogy particularly works against school regulation of newspapers, assemblies, and the like.

Note, "Recognition of High School Student Organizations: Constitutional Protection of Associational Rights," 52 *Indiana L.Journal* 487, Winter, 1977. Thorough review of changing judicial attitudes regarding associational rights of high school students. Concludes that the precedent of *Healy v. James* should be followed.

Note, "Term Paper Companies and the Constitution", 1973 *Duke L.Journal* 1275, June, 1973. Thorough review of the subject: contrasts free speech restriction with academic sanctions as remedies.

Martin Shapiro, *Freedom of Speech: The Supreme Court and Judicial Review* (Englewood Cliffs, N. J.: Prentice-Hall, 1966). A political scientist's discussion of the political and legal issues surrounding the freedom to dissent.

Chapter Four

Kenneth M. Dolbeare and P. E. Hammond, *The School Prayer Decisions From Court Policy to Local Practice* (Chicago: University of Chicago Press, 1971). This book explores the problems of obtaining compliance with the Court's prayer decisions in specific local communities.

David Fellman, *Religion in American Public Law* (Boston: Boston University Press, 1965). An excellent discussion of the political and legal values surrounding the church-state controversy and the role of religion in public life.

Eugene B. Habecker, "Students, Christian Colleges, and the Law: And the Walls Came Tumbling Down," 2 *J.Coll. & Univ.L.* 369, Summer, 1975. A discussion from the viewpoint of the religious institution of the legal consequences of Supreme Court religious decisions through the early 1970s.

Joshua J. Kancellbaum, "Shifting Currents in the Narrow Channel of State Aid to Parochial Schools," 38 *Ohio St.Law J.* 757, 1977. A discussion of *Wolman v. Walter,* its historical backdrop and implications, by the attorney who argued the case for the appellants.

Paul G. Kauper, *Religion and the Constitution* (Baton Rouge: Louisiana State University Press, 1964). An exploration of the technical legal doctrines used to explain the relationship between religion and constitutional law.

Richard E. Morgan, *The Supreme Court and Religion* (New York: Free Press, 1972). A good discussion of the political controversies that surround this constitutional issue.

Note, "Aid to Parochial Schools: The Test Flunks," 52 *Chicago Kent L. Rev.* 683, 1976. A thorough review of the cases with the intention of showing the ineffectiveness of the three-part test as a decision-making tool.

Note, "Constitutional Law—Public Regulation of Private Religious Schools," 37 *Ohio St.Law J.* 899, 1976. Good discussion of the importance of *State v. Whisner,* an Ohio Supreme Court case involving successful use of religious freedom and parental rights to challenge state efforts to regulate a nonpublic school.

Leo Pfeffer, *Church, State and Freedom,* Rev.Ed. (Boston: Beacon Press, 1967). A spirited defense of the strict separationist position by one of the prominent specialists in the field.

David J. Young, "Constitutional Validity of State Aid to Pupils in Church-Related Schools—Internal Tension Between the Establishment and Free Exercise Clauses," 38 *Ohio St.Law J.* 783, 1977. A discussion of *Wolman v. Walter,* its historical backdrop and implications, by the attorney who argued the case for the appellees.

Chapter Five

William G. Buss, "Procedural Due Process for School Discipline: Probing the Constitutional Outline," 119 *Univ. of Penn.L.Rev.* 547, Feb., 1971. An excellent conceptual essay on the contours of procedural due process in the educational environment. Various components of procedural due process are evaluated for their importance in securing fundamental fairness in student disciplinary disputes.

George F. Cole, *Criminal Justice: Law and Politics*, 2nd Ed. (North Scituate, Mass.: Duxbury, 1976). An excellent interdisciplinary text that presents most of the major problems of the criminal justice process and the rights of the accused.

Fred P. Graham, *The Self-Inflicted Wound* (New York: MacMillan, 1970). A good discussion of the major cases and problems involved in the right to counsel area.

Harry Kalven, Jr. and Hans Zeisel, *The American Jury* (Boston: Little, Brown, 1966). The definitive study on the problems of trial by jury and the notion of a fair trial.

Inequality in Education, Vol. 23, Sept., 1978. The entire issue is devoted to a comprehensive discussion of corporal punishment in American schools. Included are commentaries on *Ingraham v. Wright.*

Michael La Morte and Robert B. Meadows, "Educationally Sound Due Process in Academic Affairs," 8 *J.Law & Educ.* 197, April, 1979. Following an exploration of the developing law and an analysis of the *Horowitz* decision, the authors set forth what they regard as appropriate academic due process safeguards for students at all levels of the educational system. Highly recommended reading for teachers and academic administrators.

Note, "Coercive Behavior Control in the Schools: Reconciling Individually Appropriate Education with Damaging Changes in Educational Status", 29 *Stanford L.Rev.* 93, November, 1976. A fine review of the issue and related research. The note points out that comprehensive definitions and diagnoses related to behavior disorder lead to great abuses, and urges special protective measures be taken.

Note, "Due Process in the Public Schools—An Analysis of the Procedural Requirements and a Proposal for Implementing Them," 54 *No.Carolina L.Rev.* 41, April, 1976. An excellent review of the many situations where due process would be warranted, with special emphasis on the value of an investigative approach through an ombudsman as an alternative to the adversary system.

Michael Meltsner, *Cruel and Unusual: The Supreme Court and Capital Punishment* (New York: Random House, 1973). An interesting account of the Supreme Court's efforts to grapple with this highly controversial political issue.

Otis H. Stephens, Jr., *The Supreme Court and the Confessions of Guilt* (Knoxville, Tenn.: Univ. of Tennessee Press, 1973). A comprehensive discussion of the evolving Court doctrine on coerced confessions.

Chapter Six

Marc A. Franklin, *The Biography of a Legal Dispute: An Introduction to American Civil Procedure* (Mineola, N. Y.: Foundation Press, 1968). Examines the development of a nonconstitutional civil suit against a small town newspaper in the state court setting. It is written for the general reader as well as those who study law.

Philip B. Heymann and William H. Kenety, *The Murder Trial of Wilbur Jackson* (St. Paul, Minn.: West Publishing Co., 1975). Examines in detail the development of a criminal case in the state court setting and thus provides an interesting counterpart to the Franklin monograph.

William Zelermyer, *The Legal System in Operation* (St. Paul, Minn.: West Publishing Co., 1977). This source is more comprehensive in its examination of the development of a civil suit in the state court setting.

Chapter Seven

Norman E. Bowie and Robert L. Simon, *The Individual and the Political Order* (Englewood Cliffs, N. J.: Prentice Hall, 1977). A comprehensive textbook dealing with the major ethical problems of liberty, justice, and equality. Chapter Nine on preferential discrimination is especially relevant.

Kenneth Davidson, Ruth Ginsburg, and Herma Kay, *Sex-Based Discrimination* (St. Paul, Minn.: West Publishing Co., 1974). A comprehensive source book on the major problems of sexual equality under the Constitution.

Thomas R. Dye, *The Politics of Equality* (Indianapolis, Ind.: Bobbs-Merrill, 1971). A good discussion of the major strategies of blacks and women in their pursuit of equal justice.

"Equal Rights for Women: A Symposium on the Proposed Constitutional Amendment," *Harvard Civil Rights/Civil Liberties Law Review,* Vol. 6, March, 1971. A series of articles by major ERA advocates.

Lino A. Graglia, *Disaster by Decree: The Supreme Court Decisions on Race and the Schools* (Ithaca, N. Y.: Cornell Univ.Press, 1976). A critical discussion of the Court's major desegregation cases.

Law and Contemporary Problems, Vol. 38, No. 3, Winter-Spring, 1974. Entire issue explores the direction of school finance reform after the *Rodriquez* decision from a variety of perspectives.

Law and Contemporary Problems, Vol. 34, Nos. I and II, Winter and Spring, 1975. Both issues are devoted to an intensive examination of social science and its role in school desegregation decision-making.

Journal of Law and Education, Vol. 4, No. I, January, 1975. Entire issue offers commentary from a variety of sources on the significance of the school desegregation decisions twenty years after the *Brown* ruling. See also "Symposium on Completing the Job of School Desegregation," 19 *Howard L.Journal* 1, 1975, and "*Brown* to *DeFunis* Twenty Years Later," *The Black L.Journal,* Vol. 3, Nos. 2 and 3, 1975.

David L. Kirp and Mark G. Yudof, *Educational Policy and the Law* (San Francisco: McCutchan Publishing Co., 1974). A comprehensive text, focusing in large part on equality issues and their relationship to policy formulations.

Allan P. Sindler, *Bakke, DeFunis, and Minority Admissions* (N.Y.: Longman, 1978). A comprehensive review of these cases and the issues involved in them. See also the trilogy of articles on the same subject in the *Howard L.Journal,* Vol. 21, 1978, pp. 72–244.

Chapter Eight

P. Allan Dionisopoulos and Craig R. Ducat, *The Right to Privacy: Essays and Cases* (St. Paul, Minn.: West Publishing Co., 1976). An excellent source book on the major approaches and cases that deal with the privacy issue.

Erwin N. Griswold, *Search and Seizure: A Dilemma of the Supreme Court* (Lincoln: University of Nebraska Press, 1975). An up-to-date discussion of the Court's problem of reconciling personal privacy with the national interest.

Merle McClung, "Student Records: The Family Educational Rights and Privacy Act of 1974," 22 *Inequality in Education* 5, July, 1977. Discusses the reasons for and rationale of the law; is the lead article for this issue of *Inequality,* which is devoted entirely to the Buckley Amendment.

Note, "Legality of University-Conducted Dormitory Searches for Internal Disciplinary Purposes," 1976 *Duke L.Journal* 770, Summer, 1976. Comprehensive examination of the issue, concluding that a 1971 Supreme Court decision, *Wyman v. James,* pertaining to warrantless welfare investigations can be used to justify warrantless searches in the educational setting.

Note, "Long Hair and the Law: A Look at Constitutional and Title VII Challenges to Public and Private Regulation of Male Grooming," 24 *Kansas L.Rev.* 143, Fall, 1975. An excellent survey of the major issues and cases during the time when hair length was a major concern in and out of the educational setting.

Note, "Public School Searches and Seizures," 45 *Fordham L.Rev.* 202, October, 1976. Thorough analysis of cases involving elementary and secondary schools; particular emphasis is placed on the confusing use of *in loco parentis* and similar doctrines to uphold searches by school officials.

J. Roland Pennock and John W. Chapman (Eds.), *Privacy* (New York: Lieber-Atherton Press, 1971). A good collection of different philosophical and legal positions in this area.

Steven N. Schatken, "Student Records at Institutions of Post-secondary Education: Selected Issues Under the Family Educational Rights and Privacy Act of 1974," 4 *J.Coll. & Univ.L.* 147, Spring, 1977. Examines the issues in the higher educational context and thus complements the McClung essay and related materials cited above.

P. J. Ward, "Parietal Regulations and the University: Required Residence in Campus Dormitories," 5 *Human Rights* 215, Winter, 1976. Thorough review of all of the major cases to 1976; offers pro and con arguments associated with required on-campus housing.

Alan F. Westin, *Privacy and Freedom* (New York: Atheneum, 1967). The pioneering study on the various tools for invading privacy and the policy choices that are available to the American public.

INDEX

References are to Pages

†